S0-AQK-616

Our Social World

Donelson R. Forsyth

Virginia Commonwealth University

Brooks/Cole Publishing Company

I(T)P™ An International Thomson Publishing Company

Pacific Grove • Albany • Bonn • Boston • Cincinnati • Detroit • London • Madrid • Melbourne
Mexico City • New York • Paris • San Francisco • Singapore • Tokyo • Toronto • Washington

Sponsoring Editor: *Marianne Taflinger*
Marketing Representative: *Robert Podstepny*
Editorial Assistant: *Virge Perelli-Minetti*
Production Editor: *Laurel Jackson*
Production Assistant: *Tessa A. McGlasson*
Manuscript Editor: *Joanne Tenenbaum*
Permissions Editor: *May Clark*
Interior and Cover Design: *Katherine Minerva*
Credits continue on p. 657.

Cover Photo: *The Stock Market/Jon Feingersh © 1992*
Art Coordinator: *Lisa Torri*
Interior Illustration: *Lotus Art*
Photo Editor: *Robert J. Western*
Photo Researcher: *Joan Meyers Murie*
Typesetter: *Weimer Graphics, Inc.*
Cover Printing: *Color Dot Graphics, Inc.*
Printing and Binding: *Quebecor Printing Hawkins*

COPYRIGHT © 1995
By Brooks/Cole Publishing Company
A Division of International Thomson Publishing Inc.
The ITP logo is a trademark under license.

For more information, contact:
BROOKS/COLE PUBLISHING COMPANY
511 Forest Lodge Road
Pacific Grove, CA 93950
U.S.A.

International Thomson Publishing Europe
Berkshire House 168–173
High Holborn
London WCIV 7AA
England

Thomas Nelson Australia
102 Dodds Street
South Melbourne, 3205
Victoria, Australia

Nelson Canada
1120 Birchmount Road
Scarborough, Ontario
Canada M1K 5G4

International Thomson Editores
Campos Eliseos 385, Piso 7
Col. Polanco
11560 México D. F. México

International Thomson Publishing GmbH
Königswinterer Strasse 418
53227 Bonn
Germany

International Thomson Publishing Asia
221 Henderson Road
#05–10 Henderson Building
Singapore 0315

International Thomson Publishing Japan
Hirakawacho Kyowa Building, 3F
2-2-1 Hirakawacho
Chiyoda-ku, Tokyo 102
Japan

All rights reserved. No part of this work may be reproduced, stored in a retrieval system, or transcribed, in any form or by any means—electronic, mechanical, photocopying, recording, or otherwise—without the prior written permission of the publisher, Brooks/Cole Publishing Company, Pacific Grove, California 93950.

Printed in the United States of America
10 9 8 7 6 5 4 3 2 1

Library of Congress Cataloging-in-Publication Data
Forsyth, Donelson R., [date]
Our social world / by Donelson R. Forsyth.
p. cm.
Includes bibliographical references (p.) and index.
ISBN 0-534-24516-1
1. Social psychology. I. Title.
HM251.F636 1994
302—dc20 94-11001
CIP

To Clairese

About the Author

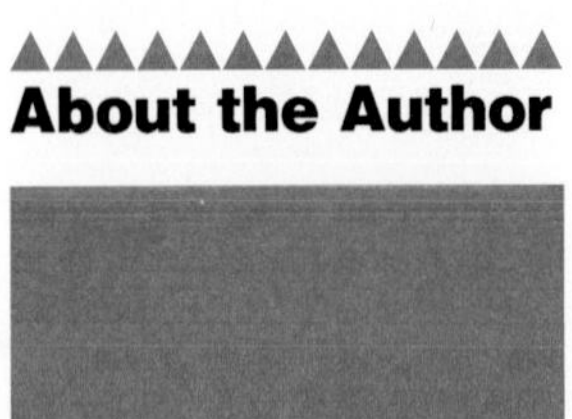

Donelson R. Forsyth is Professor of Psychology at Virginia Commonwealth University. As an undergraduate, he attended Florida State University, where he chose psychology as a major after taking a social psychology course from Russell D. Clark III. He continued his studies at the University of Florida under the guidance of Barry R. Schlenker and received his Ph.D. in 1978. He joined the faculty of Virginia Commonwealth University in that year.

Dr. Forsyth's interests include reactions to success and failure, individual difference in moral thought, applications of social psychology in clinical settings, and group dynamics. His scientific research has been published in such journals as *Journal of Personality and Social Psychology, American Psychologist, Personality and Social Psychology Bulletin,* and the *Journal of Experimental Social Psychology.* He has also written and edited several books, including *Group Dynamics* and *Handbook of Social and Clinical Psychology: The Health Perspective* (coedited with C. R. Snyder). He currently serves on the editorial board of the *Journal of Personality and Social Psychology* and is an associate editor of the *Journal of Social and Clinical Psychology.*

Dr. Forsyth is recognized as a masterful teacher. His offerings to undergraduates include Introduction to Psychology, Social Psychology, and Group Dynamics. At the graduate level, he teaches research methods in social psychology and cycles through specialty seminars on attitude theory and measurement, attribution and social cognition, group dynamics, and a practicum on teaching psychology. In recognition of his outstanding teaching, he received the Lecturer Award from the College of Humanities and Sciences in 1985 and was selected as the Outstanding Teacher at Virginia Commonwealth University in 1992.

Brief Contents

Contents

FIVE The Self 154

SIX Attitudes and Behavior 194

NINE **Influence 314**

TEN **Group Dynamics 354**

ELEVEN Personal Relationships 398

TWELVE Helping 442

Applications

Preface

Ours is a social world. It's awash with some 5.8 billion people, all of whom are busily interacting with one another. On this particular day, how many people are meeting one another for the first time, shaking hands, exchanging bows, and forming first impressions? How many times today will two people be drawn to one another and share the thought that they might become friends or lovers? How many people will decide that they ordered the wrong entrée at lunch? How many times today will someone convince someone else to try a new brand of deodorant, to donate money to a charity, or to hire him or her to do a job? How many groups will form today, how many will dissolve, how many will make excellent decisions, and how many will draw ill-founded conclusions? How many people will hurt each other, help each other, love each other, and kill each other?

These billions of social encounters are the subject matter of social psychology. Like meteorologists predicting the weather, economists charting changes in wages and prices over decades, and physicists identifying the fundamental elements of matter, social psychologists study complex, ever-changing phenomena. These phenomena, however, are social ones: They originate in the countless interactions that take place between people each day. Some of these processes are disturbing—people harming others, people isolated and alone, people failing to reach their potential. Others, though, are uplifting, for they highlight the positive side of human action: loving others, helping people, and working together to achieve important goals. Some are routine and mundane, whereas others are extraordinary and exciting. Social psychologists study such everyday actions as getting to know another person or making a decision in a group, but they also investigate phenomena that have far-reaching ramifications for our society and the world at large: violence, cooperation, prejudice, sexism, and helping. Linking all these topics—the negative, the positive, the mundane, and the earthshaking—is social psychology's fundamental interest in people interacting with other people.

Why Study Social Psychology?

If you are meeting social psychology for the first time, then you are about to embark on a journey into a new way of looking at yourself and other people. But why make this journey? Where will this social-psychological road take you? One destination is an increased understanding of social psychology's theories and findings. Once, as a neophyte teacher, my enthusiasm for social psychology led me to expect my students to put this goal above all others. I wanted them to learn everything about social psychology. If a social psychology edition of Trivial Pursuit existed, I would have used it as my final exam. With experience, however, I learned that gaining an overall view of social psychology was more important than learning all the specific details of the field. To help you achieve this goal, this book introduces you to social psychology. It isn't comprehensive; that is, it doesn't review all theory and research in social psychology. Instead, this book provides a general framework for examining social behavior while suggesting avenues for in-depth study.

Knowing the content of the field is important, but social psychology is more than just findings, facts, and theories. I hope that while studying the content of social psychology, you also learn the methods that social psychologists use to develop and test their explanations of social behavior. Social psychology offers a unique perspective on behavior, one that stresses critical thinking and scientific analysis rather than common sense and intuition. As such, it is as much a method—a way of thinking about and studying people—as it is a set of findings and theories. Long after you forget the specific facts and theories of the course, you should be able to look at a social event and say, "Here's how a social psychologist would explain what happened."

Another reason for studying social psychology is more practical. By gaining an understanding of social interactions and relationships, you may discover answers to problems you face now or will face in the future. At a personal level, insights gained by studying human interaction can be applied to your daily life, for social psychologists tend to study processes we have all experienced. For example, have you ever wondered why you sometimes let other people talk you into doing things you don't want to do? Why you like some people right off the bat but dislike others from the moment you see them? Why you have problems maintaining friendships or love relationships? Why you can or can't take charge in groups? Researchers don't have all the answers, but many people gain a deeper understanding of their own actions and interpersonal relations by applying social psychology in their everyday lives.

Social psychology also proves useful in many professional, business, and vocational settings. No matter what your professional goals, a fundamental knowledge of social interaction is helpful. Just about any time people work with other people, social-psychological processes shape their actions and outcomes. Because researchers study such phenomena as communication between people, the ways we perceive and understand each other, leadership and decision-making processes in groups, competition and cooperation, and persuasion, social psychology yields many practical suggestions for improving interpersonal relations in work settings.

Enjoyment is the final reason for studying social psychology. Learning about social interaction should not be painful and depressing, but exciting, satisfying, and even amusing. I must confess that I am embarrassingly fond of social psychology. I don't consider it simply a scientific discipline or my vocation, but a hobby and source of recreation. I am so enthusiastic about the field that I want you not only to learn its principles and findings and recognize its tremendous practical value, but also to have fun while doing so.

How to Study Social Psychology

This book does not just present social psychology; rather, it teaches social psychology by discussing ideas in a logical framework that gives you a conceptual context for absorbing the information. But if you don't use the book actively, your journey into social psychology won't be as smooth as it could be. The following are features of the text, together with suggestions for taking advantage of them:

- *Outlines and previews.* When you are studying a new area, it helps to organize the information in your own way. As you read each chapter, you will understand the material better if you can fit each bit of incoming information into an overall conceptual context. Therefore, you should build an organizational framework *before* you read the chapter. To help you accomplish this, each chapter begins with an outline of its contents. By taking a minute or two to study this outline, you can get a general idea of the organization behind the topics.
- *Cases.* A single case is used as a unifying example in each chapter. The cases are not fictitious: They describe real individuals or groups, and all descriptions are based on published descriptions of the incident and the individuals involved. The cases are included to provide a concrete example of the theoretical ideas discussed.
- *Chapter sections.* One problem with learning by reading is that your motivation dwindles long before you run out of material to read. One way to solve this problem is to read the chapter in chunks. An entire chapter may be too much to read at one time; the smaller sections within a chapter are much more digestible. Each section stands as a unit and includes a table that summarizes the material.
- *Summaries and additional sources.* After reading a chapter, be sure to study the final summary. Following the summary is a section that contains a list of sources to consult for more information about specific topics that were discussed within the chapter. As noted earlier, at certain points within the chapter, tabular summaries are also provided. If you look over the summary table and don't remember an entry, then you aren't reading the chapter as carefully as you should.
- *Headings and boldface terms.* Take advantage of the section headings and of the glossary terms listed in the margins. Headings do all sorts of good things: They indicate what you are about to encounter, they help you organize the information in the text, and they serve as memory aids when you try to retrieve information. So try to use the headings when you study the material: If you don't actively use them, they don't help much. Second, major terms are printed in **boldface type** and are defined in the margin. Use these boldface terms to identify critical ideas.
- *Figures and data tables.* Visual information, combined with the verbal information in the text, improves learning. Figures, in particular, serve as "spatial mnemonics"—visual devices that aid memory by arranging the material in an organized pattern. Study those figures, because when the time comes to remember the material, you will be able to "see" the material mentally by recalling the figure.
- *Application and In Depth sections.* Social psychology can be applied in many settings. These applications are mentioned throughout the text, but they are given extra attention at the end of each chapter in special "Application" sections. Each chapter also includes one "In Depth" section that examines some theoretical or empirical issue in more detail than is possible in the text itself.
- *Citations.* In some cases, researchers and theorists are mentioned by name in the text. In most cases, however, the citations are placed in parentheses rather than directly in the text.

I hope these features make your journey through social psychology easier, more efficient, and more enjoyable. Once you open your mind to social psychology, I think you will be mesmerized by its delights. On behalf of all my colleagues, I warmly welcome you to the field.

Acknowledgments

I could not have written *Our Social World* without the contributions and support of many colleagues, friends, family members, and students. The list of people who deserve thanks is very long, but it begins with the social psychologists who have nurtured our science. The pages of this book are filled only because thousands of people have crafted theories about social behavior and tested these theories through research. Hundreds of these social psychologists were willing to let me quote extensively from their work or present their findings in graphic or tabular form, and I appreciate very much their willingness to share their findings. Sincere thanks are also extended to the many social psychologists scattered across the country who offered myriad useful suggestions for improving earlier drafts of this book. They include Scott Allison, University of Richmond; John H. Harvey, University of Iowa; Roland Havis, Richard Bland College; Dale O. Jorgenson, California State University, Long Beach; Jon A. Krosnick, Ohio State University; Mark R. Leary, Wake Forest University; Christopher Leone, University of North Florida; Douglas Moore, Temple University; Judith Nye, Monmouth College; Tom Pyszczynski, University of Colorado; Dean Keith Simonton, University of California, Davis; Mark Stasson, Virginia Commonwealth University; and Craig Smith, Vanderbilt University. Mark Leary deserves special thanks because he read and critiqued the entire manuscript. I have lost track of how much of the book was my idea and how much was his.

Many others helped me by taking on some of the numerous tasks associated with creating a book. *Our Social World* is the fourth book I've published with Brooks/Cole, and I am always impressed by their professionalism and skill. Marianne Taflinger nurtured the project as it changed from a revision of an earlier text into a completely new book, and she always gave me the latitude I needed to develop creative ways of presenting material. With admirable skill, Laurie Jackson, my production editor, transformed the 1,200 manuscript pages, 128 figures, and 100 or so tables into a polished product. Many others, including May Clark, Tessa McGlasson, Katherine Minerva, Virge Perelli-Minetti, Bob Podstepny, Lisa Torri, and Bob Western, also deserve kudos. And here in Richmond, Diane Hunter was indispensable in linking my office to Brooks/Cole via Federal Express and the U.S. Mail.

My family, students, and work associates helped me in many ways as well. On more than one occasion, I consulted with Mark Stasson and Scott Allison to identify ways of rendering material more accessible to readers. Ray Archer not only helped me develop the material for the instructor's edition of the text, but we also worked together on the test bank and the study guide. Bethia Caffery provided both line editing for several chapters and, apparently, "writing genes." (She's both a writer and my mother.) Claire deserves sympathy perhaps more than just thanks. It's true that she read nary a word of the manuscript and just laughed when I suggested that I might need help checking the references. But she lost many a family weekend to work, and when I worked so long that my tether to our friends and family nearly came undone, she stepped in and retied it. David, who turned 17 months old today (March

22), also deserves many thanks for providing me with a wonderful distraction and my first case study of the development of a social self.

My students also helped me by giving me feedback about my success in conveying information to them. My Honors Social Psychology Class (Psy 321) in the Spring of 1993 deserves a special thanks, for they read much of the book in manuscript form and helped me identify areas for improvement. I want also to thank the students in my Introductory Psychology classes for having such interesting names. Whenever I needed first names for fictitious individuals in examples, I turned to my roster for those classes.

Last, I owe a general note of thanks to my university, Virginia Commonwealth University, for nurturing me as I developed my skills as a teacher. I could never have written this book if my colleagues did not value good teaching as much as they value good research and if they did not consider a textbook to be a bit of both.

Donelson R. Forsyth

Foundations

Why do you act, feel, and think the way you do? Why do you set goals for yourself and keep trying even when you fail? Why do you avoid eating certain foods, dress in the style you do, and champion one political cause over another? Why and when do you let others know your preferences and opinions? Why do you consider only certain people to be your friends? Why do you join some groups, avoid some groups, and even work against other groups? Why do you, at various times and places in your life, lead rather than follow, smile instead of cry, help rather than hurt, and join with others rather than remain alone? Why do you—or for that matter, why does anyone—act, feel, and think in a particular way?

social psychology
The scientific study of the way individuals' thoughts, feelings, and behaviors are influenced by the actual, imagined, or implied presence of others.

People have been pondering these kinds of questions for centuries, but a new approach has emerged in the last 60 years. This perspective, called **social psychology**, lies at the intersection of psychology and such social sciences as sociology and anthropology. Psychologists try to explain why people think, feel, and act the way they do. *Social* psychologists, however, concentrate on how our thoughts, feelings, and actions are influenced by the people around us. We humans are a social species. We spend our lives in the company of other people. We work together, relax together, sleep together, and worship together. The people around us influence us in innumerable subtle and not-so-subtle ways. Social psychologists strive to understand these interpersonal influences. The field, as defined by Gordon W. Allport, is "*an attempt to understand and explain how the thought, feeling, and behavior of individuals are influenced by the actual, imagined, or implied presences of others*" (1985, p. 3; italics are Allport's).

What can social psychology tell us about human behavior that other perspectives can't? First, because social psychologists search out the social forces underlying our actions, they often notice aspects of our social world that others may not. In a sense, social psychology offers a distinctive way of *looking* at human behavior. Second, social psychology offers a unique way of *studying* behavior. Many disciplines, such as philosophy and theology, ask the question "Why do people act the way they do?" Social psychology differs from these nonscientific approaches by evaluating its answers scientifically. This chapter introduces social psychology by examining its perspective on human action and the methods it employs to examine the adequacy of that perspective.

paradigm
Scientists' shared assumptions about the phenomena they study; also, a set of research procedures.

The Nature of Social Psychology

The philosopher of science Thomas S. Kuhn uses the term **paradigm** to describe scientists' shared assumptions about the phenomena they study

(Kuhn, 1962, 1970). Kuhn maintains that when scientists learn their field, they master not only the content of the science—important discoveries, general principles, facts, and so on—but also a way of looking at the world that is passed on from one scientist to another. The shared beliefs and unstated assumptions that make up the paradigm provide researchers with a world view that determines the questions they consider worth studying and the methods that are most appropriate.

What is social psychology's paradigm? What do social psychologists notice when they observe a social encounter? What fascinates them about people interacting with other people? To answer these questions, let us look at several rich social situations through the eyes of a social psychologist.

The Social Side of Life

The deceiver. In October of 1991 Anita Hill took her case to the public. She explained that, as a lawyer working for a government agency, her hours were long but the problems she solved were ones she felt were important. But then the harassment started. Her boss, Clarence Thomas, would call her into his office to discuss an assignment. Once they were alone he would bring up sexual subjects and ask her out on dates even when she made it clear that she was not interested. Hill also accused Thomas of talking about pornographic movies, bestiality, and his own sexual prowess. She would try to change the subject, but invariably he would return to his harassing ways.

Thomas told a different story. He claimed that he had a productive work relationship with Hill but that's all it was: a work relationship. He was bewildered and angered by the accusation of harassment, for he could not recall a single instance when he responded to his subordinate in a sexual way. He maintained that he, and not his employee, was the victim of harassment: "My name has been harmed. My integrity has been harmed. My character has been harmed. My family has been harmed. My friends have been harmed" (Thomas, 1991, p. A-6).

Who do you believe? Hill had an unblemished reputation: friends and coworkers described her as hardworking, serious-minded, principled, and conscientious. She had no reason to lie about what had happened. But Thomas marshalled a strong and impassioned argument against her. He was, after all, a nominee for a judgeship on the United States Supreme Court, and director of the agency that protected women from harassment in the workplace. The senators who were conducting the inquiry into the incident concluded, after much agitation and interrogation, that Thomas was telling the truth.

The racists. Ron Wilson's shift at the medical center was finally over. As he walked to the bus stop, his neighbor, Jim Booker, drove by. Wilson was tired, and the February night was bitterly cold, so he gladly accepted Booker's offer of a ride home.

As Wilson eased into the car, in another part of town Bob Cuneo and John Boyle were also getting ready to call it a night. They worked in a bar checking IDs and breaking up fights, and since business had been slow they had drunk as heavily as the customers. The paths of the two pairs of men crossed at a red light near Park Square. Wilson and Booker arrived first and watched the flow of street people and prostitutes down the sidewalk as they waited for the light to change. Cuneo and Boyle then pulled alongside, rolled down their windows, and began to shout a variety of insults at them. Booker offered a few derisive remarks in return, which Cuneo and Boyle answered by spitting at Booker and roaring off as the light changed. The incident might have ended there if Booker's car hadn't stalled. Cuneo noticed the problem, circled back, and confronted Wilson and Booker again. A savage fight broke out, with the four men using baseball bats, a bottle, a knife, a piece of a picket fence, jumper cables, and even a car to injure each other. Why? Were these old enemies who were settling a grudge? Gang members who had sworn a vow to defend their turf? Drug dealers fighting over territory? No. The two sets of men were strangers to one another. But Cuneo and Boyle were white, Wilson and Booker were African American, and that was reason enough (Sedgwick, 1982).

The Moonie. Jerry was doing well in college even though his classes didn't seem very meaningful to him. But then he met a young woman named Jan who was looking for volunteers to take part in a peace crusade. He was very interested in what Jan had to say, and he agreed to attend a one-day workshop dealing with poverty in the United States and abroad. Jan invited him to another workshop the next weekend. It proved to be an enjoyable mix of lively discussion, singing, sports, and short motivational speeches that referred to the "Divine Principle." When Jan invited him to a week-long retreat, Jerry accepted the offer with the thought "I found in the group some principles I could believe in and a true concern for people." In the van headed into the countryside Jerry started to wonder whether the crusade was part of any religious organization, so he asked Jan about it (Galanter, 1989, p. 52).

Jerry: Say, does the Divine Principle have something to do with the Moonies?

Jan: You mean the Unification Church?

Jerry: I don't know. Are they related?

Jan: Reverend Moon wrote the Divine Principle.

Jerry: Oh? Is he that Korean guy who spoke at Yankee Stadium?

Jan: Yes. He's a very wise man who gave us the ideas we've been talking about the last few days.

Jerry: Oh, I see. How come you didn't mention it?

Jan: People criticize Reverend Moon unfairly; they would turn you away from joining the workshop, and you would lose the chance to hear his words. We just want you to have the chance to find out what he has to say.

Jerry felt that she had a good point, and he fell silent. As the van drove on into the night and the group sang folk songs, Jerry felt very relaxed and joyful. He wouldn't be going back to college any time soon.

The wife. As Molly watched the movie, she couldn't help but remember her first date with Andrew. They had gone to a film (*Les Bonnes Femmes*, she thought), and later they critiqued it over coffee and a banana split at Howard Johnson's. They had met just the week before at a party, but Molly recognized Andrew's name immediately when they were introduced: she had been reading and enjoying his movie reviews in the *Village Voice* for years. She had imagined him to be a sensitive and clever man filled with wonderful ideas about art and literature, but on that first date he talked mostly about himself and his accomplishments. He was, it turned out, only trying to convince her not to dismiss him as a penniless critic. Fortunately, he managed to live up to Molly's expectations once he got past his first-date jitters. Two years and hundreds of movies later, they decided to marry and had enjoyed great happiness. Indeed, looking back at their lives together Molly felt that "loving Andrew had turned out to be one of the things I did best, and my idealization and romanticization of him was part of that love and part of my identity, feelings and an attitude I couldn't imagine myself without" (Haskell, 1990, p. 39). But on that winter night Molly wondered whether they would ever see another movie together again. She had rushed Andrew to the hospital the week before, and the doctors—despite all their diagnostic tests and procedures—still had no idea why he was so ill. She felt that life without Andrew might not be worth living.

The crew. The crew members of Eastern Airlines Flight 401 were looking forward to the end of the holiday flight from New York to Florida. Captain Bob Loft was on final approach to the Miami International Airport at about 11:30 at night when he noticed the indicator light on his landing gear monitor was out. Fearing that the gear for the nose of the plane was jammed, Loft pulled up from his descent and switched on the autopilot to keep the plane circling the airport at 2,000 feet.

Loft and his crewmates, First Officer Bert Stockstill and Second Officer Don Repo, went to work on the problem. Thinking the bulb was burned out, the pilots tried to replace it. Only Stockstill could reach the assembly that held the light and socket, and even after he removed it from the panel, the bulb remained jammed in the socket. The Captain then sent Repo into the bay beneath the flight deck to examine the gear and find out whether they were up or down. Meanwhile, as Loft and Stockstill continued to fuss with the light, one of them inadvertently deactivated the autopilot. As the plane dropped lower in the sky, a chime sounded a low-altitude warning, but the speaker was located near Repo's seat; the two pilots never heard the warning. Oblivious to the danger and flying over the featureless Everglades near midnight, the crew continued to work on the light until an air traffic controller noticed that they had descended to 900 feet. He radioed "Eastern, ah, four-oh-one. How are things coming along out there?" (Fuller, 1976, p. 59). Loft, deciding to land despite the unclear status of the gear, radioed back to say that Flight 401 was returning to the field for its landing. But by then it was too late. All three members of the cockpit crew, as well as 96 passengers and flight attendants, died when Flight 401 crashed in the Everglades on Friday, December 29, 1972, at 9½ seconds after 11:42 P.M.

Social-Psychological Processes

People testing the truth of a woman's claim of sexual harassment. Whites attacking African Americans, and African Americans fighting back. A young man deciding to join a radical religious group. A woman worrying about her beloved spouse. A group making a deadly error. These cases are typical of the billions of social encounters that occur routinely each day, but they are the kinds of situations that intrigue social psychologists. We do not live out our lives in isolation; rather we are enmeshed in a complex social world that continually influences us in many ways. What interests social psychologists when they examine these kinds of social situations? Where do they look for the social determinants of individuals' thinking, feeling, and acting?

Social perception and thought. Interaction between people, in many cases, becomes understandable only when we consider the psychological processes that occur within each individual in the situation. We are, after all, perceiving, judging, reasoning, and remembering animals, and all these mental processes influence our social behavior. Viewers watching Anita Hill's testimony did not weigh just her words; they also considered the way she was dressed, her facial expressions, and the tone of her voice before forming an overall impression. They also studied her actions and questioned her motives and honesty. Other cognitive factors, such as her vivid way of describing the harassment, viewers' general conceptions about the trustworthiness of men who are supervisors of women, and memories of other cases of harassment must also have influenced viewers' struggle to measure the truth behind Hill's charges.

Social psychologists assume that our reactions are determined not only by the situation, but by perceptual and cognitive processes that help us interpret the nature of the social situation. People are viewed as processors of information who constantly seek data about other people. We also seek out information about ourselves during interaction with others, and we use this information to revise or reinforce our understanding of ourselves. We aren't always careful to appraise ourselves or our situation—we can be irrational, emotional, and capricious. But even so, we do our best to process information rationally.

Attitudes and attraction. We are not just dispassionate perceivers. We are also biased evaluators whose attitudes constantly shape our reaction to the persons, places, and things that surround us. Why did Jerry decide to join in the activities of the Unification Church? Because he was a big believer in changing the world for the better, and the Church adopted that philosophy. He also liked Jan and wanted to find a way to spend more time with her. The angry white men thought of Wilson and Booker not as men but as *black* men. Their attitudes were racist, for they prejudged two strangers in a passing car simply because their skin was a different color than their own. Ardent attitudes also lie at the core of our strong friendships and love relationships. Molly initially disliked Andrew and Andrew's ways: the way he dressed, his conversational skill, his physical attractiveness, and his liking for movies. In time, however, she came to like him, and this attraction matured into a long-term, deeply intimate relationship. If we failed to take into account Molly's relationship with Andrew, we would overlook one of the most significant forces in her life.

Interpersonal relations and group processes. Like chemicals that can dramatically change the color and form of other substances, human beings are the catalysts for many reactions in other human beings. Therefore our analysis of such personal processes as social perception, cognition, and attitude formation must be complemented by the study of interpersonal processes that unfold between or among interacting individuals. We not only size up other people, like and dislike them, and fall in love with them: we also influence them, work side by side with them, hurt them, and help them. Truly most of our lives are spent with other people, and these other people influence us in a variety of ways. Jan wanted Jerry to join her group, and she used a variety of direct and indirect methods to achieve this goal. Very few of us are mindless conformists who do whatever we are told, but it can't be denied that in many social settings we find ourselves conforming to the wishes of others. We also spend much of our time in groups and organizations where we can pool our individual resources to achieve goals that would elude us if we were working alone. Yet, as the tragic case of the airline crew suggests, social forces can be so powerful that they lead to failure rather than success.

So our interpersonal relations are not always positive. The clash between the two pairs of men, one pair black and one pair white, is an example of the extreme conflict that sometimes occurs between groups. Aggression, too, is commonplace in many societies, and it has been linked to such psychological processes as frustrating events, intense emotional experiences, and opportunities to learn harmful actions by watching others. Fortunately, antisocial behaviors such as racism and aggression are often tempered by positive forms of social behavior. We help as well as hurt.

The social setting. Social encounters do not occur in empty, featureless settings, but in busy physical environments that contribute their own remarkable influence on those behaviors. The confrontation between the African American and white men took place near the bar where the whites worked. Because they were on their own turf, they may have felt that their actions were justified; in their minds, Wilson and Booker were interlopers. Similarly, picture Molly and Andrew's first date. Where did they sit when they entered the theater? Did their hands touch as they negotiated over territorial rights to the armrest between their two seats? Was the theater so crowded that they felt distracted and anxious? In the booth at Howard Johnson's, did they sit side by side or did Andrew sit across the table from Molly? People may not notice situational nuances like seating arrangements, interpersonal distances, and crowding, but these aspects of the interpersonal environment influence them nonetheless.

Social Psychology's Paradigm

What did Hill and Thomas, the Moonie, the racists, the wife, and the crew have in common? As we have seen, when viewed from a social-psychological perspective, these individuals were caught up in richly textured interpersonal encounters with a course and outcome shaped by their perceptions and cognitions, their attitudes, their relationships with one another, and by the social setting in which the encounters occurred. Social psychologists study a range of processes and phenomena, but underlying this diversity is a unifying focus on people interacting with each other. (See Table 1-1.)

The field, and its focus on the social side of the human experience, is not yet a century old (Berscheid, 1992). It emerged gradually during the 50-year period

▲ Social psychologists study how we are influenced by the people around us. If analyzing this particular group, they might first examine each member's social perceptions and thoughts: What do these people think of each other? What do they think of themselves? They might then consider the members' likes and dislikes, their attraction toward each other, and the way they work together as a team. They might even study the seating patterns of the group at the conference table and the group's tendency to split into smaller groups like those shown here.

▲ **TABLE 1-1**
Summing up: Social psychologists study a wide range of topics that include processes that occur within individuals, those that involve interacting individuals, and those that are influenced to a considerable extent by the social setting. We examine the more personal processes such as social perception and cognition before moving to more interpersonal topics such as group processes and the social environment.

Chapter	*Examples of Questions Examined*
1 Foundations	What is the nature of social psychology? What are the basic assumptions of the field? What methods are used by researchers to test their hypotheses about social behavior?
2 Impression formation and management	Can we form accurate judgments about others by noting the way they look, the way they walk, or the way they gesture? How do we control the impression we make on others? Are we accurate when it comes to judging other people's personalities and traits?
3 Social cognition	How do we organize and integrate all the information we have about another person? How do we make rapid decisions about people? What biases undermine the accuracy of our decisions?
4 Attribution	When someone sees us perform an action, will they assume that our action says something about our inner character? Do we search for the causes of our own behavior? Why do we blame our failures on the situation but take credit for our successes?
5 The self	What is the self? When are we most aware of who we are? How does the self develop, and how do we maintain our sense of self-worth when it is threatened by other people or by our own failures?
6 Attitudes and behavior	What is an attitude and how is it measured? Where do our attitudes come from? Why don't we always act in ways that are consistent with our attitudes and values? When actions and attitudes are inconsistent, do we change our actions to match our attitudes, or do we change our attitudes to match our actions?
7 Prejudice	Why do groups of people have so much difficulty getting along together? What social psychological factors lead to discrimination? What can be done to improve intergroup relationships?

from 1890 to 1940 as researchers from psychology, sociology, and related fields became increasingly interested in social processes. Indeed, the first two textbooks in the field, both titled *Social Psychology* and both published in 1908, surveyed different topics. One, written by a psychologist, focused primarily on instincts as the primary determinants of action (McDougall, 1908). The second, written by a sociologist, was an analysis of crowds and crazes (Ross, 1908).

The list of topics studied by researchers has grown considerably since 1908, but contemporary social psychology still reflects the two orientations espoused in those early texts. Over the years social psychologists became less interested in instincts, but they continued to search for psychological, *personal* processes that influence social behavior. In the 1920s and 1930s researchers recognized that our attitudes profoundly influence, and are profoundly influenced by, the social world. Considerable research effort was spent developing ways to measure and study attitudes, and eventually this purely intrapsychic process became a "primary building stone in the edifice of social psychology" (Allport, 1985, p. 37). During this same period researchers also expanded their studies beyond crowds and crazes to include many kinds of *interpersonal* processes, including interaction in small groups, leadership, and conflict.

▲ **TABLE 1-1**
(Continued)

Chapter	Examples of Questions Examined
8 Persuasion	When others disagree with you, what can you do to persuade them to take your viewpoint? When are persuasion messages effective? What can be done to help people resist persuasion?
9 Influence	Why do we sometimes go along with the group, even when we privately disagree with what the others are saying? When can a lone dissenter convince the group to change? What is social power and how is it used to influence people?
10 Group dynamics	Are individuals more productive when alone or in groups? Should important decisions be made by individuals or by groups? What is effective leadership?
11 Relationships	Why do we seek out others rather than remain alone? Are some people more social than others? Why do we like some people and dislike others? How do friendships develop between people? Is commitment a necessary condition for true love? Why do so many relationships fall apart?
12 Helping	Why are some people reluctant to help others during emergencies? Are humans biologically programmed to be helpful? How can we encourage positive forms of social behavior, such as charity, helping, and cooperation?
13 Aggression	Is aggression caused by biological urges or by social forces? Does violent television teach viewers to be aggressive? What can be done to decrease the violent nature of our society?
14 Social environment	Are human beings a territorial species? Does overcrowding lead to marked changes in social behavior? Can anything be done to increase people's willingness to protect the environment?

Some researchers restrict their investigations to the interpersonal realm by examining only naturally forming social groups or interaction among individuals (Carlson, 1984). Most social psychologists, however, believe that both personal and interpersonal processes must be considered when explaining behavior (Kenrick, 1986). Social psychologists, like sociologists, are interested in social values, cultures, and groups. They focus, however, on the individual in the social context rather than the social context per se. Social psychologists, like psychologists, are also interested in personal processes, including personality, perception, memory, and learning. They prefer, however, to focus on the way the social context and psychological processes influence each other.

interactionism
A general conceptual orientation that assumes each person's behavior is a function of his or her personal qualities, the nature of the situation, *and* the interaction of these personal qualities with factors present in the particular situation.

***B* = *f*(*P*, *E*)**
Lewin's formula for the concept of interactionism, which states behavior is a function of the person and the environment.

This perspective on social behavior is known as **interactionism** because it assumes that an individual's actions, thoughts, and feelings are produced by the combination of two sets of causes: personal factors within the individual and social factors operating in the situation. By 1936, Kurt Lewin, one of the major shapers of the field of social psychology, put this assumption into words: "Every psychological event depends upon the state of the person and at the same time on the environment" (1936, p. 12). He summarized this idea in the equation $B = f(P, E)$: Behavior is a function of the Person and the Environment.

The principle of interactionism pervades social psychology, for researchers continually strive to understand both the personal and the interpersonal factors that cause us to act the way we do. Studies of moral behavior provide an example. For many years researchers searched for the personality traits that determine who is moral and who is immoral. But their search proved futile, for they more frequently discovered that the situation was a powerful cause of moral actions. Children who did not cheat in school, for example, would lie to their friends on the playground (Hartshorne & May, 1928). But in time researchers recognized the limitations of theories that included only personality variables or situational variables, and they began to advocate an interactional view of morality (Haan, 1986; Kurtines, 1986; Waterman, 1988). People who hold themselves to a high moral standard when alone may be unable to act on these values when they become part of a group (McGraw & Bloomfield, 1987). People who believe "Lying is wrong" may lie nonetheless unless something in the situation reminds them to look to their personal values before they act (Forsyth & Nye, 1990). So when will people act morally rather than immorally? Interactionism argues that the answer depends on the joint impact of personal factors and situational factors (Bem & Allen, 1974; Kenrick et al., 1990; Mischel, 1984).

IN DEPTH

What Is the Value of Social Psychology?

When astrophysicists tell us that black holes occur when matter becomes so dense that light cannot escape its gravitational pull, we don't respond by saying, "Well, that's just common sense." Albert Einstein might have predicted the existence of black holes, but common sense never did. Yet when social psychologists report their findings, listeners often answer, "I already knew that." Social psychologists justify their research by arguing that their studies uncover new information about human social behavior, but some critics answer, "We already know the answers." Does social psychology's research tell us anything new?

Most people are already familiar with the topics that social psychologists study. In fact, through years of interaction with other people you have probably developed your own theories to explain how and why people act the way they do in various situations. It may already have occurred to you that attitudes influence behavior, that people who fail often deny responsibility for their performance, that men like women who play hard to get, and that people don't always work very hard when they are in groups. Unfortunately, these kinds of commonsense assumptions are limited in several ways. First, common sense may contain a kernel of truth, but it doesn't apply in all situations and to all people. Attitudes influence behavior only in certain limited ways, and in some instances it is the behavior that influences the attitude (Ross & Nisbett, 1991). Some individuals—such as teachers and high achievers—take more responsibility for their failures than for their successes (Miller & Ross, 1975). Playing hard to get works only under very specific conditions (Walster et al., 1973). People don't expend much effort when they feel anonymous in their group, but they work even harder when their efforts are identifiable (Harkins, 1987). Without social-psychological research, these limiting conditions can't be accurately specified.

Second, common sense often yields inconsistent conclusions. For example, if social psychologists report that people who fall in love tend to have similar characteristics, critics can answer, "Of course. Don't birds of a feather flock together?" If researchers find that lovers are often very different from one another, the same critics reply, "Of course. Don't opposites attract?" Indeed, the opposites of most commonsense maxims and proverbs seem as plausible as the originals. One investigator cleverly verified our faith in maxims and proverbs by asking people to evaluate the validity of a list of proverbs. Some of the proverbs were stated accurately, but others were the exact opposite of the original. "Love is stronger than fear" was rewritten as "Fear is stronger than love." "Wise men make proverbs and fools repeat them" became "Fools make proverbs and wise men repeat them." No matter which versions people read, they rated them as valid (Teigen, 1986).

Third, common sense may lead us to accept ideas that are erroneous. Common sense tells us the following:

- People feel better when they can blame negative outcomes on factors beyond their control.
- Brainstorming is one of the best methods for making informed group decisions.

A detailed understanding of social psychology's paradigm can be developed only over a long period of study. We were introduced to elements as we examined the content of the field: we saw that social psychologists are intrigued by how people interact with each other. The effort to understand these encounters leads them to study the interaction of personal factors and interpersonal factors. The insights gained by these studies often have implications for solving important problems and for refining our personal understanding of our own and others' behaviors (see "In Depth: What Is the Value of Social Psychology?").

Do not, however, overlook the second aspect of social psychology's paradigm, its methods. We tend to think first of a science's contents—the facts, findings, and theories assembled by investigators—but the methods used by scientists when they carry out their research are equally important. To understand social psychology's paradigm, we must consider not only the content and assumptions of social psychologists, but also the methods that researchers use to investigate these topics. We turn to these issues in the next two sections.

- In an emergency, the more bystanders who are present, the more likely you are to be helped.
- The average American citizen would refuse to obey an authority who asked him or her to harm an innocent person.
- The most important determinant of behavior is personality.

Yet research indicates that these statements are less then accurate. Even the most obvious truths must be scientifically tested. (See respectively, Thompson, 1981; Bouchard, Drauden, & Barsaloux, 1974; Latané & Darley, 1970; Milgram, 1974; Mischel, 1984).

Fourth, common sense doesn't explain *why* things happen. The platitude "Absence makes the heart grow fonder" may be generally accurate: When we are separated from the ones we love we may grow to love them more. Why does this deepening of affection occur? How does this tendency relate to other processes that strengthen or weaken our relationships? Social psychologists go beyond clichés. They develop integrating explanations that identify the social processes that produce the observed effects. Common sense offers us platitudes; social psychology offers us comprehensive theories.

So why are we so confident in the validity of common sense? Researchers have found that we rarely notice when our commonsense ideas are inaccurate because they are protected by the **hindsight bias:** our tendency to react to new information by saying, "I knew it all along." After the pitcher walks another batter we exclaim, "Why did the coach let him pitch to another batter? I knew he was tired!" When we hear about a couple getting divorced, we think, "That's too bad, but you could see it coming a mile away." Looking back at historical events, we can't understand how people could have made such poor decisions, or why events were not easily anticipated. Our revision of our predictions once the event occurs illustrates this process. When voters predicted the outcome of the 1980 presidential election prior to the election, the average person predicted Ronald Reagan would win 44.3% of the popular vote. But Ronald Reagan won with 51% of the vote. So, after the election, when people were asked to recall their original predictions, most added a few points to more closely approximate the actual outcome. The average post-election estimate was nearly 47%. Thus, hindsight is 20-20: After the fact it's perfectly clear that communism would fail in the Soviet Union and that Iraq could not win the Persian Gulf conflict. In fact, now that you know about hindsight bias, you can say to yourself, "That's just common sense; I knew that all along" (Leary, 1982a; Wasserman, Lempert, & Hastie, 1991).

Common sense is often useful and accurate. It organizes our knowledge of people and helps us in our day-to-day lives (Fletcher, 1984). But we need research to test and refine our understanding of people. Through research we can identify conditions under which common sense is accurate, identify which one of several conflicting beliefs is most accurate, and discard mistaken beliefs that have been too long protected by hindsight bias.

hindsight bias: The tendency for people to think that they knew the correct answer or could predict some event once they are told the correct answer or they witness the event; sometimes termed the *I-knew-it-all-along phenomenon.*

▲ The commonsense saying "Opposites attract" explains why Lyle Lovett and Julia Roberts fell in love, but what about the equally popular saying "Birds of a feather flock together"? Social psychology, rather than relying on folklore and common sense, tries to explain social phenomena (including the unlikeliest of lovers) by developing comprehensive explanations for all forms of social behavior and then testing these explanations through research.

▲▲▲▲▲▲▲▲▲▲▲▲▲▲

Research Methods in Social Psychology

Russell T. Johnson of Temple City, California, offers a clever test of friendship: "If you want to discover your true friends, ask them to help you move" (Parker, 1990, p. 154). The philosopher Friedrich Nietzsche wrote that "whoever despises himself still esteems the despiser within him." David Lyon, a writer and advertising authority, believes that "in any group, the person doing the least talking is the one with the most power" (Parker, 1990, p. 232). Author Mark Twain wrote that "we are discreet sheep; we wait to see how the drove is going, and then go with the drove" (Seldes, 1960, p. 698). And Jimmy, who is in Mrs. Cohen's fourth grade class in Placerville, California, warns, "Never trust a woman who smiles at you" (Parker, 1990, p. 156).

Most of us are intuitive social psychologists; we carry around theories and beliefs about why people do the things they do in social settings. These beliefs often reveal our remarkable insight into human affairs, but they are limited in one important way: they have not been tested systematically. Even though we think we understand people, we don't develop objective indexes for measuring social processes, search for continuities in people's reactions across various social settings, or set up test situations that will definitively validate or cast doubt on our hunches. It may well be true that people who talk the least in groups are very powerful, that we often conform to the group's opinion, or that women who smile are untrustworthy, but without research we cannot be certain.

Doing research in social psychology, as in any science, requires two interrelated activities: measuring and testing. First, we must develop ways to quantify the social processes and phenomena that interest us. If we are studying such things as friendship, self-esteem, or conformity, we will require an objective index of these processes. Second, we must develop a way to test our assumptions, ideas, and hypotheses about these processes. If, as Twain proposed, people follow the herd, then we must test this prediction by studying how people react when a group disagrees with their opinions. Similarly, if we think that people who are powerful talk the least during meetings, then we might want to set up a test situation where the vocality of people who are given more power than others can be assessed. We examine both of these aspects of research—measuring and testing—in this section.

Measuring Social Phenomena

What happens when materials such as wood or coal burn? Chemists in the 18th century, after puzzling over this question, offered an explanation: An invisible substance, called *phlogiston*, is present in all burnable materials. When these materials are heated, the phlogiston escapes and generates heat and light. This hypothesis, although interesting, proved difficult to test due to one major problem. The key element in the theory, phlogiston, could never be isolated and measured.

Social psychologists deal with a variety of phlogiston-like phenomena, including social perception and cognition, attitudes, attraction, and social influence. Unlike the early chemists, however, researchers in social psychology document these phenomena through careful, objective measurement. In most cases, social psychological terms and processes have both a theoretical definition and an **operational definition**. The theoretical definition gives a conceptual description of the term. Conformity, for example, is "a change in beliefs and/or behaviors brought about through social influence." The operational definition, in contrast, specifies the measurement operations that are used to quantify the concept. Conformity, operationally defined, is changing one's vote from no to yes when the rest of the group votes yes on the question "Is sexual harassment a major problem in contemporary society?" Here we consider several ways that researchers operationally define their concepts by using self-report, behavioral, physiological, and nonreactive measurement methods.

operational definition
The specific measurement operations a researcher uses to quantify a theoretical concept.

Self-report measures. Researchers are often interested in subjects' own views of their personal thoughts, feelings, and actions. These **self-report measures**, despite their variations, are all based on a simple premise: If you want to know what someone is thinking, feeling, or planning, then just ask him or her to report that information to you directly. *Opinion polls* often ask respondents to state their political beliefs or describe their stance on contemporary social issues. During *interviews* the researcher records the respondent's answers to various questions, but *questionnaires* ask respondents to record their answers themselves. *Tests, inventories*, and *scales* are similar to questionnaires, but they are usually more extensive and detailed. Self-esteem may be too complicated to assess by just asking "Do you hold yourself in high esteem?" By including many items researchers can also be more confident that the wording of the items isn't biasing their results. When the items are selected and pretested for accuracy, the measure is usually termed a test or a scale. The *Rosenberg Self-Esteem Scale*, which is shown in Table 1-2, is an example of a multiple-item index of self-worth (Morris Rosenberg, 1965).

self-report measures
Assessment procedures, such as questionnaires, tests, or interviews, in which respondents are asked to describe their feelings, attitudes, or beliefs.

Behavioral measures. Social anthropologist Erving Goffman tells of a visitor to the Shetland Islands dining with a local family. When the well-mannered visitor politely compliments his hostess on her fine soup, she nods in appreciation. But because he eats the soup very slowly and with great deliberation, the hostess decides that her guest really didn't like the soup at all (Goffman, 1959).

Behaviors sometimes provide more information than words alone, so researchers often prefer to record the actions undertaken by people in social

▲ **TABLE 1-2**
The Rosenberg Self-Esteem Scale. This scale measures general feelings of self-worth. Half of the items (1, 2, 6, 8, and 10) are positively worded; agreeing with these items indicates *higher* self-esteem. The remaining items (3, 4, 5, 7, and 9) are negatively worded; agreeing with these items indicates *lower* self-esteem. The items must be recoded before summing by reversing their values (for example, 1 is rescored as 4, 2 is rescored as 3, and so on). Scores can thus range from 10 to 40, with higher scores indicating higher self-esteem.

Please indicate your degree of agreement with each of the following statements where:

4 = Strongly agree
3 = Agree
2 = Disagree
1 = Strongly disagree

____ 1. I feel that I'm a person of worth, at least on an equal plane with others.
____ 2. On the whole, I am satisfied with myself.
____ 3. I wish I could have more respect for myself.
____ 4. I certainly feel useless at times.
____ 5. At times I think I am no good at all.
____ 6. I feel that I have a number of good qualities.
____ 7. All in all, I am inclined to feel that I am a failure.
____ 8. I am able to do things as well as most other people.
____ 9. I feel that I do not have much to be proud of.
____ 10. I take a positive attitude toward myself.

Source: From Morris Rosenberg, 1965.

observation
Any measurement method that involves watching and recording another individual's actions; "sustained, explicit, methodical observing and paraphrasing of social situations" (Weick, 1985).

settings. **Observation** requires watching and recording social behavior with subjects' knowledge (overt observation), from a hidden vantage point (covert observation), or as a member of the interaction itself (participant observation). When researchers count the number of times a person smiles when interviewing a job candidate (Deutsch, 1990), watch pedestrians jaywalking on a city street (Mullen, Copper, & Driskell, 1990), or pretend to be trainees in order to discover the influence tactics taught to door-to-door salespeople (Cialdini, 1993), they are using observational methods.

Structured observation is a specialized form of observation; it guides observers' perceptions by identifying classes of target behaviors that are of particular interest to the researcher (Weick, 1985). A recent study of boy-meets-girl encounters nicely illustrates this procedure. College-student subjects waiting for an experimenter were secretly videotaped. These encounters were then analyzed in detail, with researchers coding such behaviors as body orientation, gaze, mutual gaze, hand gestures, smiles, laughter, and amount of time spent talking. The researchers discovered that these behaviors varied systematically depending on how shy the men were and how attractive the women were. Shy men were quieter and more likely to avoid eye contact; attractive women talked more, for longer periods of time, and made more eye contact with their partners. Note, too, that the researchers protected the privacy of the subjects by offering to erase the videotape before it was studied or reviewed in any way (Garcia et al., 1991).

reaction time
The amount of time it takes a person to respond to a stimulus; an indirect indicator of cognitive processing speed and structure.

Behaviors can also be measured through the use of mechanical recording devices, such as response counters, timers, and computers. Researchers assess aggression by arranging for pairs of subjects to give each other mild electric shocks (Baron, 1972) and productivity by counting the number of nonredundant ideas generated by brainstorming groups (Diehl & Stroebe, 1991). Social psychologists also use computers in their research when they need to precisely measure **reaction time**: the amount of time it takes a person to respond to stimulus information under controlled conditions. Reaction time is an indirect way to discover how people process information. If people take longer to respond to a question, we can assume that their memory had to work harder to locate the answer.

Physiological measures. We are not robots. Changes in our overt actions are matched by changes at the physiological level. When we see other people in distress and feel sympathy for them in their plight, our heart rates slow and blood pressure drops (Eisenberg et al., 1989). When we compete with others, our muscles relax and contract in distinctive ways, our body temperature and heart rate increase, and we tend to sweat more (Blascovich, Nash, & Ginsburg, 1978; Lanzetta & Englis, 1989; Van Egeren, 1979). When we find ourselves in stressful situations, our blood pressure and heart rate increase (Contrada, 1989), and merely watching videotaped scenes of violence and aggression are enough to trigger changes in heart rate (Bushman & Geen, 1990). **Social-psychophysiological measures** identify physiological correlates of social behavior, including the neurological, muscular, and respiratory systems that operate as we deal with other people.

social-psychophysiological measures
Assessment procedures, such as blood pressure and heart-rate recordings, that index an individual's physiological response to a social stimulus.

Physiological systems can be difficult to measure for technical reasons, but many social psychophysiologists feel that the results justify the effort (Blascovich & Kelsey, 1990). Physiological changes can, for instance, be important *outcomes* of social processes; when we are fearful, heart rate increases, and when we are relaxed, it slows. Physiological changes can also be *markers* for hard-to-detect phenomena; by measuring the muscle activity of the face using an electromyograph (EMG), we can tell when a person experiences anger or happiness (Cacioppo et al., 1988; Cacioppo & Tassinary, 1990). Social-psychophysiological measures are particularly useful when subjects' self-reports or overt actions might be distorted by social pressures. In studies of prejudice, respondents often deny that they are biased against other races of people. Yet, when their physiological responses are assessed, they show telltale signs of arousal and distress when touched by a member of another racial group (Rankin & Campbell, 1955).

Nonreactive measures. Researchers also use measures that have little or no impact on the participants in the research. Such measures are so unobtrusive that they are hidden in the background of social settings. These **nonreactive measures** are most useful when subjects may act strangely if they are aware that their behavior is being investigated. Researchers have assessed compliance with a local law prohibiting the consumption of alcoholic beverages by sifting through residents' garbage cans (Webb et al., 1981) and obedience to signs prohibiting graffiti by counting the number of messages scrawled on the signs themselves (Pennebaker & Sanders, 1976; Sechrest & Belew, 1983).

nonreactive measures
Research techniques that cause little or no disruption of people's ongoing social behaviors; these methods often minimize subjects' awareness that they are being studied.

Archival analysis is a special type of nonreactive measure that takes advantage of existing records. Often these records are in public archives—the reports and statistics that are routinely collected by government agencies. Other sources of archival data include old newspapers, personal documents, and the public speeches of politicians. In an application of this method to social psychology, researchers compared the number of times two theoretically important works—Leon Festinger's 1957 book, *A Theory of Cognitive Dissonance*, and Fritz Heider's 1958 book, *The Psychology of Interpersonal Relations*—were cited by other social psychologists in scientific articles published from 1958 to 1988. They discovered that, while references to Festinger's book have dwindled in the last 15 years, references to Heider's book on attribution and

▲ **FIGURE 1-1**
Who is the more influential social psychologist: Leon Festinger or Fritz Heider? Researchers routinely give credit to past theorists and researchers when they publish their work, so these citations are an unobtrusive indicator of which theories are being discussed and which are not. The figure shows the average number of references to Festinger (1957) and Heider (1958) from 1958 to 1987. It suggests that Heider's book on social perception is currently being referenced more than Festinger's book on attitudes. (From Bagby, Parker, & Bury, 1990)

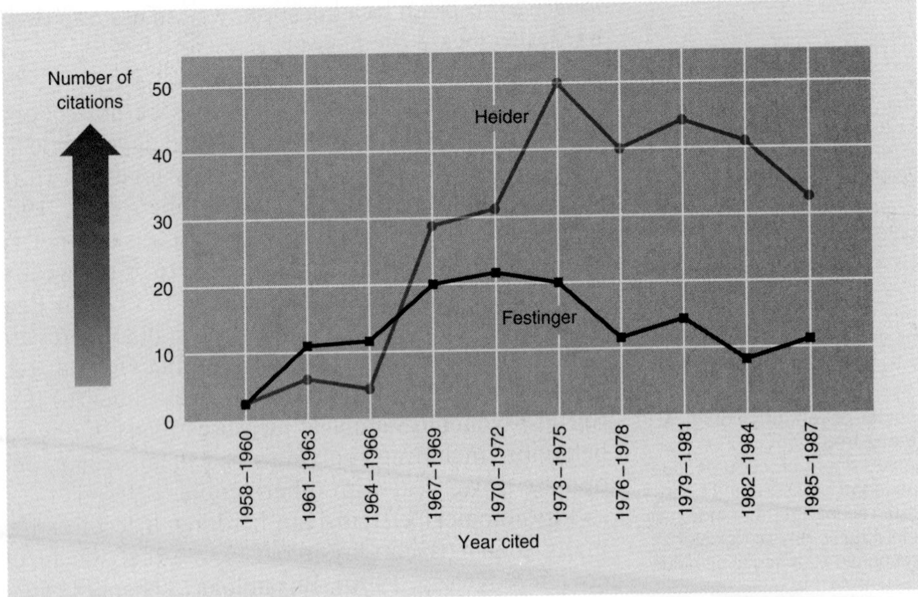

social cognition have remained numerous and constant. Figure 1-1 summarizes their findings (Bagby, Parker, & Bury, 1990).

Evaluating measurement methods. When social psychology was a fledgling discipline, many believed that it would never become a science because social processes such as impression formation, attitudes, love, conformity, and group behavior couldn't be measured. Over the years, however, researchers proved the pessimists wrong by developing the self-report, behavioral, physiological, and nonreactive measurement techniques listed in Table 1-3.

How can we evaluate the adequacy of these various methods? No matter which approach is used, it must have two basic qualities: reliability and validity. **Reliability** describes the consistency of the measure across time and across its components. If the self-esteem questionnaire (see Table 1-2) you take today indicates that you have high self-esteem, when you retake the test next week it should again indicate that your self-esteem is high (provided you experience no tumultuous insult to your self-esteem during the week). Also, your answers across the 10 questions should be relatively consistent; if you have high self-esteem you should agree with most of the positively worded items (such as items 1 and 2) and disagree with most of the negatively worded items (such as items 3 and 4).

reliability
The degree to which a measurement technique consistently yields the same conclusion at different times; also, if a measurement technique includes two or more components, reliability is the degree to which the components all yield similar conclusions.

Validity, in contrast, describes the extent to which the technique measures what it is supposed to measure. To be valid, the Rosenberg Self-Esteem Scale must measure the respondent's feelings of self-worth. If subjects routinely misrepresent their thoughts, feelings, and intentions, or they simply have difficulty describing them, the measure will not be valid. Validity can also be undermined by the **social desirability bias**, the tendency to answer questions in a socially acceptable way. If respondents think that feeling a lack of self-worth is an embarrassing personal flaw, they might claim they feel better about themselves than they actually do.

validity
The degree to which an assessment technique measures what it was designed to measure.

social desirability bias
The tendency to respond in socially appropriate ways to avoid appearing odd, foolish, or unattractive.

No index of social processes is perfect. Self-report methods are well suited for studies of personal processes, such as thoughts, feelings, or attitudes. Unfortunately, these methods assume that people are aware of their intrapersonal processes and are willing to report them. If people can't gauge their personal

▲ No single technique is best for measuring social-psychological phenomena. Some researchers rely on self-report methods, including questionnaires and face-to-face interviews and polls. Others choose to measure behaviors, often by watching people in naturalistic settings or in the laboratory through one-way mirrors. Still others examine physiological processes that serve as markers of social-psychological phenomena.

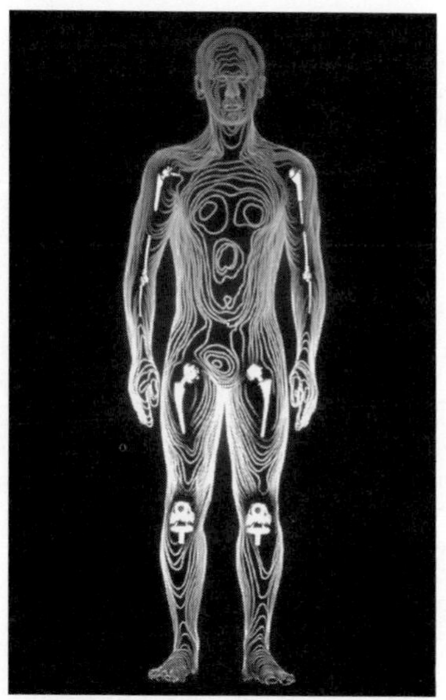

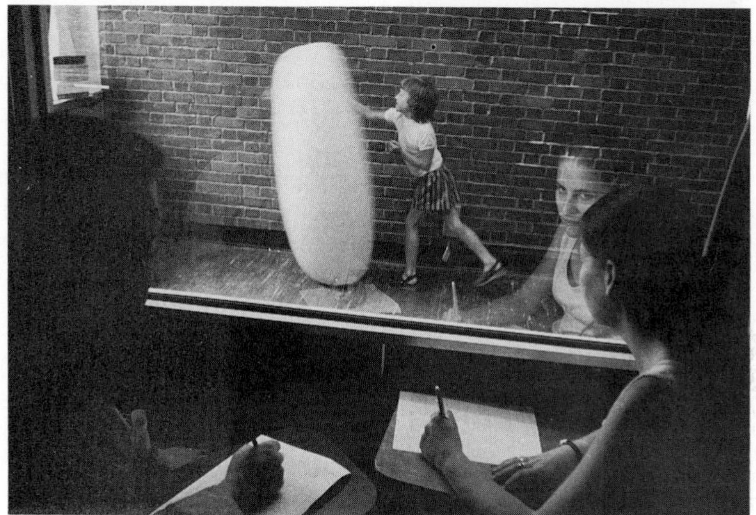

responses, or if they don't want to admit them, researchers may want to turn to the study of behavioral processes. Observational techniques are excellent tools for studying human interaction, but if observers' attitudes and motivations influence their observations, the results may be biased. In this case, structured observations carried out by uninvolved, highly trained observers yield more objective information. Furthermore, when direct measures make subjects feel self-conscious, physiological and nonreactive measures may be the most appropriate approaches.

Testing Hypotheses about Social Phenomena

Imagine that one day you go to a movie theater and see a violent action-adventure movie. When you leave, another moviegoer pushes his way out of the crowded theater with more haste and rudeness than appropriate. Just as he elbows his way out the door, one of his victims shoves him in the back. The two begin fighting, and the battle expands as several other spectators begin

▲ **TABLE 1-3**
Summing up: Types of measurement methods that social psychologists use

Method	*Example*
Self-report	Attitude surveys; opinion polls; rating one's own emotional state on a questionnaire; describing a personal experience to an interviewer.
Behavioral	Number of shocks administered; choice when offered one of two toys; running a stop sign; ratings of the leader's dominance; the number of head nods and eye blinks that occur during a videotaped interaction.
Physiological	Heart rate and blood pressure during social interaction; changes in size of pupils; small movements of facial muscles recorded by surface electrodes.
Nonreactive	Number of times a book has been checked out (index of popularity); energy consumption before and after seeing a TV program on ecology; number of students who wear clothing bearing their university's emblem (index of school pride).

shoving each other. Puzzled by the men's violence, you wonder whether the movie's aggressive tone set the stage for the outbreak.

If you wanted to study the relationship between movie violence and the viewer's aggressiveness, you would face many decisions. You would first need a way to measure aggression precisely, using self-report, behavioral, physiological, or nonreactive measures. Next, armed with sound measurement methods, you would need to test your hypothesis using rigorous scientific procedures.

Hypotheses can be tested in a variety of ways. Consider these two hypothetical studies. In Study A you bring people into the laboratory every day for a week. Some subjects are shown violent movies: *Terminator, Lethal Weapon, RoboCop*, and the like. The others watch relatively nonviolent movies such as *Fantasia, The Muppet Movie*, and *The Little Mermaid*. After one week, you measure aggressiveness by asking the subjects to give electric shocks to a stranger. In Study B you send questionnaires to 1,000 people living in Tulsa, Oklahoma. The questionnaire asks them to record all the movies they viewed during the preceding 2 months. It also includes a number of questions about violent behavior, such as "Have you, in the last 2 months, punched, slapped, or kicked someone else?"

These two studies differ in several ways. One is a laboratory study and the other is a field study. One records aggression behaviorally; the other relies on self-report measurements. More importantly, the two studies are based on different research designs. Both studies examine the same question: What is the relationship between watching violence and the viewer's aggressiveness? In the first study you examine this relationship *experimentally* by manipulating aspects of the situation and then measuring the impact of these manipulations. In the other, you examine the naturally occurring *correlation* between violence and aggression, but you don't manipulate the situation. This difference between the studies has very important implications.

Experimental designs. Why are people aggressive? Albert Bandura, Dorothea Ross, and Sheila Ross hypothesized that seeing someone else perform a violent act increases the likelihood that the viewer will subsequently act aggressively. To test this hypothesis, they set up conditions in their laboratory that would allow them to expose some children to an adult who modeled aggressive behavior, and then record whether or not the children mimicked the actions they had just witnessed. The subjects were 96 young boys and girls;

each one was randomly assigned to one of four different conditions. Children in the *control condition* were simply left alone at a table to play with crayons, stickers, and colored paper. Children in the *real-life aggression condition* watched a man or woman go through an elaborately rehearsed and standardized sequence of aggressive play with a plastic clown, the Bobo doll. Bandura and his colleagues (1963a) described the sequence as follows:

> The model sat on the Bobo doll and punched it repeatedly in the nose. The model then raised the Bobo doll and pommeled it on the head with a mallet. Following the mallet aggression, the model tossed the doll up in the air aggressively and kicked it about the room. This sequence of physically aggressive acts was repeated approximately three times, interspersed with verbally aggressive responses such as, "Sock him in the nose . . . ," "Hit him down . . . ," "Throw him in the air . . . ," "Kick him . . . ," and "Pow." (pp. 4–5)

Children assigned to the *film-aggression condition* were exposed to the same adult models who performed the same aggressive behaviors, but in this case the actions were part of a movie shown on a screen approximately 6 feet from the subjects' play table. Finally, children in the *cartoon-aggression condition* watched a simulated television cartoon of Herman the Cat attacking the Bobo doll with the same sequence of punching, kicking, and hammering.

Did these experiences increase the children's level of aggressiveness? To answer this question, observers watched the children as they played in a test room and recorded such behaviors as striking a Bobo doll with the mallet, sitting on the doll and punching it in the nose, striking other objects with the mallet, verbally attacking the Bobo doll ("Shoot the Bobo," "Stupid Bobo"), and aggressive gun play. As Figure 1-2 indicates, the subjects in all three experimental groups displayed significantly more aggressive activity than the subjects in the control condition. In fact, many of the children perfectly mimicked the exact behaviors they had seen earlier, including sitting on, hitting, and insulting the Bobo doll. Overall, boys were more aggressive than girls, and subjects who were exposed to a male modeling aggression were more violent than subjects who were exposed to a female model (Bandura, Ross, & Ross, 1963a).

experiment
A research design in which the investigator manipulates at least one variable by randomly assigning participants to two or more different conditions.

independent variable
The aspect of the situation manipulated by the researcher in an experimental study; the causal variable in a cause-effect relationship.

This study illustrates the three key qualities necessary for an **experiment**. First, Bandura and his colleagues identified the variable they believed *caused* changes in obedience. Any aspect of the situation that fluctuates can be considered a *variable*; when the variable is manipulated by the researcher it is called an **independent variable**. When researchers manipulate a variable, they literally change its value by creating different situations or conditions. In Bandura's study the independent variable was exposure to aggressive behavior. He deliberately fixed the value of this variable at four different levels by creating four conditions: control, real-life aggression, film aggression, and cartoon aggres-

Reprinted with special permission of King Features Syndicate.

▲ A hypothesis only begins the scientific process. Anyone can state a hypothesis, but it takes carefully designed research to test its validity.

▲ **FIGURE 1-2**
Are children who witness aggressive behavior more likely to become aggressive themselves? Bandura, Ross, and Ross (1963a) studied aggression experimentally: they manipulated exposure to aggressive behavior (the independent variable), controlled other variables, and then measured aggression (the dependent variable). Their results indicate that children in the three experimental conditions performed more aggressively than children in the control condition. (Based on Bandura, Ross, & Ross, 1963a)

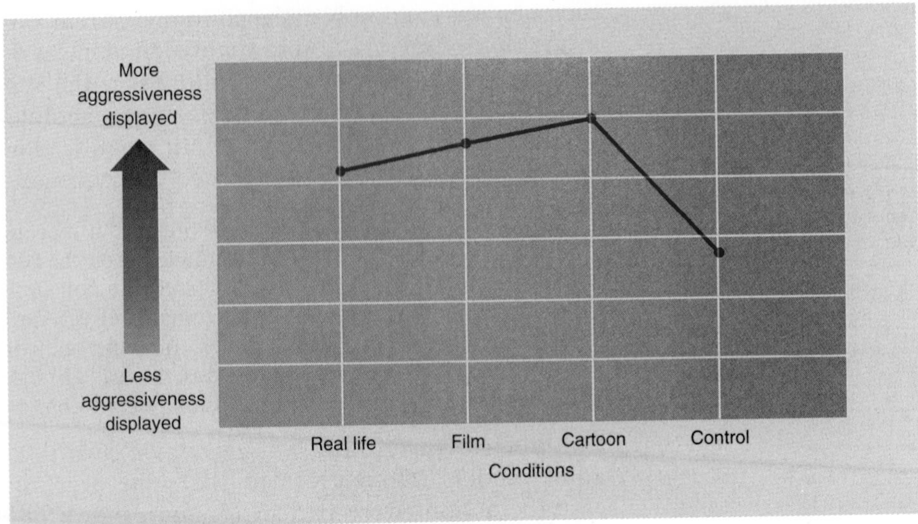

sion. Bandura chose to study a single independent variable; some experiments include several independent variables.

Second, all experiments necessarily include one or more variables that are measured rather than manipulated. The investigator wants to know the impact of the independent variable on one or more other variables. These variables are termed **dependent variables** because their magnitude depends on the strength and nature of the independent variable. In Bandura's study the dependent variable was violent play behavior, which he measured through observation. The independent variable is the hypothesized *cause*, and the dependent variable is the *effect*. Bandura wanted to know whether changes in exposure to violence caused changes in aggression.

dependent variable
The responses of the subject measured by the researcher; the effect variable in a cause-effect relationship.

Last, Bandura maintained strict *experimenter control* over any other variable that could have caused aggression. Bandura was most interested in the impact of exposure to violence on aggression, but other factors also make people more or less aggressive. If any of these factors had a stronger influence

▲ Scenes from Bandura's Bobo doll experiment. Bandura exposed some children to an aggressive model who played violently with an inflated "Bobo the clown" doll. He then left the children in a room with crayons, stickers, and the Bobo doll. The children who had been exposed to an aggressive model mimicked the model by kicking, hammering, punching, and throwing the Bobo doll.

▲ **FIGURE 1-3**
Why is the random assignment of subjects to conditions crucial in an experimental study? Researchers use randomization to control for extraneous differences among their subjects when the experiment begins. Experimenters realize each person is unique, but unique qualities shouldn't influence research results if they distribute all types of subjects evenly across both conditions.

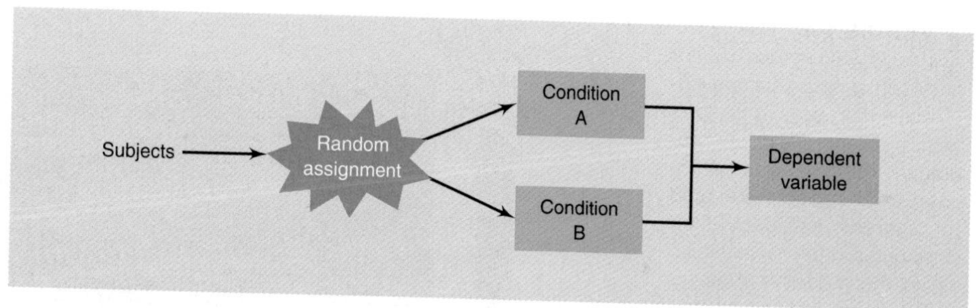

in one condition rather than another, they could have influenced aggression, too. So Bandura tried to keep all variables constant except the independent variable, which he manipulated. All subjects reported to the same room and were greeted by the same experimenter. They all were seated at the same table, and those in the experimental conditions watched identical sequences of violent actions. If he had not controlled the situation, he could not have been certain that the changes in aggression he observed were produced by the independent variable or by some other factor.

Bandura also realized that, before coming in for the study, the children differed markedly in overall aggressiveness. Some preferred to play quietly; others were more energetic and prone to quarreling with other children. Bandura couldn't eliminate these differences—he couldn't study just those children who were identical in their temperament, intelligence, ability, and so on. But he could control the impact of these differences by assigning subjects to the four conditions randomly. Instead of running the first 10 people in the control condition, the next 10 in the real-life condition, and so on, Bandura may have rolled a die to determine which one of the four situations each subject would face. This **random assignment** of subjects to conditions guarantees that differences between conditions are due to differences in the manipulated independent variable rather than to unrecognized, preexisting variations among subjects (see Figure 1-3).

random assignment
A research technique used in experiments that involves placing people in different conditions at random.

Did Bandura's manipulations influence the subjects' aggressiveness? The results graphed in Figure 1-2 suggest they did, for subjects in three experimental groups had higher scores on the dependent variable. Is this difference *significant*, statistically speaking? To find out, Bandura conducted statistical analyses that compared each condition to each other condition. These analyses took into account both the overall differences between subjects in the four conditions, but also the differences among subjects within each condition. These analyses led him to conclude, with 95% certainty, that the groups were different.

Experimental designs, then, allow researchers to probe into causal relationships—to answer questions about the factors that cause us to behave as we do. Many studies carried out by researchers are not experiments. In some cases experimental studies aren't possible; if the researcher can't structure and control the situation, an experiment will not yield meaningful findings. Also, many important questions don't require an answer that identifies causes; knowing that certain variables are systematically linked to aggression—such as childhood experiences, hormonal influences, the temperature, and cultural background—may be sufficient to extend a particular theoretical viewpoint. Consequently, social psychologists also use nonexperimental methods in their research.

nonexperimental design
A research technique that involves systematically measuring two or more variables and then examining the relationships among these variables.

Nonexperimental designs. Many different methods are categorized as **nonexperimental designs**, but all are similar in that researchers *don't* manipulate an independent variable. Instead, they systematically measure

▲ **FIGURE 1-4**
Are boys who watch violent television programs more aggressive than boys who don't watch violent television programs? The boys who participated in the project were rated for aggressiveness by their classmates. Interviewers also asked the children's mothers and fathers to name their sons' favorite programs. Boys whose favorite programs were violent were rated as more aggressive by their classmates. (Adapted from Eron, 1963)

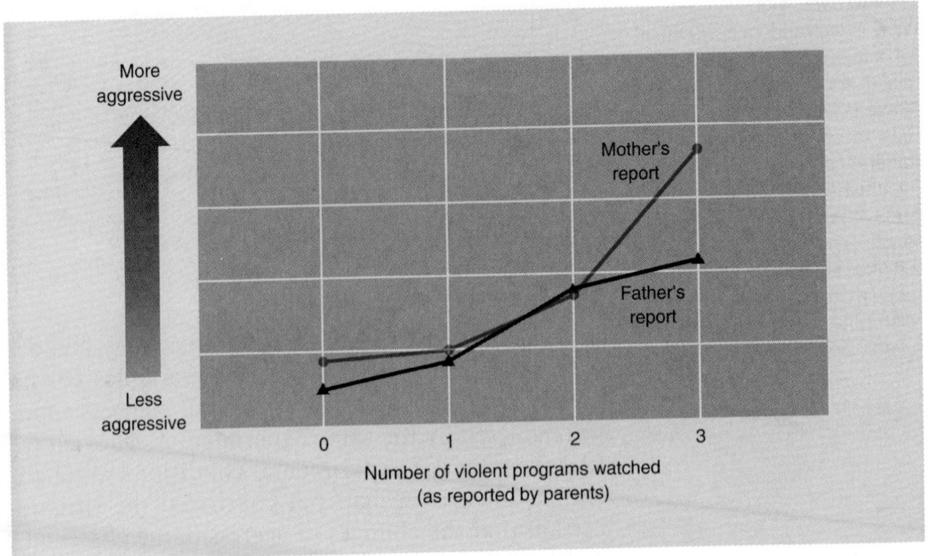

all variables of interest and examine the relationship among the measures statistically.

Leonard D. Eron (1963) was convinced that violent television programs influence young viewers, pushing them to become more violent in their own lives. He tested this hypothesis in a study of 644 boys and 567 girls attending the third grade in a school system in a semirural area of New York. First, he had the children describe one another's aggressiveness using a checklist of negative behaviors such as teasing and hitting other children. Second, he interviewed each child's parents, asking them to estimate the number of hours their son or daughter watched television per week, and asking the names of the child's three favorite programs. He then totaled up the number of favorite programs that included antisocial aggression.

Eron found evidence of a small but significant relationship between acting aggressively and watching violent television programs for boys but not for girls (Figure 1-4 presents the results for boys). Boys whose TV favorites included zero or one violent program had the lowest aggression scores, those with two violent favorites had higher scores, and those with three violent favorites had the highest scores.

This study relies on a nonexperimental design. Eron did not manipulate TV viewing or exposure to violence. Subjects themselves chose the programs they watched, and their classmates rated their naturally occurring levels of aggressiveness. Such studies are also referred to as **correlational studies** because the relationship between variables is often summarized with a **correlation coefficient** (symbolized by *r*). This statistic measures the strength and direction of the relationship between two variables. As Figure 1-5 indicates, correlations can vary in magnitude from −1.0 to +0.0 to +1.0. A correlation of zero means that the variables being measured showed no pattern of relationship with each other. Suppose Eron compared the kinds of TV programs boys watched to their aggressiveness and found that the correlation between these variables was zero. In this case, knowing a boy's favorite TV programs would tell us nothing about how aggressive he would be. Suppose, however, that the correlation turned out to be +1.0—a perfect positive correlation. This finding would mean that, without exception, the more violent programs

correlational study
A nonexperimental study that uses statistical procedures to examine the nature of the relationship between variables of interest.

correlation coefficient
A statistic that measures the strength and direction of a relationship between two variables; often symbolized by *r*, correlations can range from −1.0 to +1.0.

▲ **FIGURE 1-5**
What is a correlation? Correlations summarize the degree of relationship between two variables. A correlation (or *r*) near 0.0 indicates that the two variables are not closely related. As the value of *r* approaches either −1.0 or +1.0, the statistic indicates that the variables are closely linked.

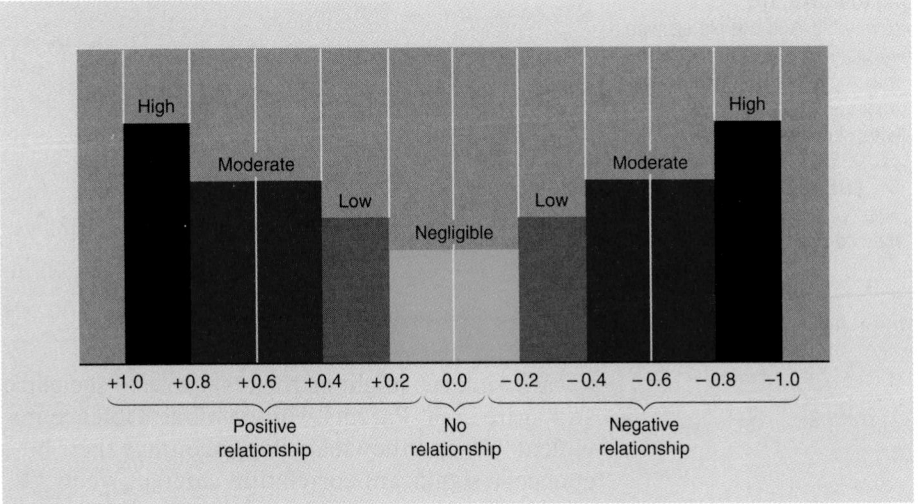

a boy watched, the more aggressive he would be in class. Finally, suppose the correlation was −1.0. In this case, watching violent TV would be negatively, or inversely, correlated with aggressiveness: As the boy watched more violent TV, his level of aggressiveness would decrease. The sign of the correlation (plus or minus) tells us whether this relationship is positive (direct) or negative (inverse). If the correlation is positive, then both variables increase and decrease together. If, however, the correlation is negative, then increases in one variable are associated with decreases in the second variable.

Between these extremes of +1.0 and −1.0 are the intermediate values investigators commonly find. In fact, Eron found that the number of violent TV programs watched and aggressiveness correlated at +.21. As Figure 1-5 indicates, this correlation shows that the two variables are only slightly related to one another. If, in contrast, the correlation had been closer to +1.0, this correlation would indicate that TV violence and aggression are more closely related to one another. In general, the greater the magnitude of the correlation (the farther it is from zero in either a positive or negative direction), the stronger the relationship between the variables. Researchers can also use statistical tests to determine whether the correlations are far enough away from zero to be significant. Eron found that even though the correlation between violent TV and aggression was only +.21, this relationship was not a chance occurrence.

A correlation is a handy way of summarizing the strength and direction of the relationship between two variables. But don't be misled into thinking that correlations demonstrate causality. Consider Eron's finding that the amount of violence in a boy's favorite TV programs correlates with his own aggressiveness. It is tempting to conclude that watching violence causes the boys to become more aggressive, but the relationship may be just the reverse. Boys who are, for whatever reason, more aggressive may seek out and prefer violent television programs. In this case, watching TV violence does not cause aggressiveness; rather, aggressiveness causes boys to watch violent TV programs. Because of this *directionality problem,* we cannot always tell in which direction causal forces flow; from A to B or from B to A (see Figure 1-6).

A correlation between two variables may also be produced by a third variable that the investigator did not take into account. The parents' attitudes

▲ **FIGURE 1-6**
If variable A is correlated with variable B, can we conclude that A causes B? Correlational findings must be interpreted with caution. Although A may cause B, B may also cause A. Or, just as likely, a third variable (C) that wasn't measured may be causing both A and B.

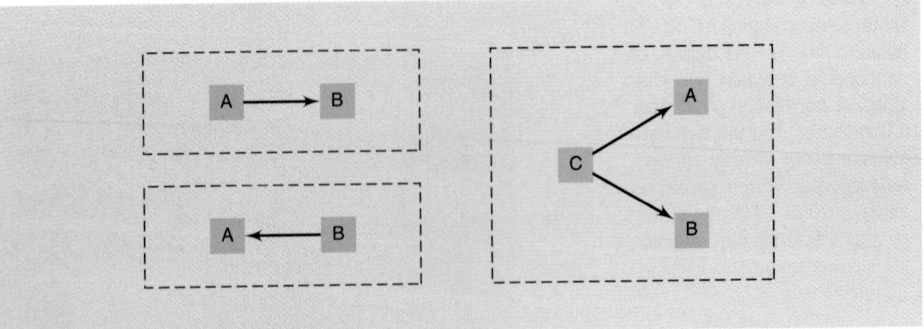

toward violence might be the real cause of the correlation between TV violence and aggression. Parents who condone violence may allow their boys to watch violent TV, and they may also encourage their boys to be aggressive. In consequence, a significant correlation emerges when TV violence and aggression are measured, even though these two variables aren't causally related. This example and those shown in Table 1-4 demonstrate that to infer causality from correlational studies is risky at best (Stanovich, 1992). An investigator may believe that one variable *caused* changes in another variable—Eron himself may think that watching violent TV programs caused the boys to become more aggressive. He cannot, however, make conclusive causal inferences without manipulating the amount of violent TV the boys watched.

Selecting a research design. Social psychologists use both experimental and nonexperimental designs in their studies of social behavior (see Table 1-5). When they want to investigate a causal relationship, an experimental design is needed. When researchers carry out the study properly by manipu-

▲ **TABLE 1-4**
Correlations and causal inference. Interpret correlational findings carefully. No matter how plausible a particular causal inference may be, other interpretations can account for correlational findings.

Correlation	*Interpretation A*	*Interpretation B*
Cigarette smoking is negatively correlated with grades in college.	Smoking reduces brain power.	Anxiety over low grades causes increased smoking.
The number of body lice on natives in the New Hebrides is positively correlated with good health.	Having a large number of body lice makes one healthy.	Lice leave the bodies of extremely ill natives in preference for healthy hosts.
The cost of rum is positively correlated with Presbyterian ministers' salaries.	Ministers are rum drinkers, so as their salaries increase, the seller raises prices.	Inflation over many years causes the cost of rum to increase as well as ministers' salaries.
The number of storks in an area of Holland is positively correlated with the area's birth rate.	Storks bring the babies, so more storks mean more babies.	The birth rate is higher in rural areas, where most storks nest.
The number of deaths by drowning is positively correlated with the amount of ice cream sold on any given day.	People eat too much ice cream, go swimming, get cramps, and drown.	People eat more ice cream on hot days, and they are more likely to go swimming (and possibly drown).

Source: Adapted from Huff, 1954.

▲ **TABLE 1-5**
Summing up: Research designs in social psychology

Design	Characteristics	Example
Experimental	The researcher manipulates the independent variable(s), measures the dependent variable(s), and maintains control over other variables. Statistical tests are used to determine if the differences between conditions are due to chance or the impact of the independent variable(s). This design yields information about cause-effect relations.	Bandura et al. (1961) arranged for children to witness an adult acting aggressively. They then watched the children play in a test room. Children who were exposed to the aggressive model displayed more aggression than children who saw no model (the control condition).
Nonexperimental	The researcher measures all variables of interest and examines the relations among the measures statistically. The strength of the relationship between variables is often summarized with a correlation coefficient, which can vary from +1.0 to −1.0. This design yields precise estimates of the strength of relationships between variables, but it yields only limited information about cause-effect relations.	Eron (1962) measured the types of programs boys watched and the amount of aggressiveness the boys displayed at school. The correlation between watching violent TV programs and aggression was +.21 for boys.

lating the independent variable, measuring the dependent variable accurately, and controlling extraneous variables, they can be fairly certain that any changes in the dependent variable were caused by the independent variable. Because experiments yield information about causality, social psychologists prefer this technique. Indeed, 1898 is remembered as a critical date in the history of social psychology, for it marks the first experimental study of a social-psychological process: Norman Triplett's study of the facilitating effect of an audience on children's performance of a simple task. Today nearly 75% of all studies published in major social psychology journals use experimental designs (Higbee, Millard, & Folkman, 1982).

The experimenter's need to control the experimental situation, however, leads to the major weakness of experimentation, artificiality. Experiments usually require controlled conditions, so they sometimes fail to approximate the complexities of behavior in naturally occurring situations. In such cases, researchers can turn to nonexperimental designs. Correlational studies don't require manipulations and elaborate controls, and they provide precise estimates of the strength of the relationship between variables. They are limited, however, because they cannot clearly demonstrate causal relationships among variables. These studies answer such questions as "Are people who watch violent television programs aggressive?" but not such questions as "Does watching violent programs cause people to become aggressive?"

Challenges and Issues

The importance of research cannot be overemphasized. By collecting information relevant to their hypotheses and questions, social psychologists extend our understanding of human behavior. The studies carried out by Bandura and Eron exemplify this process. Beginning with a hypothesis about aggression, they worked out a way to measure critical variables and assess their interrelationships. They eventually discovered other variables that were related to aggression, such as the sex of the person acting aggressively and the subject's parents' own level of aggression. These findings helped the researchers explain the origins of aggression and the factors that sustain it. This pattern of *hypothesis → data → hypothesis → data* often characterizes progress in scientific research. We begin with a hypothesis. We collect data to support the hypothesis. Next, we revise the hypothesis based on the data we collected. We gather more data to test the revised hypothesis, and the cycle begins again.

theories
Logically integrated explanations that systematize current knowledge about social phenomena and provide a framework for interpreting data and generating predictions.

Social psychologists strive to develop comprehensive, integrating explanations that identify the processes that produced the observed effects. These explanations are known as **theories**. Rather than identifying and testing one hypothesis after another, both Bandura and Eron constructed theories of human behavior and then tested hypotheses that they derived from these theories. As a science, social psychology stresses the long-term goal of increasing and systematizing our knowledge about the subject matter. It requires relating observations back to theoretical constructs that provide the framework for interpreting data and generating predictions. Hypotheses must be empirically testable, using methods that other scientists accept as adequate.

Because social psychologists study human behavior, their findings shed light on important social problems. For instance, Bandura's research warns us that people who watch too much violent television may become violent themselves. Applications of social psychology are presented throughout this book and at the end of each chapter in "Application" sections (for example, see "Social Psychology as Action Research" at the end of this chapter). This focus on people makes social psychology a tremendously useful pursuit, but it also creates unique problems for researchers. How do people react when they know they are being studied by researchers? How do we know our findings are valid? Are researchers justified in deceiving their subjects? These questions and possible answers are considered next.

Is Social-Psychological Research Valid?

internal validity
The degree to which the results obtained in a study accurately reflect the social processes that occurred in the situation under investigation.

external validity
The degree to which findings can be generalized to other populations and settings.

Bandura and his colleagues concluded that their data supported their initial hypothesis: exposure to violence leads to increased aggression. But was their study valid? When trying to assess the validity of any study, social psychologists usually distinguish between **internal validity** and **external validity** (Campbell & Stanley, 1963; Cook & Campbell, 1979). For a study to be internally valid, the results must accurately describe the true relationship between the variables under study. Bandura's study is valid if the differences in the children's behavior were caused by differences in the violent actions they watched rather than by another unknown factor. External validity, in contrast, "asks the question of generalizability: To what populations, settings, treatment variables, and measurement variables can this effect be generalized?" (Campbell & Stanley, 1963, p. 5). Bandura studied a single group of children and measured their aggression through observation. Would his results hold if he studied other children and used other measurement methods?

Even though researchers take steps to make certain their studies are valid, no scientific study is perfect; every study has both strengths and limitations. You must therefore become a critical consumer of social psychological research by training your eye to look for the following flaws and strengths, and decide for yourself whether or not the study is valid.

Assessing internal validity. Many factors threaten the internal validity of research, including confounds, evaluation apprehension, demand characteristics, and experimenter effects.

confounds
Factors that vary systematically with the independent variable and therefore might influence the dependent variable.

Confounds are factors that vary systematically with the independent variable. Bandura may have accidentally varied other factors when he exposed some of the children to an aggressive model. He may have simply provided more entertainment for the children in the experimental conditions, and because they were happier, they tended to be very active when they played with the toys in the test room. Bandura thought that they were learning to be aggressive, but actually they were only more playful.

evaluation apprehension
An anxiety-creating concern to appear normal; when research participants experience evaluation apprehension, their responses may be artificial and constrained.

Evaluation apprehension—an anxiety-creating concern to appear normal that subjects often experience when they take part in research—also undermines the internal validity of a study (M. J. Rosenberg, 1965). If Bandura's subjects experienced evaluation apprehension, they may have worried about the impression they were making. To appear helpful and normal, they may have acted aggressively because they thought they were supposed to. How do they decide what they are supposed to do? In some cases researchers unintentionally include in the situation subtle cues that can sway subjects' responses. A researcher studying aggression, for example, may include so many combat toys in the test room—toy guns and knives, boxing gloves, plastic soldiers, and so on—that the children realize they are supposed to be aggressive. These accidental hints are **demand characteristics**—cues that practically demand responses that will confirm the researcher's hypothesis (Orne, 1962).

demand characteristics
Implicit and explicit cues that convey information about the type of response expected in the situation.

experimenter effects
The impact of the experimenter on the research participant, including the unintentional tendency for researchers to obtain responses from a subject that confirm their initial expectations.

Experimenter effects can also bias the results of any investigation. Subjects sometimes respond differently to male and female, black and white, old and young, or attractive and unattractive experimenters, and experimenters may also respond differently to different sorts of subjects. Experimenters may also unintentionally bias their findings just by developing expectations about what they expect to find. Suppose two researchers who are conducting the same experiment expect opposite findings; one experimenter thinks that the control subjects will be more aggressive than the subjects assigned to the experimental condition; the second experimenter thinks the experimental group will be more aggressive than the control group. Studies of *expectancy effects* (which are discussed in Chapter 5) suggest that these expectancies will likely be fulfilled; the group that is expected to be aggressive will in fact outdo the other group (Rosenthal, 1966, 1969; Rosenthal & Fode, 1963). Fortunately, the expectancy effect can be minimized by automating the role of the researcher, making certain the research personnel are unaware of the hypotheses, and rigorously standardizing the behaviors of the research staff. (Compare Rosenthal & Rosnow, 1991, with Barber, 1976, and Barber & Silver, 1968a, 1968b.)

Assessing external validity. Even if a study is judged to have high internal validity, you must still consider its external validity: will the conclusions generalize to other people, places, and situations? Some researchers use *systematic sampling procedures* to increase the external validity of their results. If opinion pollsters want to know how many people in a country are opposed to abortion, they need a *representative sample*: a subgroup of participants who have the same characteristics (gender, race, religious, political preference) as the general population. For surveys and many nonexperimental studies, the more representative the sample, the greater the study's external validity (Mook, 1983).

Replications also enhance external validity, provided the original results are obtained when the study is carried out a second time. Also, most replications don't exactly mimic the original study, for the researchers usually change aspects of the study to determine the limits of the original findings (Neuliep & Crandall, 1993). Bandura's study, for example, has been replicated in field settings, and the overall pattern of results is similar to Bandura's (Liebert & Sprafkin, 1988). Similarly, Eron's discovery of a correlation between TV violence and aggression has been replicated in several other countries, including Finland, Poland, and Australia (Eron, 1982). In recent years social psychology has gradually increased its focus to include social behavior across cultures. This **cross-cultural research** has become increasingly important in the field as researchers strive to make comparisons of findings in different cultures and in different groups within the same culture.

cross-cultural research
Studying people from different cultural backgrounds to determine whether findings are universal (they generalize across other cultures) or culture specific.

meta-analysis
A procedure that allows a reviewer to summarize the results of multiple studies of a phenomenon statistically.

How do researchers integrate the results of all these studies to reach an overall conclusion? The most traditional approach is the *narrative review*: a comprehensive inventory of the results obtained in various studies that pinpoints consistencies and inconsistencies. Another method, **meta-analysis**, combines the results of different studies using statistical procedures. When carrying out a meta-analysis, the reviewer must not only note the results of the study, but also keep a record of the features of the study that may influence those results (for example, Were the experimenters men? Was aggression measured through self-report or observation?). Through statistical analysis, the reviewer can then determine the overall strength of the relationships between variables across studies and identify any factors that influence the strength of the relationship. Both narrative reviews and meta-analyses are essential tools, for they help researchers revise and extend their theories to incorporate or discard hypotheses that did or did not pass muster (Beaman, 1991; Johnson, 1991; Larsen & Sinnett, 1991; Maruyama, 1991; Mullen, Salas, & Miller, 1991).

Is Social-Psychological Research Ethical?

Because social psychologists study people rather than rocks, plants, atomic particles, or planets, they run up against challenges and problems that other scientists never encounter. When astronomers focus their telescopes on a passing comet, the comet takes no notice. People, however, sometimes change their behavior when a social psychologist looks their way. Likewise, when physicists examine nuclear particles by exposing a beryllium target to high-energy X rays, they don't have to worry about what will happen to the beryllium. Social psychologists, in contrast, must make certain that no harm befalls the participants in their research.

Social-psychological studies often raise many questions about ethics and human rights. In some cases researchers, in their quest to study some social process, may intrude on the right to privacy of others. Do researchers have the right to watch people as they go about their social lives in grocery stores, on street corners, in classrooms, and in public restrooms? In some cases, researchers also deliberately deceive their subjects by giving them a *cover story* that provides a rationale for the manipulations and measurements. A survey of 1,188 research reports published over 20 years indicates that more than 60% of all research studies that appeared in the leading social-psychological journals involved at least one of the techniques shown in Table 1-6 (Gross & Fleming, 1982).

Moral judgments about social-psychological research are a personal matter; your reactions depend on your own moral beliefs and values. Many researchers, however, evaluate the ethics of research studies by balancing the *risks* that studies create for subjects against the *benefits* to be gained for subjects, society, and science. Possible risks include physically or psychologically harming subjects, invading their privacy, upsetting subjects, and wasting their time. Some have even suggested that habitual deception of subjects engenders distrust and suspicion and that manipulation and deception can lead to the dehumaniza-

▲ TABLE 1-6
Percentages of social-psychological studies using different forms of deception

Type of Deception	*Description*	*Percentage*
Cover story	Giving a false rationale for the procedures and measures	81.5
Misleading instructions	Providing incorrect information concerning materials (such as tasks to be completed, questions asked)	42.0
Confederate	Using a confederate or actor without subjects' knowledge	29.2
False feedback	Giving subjects false information about their performance, personality, and so on	17.5
Covert study	Not informing participants that they are in a study	13.7
Bogus separation	Presenting two related studies to subjects as though they are unrelated	9.1
False interpersonal feedback	Giving subjects incorrect information about other interactants in the setting	5.3
Covert measurement or manipulation	Misleading participants so they think the study is completed before the time of manipulation or measurement	4.1

Source: From Gross & Fleming, 1982.

tion of research subjects (Geller, 1982; Kelman, 1982). People who have participated in research projects that used deception, however, don't report any negative feelings about the experience after they are told about the study's true purpose (Sharpe, Adair, & Roese, 1992). Participation also yields benefits for subjects, including payment, educational gains (such as an increased understanding of scientific research), and increased self-understanding and feelings of self-worth for having helped further scientific research. Benefits for social psychology and society include increased understanding of social behavior and the growth of scientific knowledge.

This risk-benefit approach has been adopted by the American Psychological Association in its code of research ethics, which states that researchers must decide if "there is a negative effect upon the dignity and welfare of the participants that the importance of the research does not warrant" (Ad Hoc Committee, 1973, p. 11). If the cost attached to a study is high, as when participants are deceived about the true purpose of the research, then the investigator must try to develop an alternative method for studying the question. Researchers must also submit their research plans to impartial reviewers before they carry out their research. Often referred to as *institutional review boards* (IRBs), these reviewers objectively weigh risks and benefits before sanctioning any study involving human participants. Yet even IRBs tend to be biased against research that examines sensitive social issues, such as racism and sexism (see Ceci, Peters, & Plotkin, 1985).

informed consent
A required statement of the research procedures, risks and benefits, and subjects rights that participants in research must review before they agree to participate in a study.

Because virtually all studies involve some risk, researchers usually make certain to use proper safeguards when carrying out their studies. In most studies subjects are first given a brief but accurate description of their duties in the research and then given the choice to participate or not. This practice is known as **informed consent**, and it serves to remind subjects that they can terminate their participation in the study at any time if they choose to do so. Most researchers also fully clarify the hypotheses once the study is over. This phase of

▲ Social psychologists sometimes withhold information from participants, but their deceptions are rarely long-lasting or harmful. This debriefing might not be enough to return Edward to his preexperimental state.

FAR SIDE copyright 1993 FARWORKS, Inc./Dist. by UNIVERSAL PRESS SYNDICATE. Reprinted with permission. All rights reserved.

debriefing
A session, held after the subjects have participated in the research project, in which the experimenter asks subjects about their reactions to the experience and informs them of the purpose of the research.

the research process is typically known as **debriefing**, and it involves reviewing the hypotheses with participants, answering their questions, revealing any deceptions that took place, and removing any harmful effects of the experience.

When risks to subjects are too great, researchers turn to low-risk alternatives such as simulations or role-play studies. In such studies they ask people to play the part of an individual in a certain kind of situation. Subjects in a role-play study of aggression would be fully informed about the purposes of the research and the roles they will play. They would, however, be asked "to suspend reality and act spontaneously" by "creating their own roles with full awareness that they are the focus of study" (Geller, 1982, p. 49; see also Hendrick, 1977; Krupat, 1977; Mixon, 1977, 1979). By adopting these and other precautions, social psychologists strive to acquire information about social behavior in ways that will be both scientifically valid and ethically acceptable (Forsyth & Pope, 1984).

Answering the Challenge

In its brief history, social psychology has established a reputation for meeting issues and challenges head-on (see Table 1-7 for a summary). When researchers realized that their findings could be distorted by evaluation apprehension and other social-psychological processes, they developed ways to deal with these problems. In some cases their methods involved deceiving subjects about the purposes of the research, but once again social psychologists openly examined

▲ **TABLE 1-7**
Summing up: Research issues in social psychology

Topic	*Issue*	*Influencing Considerations*
Internal validity	Do the results accurately describe the true relationship between the variables under study?	Confounds, evaluation apprehension, demand characteristics, and experimenter effects limit internal validity.
External validity	Can the results be generalized to other situations, people, and cultures?	Inadequate samples and failures to replicate limit external validity.
Ethics	What are the ethical responsibilities of a researcher?	Researchers must protect subjects from harm. Researchers use controversial methods (for example, deception) only when the benefits of the research clearly outweigh the risks. Informed consent and debriefing are required in most studies.

their procedures and explored alternatives. Also, through research social psychologists have uncovered a wealth of information that extends our understanding of each other—information that supplements and corrects everyday, commonsense notions about the social world. Social psychology is not simply a collection of scientific facts, theories, and methods, but thousands of researchers striving to improve our understanding of one another.

Summary

Social psychology explores the roots of social behavior by studying the way individuals' thoughts, feelings, and behaviors are influenced by other people. The discipline's *paradigm*, or core assumptions, stresses the analysis of social processes that unfold during everyday encounters between individuals. Since social psychology's inception, the topics studied and methods used by social psychologists have grown. Now investigators use a variety of methods to study both interpersonal processes—norms, aggression, interaction in small groups, leadership, helping, and so on—as well as such personal processes as attitudes and social cognition. Moreover, because the field emerged at the intersection of psychology and sociology, the concept of *interactionism* is a central principle in the field: Social behavior is a function of both the person and the social environment, or $B = f(P, E)$. This scientific approach offers advantages over intuition and common sense. Explanations of social behavior based on common sense alone don't apply in all situations and to all people, can yield inconsistent or false conclusions, and are too often safeguarded by the *hindsight bias*.

Understanding social psychology's paradigm requires more than learning the content of social psychology. Social psychology is not simply a body of scientific facts and theories, but also a way of accumulating information about people. The research process is complex, but it generally involves measuring social processes and testing hypotheses about these processes. A measure is, in a sense, an *operational definition* of a concept, and it can be achieved through the use of the following:

- *Self-report measures* that elicit subjects' own descriptions of their reactions (opinion polls, interviews, tests, inventories)

- Behavioral measures such as *observation* and *reaction time*
- *Social-psychophysiological measures*
- *Nonreactive measures* such as archival analysis

Any measurement method must be high in both *reliability* and *validity*: The measurement method should be a consistent indicator of what it is supposed to measure. Questionnaires are not valid measures when respondents answer in socially appropriate, but misleading, ways (the *social desirability bias*).

Researchers test their hypotheses in experimental or nonexperimental studies. Bandura and his colleagues studied aggression in an *experiment*: They manipulated exposure to aggressive behavior (the *independent variable*), measured aggression (the *dependent variable*), and controlled other variables by standardizing procedures and using *random assignment*. *Nonexperimental designs* require no manipulation of variables but instead establish the relationship between two or more measured variables. Such *correlational studies* summarize the strength of the relationship between variables with a *correlation coefficient*, which can vary from −1.0 to 0.0 to +1.0. Eron found that the correlation between watching violent TV programs and aggression was +.21 for boys.

Social psychologists strive to develop comprehensive, integrative *theories* that explain social phenomena. Experimental studies are preferred over nonexperimental studies when cause-effect hypotheses are tested, but both designs are useful provided they have *internal validity* and *external validity*. Internal validity can be enhanced by minimizing *confounds* (factors that vary systematically with the independent variable), *evaluation apprehension* (an anxiety-creating concern to appear normal), *demand characteristics* (cues that reveal the researcher's hypothesis) and *experimenter effects*. External validity can be increased through systematic sampling procedures, replication, *cross-cultural research*, and *meta-analysis*. No matter what procedures are used, however, steps must be taken to protect subjects from harm. Although researchers sometimes invade subjects' privacy or mislead subjects with a cover story, such procedures may be justified by the study's benefits. They must also use safeguards—such as *informed consent, debriefing,* and role-play studies—to minimize risks to participants.

For More Information

- *Applied Social Psychology*, by Stuart Oskamp (1984), describes dozens of successful applications of social psychology to practical problems.
- *The Common and Uncommon Sense of Social Behavior*, by Francis Dane (1988), is a down-to-earth, personalized look at the way one social psychologist conceptualizes and studies human behavior.
- *The Cross-Cultural Challenge to Social Psychology*, edited by Michael Harris Bond (1988), examines the generalizability of social psychology across the world's cultures.
- *Deconstructing Social Psychology*, edited by Ian Parker and John Shotter (1990), is a collection of critical essays exploring alternative means of exploring social-psychological processes.
- *Dialogues and Debates in Social Psychology*, edited by Jeannette Murphy, Mary John, and Hedy Brown (1984), presents original readings and commentary on various issues in social psychology, including choice of topics, applications, and ethics.

• *Handbook of Social Psychology*, edited by Gardner Lindzey and Elliot Aronson (1985), is a valuable sourcebook of social-psychological knowledge. Volume 1 deals with theory and methods; volume 2 examines specific topics. (Not for the dilettante.)

• *How to Think Straight about Psychology*, by Keith E. Stanovich (1992), explores the scientific side of psychology in a down-to-earth, amusing style.

• *Journal of Personality and Social Psychology* publishes theoretical papers and research reports in three areas of social psychology: attitudes and social cognition, interpersonal relations and group processes, and personality and individual differences. An excellent source of information on the current findings and directions in the field.

Application: Social Psychology as Action Research

Philosophers of science often distinguish between **basic science** and **applied science**. In basic research (sometimes called pure research), scientists extend our general understanding by testing theoretically important hypotheses. They ask, "Let's compare what is with what should be to see if the theory is adequate." Applied researchers, in contrast, seek information that will let them solve practical problems. They ask, "Let's understand the nature of this problem so we can do something to solve it" (Snyder & Forsyth, 1991b).

This division of effort can lead to problems. On the basic side, researchers often build more and more elaborate theories that have little or no applicability, or they simply lose sight of the social value of their findings. Applied research, in contrast, tends to be too problem-focused and atheoretical. When research becomes wholly applied, it drifts toward technology. In science, applied problems may be the initial source of research questions, but these applied concerns are ultimately placed into a theoretical context. The long-term goal of such research includes testing the adequacy of assumptions and hypotheses that make up the theory. In technology, on the other hand, theory and methods are used solely to develop some product—such as a new personality measure, a new way to manage workers, or a more effective advertising campaign. Technological researchers may borrow the theories of science to guide their problem solving, but they don't test generalizable propositions derived from these theories (Forsyth & Strong, 1986).

Recognizing the limitations of each form of research, social psychologists strive to combine elements of both basic and applied research in their studies of social behavior. Kurt Lewin, whose contributions to social psychology are noted in this chapter, labeled this mixture **action research**. He felt that social problems, including conflict, leadership, and group performance, should be solved scientifically for there "is no hope of creating a better world without a deeper scientific insight into the function of leadership and culture" and other essentials of social life (Lewin, 1948, p. 113).

Social psychologists have heeded Lewin's plea for action research in several ways. First, social psychologists study not only mundane, commonplace aspects of social life, but also major problems that seriously detract from the quality of our social lives: aggression, air pollution, child abuse, collective violence, cults, destructive obedience, divorce, domestic violence, intergroup conflict, littering, loneliness, mental illness, murder, noise, overcrowding, pornography, prejudice, racism, rape, riots, sexism, suicide, terrorism, vandalism, and violent crime. Much of social psychology is directly focused on increasing our understanding of social issues and proposing ways to alleviate them.

Second, even when social psychologists pursue primarily basic science goals, their theories and findings can often be applied in many settings. Although social-psychological theories are usually built on logical rather than practical grounds, they can explain problems in a variety of settings (see Table 1-8). Business nearly always involves communication among people, forming impressions of others and their actions, leadership and decision-making processes in groups, competition and cooperation, and persuasion. All of these processes are actively studied by social psychologists. Similarly, social-psychological theories suggest ways to increase patient compliance with doctors' treatment regimens, offer insight into the processes that underlie therapeutic change in psychotherapy, and explain how students react to success and failure in academic settings. Thus, even though social psychology's theories are often developed by academic researchers who test them through laboratory experimentation, these theories can have great practical significance. As Lewin remarked, "There is nothing so practical as a good theory" (1951, p. 169).

Last, social psychology is not simply a body of scientific facts and theories, but also a group of methods for

basic science: Research conducted to increase scientists' understanding of theoretically significant hypotheses.

applied science: Research conducted to increase scientists' understanding of practical and social problems and to identify possible solutions.

action research: Lewin's term for research that tests theoretically interesting ideas, yet at the same time yields insights into and solutions for practical problems.

▲ **TABLE 1-8**
Examples of the practical application of social psychology in a variety of disciplines and settings

Application	*Questions Asked by Social Psychologists*
Advertising and sales	How do consumers process information about a product? When is a spokesperson for a product persuasive? What influence tactics do salespeople use to influence buyers?
Business and industry	What behaviors comprise effective management? When should personnel work in groups rather than alone? How can organizations be reshaped to enhance productivity?
Communication and mass media	What are the essential elements of a persuasive political speech? What factors determine the credibility of a TV news anchor? Does pornography increase aggression against women?
Ecology and the environment	Why do people litter and pollute? What steps can be taken to encourage environmental conservation? How should neighborhoods be designed?
Education	Can students be taught effective ways to deal with failure? What can be done to improve teacher-student interactions? Do integrated schools reduce prejudice?
Law and justice	What factors determine parole and sentencing decisions? How do jurors judge the credibility of a witness? How do juries make decisions?
Medicine and health	Are people with many friends and loved ones healthier? What steps can be taken to increase patient compliance with physicians' prescriptions? Does stress undermine health?
Mental health	What are the necessary ingredients of effective psychotherapy? What social processes contribute to depression? What are the therapeutic factors that operate in group therapy?
Sports and recreation	Why do people join amateur sports teams? What factors lead to violence at sporting events? What is effective coaching?

expanding our understanding of social behavior. These methods can also be used to solve problems of practical significance (Gregory, 1989; Oskamp, 1984). Many organizations, including hospitals, psychiatric treatment facilities, industries, and government agencies, often call on researchers to evaluate the effectiveness of their programs. Such **program evaluations** might include a study to determine whether a new assembly-line procedure is more efficient than the old one, whether new regulations governing the distribution of welfare benefits have reduced the number of fraudulent users, or whether special education programs, such as Head Start, lead to increases in students' reading skills (Sechrest & Figueredo, 1993).

Researchers also create new programs and other innovations through **social experimentation** (Fairweather & Tornatzky, 1977; Riecken & Boruch, 1975; Saxe & Fine, 1981). To study the effects of training on police officers' job performance, for example, one researcher randomly assigned trainees to one of two treatment groups. All trainees took the same courses, but those in the high-stress group trained in a military atmosphere; those in the low-stress group trained in a relaxed, campuslike atmosphere. Because the low-stress subjects outperformed the high-stress subjects in virtually all categories, the program was incorporated in the police department's regular training program (Earle, 1973).

Thus both the content and method of social psychology are powerful tools for understanding, and possibly solving, practical problems. These applications will be examined throughout the book, but will be given particularly close scrutiny in special sections at the end of each chapter. These sections all reflect the creed of the action researcher (Forsyth, 1988, p. 65):

> Knowledge does not prosper,
> When science is one-sided,
> The basic and applied must be,
> United, not divided.

program evaluation: Research designed to assess the effectiveness of social interventions, such as drug treatment programs, community service delivery systems, or crime prevention programs.

social experimentation: Program evaluation projects that compare the effectiveness of social interventions by randomly assigning participants to two or more different community intervention procedures.

Forming and Managing Impressions

You are a member of the United States Judiciary Committee in 1991. For the last few days you have been examining Clarence Thomas, a nominee for a judgeship on the U.S. Supreme Court. Your review has uncovered an extraordinarily serious problem. Anita Faye Hill, a law professor at the University of Oklahoma, has come forward with charges that Thomas sexually harassed her when she worked as his assistant in the Department of Education.

All day you watch and listen to Hill and Thomas. Hill, sitting a few feet from you, looks directly into your eyes as she describes how Thomas discussed sexual matters whenever they were alone (Hill, 1991, p. A-6):

> His conversations were very vivid. He spoke about acts that he had seen in pornographic films involving such matters as women having sex with animals and films showing group sex or rape scenes.
>
> He talked about pornographic materials depicting individuals with large penises or large breasts involved in various sex acts. On several occasions, Thomas told me graphically of his own sexual prowess.
>
> Because I was extremely uncomfortable talking about sex with him at all and particularly in such a graphic way, I told him that I did not want to talk about these subjects. I would also try to change the subject.

Judge Clarence Thomas denies the charges clearly and emphatically. He sits in the same chair Hill had occupied earlier, but he doesn't show her cool candor (Thomas, 1991, p. A-6):

> Throughout the time that Anita Hill worked with me I treated her as I treated my other special assistants. I tried to treat them all cordially, professionally, and respectfully, and I tried to support them in their endeavors and be interested in and supportive of their success. I had no reason or basis to believe my relationship with Anita Hill was anything but this way until the FBI visited me a little more than two weeks ago. . . .
>
> I am proud of my life, proud of what I have done and what I have accomplished, proud of my family and this process, this process is trying to destroy it all. No job is worth what I have been through, no job. No horror in my life has been so debilitating. Confirm me if you want. Don't confirm me if you are so led, but let this process end. Let me and my family regain our lives.

Whom do you believe? Hill's background is beyond reproach. Deeply religious and sure of her own personal values, she never waivers during questioning and describes the events in explicit terms. Thomas, too, is a man of great integrity. He headed the office that enforces laws to protect people from sexist and racist treatment and had earned a reputation as a man who stood for women's rights. Could Hill be deliberately fabricating a lurid tale of sexual intrigue to ruin Thomas's career? Or did Thomas harass his subordinate repeatedly in 1982 and 1983?

social perception
The perceptual and cognitive processes that produce and sustain our conceptions of other people.

The Hill-Thomas incident only hints at the intricacies of **social perception**: the processes that sustain our conceptions of other people. Just as we can perceive aspects of our physical world—the hue of a color, the pitch of a sound, or the texture of a surface—we can perceive aspects of our social world. Each senator, and every viewer who watched Hill on national television, gleaned clues from her articulate answers, neat-as-a-pin appearance, and tone of voice. We remained just as vigilant as Thomas recounted the details of his relationship with Hill, searching for new hints that would help us test our hunches about his personality and proclivities.

impression formation
Formulating tentative conceptions about others' emotions, motivations, and personalities by gathering and interpreting situational and behavioral cues.

We are all psychologists of a sort, for whenever we meet other people we set to work deciphering them. Through social perception you decide whether your new neighbor is someone you would accept as a friend; whether your social psychology teacher is stern and demanding; whether your classmate is intelligent, average, or struggling to keep up. Each of these examples involves **impression formation**, for you are making inferences about, or forming impressions of, others' emotions, motivations, and personalities. You need not interview someone for hours to get an idea of their qualities and characteristics. In many cases, just watching someone walk across the room, listening to the way they introduce themselves, or seeing their photograph is enough to set the impression formation process in motion.

impression management (or self-presentation)
Influencing other people's social perceptions by selectively revealing personal information to them; includes both deliberate and unintentional attempts to establish, maintain, or refine the impression others have.

Your ability to *form* impressions of other people, however, equals their ability to *manage* the impressions they make. While you watched Hill, she doggedly regulated her outward actions in order to project a particular image. She did not simply let you, the perceiver, draw your own conclusions about who she was and what emotions she was experiencing. Instead, she actively controlled her outward statements and actions to guide you in directions she preferred. This **impression management** is often calculated, but it can also be sincere. Perceivers' attempts to understand you will be for naught if you refuse to provide them with grist for their perceptual mills. If you did not correct their impressions, they might take offense when none was meant, see flirtation in your boredom, or rejection when you want to befriend them.

Social perception, then, is a two-way process, with a perceiver formulating impressions of the target, and a target busy managing the perceptual cues he or she displays. How accurate is this perceptual exchange? What happens when an individual who is cold wants to project an image of warmth and friendliness? Will the impression manager succeed or will the perceiver see through the charade and accurately label the interpersonal claims as fraudulent? As we will see in the final section of this chapter, new understandings are often forged when the perceiver meets the one perceived.

Forming Impressions

We marvel at the observational skill of detectives like Arthur Conan Doyle's Sherlock Holmes, but we ourselves are insightful observers of other human beings. When we encounter someone for the first time—a professor giving a guest lecture, a stranger standing beside us in line, a newly hired employee at work, or a potential romantic interest at a party—we ferret out all the clues we need to form an impression of that person. Thomas offered viewers an enormous variety of perceptual cues. He verbalized many of his claims: "I cannot imagine anything that I said or did to Anita Hill that could have been mistaken

▲ Social perception is a dynamic, reciprocal process. Perceivers (like the senators at Clarence Thomas's confirmation hearings) formulate impressions of others and then revise their impressions as they gather more information. But the person whom these perceivers are trying to understand also plays an active role in this perceptual interchange. Clarence Thomas, by controlling the information he provided to onlookers, managed the impression he created in the social situation. Social perception thus depends on both impression formation (the senators) and impression management (Thomas).

for sexual harassment." But he also expressed himself without words: He glared at the committee; small twitches flowed across his face from the corners of his mouth to his eyebrows; his voice took on a choked, deep tone, and he spoke haltingly at times. He sat rigidly erect, and his hands always rested on the table.

nonverbal cues
Actions and appearances that communicate without words; facial expressions, styles of dress, and body postures are examples.

These **nonverbal cues** are profoundly important sources of information about others' feelings and emotions. As Sherlock Holmes noted, "by a momentary expression, a twitch of a muscle, or a glance of an eye," one can "fathom a man's inmost thoughts" (Doyle, 1938, p. 12). Holmes may have exaggerated, but he was right when he claimed that nonverbal cues betray our friendliness, power, and honesty. Because such cues "provide a qualitative 'script' without which verbal cues cannot be interpreted accurately," they play a critical role in regulating our social interactions (Archer & Akert, 1977, p. 449; Patterson, 1991). Nonverbal information flows from one person to another through a number of *channels,* but the four most important ones are physical appearance, facial cues, movements of the body, and voice cues that accompany or parallel spoken language (paralanguage).

Physical Appearance

Most of us do not heed the warning, "You can't judge a book by its cover." When we see others for the first time, we form snap judgments of their inner characteristics and qualities based on their physical appearance. A glance at Thomas tells you that he is an African American man in his mid-forties, that he wears a moustache and glasses, that his hair is cut short, and that he prefers a dark suit with a fashionable but conservative tie. His physical appearance may seem to be a trivial quality that says nothing about the inner man, yet evidence confirms its impact on our perceptions (Cash & Janda, 1984; de Meuse, 1987). When we look at people who are physically attractive, we tend to assume that they are more socially competent, better adjusted, more intelligent, and more likable than people with average looks (Eagly et al., 1991). Similarly, because Thomas is a man, an onlooker might guess that he is confident rather than insecure, aggressive rather than meek, and tough rather than weak (Ashmore, Del Boca, & Wohler, 1984). His moustache and full head of hair make him seem more attractive (Cash, 1990; Reed & Blunk, 1990). His glasses project an air of intelligence and authority (Bartolini et al., 1987; Edwards, 1987). His conservative business suit tells us that he knows and accepts the norms for dressing in the situation he faces (Damhorst, 1990).

stereotypes
Socially shared generalizations about the people who are members of a particular group or social category.

"what is beautiful is good" stereotype
The general belief that people who are physically attractive possess other socially attractive qualities, such as social poise, friendliness, and intelligence.

Why do perceivers assume that physical appearances reveal the inner person? In many cases these appearance cues—sex, race, age, dress, hairstyle, and the like—influence our perceptions because they activate our **stereotypes**: generalizations about people who are members of a particular group or social category (Hamilton, Sherman, & Ruvolo, 1990; McArthur, 1982). Our stereotypes may tell us that the average man is different from the average woman. He is aggressive, and she is affectionate; he is loud, and she is quiet. Our stereotypes about eyeglass-wearers might suggest that the bespectacled are bookish, intelligent, work oriented, and friendless. The **"what is beautiful is good" stereotype** may suggest that attractive people possess many positive attributes, such as intelligence and friendliness (Eagly et al., 1991).

Such stereotypes are useful when we must form judgments about other people when information is scarce, but too often they are unrealistic and extreme. We may think that attractive people are more intelligent, more well adjusted, and more sociable than unattractive people, but these assumptions are groundless. Feingold (1992) found that "good-looking people [are] . . . more popular, more socially skilled, and more sexually experienced," but they don't have any of the more far-reaching qualities we tend to associate with good looks. As we will discuss in more detail in Chapter 7, stereotypes can bias our perceptions of other people.

The Face

Our attention is often drawn immediately to others' faces. Human newborns, tested when less than one hour old, will track a moving human face farther with their eyes than they will track a blank outline of a head (Morton & Johnson, 1991). If we are shown photographs of people and then retested at a later date, we can usually pick out the people we saw previously (Diamond &

▲ Just one glance at a person is often enough for us to make snap judgments about his or her attitudes, personality, and interests. Are the people pictured here confident or insecure? Healthy and hardy or delicate and sensitive? Friendly or cold? Trustworthy or undependable? Athletic or bookish? Involved in environmental issues or apathetic? We often assume that physical appearance, clothing, facial expressions, and posture say much about the inner person.

Carey, 1986; Valentine, 1991). When we look at a picture of a group of nine people, eight of whom have the same facial expression (either a smile or a frown), we can find the individual with the unique facial expression in one second or less. We are especially fast at finding an angry face in a crowd of smiling faces and slightly slower when searching for a happy face in an angry crowd. The difference, though, is only half a second (Hansen & Hansen, 1988a). Just a glance at a face is enough to prompt some people to form a host of detailed, sometimes surprisingly accurate, conclusions about the person (Berry & McArthur, 1986). Faces are gold mines of perceptual information about others' traits, intentions, and emotions.

Babyfaces. People have long considered the face to be a clear statement of a person's inner personality. Like the orator Cicero, we naturally assume that "the countenance is the reflection of the soul." When perceivers see a man with a broad jaw and a receding hairline, they surmise that he is powerful (Keating et al., 1981). A narrow chin, on the other hand, creates the impression of naiveté, warmth, honesty, and kindness (Berry & McArthur, 1985). People with large, round eyes are also viewed as warmer and kinder than those with smaller, more narrow eyes, and people who smile are routinely viewed as more attractive and approachable than those who frown (Berry & McArthur, 1986; Gifford, 1991). Perceivers even take the shape of the head into account when formulating impressions. Individuals with sloping foreheads and smaller heads are viewed as less alert, reliable, intelligent, and strong, although they are viewed as kinder and more lovable (Berry & McArthur, 1986).

Why do we let these facial qualities influence our judgments? Diane S. Berry and Leslie A. Zebrowitz reviewed dozens of studies of impression formation before concluding that perceivers are most influenced by facial features that they associate with a baby's or child's face. Babyish facial features, they argue, elicit strong reactions from perceivers at an instinctive level. Large, round eyes, a narrow chin, high eyebrows and a sloping forehead all say to the perceiver: "I am helpless but lovable: please care for me" (Berry & McArthur, 1985). Perceivers of various ages and from different cultural backgrounds all agree that adults whose faces retain some of these babyish features, like the woman on the left in Figure 2-1, have more childlike qualities than individuals with more mature faces. They are judged to be more honest, naive, warmer,

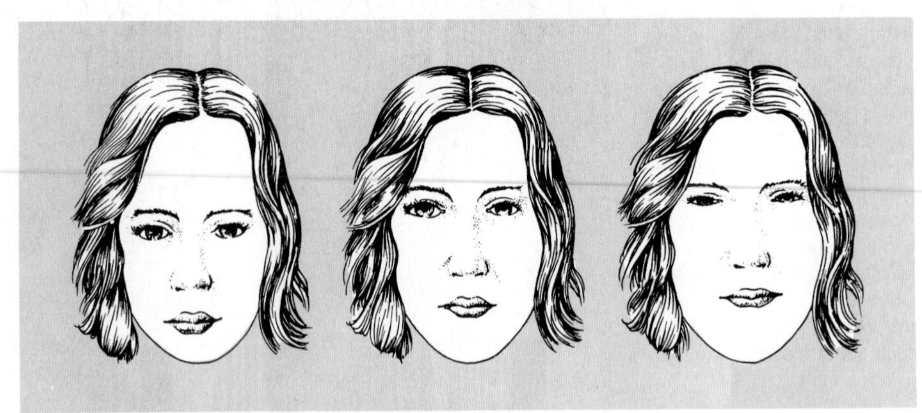

▲ **FIGURE 2-1**
Which woman is more honest? Naive? Kinder? Submissive? These faces vary in maturity. The face on the left has babyish features (narrow, shorter chin; shorter nose, larger eyes, expansive forehead); the middle face is an average adult face; the face on the right is the most mature of the three (large chin, longest nose, small eyes and forehead). Perceivers attribute more childlike qualities to the woman on the left, although they generally consider the middle face to be the most attractive. (From McArthur & Apatow, 1983/1984)

and kinder than those with mature faces, but they are also seen as weaker and more submissive. People with babyfaces aren't necessarily seen to be more attractive, but they are often viewed as less responsible for their actions. Berry and Zebrowitz-McArthur (1988) asked people to judge a person accused of a minor crime, such as inadvertently filing a false income tax report. Only 50% of the perceivers who read about a crime perpetrated by a baby-faced person believed he was guilty, whereas 85% believed that the mature-faced man was guilty. As most trial lawyers know, looking innocent is as important as being innocent (Berry, 1990; Berry & Brownlow, 1989; Berry & McArthur, 1985, 1986; Berry & Zebrowitz-McArthur, 1988; Brownlow & Zebrowitz, 1990; McArthur & Berry, 1987; McArthur & Montepare, 1989; Zebrowitz, 1990).

eye contact (or mutual gazing) A form of nonverbal communication that takes place when two people look into one another's eyes.

The eyes. The eyes have been called the "windows of the soul," for much of our communication with one another involves **eye contact**. We express our desire for interaction by signaling with our eyes; when you want to ask a question in class, you try to catch the professor's eye. Conversely, during a discussion your averted eyes tell the professor you aren't prepared. We also make judgments about other people's feelings by observing the amount and direction of their gaze. We generally assume that people who avoid our eyes are embarrassed, ashamed, or disinterested, whereas a high level of gazing implies involvement, intimacy, attraction, and respect (Burgoon et al., 1989; Kleinke, 1986). Perceivers also use gaze as evidence of certain personality traits. People who gazed at others only 15% of the time were judged to be cold, pessimistic, cautious, defensive, immature, evasive, submissive, and indifferent. Those who maintained eye contact 80% of the time were seen as friendly, self-confident, natural, mature, and sincere (Exline & Messick, 1967). Sunglasses can foster a negative impression by making eye contact impossible; individuals who wear dark glasses are usually viewed as less honest than people who do not hide their eyes (Bartolini et al., 1988).

We usually respond positively when people look us in the eye. Be warned, however, that a constant gaze (a stare) can culminate in negative perceptions. Like many animals, humans communicate aggressiveness and dominance by staring (Burgoon, Coker, & Coker, 1986). Perceivers describe starers as tense, angry, embarrassed, passive, and unintelligent, and report angry, unfriendly feelings when they are the target of a stare (Strom & Buck, 1979). Unless a stare occurs in conjunction with a more positive signal, such as a smile or positive remark, people often respond by terminating the interaction and leaving the area. Thus eye contact often serves to intensify the dominant mood, whatever it may be (Ellsworth, Carlsmith, & Henson, 1972; Fukuhara, 1990; Keating et al., 1981).

Blushing. The face sometimes broadcasts the message "I am embarrassed" to onlookers by blushing: by spontaneously darkening or reddening across the cheeks, forehead, ears, and neck. People tend to blush when they act in ways that threaten the impression they are trying to create. We blush, for example, when we do something wrong, stupid, or inappropriate in front of other people (Miller, 1992). We also blush when we are singled out for intensive scrutiny by others. When a teacher praises us in front of the entire class or the boss thanks us for a job well done, we are as likely to blush as when we are caught doing something improper or silly. Knowing that others are forming impressions of us is, in many cases, sufficient to prompt us to begin blushing. Blushing is a social event: we don't often blush when we are alone (Leary & Meadows, 1991).

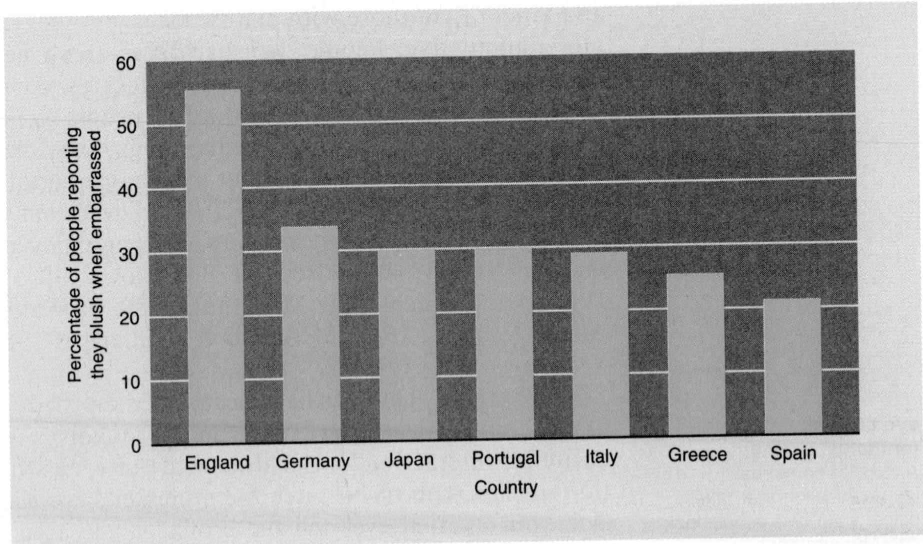

▲ **FIGURE 2-2**
Is blushing a universal phenomenon? When researchers asked people the question "Do you blush when you are embarrassed?" they found that the percentage of people who blushed varied across cultures. The Spanish reported blushing the least, and the British reported blushing the most. Some blushing was reported in every country, however, suggesting that blushing when embarrassed is commonplace. (From Edelmann et al., 1989)

People vary considerably in how much they blush. People who are anxious in social settings are more likely to blush, as are those with low self-esteem (Leary & Meadows, 1991). Cultural background also influences blushing. When researchers surveyed residents of the countries listed in Figure 2-2, they found that the English reported blushing the most, whereas the Spanish reported blushing the least (Edelmann et al., 1989). Both light-skinned and dark-skinned people blush, although blushing is much more visible in those with fairer complexions (Leary et al., 1992). Senator Biden and Anita Hill may have both blushed when they discussed the sexual details of Thomas's alleged harassment, but Biden's blushing was far more noticeable than Hill's because his skin is lighter than hers. Blushing may not, however, be a universally recognized emotion cue, like those discussed in the section, "In Depth: Cues, Culture, and Emotions."

Why do people blush? Although Charles Darwin believed that blushing served no useful social purpose, a red face clearly communicates to others that we are embarrassed and ashamed of what we have done. Blushing lets observers know we realize that we have erred and regret our mistake. The person who does something embarrassing and does not blush leaves a negative impression; the person who commits a faux pas but blushes is forgiven (Leary et al., 1992). As Mark Twain commented, "Man is the only animal that blushes. Or needs to."

Body Movements

We are usually in motion during our interactions with other people. Even though he sat in a chair before a microphone, Judge Thomas crossed and uncrossed his arms as he spoke, pointed a finger on occasion, shifted his posture, shook his head, and tapped on the table. What did these movements, these **kinesic cues** (kinesic means movement), communicate (Edinger & Patterson, 1983; Patterson et al., 1984)?

kinesic cues
Body movements that convey information to others; includes gestures, postures, facial expressions, gazing, and touching.

Posture and gait. The student slouched in a chair, the cadet standing ramrod straight, and the young woman who tilts her head to one side are all conveying information about their attitudes and emotions to onlookers. Consider the difference between an *open posture* and a *closed posture.* When we adopt an open posture, our knees and feet are spaced apart, we extend our arms out from our bodies, we keep our hands open, and we lean forward slightly as we face the perceiver. When we adopt a closed posture, we keep our legs and feet together, our arms against our bodies or crossed on the chest, our hands in our pockets or behind our backs, and our body angled away from the perceiver. A person in an open posture is usually seen as friendly, warm, and outgoing, while a person in a closed posture is viewed as unfriendly, cold, and nervous (Mehrabian, 1972).

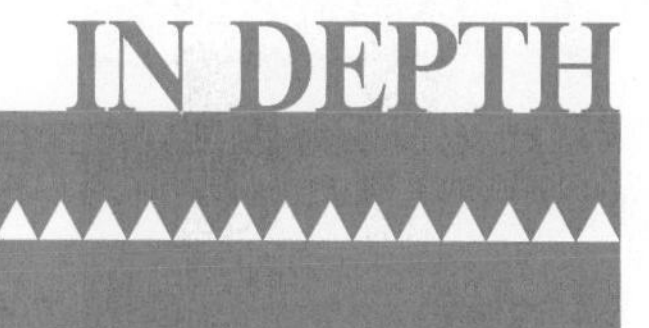

Cues, Culture, and Emotions

When one of the senators asked Judge Thomas about Hill's accusations, he sat silently for a moment. His eyes stared at the senator and seemed to bulge out from his face. His eyebrows lowered and drew together. His lips pressed together, their corners turned downward, and his chin pushed out. His nostrils flared slightly. Thomas said nothing, but those who saw him knew what he was feeling: Judge Thomas was angry.

Can we read emotions from the subtle changes in the face: a glint in the eyes, a twitch at the corners of the mouth, a pinch of the eyebrows, or the jut of the chin? Paul Ekman and Wallace V. Friesen say we can. They recognize that our emotions vary greatly in quality and intensity, but they argue that most are variations on the six primary emotions: *surprise, fear, anger, disgust, happiness,* and *sadness.* They also believe that specific facial cues are associated with each of these basic emotions. When we are happy, crow's-feet appear at the corners of the eyes, our cheeks rise, we expose our teeth, our lips turn up, and lines run from the nose to the corners of the lips. When we are disgusted, however, we lower our brows, wrinkle our noses, and raise our upper lips. To test this hypothesis, Ekman and Friesen asked perceivers to guess the emotions of people who deliberately assumed these facial cues in a photograph. As expected, perceivers were very accurate in deciphering these emotional messages (Ekman & Friesen, 1975; Ekman, Friesen, & Ellsworth, 1972). Ekman then repeated this study with photographs of unposed, spontaneous displays of emotion, and he again found that people could accurately detect emotions, with one exception: in this second study, surprise was sometimes confused with fear (Buck, 1984; Izard, 1980; Russell, 1991, 1994).

Ekman also found that the language of the face is not limited by culture or national borders. When Estonians, Germans, Greeks, Chinese, Italians, Japanese, New Guineans, Scots, Sumatrans, and Turks studied Ekman's pictures, they easily identified the emotions (Ekman et al., 1987; Levenson et al., 1992; Russell, 1991). Likewise, people living in the United States could identify emotions expressed in faces of people from other countries. Ekman photographed members of an isolated, preliterate tribe living in New Guinea as they acted out the emotions they would feel in such situations as the following:

- Your friend has come and you are happy.
- Your child has died.
- You are angry and about to fight.
- You see a dead pig that has been lying there for a long time.

When he showed people from other cultures these pictures, they could easily read the emotional message the New Guinea men were sending (Ekman, 1992a).

Culture did play a role in determining judgments of the intensity of emotions. Individuals raised in Asian countries, such as Japan and Sumatra, rated the emotions in some photographs (happiness, surprise) as less intense than did individuals raised in non-Asian countries (Ekman et al., 1987; Matsumoto & Ekman, 1989). Ekman also found that different cultures have different **display rules:** norms about how and when different emotions should be displayed. When Japanese and American subjects were secretly observed as they watched a gruesome film, both sets of subjects displayed the facial cues associated with disgust. When an experimenter was present in the room, only the American subjects looked disgusted; the Japanese masked their feelings with an outward smile (Ekman, 1992b).

Sex differences, like the cultural differences noted by Ekman, also shape our interpretation of emotional messages (Hall, 1984, 1985). In one recent study, 1,000 men and women were shown dozens of slides of various emotion-laden faces. Women usually emerged as more accurate judges than men across all the emotions save one: men were more accurate at detecting displays of anger (Rotter & Rotter, 1988). This effect may reflect sex differences in social skills, for superior social skills and communication effectiveness tend to go hand in hand (Feldman, Philippot, & Custrini, 1991; Tucker & Riggio, 1988).

display rules: Culture-specific norms that dictate how and when different emotions should be displayed by members of that culture.

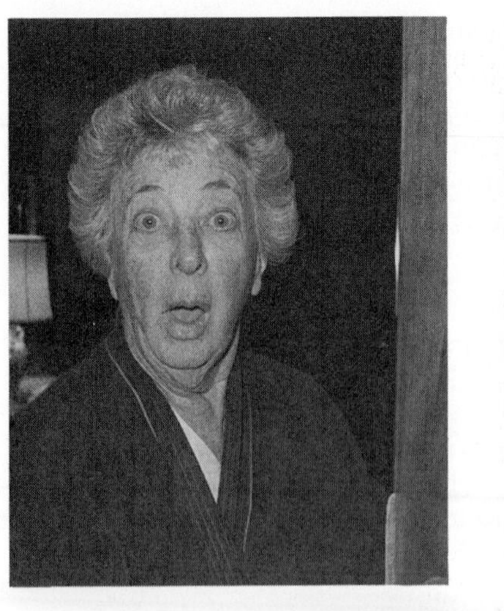

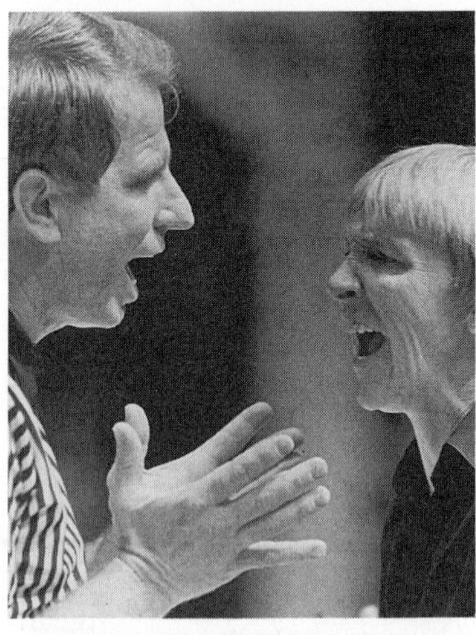

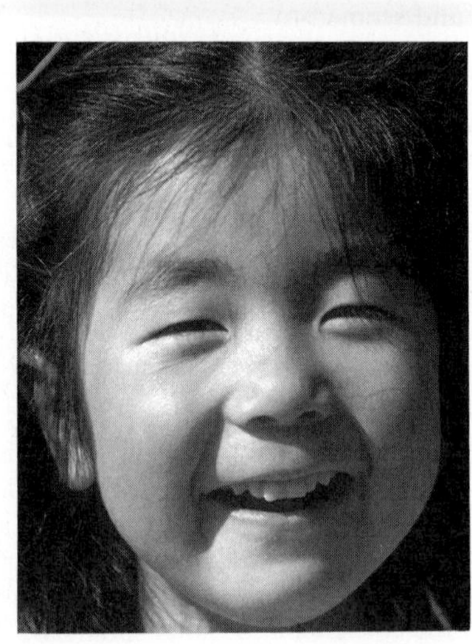

▲ What emotions are these people experiencing? Ekman and his colleagues find that people the world over can read six basic emotions from facial cues alone: surprise, fear, anger, disgust, happiness, and sadness.

The way we walk, too, can reveal information to others if they are careful to take notice. In one study researchers videotaped people as they acted out situations that would cause anger, sadness, or happiness. Sadness was simulated by having them imagine they were walking down a hospital corridor after visiting a friend who was seriously injured in an accident. When these videotapes were shown to other subjects, they could identify the emotion on the basis of gait alone. Long strides and heavy steps conveyed anger. A fast pace? Happiness. A slow pace with small arm swings? Sadness (Montepare, Goldstein, & Clausen, 1987). In related work investigators found evidence of both a "happy walk" and a "power walk." People who adopted a youthful gait that included more sway in the hips, knee bending, arm swinging, loose-jointedness, a bouncier rhythm, and a rapid pace were judged to be both happier and more powerful. A masculine gait characterized by a longer stride and forward body lean was viewed as a sign of power, but not of happiness. Observers didn't consider either gait to be particularly sexy (Montepare & Zebrowitz-McArthur, 1988).

▲ In 1968 North Korea captured the *Pueblo*, a vessel they claimed was on a spy mission for the United States. The crew eventually confessed to crimes against Korea; the Koreans released this photograph to show that the confession had not been coerced. The men in the photograph, however, broadcast a strong nonverbal message. Their faces reveal signs of tension, nervousness, and rigidity. Moreover, three men (*front row: far left, far right, and second from right*) display the insulting middle-finger gesture, which communicates contempt and anger in Western cultures but is not widely recognized in Eastern cultures.

Gestures. Some of our body movements convey relatively specific messages about ourselves, our meanings, and our feelings for the people who surround us. When we think our friend's idea is crazy, we make a rapid circular motion with our forefinger next to our ear. To express anger we clench our fists or display the *digitus impudicus.* When we describe the size of the one that got away, we hold up an imaginary fish between our hands. To seem pensive we tilt our heads back and stroke our chins. When we want someone to precede us into the room, we place one hand on our chest and motion to the open door with the other hand.

gestures
Movements of the body that convey relatively specific information; usually used as a supplement to verbal communication or when verbal channels are blocked.

These movements of the face, arms, and hands are **gestures**, and they serve a variety of useful functions. As Table 2-1 indicates, *emblems* convey specific messages, *illustrators* clarify our verbal statements, *manipulators* adjust our body or objects around us, and *regulators* guide and organize social interactions—who speaks next, who enters a doorway first, and the like (Ekman, Friesen, & Bear, 1984; Johnson, Ekman, & Friesen, 1975; compare with Rime & Schiaratura, 1991). Our gesticulations also serve a linguistic function, for recent evidence indicates that gestures help us formulate verbal statements by improving the way we retrieve and process verbal information (Krauss, Morrel-Samuels, & Colasante, 1991). Some researchers think gestures are so specific in meaning that they qualify as linguistic communication (McNeill, 1985).

Gestures, however, lack the cross-culture universality of the basic emotional expressions noted earlier. The "thumbs-up" gesture, which was used by Roman emperors to spare gladiators and now means "all right" in the United States, means "up yours" in northern Greece. The "A-OK" gesture formed when the forefinger and thumb are pressed together to form a circle means "you asshole" in southern Italy, "you're worth zero" in France, and a desire for anal sex in some other parts of Europe. Some cultures have unique gestures that have no clear meaning to outsiders. The French express "he's drunk" by putting the fist to the nose, and then twisting it; the Germans say "good luck" by balling up their hands into fists (with the thumbs tucked inside) and then making a downward pounding motion. So if you travel to a foreign country, be sure to speak as carefully with your hands as you do with your mouth (Ekman, Friesen, & Bear, 1984; Ricci Bitti & Poggi, 1991).

▲ **TABLE 2-1**
Varieties of gestures. Ekman and his colleagues have identified four basic kinds of gestures: emblems, illustrators, manipulators, and regulators.

Type of Gesture	*Definition*	*Examples*
Emblem	A signal, often made with the hand, that conveys a specific meaning	"Thumbs up" (fist clenched, thumb sticking up); the "bird" (middle finger extended)
Illustrator	An action that explains verbal communication but has no meaning alone	Pointing, outlining an object's shape, indicating age with fingers
Manipulator	Touching or rubbing an object or one's own body	Fidgeting with a button, picking the nose, rubbing the eyes
Regulator	An action that structures and organizes social behavior	Pointing to the next speaker; inviting a person to enter

Source: Adapted from Ekman, Friesen, & Bear, 1984; Johnson, Ekman, & Friesen, 1975.

Touching. A touch is one of the most intimate, most closely guarded, forms of nonverbal communication (Thayer, 1988). On any day you might shake hands with an acquaintance, kiss your lover's lips, touch a coworker lightly on the arm, push down a threatening stranger, hold hands with a child, or put your arm around a friend's shoulder. Indeed, one study of 1,500 instances of touching in everyday encounters revealed 12 different uses of touch, including support, appreciation, inclusion, sexual interest or intent, affection, demonstration of affection, playful aggression, compliance, attention-getting, announcing a response, greetings, and departure (Jones & Yarbrough, 1985).

Men and women differ, to a degree, in their initiation and response to touching. Women are more comfortable than men when giving and receiving touches in intimate settings, but women respond more negatively when unexpectedly touched by men (Andersen, Andersen, & Lustig, 1987; Derlega et al., 1989; Fromme et al., 1989). In nonintimate settings the sexes differ little in the amount of touching they do. One study of 4,500 dyads interacting in public places found that, in young couples, more of the males touched the females than the females touched the males. This tendency reversed in older couples (Hall & Veccia, 1990).

An interpersonal touch, provided the situation is friendly, usually fosters a positive impression (Burgoon et al., 1989; Stier & Hall, 1984). Clerks in a library were rated more positively when they momentarily touched a patron's hand when checking out books than when they did not—even though many of the patrons never even noticed the touch (Fisher, Rytting, & Heslin, 1976). Similarly, a handshake accompanied by a gentle squeeze of the upper arm usually makes a better impression than a handshake alone (Silverthorne et al., 1976). Also, a person who has been touched is more likely to do small favors for the toucher than someone who has not been touched (Brockner et al., 1982; Hornik & Ellis, 1988).

An unwanted touch, however, is aversive. When people we do not know well touch us, they violate implicit norms that govern intimacy and privacy (Burgoon & Walther, 1990). In these cases we view the toucher negatively and, if possible, we may seek to withdraw from the situation. A touch that is used to demonstrate status or control—as when a high-status man demeans a lower-status woman by putting his arm around her—also creates a negative impression (Henley, 1977; LaFrance, 1985; Major, 1981). Touching, when unwanted, is a form of sexual harassment, both legally and in most people's minds: A recent poll found that 64% of the respondents felt that when "a man who is a woman's boss or supervisor frequently puts his arm around her shoulders or back," he is harassing that woman (Gibbs, 1991). Clearly care should be taken when using touch, or any other nonverbal or verbal signal, during an interaction with colleagues to avoid sexual misunderstandings and ethical violations (Cooper, 1990).

Paralanguage

Many of our perceptions depend on *how* something is said, rather than *what* is said. When Judge Thomas said, "She never raised any hint that she was uncomfortable with me," he stressed the word *never* to convey his surprise at her charges. Had he stressed *she,* however, he would have implied that someone else had hinted, but Hill had not. And if he had ended the sentence with inflection ("She never raised any hint that she was uncomfortable with me?"), he would have expressed surprise. Voice cues that accompany spoken language, the stress put on words, intonation, pitch of the voice, and even sounds that have no verbal meaning (crying, mumbling, and the like) are often called **paralanguage**. Unlike visual cues found in appearance, eye gaze, and body movement cues, paralanguage is an auditory cue.

paralanguage
Voice cues, such as intonation, pitch, and pauses, that accompany spoken language; how something is said, rather than what is said.

Researchers study the impact of paralanguage on perceptions by separating voice and verbal information experimentally (Ambady & Rosenthal, 1992; Ekman et al., 1980; O'Sullivan et al., 1985; Perlmutter, Paddock, & Duke, 1985). The subjects in one study of this type reviewed a videotape or transcript of women answering questions dealing with topics that were either positive (friendship, happiness) or negative (dislikes, sadness). The subjects' task was to guess what kind of question the woman in each segment was answering (Krauss et al., 1981).

The researchers varied the type of information given to the subjects by creating the following five experimental conditions:

- *Transcript only.* Subjects read a written transcript of each segment but couldn't see or hear the segment.
- *Audio-video.* Subjects watched a videotaped recording of each segment.
- *Audio only.* Subjects listened to a tape recording of each segment.
- *Content-filtered audio.* Subjects listened to a tape recording of each segment that had been electronically filtered to blur the words but retain the paralinguistic cues. Like muffled conversations heard through a wall, these tapes are not intelligible, but changes in pitch, pauses, tone, and so on can be detected.
- *Video only.* Subjects watched a videotape of each segment with no sound track.

Subjects were very accurate when they were given the verbal message; they correctly identified the question over 95% of the time in the transcript, audiovisual, and audio conditions (see Figure 2-3). When the subjects listened to the filtered tape recording, their accuracy rate dropped dramatically (41.4% correct), but this score was still higher than any they could have achieved by random guessing. Their performance in the last condition, in which they could base their responses only on kinesic nonverbal cues, was not much better than chance guessing (32.4%). Thus, even though the filtered tape recording contained only vocal information, it was more informative than a silent videotape.

In this study, a picture *wasn't* worth a thousand words; people were more accurate when they had access to audio information than to visual information. The findings would probably have been different, however, if the subjects had watched people who were discussing more involving, exciting topics that

▲ **FIGURE 2-3**
Is a picture worth a thousand words? Not always. When people were shown a videotape of a person, they couldn't judge her accurately. When they could hear the tone of her voice, they became more accurate, but they were most accurate when they could hear the words she was speaking. (Data from Krauss et al., 1981)

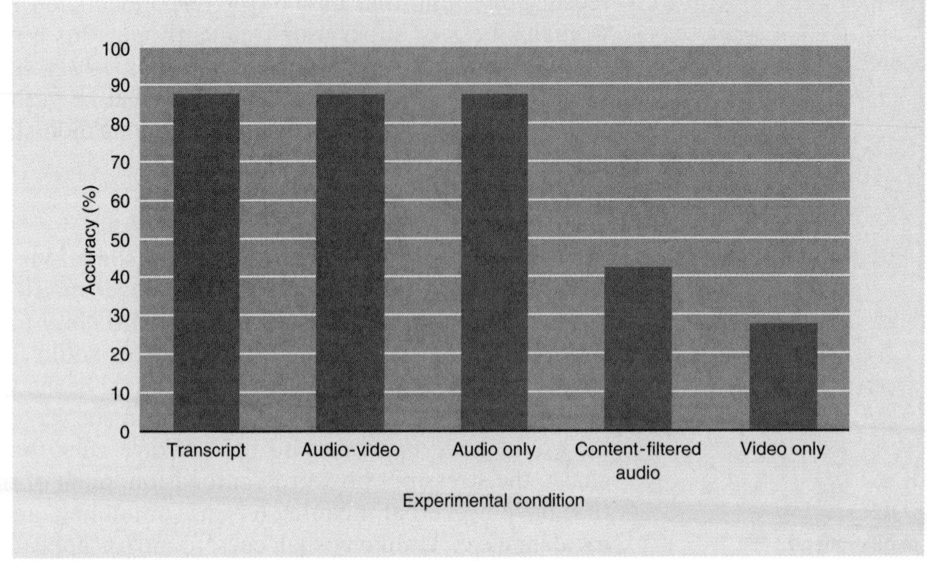

stimulated greater nonverbal communications. Also, as the section "Application: Detecting Deceivers" at the end of the chapter explains, the relative impact of verbal and nonverbal information depends on whether or not people are speaking frankly or deceptively (DePaulo, 1991; Zuckerman et al., 1982). In such situations, paralinguistic cues may tell us more than either kinesic cues or verbal cues (Berry, 1991; Krauss, Morrel-Samuels, & Colasante, 1991; Noller, 1985; see Table 2-2).

Managing Impressions

The ability to understand other people may be a remarkable gift, but it is one we have all received. We appraise other people's personalities, traits, and motives at a glance by considering their looks, body movements, and the way they express themselves.

But social perception is not a one-way process in which a detached observer records impressions of a passive stimulus person. Perceiving people isn't like sensing colors, sounds, or inanimate objects. If we decide that a shade of red should be called "puce," the color can't argue with us. If we decide a car is ugly, the car's feelings can't be hurt. People, however, play an active role in their own perception. When you know that you are the object of another's scrutiny, you can take steps to make certain the observer reaches a conclusion acceptable to you. The man who wants everyone to know he is waiting for a bus rather than just loafing scans the road in anticipation. The woman on her way to lunch who remembers that she left a letter behind on her desk pauses and snaps her fingers, then retraces her steps. The professor who seeks to project an intellectual image uses elegant phrasings and dresses shabbily. Even in these simple situations we engage in *impression management*: we steer others' impressions of us by selectively displaying social behaviors that establish, maintain, or refine our social identity (Goffman, 1959; Leary & Kowalski, 1990; Schlenker, 1980).

self-presentation (or impression management) Revealing information about one's personal qualities, such as emotions, personality traits, dispositions, and abilities, to others through both verbal and nonverbal means.

Impression management is often referred to as **self-presentation**, for it requires the exhibition of personal characteristics before a public audience. This viewpoint, which was championed repeatedly by anthropologist Erving

▲ TABLE 2-2
Summing up: Channels of nonverbal communication

Channel	*Examples*
Physical appearance	Skin color and tone, body size, hairstyle, dress, beauty, physique
Facial cues	Maturity of the face (babyishness), blushing, eye contact (staring, gazing), and facial displays of emotions
Kinesic cues (body movement)	Gestures, gait, closeness, slouching, nodding the head, touching
Paralanguage (voice cues)	Tone of voice, mumbling, stuttering, pauses, coughs

Goffman (1959), assumes that the interplay between the individual and the perceiver is analogous to the exchange between an actor and an audience. Just as an actor has a part to play, each of us has a **face**, or social image, that we are trying to foster. And just as actors must recite their lines and carry out the roles assigned them, so we must maintain our face by revealing selective aspects of ourselves through self-descriptions, body postures, styles of dress, statements of opinions, and the like. As Shakespeare proclaimed, "All the world's a stage," and "all the men and women are merely players" on that stage. The nuances of this delicate interpersonal process are considered in the next section.

face
Goffman's (1959) term for the social image that a person attempts to claim and maintain in a given situation.

Tactics for Managing Impressions

Consider Judge Thomas's testimony before the Senate subcommittee. Thomas wanted to be a Supreme Court judge, so he did all he could to claim that identity. When he answered questions thoughtfully and articulately, he was indirectly proclaiming, "I am an intelligent man." When he described his political beliefs, he was telling viewers that he was a conservative person with traditional values. But when he was accused of sexual harassment, suddenly he was *out of face*: His public image was in danger of being destroyed. He therefore redoubled his self-presentational efforts, or *facework,* to claim, "I am an innocent man who has been unjustly accused of a great crime." Thomas took an active role in this perceptual process by shaping others' perceptions of him.

Even though each of us plays a unique part on the stage of social life, most of us share a common set of self-presentational goals. Thomas needed to create the public image of a judge, but on his way to this goal he also needed to create other, more general, impressions. He needed others to see him as an attractive man rather than as a man who was socially offensive. He needed to appear competent and able rather than bumbling and stupid. He needed to avoid the appearance of weakness and stress instead his strength of will. These goals are among those identified by Edward E. Jones and Thane Pittman (1982) in their classic analysis of strategic impression management: ingratiation, self-promotion, intimidation, supplication, and exemplification.

Ingratiation: "I am likable." Dale Carnegie's book *How to Win Friends and Influence People* was first published in 1937 in an edition of only 5,000 copies. His publishers never expected a book filled with suggestions for increasing one's likability to be a best-seller. But a half-century later, the book is still in print, a testimony to our common need to be liked and admired by the people around us.

Carnegie's book is a how-to manual on **ingratiation**: winning others' affection through strategic self-presentation (Jones, 1964, 1990; Jones & Wortman,

ingratiation
Creating an attractive, audience-pleasing identity through strategic self-presentation.

1973). What do you do when you are talking to a potential romantic partner at a party, meeting a friend's parents for the first time, or lunching with a business client, and you want to be liked? First, create an impression of great interest in the other person. Rather than talking about yourself or your own interests, encourage the others to discuss themselves and their interests. When Jones and his colleagues asked people to describe what they would do if they needed to get another person to like them, nearly all of them mentioned "show interest" in the person and "draw the other person out" (Godfrey, Jones, & Lord, 1986).

Your nonverbal displays are also important in ingratiation (DePaulo, 1992). To make a good impression, be careful to look at the other person, use your eyebrows and mouth expressively, and avoid yawns and stares (see Table 2-3). Smiling is especially important, for people who are smiling are usually rated as more attractive than people who aren't smiling, even when raters are told to compensate for the impact of the smile (Mueser et al., 1984). People smile at people who smile at them (Hinsz & Tomhave, 1991). Next, position your body appropriately. Adopt a relaxed (but not too relaxed) posture by turning your head and shoulders in his or her direction and leaning forward slightly: don't slouch. In addition, you may want to adopt an open rather than closed posture, and touch the person on the hand, arm, or shoulder if a touch is appropriate in the situation (Stier & Hall, 1984).

These nonverbal actions are powerful impression management tools because they symbolize involvement and friendliness; they seem to say "I'm interested in what you have to say" (Edinger & Patterson, 1983). These behaviors should be used only when they match the display rules of the situation. Different behaviors are considered appropriate in different situations. If you violate these implicit norms, you may earn yourself a swift rejection. When you're discussing extremely intimate subjects, a high level of gaze may be inappropriate, so by staring at someone you may ensure your own rejection (Argyle & Dean, 1965). The impact of nonverbal cues also depends on the sex of the sender. For example, in one study women were judged more favorably the more they smiled and used facial expressions. Men's facial expressions did not influence their attractiveness (Riggio & Friedman, 1986).

▲ Thomas faced a complex impression management situation when he testified before the Senate subcommittee. He not only had to demonstrate that he possessed the skills needed in a justice of the Supreme Court, but he also had to convince the senators that he was innocent of all Hill's charges. Through careful impression management, he achieved both objectives. (Note the expressiveness of Thomas's face and his use of hand gestures.)

▲ **TABLE 2-3**
Nonverbal ingratiation: Behaviors that communicate friendliness and unfriendliness to others

Positive Behaviors	*Negative Behaviors*
High eye contact	Low eye contact
Leaning forward	Leaning away
Smiling	Frowning
Moving toward	Moving away
Touching hands	Touching own hair
Broadly smiling	Looking away
Grinning	Sneering
Nodding head	Cold stare
Raising eyebrows	Picking the teeth
Facing forward	Cracking the fingers
Gesturing with hands	Picking at the hands
Showing happiness	Yawning
Open body position	Closed body position
Straightening one's back	Slouching

Sources: From Burgoon et al., 1984; Mehrabian, 1972.

Other tactics, such as opinion conformity, compliments, and doing favors for the person, can also increase likability. What should Clarence Thomas do when asked about his views on abortion? If he privately believes that abortion should be outlawed, but he feels that the observers disagree with this position, to ingratiate he might publicly claim that he is ambivalent on the issue of abortion rights. Similarly, if you are discussing some topic with a new acquaintance, it's wiser to stress areas of agreement than disagreement. If the target person likes the Republican candidate, rap music, and the Mets, you might claim that you, too, vote Republican, have dozens of rap CDs, and root for the Mets (Tetlock, Skitka, & Boettger, 1989).

ingratiator's dilemma
People who most need to impress others are the least likely to be successful because observers become increasingly suspicious of others' self-presentational claims as the need for successful self-presentation increases.

Opinion conformity increases your attractiveness, but this tactic—like all ingratiation tactics—may backfire if your target realizes that your conformity is an ingratiation ploy. Jones labeled this problem the **ingratiator's dilemma**: "The more important it is to be liked, the more sensitized the target person will be to any cues suggesting deceit or inauthenticity" (Jones, 1990, p. 180). So the more you have to gain by ingratiating, the less effective your ingratiation will be. In Thomas's case, observers were skeptical of his claims because pressures to ingratiate were great. Everyone watching knew he was trying to put on his best face for the senators.

Jones noted several ways to escape from the ingratiator's dilemma. First, be sincere—if you really do admire the other person and agree with his or her opinions, your self-presentational claims will be more believable than if you are lying. Even a sincere compliment or statement of agreement can be misinterpreted, however, so you may need to use other tactics to increase the power of a compliment. Avoid seeming too dependent on the target person, and make your claims positive but plausible. Also, when complimenting others, focus on attributes that the target person is unsure about. If you compliment extremely beautiful people on their good looks you will have little impact: They probably already know they are beautiful, and other people tell them so all the time. Instead, deliver a compliment that erases their doubts about their own standing on another attribute. As Lord Chesterfield wrote several centuries ago,

"Very ugly or very beautiful women should be flattered on their understanding, and mediocre ones on their beauty" (Chesterfield, 1774/1901, p. 27).

Opinion conformity, compliments, and other ingratiation tactics are often effective, but are they ignoble? Intuitively, we tend to see ingratiation as reprehensible because the people who practice it manipulate others' perceptions rather than letting them reach their own conclusions. But what happens when other people misunderstand us, taking us for someone who is cold and rejecting when we are really warm and friendly? As Jones and his colleagues point out, "Adaptive social life requires a little blarney now and then to mute the impact of disagreement, antagonism, and even love" (Jones & Wortman, 1973, p. 52).

Self-promotion: "I am competent." We aren't always trying to convince others we are attractive people. Sometimes we willingly sacrifice likability to convince others that we are competent. Students want their teachers to view them as intelligent. Employees want the boss to see them as skilled at their jobs. Your social psychology teacher wants you to conclude that he or she is knowledgeable and effective. Judge Thomas may want you to think he will be a masterful jurist. It doesn't matter to him whether you like him or not.

self-promotion
Claiming positive personal qualities, abilities, and competencies through self-presentation behavior.

Self-promotion tactics allow us to create an impression of competence and effectiveness. Unlike ingratiators, self-promoters are proactive rather than reactive. They tend to initiate conversations, shift topics to their own areas of competence, and use attention-getting nonverbal behaviors (Godfrey et al., 1986). Self-promoters also stress their strengths and accomplishments and downplay their weaknesses and failures. Students who are failing math will talk instead about their good grades in psychology (Forsyth & McMillan, 1981a); politicians will emphasize their policy successes rather than their programs that ended in failure (Tetlock, 1981, 1985); and group members will mention the role they played in successes rather than failures (Miller & Schlenker, 1985). We also tend to tailor our self-description to fit the characteristics our audience seeks. When the leaders of small groups described their personal qualities, they stressed their competence, efficiency, and directiveness when they were told that a good leader should be task oriented. When the leaders were told that good leaders should be interpersonally supportive, they then described themselves as approachable, understanding, and sociable (Leary, Robertson, et al., 1986).

Self-promotion, however, is tricky. When we brag about our good qualities or accomplishments, others become skeptical of our claims and likability. Self-promoters also run the risk of being found out if their performances fail to match their self-presentational claims. Individuals who loudly proclaim their competence after they have performed poorly at a task do not make a particularly good impression (Schlenker & Leary, 1982a).

Skilled impression managers are cognizant of this danger, so they often use more indirect tactics when trying to influence others' impressions. Modesty is often a more skillful self-promotion tactic than self-aggrandizement, for it lends support to an impression of social competence, honesty, *and* likability (Tetlock, 1980). When the audience already knows we have impressive personal qualities, or even knows that we are incompetent oafs, the best policy may be downplaying our strengths and admitting to a few limitations (Forsyth, Berger, & Mitchell, 1981; Tetlock, 1980). **Basking In Reflected Glory**, or BIRGing, also offers a more indirect pathway to self-promotion. When BIRGing, we draw the observer's attention to our association with other competent or attractive people. Clarence Thomas was BIRGing when he linked himself to the

Basking In Reflected Glory (BIRGing)
Associating with, or drawing others' attention to, our association with prestigious groups or individuals.

▲ Curtis, the savvy ingratiator, knows that an effective way to create a likable image in Michelle's eyes is to focus the conversation on Michelle and not on himself. In the words of Disraeli: "Talk to a man about himself and he will listen for hours."

©1993 King Features Syndicate, Inc. World rights reserved.

Reprinted with special permission of King Features.

president: "When I stood next to the President in Kennebunkport being nominated to the Supreme Court of the United States, that was a high honor" (Thomas, 1991, p. A-6). Similarly, college students BIRG when their school accomplishes a noteworthy feat (Cialdini et al., 1976). When their football team wins, more students wear clothes bearing their university's name or mascot. Students also use the word *we* more when talking about their school after a win ("We are a good school") and the word *they* more after a loss ("They lost that game"). People even BIRG by mentioning that they have the same birthday as someone who is famous or has other positive social and intellectual qualities (Cialdini & De Nicholas, 1989; see also Cialdini & Richardson, 1980; Snyder, Lassegard, & Ford, 1986).

Intimidation: "I am powerful." Virtually all social animals know how to communicate the message "I am powerful." The dominant chimpanzee chatters loudly at potential rivals and waves his arms in the air. The lead wolf in the pack growls and bares his teeth when a low-ranking wolf passes by too closely. The ranking lioness in the pride rebuffs a rank-and-file member with a swat of her paw and a roar. Humans, too, can lay claim to a powerful social identity by using **intimidation** tactics (Lee & Ofshe, 1981; Mazur, 1983). Clarence Thomas did not seem meek or uncertain when he answered the senators' queries. Rather, he projected an image of strength and self-assuredness.

intimidation
Claiming power by making demands, confronting others, bullying, making threats, showing anger, and otherwise behaving aggressively.

People signal their power to others verbally and nonverbally. Verbally, instead of asking what should be done, intimidators tell other people what to do. They interpret, confirm, and dispute the views of others, but keep their own feelings or worries to themselves. They don't ask questions that reveal their uncertainty. Instead, they summarize what others have said and reflect on others' contributions (Stiles et al., 1984). They also use strong rather than weak tactics when they try to influence others (Kipnis, 1984). Instead of pleading with others or evading issues, intimidators demand, confront, persist, and even bully and threaten (Cowan, Drinkard, & MacGavin, 1984; Falbo & Peplau, 1980). Powerful people also talk the most when they are in a group or other social setting (Cappella, 1985; Dovidio, Brown, et al., 1988).

Nonverbally, intimidators usually dress in ways that match the display rules of the situation they face. A dark, well-tailored suit is often called a *power suit,* for it suggests the wearer is influential. Powerful people also maintain more eye contact with others when they speak; when others speak, they tend to look away (Dovidio, Ellyson, et al., 1988). They also use large, sweeping movements of their hands and head when they speak, they extend their legs outward when seated, and they seem relaxed and comfortable whether they are standing or sitting. They thrust their chins outward, their handshakes are vice-like rather than limp, and they avoid smiling (Gifford, 1991; Leffler, Gillespie, & Conaty, 1982).

Do these impression management tactics work? In one study of this question, male subjects role-played members of a jury reviewing the evidence in a personal injury lawsuit. Initially, all of the subjects felt that the plaintiff should be awarded at least $10,000. Before making their final decisions, however, they watched a videotape of a man who argued that a settlement of $2,000 was quite fair. For some subjects, the man who made the arguments created an impression of power by speaking in a firm, rapid, and loud voice. He rarely hesitated or stumbled over his words, and he appeared to be relaxed. He also wore a tie and sport coat. Other subjects saw a more deferential speaker. Although he made exactly the same verbal arguments, he spoke softly, slowly, and hesitantly. He paused, often searched for words, and occasionally said "umm" and "uh." He fidgeted with his hands, and he wore a T-shirt. A third group of subjects listened to a man who fell between these two extremes: He spoke at a moderate rate, he seemed fairly relaxed, and he wore a sport shirt (Lee & Ofshe, 1981).

After listening to the speakers, all three groups changed their initial award. Those who watched the first speaker were sufficiently impressed to cut their settlement down by an average of $4,273. Those watching the third speaker reduced theirs only slightly, by $2,426. Those who listened to the second speaker—the one who displayed weak rather than strong nonverbal cues—*increased* the sum they wanted to give the plaintiff by an average of $2,843. So when it comes to influencing others through impression management, it often pays to strike a powerful pose.

supplication
Claiming a lack of power through such self-presentation tactics as self-criticism, displays of submissiveness, and appearing to be easily influenced.

Supplication: "I am weak." **Supplication** is the opposite of intimidation. Supplicants, instead of projecting an image of power and dominance, try to convince others that they are weak and dependent. Instead of stressing their strengths and assuming a look of self-confidence, supplicants exaggerate their problems, bemoan the hopelessness of their situations, criticize themselves unmercifully, and acknowledge their need for help from others. They create this image for two reasons (Jones & Pittman, 1982). First, by admitting their limitations from the outset, they protect themselves from attack. Who can criticize a person who has already admitted his or her worthlessness? Second, supplication also exploits our natural tendency to help others in need. When supplicants tell us their problems, we offer to help solve them. When they criticize themselves, we respond by reassuring them of their worth. When they say all is hopeless, we do what we can to cheer them up. We tend to care for people who are weak and dependent on us.

complementarity principle
The assumption that certain interpersonal behaviors elicit certain complementary behaviors from other people. The principle assumes that people tend to respond positively to positive actions and negatively to negative actions. In contrast, coercive, powerful actions tend to elicit weak, submissive responses; submissive responses elicit strong, powerful reactions.

Putting on a front of weakness, however, is perhaps the riskiest of all impression management strategies. First, supplication does not always elicit nurturance from others. According to the **complementarity principle**, the most natural response to weakness is dominance. This principle maintains that certain interpersonal behaviors tend to pull the complementary behavior from others. When someone is friendly to us, we tend to respond to them in a friendly way, too. The complementary response to friendliness is friendliness. When someone acts in a self-deprecating, meek way, however, the complementary response tends to be domination rather than nurturance (Horowitz et al., 1991; Powers & Zuroff, 1988; Strong, 1991a). Moreover, over the long term any nurturance that supplication does evoke usually gives way to rejection. When we interact with people who seem weak and helpless, we often experience negative affect ourselves: tension, anxiety, hostility, and dislike. Indeed, studies of depressed individuals—who often display many of the same interpersonal qualities as the supplicant—indicate that their intimates eventually withdraw their nurturance if the depression continues for any length of time (Coyne, Burchill, & Stiles, 1991). Supplication, then, is the tactic of last resort, "the preferred strategy for low-power persons who have little else going for them" (Jones, 1990, p. 196).

exemplification
Claiming high moral worth by acting selflessly and describing oneself moralistically.

Exemplification: "I am worthy." Jones and Pittman (1982) close their taxonomy of impression management tactics with **exemplification**: laying claim to high moral worth by performing selfless actions and through moralistic self-descriptions. A volunteer who helps charities or a politician who has not been accused of any moral wrongdoing may draw observers' attentions to their actions in order to establish a sterling moral reputation. Again, Clarence Thomas (1991) provides an example in defending himself against Hill's charges. He stated, repeatedly, that he had an unblemished record of service in fighting against sexual harassment. Moreover, he was devoted to family values and had the support of all the other women in his office. Finally, he expressed the moral and personal anguish that the charges had produced:

> I have never in all my life felt such hurt, such pain, such agony. My family and I have been done a grave and irreparable injustice.
>
> It has got to stop. It must stop for the benefit of future nominees and our country. Enough is enough. I'm not going to allow myself to be further humiliated in order to be confirmed.
>
> In my 43 years on this Earth I have been able, with the help of others and with the help of God, to defy poverty, avoid prison, overcome segregation, bigotry, racism, and obtain one of the finest educations available in this country, but I have not been able to overcome this process. (p. A-6)

Exemplifiers, like all impression managers, must avoid this particular, avoid the appearance of *hypocrisy*: claiming to be morally virtuous, then acting in ways that are immoral. Most of us usually condemn people who act immorally anyway, but such lapses are particularly damaging for exemplifiers. In a study of such lapses some subjects watched an interview with an individual who claimed a solid moral character. This exemplifier stated that he always told the truth, that he always resisted the temptation to act immorally, and that moral codes should be followed. Others listened to an individual profess the moral values of a pragmatist: He claimed that he sometimes behaved immorally when the situation required it. Next, the subjects were led to believe that the interviewee later cheated or did not cheat on a test. As expected, the exemplifier who cheated was roundly condemned as a hypocrite (see Figure 2-4). Ironically, the pragmatist who failed to live up to his claims of moral looseness was also viewed as hypocritical when he *didn't* cheat. In this study, at least, remaining true to one's word appeared to be the most effective impression management strategy (Gilbert & Jones, 1986a).

When Impression Management Misfires: Accounts

accounts
Self-presentational claims designed to explain away an embarrassing or identity-threatening event or action.

No matter how adept we might be in using the various tactics summarized in Table 2-4, we will make mistakes from time to time. We may mistakenly violate social norms of propriety. We might accidentally insult others without realizing it. We can fail publicly or say things that are embarrassing (Miller & Leary, 1992). When we find ourselves in such situations, we often struggle to restore the impression we are trying to create by offering **accounts**: "explanations of a predicament-creating event designed to minimize the apparent severity of the predicament" (Schlenker, 1980, p. 136; see also Harvey, Orbuch, & Weber, 1990; Schönbach, 1980).

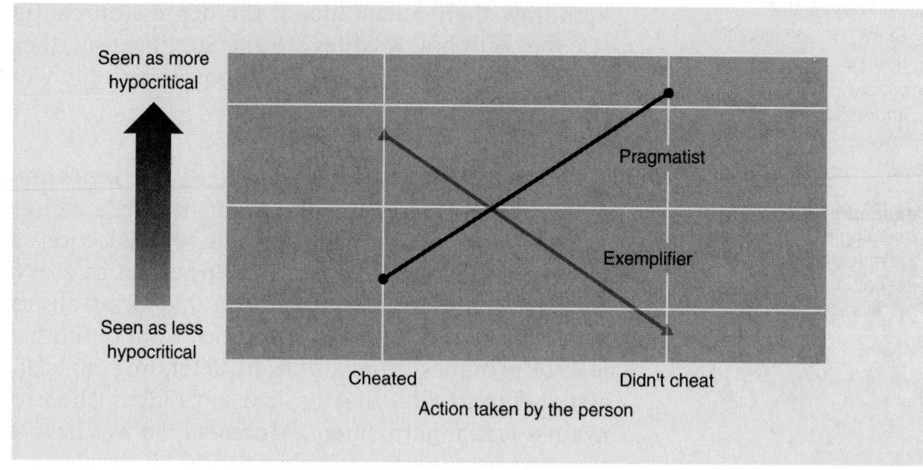

▲ **FIGURE 2-4**
When do we decide that another person is a hypocrite? People who claimed they were morally upright—exemplifiers—were seen as hypocrites if they cheated when they got the chance. Ironically, people who claimed that they weren't particularly moral—pragmatists—were seen as very hypocritical when they passed up an opportunity to cheat. Hypocrites, then, are people who fail to live up to their self-presentational claims, whether these claims are positive or negative. (From Gilbert & Jones, 1986a)

Accounts take many forms. *Excuses* reduce our responsibility for failures, blunders, faux pas, or immoral behavior. Students who fail a test often attribute their performance to external factors that were beyond their control: poor lighting, difficult material, sickness, or test anxiety (Kernis & Grannemann, 1990; Strube, 1985). Men who fear that they will behave in a socially awkward way blame their actions on their shyness (Snyder et al., 1985). *Justifications* redefine the events as positive or, at least, less harmful than might be expected. Terrorists can claim their ends justify their means, a man who harasses his secretary can claim that he has a right to flirt with her, and parents who physically punish their children can explain that it is for the children's own good. In contrast, a man who says, "It never happened" when accused of sexual harassment and the criminal who says, "I was at home when the bank was robbed" are using *denial*; they seek to absolve themselves of any responsibility by claiming that they didn't commit the behavior in question. Finally, when situations are such that we must admit we are responsible, and the action has undeniable negative consequences, we fall back on *apologies*: We admit we did it, but we say we are sorry. No matter what tactic we choose, our goal is the same: to regain a positive social identity by refuting other people's mistaken beliefs about us (Gonzales, Manning, & Haugen, 1992; Gonzales et al., 1990; Tedeschi & Riess, 1981; Tedeschi et al., 1983).

Are We All Effective Impression Managers?

We are all actors in the drama of social life, but some of us seem to be more adept in our performances than others. Poised and tactful, such people always seem to be ready with just the right action or word to set any social situation flowing smoothly. Others seem to disregard the constraints of the situation, and usually do and say whatever is on their minds.

self-monitoring
The degree to which individuals monitor and regulate their behavior to fit the situation. High self-monitors tend to regard themselves as shrewd, adaptable individuals who alter their actions to fit a given situation; low self-monitors value congruence between their private attributes and public actions.

Mark Snyder believes that these variations are caused by individual differences in **self-monitoring**: the degree to which people monitor and regulate their behavior to fit the situation. Some people are high in self-monitoring; they generally "regard themselves as rather flexible and adaptive creatures, who shrewdly and pragmatically tailor their social behavior to fit situational and interpersonal specifications of appropriateness." Low self-monitors, in contrast, "regard themselves as rather principled beings who value congruence between their actions in social situations and relevant underlying attitudes, feelings, and dispositions" (Snyder & Campbell, 1982, pp. 186–187). Snyder

▲ **TABLE 2-4**
Summing up: Five strategies that people commonly use to create various types of impressions during social interaction

Strategy	*Impression*	*Tactics*	*Risks*
Ingratiation	"I am likable."	Opinion conformity, compliments, favors, attentiveness	Sycophantic, obsequious
Self-promotion	"I am competent."	Positive self-descriptions, performance claims	Boastful, conceited
Intimidation	"I am powerful."	Threats, showing anger, displays of aggression	Blustering, bullying
Supplication	"I am weak."	Self-deprecation, submissiveness, pleading	Lazy, needy
Exemplification	"I am worthy."	Claims of moral worth, self-denial, helping, suffering	Hypocritical, sanctimonious

Sources: Data from Jones, 1990; Jones & Pittman, 1982.

developed the *self-monitoring scale* to measure this difference between people (see Table 2-5; Snyder, 1987).

These personality differences lead to important differences in the interpersonal realm. Like dedicated actors who spend long hours rehearsing their lines and making certain they have their parts down just right, high self-monitors work harder to manage other people's impressions. Since they strive to make certain their self-presentations match the demands of the situation, they are quite attentive to social cues. When they meet new people, men and women who are high in self-monitoring are more likely than low self-monitors to notice and accurately remember information about the new acquaintances. They are also quicker to form an impression of the people they meet (Berscheid et al., 1976). They will, in fact, go out of their way to acquire information that will help them to guide and manage their self-presentations (Elliott, 1979). And as they think of themselves as flexible, they willingly make use of strategic impression management strategies: "words and deeds chosen not so much for what they say about private attitudes and feelings, but rather for their tactical value in setting up appearances" (Snyder, 1987, pp. 35–36). As Snyder explains, they tend to be chameleonlike: they change their social identities to match the demands of the social situation. If the situation calls for conformity, they tend to be conforming; if it calls for autonomy, they become resolute nonconformists (Snyder & Monson, 1975). High self-monitors constantly scrutinize the fit between the self and the situation.

Low self-monitors, in contrast, are more like character actors who tend always to be cast in the same basic role, no matter what the movie or play. They rarely change their self-presentations to fit a situation. Because they act on the basis of their own dispositions—their feelings, attitudes, and self-perceptions—they have little need to pay as much attention to social cues as guides to action. Low self-monitors are not as careful as high self-monitors when it comes to controlling their nonverbal displays of emotions. When high self-monitors win a competition against a peer, they conceal their spontaneous expressions of happiness. Triumphant low self-monitors, in contrast, make no attempt to hide their happiness (Friedman & Miller-Herringer, 1991). Low self-monitors know who they are, and they try to act in ways that are consistent with their self-images. Low self-monitors tend to be more aware than high self-monitors of the nature of their self-concept, and they use this information to guide their actions across situations (Snyder & Ickes, 1985).

▲ **TABLE 2-5**
Some representative items from Snyder's self-monitoring scale. For all but the first item, people who agree are higher in self-monitoring.

Category	*Description*	*Example Item*
Motivation	Is the person motivated to create an appropriate social identity in this situation?	At parties and social gatherings, I do not attempt to do or say things that others will like.
Attention	Does the person pay attention to social cues that define what sort of impression is most appropriate?	When I am uncertain how to act in social situations, I look to the behavior of others for cues.
Ability	Can the person control and modify self-presentational and expressive behavior?	I can look anyone in the eye and tell a lie (if for a right end).
Planning	Is the person willing to use impression management strategies in particular situations?	I may deceive people by being friendly when I really dislike them.
Flexibility	Can the person tailor expressive behavior and self-presentations to fit particular social situations?	In different situations and with different people, I often act like very different persons.

Source: From Snyder, 1974.

Is Impression Management Good or Bad?

High and low self-monitors view social interaction differently. Is one viewpoint superior to the other? Is self-presentation a negative form of social behavior to be avoided?

Most social psychologists believe that self-presentation is neither good nor bad, for it can serve to communicate as well as mislead. Granted, *strategic self-presentations* are tactical, deliberate attempts to control others' impressions of us. Thomas had clear goals in mind when he testified, and he controlled his verbal and nonverbal expressions so he could create the impression he wanted to create. He may even have used his impression management tactics to mislead observers deliberately. His self-presentations, however, may have been genuine rather than tactical. Observers must have information if they are to form impressions. Therefore, Thomas provided the senators with information they needed by revealing his true self to them during the testimony. Indeed, impression management theorists believe that social life is a remarkably cooperative enterprise, with people doing what they can to sustain the smooth flow of social information. Because we know that perceivers are trying to form impressions, we help them by engaging in self-presentation. We aren't necessarily trying to manipulate them or mislead them; we are just trying to let them know who we are. We may want to make a good impression, but we also want to make certain that other people know who we are. *Authentic self-presentations* help us achieve this goal (Goffman, 1959; Schlenker, 1980).

William B. Swann, Jr., studied authentic self-presentation by putting people into situations in which observers seemed to be forming the wrong impression of them (Swann, 1987). In one study, people who considered themselves to be either dominant or submissive worked with a partner on a simple task. About halfway through the session, the partner, who was working with Swann, gave the subject some perceptual feedback. Some subjects were told they seemed dominant: "You really seem to be the forceful, dominant type." Others were told they seemed submissive: "You really don't seem to be the forceful, dominant type" (Swann & Hill, 1982). When the feedback clashed with their self-concepts, the subjects redoubled their impression management (see Figure 2-5). Subjects who considered themselves to be dominant but were labeled submissive by the confederate behaved more dominantly. Submissive subjects who thought they had been mistakenly labeled dominant became particularly submissive. Swann calls this reaction *self-verification* since it is an attempt to reaffirm or verify oneself behaviorally. When the feedback matched their self-concept, however, the subjects were more reserved in their behavior. When we believe we are perceived accurately, we have no need to resort to impression management strategies (Swann, 1987).

As an active participant in interpersonal settings, you must often choose between strategic and authentic self-presentations (Baumeister & Tice, 1985). During a job interview, a first dinner with your fiancé's parents, or a chance encounter in a bar, you may want to be honest and open, but you also want to establish as attractive a public image as possible. Determining which of these two motives is dominant has proved to be a difficult and challenging task for researchers (Leary & Kowalski, 1990). We do know, however, that strategic impression management increases when the audience is very attractive to us and the consequences of a failed presentation are very negative. Other factors, such as the importance of the attribute to our self-concept, tend to prompt authentic self-presentations. If you are personally committed to a particular career, such as journalism, mathematics, or business, but others tell you that you lack the skills to compete in these fields, you would probably react by correcting their misperceptions (Gollwitzer & Wicklund, 1985). The perceiver must always ask the question, Am I observing a strategic self-presentation or an authentic one? (Schlenker, 1985a; Tedeschi & Riess, 1981). We turn to questions of accuracy and identity negotiation in the final section of this chapter.

Impression Accuracy

Studies of impression formation and management highlight the interpersonal nature of social perception. We often think of perceivers as passive spectators

▲ In many situations, you may want to be honest about who you are, yet at the same time you want to make as good an impression as possible. People out on a date, for example, will most likely be at their self-presentational best. They want their date to know more about them, but they will also do all they can to create a favorable image. Such situations call for both authentic and strategic impression management.

who record their impressions of the people they meet, but perceivers actively construct the people they observe. The targets of our perceptions also play active roles in the process by managing the hints and clues they provide to onlookers.

How successful is this interchange? Are most of us Sherlock Holmeses, able to intuit hidden traits, emotions, and attributes at a glance, or are we Doctor Watsons, doomed to misunderstand and miscalculate at every turn? Consider, as an example, three perceivers—Senator Spector, Senator Biden, and Clarence Thomas. All three perceivers watch Anita Hill as she testifies before the Senate Judiciary Committee; then all three form impressions of Hill (see Figure 2-6). Before we can assess their accuracy, we must deal with a few preliminary questions. First, who is the target? If we cannot objectively assess Hill's qualities, we cannot tell whether or not the observers are accurate. Second, who are the observers? Spector may be a very astute judge of character, but Thomas may be a nondiscerning evaluator. We must take variations in judges into account in some way. Third, what kinds of qualities are observers' perceiving: Hill's emotions, her personality, her likes and dislikes, her goals and aspirations? Observers may be accurate when describing certain qualities but inaccurate when describing others. Only when these questions are settled can we turn to our original question: How accurate are these perceivers?

Who Is the Target?

When we estimate the size of a room, we can verify our guess by taking out a tape measure and checking our accuracy. But in the realm of person perception, no standard exists for verifying the accuracy of our judgments. If Spector argues that Hill is manipulative and unintelligent, how can we determine whether this perception is right or wrong?

Researchers have tried to solve this *criteria problem* in a variety of ways. Investigators who prefer a behavioral criterion record the target's actions and then compare these records to predictions offered by perceivers. Others may prefer to compare perceivers' evaluations to the target person's scores on standardized personality tests or to the judgments made by an expert perceiver (for example, a skilled therapist or interviewer). Consensus in perceptions is also often taken to be a sign of accuracy (Kenny, 1991). If Spector, Biden, and

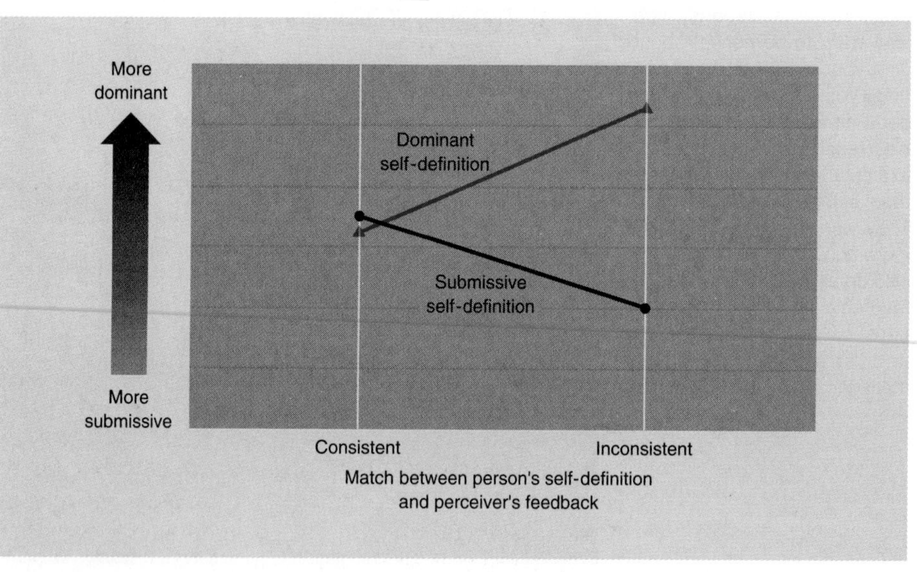

▲ FIGURE 2-5
How do we react when others misjudge us? Some subjects received feedback that matched their own self-conception; for example, people who considered themselves dominant were told that they seemed assertive and strong. Others, however, received feedback that conflicted with their self-views. A dominant person, for example, may have been told, "You don't seem to be the forceful type." People who felt misjudged tried to correct the perceiver's mistaken impression by behaving even more dominantly or even more submissively. (From Swann & Hill, 1982)

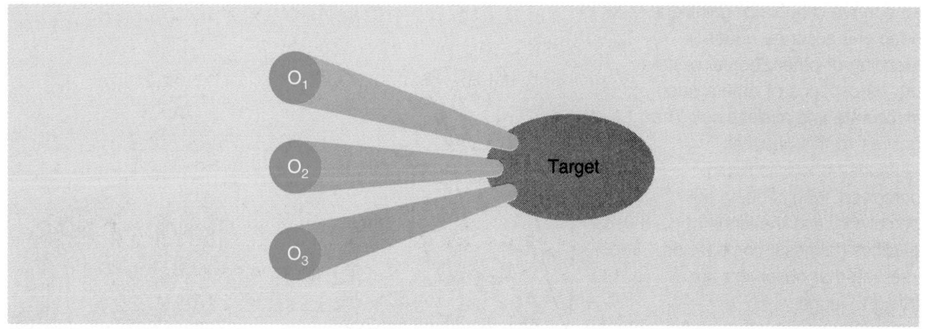

▲ **FIGURE 2-6**
Can we ever really know and understand other people? Social perception involves a person being perceived (the target) and one or more perceivers ($Observer_1$, $Observer_2$, $Observer_3$). The accuracy of social perception is often calculated by comparing observers' judgments with the target's self-ratings and by checking the level of agreement among observers. Some observers, however, may be more accurate than others, and some of the target's qualities may be more readily recognized than others.

Thomas all agree that Hill is intelligent and manipulative, this consensus lends credence to their accuracy. Perhaps the most commonly used criterion, however, is the target's own self-ratings. Once Hill evaluates her own manipulativeness and intelligence, her self-ratings can be compared to the senators' and Thomas's perceptions (Funder, 1987).

None of these solutions is perfect. Because our actions are influenced by both personal qualities and situational factors, our behaviors don't always reflect our personalities (Mischel, 1984). Psychological tests are often inaccurate, and even an expert interviewer can make mistakes (Salovey & Turk, 1991). Different people will disagree when rating the same person if they have known the target person different lengths of time, if they have observed the target person in different situations, and if they have different extraneous information about the target (Kenny, 1991; Paunonen, 1991). Last, we ourselves may not be the best judges of who we are; we are sometimes the last ones to know that we are manipulative, oafish, or unattractive (Paulhus, 1984). We also tend to rate ourselves more positively than other people do (Kenny & Albright, 1987). Given these limitations, researchers cannot always tell whether discrepancies between observers' perceptions and the target's qualities reflect a lack of acuity on the part of the observers or spring instead from faulty measures of the target's attributes (Zebrowitz, 1990).

Who Is the Observer?

People differ in their sensitivity to both the physical and social world. Some people have 20-20 vision; others can't see well enough to read the words on this page. Some people can sense the slightest change in temperature; others can't tell the difference between 85°F and 95°F. Similarly, some people are more accurate judges than others. If we compared Spector, Biden, and Thomas, we would probably find that one of them is a better judge of character than the others.

Accuracy depends, to some degree, on the perceiver's age, culture, and sex. Infants can detect changes in emotional expressions, but our ability to make inferences about others' dispositions and motives increases as we mature (Feldman & Ruble, 1981). Culture also plays a role in sensitivity to others' personal qualities. Perceivers reared in Western cultures—with their great emphasis on individuality—tend to attune more to each person's unique nuances; perceivers reared in Eastern cultures are less concerned with ferreting out the specific qualities of each individual they encounter (Triandis, 1990). Sex, too, plays a role in sensitivity. Women tend to be more accurate perceivers, particularly when they are appraising emotions (Hall, 1984).

Accuracy also depends upon the perceivers' personal qualities: their general perceptual outlook, their implicit assumptions about others, and even their moods (Forgas & Bower, 1987; Isen, 1987). Some people are simply more

▲ Are we capable of gaining a deep and accurate understanding of other people, or are our perceptions of others often inaccurate and misleading? The answer to this question depends on who is being perceived, who is doing the perceiving, and the kinds of qualities (fairness, compassion, intellect) that observers are trying to judge.

"You are fair, compassionate, and intelligent, but you are perceived as biased, callous, and dumb."

Drawing by Mankoff; © 1985 The New Yorker Magazine, Inc.

negative when they appraise others, so they tend to see more faults and limitations than people with a more positive perceptual style. The adults in one study differed dramatically when they reported their perceptions of a child they watched playing while supervised by a young adult. These observers were given a list of 25 positive and 25 negative behaviors and were asked to check off any behaviors that the child displayed during the session. All the subjects saw the same videotapes, but negative perceivers saw over 16 more negative behaviors than positive behaviors, while positive perceivers saw nearly 8 more positive behaviors than negative behaviors. Unbiased individuals saw an equal number of positive and negative behaviors (Messé et al., 1979).

One's implicit assumptions about people can also influence judgments. If Spector believes that friendliness is a fundamentally important quality in other people, he will probably judge others in terms of their apparent friendliness. Thomas may be perceptually ready to find evidence of intelligence in others, so he overlooks signs of friendliness in his quest to appraise the target's intellect. In many cases one observer's descriptions of several targets overlap more than several observers' descriptions of a single target. If Spector, Thomas, and Hill all evaluated one another, Spector's ratings of Thomas and Hill would overlap more than Spector's rating of Hill and Thomas's rating of Hill. This tendency is sometimes called the **eye-of-the-beholder effect** because it occurs when judgments are driven more by our perceptual assumptions than by the qualities of the person observed. The eye-of-the-beholder effect suggests that "the most powerful influence on interpersonal description is the manner in which the perceiver structures his interpersonal world" (Dornbusch et al., 1965, p. 440; also Bourne, 1977; Park, 1986).

eye-of-the-beholder effect The general tendency for observers' perceptual assumptions to influence their perceptions more than the characteristics of the person who is being observed.

Perceivers' evaluations of others, however, contain a kernel of truth (Jussim, 1990). Even though we bring many perceptual expectations to the situation, these assumptions do not hopelessly bias our perceptual conclusions.

Most of us can size up other people rapidly and accurately. Even after a fleeting encounter, we can discern elements of sociability, conscientiousness, and even attractiveness in others (Albright, Kenny, & Malloy, 1988). And the more time we spend with the target person, the more our perceptions come to match others' perceptions of the target. Bernadette Park (1986) examined consensus among perceivers by having the members of a small class describe each other over a 7-week period. She found that, at first, people's descriptions stressed behaviors for the most part: "Ed is usually late" or "Jean talks a great deal." By the end of the 7 weeks, however, descriptions became more abstract and referred to personality traits and dispositions: "Ed is self-centered" or "Jean is domineering." She also found that each judge applied certain idiosyncratic criteria when judging multiple targets. One subject, for example, would look for signs of shyness and intelligence in all her classmates; another subject would be more attuned to kindliness and humor. The perceivers, however, showed considerable agreement when judging where each classmate stood on these attributes. The perceivers agreed on who was smart, who was dumb, who worried, who was carefree, and so on. Because the observers agreed in their appraisals, Park concluded that these social perceptions reflected the target's actual characteristics and were not merely imagined qualities that could be traced back to the perceivers' expectations. A similar investigation confirmed these conclusions by finding that correlations between self-reports and observers' judgments increased from .21 to .26 to .30 over a 7-week period (Paulhus & Bruce, 1992).

What Is Perceived?

Our ability to sense our social world is limited, as is our ability to sense the physical world. We can only see lightwaves with wavelengths between 400 and 700 nanometers. Our dogs can hear sounds with frequencies above 20,000 Hz, but we can't. Similarly, there are some aspects of others that we can perceive, but other aspects that remain unknown to us no matter how closely we study them. Spector, Biden, and Thomas might be accurate when judging Hill's basic emotions. We are usually excellent judges of the primary emotions: surprise, fear, anger, disgust, happiness, and sadness. The onlookers might be inaccurate, however, when they try to appraise Hill's other qualities.

This variability across traits is considerable. When people who have just met one another rated themselves and their new acquaintance, the correlation between self-ratings and observers' ratings varied from a high of .52 for ratings of "responsible" to a low of .00 for ratings on the trait "good-natured" (Albright, Kenney, & Malloy, 1988). In fact, self-ratings for the trait "intellectual" were negatively correlated with observers' ratings; individuals who gave themselves high ratings on intellect were often perceived as intellectually inferior by others! David C. Funder and his colleagues obtained similar results when they compared subjects' self-ratings to ratings collected from their peers. As Table 2-6 indicates, for some qualities the match between the perceiver and the perceived is impressive. For others, however, the two do not agree (Funder, 1987; Funder & Colvin, 1988; Funder & Dobroth, 1987). This variability emerges even when observers know the target persons intimately. When researchers compared people's ratings of themselves on such qualities as competitive, neat, feels misunderstood, persistent, considerate, and virtuous to their spouses' ratings of them on these same attributes, the correlations ranged from .59 to .00 (Edwards & Klockars, 1981).

This variability does not mean that perceivers are cautious when evaluating some attributes but careless when appraising others. Some of the disparity can

"big five" personality factors
Five fundamental aspects of personality, including extraversion, agreeableness (friendliness), conscientiousness (responsibleness), emotional stability, and intelligence. Perceivers tend to base their impressions of other people on these five factors.

be attributed to the targets. First, targets do not always send clear messages to the perceivers. They sometimes take great pains to make certain their most important qualities are advertised to others in no uncertain terms, but they don't work as hard when presenting attributes that they don't think are central to their self-definition (Gangestad et al., 1992; Swann, 1984). Second, targets may not be aware of all their personal qualities, or they may not be willing to admit these qualities publicly. A target person who is dishonest or lazy will probably hide these qualities from themselves and from other people (Paulhus, 1984; Paulhus & Reid, 1991).

Variability across traits also occurs because some of our qualities are more *visible* to the perceiver's eye than others. Consider the so-called **"big five" personality factors** identified by dozens of different researchers: extraversion, agreeableness (friendliness), conscientiousness (responsibility), emotional stability, and intelligence (see Table 2-7). Two of these five factors—extraversion and conscientiousness—can be intuited almost immediately. When David Kenny and his colleagues tested the perceptual talents of their subjects by asking them to size one another up at *zero acquaintance*—before even interacting with each other—they found that perceivers' and target persons' appraisals correlated at .44 for extraversion and .52 for conscientiousness (Albright, Kenny, & Malloy, 1988). Nonverbal cues, such as smiling, style of dress, and rapid movements of the body, provided sufficient information for observers to appraise targets accurately (Kenny et al., 1992). Moreover, as perceivers spend more time with the target, their judgments may become more accurate (McCrae & Costa, 1987; Park & Judd, 1989).

Our observers, Spector, Biden, and Thomas, should be able to apprehend Hill's more socially visible personality traits and characteristics. However, our observers may not be able to judge her hidden qualities even after prolonged exposure. Is Hill "subtly negativistic"? Does she "engage in personal fantasy and daydreams"? Does she have "repressive tendencies"? These qualities all appear toward the bottom of Table 2-6; they are the ones on which observers and targets rarely agree. These qualities are also rarely observed, difficult to imagine, and ambiguously linked to overt behavior (Funder & Dobroth, 1987; Rothbart & Park, 1986). Not even Sherlock Holmes would try to guess a person's inner qualities when these qualities are never expressed in any outward way.

How Accurate Are Perceivers?

Many factors influence perceivers' accuracy: the criteria used for comparison, the characteristics of the perceiver, and the particular quality being appraised. Despite the number of factors, however, we appear to be astute observers of others. We can often predict targets' behaviors across a range of situations. We know which of our friends will become impatient when waiting in lines, who will score highest on a test, and who will be the center of attention at a party. Our perceptions of people also overlap to a considerable degree with their own self-ratings. Fraternity members' evaluations of their brothers on such attributes as extraversion, agreeableness, and conscientiousness correlated .44 with the target persons' self-ratings on these attributes (Cheek, 1982). When spouses' ratings and the targets' own ratings were compared for such qualities as persistence, leadership, perfectionism, and consideration, they correlated at an average of .32 (Edwards & Klockars, 1981). Consensus in observers' perception is also the norm rather than the exception (Kenny, 1991). If we compared the perceptions of Senator Spector, Senator Biden, and Judge Thomas, we would likely find correlations ranging from .30 to .60 (Funder, 1987).

▲ **TABLE 2-6**
Accuracy across attributes: Variations in the magnitude of the correlation between self-ratings and peers' ratings across a variety of qualities

Quality	*Correlation*
Tends to arouse liking and acceptance	.45
Is cheerful	.38
Responds to humor	.37
Initiates humor	.37
Is calm, relaxed	.37
Is a talkative individual	.36
Sex typed	.34
Social poise and presence	.33
Behaves in an assertive fashion	.33
Physically attractive	.31
Has rapid personal tempo	.29
Interested in opposite sex	.28
Facially or gesturally expressive	.27
Personally charming	.26
Unconventional thought processes	.26
Evaluates motives of others	.25
Lack of personal meaning in life	.21
Has insights into own motives and behavior	.21
Uncomfortable with uncertainties and complexities	.20
Clear-cut consistent personality	.20
Has readiness to feel guilt	.20
Creates and exploits dependency	.20
Introspective	.18
Concerned with own adequacy	.12
Arouses nurturant feelings	.08
Repressive tendencies	.07
Subtly negativistic	.06
Appears straightforward and candid	.04
Engages in personal fantasy and daydreams	.03
Projects own feelings onto others	.00

Source: From Funder, 1987.

social relations model
A research procedure that assesses the degree to which several judges agree when rating the same person and the degree to which these ratings correspond to the individual's self-ratings on these attributes.

response sets
A perceiver's tendency to respond to others similarly, irrespective of their particular personal qualities. Examples include rating all people negatively no matter how they act or giving all people high ratings on one particular trait.

Additional evidence of our perceptual skill comes from studies of David A. Kenny's **social relations model** (Kenny, 1991; Kenny & Albright, 1987). This model makes use of a round-robin rating design in which all targets and all perceivers rate one another. Spector, Biden, and Thomas wouldn't only rate Hill; all four would also rate each other. Because it calls for multiple targets and multiple perceivers, this design yields a more detailed analysis of our perceptual accuracy. First, it facilitates the identification of **response sets**: a perceiver's tendency to respond to others in a set way, regardless of the target's particular personal qualities. Some perceivers give favorable or unfavorable ratings no matter what the target does. If Spector displayed this response set, he would give generally favorable (or unfavorable) ratings to everyone he rated, including himself. A second type of response set occurs when a perceiver gives all the targets an elevated rating on a particular attribute. Biden might distinguish between targets when he rates them on honesty, attractiveness, and

▲ **TABLE 2-7**
The "big five" factors of personality: Studies of the way we perceive people, and studies of people's self-descriptions, identify five general clusters of qualities.

Factor	*Content*
Extraversion	Outgoing, sociable, interpersonal, expressive, not introverted, gregarious
Agreeableness	Friendly, warm, likable, generous, kind
Conscientiousness	Responsible, achievement oriented, dependable, self-controlled
Stability	Emotionally controlled, assured, not anxious, balanced
Intelligence	Intellectually able, open to ideas

Sources: Adapted from Digman, 1990.

humor, but when he turns to intelligence he might give them all a high rating (Cronbach, 1955). If unrecognized, these response sets can make observers seem more accurate than they actually are. If Spector responds positively to all the targets, he will seem to be quite perceptive if the targets give themselves overly positive ratings, too.

The social relations model can also determine the extent to which the perceivers agree or disagree when evaluating a single target. Kenny terms this component *target accuracy* or individual accuracy, for it refers to perceivers' overall consensus concerning a single target individual. If all four observers described Hill as intelligent, then target accuracy would be high. The model can also determine each perceivers' unique perceptions of a target person. This component is termed *relationship accuracy* because it is based on the perceptual relationship between a single pair of perceiver and target. If Biden is the only perceiver who thinks that Hill is honest and Hill also considers herself to be honest, then Biden will have a high relationship accuracy score.

Even when perceivers are tested under the strict conditions required by the social relations model, they still get high accuracy marks (Albright et al., 1988; DePaulo, Kenny et al., 1987; Kenny, 1988; Kenny & Albright, 1987; Kenny et al., 1992; Malloy & Albright, 1990; Park & Judd, 1989). Kenny has shown that perceivers who have just met the targets achieve target accuracy scores of .22

▲ Who is Anita Hill? Some perceivers believed her to be an intelligent, competent, and emotionally reserved woman who did all she could to present a fair picture of her dealings with Clarence Thomas. Others attributed more sinister characteristics to her, suggesting that she repressed her sexuality, doubted her own competency, and harbored resentment against those in authority. These qualities, however, are ones that are very difficult for social perceivers to detect accurately.

when judging extraversion and scores of .13 when appraising conscientiousness (Kenny et al., 1992). These scores become even more impressive when subjects have the opportunity to interact with one another several times. In one project 10 subjects shared information about themselves for about 30 minutes on four consecutive days. When researchers examined the subjects' ratings of one another, they found that response sets accounted for only about 10% of their perceptions. Target accuracy accounted for approximately 60% of their perceptions, and relationship accuracy accounted for the remaining 30%. These accuracy scores, however, held only for ratings of extraversion. As in other studies, subjects had a far more difficult time evaluating more hidden characteristics, such as intelligence and honesty (Park & Judd, 1989).

As Table 2-8 concludes, the answer to the question "Are we accurate perceivers?" appears to be a qualified yes. Perceivers' appraisals usually correspond to the target's own self-ratings. Also, more stringent tests of accuracy that make use of the social relations model find considerable consensus when several perceivers judge the same target. And even these tests of perceivers' talents may be too stringent. In many cases social psychologists have tested perceivers in controlled situations that didn't permit extensive interaction between the perceiver and the target person. Such conditions may stifle the impression formation processes and impression management processes that work together to generate social perceptions. As David Funder (1987) puts it, perceivers in controlled studies may make *errors* when judging others, but these errors may not produce *mistakes* in judgment during everyday social interaction. We may, it seems, be Sherlock Holmeses after all.

Summary

Our perceptual receptiveness is not limited to the physical world. The people who populate our social world are also targets for our perceptual efforts, for we constantly formulate and revise our understanding of others. In *social perception,* however, the perceiver and the person perceived play equally active roles. The *impression formation* process may begin with a perceiver who is seeking insight into another individual's emotions, motivations, and personality, but the target can use *impression management* to influence the outcome of this perceptual process.

From the perceiver's perspective social perception requires close scrutiny of any *nonverbal cues* displayed by the target person. By relying on *stereotypes,* perceivers can make inferences about people simply by considering their physical characteristics, such as race, sex, age, and physical attractiveness (the *"what is beautiful is good" stereotype*). Facial cues, including maturity, blushing, and degree of *eye contact,* are also important sources of information. Observers in cultures all over the world can identify basic emotions (surprise, fear, anger, disgust, happiness, and sadness) from facial cues alone, although cultural *display rules* regulate such emotional expressions. *Kinesic cues* (movements of the body such as posture, gait, *gestures,* and interpersonal touching) and *paralanguage* (the voice cues that accompany spoken language) are also major sources of information, particularly when observers are trying to determine whether the target is speaking truthfully.

Social perception, from the target's perspective, requires active impression management (or *self-presentation*): displaying social behaviors that establish and maintain a particular social image, or *face.* When the goal is *ingratiation,* impression managers create an attractive, audience-pleasing image by showing

▲ **TABLE 2-8**
Summing up: Perceptual accuracy depends on the criteria used to establish accuracy, the perceiver's characteristics, and the characteristics being evaluated.

Issue	*Impact on Accuracy*
What is the criterion?	Observers' perceptions of the target person must be compared to some other measure of the target person's qualities. No single criterion measure of the target's qualities is definitive, however.
Who is the perceiver?	Accuracy depends on the perceivers' demographic and personal qualities, including cultural background, sex, general perceptual outlook, and their implicit assumptions about others. The eye-of-the-beholder effect occurs when the perceivers' judgments are based more on their perceptual assumptions than on the qualities of the person observed.
What is perceived?	Perceptual acuity varies across attributes. We are usually excellent judges of the primary emotions, extraversion, and conscientiousness, but other qualities are difficult to discern.
How accurate are perceivers?	Accuracy estimates vary across attributes, but perceivers' judgments often correlate with the target person's self-ratings, and observers evaluating the same target person generally agree in their evaluations. Even when accuracy estimates are corrected to take into account *response sets* and the unique relationship between the perceiver and the person perceived, significant accuracy remains.

interest in the perceiver, giving off positive nonverbal cues, and using verbal tactics such as *opinion conformity* and compliments. Few ingratiators, however, are entirely successful since they cannot escape the *ingratiator's dilemma*: the greater their need to be liked, the more incredulous the perceivers will be. When the goal is *self-promotion,* targets try to create an impression of competence and effectiveness by describing themselves in positive terms and by behaving competently. More subtle means can also be used to achieve self-promotion, including understating one's abilities (modesty) and noting one's association with other competent or attractive people (whimsically referred to as *Basking In Reflected Glory,* or *BIRGing*). Targets can also use *intimidation* to appear powerful and *supplication* to appear weak. As the *complementarity principle* suggests, these two interpersonal styles complement each other: when the target presents an image of weakness, others respond with dominance and, to a lesser extent, caring. *Exemplification,* the final tactic, requires laying claim to high moral worth through selfless actions and moralistic self-descriptions. Exemplifiers run the risk of appearing hypocritical.

When we do something that threatens the impression we are trying to create, we often use *accounts* that excuse us or justify our actions. Not everyone is a facile impression manager, however. Those who are high in *self-monitoring* can regulate their behavior to fit the situation; they are more likely to engage in strategic self-presentations. Low self-monitors strive for more authentic self-presentations; they rarely change their faces to fit the situation.

The accuracy of this perceptual interchange is difficult to assess since there is no standard for verifying the correctness of the perceivers' judgments (the criterion problem). Individuals also vary in their interpersonal acuity. The negativistic perceiver tends to see inadequacies that don't exist, and some perceivers' conclusions are driven more by their perceptual assumptions than by the qualities of the person observed (the *eye-of-the-beholder effect*). Some aspects of people are easy to perceive; others remain unknown to us no matter how closely we study them. For example, two of the *big five personality factors*—extraversion and conscientious—are fairly easy to detect in others, but agreeableness (friendliness), emotional stability, and intelligence are more difficult to assess. Despite these complexities, when perceivers' appraisals are compared to the targets' own self-ratings, the correspondence is often very high. More stringent tests of accuracy that use the *social relations model* also find consensus when several perceivers judge the same target. Even when accuracy estimates are corrected to take into account *response sets* and the unique relationship between the perceiver and the person perceived, the estimates are still impressive. We are, it seems, insightful observers of other people.

For More Information

- *Fundamentals of Nonverbal Behavior,* edited by Robert S. Feldman and Bernard Rime (1991), includes a number of cutting-edge analyses of how our perceptions of others are shaped by their nonverbal actions.
- *A General Model of Consensus and Accuracy in Interpersonal Perception,* by David A. Kenny (1991), offers a theoretical analysis of the six basic factors that determine the accuracy (or, more specifically, the consensus) of our social perceptions.
- *Impression Management: The Self-Concept, Social Identity, and Interpersonal Relations,* by Barry R. Schlenker (1980), is a marvelous review of the many strategies we use to influence other people's perceptions of us.
- *Nonverbal Behavior and Self-Presentation,* by Bella M. DePaulo (1992), synthesizes theory and research that considers the impact of nonverbal cues on perceivers' impressions.
- *Nonverbal Communication in Human Interaction,* by Mark L. Knapp (1978) remains an excellent source of information on all forms of nonverbal behavior.
- *Public Appearances, Private Realities: The Psychology of Self-Monitoring,* by Mark Snyder (1987), summarizes our current understanding of the differences between people who strive to control the images they convey to others and those who make certain their public appearances match their private self-conceptions.
- *Social Perception,* by Leslie A. Zebrowitz (1990), provides a concise but up-to-date overview of the many perceptual and cognitive processes that undergird interpersonal perception.
- *Telling Lies: Clues to Deceit in the Marketplace, Politics, and Marriage,* by Paul Ekman (1985), reviews what we currently know about deception: the nature of lies, the reasons we lie (and perhaps should lie), and how liars betray themselves nonverbally.

Application: Detecting Deceivers

The great detectives of fiction are skilled observers of their fellow human beings. Arsène Dupin, the amateur sleuth of Edgar Allan Poe's *Murders in the Rue Morgue,* anticipated others' thoughts and actions. Television's Jessica Fletcher of *Murder, She Wrote* solves absurdly complicated crimes by noting small nuances and inconsistencies. And Sherlock Holmes, the greatest detective of all, divined emotions and motivations at a glance.

We need the talents of these fictional detectives whenever our work depends on accurately perceiving

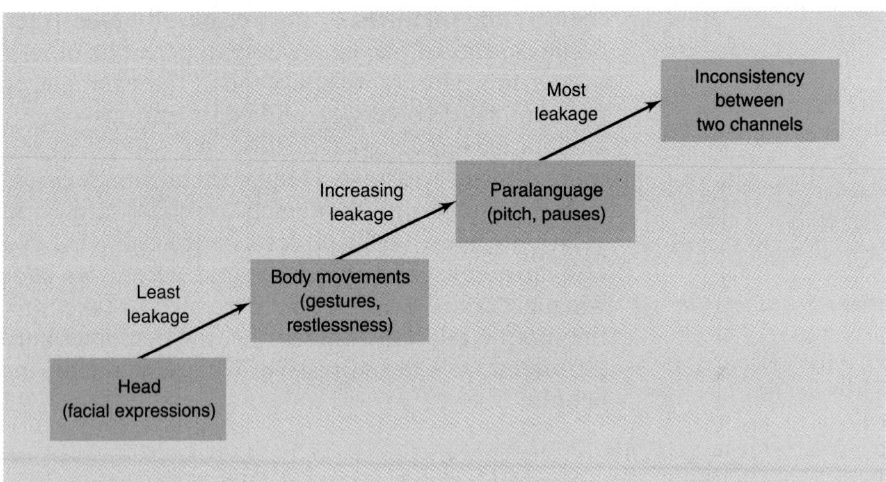

▲ **FIGURE 2-7**
Are there tell-tale signs of lying? According to the concept of the leakage hierarchy, voice cues are better indicators of deception than the face. Nonverbal face and body cues are relatively easy to control, so these channels leak the least during deception. Voice cues are more informative, as is an inconsistency between two channels (either verbal or nonverbal).

other people's plans, motives, and meanings. Supervisors must decide whether their subordinates are sincere when they promise to increase their productivity. A financial officer in a bank must decide whether borrowers possess the financial assets they claim. A company's personnel officers must separate truth from fiction in a job applicant's résumé. Police officers size up a suspect at a glance. Customs agents watching tourists declaring their property take note of anything out of the ordinary. Judges must listen to each witness's testimony before deciding who is telling the truth and who cannot be believed. Success in many occupations depends on the ability to discriminate between people who are telling the truth, people who are withholding information, and people who are lying outright.

How well do people function as lie detectors? Few of us can unerringly tell the difference between someone who is lying and someone who is speaking honestly. Studies of people who have no special training suggest that they can detect a liar about 60% of the time, which only slightly exceeds the 50% detention rate that would occur by chance alone (Zuckerman, DePaulo, & Rosenthal, 1981). Police officers are no more accurate, although they tend to be more confident in their lie detection skills (DePaulo & Pfeifer, 1986). And U.S. Customs inspectors performed particularly poorly when their skills were tested in a mock inspection. Researchers, with the consent of the Customs Service, gave some travelers a contraband item and asked them to try to sneak it through an inspection. When Customs inspectors were asked to identify the smugglers by watching a videotape of the inspection, they tended to accuse innocent travelers and overlook the simulated smugglers (Kraut & Poe, 1980).

Why is deception so difficult to detect? First of all, people are usually too lenient when appraising others' truthfulness. Even when people do things that should arouse our suspicions, we give them the benefit of the doubt (DePaulo et al., 1989). Second, we sometimes mistake nervousness for deceit. Nervous people sometimes fail to maintain eye contact, they touch themselves with their hands on their arms and face, they shift their bodies restlessly, and they blink their eyes. They also use such sounds as "er," "ah," or "ya know" to fill pauses, they have to start sentences over again, and they take too long to answer questions. These nonverbal behaviors create a false impression of dishonesty, because observers believe that liars often avert their gaze, fidget, and speak haltingly (DePaulo, Stone, & Lassiter, 1985). Over 80% of the Customs inspectors wanted to search an innocent lawyer who didn't look directly at the Customs official as he fumbled with a scarf and overcoat that he had folded over his arm (Kraut & Poe, 1980).

Third, many skilled liars have mastered controlling the nonverbal cues that perceivers use to detect deception. Expert liars show no sign of nervousness; instead, they maintain eye contact, hold their hands still, and speak clearly and concisely while telling tall tales or denying their wrongdoings. Skilled liars also mask their nervousness by displaying a covering emotion; they may smile broadly or snarl angrily when they are worried that their nervousness might be observed. Moreover, dire warnings about what will happen to liars makes them nervous and emotional, but it also inspires them to work harder to make sure they get away with their deceptions (DePaulo et al., 1988; Ekman, 1988). Asking probing questions can also backfire; probing warns liars that you are suspicious and makes truthful people so nervous that they begin to act as though they are lying (Buller et al., 1989). As Paul Ekman (1988, p. 165) laments, nonverbal signs of nervousness "are *not* signs of lying per se. There is no behavioral sign of lying itself."

Because expert liars plug the obvious nonverbal leaks, to catch them consider nonverbal cues that are more difficult to control. To tell a false smile from a genuine smile, for instance, look at the eyes rather than the lips. A genuine smile of enjoyment, or Duchenne smile (named for the 19th-century anatomist Duchenne de Boulogne who studied smiles extensively), involves upturned lips and the wrinkling of the skin around the eyes. The muscles that control the curve of the lips can be easily controlled; the muscles that cause puckering around the eyes cannot. Therefore, if the wrinkling around the eyes is absent, this non-Duchenne smile is hiding another emotion (Ekman, Davidson, & Friesen, 1990; Ekman, Friesen, & O'Sullivan, 1988). Vocal cues are also difficult to control, so study these paralanguage cues. Listen for pauses between sentences or before answering questions (silent pauses), errors in grammar or choice of words, and unexpected changes in voice tone and quality (Ekman, 1988; Zuckerman & Driver, 1985).

These suggestions are summarized by the concept of a *leakage hierarchy*. As Figure 2-7 shows, leakage increases as we move from the face to the body and then to vocal cues. Concentrate on the leakiest of channels (the lower body and the voice) before considering the more secure channels (the face and hands). Also be on the lookout for an inconsistency, or *dissynchrony,* between two channels. A smiling face and shaking hands, or constant eye contact paired with restless feet are excellent indicants of deception. Once you have drawn conclusions from nonverbal cues, turn to verbal information: truthful messages are usually more concise, plausible, and consistent than misleading messages (DePaulo, 1988; Ekman, 1988; Stiff et al., 1989; Zuckerman et al., 1982).

The leakage hierarchy can be put to good use in training people to be more accurate social perceivers. First, observers who are trained to pay more attention to the target's tone of voice and speech patterns will outperform observers who follow their natural inclination to focus on facial cues (Littlepage & Pineault, 1981). In one study people watched videotapes of six men and six women who were lying or telling the truth. Observers who were told to concentrate on the speaker's tone of voice or the speaker's choice of words were more accurate when rating the speaker's deceptiveness than people who were told to pay attention to "how the speakers look" and people who were given no special instructions (DePaulo, Lassiter, & Stone, 1982). Second, observers should also be taught that the *absence* of any nervousness is as valid an indicator of deceit as shaky hands and an averted gaze. Liars who are motivated to escape detection sometimes become so nonverbally guarded that they appear to be rigid; they don't blink much, avert their gaze, fidget, or move their heads as frequently as people telling the truth. Their statements are also shorter, and they speak more slowly. When they try not to seem nervous, their nonverbal behaviors become inappropriate. A person who is being interviewed on *60 Minutes* should be nervous. If he or she isn't, something is amiss.

Last, experience in judging the particular individual under observation is crucial. When observers were asked to make judgments about a person who told several lies and several truths, they became more proficient in their judgments with each exposure. Initially they could correctly identify lies about 50% of the time. But with practice their judgments climbed to 61%, and if they were given feedback about the accuracy of their judgments their accuracy rates climbed to 70%. This training, however, did not increase their overall lie detection ability. They became more accurate when judging someone they had seen lie before, but when they were exposed to a new set of liars, their accuracy dropped back down to the 50% level. Practice, then, in judging a particular person may be crucial for detecting deception. Although we may not be able to tell whether someone we have just met is lying to us, we are more successful when it comes to detecting the lies told to us by people we know well. The new applicant for the job may be able to bluff his or her way through the interview, but at least we will be able to tell when our friends and family members lie to us.

Social Cognition

On Monday, November 25, 1968, Professor Henry Kissinger of Harvard University sat in a spacious hotel room in Washington, D.C. Kissinger was waiting to meet U.S. President-elect Richard M. Nixon, who had called him earlier in the week to set up the conference. The president-elect hadn't said much about the meeting, but Kissinger figured that Nixon had decided to offer him a position in his administration. Kissinger was ambivalent about working with Nixon. He had once said "that man Nixon is not fit to be president" and "Richard Nixon is the most dangerous, of all the men running, to have as president" (Kalb & Kalb, 1974, pp. 15–16).

But Nixon surprised Kissinger. The president-elect didn't act like a savvy politician with a clear personal agenda; if anything, he was soft-spoken and deferential. The two men spent several hours discussing trade relations, nuclear arms, Vietnam, and varying ways the United States could encourage world peace, and by the interview's end Kissinger had changed the way he thought of Nixon: "I was struck by his perceptiveness and knowledge so at variance with my previous image of him" (Kissinger, 1979, p. 12). When Nixon later asked Kissinger to become his advisor, Kissinger agreed.

This historic encounter highlights the cognitive side of social life. All during the meeting, Kissinger absorbed the information he needed to understand Nixon and make a decision about joining his administration. But Kissinger's mind was not a dry sponge that soaked up whatever transpired. He passed the days before his meeting reviewing his storehouse of memories about Nixon, making mental lists of Nixon's strengths and weaknesses, and estimating the chances that Nixon would offer him an important post. Then, during the meeting itself, he gathered even more data from the things Nixon said and the way he said them. By the time the meeting ended, Kissinger came to a new decision about working with Nixon: if the president-elect offered him a post, he would take it.

Few of us ever have the chance to meet a president-elect, but all of us actively seek, process, and store information about ourselves and other people. We are mentally prepared for each social encounter. When we meet our friends on the street, our appraisal of their appearance, their moods, or their greetings is shaped by our memories of past encounters, conversations, and conclusions. We may take note of some new attribute or quality—a fresh tattoo, a previously concealed streak of dogged stubbornness, or a glimmer of cleverness that had escaped our notice until now—but this information must be integrated with information we already possess. Moreover, just as Kissinger decided to join Nixon, each day we must make a variety of inferences about the people we

▲ We constantly process information about the people we encounter. Each time Kissinger talked about affairs of state with President Nixon, he collected information about Nixon's mood, ideas, personality, and political aspirations. Kissinger organized, structured, and integrated this newly acquired data with information drawn from his memories of past encounters with Nixon, politicians, presidents, and people in general. Through social cognition, he succeeded in generating an overall understanding of Richard Nixon.

meet, the situations we face, the choices available to us, and the problems we must solve. We aren't just social animals, but *cognitive* social animals who reason, infer, judge, choose, and decide (Baron & Harvey, 1980; Fiske, 1992; Fiske & Taylor, 1991).

We charted a portion of the cognitive bedrock on which our social interactions rest in Chapter 2. Although no line marks the end of social perception and the beginning of social cognition, in Chapter 2 we ask, "How do perceivers form an initial impression of others?" This chapter continues the analysis by examining **social cognition**: It asks, "What mental processes sustain perceivers' understanding of the social world?" In Chapter 4 we examine attributions: "When do perceivers use behavioral data to make inferences about other people?"

social cognition
The inferential processes that organize, structure, and integrate information about people and social settings; includes memory systems that store data and the cognitive mechanisms that process this information.

Our analysis of social cognition has three parts. First, we scrutinize social thought and its various components: the attentional elements that are responsible for gathering information about the social world, the memory systems that store data for later use, and the perceptual and cognitive mechanisms that process this information. Second, we consider the cognitive processes that we use to make rapid, rule-of-thumb inferences about the people we meet, the situations we face, the choices available to us, and the problems we must solve. Our effectiveness as judges, analysts, choosers, and problem solvers is considered in the chapter's final section.

The Nature of Social Thought

Kissinger's mind must have been flooded with questions when he sat waiting for Nixon. What sort of man is Nixon? Is he a patriot or is he seeking fame? What are his plans for ending the war in Vietnam? What does he think of me? Will he be a successful president? By the time the meeting ended, he had formulated tentative answers to all these questions. How did he manage it?

The answer lies in Kissinger's ability to process information about the social world. We are not emotion-laden animals or robotlike machines who respond to events in a predetermined way. We are information processors who gather data, process that data, and respond based on the results of that processing

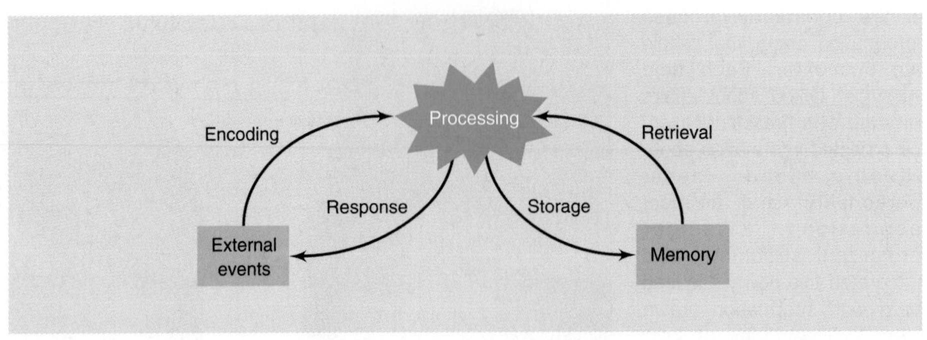

▲ **FIGURE 3-1**
What mental processes sustain perceivers' understanding of the social world? The information-processing model stresses the flow of information through several components. Environmental information is encoded; stored information is retrieved from memory. Information is then processed, and the results are exported to the environment in the form of action and stored in memory.

information-processing model
A general theoretical explanation of cognition that assumes new information acquired by the senses is combined with information we already possess to yield an updated understanding.

retrieval
The process of searching for and finding information stored in memory.

encoding
The translation of an external event into an internal, psychological representation.

(Atkinson & Shiffrin, 1968). This **information-processing model** suggests that information enters the processing system through two basic routes (see Figure 3-1). Nixon's appearance on the day he met Kissinger or the things he said during the discussion must be noticed and translated into an internal, psychological representation. The information-processing system also extracts data from long-term memory stores through a process known as **retrieval**. Kissinger, for example, followed Nixon's career closely, so he had a rich store of memories about him. Kissinger's memory also contained his beliefs about politicians, about men, and about people in general, and he could have retrieved these memories as he sat sizing up Nixon during that first interview. (For more information on Kissinger's analysis of political events, see Cleva, 1989; Eldridge, 1983; Elms, 1986; Starr, 1983, 1984).

Even though far more sophisticated conceptualizations have been offered by cognitive psychologists, most are refinements of this basic model (Anderson, 1990; Massaro & Cowan, 1993). To understand our social world, we must procure information about that world (**encoding**) and any information relevant to the current situation must be recalled from memory (retrieval). As we will see, however, these two processes commingle. Our memories influence what we encode just as the information we encode influences our search through our memories (Sherman, Judd, & Park, 1989).

Encoding Social Information

In his book *The White House Years*, Kissinger recounts his first meeting with the president-elect (1979, p. 11):

> When at last Nixon entered the room, it was with a show of jauntiness that failed to hide an extraordinary nervousness. He sat on a sofa with his back to the window overlooking Fifth Avenue, and motioned me to an easy chair facing him. His manner was almost diffident; his movements were slightly vague, and unrelated to what he was saying, as if two different impulses were behind speech and gesture. He spoke in a low, gentle voice. While he talked, he sipped, one after another, cups of coffee that were brought in without his asking for them.

We do not notice every minute detail of our social world. Attention is a very limited cognitive resource, so we allocate it sparingly and judiciously. If we decide to pay attention to the person sitting next to us in class, we may not hear what the lecturer is saying. If we are tuning the car radio, the change of the traffic light may go unnoticed. When Kissinger encountered Nixon, he took little notice of the shape of his earlobes or the color of his eyes. His attention was instead drawn to other aspects of his actions and appearance—his nervousness, his hand movements, and how much coffee he drank.

When will a bit of data be encoded rather than ignored? First, some stimuli demand our attention. Nixon's nervousness, for example, was so extreme that

bottom-up processing (or data-driven processing)
Inferential processes that are initiated and guided more by the incoming perceptual data than by the perceiver's existing cognitive structures.

top-down processing (or conceptually driven processing)
Inferential processes that are initiated and guided more by the perceiver's expectations and cognitive structures than by the characteristics of the object being perceived.

automatic processing
Involuntary, unintentional, and uncontrolled cognitive processes that require little or no effort or awareness.

salience
The relative distinctiveness of a stimulus event in the given social context.

vividness
The intensity of a stimulus event, irrespective of the social context.

anyone watching him would have noticed that he was high-strung and edgy. In this case, encoding resulted from data-driven, or **bottom-up processing**, because the stimulus (Nixon) controlled the allocation of attention. Second, perceivers' expectations, goals, and other conceptual elements sometimes determine what will be noticed and what will be overlooked. Kissinger's preconceptions about politicians and Nixon provided a structure that shaped his search for verbal and nonverbal cues when he met with Nixon. He expected, for example, a calm, self-assured man, so Nixon's restlessness was particularly noteworthy to him. In this case encoding was sustained by conceptually driven, or **top-down processing**. Third, encoding sometimes proceeds without any conscious allocation of attention. Kissinger undoubtedly shook hands with Nixon when he first met him. Did he notice the ring on Nixon's outstretched hand, deliberate over extending his own hand, or think about how to pump his hand up and down in a handshaking motion? No, because these thoughts and actions were driven by **automatic processing** (Bargh, 1984; Fiske & Taylor, 1991; Greenwald, 1988).

Bottom-up processing. When we walk down a crowded street, why do we notice the person with spiked green hair rather than someone with blonde hair? Why do the gyrating dancers in the music video capture more of our attention than the studied movements of the keyboard player? Because our limited attention favors one stimulus over another depending on relative **salience**: the distinctiveness of the stimulus event in its social context. Watching an NBA basketball game, we take no notice of the 7-foot player, but when we see him talking to a group of fans, he seems a giant. His height is a salient stimulus that becomes a perceptual novelty to us. Behaviors or qualities that are unusual for a particular person, for people in a particular situation, or for people in general are also salient. If Ed usually dresses in jeans and a T-shirt, we notice him when he sports a coat and tie. If all the presidents we have met have been confident and self-assured, we notice Nixon's nervousness and insecurity. If people usually speak French in our country, we notice a couple walking by speaking English. Our attention gravitates to the unexpected and unusual rather than to the expected and mundane (McArthur, 1981; Taylor & Fiske, 1978). Salient events are more likely to lodge themselves in our memories (Pryor & Kriss, 1977; Rholes & Pryor, 1982).

Our attention also favors vivid stimuli rather than pallid ones. Salience depends upon the relative novelty of the stimulus—even a whisper can be salient in a silent room. **Vividness**, in contrast, refers to the absolute intensity of the stimulus event. A shout, a loud colorful shirt, and our own names heard from across the room are vivid stimuli, because they arouse us emotionally, stimulate our imaginations, or appeal to our senses (Nisbett & Ross, 1980). Negative social information also tends to grab our attention. Although seeing a good friend in a crowd or noticing a dollar on the sidewalk may make us happy, we will likely survive if we overlook them. An enemy in the crowd or a scorpion in our shoe, on the other hand, demand our attention. If we overlook them, our information-processing days may be over (Pratto & John, 1991).

Because salient, vivid, and negative stimuli are more likely to be noticed, they are also more likely to make their way into our long-term memories. Imagine you were a member of a jury in a drunk-driving trial trying to decide whether the defendant, Sanders, was intoxicated when he left a party. Which version of a witness's evidence would influence you the most?

- Sanders staggered against a serving table, knocking a bowl to the floor.
- Sanders staggered against a serving table, spattering guacamole on the white shag carpet.

Sanders was just as drunk no matter what was in the bowl he knocked over. Perceivers, however, could recall more of the evidence and they were more likely to find Sanders guilty when they were told about the spattering guacamole (Reyes, Thompson, & Bower, 1980, p. 4). Similarly, who would you judge to be the better mother: Mrs. Johnson, who "sees that her son brushes his teeth," or Mrs. Jackson, who "sees that her son brushes his teeth with his Star Wars toothbrush that looks like Darth Vader"? Mrs. Jackson, naturally (Shedler & Manis, 1986. Taylor & Thompson, 1982, provide additional information about the sometimes-inconsistent impact of vividness on perceptions.)

Top-down processing. We bring an assortment of cognitive baggage with us to every social situation—expectations, goals, plans, preconceptions, attitudes, beliefs, and so on—and this baggage often determines how we direct our attention. If we expect to see a letter but instead we are shown a number for a brief instant, we report seeing a letter. We think that 13 is a *B*, or a 5 is an *S* (Neisser, 1967). If we are trying to estimate a person's age, we notice different things about them than we would if we were trying to remember their clothing (Yarbus, 1967). If we are led to believe that the people we are interviewing are depressed, we notice their lack of energy and low self-confidence but pay little attention to their sense of humor or social poise (Coyne, Burchill, & Stiles, 1991). When asked to record the number of infractions committed during a game, sports fans fail to notice many of their own team's infractions but pay close attention to the other team's every transgression (Hastorf & Cantril, 1954).

Antonia Abbey (1982) has documented a particularly disturbing case of top-down processing: the tendency for men to misunderstand the sexual meaning of women's objectively neutral behaviors. Abbey herself came face to face with this problem when listening to a band in a club. The band was good, the club was crowded, and so Abbey and her female companion asked two male strangers if they could share their table. But as the night wore on, the men, instead of recognizing that the women were forced by the crowded situation to sit with them, erroneously ascribed romantic motives to Abbey and her friend. They insisted that the women had acted in a flirtatious way, even though the women explained they never flirted with the men at any time.

Abbey explored this process by asking pairs of college students—each pair consisting of one man and one woman—to discuss their experiences in college while a hidden man and woman observed them. Although the couples talked only 5 minutes and the topic was innocuous, both men managed to see signs of sexuality in the women's actions. Whether watching or conversing, men tended more than women to interpret the other's behavior as promiscuous and seductive. The conversing men also reported feeling more sexually attracted than the women did, and even rated themselves as more flirtatious. The men's perceptions were apparently driven by their beliefs about women and sex. According to Abbey, "men are more likely to perceive the world in sexual terms and to make sexual judgments than women are" (1982, p. 836). Their assumptions about women caused social hallucinations: they saw emotions, motives, and behaviors that simply were not there.

Automatic processing. We do not waste our mental resources. When we concentrate our attention on one aspect of our environment, we pay less attention to others. For example, Kissinger couldn't listen to Nixon, plan his own answer, and take notes all at the same time. Therefore, to stretch his mental resources further, some encoding took place without his attention or awareness. He may have followed Nixon's words closely, but did he note the features of his face with care? Probably not, for he had seen human faces so many times that he could perceive Nixon's automatically, without any mental effort or conscious control (Shiffrin & Schneider, 1977).

controlled processing
Cognitive processes that can be intentionally and deliberately initiated, monitored, and terminated.

Such cognitive mechanisms are sustained by automatic processing rather than **controlled processing**. When controlled, we initiate, monitor, and terminate our information search at will. The first time we meet our new friend's parents, when we listen to a lecture, or watch ourselves on video we control our attention—we focus it on particular stimuli and ignore others that are competing for our attention. Your friend's greeting of "Hi, good to see you," a scowl, your toothbrush lying by the sink, or your mother's face, on the other hand, are such well-known stimuli that you can encode them without any mental effort. Unlike controlled processing, automatic processing tends to have the following characteristics (Bargh, 1984, 1990):

- *Rapid*: Processing is so routinized it can be carried out very quickly.
- *Autonomous*: Processing proceeds independently of other cognitive processes.
- *Effortless*: It requires little or no cognitive resources and can be carried out even when other cognitive tasks are being performed.
- *Involuntary*: It begins spontaneously and terminates automatically.
- *Unintentional*: Deliberation is not required for processing to occur.
- *Outside awareness*: The individual is not aware that processing is taking place.

Automatic processes conserve our valuable mental resources, but they also limit our ability to control—or even to understand—our own reactions and perceptions. When we are very practiced at making judgments about a person's intelligence rather than his or her friendliness, we may find ourselves instantly taking a liking to an intelligent person who is unfriendly (Smith, Stewart, & Buttram, 1992). We may automatically notice a person's skin color is different from our own, and this perception may ferret its way into our subsequent treatment of that person (Devine, 1989; compare with Stangor et al., 1992).

priming
The activation of preexisting beliefs, concepts, or other cognitive structures by an environmental or cognitive cue.

Priming is a particularly influential automatic process. Priming occurs whenever preexisting beliefs, concepts, and other cognitive structures are activated by an environmental or cognitive cue (Sedikides & Skowronski, 1991). Imagine, for example, that one day you are relaxing at the park when you see a man talking to a little boy. As you watch, the little boy shakes his head and points to a nearby bicycle. The two continue to talk, and eventually they walk off together. Would you have seen the child being abducted, or would you have seen the boy playing with his father? When perceivers watched a videotape of an ambiguous interaction between an adult and a little boy, only 43.75% thought the boy was in danger. Subjects who had passed a poster asking for information about a lost child while walking to the study, however, were much more suspicious; 71.9% thought the child was being kidnapped (James, 1986).

Priming has been documented in many situations. People who watched sexist music videos later interpreted interactions between men and women in sex-stereotyped ways (Hansen & Hansen, 1988b). People who played a name-recognition game became more hostile in an unrelated situation if their puzzles contained names of hostile people (Menachem Begin, Indiana coach Bobby Knight) rather than nonhostile types (Daniel Boone, Henry Kissinger) (Herr, 1986). Similarly, Kissinger's perception of Nixon could have been influenced if something had primed his interest in foreign affairs—Nixon's forte—rather than his interest in domestic affairs. People who were primed with a list of words that included *diplomat, ambassador,* and *consulate* rated the president more positively when he was accomplished in foreign affairs than domestic affairs. Others who read a list with words that primed knowledge of economic matters (for example, *capital, treasury, financial*) rated him most positively when he demonstrated economic expertise (Sherman, Mackie, & Driscoll, 1990). Even our own inferences about other people may, in some cases, function as primes. We may unintentionally make inferences about people's traits seconds after we meet them, and these spontaneous trait inferences may guide our conscious appraisals of these individuals from that point on (Moskowitz & Roman, 1992; Newman & Uleman, 1989; Winter, Uleman, & Cunniff, 1985).

subliminal perception Apprehending a stimulus without awareness of the stimulus.

Perceivers need not consciously connect the prime and the subsequent stimulus for priming effects to take place. **Subliminal perception**—encoding without conscious awareness—may be a form of automatic processing (Bargh et al., 1986; Greenwald, 1993; Neuberg, 1988; Robles et al., 1987). In one study, subjects watched for spots to appear on a blank computer screen; if they saw any, they were to press a switch to indicate whether the spot was on the right or left side of the screen. The spots, however, were actually words, but they were presented so briefly (for 125 milliseconds) that they looked like dark splotches. To prime the subjects, the researchers varied the meanings of the words. Some subjects were exposed to words related to honesty (*honest, sincere, liar*), others were shown words related to meanness (*kind, considerate, mean*), and control subjects saw neutral words (*what, little, many*).

The subjects saw the spots, and they could tell whether the dots appeared on the right or left side of the screen. But they didn't think that the spots were words, and they couldn't discriminate between words they were shown and words they were not shown. Yet, when the subjects evaluated a woman named Donna as part of another study, the unrecognized primes influenced their judgments. As Figure 3-2 indicates, people who were primed with honesty terms thought Donna was more honest, but people who were primed with meanness terms thought she was meaner (Erdley & D'Agostino, 1988).

These findings are relevant to the debate about subliminal advertising. In the late 1950s the public was outraged when advertisers began to place subliminal advertising messages in films and magazines. In one case, messages like "Drink Coca-Cola" and "Eat popcorn" were presented to moviegoers so briefly that they were never consciously noticed. Even though the viewers were never aware of the messages, the advertisers claimed that the sales of Coca-Cola and popcorn skyrocketed (see Moore, 1982). Researchers continue to question advertisers' claims concerning the use of these hidden persuaders, but recent studies of priming suggest that subliminal advertising works only under very specific conditions (Fiske & Taylor, 1991). First, primes sometimes influence perceptions as much as a week after the initial coding, but in most cases they lose their power very rapidly (Sinclair, Mark, & Shotland, 1987; Srull & Wyer, 1980). Subliminal advertising, then, will be most effective if consumers make their choices soon after they are primed. Second, if supraliminal cues

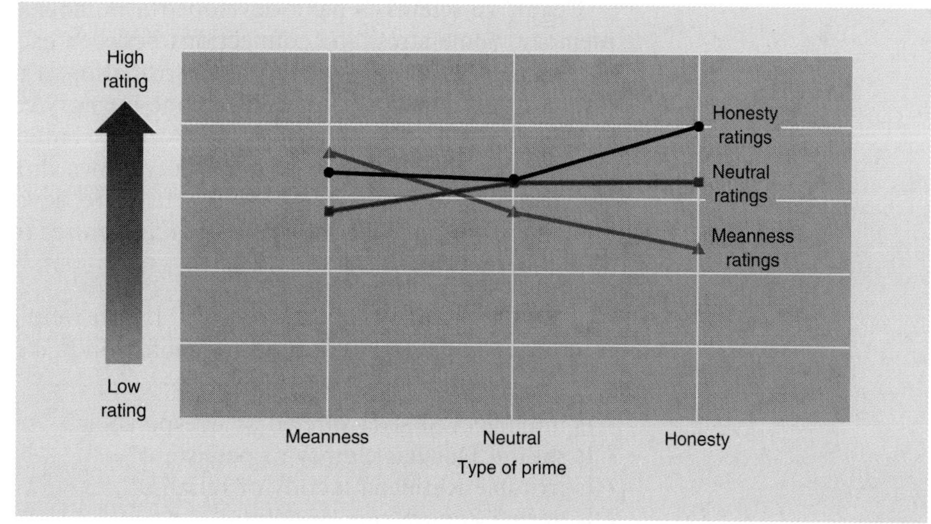

▲ **FIGURE 3-2**
Do subliminal primes influence the way we perceive others? Subjects who were unwittingly exposed to honesty-related words, meanness-related words, or neutral words later described a woman named Donna in ways that were consistent with the subliminal primes. (Data from Erdley & D'Agostino, 1988)

(ones that people are aware of) suggest a clear interpretation of the subsequent stimulus event, priming probably won't influence us. If a product looks shoddy, a person we meet is obviously obnoxious, or a situation is rife with danger, our perceptions won't be influenced even if we were primed with positive cues (see Table 3-1).

Social Memory: The Representation of Social Knowledge

Kissinger did not base his analysis of Nixon on only the cues he gathered during their conversation. Over the course of his life, Kissinger had met thousands and thousands of people. Each encounter had left its mark on him. Kissinger already had certain preconceptions about people, politicians, and Nixon, and these assumptions shaped his interpretation of Nixon's qualities and characteristics. To understand who Kissinger saw when he looked at Nixon that day in 1968, we must understand Kissinger's **social memory**: the mental structures and processes that store and retrieve information about people and social events (Mullen & Copper, 1989; Schneider, 1991; Sedikides & Ostrom, 1990).

social memory
Any past experience and information pertaining to people and social events that can be recalled; also, the psychological structures and processes that organize this information and make its retrieval possible.

▲ **TABLE 3-1**
Summing up: Three processes that influence the allocation of attention

Process	*Characteristics*	*Application*
Bottom-up	The object of perception controls the allocation of attention; perception is data-driven.	Salient, vivid stimuli are noticed more than inconspicuous, pallid ones.
Top-down	The perceivers' expectations, goals, and other conceptual elements determine what is noticed; perception is conceptually driven.	Sexually active men tend to interpret women's behaviors as sexually provocative.
Automatic	Encoding occurs almost effortlessly as information is rapidly processed outside of awareness; perception is no longer a controlled process.	Stimuli that are not noticed or perceived prime existing conceptualizations, which then influence perception.

Cognitive scientists have developed a number of models that account for memory. Some stress the connections between each element in our memory. Others describe the way incoming information is matched to stored information. Still others emphasize the way one memory can activate other memories (Solso, 1991). All these theories, however, are based on the idea that our memories are organized. Information is not thrown in haphazardly, but is instead stored in ordered patterns that allow us to retrieve the information at a later date. Here we consider two of these architectures of memory: implicit personality theories and schemas.

Implicit personality theories. If you were given just a single piece of information about another person, could you make inferences about that person's other qualities? For example:

- Is intelligent Sharifa shrewd or irresponsible?
- Is skillful Douglas clumsy or persistent?
- Is irritable Kathleen moody or reliable?
- Is boring Zainab vain or helpful?
- Is warm Latonia sentimental or superficial?

implicit personality theory Each individual's personal assumptions about the naturally occurring relationships among various traits and attributes.

We can answer these questions because our knowledge of these various traits is organized by our **implicit personality theories**: intuitive assumptions about the naturally occurring relationships among various traits and attributes. An intuitive personality theory like the one shown in Figure 3-3 tells us that intelligence is linked to shrewdness, but not to irresponsibility; that skill implies persistence, but not clumsiness; that irritability goes with moodiness, and dullness goes with vanity. Moreover, some traits are connected to many other traits, whereas others are not firmly embedded in the trait network. In Figure 3-3, for example, the term *warm* is linked to many other terms, whereas vain is relatively isolated. Therefore, knowing that a person is vain tells us very little

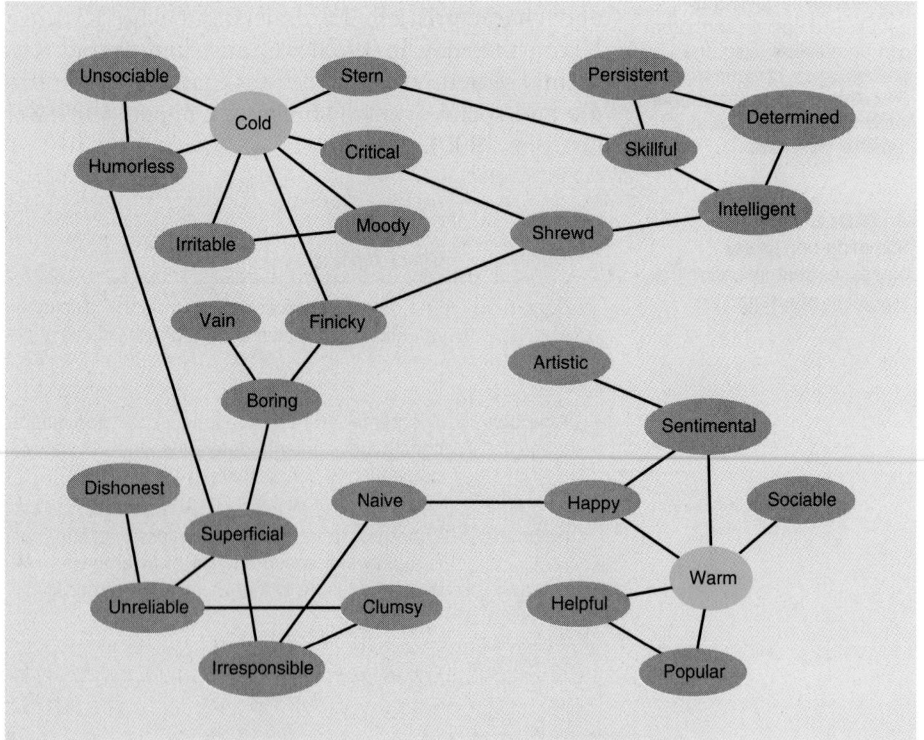

▲ **FIGURE 3-3**
What is the architecture of social knowledge? This representation of an implicit personality theory suggests that we intuitively recognize and remember interrelationships among various traits and attributes. In this example, intelligence is linked to shrewdness but not to irresponsibility; skill implies persistence, but not clumsiness. Warm and cold are central traits.

▲ **TABLE 3-2**
What themes organized Kissinger's implicit personality theory of leaders? Researchers who studied Kissinger's book, *The White House Years*, concluded that he based his understanding of world leaders on the five key dimensions shown.

Trait Theme	*Sample Attributes*
Professional anguish	Insecure, strained, lonely, uneasy, tough, senior, public, obsessive, instinctual, hard, tense, private, hopeful
Ambitious patriotism	Patriotic, suspicious, hated, dependent, ambitious, incapable, restless, isolated, fearful, military
Revolutionary greatness	Great, psychological, had faith, revolutionary, self-assured, had vision, ruthless, detailed, had grasp
Intellectual sophistication	Humorous, knowledgeable, skilled, experienced, repetitious, ambiguous, subtle, aloof, dignified, intelligent, professional, self-confident
Realistic friendship	Ambivalent, decisive, friendly, skeptical, close, dominant, unsentimental, confident, emotional, liking, warm

Source: From Swede & Tetlock, 1986.

central trait
A trait that conveys considerable information about a person due to its close connection with a large number of other traits; warm-cold is an example.

about the person, whereas knowing that a person is warm tells us a great deal. A trait that is linked to a large number of other traits is termed a **central trait** (Hampson, John, & Goldberg, 1986; Kim & Rosenberg, 1980; Schneider, Hastorf, & Ellsworth, 1979; Sternberg, 1985).

Different people adopt different implicit personality theories depending on their ages, cultural backgrounds, and experiences. Take Henry Kissinger, for example. In his book, *The White House Years* (Kissinger, 1979), he uses 3,700 traits to describe different politicians. The terms range from *ambitious, ambiguous,* and *aloof* all the way to *wary, youthful,* and *zealous.* These specific traits, however, were linked by his implicit personality theory of leadership. Kissinger believed, for example, that leaders who were insecure and strained also tended to be lonely and frustrated; that humorous individuals tended to be knowledgeable and skilled; that decisive leaders were friendly and confident. Moreover, professional anguish was, for Kissinger, a central trait. In fact, the thousands of trait terms that he used in his descriptions could be distilled down to the five fundamental beliefs about leaders shown in Table 3-2: professional anguish, ambitious patriotism, revolutionary greatness, intellectual sophistication, and realistic friendship (Swede & Tetlock, 1986).

Implicit personality theories perform a vital cognitive function: they help us turn a small amount of information into a general understanding of the total person. Kissinger did not view Nixon as a man who was nervous, knowledgeable about world affairs, uncertain, and patriotic. Rather, he combined this information in a unified impression of Nixon's personality that went well beyond the immediate information that he had gathered in his brief interview. As Solomon Asch (1946), a pioneer in the field of person perception, explains:

> We look at a person and immediately a certain impression of his character forms itself in us. A glance, a few spoken words are sufficient to tell us a story about a highly complex matter. We know that such impressions form with remarkable rapidity and great ease. Subsequent observations may enrich or upset our first view, but we can no more prevent its rapid growth than we can avoid perceiving a given visual object or hearing a melody. (p. 258)

Asch (1946) studied the impact of implicit personality theories on our perceptions using a simple but elegant procedure. He asked perceivers to form an impression of a person who possessed a certain set of traits; for example, "intelligent, warm, and practical" or "stubborn, careless, and stupid." Then, by

▲ This woman is intelligent, skillful, industrious, cold, determined, practical, and cautious. Given this information, do you think she is sociable or withdrawn? Generous or stingy? Happy or unhappy? Friendly or unfriendly? Witty or cynical? In answering these questions, you rely on your ability to synthesize perceptual information to form a unified impression of a person.

systematically varying the attributes in their lists, he could determine how perceivers combined these discrete qualities into a single impression. Consider, for example, these two individuals:

Person A: intelligent, skillful, industrious, warm, determined, practical, and cautious

Person B: intelligent, skillful, industrious, cold, determined, practical, and cautious

Even though the lists for Person A and Person B are nearly identical, Asch found that perceivers rated A much more positively than B. Only one word was changed—*warm* was replaced by *cold*—yet B (the cold individual) was more frequently described as ungenerous, unhappy, irritable, unsociable, unpopular, and humorless (Asch, 1946; see Figure 3-4). One representative subject described Person A as "a person who believes certain things are right, wants others to see his point, would be sincere in an argument and would like to see his point won" (p. 263). Person B, though, was described as "a very ambitious and talented person who would not let anyone or anything stand in the way of achieving his goal. Wants his own way, he is determined not to give in, no matter what happens" (p. 263).

Why did the warm-cold trait have such a significant impact on perceivers? Asch and the researchers who followed up his initial efforts note two possibilities (Anderson & Sedikides, 1991). First, although people's implicit personality theories are idiosyncratic, warm-cold or its synonym tends to be among the top five traits mentioned by most people when describing others' personalities (Goldberg, 1993; Peabody & Goldberg, 1989; Rosenberg & Sedlak, 1972; Zebrowitz, 1990). As a central trait, when *warm* is activated, it triggers the activation of a large number of related positive traits such as friendliness and happiness. As one subject explained, warmth "initiates other qualities. A man who is warm would be friendly, consequently happy" (Asch, 1946, p. 277). Activating *cold*, in contrast, triggered negative qualities such as pessimism and practicality (Collins & Loftus, 1975).

Second, Asch himself argued that central traits like warm-cold can change the meaning of the person's other qualities. Imagine, for example, that when

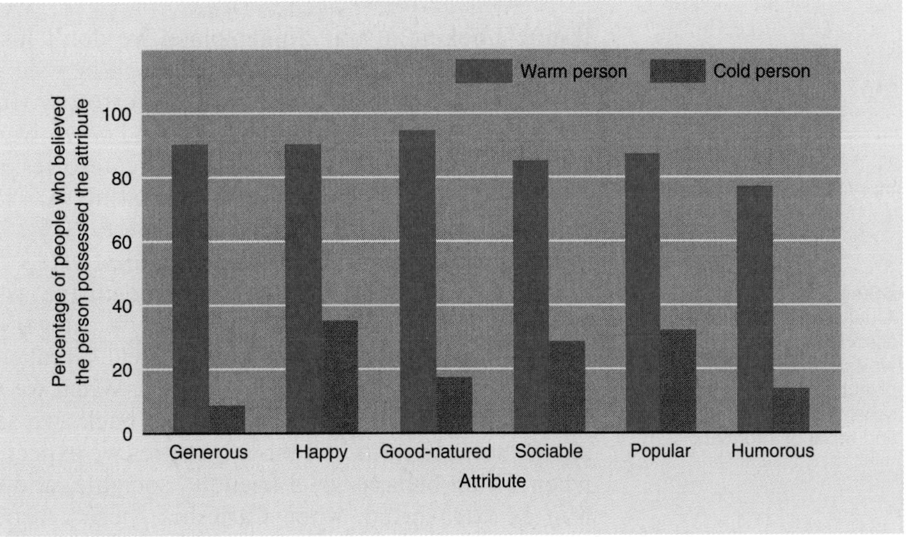

▲ **FIGURE 3-4**
What qualities do we attribute to a warm person and a cold person? Even when two individuals are described identically in all ways save one—one is called warm and the other is called cold—perceivers formulate radically different impressions of the two. A larger percentage of people attributed these positive qualities to the warm person rather than to the cold person. (Adapted from Asch, 1946)

you first meet Hal he seems cold rather than warm. Now imagine that you have discovered that Hal is also calm and discreet. When you interpret the word *calm,* does it mean poised and serene or cool and calculating? Does *discreet* mean tactful or secretive? Using these procedures, Asch found the adjective *calm* meant serene, peaceful, gentle, or tolerant only when it described a kind person. When applied to a cruel person, *calm* was reinterpreted to mean icy, calculating, or shrewd. Transformations like those shown in Table 3-3 have been obtained in other studies (Asch, 1946, Study 5; Hamilton & Zanna, 1974; Zanna & Hamilton, 1977; compare with Kaplan, 1975; Watkins & Peynircioglu, 1984).

The change-of-meaning process can also be seen at work when subjects use various strategies to form unified impressions of people who possess two apparently inconsistent traits, such as sociable and lonely or hostile and dependent. A sociable-lonely person, for example, was seen as "outwardly friendly, but inwardly shy and lonely," and a hostile-dependent person was "dependent on his or her parents, but hostile towards everyone else" (Asch & Zukier, 1984; Burnstein & Schul, 1982, 1983; Schul, 1983).

▲ **TABLE 3-3**
Why does a central trait have such a large impact on our impressions? The change-of-meaning hypothesis maintains that central traits, like warm-cold, can change the meaning of other attributes. The word *calm,* for example, means serene when used to describe a warm person, but calculating when applied to a cold person.

Attribute	*Warm Person*	*Cold Person*
Calm	Serene	Calculating
Witty	Cynical	Satirical
Discreet	Tactful	Secretive
Proud	Self-respecting	Conceited
Excitable	Lively	Touchy
Obedient	Cooperative	Submissive
Daring	Courageous	Reckless
Righteous	Virtuous	Dogmatic
Crafty	Clever	Sly
Outspoken	Frank	Blunt

Source: Based on Asch, 1946.

Schemas and cognitive categories. We are constantly classifying things. Looking at our dinner plate, we don't just see asparagus, steak, and cake but vegetables, meat, and dessert. When we walk into a room, we know that the chairs and tables fit into one category (furniture), and the paintings and sculpture fit into another (art). And when we meet people, they, too, are perceptually classified into the relevant categories: man or woman; child, adult, or elder; professor or student; white, Latino, African American, Asian American; hero or villain; introvert or extravert.

schema
A network of cognitive associations that define the typical characteristics of objects in a category; schemas guide the processing and recall of information.

We could not achieve even the simplest categorizations if we did not have **schemas**. A schema is a system of cognitive associations that defines the typical characteristics of objects in each category. We know that the sweet, squarish confection served after a meal is cake because it has the typical qualities of all objects in this category. When we walk into a room and see a wooden object with legs, a seat, and back, we say to ourselves, "This is a chair" because it has the basic qualities we expect to find in chairs. Similarly, when Thien behaves in a friendly, sociable, and exuberant way, we classify him as extraverted; when Carleshia speaks earnestly of her work with the Save the Whales Foundation, we decide she is a do-gooder, and when Patrick makes sarcastic remarks about the women in his office, we conclude that he is sexist. In each case, these individuals have the attributes we associate with each of these categories.

Different kinds of schemas organize and structure different kinds of social information. *Person schemas* summarize our intuitive understanding of other people, including their typical behaviors, traits, and goals. An implicit personality theory is a kind of person schema, for it describes how various attributes are interrelated and facilitates the classification of people into categories. Kissinger met hundreds of political leaders, but by considering their traits, behaviors, and goals, he could categorize them into the six types shown in Figure 3-5: the revolutionary, the patriot, the personal friend, the professional friend, the able adversary, and the professional competitor. *Self-schemas,* in contrast, organize our perceptions of our own qualities. In Kissinger's case, his self-schema stressed his intellectual ability, his ability to establish cordial working relations with others, and his feelings of stress and tension. He also made use of *stereotypes*, which are schemas that describe the typical characteristics of people in various social groups, and *event schemas,* or *scripts*: schemas that defined and structured his perceptions of social settings (Fiske & Taylor, 1991).

Schemas are indispensable cognitive tools (see Table 3-4). If Kissinger had been stripped of his schemas just before his meeting with the president-elect, his understanding of Nixon would have been meager at best. Sitting across from Nixon, Kissinger would have been besieged by a flood of information, each bit of information disconnected from the next. He would have been unable to distinguish between important and trivial information or to settle on an interpretation of any particular cue. And how could he remember what he had learned in the meeting if he couldn't integrate that information with his preexisting knowledge of people, politicians, and men? We could not function without schemas (Andersen, Klatzky, & Murray, 1990; Andersen & Klatzky, 1987; Schneider & Blankmeyer, 1983).

Schematic Information Processing

Our social cognitions help us sift through and organize a buzzing, blooming confusion of social data. Without implicit personality theories and schemas to structure information, we would spend our entire lives trying to understand other people. But schemas serve this cognitive purpose at a cost. Kissinger

▲ **FIGURE 3-5**
What kinds of leaders did Kissinger meet when he served as Nixon's foreign affairs advisor? Analysis of Kissinger's writings suggests that he identified six types. Revolutionaries and patriots were two distinct groups, as were friends and opponents. The friends category included personal friends whom he knew before joining the Nixon team and professional friends whom he liked and admired. Similarly, he recognized two types of opponents: able adversaries, who were intellectually sophisticated; and professional competitors, who were high in professional anguish. (Based on Swede & Tetlock, 1986)

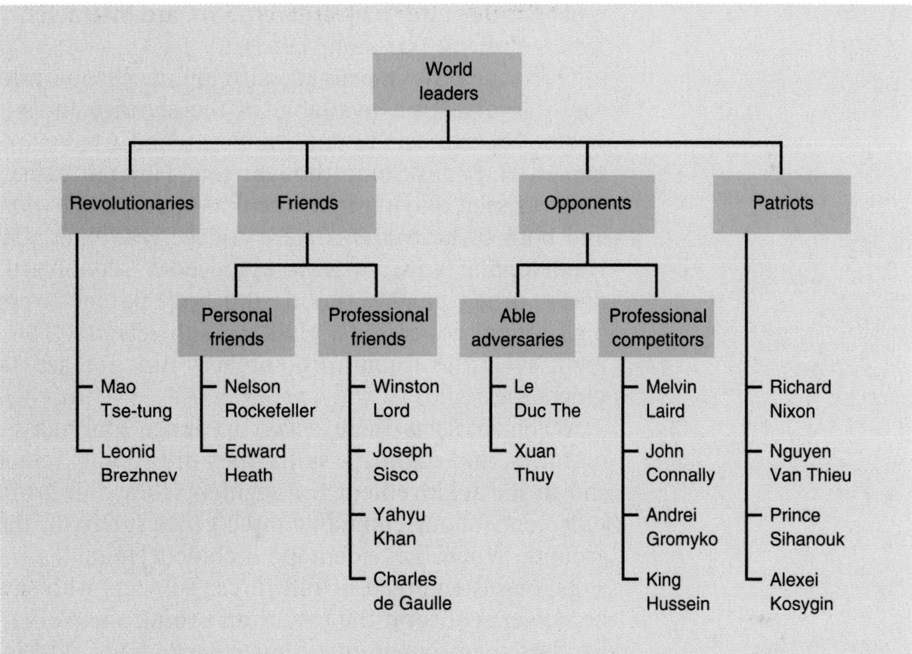

knew that Nixon was a leader, so his schema about world leaders was primed and ready to be used as a structure for incoming information (Bargh & Pietromonaco, 1982; Higgins, Rholes, & Jones, 1977). Nixon's physical features—his sex, his age, and his race, for example—also allowed Kissinger to place Nixon in a social category. Once categorized, Kissinger's stereotypes about such groups guided his analysis of Nixon's qualities (Deaux et al., 1985). Schemas, as we will see, can be cognitive bullies: they push around our perceptions as well as our memories.

Schematic perception. Abbey's study of men and women, discussed earlier in this chapter, revealed the impact of schemas on perceptions. In that study men's assumptions about women influenced what they noticed when interacting with a woman and led them to misunderstand the nature of the social interaction. Schemas, it seems, influence our perceptions by guiding our attention to some stimuli and away from others. In general, when we encounter a stimulus that matches our expectations, we encode that stimulus very rapidly. If we encounter an unexpected stimulus, encoding still takes place but at a

▲ **TABLE 3-4**
Summing up: Two cognitive structures of memory

Structure	*Attributes*	*Cognitive Function*
Implicit personality theory	The perceiver's intuitive assumptions about the relationships among various traits and attributes; central traits are linked to a large number of other traits.	Any trait, once noted, activates related traits; central traits can alter the meaning of the other perceived qualities.
Schema	A system of associations that defines the typical characteristics of objects in each cognitive category.	Schema-consistent information is more easily noticed and stored in memory; schema-inconsistent information requires more time to process and store.

much slower rate, particularly if we are distracted (Klatzky, Martin, & Kane, 1982; White & Carlston, 1983).

Our schemas, if primed, also influence our interpretations of ambiguous social information available in the setting (Jones, 1983; Sagar & Schofield, 1980). The subjects in one study watched a videotape of a 9-year-old white girl named Hannah. Some thought that Hannah came from a well-to-do family. She was seen playing in a tree-lined park, she lived in a large suburban home, and both of her parents were college graduates. Other subjects saw a poorer Hannah. She played in a stark, fenced-in schoolyard, her home was in a dilapidated, urban neighborhood, and both parents were blue-collar workers with high school educations. Half the subjects saw Hannah take a short achievement test; the remaining subjects did not see the testing portion of the videotape.

When subjects were asked to judge Hannah's work habits, motivation, maturity, and cognitive skills, they did so only reluctantly if they had not been shown the achievement test segment; they didn't think they should make snap judgments about Hannah's intelligence solely on the basis of her family background. When the videotape included Hannah's performance, however, subjects' biases emerged in full force. Subjects who saw the poorer Hannah gave her lower scores on the test, didn't think she worked as hard, and thought she had less cognitive ability. Subjects who knew nothing at all about Hannah had no evidence to reinterpret, so they were unbiased. Those who were given just a smidgen of information, however, misinterpreted that information to conform to their schematic preconceptions. In this case a little knowledge was a dangerous (or biasing) thing (Darley & Gross, 1983).

Schematic memory. Our schemas influence what we notice (and don't notice); do they also influence our memories? Do we tend to forget things that are inconsistent with our schemas? When we try to recall events, are the memories we retrieve slanted in ways that confirm rather than challenge our schemas (Alba & Hasher, 1983; Bartlett, 1932; Brewer & Nakamura, 1984)?

Claudia E. Cohen (1981) examined these questions in a study of occupation-based stereotypes. First, she identified the qualities that most people expect in

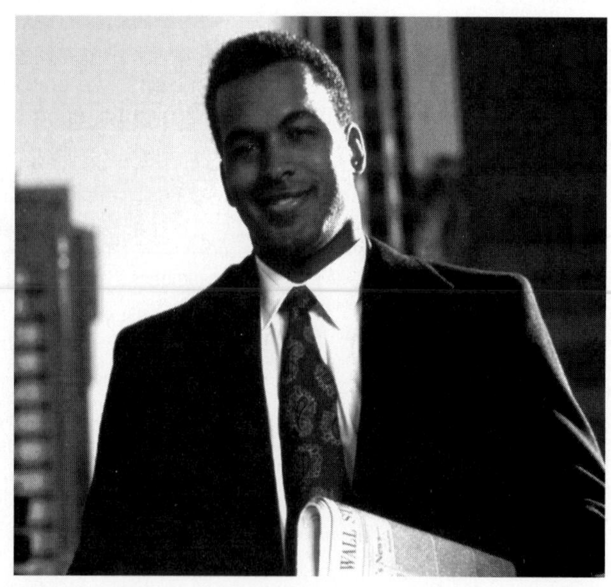

▲ Our cognitive schemas allow us to classify the people we meet into categories. Just a glance at this person might prompt us to assume that he belongs in the categories of African American, businessman, extravert, young professional, and city dweller. After we have classified a person, we rely on our cognitive schemas to make other inferences about the qualities and characteristics we expect to find in people who belong in these categories.

a woman who is a librarian and in a woman who is a waitress. She discovered, for example, that we expect a librarian to eat salad, play the piano, wear glasses, and drink wine. We expect a waitress to eat hamburgers, watch TV, bowl, and drink beer. Next, Cohen created videotapes of a woman who was supposedly celebrating her birthday with her husband. In these videotapes she carefully included features from both occupational stereotypes. The woman, for example, played the piano and wore glasses, but she also drank beer and watched TV. Cohen then showed these tapes to subjects, but before starting the tape she mentioned that the woman was either a waitress in a local restaurant or a city librarian. As predicted, when subjects were asked to recall what they had seen with such questions as "What did the woman drink?" and "What kind of music did she listen to?" they tended to remember features that were consistent with their stereotypes of librarians and waitresses. If they thought they were watching a librarian, for instance, they remembered that she listened to classical music, but thought she drank wine rather than beer (Cohen, 1981; see Figure 3-6).

Recognizing and remembering the unexpected. Cohen's subjects recalled more schema-congruent cues than schema-incongruent cues. Subsequent studies, however, indicate that we don't always overlook the unexpected or forget bits of information that contradict our schemas (Srull & Wyer, 1989). One study demonstrated our sensitivity to schema-incongruent data by asking people to listen to a tape recording of a child taking an oral test. The researchers told some of the listeners that the child came from an affluent family; others were told that he came from a disadvantaged background. They assumed that this information would create different expectations, for people listening to a child from affluent circumstances would expect him to perform well. The researchers also manipulated the child's performance. In one condition he missed many questions initially, although his performance improved over the course of the questioning (going from 30% correct to 90% correct on the final ten questions). In the other condition he performed very well at first, but his performance declined (going from 90% correct to 30% correct). When the subjects later estimated the number of questions the boy answered correctly, they were more accurate when his performance didn't match their expectations. They more accurately recalled the percentage of questions the child answered correctly when their expectations were negative and the boy per-

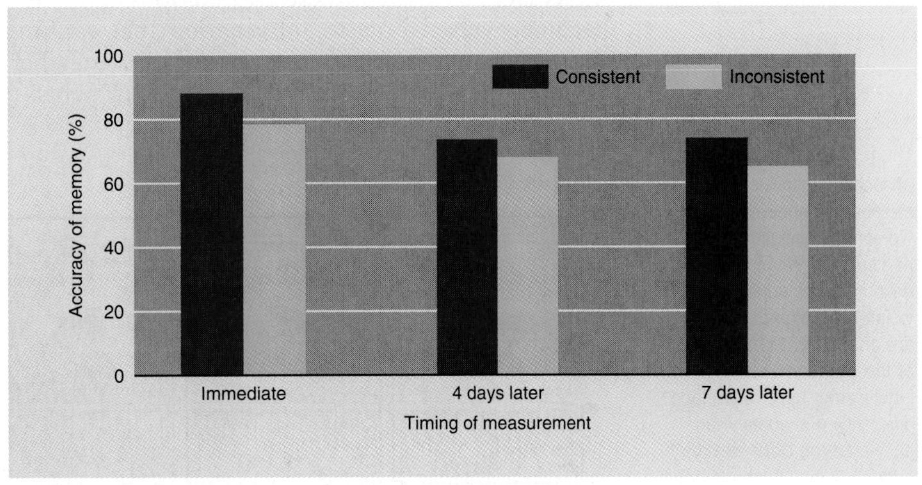

▲ FIGURE 3-6
Is memory schematic? Subjects who watched a videotape of a woman, identified as either a waitress or a librarian, playing the piano, listening to classical music, drinking beer, and watching television could recall 88% of the features that were consistent with their stereotypes, but only 78% of the stereotype-inconsistent information. This effect remained stable over time. (Adapted from Cohen, 1981)

formed well at first and when their expectations were positive and the boy performed poorly at first (Hilton, Klein, & von Hippel, 1991).

When do we recognize and remember the unexpected? The answer depends, in part, on the strength of our expectations, for strong, long-established schema usually promote confirmation rather than disconfirmation. Kissinger was a political scientist, so his schemas about politicians were richly detailed and well defined. Kissinger would therefore be more likely to remember Nixon's ambitiousness and patriotism since they are consistent with this schema. Second, he would be more likely to forget characteristics that were inconsistent with his schema (for example, being timid, friendly). Third, he would be more likely to complete his schema by remembering traits or characteristics that he never even observed (being tough, obsessive). People with weaker schemas for politicians would, instead, pay more attention to information that was incongruent with their expectations (Howard & Rothbart, 1980; Park & Rothbart, 1982; Stangor & McMillan, 1992). The impact of schema-incongruent information also tends to be greater during encoding. Although it takes us longer to encode the unexpected, once we notice such information, it has more impact on our inferences than expected information. Schema-congruent information, in contrast, is more influential at subsequent stages of information processing (Fiske, 1993). Last, a variety of situational factors determine the relative impact of congruent versus incongruent information. For example, we seek schema-consistent information when we are trying to place an individual within a global category (such as leader or artist), but we seek disconfirming, surprising data when we are trying to develop an understanding of a single individual (Srull, 1983; Stern et al., 1984). We also tend to escape the restraints of schematic biases if nothing in the situation primes our expectations (Bargh, 1984; Higgins, 1989; Higgins, King, & Mavin, 1982; Srull, 1983), when we feel the disconfirming evidence will provide important diagnostic information (Trope & Bassok, 1982), when we are motivated to form a clear, unbiased impression of the other person (Erber & Fiske, 1984; Strohmer & Chiodo, 1984), and when the situational information is incongruous (Lingle, Dukerich, & Ostrom, 1983).

Social Thought: An Up-Down Process

Sherlock Holmes warned, "It is a capital mistake to theorize before you have all the evidence. It biases the judgment" (Doyle, 1938, p. 18). But each of our social encounters is shaped by the thoughts and expectations that we carry into it. As Holmes argued, these expectations can bias our perceptions so that we become oversensitive to information that confirms our initial expectations. They also determine, in part, what we remember and what we forget. But social thought is not always top-down. Our beliefs may prompt us to expect a

DOONESBURY copyright G. B. Trudeau. Reprinted with permission of UNIVERSAL PRESS SYNDICATE. All rights reserved.

▲ Schemas, including our stereotypes about men and women, can influence our perceptions. When we encounter someone who violates our expectations, we are often slow to make sense of the situation. Would this letter carrier have responded differently if a woman had answered the Doonesburys' door?

president-elect to act confident and vainglorious, but in spite of our belief we will notice actions that are inconsistent with our expectations. Moreover, in some situations we fairly test our beliefs about people and groups, and we are capable of casting them off if the evidence weighs heavily against them. When we have no schematic information that applies, we must integrate bits of information piecemeal (Brewer, 1988; Fiske & Neuberg, 1990; see "In Depth: Mathematical Models of Social Thought"). Top-down processes are powerful, but they do not always overwhelm other, more data-driven, processes. As Figure 3-7 indicates, top-down and bottom-up processes work together to shape our understanding of other people (Higgins & Bargh, 1987; Hilton & Fein, 1989; Rasinski, Crocker, & Hastie, 1985).

Heuristics and Social Inference

We generate social knowledge through processes that are both active and complex. We gather and decipher information, formulate initial impressions by organizing and structuring this information, and then revise our understanding of other people and ourselves if the facts or our preconceptions warrant it. As Sherlock Holmes said, once we are "shown a single fact in all its bearings" we can "deduce from it not only all the chain of events which led up to it, but also all the results which would follow from it" (Doyle, 1938, p. 253).

Sometimes, however, this studied analysis gives way to a more rapid, more intuitive analysis. What should we do, for example, when we must draw inferences even though we lack critical bits of information? Will Nixon be successful as president? Is the movie showing at the theater down the street worth seeing? Will our friend keep her promise? Only time will tell, but we can't postpone our decisions until we are certain. Conversely, in some

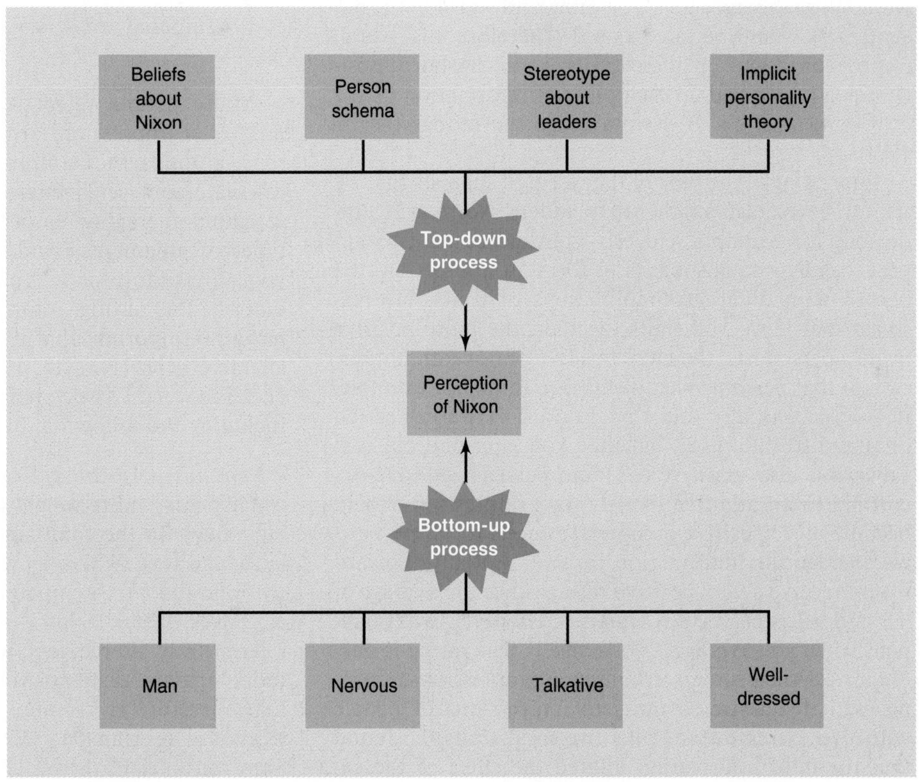

FIGURE 3-7
How do we develop an understanding of other people? Cognitive psychologists stress the integrative functioning of both data-driven and conceptually driven processes. Kissinger's observations may tell him that Nixon is knowledgeable about foreign affairs, tense, uncertain, and patriotic, but his previous experiences with politicians and world leaders may have convinced him they have certain traits and qualities. These two types of processes worked together to determine his overall reaction.

IN DEPTH

Mathematical Models of Social Thought

Kissinger considered Prime Minister of England Edward Heath to be intelligent, warm, and gentle (1979, p. 933). William Scranton: selfless and able (p. 50). Queen Elizabeth: witty, knowledgeable about world affairs, and insightful (pp. 93–95). Nelson Rockefeller, in contrast, had courage, vision, and persistence, according to Kissinger, but he was also cold-blooded and only average in intelligence (1979, p. 5).

How did he combine this information to form an overall impression of these individuals? Asch assumed that he synthesized each bit of information to form a unique configuration that goes beyond the content of the individual traits. As the well-known dictum of the early Gestalt psychologists argues, the whole is greater than the sum of its parts. Some social psychologists, however, favor a data-driven, **information-integration model** interpretation that assumes perceivers intuitively *add* or *average* pieces of information to yield an overall conclusion. For example, in evaluating Edward Heath, Kissinger may have felt that being intelligent is a very positive trait and that being warm is a slightly positive characteristic, but that being gentle is a neutral quality in a political leader. If he were asked to rate each of these attributes on a scale from +3 to −3, intelligence would probably receive a +3 rating and warm a +1, but gentleness would be rated as a 0. Therefore, his overall impression based on these traits would be fairly positive: a +4 if we add up each piece of information (3 + 1 + 0 = 4) or a +1.33 if we average the ratings (4/3 = 1.33).

Interestingly, the bulk of the research suggests that we tend to be averagers rather than adders. Norman H. Anderson, for example, cleverly contrasted the two approaches by asking subjects to form an impression of a person with different combinations of traits. He reasoned that if we add traits together, the more positive traits a person has, the more positive our overall impression of that person. What would you think, for example, if you are initially told that Edward is warm-hearted (+3) and truthful (+3), but then you later find out that Edward is also sensitive (+1) and persuasive (+1)? According to an additive model, your impression should become more positive, jumping from +6 to +8. What if we average this information instead? Initially, Edward would receive a very positive rating, since the average of +3 and +3 is 6/3, which equals 3. However, what happens when you average 3, 3, 1, and 1? The rating is only 8/4, or 2. When Anderson compared impressions of people with two extreme traits to impressions of people with two extreme traits plus two mild traits, he found that the mild information diluted the effect of the extreme information (see Figure 3-8). A person who was described as warm-hearted and truthful received a higher rating than a person described as warm-hearted, truthful, sensitive, and persuasive. Similarly, a person who was spiteful and abusive received a more negative evaluation than a person who was spiteful, abusive, unpopular, and critical (Anderson, 1965; see also Anderson, 1991; Birnbaum, 1974; Gollob, Rossman, & Abelson, 1973; Sloan & Ostrom, 1974; Wyer, 1974; Yamagishi & Hill, 1981).

Subsequent research conducted by Anderson and other researchers supported the averaging model, but added a significant refinement. Although evidence indicates that perceivers average the information available to reach an overall judgment, in most cases they weight one or more of the cues more heavily than the others. To apply this **weighted-averaging model,** imagine that you are asked to form an impression of a person who is intelligent (+3), truthful (+3), and ill-tempered (−2). Before averaging these values, however, you intuitively assign heavier weights to the trait or traits that you think are more important. If you feel that a bad temper is a particularly important bit of data, you might double its weight in relation to the other traits: −2 multiplied by its weight (2 since it will weigh twice as much) equals −4. So, according to the weighted-averaging model your opinion of the person would be calculated as follows:

Intelligent	+3
Truthful	+3
Ill-tempered $-2 \times 2 =$	$\underline{-4}$
	$+2 \div 3 = 0.66$

Many people reject Anderson's cognitive algebra models of impression formation on intuitive, commonsense grounds: they simply don't believe that they coldly calculate and weigh interpersonal information. Yet the weighted-averaging model successfully predicts many types of judgments (Anderson, 1991). If, for example, you were to formulate a judgment of a person who was described as untidy, informal, and murderous, *murderous* is so important that it will overshadow all the other characteristics (Forsyth, 1985). Other factors also influence the weight associated with each bit of information, including the following:

- *Extremity.* Traits and qualities with extreme values usually carry more weight than traits with more moderate values. In the combination warm (+1), ill-tempered (−2), and sexy (+3), sexy would be weighted more heavily, followed by ill-tempered and warm (Manis, Gleason, & Dawes, 1966).
- *Negativity.* Perceivers weight negative information more heavily than positive information. Ill-tempered may therefore carry more weight than warm and sexy (Kanouse & Hanson, 1972; Ronis & Lipinski, 1985; Skowronski & Carlston, 1989).

• *Order effects.* The position of the element in the set of information can influence its weight. A **primacy effect** occurs if information at the beginning of a sequence has a greater impact on our impression. If, in contrast, the elements at the end of the sequence are more influential, a **recency effect** occurs. In support of the wisdom of making a good first impression, primacy effects usually overwhelm recency effects. Hence *warm* would receive greater weight than *sexy* (Burnstein & Schul, 1982).

Anderson's studies suggest that, in many cases, quality counts more than quantity. If you are going to give a piano recital, it is probably wiser to perform only two pieces that you know very well rather than adding a third piece that you perform only adequately—unless, of course, the piano piece you perform only adequately would challenge a virtuoso. In this case, it might create a more favorable impression than your astounding rendition of "Chopsticks." Likewise, if two of your three letters of reference for a job are extremely positive, but the third is only above average, send only the positive ones—unless, of course, the lukewarm letter is from a famous dignitary such as Henry Kissinger. Such a letter might have a much greater impact than extremely positive letters from unknown people.

information-integration model: A theory that assumes social perceivers form impressions of others by combining information about other people piecemeal, either by adding each bit of information to other available information or by averaging available information to yield an overall conclusion.

weighted-averaging model: An information-integration theory that argues social perceivers form impressions of others by combining information about other people after first giving extra weight to certain bits of information.

primacy effect: The tendency for information presented early in a series to have greater impact than information presented later in the series.

recency effect: The tendency for information presented most recently to have greater impact than information presented earlier in the series.

cases we have so much information that we can't possibly integrate it all to reach a decision. We want to weigh all the relevant factors carefully when we buy a new car, select a college to attend, or decide to get married, but we are cognitive misers: we strive to increase our wealth of information about other people, but we can't spare the time or cognitive energy to do so (Fiske & Taylor, 1991).

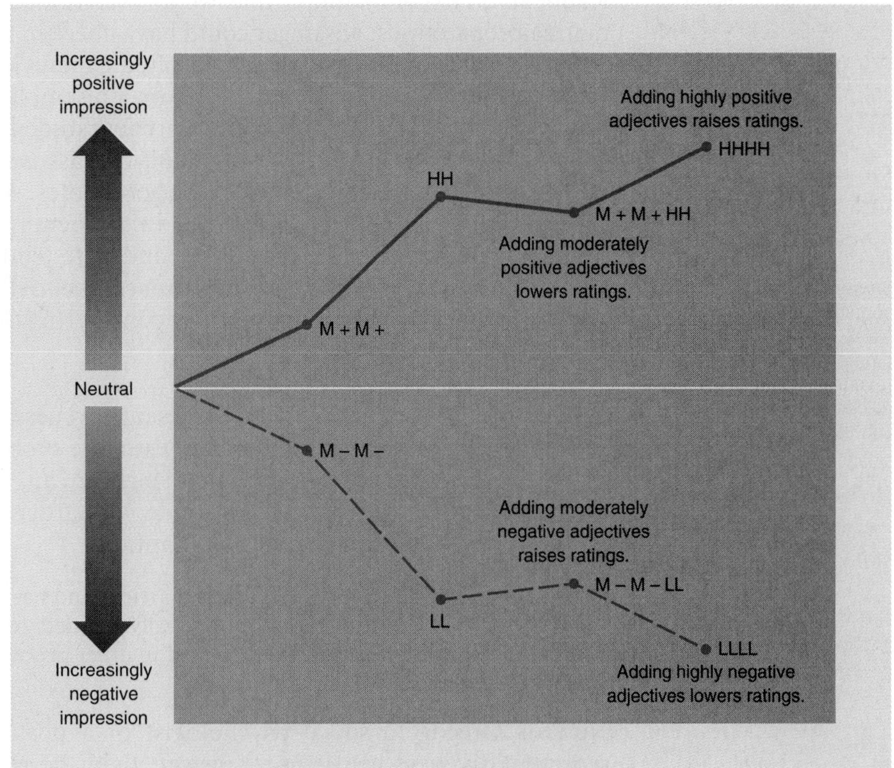

▲ **FIGURE 3-8**
Do we integrate information by averaging or by adding? Anderson's study supported an averaging model of information integration. When two moderately positive adjectives (M+M+) were combined with two highly favorable adjectives (HH), subjects' impressions became less positive. Conversely, when two moderately negative adjectives (M–M–) were combined with two highly negative adjectives (LL), subjects' impressions became less negative. Some signs of adding were also noted, however. Subjects' ratings were more positive, for example, when four positive adjectives were used (HHHH) rather than two (HH). (Based on Anderson, 1965)

heuristics
Inferential principles or rules of thumb that perceivers use to reach conclusions when the amount of available information is limited.

Cognitive psychologists Daniel Kahneman and Amos Tversky (1972, 1973, 1984) believe that we cope with these information-processing demands by making use of cognitive **heuristics**: simplifying inferential principles or rules of thumb that help us process information efficiently and rapidly. Consider, as an example, Sherlock Holmes estimating the height of the murderer in his case *A Study in Scarlet*. First, because "the height of a man, in nine cases out of ten, can be told from the length of his stride," he measured the distance between footprints the culprit had left in the mud. Second, to check his calculation, he noted the position of a message scrawled on the wall, reasoning that "when a man writes on a wall, his instinct leads him to write about the level of his own eyes" (Doyle, 1938, p. 24).

Holmes' heuristics worked marvelously; he solved the crime and dazzled the police with his skills. His heuristics, however, could have misled him if the perpetrator had been craftier. Similarly, our heuristics often help us draw accurate inferences: They speed the time it takes to make decisions, they simplify our search for information, and they usually yield results that are just as accurate as more complex strategies (Kleinmuntz, 1985; Paquette & Kida, 1988). Heuristics are, however, "quick and dirty" cognitive processes that push information through our processing systems quickly rather than thoroughly. Hence, each of the heuristics that we consider in the next section offers costs as well as benefits; they help us make rapid judgments, but they sometimes bias these judgments (Arkes, 1991; Dawes, 1988).

Representativeness

Gamblers, forecasters, and stockbrokers aren't the only people who must make judgments about probabilities. How did Kissinger calculate the odds in favor of and against Nixon's presidency? When you miss a day of class, how do you identify the person who will lend you his or her class notes? Tversky and Kahneman (1974) maintain that we answer these kinds of questions by estimating probabilities. Kissinger could have checked to see how many U.S. presidents have been outstanding or consulted experts in politics back at Harvard. But why not just intuitively gauge Nixon's resemblance to outstanding leaders in general. Similarly, it may be that very few students take adequate notes, but what if the woman who sits next to you in class is quiet and attentive? These two qualities seem essential for taking good notes, so the chances are high that she has good notes. Moreover, if she is also friendly to you, she will be a good representative of both the note taker and note lender categories. These judgments are based on the **representativeness heuristic**. We often estimate the probability of outcomes and events by considering their resemblance to a more general category or case.

representativeness heuristic
A cognitive heuristic that enables the perceiver to estimate the probability of an event or outcome by considering the degree to which the event or outcome is similar to most such events or outcomes.

The base-rate bias. The representativeness heuristic is an indispensable cognitive tool, for it allows us to estimate probabilities without gathering great amounts of information. This heuristic can, however, lead to mistakes when misapplied. Suppose, for example, you are asked to guess Gregory's occupation based on the following description:

> Gregory lives in the United States, is married, and has two children. He is liberal and ambitious. Gregory is also scientifically minded, for he enjoys solving mathematical puzzles, but he is also interested in other people. His major form of recreation is reading.

Now, is Gregory a social psychologist or a postal worker? If you use the representativeness heuristic to answer, then the resemblance between Gregory's qualities and your schemas pertaining to the two occupations might mislead you. Certainly Gregory has some qualities that match up to the social psychologist category, but many postal workers are also scientifically minded, interested in people, and bookish. Objectively, the personality sketch doesn't convey much information, so it is wiser to dismiss it and rely, instead, on base-rate data. How many people in the United States are social psychologists? Maybe 5,000. And how many people in the United States are postal workers? More than 816,000. Because postal workers far outnumber social psychologists as an occupational group, Gregory is likely to be a postal worker (even though, psychologically, he is more representative of social psychologists). If you are like most people, however, you fell prey to the **base-rate bias** by failing to make full use of the general base-rate information that was available to you.

base-rate bias
The *base rate* describes the prevalence of a characteristic in the general population or the usual probability of some event occurring. The base-rate bias occurs when individuals make insufficient use of base-rate information in forming judgments or estimating probabilities.

Richard Nisbett and his colleagues have conducted extensive studies of the weak impact of base-rate information on our inferences. They repeatedly find that, rather than recognizing the informational value of general statistical summaries, we tend to rely on our intuitive assumptions and specific single cases. In one investigation Nisbett's research team asked subjects to read a case study of a ne'er-do-well 43-year-old woman who collected welfare for 13 years. Constantly pregnant but never married, she supposedly spent her welfare money on expensive foods and gambling. The subjects, however, were also given factual information that disconfirmed the societal myths suggested by the case: the base-rate data indicated that 90% of all welfare recipients are off the rolls in 4 years. Yet when subjects described their feelings about people on welfare, the base-rate information had little influence on them. The case data were so representative that they prompted a negative reaction, even though the subjects had been told that the case was atypical (Hamill, Wilson, & Nisbett, 1980; Nisbett & Borgida, 1975; Nisbett et al., 1976).

The dilution effect. Kahneman and Tversky have traced other inferential biases back to representative thinking. Suppose that a panel of psychologists has developed short personality sketches of 100 successful male professionals. Their sample included exactly 70 engineers and 30 lawyers.

▲ This is Gregory. He lives in the United States, is married, and has two children. He is liberal and ambitious. Gregory is scientifically minded and enjoys solving mathematical puzzles, but he is also very interested in other people. His major form of recreation is reading. Is Gregory a social psychologist or a postal worker?

Case 1: You are given no information whatever about an individual chosen at random from the sample. What is the probability that this man is one of the 70 engineers in the sample of 100?

_______ chances out of 100

Case 2: Dick is a 30-year-old man. He is married and has no children. A man of superior ability and motivation, he promises to be quite successful in his field. He is well liked by his colleagues. What is the probability that this man is one of the 70 engineers in the sample of 100?

_______ chances out of 100

dilution effect
The perceiver's insufficient use of relevant information that is presented along with irrelevant information.

When Kahneman and Tversky gave their subjects these problems, they discovered the **dilution effect**: the tendency for irrelevant information to weaken the effect of relevant information. Most subjects got the first case correct. As nothing was known about the person, they relied on base rates. The sample consisted of 70 engineers, so they assumed that the chances were 70 out of 100 that a randomly selected individual would be an engineer. When subjects encountered Case 2, however, they abandoned the base-rate information. In this case, the data were not representative of either group, so they were irrelevant, but they diluted the impact of base-rate information. On this question, most subjects estimated the chances were 50 out of 100 (Kahneman & Tversky, 1973; see Kruglanski, Friedland, & Farkash, 1984).

Representative thinking can undermine the value of even anecdotal case data. When subjects made predictions about a student who was extremely punctual, most of the subjects assumed that Henry, who "never arrives late to appointments or meetings," would achieve a grade point average (GPA) of about 3.3. When, however, irrelevant information was added—Henry has a brother and two sisters, he visits his grandparents occasionally, and he goes to sleep around midnight—subjects felt that Henry's GPA must be closer to 3.0. Apparently the irrelevant information diluted the value of the relevant (Zukier, 1982; see also Nisbett, Zukier, & Lemley, 1981).

The gambler's fallacy. Representative thinking may also generate misunderstandings about random and nonrandom events. Most adults understand that certain events are random. If we flip a coin, chances are 50-50 that it will land heads. If you roll fair dice, each number should, on average, come up an equal number of times. Some sequences of events, however, are more representative of randomness than others, so we mistakenly assume they are more probable. Imagine that you flip a coin six times, obtaining the following sequence of tails (T) and heads (H): T H T T T T. On the next flip, which do you predict: tails (T) or heads (H)? If we assume that the coin is fair, then past outcomes don't change the fact that the probability of a head on the next flip is the same as the probability of a tail. However, the sequence T H T T T T H is more representative of randomness than T H T T T T T, so we mistakenly assume the former outcome is more probable.

gambler's fallacy
Mistaken beliefs about random events, including (a) the assumption that sequences of random events are irregular and without pattern and (b) the assumption that randomly determined events that haven't occurred for some time are likely to occur in the near future.

This **gambler's fallacy** explains why people misjudge their chances of winning at games of chance, such as craps or slot machines. Consider David, who is gambling at dice. To win, he must roll a 4, but he hasn't rolled a 4 for ten turns in a row. This string of misses, however, only encourages David because he figures, "Four hasn't come up in ten rolls, so by the law of averages, it has to come up now." The dice, however, have no memory; the probability of 4 is always the same, no matter what the outcome has been before. David is mistaken in thinking that a random event that hasn't occurred for some time is likely to occur in the near future (Dawes, 1988).

The conjunction error. Representativeness may also prompt us to mistakenly assume that outcomes or events are more likely when they occur together rather than separately. Consider, for example, Courtney, who is reserved and literary. Which of the following is more likely?

a. Courtney is an engineering major.
b. Courtney is majoring in engineering and minoring in English.

In answering this question, people are often distracted by the lack of representativeness between the trait description (reserved and literary) and their stereotypes about engineers (Slovic, Fischhoff, & Lichtenstein, 1977). It seems likely to them, however, that if Courtney did major in engineering, certainly she would want to take some English courses. Unfortunately, the two bits of data provide relatively little information. Also, the laws of probability tell us that the likelihood of a conjunction—two things occurring together—is less probable than the likelihood of just one of the things occurring. People who major in engineering and minor in English are just a small subset of people who major in engineering (see Figure 3-9), so certainly the probability of (a) is greater than (b). People, however, frequently make a **conjunction error**: they show a marked preference for conjunctive explanations of events even when the rules of probability suggest that these explanations are highly unlikely (Leddo, Abelson, & Gross, 1984; Read, 1988, 1989; Wells, 1985).

conjunction error
A *conjunction* is an explanation or description that combines two or more elements; for example, Person A is smart *and* in college. The conjunctive error occurs when individuals think that a conjunctive explanation is more probable than an explanation that includes just one of the elements included in the conjunctive explanation.

Availability

Our inferences and decisions are often determined by the information we happen to have at any moment. If Kissinger were asked to estimate how many diplomats tend to be emotional, for example, he might sift through his memories of all the diplomats he has known to total up the emotional types and the unemotional types. Similarly, if we are asked if it's safer to travel by car or by air, we might rapidly recall cases of auto and air accidents that we know about through personal experience or from media coverage. This **availability heuristic** allows us to base our estimates about frequencies or probabilities on information that is readily available in our own memory or imagination.

availability heuristic
A cognitive heuristic that prompts perceivers to base their judgments on information readily accessible in memory or imagination.

Kahneman and Tversky (1973) note that this heuristic works well when we have better memories for more frequent events and occurrences. In many

▲ This is Courtney. She is reserved and literary. Is Courtney an engineering major, or is she majoring in engineering and minoring in English? People often fall prey to the conjunction error when they answer this question.

▲ **FIGURE 3-9**
If you are told a person is reserved and literary, which do you think is more likely: (a) He or she is an engineering major *or* (b) He or she is majoring in engineering and minoring in English? People tend to think (b) is more likely, even though the probability of two events occurring together (a conjunction) *can't* be greater than the probability of one of the events occurring separately.

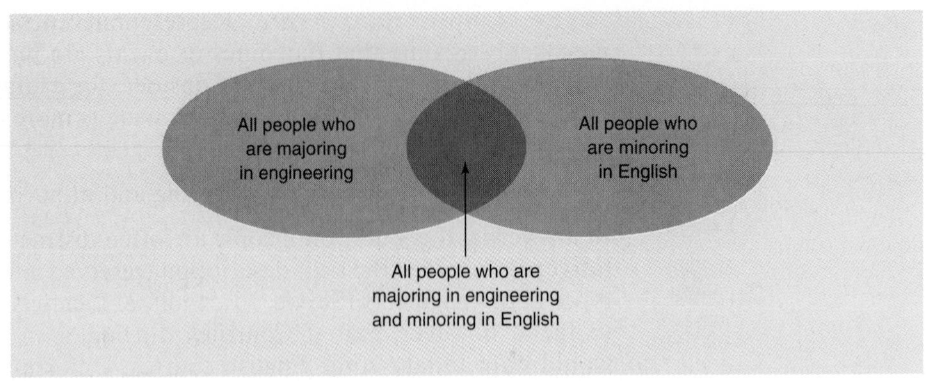

cases, however, the sheer ease of recall or ability to imagine events biases our estimates. If we see a vivid news broadcast describing the aftermath of a fiery plane crash, the incident will be much more available when we search our memories. If we are later asked the question "Which is more dangerous: travel by air or travel by automobile?" we may mistakenly answer "air travel." Similarly, when answering the question "Is the letter *R* more likely to appear as the first letter in a word or the third letter in a word?" people must generate two sets of words (ones that start with *R* and ones with *R* as the third letter) and then compare the size of the two sets. Most of us, however, have an easier time generating words starting with *R* (*run, rabbit, raunchy*) than words with *R* in the third position (*her, perceive, our, more*). But far more words in English have an *R* in the third position than start with *R*.

Ease in imagining also biases availability. When asked to estimate the major causes of death in the United States, subjects overestimated the number of fatalities that resulted from vivid, easily imaginable events such as fires, car accidents, shootings, and bee stings, but underestimated the number of fatalities caused by less easily imagined events, such as strokes, asthma, and tuberculosis (Slovic, Fischhoff, & Lichtenstein, 1982).

False consensus. The availability heuristic can lead us astray when we are trying to estimate other people's beliefs and attitudes. If, for example, you were Kissinger and it was 1971, how would you estimate the U.S. population's opinion on the war in Vietnam? You could try to recall the opinions of people you met on a daily basis. Even better, you could ask a public opinion pollster to collect the data. But if you were pressed for time, you would probably turn to your most available source of information: your own viewpoint. We tend to base our estimates of the population's opinions on our own personal opinion.

false-consensus bias
Perceivers' tendency to assume that their personal qualities and characteristics are common in the general population.

Lee Ross and his colleagues initially documented this **false-consensus bias** by asking college students at Stanford University to describe their personalities, preferences, fears, daily activities, and expectations: Are you shy? Do you like brown bread? Do you think about dying? Do you have difficulty controlling your temper? Do you play tennis once a week? They then asked these same students to describe "college students in general": How many college students are shy? How many think about dying? How many play tennis at least one time per week? In almost every case, the students felt that their viewpoints and characteristics were shared by many others. Shy people thought that 45.9% of college students were shy. Outgoing people, on the other hand, felt that only 35.9% were shy. Similarly, those who preferred brown bread estimated that more than 50% of all other college students preferred brown bread. White-bread eaters fixed the estimate at 37%. Similar biases were found for choices between two alternatives. When the researchers asked subjects if they would be willing to walk around campus wearing a sign that read "REPENT," 50% agreed to do so, and 50% refused. When they then asked the subjects to estimate the percentage of college students who would agree or refuse, subjects maintained that the consensus would favor their choice. As Figure 3-10 indicates, those who agreed felt that 63.5% would also agree, but those who refused felt that 76.6% would refuse (Ross, Greene, & House, 1977; for a review, see Marks & Miller, 1987, and Mullen et al., 1985).

Egocentrism. Availability may also prompt us to overestimate our personal contributions to collective endeavors. When asked who does more of the household chores, spouses usually overestimate their own contributions. When, for example, Janice estimates the percentage of time she spends washing the dinner dishes, taking out the garbage, resolving arguments, or even starting arguments, she assumes her contribution exceeds her partner's. But when Brian is asked the same questions, he claims that he does more around the house than Janice does (Ross & Sicoly, 1979; Thompson & Kelley, 1981). When trying to recall a turning point in a game, athletes usually point to something their own team did rather than to something the other team did (Ross & Sicoly, 1979), and they remember their own contributions more clearly than the contributions of others (Brawley, 1984). Similarly, when students who worked closely with a professor on a joint project estimate their own responsibility for the project, they usually attribute the lion's share (83.5%) to themselves rather than their mentor (Ross & Sicoly, 1979). Apparently, when we are working with others on collective tasks, our perceptions are distorted by an **egocentric bias** (or **self-centered bias**): we tend to overestimate our responsibility for joint outcomes.

egocentric (or self-centered) bias
The tendency to overestimate one's own contributions to collective endeavors.

Egocentrism is partly motivated by our need for self-esteem. When deciding who deserves the credit for our team's victory, or who does the most for the relationship, or who worked hardest in the study group, we can increase our feelings of self-worth by thinking "me" (Schlenker & Miller, 1977). Availability, however, also plays a role in producing this effect. We have more information about our own contributions than we have about the contributions of others, we are more likely to encode this information, and we undoubtedly spend more time thinking about what we are doing than what

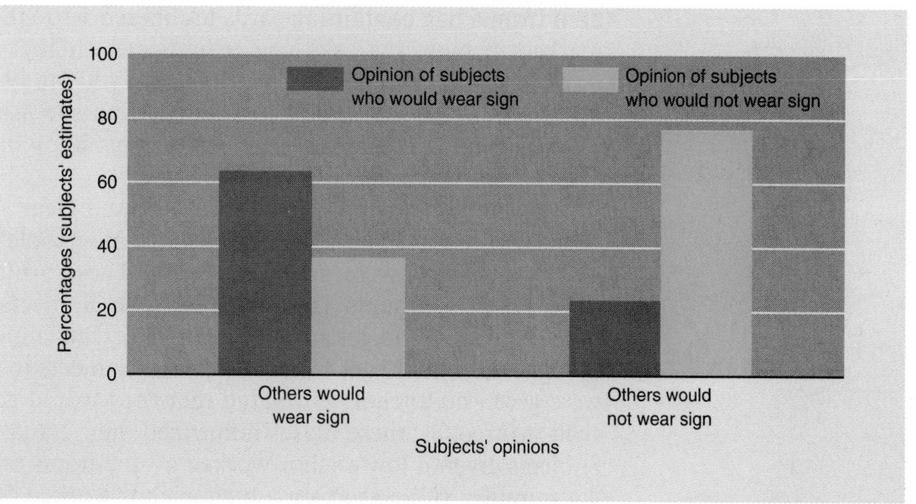

▲ **FIGURE 3-10**
When we try to estimate others' attitudes, do we assume our own opinions are very common? In this study, individuals who agreed to perform a simple behavior (wear a sign) believed that most other people (63.5%) would agree, too. Individuals who refused thought just the opposite: they assumed that, on average, 76.6% would refuse. (Based on Ross, Greene, & House, 1977)

others are doing. As a result, when we try to recall each person's contribution to the group endeavor, our own contributions are easier to remember (Ross & Sicoly, 1979).

Anchoring and Adjustment

Kahneman and Tversky (1972) argue that we often make judgments by first forming an initial estimate, and then gradually revising this estimate over time. When shopping for a new oven, you might anchor your cost estimate at $500, and then revise this estimate as you visit various appliance stores. If asked, "What are the chances that Nixon will be an outstanding president?" you might set your guess at four changes out of ten, then revise your estimate upward or downward as you consider Nixon's specific qualities. If trying to predict your success on the next psychology test, you might anchor your prediction at B+, then revise this estimate depending on whether or not you have been studying, reading, and coming to class. Kahneman and Tversky (1972) call this process the **anchoring-adjustment heuristic**.

anchoring-adjustment heuristic
A cognitive heuristic that involves making an initial judgment (which serves as a reference point or anchor) and then adjusting this estimate as more information is obtained.

Cognitive conservatism. The anchoring-adjustment heuristic is very useful when our initial estimate is accurate and we fairly adjust this initial estimate as we acquire new insights and information. It leads us astray, however, when our anchor is inaccurate or when we fail to revise our estimate sufficiently during the adjustment phase. In one study, Kahneman and Tversky (1972) asked subjects to estimate the percentage of African countries that were members of the United Nations (at that time, 35%). Before they guessed, Kahneman and Tversky made an elaborate show of spinning a game wheel to get an initial percentage estimate. The rigged wheel came up with either 10% or 65%, and subjects were asked whether their own estimates were above or below the wheel's estimate. When subjects then made their own estimates, they let the number from the wheel anchor their judgments even though they knew the number was randomly selected. Subjects who were given the arbitrary anchor of 10% estimated 25% on average, but subjects given the anchor of 65% estimated 45%.

conservatism
The failure to adjust estimates sufficiently when additional information is acquired that indicates initial estimates were too low or too high.

Other researchers have found similar evidence of this cognitive **conservatism** (Edwards, 1968; Greenberg, Williams, & O'Brien, 1986; Plous, 1989). Imagine, for example, that you are a subject in such a study (Cervone & Peak, 1986). You are asked to work on 20 anagram or graphing problems, but just before you begin, the researcher shows you a card apparently selected at random from a bag containing cards numbered 1 to 20. The card she shows you is marked *4*. Now she asks you to indicate whether you will solve 4 or more problems, 4 problems, or fewer than 4. If you are like most people, you probably would say more than 4 problems. Then she asks you to be more precise: "How many of the problems are you capable of solving?" (Cervone & Peak, 1986).

Subjects' judgments in this study showed clear signs of conservatism. The drawing of the numbers was rigged, so some people's estimates were anchored at 4, but others' were anchored at 18. These arbitrary anchors nevertheless influenced judgments (see Figure 3-11). Subjects given a low anchor (4) thought they would get an average of 8 correct; subjects given the anchor of 18 thought they would get 12 items correct. Subjects in the control condition, who were given no anchor, estimated that they would get about half the problems right. Moreover, these biases influenced their actual performance on the tasks. Subjects given a low anchor worked on the items only for an average of about 4.4 minutes; subjects given a high anchor worked for over 7.5 minutes.

Order effects. As noted earlier, first impressions often count more than later impressions. First dates, initial interviews, and early pleasantries can be critical, as Solomon Asch discovered many years ago. He asked one group of subjects to form an impression of Person A, who was intelligent, industrious, impulsive, critical, stubborn, and envious. Another group of subjects judged Person B, who was described with the same adjectives, but in the opposite order: B's list began with *envious* but ended with *intelligent*. Asch (1946) discovered that order was everything: Person A (the intelligent-to-envious sequence) was rated much more positively than Person B (the envious-to-intelligent sequence): "The impression produced by A is predominantly that of an able person who possesses certain shortcomings which do not, however, overshadow his merits. On the other hand, B impresses the majority as a 'problem,' whose abilities are hampered by his serious difficulties" (p. 27). Asch thus found evidence of a *primacy effect* rather than a *recency effect*.

The anchoring-adjustment heuristic offers insight into Asch's findings. When we receive information sequentially, the initial information anchors our initial judgments. When we hear that a person is intelligent and industrious, we may immediately formulate a relatively positive evaluation of the person. If, though, we hear someone is envious and stubborn, we set our anchor on the negative side of the scale. As we acquire more information, we adjust this initial estimate, but insufficiently (for an alternative view, see Anderson, 1991).

Overconfidence and Inference

We are information processors, but we are still human. Representative thinking steers us away from relevant information and distorts our understanding of random events. The availability heuristic prompts us to use whatever information we have at hand, and the anchoring-adjustment heuristic further undermines our accuracy. We make mistakes (see Table 3-5).

To make matters worse, we have little awareness of our fallibility (Einhorn & Hogarth, 1978; Lichtenstein, Fischhoff, & Phillips, 1982). We seem to be a little like the endearing but bumbling Scotland Yard detectives in the Sherlock Holmes tales. "It's an open and shut case," they announce before proclaiming their erroneous interpretation of the available evidence. Like those detectives, we are invariably confident, and invariably incorrect. Eyewitnesses picking out

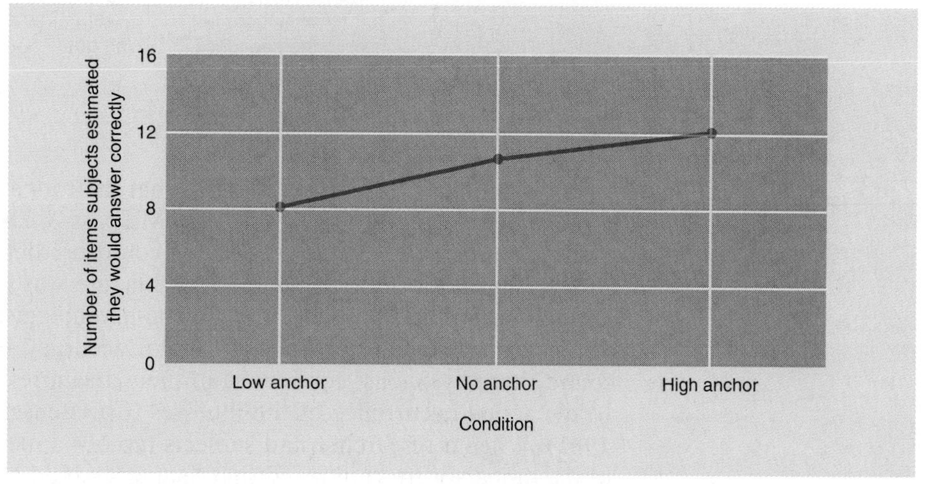

FIGURE 3-11
Are people too conservative when they adjust their initial estimates during decision making? The subjects in this study who were given arbitrary anchors subsequently underestimated or overestimated when predicting their scores on an upcoming test. (Adapted from Cervone & Peake, 1986)

▲ **TABLE 3-5**
Summing up: Heuristic-based processes that can bias our decisions and inferences (the percentages used in the examples are hypothetical)

Process	*Description*	*Application*
Base-rate bias	Underutilizing general statistical information about the overall population when evaluating an individual	You are told that 80% of the class rated your teacher as "outstanding," but one student said, "That teacher is the absolute worst." You decide to drop the class.
Dilution effect	Underutilizing useful data that are presented along with useless data	When you are told 82% of all social psychologists are men, you guess that your social psychology professor will be a man. When you are also told your professor likes to read and talk about research, you become uncertain of the professor's sex.
Gambler's fallacy	Thinking a random event that hasn't occurred for some time is likely to occur in the near future	You flip a coin five times and get heads each time. When asked to estimate the probability that you will get heads again, you underestimate the likelihood because tails is due.
Conjunction error	Assuming that the conjunction, or co-occurrence, of two outcomes or events is more likely than either occurring alone	One person in 8 has red hair. One person in 20 has a bad temper. Individuals, however, assume the likelihood is very high that a person with red hair will also have a bad temper.
False-consensus error	Assuming one's personal qualities are common in the population	A poll indicates that 40% of the people like Brand X. But when people who like Brand X are asked to estimate the poll's results, they predict that 60% of those surveyed will like Brand X.
Egocentrism	Overestimating our responsibility for joint outcomes	Two individuals work together on a project. Both estimate that they did about 62% of the work.
Cognitive conservatism	Failing to sufficiently revise initial judgments when important new information is acquired	Local forecasters predict a 20% chance of rain. But weather conditions changed and the National Weather Service posts a 60% chance of rain. The forecasters change their predictions to 35%.
Primacy effects	Basing conclusions on information presented early in the sequence rather than later in the sequence	The professor reads the student's five essays. The first is excellent, the second is very good, and the last three are below average. The professor gives the student a high grade.

the suspect in a lineup were confident that their identification was correct even when they selected the wrong person (Malpass & Devine, 1984; Wells, 1993). College students were convinced they could predict their roommates' behaviors 78% of the time, but their actual hit rate was only 68% (Dunning et al., 1990). One researcher found that clinical psychologists' estimates of their accuracy were twice as high as their actual accuracy (Oskamp, 1965). Another found that physicians' confidence in their diagnoses of illnesses was unrelated to the actual occurrence of the illnesses (Christensen-Szalanski & Bushyhead, 1981). When a researcher had subjects tap out a melody on the tabletop, 50% of the tappers were convinced that listeners would be able to identify the song they were playing. Only 2.5% of the listeners, however, successfully identified the song (Newton, 1990).

We even misjudge our ability to predict our own behavior. First-year college students were asked to predict what actions they might take over the next year—would they join a fraternity or sorority, vote in an election, feel homesick, change career goals, and so on—and to indicate how confident they were in their predictions. When their predictions were appraised at year's end, the confidence-accuracy gap yawned wide. Their confidence ratings averaged 82.3%, but their accuracy ratings reached only 68.2% (Vallone et al., 1990).

Why don't we recognize that our judgments are fallible? First, when we review our track record as social perceivers, our original predictions and beliefs are often forgotten and replaced with ones that exactly match the facts. Second, if we do review the validity of our inferences, we do so in ways that tend to confirm, rather than disconfirm, those inferences. Third, even when we come face to face with evidence that disconfirms our inferences, we generate new beliefs and viewpoints that bolster the original inferences. A false inference seems to take on a life of its own once it becomes enmeshed in our cognitive systems. Last, we have difficulty accessing the cognitions that sustain our inferences, so we cannot tell when we have processed the available information adequately.

Hindsight Bias

Writing in 1979, Henry Kissinger looked back to 1970 and his thoughts on escalating the war in Vietnam ("Vietnamization") and concluded:

> In retrospect the reasoning behind my . . . criticism of Vietnamization in September and October was almost certainly correct. . . . Once we embarked on it, there was no looking back. I knew that it would be painful and long . . . and that it might ultimately fail. (p. 308)

Our predictions about what will happen often seem more accurate once the event has moved from the future to the past. As we learned in Chapter 1, people often feel as though they "knew it all along": when recalling our predictions about such matters as historical events, psychiatric cases, athletic contests, scientific experiments, medical and legal cases, fluctuations in the stock market, knowledge of trivia questions, and election outcomes, we are confident that we predicted the outcome well in advance. Yet these retrospective surveys of accuracy are usually distorted by the hindsight bias: "a projection of new knowledge into the past accompanied by a denial that the outcome information has influenced judgment" (Hawkins & Hastie, 1990, p. 311). We recall being cleverly accurate even when our original predictions are well off the mark.

The hindsight bias appears to be robust and difficult to disable. Even when one researcher told his subjects "on previous occasions . . . we have found that [people] exaggerate how much they would have known without being told the answer. . . . Please do everything you can to avoid this bias" (Fischhoff, 1977, p. 354), the hindsight bias emerged unscathed. However, the bias does occur less frequently when people recall their answers to extremely difficult questions. When asked, for example, "Who had a longer life: the Spanish philosopher Raymond Lully or American novelist James Fenimore Cooper?" we don't say, "I knew that all along" when we find out the answer is Lully. Rather, we conclude, "I never would have known that" (Hoch & Loewenstein, 1989).

Confirmatory Bias

Just as scientists scrutinize their hypotheses and theories with critical eyes, social perceivers often test their inferences before they accept or reject them. The testing process helps us weed out our erroneous assumptions when it is done fairly, but in many cases our tests are slanted in favor of accepting hypotheses rather than rejecting them. If we believe that Nixon is a brilliant diplomat, that most people are selfish, or that we are insightful observers, the **confirmatory bias** may prompt us to seek information that confirms our inferences rather than disconfirms them (Chapman & Chapman, 1967; Gilovich, 1981).

confirmatory bias
The tendency to seek out information that confirms one's inferences rather than disconfirms them.

Mark Snyder and William Swann (1978) studied this process by giving interviewers a hypothesis about an interviewee, and then watching the interviewer struggle to confirm the hypothesis. Snyder and Swann first manipulated the interviewers' hypotheses about the interviewee's possible characteristics by giving some people a list of statements that focused on introversion and others statements that focused on extraversion. Next, the interviewers were told to select the questions they wanted to ask during the interview, and they were given a list that included items that probed for both extraversion ("What would you do if you wanted to liven things up at a party?" or "What kind of situations do you seek out if you want to meet new people?") and introversion ("In what situations do you wish you could be more outgoing?" or "What things do you dislike about loud parties?"). Snyder and Swann found that their subjects did not carry out a fair test of their inferences. Subjects who were testing the "Is this person an extravert?" hypothesis chose questions that presupposed extraversion. Interviewers who were testing the "Is this person an introvert?" hypothesis chose questions that one would normally ask an introvert. Furthermore, because the biased questioning limited their partners' responses, interviewers' expectations functioned as self-fulfilling prophecies. The interviewees were asked only questions that would confirm the interviewer's hypothesis, so they had no choice but to act in ways that confirmed the interviewer's false expectations (Haverkamp, 1993).

Belief Perseverance

An erroneous belief is not totally protected from attack. By now, most of us know that some beliefs we once held to be true—the Tooth Fairy leaves a quarter under our pillow when she takes a tooth; Russians are evil; the Bee Gees were a great band—were false. The process by which we relinquished these beliefs, however, was probably gradual. A belief, once formed, gathers so much cognitive momentum that it keeps running through our minds even when we stumble across evidence that disconfirms it (Koehler, 1991; Ross & Anderson, 1982).

Lee Ross, Craig Anderson, Mark Lepper, and their colleagues call this recalcitrant revision process **belief perseverance**. They discovered this bias when they checked on the adequacy of debriefing procedures in studies that gave subjects false information about their abilities. Under the guise of studying perceptual ability, their subjects reviewed a series of suicide notes and identified which ones were genuine and which ones were fakes. Some were told they did very well at the task, others were told they did poorly, and still others were given neutral feedback. Then, after a five-minute delay, the researcher returned and confessed that the testing phase was a sham, that their answers hadn't been graded, and that the feedback was not based on their ability. He apologized for deceiving them, and the subjects all acknowledged that they understood why they were misled. Yet when they later completed a questionnaire about their performance, the false feedback—which they knew was false—still influenced

belief perseverance
The tendency for individuals who have generated an explanation for a social event or phenomenon to continue to accept this explanation even when the evidence that initially supported the explanation has been shown to be false.

▲ Why do you suppose that people who enjoy taking risks make good fire fighters? Why do they perform so much better in this career than people who are cautious? After researchers asked people to answer these questions, they revealed the truth to them: risk taking isn't associated with success as a fire fighter. People who had generated a cogent explanation for the false fact, however, continued to embrace it, saying, "but I really think it's true that risk takers do make better fire fighters."

their self-evaluations. Subjects given positive feedback thought they got 68% correct, those given neutral feedback estimated their scores at 63%, and those given negative feedback estimated their scores at 51% (Ross, Lepper, & Hubbard, 1975).

Anderson, Ross, and their colleagues have found that belief perseverance is particularly robust when subjects must generate explanations for the data they have been given. In one study they first asked subjects to write an essay that explains the following fact: "People who enjoy taking risks make good fire fighters." Once the false belief was justified, the researcher then explained that the information was completely fictitious, manufactured solely for the experiment. Yet even when the evidence that formed the basis for the belief was discredited, belief perseverance gave the inference a life of its own. "I realize that you made up these data for this study," subjects would say, "but I really think it's true that risk takers do make better fire fighters" (Anderson, Lepper, & Ross, 1980). About the only way to remove this false belief from subjects' cognitive systems was to ask them to generate an explanation for the *opposite* relationship: in this case, subjects would be asked to explain why cautious people make better fire fighters (Anderson, 1982; Anderson & Sechler, 1986; Hoch, 1985).

Most theorists believe that several related cognitive mechanisms combine to generate belief perseverance (Koehler, 1991). First, once we explain the faulty fact or hypothetical outcome, it becomes more representative of plausible facts and outcomes. A conjunctive statement, such as "Fire fighting requires bravery, quick action, and a lack of regard for one's own well-being, so risk takers make better fire fighters," is viewed as more plausible than the statement "Risk takers make better fire fighters" because it is more representative of the category "good explanations" (Kahneman & Tversky, 1982). Second, the information that supports the fact may be more available in memory than the information that disconfirms the fact. Indeed, in some cases individuals cannot distinguish between supporting evidence that they actually gathered and supporting evidence that they only imagined (Slusher & Anderson, 1987). Third, Dan Gilbert suggests that perseverance occurs because the mere comprehension of a statement causes temporary acceptance of that statement. After comprehension we review the evidence, decide whether it supports or refutes the statement, and only then discard the statements we feel are untrue. Gilbert has found that this review process can be easily interrupted, so we never manage to review all the false statements that we comprehend (Gilbert, 1991; Gilbert, Krull, & Malone, 1990).

Accessibility of Cognitive Processes

declarative memory Memory for factual information, including general information (for example, "What is Kissinger's first name?") and personal experiences (for example, "What did you do on your last birthday?").

procedural memory Memory for doing things, including actions, skills, and information processing.

Most information-processing theories draw a distinction between **declarative memory** and **procedural memory**. Declarative memory allows us to answer such questions as "What color is Nixon's hair?" "Was Kissinger a warm person?" and "What is a schema?" because it includes our content-oriented memories. Procedural memory, in contrast, is our memory of skills and abilities. If you can ride a bicycle, then you have stored the actions that comprise this ability in your procedural memory (Schacter, 1987). Procedural memories, however, cannot be retrieved like declarative memories. You may know how to ride a bicycle, but you cannot retrieve and articulate clearly, in words, the precise actions required for bike riding. Similarly, you may know how to make a decision, but you may not be able to monitor the procedures that make this decision making possible. Although we are conscious of our thoughts and feelings, we cannot gain access to the processes that created these cognitive products. We can guess at an answer to such questions as "How did you form your impression of Jill?" and "Why did you make that decision?" but our answers may not be accurate (Nisbett & Wilson, 1977).

The inaccuracy of people's self-reports of their cognitive processes was demonstrated in one study by asking people to form an impression of the individual in the following vignette:

> Jill is applying for a job at a crisis intervention center. She is quite physically attractive and graduated from college with a very good academic record. During her job interview, however, she spilled a cup of coffee, and, in response to a question about personal stresses, described a recent automobile accident in which her pelvis was crushed.

Only after they had rated Jill's likability, intelligence, poise, and other attributes were subjects asked to describe the factors that had influenced their decisions. Was it her physical attractiveness? Her academic credentials? Her slip with the coffee? Her accident? The subjects weren't particularly accurate. Many said they liked Jill because of her good academic credentials and her honest description of her automobile accident, but their evaluations told a different story. She was liked less when the subjects found out she had good academic credentials and had been in an accident. Similarly, subjects said they weren't influenced by the coffee-spilling incident, but this blunder increased their ratings of Jill's likableness and flexibility (Nisbett & Bellows, 1977).

These findings have not gone unchallenged. Some investigators agree that we may not be aware of our perceptual or memory processes, but argue that our thinking on important matters is accessible (Kraut & Lewis, 1982; Smith & Miller, 1978; White, 1980). Recent work, however, suggests that even our attempts to observe our internal cognitive processes can disrupt the flow of information processing. If people are asked to explain why they made a decision, they sometimes change their minds and make an even less effective decision (Wilson & Schooler, 1991).

Debiasing and Increased Accuracy

The picture painted by biases, summarized in Table 3-6, is not as bleak as it seems. First, heuristics may bias the inferences we make, but a bias is not

▲ TABLE 3-6
Summing up: Why do people overestimate their judgmental abilities? The following four factors can, in some cases, prevent us from accurately calibrating our accuracy.

Factor	*Description*
Hindsight bias	Our original predictions and beliefs are often forgotten and replaced with ones that exactly match the facts.
Confirmatory bias	We seek information that confirms, rather than disconfirms, our beliefs.
Belief perseverance	We maintain our beliefs and expectations even when the evidence that initially supported the inference has been shown to be false.
Accessibility of cognitive processes	Our descriptions of the cognitive processes that sustain our perceptions, judgments, and decisions do not accurately depict those processes.

always a mistake. A bias is simply a judgmental tendency or strategy. The availability heuristic, for example, may prompt you to use your own attitudes when trying to estimate other people's attitudes. If the people you are scrutinizing are similar to you, this bias will work marvelously. Instead of saying, "I can't even guess what their attitudes might be," you can reason, "I feel this way, so I imagine they feel that way, too." Granted, if they disagree with you, your heuristic will lead you to make a mistake in judgment, but until we consider the qualities of the people you are judging, we cannot determine whether your bias will increase or decrease the accuracy of your judgments (Funder, 1987).

debiasing
Teaching individuals to minimize their reliance on error-producing heuristics when making decisions.

Second, even though biases can undermine the accuracy of our inferences, **debiasing** procedures can overcome these errors (Arkes, 1991). When people are trained to reason statistically, they show greater immunity to heuristic-based biases (Fong, Krantz, & Nisbett, 1986). Individuals who are reminded of their initial thoughts about a question before they are told the correct answer often avoid the hindsight bias. They are usually more accurate when they recall their original answer (Davies, 1987). When subjects are asked to adopt a scientific orientation rather than a clinical orientation when making decisions, they are more likely to use base-rate data properly (Zukier & Pepitone, 1984). Giving individuals feedback about their accuracy on a series of problems is also a simple but effective way to improve their performance over the long term (Klayman & Ha, 1987).

Third, in many cases the mistakes caused by heuristics are self-correcting. If we repeatedly rely on a heuristic and it repeatedly leads us astray, over time we will correct our error on our own. Novice gamblers may initially misunderstand random events, but experts have learned to assess odds and probabilities accurately. Because we learn to avoid mistakes, inaccurate judgments may be the exception rather than the rule (Christensen-Szalanski & Beach, 1984; Klayman & Ha, 1987, 1989; Robins & Craik, 1993). When, for example, individuals perform inferential tasks that are both familiar and meaningful to them, they are usually less biased (Edwards, 1992; Shanteau, 1992). College students trying to test a hypothesis, for example, usually look for confirming instances and ignore disconfirming instances, but if the hypothesis is personally relevant to them (for example, "Does this person want to go out on a date with me?"), they consider all types of data (Harkness, DeBono, & Borgida, 1985). When tempted to base their judgments on heuristics rather than close inspection of the data, professional auditors usually pick the data (Smith & Kida, 1991). Weather forecasters show virtually no overconfidence: the accuracy of their predictions and their certainty in these predictions correlate at

.985 (Lichtenstein et al., 1982). Scientists and physicians who have been trained in statistical principles are more skilled when making decisions that require calculating probabilities than individuals who are not trained (Lehman, Lempert, & Nisbett, 1988). These findings are comforting: perhaps such experts as air traffic controllers, bridge builders, automobile designers, and secretaries of state are less prone to err than the studies of heuristics might suggest (see "Application: Social Cognition in the Courtroom").

Summary

Social cognition provides the basis for understanding ourselves and other people. We search for information that will help us understand the people who populate our social world, and we organize the clues we have uncovered in our memories and cognitions. We also formulate complex social inferences. We don't merely perceive; we also test, judge, choose, analyze, and solve.

The *information-processing model* of social cognition describes several processes that sustain our understanding of other people, including *bottom-up processes, top-down processes,* and *automatic processes.* First, situational information must be *encoded,* or translated, into an internal, psychological representation. Many stimuli vie for our attention, but we disregard most to focus on the *salient* (distinctive in the social context) or vivid (attention-grabbing) ones. Our expectations, goals, plans, preconceptions, attitudes, beliefs, and the like also influence our inferences, as does automatic processing (rather than *controlled processing*). *Priming*, for example, can influence us even when the prime is *subliminal*—so unobtrusive that we don't even notice it.

The information, once encoded, is organized in our *social memory*: the mental structures and processes that store and retrieve information about people and social events. These cognitive structures include our *implicit personality theories*, with their *central traits*, and our *schemas*: networks of cognitive generalizations that organize and guide the processing of social information. Person schemas, self-schemas, stereotypes, and event schemas (scripts) facilitate social inference, but they can bias the encoding and retrieval of information. Overall, however, our understanding of others is shaped by both data-driven cognitive processes and conceptually driven cognitive processes. The *information-integration model* even suggests that we sometimes combine information in processes that resemble adding or averaging, and that some bits of information may be weighted more heavily than others (*weighted-averaging model*). *Primacy* and *recency effects* may be caused by this differential weighting.

We usually strive for accuracy as we study ourselves and other people, but in some cases we are unwilling to spend our resources processing data. Instead we rely on simplifying inferential principles or rules of thumb that help us process information efficiently and rapidly. These *heuristics* are a sensible cognitive tool, but in some situations they can distort our social inferences. The *representativeness heuristic* allows us to estimate the probability of outcomes and events by considering their resemblance to a more general category or case, but it can also bias our inferences in the following ways:

- *Base-rate biases*: people fail to use base-rate information appropriately.
- *Dilution effects*: irrelevant information tends to weaken the effect of relevant information.
- *Gambler's fallacy*: the belief that a random event that hasn't occurred for some time is likely to occur in the near future.

- *Conjunction errors*: outcomes or events are considered to be more likely when they occur together rather than separately.

The *availability heuristic* allows us to base our estimates about frequencies or probabilities on information that is readily available in our own memory or imagination, but it contributes to (1) *false consensus errors* (assuming one's personal qualities are common in the population) and (2) *egocentrism* (overestimating our personal contributions to group endeavors). We revise our initial estimates as the *anchoring-adjustment heuristic* dictates, but this heuristic can contribute to (1) *cognitive conservatism* (the tendency to make insufficient revisions during the adjustment phase) and (2) primacy effects rather than recency effects (basing conclusions on information presented early in the sequence). Finally, other biases contribute to our inability to calibrate our own accuracy:

- *Hindsight biases*: original predictions and beliefs are often forgotten and replaced with ones that exactly match the facts.
- *Confirmatory biases*: seeking information that confirms, rather than disconfirms, our beliefs.
- *Belief perseverance*: maintaining an inference even when the evidence that initially supported the inference has been shown to be false.
- *Accessibility of cognitive processes*: individuals' descriptions of the cognitive processes that sustain their inferences (*procedural memory* rather than *declarative memory*) are usually inaccurate.

Debiasing, however, can undo these negative effects of our heuristics, thereby improving our ability to make accurate social inferences.

For More Information

- "The Cognitive Perspective in Social Psychology," by Hazel Markus and R. B. Zajonc (1985), provides an insider's view of research and theory dealing with the mental processes that guide our perceptions. This article is a chapter in the *Handbook of Social Psychology* (Lindzey & Aronson, 1985).
- *Decision Making in Action: Models and Methods*, edited by Gary A. Klein, Judith Orasanu, Roberta Calderwood, and Caroline E. Zsambok (1993), contains nearly two dozen chapters by researchers who are exploring the way people solve problems and formulate decisions in everyday settings.
- *Human Inference: Strategies and Shortcomings in Social Judgment*, by Richard E. Nisbett and Lee Ross (1980), is a fascinating look at the pitfalls and problems human beings encounter when they try to make decisions and judgments about themselves and other people.
- *The Psychology of Judgment and Decision Making*, by Scott Plous (1993), integrates classic research findings and recent evidence in a masterful analysis of the limitations and strengths of human decision makers.
- *Rational Choice in an Uncertain World*, by Robyn M. Dawes (1988), is an engaging overview of the strengths and weaknesses of our inference-making abilities.
- *Social Cognition*, by Susan T. Fiske and Shelley E. Taylor (1991, 2nd ed.), reviews and synthesizes previous theory and research on the cognitive processes perceivers use to understand other people. Comprehensive yet engagingly written, this book is a must-read for the serious student of social cognition.

Application: Social Cognition in the Courtroom

In the early 1900s experimental psychologist Hugo Munsterberg urged lawyers and judges to recognize the psychological basis of most judicial processes. Too often, Munsterberg argued, legalists rely on "the most unscientific and haphazard methods of common prejudice and ignorance" to make their decisions, and he advised them to turn to psychology for answers (Munsterberg, 1908, p. 44). Unfortunately, Munsterberg's psychology did not offer much in the way of useful information to legal theorists and practitioners, so they did not heed his call (Wigmore, 1909).

Now, nearly a century later, the relationship between psychology and the law has changed considerably. Psychologists actively investigate many aspects of the judicial process. Some explore the causes of crime and offer recommendations for encouraging law-abiding attitudes and behaviors. Others study procedures used to train police officers, the factors that shape police officers' perceptions of suspects, and the intricacies of interrogation and arrest. Still others are more interested in factors that determine decisions about bail, charges, plea bargaining, jury selection, conviction, sentencing, and parole. Linking all these applications is the common concern for understanding the psychological processes that shape the criminal justice system.

One of the topics initially identified by Munsterberg—eyewitness accuracy—continues to be studied extensively by applied social psychologists. The testimony of an eyewitness to a crime often has a substantial impact on police, juries, and judges, but eyewitnesses often make mistakes. Aaron Lee Owens of Oakland, California, spent nine years in prison for two murders he didn't commit. Robert Dillon spent three months and $30,000 trying to clear himself of armed robbery charges. A former Baptist Sunday school teacher was released after serving five years in prison when the actual perpetrator of the crime confessed. Bernard Jackson spent years in prison for rape before the police discovered the identity of the actual rapist. All these individuals were convicted on the testimony of eyewitnesses who identified the wrong people.

Studies of social cognition offer considerable insight into the mechanisms that distort eyewitnesses' memories about the crimes they observe. During a crime, observers are exposed to a flood of unexpected and unusual information, so many of the details are overlooked. When questioned about the incident at a later date, however, witnesses often fill in the gaps in their memories by relying on general expectations about criminals and crime. Researchers have documented these biases by staging bogus crimes before unsuspecting spectators. In the midst of a lecture, for example, someone may burst into the room, berate, assault, knife, or shoot the speaker, and then escape. After the commotion dies down, the witnesses describe the assailant. Accuracy in these situations is influenced by many factors, but distortions are usually prevalent. Not only do witnesses overlook the assailant's physical appearance, such as hair color and type of clothing, but they also misremember important details of the crime itself; they may recall a weapon when none was used or a shouted curse that was never uttered (Buckhout, 1974; Marquis, Marshall, & Oskamp, 1972).

Eyewitnesses' memories can also be distorted by events that take place *after* the incident, such as the way the police phrase their questions during the investigation; the use of photographs for identification before the suspect appears in a lineup; and newspaper coverage of the event (see Wells & Loftus, 1984, for a review). Elizabeth Loftus, a leading researcher in this area, demonstrated such distortions by showing people a videotape of an automobile accident. She then asked the observers a series of questions about the accident. Some of the subjects were asked the question "How fast were the cars going when they *hit* each other?" Others were asked a more leading question: "How fast were the cars going when they *slammed* into each other?" As she expected, people asked about cars that *slammed* into each other thought the cars were traveling faster than people who were asked the more neutral question. Moreover, this biased question influenced recall a week later when Loftus asked the subjects whether they remembered seeing broken glass around the cars after the accident. Even though the accident didn't cause any glass to break, 32% of the people who had been asked about cars that *slammed* into each other recalled seeing broken glass. Only 14% of the people asked the nonleading question recalled seeing broken glass (Loftus & Palmer, 1974). Loftus and her colleagues believe that police can inadvertently bias eyewitnesses' memories by phrasing their questions in suggestive ways (Loftus et al., 1989).

Other police procedures can also contribute to eyewitness errors. If officers have a photograph of a suspect, they sometimes ask witnesses whether the person in the picture is the person they saw. Such *show-up* procedures pressure witnesses into falsely identifying incorrect suspects (Hans, 1989). Also, if the police later use a *lineup* procedure, in which the suspect and several foils are shown to the witness, people are more likely to pick out the suspect if they have seen his or her picture before. Lineups can be biased in other ways as well. In some cases the suspect is too different from the other people in the lineup. A suspect who is more physically attractive, taller, better dressed, or scowling will probably be identified as the guilty party, even by people who have no information about the crime. Lineups are also often conducted by people who know which person is the suspect. Just as the confirmatory bias can prompt perceivers to act in ways that confirm their perceptual hypotheses, so police conducting lineups can inadver-

▲ Eyewitnesses aren't infallible. Even when they are certain that they have correctly identified a suspect, they can be mistaken. William Jackson, pictured at right, was identified by a rape victim as the man who perpetrated the crime. He spent five years in prison before Edward Jackson, Jr. (*left*, no relation) confessed to the crime.

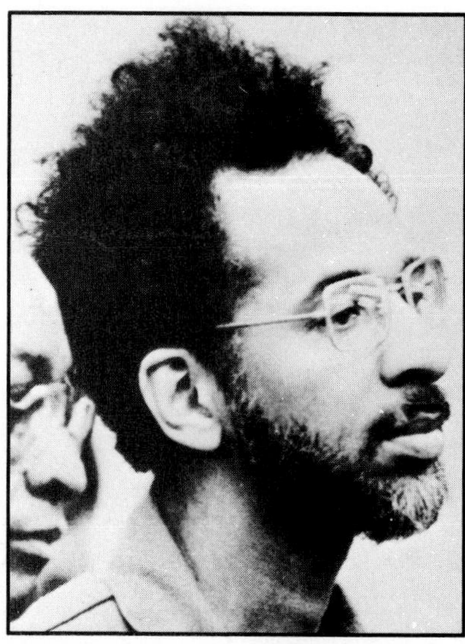

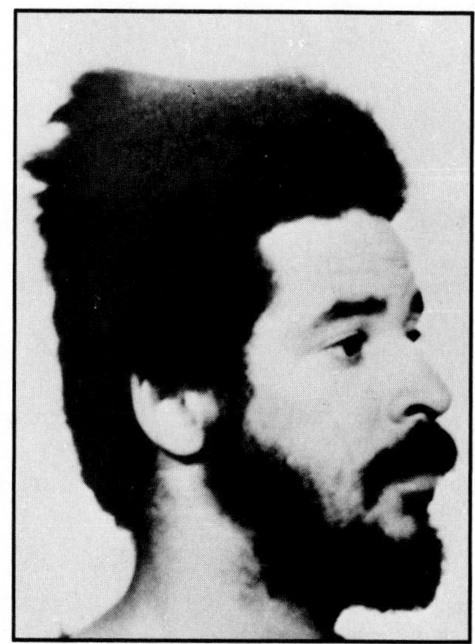

tently let witnesses know who is the suspect and who is not (Wells, 1993; Wells, Leippe, & Ostrom, 1979).

The problems caused by eyewitnesses' errors are compounded by their overconfidence in their recall. As noted earlier, even though biases can distort our decisions and inferences, we often overestimate the accuracy of our judgments. Similarly, fallible witnesses are often confident of their descriptions. Although we put more stock in the comments of a witness who boasts, "I got a good look at her; I'm absolutely certain she had red hair and wore Nike tennis shoes," studies have shown that confidence does not correlate with accuracy. In one study, the witnesses to a staged crime were asked to pick out the perpetrator's picture from a lineup of photographs. The results were sobering: right or wrong, subjects who selected someone from the lineup were confident that they were correct (Wells & Murray, 1984). The most confident witness is not always the most correct witness, even when testifying under oath (Malpass & Devine, 1984; Wells & Murray, 1984).

These findings serve as a warning that eyewitness testimony, which plays such a large role in criminal trials, can be misleading. Most jurors, however, are easily swayed by an eyewitness's testimony. In another study, Loftus (1979) asked people to listen to evidence presented in a murder trial. Most of the evidence that linked the defendant to the crime was circumstantial, so only 18% of the mock jurors believed he was guilty. When she added one more bit of evidence—the testimony of an eyewitness who identified the defendant as the murderer—judgments of guilt soared to 72%. Even more surprisingly, the eyewitness continued to influence jurors even after his testimony was discredited by the defense attorney. In this third condition, Loftus let subjects listen to the defense's cross-examination of the witnesses. The cross-examination revealed that the witness had very poor eyesight and wasn't wearing his glasses at the time of the crime. But even though this information should have discredited the eyewitness's testimony, 60% of the jurors still believed the defendant was guilty.

Because of these biases, some psychologists think that jurors should be warned about the unreliability of eyewitness testimony. Loftus (1983) even advocates the use of psychologists as expert witnesses in some cases. Their testimony could "provide jurors with additional information to better equip them to evaluate the identification evidence fully and properly" (p. 568). Jurors often display overbelief—unquestioning acceptance of a confident witness's testimony; the psychologist could remind them of factors that can undermine accuracy (Loftus, 1993). Other psychologists disagree with Loftus (Egeth, 1993; McCloskey & Egeth, 1983; Yuille, 1993). According to their view, expert testimony by a psychologist may be unnecessary; jurors are supposed to be skeptical. At present, the issue remains undecided.

Studies of eyewitness recognition are only one example of the application of social psychology to the law. The criminal justice system is complex and influential, and social psychologists are currently examining its many facets. Some researchers are examining the psychological foundations of our laws and criminal codes. Others are asking questions about the legal process itself: How do police identify suspects? What factors influence the judges' decisions about bail? What impact does a judge's instructions to jurors have on their decisions? Can jurors set aside their personal biases and examine the evidence objectively? Research in these areas extends our understanding of the social behavior, but at the same time it identifies ways the legal system can be improved. Such research enriches both social psychology and society.

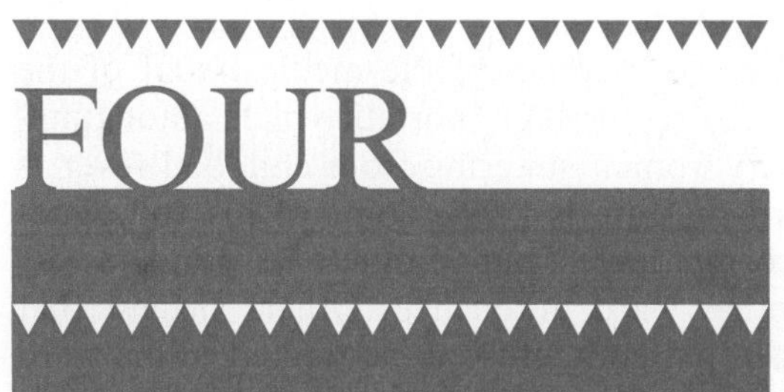

Attribution

The year is 1844. Ignaz Semmelweis, a member of the medical staff of the Vienna General Hospital, is perplexed by the high mortality rates among maternity cases. The death rate among women suffering from childbed fever is 2.3% in one ward, but in his ward the rate is 8.2%. Some of his colleagues blame the high rate on unknown cosmic forces, but Semmelweis wonders why these mystical causes leave the other ward untouched. Others suggest that overcrowding is the cause, but when patients refuse to be treated in his ward and the population dwindles, the mortality rate remains high. Semmelweis changes the delivery procedures, the routine followed by priests in their visits to the dying, and the examination procedures used by the medical students, but nothing helps. He is bewildered.

Semmelweis unravels the puzzle when he sees one of his colleagues cut himself accidentally with a scalpel during an autopsy. The unfortunate colleague soon develops the same symptoms seen in the mothers and dies. Semmelweis's science doesn't yet know that microorganisms can cause infection, yet he realizes that unseen "cadaveric matter" from the scalpel must have caused his colleague's illness. From this clue it is only one step to the conclusion that the women have been infected by staff members who have gone straight to the delivery room after performing dissections. Semmelweis tests his idea by ordering the staff to wash their hands in a solution of chlorinated lime to prevent the spread of infection. His assumption is confirmed: the mortality rate drops dramatically (Sinclair, 1909).

Semmelweis solved his problem by searching for causes. We, too, search for the causes of actions and events. When we feel feverish, we wonder, "Am I coming down with a cold?" When friends treat us harshly, we wonder, "Did I do something to upset them?" When we learn that a married couple is getting a divorce, we ask, "Why are they splitting up?" Like the scientist striving to explain an anomalous observation, a physician seeking the cure for an illness, or an engineer studying the reasons for a bridge's collapse, people in everyday situations constantly form inferences about the causes of behaviors and events. Such inferences are called **attributions**.

attributions
Inferences about the causes of behaviors or events.

Attributions are a key cog in the perceptual machinery that powers your understanding of yourself and other people. As Chapter 2 explains, *social perception* begins when you gather clues to people's emotions, motivations, and traits. You also seek, process, and integrate new information with old information to formulate an overall impression of a person in a process known as *social cognition* (Chapter 3). But your search for social knowledge does not stop there, for you also make *attributions* about other people by observing their actions. When you see Tri lose her temper, Rex smile and laugh, or Batrina take charge in the group, you don't just note these actions. You go one step further and assume that the behavior says something about the inner person: Tri is a hot-head, Rex is good-natured, and Batrina is a take-charge kind of person.

Your understanding of your *own* qualities, too, can be influenced by attributions. When you are angry, laughing, or leading, you may wonder whether these actions reflect your personal tastes and preferences or the social demands of the situation you face. These inferences yield some important practical benefits, too. By favoring one attributional interpretation over another, you can sustain and even reinforce your views of other people and yourself. Moreover, just as Semmelweis was able to prevent childbed fever once he diagnosed the cause, through attributions we can identify the causes of problematic aspects of our personal lives. Once we locate the cause, we can take the steps to rid ourselves of the problem. In this chapter, we consider all these processes—the mechanisms required to identify the causes of actions and events, self-attributions, attributional biases, and the link between attributions and health.

Perceiving Causes

Fritz Heider (1958) pioneered the study of attributions in social psychology. Heider believed that we are all "common-sense psychologists." Just as Semmelweis struggled to explain the high mortality rate in his hospital, we intuitively craft theories about the causes of others' actions. Heider assumed that this attributional work

> requires a description of the causal nexus of an environment which contains not only the directly observable facts about the behavior of another person, but also their connection with the more stable structures and processes underlying that behavior. It is an important principle of common-sense psychology, as it is of scientific theory in general, that man grasps reality, and can predict and control it, by referring transient and variable behavior and events to relatively unchanging underlying conditions, the so-called dispositional properties of this world. (p. 79)

Thus, Heider assumed that we are constantly trying to figure out other people's personalities, traits, and emotions. But because we can't directly access these qualities, we instead base our conclusions on our observations of other people's behaviors. The processes that sustain this search for dispositional causes are considered next.

From Acts to Dispositions

Our actions often betray our motives, traits, and preferences. When Kimberly decides to go to graduate school in clinical psychology rather than in social psychology, we gather she likes helping people with their problems. When we see Robert in the store wistfully studying a pint of Ben and Jerry's Chunky Monkey ice cream before reaching for the frozen yogurt, we can assume he is weight-conscious. But what can we conclude when Josh says "What a wonderful dinner" to his hostess as she clears the plates? And when we hear that Alisha continues to work for a man who harasses her, can we assume she likes this abuse? When do we feel confident that people's behavior is a fair reflection of their inner qualities?

correspondent inference theory
A theoretical framework that proposes an attributor is more likely to make attributions about people when he or she believes their actions correspond to their stable dispositional characteristics.

Edward E. Jones and Keith Davis developed **correspondent inference theory** to explain these kinds of inferences. The theory assumes that only certain behaviors have informational value. People behave in all kinds of ways in all

▲ When we see other people doing something, we often formulate inferences about the causes of their actions. If we see a boy mowing the lawn, we inevitably wonder why. Does he enjoy mowing the lawn? Do his parents make him? Does he mow lawns in the summer to earn extra money? Is he saving his money for a special vacation or a new baseball glove? This boy isn't just mowing the lawn; he is also providing us with considerable information about his motives, traits, and preferences.

sorts of situations, but as perceivers we make attributions only when we are reasonably certain that the behavior follows from, or corresponds to, a person's dispositional characteristics (Jones, 1990; Jones & Davis, 1965; Jones & McGillis, 1976).

First we must consider how much *choice* the individual had in deciding to perform the action. Kimberly considered her graduate school options and deliberately chose clinical psychology, so her actions are informative. Alisha, however, is probably constrained by the situation; maybe she can't quit her job because she has bills to pay, small children to provide for, or other obligations. If onlookers believe we did not freely choose to undertake a particular course of action, then they are reluctant to jump from acts to dispositions (Steiner, 1970).

Second, it is harder to make attributions about people who act in *socially desirable* ways. What do you think about a guest who politely thanks his host after dinner? Did he really enjoy the meal or was he just doing the polite thing? You can't be sure. But if Josh said, "I've had better meals at the school cafeteria," this socially undesirable action would convey considerably more attributional information. Indeed, any *unexpected* behavior is more informative than an expected behavior (Trope, 1986; Trope & Cohen, 1989). Wearing a coat in winter or praising oneself daringly during a job interview tells us little about a person, but walking naked through a college campus and deprecating one's ability during an interview are informative because these actions violate situational norms and are inconsistent with social roles. Consider, as examples, these two cases:

Carrie is applying for a job as a salesperson. She knows that a competent salesperson must be able to work well with others. During the interview she says, "I like to be free to do what I want, to work on my own. I usually avoid situations in which I have to rely on other people. In fact, one of my favorite summer jobs was working as a forest ranger because I didn't have to deal with people."

Stephanie is applying for a job as a computer programmer. She knows that a competent programmer must be self-reliant and independent. During the

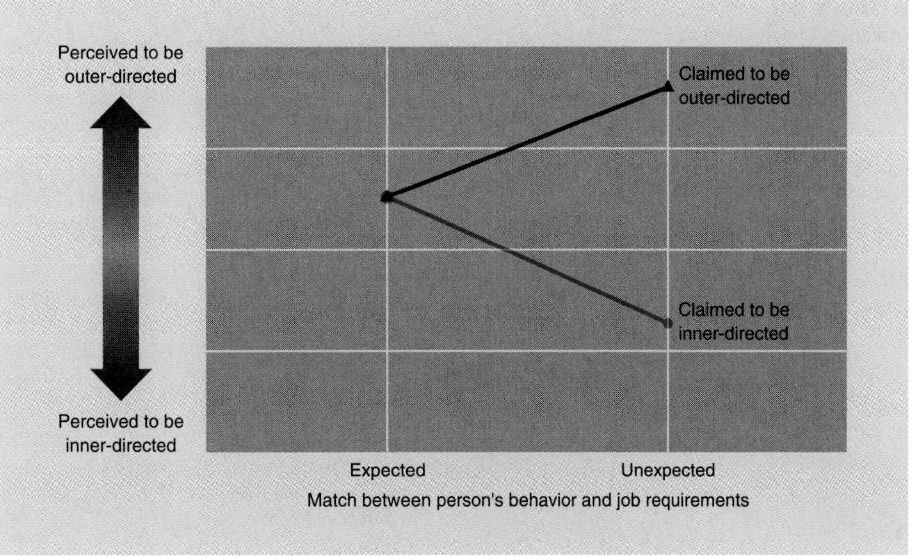

▲ **FIGURE 4-1**
When do we decide that people's actions tell us something about their personalities? When people were asked to form an impression of a man applying for a job, they made few inferences about his personality when his self-description matched the job's requirements. (For example, he said he was outer-directed when he was seeking a job that required working with others.) But when his self-description ran counter to the job's requirements, observers made correspondent inferences. (Based on Jones, Davis, & Gergen, 1961)

> interview she states, "I like to choose my own goals and work on my own. I usually avoid situations in which I have to rely on other people. One summer I really enjoyed working as a proofreader because I didn't have to deal with people."

Both women describe themselves in similar ways—as loners who are inner-directed and self-reliant. But because Carrie is applying for a job that requires someone who is outgoing and other-directed, her self-description is surprising. You can more confidently assume it corresponds to her actual personality characteristics. Jones and his colleagues confirmed this reasoning by asking subjects to form an impression of a person who described himself as inner-directed or outer-directed when he applied for a job that required working with other people (on a submarine) or working alone (as an astronaut in a one-person space capsule). Subjects made more extreme attributions when the target's self-descriptions ran counter to their expectations (see Figure 4-1).

Cause and Covariation

Correspondent inference theory provides a compelling explanation for our ability to draw inferences from a single piece of behavioral data. When we see Robert pick frozen yogurt over ice cream, Josh sexually harass Alisha, or Fred fail a calculus test, we quickly make inferences from these snapshots of social actions. In some cases, however, we can draw on additional sources of information. If we have been shopping with Robert before, we might know that he usually buys ice cream. Or we might have seen Josh harass other women besides Alisha. Or we might have seen other people fail calculus. In these situations, we have considerable information about how different people reacted at different times, and we must take this information into account before we form attributions.

Harold H. Kelley's *attribution cube theory* (1971) describes how social perceivers use information about covariation to make attributions. Covariation is the tendency for two things to occur at the same time or in the same place. In Semmelweis's hospital, assignment to his ward and infection covaried. If each time you drink alcohol you get a headache, drinking and headaches covary. If each person who took the calculus test failed, then failure and calculus covary.

▲ **TABLE 4-1**
Examples of sensitivity to covariation data

Kelley's attribution cube model maintains that people are sensitive to three types of covariation data: distinctiveness across objects, consistency across time and places, and consensus among people. In these three examples, people would consider distinctiveness, consistency, and consensus before deciding whether Devwon loves Jason, whether Fred is not smart, and whether Josh is a sexual harasser.

	Attraction	*Academic Performance*	*Sexual Harassment*
Distinctiveness			
High	Devwon has a great time with Jason, but hardly any fun when she's out with Fred or Thomas.	Fred is passing all his other courses, but he is failing calculus.	Alisha has never filed a charge before.
Low	Devwon has a good time no matter who she's with, whether it's Jason, Fred, or Thomas.	Fred is failing all his courses.	Alisha has accused other men in the office of harassment.
Consistency			
High	Devwon has dated Jason ten times. Each date has been wonderful.	Fred has failed every calculus test he has taken.	Alisha has complained about Josh before.
Low	Devwon had fun on her first two dates with Jason, but lately she has felt bored.	Fred has passed some of his calculus tests, but he has also failed some.	Alisha has been working with Josh for years and has never complained before.
Consensus			
High	Devwon has talked to her friends about Jason. They all say he's a great guy.	Everyone is failing calculus.	Ten other women in the office have complained about Josh.
Low	Some of Devwon's friends like Jason, but others think he is a "2" (on a 10-point scale).	Some students are doing well in calculus, but others are failing.	No one but Alisha has complained about Josh.

covariation principle
A commonsense assumption that observed effects are most likely caused by factors that occurred at the same time or same place as the observed effects.

Chapter 1 explains that covariation does not necessarily imply causality, but Kelley believes that most people ignore this limitation and base their attributions on the **covariation principle**: "An effect is attributed to the one of its possible causes with which, over time, it varies" (p. 3).

Social perceivers attend to three sources of covariation data, which Kelley refers to as the three axes of an "attribution cube": distinctiveness, consistency, and consensus (Reynolds & West, 1989). For example, what attributions do we make when we learn that Fred has failed a calculus test? Do we decide that Fred is intellectually impoverished or do we conclude that the calculus was difficult? It depends on the three forms of covariation noted in Table 4-1:

- *Distinctiveness* describes covariation across objects (or entities). When distinctiveness is high, the action or outcome occurs only when the object is present; the object and the behavior (or outcome) appear to be linked together across many situations. When distinctiveness is low, the action occurs when the object is present and when it is absent. If Fred is failing all his classes, then his failure in calculus is low in distinctiveness. If, however, he is doing well in his other classes, then his failure is distinctive.

- *Consistency* is an assessment of behavior in similar situations in the past. Consistency is high when we always react to the object in a particular way; it is low when our reactions vary. If Fred has failed all previous tests in calculus, then his performance is highly consistent over time; if he has been doing very well in the class until now, then consistency is low.
- *Consensus* is based on covariation across people. High consensus suggests that the object affects everyone the same way; low consensus suggests that the target person is uniquely affected by it. If many of the other students in the class failed the test, then consensus is high; if Fred is alone in his failure, then consensus is low.

How do people combine all this information about covariation? According to Kelley (1967), attributors who are well-calibrated social perceivers will emphasize external causes "when evidence exists as to the distinctiveness, consistency, and consensus of the appropriate effects" (p. 196). As Figure 4-2 indicates, if Fred is passing his other classes (high distinctiveness), but he has failed all his calculus tests (high consistency), and if everyone else in the class is failing (high consensus), then an observer would probably conclude that his failure is caused by an external factor: The course is extraordinarily difficult. When do people attribute Fred's failure to Fred himself? According to research, people make internal attributions when both distinctiveness and consensus are low, but consistency is high. If Fred is failing his other classes (low distinctiveness), he has failed all the previous tests in calculus (high consistency), but none of the other students are failing (low consensus), then perceivers would be more likely to attribute Fred's failure to him rather than to the situation. As Figure 4-2 suggests, high consistency is needed before either an internal or external attribution can be made. When consistency is low, factors vary so much over time that the action is attributed to fluctuating situational factors (Forsyth & McMillan, 1981a; Hilton & Slugoski, 1986; McArthur, 1972, p. 172; Orvis, Cunningham, & Kelley, 1975).

Kelley's theory is complex but, then again, so is attributional thought. Across a variety of research contexts, including students searching for the cause of a poor exam performance (Kernis & Granneman, 1990; Lunt, 1988), politicians explaining the source of social problems (Chebat & Filiatrault, 1986), individuals trying to decide whether a person they have just met is

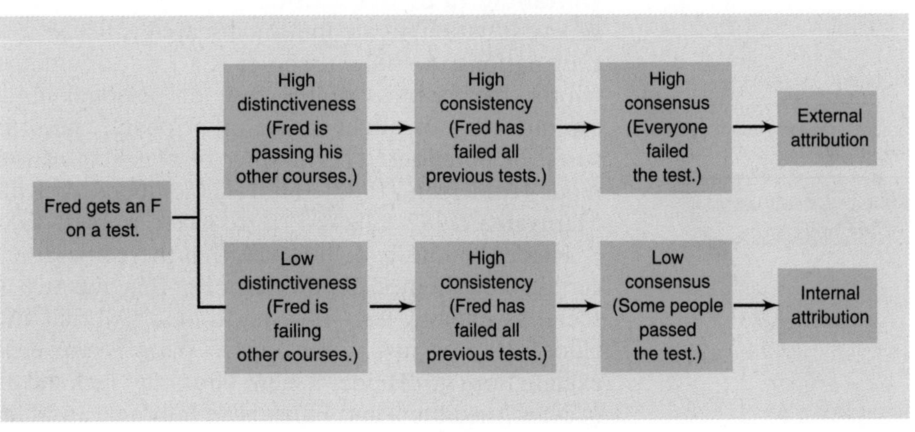

▲ **FIGURE 4-2**
What leads us to make an internal rather than an external attribution? According to Kelley's attribution cube model, if Fred is a good student (high distinctiveness), but he and the rest of the class keep failing their tests (high consistency and consensus), then the course is unusually difficult. But Fred is responsible for his own failure if he is failing all his courses, he has failed all tests in this class, and other people are passing the course.

likable (Kimble, Arnold, & Hirt, 1985), or even cheaters asked to account for their actions (Mitchell, 1985), attributions usually match the patterns predicted by the theory. The theory has also stimulated the development of a number of related models of attributional inference (Cheng & Novick, 1990; Forsterling, 1989; Hewstone & Jaspars, 1983, 1987; Hilton & Slugoski, 1986; Iacobucci & McGill, 1990; Lipe, 1991).

These efforts, however, have pinpointed one notable exception to Kelley's original predictions: Attributors underutilize consensus information. When people read brief descriptions of a person performing such simple behaviors as laughing at a comedian, displaying fear when a dog approached, and performing a task incorrectly, they usually made internal attributions. If they were given more information about the distinctiveness, consistency, and consensus of the behavior in the situation, however, many concluded that the situation also played a role in producing the reaction. Information about consensus, however, accounted for only 2.9% of their attributions, whereas distinctiveness and consistency accounted for 10.2% and 20.0%, respectively (McArthur, 1972). This tendency to discount consensus information parallels the *base-rate bias* discussed in Chapter 3. Perceivers often rely on the representativeness heuristic rather than on base rates when they make judgments. Similarly, attributors rely on their intuitive theories of causality rather than on consensus information when they formulate attributions (Borgida & Brekke, 1981; Hewstone & Jaspars, 1987; Jaspars, Hewstone, & Fincham, 1983; Zukier & Pepitone, 1984).

Even though people use consensus information imperfectly, our attributional skills remain impressive. Just as Semmelweis was able to study the covariation between illness and the medical procedures used in his hospital, the attributor takes note of distinctiveness, consistency, and (to a lesser degree) consensus to decide whether an action is likely to be caused by the individual or by factors present in the external environment. Our search for causes does not stop, however, when we identify either an internal or an external cause. Semmelweis, for example, wanted to know whether the symptoms were caused by his patients' frailties or by the hospital procedures, but he also wanted to know whether he could control the causes of the illness. Perceivers, as we will see in the next section, don't stop when they answer the question "Is this behavior caused by internal factors or external factors?" They also wonder, "Is this behavior caused by factors that change over time?" and "Is this behavior caused by factors I can control?"

Dimensions of Attribution

In any situation an attributional search is likely to turn up dozens of plausible explanations. A student who aces a test can credit good luck, intensive study efforts, the easiness of the test, or personal ability. A person who drinks too much liquor might blame other people, personal weaknesses, social pressures, or boredom. The number of plausible causes of our behavior is enormous (Anderson, 1983; Bar-Tal, Goldberg, & Knaani, 1984; Benson, 1989; Maruyama, 1982; Elig & Frieze, 1979; Weiner, 1985a).

Heider maintained, however, that these myriad causes are organized around certain key themes, or dimensions. Imagine two students who get As on a social psychology test; Takesha thinks, "All that studying paid off!" Lisa concludes "It was just dumb luck." What is the difference between these two explanations? In Heider's view, effort and luck fall at opposite ends of the *locus of causality* dimension. Effort is an internal causal factor; it reflects the individual's internal, or dispositional, qualities. In contrast, situational or environ-

▲ **FIGURE 4-3**
What dimensions organize our attributional thoughts? Weiner (1980) maintains that we intuitively categorize causes using three dimensions: locus, stability, and controllability. Applied in an academic setting, his model suggests that specific causes such as study habits, teacher bias, effort, study sessions, ability, difficulty, mood, and luck differ from one another in three ways: Are they internal or external? Are they stable or unstable? Are they controllable or uncontrollable?

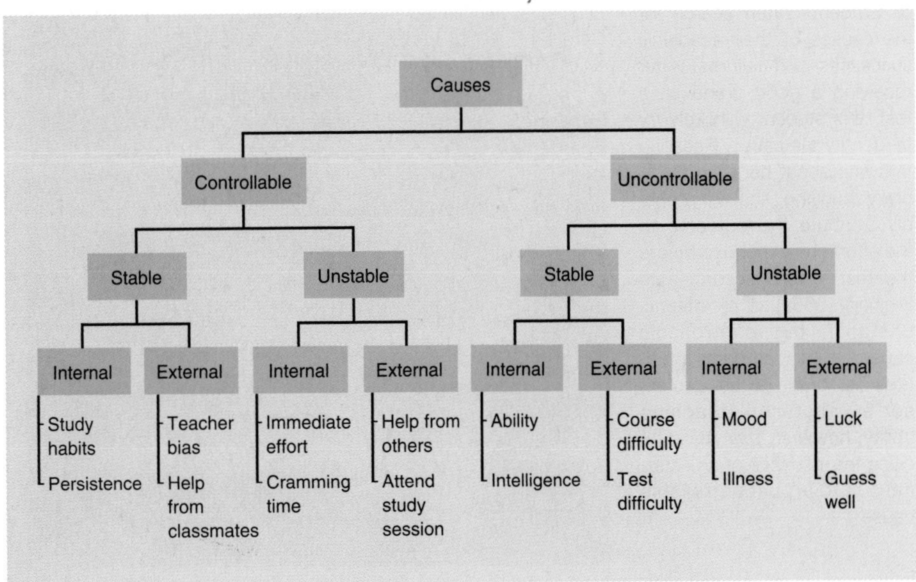

mental factors, such as good luck, are external causes (Heider, 1958; Miller, Smith, & Uleman, 1981).

Attributors make other distinctions in addition to separating internal causes from external causes (Falbo & Beck, 1979). Bernard Weiner (1985a), for example, believes that locus, stability, and controllability are the key dimensions that structure the way we think about causes (see Figure 4-3). If Takesha thinks, "I studied for 10 hours," but Lisa concludes "I really am pretty intelligent," both are making internal attributions—effort (studying) and ability (intelligence) are within the person. Their attributions vary, however, along the *stability* dimension. Unstable causes, such as effort, fluctuate over time and situations. Stable causes, such as ability, are relatively enduring. Moreover, their attributions cite causes that differ in *controllability.* Some causes, such as our basic level of ability, cannot be modified; they are uncontrollable. Others, in contrast, are controllable. We can choose to work hard or to work very little, so effort is a controllable cause (Weiner, 1980, 1983, 1985b; Weiner & Brown, 1984).

The descriptive adequacy of Weiner's three-dimensional theory has been supported in a number of laboratory and field studies (Bar-Tal, Goldberg, & Knaani, 1984; Hayamizu, 1984; Russell, 1982). When students describe the cause of their performance in their own words (the *open-ended* measure), nearly all of their responses can be classified into one of eight categories generated by Weiner's locus × stability × controllability model. Moreover, when these same students rate the causes of their performance on each of the dimensions identified by Weiner, their ratings tend to match the attributions they made on the open-ended measure (Russell, McAuley, & Tarico, 1987). The number of causes that people identify when they explain their actions may be enormous, but by taking dimensions into account, we can describe similarities and differences among these attributions.

Dimensions also seem to play a critical cognitive mediational role in determining the consequences of causal attributions, including affective reactions, shifts in expectations, and changes in behavior. Individuals who attribute a failure to internal causes, for example, often experience more shame than individuals who attribute a failure to external causes. The stability dimension, in

▲ Students often search for the causes of their academic successes and failures. After receiving a good grade on a test, this student will likely try to identify the cause. Recalling that she spent hours in the library studying, she will probably attribute the outcome to the effort she expended before the test. Effort, according to Weiner (1985a), is an internal, unstable, but controllable cause. If this student attributes her grade to her professor's masterful teaching ability, however, she would be citing the influence of an external, stable, uncontrollable cause.

contrast, is a significant determinant of individuals' expectations, for people who attribute their outcomes to unstable causes are reluctant to make predictions about their future outcomes. And individuals who attribute their performances to controllable factors are more satisfied with their successes and more willing to expend effort to overcome their failures (Weiner, 1985a).

These studies suggest that the locus, stability, and controllability dimensions organize our attributions across a variety of different situations. But they also indicate that we often prefer one kind of attributional conclusion to another. After a failure, we are loath to blame our internal, stable qualities (for example, intellect), but we readily allocate responsibility to external, uncontrollable causes. In some cases we are less-than-perfect, naive scientists; rather than seek the real cause of behavior, we sometimes err in our attributions. We return to these flaws in the last section of this chapter.

Self-Attribution

Without attributions, our social world would seem chaotic, a series of inexplicable events occurring at random. Once we formulate attributions, this flood of interpersonal encounters becomes a predictable unfolding of meaningful social life (see Table 4-2).

Our attributional machinery does more, however, than just make sense of other people's behaviors. When we turn it to focus on our own actions, we ourselves become less of a mystery. Even though common sense tells us that we know ourselves far better than any external observer could, our private stock of information is often ambiguous, inconsistent, and weak. I may feel angry, but I may not know why. A women's rights activist may be able to state "I am pro-choice" without hesitation, but she may not know whether she likes reggae music. We aren't always attuned to our inner qualities.

self-perception theory A theoretical model that assumes people gain knowledge about their personal attitudes, emotions, and other internal states by observing their own actions across different situations.

Unlike other attribution theorists, Daryl J. Bem (1972) is far more interested in the attributions we make about ourselves than in the attributions we make about others. According to his **self-perception theory**, people often "come to 'know' their own attitudes, emotions, and other internal states by inferring

▲ **TABLE 4-2**
Summing up: Theoretical analyses of perceivers' ability to make inferences about the causes of behaviors and events

Theory	*Assumptions*
Commonsense psychology (Heider, 1958)	Perceivers seek to identify the more stable dispositional structures that cause behaviors and events. Heider believed that individuals are intuitive psychologists who frequently distinguish between internal causes (such as effort and ability) and external causes (such as luck or task difficulty).
Correspondent inference theory (Jones & Davis, 1965)	Perceivers formulate attributions when they believe that an action corresponds to a person's dispositional characteristics. Freely chosen behaviors and unexpected actions are more informative than required, expected actions.
Attribution cube theory (Kelley, 1972)	Perceivers attend to three sources of covariation data: distinctiveness across objects, consistency across time and places, and (to a lesser extent) consensus among people. Attributors make external attributions when distinctiveness, consistency, and consensus are high, and internal attributions when distinctiveness and consensus are low but consistency is high.
Three-dimensional model of attribution (Weiner, 1980)	Perceivers can distinguish among various types of causes by considering such dimensions as locus (internal-external), stability (stable-unstable), and controllability (controllable-uncontrollable). Effort, for example, is an internal, unstable, controllable cause, whereas help from others is external, unstable, and uncontrollable.

them from observations of their own overt behavior and/or the circumstances in which this behavior occurs" (p. 2). Instead of searching our thoughts and memories for self-information, we scrutinize our own actions and derive knowledge from these behavioral data. If we see ourselves talking, laughing, and complimenting others, we might conclude that we are friendly, outgoing people. But if we behave in a critical or hostile manner, we infer something quite different about ourselves. Bem did not agree with the philosopher who believed, "I think, therefore I am." He believed, "I do, therefore I must be."

The Overjustification Effect

Bem's self-perception theory is, at core, an attribution theory; it argues that we actively search for the causes of our own behavior. If we decide that our behaviors are caused by internal factors, then we make inferences about ourselves. If, however, factors present in the situation "are the apparent controlling variables of the behavior" (1972, p. 6), then we don't use our actions as information about ourselves. When our behavior appears to be caused by external factors, we can't draw any inferences from it about our internal motives or desires (Bandler, Madaras, & Bem, 1968; Jones, 1990; Olson, 1992).

This attributional analysis explains why we sometimes become less motivated in work or study the more we are rewarded for working or studying (Amabile, Hennessey, & Grossman, 1986; Condry, 1977; Deci & Ryan, 1985). People have puzzled over this **overjustification effect** for centuries, as the following folktale illustrates.

overjustification effect Imposing such powerful external reasons for performing an action that any preexisting personal reasons for action (such as goals, needs, and so on) lose their motivational significance.

> Each day the children harassed the old woman. After school they would play outside her window; if she asked them to be quiet, they only called her obscene names and shouted more loudly.

> One day as the children approached, she called to them. "I have grown fond of listening to you play, but my hearing isn't what it used to be. If you will play in front of my window, I will pay each of you fifty cents."
>
> The children laughed at the woman's foolish request, but they agreed to play as noisily as they could. For a week, they collected their payment each day after school and raised a tremendous din.
>
> The next week, however, the woman greeted the children with a frown. "Times are hard. I can pay you only a quarter for playing outside my window."
>
> The children complained, but they agreed to her offer. Then, after three days, the woman met them again. "Times are hard. I can pay you only ten cents," she told them.
>
> "Ten cents? That's not enough," they said. And they left her in peace.

intrinsic motivation
Doing something for its own sake rather than to achieve some reward or to avoid a punishment; for example, studying for the pleasure of learning new things.

extrinsic motivation
Doing something to secure some reward or avoid a punishment, rather than for the satisfaction of performing the behavior per se; for example, studying to earn a grade rather than studying for the joy of learning new things.

Why did the children stop? Self-perception theory suggests that the money undermined their **intrinsic motivation**. Intrinsically motivated behavior is done for its own sake, for no apparent ulterior motive or goal. People who are intrinsically motivated study for the sheer joy of learning or help others because they find pleasure in doing so. **Extrinsic motivation**, in contrast, can be created by offering people rewards. When we are extrinsically motivated, our behavior is only a means to an end. We don't want to just work or just study; rather, we are interested in earning money or graduating from college. As the story of the old woman and the noisy children demonstrates, extrinsic rewards can destroy intrinsic motivation. When we are rewarded for behaving a certain way, we forget our original motivations and assume that external inducement is the cause of our actions (Deci & Ryan, 1985).

When the boss gives us a raise, is she actually dampening our work motivation? When the teacher puts a gold star on Johnny's arithmetic homework, will Johnny begin to lose interest in math? A study of nursery-school children says yes. Investigators watched 3- to 5-year-olds during their free-play period in nursery school and identified the children who liked to play with felt-tip markers (most did; felt-tip markers have replaced crayons in the hearts of small children). Two weeks later the researchers returned and asked the children to use felt-tip markers when they drew their pictures. One group of children expected and received a reward when they finished: a colored card with a large gold star, a red ribbon, and the phrase "Good Player Award" in large letters. A second group of children was surprised with an award; these children had not been told beforehand that they would receive one. The researchers asked a third group of children "Would you like to draw some pictures?" No reward was mentioned or given.

What did the children do during their free-play period one week later? Those who had been given the promised award used the markers less than the children in the other conditions. Before the reward, they had spent 17% of the time playing with the markers. Now they spent only 9% of their time using markers. They drew more pictures when they were expecting a reward, but their pictures were judged to be less creative than those drawn by the children in the other conditions. Extrinsic rewards, the researchers concluded, "turn play into work" (Greene & Lepper, 1974; Lepper, Greene, & Nisbett, 1973).

These findings are consistent with Teresa Amabile's analyses of motivation and creativity (1983b, 1985). She maintains that creativity is based on three components: domain-relevant skills, creativity-relevant skills, and motivation. Painters, for example, must possess the technical skills required to combine colors, sketch, and draw (domain-relevant skills). They must also be capable of generating new styles and techniques for translating their ideas into painted images (creativity-relevant skills). Amabile believes, however, that these

▲ Studies of motivation suggest that teachers can inadvertently damage children's intrinsic interest in learning when they assign homework, watch children as they work, encourage competition in the classroom, and give grades. Extrinsic motivators can "turn play into work."

skills will be useless if the artist isn't intrinsically motivated. Amabile (1985) tested this hypothesis with a group of writers recruited from local colleges. These individuals were intrinsically motivated to express themselves creatively through their writing: They had taken advanced courses in writing, many had published poetry and fiction, and on average they spent more than 6 hours a week writing creatively. Before Amabile asked them to write a haiku-style poem, she had each one rank a number of "reasons for writing" from most to least personally important. Amabile manipulated the list, so that some of the subjects reviewed only intrinsic motivators (for example, "You get a lot of pleasure out of reading something good that you have written"; "You like to play with words"); others were given a list of extrinsic motivators (for example, "You know that many of the best jobs available require good writing skills"; "Your teachers and parents have encouraged you to go into writing"). As expected, writers who were reminded of their extrinsic motivations wrote less creative poems (as judged by a panel of poets) than writers who ranked intrinsic motivators and writers in a control condition who did not perform a ranking task.

What can be done to avoid damaging creativity through overjustification? First, be sensitive to your use of extrinsic motivators. Although money and gold stars are obvious extrinsic motivators, watching people while they work, setting deadlines, encouraging competition between people, assigning tasks, and making one activity contingent on the completion of another activity all undermine motivation (Flink, Boggiano, & Barrett, 1990; Lepper et al., 1990). Second, eschew the use of extrinsic motivators whenever you see signs of high intrinsic motivation. If people are working hard, enjoying the task, and striving for quality, adding extrinsic motivators may prove devastating (Hennessey, Amabile, & Martinage, 1989). Third, if you do offer rewards, be certain to make them contingent on quality rather than quantity. When people are given rewards for good performance, rather than simply for doing the task, the negative effects of extrinsic motivators are lessened (Ryan, Mims, & Koestner, 1983).

Attributions and Emotions

Bem's self-perception theory is consistent with William James's 19th-century analysis of emotions. James (1892/1961) argued that emotions do not precede

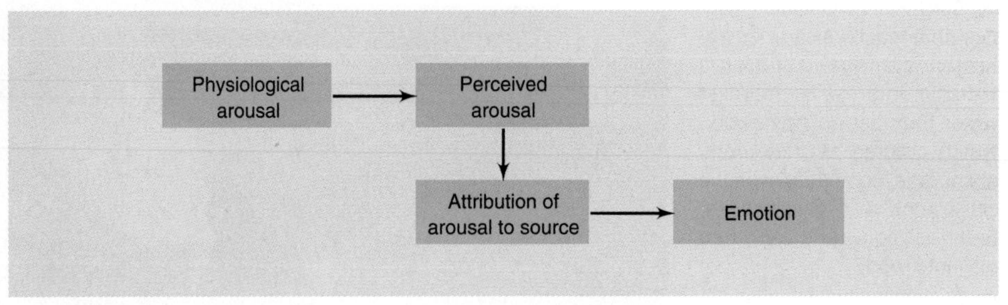

▲ **FIGURE 4-4**
How do we identify the emotion we are experiencing? Schachter and Singer (1962) propose that our emotional experiences begin when something arouses us physiologically. Once we notice we are aroused, we examine the situation to learn the cause. When we find it, we assign it an emotional label.

our behavioral reactions. We do not feel angry and then shout. Rather, we often shout, and then label our emotion *anger*. He wrote:

> Common sense says, we lose our fortune, are sorry and weep; we meet a bear, are frightened and run; we are insulted by a rival, are angry and strike. The hypothesis here to be defended says that this order of sequence is incorrect, that the one mental state is not immediately induced by the other, that the bodily manifestations must first be interposed between, and that the more rational statement is that we feel sorry because we cry, angry because we strike, afraid because we tremble, and not that we cry, strike, or tremble because we are sorry, angry, or fearful. (pp. 242–243)

two-factor theory of emotions
A framework that argues emotions are based on the interaction of level of general physiological arousal and attributions about the cause of that arousal.

This basic notion—that emotions may follow our physiological reactions rather than precede them—provided the foundation of Stanley Schachter and Jerome E. Singer's **two-factor theory of emotions**. Schachter and Singer maintain that we don't automatically know when we are happy, angry, or jealous. Instead, we make attributions about the causes of our physiological and behavioral reactions before attaching labels to our experiences. This labeling process, they maintain, depends on two factors. First, some element in the situation must trigger a general, nonspecific arousal marked by increased heart rate, tightening of the stomach, and rapid breathing. Second, we must search the situation for cues that tell us what has caused our reaction. If we are with someone who we think is physically attractive, we may label our feelings as love or sexual excitement. If we are arguing with someone, we may conclude we are angry. If we are at a party, we may decide that we are happy or euphoric. Because they assume that "emotional states are a function of the interaction of such cognitive factors with a state of physiological arousal," Schachter and Singer's approach has been called the two-factor theory (Schachter & Singer, 1962, p. 381; see Figure 4-4).

Schachter and Singer conducted an ingenious analysis of their theory in the early 1960s. They told the men who volunteered for their study that they were studying a vitamin supplement called Suproxin. The men were asked if they were willing to take the supplement, and those who consented were injected with epinephrine or a placebo. Epinephrine, which is also called adrenaline, is released by our hormonal system whenever we face stressful situations; it increases blood pressure, heart rate, and respiration. Thus the men who received the epinephrine were more physiologically aroused than those who received the inert placebo.

Schachter and Singer also manipulated subjects' interpretations of their physical sensations. They told some of the epinephrine-injected subjects that even though the drug wasn't harmful, side effects were quite common: They might feel flushed, their hands might shake, and their hearts might pound. The other subjects were given no information about the effects of the drug.

▲ **FIGURE 4-5**
Do people rely on situational cues to label their feelings? To test their two-factor theory of emotions, Schachter and Singer manipulated two variables: (1) subjects' arousal and perceptions of that arousal and (2) situational cues. Some subjects took an arousing drug and were told it would arouse them. Others took the drug but weren't warned. Others took a placebo. Some subjects worked with an angry person; others, with a euphoric one. The mood of the aroused, unwarned subjects matched that of their partners. (From Schachter & Singer, 1982)

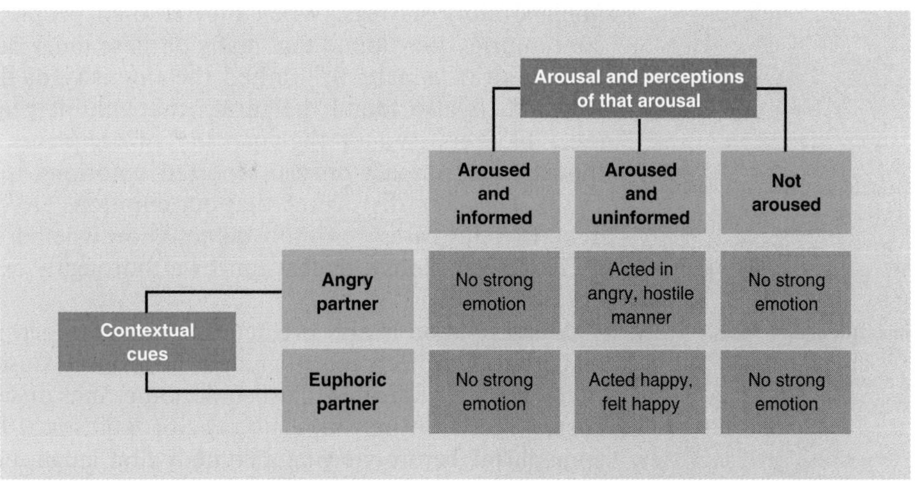

Schachter and Singer reasoned that once the epinephrine kicked in, subjects would begin to search for the cause of their arousal. People who had been told that the drug would arouse them should have assumed the drug was causing their hands to shake and their hearts to pound. If they hadn't been warned about the drug's effects, then they would be more likely to interpret their arousal as emotion.

What kind of emotion would these uninformed subjects experience? Schachter and Singer believed their reactions would depend on the available situational cues. They therefore manipulated this variable as well. They arranged for their subjects to wait for Suproxin's effects in a small room with one of Schachter and Singer's accomplices. The accomplices were trained to behave in either a euphoric or angry fashion. The euphoric confederate clowned around during the 20 minutes, doodling on scratch paper, playing a game of "basketball" with wadded-up balls of paper, making and flying a paper airplane, building a tower out of file folders, and playing with a hula hoop. The angry confederate, in contrast, became increasingly agitated during the 20 minutes. The subjects were asked to complete questionnaires that included very personal questions. After loudly criticizing questions that requested information about childhood diseases, father's income, and family members' bathing habits and psychiatric adjustment, the accomplice flew into a rage at the question "How many times each week do you have sexual intercourse?"

Schachter and Singer observed and coded the actions taken by each subject and also asked them to describe their emotional states. As they had predicted, the physiologically aroused subjects who hadn't been told about the supplement's side effects responded with emotions that matched the confederate's actions. If they were aroused and hadn't been expecting the arousal, then they felt happy when their fellow subject was happy, but angry when their fellow subject was angry. Forewarned subjects and unaroused subjects who received a placebo, however, displayed no pronounced emotion. Also, the subjects in a special control condition—people who had been given epinephrine but had been misinformed about its possible effects—also displayed the emotions enacted by a euphoric confederate (see Figure 4-5).

Schachter and Singer's experiment was only the beginning. Other researchers, intrigued by their findings, tested their model in both laboratory and nonlaboratory settings. When they studied people who suffered from spinal cord injuries, they found that many of these individuals had blunted emotions; their injuries apparently limited the intensity of their physiological arousal. Researchers also found that drugs that inhibit general physiological arousal (beta blockers) reduce the intensity of recipients' emotional behaviors, although their impact on self-reported emotions is inconsistent (Reisenzein, 1983). They also discovered that our emotions are largely situationally dependent. In many cases we simply do not know whether we are experiencing anger, excitement, jealousy, or fear until we thoroughly examine the social situation (Averill, 1990).

misattribution
The attribution of an event to a source with which it has little or no connection.

Misattribution is also predicted by the two-factor model. Just as Schachter and Singer's subjects misattributed the arousal caused by the drug to the situation, evidence indicates that people sometimes misattribute arousal caused by Factor *A* to an entirely unrelated Factor *B* (Olson, 1990). Subjects injected with epinephrine before viewing a comedy film laugh more and harder than those given a placebo; subjects given a tranquilizer laugh less (Schachter & Wheeler, 1962). Individuals who become aroused while exercising respond more aggressively or more sexually when subsequently confronted or shown erotic films (Cantor, Zillmann, & Bryant, 1975; Zillmann & Bryant, 1974). As the section "Application: Attributions and Health" reveals, insomniacs who attribute their restlessness to an external, controllable factor (such as that last cup of coffee after dinner) can sometimes get to sleep faster than insomniacs who make no misattributions (Storms & Nisbett, 1970).

The equally interesting tendency for us to experience emotions when we mistakenly think we are aroused is also consistent with the two-factor model. The effect is sometimes termed the *Valins effect,* in reference to Stuart Valins (1966), who documented this phenomenon. In his initial studies, Valins showed male college students a series of slides depicting attractive nude women while their heart rates were supposedly being monitored. Valins told the subjects that technical difficulties would cause their heart beats to be audible. Instead of their actual heart beats, however, he played one of two recordings. The first recording was of a heart beating normally; the second, of a heart occasionally beating faster. Thus some subjects heard their heart rates fluctuate as they watched the slides, but others did not. As predicted, the men reported greater attraction toward images of women that had been paired with increases in the audible bogus heart beat. Apparently, just believing that we are becoming aroused is sometimes sufficient to create emotions in us. (Studies of the Valins effect are reviewed in Parkinson, 1985.)

Other studies, however, indicate that our emotions aren't quite so labile as the two-factor theory suggests. First, subjects in later studies patterned after Schachter and Singer's experiment sometimes reacted negatively when they experienced unexplained arousal. Rather than rely strictly on the situation for clues that would help them label their emotions, they tended to be angry rather than happy (Marshall & Zimbardo, 1979; Maslach, 1979). Second, arousal may not always precede cognitive appraisal, as James and Schachter and Singer suggest. Appraisal may, in some cases, precede the physiological response or the two responses may occur simultaneously (Lazarus, 1984; Zajonc, 1984). Third, emotions can occur when only one of the two factors identified by Schachter and Singer are present. People experience happiness or anger even when they aren't physiologically excited (Reisenzein, 1983). Also, emotions do not always require the cognitive component. The **facial feedback hypothesis,** for example, argues that the muscles in our faces sometimes directly influence our emotions without any intervening attributional interpretations.

facial feedback hypothesis
The hypothesis that the muscles in our faces directly influence our emotional experiences and behavior; movements of the muscles that create a smile, for example, trigger positive feelings, whereas movements of frown muscles create negative ones.

▲ These exercisers had better be careful: According to the two-factor theory of emotions, even though their physiological arousal is produced by the exercises they are performing, they might misattribute their arousal to each other. Instead of feeling energized by the workout, they might instead conclude that they are falling in love.

People who are told to keep their lips locked in a fixed smile for a long period of time report feeling happier than individuals who fix a scowl on their faces (Matsumoto, 1987). This facial feedback effect occurs even when subjects aren't aware of their facial expressions. When subjects were told to hold a pen in their mouths—in a supposed study of how people can use their mouths for various tasks—they felt more positive when they clenched a pen in their teeth rather than hold it in their lips. If you try it yourself, you will see that holding a pen in your lips forces your facial muscles into a frown, but holding a pen in your teeth forces a smile (Strack, Martin, & Stepper, 1988). This facial feedback process is not yet clearly understood, but recent research suggests that our expressions may directly influence blood flow and body temperature in the face and head, and these changes may in turn influence the emotion centers of the brain (Zajonc, Murphy, & Inglehart, 1989).

Attribution and Action Identification

What are you doing at this moment? Are you relaxing? Exercising? Reading? Yes, you are reading the words on this page. So you are a reader. But aren't you doing more than just reading? Aren't you also preparing for the next test? So you are studious. Is studying all you are doing? Aren't you reading because you are attending college, and college courses always require reading? So you are a college student. Aren't you also learning new information about yourself and the people around you? Yes. So what are you doing? Reading, studying, going to college, or learning?

action identification theory A conceptual analysis of the way people identify the meanings of their actions; argues that individuals are less likely to accept alternative interpretations of actions identified at a high conceptual level.

Daniel Wegner and Robin R. Vallacher (1987), in their **action identification theory**, argue that your self-perceptions after an action depend, in large part, on the level at which you identify the act. If you identify your act at a low level—when you look at yourself reading and say, "I'm reading"—the action doesn't say much about you or your self-concept. High-level act identifications, in contrast, interpret the behavior in a more abstract way that includes its general meaning and purposes. When you say, "I'm learning about social behavior," this high-level identification holds "greater potential for defining one's self than do lower level act identities" (Vallacher & Wegner, 1987, p. 11; see Table 4-3).

▲ **TABLE 4-3**
Examples of low- and high-level identifications of actions

Action-identification theory distinguishes between low- and high-level identifications of actions. Actions with low-level conceptualizations are less meaningful, more easily interrupted, and more easily redefined. Actions with high-level conceptualizations, in contrast, are more meaningfully defined and understood.

Context	*Low-Level Identification*	*High-Level Identification*
Education	I'm listening to a lecture. I'm reading this book.	I'm earning a degree. I'm learning about psychology.
Sports	I'm tackling the ballcarrier. I'm kicking the ball.	I'm doing my part for the team. I'm trying to win the game.
Entertainment	I'm watching a movie. I'm listening to music.	I'm relaxing after a hard day. I'm appreciating the artist's labors.
Work	I'm filling out my time card. I'm answering the telephone.	I'm earning the money I need. I'm providing a service to customers.
Health and fitness	I'm lifting weights. I'm eating nonfatty foods.	I'm increasing my overall fitness. I'm dieting.
Household	I'm taking out the trash. I'm cleaning my room.	I'm maintaining the household. I'm expressing my personal tastes.

Because behaviors that are identified at a high level are more meaningful to us, we are less likely to accept alternative interpretations of them. If we enter a situation with a higher-order act identity clearly in mind, our self-perceptions do not change once we have carried out the behavior. Sometimes, however, we don't know what we are doing—at least in a larger sense—because our actions are identified at a low level. These actions are easy targets for reinterpretation at a higher level. If you initially defined your action as learning (a high-level act identity), then you would probably remain at that level of identification rather than redefine your behavior as merely reading or studying. If, however, you initially said you were reading, you would more readily accept a higher level identification.

Wegner and his colleagues (1984) illustrated this process in a study of coffee drinkers. Some subjects were given coffee in standard cups; others drank their coffee from oddly shaped cups that demanded considerable attention. The odd cups, they assumed, required so much attention that subjects would identify their behavior at a lower level than the subjects given standard cups. Next, all the subjects were given a high-level identification for drinking coffee. For some subjects, this identification suggested that they were drinking coffee because they sought stimulation. For others, the information subtly suggested that they drank coffee so they could avoid stimulation. As predicted, only the subjects who drank their coffee from the strange cups—and hence were very cognizant of their behavior rather than of the meaning behind the behavior—accepted the high-level act identity. These subjects had the opportunity to adjust the volume of the music in the room. They turned up the volume when coffee was defined as a way to increase stimulation, and turned it down when coffee was defined as a way to decrease stimulation.

Self-Perception versus Self-Knowledge

Table 4-4 summarizes some of the ways attributional processes can generate self-knowledge. When we act to secure a reward for ourselves, our intrinsic motivation wanes as our extrinsic motivation waxes. When we are physiologi-

▲ **TABLE 4-4**
Summing up: Even though we generally assume we have detailed information about ourselves, self-perception theory argues that we often make attributions about motivations, emotions, and the meaning of our actions.

Type	*Process*
Motivation	People don't always know why they do the things they do. Giving people rewards or prizes when they reach their goals can undermine their intrinsic desire to reach these goals. This *overjustification effect* occurs when perceivers assume that extrinsic motivators, not their intrinsic motivation, are causing their behavior.
Emotion	People don't automatically know what emotion they are experiencing. As the two-factor theory of emotion (Schachter & Singer, 1962) suggests, people who are experiencing nonspecific arousal search the situation for situational cues that will help them define the nature of the emotional experience. Misattribution occurs when arousal caused by one event is attributed to an entirely unrelated event.
Action	People don't always know what they are doing. Action identification theory argues that when people conceptualize their actions at a high level they recognize the general purpose and meaning of the behavior. Frequently, however, we perform actions that are conceptualized at a low level. These attributionally ambiguous actions change their meaning and implications depending on contextual cues (Wegner & Vallacher, 1986).

cally aroused, we search the situation for the cause of our arousal and label our emotional experiences accordingly. And when we do things without considering their significance, we readily redefine them so they become more meaningful to us.

Self-perception processes, however, do not automatically take precedence over self-knowledge. Even though Bem (1972) emphasized the impact of behavioral data on our self-perceptions, he also noted that we reject behavioral data when they conflict with well-established, private self-knowledge. What if you vote for a Republican but think of yourself as a Democrat? What if you feel very hungry but eat like a bird when you sit down to a meal? What if you feel very strongly about saving the environment but never take part in any environmentalist activities?

In general, when we possess a clear image of our personal qualities, behavioral data don't have much impact on our self-perceptions (Chaiken & Baldwin, 1981; Tybout & Scott, 1983). When prompted to recall either environmentally positive (recyling) or negative (littering) behaviors that they had performed in the past, people who possessed a well-defined personal view of environmental issues didn't change their self-descriptions. People whose attitudes about the environment were vague and inconsistent, however, were strongly influenced by the behavioral information (Chaikin & Baldwin, 1981). Similarly, people who tell others about their private thoughts and feelings conclude that they have described themselves more accurately than people who have described only their behaviors (Andersen & Ross, 1984; see also Andersen, 1984; Andersen & Williams, 1985). As shown in Chapter 5, when we answer the question "Who am I?" we often look first to our stock of private self-knowledge before turning to consider the meaning of our public actions.

Biases in Attributions

The doctors in Semmelweis's hospital did not feel responsible for the high mortality rate among maternity cases. They instead blamed unknown cosmic energies and the priests, who should have warded off these pernicious forces.

Senator Packwood, when accused of sexually harassing a dozen women, maintained that his excessive consumption of alcohol, not his lack of moral fiber, was the culprit. A mother living in Seattle drank bourbon regularly during her pregnancy and blamed the manufacturer of the liquor for her newborn's deformities. When Orval Wyatt Lyod killed his mother-in-law with an ax in his garage, he explained that in the darkness he mistook her for a large raccoon foraging for food. The motorist who ran over a pedestrian complained that he "ran into my car as I was moving through the intersection."

Heider argued that social perceivers, like scientists, strive to develop a veridical (accurate) view of the social world. But the causes that we search for are often ambiguous, so even a systematic search sometimes yields only guesses and conjectures. Moreover, we don't always function as mistake-free attribution computers. Biases sometimes distort our view of other people and of ourselves.

The Fundamental Attribution Error

Why did Anita Hill testify at the Thomas confirmation hearings? Thomas's wife Virginia felt that Hill was motivated by revenge: She believed Hill was trying to punish Thomas for scorning her. Senator Orrin Hatch was convinced that Hill was unstable and prone to fantasy. John Doggett, a Yale classmate of Hill's, attributed her reaction to her hypersensitivity about sex: He claimed she saw sexual harassment where none existed (Smolowe, 1991). These observers did not believe that she was a reluctant witness who was forced to come forward by the FBI and several members of the Judiciary Committee.

fundamental attribution error (FAE)
The tendency to overestimate the causal influence of dispositional factors while underemphasizing the causal influence of situational factors.

Virginia Thomas, Senator Hatch, and John Doggett, like most observers, had fallen prey to the **fundamental attribution error (FAE)**: the tendency to attribute behavior to internal, dispositional factors (Ross, 1977). Because of the FAE, a fast driver is called a *leadfoot* rather than someone who is late for an appointment, a student who falls asleep in class is lazy rather than exhausted by a part-time job, and a woman who files charges against a sexual harasser is vindictive rather than abused. Some researchers feel that this focus on dispositional factors is not *the* fundamental error in attribution processing, but all agree that the tendency is pervasive: We habitually underestimate how much people's behavior is influenced by the situations they face (Harvey & McGlynn, 1982; Jones, 1993; Trope & Higgins, 1993).

The FAE influences our perceptions in many situations. We use people's actions as indicators of their internal qualities even when we know all too well that they are deliberately putting on a performance for us. When the individuals in one study were told that a woman they were about to meet was trained to act in a certain way during the interview, they should have been cautious when making inferences about her personality. Yet they went right ahead and based their impressions on her actions. When she behaved in a friendly way, they assumed she was friendly; when she acted unfriendly, they supposed she was an unfriendly person (Napolitan & Goethals, 1979).

We also tend to take actions at face value, without considering the impact of the situation. In one study people were randomly assigned, with great fanfare, to one of two roles: questioner or contestant. The questioners then made up questions that would be used to test the contestants. They were asked to avoid easy questions ("What are the months of the year?") and unfair questions ("What is my brother's name?"), but such items as "What does FAE stand for?" or "What is the longest glacier in the world?" were fair game. After the hapless contestants were quizzed, both participants rated one another on general knowledge. Despite the fact that getting to make up the questions gave the questioners a huge edge, the contestants and uninvolved observers of the quiz match mistakenly assumed that the questioners were particularly knowledgeable (Ross, Amabile, & Steinmetz, 1977).

Why do we make unwarranted dispositional attributions? First, as Heider suggested, "behavior engulfs the field." When we see people moving, talking, and interacting, they are perceptually more salient than the situational field that surrounds them. Hence, when asked to explain the reason for their behavior, our attention—and our attributions—focus on the person rather than the situation (Fiske & Taylor, 1991). Second, the tendency to believe that actions reflect dispositions may be a part of Western society's emphasis on free will and individuality. People raised in non-Western cultures do not display the error as much as people raised in Western societies (Fletcher & Ward, 1988), and children learn to make dispositional attributions as they grow older (Kassin & Pryor, 1986; Rholes, Jones, & Wade, 1988; White, 1988).

Limitations in our information-processing capacity, which are examined in Chapter 3, may also contribute to the FAE. Some theorists believe that when we observe a person, we initially make a dispositional attribution. Only then do we turn to the situation and correct our dispositional attribution to take external, exogenous determinants of action into account (Quattrone, 1982; Trope, 1986; Trope & Cohen, 1989). In many cases, however, we do not sufficiently correct our initial attributions during this second stage. The action serves as an anchor for our initial judgment, and we fail to adjust this judgment to take into account other information (Fletcher, Reeder, & Bull, 1990; Lupfer, Clark, & Hutcherson, 1990).

Dan Gilbert and his colleagues have confirmed this possibility in a series of experiments. Gilbert believes that the attribution process involves three sequential stages: categorization, characterization, and correction. First, the attributor categorizes the behavior as one that reflects a particular trait or quality. Shaking one's fist at another motorist, for example, might be classified as *angry behavior.* Second, the attributor uses this behavioral label to characterize the actor—the motorist is considered to be an angry person because he has acted in an angry way. Last, the attributor corrects this characterization to take into account situational constraints that may have caused the motorist to act like an angry person. This third stage, however, requires more cognitive resources than the other stages, so we often fail to correct our dispositional inferences to take external determinants into account. Gilbert's model explains why people who are *cognitively busy*—trying do to several things at once—fall prey to the FAE even when they are aware of external factors that may be causing the action. They notice the external causes, but they don't have the cognitive resources needed to factor them into their attributional conclusions (Gilbert & Krull, 1988; Gilbert et al., 1992; Gilbert, Pelham, & Krull, 1988).

The correspondence bias. A specific type of FAE occurs when perceivers assume that people mean what they say, even when their verbal declarations are heavily constrained by the situation. Jones and his colleagues studied this **correspondence bias** by asking people to read an essay on a particular topic, such as the legalization of marijuana, racial segregation, Fidel Castro's government in Cuba, or abortion. Some subjects are told that the person who wrote the essay was free to take any position on the issue (choice condition); others are told that the essay writer was assigned a position (no-choice condition). Subjects then estimate the essay writer's true attitude. Invariably, people assume that the writer believes what he or she has written, even when they

correspondence bias
The tendency for observers to base their attributions on the content of a person's verbal communication, even when the person was forced to express certain opinions in the communication.

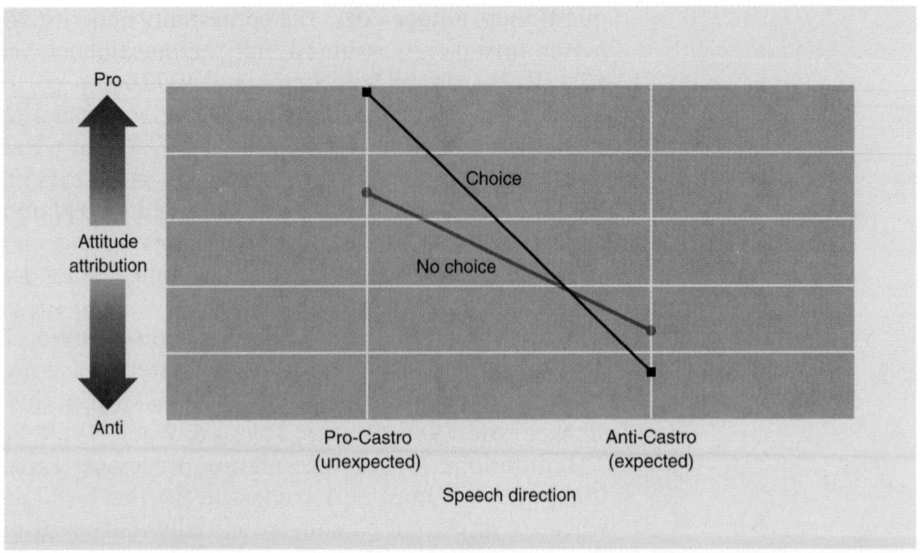

▲ **FIGURE 4-6**
Do we too often assume that people always mean what they say? Correspondent inference theory predicts that people's freely chosen actions reveal their inner character. Someone who writes a speech endorsing Fidel Castro is assumed to be pro-Castro; someone who writes a speech attacking Castro, however, is perceived as anti-Castro. But what if people cannot choose which kind of speech they write? Correspondent inference theory predicts that perceivers won't make attributions because the writer couldn't choose the essay's direction. Yet, in such situations, people still make attributions: They think the writer of the favorable speech is pro-Castro and the writer of the negative speech is anti-Castro. (From Jones, 1979)

are told that the writer was only carrying out an assignment (Jones, 1990; see Figure 4-6).

The tendency to attribute behavior-consistent attitudes to a speaker who is not acting freely violates the logic of correspondent inference theory: Perceivers should realize that actions may not correspond to attributes when behavior is constrained. But this bias occurs consistently in many studies. Jones once went so far as to arrange for subjects to write essays setting forth a particular view on a topic, then exchange essays with people in another room. Even though they had just written essays expressing an assigned position and should have realized that the content of the essays said nothing about the writers' attitudes, overattribution still occurred (Snyder & Jones, 1974). In another study, it was the subjects who made the assignments—they literally told other individuals how to answer a series of questions dealing with abortion. Although it was the subjects who constrained the respondents, they still assumed the individuals' answers reflected their attitudes (Gilbert & Jones, 1986b). In another study, subjects read two essays supposedly written by the same student for a class. Subjects were told that one of the essays was written 9 months after the other but that the writer (named Harris Jones) had no choice in selecting which side of the issue to endorse in either essay. Even when the second essay expressed a view that was the direct opposite of the view expressed in the first essay, people still attributed an essay-consistent attitude to the writer. They assumed the writer changed his mind after writing the first essay (Allison et al., 1993). The only way researchers have found to eliminate overattribution is to have the subject simply copy someone else's essay, or read an essay that is so weak or unenthusiastic that it betrays a refusal to take the assignment seriously (Schneider & Miller, 1975; Snyder & Jones, 1974).

Many of the processes that sustain the FAE combine to produce the correspondence bias. The essay is such an arresting stimulus for perceivers that they spend more time examining, processing, and drawing inferences from it (Fiske & Taylor, 1991; Taylor & Thompson, 1982). The result: The "actor and his act form a natural cognitive, if not perceptual, unit," and perceivers end up overattributing attitude (Jones, 1979, p. 115). Attributors may also start with the assumption that actions reflect attitudes and only later revise this judgment to take into account situational constraints. If the perceiver's subsequent revisions are insufficient, however, a correspondence bias results (Fein, Hilton, & Miller, 1990; Gilbert, 1991; Miller, Ashton, & Mishal, 1990; Reeder, Fletcher, & Furman, 1989). The bias may also be due, in part, to the perceiver's belief that few situations are so constraining that they eliminate all choice (Fleming & Darley, 1989; Quattrone, 1982). Although social psychologists routinely argue that behavior is a product of both the person and the environment, perceivers tend to underestimate the impact of social forces on behavior. Only attributors who correctly acknowledge the actor's lack of choice do not evidence the correspondence bias (Miller & Lawson, 1989; Miller et al., 1977).

The actor-observer difference. When H. H. Kelley and his colleagues asked 41 dating, cohabitating, or married couples to describe times they disagreed, the couples generated nearly 700 examples of things you can do to make other people angry: fail to behave affectionately, display insensitivity, criticize, become excessively involved in outside relationships, behave ineptly, behave irresponsibly—the list was lengthy. These problematic behaviors were probably sufficient to create conflict, but to make matters worse, Kelley found that the partners typically disagreed about the causes of the problems. Those who performed the problematic actions, the actors, typically believed that the situation had constrained them. The offended parties, the observers, disagreed: They blamed the behavior on the actors' personal qualities. The dispute then worsened, for the actor and observers saw the world in very different ways (Passer, Kelley, & Michela, 1978).

actor-observer difference The tendency for actors (the people who perform the behavior) to explain their behavior in terms of situational causes and for observers to explain the actors' behavior in terms of dispositional causes.

E. E. Jones and Richard Nisbett call this divergence the **actor-observer difference**: Actors (the people who perform the behavior) tend to explain their behavior in terms of situational factors, but observers usually emphasize dispositional causes. When male college students were first asked to explain why they chose their majors or why they liked their girlfriends, they emphasized the positive qualities of the fields or the women: "Psychology is an interesting field," they said, or "Karen is a very friendly, outgoing person." Next, they were asked to explain their *best friends'* choices. Now they emphasized their friends' unique dispositional qualities. "He wants to help people," they suggested, or "He has a weakness for redheads" (Nisbett et al., 1973). Apparently, actors are more ego-involved in the particular context, and they view themselves as adapting to fit changing situations (Baxter & Goldberg, 1987; Blass & Kaplowitz, 1990; Sande, Goethals, & Radloff, 1988). Observers, in contrast, have less information about how actors have behaved in other settings, so they tend to attribute actions to stable causes (Anderson, 1985; Fischer, Schoeneman, & Rubanowitz, 1987; Zacarro & Lowe, 1985). Actors and observers also see the situation from completely different perspectives. For actors, the environment is salient, so they tend to attribute their actions to external causes. The actor is salient to observers, so they tend to attribute actions to the actor (see Goldberg, 1981; Van Heck & Dijkstra, 1985, for reviews).

What can be done to reduce actor-observer differences? One solution requires *changing your focus of attention.* In several studies, when observers looked at the situation from the actor's perspective—either literally (by arranging for observers to watch a videotape taken from the actor's vantage point) or psychologically (by asking observers to empathize with the actor)—actor-observer differences were minimized (Arkin & Duval, 1975; Storms, 1973; Taylor & Fiske, 1975). In one study, observers were told to empathize with an actor named Margaret:

> Imagine how Margaret feels as she engages in conversation. While you are watching . . . picture to yourself just how she feels in the situation. You are to concentrate on the way she feels while conversing. Think about her reaction to the information she is receiving from the conversation. In your mind's eye, you are to visualize how it feels to Margaret to be in this conversation.

When subjects were told to be empathic, they attributed Margaret's behavior more to situational factors than to dispositional factors. These findings, as well as others, lend credence to the idea that empathy helps ease tension between people (Banzai, 1983; Fiske et al., 1979; Galper, 1976; Regan & Totten, 1975; Stephan, 1975; Zucker, Worthington, & Forsyth, 1985).

Defensive Attribution

We can't hear of an accident without asking who is to blame. Consider, for example, the following case.

> Lennie had just bought a car—it was about six years old or so. He and his buddy drove up to Duluth and parked at the top of this hill. Lennie's buddy said Lennie did set the handbrake, but while they were gone the car started rolling. Some campus police who checked the car later said the brake cable was pretty badly rusted and must have broken. Anyway . . . the car really crashed through the window of this store that's right at the bottom. It hit a kid that was standing at the counter and the grocer. The kid was just dazed a little, but the grocer was hurt pretty badly. He was in the hospital all last year. Lennie didn't have any insurance at the time. (Walster, 1966, p. 76)

When the subjects later estimated Lennie's responsibility for the accident on a scale from 1 to 4, they attributed more responsibility to Lennie when the grocer was injured (the version you just read) than when the car happened to be deflected from its deadly course by a stump (Walster, 1966). Other studies obtained the same results, even when the actor's intentions, the foreseeability of the consequences, and the justification for the behavior were held constant (Chaiken & Darley, 1973; Phares & Wilson, 1972; Shaw & Sulzer, 1964).

defensive attribution
The tendency to blame individuals for actions that yield negative outcomes, even when the outcomes were unintended and unforeseeable.

just-world hypothesis
An intuitive assumption that the world is a just place where individuals receive what they deserve.

The tendency to blame individuals for actions that yield negative outcomes—even when the outcomes were unintended, unforeseeable, and accidental—is called **defensive attribution**. This response is a defensive one because, by blaming someone for an accident, observers assure themselves that a similar misfortune won't befall them. The more severe the accident, the "more unpleasant to acknowledge that this is the kind of thing that could happen to anyone" (Walster, 1966, p. 74). Defensive attributions help us insulate ourselves from the anxiety associated with the recognition that catastrophic events cannot always be avoided (see Burger, 1981; Shaver, 1970a, 1970b). We also blame people because we assume that the world is a fair place where people usually get what they deserve (Lerner & Miller, 1978). This **just-world hypothesis** leads us to think that Lennie must have deserved his misfortunes. In fact, we may even assume that the grocer, who was the victim of the accident, was also partly to blame.

Cognitive factors may also prompt us to allocate more blame than we should. Although we recognize that accidents have many causes, we tend to select the most blameworthy act as the prime cause of the accident (Alicke, 1992). A person who wrecks a car while trying to hide a vial of cocaine will be blamed more for the accident than a person who wrecks a car while trying to hide his or her parents' anniversary gift on the floor of the car. Both individuals acted recklessly, but the cocaine user seems more culpable to the social perceiver (Alicke, 1992). The *hindsight bias* also influences attributions of

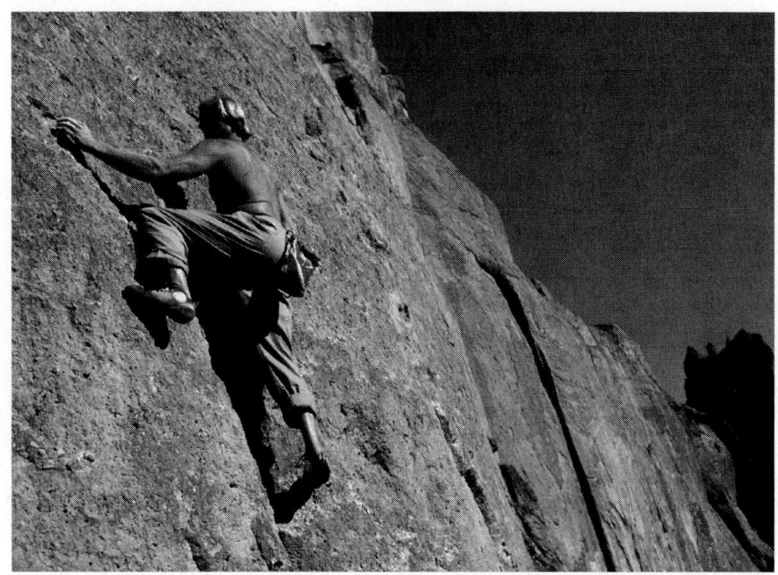

▲ Why would anyone take up rock climbing as a hobby? As observers, we would tend to attribute this climber's behavior to his personal qualities: he must be a risk taker, a daredevil, or a thrill seeker. The rock climber, as the actor, probably explains his actions by citing external, situational causes. He may explain that his roommate talked him into going rock climbing one day and he liked it, or that he does it because it's a good way to stay in shape. Because of the actor-observer difference, observers attribute behavior to internal causes, and actors attribute behavior to external causes.

blame, for once we learn about the negative consequences, we unwittingly increase our estimates of the accident's likelihood. As a result, an unforeseeable accident, when viewed in retrospect, appears to have been foreseeable (Hershey & Baron, 1992; Lipshitz, 1989; Janoff-Bulman, Timko, & Carli, 1985).

blame the victim
The tendency to blame individuals for misfortunes that befall them through no fault of their own.

These biases can prompt us to mistakenly **blame the victims** of crimes and accidents for their misfortunes (Lerner, 1970; Lerner & Miller, 1978). When individuals are told about a woman who complains of sexual harassment, they often assume that the woman contributed to the problem by dressing provocatively or by attempting to work in a setting typically reserved for men. Perceivers even tend to allocate some of the blame to women when they are raped. Such statements as "good girls don't get raped"; "any healthy woman can resist a rapist if she really wants to"; "women ask for it"; and "when a woman cries rape, you can figure she's been jilted or has something to cover up" all shift blame for the crime to the woman (Burt, 1980; McCaul et al., 1990). Women themselves can fall prey to these defensive attributions and blame themselves rather than their assailants when they are sexually harassed or raped. Indeed, one study of college women found that 42% had experienced at least one episode of sexual coercion, yet only 6% of the incidents were reported to authorities (Mynatt & Allgeier, 1990), and surveys of women who have been raped show that women often blame themselves for being attacked (Frazier, 1990; Janoff-Bulman, 1979). Evidence indicates that this bias also operates in the criminal justice system. Because women are assumed to be responsible for rape, they can be made to feel as though they are on trial for the crime (Brownmiller, 1975). When jurors fall prey to this bias, the rapist is less likely to be convicted (Borgida, 1981). These unfair biases conspire to support aggression against women.

Self-Serving Attributions

Each day's social agenda brings us many opportunities to experience the positive side of social life and an equal number of chances to find calamity. Your boss praises your work and gives you a bonus. You get a D on a term paper. You tell a joke at a party, and no one laughs. Your stocks climb. An attractive

▲ When this athlete asks, "Why did I win the race?" his explanation will likely stress internal causes. "I won," he concludes, "because I'm naturally quick and I practiced as much as I could." The losers, by contrast, would be more likely to blame their loss on bad luck, poor track conditions, or the weather. These attributions reflect the self-serving bias: People emphasize internal causes when they succeed and external causes when they fail.

stranger smiles at you suggestively. You discover an overdue library book under a pile of dirty clothes. You wreck your car.

self-serving bias
The general tendency to attribute positive outcomes to personal factors and negative outcomes to external factors.

Naturally, we often identify the causes of our positive and negative experiences. But in doing so, we display a **self-serving bias**: We attribute positive outcomes to internal, personal factors, and blame negative outcomes on external, situational factors. To cite just a few of the hundreds of studies that have documented this tendency:

- Over 60% of the married men and women who have had affairs blame their consort in the affair, claiming he or she pressured them into being unfaithful (Buunk, 1984).
- People seeking advice from newspaper advice columnists tend to blame their problems on the willful behaviors of the other people in their lives (Fischer, Schoeneman, & Rubanowitz, 1987).
- Students tend to emphasize external factors—such as the difficulty of the test or the teacher's ability—after performing poorly on an examination, but they point to internal factors—such as superior ability and effort—when they achieve a high score (Forsyth, 1986; Whitley & Frieze, 1985).
- When explaining wins or losses in professional football games, sports writers, coaches, and players mention internal factors more often after their team wins than after it loses (Gilovich, 1983; Lau, 1984).
- Individuals working in groups often claim personal responsibility for the group's successes, but they deny responsibility when the group fails (Norvell & Forsyth, 1984).
- Clinicians credit their good work when the client responds positively, but blame the client when the therapy session goes poorly (Roberts & McCready, 1987).
- People in unhappy marriages blame their problems on their spouses, but they take credit when things go well (Bradbury & Fincham, 1990; Fincham, Beach, & Baucom, 1987).
- In organizations subordinates blame negative performance appraisals on their bosses, the poor working conditions, or unfair standards, but they credit their own hard work when they receive positive reviews (Giola & Sims, 1985).

▲ Because of the self-serving bias, we prefer to blame our shortcomings and errors on external factors—bad luck, fate, poor conditions, unfair treatment, other people, or even cats.

Drawing by S. Gross; © 1994 The New Yorker Magazine, Inc.

"The cat told me to eat your homework."

• When social psychologists' research reports are rejected by a scientific journal, they tend to blame the rejection on external factors, such as the editor, the availability of journal space, luck, and the reviewers. When their papers are accepted, they credit their effort, the soundness of the research design, and their own ability and training (Crittenden & Wiley, 1985).

Some people are less susceptible to this bias than others. Women are more likely than men to attribute their success to good luck rather than to personal effort or ability (Deaux, 1984; Frieze et al., 1982). Individuals who are depressed or who suffer from chronically low self-esteem tend to take the blame for their failures, but deny responsibility for their successes (Brown, 1991). Cross-cultural research, too, suggests that people in many non-Western cultures respond in different ways to success and failure. Japanese students tend to emphasize the influence of effort in their attributional explanations, irrespective of whether they succeeded or failed (Fletcher & Ward, 1988). Overall, however, the effect is a powerful one, and is probably sustained by a number of interrelated psychological, cognitive, and interpersonal factors (see "In Depth: What Causes the Self-Serving Bias?")

The Illusion of Control

Do you personally play an essential part in creating your own destiny? Are you vulnerable to accidents and catastrophes? Do you regulate your health and happiness? Do illness and sadness sometimes overtake you no matter what steps you take to prevent their occurrence?

The world is a complex and capricious place that sometimes follows its own course in spite of our puny human efforts. Yet most attributors prefer to maintain the illusion that they are in control of their important outcomes (deCharms, 1968; Kelly, 1955; White, 1959). We don't like to think that accidents occur at random, that other people control what happens to us, or that

illusion of control
The intuitive belief that one can exercise control over his or her own outcomes, even when these outcomes are determined by chance.

nothing we do can change our destinies. We prefer, instead, to see ourselves as the controllers rather than the controlled; as agents rather than pawns. Gamblers display this **illusion of control** when they perform various rituals to influence utterly random events, like the roll of the dice or the spin of the roulette wheel (Langer, 1975). Students prefer to attribute their grades to causes they can control; better a lack of effort causes a bad grade than a lack of ability (Forsyth & McMillan, 1981a). And most of us believe that unpredictable negative events, such as heart attacks, layoffs, unwanted pregnancies, car accidents, and alcoholism, won't happen to us (Burger & Palmer, 1992; Whitley & Hern, 1991).

A sense of control, even when unwarranted, serves as a protective buffer against stressful events (Thompson & Spacapan, 1991). People who are exposed to obnoxious, annoying noises but believe they can switch off the noise experience fewer harmful aftereffects—even though they never use the switch (Glass & Singer, 1972). Students who regularly attribute their grades to factors they control are more successful than students who don't think they can control their academic outcomes (Diener & Dweck, 1978, 1980). People paralyzed by accidents who blame themselves rather than uncontrollable events cope

IN DEPTH

What Causes the Self-Serving Bias?

Why do we shrink from failure but embrace our successes? Originally researchers offered a *self-esteem* explanation for this bias. Because failure undermines our sense of self-confidence and self-worth, we seek an external factor that can be blamed for our failure. When we succeed, however, we can bolster our sense of self-worth by attributing this positive outcome to personal factors (Covington, 1992). The self-serving bias thus serves two important self-motives: it helps us avoid responsibility for negative outcomes (self-protection) and allows us to seek credit for positive outcomes (self-enhancement). Indeed, high self-esteem individuals tend to show more self-enhancement, whereas low self-esteem individuals are more concerned with self-protection (Baumeister & Tice, 1985; Baumeister, Tice, & Hutton, 1989; Tice, 1991).

Several bits of evidence lend credence to the self-esteem view. First, the self-serving bias tends to be much stronger when people are working on tasks that are personally important rather than personally unimportant (Greenberg, Pyszczynski, & Solomon, 1982; Weary, 1980). One researcher told subjects that they had failed or succeeded on a task, but he also manipulated the importance of the task: he told some subjects the test was a valid measure of social intelligence and skill and others that the test was an experimental measure with unknown validity. As the self-esteem explanation predicts, people who failed said the task was difficult and that bad luck had influenced their performance—but only when the task was a personally involving one (Miller, 1976). Second, individuals who are encouraged to make external attributions after they fail generally report higher levels of self-esteem and more positive feelings than individuals who are encouraged to make internal attributions (McFarland & Ross, 1982; Mehlman & Snyder, 1985). Third, some individuals who experience problems and hardships but fail to protect themselves through external attributions experience negative aftereffects, such as depression, poorer health, and feelings of helplessness (Follette & Jacobson, 1987; Tennen & Affleck, 1990).

Not all social psychologists, however, accept this self-esteem explanation. Some maintain that the term *self-serving bias* is a misnomer, for the self isn't served by this bias. Instead, they argue, the tendency for us to internalize success and externalize failure is caused by cold cognitive processes rather than hot motivations and needs. This *information-processing* explanation contends that expected outcomes are attributed to stable, personal factors. One researcher divided subjects into two groups: those who expected to succeed, and those who expected to fail. He then gave these two groups puzzles that varied in difficulty, so that half succeeded and half failed. As the information-processing explanation would suggest, expected outcomes, whether positive or negative, were attributed to ability, but unexpected outcomes were attributed to luck (Feather, 1969). Furthermore, in most situations we are very optimistic about success. We expect to pass tests, get good jobs, have long-lasting relationships, and live to a ripe old age rather than fail, get fired, divorce, and die young (Wein-

▲ **TABLE 4-5**
What causes the self-serving attributional bias?

The term *self-serving* suggests that we take credit for success and avoid blame to protect our self-esteem, but evidence suggests that several factors combine to influence our attributions.

Explanation	*Description*
Self-esteem maintenance	People are motivated to maintain and enhance their self-esteem. Because failure undermines our sense of self-confidence and self-worth, we seek an external factor that can be blamed for our failure. When we succeed, however, we can bolster our sense of self-worth by attributing this positive outcome to personal factors.
Information processing	People generally expect to succeed rather than fail, so they attribute success (which they anticipated) to stable, personal factors and failure (which is unexpected) to fluctuating situational conditions.
Social identity	People are motivated by a need to protect their public social identity rather than their private image. Because failures threaten our image of competence, we blame them on external factors. Because successes bolster our public image, we try to take credit for them.

stein, 1980, 1982). Hence, our failures take us by surprise, so we attribute them to external factors (Miller & Ross, 1975; Ross & Sicoly, 1979; Riess & Taylor, 1989).

Yet a third explanation of the self-serving bias has also been offered. This view maintains that most of us hope that others consider us to be competent, successful people rather than incompetent boobs. Failures or blunders threaten this social identity, so we protect our public images by attributing poor performances to external factors and successes to our own personal efforts or abilities. According to this *social identity* explanation, attributional distortions are motivated by a need to protect our public social identities rather than our private images (Backman, 1985; Tetlock, 1985; Weary, 1979).

Considerable empirical evidence supports this explanation as well. First, internalization of success and externalization of failure are greatest when these claims are likely to go unchallenged by others and by future events (Schlenker & Weigold, 1990; Schlenker, Weigold, & Hallam, 1990). If we are in groups, we are less likely to claim all the responsibility for a success when the other group members are around (Miller & Schlenker, 1985), and we make very guarded attributional claims when we must face the same testing situation again in the future (Weary et al., 1982). Second, people often tailor their attributions to fit the norms of the situation. When the situation calls for self-blame, then people usually attribute their failures to themselves rather than trying to convince their audience that they are guiltless (Ames, 1975; Ross, Bierbrauer, & Polly, 1974). Last, when researchers use special measurement methods that force subjects to be as accurate as possible when reporting their attributions, the self-serving bias is reduced (Arkin, Appelman, & Burger, 1980; Riess et al., 1981).

Which one of these three explanations best accounts for the self-serving attributional bias? Most researchers now believe that it would be a mistake to assume that one explanation is clearly superior to the others. Only in rare cases are self-esteem, information processing, and social identity processes mutually exclusive (see Table 4-5). Just because an attribution makes us appear competent to others doesn't mean that it can't also bolster our self-esteem. Hence, in many situations, motivational, cognitive, and interpersonal processes operate jointly to determine our attributions. In addition, different processes may become particularly influential in different social situations. When working on tasks that are central to our self-images, our attributions may be biased by self-esteem motivations. When we need to understand the actual causes of our performance because we will be repeating the task in the future, then rational information-processing mechanisms guide our perceptions. And when our performances are public, we want to make certain that others won't blame us for our failures but will credit us for our successes. As is so often the case in scientific research, the most progress is achieved by synthesizing theories that were once thought to be incompatible rather than continuing to champion one viewpoint over another (Anderson & Slusher, 1986; Leary & Forsyth, 1987; Tetlock & Levi, 1982; Tetlock & Manstead, 1985).

more constructively with their disabilities (Bulman & Wortman, 1977). Patients with cardiac disease, rheumatoid arthritis, and some forms of cancer show greater improvement when they believe they can exert control over the course of their illnesses (Taylor et al., 1991). Rape victims who identify ways to prevent repeated victimization cope better than those who feel no sense of control (Frazier, 1991; Janoff-Bulman & Schwartzberg, 1991). People who routinely locate the cause of their outcomes in factors they personally can control (an internal-locus-of-control orientation) are healthier, happier, and lead more vigorous lives than individuals who believe that external forces determine their outcomes (externals; Lefcourt & Davidson-Katz, 1991). In all these instances, the *perception* of controllability is more important than controllability itself. People who experience a negative event but think they can control it tend to cope effectively with their problems.

Just as feeling in control is a healthy attributional outlook, the loss of this illusion can be devastating. Depression and feeling out of control go hand in hand, particularly when we experience negative outcomes (Brown & Siegel, 1988; Hull & Mendolia, 1991). Failing students, burn victims, cancer patients, the overworked staff of companies, and the elderly all respond more negatively to their plights when they feel they have no control over the cause or course of their difficulties (Boggiano & Katz, 1991; Greenberger et al., 1991; Lachman, 1991). Uncontrollability can lead to feelings of hopelessness, with the result that we cannot identify solutions to our problems or summon up the energy needed to solve them (Snyder, Irving, & Anderson, 1991).

learned helplessness A psychological state that occurs when individuals believe important events in their lives are uncontrollable.

Martin E. P. Seligman explains this reaction in his theory of **learned helplessness** (Abramson, Metalsky, & Alloy, 1989; Burns & Seligman, 1991). Seligman first became interested in maladaptive reactions to stressful events when he was studying learning in dogs. As part of a controlled laboratory study, he trained several dogs to jump over a small partition whenever they received an electric shock. Some of the dogs proved to be extremely difficult to train. Rather than escape the shock by jumping over the barrier, they accepted the

▲ Learned helplessness occurs when people lose their illusion of control.

ZIGGY copyright ZIGGY AND FRIENDS, INC. Dist. by UNIVERSAL PRESS SYNDICATE. Reprinted with permission. All rights reserved.

shock passively. When Seligman investigated further, he found that the dogs had been used in a previous experiment that involved inescapable shock. As a result of this experience, they had apparently learned that shocks couldn't be avoided. They had learned to be helpless (Overmier & Seligman, 1967; Seligman & Maier, 1967).

attributional style An individual's consistent tendency to attribute outcomes and problems to certain types of causes, internal, stable, and global causes.

Seligman suggests that each of us has a particular style of formulating attributions and that some styles are more likely to lead to helplessness than others. Imagine that you have just broken up with your lover or divorced your spouse. As you search for the cause of this negative event, you will tend to focus on different types of causes depending on your **attributional style**. Seligman believes that it is the person who gravitates toward internal, global, and stable causes who is the most likely to become helpless. If you adopted such an attributional style, you would make *internal* attributions when assigning blame for the breakup ("I'm the one who is to blame for everything—it's all my fault"), you would feel that the breakup has *global* implications for your self-esteem ("I'm incapable of doing anything right"), and you would assume that the problem was caused by factors that are so *stable* that it will never improve ("I always mess up relationships; I'm no good at them"). Seligman and his colleagues found that those who adopt a pessimistic attributional style not only blame uncontrollable causes for their problems, but they also experience more depression, are less productive on their jobs, show poorer recovery from illnesses, and die at younger ages than those who adopt a more optimistic attributional outlook (Burns & Seligman, 1991; Zullow et al., 1988).

Adaptive Illusions

Our attributional biases can distort our perceptions of social reality. We misunderstand other people's natures when we fall prey to the fundamental attribution error, and we assume that the innocent are guilty when defensive attribution steers our perceptions. If we externalize all of our failures or insist that we can control the uncontrollable, then we may never recognize our own shortcomings, and we may set goals that we can never achieve (see Table 4-6).

These biases, however, are adaptive in many ways. If we couldn't make inferences about others' personalities and traits, the swirl of interpersonal

▲ Attributions help us overcome negative events. If we were to blame all our failures on our shortcomings and personal limitations, in time we would lose interest in trying to overcome those limitations. But by blaming our failures on external causes, we shield our vulnerable selves from self-doubt and convince ourselves to try again.

▲ **TABLE 4-6**
Summing up: Biases and illusions in the attribution process

Bias	*Description*	*Examples*	*Sustaining Mechanisms*
Fundamental attribution error	Attributing behavior to internal, dispositional factors rather than to external, situational pressures	• A lecturer who forgets to keep an appointment is an "absent-minded professor." • A man assumes that a woman smiles at him because she is attracted to him.	Behavior is perceptually salient; our society stresses the causal impact of personality on behavior; we insufficiently adjust for our natural tendency to formulate dispositional attributions.
Correspondence bias	Assuming that people believe what they say or write, even when their verbal declarations are heavily constrained by the situation	• A teacher who must give a lecture on Freud is thought to believe in Freud's theories. • A person who is told to write an essay encouraging recycling is assumed to be an environmentalist.	Expressions of attitudes are salient; dispositional attributions are automatically formulated when we see someone express an attitude; attributors underestimate the power of social situations.
Actor-observer difference	Assuming that one's own actions are caused by situational factors but attributing other people's actions to dispositional causes.	• The tardy employee blames the heavy traffic, but the boss thinks he or she is irresponsible. • The student thinks her or his failure was caused by the ambiguous test questions, but the teacher attributes it to lack of effort.	Actors view themselves as adapting to fit changing situations; observers have less information about how actors have behaved in other settings; actors and observers have different perspectives.
Defensive attribution	Blaming individuals for accidental, unintended, or unforeseeable outcomes	• Homeless people are blamed for their plight. • A woman who is raped is criticized for dressing in a provocative style.	Observers do not want to admit that accidents can happen to them; we assume that people get what they deserve; post hoc estimates of the likelihood of the accident are inflated.
Self-serving bias	Attributing positive outcomes to internal, personal factors and attributing negative outcomes to external, situational factors	• The failing student blames the confusing textbook. • The award-winning actor credits her acting ability. • The player takes the credit for the team's victory.	People are motivated to protect and maintain their self-esteem; people expect success rather than failure; attributors are motivated to project an image of competence.
Illusion of control	Believing that we can personally control our outcomes	• Gamblers believe they can control the roll of the dice. • Cancer patients think that they can overcome their disease.	Most people are unrealistically optimistic about their future; people cope with problems by convincing themselves they can control them.

events in our lives would leave us baffled and unsure of ourselves. Our attributions make the world more predictable and help us estimate (if somewhat inaccurately) the likelihood of future events. Moreover, and as the section, "Application: Attributions and Health," at the end of the chapter notes, attributions play an important role in helping us overcome negative events. We commonly assume that well-adjusted individuals are objective and accurate when perceiving themselves and the world around them, but these attributional biases and illusions appear to promote mental health. Indeed, when depressed people and nondepressed people's attributions are compared, it is the depressed people who are bias free. They take responsibility for their failures, and they don't exaggerate their control over uncontrollable events (Brown, 1991; Snyder & Higgins, 1988; Taylor & Brown, 1988). Depressive realism about causality and control may be more accurate, but it erodes our ability to cope with the negative experiences that inevitably await us (Alloy & Abramson, 1988). Our attributional biases, then, are *adaptive*: they "help make each individual's world a warmer and more active and beneficent place in which to live" (Taylor & Brown, 1988, p. 205).

Summary

The ability to formulate *attributions* about the causes of behaviors and events is a vital component of social perception, for we must know when others' actions are caused by their personal qualities rather than by outside pressures. In the years since Heider described his "common-sense psychology," other theorists have extended his ideas in several different directions. Jones and Davis's *correspondent inference theory* assumes that we use behavioral data to make inferences only when we feel that the behavior follows from or corresponds to the disposition. Kelley's cube model, in contrast, is based on the *covariation principle*: it assumes that people attribute an effect to the cause with which it covaries over time. Covariance information is drawn from three sources—distinctiveness, consistency, and consensus—but people tend to undervalue consensus information. Weiner's three-dimensional model is based on *locus of causality* (internal-external), *stability* (stable-unstable), and *controllability* (controllable-uncontrollable).

Bem's *self-perception theory* suggests that we also make attributional inferences about our own actions. Consider, for example, the *overjustification effect*: the tendency for increases in *extrinsic motivation* to undermine our *intrinsic motivation.* Children at play, college students, and even highly creative individuals such as poets and artists, when given an extrinsic reason for doing something, often lose their intrinsic interest in the subject. Bem's theory is also consistent with Schachter and Singer's *two-factor theory of emotions.* In their classic study of anger and euphoria, Schachter and Singer found that subjects make attributions about the causes of their physiological reactions before attaching labels to their experiences. Subsequent researchers, expanding on this premise, have also found that arousal caused by one factor can be misattributed to an entirely unrelated factor, and that individuals who only think they are physiologically aroused sometimes experience emotions (the Valins effect). Not all emotions require an attributional search, however. The *facial feedback hypothesis,* for example, argues that the muscles in our faces sometimes directly influence our emotions without any intervening attributional interpretations. In addition, Wegner and Vallacher's *action identification theory* maintains that self-perception is most likely when an action is identified at a low rather than high level of conceptualization. Thus, even though Bem emphasized the impact of behavioral data on our self-perceptions, in many cases we reject behavioral data when they conflict with well-established private self-knowledge.

Several biases systematically distort our causal inferences. When we make attributions about other people, we underestimate how much that person's behavior is influenced by the situation and overestimate the causal influence of dispositional factors. Because of this *fundamental attribution error,* we often assume that people mean what they say, even when their verbal declarations are heavily constrained by their situations (the *correspondence bias*), and observers frequently emphasize personal causes more than actors do (the *actor-observer difference*). Moreover, perceivers also tend to fall prey to *defensive attribution,* for they attribute too much responsibility to people whose actions yield unforeseeable negative consequences. This tendency apparently arises from our intuitive belief in the *just-world hypothesis,* but it can cause us to unfairly *blame the victim* of crimes and other negative events rather than the perpetrator or circumstances. When we make attributions about our own actions and experiences, in contrast, we usually seek out internal causes when outcomes are positive (self-enhancement) and external causes when outcomes are negative (self-protection). This tendency, known as the *self-serving bias,* is probably produced by the need for self-esteem, a tendency to process information logically, and a desire to present oneself in a favorable light. Finally, when we make attributions, we often exaggerate our control over the causes of our outcomes. Although this *illusion of control* is a bias, it is probably adaptive. Individuals who believe they can personally produce and regulate their own outcomes are less likely to experience depression following negative events. As Seligman argues in his theory of *learned helplessness,* people with pessimistic *attributional styles* that stress their inability to control events and outcomes are most likely to suffer a decline in mental and physical health following a stressful event.

For More Information

- *Attribution,* by Gifford Weary, Melinda A. Stanley, and John H. Harvey (1989), is an excellent update of Harvey and Weary's 1981 sourcebook on attribution, and it focuses on applications in clinical, educational, and related settings.
- *Attribution Theory: Applications to Achievement, Mental Health, and Interpersonal Conflict,* edited by Sandra Graham and Valerie S. Folkes (1990), offers many examples of how attribution theory can be applied in educational, business, and mental health settings.
- *Interpersonal Perception,* by Edward E. Jones (1990), illustrates how one well-known social psychologist conceptualized and studied the processes that influence our understanding of other people.
- *Intrinsic Motivation and Self-Determination in Human Behavior,* by Edward L. Deci and Richard M. Ryan (1985), reviews over 200 laboratory and field studies of intrinsic motivation and integrates the findings in a framework based on the concept of self-determination.
- *On Inferring Personal Dispositions from Behavior,* edited by Yaacov Trope and E. Tory Higgins (1993), is a special issue of the *Personality and Social Psychology Bulletin.* The 15 articles in the issue examine a variety of questions concerning the psychological processes that sustain our understanding of others' dispositional characteristics.

• *Perceived Control in Vulnerable Populations,* edited by Shirlynn Spacapan and Suzanne C. Thompson (1991), is an issue of the *Journal of Social Issues* that deals with the impact of control on children, medical patients, employees, and the elderly.

• *The Psychology of Control,* by Ellen J. Langer (1983), collects under one cover Langer's work dealing with perceived control.

• *The Psychology of Interpersonal Relations,* by Fritz Heider (1958), is a classic, a tour de force in theory construction filled with one insightful observation after another.

Application: Attributions and Health

The ache in his chest was painful, so the 55-year-old man decided to go to the emergency room of his local hospital to get checked by a doctor. By the time his name was called, the pains had subsided, but he decided to complete the checkup anyway. Unfortunately, the intern had problems finding an artery when trying to draw blood:

> As the intern persevered in his fruitless endeavor, the patient became apprehensive, concerned about the doctor's competence, and then overwhelmed with a sense of impotence to do anything about his situation. During these several minutes he first felt hot and flushed, his chest pain returned, and then . . . the patient became weak and then suddenly passed out. (Engel, 1978, p. 403)

The patient suffered a stress-induced myocardial infarction, or heart attack. He survived, but his case raises many questions: Did his belief that the incompetent doctor was in control in the situation contribute to his heart attack? Would the outcome have been different if he had attributed his reaction to anger at the doctor rather than to the pain of an oncoming heart attack? Can our psychological interpretations of the causal forces at work in a situation—our attributions—influence our physical well-being?

Attributions provide us with insights into our own and other people's traits and characteristics, but they also influence the general soundness of our physical, mental, and emotional health. Although we tend first to consider physical and biological factors when exploring illness and health, social psychological factors in general—and attributions in particular—can contribute to our well-being as well. Consider, for example, your reactions to **stress**: life circumstances that threaten your sense of well-being and safety. Illnesses, accidents, traumas, frustrations, and the little hassles that pepper your days are unavoidable, but will they undermine your health? Their impact depends, in part, on the processes diagrammed in Figure 4-7. First, when you experience an event, you initially evaluate its impact on you; essentially, you decide whether it is a stressor or not. This stage is termed *primary appraisal.* Next, if you perceive the event to be a threat, then you consider your ability to cope with the event. This stage is termed *secondary appraisal.* Importantly, your reaction during both stages depends on your attributional analysis of the situation (Folkman & Lazarus, 1988; Lazarus & Folkman, 1984; Smith, 1991).

What makes an event seem stressful to us? Clearly, negative events tend to be more stressful: physical injuries, visits to the dentist, and traffic jams are more stressful than birthday parties, watching a good movie, and gentle kisses. Events that are perceived to be uncontrollable or unpredictable, however, also tend to generate stress (Folkman, 1984). Your next-door neighbor's loud music will be particularly irritating if you never know when he'll crank up the volume and he always refuses your requests to tone it down (Glass & Singer, 1972). People who live through natural disasters, such as

stress: Negative physiological, emotional, cognitive, or behavioral responses to circumstances that threaten, or are thought to threaten, one's sense of well-being and safety.

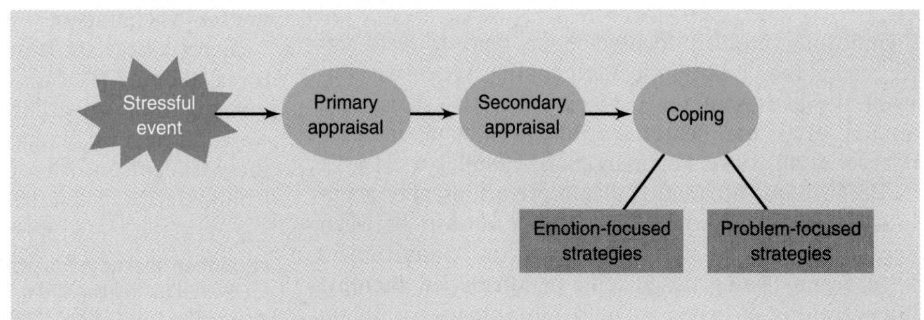

FIGURE 4-7
Can attributions influence your well-being? Your reaction to stressors depends on your perceptions of the nature of the event, your capacity to cope with the event, and the coping strategies you use. (Based on Lazarus, 1991)

tornadoes, hurricanes, and floods, report more stress when they view these events as unpredictable and uncontrollable (Lefcourt & Davidson-Katz, 1991). The likelihood of soldiers' experiencing posttraumatic stress disorder is negatively correlated ($r = -.38$) with their general beliefs about personal control over their outcomes (Solomon, Mikulincer, & Avitzur, 1988). Indeed, even a benign event can generate feelings of stress when predictability and controllability are low. Nursing home residents enjoy visits from their friends, but these visits can become stressful when they occur sporadically and without invitation by the individual being visited (Reich & Zautra, 1991; Schultz & Hanusa, 1978).

Secondary appraisal—the identification of ways to cope with the problem—also depends, in part, on our attributional interpretation of events. When people doubt that they can do much to change the situation they face, they tend to use *emotion-focused coping strategies.* They report using such strategies as the following (paraphrased from Carver, Scheier, & Weintraub, 1989, p. 272):

- I get upset and let my emotions out.
- I refuse to believe that it has happened.
- I give up the attempt to get what I want.
- I admit to myself that I can't deal with it, and quit trying.
- I daydream about things other than this.
- I sleep more than usual.

When people believe they know what is causing their problems, and they think they can control these causes, they tend to use *problem-focused coping strategies.* People in one study, who felt they could do something about the stressful situations they faced, took active steps to solve their problems, spent more energy planning solutions, and often reinterpreted the situation in positive terms. They reported using such strategies as the following:

- I take additional action to try to get rid of the problem.
- I do what has to be done, one step at a time.
- I make a plan of action.
- I think about how I might best handle the problem.
- I look for something good in what is happening.
- I try to grow as a person as a result of the experience.

Significantly, problem-focused coping tends to yield better results than emotion-focused coping. When we confront the causes of the problems directly, stress and anxiety drop, and self-esteem and well-being increase (Carver et al., 1989; Folkman et al., 1986).

Because our attributional interpretations play a significant role in moderating the relationship between negative events and stress, researchers and practitioners have begun testing the benefits of **attribution therapy**: interventions designed to help individuals formulate adaptive causal explanations for their problems. Ellen Langer and Judith Rodin (1976) indirectly modified the attributional outlook of elderly people living in a nursing home by giving them more control over their environment. Langer and Rodin gave the residents of one floor more responsibilities; they were given small plants to care for, and they had to decide for themselves when they would participate in various nursing home activities. Residents on a second floor were given plants, too, but the staff cared for the plants. These residents also took part in various activities, but they were assigned to particular sessions by the staff. Eighteen months later, the residents who were given responsibilities were rated as happier and more active, sociable, and vigorous than the control subjects. Moreover, 30% of the subjects in the control group died during the 18-month period compared to only 15% in the added-responsibility condition (Langer & Rodin, 1976; Rodin & Langer, 1980; see Forsterling, 1985; Murdock & Altmaier, 1991, for reviews).

Attribution therapy has also been used in educational settings. Carol Dweck (1975) identified 12 children who showed extremely maladaptive responses after failure: negative expectations about their performance, performance deficits following negative feedback, and low persistence on difficult tasks. She then trained 6 of these children to attribute their failures to lack of effort rather than lack of ability. For a 25-day period, these students worked on a series of arithmetic problems while the experimenter-teacher watched. The teacher usually told the students they were doing well. Occasionally she told the students they had taken too long to solve the problems before adding "you should have tried harder." The remaining 6 students were exposed exclusively to success feedback; they were never told they had failed or taken too long.

Dweck measured the students' reactions to negative feedback before the experiment, halfway through it, and again at its conclusion by asking them to solve sets of difficult math problems. As she had predicted, when the students in the control group made mistakes on these problems, their persistence evaporated. The students who had been trained to accept failure and overcome it, however, persisted at these difficult problems, and when they did receive failure feedback they attributed their poor performance to lack of effort. These findings lend support to that ever-popular educational maxim "Failure builds character."

Even college students have been helped with attributional therapy (Wilson & Linville, 1982, 1985). In one investigation researchers identified 36 students who were failing a psychology class. They then gave some of these students information that shifted their attributions from external, uncontrollable factors (such as the test's

attribution therapy: Helping individuals cope with stressful life events by training them to formulate attributions that promote healthy psychological functioning.

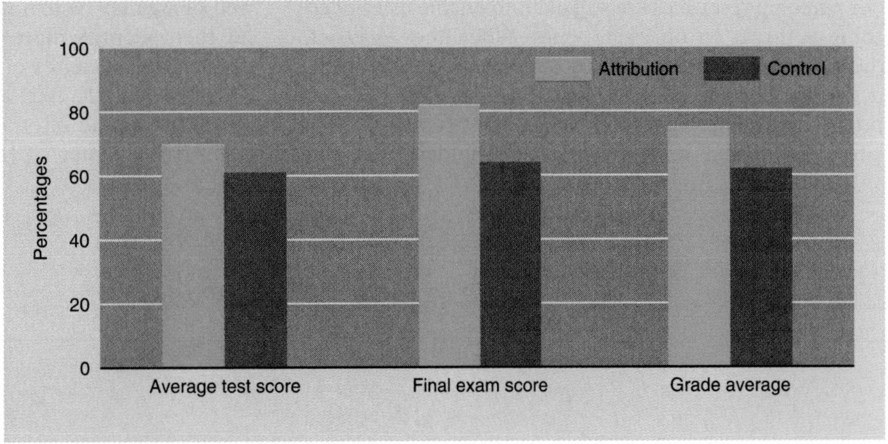

▲ **FIGURE 4-8**
Do attributions help us perform better in achievement settings? When researchers encouraged students to attribute their failures to internal, controllable causes, they earned higher grades than students who received no attributional retraining. (From Noel, Forsyth, & Kelley, 1987)

difficulty) to internal, controllable causes (such as effort and motivation). On subsequent tests and on the final examination, subjects in the experimental condition earned higher grades than control students who received no attributional information. Indeed, at the end of the course the students in the experimental condition earned Cs, but most of the students in the control group received Ds and Fs (see Figure 4-8; Noel, Forsyth, & Kelley, 1987).

Practitioners have also used misattribution to reshape clients' reactions to stressful situations. As noted in Chapter 3, misattribution occurs when an individual attributes arousal caused by one factor to another, unrelated factor. By shifting arousal and tension away from the initial cause to a more controllable cause, the therapist can ease the client's distress. Michael D. Storms uses this technique to help people overcome insomnia. Storms believes insomnia is caused by our tendency to attribute a momentary inability to fall asleep to insomnia. Once we decide we are experiencing insomnia, we become more and more aroused and less and less likely to fall asleep. The more we worry about our insomnia, the worse it gets. Storms calls this escalating attribution process an *exacerbation cycle* and believes that it causes a number of stress-related disorders, including insomnia, stuttering, and impotence (Lowery, Denney, & Storms, 1979; Storms & McCaul, 1976; Storms & Nisbett, 1970; Storms et al., 1979).

Storms uses misattribution processes to interrupt this exacerbation cycle. In a study conducted with Richard Nisbett (1970), he gave mild insomniacs pills to take before retiring. All the pills were inert placebos, but some subjects were led to believe that the pills would relax them; others were told that the pills would increase their physiological arousal. As predicted, the subjects given the "relaxing" pill took longer to fall asleep than the subjects given the "arousing" pill and control subjects given no pills at all. Although these findings seem to conflict with our intuition, they make sense when we consider the insomniacs' attributions. When they expected the pill to relax them but still felt restless, they concluded that their insomnia was particularly bad that evening. Hence the relaxing pill contributed to the exacerbation cycle. When, in contrast, subjects thought they had taken an arousing pill, they misattributed their arousal to the pill. This misattribution broke the exacerbation cycle, and they fell asleep more quickly.

Subsequent studies suggest that this treatment for insomnia doesn't always work, as people sometimes feel more aroused when they think they have taken an arousing pill, and they don't always attribute their arousal to the pill (see Storms et al., 1979, for a review). In consequence, Storms now recommends less threatening misattribution methods for treating insomnia. In one approach, insomniacs are told that their sleep difficulties are caused by their unusually high levels of bodily functioning rather than by stress or maladjustment. Once they realize that their inability to fall asleep is normal, they don't lie in bed worrying about their insomnia. Therefore, the exacerbation cycle is cut short, and they can slowly drop off to sleep.

Storms's work and the other investigations of attributions and adjustment that we've considered all attest to the value of applying social psychology in health-related fields. Social psychology, it seems, is also in large part **health psychology**. Like medical experts, social psychologists search for ways to promote health and adjustment, to improve methods for treating illnesses, and to identify the causes and correlates of health and illness. Rather than focusing on biological causes and cures, social psychologists consider the impact of both personal and interpersonal factors on health. The social-health psychologist assumes that individuals actively react to health problems and stressful events by identifying the causes of their problems, exerting control over their symptoms, or regulating their behaviors to avoid outcomes that are harmful to their health. In many cases,

health psychology: A branch of psychology that studies ways to promote health and adjustment, to improve methods for treating illnesses, and to identify the causes and correlates of health and illness.

our personal resources are sufficient to enable us to overcome a threat to our well-being. When they are not, these personal resources are supplemented by interpersonal sources of information, social support, and professional help. Individuals who consistently formulate attributional interpretations that undermine their well-being may benefit if other people intervene by helping them identify more positive, health-promoting ways of viewing the causes of their problems. To a social psychologist, health, like most processes, is a function of our personal and interpersonal resources, or, in Lewin's terms (see Chapter 1), *Health* = *f*(*Person, Environment*).

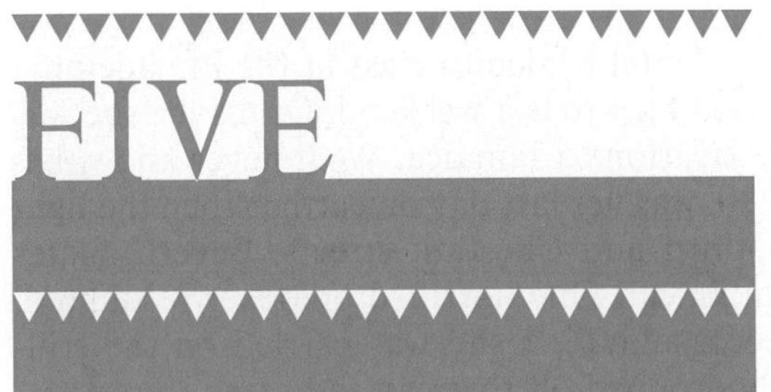

FIVE

The Self

Perhaps she was thinking about her dental hygienics class at the Philadelphia Training School or the chores she didn't get to last weekend. Or maybe she was daydreaming about her upcoming vacation to Jamaica. We'll never know, because Wednesday, February 13, 1980, was her last day on earth. When the light changed at the corner of Twenty-third and Chestnut streets, Beverly Slater stepped into the path of an oncoming car. One horrified onlooker recounted, "All I can remember is that screech sound . . . she was carried on the still-moving car and she was eventually dropped off that car and came to rest . . . just a couple of feet in front of the front end. . . . I thought she was dead" (Slater & Leighton, 1984, p. 143). Her injuries were life-threatening—her skull was cracked, blood oozed from both her ears and nose, and her entire body was bruised and swollen. But, miraculously, she survived the trauma, and after two days in a coma, she gradually regained consciousness.

Tests revealed no permanent physical damage. Slater had complete feeling in her limbs. She could hear, see, and talk. She could move her fingers and toes. But when a nurse asked her, "What is your name?" she replied, "I don't know, what's *your* name?" She had no idea who she was, where she lived and worked, or how she came to be in the hospital. She denied knowing her husband when he visited and told him to get out of her room. She cursed her son when he visited. Her daughter Joanie received a particularly negative reception. When Joanie walked into her mother's room, Slater roared, "Who the hell are you?" Shaken, Joanie answered, "Mother, I'm your child. I'm Joanie. Don't you recognize me?" Slater had no memory at all of Joanie. "Go to hell, bitch" was her only answer (Slater & Leighton, 1984, p. 24).

Slater's case, although atypical, raises questions that apply to all people—whether amnesiac or not. First, exactly what was she missing? In Slater's case, the memories of 48 years of life were gone. Her husband and children were strangers to her. She knew nothing of her own strengths and weaknesses, she didn't know what she liked and disliked, and she didn't recognize her own face in the mirror. She couldn't review her motives, plans, or daydreams or answer such questions as "Who am I?" and "What are my goals in life?" Slater's amnesia took her **self**—her personal conception of who she was. Like most of us, Slater took her sense of self for granted until it was torn from her. Heeding Socrates' advice to "know thyself," we examine the nature of the self in the first section of this chapter.

self
One's sense of personal identity; the individual as viewed by himself or herself.

Slater's case raises a second question. She never regained her memory—her original self never returned. She did, however, develop a new personal identity as she recovered from the accident. The original Slater was a serious career woman who dressed conservatively and doted on her son. The new Slater is more outgoing, emotional, and energetic. The old Slater liked brown and beige; the new Slater prefers reds and yellows. The old Slater enjoyed fine foods and quiet evenings; the new Slater loves to gamble. What was the source of Slater's new self? In answering this question, the second section of this chapter argues that we frequently learn who we are—and alter the way we see ourselves—in the course of interacting with others. The self is, to a surprising degree, a social creation.

Once we consider the nature and source of Slater's new self, one final question remains: How did she sustain her self? At first, each setback—each forgotten name, each personal inconsistency, each failure to understand the world around her—made her question herself and her worth. As she recovered, however, she came to protect her fledgling self. She maintained her self-esteem even when others belittled her or she failed to reach her goals. She maintained her grasp on who she was over time, so that the Slater of today was consistent with the Slater from the week before. As we will see in the final section of this chapter, Slater's self became an unseen party to all her social interactions, and its motives intimately affected her interactions with others.

What Is the Self?

Scholars have pondered the nature of the self for centuries. Plato equated the self with the soul and felt that it was the seat of wisdom. Buddha believed that each of us creates our own sense of personal identity, but this self-understanding is often distorted and incomplete. Descartes traced the self back to our ability to think, Hume equated the self with perceptual experiences, and Kant noted that the self is our view of who we *believe* we are rather than who we *truly* are (Baumeister, 1987; Hattie, 1992).

William James (1892/1961) offered one of the first psychological analyses of the self in his *Principles of Psychology.* He asserted that our sense of self is based on two components. We encounter the qualities and characteristics that we believe we possess when we direct our attention inward. This aspect of self, which James called the *me* or the *known,* is usually called the **self-concept**. However, if the self-concept is that aspect of your self that is perceived, who is doing the perceiving? Obviously, part of you must guide your attention as you search through the contents of the self-concept. James called this aspect of the self the *I* or the *knower,* but contemporary theorists prefer the term **self-awareness** or consciousness (Gordon, 1968; Yates, 1985). In the sections that follow, we examine these two sides of the self.

self-concept
An individual's conception of his or her personal qualities and characteristics. The individual's answer to the question "Who am I?"

self-awareness
The psychological state in which one's attention is focused on one's self, one's personal standards, or one's inner experiences.

Self-Concept

We are, in a sense, historians who are writing and rewriting our own autobiographies (Greenwald, 1980; Greenwald & Pratkanis, 1984). Each time we acquire new information that we feel defines who we are, we store this information in our self-concept: our perception of our enduring personal qualities and characteristics. The self-concept does not necessarily describe our true characteristics, but it does summarize and organize our *assumptions* about our qualities (McGuire & McGuire, 1988; Rosenberg, 1979, 1986).

Self-concepts, like snowflakes, are unique; no two people define themselves in exactly the same way. Common themes, however, tend to recur when people are asked to describe themselves in their own words. Consider these examples.

▲ **TABLE 5-1**
Five themes often found in people's answers to the question "Who am I?"

Type of Attribute	*Contents*	*Examples*
Physical qualities	Personal attributes, such as hair color, height, weight, strength, physical beauty, and overall body image.	I have red hair. I weigh too much. I am very tall.
Demographic qualities	Membership in general social categories based on such qualities as sex, age, race, nationality, social status, and religion.	I am a black woman. I come from a wealthy family. I am a Baptist.
Roles and group memberships	Function and position in social relationships, including family, occupation, educational roles, and membership in interacting groups.	I am a father. I am a student. I am on the football team.
Traits and core beliefs	Dispositional qualities, personality characteristics, and ideological beliefs.	I am very shy. I am moody. I never tell lies.
Interests and activities	General preferences and orientations, including tastes, likes and dislikes, recreational activities, and hobbies.	I enjoy baseball. I love social psychology. I am interested in literature.

> *Nine-year-old*: I have dark brown hair, brown eyes, and a fair face. I am a quick worker but often lazy. I am good but often cheeky and naughty. My character is sometimes funny and sometimes serious. My behavior is sometimes silly and stupid and often good. It is often funny, my daddy thinks. (Livesley & Bromley, 1973, pp. 237–238)
>
> *Lyndon Johnson, former U.S. president*: I am a free man, an American, a United States Senator and a Democrat, in that order. I am also a liberal, a conservative, a Texan, a taxpayer, a rancher, a businessman, a consumer, a parent, a voter, and not as young as I used to be nor as old as I expect to be—and I am all those things in no fixed order. (quoted in Gordon, 1968, p. 123)
>
> *College senior*: I am a woman of average intelligence. I am a college student now, but will be graduating soon. When I finish school, I will be getting a job and getting married. I am a psychology major, but I am pretty disgusted with the university. I am tired of being tied to my mother's apron strings. (adapted from Kuhn, 1960, p. 42)
>
> *Beverly Slater*: Who am I? I'm afraid to find out. The new Beverly loves playing craps at the casino. . . . The new Bev says whatever is on her mind, no matter how outrageous. . . . To the new Bev, there are no strangers. (Slater & Leighton, 1984, p. 243)

Despite their divergent self-concepts, these individuals mention similar kinds of characteristics in their answers to the question "Who am I?" (See Table 5-1.) They allude to *physical qualities* that they personally feel are important, such as their height, weight, strength, and physical appearance ("I have dark brown hair, brown eyes, and a fair face"). They also refer to *demographic qualities* that place them in social categories. The politician refers both to his sex ("a free man") and his nationality ("an American"), and the college senior mentions that she is a woman. The self-concept also includes social *roles and memberships,* for we often view ourselves in terms of the function and position we occupy in social relationships and groups; the 9-year-old refers to her father, assigning herself the role of daughter, and the college student refers to many

▲ When children and adults answer the question "Who am I?" they usually mention their names ("My name is Ted"), physical qualities ("I'm 11"), demographic qualities ("I live in Richmond"), roles and memberships ("I go to Carver School"), traits and beliefs ("I make friends easily"), and interests and activities ("I like to swim"). In addition, as the distinctiveness postulate suggests, they tend to mention qualities that set them apart from others. According to this postulate, the boy on the left should therefore be more likely to mention his race when he describes himself.

roles: psychology major, daughter, wife. These people also mention their perceptions of their relatively enduring personality *traits and beliefs.* The 9-year-old confesses she is often lazy; the college student describes herself as average in intelligence; and Slater stresses her friendliness. These self-views may not correspond to their actual personality characteristics. The 9-year-old may be a very hard worker and Slater may be unfriendly, but in their own eyes they are lazy and friendly, respectively. *Interests and activities* are also included in the self-concept, for we often define ourselves in terms of our likes, dislikes, and the activities we remember doing in the past. Slater, in particular, defines herself in terms of her likes and dislikes, as did the college student when she said, "I am disgusted with the university" (Kuhn, 1960; Kuhn & McPartland, 1954; Rosenberg, 1979).

The working self-concept. You do not always give the same answer to the question "Who am I?" because only a portion of the self can be cognitively accessed at any given time. You have, after all, been collecting information about yourself for many years, so your **working self-concept** includes only the attributes that are activated by the current social situation (Markus & Kunda, 1986; Markus & Nurius, 1986).

working self-concept
The aspects of the self-concept that are currently available in active memory.

William J. and Claire V. McGuire believe that the working self-concept usually includes your more uncommon characteristics. They asked children to describe themselves using whatever words came to mind. As they expected, the children stressed qualities that set them apart from the people around them. Overweight or underweight children mentioned their size. If they were born in another state, they mentioned their birthplace. Members of racial minorities (either African-Americans or Hispanic) mentioned their race. Boys living in female-majority homes and girls living in male-majority homes mentioned their sex more frequently (see Figure 5-1).

The McGuires summarize their findings in the *distinctiveness postulate*: "A given trait is salient in a person's self-concept to the extent that this trait is distinctive for the person within her or his social groups" (McGuire & Padawer-Singer, 1976, p. 743; McGuire & McGuire, 1988). This postulate reaffirms the social nature of the self. Your self-concept stores a vast array of

▲ **FIGURE 5-1**
Do we stress our relatively unique qualities when we answer the question "Who am I?" Children living in households where they were outnumbered by members of the opposite sex were more likely to mention their biological sex in the self-descriptions. In male-majority households, more girls than boys mentioned their sex when they described themselves. In female-majority households it was boys who tended to mention their sex. (Based on McGuire, McGuire, & Winton, 1979)

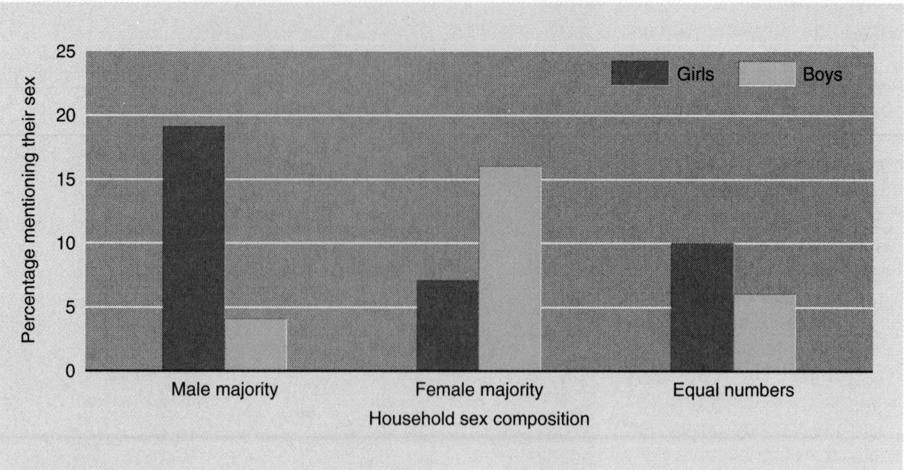

information about your experiences and social relationships. However, qualities that set you apart from other people tend to be more salient than your more ordinary attributes. Thus we are all a bit like Gulliver, who felt very tall when he was in the land of the Lilliputians but very short when he was surrounded by the giants of Brobdingnag.

Self-schemas. The self-concept does more than just catalog all your attributes; it also organizes them. Former U.S. President Lyndon Johnson's self-concept was organized around a political theme: He was a Democrat, a conservative, and a senator rather than strong, brusque, or a father. Similarly, openness lay at the heart of Slater's emerging self-concept. She knew she was a mother, that she was a college graduate, and that she had many friends, but the first thing that came to her mind when she thought of herself was her candidness: "The new Bev says whatever is on her mind, no matter how outrageous." The self-concept is not a disorganized jumble of qualities; instead, it is organized around **self-schemas**: "cognitive generalizations about the self, derived from past experience, that organize and guide the processing of self-related information contained in the individual's social experiences" (Markus, 1977, p. 64; Breckler, Pratkanis, & McCann, 1991; Higgins, Van Hook, & Dorfman, 1988).

self-schemas
A network of cognitive associations that integrate one's most important personal characteristics and qualities.

As noted in Chapter 3, self-schemas seem to organize self-knowledge in a system of cognitive associations or networks. These networks consist of memory nodes pertaining to specific self-relevant concepts and pathways that link these nodes to one another (Collins & Loftus, 1975). Consider the portion of a hypothetical self shown in Figure 5-2. The figure suggests that this individual has many pieces of self-information stored in her self-concept, but only some qualities are connected directly to the self. She knows that she graduated from college and is a teacher, but these attributes are linked to the self through the more central attribute, "intelligent." Similarly, several qualities ("caring" and "gentle") are connected to the more general concept, "feminine," which in turn is connected to the self via an even more general concept—woman. Accordingly, "intelligent" and "woman" are both *schematic* self-qualities because they are embedded in an organized, well-elaborated system of interrelated attributes. Qualities such as "forgetful" or "likes flowers" are *aschematic* qualities. Although they are recognized as part of the self, these peripheral elements

▲ **FIGURE 5-2**
How is information organized in the self-concept? Self-information seems to be organized into distinct clusters, or schemas, that pertain to specific domains. In this model of a portion of a hypothetical self-schema, the ovals correspond to various memory nodes containing information about the self; inter-connections between these elements are represented by lines between the ovals. Only ovals that are directly linked to the self (oval in the center of the figure) are schematic attributes.

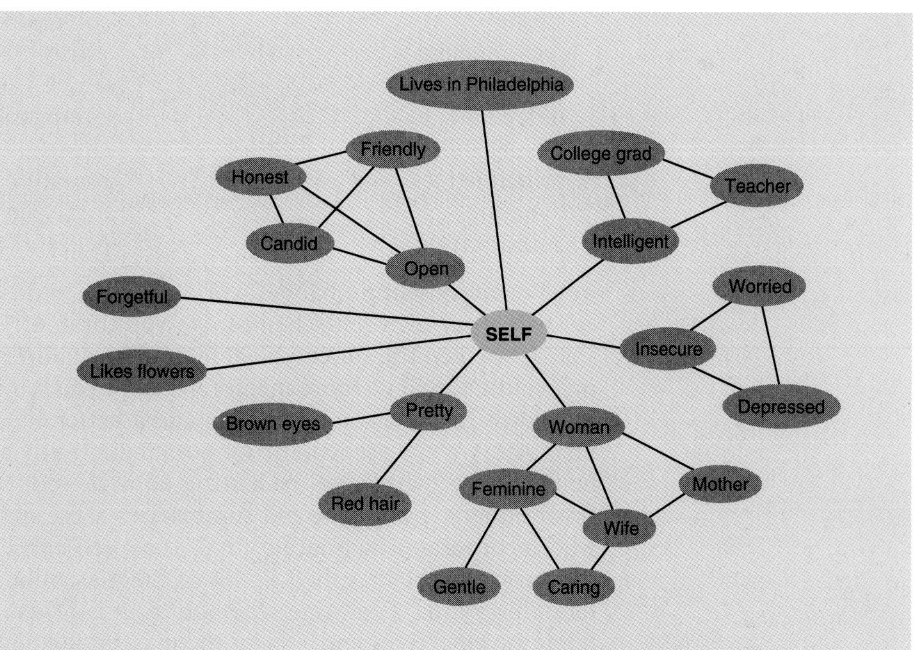

aren't associated with any other aspects of the self (Cantor & Kihlstrom, 1987; Kihlstrom et al., 1988; Markus, Smith, & Moreland, 1985).

How can you tell whether one of your attributes functions as a self-schema? In general, your schematic qualities are well articulated. You may consider yourself to be a "liberal," but if your political views are only peripheral elements in your self-concept, then you might not be able to give a very elaborate description of your politics. Schematic liberals, in contrast, will have a plethora of political knowledge that they actively maintain (Fiske, Lau, & Smith, 1990). Your schematic qualities are also the ones you think are central to your self-concept. You might be a student, you might be shy, and you might like jazz, but if you don't think these qualities are particularly important ones, then they probably aren't self-schemas (Fiske & Taylor, 1991; compare with Burke, Kraut, & Dworkin, 1984; Nystedt, Smari, & Boman, 1991). You can also identify your schematic qualities rapidly and confidently (Markus, 1977). People who think of themselves as exercisers describe themselves with words and phrases related to exercising, and they take less time to make such judgments. People who exercise regularly but don't define themselves as exercisers, use fewer exercise-related adjectives and respond more slowly (Kendzierski, 1990). Similarly, people who underscore their "feminine" attributes in their self-concepts (feminine schematics) require less time when they are asked to rate themselves on "feminine" adjectives (for example, *soft-spoken, gentle*) rather than "masculine" adjectives (for example, *ambitious, takes a stand*). Masculine schematics show the reverse tendency, and individuals who are aschematic on both masculinity and femininity respond with equal rapidity and confidence to both sets of adjectives (Markus et al., 1982; Forbach, Evans, & Bodine, 1986).

The self-reference effect. Self-schemas not only structure our self-knowledge, they also facilitate the encoding and retrieval of this information. Will you remember any of these words five minutes from now (Tzuriel, 1984, p. 445)?

strong	soft-spoken
self-sufficient	warm
dominant	gentle
independent	compassionate
courageous	cheerful
principled	romantic
dynamic	forgiving
authoritative	peaceful

Your memory will probably favor any of the words in the list that are congruent with your own self-schemas. Do you think of yourself as a masculine person? If so, then the stereotypical masculine qualities on the list (all items in the first column) will be more memorable. Are you feminine-schematic? If so, then the words in the second column stand a better chance of being lodged in your memory. Are you aschematic for both masculinity and femininity? In this case, neither set of words will be associated with your self, so your memory won't favor either type. Figure 5-3 summarizes these differences. When individuals who incorporated masculinity into their self-concepts completed this kind of memory test, they recalled 17.1% of the masculine words but only 13% of the feminine words. Feminine schematics, in contrast, remembered 19.5% of the feminine adjectives and 13% of the masculine adjectives. Aschematic individuals, in contrast, remembered 15% of the masculine adjectives and 16% of the feminine adjectives (Markus et al., 1982).

self-reference effect
The tendency for people to show superior memory for information that pertains to their self-schemas.

Researchers now believe that several cognitive processes act in concert to produce this **self-reference effect** (Higgins & Bargh, 1987; Kihlstrom et al., 1988; Klein, Loftus, & Burton, 1989). First, level-of-processing theory maintains that self-referent information is processed at a deeper level than non-self-referent information. If, for example, you were asked "Does the word *strong* contain fewer than three letters?" you could respond without processing the word very deeply. You would need to consider only the word's appearance rather than its meaning. Such shallow processing wouldn't lead to particularly durable memories. In contrast, the question "Does the word *strong* mean the same as *powerful*?" would require deeper processing, for you would need to think about the relationship between the word and other concepts in your semantic network. Such semantic encoding improves memory for the word

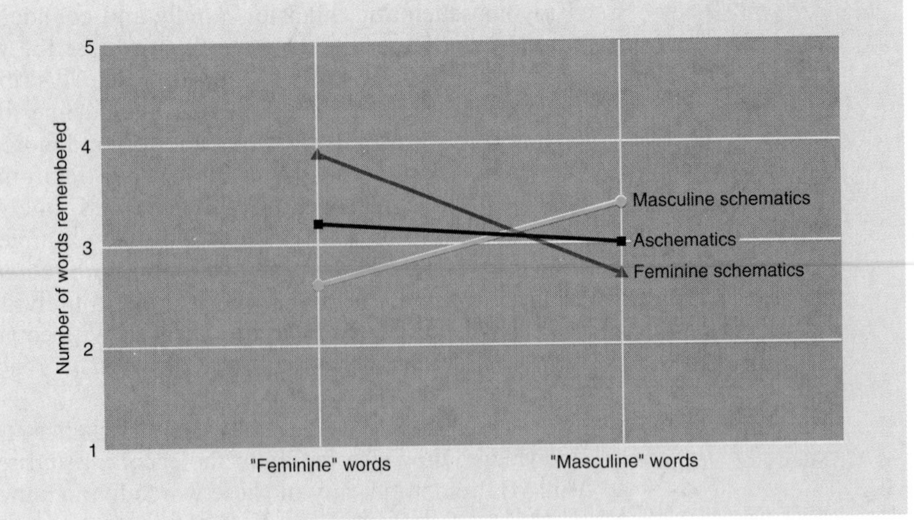

▲ **FIGURE 5-3**
Do self-schemas influence what we see and remember? When researchers asked subjects to rate themselves on a series of adjectives, some people described themselves in mostly "masculine" terms (masculine schematics); others used mostly "feminine" descriptors (feminine schematics). Still others, who showed no preference, were labeled *aschematic.* When subjects were later asked to recall the adjectives, they could remember more of the words that matched their self-schemas. Aschematics remembered masculine and feminine words equally well. (Data from Markus et al., 1982)

▲ The self-reference effect (in dogs). We are more likely to notice and remember things that are related in some way to our self-schemas.

The Far Side cartoon by Gary Larson is reprinted by permission of Chronicle Features, San Francisco, CA. All rights reserved.

but not as much as self-referent encoding. When subjects were asked questions such as "Does the word *nice* mean *pleasant*?" they remembered 13% of the words they had rated, but when they were asked "Does the word *nice* describe you?" they remembered 27% of the words (Klein & Kihlstrom, 1986). Self-referent processing is deep processing.

Second, schema theories of memory suggest that the more elaborate the schema that will hold the incoming information, the better our ability to recall that information later. Since self-schemas may be the most complex and intricate associative networks in our memory systems, self-referent information is particularly memorable. One researcher illustrated the memory benefits of complex schemas by asking individuals to rate the former news anchor Walter Cronkite on a series of adjectives (friendly, ambitious, and orderly). When they finished their ratings, he asked them to list as many of the adjectives as they could remember. On average, subjects recalled fewer than 20% of the items. In comparison, when subjects used the adjectives to rate their fathers, their recall scores averaged nearly 25%, and when they rated themselves, they remembered over 31% of the items (Lord, 1980). The father schema was probably more elaborate than the Cronkite schema, so it improved memory to some extent. When the most elaborate schema was used—that pertaining to the self—memories were most durable (Prentice, 1990).

Self-Awareness

When the nurse asked Slater, "Who are you?" Slater turned her attention inward to concentrate on the contents of her self. In that instant she became aware of herself as an object and could monitor her thoughts, review her attributes, and describe her emotions and sensations. This inner search yielded little information about her past experiences, but it did reveal her pain, confusion, and anger. Slater had lost her self-concept, but she had not lost her capac-

▲ Is *Homo sapiens* the only self-aware species—the only animals capable of focusing their attention on their inner states, of pondering meanings and interpretations, of recognizing their image in a mirror? Researchers have found evidence of some self-awareness in chimpanzees, orangutans, and gorillas.

ity for self-awareness (Carver & Scheier, 1990, 1991; Duval & Wicklund, 1972).

Self-recognition. Self-awareness is one of our most unique qualities. Indeed, Slater's doctors feared she had lost this ability until one day she demanded a mirror. Looking into the glass, she saw her features as if for the first time; nonetheless, she knew that she was seeing herself. She displayed self-recognition.

Gordon G. Gallup, Jr. (1977, 1991) believes that self-awareness cannot exist unless the individual is capable of self-recognition. When we look at our reflections in mirrors or see our images in pictures, we realize that the images we see are our own. Most other animals, in contrast, react as though images of themselves were members of their species. Rhesus monkeys, for example, can't be trained to use a mirror for self-examination. When they see their images, they respond socially—they grimace, vocalize, posture, and stare at their own images just as they would when they confront another monkey. They do not recognize their own images, because they have no awareness of themselves as objects. As Gallup points out, "an organism that can recognize itself is one that can also conceive of itself" (1991, p. 123).

Humans, however, are not the sole possessors of self-awareness. When Gallup tested chimpanzees for mirror self-recognition, they initially acted as though they were seeing other chimpanzees. Over the course of several days, however, the chimps seemed to realize that they were seeing their own images in the mirror. As Figure 5-4 indicates, over a ten-day period the number of social responses dwindled, and self-directed responses increased dramatically. The chimps stopped greeting their images and began to use the mirror to gain information about parts of their bodies they couldn't directly observe; they would stare into the mirror, picking bits of food from between their teeth, blowing bubbles, and making faces for their own amusement.

Gallup then took the test one step further. He anesthetized the chimps and painted one eyebrow and one ear with bright red, odorless, nonirritating dye. When the chimps awoke in a room with a mirror, they engaged in spontaneous self-examination. The painted chimps touched and rubbed their dyed ears and

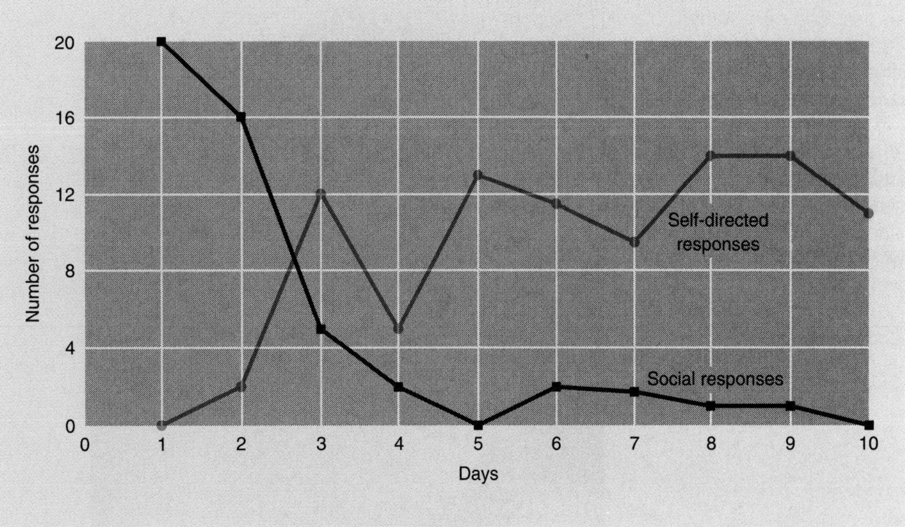

▲ **FIGURE 5-4**
Are chimpanzees capable of self-awareness? When Gallup tallied the number of social responses (greeting the mirror image as if it were another chimp) and self-directed responses (using the mirror for self-examination) over ten days, he discovered that social responses decreased steadily, while self-examination increased dramatically. (From Gallup, 1977)

brows and rubbed the spots to see whether the dye rubbed off on their fingers. Chimps who had never been exposed to mirrors, and whose ears and brows had been similarly dyed, didn't even notice the marks.

At present, researchers have verified self-recognition in only the great apes—*Homo sapiens,* chimpanzees, orangutans, and some gorillas. Other species can use mirrors in limited ways, but they do not seem to recognize their reflections as their own images. Gallup admits that porpoises may also be self-aware, but he has yet to devise a way of testing them (Gallup, 1977; see also Epstein & Koerner, 1986; Povinelli, 1993).

Seeking the self. Even though you are capable of self-awareness, your self doesn't always occupy center stage. When your attention is drawn to the environment—a clock ticking across the room, a radio playing in the distance, or the words on this page—then your self-awareness dwindles (Wicklund, 1975, 1978). If, however, something in your immediate environment reminds you of your individuality—a camera, a mirror, a tape recorder, or an observer—then you become more self-focused. In class, you will probably become self-aware when the instructor asks you a question, and all the other students turn in your direction (Leary & Meadows, 1991). If you are a member of a small group submerged in a large group, then your self-awareness will increase (Mullen, 1986a, 1987b). And in the library you will surely become self-focused if a photographer asks you to pose for a picture (Carver & Scheier, 1991).

Self-awareness also varies from one person to another. Do you tend to

- try to figure yourself out?
- reflect about yourself a lot?
- constantly examine your motives?
- feel concerned about the way you present yourself to others?
- feel self-conscious about the way you look?
- worry about making a good impression?

self-consciousness
The dispositional tendency to be in a state of self-awareness; individuals who are high in self-consciousness tend to be more self-focused across all situations.

If you do, your overall level of self-awareness may be higher than most people's. The dispositional tendency to be self-aware is generally called **self-consciousness** to distinguish it from self-awareness brought about by situational factors (Fenigstein, Scheier, & Buss, 1975).

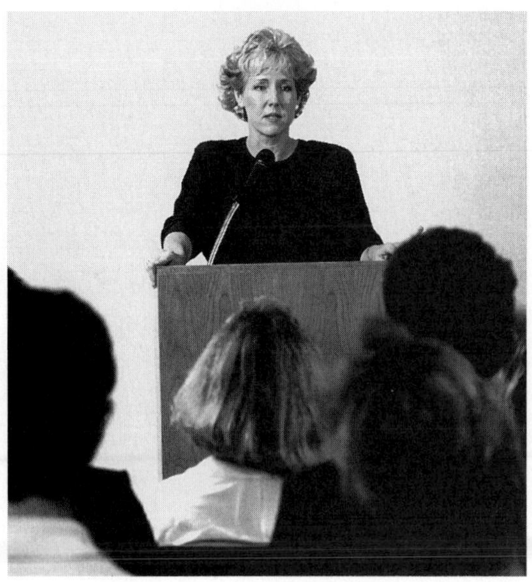

▲ Self-awareness varies across settings. When our attention is focused on the situation, our personal qualities, motives, and thoughts may fade into the background. But when something in the situation reminds us of our self—for example, when we stand before a group of people who are watching us closely—we will probably become extremely aware of our self (and our self's shortcomings).

When your attention is focused on the environment, the self is like a radio with the volume turned down. Even if you can hear the music, you can't make out the words or recognize the songs. But when you are self-aware, your inner radio plays loudly (Pyszczynski et al., 1991). As a consequence, you can access information stored in your self-schemas more rapidly and efficiently. Self-aware individuals describe themselves more elaborately, and they don't take as long to decide whether a particular adjective does or does not describe them (Turner, 1978). Self-awareness can also enhance the accuracy of our recall. Did you, for example, take the SAT test? Do you remember your score? When researchers asked undergraduate men about their scores, most of them remembered scoring higher than they actually did. The average discrepancy between actual score and self-reported score was about 50 points. If, however, subjects sat in front of a mirror when they reported their scores, the discrepancy dropped to a mere 16 points (Pryor et al., 1977).

Self-awareness also intensifies emotional experiences. When people who were already in a good mood rated their emotions while seated in front of a mirror, their self-ratings were more positive than when they were seated in front of a blank wall. In contrast, as Figure 5-5 indicates, people in bad moods became even more negative. Moreover, people who were high in self-consciousness reacted just as subjects sitting before a mirror did, but subjects who were low in self-consciousness were more similar to the subjects seated in front of a wall. A self-aware person, then, might be a happier person, but a self-aware person might also be a much sadder person: annoyance turns to anger, and worry becomes anxiety when we are self-aware (Scheier & Carver, 1977).

Regulating the self. When we encounter our selves, we aren't always pleasantly surprised by what we find. We may want to think that we are brilliant, wealthy, and popular, but when we review our week's exploits, they may include a failed examination, a bounced check, and a lonely Friday night. When our self-concepts are discrepant with our images of who we would like to be—the *ideal self*—we experience dejection and guilt (Higgins, 1987, 1989; Higgins & Tykocinski, 1992; Newman, Higgins, & Vookles, 1992).

▲ **FIGURE 5-5**
Is self-awareness positive or negative? When subjects who were already in a good mood sat before a mirror, they experienced more positive emotions. Subjects in a bad mood, in contrast, felt more negative. Similar effects held when subjects who were low in self-consciousness were compared to those who were high in self-consciousness. These results suggest that self-awareness is neither positive nor negative; rather, it intensifies the emotions we are currently experiencing. (Adapted from Scheier & Carver, 1977)

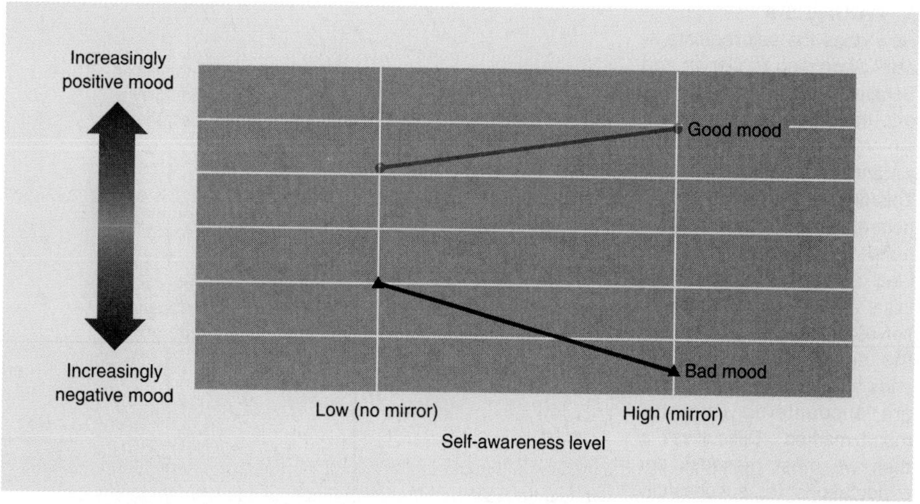

Evidence indicates that our awareness of a discrepancy between our selves and ideal selves provides a foundation for self-regulation: the ability to modify one's behavior so that it more closely matches a relevant standard (Higgins, 1987; Karoly, 1993; Markus & Nurius, 1986). Charles S. Carver and Michael F. Scheier, in their **self-regulation theory**, liken this self-regulation process to the thermostat in a heating system. A thermostat compares the temperature in the room to the temperature setting you have selected. If the temperature in the room drops too low, then the thermostat turns on the furnace that supplies heat. The thermostat continues to compare the ambient temperature to the setting, and when the two match it switches off the furnace. Carver and Scheier propose that self-awareness sets in motion a similar kind of adjustment process (see Figure 5-6). Slater, for example, had a strong need for other people to like her and accept her, but she was often very blunt. She wouldn't hesitate to tell a friend that her dress was an ugly color or to ask about matters that were very personal. Each time she erred, however, the incipient increase in self-awareness prompted her to compare her behaviors to her standards. When she discovered a discrepancy, she tried to reduce it by changing her behavior (Carver & Scheier, 1981, 1991).

self-regulation theory
A conceptual model that describes the psychological processes that allow individuals to reduce discrepancies between their actions and their behavioral standards or goals.

Self-regulation, however, is not always easily accomplished. Students strive for all As but get Bs. Dieters order high-calorie desserts. The well-meaning Slater unintentionally insults her best friend. Carver and Scheier's model indicates that when we experience problems with self-regulation, we usually react by reevaluating our expectations. "Can I ever make the Dean's List?" we may wonder, or we ask ourselves "Have I set my weight-loss goals so high that I will never reach them?" As Figure 5-6 indicates, if we remain confident, this reevaluation changes little. We remain self-aware and continue trying to reduce the discrepancy between our goals and our actual outcomes. If, however, we question our ability to reach our goals, then we may "disengage from the attempt." We give up.

The decision to persist or relent hinges, in large part, on our overall expectations for successful regulation (Duval, Duval, & Mulilis, 1992). Individuals who are high in **optimism**, for example, are likely to view their setbacks as challenges rather than threats. They don't respond negatively to their problems, but instead focus their efforts on identifying ways to achieve their goals and solve their problems. Pessimistic individuals, in contrast, lose their confidence when they face a challenge. They are more likely to deny their difficul-

optimism
The degree to which individuals tend to see discrepancies between their goals and their current actions as challenges that can be overcome rather than as threats.

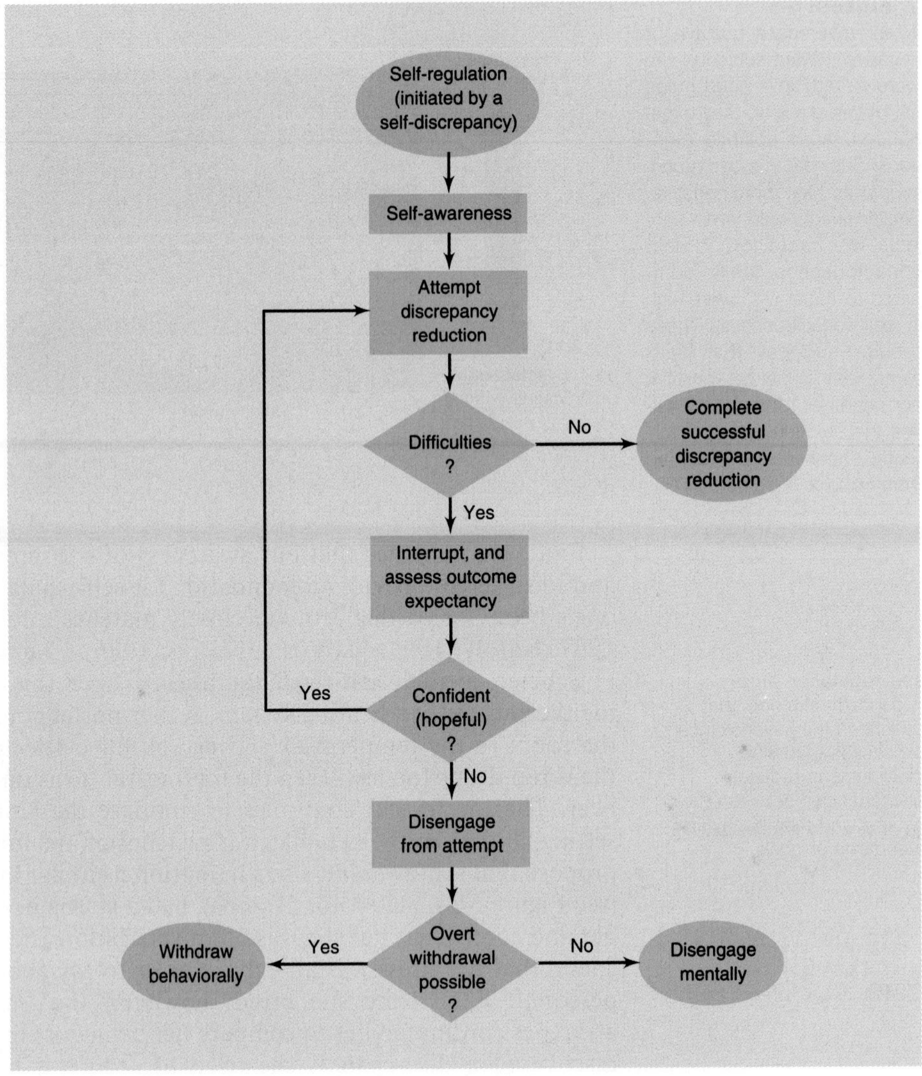

▲ **FIGURE 5-6**
How does the self regulate itself? According to Carver and Scheier's self-regulation theory, the process begins when we act in ways that are inconsistent with our ideal selves. This discrepancy leads to self-awareness and an initial attempt to reduce the actual-ideal self-discrepancy. If this initial attempt successfully resolves the discrepancy, then the self-regulation process ends successfully. If problems are encountered (the diamond marked "Difficulties?"), then we must reassess our expectations for successfully resolving the discrepancy. If we are confident that the problems will be overcome, then we loop back to the discrepancy-reduction box. If we are not confident, then we disengage from the attempt at self-regulation and withdraw either behaviorally or mentally. (From Scheier & Carver, 1988)

ties, focus on their negative feelings, and fail to find alternative ways to overcome obstacles (Carver & Scheier, 1991; Snyder, Irving, & Anderson, 1991). Is it any wonder optimistic individuals persevere longer after failure (Scheier, Weintraub, & Carver, 1986), remain abstinent after completing a treatment program for alcoholism (Strack, Carver, & Blaney, 1987), and recover more completely following major surgery (Scheier et al., 1989). Pessimists, in contrast, react by disengaging—from the situation and even from themselves. When pessimistic people who are very self-aware experience failures and other negative outcomes, they often respond by escaping from the immediate situation (Duval & Wicklund, 1972). Alternatively, they may cope by shifting their focus of attention away from themselves. They may go to the movies, watch TV, or sleep to get their mind off their problems rather than try to solve them (Carver et al., 1989; Scheier & Carver, 1993).

Escaping the Self

Without self-awareness you could never gain access to your self-concept. You would never know who you were, and you would have difficulty regulating your behavior, for you wouldn't know what your personal standards were or what goals you wanted to seek (see Table 5-2). A sense of self may be vital to your psychological well-being, for it may serve to buffer you from such existential worries as "What is the meaning of life?" and "Is there life after death?" (Solomon, Greenberg, & Pyszczynski, 1991).

A sense of self can, however, be a burden as well as a boon. Evidence suggests that the profoundly negative emotions of depressed people may stem, in part, from self-awareness. Because self-awareness polarizes reactions to outcomes, most people avoid self-awareness when they fail a task or are given negative feedback about themselves. Depressed people, in contrast, tend to engage in *depressive self-focusing*; instead of avoiding the self, they maintain a high level of self-awareness that prompts them to dwell on their shortcomings and limitations. This inability to escape from self-awareness may contribute to their dysfunction (Ingram, 1990, 1991; Pyszczynski et al., 1991).

More extreme forms of self-injurious behavior, such as alcohol abuse, suicide, masochism, and eating disorders like bulimia, may also reflect the need to escape from oneself (Baumeister, 1989, 1990a, 1990b, 1991; Heatherton & Baumeister, 1991). Roy Baumeister's (1990) study of suicide, for example, argues that some people take their own lives because they want to "unmake the self." He notes that suicide is more prevalent among individuals who set high standards for themselves or who live with people who expect a great deal of them. Although they may struggle with the discrepancy between the self and ideal self for years, a significant adverse event—divorce, job loss, financial ruin, or illness—may undermine all their efforts. Baumeister theorizes that suicidal individuals take all the blame for their failures and in doing so experience a number of negative psychological consequences: Their emotions become extremely negative, they avoid self-awareness at all costs, and they stop trying to make sense of their life circumstances. In this confused state, the oblivion of death seems comforting rather than terrifying.

The Social Self

Beverly Slater's doctors hoped that her memory would come back when she returned to her home. It did not. She retained her capacity for self-awareness,

TABLE 5-2
Summing up: The cognitive foundations of a sense of self

Element or Process	*Characteristics*
Self-concept	Individuals' perceptions of their enduring personal qualities and characteristics, including physical and demographic qualities, roles and memberships, and traits, beliefs, interests, and activities.
Self-schema	A network of cognitive associations that organize self-related information.
Self-reference effect	The tendency for individuals to show superior memory for information that pertains to their self-schemas.
Self-awareness	The psychological state in which one's attention is focused on the self, personal standards, or inner experiences.
Self-consciousness	The dispositional tendency to be self-aware. People who are high in self-consciousness tend to be more self-focused across situations.
Self-regulation	The cognitive process responsible for monitoring and maximizing the degree of fit between the actual self and the ideal self.

but because she had no self-concept, she could find no answer to the question "Who am I?" Looking at her wardrobe, she wondered why her clothes were so colorless. When her husband pointed out that she had selected all of her clothes herself, she answered, "No, I didn't. That was some other lady. I don't know her and I don't like what she picks" (Slater & Leighton, 1984, p. 68).

Slater's memories never came flooding back over her, but she developed a self nonetheless. It was not, however, based on her pre-accident experiences, which had been permanently erased from her autobiographical memory. Instead, she constructed an answer to the question "Who am I?" by drawing on interpersonal sources. She listened to what other people told her about herself. She watched how they treated her. When her husband called her a dummy, she doubted her intelligence. But when her friends treated her as an equal, she felt competent and normal. When her doctor said, "Hi, Beverly Slater. You are Beverly Slater and I am Dr. O'Connor. How is Beverly Slater today?" she decided that she must be Beverly Slater (Slater & Leighton, 1984, p. 22). To Slater, other people were mirrors she could use to catch glimpses of herself.

In some ways all of us are like amnesiacs who must reconstruct who we are. We aren't born with a clear and detailed sense of who we are. Rather, we learn about ourselves as we go through life. As we acquire new information, our sense of who we are changes and grows. But where do we find self-knowledge? Like Slater, we live surrounded by other people, and in large part our sense of who we are can be traced back to their direct and indirect influences. Far from being well-defined selves who interact with other well-defined selves, we learn who we are—and alter the way we see ourselves—in the course of interacting with others. We compare ourselves to others. We use others' reactions to tell us who we are. And we stake claims to identities in others' eyes and seek to defend them. As we see in the following sections, the self is as much an interpersonal process as it is a personal possession.

Social Comparison

Slater acquired considerable information about herself by comparing herself to others. She often felt ignorant because she didn't understand things other people did. She asked her friends questions about sex because she wasn't sure whether she liked it or not. She also compared her own case of memory loss to the other documented cases of amnesia to see whether other people coped with memory loss better than she did.

social comparison
Evaluating the accuracy of personal beliefs and attitudes by comparing oneself to others.

Social comparison begins when you feel uncertain of some aspect of yourself—your skill on a task, the accuracy of a belief, the appropriateness of your opinions. You might reduce this uncertainty by consulting objective sources of information, but you can also evaluate yourself by drawing comparisons between yourself and others (Festinger, 1954; Kruglanski & Mayseless, 1990). College students can determine how well they are doing in their courses by consulting their teachers or reviewing their grades, but they can supplement this objective information by discussing their progress with their friends, roommates, and classmates. When students recorded all of the social comparisons they made over a 2-week period, more than 25% of these comparisons focused on academic matters: how well am I doing relative to the other people in my classes? As Table 5-3 indicates, other areas that students explored through comparison included their personality traits, their looks, their lifestyles, and their abilities (Wheeler & Miyake, 1992).

We rely on social comparison when physical reality fails to give us enough information about our personal attributes, qualities, and abilities. If we have taken math tests for 12 years and have always failed them, then we have little

▲ **TABLE 5-3**
Percentage of social comparisons reported by men and women in ten types of qualities

These statistics suggest that students are most likely to engage in social comparison when evaluating their academic skills or personality characteristics. Men and women differed significantly in only three of the categories: physical appearance, opinion, and eating habits.

Type of Quality	*Men*	*Women*
Academic	25.0	27.2
Personality	13.6	14.9
Physical appearance	11.7	15.9
Lifestyle	14.0	10.9
Abilities	14.0	12.4
Social skills	7.7	6.1
Wealth	4.7	3.7
Opinion	3.9	1.6
Relationships	0.8	1.6
Eating habits	0.0	1.5

Source: Wheeler & Miyake, 1992.

need for social comparison information. If, in contrast, we are uncertain of some aspect of ourselves or the situation, then we engage in social comparison. When people are placed in situations that are ambiguous or threatening, they tend to seek out other people so they can make comparisons (Cottrell & Epley, 1977). Competitors evaluating their athletic ability, workers judging the fairness of their pay rates, and hospitalized patients estimating the severity of their illnesses all rely on social comparison when they are uncertain of their skill or situation (Suls & Wills, 1991). Even scientists use social comparison. Researchers working in fields that lack a clear paradigm, such as psychology and sociology, face more ambiguity when evaluating the worth of their efforts than researchers in fields with long-established paradigms (for example, physics and chemistry). In the acknowledgement footnotes that accompanied their pub-

▲ Where can you turn when you need information about your personal worth, your strengths and weaknesses, and the accuracy of your perceptions? Other people, by providing us with social comparison information, help us develop and refine our understanding of social reality.

lished scientific reports, sociologists thanked an average of 2.0 individuals, psychologists thanked an average of 1.2 people, and researchers in the physical sciences thanked an average of about 0.5 people (Suls & Fletcher, 1983). Social comparison eases ambiguity.

The self based on social comparison is a relative self: it can change when the people around us change. In one study, students who were applying for a research job completed their application forms in the same room as the researchers' accomplice. In the Mr. Clean condition, the accomplice was nicely dressed and appeared competent in every way. In the Mr. Dirty condition, the accomplice was unkempt, sloppy, and had difficulty completing the application. As predicted, applicants who sat with Mr. Clean experienced a momentary drop in self-esteem, whereas people who sat with Mr. Dirty felt more confident in themselves (Morse & Gergen, 1970). Similar results have been found when people judge their physical attractiveness. Women feel more beautiful after seeing a picture of an unattractive woman rather than an attractive woman. Men's self-ratings, in contrast, don't change (Brown et al., 1992).

Interpersonal Feedback

Early theorists in both the sociological and psychological traditions claimed that other people significantly influence our self-concept (Cooley, 1902; James, 1892/1961; Mead, 1934). In some cases, other people directly give us explicit information about our personal qualities. Slater's husband repeatedly told her she was a dummy, and the doctors told her she was feisty. But people also give us feedback about our qualities by responding to us in certain ways. Slater's husband didn't let her remain alone in the house without supervision, so she concluded that she must be incapable of taking care of herself. Her friends never said explicitly, "You are intelligent," but they treated her as though she were quick-witted and savvy. By providing her with both direct and indirect feedback about her personal qualities, people told her who she was. As one theorist puts it, other people are mirrors we use to understand our selves:

> As we see our face, figure, and dress in the glass, and are interested in them because they are ours . . . so we perceive in another's mind some thought of our appearance, manners, aims, deeds, character, friends, and so on, and are variously affected by it. (Cooley, 1902, p. 231)

symbolic interactionism
A sociologically oriented theory that assumes individuals' conception of self develops as they interpret and selectively internalize others' symbolic gestures.

This *looking-glass conception of the self* is consistent with a general theory of social behavior known as **symbolic interactionism** (Stryker & Stratham, 1985). This theory assumes that social life is based on interactants' interpretations of the symbolic gestures—words, actions, and appearances—displayed by other people. To the symbolic interactionist, the self isn't a fixed entity, but a fluid process that changes continually in the course of daily encounters with other people. During such encounters we engage in *role-taking*: we step into other people's roles and look at ourselves from their perspectives. If a friend compliments you, she may or may not be sincere. If a coworker criticizes your work, he may be in a bad mood, or your work may actually need improvement. To make sense of such symbolic interactions, you must imagine how you would react if you were in their positions. By taking the role of the other person, you can decide whether your friend likes you and whether your coworker thinks your work is flawed (Ryan, Plant, & Kuczkowski, 1991).

Next, sometimes you internalize the information you gather through role-taking in your conception of yourself. Not only do you realize that your complimentary friend likes you, but you also conclude that you are a likable person. If you guess that your coworker feels your work is below par, you may end up agreeing with his appraisal. Thus you come to know and understand your self by (a) imagining how others see you and (b) incorporating (or internalizing) this feedback in your own concept of your self.

This view underscores the interpersonal foundations of the self. We intuitively believe that the core of the self is fixed and stable, but symbolic interactionists believe that your self changes as others' perceptions of you change. Students entering medical school, for example, don't define themselves as physicians. But when their training is complete, their self includes the component *physician* and many of its associated qualities (Preiss, 1968). Conservative people who joined a group that turned out to be relatively liberal eventually came to view themselves as liberal as well (Newcomb, 1943). Individuals who join nudist colonies alter their self-conceptions until they affirm the values associated with nudism: friendliness, need for relaxation, freedom from social constraints, and so on (Weinberg, 1966). Mental patients, once they realize they are members of this category, tend to adopt stigmatized self-concepts that reflect their psychological difficulties (Goffman, 1961).

Are you, then, a social chameleon who changes to match the perceptions of the people around you? Yes and no. As we will see, others' perceptions can be very influential, but we can control their effects on us through self-verification.

Self-fulfilling prophecies. Can other people's perceptions of us actually change us? Can perceptions create social reality? Mark Snyder, Elizabeth Decker Tanke, and Ellen Berscheid's (1977) study of men and women getting to know one another offers an answer. As part of a study of the acquaintance process, subjects were told that they would talk to another student for a few minutes by telephone. Before the start of the conversation, each man was given a picture of a woman. He was told it was a snapshot of his partner, but the picture was actually one of several prepared in advance by the researchers. Some subjects were given a picture of a very attractive woman (an 8 on a 10-point scale). Others were shown a picture of an unattractive woman (a 2.5 on a 10-point scale). The women who were the men's actual partners weren't told anything about the photographs, and they weren't given pictures of men.

As the "what is beautiful is good" stereotype would suggest, a man who thought his partner was physically attractive rather than unattractive rated her more positively even before he had the opportunity to converse with her. His false beliefs about his partner, however, also influenced *her* behavior. Snyder and his colleagues arranged for independent judges who knew nothing about the research to rate the subjects' comments. These raters were unbiased by any expectations, yet they felt that a woman talking to a man who thought she was attractive *sounded* more attractive—more sociable, poised, sexually warm, outgoing—than a woman talking to a man who thought she was unattractive. The man's false expectation about his partner acted as a **self-fulfilling prophecy** by causing the woman's behavior to change to confirm his expectation.

self-fulfilling prophecy
A perceiver's inaccurate belief that can evoke new behaviors in the person being observed, which confirm the perceiver's original inaccurate conception.

In other studies, subjects who were perceived to be aggressive became hostile, individuals who were viewed as extraverted became sociable, and people who were perceived to be bright became more intelligent (Snyder, 1984). This last, and most controversial, effect was reported in 1968 by Robert Rosenthal and Lenore Jacobson. They told elementary school teachers that certain students in their classes were late bloomers who would soon shine intellectually. Although these late bloomers were selected at random by the researchers, the positive expectations the label created were soon translated into behavioral changes and intelligence gains. The teachers became more positive in their interactions involving the labeled pupils, they gave late bloomers more feedback about their progress, and even taught them more information (Rosenthal, 1986). The students, in turn, responded to this preferential treatment by asking more questions, working harder, and becoming better behaved. Eventually the false prophecy was fulfilled when the students altered their self-concepts to match their newly gained academic abilities (Cooper, 1983; Rosenthal, 1986). As the section, "Application: Expectancies and Educational Outcomes," at the end of this chapter explains, other people's answers to the question "Who is she?" (or "Who is he?") can influence our answer to the question "Who am I?"

Self-verification. Self-fulfilling prophecies provide striking confirmation of the *constructivist perspective.* According to this view, perceivers *create* social reality as much as they *perceive* it. They bring their prejudices, biases, and expectations to every social situation they face, and these social beliefs sometimes create changes in social reality (Jussim, 1991). We do not create our own images—rather, we are created by the people around us.

significant others
Influential individuals, such as friends, family members, and loved ones, whose beliefs about us influence our own self-conception.

We are not, however, mere foils for others' perceptual prophecies. For one thing, we internalize feedback only from **significant others**—people (friends, family members, loved ones, peers, and leaders) who play particularly important roles in our lives (Hoelter, 1984). Interpersonal feedback is also filtered through our perceptions before it is stored in the self. For example, athletes' personal opinions about their athletic ability and their perceptions of their teammates' ratings of their ability are highly correlated ($r = .55$). These athletes' self-ratings and their teammates' actual judgments weren't correlated at all, however (Felson, 1981). In general, our self-ratings tend to match only our *perceptions* of others' appraisals, not the others' *actual* ratings. Thus, you may use others as your looking glass, but your reaction depends more on the image you see than on the reflections others cast (Shrauger & Schoeneman, 1979).

Nor do you react passively when other people give you feedback. If someone tells confident Claire that she doubts herself, will she abandon her self-view? If a friend tells dominant Don that he's easy to manipulate, will he agree? William B. Swann, Jr.'s (1987) studies of *self-verification*, which are discussed in Chapter 2, suggest that Claire and Don will probably try to change other people's views of them before they relinquish their own. Swann and his colleagues asked people who considered themselves to be likable or dislikable to talk with another person. Some people thought their partner viewed them in either a favorable or an unfavorable light. This information, which was fabricated by Swann, had little impact on the subjects so long as it matched the subjects' self-views. People who thought of themselves as dislikable, for example, didn't try to dispel a negative partner's perceptions. But when people thought their partners misunderstood them, they acted in ways that reaffirmed their own views of who they were. People who considered themselves to be likable worked to elicit favorable reactions, whereas people who thought of themselves as dislikable worked to elicit unfavorable reactions (Swann & Read, 1981a). Swann found a similar effect when he told people who thought of themselves as dominant or submissive, "You really seem to be the forceful, dominant type," or "You really don't seem to be the forceful, dominant type." Misjudged dominant people, as noted in Chapter 2 (see Figure 2-5), displayed behaviors that were particularly forceful, and misjudged submissive people bent over backward to seem less dominant (Swann & Hill, 1982; see also Darley et al., 1988).

Swann's findings confirm the interpersonal nature of the self. Perceivers construct the people they perceive, but the targets of their perceptions play an equally active role in the process. Sometimes they change their identity so it matches the perceivers' judgments. At other times, however, they battle for their own view of who they are and force perceivers to alter their judgments. We shouldn't forget that self-perceivers have their prophecies to confirm, too (Swann, 1984, 1987).

Collective Identity

Slater's self-concept expanded as she realized that she was not just an isolated person but the member of many groups. She was married, so she and her husband—even though she didn't recognize him—were a couple. She was part of an informal clique of women who got together regularly for lunch and tennis. She was also a woman, a resident of Philadelphia, an amnesia victim, and a hospital patient.

social identity theory
A theoretical framework that assumes individuals' self-conceptions include their personal qualities *and* qualities they share in common with members of their social groups.

collective self
The portion of the self that contains qualities that reflect one's membership in social groups, including families, cliques, neighborhoods, tribes, cities, countries, and regions.

As **social identity theory** notes, the self-concept is dualistic (Tajfel & Turner, 1986). One component, the personal self or identity, encompasses our unique qualities—traits, beliefs, skills, and so on. The second component, the **collective self**, includes all the qualities that spring from our membership in social groups—families, cliques, neighborhoods, tribes, cities, countries, and regions. Even our demographic qualities, such as sex or age, can influence the collective self when we categorize ourselves on the basis of these qualities. Once Slater thought of herself as a woman, her self-concept took on some of the general characteristics of the members of that group (James, 1993). Our selves, then, are defined in part by the people to whom we are connected (Baldwin, 1992). When people are asked to assemble a display of photographs that answer the question "Who are you?" 88% include at least one picture of themselves with other people (Dollinger & Clancy, 1993).

The relative sizes of the personal and collective selves vary among people, situations, and cultures. When they describe themselves, collectivists are more likely to mention the groups to which they belong and their family responsibilities. Individualists, in contrast, stress their personal attributes and are less likely to refer to other people when they describe themselves (Triandis, 1990; Triandis, McCusker, & Hui, 1990). Gender and culture can also influence collectivism. Women tend to stress connections and interdependence in their self-conceptions, whereas men stress independence and autonomy (Josephs, Markus, & Tafarodi, 1992). The collective self also plays a more pivotal role in some cultures than in others (Baumeister, 1986; Triandis, 1990). Indeed, the view of the self as a unified, integrated whole may be peculiar to Western societies, for such cultures typically stress **individualism**. Other cultures—those of Bali and Japan, for example—emphasize the unity of all people rather than each person's individuality. As a result, members of such societies don't consider themselves to be unique, autonomous people who exist separately from other people. As one Japanese psychologist writes, "the concept of a self completely independent from the environment is very foreign" to Japan, as that culture tends to view people as embedded in a social context (Azuma, 1984, p. 973). Such cultures stress **collectivism**, and some researchers believe that individuals in those cultures tend to be more aware of their collective selves than of their personal or private selves (Trafimow, Triandis, & Goto, 1991). In consequence, Japanese people's self-descriptions vary depending on who they are with and the nature of their social context. Americans' self-descriptions, in contrast, are more consistent across different situations (Cousins, 1989).

individualism
An ideology that places greater emphasis on the individual, including his or her rights, independence, and relationships with other individuals.

collectivism
An ideology that focuses on the group rather than on the individual in the group, and stresses the importance of cooperation and constructive interdependence.

Sources of the Self

Common sense tells us that our sense of identity is relatively constant and independent of changing situations. Most of us consider our basic qualities to be highly private, personal possessions that don't change much from one day

▲ Asian cultures tend to be more collectivistic than Western cultures because they stress social unity rather than the unique personal qualities of each individual.

to the next or from one situation to another. But our answers to the question "Who am I?" change when our circumstances change. Each social encounter offers an opportunity to redefine and refine your sense of self through the processes summarized in Table 5-4. Because the self is an outgrowth of social processes, it is more dynamic than static, more flexible than rigid.

The self is not, however, a feather than can be blown about by interpersonal forces. Extraordinary changes in our lives can lead to extraordinary changes in our self-concepts, but the self is marked more by continuity than by discontinuity. We are committed to a view of who we are, and we defend that view against incursions (Markus & Kunda, 1986). When we are confronted with new information that conflicts with our stock of private thoughts and feelings, we assume that our private self-knowledge is more accurate (Andersen & Ross, 1984). We recognize that we may change in the future, but we usually set our courses so that tomorrow's selves are not too discrepant from today's (Markus & Nurius, 1986).

Maintaining Self-Esteem

We have seen that the self is part history and part historian. As history, your self offers an answer to the question "Who am I?" for it summarizes your perceptions of your qualities and characteristics. As historian, the self extracts information from other people and from each day's experiences. But this historian is also part critic. The self-concept includes both a description of your characteristics *and* an evaluation of them. Thus you are not just a student, but a *good* student or a *bad* student. Similarly, Beverly Slater was not just a cook, a teacher, a mother, a wife, and a friend. Rather, she considered herself to be the "frustrated cook, the would-be teacher, the confused mother, the bumbling wife, and the stumbling friend" (Slater & Leighton, 1984, p. 158). We possess not merely a self, but a *positive* self or a *negative* self.

self-esteem
Individuals' personal appraisal or evaluation of their attributes; the evaluative component of the self-concept.

The evaluative side of the self is known as **self-esteem**, and it comes in two varieties. Your overall evaluation of yourself and your attributes across times

▲ **TABLE 5-4**
Summing up: The interpersonal nature of the self

Process	*Description*	*Result*
Social comparison	We evaluate the accuracy and adequacy of personal beliefs and attributes by comparing ourselves to other people.	The self is relative; it can change when the people around us change.
Symbolic interactionism	We use other people's reactions to us as mirrors to examine our own attributes.	The self is socially constructed.
Self-fulfilling prophecies	Others' beliefs about us, even if erroneous, can prompt us to act in ways that are consistent with those erroneous beliefs.	Other people can change our self-definitions.
Self-verification	When others misperceive us, we attempt to correct their misperceptions through tactical self-presentation.	We communicate self-information to others.
Collective identity	A portion of the self is based on qualities that we share in common with other members of our social groups.	The self is part of a larger collective; all selves are interconnected.

and situations is your *trait self-esteem.* If you possess high trait self-esteem, then you respect, accept, and positively evaluate your self. You would tend to agree with statements such as "I feel that I'm a person of worth, at least on an equal plane with others." If, in contrast, you have low trait self-esteem, then you tend to negatively evaluate your self. You would be likely to agree that "All in all, I am inclined to feel that I am a failure." (These statements are drawn from the Rosenberg Self-Esteem Scale (1965), discussed in Chapter 1; see Table 1-3.) Your *state self-esteem,* in contrast, depends on your self-appraisal in a given situation. A failed test or a lonely evening may lower normally high levels of self-esteem, just as a promotion or compliment may raise low self-esteem temporarily (Heatherton & Polivy, 1991; Kernis & Johnson, 1990).

People vary considerably in their appraisals of their self-worth: the depressed individual feels inferior, discouraged, or even worthless, whereas the narcissist is consumed with self-adoration. Most people, however, usually manage to maintain a positive sense of self. As Hazel Markus (1980) explains, the "notion that we will go to great lengths to protect our ego or preserve our self-esteem is an old, respected, and when all is said and done, probably one of the great psychological truths" (p. 127). We are motivated to maintain our self-esteem, and we have many tools at our disposal to help us achieve this goal.

Framing the Self

Few people are successful in everything they do. I may wish to be a great teacher, a brilliant researcher, an engaging author, and a wonderful spouse, but I may fall short of success in some of these endeavors. If I do, however, I can always compensate for my shortcomings by reassessing the importance of each role when I formulate my self-definition. If I receive an award for my contributions as a teacher, I can remind myself that good teaching is one of my primary goals. If my spouse divorces me, then I may begin to think, "My career is more important to me than my success in marriage." Because my self has many characteristics, I can selectively focus on some features while ignoring others. This selective shifting of attention and emphasis from one attribute to another is called *framing.*

Those of us with high self-esteem frame our self-views in ways that highlight our positive features (Pelham & Swann, 1989). When we describe our qualities, our most positive attributes are also the ones we think are the most important ones in defining who we are (Lewicki, 1983; Pelham & Swann, 1989). When we indicate how bad or good we are in such roles as student, son or daughter, friend, and religious person and the importance of each of these roles for self-definition, the two sets of ratings are correlated (the *r*'s ranged from .44 to .78 in Hoelter, 1983). When we rate our various strengths and weaknesses, we are more certain that our ratings of our strengths are accurate than our ratings of our weaknesses (Pelham & Swann, 1989). When we describe ourselves to other people who already know we possess certain weaknesses, we acknowledge these weaknesses but then highlight our strengths. "I may be insensitive," we admit, "but did you know that I am intelligent, warm, creative, and reliable?" (Baumeister & Jones, 1978).

self-complexity
The degree to which self-knowledge is elaborately organized and differentiated.

Because our self-esteem prospers when we can select and highlight our positive attributes and ignore our negative qualities, self-esteem is often closely linked to **self-complexity**. People with complex self-concepts use a large number of schemas to represent their self-knowledge. They also maintain clear distinctions between these self-aspects. People who are low in self-complexity, in contrast, use fewer and more closely interrelated schemas to represent themselves. Although a simple view of the self may be just as valid as a complex one, these differences in complexity influence our ability to frame the self selectively. First, when people who are high in self-complexity experience a negative event in their lives, they can cope by focusing on the more positive aspects of their lives. A lawyer who thinks of herself as a woman, a wife, a mother, and a friend can emphasize these other parts of her self when she loses an important case. A person who is low in self-complexity—a lawyer who thinks of herself as, say, a lawyer and a wife only—is limited by her two-dimensional self-concept. Second, because individuals who are high in self-complexity differentiate among their various self-views, a catastrophe in one arena is less likely to spill over and contaminate their other self-views. The high-complexity lawyer who loses a case may wonder whether she is a good lawyer, but these self-doubts won't undermine her image of herself as a woman, wife, mother, and friend. The low-complexity lawyer who loses, however, will experience more spill-over effects. Her overall level of self-esteem declines, particularly if she can't avoid focusing on her failure. A complex self-concept, then, serves as a buffer that protects us from the stresses and strains of everyday life (Linville, 1985, 1987; Niedenthal, Setterlund, & Wherry, 1992).

Researchers tested these hypotheses by telling people who differed in self-complexity that they performed well or poorly on a test of verbal intelligence. The researchers then asked the subjects to write essays about their personal goals while they were seated before a large mirror. People with complex selves who failed didn't seem to be bothered by the mirror; they spent an average of 10.4 minutes in front of the mirror. People with simple selves who failed, however, spent an average of only 6.7 minutes in the self-focusing situation. They also wrote shorter essays that were lower in quality. A complex self-concept apparently offers advantages over a simple self-concept. When people with complex selves fail in one context, they can review their accomplishments in other, unrelated contexts. People who are lower in self-complexity, in contrast, must take each failure to heart (Dixon & Baumeister, 1991).

▲ A complex self may protect us from the negative consequences of life's setbacks and disasters. If this woman experiences a negative event, such as the trauma of a divorce, she can reframe her view of herself to focus more on her career and on her role of mother. A woman with a less complex self may not be able to reframe her identity so successfully, and the negative emotions produced by the failed marriage may influence her overall level of self-esteem.

Accepting and Rejecting Feedback

An entrepreneur once took out advertisements in several newspapers offering readings of astrological charts for a small fee. He did not bother to develop individualized horoscopes, however. He just sent all of his customers the same general description of their personality and prediction for their future. He received more than 200 letters thanking him for his perceptive, accurate analyses (Snyder, Shenkel, & Lowery, 1977).

Barnum effect
The tendency to accept global and ambiguous feedback about ourselves, even if the source of the information lacks credibility.

We tend to accept global and ambiguous feedback about ourselves, even if the source of the information lacks credibility. This tendency is known as the **Barnum effect**, in honor of showperson P. T. Barnum; Barnum, whose circuses and theatrical extravaganzas were immensely popular, is reputed to have credited his success to the fact that "there's a sucker born every minute."

To demonstrate the Barnum effect, simply ask someone you don't know very well if you can read their palm, cast their horoscope, or study their handwriting. Next, give them the following personality description:

> You have a great need for other people to like you and admire you. You have a tendency to be critical of yourself. You have a great deal of unused capacity which you have not turned to your advantage. While you have some personality weaknesses, you are generally able to compensate for them. Your sexual adjustment has presented problems for you. Disciplined and self-controlled outside, you tend to be worrisome and insecure inside. At times you have serious doubts as to whether you have made the right decision or done the right thing. You prefer a certain amount of change and variety and become dissatisfied when hemmed in by restrictions and limitations. You pride yourself on being an independent thinker and do not accept others' statements without satisfactory proof. You have found it unwise to be too frank in revealing yourself to others. At times you are extraverted, affable, and sociable, while at other times you are introverted, wary, and reserved. Some of your aspirations tend to be pretty unrealistic. Security is one of your major goals in life. (Forer, 1949, p. 120)

Your acquaintance will probably marvel at your insight.

The Barnum effect becomes even stronger when the feedback is primarily positive (Snyder, Shenkel, & Lowery, 1977; compare with Johnson et al.,

1985). We do not believe that negative information is accurate, but we wholeheartedly accept the validity of positive feedback. The student who fails the test says, "What an ambiguous, invalid test." The A student replies, "I thought it was an excellent, comprehensive exam." The professor who receives a poor evaluation from the students asks, "What do those kids know about good teaching?" The highly rated professor replies, "Students are excellent judges of quality in teaching." The parent of the child who gets a low score on an intelligence test argues that "IQ scores are meaningless," but the parent of the high-scoring child smiles and says, "Perhaps, but IQ scores do predict academic success" (Ditto & Lopez, 1993; see "In Depth: Which Motive Is Stronger: The Need for Self-Esteem or the Need for Self-Consistency?").

As testimony to the power of this bias, one team of researchers went to great lengths to destroy the credibility of positive feedback by giving subjects one of two tests that purportedly measured their personalities. Some subjects took an impressive, valid-sounding psychological test. Others completed the North Dakota Null Hypothesis Brain Inventory: a patently absurd instrument developed

IN DEPTH

Which Motive Is Stronger: The Need for Self-Esteem or the Need for Self-Consistency?

Whereas the injunction "Love thyself" encourages self-enhancement, we often feel the pull of a second self-motive: "To thine own self be true." We don't always want to discover something good about ourselves. We sometimes seek to conclude that, good or bad, we knew it all along. We seek self-consistency (Secord & Backman, 1961).

The need for self-consistency is the cornerstone of Swann's self-verification theory (1983, 1987). Swann insists that we seek, process, and remember information in ways that confirm, rather than bolster, our conception of ourselves. Earlier in the chapter we saw that individuals who believe they are misperceived by other people will redouble their self-presentational efforts. If others seem to think you are shy, but you think of yourself as outgoing, then you will be particularly sociable and extraverted (Swann & Hill, 1982). People also go out of their way to acquire feedback that fits their current view of themselves. In one study, Swann and his colleagues offered people who considered themselves to be assertive or nonassertive some feedback about their personalities. The information that was offered consisted of 16 items, 8 dealing with assertiveness and 8 with unassertiveness. Swann's subjects showed a preference for feedback that confirmed their self-conception: assertive individuals chose items dealing with assertiveness, and unassertive individuals preferred items dealing with unassertiveness. Subjects responded in similar ways when emotionality served as the personality trait, and when they had to pay a small amount of money to gain access to the feedback (Swann & Read, 1981b). Swann (1983) writes: People "will engage in a wide array of mental gymnastics to dismiss discrepant feedback" (p. 44).

For most people, the need for self-consistency and the need for self-esteem go hand in hand. We usually hold ourselves in high regard, so positive feedback both confirms and bolsters our already positive view. But how do we react to feedback when our self-esteem is low? How would you react, for example, if all your life you have felt incompetent when dealing with math and numerical computations? Then, when you entered college, you performed very well on a math placement test. Would you reject this feedback, as self-consistency theory predicts? Or would you be particularly appreciative of this esteem-building feedback because you have been denied it all your life?

Many theorists side with Swann (1990), who argues that the need for self-consistency triumphs over the need for self-esteem. If we expect negative information, we tend to accept it, and if positive information is unexpected, we are often critical of its validity and accuracy (Deutsch & Solomon, 1959; Feather & Simon, 1971). People with chronically low self-esteem are also less likely to use many of the self-enhancing mechanisms, such as self-serving attributions, to protect their self-esteem (Pyszczynski & Greenberg, 1985; Swallow & Kuiper, 1987; Tabachnik, Crocker, & Alloy, 1983). When people with high self-esteem fail, for example, they blame the results on the difficulty of the test. Individuals with low self-esteem, in contrast, blame themselves. Low self-esteem individuals also tend to overgeneralize their failure. When high self-esteem individuals fail a test, they may say, "I'm not doing well in that class," but low self-esteem individuals conclude "I'm stupid" (Kernis, Brockner, & Frankel, 1989).

▲ Why do people uncritically accept the predictions and personality descriptions that astrologists offer? Is it because these so-called experts are careful to speak in positive generalities, such as "You have a great need for others to like you and admire you," "You tend to be critical of yourself," and "You pride yourself on being an independent thinker"?

Other theorists, however, favor self-esteem theory. They note that in many instances people show a marked preference for feedback that exceeds their expectations; even individuals who expect to fail and those with low self-esteem are more satisfied after success than after failure (Jones, 1973). Similarly, no matter how we feel about ourselves, when other people treat us in positive, accepting ways, we tend to like them; we reject people who treat us in a negative manner (Regan, 1976).

As is so often the case with scientific controversies, researchers now believe that both views are correct. If we look closely at all the earlier studies that tested people's reactions to positive and negative feedback, we can discern two general patterns. People who receive the feedback they expect usually believe the feedback is accurate, even if it is negative (Shrauger, 1975). These effects of self-consistency hold true only at the cognitive level, however. When people describe their emotional reactions to the feedback—"How much did you like the test-giver?" or "Did you enjoy work on the test?"—self-esteem motives dominate. People clearly dislike negative feedback and the people who give it to them, especially if they had negative expectations. Information that is expected may be viewed as more valid, but self-enhancing information is more satisfying (McFarlin & Blascovich, 1981; Moreland & Sweeney, 1984).

Swann and his colleagues (1987) tested this possibility directly by measuring subjects' cognitive *and* emotional reactions to feedback. All the subjects completed a measure of social self-esteem during a pretest session. People who scored very high or very low on the measure were then scheduled for a laboratory session during which they read a short excerpt from the book *The Naked Ape* as an observer looked on. This observer, instead of rating the subject, gave the subject one of two standard feedback sheets. The positive feedback sheet was laudatory, describing the subject as very competent; the negative feedback sheet was more disapproving. Subjects then got the chance to rate their feedback, and their moods, on a series of questionnaires. As the results shown in Figure 5-7 indicate, subjects thought the feedback was more accurate when it matched their own expectations. They felt better emotionally, however, when they received positive rather than negative feedback (Swann et al., 1987).

Swann's findings suggest that we are not always of one mind when it comes to evaluating ourselves. If we possess low self-esteem or evaluate ourselves negatively in a specific domain but receive positive feedback about the self, then we are caught in a cognitive-affective crossfire: the cognitive side wants to reject inconsistent information because it is inaccurate, but the emotional side wants to accept positive information because it is reassuring. Immediately after the feedback, our emotions probably dominate our responses, since this system is designed for rapid decision making. In the long term, however, the cognitive system should emerge as more influential, provided we have the time and cognitive resources needed to consider the feedback thoroughly (Swann et al., 1990). Swann and his colleagues conclude:

> To be sure, the assumption of psychological unity is appealing in many ways. It is simple, elegant, and phenomenologically compelling. . . . Yet our data suggest that at least with respect to reaction to social feedback, people are not nearly as single minded as the unity assumption would have us believe. (Swann et al., 1987, p. 887)

FIGURE 5-7
Which motive is stronger: the need for self-esteem or the need for self-consistency? Individuals who received feedback that matched their self-concepts felt the feedback was more accurate than those who received feedback that ran counter to their self-concepts. Overall, however, people felt more positive emotions when they received favorable rather than unfavorable feedback. Thus, self-consistency prevailed at the cognitive level, and self-esteem prevailed at the affective level. (From Swann et al., 1987)

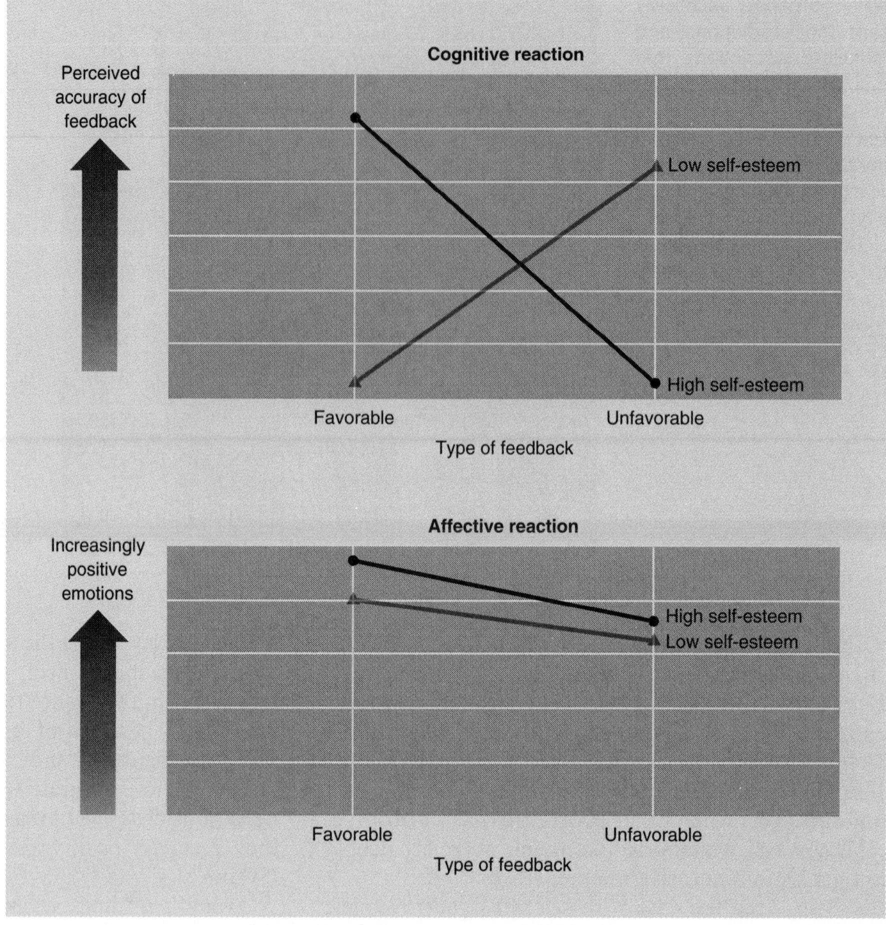

by the humorist Art Buchwald. This test included such items as "I am never startled by fish," "I think beavers work too hard," and "I would never shake hands with a gardener." Who believed the test results? Subjects who received uniformly positive feedback, no matter what the source (Collins, Dmitruk, & Ranney, 1977).

Remembering the Good

Slater's inability to remember the details of her accident is not unique. People who are injured in accidents or are victims of violence often cannot remember the event (Bower, 1981). This selectivity in memory, to use Sigmund Freud's (1920) term, is **repression**. When thoughts, memories, or impulses threaten our sense of well-being, we push them out of our awareness. We are motivated to forget the bad and remember the good.

repression
Motivated forgetting of negative thoughts, memories, or impulses.

A mild form of repression influences our memories for the bad events and experiences that pepper our everyday lives. Our memories of esteem-damaging information—being stood up by a date, failing a course in college, getting fired from a job, losing an important game—tend to fade faster than our memories of positive events—a successful interview, a pleasant first date, achieving the highest average in a course (Conway, 1991; Skowronski et al., 1991). When returning to college after the winter holiday break, students remembered more of the pleasant than unpleasant things about the holiday. Six weeks later, when their memories were retested, even more of the unpleasant events had been forgotten (Meltzer, 1930). People usually recall interrupted tasks better than they recall tasks they have completed (the *Zeigarnik effect*); but if they were failing on the interrupted task and they succeeded on the completed task, then their recall of the completed task is superior (Greenwald, 1980). Also, when we experience a mixture of successes and failures, we tend to overestimate the frequency of our successes and underestimate the frequency of our failures (Vreven & Nuttin, 1976).

The self is usually best served when past failures and shortcomings are forgotten. An interesting exception, however, occurs when we are trying to improve some aspect of ourselves. A dieter, for example, may say "I'm overweight, but I used to be really heavy," or a client in psychotherapy may conclude "I'm still very anxious, but I used to be really crazy." When we hope we are changing, we tend to remember how badly off we used to be. In one study of this process, college students who wanted to improve their grades took part in a study-skills program. The program didn't help them a bit, but participants convinced themselves that their skills had improved by exaggerating how poorly they had studied before they joined the program. Apparently, people who are trying to change—perhaps striving to be thinner, friendlier, sexier, better adjusted, or stronger—but who fall a bit short of their goals sometimes say to themselves, "I may not be perfect now, but I was much worse before" (Conway & Ross, 1985).

The Mere Ownership Effect

We could not hold ourselves in high regard if we did not positively appraise the specific components of our self-concepts (Woike & Baumgardner, 1993). The introvert thinks that a shy, retiring lifestyle is more attractive than a boisterous, raucous one. The student who majors in psychology thinks it's a great field (Rosenberg, 1979).

People admire even their most trivial characteristics. We show a distinct preference for letters that appear in our own names (Hoorens et al., 1990), and we evaluate the things we own—our cars, our houses, our clothes, and our books—more favorably than things we don't own (Beggan, 1992). In a study of this *mere ownership effect*, female college students evaluated a number of inexpensive objects: a candy bar, a key holder, a ministapler, a plastic comb, a drink insulator (one of those foam rubber things people put around cans to keep them cold), and the like. Some of the women were given the drink insulator before they made their ratings, others were given the key holder, and still others received nothing. As expected, the women who had suddenly become the owners of the drink insulator rated the insulator more positively than did the owners of the key holder and the women in the control condition. Women who had recently failed displayed the strongest mere ownership effect, for they most needed to bolster their self-esteem (Beggan, 1992).

Self-Serving Attributions

From time to time Slater would experience a setback during her recovery. She might, for example, insult a friend without meaning to or lose her temper when talking to her husband. These incidents, however, did not have much impact on her self-esteem or confidence because in many cases she blamed them on "Little Bev," her childlike side that was very immature, short-tempered, and couldn't tolerate boredom.

Our attributions, as noted in Chapter 4, often provide us with an excellent means of protecting or enhancing our self-esteem. When things go well, self-serving attributions emphasize our responsibility for the outcome, and when things go wrong, we can minimize our responsibility by blaming someone or something else (Pyszczynski & Greenberg, 1987). People who get caught cheating on a test claim they were forced to cheat by situational pressures, and students who don't cheat emphasize their personal moral scruples (Forsyth, Pope, & McMillan, 1985). Individuals whose decisions lead to unpleasant consequences claim they had no choice in the matter, but they emphasize their freedom of choice when pleasant consequences follow (Harris & Harvey, 1975). These biases, as discussed in Chapter 4, don't spring solely from our need for self-esteem. Self-serving attributions do, however, contribute to self-esteem, and their absence is often associated with low self-esteem (Brown, 1991).

Self-Handicapping

What can Slater do when, on the night before her first dinner party after the accident, she is overcome by worries that the party will be a flop? What can we do if we want our classmates to see us as successful and intelligent students, but we anticipate failing the midterm examination?

self-handicapping Actively seeking or creating impediments for performance.

Self-handicapping offers us a way to escape from such dilemmas. Rather than working hard to overcome factors that might ruin our performance, we set the stage for our self-serving attributions by deliberately seeking out impediments. Swimmers cut practices so they can blame a poor showing on lack of preparation (Rhodewalt, Saltzman, & Wittmer, 1985). Men who fear they will be unable to act in a socially competent manner drink more heavily in social settings (Higgins & Harris, 1988). And students who expect to fail an important test take drugs before the test so they can blame the drugs (Jones & Berglas, 1978). The college students in this last study were led to believe that they would be participating in a "clinical trial" designed to test the influence of two drugs on intellectual performance. The cover story for the study claimed that they would first take a 20-item test of analogies. They would then be given one of two drugs: either Actavil, which would probably improve their intellectual performance, or Pandocrin, which would impair it. Last, they would be given a second 20-item analogy test. Actually, no drugs were given, for the investigators only wanted to see which drug the subjects would choose. As they had anticipated, subjects who didn't think they would pass the second test usually chose the performance-inhibiting Pandocrin. This effect was particularly pronounced among men, a finding that suggests that men may be more likely to handicap themselves than women (Berglas & Jones, 1978, Study 1; see also Arkin & Baumgardner, 1985; Leary & Shepperd, 1986; Higgins, Snyder, & Berglas, 1990; Self, 1990; Shepperd & Arkin, 1991).

Self-handicapping can be used to avoid the attributional implications of failure (self-protection) as well as to garner credit for success (self-enhancement). The dual purposes of self-handicapping were studied by having individuals who were high or low in self-esteem take a test (Tice, 1991). The researcher manipulated subjects' involvement in the situation by telling some people the test was an important one: it measured a cognitive ability and predicted career success. She told others the test tapped a relatively trivial ability. The researcher also made salient the need to protect the self or the need to enhance the self by describing the task differently. She told some of the subjects that only a low score on the test would be meaningful because most people performed well. She told others that only a high score would be meaningful because it was extremely difficult. Tice then let subjects practice before their testing session and assumed that people who practiced for a very short period of time were handicapping themselves. As expected, high self-esteem individuals self-handicapped when a high score was meaningful (self-enhancement) and low self-esteem individuals handicapped when a low score was meaningful (self-protection).

Self-handicapping becomes more likely when people are working on tasks that are central to their social identities, and when other people will be scrutinizing their performance. Hence, most researchers believe that self-handicapping enhances both our private self-esteem and our public social identity (Arkin & Shepperd, 1988; Baumgardner, Lake, & Arkin, 1985; Shepperd & Arkin, 1989). But whether or not self-handicapping is an effective means of protecting one's public identity is debatable (Luginbuhl & Palmer, 1991).

Downward Social Comparison

When Slater recovered from her physical injuries, she became interested in other cases of permanent amnesia. She began to search the medical literature for cases and read her own file thoroughly. Her studies brought her some solace, for she noted that her memory loss was one of the most severe losses ever documented. Other individuals had forgotten their memories of past experiences, but only a few had forgotten their own personal qualities as well. Considering the seriousness of her case, Slater felt as though she were recovering quite nicely.

upward social comparison Comparing oneself to others who are performing more effectively than oneself.

downward social comparison Comparing oneself to others who are performing less effectively than oneself.

We compare ourselves to others when we lack information about ourselves and the situations we face. We are not, however, indiscriminate when selecting targets for comparison. When we want information, we compare ourselves to people who are similar to us; men might compare themselves to other men, and psychology majors might compare themselves to other psychology majors. When our self-esteem is on the line, however, similarity becomes a less important criterion. In such cases we avoid **upward social comparison**—comparing ourselves to people who are more fortunate than we are. We opt instead for **downward social comparison**—comparing ourselves to others who are performing more poorly, experiencing more negative outcomes, or coping less well than we are. Slater compared herself to other patients who had suffered the same injury but were faring less well than she was. She avoided drawing comparisons between herself and patients who had completely recovered from identical medical problems (Wood, 1989).

Downward social comparison becomes more prevalent when our self-esteem is threatened (Wills, 1991). If you have just been told that you got an A on an examination, downward social comparison is unnecessary because your self-esteem is already secure. But what if your grade was a D? To counter this threat to your self-esteem, your need to compare yourself to others—particularly low-scoring others—should be much greater. Researchers created this situation by telling subjects that they earned either high or low marks on a test of social sensitivity. They then asked the subjects if they wanted to look at some other test-takers' papers. As Figure 5-8 indicates, those who had done poorly wanted to see others' scores, but only if they had been led to believe that these scores would be relatively low. If they thought that the other subjects had outscored them, then they showed little interest in the other subjects' tests (Pyszczynski, Greenberg, & LaPrelle, 1985). When subjects in a similar study, who thought that their scores on a personality test revealed some psychological abnormalities, were given the opportunity to see other people's personality tests, 95% of these subjects picked someone who scored more negatively than they did (Hakmiller, 1966; Levine & Green, 1984).

Downward social comparison is particularly important when we are suffering through some painful or harmful experience. How do we cope when people

▲ **FIGURE 5-8**
When do we engage in downward social comparison? Individuals who succeeded at the task did not show very much interest in seeing other students' papers. Those who failed, however, were much more likely to request copies of other students' tests—provided they had been led to believe that most students' scores were fairly low. (From Pyszczynski, Greenberg, & LaPrelle, 1985)

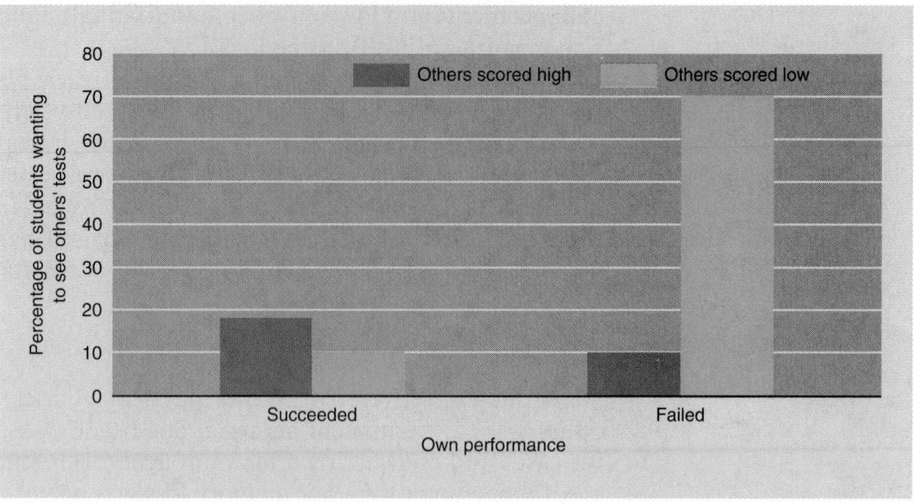

we love, or we ourselves, become very ill? How do we react to a natural disaster, such as a tornado or flood? What if we are injured in an automobile accident or are victims of a crime? In such problematic situations we often prefer to associate with people who are coping well with their problems—their valiant efforts make us feel more optimistic about our own chances of recovery. Note, however, that *contact* with such people is reassuring but *comparison* with them is not (Taylor & Lobel, 1989). Our own plights often seem more bleak and our coping less effective in comparison with their heroic efforts (Wood, Taylor, & Lichtman, 1985). We therefore prefer people who are less fortunate than ourselves when we engage in social comparison. By comparing ourselves to others who are experiencing even more severe hardships or to those who can't cope with their problems, we can minimize our sense of victimization and often recover more quickly (Gibbons & Gerrard, 1989; Wood, Taylor, & Lichtman, 1985). Dwelling on other people's misfortunes may seem callous, but our self-esteem is best served when we look down rather than up (Affleck et al., 1988; Schultz & Decker, 1985).

Maintaining Collective Self-Esteem

To maximize her sense of self-worth, Slater questioned the validity of negative feedback, attributed setbacks to external factors, and compared herself to people who were recovering more slowly than she was. But she also bolstered her self-esteem by increasing her collective self-esteem. Because the self includes both a personal component and a collective component, our sense of self-worth prospers when we associate with people we respect or admire (Luhtanen & Crocker, 1992). When we join prestigious groups, we usually feel more satisfied with ourselves and our attributes (Brown & Lohr, 1987). Studies of BIRGing, or basking in reflected glory, suggest that people draw attention to their memberships in successful groups in an indirect attempt to raise their self-worth (see Chapter 2). When the teams that we root for win, for example, our self-esteem swells, and we feel more confident (Hirt et al., 1992). We also protect our collective self's worth by exaggerating the caliber of the groups we belong to, by derogating members of other groups, and by blaming our group's failures on external causes (Crocker & Luhtanen, 1990; Deaux, 1993; Leary & Forsyth, 1987).

Bolstering our collective self-esteem by associating with attractive, successful people has its drawbacks, however. When we associate with competent

DOONESBURY copyright G. B. Trudeau. Reprinted with permission of UNIVERSAL PRESS SYNDICATE. All rights reserved.

▲ Downward social comparison in support groups. When we compare ourselves with people whose predicaments are even bleaker and drearier than our own, our situation seems more hopeful.

people, our own talents pale by comparison. Slater felt a surge of pride when she played tennis at the club with her friends, but she also felt humbled because she played so poorly in comparison to them.

self-evaluation maintenance Maintaining and enhancing self-esteem by associating with high-achieving individuals who excel in areas irrelevant to our own sense of self-esteem and avoiding association with high-achieving individuals who excel in areas that are important to our sense of self-esteem.

Abraham Tesser, Jennifer Campbell, and their associates believe that **self-evaluation maintenance** processes help us deal with this kind of problem. Their theory proposes that we seek out associations with people who are our superiors, but only if they are superior in ways that aren't relevant to our own self-concept. Imagine that you are a B student who wants to be an A student and go to medical school. Will you associate with a group of Dean's List students who earn As on all their papers and projects with little effort? Probably not. What if you are more interested, however, in your athletic skills than in your academic skills? In this case, you might feel very comfortable associating with students who earn higher grades. Indeed, Tesser and Campbell's self-evaluation maintenance model (SEM) assumes that the ideal co-member or friend is someone who performs less well than you do on tasks that you think are important but very well on tasks that you don't think are important. Such associates provide you with targets for downward social comparison, and you can also bask in the glory of their accomplishments in areas that don't interest you (Tesser, 1988; Tesser & Campbell, 1983; Tesser, Campbell, & Smith, 1984).

Tesser and Campbell tested the model by giving elementary school students a list of activities (sports, art, music, math, and the like) and asking them to pick out activities they considered to be important and unimportant. The students also identified their most and least preferred classmates. One week later, the students rated their ability, their close classmate's ability, and their distant classmate's ability in an area they felt was important and one they felt was unimportant. If the students thought the task was important, they judged their performances as superior to their close friends' (see Figure 5-9). If, however, the task was not important to them personally, they felt that they had not performed as well. The performances of disliked classmates were derogated for both important and unimportant tasks (Tesser et al., 1984).

Return to Selfhood

Despite her loss of a self she had spent 48 years building, Beverly Slater was able to return to selfhood. She retained the capacity for self-awareness and succeeded in gradually recreating her self-concept. Slater also learned to secure her self's value by using the methods summarized in Table 5-5 (Brown & Mankowski, 1993). Indeed, she eventually became completely satisfied with her new self. When asked, "Do you want your old self back?" she answered, without hesitating:

> I *know* myself now. You're asking me if I want to remember and know an image that's a stranger to me. I don't know her. I only know myself. So maybe I don't

▲ **FIGURE 5-9**
Does our desire to maintain our self-esteem influence who we pick to be our friends? The self-evaluation maintenance model argues that people will prefer to outperform their friends in areas that are important to their self-definitions. Therefore, on personally important tasks the students in this study felt that they outperformed their closest friend. If, however, the task was not important to them personally, they felt that they performed relatively less well. The performances of distant classmates were derogated for both important and unimportant tasks. (Adapted from Tesser, Campbell, & Smith, 1984)

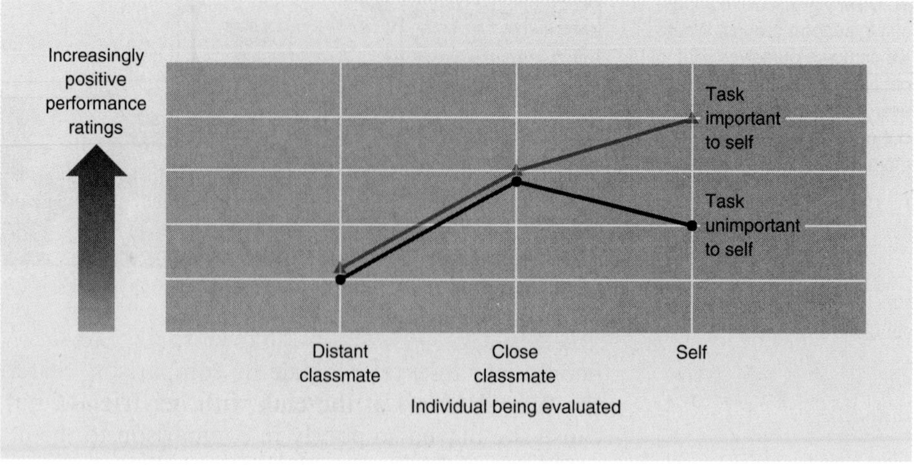

want to remember her because I don't *know* her. What I want is to remember *both*, or forget the past. I like myself today and I won't give myself up willingly. (p. 231)

Her return to selfhood was complete.

Summary

William James described the duality of the *self* when he distinguished between the *self-concept* and *self-awareness*. The self-concept is a comprehensive record of our assumptions about our enduring personal qualities and characteristics. The *working self-concept* includes only attributes that are activated by the current social situation, and the cognitive structures that organize this information are termed *self-schemas*. In general, self-schematic information is processed more rapidly and efficiently, and any material that is associated with the self, even in a superficial way, is more easily remembered (the *self-reference effect*). Even though human beings and a small number of other species are capable of self-awareness, we are not always self-aware. If environmental stimuli do not focus attention on the self or if we are low in dispositional *self-consciousness*, we may not monitor the self closely. Indeed, as Carver and Scheier's *self-regulation theory* suggests, we take steps to reduce the discrepancy between the ideal self and the actual self only when we are self-aware, and our *optimism* regarding the outcome is high.

The self is as much an interpersonal process as it is a personal possession. When we feel uncertain of some aspect of ourselves, and physical reality provides insufficient information, we seek *social comparison* information: we compare ourselves to the people who surround us. We also use other people as social mirrors to catch a glimpse of our selves as others perceive them. Advocates of *symbolic interactionism* assume that we develop an understanding of ourselves by imagining how others see us and then internalizing these perceived appraisals in our self-concepts. Others' perceptions can become *self-fulfilling prophecies*—mistaken beliefs that can evoke new behaviors in the person being observed, which confirm the perceiver's original inaccurate conception. Although we often accept interpersonal feedback from *significant others*, in most cases we strive to manage their views of us through *self-verification*. Our selves are also derived, in part, from our group memberships. As *social identity theory* notes, the *collective self* (or social identity) includes all

▲ **TABLE 5-5**
Summing up: Some methods for maintaining self-worth

Process	*Description*	*Example*
Framing the self	Selectively emphasizing the most positive attributes in our self-descriptions while downplaying any central, but negative, attributes	The teacher who receives poor evaluations from his students exclaims, "Performing good research is more important to me than teaching."
Selective acceptance of feedback	Accepting favorable feedback as accurate but rejecting unfavorable feedback as invalid	Students question the validity of the test questions they miss but recognize the quality of questions they answer correctly.
Repression	Remembering positive self-information but forgetting negative information about the self	Dozens of failed first dates are forgotten, but the first date that resulted in a long relationship is remembered vividly.
The mere ownership effect	Selectively overvaluing the qualities or objects we possess or hope to possess	Ed Smith thinks the letters *E* and *S* (his initials) are more attractive than the letters *F* and *Z*.
Self-serving attributions	Emphasizing one's personal responsibility for positive events and outcomes but minimizing responsibility for negative events and outcomes	The employee who is passed over for a promotion blames the failure on the boss's stupidity and biases rather than on her own incompetency.
Self-handicapping	Setting the stage for self-serving attributions by deliberately seeking out impediments to performance	The professor who fears that she will give a boring lecture deliberately leaves too little time to prepare for the presentation.
Downward social comparison	Comparing ourselves to others who are worse off than we are	The student who gets a D on a paper compares herself to her roommate, who is failing the course.
Maximizing collective self-esteem	Maintaining and enhancing a high level of collective self-esteem	The struggling A student is best friends with the C-average track team star.

the qualities that spring from our memberships in social groups. Emphasis on our personal identities is known as *individualism*, whereas awareness of the collective self heightens our feelings of *collectivism*.

Most of us are motivated to maintain or enhance our current feelings of self-worth, or *self-esteem* (both trait and state). Because our self-esteem prospers when we can frame our positive attributes and discount our negative qualities, self-esteem is often closely linked to *self-complexity*. We are predisposed to accept global, ambiguous feedback about ourselves (the *Barnum effect*), but we more readily embrace favorable feedback than unfavorable feedback. Even individuals with low self-esteem react negatively to unfavorable feedback. Cognitively, they may seek information that verifies their negative self-conceptions, but emotionally, they respond more positively to favorable than unfavorable information. Through *repression* we push negative memories out of our awareness. We positively evaluate characteristics we possess and objects we own (the *mere ownership effect*). When we fail, we often attribute our poor performances to external factors (the self-serving bias), and we even set the stage for failure by *self-handicapping*. We also avoid comparing ourselves to people who are performing more skillfully than we are (*upward social comparison*), and who seek out targets who are less fortunate than we are (*downward social comparison*). According to *self-evaluation maintenance* theory, we seek out associations with people who outperform us only if they are superior in ways that aren't relevant to our own self-concepts.

For More Information

• *Advances in Experimental Social Psychology*, Volume 21, edited by Leonard Berkowitz (1988), contains a number of excellent articles dealing with the self, its contents, and its motives.

• *Encounters with the Self*, by Don E. Hamachek (1987), uses some of the concepts examined in this chapter to explore the link between the self and personal adjustment. An excellent choice for people who want more information on self-improvement.

• *Escaping the Self*, by Roy F. Baumeister (1991), presents a comprehensive social-psychological analysis of intriguing oddities in human behavior, including alcoholism, masochism, and eating disorders.

• *The Self: Interdisciplinary Approaches*, edited by Jaine Strauss and George R. Goethals (1991), contains over a dozen cutting-edge analyses of the self that were presented at the G. Stanley Hall symposium in 1989.

• *Self-Esteem at Work*, by Joel Brockner (1988), is a thorough analysis of the impact of high and low self-esteem on employees' reactions to organizational changes.

• *Self-Handicapping: The Paradox That Isn't*, by Raymond L. Higgins, C. R. Snyder, and Steven Berglas (1990), furnishes a comprehensive review of what is known about self-handicapping and suggests avenues for future study of this paradoxical process.

Application: Expectancies and Educational Outcomes

When children reach age 5 they begin a uniquely influential and long-lasting experience: school. For the next 12 years they will spend one-third of their waking hours listening to their teachers, playing with their friends, acquiring new skills and interests, and experiencing the joy of success and the anguish of failure. These experiences will change them intellectually, emotionally, and socially. Will they develop basic skills such as reading and writing? Will they learn to work cooperatively with other people? Will they develop insight into their own characteristics and learn to regulate their actions? The answers to these questions depend, in part, on social psychological factors, for education is undeniably an interpersonal process (Bickman, 1983; Feldman, 1986).

Studies of self-fulfilling prophecies provide a compelling illustration of social psychology's relevance to the field of education. The idea that perceivers' mistaken expectancies can become self-confirming was first discussed in 1948 by Robert Merton. He speculated that a perceiver's inaccurate beliefs about other people can evoke new behaviors that make the original inaccurate conceptions come true. According to Merton, a vivacious woman who is perceived as boring can become a bore. An honest man who is judged to be a criminal can become a criminal. Perhaps even a dullard who is perceived to be brilliant will become intelligent.

Over the years, Merton's thoughts on self-fulfilling prophecies were questioned by social psychologists, but little progress was made toward understanding the puzzling phenomenon. All this changed in 1968, when Robert Rosenthal and Lenore Jacobson published the results of a remarkable study carried out with elementary school teachers and their pupils. After supposedly testing the students using a newly developed test ("The Harvard Test of Inflicted Acquisition"), Rosenthal and Jacobson claimed that some of the pupils were "late bloomers"—students who had seemed average during their early school years but were now poised on the brink of great academic progress. Unbeknownst to the teachers, these students were selected at random and therefore were no more likely to gain intellectually than their classmates. Yet, when the researchers returned

▲ **TABLE 5-6**
How do perceivers' beliefs about other people (targets) become fulfilled during interaction?

Perceivers often treat targets differently depending on their perceptions, and this differential treatment changes the targets.

Stage	*Process*	*Example*
1	Perceiver develops expectations concerning the target.	Teachers believe that some of their students are late bloomers.
2	Perceiver acts on the basis of this expectation.	Teachers show more warmth toward late bloomers; teach late bloomers more material.
3	Target person changes his or her behavior in response to perceiver's behavior.	Late bloomers study more, put forth more effort, get higher test scores, show more improvement.
4	Target internalizes the dispositions implied by perceiver's behavior.	Late bloomers redefine themselves as more intelligent and as better students.

eight months later, the late bloomers had changed. Relative to students in a control condition, their scores on tests of verbal ability rose by 2 IQ points, whereas their scores on a test of reasoning rose 7 points. Some students showed even more remarkable change, improving their scores by as much as 30 points. The teachers also rated the late bloomers more positively than they rated students in a control condition.

Rosenthal and Jacobson titled their report, *Pygmalion in the Classroom*. Pygmalion, according to Greek lore, could find no one worthy of his affections. He was a gifted sculptor, however, so he carved a statue of his ideal mate out of ivory. When he fell in love with his statue, the goddess Aphrodite answered his prayers by bringing the statue to life. Rosenthal and Jacobson's study suggested that teachers can turn ordinary students into high achievers, just as Pygmalion created the ideal lover out of ivory. The impact of a teacher's false expectations on student learning was promptly dubbed the *Pygmalion effect*.

Their findings stirred a considerable controversy, for many people did not think that expectations could have such powerful effects on students' achievements. But when other researchers set out to reexamine their hypothesis, they, too, found that teachers' expectancies can substantially influence student achievement. When Rosenthal combined the results of the 400 studies carried out between 1968 and 1985, he concluded that most confirmed the Pygmalion effect. The effect also appears to operate in a range of settings. Evidence indicates that adolescents who are treated like criminals when they violate laws are more likely to engage in more serious forms of delinquent activity (Oyserman & Markus, 1990). Negotiators who expect that the other party will be hostile and uncooperative indirectly encourage the display of these very behaviors (Rubin, Kim, & Peretz, 1990). People who work for companies with affirmative action policies may mistakenly assume that minority members who work for the company were hired because of their ethnic status rather than their capabilities. The minorities, in turn, may respond by doubting their own potential and by denigrating their own performance (Nacoste, 1987, 1989).

A self-fulfilling prophecy does not become confirmed by mystical means, however (Cooper & Hazelrigg, 1988; Harris & Rosenthal, 1985). Rather, it is mediated by interpersonal processes like those described in Table 5-6. The process begins when the perceiver develops expectations concerning another individual (the target). Whether they are based on stereotyped thinking or initial misunderstandings, these expectations are false: they misrepresent the individual who is being perceived. These false beliefs, however, influence the way that the perceiver acts toward the target. The police officer who assumes urban youth are dangerous treats them like criminals. The boss who thinks people are lazy treats them with contempt. In the Pygmalion study, the teachers created a warmer, more positive learning climate for the late bloomers. They also gave late bloomers more feedback about their progress and even taught them more information (Cooper, 1983; Harris & Rosenthal, 1986). Third, the target person changes his or her behavior to respond to the expectations held by the perceiver. The students responded to their teachers' expectation-based efforts; they asked more questions, worked harder on assignments, and literally learned more information. In the final stage, the target internalizes the dispositions implied by his or her behavior. The prophecy was fulfilled when the students altered their self-concepts to match their newly gained academic abilities (Darley & Fazio, 1980; Fazio, Effrein, & Falender, 1981; Jussim, 1986, 1990, 1991; Miller & Turnbull, 1986; Snyder, 1984).

The Pygmalion effect has important educational implications. Although teachers who think their students are capable of great success may stimulate achievement, teachers who bring negative expectations to the classroom can undermine student achievement. Tracking systems, for example, can adversely affect students. Educators often justify tracking students into different classes on the basis of their ability because teaching is easier when the class is homogeneous. They also assume that tracking shields slower students from esteem-damaging comparisons with faster students. Yet evidence indicates that students suffer more when they realize that they have been classified as slow learners. Also, teachers tend to respond differently to children in the slow tracks; they set easier goals, teach less material, and are less likely to respond positively to these children (Covington, 1992; Harris & Rosenthal, 1986).

Researchers have identified a number of ways to eliminate the negative influence of self-fulfilling prophecies. Some interventions help teachers recognize how their implicit expectations influence their teaching. Teacher Expectations and Student Achievement (TESA) workshops (Kerman & Martin, 1980), for example, warn teachers of the dangers of false expectations. The workshop also identifies 15 specific teaching behaviors that mediate the impact of expectations and trains teachers to be careful when rewarding students, when asking questions, when responding to troublesome pupils, and so on. A similar program, the Student/Teacher Interactive Learning Environment (STILE) (Banuazizi, 1981), also begins with a discussion of the Pygmalion effect. Teachers are then observed when interacting with students, and they are given detailed feedback on how they use rewards, questions, and nonverbal cues. If this observation suggests that they are responding differentially to students, the teachers take part in an additional training session in which they role-play various teaching situations. Parents, too, are sometimes included in the intervention since their expectations can also influence their children's accomplishments. Preliminary findings suggest that these kinds of programs are effective ways of minimizing unequal treatment of students by their teachers (Harris & Rosenthal, 1986).

Other interventions focus on students by raising their self-esteem and their expectations for success. One of the most promising of these approaches is based on Albert Bandura's theory of **self-efficacy** (Bandura, 1986). According to Bandura, students who are high in self-efficacy believe they are capable of performing the actions needed for success in any given situation. Rather than try to bolster individuals' overall feelings of self-esteem, Bandura and his colleagues focus on feelings of self-efficacy with regard to specific tasks. One study manipulated children's feelings of self-efficacy with regard to a math test. Some children were given specific, attainable goals to work for; others were not. When they were tested later, the children who were working toward attainable goals had higher feelings of self-efficacy, solved more problems on the test, and also were more interested in the test (Bandura & Schunk, 1981). In a variety of settings, Bandura and his colleagues have found that any intervention that increases students' levels of self-efficacy improves their persistence, satisfaction, and performance (Multon, Brown, & Lent, 1991; Schunk, 1984).

These studies suggest that educators should not ignore the social nature of the classroom. As active participants in the social setting, teachers often expect to see certain qualities in their students, and these expectations influence the way they teach. Students may struggle to disconfirm their teachers' mistaken assumptions, but if contact with the teacher is prolonged, the student may eventually accept the teacher's definition of his or her qualities. Fortunately, however, this expectation-confirmation can be interrupted by helping teachers develop positive expectations about students' chances of success, and by encouraging feelings of efficacy in students.

self-efficacy: The belief that one can personally produce and regulate one's outcomes.

KEEP
ABORTION
LEGAL
KEEP
ABORTION
LEGAL
TEEN

Attitudes and Behavior

Janet is a happy new mother. She's become expert at the many baby-maintenance tasks that crowd her days, and if pressed she might even admit that she enjoys them. Her baby is healthy, happy, and growing into his own person a bit more every day. But now, only two months after the birth, she is pregnant again. It's a shock. She is devoted to her husband and son, but they take all her time and energy. A second baby would tie her down completely, and she knows it. A second baby would also drain the family's limited economic and emotional resources, and she wonders whether she can handle the added responsibility. Her body hasn't recovered physically from her first pregnancy, and her doctor opposes her carrying the child to full term. All these factors weigh in favor of an abortion, but her attitude about abortion is decidedly negative. Janet is Catholic, and she believes that abortion is wrong: "It is taking a life. Even though it is not formed, it is the potential, and to me it is still taking a life" (quoted in Gilligan, 1982, p. 83).

attitude
An affective feeling of liking or disliking toward an object; positive or negative cognitive representations of social objects that exert a directive or dynamic influence on behavior.

Janet's predicament arises, in part, from the push and pull of her own **attitudes**. She dislikes some of the mundane chores that come with parenting, but she likes staying at home to care for her son. She dislikes being tied down with obligations, but she loves her husband and son. She believes abortion is morally wrong, yet she also believes it would be selfish of her to have another child at this time. She does not simply perform the actions of a mother; she also evaluates and appraises motherhood. She does not coldly calculate the need for an abortion; instead she is repulsed by the thought of aborting her unexpected pregnancy. These attitudes, like all attitudes, reveal the universal human tendency to react in a positive or negative way to aspects of our social world. We don't just observe and perceive; we also evaluate, praise, and criticize.

But why should we, as social psychologists, be concerned with Janet's attitudes? The sections of this chapter offer an answer in three parts. First, attitudes fulfill a number of critical functions for human beings. They are vast repositories of information about many aspects of our social world, which we update regularly as we learn new data from others or through personal experience. Janet's attitudes, for example, summarize her likes and dislikes for thousands of social objects ranging from abalone earrings and abortions all the way to zoos and zygotes. As we see in the first section of this chapter, if we are to understand how people mentally represent and evaluate themselves, other people, places, objects, or issues, then we must understand their attitudes (Greenwald, 1989a).

Second, attitudes are a fundamental component in a complex system that links our personal preferences to our actions. We act, in most cases, in ways that are consistent with our attitudes. Janet does not respond randomly to social events; instead, her attitudes guide her toward objects and choices she favors and away from objects and choices she dislikes. Once we understand her attitudes, we can predict her behavior more accurately (Ajzen, 1988; Eiser & van der Pligt, 1988).

Third, just as our attitudes often influence our actions, so our actions can influence our attitudes. If, after weighing her options, Janet decides to have an abortion, this action will in all likelihood influence her attitudes toward abortion and her self. As we discover in the final section of this chapter, if we can't change our behavior to match our attitudes, we sometimes change our attitudes to match our behavior (Olson & Zanna, 1993).

The Nature of Attitudes

Artists were perhaps the first people to talk of attitudes. They used the word to describe the pose taken by a figure in sculpture or painting. A model was said to strike an attitude, and artists were urged to vary their colors, their subjects, and their attitudes (*Oxford English Dictionary*, 1970, p. 553). Charles Darwin, the evolutionist, echoed this usage when he labeled any overt expression of strong emotion an attitude. A wolf, he suggested, takes on an aggressive attitude by snarling and arching its back (Darwin, 1872/1955).

Social psychologists turned their attention to attitudes early in this century. They were puzzled by our tendency to seek out some things while avoiding others, and so they theorized that some unseen psychological process—an attitude—may be the hidden mediator. The concept of attitude, however, raised nearly as many questions as it answered: What is the nature of an attitude? How do we acquire our attitudes? Why do we even have attitudes? The answers to these questions, which are considered in the following sections, led to one undeniable conclusion: Attitudes are far more complicated than Darwin and the artists had imagined (Eagly, 1992; Eagly & Chaiken, 1992; Tesser & Shaffer, 1990).

What Is an Attitude?

People use the word *attitude* in dozens of different ways every day. A teacher tells a sulking student that he has a "bad attitude." A boss compliments her employee on his "good work attitude." Coaches commend their players for showing a "team attitude." Social psychologists, in contrast, prefer to use the term *attitude* in a more narrow sense—to describe affectively valenced (that is, positive or negative) cognitive representations that exert a directive or dynamic influence on behavior (Breckler & Wiggins, 1989a, 1989b; Greenwald, 1989b). An attitude, then, is not a feeling, a cognition, or a form of behavior; instead, it combines all three components in an integrated affect-cognition-behavior system (Rosenberg & Hovland, 1960).

Consider Janet's attitudes: "I condemn abortion," "I love my son," "I dislike doctors." First, all these attitudes are affectively valenced: they include an emotional component that is either positive (liking, love, desire, wanting, admiration) or negative (disliking, hatred, abhorrence, contempt, rejection). Second, each of these attitudes includes a cognitive representation that summarizes Janet's assumptions and beliefs about aspects of her social world (Pratkanis, 1989). They are her internalized, mental images of objects, people, social groups, and social issues (Greenwald, 1989b). Last, Janet's attitudes exert a directive or dynamic influence on her behavior. She does not just

▲ **FIGURE 6-1**
What is the structure of an attitude? The tricomponent theory emphasizes the so-called ABCs of attitudes: affect, behavior, and cognition. R_{ab} is the relationship between affect and behavior. R_{ac} is the relationship between affect and cognition. R_{bc} is the relationship between behavior and cognition.

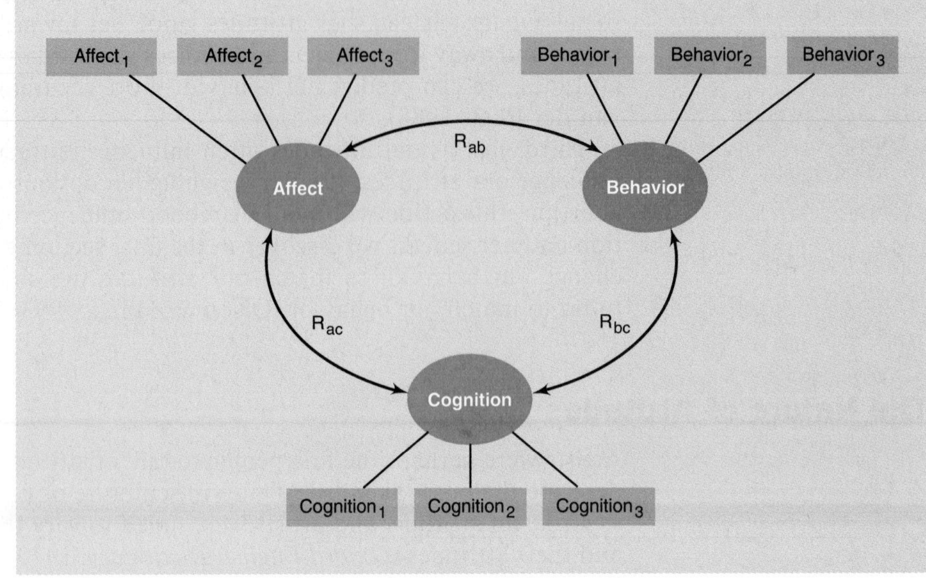

harbor her ill-will toward doctors, and she does not treat her son in harsh, unfair ways. Instead, her overt actions are consistent with her feelings and cognitions on both matters. This behavioral component of an attitude includes not only overt actions but predispositions to respond in certain general ways. This readiness to respond is often termed a **behavioral intention** (Fishbein & Ajzen, 1975).

behavioral intention
A person's intention to respond in either a positive or negative way to an object.

tricomponent model
A theoretical perspective that argues that an attitude forms when three components—affect, cognition, and behavior—become linked in an organized structure.

This analysis of attitudes is often termed the **tricomponent model**, for it hypothesizes that attitudes form when all three components—affect, cognition, and behavior—become linked together in an organized structure like the one shown in Figure 6-1. What is your attitude, for example, toward snakes? Do you like them, dislike them, or do you have no attitude one way or another? Steven J. Breckler (1984) studied the underlying structure of such an attitude by measuring each of the components specified in the tricomponent model. When his subjects arrived for the experiment, he asked them to sit in front of a live, caged, corn snake. He measured their affective responses to the snake by monitoring their heart rates and by asking them whether they felt tense, fearful, jittery, elated, playful, pleased, and so on. He measured their cognitive responses to the snake by asking them to describe their snake-related beliefs (for example, "Snakes are soft and smooth" and "Snakes control the rodent population") and by asking them to list all their thoughts when they were in the presence of the snake. Last, he measured behavior by asking subjects to indicate how they usually act around snakes (for example, "I scream whenever I see a snake" or "I like to catch snakes") and how closely they approach them. He also gave subjects the opportunity to pet and hold the snake.

Breckler used an advanced statistical procedure known as *structural equations modeling* to examine the interrelationships among the three components. This procedure indicated that the three components were distinct from one another but that they were also interlinked. The correlation between affect and cognition was .38, the correlation between affect and behavior was .50, and the correlation between cognition and behavior was .70. These data suggest that individuals who have strongly positive feelings about snakes also tend to have favorable beliefs about snakes and are willing to touch them. The relationships among the various components, however, were not equal in strength. Indeed,

▲ Attitudes link our emotions, cognitions, and behaviors together in an organized structure. In some cases, however, these components are not completely consistent with one another. For example, you may know that a snake is harmless (cognition), but at the same time you may experience an intensely negative emotional reaction (affect) and scream (behavior) when you encounter one.

the affect-cognition link was the weakest, suggesting that quite a few of Breckler's subjects who felt that snakes were harmless still felt upset when they sat by one. In contrast, most of the individuals who reported positive cognitions about snakes were willing to approach a snake closely or even to handle one.

Do these findings hold only for snakes? Apparently not, for studies of attitudes pertaining to religion, contraceptives, and even other racial groups indicate that affect, cognition, and behavior combine to form attitudes (Bagozzi & Burnkrant, 1979, 1985, Campbell, 1950; Kothandapani, 1971; compare with Dillon & Kumar, 1985). In one such study, Donald Campbell arranged for white high school and college students to rate five social groups—black, Jewish, Japanese, Mexican, and English—on five scales. He measured affect by asking the subjects to indicate how much they liked or disliked each group. He measured cognitions by collecting ratings of each group's competence, morality, and responsibility for social problems. Last, he measured behaviors indirectly by asking subjects if they would be willing to interact with members of the groups in a variety of social settings. Like Breckler, Campbell found substantial affect-cognition-behavior linkages. People who disliked Mexicans, for example, also reported many negative beliefs about them and were unwilling to interact with them. The average of the correlations among the three components was about .50 (Campbell, 1950; see Table 6-1).

Learning Attitudes

Some of our most basic attitudes may be instinctive. Some theorists have suggested that certain negative attitudes, such as our fear of snakes or the nearly universal revulsion for bodily wastes and decaying matter, may be so useful to our survival that they are part of our genetic heritage (McGuire, 1985; Rozin & Fallon, 1987; Tesser, 1993). Most of our attitudes are learned, however. In some cases, our attitudes form as we learn about the object through direct experiences with it. In others, the people around us may teach us our attitudes through direct and indirect instruction. In either case, we learn to like and love, just as we learn to dislike and hate.

▲ **TABLE 6-1**
Summing up: The tricomponent model of attitudes

Component	*Definition and Characteristics*	*Examples*
Affect	Emotional reaction to the attitude object; positive or negative feelings aroused by the attitude object	"I dislike correlational designs." "Seeing homeless people upsets me." "Polluters make me angry."
Cognition	Internalized mental representation of objects, people, social groups, and social issues; beliefs, ideas, thoughts, and other bits of information pertaining to the attitude object	"Experiments yield conclusions about causality." "The government should do more to help the homeless." "Littering hurts the environment."
Behavior	A tendency to respond to the attitude object in a particular way; overt actions and predispositions	"I only conduct experimental research." "I donate money to a shelter for the homeless." "I recycle my newspapers."

Direct experience. Like most people, Janet acquired some of her attitudes through direct experience with various objects. During her pregnancy she probably became very fond of certain kinds of foods because these foods tasted wonderful when she ate them. In contrast, she probably disliked foods that seemed to have an unpleasant taste or made her feel nauseous. She grew to like some foods and dislike others through direct contact with them (Fazio, 1989; Fazio & Zanna, 1981).

mere exposure
The formation of a positive attitude through repeated exposure to the object.

Direct experience with an object sets the stage for several attitude-building processes. Direct experience increases our overall familiarity with an object, and in most cases, the more familiar an object, the more we like it (Bornstein, 1989). The **mere exposure** process explains many of the attitudes we take for granted. English-speaking people judge words that occur frequently in the English language (*together*, *good*, *add*, *upward*) more positively than words that occur less frequently (*apart*, *better*, *subtract*, *downward*). When people were shown nonsense words—such as *iktitaf*, *afworbu*, and *saricik*—once, 5 times, 10 times, or 25 times, they became more positive toward the words they heard more frequently (Zajonc, 1968). When people see a photograph of themselves and a photograph developed from a reversed negative, they generally prefer the reversed image. It corresponds to the image they see of themselves every day when they look in the mirror. When they look at pictures of friends or loved ones, they prefer the true images to reversed images (Mita, Dermer, & Knight, 1977). Exposure apparently makes the heart grow fonder.

classical conditioning
A learning-through-association process that takes place when a neutral stimulus is paired repeatedly with a stimulus that already evokes a response. After sufficient pairings, the formerly neutral stimulus will evoke the response when presented by itself.

Direct experience also increases the likelihood that an attitudinal response can become conditioned, either through classical conditioning or instrumental conditioning. When **classical conditioning** occurs, the attitude object becomes associated with objects or experiences that are pleasant or unpleasant (Zanna, Kiesler, & Pilkonis, 1970). In one study, the nonsense syllables *las*, *ike*, *yof*, and *wuh* were paired with emotionally toned words. Initially, *yof* and *wuh* had no meaning at all for subjects; but when *yof* was repeatedly paired with such positive words as *gift*, *sacred*, and *happy*, people ended up liking *yof*. In contrast, when *wuh* was paired with such words as *bitter*, *ugly*, and *failure*, subjects eventually acquired a negative reaction to *wuh* (Staats & Staats, 1958). Janet's attitudes may have developed through this kind of associative learning. Her attitudes toward foods may have developed because she experienced pleasurable

▲ Do you see any differences between these two pictures? The photo on the left is a true image—a picture of the woman as other people see her. The photo on the right, in contrast, is a reversed image; it corresponds to the reversed image the woman would see if she looked at herself in a mirror. Although the two photographs seem identical, researchers have found that people tend to prefer reversed-image photos of themselves. We see our reversed image each time we look in the mirror, but we rarely see our true image. Because of this repeated exposure, we come to regard the reversed image more favorably.

sensations when she ate mashed potatoes, but unpleasant sensations occurred when she smelled coffee. This type of conditioning can occur even if Janet fails to recognize the association (or contingency) between the object and her emotional reaction (Coleman & Gormezano, 1979; Krosnick et al., 1992).

instrumental conditioning (also called operant conditioning)
A learning process that takes place when a response is immediately followed by a reinforcer or a punishment. Responses followed by reinforcers become more frequent in the future, whereas responses followed by punishments become less frequent.

Instrumental conditioning occurs when attitudinal reactions are followed by rewards or punishment. The behaviorist B. F. Skinner (1975) argued that whenever our responses are immediately followed by rewards (Skinner called them *reinforcers*), these responses become more frequent in the future. Responses that are followed by punishments, in contrast, become less frequent. If, immediately after she nurses her son, Janet feels peaceful and happy, she will develop a positive attitude toward nursing. Similarly, the girl who gets gold stars for passing her math tests may develop a fondness for math, whereas the boy who is ridiculed each time he strikes out at softball may come to hate the sport (Insko, 1965; Lott & Lott, 1985).

socialization
The gradual acquisition of language, attitudes, and other socially approved values through reinforcement, observation, and other learning processes.

Socialization. We learn many of our attitudes in the same way that we learn our language, social norms, and cultural values: through **socialization**. Society's socializing agents—parents, peers, teachers, relatives, newspapers, books, television, religious groups, and so on—teach us how to interact with other people, what behaviors are expected of us in various situations, and what things are valued in our society. These sources sometimes explicitly define, through instruction and persuasion, what is considered good and what is considered bad. Janet was raised in the Catholic faith and had been taught to believe that abortion is morally wrong. If Janet's family had some other religious background, or if she had grown up in a different culture, her attitudes about abortion might have been positive rather than negative.

Socializing agents also transfer attitudes from one generation to the next through conditioning. Our parents not only tell us what is good or bad, they also reward us when we later express the attitudes they prefer. Chet Insko (1965) demonstrated just how easy it is to condition people by telephoning students and asking them a series of questions pertaining to a festival week of bands and outdoor events held at the university. Half of the students were reinforced with a "Good" each time they expressed a favorable opinion about the festival, whereas the others were reinforced only when they criticized the festival. Insko waited a week and then measured their attitudes in a completely different context. Sure enough, students whose positive statements had been reinforced expressed more favorable attitudes than students whose negative comments had been reinforced. Like an experimenter giving a rat a reward for learning a maze or a trainer giving a dog a bone when the dog fetches the stick, socializers can create and destroy attitudes by selectively rewarding or punishing us.

social learning theory
A model of learning which argues that new behaviors are acquired by observing and imitating the actions displayed by models, such as parents and peers.

According to Albert Bandura's **social learning theory**, socializing agents also influence us by modeling behaviors, which we then imitate. Imagine Janet, her mother, and father discussing *Roe* v. *Wade*, the Supreme Court case that legally sanctioned abortion in the United States. As the discussion unfolds, Janet's father remarks that the Court made a terrible decision because abortion is immoral. Janet then watches as her mother smiles at her father, touches his hand, and nods her head in agreement. According to social learning theory, Janet would be more likely to express a similar attitude toward abortion and *Roe* v. *Wade* in the future (Bandura, 1969, 1977).

Unlike theories based on classical and instrumental conditioning, social learning theory maintains that people can acquire attitudes by observing others' actions. We don't imitate all that we observe, however. Because Janet's father was reinforced for his anti-abortion remarks, she would be likely to adopt his position. Had her mother risen from the table and said in an angry voice, "I'm tired of men thinking that they have the right to even discuss an issue that is solely the concern of women," then Janet would have learned to avoid her father's behavior. Janet didn't directly experience the consequences her father did; they were vicarious consequences. But, according to Bandura, learning is more likely to occur when the vicarious consequences are positive than when they are punishing.

Acquiring political attitudes. In sum, our attitudes spring from a number of sources, including direct experience and socialization. Consider, for example, your attitudes about political issues: Are you Republican, Democrat, or Independent? Do you think the government should do more for poor people? What is your opinion of President Clinton? Do you think the health care system in the United States should be changed? Should capital punishment be banned?

The social-psychological forces summarized in Table 6-2 probably played a role in creating your opinions on these issues. Through exposure you may have learned to like Bill Clinton, even though you had no opinion about him in 1990. Perhaps your friends rewarded you each time you mentioned your negative feelings about capital punishment, so these attitudes became stronger and stronger over time. You may also endorse the same political beliefs as your parents, for when you were growing up they may have talked about politics at the dinner table (Kinder & Sears, 1985).

These social-psychological processes explain the dramatic shifts in attitude that Theodore Newcomb (1943) documented in his classic study of political attitudes. Newcomb noticed that most of the students at Bennington College, where he taught, came from politically conservative families, so students in the incoming class usually expressed conservative attitudes. The graduating seniors, in contrast, tended to express more liberal attitudes. Why such a disparity? When Newcomb examined students' attitudes over a four-year period, he found that students acquired new attitudes from their classmates and the

▲ TABLE 6-2
Summing up: The sources of our attitudes

Source	*Definition*	*Examples*
Mere exposure	Repeated exposure to an object generally increases our overall favorability toward the object.	• Songs we hear frequently on the radio are liked more than songs we hear rarely. • Politicians whose names are easily recognized receive more votes than low-profile candidates.
Classical conditioning	If the attitude object is paired repeatedly with a stimulus that already evokes a positive or negative response, the object will evoke the response when presented by itself.	• Consumers buy tires after watching advertisements that repeatedly pair the tires with cute babies. • A hungry dog salivates to a bell ring if the bell has previously been paired with food.
Instrumental conditioning	Attitudinal reactions, including affect, cognition, or behaviors, that are immediately followed by a reinforcer occur more frequently in the future; responses that are followed by punishments become less frequent.	• The pupil who gets gold stars for passing math tests likes mathematics. • The diner who gets food poisoning after eating a pizza dislikes pizza for several years.
Socialization	The acquisition of language, attitudes, and other socially approved values through direct instruction, reinforcement, and other learning processes.	• Hindus are taught to eat pork but not beef; Jews eat beef but not pork. • Catholics are taught that abortion and birth control are immoral.
Social learning	New behaviors and attitudes are acquired by observing and imitating the actions displayed by models, such as parents and peers.	• Children prefer wearing their seat belts after watching TV shows in which the heroes wear seat belts. • A son advocates the death penalty after listening to his father make pro-death-penalty statements.

college faculty. Their families taught them to be conservative, but the college community supported only liberal attitudes. So students who were actively involved in campus life shifted toward liberalism, especially if they associated with students who tended to be liberal. Individuals who were very family oriented and didn't take part in campus events remained conservative. The impact of this socializing experience was considerable, for the more liberal attitudes created by the group remained a part of the beliefs of many of the graduates some 25 years later (Newcomb et al., 1967).

Attitude Functions

Attitudes are universal. Only some people have a million dollars, red hair, or social poise, but we all have attitudes. Given their prevalence, the natural question that comes to mind is, "Why?" Of what use are they to us? How do they benefit us? In answering these questions, several theorists describe the useful things attitudes do for us (Abelson & Prentice, 1989; Herek, 1987; Katz, 1960; Shavitt, 1989; Smith, Bruner, & White, 1956; Snyder & DeBono, 1989). Daniel Katz (1960) described four key functions that attitudes fulfill for us: organizing information (knowledge function), identifying positive and negative objects (instrumental function), self-expression (expressive function), and self-protection and enhancement (defensive function).

▲ **TABLE 6-3**
A hierarchical model of attitudes

This model suggests that attitudes organize our knowledge across four different levels of specificity: objects, categories, propositions, and schemas.

Level	*Definition*	*Examples*
Object	Evaluation of specific social objects	"I like *Gone with the Wind*." "I enjoy Jiffy peanut butter."
Category	Identification of evaluatively positive and negative abstract categories	"I hate game shows." "I like Koreans."
Proposition	Description of actions and states that range from desirable to undesirable	"Abortion is wrong." "Live free or die."
Schema	Rule-governed groupings of propositions that are evaluative	One's conception of democracy. One's moral ideology.

Source: Greenwald, 1989b.

The knowledge function. Some attitudes help attitude-holders keep track of all the information they have about thousands of individuals, objects, places, and issues. Such attitudes can summarize information about a specific object, or they can be more general (Greenwald, 1989b; see Table 6-3). Some of Janet's attitudes, such as "I love my son" and "I dislike yogurt," are examples of object-specific attitudes. Others, such as "I dislike doctors," summarize her overall appraisal of entire categories, and still others pertain to general propositions (for example, "Abortion is wrong"). The most general attitudes organize a variety of arguments, beliefs, values, and facts in a cognitive schema like the one shown in Figure 6-2 (Judd & Kulik, 1980; Pratkanis, 1989).

Like the cognitive structures discussed in Chapter 3, attitudes allow Janet to process incoming information rapidly, but they also influence her ability to later retrieve information from memory. When pro-abortion, anti-abortion, or neutral subjects were shown a series of negative and positive statements pertaining to abortion their attitudes influenced their ability to remember this information. Individuals with well-defined schemas pertaining to abortion could accurately identify pro- and anti-abortion information that they had previously been shown, but individuals who did not have a well-formed attitude pertaining to abortion made significantly more mistakes (Hymes, 1986). When attitudes fulfill an informational function, they influence what we notice, encode, and remember (Lord, Lepper, & Mackie, 1984; Pratkanis & Greenwald, 1989).

The instrumental function. According to Katz, an individual typically develops "favorable attitudes towards the objects in his world which are associated with the satisfactions of his needs and unfavorable attitudes toward objects which thwart him or punish him" (Katz, 1960, p. 171). Such attitudes fulfill an instrumental function in that they guide behavior in the direction of desirable, useful objects and away from punishing objects that lack any instrumental value to us. Why, for example, when people are asked to name their "favorite material possessions," does the list include their stereos, television sets, clothing, personal computers, credit cards, watches, refrigerators, beds, telephones, and their home? Because we use these objects to meet our everyday, practical needs (Prentice, 1987). In contrast, objects and events that prevent us from meeting our basic needs are disliked; we avoid traffic jams,

▲ **FIGURE 6-2**
Are attitudes schemas? This model of a hypothetical attitude assumes that attitudes function like schemas by organizing our beliefs, values, ideas, opinions, and feelings about certain issues and objects. This model suggests that attitudes about abortion are bipolar; they have both positive and negative elements. Other attitudes might be unipolar instead.

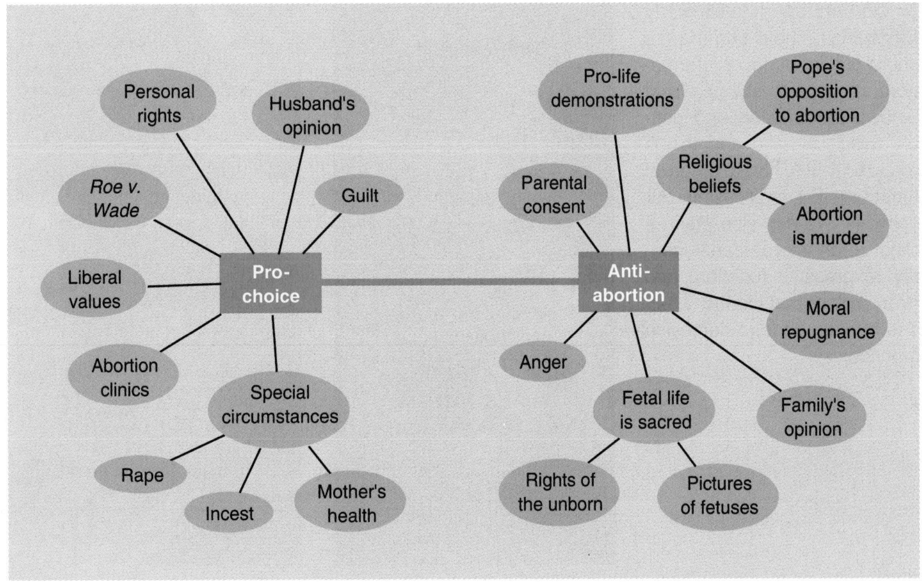

incompetent co-workers, and unreliable alarm clocks because they are worse than useless; they undermine our ability to meet our goals.

The expressive function. Our attitudes are often the means by which we express ourselves and our identities. A large part of our self-conception is determined by our attitudes, for we often answer the question "Who am I?" by listing our likes and dislikes (see Chapter 5). A person who thinks of herself as "cultured," for example, when asked to name her likes, would be more likely to list art books, poetry books, paintings, formal clothes, and pearls, whereas a sports enthusiast would list his baseball bat, basketball, catcher's mitt, and so on (Prentice, 1987). We also use our attitudes to increase our association with social groups: "I am a Catholic" or "I am pro-choice on the issue of abortion" are both examples of the use of an attitude to express our alliance with a group or political outlook. Moreover, when we express such attitudes to others, they serve a communicative, self-presentational function. When we first meet other people, we often let them know who we are by telling them about our basic attitudes (Schlenker, 1980).

The defensive function. The individual may also use attitudes to protect "himself from acknowledging the basic truths about himself or the harsh realities in his external world" (Katz, 1960, p. 170). This function, which has roots in psychoanalytic theory, suggests that attitudes sometimes help us deal with internal conflicts and personal insecurities. Janet faces a difficult decision regarding her pregnancy, and she may cope by saying she has no choice in the matter because abortion is immoral. Individuals who feel uncertain of their own worth also use prejudicial attitudes defensively; by condemning other groups, they feel more secure about the value of themselves and their own group (Allport, 1954). Katz points out that defensive attitudes can be aroused in many ways—through external threats, by increasing internal conflicts and anxieties, or by frustrating the individual—but that successfully changing defensive attitudes can be difficult. (Chapter 7 deals with prejudicial attitudes and their functions in more detail.)

These four functions, which are summarized in Table 6-4, don't represent four mutually exclusive categories; most attitudes serve more than one pur-

▲ Our attitudes fulfill many functions. They summarize enormous amounts of information about our social world (knowledge function) and identify things we like and things we don't like (instrumental function). By expressing our opinions, we can also stake a claim to an interpersonal identity (expressive function) and even protect that identity when it is threatened (ego-defensive function).

pose. Take your attitudes about various types of music. First, by serving a knowledge function, these attitudes help you understand and organize the new songs you hear. Your attitudes help you classify a song as to type—jazz, metal, rap, country, rock, or easy listening—while also influencing your reactions to it (for instance, "It's metal; I don't like it" or "This is Pearl Jam; I like their songs"). Second, attitudes are instrumental in guiding your behavior; how will you know which CDs to buy when you enter a music store if you don't have any attitudes? Third, your attitudes about music may play a part in defining who you are—a sophisticated socialite who likes the opera and symphony, a fun-loving alternative music fan who likes rap and hip-hop, a soft-spoken intellectual who likes jazz—by summarizing your values and interests. Last, your attitudes about music might be defensive. If you feel threatened by rapid changes in the world, you may condemn any kind of music with which you are not familiar, whether it be new forms of contemporary music, such as rap, modern orchestral pieces, or remakes of old songs by new artists. In sum, where would you, or anyone for that matter, be without attitudes?

Attitudes and Behavior

Would life without attitudes be possible? Gordon W. Allport (1935, p. 806), one of social psychology's founders, doesn't think so.

▲ **TABLE 6-4**
Summing up: Four possible functions of attitudes

Function	*Definition*
Knowledge	Attitudes summarize information about objects in the social world; they organize our feelings and beliefs while providing a frame of reference.
Instrumental	Attitudes guide behavior by identifying what is good and bad, desirable and undesirable.
Expressive	Attitudes help define the self-concept by defining our likes and dislikes and representing our views on various issues.
Defensive	Attitudes protect us from inner conflicts that could threaten our world view. They protect and bolster self-esteem.

> Without guiding attitudes the individual is confused and baffled. Some kind of preparation is essential before he can make a satisfactory observation, pass suitable judgment, or make any but the most primitive reflex type of responses. Attitudes determine for each individual what he will see and hear, what he will think and what he will do.

But the relationship between attitudes and behaviors is neither so simple nor so uniformly powerful as Allport suggested. If we love Oreo cookies, do we always buy Oreo cookies at the store? Does a bigot always discriminate against racially different people? If Janet is opposed to abortion on moral grounds, can we be certain she will decide to carry her baby to full term rather than seek an abortion? What is the relationship between our attitudes and our actions?

Do Attitudes Guide Behavior?

Even as Allport argued that attitudes determine what we "will think and do," Richard T. LaPiere reported the results of a study that indicated attitudes are not always connected to behavior (LaPiere, 1934). LaPiere, who was white, enlisted the help of two Chinese friends, and the threesome spent their vacations driving across the United States. LaPiere expected to find great hostility, for prejudice against Asians was widespread in the United States at that time. Yet only one establishment out of the 251 restaurants, hotels, and campgrounds they visited turned them away. When LaPiere sent questionnaires to these same establishments asking them about their attitudes toward Chinese, they responded very differently—90% of them claimed that they did not serve Chinese. LaPiere thus answered the question "Do attitudes guide behavior?" with a resounding "No."

LaPiere's findings sparked the *consistency controversy*: a prolonged debate among researchers who disagreed about the strength of the attitude-behavior relationship (Liska, 1975). Some participants in the debate took issue with LaPiere's methods. He assessed attitudes several months after the behaviors, and during that time attitudes may have changed. He had no way of knowing whether the person who greeted his group was the same person who answered the letter or whether responding to a letter asking, "Will you accept members of the Chinese race as guests in your establishment?" adequately measured attitudes. Also, the object of the behavior was an English-speaking Chinese couple accompanied by a white man, whereas the object of the attitude was the very nonspecific "members of the Chinese race" (Ajzen & Fishbein, 1977).

Even when researchers corrected these problems, the attitude-behavior relationship did not emerge consistently across studies. Some researchers reported relatively strong correlations between actions and attitudes—political attitudes predicted voting behavior, attitudes about other racial groups influenced the willingness to be seen with members of that group, and attitudes toward drinking alcoholic beverages predicted drinking behavior (Campbell et al., 1960; DeFleur & Westie, 1958; Veevers, 1971, respectively). Others, in contrast, reported negligible attitude-behavior correlations—attitudes toward birth control didn't influence the use of birth control pills, whites' attitudes about blacks were unrelated to their reaction to a black person, and mothers' attitudes toward various child-rearing practices did not predict their behavior when they were with their children (Davidson & Jaccard, 1979; Himelstein & Moore, 1963; Zunich, 1961, respectively; Ajzen, 1988; Oskamp, 1991; and Wicker, 1969, review these studies in detail).

The consistency controversy raged on until researchers eventually realized they were asking the wrong question. Even if you prefer Oreo cookies, this preference may not be very strong. You might be prejudiced, but this attitude might not influence the way you treat specific individuals. Janet may be opposed to abortion in principle, but for medical and personal reasons, she may find that she must abort her pregnancy. These inconsistencies, however, don't necessarily mean that people are hypocrites who say one thing and do another. Rather, the link between attitude and action depends on many attitudinal, personal, and situational factors. LaPiere asked, "*Do* attitudes guide behavior?" He should have asked, "*When* do attitudes guide behavior?"

When Do Attitudes Guide Behavior?

We often act just as our attitudes dictate: the cookie lover gorges on Oreos, the bigot discriminates against people from different racial backgrounds, and the Catholic protests abortion. But in other cases our attitudes remain dormant. The attitude-behavior relationship can be robust or frail, depending on the nature of the attitude and the situation in which we find ourselves (Zanna, Higgins, & Herman, 1982).

Strong attitudes guide behavior. All attitudes are not created equal (Scott, 1968). Some attitudes are only subtle preferences; these attitudes are often ignored. Other attitudes—those that are central elements in our belief systems—may be so important that they influence actions across a wide range of settings (Rokeach, 1968). If your preference for a political candidate is weak or ambivalent, then your vote at the polls will be difficult to predict. If political attitudes are important to you, however, then your attitudes will guide both your perceptions of the candidates and your actual voting behavior (Krosnick, 1988). In general, people who are well-informed about issues usually let their attitudes guide their behaviors (Davidson et al., 1985; Zanna, Olson, & Fazio, 1980).

We are also more likely to act on our attitudes when we have a *vested interest* in the issue. When investigators polled college students concerning a proposal that would have raised the legal drinking age from 18 to 21, they found that most objected to the proposal. Few, however, were willing to campaign against it by making telephone calls. The investigators then split the students into two groups—students under 19, who would be denied alcoholic beverages for 2 or more years if the proposal passed, and students 21 and over, who wouldn't be affected by the change. The connection between students' attitudes toward the proposal and their behavior (as measured by the number of campaign phone calls they volunteered to make) was much stronger among younger subjects, who had a personal interest in the issue's outcome, than for older subjects. The attitude-behavior correlation was .61 for the younger students and only .16 for the older students (Sivacek & Crano, 1982).

Specific attitudes guide behavior. Our specific attitudes tend to be more potent guides for behavior than our diffuse attitudes and values. You might have a generally pro-environment attitude, but will this attitude prompt you to perform specific behaviors, such as attending Earth Day or recycling aluminum cans? In a study of just this question, researchers assessed subjects' attitudes concerning four issues: the environment, conservation, pollution, and the environmental interest group, the Sierra Club. Five months later, the subjects were asked to assist the Sierra Club by writing a letter to the local newspaper, joining the organization and paying dues, and so on. As Figure 6-3 shows, subjects' general attitudes toward the environment, conservation, and pollution proved to be poor predictors of their behavior. Their attitudes toward the Sierra Club, however, were highly correlated with their willingness to help

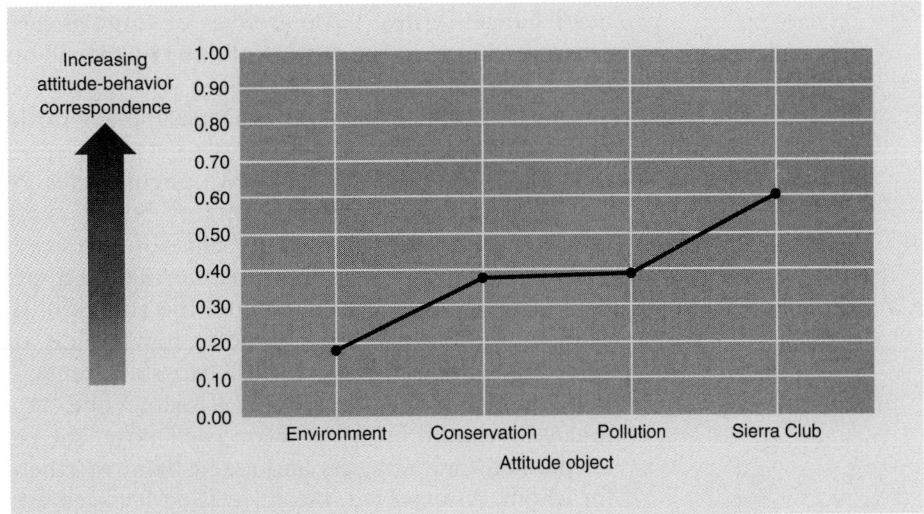

▲ **FIGURE 6-3**
What is the relationship between our attitudes and our behaviors? Researchers found that general conservation attitudes weren't linked to behavior, but specific attitudes toward the Sierra Club were correlated with willingness to assist the Sierra Club. (From Weigel, Vernon, & Tognacci, 1974)

the organization (Weigel, Vernon, & Tognacci, 1974). Evidence indicates that highly specific attitudes—those that pertain to specific objects in specific contexts and at specific times—are excellent predictors of specific behaviors (Ajzen & Fishbein, 1977). Very general attitudes can influence behavior, but their influence seems to be channeled through specific attitudes. Individuals who have pro-environment values usually have specific attitudes about recycling and saving water, and these specific attitudes, rather than general attitudes, guide behaviors (Homer & Kahle, 1988). As the section "Application: Promoting Healthy Behavior" explains, changing people's positive attitudes toward maintaining their health in general may not lead to changes in specific behaviors.

Attitudes formed through direct experience guide behavior. Studies conducted by Russell Fazio, Mark Zanna, and their associates indicate that our most behaviorally potent attitudes are ones that we acquire through direct experience with objects (Fazio & Zanna, 1978, 1981; Regan & Fazio, 1977). When subjects picked which problem they would complete in an experiment, did they choose the one they liked the best? Yes, provided they had formed their opinion of the task after actually working the problems earlier. Did students who felt that campus overcrowding was a serious problem volunteer to help change the system by handing out petitions and writing protest letters? Yes, provided they themselves had experienced problems finding housing on campus (Regan & Fazio, 1977). Attitudes acquired through direct experience are more specific, held with greater confidence, more easily recalled, more resistant to change, and more likely to influence our subsequent behavior (Fazio, Powell, & Herr, 1983; Fazio et al., 1986; Fazio & Zanna, 1978; Sherman et al., 1982; Wu & Shaffer, 1987).

Accessible attitudes guide behavior. Ellen Langer (1989) notes that we often behave first and think second. Even though we tend to think of ourselves as careful information processors who weigh various factors before selecting a course of action, when we fall prey to **mindlessness**, we perform behaviors without considering their meaning. Who among us hasn't answered an acquaintance's "How are you?" with a "Fine" even when we were ill, or watched our usual TV program even though we had decided to try something

mindlessness
A state of reduced cognitive activity in which individuals respond without considering the meaning of their behavior or its possible consequences.

new? Langer writes, "The grooves of mindlessness run deep. We know our scripts by heart. In the routine of daily life we do not notice what we are doing unless there is a problem" (p. 43).

Langer's concept of mindlessness, applied to the consistency controversy, suggests that our attitudes will have a strong impact on our actions only when they are accessible in memory. We might prefer Pepsi to Coke, poetry to fiction, or the seashore to the mountains, but these attitudes aren't always accessible to us when we are making behavioral choices. Fazio and Carol Williams (1986) studied this process during the 1984 U.S. presidential election. Months before the election, they measured the accessibility of attitudes pertaining to presidential candidates by recording how rapidly subjects could indicate their agreement or disagreement with two statements: "A good president for the next four years would be Ronald Reagan," and "A good president for the next four years would be Walter Mondale." After the election, Fazio and Williams telephoned their subjects and asked them whether they had voted and, if so, for whom. As expected, the correlation between attitude and behavior was .83 for subjects who responded very rapidly to the attitude measure, but only .64 for subjects who responded more slowly. Similar findings have been obtained when the attitude topic was subjects' opinion toward the environment (Kallgren & Wood, 1986).

Self-awareness, discussed in Chapter 5, can also increase the availability of our attitudes (Gibbons, 1990). Frederick X. Gibbons (1978) illustrated this process by measuring male college students' opinions concerning erotic books, movies, and magazines. To do so, he asked whether they agreed or disagreed with such statements as "I think laws should be passed preventing the sale of pornography," and "I enjoy reading magazines like *Playboy* and *Penthouse*." One month later he showed these same men pictures of nude women and asked them two questions about each one: "How attractive is she?" and "How exciting is she?" When subjects made their ratings while seated in front of a mirror, their attitudes toward erotica were correlated with their ratings of the women; the more the subject liked erotica, the higher his ratings of the nudes (especially when the ratings focused on excitement). When the mirror was removed, subjects' attitudes concerning erotica were not significantly related to their ratings of the women. Only the self-aware subjects, who were reminded of their personal standards concerning erotica, used these standards to regulate their ratings. Self-awareness and hypocrisy are often antithetical (Ajzen, Timko, & White, 1982; Borgida & Campbell, 1982; Cacioppo et al., 1986; Carver & Scheier, 1981, 1990, 1991).

Norms can mute the effects of attitudes. Some situations can be more powerful than our attitudes (Ross & Nisbett, 1991). Although our attitudes prompt us to buy another bag of cookies or treat others unfairly, **norms** in the situation can prevent us from acting out our attitudes (Fishbein & Ajzen, 1975). Norms provide us with guidelines for action, for they are the implicit standards that describe what behaviors should and should not be performed in social situations. If our attitudes lead to actions that will conform to social norms, then acting out our attitudes poses little problem. If, however, our attitudes call for counternormative behaviors, then we may decide to go against our private feelings to avoid negative social sanctions. One early study of racism found that most prejudiced whites in a West Virginia mining town discriminated against African Americans; they avoided interacting with African Americans in social settings, and only 20% of the whites reported having

norms
Consensual standards that describe behaviors people should and should not perform in a given context; they prescribe the socially appropriate way to respond in the situation—the *normal* course of action—as well as proscribing actions to avoid if at all possible.

▲ When people confront powerful social situations, these situations sometimes uncouple the relationship between their attitudes and behaviors. A woman who is pro-choice and recognizes her legal right to have an abortion if she makes that choice may not be able to act on that belief. The woman pictured here required considerable support from the clinic's staff before she could pass the pro-life protesters and enter the building.

any African American friends (Minard, 1952). In the mines, however, attitudes did not guide behavior. African Americans and whites worked together without conflict, and 80% of the whites expressed friendship toward African Americans.

These findings are understandable if we take into account the difference between the norms of the town and of the mine. The town norms discouraged interracial contacts, and therefore promoted a high incidence of discrimination. In the mine, however, work norms emphasized cooperation and productivity, so racial discrimination was discouraged. Hence social norms, rather than attitudes, tended to be the primary determinants of the miners' actions (Campbell, 1963; Green, 1972; Warner & DeFleur, 1969).

Not all individuals, however, are susceptible to normative influence. Mark Snyder's concept of self-monitoring, introduced in Chapter 2, assumes that people differ in their ability to monitor and regulate their behavior to fit the situation. High self-monitors try to tailor their social behavior to fit the situation, whereas low self-monitors base their actions on relevant underlying attitudes, feelings, and values (Snyder & Campbell, 1982). Since high self-monitors strive to make certain their behavior fits the demands of the situation, they change their behavior to match the situation (Snyder & Monson, 1975). Low self-monitors, in contrast, are more likely to act in ways that are consistent with their attitudes (Miller & Grush, 1986; Jamieson & Zanna, 1989; Snyder & Kendzierski, 1982).

How Do Attitudes Guide Behavior?

When researchers began asking the question "When do attitudes guide behavior?" they found many answers: when the attitudes are strong, specific, formed through direct experience, and accessible, and when the situation or the individual permits them to exert an influence (see Table 6-5). But, as Russell Fazio notes (1986, 1989, 1990), these studies raised yet a third question. Yes, attitudes sometimes guide behavior, but *how* do they guide behavior? What psychological mechanisms and processes mediate the strength of the attitude-behavior relationship?

▲ **TABLE 6-5**
Summing up: Factors that influence the correspondence between attitudes and behavior

Factor	*Impact on Attitude-Behavior Consistency*
Attitude potency	Strong, important attitudes that are central to our belief system guide behavior. Individuals who have a vested interest in the issue and are well informed tend to act on their attitudes.
Attitude specificity	Attitudes that pertain to specific objects in a particular context are more potent guides for behavior.
Attitude formation	Attitudes formed through direct experience are more specific, held with greater confidence, more easily recalled, more resistant to change, and more likely to influence our subsequent behavior.
Accessibility	Attitudes that are accessible in memory are more influential.
Situational norms	If situational norms are powerful and inconsistent with private attitudes, then attitude-behavior correspondence will decrease.
Personality factors	Self-awareness increases and self-monitoring decreases attitude-behavior correspondence.

Fazio's mode of processing model. Russell Fazio (1990) theorizes that the link between our attitudes and our actions is sustained, in part, by the two interdependent systems for processing information discussed in Chapter 4: automatic cognitive processing and controlled cognitive processing. When Janet sees a picture of her baby, she may immediately experience a warm, positive feeling. When the sexist man meets a woman, he unintentionally treats her in stereotyped ways. When we are offered a meal of fried worms, we spontaneously experience disgust. In these situations, attitudes automatically guide our cognitive and behavioral reactions. Once we recognize the object (the baby, the woman, the worms), we then encode, categorize, and evaluate the object in ways that are consistent with our attitudes. Automatic processing takes place outside of our awareness and very rapidly, so we act without careful deliberation (Fazio, 1990; Jamieson & Zanna, 1989; Sanbonmatsu & Fazio, 1990).

We do not, however, always respond automatically to attitude objects. When we have time, or we are motivated to make the best choice possible, we think things over before acting (Sanbonmatsu & Fazio, 1990). In these and other cases, the attitude → action sequence depends on controlled cognitive processes. Janet did not rapidly and effortlessly decide to have an abortion. When researcher Carol Gilligan (1982) asked her how she felt about seeking an abortion, she answered, "To me it is taking a life, and I am going to take that decision upon myself, and I have feelings about it, and talked to a priest" (p. 84). In this instance, Janet initiated, monitored, and terminated her search for information at will. Her attitudinal and behavioral response was controlled and intentional rather than automatic and unintentional (Bargh, 1984, 1990; Bargh et al., 1992).

Controlled cognitive processing strengthens the attitude-behavior relationship if we generate information that supports our attitudes. Men's attitudes toward affirmative action programs, for example, predicted their subsequent judgments about a court case involving sex discrimination only when they were told to focus their attention on their "thoughts and views on the affirmative action issue" (Snyder & Swann, 1976). If, however, our search for information turns up information that conflicts with our attitudes, then the attitude-behavior relationship will be disrupted. Timothy Wilson and his colleagues have documented just such a disruption in a series of studies (Wilson

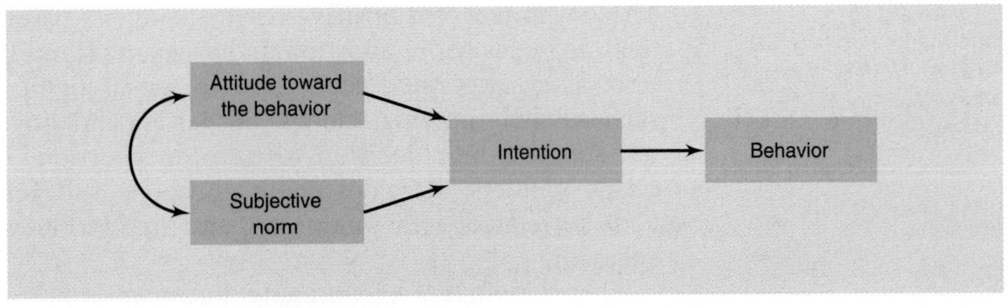

▲ **FIGURE 6-4**
When does attitude match action? According to the theory of reasoned action, two factors affect people's decisions about intent to engage in a behavior: attitudes toward the behavior and perceptions of norms regarding it. These factors determine intentions, which influence behaviors. (From Ajzen, 1988)

& Dunn, 1986; Wilson et al., 1984, 1989; Wilson & Kraft, 1989). They found that asking individuals to explain their reasons for holding a particular attitude uncouples attitudes and behaviors, particularly when the attitude is based on scanty information.

Thinking about our attitudes also disrupts behavior when the affective and cognitive components of the attitude aren't entirely consistent with one another. Many people may know that a garden snake is harmless but still feel upset when one crawls by. If such people spend time considering their emotions, then their subsequent behaviors will reflect their feelings about the snake, rather than their thoughts. Thus, when affective and cognitive components are in good evaluative agreement, then thought emphasizing either component leads to attitude-behavior correspondence. However, if the affective and cognitive components are not in agreement, then thought emphasizing different components leads to inconsistencies (Edwards, 1990; Millar & Millar, 1990; Millar & Tesser, 1986a, 1989; Shavitt & Fazio, 1991).

Fishbein and Ajzen's theory of reasoned action. Martin Fishbein and Icek Ajzen stress controlled reasoning processes in their analysis of attitude-behavior relation. According to their theory of reasoned action, shown in Figure 6-4, attitudes don't cause behavior directly. Rather, attitudes influence our intention to perform the behavior, and then this intention determines the action. Imagine that we want to know whether Janet will have an abortion. Fishbein and Ajzen believe that her general attitudes about the unborn child's life, *Roe* v. *Wade*, or religious beliefs may have little to do with her decision to end her pregnancy. Instead, her behavior is determined by her attitude toward the action itself: aborting this specific pregnancy. Janet may endorse pro-life attitudes, but she might also have a positive attitude toward getting an abortion. Fishbein and Ajzen also maintain that Janet's actions will be influenced by her subjective perceptions of the norms surrounding this action. Even though she may have a positive attitude toward having an abortion in this case, she may not want to violate social standards that condemn abortion. Fishbein and Ajzen believe that these two factors—her attitude toward the action and her subjective beliefs about norms—combine to form her behavioral intention. When will she plan to have an abortion? Only when (1) she has a positive attitude toward the abortion and (2) situational norms support this action (Ajzen, 1988; Ajzen & Fishbein, 1980; Fishbein & Ajzen, 1975).

Researchers have used the theory of reasoned action to examine many kinds of actions—voting, donating blood, dieting, family planning, and career choices (Burnkrant & Page, 1988; Pagel & Davidson, 1984; Schifter & Ajzen, 1985; Sheppard, Hartwick, & Warshaw, 1988; Stasson & Fishbein, 1990; Vallerand et al., 1992). One team of investigators, for example, studied women who were visiting a health center for pregnancy tests (Smetana & Adler, 1980).

Those who received positive results completed a questionnaire that measured their attitudes about abortion and their intentions concerning a possible abortion. They also rated the extent to which significant people in their lives, such as their parents, clergy, husbands, and boyfriends, would support or not support their decision to have an abortion. As the theory of reasoned action predicts, attitudes about abortions and perceived social norms were both correlated with intentions, and intentions were correlated with actual behavior.

These results are encouraging, but much more information about the relationship between attitudes and behaviors is still forthcoming. Ajzen (1988) recently suggested that one's perception of control may be an important third determinant of planned behavior (Madden, Ellen, & Ajzen, 1992). Researchers have also found that when moral concerns are particularly pronounced, then moral obligation may overwhelm behavioral intentions (Gorsuch & Ortberg, 1983). Dutch tax evaders, for example, didn't respond as the theory predicted because attitudes toward the action and ratings of subjective norms correlated with self-reported tax payments, but not with actual tax payments (Hessing, Elffers, & Weigel, 1988). Overall, however, Ajzen and Fishbein's theory of reasoned action, and Fazio's mode of processing model as well, have yielded considerable insights into the question "How do attitudes guide action?" (Ajzen, 1988; Bentler & Speckart, 1981; Davidson & Morrison, 1983; Dillon & Kumar, 1985; Fredrick & Dossett, 1983; Kahle & Berman, 1979).

Behavior and Attitudes

Attitudes can and do influence our behaviors. But does the opposite process hold true as well? Do our behaviors influence our attitudes? If a bigoted politician makes a speech championing racial equality will he or she become less racist? If an apathetic college student strays into a pro-ecology rally will he or she become more concerned about protecting the environment? If Janet has an abortion, will her belief that abortion is murder change? Can the attitude → behavior sequence be turned on its ear, so that behavior → attitude?

Does Behavior Generate Attitudes? A Theory of Cognitive Dissonance

Many theorists believe we have a powerful need to maintain consistency across our emotions, cognitions, and behaviors. When we feel a certain way, we expect our cognitions and actions to match this feeling. If we act a certain way, then our cognitions and emotions should match our behaviors. Our emotions, cognitions, and behaviors aren't isolated from one another, but instead they are interconnected and integrated, fitting together like the pieces of a puzzle. Consistency, however, exacts a cost. Consistency theorists believe that, in order to achieve harmony among our various emotions, actions, and cognitions, we must sometimes modify them so they fit the overall pattern (Abelson, 1983; Abelson et al., 1968).

cognitive dissonance An aversive psychological state that occurs when an individual simultaneously accepts two conflicting cognitions.

This view is perhaps best elaborated in Leon Festinger's theory of **cognitive dissonance** (Festinger, 1957). Festinger uses the term *cognition* very broadly to refer to a variety of internal processes, including emotions, perceptions, and attitudes. He believes that in most cases all of our cognitions are *consonant* with one another; they fit together psychologically, with one implying or following from the other. For example, Hunter's preference for the color blue is consistent with the fact that his closet contains lots of blue clothes. Julie's

▲ **TABLE 6-6**
Modes of dissonance reduction

Festinger maintains that people can decrease the inconsistency between their cognitions by using one or more *modes* of dissonance reduction. The five modes listed here would all help a cigarette smoker reduce the dissonance caused by the two cognitions "I smoke cigarettes" and "Smoking isn't healthy."

Mode	*Description*	*Example*
Attitude change	Adopting a more extreme attitudinal position	"I like smoking too much to quit."
Adding consonant cognitions	Stressing the positive side of smoking	"Smoking relaxes me." "I smoke low-tar cigarettes."
Rationalization	Changing the importance of the cognitions	"I want to enjoy life while I can."
Denial	Claiming to stop, but continuing to smoke	"I've quit, but may I borrow one of yours?"
Behavior change	Smoking less or stopping altogether	"I've quit."

Source: Adapted from Festinger, 1957.

desire to lose weight is consistent with her habit of working out daily. *Dissonant* cognitions, in contrast, clash with one another; they are inconsistent, with one implying the opposite of the other. Julie's desire to lose weight is inconsistent with her love of Oreo cookies. Similarly, Janet's decision to abort her pregnancy is dissonant with her belief that abortion is immoral. *Irrelevant* cognitions, on the other hand, have nothing to do with one another: Hunter's preference for blue is not related to his stance on abortion.

Festinger maintains that consonance and irrelevance are comfortable psychological states, but that *dissonance* is so unpleasant that we try to avoid it when possible. "Just as hunger is motivating, cognitive dissonance is motivating. Cognitive dissonance will give rise to activity oriented toward reducing or eliminating the dissonance" (Festinger, 1957, p. 70). Consider people who smoke cigarettes despite the medical evidence linking smoking with cancer. Their two cognitions, "I smoke cigarettes" and "Smoking isn't healthy," are dissonant, and hence they will be motivated to reduce this dissonance in one of the ways listed in Table 6-6. They might become more positive toward smoking as they decide that the pleasures of smoking are so great that the risk to their health is worth the cost. They might also focus their attention on cognitions that are consonant with smoking cigarettes, such as "I smoke a low-tar brand" or "All that research on smoking is strictly correlational—it says nothing about causes of cancer." Alternatively, they can rationalize their behavior by excusing their actions, denying the inconsistent behavior, or cutting down on how much they smoke. But no matter what mode of dissonance reduction they use, the end result will be the same—the clash between cognitions will be eliminated and a state of psychological comfort regained—even at the cost of rationality. Festinger sees us as consistency seekers who embrace attitudes that ensure our psychological comfort. We sacrifice rationality in the pursuit of consistency.

Actions can change attitudes. We cannot always follow our hearts and perform only actions that match our tastes and preferences. Sometimes, due to the press of circumstances, we find ourselves doing things that conflict

▲ Dissonance in a box: How do smokers cope with the conflict produced by the cognitions "I smoke cigarettes" and "The box they come in states 'The Surgeon General has determined that cigarette smoking is dangerous to your health.' "?

counterattitudinal behavior Any action that contradicts, or is inconsistent with, one's attitudes.

with our private attitudes and beliefs. But these **counterattitudinal behaviors**, Festinger argues, can engender cognitive dissonance, which we reduce by changing our attitude to match our behavior.

Imagine that you have agreed to take part in a study described as an investigation of "personality and task performance" (Comer & Laird, 1975). The study sounds simple enough, but when you arrive for your session, you discover the task requires eating a dead worm. As you sit at the table set with a napkin, fork, cup of water, and a plate with a worm on it, the young man who is conducting the study reminds you that "You are free to refuse or to terminate participating at any time in the study." But before you can say anything, he asks you to wait a few minutes while he takes care of an unrelated chore in the next room. He leaves you suffering silently as you prepare to choke down the unappetizing tidbit.

Festinger would suggest your two cognitions, "I agreed to eat a worm" and "I don't like worms," should create considerable dissonance for you (Aronson, Carlsmith, & Darley, 1963; Foxman & Radtke, 1970). You could convince yourself that you did not agree to eat the worm, but the experimenter was careful to create the *illusion of choice* by explaining that the decision to eat the worm was up to you. So, rather than blame the experimenter, you reduce your dissonance by reappraising worms. Supporting Festinger's theory, many of the subjects (40%) changed their attitudes; they claimed that eating a worm might be fairly pleasant. The remaining subjects, however, offered up alternative dissonance-reducing rationalizations. Some concluded that they were heroes suffering to help in a scientific experiment ("I am brave"), and others condemned themselves, concluding that they deserved to suffer. These psychological gyrations even influenced subsequent behavior, for when the experimenter later told the subjects that they could switch to a simple perceptual task instead of eating the worm, 80% of the subjects asked to eat the worm. One subject was so resigned to his fate that he "cut his worm up into bite-size pieces during the waiting period" (Comer & Laird, 1975, p. 99).

Saying can lead to believing. Misrepresenting our beliefs to others—lying, if you will—is a special type of counterattitudinal behavior termed *counterattitudinal advocacy*. But do we ever come to believe the lies we have told others?

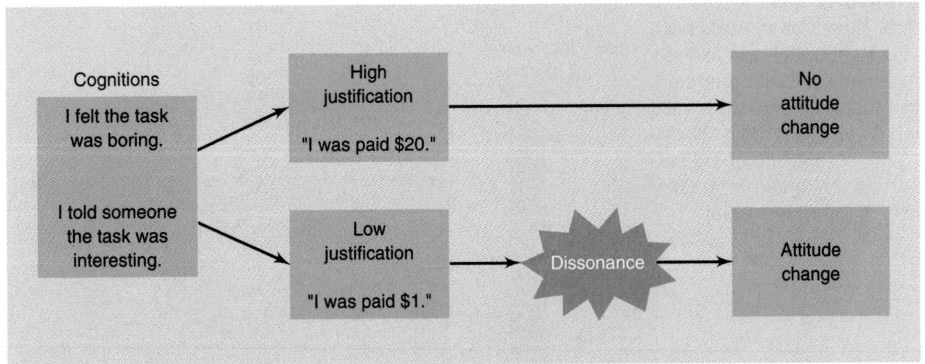

▲ **FIGURE 6-5**
When does counterattitudinal advocacy lead to attitude change? Festinger and Carlsmith (1959) predicted that only individuals who had insufficient justification for acting in a counterattitudinal way would change their attitudes.

Festinger, with his colleague J. Merrill Carlsmith (1959), studied this question by asking male college students to perform two exceedingly boring tasks: putting 12 spools onto a tray over and over again and turning 48 square pegs a quarter of a turn clockwise. The subjects spent 30 minutes working at each task, so by the hour's end they had probably formed the cognition, "This is the most boring and monotonous experiment imaginable." The experimenter then gave subjects a bogus debriefing.

Subjects assigned to the control condition were dismissed at this point. Before experimental subjects could leave, however, the researcher made one last request of them. He claimed that he was studying the impact of motivation on performance, so some subjects were led to believe that the task would be enjoyable before they went to work. Indeed, the next subject was supposed to receive this misinformation, but the researcher's confederate had been detained. The researcher then asked the subjects whether they would be willing to play the role of the "fellow who usually meets the waiting subject." All they needed to do was tell the person waiting in the next room that the study was interesting and enjoyable and to remain on call in case they were needed again in the future. The experimenter would even pay them for their trouble—either $1 or $20. Most subjects agreed after a little prodding. When they met the waiting subject (who was really the confederate), they described the experiment as interesting, enjoyable, and involving.

This elaborate hoax subtly forced subjects into counterattitudinal advocacy. Participants undoubtedly considered the entire study to be a bore, but they voluntarily agreed to tell the waiting confederate that it was, in fact, interesting. According to Festinger, behaving in such a counterattitudinal manner should create dissonance, but only when the subject was paid $1. As Figure 6-5 indicates, both the $1 and $20 subjects should display the dissonant cognitions, "I felt the task was boring" and "I told someone that it was interesting." But the subjects paid $20 had sufficient justification for lying about the task; they could think to themselves, "I made a lot of money by telling a little white lie about the study." Because this justification should eliminate their dissonance, Festinger and Carlsmith predicted that they would not change their attitudes. Subjects who were paid only $1, however, had *insufficient justification* for lying. Therefore, they should have experienced dissonance and attitude change. The results shown in Figure 6-6 confirmed Festinger and Carlsmith's hypothesis. All subjects, including those in the control condition, were interviewed immediately after the study. Those who were paid $1 thought the task was more enjoyable than subjects in the other conditions, and they were also more willing to participate in a similar experiment.

▲ **FIGURE 6-6**
What impact do rewards have on our attitudes? Just as Festinger and Carlsmith predicted, the subjects who were paid only $1 were the most positive in their evaluations of the boring task. (Adapted from Festinger & Carlsmith, 1959)

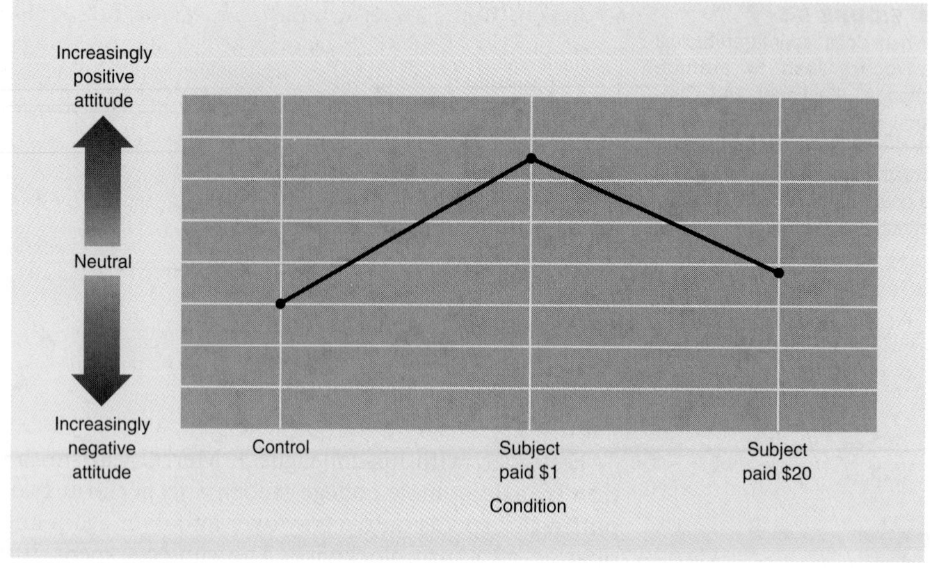

These findings are counterintuitive. We usually think of money as an incentive and expect the greatest change in people who are paid more (Elms, 1967; Rosenberg, 1965). The $20, however, was so substantial a reward that it justified the counterattitudinal behavior, and thereby eased subjects' feelings of dissonance. Indeed, many factors besides money can increase justification for counterattitudinal behavior and thereby eliminate dissonance. When we act counterattitudinally at the behest of an attractive experimenter, our attitudes don't change (Forsyth, Riess, & Schlenker, 1977; Rosenfeld, Giacalone, & Tedeschi, 1984; Zimbardo et al., 1965). Similarly, if the experimenter threatens us with dire punishment, our attitudes don't change (Freedman, 1965). If our work on a boring task is rewarded with positive feedback, we don't decide the task is interesting (Beauvois & Joule, 1982). But when these justifications are stripped away—when we act counterattitudinally with insufficient justification—then acting in a new way can lead to thinking in a new way.

Justifying our choices. Janet's decision to have an abortion was not a thoughtless one. She struggled for days before making her choice as she weighed her feelings, her responsibility to herself, and her responsibility to her family. Even after she had reached a decision, she painstakingly reexamined it to make certain that it was justified. As Gilligan (1982) notes, the "outward justification, the concern for 'good reasons' " (p. 85) for her behavior remained critical for Janet.

According to Festinger, important decisions are the breeding ground for cognitive dissonance. Whenever we make choices, all the positive aspects of the rejected alternative haunt us, as do the negative aspects of the alternative we have picked in its place—until, that is, dissonance-reduction processes come to our rescue. Immediately after the choice, we are beset by feelings of regret, but given enough time we will begin to justify our decision by discovering new arguments to support our choice (Walster, 1968). These postdecision justifications result in a **spreading of alternatives** as our attitude toward the chosen alternative becomes even more positive, and our attitude toward the rejected alternative becomes more negative (Gerard & White, 1983; Knox & Inkster, 1968; Rosenfeld, Kennedy, & Giacalone, 1986; Younger, Walker, & Arrowood, 1977).

spreading of alternatives
The postdecision tendency to become more favorable toward a chosen alternative and less favorable toward unchosen alternatives.

Jack Brehm (1956) studied this spreading-of-alternatives phenomenon by telling women recruited from college classes that if they participated in a study of consumer attitudes, they would receive a product as a gift. The women then rated the desirability of the products, which included records, an art print, a stopwatch, and a radio. Brehm established three experimental conditions to vary the amount of dissonance created by the selection. The women in the control condition were simply given a product; they had no choice, and therefore should have experienced little dissonance. The women in the low dissonance condition were given their choice of two gifts, one of which was much more desirable than the other. Because the two choices were already very different in terms of desirability, Brehm felt that such a choice would arouse little dissonance, and postdecisional spreading should be minimal. Subjects in the high dissonance condition were asked to choose between two products that were very similar in desirability. As predicted, spreading was much more pronounced when the alternatives were very similar in desirability than when they were dissimilar or when no choice was involved. By inflating the desirability of the chosen product, the women could later reassure themselves that they had made the right decision.

Even after the decision is made and the chosen alternative is recast in a more positive light, people continue to ease the stress of decision making by engaging in **selective exposure**: They seek out information that supports their decision and avoid information that suggests they made a poor choice (Frey & Wicklund, 1978; Wicklund & Brehm, 1976). A woman who decides to abort her pregnancy would probably avoid discussing the matter with her priest. Instead, she might read over the literature given her by Planned Parenthood or discuss the decision with her physician.

selective exposure
The tendency for people to seek out information that is consistent with their choices while avoiding information that is inconsistent with their choices.

Festinger originally suggested that both types of selective exposure—a search for consonant information and avoidance of dissonant information—were equally likely in any given situation. Subsequent studies, however, indicated that the strategy chosen depends on a number of factors. If we think that the information we may get—whether consonant or dissonant—will be easy to refute, then we tend to seek out the dissonant information. If, however, we think the information will be difficult to refute, then we usually selectively seek the consonant information and avoid the dissonant (Frey, 1981). Selective exposure is also strongest when we experience a moderate amount of dissonance (rather than extremely high or low dissonance) over the choice (Converse & Cooper, 1979; Frey, 1982) and when the decision is irrevocable (Frey et al., 1984).

Rationalizing our efforts. We rarely work hard only to discover that the goal we seek is not worth having. If we struggle to learn a sport, we later prize our athletic skills. If we must pass an initiation before joining a club, we value our membership that much more. If we persevere to win another's affections, that friendship becomes very important to us. Are we so careful that we set our sights on only the most worthy goals? Or, as Festinger's cognitive dissonance theory (1957) slyly suggests, do we reevaluate our goal to justify the effort we expend in reaching it (Tiller & Fazio, 1982)?

Elliot Aronson and Judson Mills (1959) examined this issue by making women expend considerable effort before they were allowed to join a worthless group. A male experimenter greeted each subject individually, and told her that she had been chosen to take part in a group discussion of the psychology of sex. He noted, however, that only women who could discuss sex without embarrassment would be welcome in the group, so all prospective members

▲ Important decisions, such as choosing a college, deciding to marry, or purchasing a house, can generate considerable dissonance. When people face such momentous choices, they try to weigh all the available options before making up their minds. But once they make a decision, they will likely be beset by misgivings about their choice and the alternatives they passed up—until dissonance reduction helps by exaggerating the positive features of the chosen alternative and the negative features of the rejected options.

had to pass an "embarrassment test." Some of the women were then subjected to a severe initiation: they were required to read descriptions of sexual interludes and a series of obscene words aloud to the male experimenter. (In 1959, women were presumably mightily embarrassed by such vulgarities.) Women who experienced a mild initiation read some mildly provocative passages and words (*prostitute*, *petting*, *virgin*), and women in the control group agreed only to be screened.

The women were told they passed their initiation. They then listened to a group discussion on an intercom system. They were led to believe that they were eavesdropping on their future fellow group members' conversations, but they actually heard a tape recording of a discussion that had been deliberately designed to be boring and banal. This bit of subterfuge was designed to create two inconsistent cognitions for subjects who suffered the severe initiation: "I worked hard to join this group" and "The group is boring." Aronson and Mills predicted that, to reduce the dissonance aroused by this inconsistency, these women would assume that the group was more interesting and enjoyable than the women who experienced a mild initiation or no initiation at all. As Figure 6-7 indicates, these predictions were confirmed. The greater the effort expended in joining the group, the more the women liked the group.

A replication of this study, in which electric shocks rather than obscene readings were used to manipulate the severity of the initiation into the group, yielded very similar results: people who received stronger shocks liked the group the best (Gerard & Mathewson, 1966). Researchers have also shown that the mere anticipation of expending effort in pursuing a goal is, in some cases, sufficient to generate effort-justifying change (Axsom, 1989; Axsom & Cooper, 1985). It seems the opposite of the old saw, "That which is worth having is worth working for," is also true: That which is worth working for is also worth having.

These findings offer a potential explanation for the curious tendency of groups to initiate new members. Initiations demand an investment from inductees, even before they have had a chance to become full-fledged members. These investments may work to bind the initiates to the group, for they become more favorably disposed to it in order to reduce cognitive dissonance. A

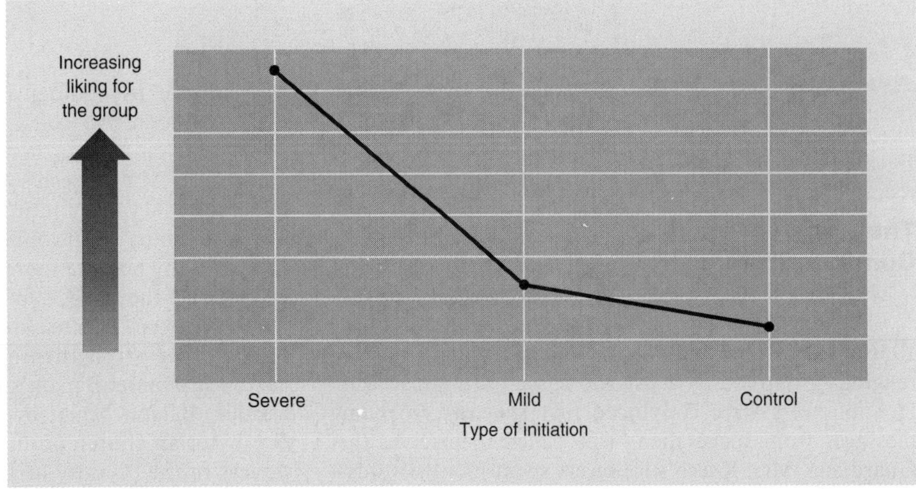

▲ **FIGURE 6-7**
If you had to suffer through a severe initiation to get into a group, would you still like the group when it turned out to be boring? Aronson and Mills found that the more severe the initiation, the more the members liked their group. (From Aronson & Mills, 1959)

similar process may bind people to other emotionally involving groups, such as social movements or cults (Atlas, 1990; Bliese, 1990). As the group demands more and more in the way of personal commitment, individuals become more enamored of the group to justify their investment in it (see "In Depth: The Road to Commitment").

Why Do Actions Influence Attitudes?

Festinger maintained that we don't always think before we act or change our minds when we uncover evidence that challenges our beliefs. When we find ourselves performing counterattitudinal actions, we change our attitudes to match the behavior. We reduce our misgivings about our decisions by exaggerating the desirability of the alternatives we choose, and we value goals and outcomes that we must suffer to obtain. Sometimes our beliefs become stronger after they have been convincingly refuted. Actions do, indeed, lead to attitudes (see Table 6-7).

In the years since Festinger offered up his theory, however, many researchers have asked the "Why?" question. Festinger originally answered this question with his concept of dissonance: inconsistency is so irritating that we will change our cognitions to achieve consistency. Other theorists, however, remained skeptical. They noted that dissonance itself—that troublesome tension caused by inconsistency—was rarely measured in any direct way. Researchers also had difficulty predicting when dissonance would occur and which mode of dissonance reduction people would use to ease their inconsistencies (Aronson, 1968, 1989; Cooper & Fazio, 1984; Joule, 1986). These researchers, in time, developed alternative views that offered new answers to the question "Why do actions influence attitudes?" Three of these perspectives, self-perception theory, self-presentation theory, and self-affirmation theory, are considered next.

Self-perception theory: The rational factor. Cognitive-dissonance theory often yields counterintuitive hypotheses—they violate our commonsense assumptions about the rationality of human beings. As a result, it takes a little practice to learn to think like a dissonance theorist. Daryl J. Bem (1965), however, doesn't think the effort is worth it. Bem believes that the attitudes people report after they engage in counterattitudinal behavior result from self-perception rather than from the arousal of cognitive dissonance. As noted in Chapter 4, Bem's theory assumes that we infer our attitudes, emotions, and

IN DEPTH

The Road to Commitment

Festinger's research legacy offers one final example of the triumph of consistency over rationality. In the mid-1950s Festinger and his colleagues undertook a rare field study of cognitive dissonance (Festinger, Riecken, & Schachter, 1956). They began their study by infiltrating a radical religious group led by a psychic named Marian Keech. Her followers were convinced that she was receiving messages from space aliens who called themselves the Guardians. Mrs. Keech's followers spent months studying the Guardians' messages, which turned out to be a warning: the planet Earth was about to be destroyed by flood!

The cataclysm was scheduled for December 21, but the Guardians promised to pick up Mrs. Keech's followers at midnight. They gathered in readiness in her living room (Mr. Keech, a nonbeliever, went to bed), bags packed, all metal—zippers, buttons, snaps—removed from their clothing (metal does strange things in flying saucers), passwords all memorized. Unfortunately, midnight came and went with no sign of a flying saucer. The bad news was that Mrs. Keech was wrong when she predicted they would be rescued; the good news was that she was also wrong about the flood.

So how did her followers respond? Did they denounce Mrs. Keech as a fraud? Did they try to contact the Guardians themselves? Did they sew all their zippers back into their clothes? No, they became more committed to Mrs. Keech's teachings. They accepted her rationalization that the tremendous faith and devotion of the group was so impressive that God had decided to call off the flood, and they spread this important message to news reporters. They refused to abandon their central beliefs, even though they had been undeniably disconfirmed. They clung tenaciously to the irrational hope that the space travelers would come.

Festinger maintained that this reaction was explicable if we assume that the members wanted to keep all their cognitions (attitudes, beliefs, perceptions) and behaviors consistent with one another. If they admitted that Mrs. Keech was a false prophet, they would also have to admit that they were wrong in believing in her teachings. Furthermore, they would have no justification for their actions over the previous months; many had quit their jobs, dropped out of school, moved hundreds of miles to be closer to Mrs. Keech, and alienated their friends and relatives. If, however, they became more firmly committed to Mrs. Keech, their cognitions and behaviors would all be consistent with one another, and they could avoid the dissonance that arises from inconsistency.

As these psychological machinations reveal, the need for cognitive consistency is a powerful human motive. Even though her prophecy was directly disconfirmed, Mrs. Keech's followers still clung to their beliefs. In fact, they rationalized the failure by generating so many additional consonant cognitions that they actually became more strongly committed to their group, and they began to seek out new recruits (Festinger, Riecken, & Schachter, 1956; Hardyck & Braden, 1962). This strengthening of commitment also occurred in Daniel Batson's (1975) study of religious attitudes. Batson began by splitting the members of a Presbyterian church group into two groups: strong believers in the divinity of Jesus Christ and people who, while accepting Jesus' teaching, denied his divinity. Batson showed both groups a bogus newspaper article. The article had supposedly been "denied publication in *The New York Times* at the request of the World Council of Churches because of the obvious crushing effect it would have on the entire Christian world" (p. 180). It claimed that researchers had recently discovered a large collection of letters written by the disciples, which clearly indicated that the New Testament writings were fabricated. One letter supposedly stated: "Since our greater teacher, Jesus of Nazareth, was killed by the Romans, I am sure we were justified in stealing away his body and claiming that he rose from the dead."

Batson found that people who initially denied Jesus' divinity became even more doubtful. Believers, however, displayed one of two different reactions. As Table 6-8 indicates, one group of subjects rejected the dissonant information; they reduced their cognitive dissonance by questioning the veracity of the article. A second group reacted more irrationally. Despite their reluctant acceptance of the truth of the article, their belief in Jesus' divinity actually intensified. Like the members of Mrs. Keech's group, these subjects emerged "not only unshaken, but even more convinced . . . than before" (Festinger, Riecken, & Schachter, 1957, p. 3). Batson, of course, carefully debriefed all his participants, and their teachers spent several sessions reviewing the experience.

Batson (1975) points out the irrationality of the attitude intensification he observed and applies his findings to the problems faced by anyone trying to persuade committed believers to change their attitudes: "If, on the one hand, the believer does not accept the facts as facts, then clearly one's arguments are without impact. But, on the other hand, if the believer accepts them as true, this may actually drive him into even more fervent adherence to his initial position" (p. 184).

▲ **TABLE 6-7**
Summing up: Just as our attitudes often guide our actions, in some cases our actions can influence our attitudes.

Process	*Characteristics*	*Example*
Counterattitudinal behavior	When we perform an action that runs counter to our private attitudes, and we feel that we freely chose to behave in this way, we adopt attitudes that are consistent with the behavior.	Individuals who agree to eat a worm express positive worm-eating attitudes (Comer & Laird, 1975).
Counterattitudinal advocacy	When we argue against a position that we actually believe in, we adopt the attitude expressed in the essay or speech.	Individuals who are paid only $1 to tell a waiting confederate that a boring task is actually interesting become more positive toward the task (Festinger & Carlsmith, 1959).
Spreading of alternatives	After a decision, we reassure ourselves as to the correctness of our choice by increasing the value of the chosen alternative and decreasing the value of the rejected alternative. This change is facilitated by selective exposure: seeking out information that supports our decision.	Individuals who choose one record over another rate the chosen record higher and lower their rating of the unchosen alternative (Brehm, 1956).
Effort justification	After investing energy or personal resources in an activity or in seeking a goal, we become more positive in our appraisal of the activity or the goal.	Women who underwent a severe initiation in order to join a boring group became more favorable toward the group (Aronson & Mills, 1959).

other internal states by observing our own overt behaviors. If we observe ourselves working hard to join a group, then we infer from this behavior that we must like the group. If we diligently prepare to be rescued by people from outer space, we assume that we believe in the existence of extraterrestrial life. If we agree to have an abortion, then we assume that abortion is allowable in some circumstances (Bem, 1965).

We do not, however, always assume that our attitude matches our behavior. Bem notes that we are sensitive to external pressures that may influence our actions. If you are forced to join a boring group, then you may not infer that you like the group all that much. Similarly, if you observe yourself telling someone a task is interesting, why infer a positive attitude toward the task if you know you are telling the lie only because someone has promised to pay you $20 (Freedman, Cunningham, Krismer, 1992)? Self-perception theory can account for findings obtained in many dissonance experiments, but it denies the existence of aversive motivational pressures; people change their attitudes, not to reduce dissonance, but because they logically infer their attitudes from their overt behaviors. Bem offers a cold, cognitive, information-processing model that contrasts with Festinger's hot, dynamic, motivational model.

Bem initially tested his hypothesis in a number of simulation studies of counterattitudinal behavior experiments (Bem, 1972). He arranged for uninformed observers to read about or watch the procedures used in counterattitudinal behavior studies, and then he asked the observers to predict the actual subjects' reactions. Even though these observers probably experienced

▲ **TABLE 6-8**
Effects of disconfirming information on religious beliefs

Batson measured belief in the divinity of Jesus before exposure to the disconfirming information and after exposure across three groups: nonbelievers, believers in Jesus' divinity who doubted the disconfirming information, and believers in Jesus' divinity who accepted the disconfirming information (higher scores indicate stronger beliefs).

Groups	*Number of Subjects*	*Pretest*	*Posttest*	*Type of Change*
Nonbelievers	8	3.37	2.91	Believed even less in Christ
Believers doubting the information	31	3.97	3.90	No change in beliefs
Believers accepting the information	11	4.07	4.30	Believed even more in Christ

Source: Batson, 1975.

none of the psychological arousal hypothesized by cognitive-dissonance theory, they could nonetheless predict the actual subjects' responses. Self-perception theory also explains the *overjustification effect* discussed in Chapter 4: when people are rewarded for engaging in pro-attitudinal behavior, their attitudes often become less positive (Benware & Deci, 1975; Kiesler, Nisbett, & Zanna, 1969; Schlenker & Riess, 1979). Acting in ways that are consistent with our attitudes shouldn't induce dissonance. Self-perception theory, however, offers a tidy explanation for the overjustification effect: if we must be paid to do something, chances are we didn't really want to do it in the first place.

Self-presentation theory: The interpersonal factor. Self-presentation theory also offers another explanation for the impact of behavior on attitudes. This theory assumes that our public expressions of our attitudes often serve a self-presentational function. Just as we strive to construct and maintain a particular impression by managing our self-descriptions, actions, and appearances, we also try to express attitudes that are consistent with the social identity we seek to establish (Goffman, 1959; Schlenker, 1980, 1985; Schlenker, Weigold, & Doherty, 1991).

Situations like those studied by dissonance researchers, however, threaten our social identities. When researchers prompt us to eat worms, lie, work hard for no purpose, or refrain from doing what we would naturally prefer to do, we appear to be immoral, unintelligent, weak-willed, and irrational. We therefore use our attitudes as self-presentational devices to rebuild our damaged identities. "I'm no patsy who you can force to eat worms: I like worms." "I didn't tell a lie for a mere $1 bribe: I really do think turning spools is interesting." "I didn't embarrass myself just so I could join a boring group: I think the group is interesting." Our attitude claims, then, are more often public rationalizations than private ratiocinations (Tedeschi & Riess, 1981b; Tedeschi, Schlenker, & Bonoma, 1971).

This self-presentational interpretation has fared well when subjected to empirical tests (Schlenker & Weigold, 1992). High self-monitors, who are more attuned to the self-presentational demands of situations, show greater attitude change following counterattitudinal behavior (DeBono & Edmonds, 1989). Also, people are more likely to maintain consistency between their actions and their attitudes when their responses are made publicly rather than anonymously (Baumeister & Tice, 1984; Hirose & Kitada, 1985: Schlenker et al., 1980). Inconsistencies are also disregarded when people are led to believe that other people in the situation won't hold them accountable for their actions (Gaes, Melburg, & Tedeschi, 1986; Riess & Schlenker, 1977), or will even approve of their actions (Forsyth, Riess, & Schlenker, 1977; Riess et al., 1977; Schlenker, 1975). Last, when special procedures are used to prevent people from misrepresenting their attitudes, the attitudes they report don't necessarily match their behaviors (Gaes, Kalle, & Tedeschi, 1978; Malkis, Kalle, & Tedeschi, 1982; Paulhus, 1982; compare with Stults, Messe, & Kerr, 1984).

Self-affirmation theory: The self-esteem factor. Counterattitudinal behaviors don't just threaten our social identity. When we perform counterattitudinal behaviors, waste our effort, or make poor decisions, our private self-esteem is just as threatened as our public image. Who feels competent when they are doing things that conflict with their own values and attitudes? Who feels moral when they are expressing attitudes that don't match their true attitudes? Who feels clever when working hard for no good reason? Self-esteem theory agrees with Festinger that these situations are unpleasant, but not because they create cognitive inconsistencies. Rather, these situations are disturbing because they threaten our positive view of our selves (Aronson, 1968; Bramel, 1968; Zimbardo, 1969a).

self-affirmation theory
A theoretical explanation of the tendency for attitudes to change to match behavior; argues that such change is motivated by a desire to protect and enhance self-esteem. This theory also argues that attitude change is only one way individuals can affirm their self-esteem after behaving counterattitudinally or inappropriately.

Claude M. Steele's **self-affirmation theory** is based on this assumption, for he argues that we are more interested in protecting and enhancing our sense of self-esteem than we are in resolving cognitive inconsistencies. He contends that cigarette smokers aren't disturbed by the cognitions "I smoke cigarettes" and "smoking is unhealthy." Rather, they are disturbed because they consider themselves to be intelligent, rational, competent people, yet they engage in a life-threatening behavior. Therefore, rather than stop smoking, all they need to do is "engage in some affirmation of general self-integrity, even when that affirmation bears no relationship to smoking or to the inconsistency that smoking produces" (Steele, 1988, p. 262). If they can reassure themselves of their value, say by writing poetry, attending church, making a donation to a charity, or passing a test, then their unhealthy habit becomes a weaker threat to their sense of self-esteem.

Steele and his colleagues have found that people rarely worry about inconsistencies between their attitudes and their behaviors if they are given the opportunity to affirm their self-integrity in some way (Steele, 1975, 1988; Steele, Hopp, & Gonzales, 1986; Steele & Liu, 1981, 1983). When college students were asked to write an essay arguing in favor of a tuition hike at their university, subjects who freely agreed to write the essay softened their opposition to the hike more than subjects who were assigned the essay without any choice. This effect, however, was eliminated if the subjects were given the opportunity to express their personal opinions on another, unrelated issue immediately after they wrote their essays (Steele & Liu, 1983). Similarly, in a study of postdecisional stress, Steele and his colleagues (1986) found that subjects who expressed their personal values by wearing particular kinds of clothes were immune from the spreading of alternatives demonstrated by Brehm (1956). Steele (1988) concludes that "people cope with the meanings conveyed by the inconsistencies rather than the inconsistencies themselves" (p. 281).

Dissonance theory responds: The arousal factor. Cognitive-dissonance theorists noted the objections and arguments raised by these alternative perspectives, but they did not abandon their theory. Rather, they responded to the challenge by refining and extending their theory through

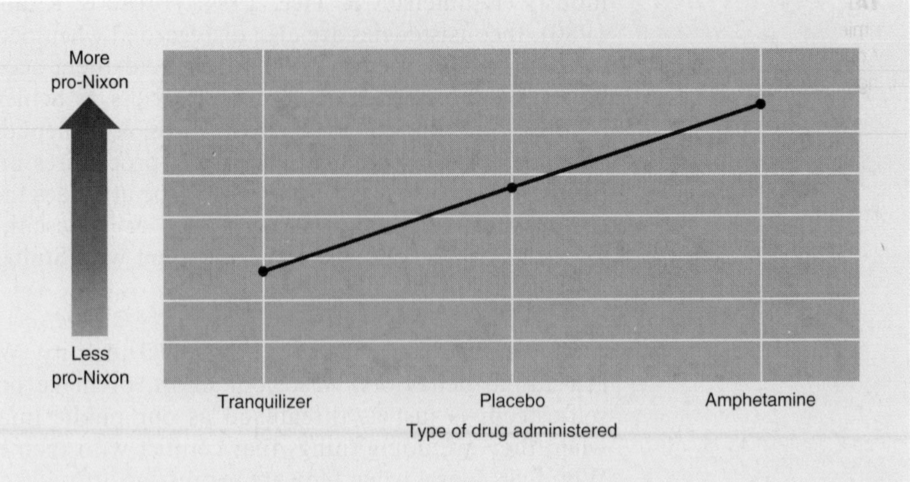

▲ **FIGURE 6-8**
Is cognitive dissonance an arousing, motivating experiential state? When researchers tranquilized subjects, thereby limiting their arousal, the attitudes they reported did not match the arguments they made in a counterattitudinal essay. Subjects given a placebo did express attitudes that were consistent with their actions, and those given a stimulant showed the most change. (From Cooper, Zanna, & Taves, 1978)

research. They managed to identify a number of factors that Festinger did not mention in his original theory and that must be present before dissonance is aroused by counterattitudinal behavior (Wicklund & Brehm, 1976). The *illusion of choice*, for example, is critical: the cognitions "I believe in *X*" and "I was forced to say I do not believe in *X*," do not generate dissonance. The action, too, must lead to *foreseeable negative consequences*. We do not change our own opinions after we write an essay arguing that wearing seat belts is dangerous if we believe that no one is going to be convinced by our claims. Feelings of *personal responsibility* for any harm that arises from the counterattitudinal action also seem to be prerequisites for cognitive dissonance (Collins & Hoyt, 1972; Cooper & Fazio, 1984; Scher & Cooper, 1989).

Researchers also searched for direct evidence of the *arousal properties* of dissonance (Joule, 1987; Kiesler & Pallak, 1976). If, they argued, dissonance is the arousing, motivating, dynamic state of tension that Festinger (1957) described in his original theory, then they should be able to document this tension through physiological measurement (Croyle & Cooper, 1983; Elkin & Leippe, 1986; Zimbardo, 1969a). In one project, researchers carefully monitored subjects' galvanic skin response (GSR) as they wrote an essay arguing that their university should start charging a fee for parking (obviously, a counterattitudinal behavior). As expected, subjects who were give no choice in selecting their essay topic did not become aroused, whereas subjects who were free to choose the essay topic showed elevated arousal levels. Overall, the correlation between attitude change and arousal was .73 (Elkin & Leippe, 1986, Experiment 1).

Researchers also discovered that any factor that limits or redefines arousal will eliminate dissonance (Cooper, Zanna, & Taves, 1978; Frey, Fries, & Osnabrugge, 1983; Steele, Southwick, & Critchlow, 1981; Tedeschi et al., 1986). One team of researchers interrupted the behavior → attitude sequence by convincing subjects that the arousal produced by their dissonance was actually caused by a pill they had taken. These researchers first secured subjects' agreement to take either a tranquilizer, a placebo, or an amphetamine for research purposes. The subjects were indeed given a placebo, a tranquilizer, or an amphetamine, but all were told that the drug they received was a placebo. They then wrote counterattitudinal essays favoring the pardoning of Richard M. Nixon (an unpopular opinion at the time). The researchers then measured the essay writers' attitudes on the topic and discovered the pattern shown in Figure 6-8: tranquilized subjects showed very little change, and the

▲ TABLE 6-9
Summing up: Four reasons why our attitudes sometimes change to match our behavior

Theory	*Assumptions*
Cognitive-dissonance theory	Inconsistencies among our cognitions can, in certain cases, lead to dissonance, an aversive psychological state that we are motivated to avoid. This hot, motivational model highlights the irrational side of attitudes and behaviors.
Self-perception theory	We make inferences about our attitudes by observing our own behavior in situations where we are able to act freely. This logical information-processing model stresses cold cognitive processes.
Self-presentation theory	Behaving in ways that are inconsistent with our attitudes threatens our social identities, so we use our public statements of attitude to protect our identities. This interpersonal model stresses the strategic uses of attitudes.
Self-affirmation theory	Actions that run counter to our attitudes threaten our self-esteem, so we change our attitudes or display other types of defensive reactions to maintain and protect our sense of self-worth. This intrapersonal model stresses the functional uses of attitudes.

highly aroused subjects who had received an amphetamine showed substantial change (Cooper, Zanna, & Taves, 1978). Dissonance and dissonance-reduction tactics such as attitude change were also eliminated in a study in which college students drank several beers or mixed vodka drinks after writing a counterattitudinal essay favoring an increase in tuition (Steele, Southwick, & Critchlow, 1981). Apparently, the sedative effect of the alcohol blocked the arousing effect of the counterattitudinal behavior. Dissonance, as Festinger maintained, is indeed arousing, although the experience may not be as negative as Festinger first proposed (Cooper, Fazio, & Rhodewalt, 1978; Higgins, Rhodewalt, & Zanna, 1979; Losch & Cacioppo, 1990; Rhodewalt & Comer, 1979).

Dissonance Revisited: Toward Theoretical Synthesis

No one theory can account for all we now know about the complex interrelationships between our behaviors and our attitudes (see Table 6-9). Festinger originally stressed the dynamic impact of actions on attitudes, but alternative approaches soon offered opposing interpretations (Aronson, 1989; Berkowitz & Devine, 1989a, 1989b; Cooper & Fazio, 1989; Westermann, 1988). Because these approaches have been supported empirically, some investigators feel that these alternative explanations should not "be regarded as 'competing' formulations but as complementary ones" (Fazio, Zanna, & Cooper, 1977; Lord, 1989; Paulhus, 1982). Although researchers have spent many years striving to disconfirm one theory while confirming another, each approach adds another piece to the puzzle (compare with Greenwald, 1975b; Greenwald & Ronis, 1978; Ronis & Greenwald, 1979). When people are keenly aware of their attitudes—like Janet and Mrs. Keech's followers—we probably need cognitive-dissonance theory to explain their intense emotional reactions. When initial attitudes are weak, unclear, or not yet formed, however, then self-perception theory probably offers a simpler explanation for the behavior-to-attitude sequence (Fazio, 1987). Similarly, when we act in ways that threaten our social identities, we use our attitude statements to shore up our damaged identities—as self-presentation theory would predict. Finally, when our sense of who we are and the value we put on ourselves are threatened, then our attitudes reflect our need to protect and enhance our private selves as well as our public images. We are, after all, complicated creatures who can feel, reason, communicate, and affirm our worth at will. Janet, once again, provides us with a final example:

> I think in a way I am selfish, and very emotional, and I think that I am a very real person and an understanding person, and I can handle life situations fairly well, so I am basing a lot of it on my ability to do the things that I feel are right and best for me and whomever I am involved with. I think I was very fair to myself about the decision, and I really think that I have been truthful, not hiding anything, bringing out all the feelings involved. I feel it is a good decision and an honest one, a real decision. (quoted in Gilligan, 1982, p. 84–85)

Summary

Individuals react to the social world in both positive and negative ways. These reactions are guided by *attitudes*: affectively valenced cognitive representations that exert a directive or dynamic influence on behavior. Our attitudes can pertain to virtually any aspect of the social environment, and most include three basic components: an affective component (the positive or negative feeling), a cognitive component (thoughts and beliefs), and a behavioral component (overt actions and *behavioral intentions*). This view is known as the *tricomponent model* of attitudes.

Most attitudes are learned through direct experience with the attitude object. This learning may take place gradually through *mere exposure*: frequent exposure to an object tends to increase our liking for that object. Alternatively, when an object is repeatedly paired with a stimulus that creates positive or negative feelings on its own, the object may come to evoke similar feelings. This process is known as *classical conditioning*. *Instrumental conditioning*, in contrast, occurs when we are reinforced after we have expressed an attitude or reacted to an object in a certain way. We also acquire our attitudes through *socialization*: our parents and peers influence us through direct instruction, by conditioning us, and through *social learning*—we observe and imitate their actions and expressed attitudes.

What functions do attitudes serve? Katz identified four, including organizing information (knowledge function), identifying positive and negative objects (instrumental function), self-expression (expressive function), and self-protection and enhancement (defensive function). Attitudes also guide behavior—in some circumstances. Although a classic study by LaPiere suggested that our self-reports about attitudes say little about our actual behaviors, recent research indicates that many factors influence the attitude-behavior relationship. Strong, important attitudes are most influential, especially when we have a vested interest in the situation. Attitudes that pertain to specific objects in a particular context are also more potent guides for behavior, as are attitudes formed through direct experience that are accessible in memory. When situational norms are powerful and inconsistent with private attitudes, attitude-behavior correspondence decreases. Self-awareness increases attitude-behavior correspondence, whereas self-monitoring and *mindlessness* decrease it.

Several theories have been offered to explain how attitudes guide behavior. Fazio's mode of processing model stresses both automatic and controlled cognitive processes. Controlled cognitive processing strengthens the attitude-behavior relationship if we generate information that supports our attitude. Fishbein and Ajzen's theory of reasoned action, in contrast, argues that attitudes don't cause behavior directly. Rather, attitudes influence our intention to perform the behavior, and then this intention determines the action.

Just as attitudes guide behavior, behavior sometimes influences attitudes. Festinger's theory of *cognitive dissonance* argues that cognitive inconsistency creates a state of psychological tension that we are motivated to reduce. When we engage in *counterattitudinal behavior*, we reduce the ensuing dissonance by changing our attitudes to match our behavior. Dissonance offers an explanation for a number of tendencies of actions to influence our attitudes, including change following counterattitudinal advocacy, *spreading of alternatives, selective exposure* after making choices, the tendency to justify the effort we expend to reach our goals, and reactions to information that disconfirms our beliefs. Other theorists, however, offer alternative interpretations of these fascinating tendencies. Bem's self-perception theory takes a more rational, information-processing approach, for it assumes that we make inferences about our attitudes by observing our own behavior in situations in which we are able to act freely. Self-presentation theory's emphasis on interpersonal processes maintains that behaving in ways that are inconsistent with our attitudes threatens our social identity, so we use our public statements of attitude to protect our identity. Self-esteem theories, such as *self-affirmation theory*, argue that actions that run counter to our attitudes threaten our self-esteem, so we change our attitudes or display other types of defensive reactions to maintain and protect our sense of self-worth. Hypotheses derived from all four of these perspectives have been supported empirically, prompting many researchers to suggest that motivational, cognitive, interpersonal, and self-esteem processes combine to influence behavior → attitude sequences.

For More Information

• "Attitude and Opinion Measurement," by Robyn M. Dawes and Tom L. Smith, provides an advanced but succinct review of the basic ways to measure attitudes. This selection is a chapter in the *Handbook of Social Psychology* (Lindzey & Aronson, 1985).

• *Attitude Structure and Function*, edited by Anthony R. Pratkanis, Steven J. Breckler, and Anthony G. Greenwald (1989), revitalizes the study of attitude structures and functions by bringing together 17 chapters by leading experts in the field.

• *Attitudes*, by D. W. Rajecki (1990), provides a broad overview to the field of attitudes, with in-depth coverage of measurement, attitude-behavior relationships, and polarization.

• *Attitudes and Opinions*, by Stuart Oskamp (1991), is a sturdy synopsis of decades of research dealing with attitude formation and change.

• *Attitudes, Personality, and Behavior*, by Icek Ajzen (1988), investigates areas of consistency and inconsistency in human affairs and provides an updated version of the theory of reasoned action.

• *Consistency in Social Behavior: The Ontario Symposium* (Volume 2, 1982), edited by Mark P. Zanna, E. Tory Higgins, and C. Peter Herman, presents papers from a symposium held at the University of Waterloo in Canada. The symposium focused on one basic question: When do attitudes and personality traits influence behavior? The 12 papers are most suitable for advanced students.

• "Multiple Processes by Which Atitudes Guide Behavior: The MODE Model as an Integrative Framework," by Russell H. Fazio (1990), is one of the most comprehensive and theoretically sophisticated analyses of the question:

How do attitudes guide action? This selection is a chapter in *Advances in Experimental Social Psychology* (Zanna, 1990).

- "Public Opinion and Political Action," by Donald R. Kinder and David O. Sears, provides a comprehensive review of research and theory applying the social psychology of attitudes to political processes. This selection is a chapter in the *Handbook of Social Psychology* (Lindzey & Aronson, 1985).

Application: Promoting Healthy Behavior

The discrepancy between people's attitudes pertaining to their health and their health-sustaining behaviors is striking. People who drink alcohol excessively realize alcohol abuse is harmful, yet they continue to overindulge. Nearly three-quarters of all people who smoke cigarettes report that they have tried to break this unhealthy habit but have failed (Wood, 1990). Most adults realize that seat belts reduce the likelihood of serious injury or death in automobile accidents, yet only about 40% of us wear seat belts regularly (Decision Making Information, 1986). People who believe they are at risk for contracting AIDS are no more likely to take steps to reduce their vulnerability to the disease than those who don't believe they are at risk (Aspinwall et al., 1990). Health-promoting attitudes are no guarantee that people will engage in healthy actions.

This attitude-behavior discrepancy, although puzzling on the surface, becomes more understandable once we realize that no one-to-one relationship links an attitude to a behavior. Consider, for example, people's knowledge of AIDS and their willingness to take precautions to avoid the disease. AIDS was initially diagnosed in the spring of 1981 at several medical centers in metropolitan areas of the United States. The patients were all young men whose immune systems failed to protect them from infections and viruses. By 1983, the disorder was traced to the human immunodeficiency virus (HIV), and the disease itself was named the acquired immunodeficiency syndrome, or AIDS. At this time AIDS is incurable and is nearly always fatal. It is the leading cause of death for men between the ages of 25 and 45 in the United States.

Initially, AIDS was a disease more feared than understood. Most cases were reported for two subgroups in the U.S. population—homosexual men and intravenous drug users—and these associations increased heterosexuals' and nonusers' negativity toward the disease. The prevalence of the disease in subgroups rather than in the general population was also reassuring for many people because they assumed that AIDS was a "gay disease" or "drug addict's disease." Many myths also circulated about the origins and transmission routes of the disease, and these myths interfered with public health programs designed to control its spread. Even today, some 20% of all people in the United States believe that people who suffer from AIDS have "only themselves to blame" (Herek & Glunt, 1993, p. 241).

Public knowledge of AIDS has increased dramatically in recent years (Herek & Glunt, 1993). Although some myths persist, most adults now know AIDS is typically transmitted in one of three ways. A mother can pass the virus to her unborn child perinatally. AIDS is also transmitted through contact with contaminated blood. Intravenous drug users, for example, can pass the virus on to others when they share contaminated hypodermic needles. AIDS is also a sexually transmitted disease (STD): when a person with AIDS engages in sexual behavior with a healthy person, that person may become infected with the HIV virus. Adults can therefore reduce the likelihood of infection if they avoid risky behaviors. They can stop using intravenously injected drugs or at least stop sharing hypodermic needles with other people. They can stop having sex, or they can at least make their sex behaviors safer by using a condom and limiting casual sex encounters with unfamiliar partners.

Extensive knowledge of AIDS and generally favorable attitudes toward safe sex, however, don't always translate into healthy actions. People often claim that the threat of AIDS has made them more cautious when it comes to sex, but self-reports of change don't always correspond to behavioral changes (Gerrard et al., 1993). College students who know that sex with multiple partners and without a condom increases their chances of infection don't refrain from casual sex or use condoms regularly (Baldwin & Baldwin, 1988). Over 50% of all adolescents in the United States have engaged in sexual intercourse by the time they reach the age of 18, but fewer than 10% of these adolescents use condoms during sex (Centers for Disease Control, 1991a; Kegeles et al., 1988). Gay men who realize that certain sexual practices increase their vulnerability to AIDS do not always avoid such sexual practices (Gerrard et al., 1993).

Given the severely negative consequences of AIDS, why don't people take more precautions to avoid it? First, as the theory of reasoned action, discussed earlier in the chapter, suggests, positive attitudes about health don't guarantee positive attitudes about healthy behaviors (Jemmott & Jones, 1993; Terry, Gallois, & McCamish, 1993). Individuals may value their health and well-being, but their attitudes toward actions that will minimize their risk of infection with AIDS may be distinctly negative. Many individuals do not like to use condoms, for they believe that they interfere with sexual pleasure. Nor do they want to limit their sexual liaisons to a single partner or discuss the possibility of AIDS before having sex with a partner. These behaviorally specific attitudes thus encourage unhealthy rather than healthy practices.

Second, social norms pertaining to sexuality also influence people's willingness to use precautions. Until recently, some gay communities encouraged unsafe sexual practices, such as casual sex relations with unfamiliar partners. Similarly, the norms on many college campuses are either silent on the issue of condom use or openly antagonistic. Few individuals can consistently avoid risky sexual behaviors if their peers and partners do not support safe sexual practices (Jemmott & Jemmott, 1991).

Third, even though people may have positive attitudes toward AIDS-preventative behaviors, and social norms may encourage healthy actions, behavioral skills are still required if these attitudes are to be put into action. An effective *AIDS risk-reduction behavior sequence* includes several critical components (Fisher & Fisher, 1993). People must be able to do the following:

- Accept their own sexuality and recognize the need for safe sexual practices
- Acquire information about techniques and methods that can be used to reduce their vulnerability to AIDS
- Expand their own sexual agenda to include not only personal pleasure and increased intimacy but also the avoidance of AIDS
- Discuss their AIDS-prevention agenda with their partners before sexual intimacy and leave situations that will defeat their protective agenda
- Perform behaviors in public settings that are essential for carrying out their AIDS-prevention agenda, including purchasing condoms
- Monitor the effectiveness of their AIDS-preventing actions

The ability to talk openly about sexual matters or express one's personal opinions about condom use may seem like insignificant skills, but people who possess these skills are more likely to act in health-promoting ways (Cantania et al., 1989).

Last, situational factors may disrupt people's ability to access their pro-health attitudes, while undermining their behavioral skills. A person who is preoccupied with feelings of intense loneliness may do things that he or she would usually avoid. When two people become sexually aroused, this intense emotional experience may inhibit their access to their pro-health attitudes and interfere with even a well-learned AIDS risk-reduction sequence (Miller et al., 1993). Alcohol and other drugs, too, can short-circuit an otherwise effective AIDS risk-reduction sequence. People who are intoxicated are much more likely to engage in unsafe sex, presumably because they underestimate the risk of infection and fail to follow their behavioral agenda (Leigh & Stall, 1993).

This recognition of the uncertain link between knowledge of AIDS and the use of precautions during sex offers clear recommendations for building effective prevention programs (Kelly et al., 1993). Such programs must do more than just warn people about the dangers of AIDS. They must also motivate people to take precautions and teach them the behavioral skills they need to reduce their risk. One successful treatment program used with college students, the AIDS Risk Reduction Project, directly attacks negative attitudes toward condoms and anti-condom norms by exposing students to videotaped testimonials of medical experts and other students (Fisher & Fisher, 1993). The speakers in these testimonials argue that condoms don't adversely affect sexual pleasure. The testimonials also point out the benefits of using condoms (for example, "Now that I use condoms I can relax and enjoy sex," p. 145) and stress pro-condom social norms (for example, "If my roommate was sexually active, and I found out she was not using condoms, I'd think she was out of her mind," p. 146). Participants are also shown videotapes of couples discussing safe sexual practices, negotiating the use of condoms, and leaving threatening situations. They are also given the opportunity to role-play these behavioral skills with other members of the group, who provide them with encouragement and social support. This program, and others that include similar components, appear to be effective means of controlling the spread of AIDS (Fisher & Fisher, 1992).

People's failure to protect themselves from AIDS is only one example of self-destructive behaviors that become less enigmatic when reexamined within a social-psychological framework. Most people know that smoking and cancer are linked, but this realization may be overwhelmed by the more immediately pleasurable aspects of smoking. Even though we have been told time and again that "seat belts save lives," this global value may not be readily accessible as a guide for action when we enter our cars. Situational norms may also prevent us from following the healthy course of action by eating properly and avoiding alcohol. Although it might be tempting to attribute such unhealthy actions to unknown causes or human irrationality, the social-psychological factors that sustain health-promoting behaviors also maintain unhealthy ones. Moreover, since social processes sustain these health problems, social processes also hold the key for their alleviation (Coie et al., 1993).

Prejudice

The four men were about to become antagonists in a violent drama on the frozen winter streets of Boston. Cuneo was driving a battered Comet, and his buddy Boyle sat by his side. They were keyed up after working as bouncers at a local bar, very drunk, and white. On a nearby street, Booker was driving a maroon Buick with a weak battery. Wilson, Booker's neighbor, was sitting next to him: the two of them were headed for home after working a shift at the nearby medical center. They were tired, sober, and black.

The Comet and the Buick were sitting side by side at a red light at Park Square when Boyle rolled down his window and began shouting insults at Booker; his language was obscene and laced with racial epithets. When Booker answered back with his own opinions of Boyle and his heritage, Cuneo waded into the melee by spitting at Booker. The incident would have ended when the light changed and Cuneo sped off if Booker's Buick hadn't stalled. Cuneo made a U-turn on the dark street so he could drive back and renew the conflict. By then, Booker was connecting jumper cables to his stalled car. Wilson stood by his side. Boyle immediately rushed the pair, and Booker responded by pulling out a baseball bat from under the Buick's front seat. Boyle then snatched up the jumper cables and began to swing them in Booker's face. Meanwhile, Cuneo, still in his car, tried to run over Wilson, who ran down the street and around the corner.

The white men were winning the battle. One witness explained, "It was all their show" (Sedgwick, 1982, p. 158). But when the jumper cables slipped from Boyle's February-frozen fingers, Booker closed in. Pulling a knife from his coat, he buried the blade in Boyle's liver:

> Boyle stumbled back a few steps, then straightened and hobbled back to the Comet. He told Cuneo his side hurt, then passed out. Thinking Boyle had been clubbed with the bat, Cuneo reached under his friend's sweater to feel his ribs. When he pulled out his hand, it was covered with blood. (Sedgwick, 1982, p. 158)

Cuneo rushed Boyle to a nearby hospital, but Boyle didn't live through the night.

prejudice
Liking or disliking people because they belong to an ethnic, racial, or other social category one likes or dislikes; prejudice usually refers to a negative bias rather than a positive one.

Boyle was killed by his own **prejudice**: his intense rejection of another person simply because that person belonged to a group he disliked. Countless groups comprise modern society—young, old, blacks, whites, Anglos, Latinos, men, women, Arabs, Israelis, Catholics, Protestants, gays, straights, Coke drinkers, Pepsi drinkers, and on and on. In many cases, people develop strong attitudes toward the members of these groups. In theory, prejudicial attitudes can be positive biases, but the term usually carries a negative connotation. As we see in the first section of this chapter, prejudice implies an unfavorable rejection of others that is both unfair and irrational. It prompts us to *prejudge* people solely on the basis of their membership in a group or category. Boyle did not see two individuals with unique personality traits, interests, and goals when he looked out his car window and saw Booker and Wilson. Instead, he saw two black men, and he hated them.

Recognizing the prejudiced nature of Boyle's attitudes and actions is not enough, however. We must also explore the roots of his prejudice and attempt to discover why, across many societies and many eras, the people in one group have hated the people in other groups. Was Boyle's antagonism part of his basic personality—a closed-minded person who resisted new ideas and social change? Did his intolerance spring from a general antipathy for anyone who didn't belong to the same social group or category that he did? Or did he reject black people because white society had taught him to think of African Americans as targets of abuse and hatred? Prejudice has many causes, but once we enumerate them, we can turn to a more hopeful topic—cures for prejudice.

The Nature of Prejudice

The 19th-century English author Charles Lamb admitted, "I am, in plainer words, a bundle of prejudices—made up of likings and dislikings—the veriest thrall of sympathies, apathies, and antipathies." Mark Twain, however, claimed that he was completely unprejudiced: "I have no race prejudices, and I think I have no color prejudices nor creed prejudices. Indeed, I know it. I can stand any society."

Are you prejudiced? Before deciding, consider the meaning of the term to a social psychologist. Experts do not agree on how to define the term most clearly, but prejudices are, above all else, attitudes. So, as the tri-component model of attitudes discussed in Chapter 6 suggests, prejudices actuate our feelings, our thoughts, and our actions (see Figure 7-1). The *affective component* of prejudice is characterized by emotions that range from mild nervousness to outright hatred. Such statements as "I hate whites," "Allowing gays in the army makes me angry," "Blacks frighten me," and "I can't stand pushy women" all illustrate the emotions in our prejudices. Indeed, our strongest negative emotions are often reserved for groups rather than individuals. As Gordon W. Allport (1954) noted in his classic treatise, *The Nature of Prejudice,* "anger is customarily felt toward individuals only, whereas hatred may be felt toward whole classes of people" (pp. 340–341).

Prejudice also includes a *cognitive component*: assumptions and beliefs about the members of other groups. These cognitions can be as inaccurate as our emotions are ardent, but we feel that these beliefs are supported by facts and objective observations. An American citizen who is prejudiced against Russians, for example, may assume Russians deserve this rejection because they are untrustworthy, aggressive, and unintelligent. A racist Anglo may believe that Latinos are lazy. Such overgeneralizations about the members of other social groups are **stereotypes**. As discussed in Chapter 3, stereotypes are cognitive schemas, so they can systematically influence our perceptions and memories.

stereotypes
Socially shared generalizations about people who are members of a particular group or social category.

discrimination
Differential treatment of a person based on his or her membership in an ethnic, racial, or other social category.

Discrimination constitutes the *behavioral component* of prejudice. A sexist man, for example, may quit his job when he is transferred to a department managed by a woman. A prejudiced black may discriminate against whites by treating them unfairly. The behavioral component of an attitude, however,

▲ **FIGURE 7-1**
What is prejudice? The tricomponent theory of attitudes argues that prejudice, like any other attitude, includes emotions, thoughts, and actions. This model suggests that prejudices such as sexism occur when individuals experience negative feelings toward women, endorse unfavorable beliefs and assumptions about women, and act in ways that discriminate against women.

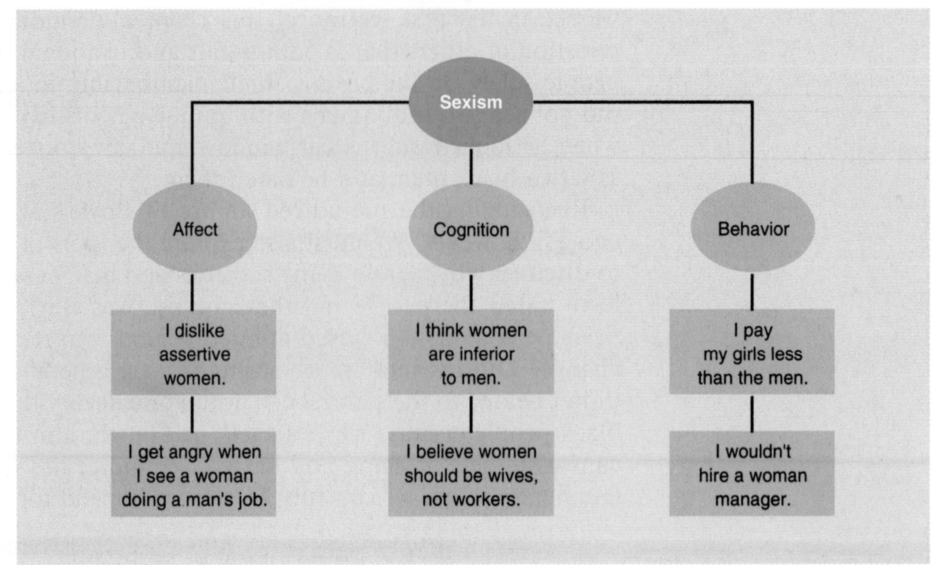

also includes predispositions to respond in certain ways. A white person who is prejudiced against African Americans could plan to live in segregated housing areas and decide to vote for only white candidates in all elections. (Varying views on the definition of prejudice are offered by Ashmore & DelBoca, 1981; Brewer & Kramer, 1985; Duckitt, 1992; Simpson & Yinger, 1985.)

Prejudice can be directed at virtually any one of the innumerable groups that make up our heterogeneous society. Even today, Catholics, Jews, Muslims, and other religious groups are persecuted for their beliefs. Those who adopt alternative lifestyles, such as gays and lesbians, are often the victims of prejudice-motivated violence: so-called *hate crimes* or *bias crimes*. People who are physically challenged are viewed in stereotypical ways that are both demeaning and unfair. Latinos, Asian Americans, Native Americans, and other ethnic and racial groups experience systematic persecution because they are different from others. All of these forms of prejudice demand close study, but we cannot survey the vast literature on all these forms of prejudice in one chapter. We therefore concentrate on only two of these many forms of prejudice, in detail: **racism**, which is prejudice based on race, and **sexism**, or prejudice based on biological sex. This emphasis on racism and sexism does not mean that other forms of prejudice are less important or less worthy of study.

racism
Prejudice against people based on their membership in a racial category.

sexism
Prejudice against people based on their biological sex (either male or female).

Racial Prejudice

Racial tensions and prejudices have long been a part of American society. In colonial times African men, women, and children were enslaved by European whites, who denied them any rights of justice or equality. The passage of three amendments to the U.S. Constitution restored some of their civil rights, but African Americans were still systematically oppressed by unfair labor laws, voting restrictions, and exclusionary practices. Throughout the early 1900s, black people were considered to be inferior in many ways, and **apartheid** laws prohibited equal status or intimate contact between the two groups. Then, in 1954, the U.S. Supreme Court struck down many of these unfair laws in *Brown v. Board of Education of Topeka, Kansas*. The Court mandated the desegregation of public schools, but progress was negligible until the social movements of the early 1960s forced the passage of new civil rights legislation. Now, some

apartheid
A political system based on racial segregation and discrimination.

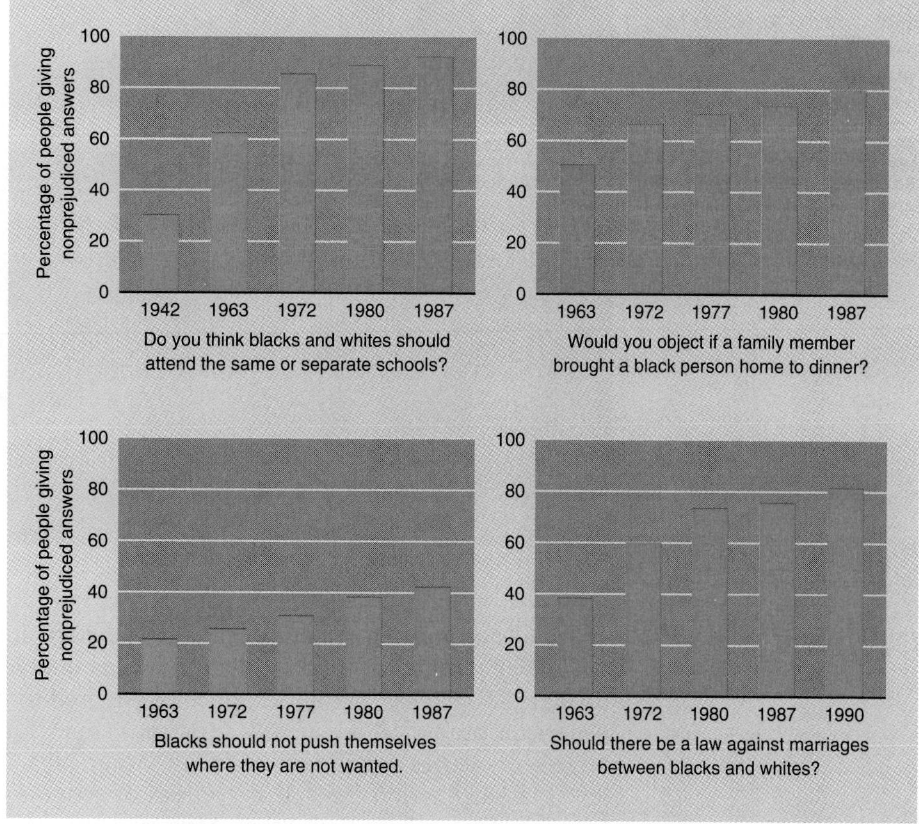

▲ FIGURE 7-2
Have white Americans' attitudes toward blacks changed in the last 50 years? Public opinion polls suggest that whites were highly prejudiced in the early 1940s: most felt that blacks and whites should attend separate schools, that contact between the two groups should be minimized, and that intermarriage should be illegal. Over the years, however, whites' attitudes have become increasingly egalitarian. (Data from Davis & Smith, 1990)

40 years after the Court's ruling, treating a person unfairly because of his or her race or color is neither legal nor condoned.

Have white people's attitudes kept pace with these changes in civil rights? Polls taken between 1942 and 1990 are heartening. In 1942, most white Americans favored segregated schools and separate seating areas on streetcars and buses (see Figure 7-2). In 1944, most white people felt that a white should be given the chance to take a job before it is offered to a black. In 1958, only 37% of white voters said they would vote for a black man for president if their party nominated him. In 1963, 50.4% of white Americans surveyed claimed they would object if a member of their family brought home a black friend to dinner; 63.6% felt that interracial marriage should be against the law; and 78.2% felt that blacks shouldn't "push themselves where they're not wanted." These numbers, however, changed dramatically during the 1970s and 1980s. Now, well over 90% of white people accept black people in schools, their homes, neighborhoods, and public office. White racists, once the majority in America, are now the minority (Schuman, Steeh, & Bobo, 1985; Wood, 1990).

Other evidence, however, is less encouraging. As Figure 7-2 indicates, some whites still express openly negative attitudes toward African Americans. As recently as 1992, 36% of the white Americans polled by Gallup (1993, p. 92) agreed that "many whites dislike blacks," and 35% of the African Americans agreed that "many blacks dislike whites." Second, hostile encounters between blacks and whites—like the savage attack perpetrated by Boyle—may be increasing rather than decreasing. Police officials recorded 15 separate bias incidents during a 9-day period in January of 1992 in New York City alone. The vicious beating of Rodney King by police officers reaffirmed to many the lack

▲ White Americans' attitudes toward African Americans have become more positive over the years, but conflict between the two groups still remains. Nearly 20% of all white Americans are prejudiced against African Americans, and many African Americans report feelings of economic, social, and political oppression.

of racial harmony in America, and set the stage for the Los Angeles riots of 1992. The number of blacks killed by whites doubled between 1978 and 1988 (FBI, 1988). College campuses, once considered to be safe harbors in a sea of American prejudice, frequently serve as venues for racial conflicts. Last, the targets of whites' prejudice—African Americans—continue to report lower levels of satisfaction, as well as feelings of economic, social, and political oppression. One survey found that African Americans continue to feel discriminated against when seeking housing, jobs, and a good wage (Sigelman & Welch, 1991). In another survey, 42% of the black respondents opined that whites want to keep blacks in their place; 36% stated that white people do not care what happens to black people. Most blacks in the United States identify more closely with African blacks than with whites in America (Institute for Social Research, 1983).

These figures suggest that anti-black racism in America has changed during the last 30 years. The white racist who openly denounces blacks and favors segregation may be a rarity, but many experts believe that new forms of prejudice have supplanted traditional prejudice (Kleinpenning & Hagendoorn, 1993). Contemporary forms of white racism, including covert racism, aversive racism, symbolic racism, and regressive racism, are examined next.

Covert racism. The white salesclerk doesn't like waiting on African Americans but knows that it's just part of the job. The white grandmother believes schools should be segregated, but talks about these ideas only with her daughter. The honors student thinks the blacks in his classes are stupid, but he does not say so. Such **covert racism** occurs because some whites continue to be prejudiced against blacks, but they keep their sentiments hidden from public scrutiny to avoid the appearance of racism (Batson et al., 1986).

covert racism
Prejudice against members of other racial categories, which is not expressed openly.

Researchers must use more sensitive methods of measurement than opinion polling to detect covert racism. One such method, the *bogus-pipeline procedure,* involves convincing people that their truthfulness is being monitored by a highly accurate lie-detector machine. Subjects first fill out a questionnaire pertaining to such innocuous issues as movies, sports, and music.

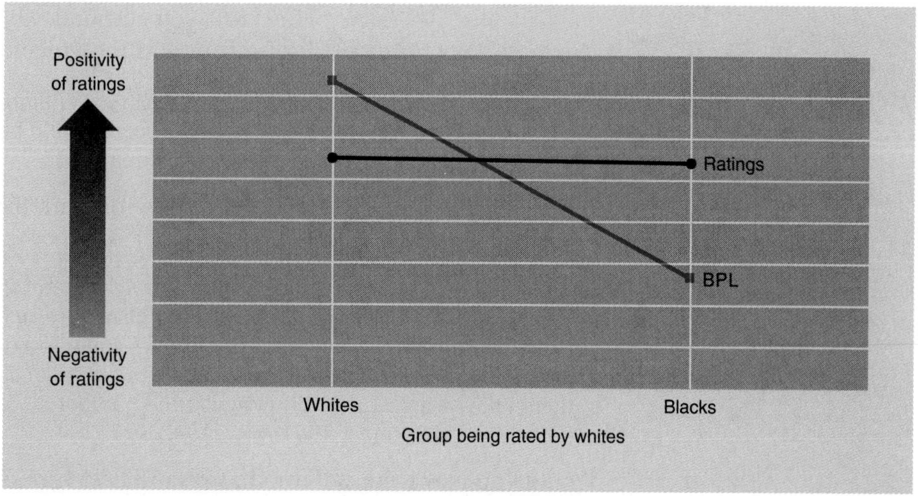

▲ **FIGURE 7-3**
Do white people claim to be less prejudiced than they actually are? When whites rated blacks' and whites' intelligence, stupidity, sensitivity, dirtiness, and other qualities, they showed no signs of prejudice. The overall index of their ratings for blacks was as positive as their overall ratings of whites (as the line labeled "Ratings" indicates). But when they thought dishonesty would be detected by a lie-detector machine (the BPL), their ratings of whites were much more positive than their ratings of blacks. (From Sigall & Page, 1971)

Next, the experimenter connects them to a maze of sophisticated equipment. The researcher claims the machine measures attitudes as accurately as a lie-detector test. He or she then demonstrates the machine's precision by asking subjects a few questions about movies, sports, and music. After each question, the machine buzzes momentarily, then spits out its reading of their opinion. Amazing space-age technology? Not really. The machine's dials and buzzers are controlled by a confederate in the next room who has a copy of the subjects' responses to the original questionnaire (Jones & Sigall, 1971; Roese & Jamieson, 1993).

When connected to the bogus pipeline, people give more prejudiced answers than people who fill out questionnaires or answer a pollster's questions. The white college students in one study were asked whether African Americans are intelligent, honest, lazy, talkative, musical, ambitious, and so on. They rated white Americans as well. A second set of subjects completed the same ratings while connected to the pipeline. The method of measurement made a critical difference, as Figure 7-3 indicates. Students who thought that any dishonesty would be detected by the bogus pipeline rated blacks more negatively than whites, whereas students who used the paper-and-pencil methods rated the two groups identically. The researchers concluded, "Current stereotypes: A little fading, a little faking" (Sigall & Page, 1971, p. 247).

Covert racism also surfaces when people believe they are interacting with like-minded individuals. When whites in one study watched two people debate the issue "the value of nuclear energy," they rated a black who lost the debate as favorably as a white who lost the debate. A different pattern emerged, however, when a confederate in the audience made a racial slur just before the ratings were taken. When the accomplice used a racist word to describe the black man, the subjects rated the losing black debater more negatively than the losing white debater (Greenberg & Pyszczynski, 1985). Similarly, when students gave their opinions about a series of racial incidents on campus after hearing another person condemn those involved, they agreed that the perpetrators should be punished. If, however, the other person condoned the mistreatment of black people, then the students were much less likely to condemn the perpetrators. Indeed, in some cases, these students expressed approval of white students who harassed black students (Blanchard, Tilly, & Vaughn, 1991).

Aversive racism. How will you respond when you pick up the ringing phone in your home or dorm room and the voice on the line says:

> "Hello . . . Ralph's Garage? This is George Williams. . . . Listen, I'm stuck out here on the parkway . . . and I'm wondering if you'd be able to come out here and take a look at my car." (Gaertner & Bickman, 1971, pp. 219–220)

When you tell George that he has the wrong number, he exclaims:

> This isn't Ralph's Garage! Listen, I'm terribly sorry to have disturbed you, but listen . . . I'm stuck out here on the highway . . . and that was the last dime I had! I have bills in my pocket, but no more change to make another phone call. . . . Now I'm really stuck out here. What am I going to do now?
>
> Listen, do you think you could do me the favor of calling the garage and letting them know where I am? I'll give you the number. . . . They know me over there. (Gaertner & Bickman, 1971, pp. 219–220)

Would you make the call for George and help him out, or would you just forget about it?

Samuel Gaertner, John Dovidio, and their colleagues believe that your response may be tinged by your racial prejudices. Using this *wrong-number technique,* they called 1109 residents of Brooklyn, New York, between 6:30 and 9:30 P.M. and made the request. After hanging up, the researchers waited for the subjects to call the number for Ralph's. They identified their subjects' sex and race using location of residence, last name, and voice characteristics. Seven blacks, who purposely spoke in a southern black dialect, and 7 whites made the telephone calls. White listeners, as Figure 7-4 shows, discriminated more than blacks. They helped whites 12% more frequently than blacks, whereas blacks helped whites 7% more frequently than blacks (Gaertner & Bickman, 1971).

Gaertner and Dovidio believe that many whites are fair-minded: they sincerely strive to treat others justly. Many, however, continue to experience aversive emotions when they interact with African Americans. These negative feelings, which include nervousness, stress, tension, and concern, are vestiges of nearly forgotten racial fears and anxieties, and in many cases they aren't even consciously recognized. Such individuals may swear that they are unprejudiced—that they are color-blind when it comes to race—yet they respond

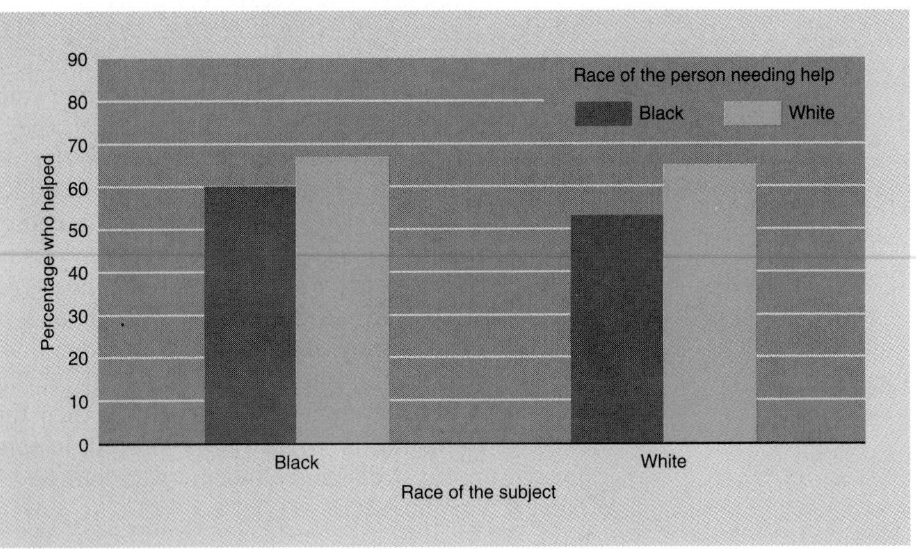

▲ **FIGURE 7-4**
If a man calls you on the phone and asks for help, would you be more likely to agree if he was a member of your racial group? When a white asked for help, race made no difference. He was helped by equal numbers of African Americans and whites. But when an African American asked for help, white racism surfaced. Whites were more likely to help a white person than a black person. (From Gaertner & Bickman, 1971)

▲ Blatant racism has declined in recent years, to the point that overtly racist acts (such as KKK cross-burnings) are relatively rare. This old-fashioned, overt racism has been replaced by more subtle forms of racism, such as aversive racism. Whites who experience aversive racism don't express their prejudice overtly, but they nonetheless experience negative emotions when they encounter African Americans in public places. As Kenneth B. Clark concludes, modern prejudice is "more complicated and more subtle."

aversive racism Prejudice experienced by individuals who accept egalitarian values but nonetheless experience negative emotions in the presence of members of other racial groups.

negatively to black people. Gaertner and Dovidio call this bias **aversive racism**: a negative emotional reaction to members of another group experienced by people who endorse nonprejudicial values. Like the subjects in the wrong-number study, aversive racists may hang up the phone without listening when the caller is black. They help a white who has fallen down, but they overlook a black person who needs help (Gaertner & Dovidio, 1986). They brusquely shake off the request of a black petitioner, but they stop and listen to the white petitioner's request for a signature (Crosby, Bromley, & Saxe, 1980). They are animated and personable when they are interacting with a black person, but privately they feel upset and uncomfortable (Ickes, 1984). When asked whether they are prejudiced, these individuals claim that they are not; yet they choose to sit by a white rather than a black on a crowded bus or pass by a black panhandler to give a coin to a white one (Dovidio & Gaertner, 1986, 1991).

symbolic racism Prejudice displayed by individuals who claim they reject other racial groups, not because of their color or background, but because these other groups don't accept traditional social values.

Symbolic racism. Dick argues that blacks have only themselves to blame for their poverty—if they just worked harder, they could overcome their problems. Darlene and Roberta think that African Americans, as a group, don't value a good education, so they often end up in dead-end jobs. John insists that anyone in America can succeed if they apply themselves (from interviews in Wellman, 1977). These individuals all show signs of **symbolic racism**, "a blend of anti-black affect and the kind of traditional American moral values embodied in the Protestant Ethic" (Kinder & Sears, 1981, p. 416). Symbolic racists tell themselves that they don't condemn a person based on his or her color or creed. They do, however, dislike people who reject traditional American values of individualism, self-reliance, discipline, and hard work. And blacks, they feel, fit this category (McConahay & Hough, 1976; Sears, 1988; Sears & Kinder, 1985).

The concept of symbolic racism explains why many white Americans enthusiastically endorse principles of racial equality but refuse to support the programs needed to implement these principles. They claim to bear no grudge against black people, but they object to government welfare programs ("Most people on welfare are just lazy"), hiring quotas based on race ("The government shouldn't interfere in a company's hiring practices"), and busing to

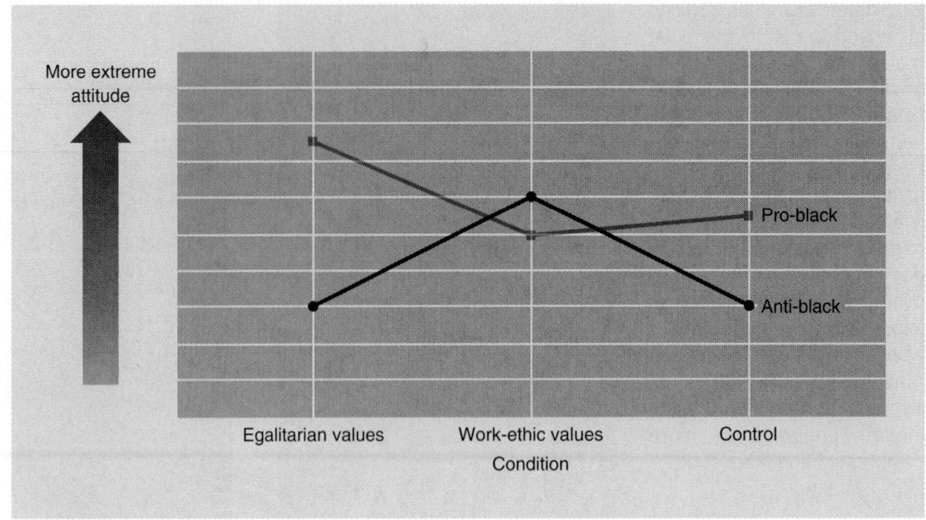

▲ **FIGURE 7-5**
Why are some whites so inconsistent in their dealings with blacks? Studies of symbolic racism suggest that some whites hold two sets of conflicting values—egalitarian and work ethic—and think blacks don't work hard enough. When symbolic racists consider egalitarian values, they rate blacks more highly and reject anti-black sentiments. But when they reflect on work-ethic values, their anti-black ratings increase, and pro-black scores fall slightly. (Data from Katz & Hass, 1988)

achieve integrated schools ("Kids should be able to go to neighborhood schools"). This principles-implementation gap stems, in part, from a general dislike of government regulations. However, it also reflects the belief that governmental assistance to blacks is unfair and undeserved (Institute for Social Research, 1985; Kinder & Sears, 1981).

Some researchers believe that symbolic racists unconsciously use their political values as justification for rejecting blacks. When people who don't want to be prejudiced find themselves reacting negatively to blacks, they explain away their responses by attributing them to their traditional values rather than to racial prejudices (McConahay, 1986). Other researchers, however, believe that many whites are continually struggling to balance their belief that everyone should be treated fairly and their belief that black people don't do enough to help themselves. These competing sets of values leave whites feeling profoundly ambivalent about African Americans, for they simultaneously feel that blacks are victims of decades of mistreatment *and* are undeserving of any assistance (Hass et al., 1991, 1992; Katz, 1981; Katz, Wackenhut, & Hass, 1986).

This ambivalence often translates into inconsistent patterns of discrimination and fairness when whites interact with blacks. When whites' egalitarian values (that is, principles of fairness) direct their reactions, they treat blacks fairly and without prejudice. When, however, their work-ethic values (such as individualism, self-reliance, discipline, and hard work) are dominant, then they respond negatively to blacks (see Figure 7-5). When whites first reflected on their egalitarian values before completing a measure of anti-black sentiment and pro-black sentiment, their pro-black scores climbed, and their anti-black scores fell. When they first reflected on their work-ethic values, however, the reverse occurred. Anti-black scores increased, and pro-black scores fell slightly (Katz & Hass, 1988).

Regressive racism. Why, to this day, does racism "bind the mind in such a way that democratic relationships in adult life are impossible" (Allport, 1954, p. 99)? Why, in 1989, did working-class whites in Brooklyn shoot a 16-year-old black youth who was visiting the neighborhood to buy a used car? Why did white police officers brutally beat Rodney King in 1991? Why did Boyle attack Booker?

▲ **FIGURE 7-6**
Will otherwise fair-minded whites react violently when angered by a black? When the whites in this study were insulted by a confederate of the researcher, they administered stronger and longer electric shocks when the insulter was black rather than white. Unangered whites treated blacks more favorably than whites. (From Rogers & Prentice-Dunn, 1981)

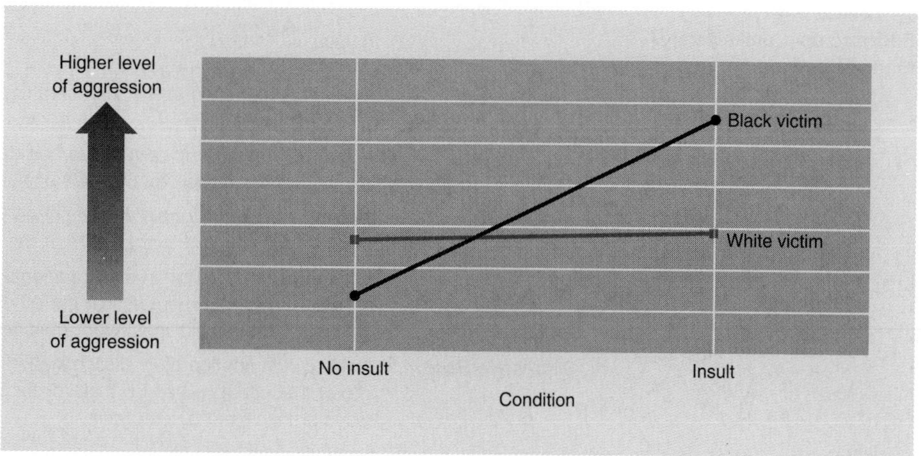

Ronald Rogers and Steven Prentice-Dunn (1981) theorize that most whites in America do not want to treat others unfairly, nor do they want to foster the impression that they are racists. Therefore, in most everyday situations, whites' personal prohibitions against acting in racist ways and the possibility that others will perceive them to be racist keep them from discriminating against blacks. When, however, these restraints are stripped away by feelings of anger, fear, or other arousing circumstances, whites act more impulsively. In extreme cases, they may even regress to an outmoded pattern of racial aggression that Rogers and Prentice-Dunn label **regressive racism**.

regressive racism
Open condemnation of or discrimination against members of another group that occurs when personal prohibitions against acting in racist ways are inhibited by emotions.

Rogers and Prentice-Dunn succeeded in documenting the link between anger and regressive racism in their laboratory. They told their white college student subjects that, as part of a study of behavior modification, the students would be asked to give painful electric shocks to another student. This other student, who was actually a confederate, had been sitting in the waiting area with the subjects before the study began. In some cases, a black student played the role, but in others, a white student took his place. Then, as the confederate was apparently being wired up to receive shocks, a second variable was manipulated. Sometimes the confederate deliberately insulted the subjects: He mentioned that the equipment looked complicated, and he wondered whether people who looked as dumb as the other subjects could use it properly. Sometimes he said nothing negative about the others. The confederate actually received no shocks, but the number and duration of the shocks meted out by the subjects was carefully recorded.

Rogers and Prentice-Dunn found that unangered whites responded very differently from angered whites (see Figure 7-6). Unangered white subjects treated whites more shabbily than blacks; they displayed a pattern of reverse discrimination (Baron, 1979; Donnerstein & Donnerstein, 1973; Griffin & Rogers, 1977). Angered whites, however, displayed regressive racism. They administered stronger and longer electric shocks to the black victim than to the white victim. Once their anger inhibited their personal prohibitions against acting in racist ways, they acted impulsively rather than rationally.

Contemporary white racism. Whites' attitudes toward blacks have changed a great deal since the early 1960s. Yet remnants of prejudice remain (see Table 7-1). Overt, blatant prejudice has decreased, but covert prejudice remains. Despite their best attempts to respond to others fairly, some whites experience aversive emotions when they interact with blacks. Still others fall

▲ **TABLE 7-1**
Summing up: Contemporary forms of racism

	Definition
Overt Racism	Open condemnation of the members of another group
Covert Racism	Public tolerance of the members of another group paired with rejection of this group privately, when detection is unlikely, or when prejudice is condoned by others
Aversive Racism	Acceptance of egalitarian values paired with unexamined negative emotional responses to members of the other group
Symbolic Racism	Acceptance of egalitarian and traditional work-ethic values combined with the belief that members of the other group do not act in accordance with traditional work-ethic values
Regressive Racism	Open condemnation of or discrimination against members of another group that occurs when personal prohibitions against acting in racist ways are inhibited by emotions

prey to symbolic racism because they assume that blacks' values differ from theirs. And some lose the fight against bigotry when their anger obscures their good judgment, and they display regressive forms of prejudice. As Kenneth B. Clark, a leading social psychologist in the field of racism, concludes, modern prejudice is "more complicated and more subtle" (quoted in Winston, 1983, p. D-3). Whites' attitudes are changing, but prejudice remains.

Prejudice Against Women

When Boyle died, the police arrested Booker *and* Wilson. Wilson explained that he was down the street fighting with Cuneo when Boyle was stabbed, but the police knew better. An attendant at a parking deck, who happened to be white, told a different story. He was nearly a block away, but he claimed that Wilson yelled, "Dig him" just before the stabbing. A second witness offered a different story, but the police did not believe her. Laura Mitchell explained that she watched the entire incident from just across the street. She claimed that the whites were the aggressors and that it was Cuneo who yelled, "Get him, get him." But the police dismissed her evidence entirely. She was, after all, contradicting the testimony of a man.

Attitudes about men and women have changed in many ways since the early 1900s. Women can now enter into contracts and own property without the consent of their fathers or their husbands. Women can also vote in elections, serve on juries, and run for public office. Indeed, as Figure 7-7 indicates, most Americans now claim that (a) they would vote for a woman for president if she were nominated by their party, and (b) they approve of a married woman who works even though her husband is capable of supporting her. Yet, just as the police officers assumed that Laura Mitchell was confused by the violence she witnessed, people continue to embrace stereotypes about women and men. These stereotypes, as we will see next, influence both perceptions of men and women *and* the treatment of men and women.

Stereotypes about men and women. The ancient book *I Ching* describes the fundamental forces of nature as yin and yang. Yin is woman: dark, the negative, emotionality, the passive, the feminine. Yang, in contrast, is man: light, the positive, rationality, the active, the masculine. Aristotle described women as more humane, more envious, more disagreeable, more moody, more "false of speech," and less self-respecting than men. In 1933, Sigmund Freud

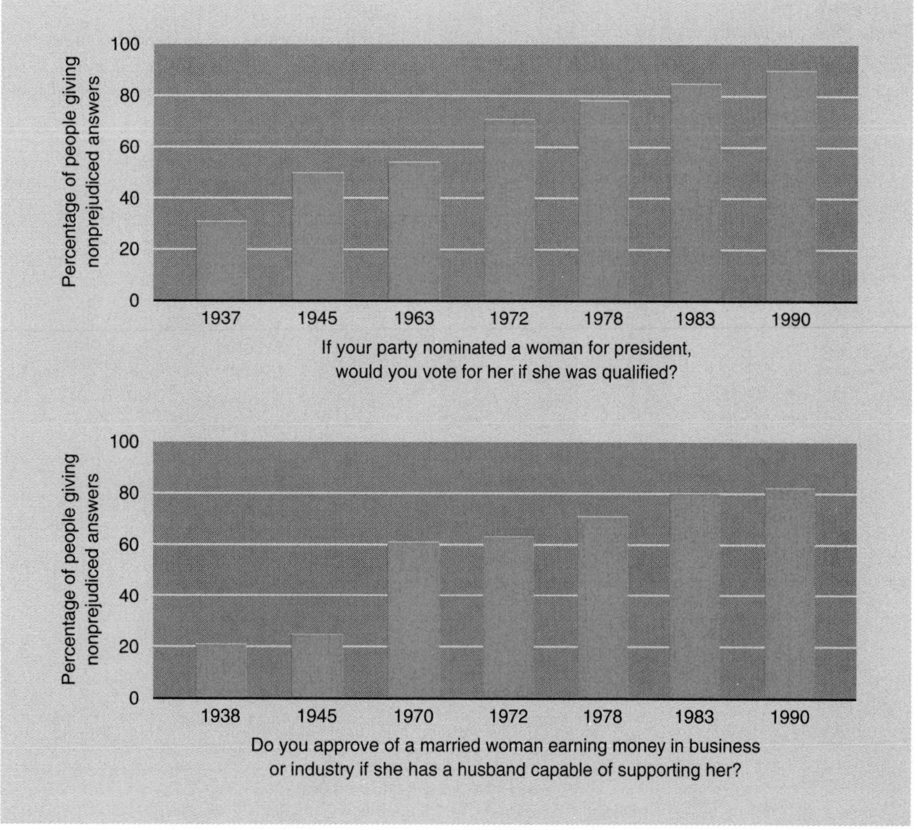

▲ **FIGURE 7-7**
Have Americans' attitudes toward women changed in the last 50 years? Public opinion polls suggest that opposition to women's taking active roles in politics and business has waned over the years. In the late 1930s, most Americans were opposed to the idea of a woman candidate for president or a woman business leader. By the 1990s, these attitudes gave way to become more and more egalitarian. (Data from Davis & Smith, 1990)

wrote: "It must be admitted that women have but little sense of justice, and this is no doubt concerned with the preponderance of envy in their mental life" (p. 183).

For centuries now, people have assumed that men differ from women in predictable ways. If we have never met a person before, but we know the person's sex, we can offer up a number of guesses about his or her other characteristics. Will Brian be indecisive or competitive? Will he be physically strong or weak? Will he enjoy shopping or watching sports? Do you think Tonya is independent or nervous? Is she athletic or frail? Is she skilled in business or an excellent cook? Even though we realize that sex differences are fading, we nonetheless use people's sex as a heuristic index of their personality traits, their physical attributes, and the roles they occupy in society (Deaux & Lewis, 1984).

Table 7-2 presents the 20 traits that were most frequently mentioned by people in their descriptions of men and women in 25 different countries (Williams & Best, 1990). Although gender stereotypes varied among the different cultures, two basic themes emerged with impressive consistency. When asked to describe women, people in virtually all cultures spoke of their *expressive* qualities, including nurturance, emotionality, and warmth. They expected a "she" to be sentimental, affectionate, sympathetic, soft-hearted, talkative, gentle, and feminine. When describing men, they stressed their *instrumental* qualities, including productivity, energy, and strength. Most expected a "he" to be boastful, ambitious, independent, strong, forceful, dominant, and masculine (Martin, 1987; Spence, Deaux, & Helmreich, 1985).

▲ **TABLE 7-2**
Terms most frequently used to describe men and women

When people in 25 countries were asked to describe sex-related qualities of men and women, the majority mentioned these qualities. Those listed at the top of the columns were mentioned more frequently than those further down the list, although all the adjectives were frequently mentioned.

Adjectives Used to Describe Women	*Adjectives Used to Describe Men*	*Neutral Adjectives*
feminine	handsome	adaptable
sentimental	enterprising	resentful
affectionate	tough	suspicious
sympathetic	opportunistic	withdrawn
soft-hearted	rational	peculiar
talkative	logical	dissatisfied
flirtatious	egotistical	bossy
attractive	assertive	hasty
gentle	courageous	bitter
appreciative	confident	intelligent
dreamy	daring	vindictive
fussy	boastful	alert
sensitive	ambitious	interests wide
excitable	independent	interests narrow
frivolous	strong	defensive
sexy	forceful	good-natured
warm	dominant	dependable
submissive	adventurous	clever
cheerful	aggressive	forgetful
fickle	masculine	planful

Source: Williams & Best, 1990.

Stereotypes aren't limited only to presumptions about personality traits. People also expect men and women to act differently and take on different kinds of social roles (Deaux & Lewis, 1984). Stereotyped thinking causes people to assume that men are more likely to be task- and activity-oriented: Men change the car's tire when it goes flat, they play competitive sports, they take charge and lead, and they are the financial providers for their families. Women, in contrast, are often thought to be interpersonally oriented: They cook the meals and clean the home, they take care of the children, and they resolve conflicts between family members (Deaux, 1984; Deaux & Major, 1987).

Do these stereotypes mirror real differences between men and women, or are they unfair myths? First, many stereotypes about women and men are simply false: the differences they describe don't exist. Systematic studies of sex differences in such areas as intelligence, leadership, and emotionality have failed to find differences between men and women (Eagly, 1987).

Second, even though gender stereotypes may contain a kernel of truth, these differences are not so profound that they can be used as a basis for making judgments about any specific man or woman. The sexes are different in some ways. Women are better at reading nonverbal messages (Hall, 1984), they are more sensitive to feedback from others (Roberts, 1991), and they tend to be happier than men (Wood, Rhodes, & Whelan, 1989). Men are more autocratic leaders than women (Eagly & Johnson, 1990), more aggressive (Hyde, 1986), and physically stronger (Thomas & French, 1985). These differences are a matter of degree rather than kind, however. Many men are sensitive to nonverbal messages, and many women are not. Similarly, many women are autocratic

▲ You have just met this woman at a party. Can you form an impression of her? Do you think she is warm and sensitive, or cold and blunt? Do you think she makes decisions quickly, or does she procrastinate before committing herself? If given a choice, would she like to go to a movie or to a baseball game? Is she a homemaker or does she work at a bank? Your answers to these questions may have been influenced by your stereotypes about women.

leaders, and many men prefer to adopt a more democratic style. Women and men aren't "opposite sexes" by any stretch of the imagination.

Last, even when the differences suggested by stereotypes can be documented, a final interpretational wrinkle remains. The stereotypes themselves may be causing the sex differences. Almost from birth, we are treated differently depending on our sex. Parents of newborns think that their baby girl is weak and fine-featured, but their baby boy is big and strong. Parents who see a baby crying assume that the child is angry when they think the baby's a boy, but they think the child is fearful when they think the baby's a girl (Condry & Condry, 1976). Mothers and fathers treat their sons and daughters differently, rough-housing more with the boys and encouraging their independence, while showing more affection and protection with girls (Lytton & Romney, 1991; Siegal, 1987).

Moreover, as Alice Eagly (1987) suggests, even as adults we can't escape the restraints of social conventions regarding the sexes. The woman who marries and has a child, for example, may not be very nurturant or caring. Once in the role of mother, however, she may become more nurturant as she meets the role's requirements. Similarly, a man may not be aggressive or competitive by nature, but if he enters a profession or occupation, his role may require him to act in these ways. Thus, stereotypes don't necessarily arise because people notice differences between men and women. Rather, differences between men and women arise because social roles and stereotypes create these differences.

Contemporary forms of sexism. The police officers' stereotypes about women and men didn't influence only their perceptions of Laura Mitchell. They also influenced the way they responded to her. They discriminated against her by dismissing her statements but wholeheartedly accepted the claims of the man who witnessed the fight. Sex stereotypes are not harmless misconceptions. They reinforce the continuing discrimination against women in contemporary society.

Just as the police officers devalued Mitchell's evidence, society in general tends to place a lower value on the qualities, actions, accomplishments, and roles that are associated with women rather than men.

Qualities ascribed to men are judged to be more socially desirable than those attributed to women. Stereotypical masculine qualities, such as independence, objectivity, rationality, and ambition, are more valued in many societies than are stereotypical feminine qualities, such as emotionality, warmth, and sentimentality (Rosenkrantz et al., 1968).

Actions performed by men are evaluated more positively than the identical actions performed by women. When, for instance, people are asked to evaluate men and women leaders, they give higher scores to the men, even when the men and women being reviewed performed identical behaviors (Brown & Geis, 1984; Butler & Geis, 1990; Geis, Boston, & Hoffman, 1985).

Accomplishments of women are evaluated more critically than men's accomplishments. For instance, in one study people who read an article that was supposedly written by Joan T. McKay rated it more harshly than people reading the same article attributed to *John* T. McKay (Goldberg, 1968). Meta-analyses of subsequent studies indicate that such blatant bias is relatively rare (Swim et al., 1989). More frequently, women's accomplishments are diminished only indirectly. When, for example, people hear that a woman has performed a task well, they often assume that her success was more a matter of luck rather than ability. Men's successes, however, are attributed to their abilities (Deaux & Emswiller, 1974).

Roles more frequently occupied by women tend to be viewed as less important than roles occupied by men. In most societies, the division of labor is based on sex: men usually generate income by working outside the home, whereas women carry out domestic tasks such as child-rearing and food preparation within the home. Note, however, that work outside the home is viewed as more difficult and more worthy of financial reward than work inside the home (Nielsen, 1990).

Sexism leads to economic disadvantages for women. Even though the number of women working outside the home has risen steadily over the years, men hold a near monopoly on the most financially lucrative professions and occupations (Roos, 1985). Women tend to be nurses rather than physicians, schoolteachers rather than administrators, legal secretaries rather than lawyers, and dental hygienists rather than dentists. In every case, occupations dominated by women are lower in prestige and salary than those occupied mostly by men. Moreover, even when women manage to enter a male-dominated field, their advancement in their profession is often slower than men's. A glass ceiling seems to block women's rise into top management positions. Women make up about 5% of the middle management and only 1% of the top management. A survey of corporate heads located 15 female chief executive officers (CEOs) and 2,500 male CEOs (Nielsen, 1990). In the well-known case of *Hopkins* v. *Price Waterhouse,* Ann Hopkins outperformed most of the men in her accounting firm, yet she was denied a partnership. One of her superiors urged her to "walk more femininely, talk more femininely, dress more femininely, wear make-up, have her hair styled, and wear jewelry" (Fiske et al., 1991, p. 1050). With the help of social psychologist Susan Fiske, who gave expert testimony on her behalf, Hopkins was able to convince the Supreme Court that the company had discriminated against her.

The gap between men's and women's salaries is also substantial. Even when men and women do the same job, women's wages are 65 to 68% of men's wages. Do men work harder than women? Are they more productive? Do they have better credentials? No. When differences in work quality, absenteeism, or educational level are taken into account, the gap remains. The man with a college degree who takes 2 weeks of vacation, misses 7 days of work due to sickness, and brings in $200,000 worth of business for his company will be

▲ **TABLE 7-3**
Summing up: Forms of prejudice against women in contemporary society

Form of Prejudice	*Impact on Women*
Stereotypes	People perceive men and women in stereotypical ways. Women are viewed as emotionally expressive, whereas men are expected to be more instrumental. Stereotypes also suggest that certain occupations and roles are more appropriate for one sex rather than the other.
Evaluations	The qualities that comprise traditional stereotypes about women are not as positive as the qualities incorporated in stereotypes about men. Actions and accomplishments are evaluated less positively when attributed to women than to men. Roles traditionally filled by women are considered to be less important than roles occupied by men.
Economic bias	Women are underrepresented in many occupations, and their advancement through the ranks in business is slower than that of men. Women are paid 68% of what men are paid for identical work.
Victimization	Women, more so than men, are the targets of sexual harassment, domestic violence, incest, and rape. Their personal freedoms are restricted.

paid $50,000, whereas the woman with exactly the same profile would be paid, on average, $34,000 (Statistical Abstract of the United States, 1992).

Sexism even influences women's health and well-being. Women who work outside the home often experience more stress than men because they continue to do more of the domestic chores (Biernat & Wortman, 1991). Women are more likely to experience sexual harassment and its stressful consequences (Fitzgerald, 1993). Women tend to be the victims of violence, whereas men tend to be the perpetrators of violence. How many women who are murdered in the United States are killed by their husbands or boyfriends: a shocking 29%! How many men are murdered by their wives or girlfriends: 4%. Women are usually the victims in cases of domestic violence, just as they are more frequently the victims of rape. Hence, women are not as free as men are even today. Men can more freely choose when and where they will go than women can (Nielsen, 1990):

> In some life-sustaining situations, the assurance of civil rights remains problematic for women. . . . If we also take into consideration statistics on rape (most victims are female), incest (most cases are man-girl), and other forms of physical or psychological violence primarily against women (e.g., sexual harassment), there is a widespread pattern of men using physical force to control, coerce, intimidate, or otherwise limit women. (p. 59)

Prejudice in America: Conclusions

Despite decades of political and social activism, prejudice—and its pernicious consequences—persists. Many blacks in America continue to suffer indignities and disadvantages that whites do not. Most African Americans feel that they have "little or no power" in American society, and that whites' racist attitudes create barriers for them that are difficult to overcome. The strength of blacks' personal convictions has helped them cope with these social inequities, but many of the advances achieved during the 1960s and 1970s have eroded in the 1980s (Institute for Social Research, 1983; Sigelman & Welch, 1991). Similarly, sexism remains ubiquitous (see Table 7-3). Although many fields are now open to women, their wages remain about 68% of the amount paid men working similar jobs. Women are also overrepresented in low-status occupations and underrepresented in more prestigious positions (Eagly & Steffen, 1984). These status differences reinforce stereotypes about men and women and may contribute to feelings of inadequacy in women. As Geraldine Ferraro (1984) explains, for "every woman who endures the degradation and self-doubt that result from being paid less than she is worth," the gap between men's and women's wages "is an issue of human dignity" (p. 1166).

Sources of Prejudice

In *The Nature of Prejudice,* Gordon W. Allport (1954) laments the sad state of humanity. Even though we have achieved great technological feats and have cured many devastating diseases, the human race remains burdened by unwarranted animosities:

> Moslems distrust non-Moslems. Jews who escaped extermination in Central Europe find themselves in the new State of Israel surrounded by anti-Semitism. Refugees roam in inhospitable lands. Many of the colored people of the world suffer indignities at the hands of whites who invent a fanciful racist doctrine to justify their condescension. (p. ix)

Why do we seek esteem and acceptance from others but deal out rejection in return? What are the sources of prejudice?

Psychological Sources

We can't ignore the intensity of Boyle's reaction to Booker. He did not just think to himself, "A black man; he's not as good as I am." He attacked Booker because Booker was an African American. His reaction was so extreme, so irrational, that it suggests that deep-seated but powerful psychological processes sustained his bigotry. This interpretation, which owes much to Sigmund Freud's thinking, hypothesizes that Boyle broadcast his own self-hatred, frustration, and personality flaws when he belittled others (Ostow, 1991).

Prejudice as ego defense. Prejudice against African Americans is greatest among whites of low socioeconomic status (Pettigrew, 1978). People who feel insecure about their own abilities are more likely to judge others harshly (Amabile & Glazebrook, 1982). Men who are low in self-acceptance are more attracted to women who conform to gender stereotypes (Grube, Kleinhesselink, & Kearney, 1982). People who have just experienced a blow to their self-esteem are more likely to discriminate against others than are people who have just gone through an esteem-bolstering experience (Hogg & Sunderland, 1991). When we are reminded of our mortality—that we won't live forever—we become less tolerant toward people who don't accept our worldview (Greenberg et al., 1992). Why?

Individuals who feel threatened and uncertain about their own status and worth sometimes defend their egos by attitudinally rejecting others. As shown in Chapter 6, attitudes fulfill various functions for people, including ego defense. The man who worries about his own masculinity and competency may mask his lack of self-confidence by criticizing women. The white job applicant who fails to land the job can rationalize this failure by expressing hatred for blacks. In general, whites who feel that they are being surpassed economically, socially, and politically by blacks are strongest in their rejection of blacks (Bobo, 1983; Doty, Peterson, & Winter, 1991; Vanneman & Pettigrew, 1972).

▲ A sexist man would be unlikely to support Lynn Yeakel's bid for election to the U.S. Senate. An ego-defensive explanation of this rejection argues that his opposition may stem from his own feelings of inadequacy or failure. Troubled by these unrecognized self-doubts, he responds by lashing out at women who are more successful than he is.

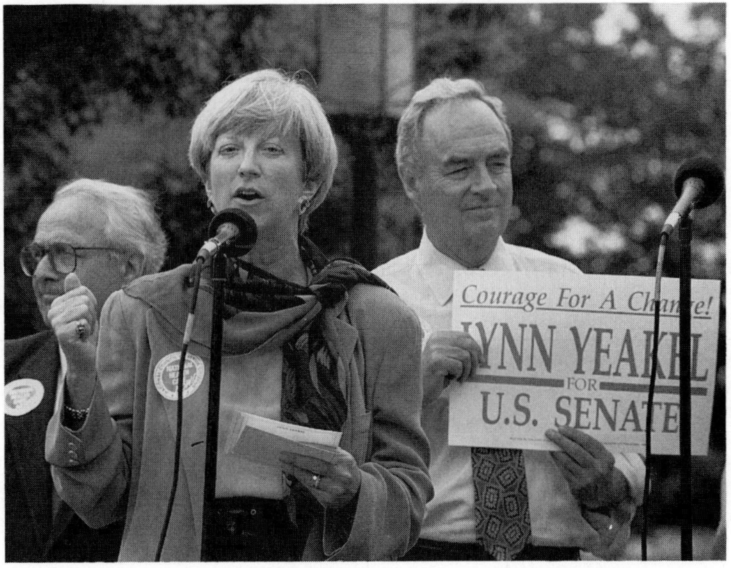

Prejudice as scapegoating. What kind of day did Boyle have the day he accosted Booker? Did he get a parking ticket? Did his boss call him into the office and tell him to improve his work performance? Did he argue with his girlfriend?

scapegoat theory of prejudice
An explanation of conflict between racial groups that argues hostility caused by frustrating environmental circumstances is sometimes released by taking hostile actions against members of other social groups.

The **scapegoat theory of prejudice** argues that tensions build up in people when they experience frustrations, and these tensions must eventually find release. When people like Boyle fight with their girlfriends, are criticized by their bosses, or are reminded that their chances for a prosperous life are next to nil, they sometimes respond by attacking people who have nothing to do with their situations. These scapegoats are not the sources of the individuals' misfortunes, but they serve as outlets for frustrations when hostility toward the actual frustrator is blocked.

The scapegoat theory explains why frustrating economic conditions often stimulate increases in prejudice and violence. Studies of anti-black violence in southern areas of the United States between 1882 and 1930 indicate that outbreaks of violence tended to occur whenever the economy of that region worsened (Hovland & Sears, 1940). Indeed, the correlation between the price of cotton (the main product of that area at the time) and the number of lynchings of black men by whites ranged from −0.63 to −0.72, suggesting that when whites were frustrated by the economy, they took out their frustrations by attacking blacks (see also Mintz, 1946, for a more sophisticated analysis of the Hovland-Sears data). Similar explanations have been offered to account for riots that began in the 1960s and have carried through to the Los Angeles riots of the 1990s. Even though African Americans are angered by their mistreatment by employers, property owners, and police, they can not express their hostility through direct attacks on these groups. They therefore vent their hostility by attacking scapegoats—shop owners, passing motorists, and firefighters—rather than the source of their frustrations (Harding et al., 1969).

Prejudice as a personality trait. What was Boyle like, as a person? Was he a nonconformist, or did he have respect for middle-class American values? Did he comply when his boss told him to tuck in his shirt? Was he sentimental? Did he enjoy exerting authority over others? What are the typical personality characteristics of a prejudiced person?

A team of researchers investigated this question at the University of California at Berkeley in the 1940s (Adorno et al., 1950). Responding to the flood of anti-Semitism (prejudice against Jews) sweeping Nazi Germany, these researchers explored the personalities of highly prejudiced persons through in-depth interviews, clinical case studies, and questionnaires. Their analyses revealed a distinctive pattern of values and beliefs that researchers labeled the **authoritarian personality**. The three most important earmarks of authoritarianism are listed in Table 7-4. First, authoritarians tend to be high in *conventionality*. They feel that the status quo should be maintained at all costs and that conventional social standards should not be challenged. Second, they display signs of *respectful submission* to authority; they believe that children should mind their parents and that obedience is a virtue. Third, authoritarians endorse *punitive aggression* as a means of dealing with many social problems. They believe that the "world is a dangerous place" and that people should be punished harshly when they do things that threaten society's values (Altemeyer, 1981, 1988, p. 146).

authoritarian personality
An overall system of values, beliefs, and preferences characterized by conventionalism (adherence to traditional social values), respectful submission (uncritical acceptance of authority), and aggression (hostile rejection of nonconformists).

The Berkeley researchers measured authoritarianism with a questionnaire that they called the **F-scale**; *F* because high scorers tended toward fascist political and social values. This scale has been used in hundreds and hundreds of studies, yet its meaning remains controversial (Christie, 1991). However, the basic premise of this approach to prejudice—that some attitudes are deeply rooted in the individual's personality—has been supported in a wide range of studies. Authoritarians, for example, tend to be very envious of people who are successful in school or in business, and they are more likely to express satisfaction when these "tall poppies" fail (Feather, 1993). They are also more likely to view people with AIDS, the homeless, and homosexuals as members of the outgroup who should be punished. They tend to agree to such statements as "They should quarantine everyone with AIDS, just like they would do with the plague or chicken pox," "AIDS is a plague that homosexuals pass on to the decent people," and "The homeless are basically lazy" (Peterson, Doty, & Winter, 1993, pp. 182–183; Witt, 1989). Other studies have linked authoritarianism with prejudice against blacks (Schuman, Bobo, & Krysan, 1992), right-wing political attitudes (Altemeyer, 1988), obedience to authority (Milgram, 1974), and an intolerance of new political ideas (McFarland, Ageyev, & Abalankina-Paap, 1993). These findings suggest that some people, given the nature of their personalities, are prone to be prejudiced against others.

F-scale
A self-report measure of authoritarianism, so named because high scorers tend to adopt extremely conservative (fascistic) political views.

▲ **TABLE 7-4**
Three basic components of the authoritarian personality

Component	*Interpretation*
Conventionalism	Rigid adherence to traditional social values and standards of behavior; uncomfortable with people or ideas that violate conventional values
Respectful submission	Uncritical acceptance of authority; emotional need to submit to others who are dominant or powerful
Authoritarian aggression	Feelings of hostility and anger; condemnation of anyone who violates conventional norms

Source: Adorno et al., 1950.

▲ Social categorization prompts us to classify people into groups. One of the most basic distinctions made is "in my group" and "not in my group." Michael, the boy in the cartoon, categorizes differently than his mother does: he notices age rather than race.

For Better or for Worse copyright Lynn Johnston Prod., Inc. Reprinted with permission of Universal Press Syndicate. All rights reserved.

Cognitive Sources

We are a thinking, reasoning species. When we meet someone for the first time, we rush to put them into a *category* where their idiosyncratic qualities are soon forgotten. We also use *stereotypes* to round out our impressions when specific information about a person is sketchy. These mental abilities, although undeniably adaptive in the long run, nonetheless provide a cognitive foundation for our prejudices. As Allport (1954) concluded, "Given a thimbleful of facts we rush to make generalizations as large as a tub" (p. 9).

Social categorization. As Chapter 3 explains, we are categorizers. When we see a feathered animal that flies, we assign it to the category "birds." If we trip over a piece of granite, we might say to ourselves "Ah, an igneous rock." And, in Boyle's case, if he meets a young man on a dark city street who has more pigment in his skin than he does, he puts him in the category "black." Categorization is, in all likelihood, an automatic cognitive process; without much effort we rapidly pigeonhole the people we encounter each day. But once we fit people into a category, we no longer look at them as separate people with unique qualities. The individual is recognized as a member of our group—the ingroup—or as a member of some other group—the outgroup (Messick & Mackie, 1989; Stephan, 1985).

When we decide someone is one of "those people," we look at him or her in a different way. They lose their individuality and become more similar to other people in their group—at least in our eyes. This tendency is called the *outgroup homogeneity bias,* for it leads to the erroneous belief that people in other groups possess similar qualities and characteristics. Women's descriptions of men, for example, are less variable than their descriptions of women. Physics majors assume dance majors are all alike, but they think of physics majors as a hodgepodge of different types. Students at Princeton consider Rutgers students to be all cut from the same cloth, but they deem Princeton students to be a diverse lot.

The outgroup homogeneity bias may even lead to errors in recognizing people in other groups. We have a remarkable ability to identify faces we have seen, but our accuracy diminishes when we must make judgments about people in other racial groups (Brigham, 1986; Brigham et al., 1982). In one study, people from various racial groups looked at 20 photographs of people from their racial groups or from other racial groups. When they were tested a minute later, people were much more likely to recognize members from their own racial group than people from other groups. Whites had trouble recognizing blacks, blacks had trouble recognizing whites and Asians, and Asians had trouble recognizing whites (Luce, 1974). Other evidence suggests that we have the capability of distinguishing people from other groups. When, for example, we see a person from another group, we can intuitively appraise his or her attractiveness or friendliness, just as we appraise members of our own group (Zebrowitz, Montepare, & Lee, 1993). Yet we don't always live up to our capabilities (Anthony, Copper, & Mullen, 1992). Many different types of people may belong to a group, yet we conclude that "they all look alike to me" (Park & Rothbart, 1982; Quattrone & Jones, 1980; Tajfel, Sheikh, & Gardner, 1964; cf. Simon & Brown, 1987).

The homogeneity bias is complemented by the *ingroup differentiation bias* (Linville, Salovey, & Fischer, 1989). Our views of other groups may be simplistic and undifferentiated, but when we turn our eye to our own group, we are struck by its diversity and complexity. Ask a man to describe men in general or a woman to characterize the typical woman and most likely they will use far more concepts and qualities than they would if they were describing the typical member of another group (Linville, 1982; Linville & Jones, 1980; Park & Rothbart, 1982; Quattrone, 1986).

Our judgments about people aren't necessarily more negative once they have been categorized, but they do tend to become more extreme. A white bystander, for example, might say that Boyle (who was white) seemed "angry," but that Wilson (who was black) was "scared to death." A black bystander, in contrast, would say that Boyle was "furious," whereas Wilson was "frightened." In one study of this *extremity bias,* college-age men read a favorable or unfavorable story about a person who was not in their age group (an elderly person) or a person who was in their age group (a young person). When they later rated the person in the stories they had read, they rated the older person more positively when the story was favorable and more negatively when the story was unfavorable (Linville, 1982). Categorizing people can polarize our opinions of them.

The racially toned phrase, "You seen one, you seen them all," illustrates another category-based bias: the tendency to make sweeping statements about the entire outgroup after observing one or two of the group's members. If a black is victimized by a white employer, he or she may decide that all whites are racists. Similarly, a visitor to another country who is treated rudely by a passerby may leap to the conclusion that everyone who lives in that country is discourteous. We fall prey to the **law of small numbers** whenever we assume that the behavior of a large number of people can be accurately inferred from the behavior of a few people.

law of small numbers The tendency for people to base sweeping generalizations about an entire group on observations of a small number of individuals from that group.

Even students at such prestigious universities as Rutgers and Princeton aren't immune to this bias. Men recruited from these schools watched a videotape of a student making a simple decision, such as deciding to wait alone or with others before the start of an experiment. They then estimated how many other students would make the same choice as the person on the videotape. Students obeyed the law of small numbers when they were initially uncertain about how most people would react (see Figure 7-8). When they thought they were watching a student from another school, they used this single person as a guide for estimating the entire group's response. If, for example, the Rutgers student saw a Princeton student decide to wait alone, he then decided that most Princeton students would want to wait alone. When they thought they were watching a student from their own school, however, they were more conservative in estimating how many people would make the same decision (Quattrone & Jones, 1980).

The opposite process—assuming that the characteristics of a single individual in a group can be inferred from the general characteristics of the whole group—can also lead us astray. If we know our group's position on an issue, we

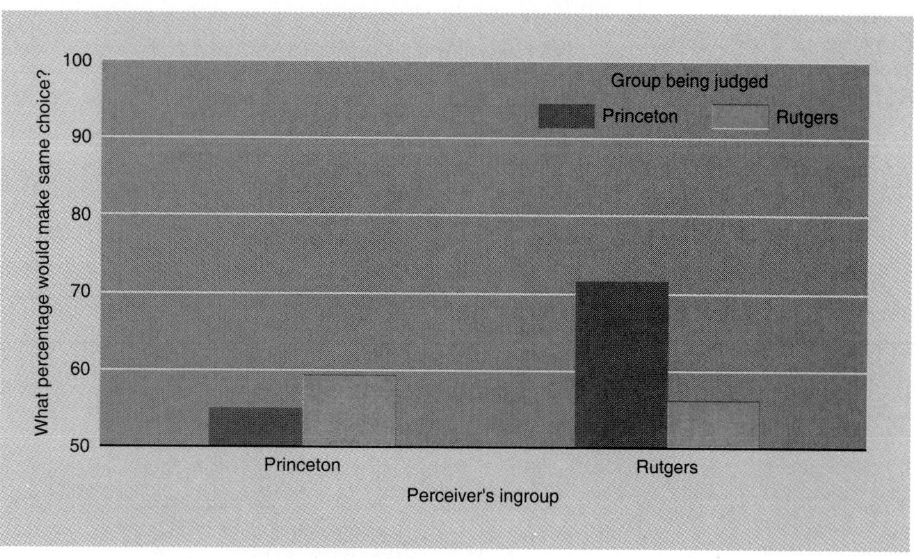

▲ **FIGURE 7-8**
Do people intuitively believe the racist phrase, "You seen one, you seen 'em all"? When Rutgers students watched a Princeton student make a choice, they assumed that most Princeton students would make the same choice as the person they watched. The Princeton students, to a lesser degree, showed the same tendency to infer the entire group's choice after seeing one individual make a choice. (Data from Quattrone & Jones, 1980)

are reluctant to assume any one of us agrees with the majority. When we know another group's position, however, we are much more willing to assume each person in that group agrees with that position. Scott Allison and his colleagues studied **group attribution error** by telling their college-student subjects that an election had recently been held at their college or at another college to determine how much funding should be given to the colleges' athletics programs. They then told the students the results of the vote, and asked them to estimate the opinion of the "typical student" at the college where the vote was taken. When the students thought the vote had been taken at their own college, they didn't want to assume that the individual's opinion would match the group's opinion. But when they thought the vote was taken at another college, they were much more confident that the individual's opinion would match the group's opinion (Allison & Messick, 1985; Allison, Worth, & King, 1990).

group attribution error
The tendency for perceivers to assume that individual group members' beliefs and characteristics can be inferred from their group's decisions and general characteristics.

Stereotyping. Stereotyping goes hand in hand with the categorization processes summarized in Table 7-5. Once we classify a person into a group, we assume that they will possess the qualities and characteristics that typify people in that group. Stereotypes are not intrinsically prejudicial. Like all cognitive schemas, stereotypes summarize large amounts of information about other people, structure our perceptions of others, and reduce the load placed on our fallible memories (Judd & Park, 1993; Macrae, Milne, & Bodenhausen, 1993; Swim, 1994). Unlike many other schemas, however, stereotypes are widely adopted by many people rather than by single individuals (Simon, Glässner-Bayerl, & Stratenwerth, 1991). They also tend to be exaggerated rather than accurate, negative rather than positive, and resistant to revision even when we encounter individuals who directly disconfirm them (Stephan & Rosenfield, 1982). We cling to our stereotypes so resolutely that they become unreasonable beliefs rather than honest misconceptions. Allport (1954) writes: "prejudgments become prejudices only if they are not reversible when exposed to new knowledge" (p. 8).

If stereotypes have all these perceptual and cognitive limitations, why do they persist? Walter Lippmann (1922), who first used the word *stereotype* to describe our intuitive assumptions about people, argued that the stereotype resists disconfirmation because "it stamps itself upon the evidence in the very

▲ **TABLE 7-5**
Summing up: Categorization processes in social perception

Process	*Description*	*Common Expression*
Outgroup homogeneity bias	People assume that individuals in other groups all possess similar qualities and characteristics.	"They all look alike to me."
Ingroup differentiation bias	People think their own group is complex and diverse.	"We are all individuals who can't be easily described."
Extremity bias	People are more extreme when making judgments about people in other groups.	"We are thrifty, but they are miserly."
Law of small numbers	People assume that valid judgments about another group can be based on observations of a small number of individuals from that group.	"You seen one, you seen them all."
Group attribution error	People assume that valid judgments about individuals can be inferred from the general characteristics of the whole group.	"He (or she) is just like all the rest."

act of securing the evidence." When we see people through eyes clouded by stereotypes, we misperceive and misremember people and events. Yet only rarely do we notice these errors, for our stereotypes are protected by confirmatory biases that serve to affirm their validity.

We sometimes reinterpret ambiguous information so that it matches our expectations. Prejudiced white people, for example, when asked to make up a story about a picture of a black person interacting with a white person, usually assumed the whites and blacks were arguing with one another, and they usually blamed the black for starting the dispute (Allport & Postman, 1947). White college students who observed a staged argument between a black and a white in which one person shoved the other described the push as "violent" when the perpetrator was black, but "playing" or "dramatizing" when the perpetrator was white (Duncan, 1976). Junior high school boys described the actions committed by a black male in a drawing as "meaner" and more threatening than the identical behavior performed by a white male (Sagar & Schofield, 1980). Stereotypes resist disconfirmation because we reinterpret the evidence until we see what we expect. (See Chapter 3 for more information about the complex relationship between our schemas, expectations, and perceptions.)

Stereotypes also influence what we remember and forget. The white parking lot attendant remembered that Wilson had shouted "Dig him" during the fight. Anti-black teachers may not remember how many white students failed the last test, but they may clearly remember how many black students failed. The person who believes that accountants are timid and waitresses are loud won't remember the extraverted accountant but will remember the boisterous waitress (Hamilton & Rose, 1980). People even forget the negative behaviors that members of their own group performed but recall with great acumen the objectionable actions undertaken by people in other groups (Howard & Rothbart, 1980; Park & Rothbart, 1982; Rothbart et al., 1978; Rothbart, Evans, & Fulero, 1979). These stereotype-based memory

illusory correlations Assumed relationships between two variables that are not related to one another; for example, erroneously assuming that a certain characteristic (such as skin color) is related to some other characteristic (such as hostility).

biases have been implicated as one of the key causes of **illusory correlations**: overestimations of the strength of the relationship between unrelated characteristics. (For more information, see the section, "In Depth: Illusory Correlations and Misperceptions.")

Interpersonal processes also insulate our stereotypes from disconfirmation. When we interact with others, we tend to evoke new behaviors in those persons that are consistent with our stereotype-based expectations. Allport (1954) describes an Irishman and a Jew who

> encounter each other in casual contact, perhaps in a small business transaction. Neither has, in fact, any initial animosity toward the other. But the Irishman thinks, "Ah, a Jew; perhaps he'll skin me; I'll be careful." The Jew thinks, "Probably a Mick; they hate the Jews; he'd like to insult me." With such an inauspicious start both men are likely to be evasive, distrustful, and cool. (p. 252)

Allport's anecdote suggests that stereotypes can function as *self-fulfilling prophecies* (see Chapter 3). If Boyle thinks that black people are dangerous, he may keep his eye on Booker when their paths cross. But Booker may see the suspicion in Boyle's eyes and react negatively. Boyle takes Booker's reactions as evidence that his suspicions are correct, so he challenges him. This cycle of expectation and behavioral confirmation continues until the prophecy of conflict is fulfilled (Cooper & Fazio, 1986).

One team of researchers examined this cycle of self-fulfilling prophecy in two studies of racism. In the first, white male college students interviewed white and black high school students who were interested in joining a team. The interviewers were not aware that the high school students had been trained to give certain answers and behave in a standard fashion. Despite the similarity in their actions, the white interviewers treated black interviewees more negatively than white interviewees: they sat farther away from them, displayed signs of nervousness, and terminated the interviews sooner.

Now the researchers took the situation one step further by asking, How will people react when they encounter an interviewer who displays these negative behaviors? All the subjects in this second study were white, but some encountered an interviewer who enacted the negative behaviors identified in the first study. Others met with an interviewer who treated them in a more positive manner. In essence, some of the subjects were treated like whites, and others were treated like blacks.

When an independent panel of judges rated their performance, the whites who were treated negatively (the way blacks were in the first study) were judged to be less competent, less confident, and generally less desirable as employees. The whites who were treated like the whites in the first study were rated more favorably. These findings argue that in an actual interview the interviewee will probably live up (or down) to the interviewer's stereotypical beliefs (Word, Zanna, & Cooper, 1974; see also Lord & Saenz, 1985; Skrypnek & Snyder, 1982).

Interpersonal Sources

Boyle didn't develop racist attitudes all by himself. His personality and cognitive outlook may have fed his enmity toward blacks, but interpersonal processes undoubtedly supported these personal processes as well. Growing up in the United States, he could not have avoided socializing forces that condone racism or ignored social norms that call for the differential treatment of people based on their race, sex, or ethnicity.

IN DEPTH

Illusory Correlations and Misperceptions

The white racist thinks that being black and being lazy go together. The sexist assumes that most women are manipulative. The homophobic is certain that homosexuality is linked to promiscuity. What factor sustains these illusory correlations—the tendency to see relationships between qualities that are totally unrelated to each other?

Studies of our powerful, but occasionally prejudiced, memory systems offer some answers. In an early investigation of memory errors, researchers read people long lists of word pairs, such as *lion-tiger, blossoms-notebook,* and *bacon-eggs.* Even though each word was paired with every other word an equal number of times, people insisted that common pairings, such as *bacon-eggs,* occurred more frequently than uncommon pairs (for example, *lion-eggs*). They also believed that distinctive words were more frequently paired. The words *blossoms* and *notebook,* for example, were longer than most of the other words, and many subjects overestimated the number of times these two words were paired (Chapman, 1967; Chapman & Chapman, 1967).

Social psychologist David Hamilton and his colleagues are now convinced that both of these kinds of memory biases combine to produce illusory correlations in our judgments of other people. Do you think that accountants are timid? Do you believe that women make good business leaders? To answer these kinds of questions, you must sift through your memories about accountants and women bosses to determine how many did and did not have these particular qualities. This judgment process will be biased, however, when your stereotypes about these groups expedite the recall of confirming instances while obstructing the recall of disconfirming instances (Hamilton, 1979; Hamilton & Gifford, 1976; Hamilton & Rose, 1980; Hamilton & Sherman, 1989; Stroessner, Hamilton, & Mackie, 1992).

Hamilton's research group examined this process by asking students to read a long list of statements describing various people. The statements included a person's name, his or her occupation, and two adjectives. "Ed, the accountant, is timid and talkative" and "June, the stewardess, is wealthy and attractive" are examples. Unknown to subjects, the adjectives were paired with each occupational group an equal number of times. There were as many timid accountants in the list as there were timid stewardesses. Yet, when Hamilton tested their memory by asking them to recall how many times a particular adjective such as *timid* or *attractive* was used to describe accountants and stewardesses, they overestimated the number of timid accountants and attractive stewardesses because those pairings matched their stereotype-based expectations (Hamilton & Rose, 1980). They saw a correlation between variables that were actually unrelated to each other (McArthur & Friedman, 1980).

Differences in the frequency of cases can also set the stage for illusory correlations. Imagine that you see a woman flight attendant spill coffee on a passenger. Even though this action is distinctive—you don't often see flight attendants fumble in their duties—the person who did the fumbling isn't distinctive—most flight attendants are women. What if the flight attendant had been a man? In this case, two rare events would have been linked, and they would therefore have become easier to recall. If you were asked whether men or women make better flight attendants, you would be more likely to remember the clumsy man and to state that women make better flight attendants.

Hamilton's research group examined the impact of shared distinctiveness on illusory correlations directly by giving subjects a list of 39 statements, such as "Ed, who is in Group A, complimented a stranger." Each statement included the person's name, their group membership (either A or B), and a description of either a positive or negative behavior. Negative behaviors were relatively rare: 12 of the 39 (31%) actions were negative, but 27 (69%) were positive. However, members of group B were also rare. The set of 39 statements included 26 descriptions of Group A, but only 13 statements about Group B. Hamilton made certain that the group membership did not covary with behaviors. The proportion of members of Group A who performed bad behaviors was equal to the proportion of members of Group B who performed bad behaviors. But when subjects' memories were tested later, they attributed more negative behaviors to the smaller group—Group B—than Hamilton had actually shown them. He concluded that, because Group B and bad behaviors were both infrequent, they were also more distinctive to perceivers (Hamilton & Gifford, 1976).

Hamilton's findings explain why stereotypes about minority groups tend to take on a negative tone rather than a positive one. Members of minority groups, by definition, are rarer, and therefore more distinctive. Moreover, negative events, traits, and behaviors are also more distinctive than positive events, traits, and behaviors. Hence, we tend to overestimate the covariation between negative qualities and minority group members. A white person may encounter 10 blacks and 40 whites during a typical day because whites outnumber blacks. But if 2 blacks and 8 whites display negative qualities, such as the use of offensive language or rudeness, the perceiver will still overestimate the correlation between skin color and negative characteristics. We may not want to view others in stereotyped ways, but our limited ability to process information completely sometimes distorts our perceptions anyway (Hamilton & Sherman, 1989; Mullen & Johnson, 1990).

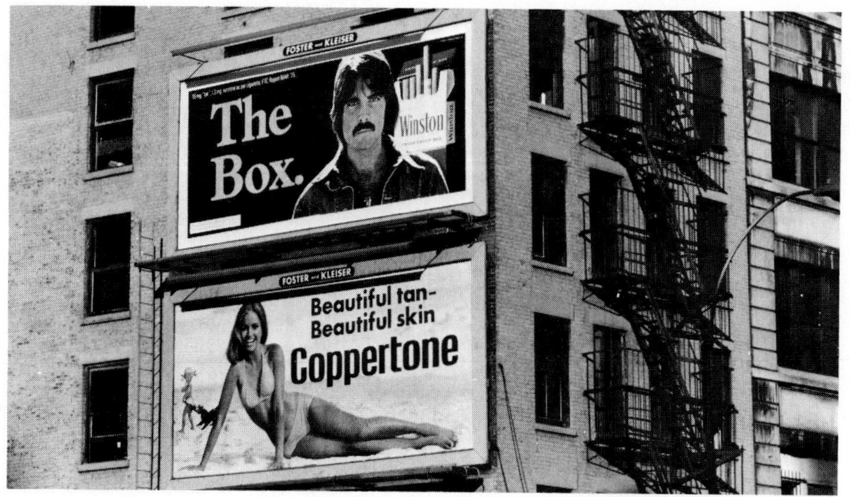

▲ Symbolic cues in the media and in advertisements define the relative value of men and women. This display of advertisements is rich with meaning. The man's image is placed above the woman's. He is dressed, whereas the woman is wearing only a bathing suit. Notice, too, the "faceism" in the two ads: the billboard featuring the man focuses on his head and upper torso, whereas the ad featuring the woman shows her entire body.

Social learning. Boyle wasn't born a bigot. Rather, as he grew up in a racially mixed society, he probably acquired his negative opinions about blacks from other people. Prejudiced parents often pass their biases on to their children. They may explicitly tell children that other groups are inferior, and forbid them from playing with them. Some parents reward children who express sexist or racist beliefs, and punish those who fail to adopt their values. Moreover, as social learning theory predicts, when parents act in ways that are prejudicial, their children tend to imitate these prejudices (Carlson & Iovini, 1985; Milner, 1983).

Peers are another significant source of prejudice. Perhaps Boyle was originally neutral toward African Americans, but after spending time with Cuneo, he may have adopted his friend's racist attitudes (Bagley & Verma, 1979; Patchen, 1982). Boyle may have also learned to be prejudiced through exposure to negative images of blacks and women in books, newspaper stories, advertisements, television programs, and cartoons. Blacks are underrepresented in children's books, comics, and on television, and the few characters that do appear often conform to whites' stereotypic notions of happy-go-lucky or aggressive blacks. These biases have diminished in recent years, but even now blacks are often cast in stereotypical roles that stress sports or entertainment (Armstrong, Neuendorf, & Brentar, 1992; Branthwaite & Peirce, 1990). Bill Cosby's character, Dr. Cliff Huxtable, is a noteworthy exception, but even *The Cosby Show* failed to portray the unique and individualizing aspects of black identity (Peterson-Lewis & Adams, 1990). News reports tend to overlook instances of peaceful coexistence between the races to highlight cases of racial conflict (Milner, 1983). Television programs also continually use the color white as a symbol of goodness and the color black as a symbol of evil (Duckitt, 1992; Elliot & Tyson, 1983).

Sexism, too, can be traced back to the symbolic cues that subtly define the value of men and women. Through the newspapers we learn that the world's affairs are shaped mostly by men. Many advertisements in magazines depict women as subservient to men and overly concerned with their physical appearance. Moreover, photographs of women in magazines often focus on their bodies, whereas photographs of men tend to center on their faces. This "faceism" sends the implicit message that women are judged by the shapes of their bodies, and men are judged by the strength of their ideas (Archer et al., 1983; Copeland, 1989).

▲ So why is it that the characters in cartoons and comics tend to be male rather than female? Does it reflect society's tendency to favor men over women?

© 1994. The Washington Post Writers Group. Reprinted with permission.

Women, like blacks, are also portrayed in stereotyped ways on television. Even though more and more women are working outside the home, in commercials they are most often depicted as housewives. Studies of commercials indicate that women are often portrayed as unintelligent, dependent on male advice, incapable of performing simple tasks, easily persuaded, eager to please men, envious of women who are better cooks or housekeepers, devoted to traditional roles of parenting, and deeply concerned with maintaining their attractiveness (Davis, 1990; Russo, Feller, & DeLeon, 1982). During sports broadcasts, commercials become more stereotypical, but prime-time commercials portray both sexes more fairly (Craig, 1992). Men outnumber women 3 to 1 in the world of television. Researchers identified 986 characters in 115 TV episodes broadcast during a two-week period. They found that 64.9% of the characters were male, and that 67.7% of the people who were portrayed in occupations were men (Vande-Berg & Streckfuss, 1992). When an off-screen voice introduces a product during a commercial, 89.9% of the time the voice is a man's rather than a woman's (Lovdal, 1989). Victims of violence are usually women rather than men (Huston et al., 1992). Most music videos feature men rather than women, and the women who do appear often seem passive and aimless (Brown, 1985). Four percent of the males, but over 30% of the females, in music videos broadcast by MTV wore revealing clothes (Seidman, 1992). Given all these prejudicial cues, it is not surprising that children who are not already sexist tend to become so if they watch large amounts of television (Gunter, 1986; Huston et al., 1992; Signorielli, 1989).

Norms and prejudice. The air force officer finds himself surrounded by people who ridicule women pilots. He begins to agree with them. Cuneo may not be prejudiced against blacks, but when he's with Boyle he goes along with his buddy's plan to harass them. The Alabama native is prejudiced against blacks, but when she goes to college in California her biases fade.

The officer, Cuneo, and the student are all responding to social norms—consensual standards that describe what behaviors should and should not be performed in a given situation. As we examine in more detail in Chapter 9, norms guide our actions in all manner of social settings. Why do you wear a particular style of clothes, eat three meals a day, smile when others smile at you, and value hard work? Because norms structure your actions and attitudes. In some of these situations, you may be following the norm just to avoid sanctions or to seem agreeable. But when you internalize a norm, it becomes a part of your total value system. You don't work hard just because you want to conform to social norms but because working hard is personally satisfying.

But can something as elusive as a social norm cause something so pervasive as prejudice? Research clearly says it can. Thomas Pettigrew (1958, 1959, 1960), for example, wondered whether the extreme amounts of racism seen in South Africa were caused by South Africans' personality traits or by social norms that demanded separation of the black and white people. He discovered that even though South Africans were far more prejudiced than Americans, they weren't more authoritarian in their personal beliefs. He did discover, however, that white South Africans who were the most prone to conform to norms were often the most prejudiced. A person who agreed with such statements as "It's better to go along with the crowd than to be a martyr" and "Adherence to convention produces the best kind of citizen" was also more likely to express the strongest anti-black attitudes (Duckitt, 1992).

Researchers have also found that prejudicial attitudes wax and wane when people move from situations that encourage or discourage prejudice. Recall the study of racism in a small West Virginia mining town discussed in Chapter 6. The norms in the town discouraged interracial contacts and therefore promoted a high incidence of discrimination. In the mine, however, work norms emphasized cooperation and productivity, so racial discrimination was discouraged (Minard, 1952). Studies of whites who move from one geographic area to another suggest that they tend to take on new attitudes to match the standards of their new residence. Whites who moved from southern regions of the United States to northern regions became less prejudiced, whereas whites who moved to the South became more prejudiced (Middleton, 1976). Even prisoners' racial attitudes change to match the predominating racial sentiments of the institution where they are confined. One researcher identified within a single prison two housing areas that adopted different norms about interracial interaction. She then tracked changes in new inmates' attitudes when they were assigned to housing in these two areas. As Figure 7-9 indicates, over two-thirds of the inmates assigned to the section with norms favoring tolerance became less prejudiced, and over one-third of the inmates housed in the less tolerant section became more prejudiced (Foley, 1976). These findings support Allport's initial insights into prejudice and norms. In 1954 he wrote, "About a half of all prejudiced attitudes are based only on the need to conform to custom, to let well enough alone, to maintain the cultural pattern" (p. 286).

Intergroup Sources

Allport points out that prejudice is an intergroup phenomenon. It does not involve a lone individual who rejects other individuals. Rather, it involves a group of individuals who reject other groups of individuals. Boyle did not simply dislike Booker. Rather, he took pride in his whiteness and the accomplishments of his race. At the same time, he also denigrated blackness and the accomplishments of black people.

ingroup-outgroup bias
The tendency to view the ingroup and its members and products more positively than the outgroup and its members and products. Ingroup favoritism is more common than outgroup rejection.

This tendency to view people in our group more favorably than those outside our group is called the **ingroup-outgroup bias**. The bias is really two biases combined: a tendency to favor our own group, its members, and products; and the tendency to derogate the outgroup, its members, and its products (Brewer, 1979; Coser, 1956; Hinkle & Schopler, 1986). In general, however, ingroup favoritism is stronger than outgroup rejection (Brewer, 1979; Coser, 1956; Hinkle & Schopler, 1986).

▲ **FIGURE 7-9**
Can prejudice be reduced by changing situational norms rather than individuals' attitudes? When inmates at a men's correctional facility were housed in a part of the jail with relatively positive norms about interracial contact, their prejudices abated. Many of the men who were housed in a part of the jail with anti-interracial contact norms became more prejudiced, however. (Data from Foley, 1976)

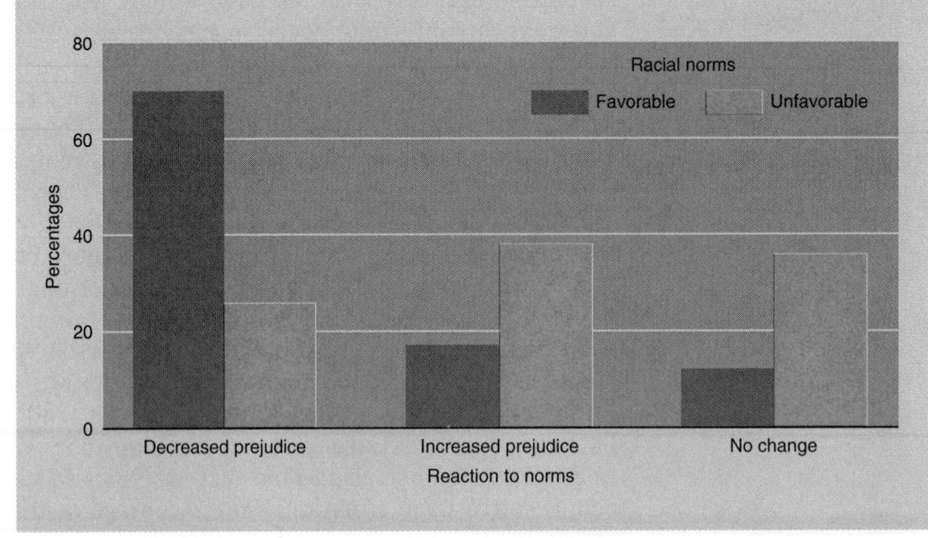

ethnocentrism
The belief that one's own tribe, region, or country is superior to other tribes, regions, or countries.

The ingroup-outgroup bias is called **ethnocentrism** when it causes tensions between members of larger social groups, such as tribes, ethnic groups, or nations. In *Folkways,* sociologist William Graham Sumner (1906) wrote:

> The insiders in a we-group are in a relation of peace, order, law, government, and industry, to each other. Their relation to all outsiders, or other-groups, is one of war and plunder. . . . Sentiments are produced to correspond. Loyalty to the group, sacrifice for it, hatred and contempt for outsiders, brotherhood within, warlikeness without—all grow together, common products of the same situation. (p. 12)

When two groups collide, the powerful intergroup processes examined next are set into motion.

Realistic group conflict. Some whites believe that blacks pose a threat to their way of life. They fear that blacks will move into their all-white suburban neighborhoods and place their children in the neighborhood schools. Whites also realize that blacks want better jobs and that they may displace white workers. Many blacks, in contrast, believe that whites strive to maintain the status quo (Institute for Social Research, 1983, p. 7).

realistic group conflict theory
A conceptual framework that argues conflict between groups stems from competition for scarce resources, including food, territory, wealth, power, natural resources, and energy.

Realistic group conflict theory claims that prejudice is caused by competition among groups over limited resources. This theory notes that the things people value, including food, territory, wealth, power, natural resources, and energy, are so limited that if the members of one group manage to acquire a scarce commodity, the members of another group will go without it. Naturally, groups would prefer to be haves rather than have-nots, so they take steps designed to achieve two interrelated outcomes: attaining the desired resources and preventing the other group from reaching its goals (Campbell, 1965; LeVine & Campbell, 1972). Groups in competition are usually groups in conflict (Rabbie & Horwitz, 1969; Rapoport & Bornstein, 1987; Taylor & Moriarty, 1987).

Realistic group conflict theory explains why the ingroup-outgroup bias emerges with a vengeance when groups compete. Groups may coexist peacefully during times of plenty, but when resources become scarce, intergroup biases escalate. Researchers in one study told some groups that they were competing with other groups. Other groups, in contrast, were told that they were cooperating with others or working independently (Worchel, Andreoli, & Folger, 1977). The groups then completed a task and were given sham feedback about their performance: Half thought they failed, and half thought they succeeded. As expected, subjects rated their own groups more favorably—the average was about 25 on the 31-point scale. The ratings of the outgroup were lower, between 19 and 20, when the two groups were cooperating or working independently, and considerably lower (the average was 15) when the groups were competing. This outgroup rejection was even more pronounced if the groups later experienced a second failure. Other studies have confirmed this effect, suggesting that ingroup favoritism is stronger than outgroup rejection and that outgroup rejection is intensified by failure (Dion, 1973, 1979; Ryen & Kahn, 1975; Wilson & Miller, 1961).

Social identity. According to the realistic group conflict theory, people become prejudiced when they feel that other groups pose a threat of some kind. Henri Tajfel and John Turner, however, argue that prejudice can occur even in the absence of conflict and threat. They believe that categorization, rather than competition, sews the seeds of conflict by creating a cognitive distinction between "us" and "them." They write, the "mere perception of belonging to two distinct groups—that is, social categorization per se—is sufficient to trigger intergroup discrimination favoring the in-group" (Tajfel & Turner, 1986, p. 13; see also Turner, 1987).

Is it possible that group membership per se—even in the absence of any competition—is sufficient to produce intergroup conflict? Tajfel and his colleagues put this hypothesis to the test in what they call the *minimal group paradigm.* They randomly assigned volunteers to one of two groups, although the volunteers were told that the division was based on some irrelevant characteristic such as art preference. Several tasks later, the subjects were then asked to divide up a small amount of money among the members of the two groups. Remember, these groups are purely cognitive; they exist in the minds of the subjects, but they have no social reality. The subjects don't know one another, can't see one another, don't expect to interact with each other, and the groups have absolutely no personal or interpersonal implications. Yet the ingroup-outgroup bias occurred nonetheless. People not only awarded more money to members of their own group, but they also seemed to try actively to keep money from members of the other group. Even when Tajfel made it clear that subjects had been assigned to the groups at random and that giving money to the outgroup would not cause any monetary loss for any ingroup member, the bias persisted. He concluded that it was the categorization process itself, rather than feelings of similarity, competition, a shared common bond, and the like, that stimulated conflict with the other group (Tajfel & Turner, 1986).

social identity theory
A conceptual explanation of prejudice that traces tensions between groups to social categorization processes (the tendency to distinguish between people who are in our group or in another group) and the need to maintain and enhance self-esteem. The theory assumes that people, by overestimating the value of their own group while derogating other groups, indirectly enhance their own self-esteem.

Tajfel's research provoked a search for the causes of ingroup favoritism in minimal groups that still continues (Aschenbrenner & Schaefer, 1980; Bornstein et al., 1983; Brewer, 1979; Brewer & Kramer, 1985; Hogg & Sunderland, 1991; Mason & Verkuyten, 1993). Many researchers, however, now believe that **social identity theory** offers an explanation for Tajfel's results. This theory, which draws heavily from prior social-psychological theorizing, is based on three basic assumptions. First, as the concept of social categorization maintains, we can readily distinguish between ingroup members and outgroup members. Second, we are motivated to maintain a positive social identity. Third, we derive much of our social identity from our group identities. These three assumptions, taken together, suggest that we favor members of our own

▲ Prejudice is an intergroup phenomenon. In this case, supporters of David Duke clash with college students who are protesting against him. Social identity theory suggests that such intergroup conflicts may indirectly enhance the group members' feelings of worth. By derogating the outgroup and revering the ingroup, individuals can find evidence of their relative superiority.

group in order to maintain and protect our own social identity. If our self-esteem is shaken by a personal setback, our group provides us with reassurance and identity (Meindl & Lerner, 1984). By praising our own group in comparison to others, we bolster our own self-esteem. By comparing our qualities to the qualities possessed by members of the outgroup, we find evidence of our superiority (Lemyre & Smith, 1985; Oakes & Turner, 1980; Turner, Sachdev, & Hogg, 1983). This explanation, although speculative, accounts for certain aspects of prejudice. For example, even though African Americans have been denied many of their civil rights and are depicted negatively in the media, they remain relatively high in self-esteem and group pride (Crocker & Major, 1989).

sociobiology
A biological approach to understanding social behavior; assumes recurring patterns of behavior in animals ultimately stem from evolutionary pressures that increase the likelihood of adaptive social actions while extinguishing nonadaptive practices.

Sociobiology of bias. The ingroup-outgroup bias is so pervasive—it is found in virtually all cultures and all eras of human history—that some experts believe it may have a genetic basis. **Sociobiology**, a branch of biology that explores the genetic roots of social behavior, suggests that favoring members of our own group and rejecting members of other groups may have given our early ancestors a distinct survival advantage. Early humans, they suggest, lived in small tribes composed of people who were genetically similar. Therefore, by helping members of one's own group, one was also helping to protect copies of one's genes that were present in these other people. Moreover, these tribes often competed violently with neighboring tribes for land, food, water, and shelter. Because outsiders were a danger, people with the ability to recognize and avoid them tended to survive, whereas those who did not tended to die off. After eons of this *natural selection* process, the earth was populated primarily by human beings with a built-in readiness to respond positively to the ingroup and negatively to the outgroup (Rushton, 1989).

Sociobiology offers a counterpoint to social psychology's emphasis on interpersonal processes as the causes of intergroup conflict (see Table 7-6). Prejudice may be an instinctive reaction to people who are unlike us genetically. Yet even sociobiology notes that biological predispositions are often strongly modified by the social situation in which the individual lives. Some aspects of our behavior may have a biological basis, but these basic patterns are not so inflexible that they cannot be altered through experience. We may instinctively react

▲ **TABLE 7-6**
Summing up: Intergroup processes that contribute to prejudice and discrimination against other groups

Process	*Characteristics*
Ingroup-outgroup bias	The tendency to favor the ingroup, its members, and its products, and the tendency to derogate the outgroup, its members, and its products. Rejection of others in larger social collectives is termed *ethnocentrism.*
Realistic group conflict	Rejection of other groups during competition for scarce resources. Members of groups that dominate other groups are less prejudiced against the outgroup than are members of groups that fail during competition with other groups.
Social identity processes	Maintaining and enhancing personal and collective self-esteem by positively evaluating the ingroup and negatively evaluating outgroups. Individuals in minimal group situations favor members of their own group even though these groups have no significance.
Sociobiology	The instinctive tendency to fear and dislike people who are unlike us genetically.

to strangers with fear and distrust, but as we see in the next section, biology's lessons can be unlearned.

Eliminating Prejudice

If prejudice were a physical disease, this pestilence could not be blamed on any one infectious germ or contagious virus. Boyle's self-doubts, his personality, his assumptions about whites and blacks, his family life, and the very existence of multiple groups in our heterogeneous society may all have played a part in making him a bigot (see Table 7-7). But this swirl of overlapping causes of prejudice also holds the key to eliminating prejudice. Because social factors sustain prejudice, perhaps these same factors can be marshalled to eliminate it.

The Contact Hypothesis

contact hypothesis
The prediction that equal-status contact between the members of different groups will reduce intergroup conflict.

Boyle was a product of a segregated society. Growing up in Boston in the 1950s and 1960s, he had very little contact with African Americans. He never had the opportunity to work with blacks, to understand and make friends with individual members of the black community, or to forge any other interpersonal ties with blacks. The **contact hypothesis** suggests that increased contact between Boyle and blacks would have cured his prejudice: If people lived in situations that promoted frequent contact between black and white people, our prejudices would be replaced by impartiality.

Robbers Cave Experiment
A field study performed by the Sherifs and their colleagues (1961) in an attempt to better understand the causes and consequences of intergroup conflict; the study derives its name from the state park that was the site for the research.

Muzafer Sherif and his colleagues carried out one of the best-known studies of the contact hypothesis at a boy's summer camp located in Robbers Cave State Park in Oklahoma (Sherif et al., 1961). They began their so-called **Robbers Cave Experiment** by separating 22 white 11-year-old boys into two groups: the Rattlers and the Eagles. They let the two groups solidify for a time before pitting them against one another in a series of competitions. Eventually, the researchers had to physically separate the two groups to prevent them from harming each other.

After creating prejudice between the two groups, the researchers then set about trying to reduce it. Hoping that contact between the groups would ease tensions, the researchers arranged for the Rattlers and the Eagles to take part

▲ **TABLE 7-7**
Summing up: Sources of prejudice

Sources	*Definition*	*Processes*
Psychological	Motivational and personality mechanisms that shift negative feelings caused by a sense of inferiority or frustration onto the members of other groups	• Ego defense • Scapegoating • Authoritarianism
Cognitive	Mental processes that facilitate social perception by making use of expectations, schemas, and other existing cognitive structures	• Social categorization • Stereotypes
Interpersonal	Social processes that facilitate the transmission of prejudicial attitudes and values from one person to the next	• Socialization • Social learning • Social norms
Intergroup	Conflict-sustaining processes that occur whenever two or more groups come into contact	• Ingroup-outgroup bias • Realistic group conflict • Social identity • Instinctive rejection of strangers

together in seven pleasant activities such as eating, playing games, viewing films, and shooting off firecrackers. Unfortunately, contact failed to cure their hostility. During all these events the lines between the two groups never broke. Pleasant experiences became rife with tension, and shared meals erupted into "food fights" and shoving matches.

The failure of contact to cure the boys' prejudices isn't surprising. When white and black schoolchildren attend the same schools, this contact doesn't necessarily reduce their prejudices. (This topic is explored in the section "Application: Reducing Prejudice Through School Desegregation," which concludes this chapter.) When rival departments in a business are moved closer together so employees must commingle during the work day, tensions between the departments don't necessarily disappear (Brown et al., 1986). College students studying in foreign countries actually become *more* negative toward their host countries the longer they remain in them (Stroebe, Lenkert, & Jonas, 1988).

Cooperation

Boyle would have probably remained prejudiced even if he had interacted regularly with African Americans. But what if the contact had occurred in a situation that required close cooperation with blacks, such as the workplace or during combat? Perhaps Boyle might have changed more if the situation had called for cooperation rather than mere contact.

The Robbers Cave Experiment provides proof of the curative contribution of cooperation over mere contact. After contact failed, the Sherifs forced the boys to work for **superordinate goals**—goals that can be attained only when groups work together. Disagreeable neighbors who unite forces when a severe thunderstorm threatens to flood their homes are working to achieve superordinate goals, as are the warring nations often depicted in science fiction who pool their technological skills to prevent the collision of the earth with an asteroid.

superordinate goals
Goals that can be attained only if the members of two or more groups work together by pooling their efforts and resources.

The Robbers Cave experimenters created superordinate goals by staging a series of crises. They secretly sabotaged the water supply so the campers awoke one morning without water. The boys became quite thirsty as they struggled to solve the problem and cheered when the problem was repaired. They told the boys that they could rent a movie, but made it clear that they could see a much more interesting movie if the two groups pooled their limited funds. When the supply truck apparently broke down, both groups of boys had to pull a shared rope to move the truck. Within days the Sherifs' efforts were rewarded: the original tensions between the groups were wiped out.

The superordinate goals were effective because, unlike the simple contact situations they created, the emergencies forced the two groups to cooperate with one another. For the preceding week, the Rattlers and the Eagles had been competitors, and this competition carried over to the simple contact situations. Even when group members tried to work with outgroup members, they earned no special rewards and were even criticized by their fellow group members. Without cooperation, the two groups continued to perceive one another as opponents who had to be rejected and defeated. They continued to discriminate against the outgroup, to view them with distrust, and even to resort to aggression and verbal abuse. When the situation called for cooperation, however, animosity was replaced by camaraderie. In general, cooperation leads to better communication, increased trust and attraction, changes in perception, and a willingness to tolerate group differences (Bodenhausen, Gaelick, & Wyer, 1987; Desforges et al., 1991; Riordan & Riggiero, 1980).

Cooperation doesn't always work, however (Worchel, 1986). First, in all likelihood several cooperative encounters will be needed before conflict is noticeably reduced. In the Robbers Cave research, a whole series of superordinate goals was required before animosity was reduced. When students from two different colleges worked together on problems, the cooperative encounter led to increased liking for members of the outgroup only when it occurred twice (Wilder & Thompson, 1980). Students who worked with the outgroup just once or not at all rated the members of the outgroup more negatively than students who worked with the outgroup twice. Similarly, in public schools a long period of cooperative intergroup contact is needed to reduce intergroup prejudice, and if cooperation is not constantly encouraged, then groups inevitably drift apart once again (Schofield, 1979; Schofield & Sagar, 1977).

Second, if the cooperative venture fails, then conflict inevitably ensues. Cooperating groups that manage to succeed like one another, but when groups fail, the negative affect associated with a poor performance spreads to the outgroup. Each group may blame the other for the misfortune, and intergroup relations may further erode. Thus, cooperation is not enough; the cooperation must also lead to success rather than failure (Blanchard, Adelman, & Cook, 1975; Blanchard & Cook, 1976; Blanchard, Weigel, & Cook, 1975; Cook, 1978, 1984; Mumpower & Cook, 1978; Weigel & Cook, 1975; Worchel & Norvell, 1980).

Undoing Categorization and Stereotyping

Norman Miller and Marilyn Brewer agree that cooperation works to dispel prejudice. They believe, however, that cooperation reduces conflict because it reverses some of the pernicious consequences of social categorization. Rather than thinking of the members of another group as "them," when working together to achieve superordinate goals, the boundary between the two groups becomes vague. Others are eventually viewed as members of our group rather than of the outgroup (Brewer & Miller, 1984; Gaertner et al., 1990; Miller & Brewer, 1986a, 1986b).

This process took place at Robbers Cave. Near the end of the project, friendships formed across the group lines, and the two groups intermingled

▲ How can this kind of interracial harmony be achieved in society at large? Researchers recommend encouraging contact between people of different races in cooperative situations.

during meals. In fact, when the researchers asked the Rattlers and Eagles if they wanted to travel home in separate buses, the boys chose a single bus. They had become Robbers Cave campers rather than Rattlers or Eagles.

Categorization can be undone in many ways. Similarities between the groups can be stressed, even if the similarities are unimportant. This technique worked well in one study when researchers asked two groups to work together on a joint task. If the researchers had the two groups wear the same color laboratory coats, then the collective effort minimized ingroup-outgroup conflict. If the two groups wore different colored coats, then the cooperative contact failed to assuage the group conflict (Worchel et al., 1978). Categorization can also be reduced by short-circuiting the outgroup homogeneity bias discussed earlier (Wilder, 1978). If people can be convinced to look at the members of the other group as individuals rather than as "them," then prejudice dwindles. When we learn that a few members of the outgroup disagree with their own group's position or have qualities that set them apart from their group, we become less likely to categorize automatically (Wilder, 1986b).

Stereotyped thinking, in contrast, has proved to be more difficult to rectify. As Patricia Devine (1989) explains, stereotyping is an automatic cognitive process. When one encounters a member of another group, or one is merely

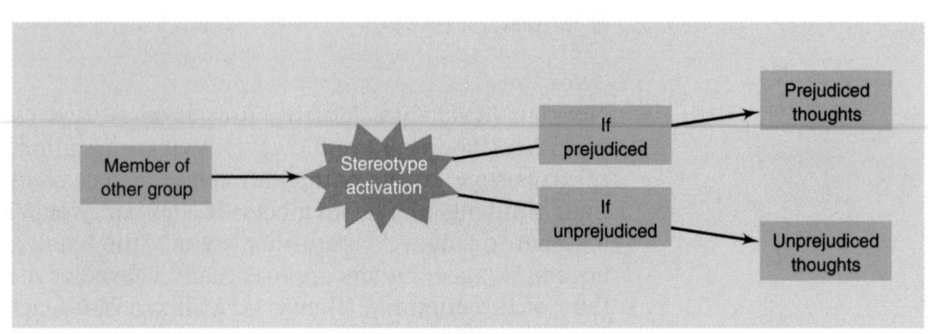

▲ **FIGURE 7-10**
Is prejudice inevitable? Patricia Devine believes that stereotypes are automatically activated when we encounter a member of another group. These stereotypes need not lead to prejudiced responses. Devine argues that unprejudiced people can't prevent stereotype activation but can inhibit its impact on thoughts, feelings, and actions. Prejudiced people cannot or do not inhibit their stereotypes.

▲ TABLE 7-8
Summing up: Factors that reduce prejudice and discrimination

Factor	*Characteristics*
Contact	The contact hypothesis assumes that frequent contact between groups reduces conflict between those groups. Empirical evidence (such as the Robbers Cave Experiment) does not support this hypothesis; contact per se is rarely sufficient to reduce intergroup conflict.
Cooperation	Situations that encourage groups to work together to achieve a common goal (a superordinate goal) can reduce conflict between these groups. Cooperation is most effective when it occurs repeatedly and results in successful goal attainment.
Inhibiting categorization	Conflict between groups can be eased by limiting the tendency to divide individuals into exclusive categories, such as "us" and "them." Categorization can be inhibited by emphasizing similarities rather than differences between members of different groups and by stressing each person's individual rather than group identity.
Controlling stereotyping	Stereotypes appear to be automatically activated. Unprejudiced perceivers can, however, inhibit the impact of stereotypical beliefs so that they won't influence their subsequent judgments and evaluations.

reminded of that other group by some symbol or other meaningful stimulus, stereotypes are activated. The color of a person's skin, the length of a person's hair, an accent, or a style of shoes may be enough to activate a stereotype, which may then influence our responses. Even cues that are so subtle we don't consciously recognize them may prime our stereotypes.

Devine does not believe, however, that prejudice is inevitable. Even though we may not be able to avoid the activation of stereotypes, we can control our subsequent thoughts to inhibit negative, unfair thinking (see Figure 7-10). Devine found that the whites she studied could easily list the contents of this culture's stereotypes about African Americans. She also found that whites who were low in prejudice could describe the stereotype as accurately as those who were high in prejudice. The unprejudiced whites, however, could control their thoughts after the stereotypes were activated. When asked to list their thoughts about African Americans, the unprejudiced subjects listed such things as "Blacks and whites are equal" and "It's unfair to judge people by their color—they are individuals." Prejudiced whites, in contrast, listed negative, stereotypical thoughts. Devine and her colleagues have also found that unprejudiced whites feel guilty when they find themselves responding to African Americans in stereotypical ways, whereas prejudiced whites do not (Devine et al., 1991).

Postscript on Prejudice

Is there a positive side to the social psychology of prejudice? Perhaps. By identifying the sources of prejudice, we also identify the ways to eliminate prejudice (see Table 7-8). If Boyle had experienced situations that promoted cooperation with African Americans, if he had learned to avoid categorizing people into groups based on their color, and if he had managed to inhibit his stereotyped thinking, he might be alive today.

But even though the case of Boyle and Cuneo versus Booker and Wilson ended tragically, it offers some glimmer of hope for the future. Booker went to jail for stabbing Boyle, but Wilson did not. He was charged by police with murder, but a private investigator named Gil Lewis decided to help him. Lewis was a white man, but he was not prejudiced. He did not think of Wilson as a black who had attacked a white, but instead considered him to be a person caught up in a bad situation. He arranged bail for Wilson, and together they reviewed the incident. They then searched the streets around the scene of the attack looking for witnesses and eventually found several people who could refute the police witnesses. Wilson would have surely gone to prison were it not for Gil Lewis—a white man who looked past skin color to what lies beneath the surface. People like Boyle remind us that prejudice is still a negative force in today's society, but people like Lewis reassure us that prejudice is not inevitable.

Summary

Prejudice is a powerful influence in contemporary society. The prejudiced person rejects other people simply because they belong to a disliked group. Prejudices are attitudes, so they color emotions, reinforce inaccurate *stereotypes* about people, and can lead to injurious forms of *discrimination.*

Because countless groups make up our heterogeneous society, prejudice can take many forms. *Racism,* for example, is prejudice based on race, and *sexism* is prejudice based on sex. Although *apartheid* laws that prohibited equal status contact between blacks and whites have been struck down, and few whites express racial views when interviewed by public opinion pollsters, anti-black racism persists in various forms. *Covert racism,* or public tolerance of a group paired with rejection of this group privately, surfaces when prejudiced whites feel that detection is unlikely. *Aversive racism* develops when whites accept egalitarian values but continue to experience negative emotions when interacting with blacks. *Symbolic racism* is characterized by ambivalence, for African Americans are considered to be both victims and undeserving of help. *Regressive racism* is blatant mistreatment of blacks that occurs when whites' personal prohibitions against acting in racist ways are stripped away by emotions. Stereotypes about the sexes continue to persist as well, for men and women are expected to display instrumental and expressive qualities, respectively. Moreover, the qualities, actions, accomplishments, and roles associated with women aren't as highly valued as those associated with men.

Psychological, cognitive, interpersonal, and intergroup processes combine to produce prejudice. Psychological processes, such as ego-defensiveness and scapegoating, help people avoid feelings of inferiority. The *scapegoat theory of prejudice,* for example, suggests that individuals vent their frustrations by blaming others and that those with *authoritarian personalities,* as assessed with the *F-scale,* are prone to be prejudiced against others. Social categorization and stereotyping provide a cognitive foundation for prejudice. Once we classify people into the category "them"—the outgroup—we overestimate their similarity (the homogeneity bias), overstate the ingroup's distinctiveness (the ingroup differentiation bias), make extreme judgments of outgroup members (the extremity bias), and generalize from one person to the entire group (the *law of small numbers*) and from the entire group to one individual (the *group attribution error*). Stereotypes, too, resist disconfirmation by influencing perceptions, producing *illusory correlations,* and initiating self-fulfilling prophecies.

Interpersonal processes, such as social learning and social norms, also promote prejudice. Society's socializing agents, such as our parents, peers, teachers, books, and television, teach us to reject others through direct instruction and by modeling negative attitudes. People also become more prejudiced when the situational norms condone negative attitudes and less prejudiced when norms condemn prejudice. Prejudice is also an outgrowth of conflict-sustaining processes that occur whenever two or more groups come into contact. People tend to view those in their own group more favorably than those outside their group. When this *ingroup-outgroup bias* causes conflict between larger societal groups, such as tribes or nations, *ethnocentrism* results. *Realistic group conflict theory* argues that competition for scarce resources fuels intergroup conflict, but social identity theory suggests that social categorization, per se, is sufficient to create the ingroup-outgroup bias. Analyses based on *sociobiology* go so far as to suggest that prejudice is an instinctive reaction to people who are unlike us genetically.

How can prejudice be eliminated? The *contact hypothesis* recommends promoting contact between groups, but this assumption has not been borne out by research. The *Robbers Cave Experiment* found that contact per se did not eliminate intergroup conflict, but that cooperation in the pursuit of *superordinate goals* did. Prejudice can also be undone by disabling the cognitive processes, such as categorization and stereotyping, that sustain it. Even though stereotyping appears to be an automatic process, people who are unprejudiced are able to control the impact of these negative beliefs on their subsequent judgments and evaluations. Social factors sustain prejudice, but these same factors can be marshalled to eliminate it as well.

For More Information

- *Black Americans' Views of Racial Inequality: The Dream Deferred,* by L. Sigelman and Susan Welch (1991), uses public opinion polls to develop an overall picture of African Americans' attitudes about the causes and consequences of racism in the United States.
- *The Content of Our Character,* by Shelby Steele (1990), is an articulate and insightful analysis of black-white relations in the United States.
- *The Nature of Prejudice,* by Gordon W. Allport (1954), was published in 1954, but it is still the best analysis of prejudice available. It offers an excellent integration of theory, case studies, research, and insight.
- *Opening Doors,* edited by Harry Knopke, Robert Norell, and Ronald Rogers (1991), examines prejudice from a variety of scientific and literary perspectives. The editors have included chapters by such noted experts on prejudice as John F. Dovidio, Samuel Gaertner, Thomas Pettigrew, Walter Stephan, and James Jones.
- *Psychology of Intergroup Relations,* edited by Stephen Worchel and William G. Austin (1986), includes chapters written by the leading researchers and theorists in the field. Entire chapters are devoted to such topics as social categorization, ingroup-outgroup perceptual biases, stereotypes, and inaccuracies in identifying outgroup members.
- *The Social Psychology of Prejudice,* by John Duckitt (1992), provides a comprehensive review of the causes of prejudice, with a particularly strong analysis of racism in South Africa.

Application: Reducing Prejudice Through School Desegregation

In 1954 the Supreme Court handed down a controversial ruling in the case of *Brown* v. *Board of Education of Topeka*. The Court ruled that all laws that required separate facilities for blacks and whites were unconstitutional, for such segregation failed to recognize the equality of races. Forced segregation became unlawful.

In making this historic ruling, the Court relied on evidence supplied by a number of social psychologists. In a brief entitled "The Effects of Segregation and the Consequences of Desegregation: A Social Science Statement," Floyd H. Allport, Kenneth B. Clark, Isidor Chein, Stuart W. Cook, and other researchers identified a number of harmful consequences of segregation, including a loss of pride and self-acceptance among blacks (Allport et al., 1953). The statement also argued that equal-status contact between the races would be needed to eliminate the mistaken assumptions and false stereotypes that sustain prejudice. This perspective, which is known as the *contact hypothesis,* recommended desegregation as the best tool for eliminating prejudice (Cook, 1984).

The Supreme Court mandate took effect slowly, but by the early 1970s a large percentage of the public schools had been desegregated. With desegregation, however, came a growing realization that contact between blacks and whites doesn't always reduce prejudice (Schofield, 1978; St. John, 1975). For nearly every study that reported reductions in prejudice following desegregation, another revealed that desegregation either had no impact on prejudice or actually increased it. One team of researchers found that before their schools were desegregated, black and white children were relatively accepting of those of other racial backgrounds. When desegregation began, however, intergroup attitudes became increasingly negative (Gerard & Miller, 1975; Rogers & Miller, 1981). Apparently, intergroup contact is no panacea for prejudice (Gerard, 1983).

Why doesn't school desegregation always lead to more positive racial attitudes? One possible answer focuses on the nature of the contact. Few people would argue that any kind of contact is sufficient to reduce prejudice. If black and white students insult, argue with, physically attack, or discriminate against one another, then certainly such contact should not be expected to yield beneficial effects (Riordan & Riggiero, 1980). Contact under such conditions may actually promote prejudice by providing blacks and whites with information that they can reinterpret to support their biases and stereotypes. Apparently, many schools fail to create the appropriate contact situation needed to reduce prejudice (Miller & Brewer, 1984).

Ironically, the social science statement presented in 1954 to the Supreme Court recognized this limitation, for it argued that contact per se is not sufficient to reduce prejudice (Allport et al., 1953; Cook, 1985). The original brief maintained that contact *can* be an effective means of reducing prejudice provided certain preconditions are met. First, the *status* of the individuals who interact in the contact situation must be equal. If, for example, the white students in a school come from middle-class families while the black students come from lower-class families, these differences in socioeconomic background can create conflicts and tensions. Differences in academic background and athletic skill can also create rifts between the two groups (Miller, Rogers, & Hennigan, 1983; Schwarzwald, Amir, & Crain, 1992).

Second, the contact should involve informal, *personal interaction* with outgroup members rather than superficial contact. As Thomas Pettigrew (1975) notes, desegregation does not always lead to integration. Blacks and whites may attend the same school without interacting with one another. When a school is first desegregated, contacts between blacks and whites increase, but within a few months the school becomes resegregated: blacks interact primarily with blacks, whereas whites interact primarily with whites (Silverman & Shaw, 1973). Also, many school systems compound this problem by grouping students on the basis of their scores on standardized achievement tests. Because of profound differences in educational experiences, whites typically outperform blacks on such tests. As a result, blacks and whites usually end up in different classes, and little contact between groups occurs (Schofield, 1979).

Third, the *norms* of the social situation must encourage friendly, helpful, egalitarian attitudes. Yet in many cases desegregation is mandated by the federal government over the objections of school officials and parents. In this atmosphere of tension and animosity, norms that discourage intergroup conflict often evolve (Stephan & Rosenfield, 1978).

Fourth, the situation must require *cooperative interdependence* in the pursuit of common goals rather than intergroup competition. Just as the Sherifs and their colleagues in the Robbers Cave Experiment found, competition between groups sets the stage for intergroup conflict. If, however, groups must work together to achieve superordinate goals, then animosity between groups can be eliminated (Sherif et al., 1961).

Intergroup contact is much more likely to lead to reductions in prejudice when these four prerequisites are satisfied. Stuart W. Cook, for example, created an optimal contact situation in his study of highly prejudiced white women. He assigned approximately half of the prejudiced women to a control condition that received no treatment; the rest were hired to "develop a training exercise to be used in industry." For 2 hours each day for 20 days, they worked with two other women on an experimental task that required them to make complex decisions in a simulation of a shipping business. The other two women were part of the research staff; one was black, and one was white.

Cook arranged the contact situation to meet the conditions just described. First, the subject and the black confederate were equal in status: they worked in jobs that were equally important, and their educational backgrounds were similar. Second, each session lasted 2 hours, with a lunch break after the first hour. The lunch break provided the black confederate with an opportunity to reveal personal aspects of her life in a friendly, open way. Third, during these lunches, both confederates discussed topics dealing with racial equality and desegregation, so the white confederate had an opportunity to express egalitarian attitudes. Last, the task itself could not be solved without close cooperation.

When the subjects rated the black confederate at the end of the study, they were uniformly positive. Moreover, when their attitudes were measured several months later in a completely different setting, many subjects reported more favorable attitudes toward blacks in general. In the original experiment and a subsequent replication, Cook found that 40% of the women in the experimental condition showed a significant reduction in prejudice in comparison with only 12% in the control group. Given the initial strong prejudice of the subjects and the limited amount of contact (subjects worked with only a single black woman), these results are encouraging (Cook, 1985).

Educators have put Cook's analysis of intergroup contact into practice in the classroom by developing educational programs that encourage cooperation among members of different racial and ethnic groups. One such approach, Elliot Aronson's **jigsaw classroom,** has proved to be remarkably successful. Aronson and his colleagues developed the program to combat a rising tide of interracial violence in desegregated public school systems in Texas. His own observations of these classrooms indicated that competition among the Anglo, African American, and Mexican American students was creating racial tension, so he developed assignments that forced students to work together. In general, a unit of study is broken down into various subareas, and each member of a group is assigned one of these subareas; students must then become experts on their subjects and teach what they learn to other members of the group. For example, in a class studying prejudice, the teacher might separate the pupils into four-person groups, with each member of the group being assigned one of the following questions: What is racism? What is sexism? What causes prejudice? How can prejudice be eliminated? When working on their assigned topics, the students would leave their groups and meet with their counterparts from other groups. Thus, everyone assigned to study the question "What is racism?" would meet to discuss it and decide how to teach the material to others. Once they had learned their material, these students would then rejoin their original groups and teach their fellow group members what they had learned (Aronson, 1982, 1990; Aronson & Gonzalez, 1988; Aronson et al., 1978).

Aronson's jigsaw classrooms improved interracial relations in the school dramatically. He concluded that, within six weeks, children who were working in jigsaw classrooms "liked one another more, liked school better, increased in self-esteem, and performed better on objective exams" (1990, p. 121). Other research supports his conclusion, for a meta-analysis of 31 separate studies found that ingroup-outgroup hostility was reduced in cooperative rather than competitive classrooms (Johnson, Johnson, & Maruyama, 1984). This positive impact is even greater when assignments are structured so that students of all levels of ability can contribute, when students are assigned their individual topics randomly, and when groups contain equal numbers of children from the racial groups being integrated. Other technical matters, such as the way grades are assigned, had little impact on the success of the intervention (Miller & Davidson-Podgorny, 1987).

In sum, although many educators initially assumed that desegregation would automatically reduce prejudice, the promise of desegregation remains largely unfulfilled. Despite decades of political and social activism, prejudice and its pernicious consequences persist. The strength of African Americans' personal convictions have helped them cope with these social inequities, but stronger interventions are needed to ensure the effectiveness of current social policies. Desegregating schools is a start, but unless the nature of the contact situation supports egalitarian attitudes, school desegregation will realize only a fraction of its potential. Schools must be integrated rather than merely desegregated.

jigsaw classroom: A team-learning technique that involves (a) creating race-heterogeneous groups, (b) assigning topics to each group member, and (c) requiring these group members to teach their topics to the other members of their groups.

JIL SANDER

Attitudes and Persuasion

David Martin sells things. Not over the counter of some store or shop, but on television screens, billboards, and the pages of magazines and newspapers across the country. David Martin is the consummate ad man. He and his staff have created advertisements that have taken products and companies from obscurity to eminence. He told car buyers, "You only live once. Do it in a Maserati!" He illustrated brochures for Colonial Williamsburg with original sketches by Norman Rockwell. When his "Barnett is Florida's bank" campaign marched across the state's billboards, bank deposits jumped from $12 billion to $20 billion. David Martin can change people's attitudes (Martin, 1989).

As shown in earlier chapters, attitudes summarize our likes, dislikes, preferences, and predilections. They are essential components of who we are, and they play a pivotal role in determining how we react across situations. But, indispensable as they are to us, our attitudes aren't set in stone. They flex, mutate, and realign over time. When we are children, our favorite possessions are stereos, TV sets, and bikes. When we are adults, our attitudes shift to favor household furnishings, art objects, and automobiles. By the time we become grandparents, our most treasured possessions are photographs (Csikszentmihalyi & Rochberg-Halton, 1981; Kamptner, 1991). Despite our desire to hold fast to our personal tastes and preferences, at times even our most cherished attitudes must be relinquished.

Many of the forces that cause our attitudes to change are examined in Chapters 6 and 7. The learning processes that lead to the formation of an attitude can also change existing attitudes. Nicole may lose her fondness for Italian food when she comes down with intestinal flu on the same night she treats herself to a large pizza. After watching his favorite talk show host complain about fast-food restaurants, Inman may condemn McDonald's. Attitudes also change when our behaviors change. George, for example, may accidentally purchase a new brand of detergent at the store, but after using it for a month he may come to prefer it. Dissonance theory (see Chapter 6) explains how our attitudes change when we make choices, after we decide to act in a new way, and when we expend effort in the pursuit of a goal.

Attitudes can change for other reasons, however. Why, for example, would a pediatrician begin prescribing a banana-flavored children's medicine called Donnagel-PG after seeing The Martin Agency's advertisement for that product? Perhaps attitudes change because we are rational, thoughtful people who revise our attitudes to take into account new information and experiences. Pediatricians who read that Donnagel-PG is an effective medicine and tastes better than all other competitive brands may decide that Donnagel-PG is a superior product. But our attitudes sometimes change for less rational, more emotional reasons. Pediatricians may not spend much time at all thinking about Donnagel-PG, but when they have to prescribe something for a patient the slogan "Kids think it's the bananas" may flash through their minds, and there they are, telling the parents to try Donnagel-PG. **Persuasion**, as we see in the first section of this chapter, has both a rational and an irrational side.

persuasion
The communication of facts, arguments, and information calculated to change another person's attitudes.

When do attitudes change? When will a physician switch from one brand of medicine to Donnagel-PG? Before we can predict when change will occur, we must examine the central elements in the persuasion process: Did the doctor think the information in the ad was accurate? Were the arguments in the ad persuasive ones that would convince a doctor, or were they weak and unsubstantiated claims? Is the doctor a long-time user of some other brand? We must know who is saying what to whom.

Last, what factors protect our attitudes against persuasive assaults? Will the doctor who prescribes Donnagel-PG continue to prescribe it after he or she reads an advertisement for a competitor's product? We examine our ability to resist a persuasive appeal in the final section of the chapter.

Theories of Attitude Change

The advertisers have us surrounded. The billboard's Marlboro man looks rugged as he lights a cigarette. On the car radio, politicians enumerate their accomplishments and ask for your vote. The Coke commercial repeats its latest slogan over and over again while youthful actors cavort on a beach. The grocery store's newspaper ad includes coupons you can clip to get extra savings on some products. The Duracell rabbit marches by, still beating his drum.

The diversity of all these ads can be bewildering, but if you study any magazine, newspaper, or television advertisement, you will probably discover a strategy behind the words, graphics, and images. As David Martin (1989) explains, many advertisements describe the qualities of the product, enumerate its advantages, and urge the consumer to purchase the product: They appeal to our rational, logical side. Other ads, in contrast, take a more indirect approach. They don't try to convince us with words, but instead arouse emotions, link their product to experiences and events we already enjoy, or make us laugh. They appeal more to emotions and impressions.

Both techniques work. Appeals to reason sell, but so do appeals to emotions, images, and actions. Why?

The Elaboration Likelihood Model

Carl Hovland and his colleagues carried out some of the earliest systematic studies of attitude change at Yale University in the 1940s and 1950s. Their **learning model of persuasion** assumed that an effective persuasive appeal must achieve four goals: First, it must capture the audience's attention, for what is ignored can hardly persuade. Second, the message must be understandable; an audience must comprehend what is being said. Third, the source should strive to make the message convincing enough so that listeners will accept it. Fourth, the argument must be memorable so that its impact will be long-lasting (Hovland, Janis, & Kelley, 1953).

learning model of persuasion
An early explanation of persuasion that assumed attitude change is a learning process and is therefore shaped by the characteristics of the source of the message, the message itself, and the target of the message. Because persuasion requires learning, a persuasive argument should be attention-grabbing, understandable, convincing, and memorable.

Richard Petty and John Cacioppo (1981) agree, in principle, with the learning model's emphasis on our rationality. In many cases we review the arguments, look for weaknesses, reexamine our own ideas on the topic, and then make changes in our attitudes if the new information warrants such changes.

▲ How did David Martin convince pediatricians to prescribe Donnagel-PG instead of some rival remedy? Through interviews with physicians, Martin discovered that the product's unique feature was its banana flavor that masked the medicine's bitter taste. So he crafted a campaign that included monkeys and the slogan "Kids think it's the bananas." Sales doubled because the campaign capitalized on both the rational and emotional sides of persuasion.

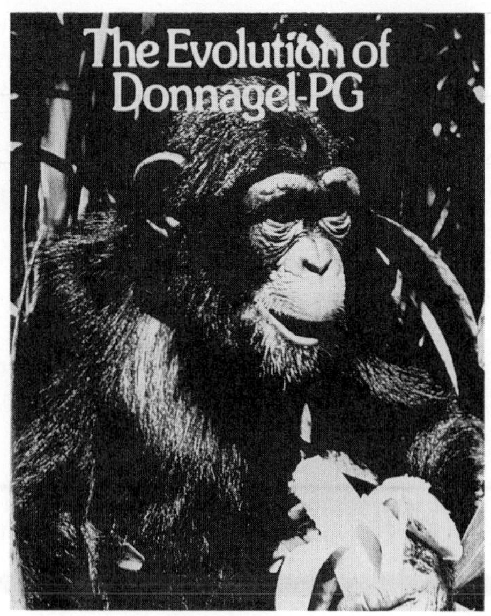

We are critical consumers of persuasive messages. At other times, however, we are less thoughtful. We don't pay much attention to what we are told, we don't really understand the arguments completely, we don't notice that the claims are weak, and we forget the original message, yet our attitudes still change.

elaboration likelihood model (ELM)
A dual-process theory of persuasion that argues attitude change occurs when persuasive arguments generate pro-message thoughts (*central route processing*) or when peripheral cues, such as the source's attractiveness or expertise, prompt acceptance of the message without thoughtful analysis (*peripheral route processing*).

This duality prompted Petty, Cacioppo, and their colleagues to develop the **elaboration likelihood model (ELM)** of persuasion. They believe that persuasive messages follow one of two routes in their quest to change our existing attitudes. The *central route* entails a thoughtful analysis, or elaboration, of the issues at hand. We consider the quality of the arguments, search our memories for information on the subject, and revise and store our attitudes as necessary. If Lisa drinks nonalcoholic beer but is disenchanted with her current favorite, she might read closely an advertisement that describes the special methods used to brew Miller Sharp's. If Golnar learns he has six cavities when he visits the dentist, he may read over a toothpaste advertisement that presents the results of a clinical trial conducted by the American Dental Association. The central route takes a *Consumer Reports* approach to persuasion.

The *peripheral route,* in contrast, doesn't require very much mental effort or elaboration. Warren develops a liking for a cold climate after spending three winters in Vermont, but he doesn't think much about it. Melissa decides to buy Nike running shoes after a sports star she admires is featured in a Nike ad. Robert prefers Crest toothpaste because his mother always bought that brand. The peripheral route requires much less cognitive activity relative to the central route (Cacioppo et al., 1991; Petty & Cacioppo, 1981, 1986a, 1986b).

When will incoming information be processed in the peripheral route rather than the central route? The ELM, as summarized in Figure 8-1, offers two answers. First, the likelihood of cognitive elaboration decreases when we aren't motivated to process information systematically. A childless couple won't carefully process a well-reasoned proposal for changing the elementary school curriculum because they don't care about the issue. Second, if we lack the cognitive resources and abilities needed for elaboration, then we will probably shift to the peripheral route. When we are distracted, when we have a prior opinion, or when we just can't make any sense out of the message, we are less likely to think carefully about the information.

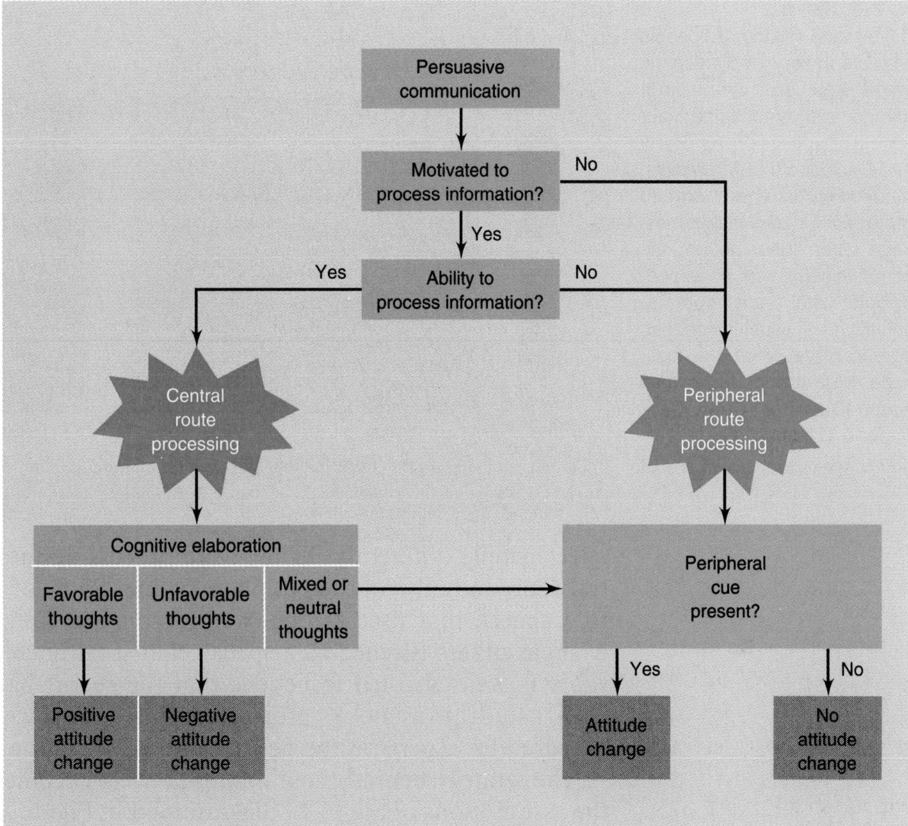

▲ **FIGURE 8-1**
What are the two basic routes that persuasive messages follow when changing our attitudes? According to Petty and Cacioppo's elaboration likelihood model, when we are motivated to process the message and have the ability to do so, it will be subjected to systematic, central processing. If the message generates favorable thoughts, our attitude will shift toward the message. If we aren't motivated to process the message, or if we lack the ability to do so, then we will shift to a peripheral processing mode. If a peripheral cue is present, then our attitude will shift temporarily. If no cue is present, then we will retain our initial attitude. (Adapted from Petty & Cacioppo, 1986a)

Once the message moves to the processing stage of the central route, its impact on our attitudes depends on the kind of thoughts it generates. Petty and Cacioppo believe that a persuasive message generates an internal cognitive response that "may agree with the proposals being made in the message, disagree, or be entirely irrelevant to the communication" (Petty & Cacioppo, 1981, p. 225). If the message prompts positive cognitive responses, the listener will be persuaded. A message that leads to negative responses, however, may produce a **boomerang effect**: The listener may become strongly opposed to the advocated position. And a message that generates neutral thoughts or both positive and negative thoughts may initiate peripheral route processing. Thus, even when a message includes many strong arguments, what matters most during central processing is the listener's cognitive response to the message. People who can list all the claims made by an advertiser may not like the product. But people who respond to an ad with many positive thoughts will like the product even if they can't remember the exact claims made in the ad (Mackie & Asuncion, 1990).

boomerang effect
Change in the direction opposite to that argued in a persuasive message.

Petty, Cacioppo, and Rachel Goldman (1981) investigated this elaboration process by asking college students to listen to a tape recording of a speech arguing that their university should institute a comprehensive examination that all seniors must take prior to graduation. Naturally, most of the students were none too pleased with the prospect of yet another graduation requirement, and the researchers made the issue even more personally relevant by telling some of them that the change would take place the very next year. Others were assured that the change wouldn't be instituted for 10 years, so they were less personally involved in the discussion. Petty, Cacioppo, and Goldman then manipulated two situational variables that should, according to the ELM,

▲ **FIGURE 8-2**
If you are talking to people who aren't very involved in the issue you are discussing, should you emphasize your special expertise? As Petty and Cacioppo's ELM predicts, uninvolved listeners agreed more with a persuasive message when they thought the communicator was an expert. People who were more involved in the issue, in contrast, agreed more when the message was strong rather than weak. (Data from Petty, Cacioppo, & Goldman, 1981)

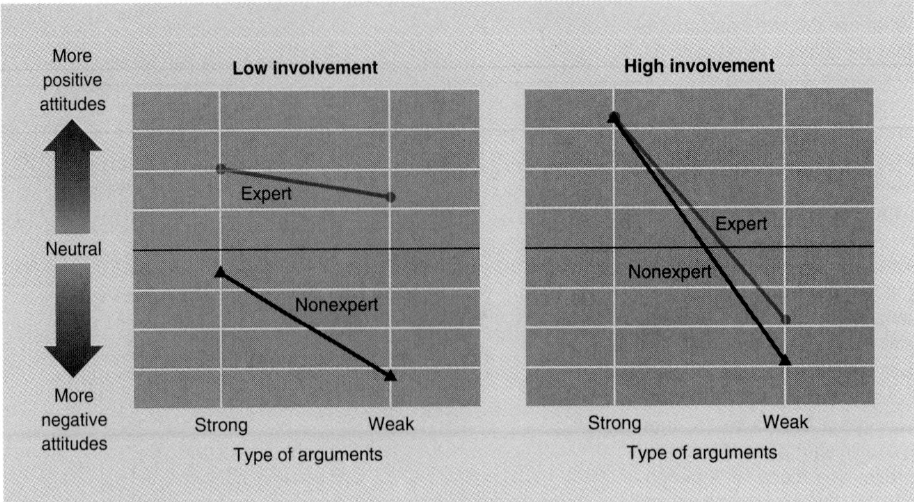

affect people differently if they were processing information through the central route rather than the peripheral route. Some of the students were exposed to a speech that used strong, well-reasoned arguments to support the point, whereas others listened to a speech that used unconvincing arguments. Some subjects were also led to believe that the report had been developed by high school students as a class project, whereas others were told that the report was prepared by experts in the field of higher education.

The strategy behind these manipulations becomes clear when you consider the assumptions of the ELM diagrammed in Figure 8-1. First, making the issue personally relevant should have increased the likelihood of elaboration and central route processing. When the issue wasn't personally relevant and subjects weren't motivated to review the arguments, then processing should have shifted to the peripheral route. Second, central processors—because they are examining the quality of arguments—should have been more influenced by the strong arguments than the weak ones. Third, the expertise of the source of the argument might influence central processors slightly, but this cue should significantly impact peripheral processors. These individuals should be much more influenced by a communication from a prestigious source, irrespective of the quality of the arguments presented.

The results of the investigation, which are presented in Figure 8-2, confirm the ELM predictions. Uninvolved students reported more positive attitudes on the topic when the report was prepared by experts rather than nonexperts. This effect was particularly pronounced when the arguments were of low quality. Involved students, in contrast, agreed with the well-reasoned speech that contained strong arguments but disagreed with the weakly argued speech. Both the central and the peripheral routes culminated in persuasion, but they did so in very different ways.

Heuristic-Systematic Model of Persuasion

Shelly Chaiken, Alice Eagly, and their colleagues, like Petty and Cacioppo, believe we process information relevant to our attitudes in one of two ways. We are often eminently logical people who carefully review information before amending an attitude. This *systematic mode* of information processing corresponds to the central route identified by Petty and Cacioppo (Chaiken, 1980, 1987; Chaiken, Liberman, & Eagly, 1989; Chaiken & Stangor, 1987; Eagly & Chaiken, 1984).

Chaiken and Eagly are particularly interested in the shortcuts we sometimes take to avoid systematic processing of information. Tara, for example, doesn't try to pick apart the arguments in an editorial condemning capital punishment because she assumes that the news media can be trusted. Christopher buys a Sony brand tape deck because it's more expensive than the others, and he figures that "more expensive things are better things." Cathleen picks out the product that a beautiful model uses. Past experience has taught these people that, in general, "experts can be trusted," "high price equals high quality," and "attractive people like what I like," so they rely on these rules of thumb to reach a conclusion or decision. This *heuristic mode* of thought sacrifices precision but improves processing efficiency.

heuristic-systematic model (HSM) of persuasion A dual-process theory of persuasion that argues attitude change occurs when individuals rationally examine the arguments presented (*systematic processing*) or when heuristics, such as "length means strength," prompt acceptance of the message without thoughtful analysis (*heuristic processing*).

Chaiken and Eagly's **heuristic-systematic model (HSM) of persuasion**, like the ELM, maintains that our reliance on heuristics escalates when we aren't motivated to process information systematically and when we lack the cognitive resources such a review requires. Systematic processing also uses up valuable cognitive resources, and we can't always afford the luxury of a detailed review of messages. If we had to spend time contemplating every persuasive appeal, every advertisement, every argument we encounter, we wouldn't be able to perform any other cognitive tasks. Therefore, the cognitive miser saves mental resources by using heuristics. They are less effortful, quicker, and accurate enough for most purposes. (See Chapter 3 for more information on heuristic thought.)

When people use heuristics rather than systematic processing, they may respond very differently to the same persuasive appeal. Danny Axsom, Suzanne Yates, and Shelly Chaiken (1987) examined the impact of the two different modes of processing on attitudes by asking college students to listen to a tape-recorded debate in which one speaker argued that probation programs are more effective than imprisonment methods. To prompt some people to use heuristic rather than systematic processing, the researchers manipulated the listeners' involvement in the issue. They created high involvement by stressing the importance of the debate and its relevance for the listeners' community, and low involvement by telling listeners to just "sit back and relax" because this study was just a preliminary analysis of the idea. Axsom, Yates, and Chaiken also varied the strength of the arguments in the message and the recorded audiences' reactions to the message. Some subjects listened to a speech that included a number of strong reasons in favor of probation rather than incarceration, whereas others listened to a speech that incorporated weak arguments. Also, subjects could hear, in the background of the tape recording, the apparent response of the original audience. In some cases, the audience responded with great enthusiasm—bursts of clapping and cheers of approval—but in others, the audience rarely clapped and even heckled the speaker.

HSM argues that these two factors—the quality of the arguments and the audience's reaction to the speech—should have very different effects on the listeners who are processing information systematically rather than heuristically. Systematic thinkers should agree more with a speaker who presents strong rather than weak arguments, but they shouldn't be influenced by the audience's responses. Heuristic thinkers, in contrast, should respond more favorably when the audience responds positively. After all, the *consensus heuristic* argues that "if other people think a message is correct, then it probably is correct" (Axsom et al., 1987, p. 31). The results, shown in Figure 8-3, provide considerable support for the heuristic model. People who were involved in the issue (and presumably were processing information systematically) were more persuaded by a speech with strong arguments rather than weak ones. They

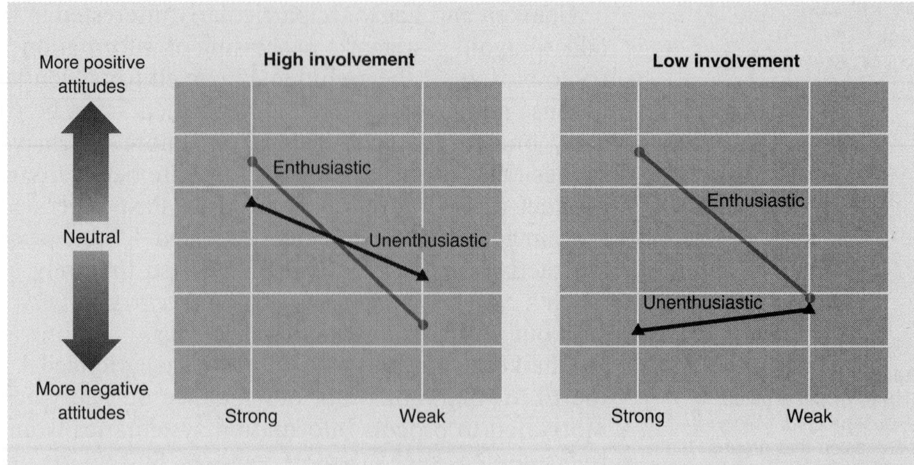

▲ **FIGURE 8-3**
Do people rely on the audience's response to a speech as a heuristic cue to estimate the speech's persuasiveness? When people who weren't very involved in the topic under discussion overheard an audience reacting very positively to a decent speech, they responded by changing their attitudes. People who were more interested in the topic, in contrast, weren't influenced by the audience's response to the speech. (Data from Axsom, Yates, & Chaiken, 1987)

weren't influenced to any great extent by the audience's response to the speech. People who weren't involved in the issue (and presumably were processing information heuristically), in contrast, were more likely to agree with a strong speaker whose ideas were well received by the audience. These heuristic thinkers weren't completely oblivious to the quality of the arguments—they didn't agree with a low-quality argument even if the audience liked it—but they did let the audience's approbation guide their conclusions when the speech was sound.

Pathways to Persuasion

The ELM and HSM differ on several points. The ELM focuses on the elaboration process that takes place when messages are processed along the central route, whereas HSM is more concerned with rapid, rule-of-thumb responses to persuasive messages. Petty and Cacioppo's ELM also includes other nonlogical processes in the peripheral route (for example, the listener's emotions and repeated exposure to the message), whereas Chaiken and Eagly's HSM focuses on heuristic thought (Chaiken & Stangor, 1987).

▲ The heuristic-systematic model of persuasion explains the influence of inspirational speakers. People who aren't involved in a speaker's ideas and arguments will let the audience's responses guide them rather than systematically process the message. If this crowd applauds and cheers the speaker, people will accept the message. If the crowd boos and jeers, they will reject it.

▲ **TABLE 8-1**
Summing up: Two contemporary theories of persuasion

Theory	*Types of Processing*	*Basic Assumptions*	*Sample Predictions*
Elaboration likelihood model (ELM) developed by Petty, Cacioppo, and their colleagues	Central route processing involves the diligent consideration of the message. Peripheral route processing relies on positive or negative cues that trigger change without the need for extensive issue-relevant thought.	Central route processing is more likely if listeners are motivated and have the required cognitive resources. Persuasion occurs if elaboration generates pro-message thoughts. Change also occurs if peripheral cues, such as the source's attractiveness or expertise, prompt acceptance of the message.	When personally involved, people are more influenced by strong arguments. People who are not involved in the issue (peripheral processors) are more impressed by an expert's claims even when these claims are weak.
Heuristic-systematic model (HSM) of persuasion developed by Chaiken, Eagly, and their colleagues	Systematic processing subjects the message to careful, rational analysis, whereas heuristic processing relies on rules of thumb that are less effortful but accurate enough for most purposes.	Individuals are more likely to rely on heuristic processing when cognitive resources are scarce and motivation to process the message systematically is low. Convincing messages generate persuasion during systematic processing. Heuristics—such as "length means strength" or "agree if the source is an expert"—lead to persuasion during heuristic processing.	When personally involved in the issue, people are more persuaded by strong than weak arguments. People who aren't interested in the issue are persuaded when the rest of the audience responds enthusiastically to the message (the consensus heuristic).

The two theories, however, agree on the fundamentals. As Table 8-1 indicates, they are both *dual-process theories.* They identify two paths that can culminate in attitude change. Both models also admit that these two paths to persuasion are not necessarily mutually exclusive. A message can generate extensive cognitive analysis while stimulating peripheral, heuristic processing. Consider, for example, David Martin's advertisements for Maserati automobiles. They stress the car's reliability, performance, and relative low cost compared to other imported sports cars. Martin asks customers to listen to his claims, weigh them, and then base their next purchase on the facts he has provided. But his ads don't just give us the facts and figures. He appeals to the feeling person as well as the thinking person. He capitalizes on the image of the Maserati as an exotic, exciting, and alluring sports car and asks us to put more excitement into our lives by driving it. Not leaving anything to chance, Martin uses both pathways to reach the goal of persuasion.

Elements of Persuasion

The American Cancer Society wants to make sure you realize that cigarette smoking is harmful, but Philip Morris, Inc., hopes you will decide to smoke

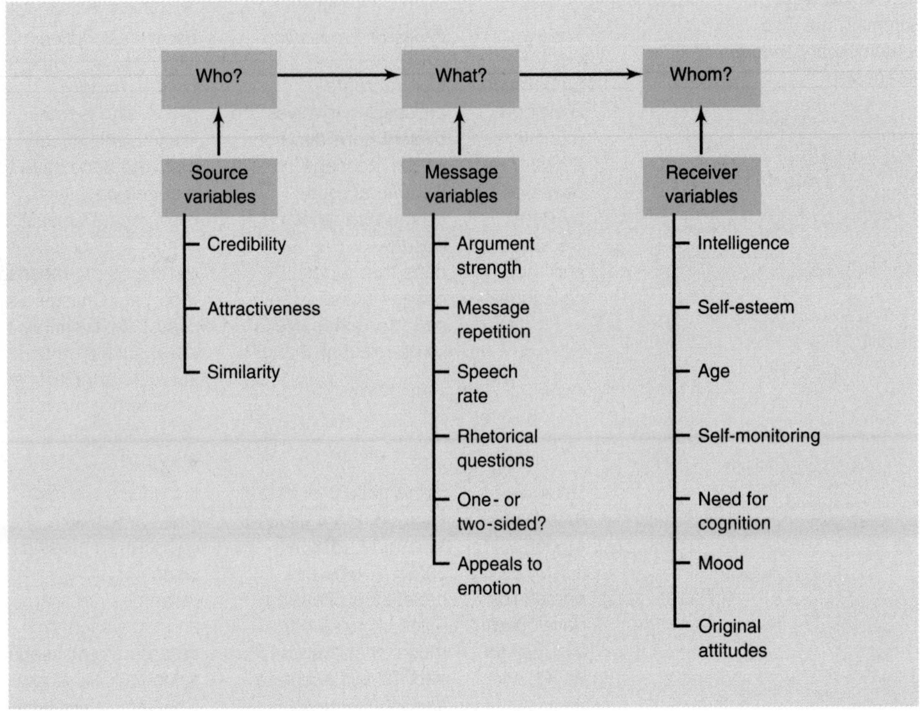

▲ **FIGURE 8-4**
What factors influence the persuasion process? Researchers in the Yale Communication and Attitude Change Program carried out at Yale University in the 1950s never developed a formal theory of attitude change, but they summarized their research with the question "Who says what to whom?" To know when persuasion will occur, we must consider three basic elements that are common to all persuasion situations: the source, the message, and the receiver.

Marlboros. One of your friends thinks you should buy a Volvo, but a coworker at the office spends an hour trying to convince you to buy an American-made car. Apple Computer, Inc., argues that its Macintosh computers are easy to operate, but IBM maintains that its machines are more useful in the business world. Politicians worry that handguns contribute to the rise in crime, but the National Rifle Association argues that Americans have a fundamental right to own weapons. Ahmad tells Tarie that they must make love for their relationship to mature, but Tarie argues that she just isn't ready for that level of physical intimacy.

The world is filled with persuaders, but some are more successful than others. Why? Many years ago Hovland's Yale research group answered this puzzle by identifying the three elements of any persuasive encounter: the source of the persuasive message, the nature of the message, and the characteristics of the receiver (Hovland, Janis, & Kelley, 1953). Before we can make a prediction about the outcome of a persuasive message, we must know *who* is saying *what* to *whom,* as Figure 8-4 shows (Olson & Zanna, 1993).

The Source

On any ordinary day you are inundated with persuasive messages from a host of sources. Advertisements urge you to change your hair color, your diet, the way you smell; newspaper editorials suggest political positions; movie reviews condemn and acclaim; junk mail fills our mailboxes, parents make clear their views, and your friends offer suggestions. With all these voices clamoring in your ears, it's no wonder that you tend to listen to some sources more than others. Who do you listen to the most? People who seem credible, people who are attractive, and people who are similar to you in some way.

Credibility. I still remember the cereal box's promise that for only one box top and $1.75, I could be the proud owner of a "self-propelled submarine that dives and surfaces." When the package arrived, I filled the bathtub with water, inserted the "propellant" (a tablet of baking soda) into the submarine, and watched. The feebly bubbling submarine slowly sank to the bottom of the tub, where it lay on its side, taking in water and teaching me about credibility.

Most of us have learned that some sources are more credible than others, and it is the message from credible sources that we accept. During the Cold War era, U.S. citizens were more likely to agree with a message favoring the further development of nuclear-powered submarines when it was attributed to a U.S. physicist rather than to the Russian newspaper *Pravda* (Hovland & Weiss, 1951). People listening to a speech arguing for more lenient treatment of juvenile delinquents change their attitudes more when the source is a judge rather than a drug dealer (Kelman & Hovland, 1953). We agree with the statement "A little rebellion now and then is a good thing" when it's credited to Thomas Jefferson, but not when it's credited to Vladimir Ilyich Lenin (Lorge, 1936). And if we are told that we can get by with far less sleep than we usually get, we tend to agree more with this recommendation when it comes from a Nobel Prize–winning physiologist than when the source is the local YMCA director (Bochner & Insko, 1966). Messages from credible sources trigger both central, systematic processing and peripheral, heuristic processing. We spend more time examining arguments when they come from credible sources, and the assumption "agree with the experts" is a useful heuristic (DeBono & Klein 1993; Verplanken, 1991).

Who is credible and who is not? First, people who seem to be *experts* are often viewed as credible sources of information. When listening to a lecture about land preservation, we would be more influenced by the speaker who has a degree in geology than by one who majored in French (Wood & Kallgren, 1988; see also Olson & Cal, 1984). Second, *trustworthy* people—those who we believe will give us unbiased information—are more credible sources than people who can't be trusted to speak honestly. Do you trust politicians, police, insurance agents, and car dealers to tell you the truth? Or would you be more likely to believe someone who is a parent, a teacher, or an ordinary person off the street? Marketing experts prefer to use trusted people in their advertisements rather than individuals with a reputation for doubtful ethics.

This is not to say that we never believe untrustworthy sources. Even individuals who are typically regarded as low in credibility—politicians running for reelection, salespersons trying to close a deal, criminals proclaiming their innocence—can be credible sources when they take an unexpected stance on an issue (Eagly, Wood, & Chaiken, 1978; Wood & Eagly, 1981). Alice Eagly, Wendy Wood, and Shelly Chaiken asked people to read a politician's speech that accused a large company of industrial pollution. When subjects were told the politician was speaking to a group of environmentalists, they questioned the credibility of the source; they assumed the politician was interested only in currying the audience's favor. In contrast, when subjects thought the politician was addressing the company's supporters, they felt he was much more sincere.

sleeper effect
A delayed increase in the persuasiveness of noncredible sources that usually occurs when the source of the message is forgotten before the message itself is forgotten.

Sometimes, too, a message from a noncredible source that is initially uninfluential can generate attitude change at a later time. This **sleeper effect** was first studied by group of researchers at Yale in 1949 (Hovland, Lumsdaine, & Sheffield, 1949). Five days after viewing a pro-U.S. film, American soldiers showed little change in their attitudes. Nine weeks later, however, attitude change had occurred. The soldiers who had seen the film were more positive than soldiers in a control group who had not seen the film.

Hovland and his colleagues advanced the *disassociation hypothesis* to account for this surprising effect. Because the message came from the U.S. Army, and the soldiers felt that the army was a biased source of low credibility, they

▲ **FIGURE 8-5**
Does a message ever become *more* persuasive as time passes? A persuasive communication that was described as inaccurate had little impact on subjects' attitudes at first. Five weeks later, however, subjects' attitudes had changed toward the communication, revealing a *sleeper effect*. (From Gruder et al., 1978)

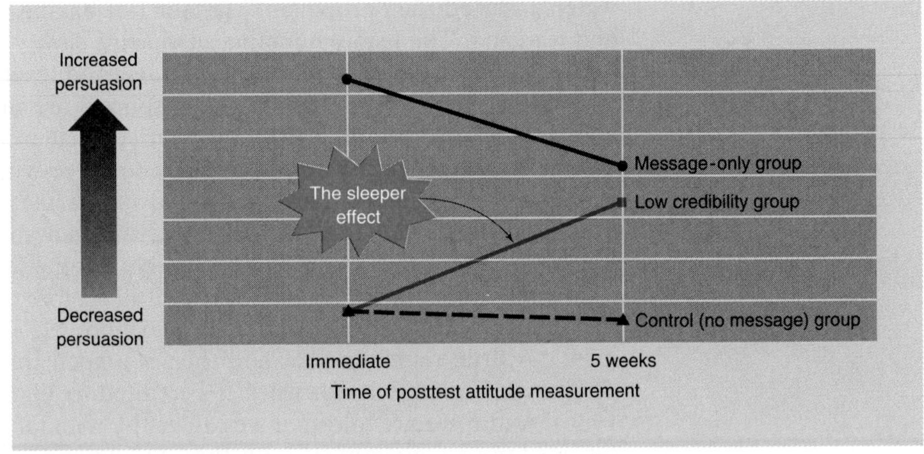

tended to discount the information presented in the film. But the passage of time erased this *discounting cue* before it erased the information itself. Because the cues that originally led the soldiers to question the credibility of the communication were gone, discounting no longer took place, and the message slowly changed their attitudes.

Subsequent investigators sought to test the discounting cue hypothesis by exposing subjects to messages from credible and noncredible sources and measuring their attitudes at different times. In many of these studies, the sleeper effect didn't occur; subjects who listened to a noncredible source showed no increase in attitude change over time. Granted, they were no less positive than subjects who had listened to a more credible source, but this effect occurred because the influence of the highly credible source decreased over time. If anything, the findings demonstrated a delayed decrease in attitude change—a reverse sleeper effect (Cook et al., 1979; Gillig & Greenwald, 1974; Greenwald, 1975a).

Recently, however, researchers have succeeded in identifying the key ingredients of the sleeper effect. First, the message itself must be persuasive enough to produce attitude change. Second, the discounting cue (for example, the low credibility of the source) must be powerful enough to inhibit attitude change. Third, attitude measurement should be delayed long enough for the subject to forget the source of the message but not so long that the subject forgets the original message as well. Last, the appropriate statistical tests are needed to detect the effect. Researchers who incorporated all these features obtained the sleeper effect shown in Figure 8-5 (Cook & Flay, 1978; Cook et al., 1979; Gruder et al., 1978).

Researchers have also revised Hovland's original explanation of the sleeper effect to stress *differential decay* rather than disassociation. As time passes, both the message and knowledge of the source are forgotten, but the source of the knowledge is forgotten more quickly. Hence, at some critical point days or weeks after exposure to a message from a suspect source, the message is remembered, but the source is forgotten (Pratkanis et al., 1988).

Attractiveness. When Madonna tells us to vote, Michael Jordan holds up a box of cereal, or Bill Cosby spoons pudding into his smiling mouth, we listen and take heed. Attractive people—the pretty, the handsome, the likable, the charming, the admired—are more persuasive than unattractive people. College students who listened to a "Mr. Holmes" discussing venereal diseases changed their attitudes on the topic if Mr. Holmes had praised students earlier in his speech. The Mr. Holmes who admitted that he thought students were immature, irresponsible, and difficult to work with swayed few students (Eagly & Chaiken, 1975). A woman who spoke tentatively was a better persuader of men than a woman who spoke assertively, apparently because men liked the tentative woman more (Carli, 1990).

Why are attractive people so persuasive? As Shelly Chaiken (1979) reports, they are better persuaders than less attractive people. She recruited a number of attractive and unattractive people to act as persuaders in a study of attitude change only to discover that physically attractive people had superior communication skills, articulateness, and self-confidence. Attractive people also stimulate more central and peripheral processing. We pay more attention to the arguments offered by attractive people, and we also employ the heuristic "agree with attractive people." Wendy Wood and Carl Kallgren (1988) tested this explanation by measuring students' opinions about environmental preservation after they were exposed to either an attractive or unattractive person who argued against stricter environmental regulations. Students who were very knowledgeable about environmental issues weren't persuaded by the communicator's good looks, but they did pay more attention to strong messages. Students who were not knowledgeable, in contrast, were more easily persuaded when the speaker was attractive. They changed more when the communicator was attractive rather than unattractive. Since they were uninformed, the communicator's attractiveness apparently functioned as a heuristic cue that triggered persuasion (Chaiken, 1979, 1980; Pallak, 1983; Petty, Cacioppo, & Schumann, 1983; Roskos-Ewoldsen & Fazio, 1992).

Similarity. You are in a paint store picking out a brand of paint to use in redecorating your bedroom; you figure you need about 3 gallons. You are pondering your choice when a clerk walks up and says, "I think Glidden is the best. I used about 3 gallons painting my living room and it worked fine." But another clerk suggests Sherwin-Williams: "I used about 60 gallons last month and liked the way things turned out." Which brand will you buy—Glidden or Sherwin-Williams?

▲ A product's fortunes often ride on the image of the person who acts as the spokesperson in its advertising. People are more likely to take note of information provided by a trustworthy, similar, and—most important—attractive source.

Surprisingly enough, customers in a paint store who were presented with these two recommendations tended to take the advice of the clerk who had used the same amount of paint that they were planning to buy. Clearly, the clerk who had used more of the paint had more experience (and therefore should have been a more credible source), but the other clerk was more similar to the subject. Even though the similarity between the clerk and the customer was based on an irrelevant characteristic—does it really matter that they both needed 3 gallons of paint?—this trivial similarity made for greater persuasiveness (Brock, 1965).

Cognizant of the similarity-persuasion effect, advertisers usually try to match the persuader to the target: Billboards in African American communities feature African American models, MTV ads for acne medicine use young people as spokespersons, and ads aimed at young mothers feature young mothers. This strategy is consistent with research that indicates people are more likely to process carefully messages that come from ingroup members than from outgroup members (Mackie, Worth, & Asuncion, 1990). Students at the University of California at Santa Barbara (UCSB) who read a speech arguing against standardized testing changed their attitudes more when the speech contained strong rather than weak arguments—but only when they thought the speech was written by a student at UCSB. Neither the strong nor the weak speech had any effect on them when the speech was attributed to a University of New Hampshire student. Apparently we are willing to listen to arguments presented by people in our own groups, but we reject without much thought the pleas offered up by outgroup members (Mackie, Gastardo-Conaco, & Skelly, 1992; Wilder, 1990).

The Message

Even communicators with all the persuasion-enhancing qualities listed in Table 8-2—credibility, attractiveness, similarity—fail as persuaders if they organize and present their arguments ineffectively. Anyone who has ever suffered through a disorganized lecture, listened to a speech that makes no sense, or read an essay that harps on mundane, trivial arguments that are largely irrelevant to the central topic can understand the importance of developing a message that communicates and persuades.

What makes a message persuasive? Hovland's cognitive approach reminds us that a persuasive message must capture our attention and be understandable, convincing, and memorable (Hovland et al., 1953). And Chaiken's (1980)

▲ **TABLE 8-2**
Summing up: Three source factors that influence persuasion

Source Factors	*Impact on Persuasion*
Credibility	Experts are perceived to be credible, as are people we think we can trust. Noncredible sources can be persuasive when they take unexpected stances on issues and when differential decay causes the listener to forget the source of information before the information itself (the sleeper effect).
Attractiveness	People who are physically or socially attractive, likable, or admired are more persuasive than less attractive people. Attractive people are also more skilled at persuasion than unattractive people.
Similarity	Similarities between the source of the message and the listener increase persuasion, even if the similarity involves superficial qualities that are not relevant in the current situation. We are more likely to be persuaded by someone in our group rather than by someone outside of our group.

HSM argues that a weak message, if properly presented, can still lead to attitude change if we *assume* it's persuasive. As we will see next, any factor that increases the likelihood that we will engage in pro-message thinking or heuristic-based acceptance of the message will increase the message's persuasive power.

Argument strength. Advertisers know how to create strong, persuasive messages. Their messages are well-organized and coherent, moving from attention-grabbing introductions to final conclusions. David Martin (1989) writes: "Advertising must be witty and wise, perhaps indirect, but sufficiently clear so that the customer himself can discover the value" of the product (p. xiii).

Advertisers' faith in our ability to tell the difference between a strong argument and a weak one has been borne out by research (Eagly, 1974; Pallak, 1983; Petty, Cacioppo, & Schumann, 1983; Petty, Harkins, & Williams, 1980). Petty and Cacioppo (1984) used two sets of arguments to create two essays that called for a comprehensive examination for all graduating college seniors. The strong essay included only cogent arguments: The exams would improve teaching, student learning, and students' earning potential (see Table 8-3). The weak essay included specious appeals to personal opinion and several logical fallacies. People who read the essay supported by strong arguments were much more positive toward the idea of comprehensive exams, particularly if they thought that change would take place very soon. Moreover, when Petty and Cacioppo increased the number of arguments from three to nine, the essay became even more persuasive if the arguments were cogent ones.

Their findings, which are summarized in Figure 8-6, suggest that strong arguments have their biggest impact on people who are systematically process-

▲ **TABLE 8-3**
Message quality counts.

Petty and Cacioppo had college students read one of two essays, both of which argued that all graduating students—before they could get their degree—must pass a comprehensive exam in their major area of study. One essay's position was backed up with strong, cogent arguments; the other relied on weak, unsubstantiated claims.

Strong Arguments	*Weak Arguments*
Prestigious universities have comprehensive exams to maintain academic excellence.	Most of my friends support the proposal.
Institution of the exams has led to a reversal in the declining scores on standardized achievement tests at other universities.	My major adviser took a comprehensive exam and now has a prestigious academic position.
Graduate and professional schools show a preference for undergraduates who have passed a comprehensive exam.	The risk of failing the exam is a challenge most students would welcome.
Average starting salaries are higher for graduates of schools with the exams.	The difficulty of the exam would prepare one for later competitions in life.
The quality of undergraduate teaching has improved at schools with the exams.	If the exams were instituted, our university would become the American Oxford.
The National Accrediting Board of Higher Education would give the university its highest rating if the exams were instituted.	The Educational Testing Service wouldn't market the exams unless they had great educational value.

Source: Petty & Cacioppo, 1984.

ing the message. When Petty and Cacioppo asked people to list all their thoughts after reading the essay, students who were personally involved in the question of senior comprehensive examinations listed more pro-exam thoughts when the essay used strong arguments. Personally involved students who read an essay supported by weak arguments listed more anti-exam thoughts, suggesting that the weak essay generated counterarguing. When people weren't involved in the topic, the number of arguments became more important to them than the quality of the arguments. These peripheral, heuristic processors apparently concluded that length means strength and simply agreed more with the essay that listed nine supporting arguments rather than just three. Thus, quality counts more than quantity, but only on the central route to persuasion.

Message repetition. Advertisers believe that any good ad is worth repeating, and repeating, and repeating. Writes David Martin (1989): "Consumers are indifferent bystanders. The mental notes they take of advertising are soon forgotten unless the product's personality and advantage points are tirelessly reinforced" (p. 97).

Message repetition capitalizes on the *mere exposure* process. Repeated exposure, as noted in Chapter 6, often creates positive attitudes, particularly when we have no preexisting feelings on the subject. One field study of this exposure process, sponsored by Seagram's & Sons, studied consumer responses to four well-known Seagram's brands and four less well-known brands. With the cooperation of Time, Inc., researchers identified households that subscribed to *Time* magazine, *Sports Illustrated,* or both magazines. Then, during a 48-week test period, they systematically varied the number of advertisements for Seagram's products placed in these magazines. Some households received magazines with no Seagram's ads, whereas others received magazines with one, two, or four ads. Seagram's found that more was better: The people who received magazines with more ads were more aware of those products, particularly if the products were new ones (*Time,* 1982).

Laboratory studies of attitude change confirm these results, although they suggest that excessive exposure hurts more than it helps. When Cacioppo and Petty (1979) repeated an argument several times, listeners thought more about the issue and generated more pro-issue thoughts each time they heard the message. However, if the message was repeated too many times (in this case, five times in one hour), the message generated more anti-issue and irrelevant thoughts. Repetition, like most things, may not be such a good thing if overdone (Anannd & Sternthal, 1990; Cacioppo & Petty, 1985, 1989; Sawyer, 1973).

Speech rate. Many commercials use voice-overs. In a voice-over, a person who never appears on the screen presents information that explains the on-screen situation or offers arguments for purchasing the product. If the voice-over is played too fast, then the viewer may miss important information. But if the voice-over is too slow, then viewers are bored.

Even though the expression *fast talker* is pejorative—it calls up the image of a slick salesperson who says a lot without really saying anything of substance—fast talkers are fairly persuasive. One team of researchers arranged for subjects to listen to a lecture that was delivered rapidly, moderately fast, or slowly. The three rates were 191, 140, and 111 words per minute. The fastest talker was more persuasive than the moderate and slow speakers (Miller et al., 1976).

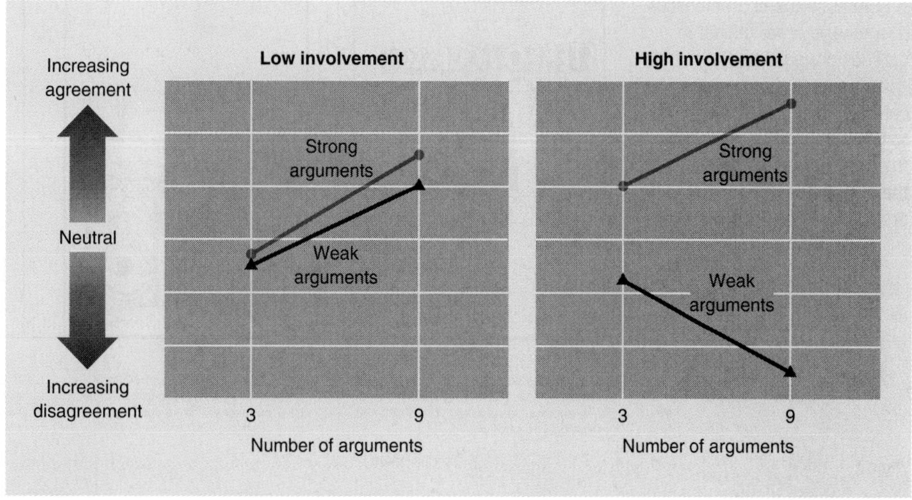

▲ **FIGURE 8-6**
When it comes to persuasion, does quality win out over quantity? People personally involved in the issue were more influenced by the arguments' quality and quantity, but nine strong arguments influenced them more than three strong arguments. People not personally involved in the issue were influenced only by quantity. (From Petty & Cacioppo, 1984)

Other studies, in which researchers have varied the speed of a message electronically without changing its other properties, have also confirmed the greater persuasiveness of rapid-fire delivery (Apple, Streeter, & Krauss, 1979; MacLachlan, 1979).

Why are fast talkers so convincing? Apparently their rapid-fire delivery convinces listeners that they are intelligent and well informed. Rapid delivery also interferes with the ability to argue against the ideas presented. If we are initially opposed to the speaker's position and he or she talks rapidly, we don't have the chance to think through the arguments for ourselves, so we tend to accept them (Smith & Shaffer, 1991).

Rhetorical questions. The Sierra Club, an environmental action organization, tries to block a dam project in the Grand Canyon with advertisements that ask "Should we also flood the Sistine Chapel so tourists can get nearer the ceiling?" An ad for Rolls-Royce automobiles asks "Should every corporation buy its president a Rolls-Royce?" Years ago Buick's ads always sang, "Wouldn't you really rather have a Buick?"

Rhetorical questions call for an answer that is so obvious it doesn't even need to be stated. In theory, such questions are persuasive because they force listeners to think about the message. Instead of passively taking in the message, a rhetorical question makes us think about the arguments and draw our own conclusions.

Unfortunately, people don't always answer the way one would expect. Readers may think that flooding the Sistine Chapel is a fine idea or that, no, they would really rather have a BMW. Petty, Cacioppo, and Marty Heesacker (1981) studied this limitation of rhetorical questions by asking college students to listen to a recording advocating comprehensive examinations for all graduating seniors. They used four types of speeches to manipulate the strength of the argument and the rhetorical style of the message. In the strong-arguments–rhetorical-style condition, for example, the message presented many strong arguments and such questions as "Wouldn't instituting a comprehensive exam be an aid to those who seek admission to graduate and professional schools?" In the weak-arguments–regular-style condition, the supporting arguments were easily refutable and summarized by direct statements. The researchers also manipulated

▲ Because the characteristics of a message are critical to persuasion, advertisers and sales personnel often use carefully constructed messages to influence consumers. But they sometimes fail to develop the right message for their products.

"... Do speakers *really* sound better with 'monster cable'? I can only tell you that in Los Angeles, when asked, 128 out of 150 Ouija boards said 'yes.'"

"I don't like to knock a competitor's product, sir, but listening to the Audak HX-7 speaker will make you impotent."

"... Another nice feature is the cross-over network, sir. It utilizes heavy gauge wire so the sounds that cross over into the mid-range speaker will have in effect, 'a safe crossing.'"

Reprinted with permission from *Stereo Review* magazine, © 1983 by Charles Rodrigues; all rights reserved.

the audiences' involvement with the issue. They told half of the subjects that the proposal was being considered by the president of a distant college (low involvement); they told the others that the new comprehensive exams were being considered for the following year at their own college (high involvement).

Figure 8-7 presents the results of this complex experiment. First, consider the results when people are not personally involved with the topic. According to the ELM, a rhetorical question prompts the listener to respond actively to the message. Thus, when strong arguments are used, rhetorical questions should help. But when the arguments are weak, rhetorical questions should hurt. These predictions were confirmed. But what happens when people are already involved with the issue? In this case, a rhetorical question interfered with persuasion. Because subjects were already paying attention to the message, the question merely distracted them (see also Howard, 1990).

These findings indicate that rhetorical questions can backfire when the listener's cognitive response to the argument is negative. If your audience is apathetic and needs to be roused, rhetorical questions may be effective. But if you already have their attention, then a simple summary is best. (Notice I didn't say, "Isn't it clear that a rhetorical question is most effective when the audience is apathetic and needs to be roused?")

One-sided versus two-sided communications. Is the beer manufacturer wise to claim "Bud is superior to Miller's"? Should the software producers state "People prefer WordPerfect to WordStar two to one"? Some experts believe ads that directly compare the client's product to the competitor's product are very effective, whereas others believe these ads just confuse consumers and even advertise the *other* brand (Ogilvey, 1983).

As with other message characteristics, the impact of one-sided versus two-sided messages depends on the context: Who is the audience, are they involved in the topic, and do they already have a preference? In general, a one-sided message is best only when the audience is relatively gullible, already agrees with you, and doesn't know that an alternative position could reasonably be taken (Hovland et al., 1949).

If a two-sided communication is chosen, be careful when deciding how to order the presentation of the two sides. Imagine you are running for public office, and a debate has been scheduled for broadcast two days before the election. During the debate you and your opponent will each present your views in a 15-minute speech. If you are given a choice, should you present your

▲ **FIGURE 8-7**
Rhetorical questions are always effective, aren't they? As the ELM predicts, rhetorical questions are more effective than regular summaries provided the message presents strong arguments and the audience is not personally involved in the topic under discussion. If the listeners are already involved and the arguments are strong, then a standard summary is more effective. (From Petty, Cacioppo, & Heesacker, 1981)

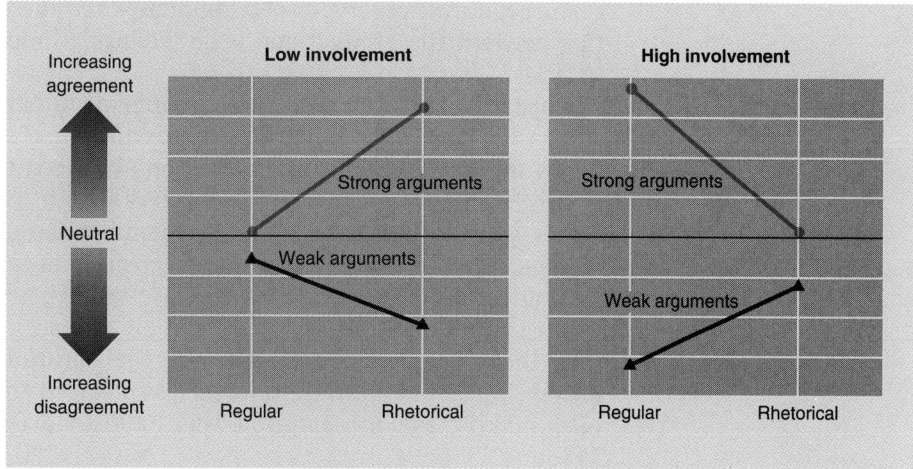

Increasing agreement
Neutral
Increasing disagreement
Low involvement
Strong arguments
Weak arguments
Regular
Rhetorical
High involvement
Strong arguments
Weak arguments
Regular
Rhetorical

views first or second? If a *primacy effect* occurs, then you will be more influential if you go first. If, however, a *recency effect* occurs, then you will garner more votes if you speak second.

Timing appears to be a critical variable in determining when primacy and recency effects will emerge (Miller & Campbell, 1959). If your audience voted immediately after the speeches, order would be unimportant; both views would be remembered equally well. Conversely, if the audience voted many months after the debate, again no order effects would be found because both messages would have been forgotten. However, if the speeches are given back to back and the vote (or measurement) is taken after a delay of only two or three days (as in the example), then a primacy effect is obtained—the first speech has a stronger impact. Furthermore, to obtain a recency effect, there should be a moderately long delay between the first and second speeches, and the vote should be taken soon after the second speech is presented.

Appeals to emotions. David Martin (1989) believes that the best advertisements are those that appeal to our basic emotions and motivations. Show parents with their happy children, friends relaxing, birthday celebra-

▲ The American Cancer Society uses many advertising methods to warn Americans about the dangers of smoking. Are messages that arouse fears more effective than milder messages?

PREGNANT MOTHERS:
PLEASE DON'T SMOKE!
If you are pregnant or planning a family, here are three good reasons to quit smoking now:
1. Smoking retards the growth of your baby in your womb.
2. Smoking increases the incidence of infant mortality.
3. Your family needs a healthy mother.
Please don't smoke for your baby's sake. And yours.
AMERICAN CANCER SOCIETY

tions, beautiful scenery, or cute animals—*and* the product. Create an association between the product and good feelings. "Emotion works," Martin states (p. 134).

Appeals to emotions take the peripheral rather than the central route to persuasion. Instead of carefully considering whether or not Coke will make us happy or Pampers will cement the bond between us and our baby, we let the positive feelings generated by the ads taint our attitudes about the product. When women read a factual set of recommendations for a particular brand of aspirin, the correlation between their positive thoughts about the product and their attitudes toward the product was +.35. They were processing the claims in the central route. When they read an ad that appealed to their emotions, their thoughts about the product and their attitudes about the product were uncorrelated. The message nonetheless changed their attitudes, provided the man making the presentation was handsome (Pallak, Murroni, & Koch, 1983).

fear appeals
Persuasive messages that frighten listeners by warning them of the dire consequences that will occur if proffered recommendations are not followed.

Negative emotions, such as fear, can also change our attitudes. Many public service announcements aimed at changing our attitudes toward unhealthy activities—such as cigarette smoking, drinking and driving, unprotected sex, and drug use—make use of **fear appeals**—persuasive messages that warn of dire consequences if recommendations are not followed. Frightening letters sent by physicians to their patients outlining the hazards of smoking goaded 30% of them into trying to quit, whereas nonthreatening letters garnered only 8% compliance with the doctors' requests (Wilson, Kaplan, & Schneiderman, 1987; Wilson, Purdon, & Wallston, 1988). Smokers who sat through a lecture on the dangers of smoking that included a film clip showing surgeons removing a cancerous lung from a smoker were far more likely to report a strong desire to stop smoking than those who saw an innocuous lecture and film clip (Leventhal, Watts, & Pagano, 1967; see also Leventhal & Niles, 1965; Leventhal, Singer, & Jones, 1965).

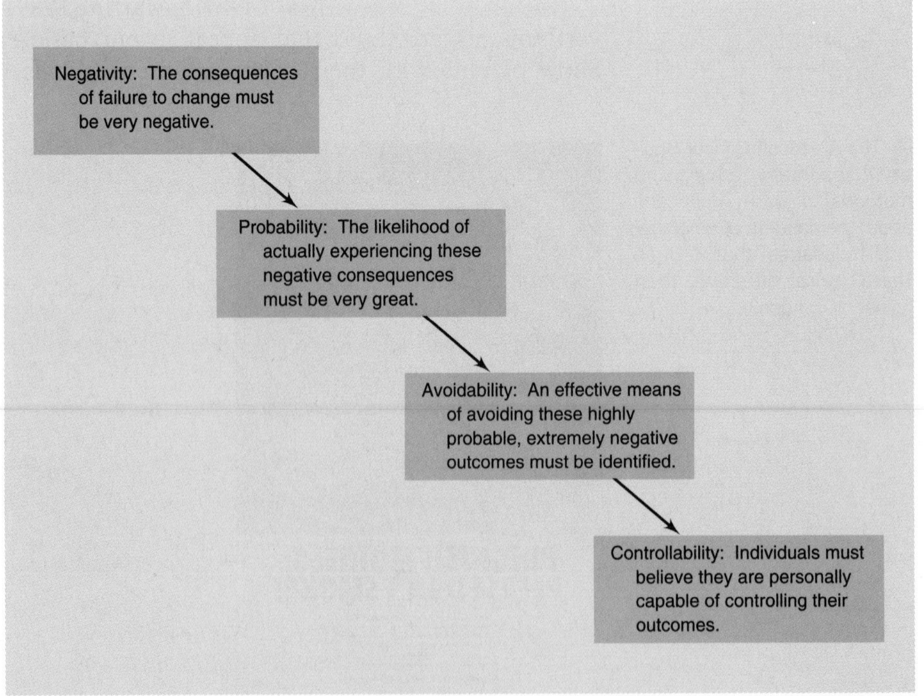

Negativity: The consequences of failure to change must be very negative.
Probability: The likelihood of actually experiencing these negative consequences must be very great.
Avoidability: An effective means of avoiding these highly probable, extremely negative outcomes must be identified.
Controllability: Individuals must believe they are personally capable of controlling their outcomes.

▲ **FIGURE 8-8**
When are fear appeals effective in stopping people from performing self-injurious actions? A successful fear appeal must convince the target person that the consequences are negative, probable, avoidable, but controllable. Without all four ingredients, the fear appeal is likely to fail. (Adapted from Rogers & Mewborn, 1976)

Simply scaring people is not always the best way to persuade them. People who smoke heavily may become so upset by anti-smoking advertisements that they cope by not thinking as much about the message or the problem. Smokers might also be much more critical of the arguments presented in threatening messages. More so than nonsmokers, they would be more likely to point out the flaws in the research cited in the ad or the quality of the writing (Liberman & Chaiken, 1992).

These persuasion-inhibiting reactions can be minimized if the message offers the listener hope for avoiding the threat. According to the *protection-motivation model* illustrated in Figure 8-8, a fear-inducing message must include four basic elements (Rogers, 1983). First, the message must make it clear to listeners that the consequences of their failure to change the attitude or the behavior will be very negative. Second, listeners must believe that the likelihood of these negative consequences will be very great if they do not accept the message. Third, the source must outline actions listeners can take to prevent the negative consequences. Last, listeners must feel they are capable of performing the recommended actions. An advertisement that describes with grim examples and statistics the dangers of AIDS, for example, should also describe ways to minimize the risk of contracting the disease (Struckman-Johnson et al., 1990). A public-service announcement about crime should tell people what steps they can take as individuals to avoid being victims (Gleicher & Petty, 1992). If the message only threatens and doesn't reassure, then the listener will become defensive and ignore the communication (Robberson & Rogers, 1988; Self & Rogers, 1990).

The Receiver

We select an excellent source person and carefully design the persuasive message to take into account the various qualities summarized in Table 8-4. Yet some members of the audience show no change in attitude. Why? Because persuasion does not depend on the source and the message alone, but also on the characteristics of the audience.

Self-esteem and intelligence. Who are easier to persuade: People with low self-esteem or those who are self-confident? Clever people or dull people? For many years researchers puzzled over these questions, for some studies indicated that self-esteem enhanced persuasion, but others found no correlation between these variables. Studies of persuasion and intelligence were equally perplexing (McGuire, 1968).

William J. McGuire (1985) offered an explanation for the inconsistency. McGuire noted that self-esteem and intelligence may influence two of the key elements of the persuasion process identified by the Yale researchers: *reception* and *yielding*. If listeners can't understand what is being said, or they refuse to yield to the arguments presented in the message, then they probably won't change their opinions. McGuire recognized that people with high self-esteem or high intelligence probably have clearer reception of the message, but they are less likely to yield to it. In contrast, those with low self-esteem or low intelligence might not be able to understand the arguments as well, but they will be more likely to yield.

Researchers recently tested McGuire's explanation by carrying out a meta-analytic review of 57 studies of persuasion (Rhodes & Wood, 1992). The investigators discovered that people who were average in their level of self-esteem—neither very high nor very low—tended to be more persuadable. Individuals with low self-esteem were less likely to remember the message, those with high self-esteem were less likely to accept the message, but those with average self-esteem remembered the message and yielded to it. In general, brighter people were less easily persuaded compared to duller people, but the researchers couldn't tell whether people of average intelligence were the most persuadable because very few researchers had identified people of high, moderate, and low intelligence. Future studies will no doubt examine this question more thoroughly.

Sex. Why did the snake ask Eve rather than Adam to try the apple? Did the snake know—on the basis of its very limited experience with humans—that women tend to be more persuadable than men? Studies of persuasion and conformity in groups substantiate the snake's choice (Eagly, 1978). In her review of 62 persuasion studies that included both men and women, Alice Eagly (1978) notes that 82% of the studies reported no differences due to gender, women were more easily persuaded than men in 16% of the studies, and men were more persuadable than women in only 2% of the studies. The differences between men's and women's persuadableness are not very large, but they are relatively consistent.

A number of explanations have been advanced to account for these differences. First, in many cultures, the feminine sex role stresses concurrence-seeking and the masculine sex role stresses independence. In such cultures women, by tradition, are supposed to be more easily influenced, whereas we expect independence and resistance from men (Eagly, 1978). Second, some evidence suggests that women may process persuasive messages more thoroughly than men. So long as the arguments presented are cogent ones, this elaboration should result in women's changing their attitudes more than men (Meyers-Levy & Sternthal, 1991). Third, women and men may use their public expressions of attitudes to create different impressions. A man may refuse to change his attitude because he wants other people to think he is independent and uncompromising. Women, in contrast, may claim that they have changed their opinions so they can appear cooperative and sensible. Relative to men, women are more likely to vary their expressed opinions in order to match the views of attractive male partners (Tuthill & Forsyth, 1982; Zanna & Pack, 1975). Last, Eagly (1978) believes that methodological problems may exaggerate the magnitude of the sex difference. Researchers often study topics that men are more familiar with than women, so women may have suffered from "an information deficit relative to males" (p. 97). Indeed, studies conducted by men tend to find that women are the more persuadable sex (Cooper, 1979; Eagly & Carli, 1981).

Age. Sales promotions for tobacco products and alcoholic beverages often target one particular population—young people. Cigarette ads feature young people who seem to find smoking socially rewarding. One company even uses a cartoon camel that says things like "I'm one cool camel." Beer promotions, too, are youth oriented, for most of the major brewers advertise in college newspapers, sponsor sporting events and rock concerts, and flood the airwaves with advertisements during spring break. Youthful consumers are considered by advertisers to be easy targets, for they are not yet locked into any particular brand. Thirty-year-olds have a favorite cigarette or beer, but 20-year-olds are thought to be formulating their attitudes and brand loyalties. Critics write: "Advertising to young people is more than just appealing to existing drinkers. Rather, youth marketing is the business of creating drinkers and brand allegiances" (Jacobson, Atkins, & Hacker, 1983, p. 49).

▲ **TABLE 8-4**
Summing up: Message factors that influence persuasion

Message Factors	*Impact on Persuasion*
Argument strength	Persuasive messages that contain cogent arguments, supporting documentation, testimonials, and research data are more persuasive than weak messages. Multiple arguments will increase the persuasiveness of a message if they stimulate pro-message thoughts and the listener assumes that length equals strength.
Message repetition	Repeating a persuasive message several times usually leads to increased attitude change. Excessive repetition during a short period of time can, however, generate more anti-message thoughts and attitudes.
Speech rate	A message that is delivered at a rapid rate is usually more persuasive than one that is delivered slowly. Fast talkers are often thought to be more intelligent and better informed, and rapid speech may inhibit counterarguing.
Rhetorical questions	Summarizing arguments with rhetorical questions is an effective way to increase the audience's involvement in the discussion provided a strong case has been made. If people are already interested, rhetorical questions interfere with their comprehension and lead to less persuasion.
One or two sides	One-sided messages are more persuasive when the audience is sympathetic to the position argued and uninformed about alternative positions. When two equally strong messages are presented to a neutral audience, the first position will be more persuasive (a primacy effect) if attitudes are assessed after a brief delay. The second position will be more persuasive (a recency effect) if the second message is delayed and attitudes are assessed soon afterwards.
Appeals to emotions	Messages that induce positive feelings in listeners are often effective even though they don't generate any pro-message thinking. Threatening messages designed to change attitudes by reminding listeners of potential dangers (fear appeals) are most effective when they also identify strategies listeners can personally use to avoid or minimize the danger.

Are younger people more easily swayed by persuasive messages? And once they endorse a position, are they likely to retain that attitude as they age? Newcomb's (1943) Bennington College study, discussed in Chapter 6, supported the *impressionable-years hypothesis*. Not only did many women change their attitudes during their college years, but many still endorsed these same attitudes years later (Newcomb et al., 1967). Other studies suggest that the impressionable years may last into the 30s, but by the time we reach the mid-30s, our attitudes may be as stable as they will ever be. When researchers examined people's political attitudes several times during a four-year period, they found more stability in older people's attitudes than in younger people's attitudes. Stability, as Figure 8-9 indicates, peaked by the age of 34 and remained stable into the 80s (Krosnick & Alwin, 1989; Zaller, 1987).

Even though attitude stability appears to be the hallmark of maturity, the mature person isn't necessarily a rigid person. Each day we learn new information, hear new ideas, and experience new things, and our attitudes often change to reflect these experiences. When researchers measured people's attitudes toward the police and court system in 1984 and again in 1985, they found that the correlation between 1984 attitudes and 1985 attitudes was about .22 for young people and .45 for older people. These findings indicated

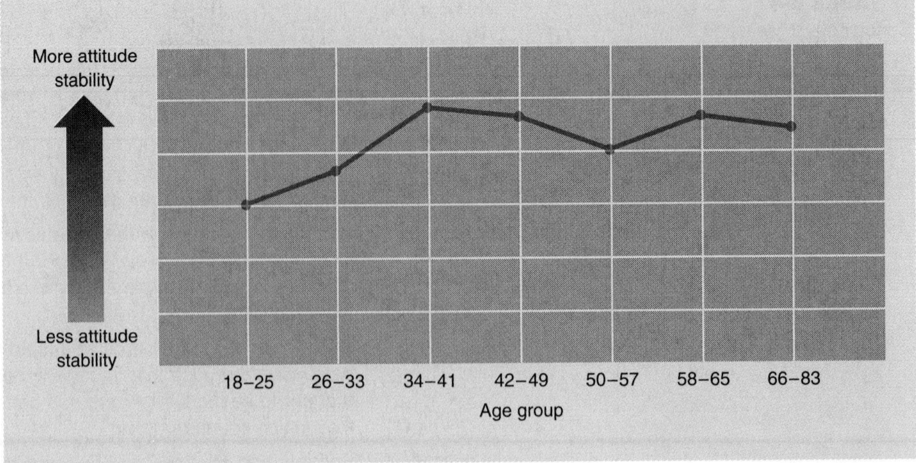

▲ **FIGURE 8-9**
As we grow older, do we pass through periods when we are more impressionable and periods when our attitudes no longer change? People who ranged in age from 18 to 25 had less stable attitudes than older people, as did people in the 26-to-33 age group. However, once people reached age 34, their attitudes stabilized and didn't show much change over time. (Data based on Krosnick & Alwin, 1989)

that older people's attitudes were more stable than young people's attitudes. Both the old and the young, however, changed their attitudes when they had experienced direct exposure to the police or legal system during the time period between the two measures. People who had gotten a quick response from the police when they called, for example, became more positive, whereas those who had been stopped by the police for speeding tended to become more negative. These findings suggest that, even though older individuals' attitudes are more stable, we are open to new experiences all our lives (Tyler & Schuller, 1991; see also Alwin, Cohen, & Newcomb, 1991).

Self-monitoring and persuasion. Advertisers often distinguish between image-oriented and quality-oriented advertising. The image-oriented approach uses vivid images to emphasize the product and highlight the positive effects of using it. Levi's commercials, for example, depict interesting people wearing their jeans, and Calvin Klein intrigues the viewer with his underwear advertisements. The quality-oriented approach, in contrast, emphasizes the quality of the product. IBM ads, for example, discuss in great detail their computers' many fine features, such as expendability and compatibility (DeBono & Packer, 1991; Snyder & DeBono, 1985).

Which kind of advertisement influences you most? Do you pay more attention to a TV commercial that promises a deodorant will enhance your lifestyle, or one that argues the product will keep you dry and odorless? Are you more influenced by an advertisement that shows people relaxing over a beer or one that emphasizes the exacting standards that are used in brewing the product? Mark Snyder and Kenneth G. DeBono (1985) believe that individual differences in self-monitoring provide an answer. Self-monitors, as discussed in Chapter 2, strive to tailor their behavior to the demands of the situation. They want to be the right person in the right place at the right time, so they pay more attention to ads that tell them how they can achieve an acceptable image. Low self-monitors, in contrast, prefer to act in ways that are consistent with their personal tastes and preferences. Therefore, they pay more attention to quality-oriented advertising.

Snyder and DeBono tested their hypothesis by asking high and low self-monitoring subjects to evaluate image-oriented and quality-oriented advertisements. One advertisement for Irish Mocha Mint coffee depicted a man and woman drinking coffee in a candlelit room. The image-oriented ad included the statement, "Make a chilly night become a cozy evening with Irish Mocha

Mint." The quality-oriented ad stated, "Irish Mocha Mint: A delicious blend of three great flavors—coffee, chocolate, and mint" (Snyder & DeBono, 1985, p. 589). Sure enough, high self-monitors reacted more favorably to the image ads, and low self-monitors preferred the quality ads. High self-monitors reported that they would be willing to spend an average of $3.43 on the product shown in the image-sell ad but only $3.28 for the product in the quality-image ad. The reverse held true for low self-monitors. They would be willing to pay, on average, $2.97 for the product after seeing an image-oriented ad but $3.50 after seeing a quality-oriented ad. As with any form of persuasion, the nature of the message was important, but so were the characteristics of the receiver.

The need for cognition. Not everyone enjoys following the arguments in a political debate, solving intellectual puzzles, or spending time thinking deep thoughts. Indeed, Cacioppo and Petty (1982) believe that people differ in how thoughtful (taken literally to mean "full of thought") they are. Some are high in the **need for cognition**. They pride themselves on their mental abilities, prefer tasks that are intellectually challenging, and prefer watching educational programs to watching entertaining programs. They tend to agree with such statements as

need for cognition
A personality dimension that describes differences in the extent to which individuals devote cognitive resources to the analysis of problems, arguments, and decisions.

- I really enjoy a task that involves coming up with new solutions to problems.
- I believe that if I think hard enough, I will be able to achieve my goals in life.
- I am very optimistic about my mental abilities.
- I would prefer a task that is intellectual, difficult, and important to one that is somewhat important but does not require much thought.
- I take pride in the products of my reasoning.

Others, however, believe that ignorance is bliss: They avoid tasks that require deliberate thought and don't spend much time contemplating life's deeper riddles. They usually agree with such statements as

- When something I read confuses me, I just put it down and forget it.
- Learning new ways to think doesn't excite me very much.
- I have difficulty thinking in new and unfamiliar situations.
- I only think as hard as I have to.

Petty, Cacioppo, and their colleagues have confirmed that people with a high need for cognition differ in their tendency to process persuasive messages centrally rather than peripherally. When shown a persuasive message, people who are high in the need for cognition extracted and recalled more information from both high- and low-quality arguments than low scorers did. People with a high need for cognition also put forth more effort in analyzing the argument, and they were also more influenced by a high-quality argument (Cacioppo, Petty, & Morris, 1983). And once people with a high need for cognition form an attitude, they are less likely subsequently to change that attitude when they receive more information (Haugtvedt & Petty, 1992).

Mood. As noted earlier in the chapter, advertisers often design their messages so as to create good feelings in the listener. They assume that a person who is in a good mood is also a person who will be easily persuaded. Indeed, attitudes change more when researchers directly manipulate listeners' moods by showing them emotion-producing slides or serving them snacks and sodas during the speech (Biggers & Pryor, 1982; Schwarz, Bless, & Bohner, 1991).

Moods connect to persuasion at several levels. First, as ELM suggests, your mood may function as a peripheral cue that triggers rapid acceptance or rejection of the message. A person who is feeling good may conclude, "I agree with what you say," whereas a person who feels grouchy would be more likely to respond, "I don't think you are right" (Petty, Gleicher, & Baker, 1991). Second, moods may influence our thinking when we consider the arguments offered in the message. During cognitive elaboration, a happy person may generate more pro-message thoughts, whereas an unhappy person may generate more anti-message thoughts (Breckler & Wiggins, 1991; Petty et al., 1993). Third, moods may generate irrelevant thoughts that interfere with the ability to process complex arguments. People who were in a good mood, for example, changed their attitudes to agree with an essay even when the essay presented weak arguments, apparently because they couldn't process the essays thoroughly. If, however, they were given an unlimited amount of time to read the essay, then they could distinguish between a strong essay and a weak one (Mackie & Worth, 1989).

Original attitudinal position. You are concerned about Alicia, a friend of yours who smokes two packs of cigarettes a day. When you talk to Alicia about your concern, you discover that she doesn't think smoking is particularly harmful. In fact, on an 11-point scale where −5 is extremely harmful and +5 is not harmful at all, she is a +1. If you want to change Alicia's attitude, what position should you take during subsequent discussions of the issue? Should you take a very extreme stance (say, a −3) in the hope that the two of you can reach a compromise position that satisfies you? Or should you select arguments that are closer to Alicia's view (say, about 0 or −1) so you can be sure they won't be rejected out of hand?

social judgment theory
A theoretical analysis that argues attitude change depends on the magnitude of the discrepancy between the listener's original attitude position and the position advocated in the message.

Social judgment theory (Sherif & Hovland, 1961; Sherif & Sherif, 1967; Sherif, Sherif, & Nebergall, 1965) offers one possible answer to your dilemma. According to this approach, Alicia's own attitude serves as an anchor or standard by which she judges incoming persuasive communications. If the discrepancy between her attitude and your message is small, then *assimilation* will take place, and your arguments will be accepted. If, however, the discrepancy between Alicia's attitude and the message is great, then a *contrast effect* will occur; your −3 argument will be seen as very extreme and unreasonable.

As Figure 8-10 indicates, assimilation usually occurs when the message falls in the hearer's *latitude of acceptance*—the area that includes all attitudes Alicia finds acceptable. This area includes Alicia's preferred position and other attitudes that aren't so different from hers that she dismisses them. A contrast effect, on the other hand, occurs when the message falls in the *latitude of rejection.* This area includes all attitudes that Alicia finds objectionable; messages in this area are so discrepant from hers that she will reject them. The buffer area between acceptance and rejection is known as the *latitude of noncommitment*; messages within this range result in neither assimilation nor contrast. Thus, to achieve maximal attitude change, the discrepancy between your arguments and Alicia's initial attitudes should be as great as possible, but your message must still fall within the latitude of acceptance. Hence a communication advocating a position of −1 would be ideal. Beyond −1, the message would become less and less effective, and if you used an extreme antismoking argument (−5), you might even produce a boomerang effect; Alicia might become even more convinced that cigarettes are not harmful (Johnson & Eagly, 1989, 1990).

Persuasion and Change

Attitude change, David Martin explains, is a complex business. So complex, in fact, that many programs of persuasion fail to succeed. Imagine, for example,

▲ **FIGURE 8-10**
Will a message that is too distant from our personal opinion be influential, or will we reject it out of hand? Social judgment theory suggests that Alicia would be willing to listen to arguments within a range of ±2 points because they fall within her latitude of acceptance but would reject arguments that are too positive or negative.

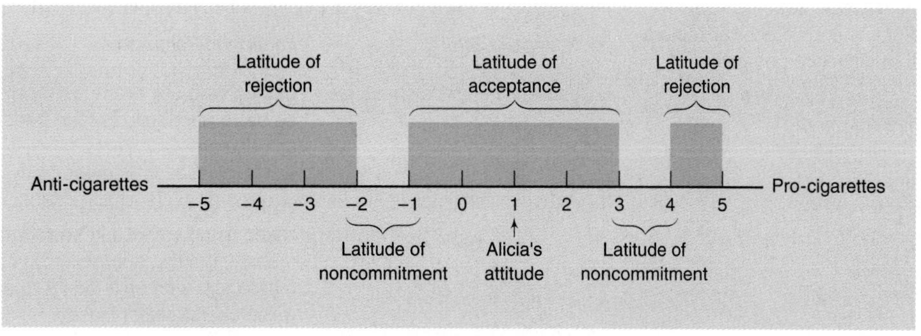

that you teach in a high school. Shocked by the prevalence of drug use among your students, you decide to conduct a series of lectures emphasizing the dangers of drugs. Unfortunately, at the end of your program of lectures you discover that the students seem to be even more interested in illegal drugs than they were before. Why? What did you do wrong?

First, who was the source of the communication? As a teacher, are you a very credible source? What do you know about the effects of marijuana, crack, steroids, or heroin? And can you be trusted to give accurate information about drugs? After all, you are an adult and therefore you may be presumed to be biased against anything that appeals primarily to the young, whether it is drugs, rock and roll, or new hairstyles. Furthermore, inasmuch as your age makes you a dissimilar source, won't students tend to dismiss your information and rely instead on the facts and opinions they get from their peers, who are more similar and more attractive to them?

Second, you may not have put together an effective message. At a fundamental level, your lectures may have been boring, difficult to understand, unconvincing, and unmemorable. For example, your slow rate of speech may have implied that you didn't know what you were talking about. Perhaps after building a weak argument against alcohol use, you closed with the rhetorical question "Now doesn't it make sense that you should never drink booze?" and all the students said "No." Even though you know students realize that some people advocate the legalization of marijuana, you presented only the negative side of the argument. Finally, your arguments may not have been organized effectively, and by telling students that "sometimes, in some cases, drug abuse leads to some highly negative consequences," you misused fear appeals.

Third, consider the audience factors listed in Table 8-5. Did you overlook the characteristics of your audience—their intelligence, self-esteem, and sex? In addition, your arguments may have been too extreme, so they fell into the listener's latitude of rejection. When you argued against marijuana, for example, you might have created such a contrast effect that your message was viewed as extreme and unreasonable. Then, when you presented information about more dangerous drugs, these messages were also discounted. Like the would-be persuaders described in the section "In Depth: Coercive Persuasion," you might think your techniques are so powerful that your listeners will be forced to change, but you may fail to persuade nonetheless.

Resisting Persuasion

People aren't patsies. They can't be readily manipulated into discarding their current attitudes and taking on new ones. Indeed, loyalty to particular brands

▲ TABLE 8-5
Summing up: Receiver factors that influence persuasion

Receiver Factors	*Impact on Persuasion*
Intelligence and self-esteem	People who are average in their level of self-esteem tend to be more persuadable than people with very high or very low self-esteem. Decreases in intelligence tend to be associated with increases in persuadability, but results are not uniform.
Sex	Women's greater persuadability relative to men has been linked to differences in socialization, the nature of the topics studied, women's superior comprehension of persuasive messages, women's desire to appear adaptable, and researchers' sexist biases.
Age	People are more impressionable during the ages 18 and 25 and less impressionable once they reach the age of 35. Direct experiences, however, continue to influence attitudes throughout life.
Self-monitoring	Because high self-monitors strive to tailor their behavior to the demands of the situation, they are more influenced by image-oriented messages. Low self-monitors are more persuaded by quality-oriented messages.
Need for cognition	People who are high in the need for cognition respond more thoughtfully to persuasive messages. The higher one's need for cognition, the more likely one will process messages in the central rather than peripheral route.
Mood	People are more easily persuaded when they are in a good rather than neutral mood. Good moods can, in certain conditions, limit individuals' ability to distinguish between strong and weak persuasive messages.
Original attitude	Messages that argue for positions that are too discrepant from the listener's attitudes are not persuasive. Social judgment theory argues that persuasive messages that fall into the listener's latitude of acceptance will influence the listener, but that no persuasion will occur if the messages fall in the listener's latitude of rejection.

is the rule rather than the exception in sales. Consumers return to purchase the same soups (Campbell), tires (Goodyear), flour (Gold Medal), film (Kodak), chewing gum (Wrigley), and soap (Ivory) year after year. Despite billions of dollars in advertising, we remain resolute in our attitudes. What factors protect our attitudes from influence?

Reactance

Advertisers usually just ask the viewer, in a polite way, to purchase their product. Rarely do they go beyond pleading to pressuring, for they realize that strong-arm tactics usually backfire. The ad that insists "Don't delay, order now," the speaker who rants "If you agree with me on this issue, then you must vote for me for president," and parents who tell their children "I forbid you to put green dye in your hair" are all perilously close to arousing **reactance** in their listeners (Clee & Wicklund, 1980).

reactance
A complex emotional and cognitive reaction that occurs when individuals feel that their freedom to make choices has been threatened or eliminated.

Reactance, as described by Jack Brehm (1966; Brehm & Brehm, 1981), is the feeling that one's freedom to choose has been threatened or eliminated. Whenever we experience reactance, we strive to regain a feeling of autonomy, often by overcoming the source of the threat. Therefore, if someone tries too hard to persuade us, we may refuse to change our attitudes, or we may even move in the opposite direction (a boomerang effect). People were less likely to

IN DEPTH

Coercive Persuasion

When the Korean War ended in 1953, the Chinese government liberated 3,500 U.S. servicemen they had captured during the struggle. Some of the liberated soldiers, however, refused to return to the United States. Why? Had the Chinese used some mysterious method of persuasion to manipulate their minds?

When Edgar H. Schein (1956, 1961) interviewed many former prisoners of war (POWs), he discovered that the Chinese had, in fact, used systematic indoctrination techniques to alter the prisoners' attitudes. The Chinese referred to their program as *hsi nao,* which literally means "to cleanse the mind." Americans called it brainwashing. Schein, however, felt that *brainwashing* was much too strong a term because the methods the Chinese used were neither unique nor exotic. Rather, the Chinese simply combined many commonplace methods into a single, unified attempt to change attitudes. Schein called this program **coercive persuasion,** for it relied on psychologically compelling techniques to change individuals' attitudes against their will.

The Chinese indoctrination strategy involved three basic phases. First, the Chinese sought to disrupt, or *unfreeze,* the POWs' current attitudes and values. The second phase involved *changing* these attitudes to conform with communist doctrine. In the final phase, new attitudes were ingrained within the POWs' overall value system. Schein calls this phase *refreezing.* To begin the unfreezing process, the Chinese subjected the men to physical hardships and stressful psychological pressures. Many of the men were forced to march for days with very little food or rest. Conditions at the camp were not much better, for the prisoners slept in huts with dirt floors, ate mostly cereals and soup, and had no access to medical facilities. These privations, which left them weak and disoriented, were reinforced by the disruption of their social relationships. The Chinese routinely undermined all relationships among the POWs. They disrupted military organization by separating the officers and enlisted men. They broke up any friendships that developed by transferring the men involved. They undermined trust among the prisoners by placing informers in each living area. No religious ceremonies were permitted, and letters from home were withheld so that bonds with loved one were also disrupted. Many of the men became convinced that only letters containing bad news were delivered.

In this second phase, the Chinese also relied on both direct and indirect techniques to change the prisoners' attitudes. Each day the POWs attended two- or three-hour classes on the basic philosophy of communism. The material also included attacks on American values, criticisms of the United Nations, and pro-communist propaganda films. Whenever possible, the men were also exposed to pro-communist testimonials given by fellow POWs: speeches on the benefits of communism, readings of pro-communist essays, public confessions to various war crimes. The Chinese repeatedly claimed, for example, that the UN forces were using germ warfare. Prisoners were told an international commission was investigating the problem, and the Chinese showed movies of Americans confessing to war crimes. They also coerced several U.S. Air Force officers into visiting each camp and explaining why germ warfare was used.

These direct persuasion tactics were relatively ineffective. The teachers were English-speaking Chinese, so their credibility was doubtful. Also, the information about America was often inaccurate and easy to refute. In fact, because the Chinese relied primarily on the works of Mao Tse-tung, men who were familiar with Karl Marx's writings were able to challenge the teachers on the communist principles they were discussing. The testimonials, in contrast, had a great impact on the men. Because they came from fellow POWs, the source was much more credible. These testimonials also undermined social supports for the prisoners' attitudes. When they banded together to reject the communist arguments, their unity reinforced their convictions. The testimonials destroyed this unity.

Just as the direct techniques of the Chinese relied heavily on persuasive methods, the indirect techniques they used were consistent with studies of cognitive dissonance (Festinger, 1957; see Chapter 6). Time and again the men were coerced into performing pro-communist actions. Often these actions were inconsequential, such as copying an essay out of a notebook or answering some questions about life in the United States. Once the men agreed to a minor request, a more significant request followed. And the Chinese insisted on some kind of active response, either written or oral. One technique required the men to discuss political questions, such as "Is the aim of the capitalist nations world domination?" After each discussion, the men were asked to write out their answer to the question. If they answered "incorrectly" (by challenging the communist doctrine), the entire group repeated the exercise. Eventually, the men decided that little harm could be done if they answered the questions the way their captors wanted. Each small concession led to a slightly larger one until the men unwittingly found themselves collaborating with the Chinese. In some cases, using such simple methods, the Chinese succeeded in extracting confessions to war crimes and pledges of allegiance to communism. (Chapter 9 contains more information on these social influence techniques.)

The Chinese also tried to create cognitive inconsistencies through interrogation. These sessions could last for days or even weeks as the Chinese questioned the men about their basic values and attitudes. After examining their prisoners' civilian lives in detail, the Chinese

coercive persuasion: Psychologically compelling techniques designed to change individuals' attitudes against their will.

would claim that many of the prisoners' past problems were caused by flaws in the capitalist system. They described the Korean conflict as a civil war and asked the men how they would have felt if a foreign power had intervened in the American Civil War. With these tactics, the interrogators often succeeded in convincing the men that U.S. involvement in Korea was inconsistent with principles of fairness.

In the final phase, men who cooperated with the Chinese were asked to make public commitments to communism. They were given jobs to perform around the camp, and they were excused from any unpleasant chores. These men were allowed to form committees that helped run the camp, and they helped prepare propaganda leaflets and testimonials. All in all, these tactics sought to provide social supports for the newly acquired attitudes.

How successful was this program of coercive persuasion? Schein points out that at one time or another nearly all of the men performed actions that helped the enemy. Their collaboration took many forms: Prisoners signed petitions protesting the war, made radio appeals, wrote letters home touting the benefits of communism, posed for misleading photographs, made false confessions, ran errands for the Chinese, and informed on fellow POWs. The Chinese clearly succeeded in disrupting social relations among the prisoners. Discipline and morale were poor, the men rarely attempted to escape, and disloyalty was rampant (Schein, 1961; Segal, 1954).

The Chinese were less successful in creating long-term change. Of the 3,500 POWs, only 21 voluntarily remained in Korea at the end of the war. Most of the others regained their confidence in America once they escaped the influence of the Chinese. Schein concludes that though the Chinese were effective in the first phase of their strategy—they succeeded in disrupting individuals' value systems—they generally failed to change those attitudes or to refreeze attitudes that they did change. Schein believes that most acts of collaboration resulted from the physical and psychological pressures of imprisonment. Living under constant threat of punishment and even death, the men cooperated in small ways. These actions rarely reflected deep changes in political attitudes. In fact, this firsthand experience convinced many of the men that the communists posed a greater threat to American values than they had originally believed.

Schein's intriguing analysis offers many insights into the social foundations of our attitudes and values. We often assume that attitudes are very private and personal, but they often reflect the beliefs accepted by the people around us. When we find ourselves in an entirely new situation, surrounded by people with beliefs that differ from ours, our attitudes may change (Newcomb, 1943). This change, however, is only a temporary one, for when we return to our social network, we revert to our original attitudinal positions.

The concept of coercive persuasion also sheds light on a disturbing contemporary phenomenon—the growth of cults. Many authorities believe that radical religious groups and social movements, such as the Unification Church (Moonies), the International Society for Krishna Consciousness (Hare Krishna), the Divine Light Mission, and the Church of Scientology, use coercive techniques to recruit and retain their members. In accordance with Schein's three-step model, recruits' beliefs are first unfrozen though a series of manipulations: They are deprived of sleep, their diet is altered, and they are persuaded to take part in physically exhilarating activities (Isser, 1991). Supports for their original attitudes are stripped away when they are isolated from parents and friends. Next, new attitudes are created though a series of lectures and discussions. Often these lectures focus on the teaching of a charismatic leader—a David Koresh or a Sun Myung Moon—who is an extremely effective speaker. Induction into the group proceeds through a series of escalating commitments. Compliance with small requests is followed by greater demands, as was the case with the Korean POWs. Last, the emphasis on group living ensures that the newly created attitudes will find strong support within the social group (Ofshe & Singer, 1986).

Radical groups sometimes succeed in exerting considerable control over their members. In 1970, 911 members of the People's Temple followed their leader's order and committed mass suicide. In 1993, 86 men, women, and children died when David Koresh told them to set fire to their besieged compound in Waco, Texas. Yet most such attempts at coercive persuasion fail to create long-lasting change among members (Bromley, 1985; Levine, 1984). Interviews with former group members suggest that they joined a group because they were initially attracted to the alternative lifestyle the group offered. They weren't psychologically seduced by special recruitment tactics. Cult members use strong tactics to control members' actions, but the dropout rate in such groups remains fairly high. By one estimate, 90% of all members leave the group within two years (Levine, 1984). Again, interviews with former members suggest that they became disillusioned with the inconsistency of their leaders' actions, by the group's failure to reach its goals, and by a lifestyle that soon became monotonous. If persuasive techniques were effective, we would expect such groups to retain far more of their members. Interestingly, when ex-members sue their former cult leaders, the courts usually conclude that the recruiters did nothing illegal (Anthony & Robbins, 1992).

People tend to think that cults brainwash their recruits, but the evidence suggests otherwise (Loewenthal, 1986; Pfeifer, 1992). The techniques used are powerful, but no more powerful than those used by advertisers, salespeople, health agencies, and our friends.

> The lure and power of the new religious groups have been exaggerated. The most telling critique of these groups is not that they capture and enslave innocent youth, but that they ultimately have not been able to provide the answers they had hoped for. (Bromley, 1985, p. 15)

change their attitudes to agree with a persuasive message when it ended with the line, "You have no choice but to agree with me" (Worchel & Brehm, 1970). Subjects who were initially offered a choice among several alternatives, but were later told that some of the choices were no longer available, became more positive toward the choices that were threatened (Brehm & Sensenig, 1966). When individuals learned that an essay or speech had been censored, they became more positive toward the position advocated in the censored message (Worchel, Arnold, & Baker, 1975). In general, people are opposed to positive social reforms—such as bans on TV advertising by politicians or mandated taxes on gasoline to prevent pollution—when they feel that these reforms will restrict their behavior in some way (Baron & Jurney, 1993).

Reactance protects our attitudes from overpowering attacks, but clever persuaders can sometimes use reactance to their benefit. The car dealer may insist that you road test the competitor's car before buying, knowing that reactance will make you want to refuse. Some ads, in bold print, state, "Do not read this ad." Naturally, we do. Even therapists occasionally use reactance to help their clients change. **Paradoxical therapy** is a curative technique in which the therapist requires clients to continue experiencing the problems they are trying to eliminate. Depressed individuals, for example, are told to practice feeling depressed. Obese people are told to continue overeating. Those troubled by obsessive thoughts are instructed to ruminate even more. This form of therapy is often effective in treating highly resistant or hard-to-control behaviors such as smoking, insomnia, depression, procrastination, overeating, phobias, or drug addiction. When the therapist attempts to reduce clients' freedom by suggesting they behave in a certain way, clients seek to reestablish their autonomy by responding in the opposite fashion. The more demanding the therapist, the more likely it is that the client will refuse to accept the paradoxical directive (Tennen & Affleck, 1991). The section "Application: The Interface of Social and Clinical Psychology," which concludes this chapter, offers other examples of the application of attitude change principles in therapeutic settings.

paradoxical therapy
A technique used during therapy that involves requiring clients to continue performing the problematic behaviors they are trying to eliminate.

Assimilation and Polarization Processes

A dedicated Chevy truck owner and a dedicated Ford truck owner both watch a news special investigating the strengths and weaknesses of American-made pickup trucks. When it's over, the Chevy owner exclaims, "See, I always knew that Chevy trucks were great." The Ford owner reacts with disbelief. "Are you kidding? They clearly showed that Fords are superior."

Our current attitudes are resistant to change because they color our perceptions of persuasive communications. If we already like Chevrolets, then we will respond to equivocal information that both supports and disconfirms our attitudes selectively. We will embrace the supportive information as persuasive, accurate, and interesting but view the critical information as unpersuasive, inaccurate, and irrelevant. In one study of this **biased assimilation** process, researchers separated people into two groups—those who favored capital punishment and those who were opposed to it. Next, they had both groups of people read the results of several studies that had investigated the impact of capital punishment on criminal behavior. Some of these results suggested that capital punishment was an effective deterrent, but others suggested just the opposite. When the researchers then asked the subjects to critique the various studies, they found clear evidence of biased assimilation (see Figure 8-11). The person who was in favor of capital punishment gave supportive studies high ratings and critical studies low ratings. The person who was against capital punishment did just the opposite (Lord, Ross, & Lepper, 1979).

biased assimilation
The tendency for individuals to accept portions of a communication that match their own attitudes while rejecting portions that do not.

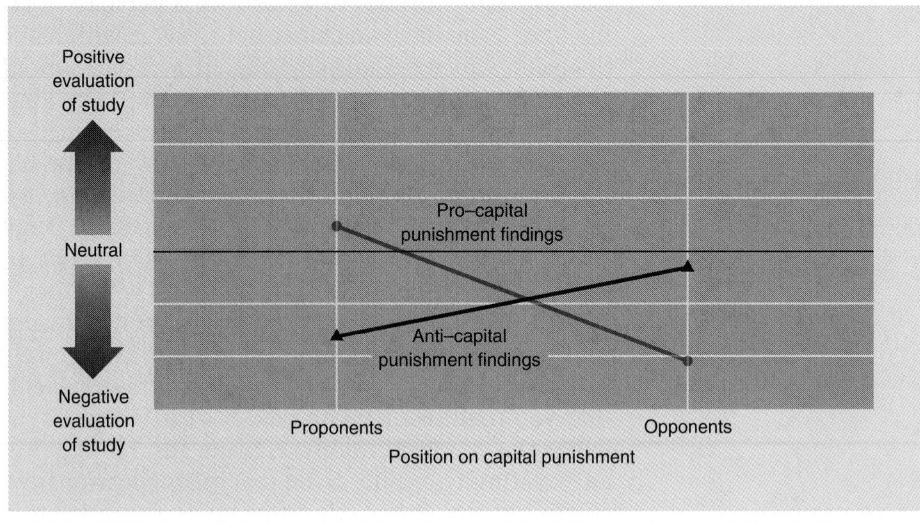

▲ **FIGURE 8-11**
Do we assimilate evidence so that it confirms rather than disconfirms our attitudes? When people who were in favor of or opposed to capital punishment reviewed a series of studies that investigated the effectiveness of capital punishment as a deterrent, they evaluated studies that supported their attitudinal position positively, but criticized studies that conflicted with their position. (Data from Lord, Ross, & Lepper, 1979)

Some researchers believe that this biased assimilation process can strengthen people's attitudes. The Chevy owner who watches the investigative program will think that the pro-Chevy elements are persuasive and may become even more convinced that Chevy trucks are superior. The Ford owner, in contrast, will think that the pro-Ford elements are persuasive and may become even more convinced that Ford trucks are superior. Thus, even though both people see the same program, their different interpretations of the message cause their attitudes to move even further apart. When **attitude polarization** occurs, persuasive messages cause people to become more extreme in the direction of their original attitudes. Hence, the person who was in favor of capital punishment in the first place reported feeling more favorable toward capital punishment after reading the results of studies that were either critical of or favorable to capital punishment. The person who was against capital punishment in the first place, however, reported becoming more negative (Leone, 1989; Millar & Tesser, 1986; Tesser & Shaffer, 1990).

attitude polarization
The tendency for individuals' attitudes to become more extreme after exposure to a message that contains arguments that both support and contradict their attitudes.

The assimilation bias explains why voters who watched the 1992 presidential debates between Bill Clinton and George Bush usually came away feeling as though their candidate won. Democrats were convinced that Clinton did a masterful job, whereas the Republican viewers thought Bush was presidential. Recent research, however, suggests that people tend to overestimate the impact of assimilated messages on their attitudes. When people who were either for capital punishment or against it reviewed studies of the effectiveness of capital punishment, assimilation occurred: People who were already in favor of capital punishment thought the favorable studies were more valid than the critical studies. Moreover, these individuals also felt that their attitudes became more extreme after they read the results of these studies. But measures of their actual attitudes revealed no significant shift. People thought their attitudes had become more extreme, but in reality their attitudes hadn't really changed that much. Polarization is more in the eye of the attitude holder (Miller et al., 1993).

Forewarning

Advertisers sometimes try to take viewers by surprise. Some hide their messages in bogus news stories that purport to be objective reports about a particular product. Others create entire series or programs based on particular products, such as the *Teenage Mutant Ninja Turtles* and "infomercials" in which miraculous new products are discussed. Many of the commercials broadcast on MTV look and sound more like music videos than advertisements.

forewarning
Situational cues that warn listeners of a future attempt to influence their attitudes.

Why the subterfuge? Studies suggest that persuasive messages we anticipate have less impact on us than those that take us unawares. **Forewarning** of persuasive intent gives us the time we need to prepare cognitively for the message. As the ELM suggests, when we know a speaker is trying to change our opinion, we are more likely to process that information through the central route. When we hear the arguments, the cognitive elaboration process is more likely to generate *counterarguments* that refute the incoming information. Forewarning also gives us time to review our own positions on the issue, and if our attitude is readily accessible in memory, then we will be more likely to rely on our personal informational resources rather than on the information from the external source (Krosnick, 1989; Wood, 1982). When it comes to persuasion, to be forewarned is to be forearmed.

Inoculation

Medical inoculations, such as flu shots and smallpox vaccines, work by stimulating the body's natural defense mechanisms. When the organisms that cause the disease are injected into the body in a weakened form, the body reacts by building up protective antibodies. Later, if the inoculated individual is exposed to more virulent forms of the disease-causing organisms, because the defensive antibodies needed to fight the infection have already developed, these antibodies immunize the individual against the disease.

inoculation theory
A theoretical position that hypothesizes resistance to persuasion can be developed by exposing individuals to weak versions of the arguments that will be used by a persuasive communicator.

According to William J. McGuire's **inoculation theory** (1964), resistance to persuasion can also be developed through an inoculationlike process. When the arguments that might be used by a persuasive communicator are presented in a weakened form, receivers defend their beliefs by developing effective counterarguments. When the "immunized" receivers later encounter stronger persuasive messages, they will be less likely to change their attitudes because (1) they have developed cognitive response strategies that facilitate counterarguing, and (2) the experience of successfully defending their attitudes against a weak attack has strengthened their confidence in their own attitudes.

McGuire tested his theory in one study by attacking subjects' acceptance of several cultural truisms—beliefs that are so widely held by a given culture that they are assumed to be true (McGuire & Papageorgis, 1961). McGuire chose the truisms, "You should brush your teeth after every meal" and "Mental illness is not contagious." He believed that very few of the subjects would ever have been asked to defend these beliefs, so they would have trouble spontaneously generating counterarguments to refute arguments that would challenge these beliefs. Like Pacific islanders who died of measles because their isolation prevented them from developing the necessary defenses against it, subjects would lack the counterarguments needed to fend off the unexpected attack. As he predicted, McGuire found that subjects who had been inoculated by a series of weak, easily refutable arguments against the truisms resisted persuasion more than (a) subjects who received no inoculation against a strong attack and (b) subjects who had been given only pro-truism information.

Some of the most outstanding advertising campaigns have used inoculation to strengthen consumers' attitudes. In the 1960s, for example, advertisements for Volkswagens pointed out the limitations of the product, but then offered strong refutations of these minor complaints. These refutations presumably increased consumers' loyalty to the brand (Bither, Dolich, & Nell, 1971;

▲ **TABLE 8-6**
Supportive and refutational appeals used to test the impact of inoculation in advertisements

Product	*Supportive Appeal*	*Refutational Appeal*
Bayer aspirin	Bayer works wonders. Relax with Bayer. Bayer is 100% aspirin.	Buffer it, square it, fizz it . . . nothing has ever improved aspirin. Bayer is 100% aspirin.
Lava soap	For real dirty hands, reach for Lava—the soap that can really clean.	Lava—world's worst bath soap! Lava users have revolted. They argue that Lava is not only a good soap for hands but for anything else, too.
Parker pens	Just one could be all you ever need. At $1.98 it's the best pen value in the world. Up to 80,000 words.	Why pay $1.98 for a ballpoint pen? You can get them for 49¢, 69¢, or for free. The kind that skip, stutter, and run out of ink. You pay $1.98 for a Parker, but you never have to buy another.
Renault automobiles	Sales are climbing. Renault's new features and fine construction are paying off.	Sure, they save money, but I wouldn't want to take a long trip in one. Foreign cars are easy on the wallet but hard on everything else. Renault is changing all that.

Source: Sawyer, 1973.

Szybillo & Heslin, 1973). The wisdom of this strategy was tested in one study in which people were shown ads that mentioned, but then rebutted, the arguments of competitors (refutational ads) or ads that presented only the positive characteristics of the product (supportive ads). When, for example, the target product was Bayer aspirin, the supportive appeal mentioned only the product's positive attributes (see Table 8-6). The refutational appeal, in contrast, subtly suggested some negative characteristics of Bayer—it's not buffered (like Bufferin) and it doesn't fizz (like Alka Seltzer)—but then belittled these characteristics. "Nothing has ever improved aspirin. Bayer is 100% aspirin." The researchers found that people who were already using the advertised brand became more loyal after reading a refutational appeal, and many nonusers reported stronger intentions to switch to the advertised brand after they saw a refutational ad. Thus, overall, refutational ads were more effective than supportive ads (Sawyer, 1973).

Protecting People Against Persuasion

The various processes that work to prevent persuasion, as summarized in Table 8-7, have been used to try to protect people from harmful advertising, from developing health-injurious habits, and from engaging in reckless, dangerous forms of behavior. The Social Psychological Deterrents of Smoking Project, for example, uses inoculation and counterarguing to prevent adolescents from developing positive attitudes toward cigarette smoking. Rather than using direct persuasion, the technique shows 7th graders videotapes of same-age models resisting the temptation to smoke (Evans, 1980, 1984). Segments include demonstrations of students refusing to smoke despite strong pressures by peers, detailed discussions of the dangers of imitating parents' smoking habits, and critiques of advertisers' claims concerning smoking. Testifying to the effectiveness of these interventions, students assigned to a no-information control con-

▲ How can people's resistance to persuasion be bolstered? Many public service messages have been developed to help people resist persuasive advertisements, yet these messages are often presented side by side with the advertisements they are trying to defeat. Can advertising be used to counter the effects of advertising?

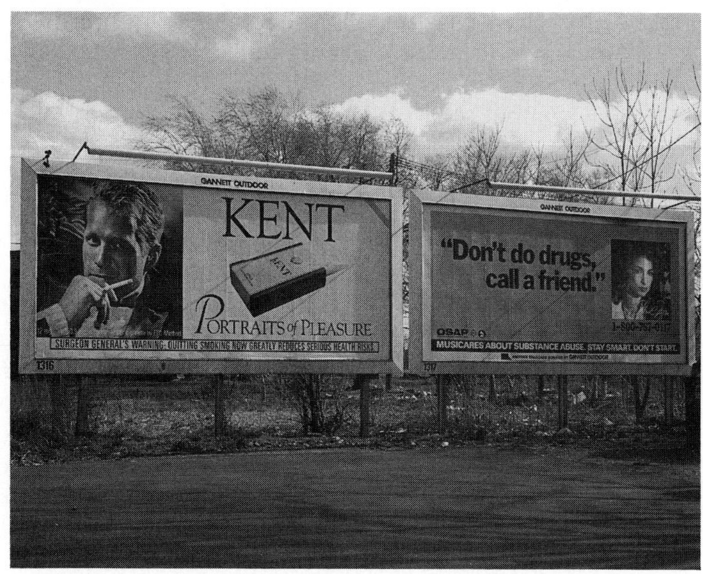

dition were found to be almost twice as likely to begin smoking than students in the experimental conditions.

These findings, and those discussed throughout this chapter, suggest that social psychology offers many suggestions for promoting mental and physical health (Chassin, Presson, & Sherman, 1990). One approach, highlighted in the section "Application: Promoting Healthy Behavior" in Chapter 6, focuses on helping people translate pro-health attitudes into pro-health behaviors. A second approach explains how people in various helping professions can use persuasion techniques to help others change (see the section "Application: The Interface of Social and Clinical Psychology" at the end of this chapter). Social

▲ **TABLE 8-7**
Summing up: Processes that can work to prevent persuasion

Process	*Impact on Persuasion*
Reactance	Reactance is a motivational state that arises when people feel that their freedom has been threatened or eliminated. When persuasive messages arouse their reactance, listeners will strive to regain feelings of autonomy, often by expressing unchanged or more extreme beliefs. Paradoxical therapy is based on reactance.
Biased assimilation	Individuals tend to accept portions of a communication that match their own attitudes, but they reject the portions that do not.
Polarization	After exposure to a message that contains arguments that both support and contradict their attitudes, individuals tend to adopt more extreme rather than more moderate attitudinal positions.
Forewarning	Listeners are less persuaded by messages that they anticipate. Forewarning increases the accessibility of current attitudes and stimulates counterargument.
Inoculation	People who have been exposed to a weakened form of an argument that they successfully repudiated are less likely to be subsequently persuaded by a stronger version of the same argument. McGuire's inoculation theory argues that immunization stimulates counterarguing and increases listeners' confidence in their opinions.

psychology recognizes that health-injurious attitudes and habits can be deeply ingrained, but these health-injurious behaviors can be replaced with health-promoting ones.

Summary

Why do attitudes change? As Chapter 6 explains, in some cases newly learned attitudes supplant older attitudes, or we act in ways that are inconsistent with our old way of looking at things. Often, however, attitude change results from *persuasion*: the communication of facts, arguments, and information intended to change another person's attitudes. The Yale research group's *learning model of persuasion* suggests that persuasion occurs when we notice, understand, accept, and remember information that disconfirms our current attitudes. But persuasion is not always an entirely logical process. Petty and Cacioppo's *elaboration likelihood model* (ELM), for example, distinguishes between the central route and the peripheral route to persuasion. Central route processing requires cognitive elaboration of the message. If this analysis generates favorable thoughts, then people are persuaded; but if the message stimulates negative thoughts, then people's attitudes may strengthen instead (a *boomerang effect*). If people lack the motivation or ability to examine the message closely, they let peripheral cues in the situation influence their attitudes. Similarly, Chaiken and Eagly's *heuristic-systematic model* (HSM) suggests that systematic processing requires careful analysis of the message but that heuristic processing relies on rules of thumb that are accurate enough for most purposes. In general, people who are personally involved in issues process messages centrally or systematically, so they are more influenced by strong arguments. When people aren't that interested in the issue, they are persuaded by less reasonable factors, such as the expertise of the source or the audience's reaction to the message.

When do attitudes change? The Yale researchers believed that the impact of a persuasive message depends on the source, the message, and the receiver—"who says what to whom." First, sources who are credible, attractive, and similar to the listener tend to be more persuasive. Credibility increases whenever the listener believes the source is an expert or can be trusted to give accurate information. Sometimes, after a delay, even a message from a person who isn't credible can influence our attitudes. This *sleeper effect* is caused more by differential decay in the listeners' memories than by the gradual dissociation of the source and the message. People are more easily persuaded by members of their own group.

Second, the message has a major impact on the outcome of persuasive encounter. Strong arguments are more influential than weak ones, and adding more arguments usually strengthens a case. Repeating the message several times and speaking rapidly are also effective persuasion tactics, provided the message is not repeated too frequently or spoken too rapidly. Rhetorical questions and one-sided messages, in contrast, are effective only in rare circumstances. When two opposing messages are presented to the listener, the position presented first outweighs the impact of information presented second (a primacy effect) if only a short amount of time separates the two messages. As the time gap increases, recently presented arguments exert a stronger influence (a recency effect). *Fear appeals,* too, often motivate people to change dangerous attitudes and behavior. These tactics are maximally effective when they describe specific tactics that the listener can use to avoid the danger.

Third, listeners' intelligence, self-esteem, sex, age, personality, and attitudes all play a role in determining their reactions to a persuasive message. Although people who are intelligent and high in self-esteem are more open to well-developed persuasive messages, they are also more confident in their initial opinions. Women are more easily persuaded than men, but this difference probably arises from a number of social, interpersonal, and procedural factors. Age, too, influences one's persuadability, for people are the most impressionable during the ages 18 and 25 and least impressionable once they reach the age of 35. And what about personality? High self-monitors are more influenced by image-oriented messages, and low self-monitors are more persuaded by quality-oriented messages. People who are high in their *need for cognition* tend to process messages systematically, whereas those who are low in the need for cognition are more influenced by peripheral cues rather than the strength of the message. People are more easily persuaded when they are in a good rather than neutral mood. Last, people who hold different attitudes initially respond differently to the same persuasive message. *Social judgment theory,* for example, argues that persuasive messages that fall within the listener's latitude of acceptance or noncommitment will influence the listener, but that no persuasion will occur if the message falls within the listener's latitude of rejection.

What factors inhibit attitude change? In some cases, persuaders may arouse *reactance* in listeners, who then strive to regain feelings of autonomy by expressing unchanged or more extreme beliefs. When, for example, a therapist insists that a client continue feeling depressed, the client may stop experiencing depression. This approach is called *paradoxical therapy.* Attitudes often remain unchanged after we are exposed to information that partially disconfirms them because the listener accepts the positive parts of a message but rejects the parts that are negative. This *biased assimilation* sometimes results in *attitude polarization*: Individuals who are exposed to an ambiguous message adopt more extreme rather than more moderate attitudinal positions. *Forewarning* also undermines the impact of persuasive messages, as does inoculation. *Inoculation theory* assumes that people who have the opportunity to generate counterarguments to a weakened form of an argument will not be persuaded by a stronger version of the same argument.

For More Information

• *Age of Propaganda: The Everyday Use and Abuse of Persuasion,* by Anthony Pratkanis and Elliot Aronson (1991), is an entertaining examination of advertising, the news media, and government propaganda from a social-psychological perspective.

• "Attitudes and Attitude Change," by William J. McGuire (1985), is a chapter in volume 2 of the *Handbook of Social Psychology.* This chapter was written for social psychologists and advanced students and presents the history of research in the field.

• *Coercive Persuasion,* by Edgar H. Schein (1961), presents theory and evidence pertaining to the effectiveness of "illicit" persuasion tactics, such as those used by the Chinese during the Korean War.

• *Handbook of Social and Clinical Psychology: The Health Perspective,* edited by C. R. Snyder and Donelson R. Forsyth (1991), comprehensively surveys current developments at the interface of social and clinical psychology.

• *The Psychology of Attitude Change and Social Influence,* by Philip Zimbardo and Michael R. Leippe (1991), is a lively yet comprehensive analysis of attitudes and why they change.

• *The Psychology of Attitudes,* by Alice Eagly and Shelly Chaiken (1992), is an up-to-date and thorough examination of theory and research in the field of attitude change.

• *Romancing the Brand: The Power of Advertising and How to Use It,* by David Martin (1989), offers dozens of insights into the field of advertising, as viewed through the eyes of an expert.

Application: The Interface of Social and Clinical Psychology

Significant advances often occur in science when researchers in different fields unite in a common effort. When biologists and chemists merged in biochemistry departments and astronomers joined with physicists in the study of astrophysics, these interdisciplinary research teams generated new insights into problems that researchers working independently could not solve. Similar gains are accruing at the boundary between social psychology and such clinically oriented fields as clinical, counseling, and community psychology. Social psychologists have recently joined with these applied researchers and practitioners to explore sources of and solutions for psychological maladjustment. Likewise, psychologists in these applied fields who recognize the role of interpersonal dynamics in adjustment and therapy have begun to synthesize social-psychological principles and clinical practice. This collaborative, cross-disciplinary movement is producing a growing *interface* between psychology's helping professionals and social psychology (Brehm & Smith, 1986; Derlega, Costanzo, & Oliveri, 1991; Higgenbotham, West, & Forsyth, 1988; Leary & Maddux, 1987; Leary & Miller, 1986; Ruble et al., 1992; Weary & Mirels, 1982).

Researchers working at the interface of social and clinical psychology are interested in many aspects of psychological adjustment. Some explore the social and personal processes that help individuals sustain their mental health, such as social support, relationships, and self-esteem. Others are more interested in the factors that undermine the balance between adjustment and maladjustment. Why, they ask, do people become depressed, suicidal, anxious, or drug-dependent? And some researchers focus specifically on treatment by examining the factors that determine clinicians' diagnoses, the therapy process, and the effectiveness of various therapeutic strategies. In each of these areas, investigators rely on social-psychological principles to enhance their understanding of clinically significant processes (Strong et al., 1992).

Consider, for example, social-psychological analyses of the psychotherapeutic process. Some experts think the psychological processes that occur during counseling and psychotherapy are unique, so they cannot be explained by social-psychological principles. Many psychologists, however, think that psychotherapy is a form of applied persuasion. Individuals seek help when they are dissatisfied or frustrated with their current behaviors but don't feel they can resolve these problems without assistance. The therapist takes the role of the psychological expert who suggests interpretations of the client's experiences and ways to deal with current problems. Clients, however, are often unwilling or unable to accept the therapist's help. People who are depressed, for example, may not recognize that their own bleak conceptualization of their problems is contributing to their negative mood, just as alcoholics are often unwilling to admit that their problems stem from their drinking. The successful therapist, then, is one who can persuade the resistant client to accept the therapeutic message (Strong, 1968, 1991a).

If therapists make use of principles of persuasion, then their success will depend on the three factors identified by social psychologists: the therapist (the source), the therapeutic interpretation (the message), and the client (the receiver). Just as certain speakers are more persuasive than others, so some therapists are more effective in influencing their clients. Which therapists are the most persuasive? Those who make use of three types of cues to convince their clients that they are experts, attractive, and competent. *Evidential cues* include primarily nonverbal stimuli such as age, physical appearance, style of dress, office location, and decor. Therapists try to look the part. *Reputational cues* pertain to the therapist's level of experience and expertise and can include degrees, titles, and other professional credentials. Many therapists carefully post their diplomas and certificates so their clients know they have been properly trained. Last, *behavioral cues* include the verbal and nonverbal actions that clients associate with effective and ineffective interventions. Effective therapists conduct sessions in an assured, self-confident manner. They can also increase their impact on their clients by using appropriate and abstract psychological terminology, by asking thought-provoking questions, and by adopting "an attentive, confident, and reassuring manner" (Corrigan et al., 1980, p. 434).

Message factors also determine the outcome of the therapeutic session. When researchers analyzed recordings of therapy sessions, they discovered that therapists respond to clients at several levels. They (a) provide information and guidance, (b) ask a variety of questions, (c) repeat and paraphrase the client's statements, (d) confront the client's interpretations of problems, (e) offer their own interpretation of the causes of the client's problems, and (f) express their approval of and support for the client. Even though clients responded more positively to messages that provided information and approval, questions tended to produce greater reductions in anxiety, and paraphrasing was associated with increases in self-esteem (Hill et al., 1988).

Questioning and paraphrasing may promote change by stimulating change-provoking thought. Specific suggestions and advice may be helpful temporarily, but most therapists believe that long-term change occurs when clients discover the source of their own problems through guided self-exploration. Applications of the elaboration likelihood model (ELM) of persuasion to therapy support this interpretation, for they indicate that messages that stimulate change-provoking thoughts are more effective than messages that don't stimulate central route processing (Cacioppo et al., 1991; Heesacker, 1989; McNeil & Stoltenberg, 1989). The researchers in one study compared a traditional assertiveness training workshop to one that incorporated several factors stressed in ELM (for example, motivation, ability, positive thoughts, and memory). Both workshops explained the concept of assertiveness training and let participants rehearse their newly acquired skills. The ELM workshop also stimulated positive thoughts about assertiveness by exposing participants to four supportive arguments about the value of assertiveness training. As predicted, the message that stimulated central route processing produced more positive thoughts and pro-assertiveness attitudes immediately after the workshop. The ELM training also had longer-lasting effects. When their roommates described the participants two weeks later, people who participated in the ELM workshop received higher ratings in assertiveness than those who participated in the traditional workshops (Ernst & Heesacker, 1993).

The characteristics of the client also influence the course of the therapeutic encounter. Paralleling sex differences in persuasion, women in therapy tend to experience more improvement than men (Nelson, 1993). Men, on the other hand, are more likely to avoid therapy, particularly if they endorse traditional masculine values that stress independence, dominance, and control (Robertson & Fitzgerald, 1992). The client's racial background also influences the outcome of the therapeutic encounter, for same-race combinations of client and therapist tend to be more beneficial than mixed-race combinations (Watkins et al., 1989). Different clients also bring different sets of expectations with them to the therapy process. Many enter therapy expecting concrete suggestions for solving their problems and are disappointed when the therapist provides them with support rather than specific direction (Tinsley, Bowman, & Barich, 1993). When clients' expectations are not met, they are likely to leave therapy before reaching their personal goals for change (Higgenbotham et al., 1988).

The social-clinical interface enriches both social psychology and the helping professions of psychology (Forsyth & Leary, 1991). At the practical level, a social-psychological conceptualization offers insight into clinically significant questions. If, for example, social psychologists discover that asking questions stimulates central route processing, then this finding informs analyses of change during therapy (Cacioppo et al., 1991). Social psychology may also be the source of novel treatment procedures. A number of current cognitive therapies were derived directly from relatively esoteric theories of the structure of causal thought (Murdock & Altmaier, 1991).

At the theoretical level, the interface stimulates the development of conceptual models that are more encompassing than those developed in either field separately. Clinicians' theories of depression, for example, could not deal adequately with cases in which people faced uncontrollable circumstances but did not perceive the setting as out of their control. When integrated with attribution theory, however, the model increased in strength and comprehensiveness (Abramson, Seligman, & Teasdale, 1978). Similarly, the large number of clinically based explanations of social anxiety and inhibition can be integrated with social-psychological perspectives that emphasize people's self-presentational concerns (Leary, 1983; Schlenker & Leary, 1982b).

In sum, the social-clinical interface is based on the premise that social and clinical psychologists share a similar goal: to develop and test generalizable principles of human behavior. When clinical psychologists explain behavior in terms of propositions that are essentially social psychological in nature, then social-psychological studies of these principles are necessarily relevant in evaluating the adequacy of these propositions. And if social psychologists are to explain the full range of human experience, then they must develop theories that can explain questions of adjustment and coping. The road between social and clinical psychology is a two-way street that social psychologists should travel often (Forsyth & Strong, 1986; Strong, 1991b).

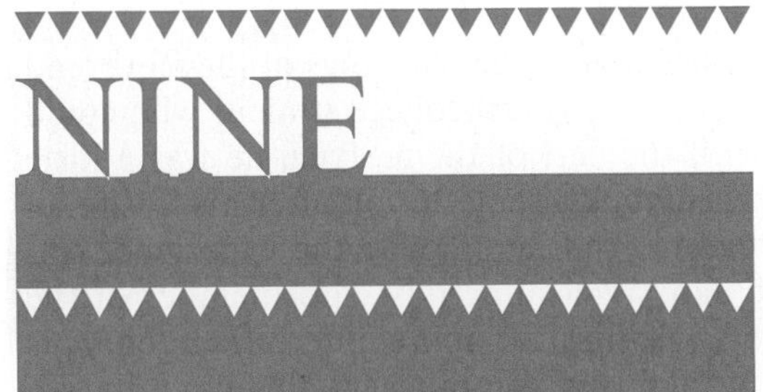

Influence

Jerry hadn't always been a dedicated believer in the teachings of the Reverend Sun Myung Moon. Just a year ago he was a typical college student who could skip a class or cram for an exam with the best of them. True, he was a little more politically involved than most. He took a semester off after his freshman year to work in an antipoverty program, and he enjoyed the experience immensely. So, when he encountered Jan, a social activist and member of the One World Crusade, he found her polemics far more interesting than his classes. Jerry's interest in college waned, his commitment to humanitarian ideals waxed, and he began spending more time at workshops sponsored by the One World Crusade.

Jan ended one particularly exhilarating session by inviting Jerry to a week-long retreat at the group's seminary in Barrytown, New York. He jumped at the chance. Up to this point he had no idea that the group was an arm of the Unification Church—colloquially known as the "Moonies." Had he known, he would have broken off all contact—he thought Moonies were kooks. But once at the seminary, he felt a growing commitment to the group and its goals. By the end of the week, he decided to remain with the Unificationists. Jerry's parents weren't pleased. They sought to have him classified as mentally incompetent so they could take him home (Galanter, 1989).

Jerry was no pushover. He considered himself to be a free thinker who was in control of his actions and decisions. But Jerry, like most people, overestimated his self-determination, for anyone who lives with other people will never be completely free from the inexorable demands a social life entails. The people who surround us influence us in ways both obvious and subtle; they shape our attitudes and feelings, sway our judgments, and convince us to stop doing some things while encouraging us to do other things. **Social influence**—interpersonal processes that lead to changes in feelings, thoughts, or behaviors—is a powerful force in our lives.

social influence
Interpersonal processes that lead to changes in the beliefs, feelings, or behaviors of another person.

The social processes Jerry faced changed him from a biology major into a Moonie in less than one month. These same processes are at work whenever we join with others rather than remain alone. Many situations call for **conformity**: We feel compelled to change our opinions, judgments, or actions to match the opinions, judgments, or actions of the people around us. The student sitting in the lecture hall, the office worker who feigns productivity while daydreaming, the driver in rush-hour traffic, the couple thanking their host for a pleasant evening are all conforming in some way to the pressures of the situation. Many situations also require **obedience** to a person in authority. When Jerry started to waver, the workshop leaders confronted him directly by urging him

conformity
Changing one's opinions, judgments, or actions to match the opinions, judgments, or actions of other people.

obedience
Changing one's opinions, judgments, or actions in response to a direct order from an authority.

to embrace Reverend Moon's teachings on faith. Similarly, the student who accepts the teacher's assignment unquestioningly, the office worker who stays late because the boss demands it, the driver who heeds the posted speed limit, and the person who dutifully follows the spouse's orders are experiencing the power of social influence. We don't control these kinds of social situations; they control us.

Conformity and Independence

The people we encounter on any given day influence our thoughts, our emotions, and our behaviors. Social psychology is based on this fundamental premise, but does this premise explain why Jerry joined the Unificationists? Is social influence so pervasive? So profound? So powerful?

Conformity Confirmed

Muzafer Sherif (1936) was one of the first social psychologists to document the power of social influence in an experiment. He believed that consensus, rather than disagreement, is the rule in most social settings: "When the external surroundings lack stable, orderly reference points, the individuals caught in the ensuing experience of uncertainty mutually contribute to each other a mode of orderliness to establish their own orderly pattern" (Sherif, 1966, pp. xii–xiii).

autokinetic effect
An optical illusion of apparent motion that occurs when perceivers observe a pinpoint of light in an otherwise totally darkened room.

Sherif examined this consensus-seeking process by capitalizing on an optical illusion known as the **autokinetic effect**. When a person looks at a pinpoint of light in an otherwise totally darkened room, the light appears to move. This illusion of movement occurs because the visual system lacks a frame of reference, so it can't correct for minor movements of the eye. When people estimate the amount of movement by themselves, they usually develop their own idiosyncratic standards. But when Sherif arranged for people to state their judgments aloud in a group, their personal estimates blended with those of other group members until a consensus was reached. A typical group's responses are shown in Figure 9-1. At first, Person A thought that the dot wandered over 7 inches. Persons B and C were more conservative; they guessed 2 and 1 inches, respectively. In the group, however, the people's three judgments converged rapidly. Person A revised his estimates downward, Persons B and C revised theirs upward, and by the study's end, the subjects had accepted a standard estimate in place of their own idiosyncratic judgments. They weren't con-

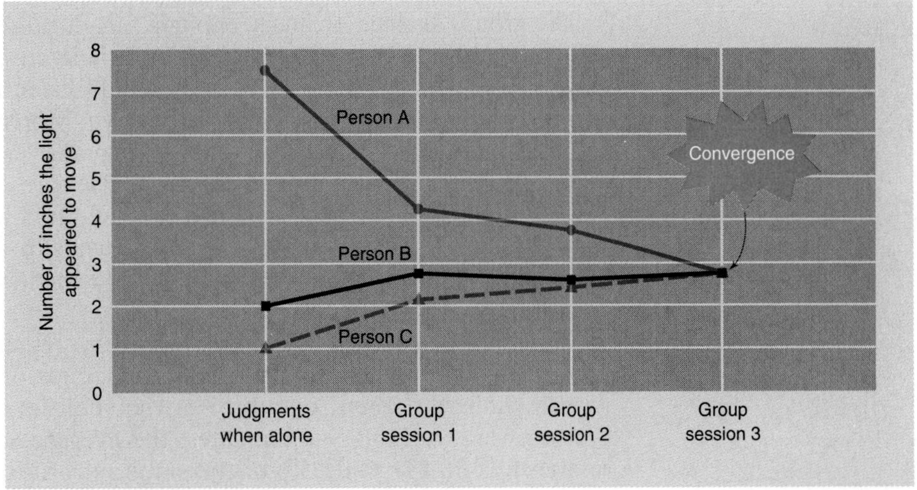

▲ FIGURE 9-1
Do people in ambiguous situations gradually modify their perceptions until they match other people's perceptions? Subjects' judgments in Sherif's study converged over time. Their private, pregroup judgments differed markedly, but when they joined with others, their judgments converged. (Data from Sherif, 1936)

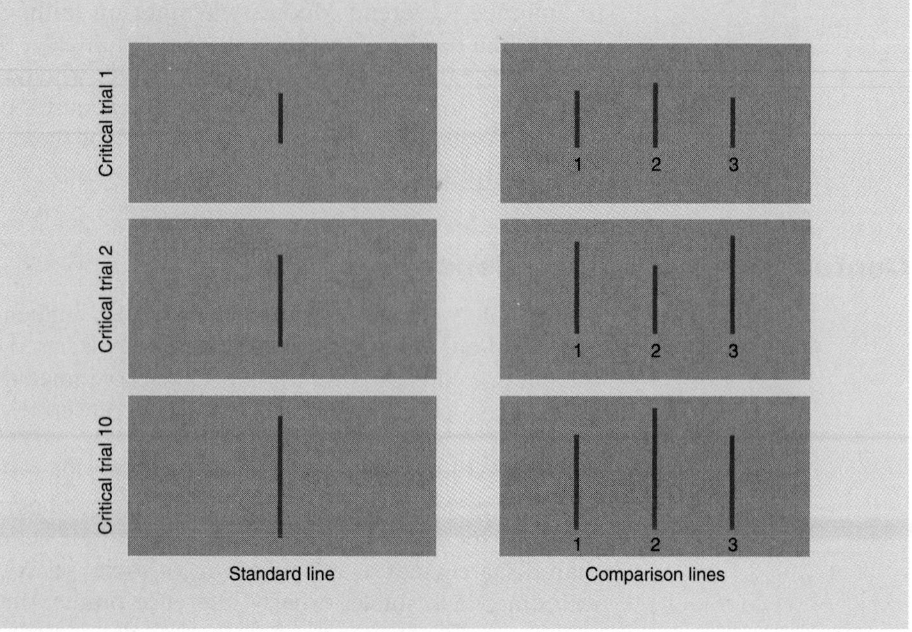

▲ **FIGURE 9-2**
Will people agree with others even when these people are clearly in the wrong? Asch used easy problems in his studies of conformity. On each trial he showed subjects two cards—one with the standard line, and the other with three test lines. The subjects were to state the number of the line on the second card that matched the standard line's length. But in 12 trials, confederates in the group deliberately chose the wrong line. In trial 1 (see top of figure), line 3 was the correct answer; the confederates chose line 1. Cards from trials 2 and 10 are also shown. (Adapted from Asch, 1955)

sciously trying to agree with each other, but they used other people's estimates to revise their own opinions and beliefs anyway.

Years later Solomon Asch (1951, 1955) extended Sherif's initial findings. Yes, he agreed, in the ambiguous autokinetic-effect situation, people conform because the task they are trying to accomplish has no clear answer. But would they still conform, Asch wondered, if they were very confident about their attitudes, opinions, or judgments? Asch set about answering this question by testing for conformity with a clear-cut task. He assembled seven-man groups in his lab and told them he was interested in visual acuity. He therefore wanted them to look at a series of lines and decide which ones were the same length. Asch then showed the subjects two cards like those in Figure 9-2; one card contained a standard line, and the other card displayed three lines of varying length. The subjects then picked the one line from the second card that was the same length as the standard line on the first card. This comparison process was repeated 18 times, or trials, and on each occasion the subjects announced their answers aloud.

The groups seemed ordinary enough, but in this case looks were deceiving: All of the subjects but one were Asch's confederates. The one real subject was always seated in the sixth chair, so he could listen to five of the other group members' judgments before he made his own. Moreover, on 12 of the 18 trials the confederates deliberately gave the wrong answer. On the first of the rigged trials, the first confederate would glance at the cards and confidently say, "The answer is line 1." The next confederate would nod his head in agreement and say, "Yes, it's line 1." After five wrong answers, it was the subject's turn. He faced a choice: agree with everyone else's judgments or give the answer that he personally thought was correct.

Judging the lengths of the lines was easy. When subjects worked alone, they rarely made errors. After the confederates had given the same wrong answer, however, about one-third of the subjects conformed by also giving that answer. As Table 9-1 indicates, the average conformity rate across the session was 36.8%. Only 5% of the subjects conformed on every trial. How-

▲ **TABLE 9-1**
Percentages of conformity and independence recorded by Asch

Item Measured	*Result*
How many items did the average subject answer incorrectly?	36.8%
How many subjects made at least one error?	76.4%
How many subjects never conformed?	24.0%
How many subjects conformed ten or more times?	11.0%
How many mistakes did the average subject make when working alone?	0.9%
How many subjects made at least one mistake when performing the task alone?	5.0%

Source: Data from Asch, 1955.

ever, over 75% of the subjects made at least one blatant error during the experiment.

Asch was surprised by his own findings, for he didn't think people would willingly go along with a group that was determined to make an obvious error. He noted, however, that some of his subjects were not simply going along with the others; they actually thought the group was correct. These people concluded, "I am wrong, and the group is right." These individuals were displaying **conversion** (or **private acceptance** or **internalization**), for their personal opinions changed in response to social influence. Others, in contrast, thought the rest of the group was mistaken, yet they decided to just go along because they did not want to seem out of step with the others, anger the experimenter, or appear stupid. This type of conformity is usually labeled **compliance**—public agreement paired with private disagreement (see Figure 9-3). But whether the individual was converted or merely complying, the result was the same—conformity. If the subjects in Asch's research had been making life-and-death decisions, their choices would have been fatal one-third of the time (Levine & Russo, 1987; Nail, 1986; Nail & Van Leeuwen, 1993; Stricker, Messick, & Jackson, 1970; Willis, 1963).

conversion (or private acceptance; internalization)
Changes in opinions, judgments, or actions that occur when individuals personally agree with the influencer's position.

compliance
Changes that occur when the targets of social influence publicly accept the influencer's position but privately continue to maintain their original beliefs.

Majority and Minority Influence

Sherif's and Asch's studies, as Table 9-2 notes, provide compelling evidence of the power of others to influence us. Both studies, however, also hint at the other side of social influence. Yes, Asch (1955) explained, "people submit uncritically and painlessly to external manipulation by suggestion," but he also pointed out that "independence and the capacity to rise above group

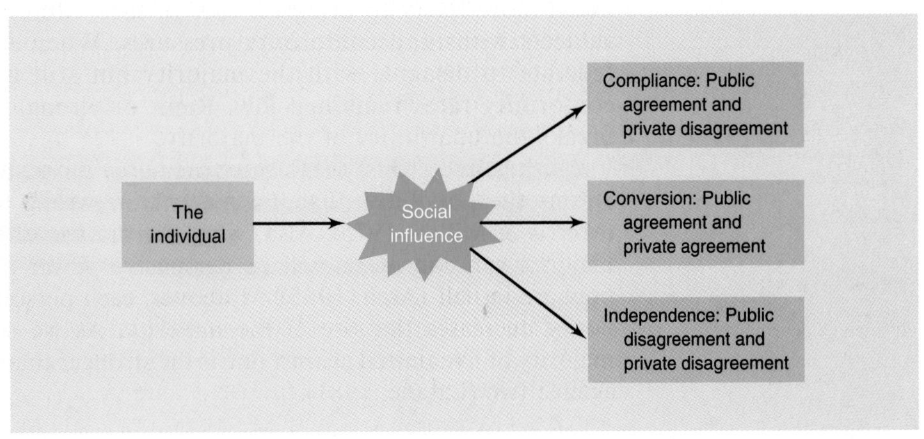

▲ **FIGURE 9-3**
How do we respond when other people pressure us to change? Some express agreement publicly but remain unchanged at a personal level (compliance). Others change both publicly and privately (conversion). Still others refuse to change (independence).

▲ **TABLE 9-2**
Summing up: Two classic studies of conformity

Study	*Basic Paradigm*	*Conclusions*
Sherif's autokinetic-effect study (1936)	Subjects first estimated the distance a dot of light moved in an otherwise dark room. They then stated their estimates aloud in a room with two other people.	Subjects' pregroup judgments differed markedly, but when they made judgments in a group, they modified their estimates to reflect the group's emerging standards. Estimates eventually converged.
Asch's line-judging situation (1955)	On each trial, subjects decided which of three lines was equal in length to a standard line. On some critical trials, confederates who announced their answers before the subject deliberately made errors.	Subjects made few errors when judging lines alone. When confederates gave the wrong answer, error rates escalated. Subjects gave the wrong answer on 36.8% of the items.

passion are also open to human beings" (p. 32). Just as the majority pushes for group unity, the minority pushes for independence and uniqueness. Which side will win the struggle for influence—the majority or the minority—depends on many factors, including the size of the minority and majority, the consistency of the minority, and members' social status (Maass & Clark, 1984).

One against many. The One World Crusaders took advantage of *unanimity* to influence Jerry. Jerry accepted Jan's invitation to dinner because he wanted to get to know her better. But during dinner, and at each subsequent meeting, Jerry was surrounded by people who announced their faith in Reverend Moon's Divine Principle and encouraged Jerry to share their commitment. They never expressed any qualms about the Principle and didn't tolerate negative opinions.

Jerry had meandered into a powerful social situation, a unanimous majority facing a minority of one. Had he been able to find a partner—a single ally who was critical of the Unificationists' teachings—then he would have been much more likely to withstand their attempts to influence him. Asch demonstrated this advantage by giving his subjects a partner, either a trained confederate or a second uninformed subject. The results were clear: When another person disagreed with the majority, subjects were much more likely to disagree, too. In fact, even an inaccurate ally helped subjects withstand conformity pressures. When Asch arranged for a confederate to disagree with the majority but still give an incorrect answer, conformity rates remained low. Right or wrong, another dissenting voice breaks the unanimity of the majority.

Allies help us resist conformity pressures for several reasons. A partner reaffirms the possibility that the majority is wrong and the minority is right (Morris & Miller, 1975). Also, when we are the only ones who disagree, the majority can concentrate all its persuasive power on us. A partner cuts this pressure in half (Asch, 1955). Moreover, each person who converts to the minority decreases the size of the majority. As we see in the next section, a majority of five united against one is far stronger than a majority of four united against two (Latané, 1981).

▲ Sherif and Asch studied people's reactions to experimental tasks, but their findings apply in many everyday situations. When groups discuss issues, individuals often change their opinions to match the group's. This man (*center*) disagrees with the others, but he faces a situation in which independence is difficult: three against one. If he gives in, this change could reflect either compliance—agreeing with others but retaining one's original beliefs—or private acceptance—true conversion to the position endorsed by the majority.

The social physics of influence. At first, Jerry was more interested in spending time with Jan than in trying to save the world. But he never had the chance to be alone with her. From the time he awoke to the time he went to sleep, he was surrounded by at least four Unificationists. He was outnumbered.

How many people does it take to create maximum conformity? Is 2 against 1 enough? Is 11 against 1 too many? This question intrigued Asch, so he carried out his line-judgment task with groups that varied in size from 2 to 17 members. His findings, shown in Figure 9-4, suggest that increasing the size of the majority increases its influence, but only up to a point. Subjects conformed on 3.6% of the trials if they faced one opponent. Two opponents, however, increased the percentage to 13.6, and a majority of three increased conformity to 31.8%. Adding even more people generated a little more conformity (conformity peaked at 37.1% in the seven-person groups), but even a majority of 16 couldn't raise conformity appreciably above the 31.8% level achieved with 3 people against 1. (Buby & Penner, 1974; Gerard, Wilhelmy, & Conolley, 1968; Milgram, Bickman, & Berkowitz, 1969; Nordholm, 1975; Reis et al., 1976; and Stang, 1976, have also examined this question.)

More influencers usually means more conformity, but the precise shape of the relationship between size and conformity is much debated (Jackson, 1987;

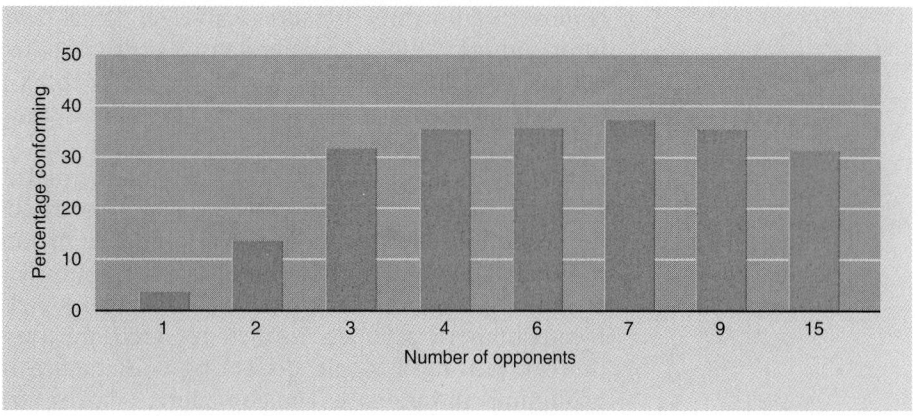

▲ **FIGURE 9-4**
How many people does it take to create maximum conformity? When Asch repeated his conformity study with differing numbers of confederates, he found that conformity increased rapidly as more people were added to the majority, but only up to a point. Conformity peaked at 37.1% in the seven-person groups. (Data from Asch, 1955)

social impact theory A conceptual analysis of social influence that seeks to identify and calibrate the psychological effect, or impact, of one or more sources of social influence on one or more targets of social influence. Argues that increasing the number of sources of social influence increases the impact of these sources, at a gradually decreasing rate.

Knowles, 1983; Tindale et al., 1990). Some have argued that few people conform when one other person disagrees with them, but that conformity rises rapidly when the majority increases to two or three (Tanford & Penrod, 1984). Others, however, think that just one opponent can have a substantial impact on us and that each additional person has less and less impact. Bibb Latané and Sharon Wolf's **social impact theory**, for example, reminds us that most psychological processes follow this pattern. Increasing the intensity of a stimulus increases the intensity of the psychological experience of that stimulus, but at an ever-decreasing rate. Imagine that you turn on a lamp in an otherwise dark room. Suddenly the room is filled with brightness. What if you turn on more lights? The room will get brighter with each light, but eventually the room will become so bright that adding another light will make no difference. Likewise, the more people who oppose you, the greater their impact—up to a point. The first light you turn on in a dark room has a greater impact on you than the hundredth light you turn on. Similarly, the first person who disagrees with you has more impact on you than the hundredth person added to a majority that disagrees with you. Thus, conformity pressures don't increase at a constant rate as more people join the majority; rather, "there is a marginally decreasing effect of increased supplies of people" (Latané, 1981, p. 344; see also Latané & Wolf, 1981; Wolf, 1985, 1987; Wolf & Latané, 1983).

Brian Mullen (1983, 1986b, 1987b) agrees with Latané and Wolf, but for different reasons. As noted in Chapter 5, when our attention is focused on our public selves, we strive to maintain a proper appearance and make a good impression. As a result, we are more likely to conform to others' expectations and opinions. Mullen thinks that disagreeing with one other person increases self-awareness slightly. But as more and more people join the majority, our self-attention increases and so does our conformity. Mullen's self-attention theory also explains why our resistance to conformity pressures increases when one or two other group members agree with our dissenting views. Mullen proposes that membership in a subgroup within the larger group reduces our overall self-awareness and eases our concern over our public self-images.

Consistency and innovation. Jerry and the other Unificationists talked for hours about the world's problems, but none of the Unificationists abandoned Reverend Moon's ideas and embraced Jerry's. Jerry didn't change anyone else's outlook; instead, they changed his.

Those with dissenting opinions rarely succeed in changing the majority's position on issues (Penrod & Hastie, 1980; Tanford & Penrod, 1984). In juries, for example, the lone holdout who opposes all the other jurors usually succumbs to conformity pressure (Kalven & Zeisel, 1966). When a majority of the jurors initially think the defendant is guilty, the jury returns a verdict of guilt 90% of the time. If a majority of the jurors think the defendant is innocent, then the defendant is acquitted in 86% of the cases. Indeed, most groups implicitly assume that as soon as a significant majority of the members (say, two-thirds) favors an opinion or decision, then the matter is settled (Davis, Bray, & Holt, 1977). (The dynamics of juries are discussed at the end of the chapter in the section, "Application: Social Influence in Juries.")

What can you do if, like Jerry, you find yourself in a situation in which you are arguing against everyone else? Serge Moscovici and his colleagues recommend stubborn defiance. In their research, they reverse the usual Asch situation by putting a single dissenting confederate into a group of otherwise unanimous individuals. The confederate makes no claim to special expertise, skill, or insight, but he or she never wavers during the discussion. This consistency is critical, for only the consistent minority will shake the confidence of the majority and thereby force the group to accept a change (Moscovici, 1976, 1980, 1985; Moscovici & Faucheux, 1972; Moscovici & Lage, 1976; Moscovici & Nemeth, 1974; Moscovici & Personnaz, 1980).

Moscovici finds that an unwavering minority can influence the majority's answers, but often in very subtle ways. When, for example, five people are arguing over some issue and one person consistently disagrees with the other four, the lone dissenter may not be able to sway the group's opinion. But when the group turns to another issue, the dissenter's arguments will begin to influence them (Nemeth & Wachtler, 1974). Eventually, Moscovici suggests, the majority will be converted to the minority's position. Moreover, because this change comes about through subtle interpersonal processes rather than blatant social pressuring, Moscovici argues that the change is more permanent—true conversion to the minority's position rather than mere compliance with someone else's view (Maass, West, & Cialdini, 1987; Nemeth, 1986).

Status and influence. Edwin P. Hollander offers another recommendation to people who find that everyone else in the group disagrees with them. He believes that dissenters who immediately begin by challenging the majority without first earning others' respect will probably be overruled by the majority. If, however, the dissenters first demonstrate their willingness to cooperate with others, then the majority will be more likely to listen to their views. Hollander thinks that early conformity to the majority builds up **idiosyncrasy credits**—psychological credits or bonuses ("brownie points"). Dissenters can spend these credits later when they take an unpopular position or view. Without any idiosyncrasy credits, the majority won't tolerate such dissent, and the deviant will be rejected. The evidence supports the wisdom of Hollander's recommendation: People who act in a group-oriented, cooperative manner during the early phases of a group problem-solving session influence the group members more than people who violate group rules from the very start (Hollander, 1958, 1960, 1961, 1981; see also Ridgeway, 1982).

idiosyncrasy credits
Psychological credits or bonuses earned when an individual makes a contribution to the group.

Moscovici's consistency approach and Hollander's idiosyncrasy credits alternative recommend different strategies but both probably work. Researchers tested the relative strengths of the two strategies by asking groups of college students to discuss three proposed ways of reducing university spending: curtailing the school newspaper, raising the prices for admission to athletic events, and increasing tuition. Four of the group members were subjects who were generally opposed to these proposals, but each group also included two confederates who took a minority position on all three issues (as Moscovici's consistency model suggests) or on the last issue only (as Hollander's idiosyncrasy credits approach advocates). The investigators found that the minority members influenced the majority no matter which approach was taken. Hollander's approach, however, was more influential in all-male groups (Bray, Johnson, & Chilstrom, 1982). These findings suggest that minorities can reach their goals by taking either of two routes: the direct path recommended by Hollander or the indirect path suggested by Moscovici (Maass & Clark, 1984; Maass et al., 1987).

Individual Differences in Conformity

Another student attended the same dinner that Jerry did. He heard the same speeches, ate the same food, and sang the same folk songs that Jerry did. But he never went back to the center. Why not? Why do some people conform more than others?

▲ Independence and nonconformity can be achieved in many different ways. The graduate who wears a message to his mother on his mortarboard stands out in the crowd at commencement, as does the young tough with the spiked hair.

The conforming personality: Fact or fiction? Richard Crutchfield carried out some of the earliest systematic studies of individual differences in conformity and nonconformity using a special procedure now known as the Crutchfield Apparatus. The subjects sat in individual cubicles containing a series of switches and lights. When asked a question—such as "Which one of the lines (A, B, or C) is the same length as the standard line?"—they answered by flipping the appropriate switch. The subjects thought their answers were being transmitted to the experimenter and the other subjects, but the experimenter actually tested for conformity by telling each subject to answer last and substituting incorrect responses on critical trials.

Crutchfield (1955) concluded that some people were conformists. They bent consistently to social influence pressures across a range of situations. They were high in "respect to authority, submissive, compliant, and overly accepting" (p. 194). Other people, in contrast, were independent types: They were "self-reliant; independent in judgment; and able to think for" themselves. Other studies support Crutchfield's conclusions (see Table 9-3). Conformists, for example, are often authoritarian: Their conventionality, conservative values, and unwillingness to confront authority increase their willingness to accept the majority's opinion (see Chapter 7). Conformists also tend to let the situation and other people influence their perceptions, opinions, and outlooks. People who rely on situational cues when making perceptual judgments (field dependents), self-consciousness individuals, and high self-monitors are more likely to make certain their actions match the group's standards (Hare, 1976). Indeed, people who conform show a greater interest, overall, in other people. They are higher in the need for social approval, more interpersonally oriented, and more fearful of social rejection (Bornstein, 1992). Factors that undermine self-confidence—low self-esteem, incompetence, low intelligence—also increase conformity (Shaw, 1981).

▲ **TABLE 9-3**
Personality characteristics typical of people who conform and people who remain independent

Characteristic	*Conformists*	*Independents*
Authoritarianism	High F-scores	Low F-scores
Field orientation	Field dependent	Field independent
Self-awareness	High public self-consciousness	Low public self-consciousness
Self-monitoring	High self-monitors	Low self-monitors
Anxiety	Anxious	Emotionally stable
Need for approval	Approval-oriented	Low need for approval
Birth order	First-born	Later-born
Dominance	Submissive	Assertive
Self-esteem	Low self-esteem	High self-esteem
Expertise	Inexperienced	Experienced
Intelligence	Unintelligent	Intelligent

Sources: From Hare, 1976; Shaw, 1981; Snyder & Ickes, 1985.

The counterconformist. Psychologists who examined U.S. soldiers who had been imprisoned during the Korean War identified two very different kinds of resisters (see the section "In Depth: Coercive Persuasion" in Chapter 8). Some of the prisoners of war reacted like the nonconformists identified by Crutchfield. They rejected indoctrination because they simply did not agree with the communists. Others, however, fought indoctrination because they resisted all forms of authority and influence, regardless of the source:

> These men were characterized by a life-long pattern of indiscriminate resistance to all forms of authority, and had histories of inability to get along in the United Nations Army just as they were unable to get along with the Chinese. They openly defied any attempt to get them to conform. (Schein, 1956, p. 166)

counterconformist
An individual who deliberately adopts views that oppose others' views.

Unlike people who dissent because they disagree with the majority and want to express their own personal views, the **counterconformist** (or anticonformist) enjoys arguing against any position the majority adopts (Nail & Thompson, 1990; Willis & Hollander, 1964). College students in Japan, for example, displayed surprisingly high levels of anticonformity in an Asch-type situation. Not only were conformity rates lower than those reported by Asch, but 34% of the subjects gave incorrect answers even when the majority gave the correct answer. The subjects were working so hard to be disagreeable that they deliberately gave wrong answers (Frager, 1970). The anticonformity was caused, apparently, by the impersonal nature of the laboratory groups. When investigators used the subjects' personal friends as accomplices in a later study, conformity was very high and counterconformity virtually nonexistent (Williams & Sogon, 1984).

Do women conform more than men? Don't women conform more than men? Isn't it true, "at least in our culture, that females supply greater amounts of conformity under almost all conditions than males" (Nord, 1969, p. 198)? That "women have been found to yield more to a bogus group norm than men" (Hare, 1976, p. 27)?

Alice H. Eagly and her colleagues don't think women are easy targets for social influencers (Eagly, 1978; Eagly & Carli, 1981; Eagly, Wood, & Fish-

▲ **FIGURE 9-5**
Do women conform more than men? Women conformed more when items concerned matters "likely to be of greater interest to and judged more accurately by males." Men conformed more than women when the items concerned matters of greater interest to women. No sex differences were noted for neutral items. (From Sistrunk & McDavid, 1971)

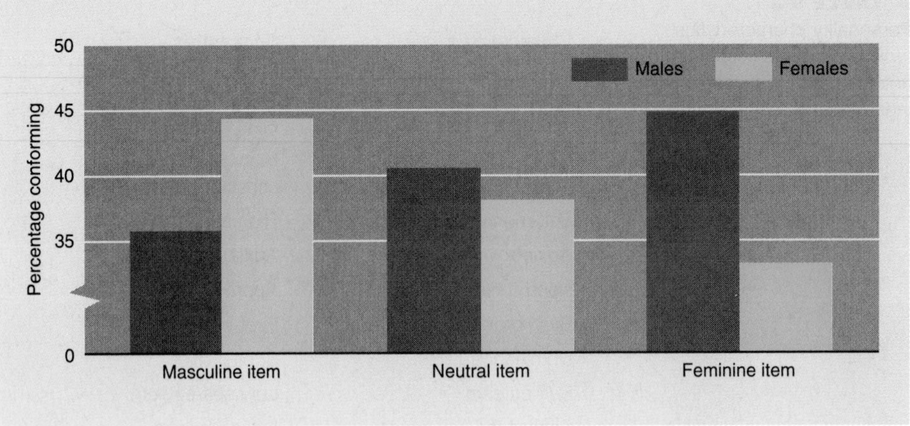

baugh, 1981). Eagly, as noted in Chapter 8's discussion of persuasion, found that many of the studies that demonstrated sex differences often stacked the deck against women by using tasks that are of greater interest to men rather than to women. As Figure 9-5 indicates, when researchers tested for conformity with items that favor neither sex, few sex differences emerged (Goldberg, 1974, 1975; Javornisky, 1979; Sistrunk & McDavid, 1971). Eagly also wonders whether the male researchers, who carried out nearly two-thirds of the research, unintentionally portrayed their own sex in a flattering way (Eagly & Carli, 1981). When Eagly examined earlier research in light of these two methodological problems, she found "true" sex differences in only one kind of situation. The sexes diverge only when group members are sitting face to face and they must state their opinions aloud. Only then do women conform more than men.

What is it about face-to-face situations that brings out sex differences? Eagly suggests that the pressure to conform to stereotypes that postulate the "proper" behavior of men and women may be stronger in public settings. If individuals feel that they should behave in a traditional way, then women may conform and men may remain independent (Eagly, Wood, & Fishbaugh, 1981). Women who do not accept the traditional role of women do not conform more than men, whereas men who adopt a feminine sex role do conform more (Bem, 1975, 1985). Women are more likely than men to agree with other group members for interpersonal reasons (Eagly et al., 1981). Men think of conformity as a weakness and use disagreement to separate themselves from the rest of the group (Maslach, Santee, & Wade, 1987; Santee & Jackson, 1982; Santee & Maslach, 1982). Women, in contrast, may use agreement as a self-presentational tactic. Instead of stressing their points of disagreement, women may prefer to stress their points of consensus and cohesion (Josephs, Markus, & Tafarodi, 1992). Thus nature did not decree men to be nonconformists and women to be conformists. Like the other situational and personal factors reviewed in Table 9-4, sex is systematically related to conformity only in certain circumstances.

Why Do People Conform?

Picture in your mind a person conforming in the Asch experiment. Whom do you see? A pale, nervous sycophant mumbling an answer he knows is wrong? A weak-kneed follower who can't make up his mind without relying on others' opinions? A nearsighted self-doubter who doesn't trust the evidence of his own perceptions? These images of people who conform are unfair exag-

▲ **TABLE 9-4**
Summing up: Situational and personal factors that influence conformity and independence

Factor	*Impact on Conformity*
Unanimity of the majority	Conformity pressure increases when a single person confronts a unanimous majority. If the lone dissenter gains an ally (another person breaks with majority), conformity declines.
Size of the majority	Conformity increases as the number of influencing agents increases, but at a declining rate. Asch found that conformity rates reached over 30% when a single person confronted three others, but adding more people to the majority didn't substantially increase conformity.
Consistency of the minority	Dissenters rarely convince majorities to change their positions, but a minority who is very consistent over time sometimes influences the majority indirectly.
Status of the minority	Dissenters who preface their disagreement with agreement during early stages of the group discussion are more influential than dissenters who have not accrued any idiosyncrasy credits.
Personality and conformity	People who conform espouse authoritarian values and rely more on situational cues and other people when formulating their judgments. They also tend to be more interpersonally oriented and less confident.
Counterconformity	People who dissent fall into two categories: independents who personally disagree with the majority's position and counterconformists (or anticonformists) who resist all forms of authority and influence regardless of the source.
Sex differences	Women conform no more than men when the task is of equal interest to the sexes and the situation does not call for sex-role-specific responses. Women may use conformity in face-to-face group settings to create a more positive interpersonal climate.

gerations. Although the word *conformity* summons up thoughts of wishy-washy people who are so intimidated by the majority's opinions that they can't stand up for their rights, conformity springs from many sources. First, conformity is often the most reasonable response in a situation: When the people around us are well-informed but we ourselves are ignorant, it's wise to use them as an informational resource. Second, we often conform because we implicitly accept the legitimacy of social norms. Last, conformity is often interpersonally rewarding: The people around us will reward us when we agree with them, but they will punish us if we dissent (Forsyth, 1990). These three causes of conformity—the informational, the normative, and the interpersonal—are examined next.

Informational influence. In familiar, everyday situations you need not consult others to make decisions or form opinions; you rely on your own judgment. Sometimes, though, when you don't have enough information to respond, you engage in *social comparison*: you check to see whether your reactions correspond to the reactions of other people present in the setting (see Chapter 5). When you attend a symphony concert for the first time, you may do what others do: clap when they clap, stand when they stand, and shout "Encore!" when they shout "Encore!" Or, if you are having dinner with some religious zealots, you may see how the other guests are reacting to figure out what is expected of you.

informational influence Social influence that results from discovering new information about a situation by observing others' responses.

Informational influence occurs when other people provide us with information, which we then use to make decisions and form opinions. In Sherif's (1936) autokinetic-effect study, subjects lacked an external standard or any experience in the situation. They were not sycophants who were agreeing just to agree; rather, they were striving for accuracy. They therefore used the information contained in others' responses to guide them (Pollis, Montgomery, & Smith, 1975).

When we learn that other people disagree with us, we reexamine the situation and, if necessary, revise our opinions accordingly. The subject in Sherif's study who initially thought that the dot of light moved a whopping 7.5 inches probably looked a bit more closely at the light after he heard everyone else estimate 1 or 2 inches. Subjects who found out that everyone else in their group agreed with the statement, "I would never go out of my way to help another person," reinterpreted the phrase, "go out of my way"; they decided it must mean "risk my life" rather than "be inconvenienced" (Allen & Wilder, 1980). In these kinds of situations, people who spend more time thinking about the issues conform more (Campbell, Tesser, & Fairey, 1986).

Minorities, too, can be sources of informational influence (Wolf, 1985, 1987). When a group's members are in complete agreement with one another, they may fail to consider all the evidence when they make a decision. A consistent dissenter, however, will force the group to reevaluate all the issues. Researchers illuminated this process by having people work a series of puzzles alone, in groups, or in groups with a consistent minority. When people worked alone, their solutions weren't very creative, and when they worked in a group, they usually just picked the solution favored by the majority. But when a minority of two confederates argued for a nonobvious solution, the group's solution was usually much more creative. The group did not necessarily accept the minority's proposal, but the minority did stimulate reevaluation of the original answer (Nemeth & Wachtler, 1983). A persistent minority, perhaps by stimulating reappraisal of the problem, spurs the group on to greater levels of effectiveness and creativity (Nemeth, 1986; Nemeth & Kwan, 1985, 1987; Nemeth, Mosier, & Chiles, 1992; Nemeth et al., 1990).

Normative influence. Theorists usually draw a distinction between informational influence and normative influence (Deutsch & Gerard, 1955; Kelley, 1952). Informational influence, as we have seen, occurs because others' responses convey information concerning the nature of the social setting and how we should behave. **Normative influence**, in contrast, occurs when we tailor our actions to fit the social norms of the situation. As noted in Chapter 7, norms prescribe the socially appropriate way to respond in the situation—the normal course of action—as well as proscribing actions that are to be avoided, if at all possible. Norms are the "cement of society" (Elster, 1989, p. 251). We are all restrained to a degree by norms, but we also benefit from the order that norms provide. Friends greeting on the street, executives discussing business strategies, strangers in queues, and even new recruits to bizarre religious organizations all recognize and respond in ways that are consistent with the norms governing their particular situations.

normative influence Social influence that results from personal and interpersonal pressures to conform to group norms.

Norms are not social shackles that we constantly strain to break. We conform to most norms because we have internalized them—incorporated them into our own personal systems of beliefs and values. General norms such as "Don't lie" and "Help other people when they are in need" correspond to such personal norms as "I don't lie to other people" and "I help people whenever I can." When we violate social norms we have accepted, we experience a range of negative emotional consequences such as embarrassment, guilt, and shame (Tangney, 1990, 1991).

Sherif studied the impact of normative influence in his studies of the autokinetic effect. He believed the gradual changes that occurred when people made judgments aloud in groups were likely due to informational social influence—people used others' estimates as guidelines. But what would happen when subjects were later asked to make judgments by themselves? Would they revert to their own idiosyncratic estimates? Or would they continue to base their judgments on the distance norm that their group had developed? As Sherif predicted, the subjects continued to base their judgments on the distance standard that emerged during the group sessions. Sherif had managed to create a norm experimentally in a laboratory setting, and his subjects internalized this norm.

Normative influence accounts for the transmission of religious, economic, moral, political, and interpersonal beliefs across generations. Recall Theodore Newcomb's (1943) study of political attitudes, discussed in Chapter 6. Many of the students entered Bennington College with conservative political values, but most of them gradually accepted the more liberal values expressed by the college's faculty and seniors. Normative influence also gives us insight into the origins of the eating disorder, bulimia—a cycle of binge eating followed by self-induced vomiting or other forms of purging. Binging and purging are considered by society at large to be abnormal, yet they are prevalent in certain groups, such as cheerleading squads, dance troupes, teams, and sororities. Rather than viewing these actions as a threat to their health, these groups apparently accept them as a normal means of controlling one's weight. In one study, college women who didn't purge began to purge when they joined a sorority in which the most popular members purged. Which women were most popular in these groups? Women who purged at the rate established by the group's norms (Crandall, 1988). A similar cycle of normative influence explains the problem of alcohol abuse on some college campuses. Most of the students who participated in one study of alcohol use didn't want to make a habit of drinking too much, but they believed their campus's norms encouraged alcohol consumption. The men in the study responded to this normative influence by gradually internalizing the misperceived norm. They began to drink more the longer they stayed at the school. The women, in contrast, responded by distancing themselves from their university and its norms about drinking (Prentice & Miller, 1993).

Interpersonal influence. We value nonconformity and independence. As Ralph Waldo Emerson (1926) proclaimed, "I must be myself. I will not hide any taste or aversions. . . . I will do strongly before the sun and moon whatever inly rejoices me and the heart appoints" (p. 53). Yet in countless everyday situations the dominant theme is "to get along, go along." Dissent is not rewarded; in fact, it is met with **interpersonal influence**: social responses that selectively encourage conformity while discouraging or even punishing nonconformity. Those who violate norms of civility are often reminded of their duty and told to change their ways (Goffman, 1971). People who break into lines are punished; they are insulted, pushed, or at least shot a dirty look (Milgram, 1992). The individual who publicly violates a moral norm is likely to meet with reproach (Sabini & Silver, 1978). And those who break society's laws—its legal norms—and are caught in the violation meet with more formal

interpersonal influence
Social influence that results from other people's selectively encouraging conformity while discouraging or even punishing nonconformity.

▲ Conformity isn't a lamentable side effect of living in a social world. We don't grudgingly dress in a certain way, stand in queues, or cross the street when the traffic light says "Walk." Rather, we conform to standards because we personally accept the need to rely on norms to structure social interaction.

sanctions—incarceration, monetary fines, public degradation, and even death. Nonconformists are punished more often than they are lauded.

Stanley Schachter (1952) studied interpersonal influence by planting three kinds of confederates in a number of all-male discussion groups: the *deviant,* who was trained to disagree with the majority; the *slider,* who disagreed at the start of the discussion but gradually came to agree with the majority; and the *mode,* who consistently agreed with the majority. Schachter was interested in seeing what kinds of pressures would be put on the deviant and also what effect two other independent variables—the cohesiveness of the group and the relevance of the topic under discussion to the group's goals—would have on conformity pressure.

Schachter gauged the amount of direct social pressure applied to each of these three confederates by tracking the number of times each subject spoke to each confederate. When he examined these patterns of communication, he found that the deviant was the target of a barrage of communications as the others tried to reason with him (see Figure 9-6). In most groups, the high rate of communication increased throughout the entire session when the target was the deviant, but decreased throughout the session when the target was the slider. Apparently, when the group members managed to talk the slider into agreeing, they shifted their efforts to the deviant. Last, when the group was cohesive and the task was relevant, Schachter found evidence of a strong rejection of the deviant by some subjects. Over 75% of the subjects in this condition reached a point where they seemed to give up on the resolute deviant and stopped communicating with him. All he did was disagree with the opinion of the others, but in the space of a few short minutes, he was cast out of the group.

Disagreeing with people is a sure way to antagonize them. Schachter found that the group members actively disliked the dissenter. When they rated each other on likability, the deviant got low marks, whereas the mode was liked the most. The deviant was also saddled with the secretarial chores of group; the mode and slider were assigned more desirable positions. Apparently, even a little disagreement with the group can lead to disaffection. By asking the members of a group discussing a legal case to vote on a recommendation five times, researchers created the six types of sliders, modes, and deviants shown in Table 9-5. When subjects later rated these six types of group members, the modes were liked the most, and the deviants were liked the least. Even the slider who began by disagreeing with the majority but eventually came around to that side was liked less than the confederate who always agreed with the majority (Levine, Saxe, & Harris, 1976; see also Levine, 1980; Levine & Ranelli, 1978; Levine & Ruback, 1980; Levine, Saxe, & Harris, 1976; Levine, Sroka, & Snyder, 1977).

Why would we reject someone whose only crime was to disagree with us? As noted in Chapter 2, we like people who agree with us and dislike people who express attitudes that clash with ours. Dissenters are also cognitive troublemakers. Just when we are trying to get closure on an issue, the deviant makes us reconsider our decision. Perhaps for that reason we are particularly negative toward deviants who express their disagreement near the end of a group's discussion rather than at the beginning (Kruglanski & Webster, 1991). In any case, these studies support the strategy of yea-saying: To be accepted in a group, agree with the group. You may earn others' respect by disagreeing with them, but you probably won't win their hearts.

Conformity Demystified

Why did Jerry agree, with remarkably little struggle, to join the Unificationists? The answer lies in the three forms of influence summarized in Table 9-6. First, Jerry felt that the One World Crusaders' ideas were very helpful to him personally. He met Jan when he was worried about his future, and the One World Crusaders offered him a clear solution that cut through all his misgivings and uncertainties. Jerry later recalled:

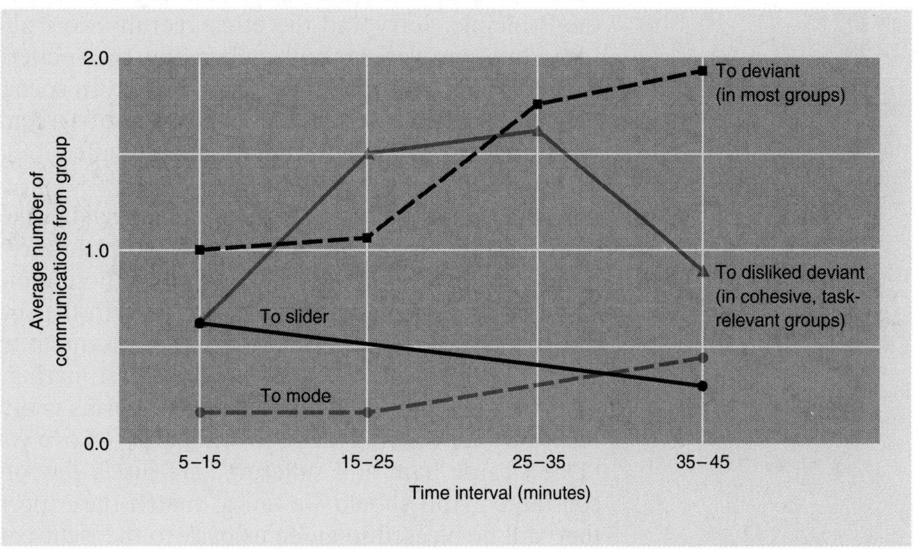

▲ **FIGURE 9-6**
How does a group react when one of its members disagrees with the rest? In Schachter's study, the person who disagreed with the others usually received the most communications at all times during the experiment. The only exception occurred in cohesive groups working on a relevant task who disliked the deviant. In this case, communications tapered off. The average number of communications addressed to the mode increased slightly over the session, while communication with the slider decreased. (Adapted from Schachter, 1951)

▲ **TABLE 9-5**
Who do we like most: people who always agree with us, people who disagree with us initially but then change their minds, or people who steadfastly disagree with us?

Levine and his associates found that the more people agree with us, the more we like them. The higher the subject's score, the more the subject was liked (recoded from the original; scores can range from 3 to 21).

Stimulus Person	*Initial Position*	*Final Position*	*Mean Attraction Score*
Mode	Agreement	Agreement	17.8
Slider	Neutral	Agreement	15.3
Slider	Disagreement	Agreement	14.0
Slider	Agreement	Disagreement	10.5
Deviant	Disagreement	Disagreement	7.8
Slider	Neutral	Disagreement	7.6

Source: Levine, Saxe, & Harris, 1976.

> It was strange, but the intensity of the two days left me much clearer about why I had been so uncertain, and where I might head for the future; it was as if a haze had been lifted. I began to understand things that had made no sense before, why most people rushed around for no reason, without any lasting sense of purpose. I had a sense that I could look for direction to my friends in the One-World Crusade. (quoted in Galanter, 1989, p. 61)

Second, Jerry felt obligated to conform to group norms that encouraged friendliness, cooperation, and total acceptance of the Divine Principle. He explains that, at first, he "went along in all the activities because they were sincere people doing things for a good cause, even though sometimes it seemed silly." Eventually, though, he internalized the group's norms. "I realized the Principle had to be important. I could see what it was doing for me" (quoted in Galanter, 1989, p. 63).

Third, Jerry was constantly surrounded by people who would not take no for an answer. They announced their faith in Reverend Moon's Divine Principle with great enthusiasm, and they encouraged Jerry to share their commitment. During group discussions of such topics as the meaning of life and the quest for happiness, the church members all expressed total agreement with the Principle. Jerry and the other recruits were allowed to express their own ideas, but they were far outnumbered by the vociferous believers. Recruits who were too negative were taken aside and given special counsel by several of the long-term members. And each expression of agreement with the group's ideals was met with a tremendous outpouring of affection and warmth. Jerry couldn't withstand the interpersonal pressure.

These three factors apply to more than just odd, unexpected social actions. In our day-to-day interactions with other people, we constantly modify our behaviors so they will fit in with the actions of those around us. In ambiguous situations, other people's actions provide us with the social proof we need to make our own choices. If it's OK for them, we assume it must be OK for us (Cialdini, 1993). As the section "In Depth: Underestimating the Power of Social Influence" suggests, the guiding influence of norms is often so subtle that we hardly realize we are obeying them. "Work hard," "Love your family and friends," and "Don't cause pain and suffering" are just a few of the norms we conform to constantly. And should we fail to match the expectations of those around us, they will be pleased to guide us back to the right path (Abrams, 1990).

▲ **TABLE 9-6**
Summing up: Three general causes of conformity

Cause	*Impact on Conformity*
Informational influence	Influence that results from discovering new information about a situation by observing others' responses to that situation. Differences of opinion in groups prompt members to reexamine the situation and, in some cases, to revise their opinions.
Normative influence	Influence that is caused by people's tendency to tailor their actions to fit the social norms of the situation. People sometimes obey norms merely to avoid sanctions or to seem agreeable, but normative action is personally satisfying when individuals have internalized the social standard.
Interpersonal influence	Influence that results when individuals are subjected to social responses that selectively encourage conformity while discouraging or even punishing nonconformity. Dissenters are often pressured by others to change their opinions, and those who do not are disliked.

Obedience

Jerry nearly agreed to go with his parents when they came to Barrytown. But the leaders of the One-World Crusade took him aside and told him what to do—slip away from the compound and seek refuge at a remote Unificationist Center. Jerry agreed, leaving his parents bewildered, angry, and behind.

The human capacity for obedience can be devastating. During World War II, Germans obediently followed Hitler's orders and exterminated millions of Jews. At the height of his church's power, Reverend Moon ordered 4,150 of his followers to marry each other during a mass ceremony held in Madison Square Gardens. Virtually all of them did. In 1978, more than 900 members of the People's Temple drank poison and died when ordered to do so by their spiritual leader, Jim Jones. Fifteen years later, David Koresh ordered his followers to set fire to their compound after nearly two months of negotiations with the FBI. Eighty-six people died. Hitler, Moon, Jones, and Koresh all possessed extraordinary social **power**—the capacity to influence others, even when these others try to resist this influence (Lewin, 1951; Wrong, 1979).

power
The capacity to influence others, even when others try to resist this influence.

What are the limits to this power? When a malevolent authority demands our obedience, do we obey? What is the source of this power? And what methods do people use to increase their power over others? We consider these questions next.

The Obedience Situation

Stanley Milgram carried out his famous studies of obedience to authority in the early 1960s. Initially he had planned to test both Americans and Germans to see who was more obedient, but he soon changed his plans. "I found so much obedience" in America, Milgram explained, "I hardly saw the need for taking the experiment to Germany" (quoted in Meyer, 1970, p. 73; for more information, see Milgram, 1963, 1965, 1974).

Consider Milgram's experiment from the subject's perspective. Imagine yourself leaving work at five o'clock and driving to the Yale University campus. Only a week ago you responded to a flyer in the mail asking for volunteers for a study of memory and learning. You sent in your name because you met all the requirements (between the ages of 20 and 50 and not currently enrolled in high school or college), but you were still surprised that the researchers called you to schedule today's appointment. Coming to the Yale campus at night is inconvenient, but the study promises to be an interesting experience. Besides, the $4.50 they're paying for the hour's time will be a nice bonus.

Hoping your nervousness doesn't show too much, you enter to find yourself in a scientific-looking laboratory room. A young man in a gray lab coat approaches and asks, "Are you here for the experiment? Fine. I'm Mr. Williams; I'll be conducting the research." The experimenter then gestures to an innocuous-looking man seated in the corner and explains, "That's Mr. Wallace. You are both subjects in tonight's research."

You shake hands with the fiftyish, overweight Mr. Wallace before sitting down. Mr. Williams clears his throat before briskly explaining the study.

> We know very little about the effect of punishment on learning, because almost no truly scientific studies have been made of it in human beings.
>
> For instance, we don't know how much punishment is best for learning—and we don't know how much difference it makes as to who is giving the punishment, whether an adult learns best from a younger or an older person than himself—or many things of that sort.

Underestimating the Power of Social Influence

Do you find a conformity explanation of Jerry's actions surprising? Do you feel that so bizarre an outcome requires an equally bizarre explanation? If so, then you may be intuitively underemphasizing the power of social norms and conformity pressures. Indeed, in 1978 a representative sample of Americans was asked, "Why do you think people become involved in cults?" (Gallup, 1978, p. 275). Few of the respondents pointed to the powerful social-influence pressures that maximize conformity and minimize independence. Instead, most people blamed the personality characteristics and flaws of the cult members. They were seeking a "father figure"; they were "unhappy" or "gullible" or "searching for a deeper meaning to life"; they were "mentally disturbed," "escapists," or "addicted to drugs." Very few people correctly noted that cults use powerful social-influence tactics that maximize conformity and minimize dissent.

Why is social influence invisible to the naked eye? The *fundamental attribution error* provides part of the answer. As noted in Chapter 4, people overlook social determinants of actions, but they overestimate the causal role played by internal, personal factors. When we read that Jerry fell victim to the cult's influence, we assume that he was a weak, gullible person who was easily influenced by Jan and her group (Ross, 1977; Safer, 1980; West, Gunn, & Chernicky, 1975). When we ourselves bend to social-influence pressures, however, we attribute our responses to our personal tastes, interests, and preferences rather than to the situation. People who yield to indirect social pressure don't typically say "I was pressured into my decision." Instead, they claim that they studied the arguments other people offered and, with logic and reason, revised their position accordingly (Cialdini, Green, & Rusch, 1992; Griffin & Buehler, 1993). Given a choice, people explain actions in psychological terms rather than in social-psychological terms.

Social-influence processes are also relatively subtle. Jerry wasn't tortured, forced to watch indoctrination films, injected with mind-altering drugs, or deprived of sleep for days. Instead, he was subjected to continual informational, normative, and interpersonal influence until he converted to the group's position. These social processes affect all manner of social situations, from the informal and intimate to the ceremonious and public, but they remain hidden in the background—ever present and influential but rarely detected. Stanley Milgram's (1992) studies of encounters between people in urban settings illustrate the paradoxical power and subtlety of social forces. He sought to explain the high degree of social order that characterizes encounters between complete strangers in public places. Even though these encounters are fleeting and relatively inconsequential, they are for the most part ordered and predictable. Milgram was particularly intrigued by the waiting line or queue. This group comprises individuals who are strangers to one another and who are not likely to meet again, yet interaction within the queue is ordered by commonly recognized norms: Do not break line; do not talk to the stranger next to you; face the

Therefore, I'm going to ask one of you to be the teacher here tonight and the other one to be the learner. Does either of you have a preference? (Milgram, 1974, p. 18)

You look at your fellow subject, who shrugs and says "No." You do the same. Mr. Williams puts two slips of paper into a hat, shakes the hat, and then asks you each to draw one slip. "Mine says 'Learner,'" announces the other subject. Yours reads "Teacher."

At this point, you and Mr. Wallace follow Mr. Williams into another room, where Mr. Wallace, who is now the learner, is strapped into a chair. Williams explains that the straps are necessary to prevent excessive movement when shocks are given. Mr. Williams then attaches a wire to Wallace's wrist and says, "This electrode is connected to the shock generator in the next room. And this electrode paste," he adds, "is to provide a good contact and to avoid blisters and burns."

"Are the shocks dangerous?" asks Mr. Wallace.

"No," answers the experimenter. "Although the shocks can be extremely painful, they cause no permanent tissue damage" (Milgram, 1974, p. 19).

Leaving the learner tied in his chair and ready to receive shocks, you follow Mr. Williams into the next room. He asks you to sit in front of a machine labeled

front; move forward to fill spaces; and so on. These norms of civility emerge spontaneously when we join with others; they change a potentially chaotic situation into an orderly social encounter (Schmitt, Dube, & Leclerc, 1992). Yet we rarely notice their impact.

How can these subtle, nearly invisible social forces be made more discernible? Try doing something that violates one of the taken-for-granted rules of your social world. When purchasing a small object in a store, barter with the salesperson—"I'll give you 35 cents for this candy bar, but not a penny more." Or ask several friends to play a game of tic tac toe, and during the game erase their marks and replace them with your own. When they challenge your actions, insist that erasures are "just a part of the game." Another method involves refusing to understand common, everyday expressions during conversations with others. If someone says, "How are you?" you answer with "Do you mean physically or psychologically?" Or you can violate the norm of "civil inattention" by staring at people when riding in an elevator (Garfinkel, 1967; Goffman, 1963).

These norm violations may seem minor, but others will probably try to punish you for not conforming. And should you refuse to change your behavior, you will probably feel very self-conscious. Even Stanley Milgram was personally surprised by his own reactions when he violated a norm. He had men and women board a New York City subway and ask someone to give up his or her seat. In this situation, all interactants recognize and accept the rule "all seats are filled on a first-come, first-served basis," so asking someone to give up his or her seat is a norm violation. Still, many people gave up their seats, apparently because the request took them by surprise, they wanted to avoid interaction, or because they normalized the situation by concluding that the requester was ill. Milgram was particularly intrigued, however, by the reactions displayed by the norm violators. Even though they were volunteers who were deliberately breaking the situational norms in the name of research, all of them experienced severe emotional turmoil as they approached the situation. They "reported that when standing in front of a subject, they felt anxious, tense, and embarrassed. Frequently, they were unable to vocalize the request for a seat and had to withdraw" (Milgram, 1992, p. 42). Milgram, who also performed the norm-violation task, described the experience as wrenching, and concluded that there is an "enormous inhibitory anxiety that ordinarily prevents us from breaching social norms" (p. xxiv).

These studies remind us not to underestimate the power of social forces. Because social processes are not readily discernable, we can easily imagine that they are inconsequential. When we read about a riot following a soccer game in England, we too easily blame the violence on the people instead of on the norms that govern their behavior in that situation. When we read about a young man who murdered his roommate, we label him vicious instead of considering the context in which he lived. When we stand in line at a fast-food restaurant, we think we are free to do whatever we please, but in reality we must follow the rules and wait with all the others who are in line. We may not notice what our social world is doing to us, but this neglect does not free us from its control.

▲ Hundreds of young members of the Unification Church take their marriage vows in a ceremony conducted by Rev. Sun Myung Moon. In many cases, the bride and groom had never met before Rev. Moon decided that they should marry, yet few disobeyed his orders to wed.

Shock Generator, Type ZLB
Dyson Instrument Company
Waltham, Mass.
Output 15 Volts–450 Volts

The generator has a row of 30 levers, marked in 15-volt increments beginning at 15 and ending at 450 (see Figure 9-7). Mr. Williams lets you take it all in and then explains:

> As the teacher, you will be asked to read a list of word pairs, such as blue-box, nice-day, and wild-duck to the learner using this intercom system. Once you have read the entire list to him, you are to test his memory by asking him a series of multiple choice questions, such as blue: sky, ink, box, lamp; nice: rose, wall, duck, day. The learner communicates his answer by pressing one of four switches in front of him, which in turn lights up one of the four numbered quadrants in the answer box on the top of the shock generator. If the learner answers correctly, then you can move on to the next multiple choice test question. However, if he gives an incorrect response, he must be given an electric shock. Start at fifteen volts, and increase the shock level one step each time the learner gives a wrong answer. Any questions? Fine. Before we actually begin, we always ask the teachers to experience a sample shock for themselves. So could you roll up your sleeve? Let me attach this electrode. Okay, now I'll flip the switch for forty-five volts and that's an example of the shock the learner will be receiving (paraphrased from Milgram, 1974, pp. 19–20)

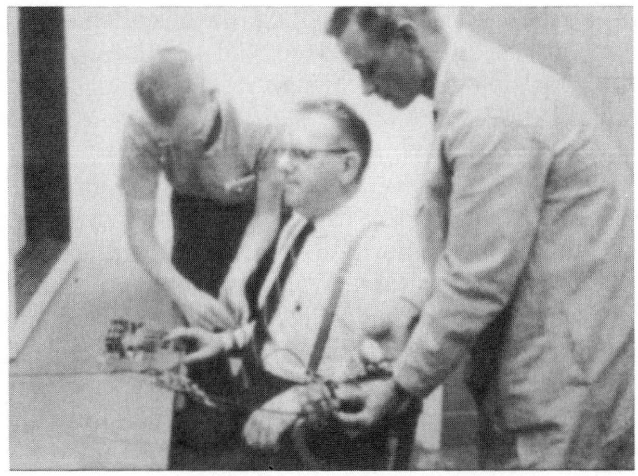

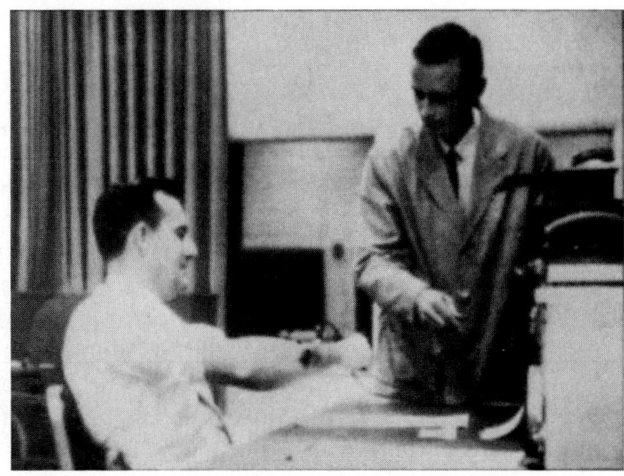

▲ (a) The "teacher" gives a helping hand as the experimenter straps the "learner" into the chair. (b) The experimenter gives the "teacher" a sample shock of 45 volts by pushing down the third lever on the shock generator.

Ruefully rubbing your arm as you recover from the sample shock, you begin teaching the learner the list: "blue-box; nice-day; wild-duck," and so on, until you reach the end. Then you test his memory with the multiple-choice questions. Before long, the learner misses one of the items.

"No," you explain into the microphone, "the answer is 'duck.' Fifteen volts." As you push down the lever for 15 volts, a small light above it flashes red, a loud buzzing noise fills the room, a series of clicks and switches sound inside the machine, a blue light flashes *voltage energizer,* and the dial labeled *voltage meter* swings far to the right. An impressive machine, you think to yourself.

Down the list of questions you go, punctuating each wrong answer with a shock of ever-increasing voltage—15, 30, 45, 60, and upward. With each step up you become more concerned about the welfare of the learner; after all, the 45 volts you received seemed painful enough. What would 255 or 270 volts feel like? Finally, as you administer 300 volts for yet another incorrect answer, you hear the helpless learner pounding on the wall.

"I think he's trying to communicate with me."

Mr. Williams looks up from his desk. "Please continue."

"Well, it's not fair to shock the guy . . . These are terrific volts."

In the same even tone, Mr. Williams once more commands, "Please go on. The experiment requires that you continue."

Reluctantly you read the next question, but the learner does not respond. "Mr. Wallace," you ask, "what is your answer?" but the response does not light up on the panel. Turning to the experimenter, you mumble, "Well, that's it." The experimenter, however, sits unmoved in his chair. As you hesitate, he tells you, "Wait five or ten seconds before considering no response as a wrong answer, and then increase the shock level one step each time the learner fails to respond correctly."

Turning back to the microphone, you tell the silent Mr. Wallace, "Wrong. The answer was 'day.' Three hundred fifteen volts." As you press the switch, above the buzzing and clicking you hear a pounding on the wall. Disconcerted by the sound, you once more confront the experimenter.

"I don't think this is very humane. I can't go on with this."

Mr. Williams answers firmly, "Please continue. The experiment requires that you continue."

"No, this isn't right," you answer. "It's a hell of an experiment."

Mr. Williams doesn't seem to listen to you. He only says, "Whether the learner likes it or not, you must go on until he has learned all the word pairs correctly. So please go on" (Milgram, 1974, p. 32).

Turning back to the control panel, you look at the long row of switches that you have flipped; 15, 30, 45, all the way up to 315. And you look at the switches that remain: 330, 345, 360, and on up to 450. Frozen with indecision, you ask yourself, "What should I do?"

Responding to Authority

Milgram was studying obedience rather than learning; he wanted to understand when and why people follow an authority's orders. Both the experimenter (Mr. Williams) and the learner (Mr. Wallace) were Milgram's accomplices, hired and trained to enact particular roles. Milgram rigged the drawing to identify shocker and shockee—both of the slips in the hat read "Teacher." The learner's responses were carefully designed to include mistakes, the shock machine hadn't really been connected, and the pounding on the wall at the 300- and 315-volt levels was prearranged. The experimenter's actions were painstakingly rehearsed to create a standard setting for the measurement of obedience. His "manner was impassive, and his appearance somewhat stern throughout the experiment" (Milgram, 1963, p. 373), and he always responded to the subject's questions with the same sequence of "prods" (Milgram, 1974, p. 21):

Prod 1: Please continue [or Please go on].
Prod 2: The experiment requires that you continue.
Prod 3: It is absolutely essential that you continue.
Prod 4: You have no other choice, you must go on.

Milgram did not think very many people would be obedient. Indeed, he went so far as to describe his procedures to a group of researchers and psychiatrists and asked them to predict how people would behave. None of these experts thought subjects would shock the learner to the 450-volt level—150 volts, maybe, but no more. To everyone's surprise, however, the majority of the subjects behaved obediently. All of the subjects shocked the learner up to

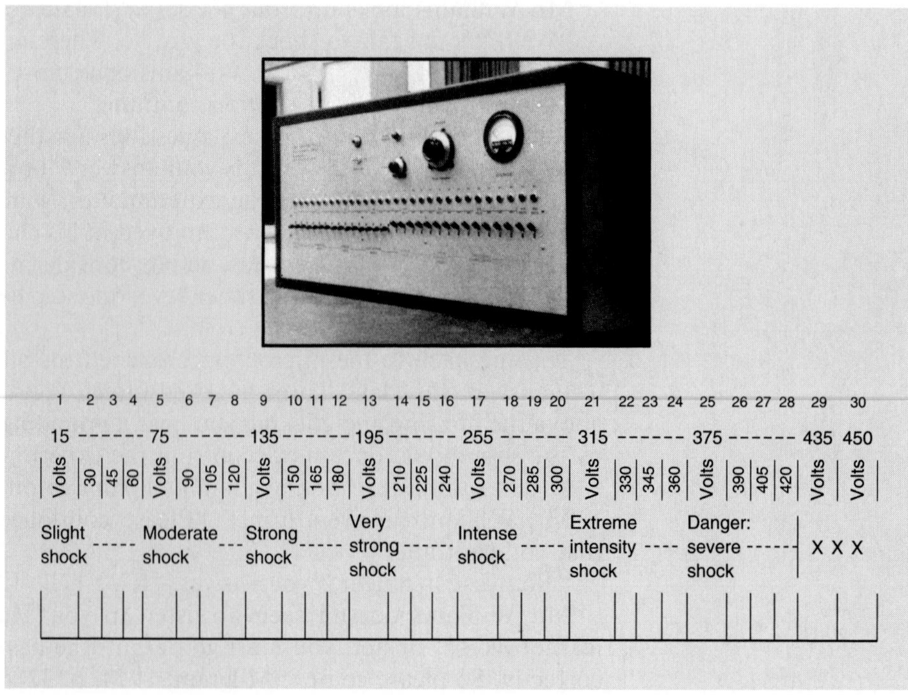

▲ **FIGURE 9-7**
How did Milgram measure obedience to authority? In his classic research Milgram arranged for individuals to deliver electric shocks to a confederate using this bogus machine. Shocks ranged from a low of 15 volts to a high of 450 volts. The subjects administered a shock by pressing one of the levers on the box. (Adapted from Milgram, 1974)

the 300-volt level, when the learner's pounding could be heard. Several people quit at this point, but many more continued. Forty people participated in that first study: Twenty-six of them—65%—obeyed completely by giving the learner a 450-volt shock (see the line labeled "Remote" in Figure 9-8).

Milgram studied the responses of nearly 1,000 people in a series of replications and extensions of his original study. In these later researches, some of which are discussed next, different aspects of the setting were systematically manipulated, allowing Milgram to assess their influence on obedience rates. Although he continued to search for the limits of obedience, again and again Milgram's subjects buckled under the pressure of the experimenter's power. His studies indicate that ordinary people, when put into an extraordinary situation, can be coerced into obedience by powerful authorities.

Harm and obedience. After Milgram tested the first group of subjects, he realized that many were confused about what was happening to the learner. They had all heard the pounding on the wall, but the signal that something was wrong was ambiguous. So Milgram intensified the experience by having the learner grunt, scream in pain, and repeatedly plead for release. Still, as the line labeled "Voice feedback" in Figure 9-8 indicates, 62.5% of the subjects obeyed. So Milgram made the victim's suffering more apparent to the subjects by placing the screaming learner in the same room as the teacher. In this "Proximity" condition, 40% of the subjects obeyed to the 450-volt level. Still fewer (30%) obeyed when they had to touch the victim each time he received a shock. In the "Touch proximity" condition, the teacher had to force the learner's hand down onto an electrical plate before giving the shocks.

When these conditions were complete, Milgram decided to change the feedback from the victim to make the harmful consequences of obedience more salient. He kept the grunts, the screams, and the anguished pleas, but he also added a new problem. When the experimenter strapped him in the chair, the learner mentioned that he had a heart problem. Then, at the 150-volt level, he complained that his heart was starting to bother him. By the 300-volt level, he was screaming hysterically about his heart condition. Still, 65% of the subjects were maximally obedient.

Obedience and conformity. In the original version of the experiment, the subject was alone when he faced the authority. Milgram wondered what would occur if the teacher were part of a group of two or three others who refused to administer the electric shocks. Would disobedience be the rule rather than the exception? Milgram found that subjects were more obedient when they were alone than when they were with others who refused to obey. The subject still gave the shocks, but two other subjects helped with related tasks, such as reading the questions and giving feedback. Only the individual giving the shocks was a real subject, however; the other two were confederates trained to refuse to continue with the shocks at the 150-volt and 210-volt levels, respectively. In this situation, Milgram found that only 10% of the true subjects were completely obedient.

Power and obedience. Milgram concluded that the situation was more constraining than he had initially intended. So he moved the study to a different location to see whether people were obeying because they respected anything associated with prestigious Yale University. The new location was an unpretentious office building in downtown Bridgeport. Obedience dropped only slightly, to 47.5%, even though the study wasn't connected to a legitimate research facility.

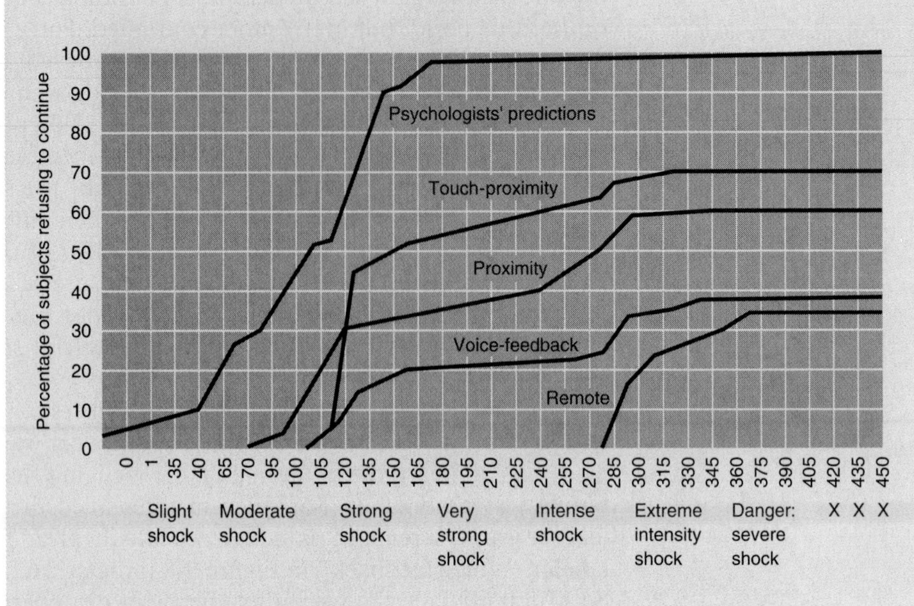

▲ **FIGURE 9-8**
Will people obey an authority who asks them to give painful, and possibly lethal, electric shocks to an innocent person? Milgram's findings for four different obedience situations suggest that people are surprisingly obedient. Obedience was highest when the victim was seated in a different room and communicated only by pounding on the wall ("remote condition"). As the victim was moved closer and closer to the subject, obedience decreased. Still, even when subjects had to push the victim's hand down on the shock plate, 30% were obedient to the 450-volt level. (Adapted from Milgram, 1974)

Obedience dwindled, however, when the experimenter left the room. If he had to give the order to shock by telephone, only 20% of the participants were obedient to the 450-volt level. Another low-obedience variation featured a second confederate who sat recording information at what had formerly been the experimenter's desk. The experimenter explained the study as in other conditions, but he gave no instructions about shock levels before being called away. The confederate, however, filled the role of the authority; he suggested that shocks be given in increasingly strong doses and ordered the subject to continue giving shocks when the learner started to complain. In this instance, obedience dropped to 20%.

Milgram found the least amount of obedience in one particularly creative episode in which the experimenter agreed to take the role of the learner supposedly to convince a reluctant subject that the shocks weren't harmful. After receiving a 150-volt shock, the experimenter shouted, "That's enough, gentlemen," but the confederate—who had been watching the procedure—gleefully insisted, "Oh, no, let's go on. Oh, no, come on, I'm going to have to go through the whole thing. Let's go. Come on, let's keep going" (Milgram, 1974, p. 102). The confederate demanded continuation, but all the subjects refused.

Why obedience? Milgram's findings, which are partly summarized in Table 9-7, generated considerable controversy. Some critics suggested that his findings were a product of some unrecognized flaw in his procedures. But his basic findings have been replicated in many studies (for example, Blass, 1991; Meeus & Raaijmakers, 1987; Miller, 1986). Others suggested that the subjects weren't duped by the procedures. They knew all along that no shocks were being delivered. Yet Milgram documents the strain under which most subjects labored as they confronted the authority. According to Milgram (1963):

> many subjects showed signs of nervousness in the experimental situation, and especially upon administering the more powerful shocks. In a large number of

> cases the degree of tension reached extremes that are rarely seen in sociopsychological laboratory studies. Subjects were observed to sweat, tremble, stutter, bite their lips, groan, and dig their fingernails into their flesh. (p. 375)

The distress of the subjects was so great that the publication of the study sparked a controversy over the ethics of social-psychological research (Baumrind, 1964; Forsyth, 1981; Schlenker & Forsyth, 1977).

Many critics also focused on the characteristics of the subjects themselves. Falling prey to the fundamental attribution error discussed earlier in the chapter, many wondered, "What kind of evil, sadistic men did he recruit for his study?" Indeed, research has shown that people tend to blame the subjects for their obedience, attributing their actions to their personal characteristics rather than acknowledging the powerful situational forces at work in the experimental situation (Sabini & Silver, 1983). Furthermore, when asked whether they would have obeyed in the same circumstances, most people claim they would have stopped at around the 150-volt level. None of the individuals polled answered that they would deliver 450-volt shocks, but Milgram's findings suggest otherwise.

These explanations all underestimate the power of social influence. When the subjects agreed to take part in Milgram's study, they became part of a social hierarchy complete with powerful norms. They no longer acted in an autonomous state where they fulfilled their own purposes and goals; instead, they conformed to the demands of the situation. Milgram himself underestimated the power of the situation: The impressive laboratory, the fancy shock machine, Yale University's campus, the impassive experimenter, the prods, the gradual increments in shock level all contributed to the high levels of obedience. As we see in the next section, each of these situational cues increased the experimenter's power over the subject.

Bases of Power

Did it take an order from Reverend Moon himself to prompt Jerry to leave his family? No, but the order carried with it the power of Reverend Moon himself. Jerry recognized the authority of the One-World Crusade leaders, for they were appointed by Moon. They had a secure power base, which they used to influence the new recruits.

John R. P. French and Bertram Raven suggest that people draw their power from a variety of sources. In their original analysis of the **bases of power**, they identified five key sources: rewards, punishments, status, attraction, and expertise. Those who control these five bases are powerful; those who do not are powerless (French & Raven, 1959; Raven, 1965).

bases of power
Sources of social power over other people; includes the capacity to reward and to punish, status, attraction, and expertise.

reward power
The ability to reinforce positively or negatively others who comply with requests or demands.

Reward power. The influencer who gives or promises rewards exercises **reward power**. Sometimes tangible, material rewards are given or promised. The supervisor who increases workers' salaries when they raise their productivity and the teacher who gives students extra credit for extra work are both using tangible rewards to influence people. In other instances, intangible, social types of rewards—such as approval, compliments, intimacy, agreement, and love—may be used. When you smile at your friends, help them with their course work, or tell them, "You look great today," you are using reward power. Milgram's experimenter relied more on this form of reward, for he was an important source of positive evaluations. Subjects wanted to win a favorable appraisal from Mr. Williams, and they did each time they administered a shock.

▲ **TABLE 9-7**
Summing up: The percentage of subjects who delivered 450-volt shocks in several versions of Milgram's studies of obedience

Condition	*Description*	*Obedience Rate*
Remote	No vocal complaints can be heard, but at 300 and 315 volts the learner pounds on the wall. After 315 volts he stops pounding and no longer answers the questions.	65.0%
Voice feedback	The learner begins to grunt in pain at the 75-volt level, and his screams, grunts, and desperate pleas for release become more intense up to the 315-volt level. After 330 volts, he stops screaming and answering.	62.5%
Proximity	The learner grunts, screams, and complains, as in the voice-feedback condition, while sitting in the same room as the subject.	40.0%
Touch-proximity	The same cues are used as in the voice-feedback condition, but the learner receives a shock only when his hand rests on a shock plate. After 150 volts he refuses to continue, so the subject (wearing a protective mitt) must force his hand down on the plate.	30.0%
Heart condition	The learner mentions that he has heart problems when he is strapped into his chair in the adjoining room. When shocked, he screams as in the voice-feedback condition, and he repeatedly claims that his heart is bothering him. He stops responding after 330 volts. Complaints about the heart condition were used in all subsequent versions.	65.0%
Disobedient peers	Three learners carry out the task. One subject gives the shocks, and the two others help with related tasks. These other subjects are confederates who refuse to continue with the shocks at the 150-volt and 210-volt levels.	10.0%
Office building	The heart condition version is replicated at a run-down office suite in a building located in downtown Bridgeport.	47.5%
Experimenter absent	In most conditions, the experimenter sits at a table a few feet from the teacher. In this version, however, the experimenter gives his instructions and then leaves the room. He delivers his prods by telephone.	20.5%
Ordinary person as authority	Two teachers give shocks to the learner, but the experimenter does not tell them to increase the voltage each time. When the experimenter leaves the room, one of the teachers (a confederate) orders the other subject to increase the voltage level each time.	20.0%
Authority as victim	When the learner expresses misgivings about the shocks, the experimenter volunteers to act as the learner for a session. At the 150-volt level, the experimenter demands that they stop, but the original learner insists that they continue.	0.0%

Source: Adapted from Milgram, 1974.

coercive power
The ability to punish or threaten others who do not comply with requests or demands.

Coercive power. The employer demotes a worker to a less desirable position as punishment for poor performance; the teacher tells the class that everyone is going to fail if the exam grades don't improve; in anger, you tell a friend, "You're acting like an idiot." These examples involve **coercive power** because they are based on threats, warnings, and actual punishment. Tangible threats and punishments include physical abuse, fines, low grades, and firings. Intangible, social threats include disapproval, insults, and expressions of contempt. Mr. Williams used coercive power in his prods. "The experiment requires that you continue"; "It is absolutely essential that you continue"; and "You have no other choice, you must go on" all warn of possible negative consequences for disobedience.

Coercive power is most effective in changing behaviors when it is applied immediately and without emotion. Even when it is used with care, however, coercive power can have negative side effects (French & Raven, 1959; Podsakoff & Schriesheim, 1985; Raven & Rubin, 1976). We simply do not like people who control us through the use of threats and punishments. We tend to counter coercive influence by avoiding the source altogether or by resorting to coercion ourselves (Schlenker et al., 1976).

legitimate power
Power that stems from an authority's justifiable right to require and demand compliance.

Legitimate power. Unlike reward and coercive power, **legitimate power** stems from the influencer's recognized right to require and demand the performance of certain behaviors. The employer has a legitimate right to demand a certain level of productivity because of the contractual relationship between employer and employee. Similarly, the teacher can insist that students refrain from talking and cheating during exams if both the students and the teacher recognize that these demands are among the teacher's prerogatives. Like normative social influence—one of the causes of conformity examined earlier in this chapter—legitimate power arises from an internalized sense of duty, loyalty, obedience, or normative obligation rather than from a desire to gain rewards or avoid punishments. Many subjects in the Milgram study felt that when they agreed to participate in the study they had entered into an oral contract that obliged them to obey. In consequence, Mr. Williams had a legitimate right to control their actions, and the learner had no right to quit the study.

referent power
Influence based on subordinates' identification with, attraction to, or respect for, the power holder.

Referent power. Many of us belong to the same political party as our parents. We purchase the same type of lawn fertilizer as our neighbors. We read the books and magazines that are praised by our best friends. Why? According to French and Raven (1959), people we like, respect, and admire—our parents, neighbors, colleagues—possess **referent power**: Their views provide us with important reference points for defining and testing our own beliefs and behav-

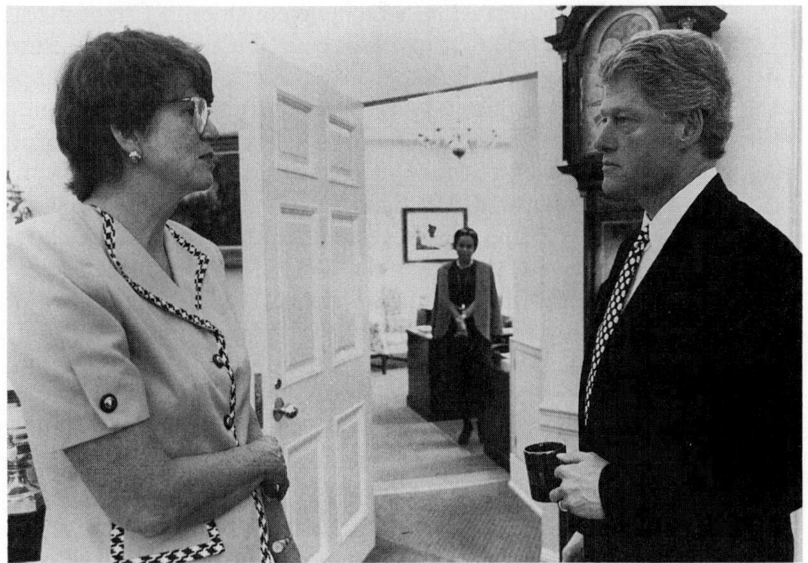

▲ A leader's ability to influence others ultimately depends on his or her bases of power. A leader who can offer rewards and promises (reward power), can make threats and administer punishments (coercive power), occupies a respected position (legitimate power), is respected and liked by his or her staff (referent power), and appears to do his or her job well (expert power) will be influential indeed.

ior. Bosses who enjoy the unswerving loyalty of their employees may be able to increase productivity simply by looking at a worker. Teachers who are high in referent power—the friendly teacher whom all the students like and the tough but well-respected teacher—may be able to maintain discipline in their classes with little apparent effort because the students obey every request. Mr. Williams's referent power was substantial. The subjects respected Yale and recognized the importance of scientific research. They trusted Mr. Williams to do the right thing and did not feel that they should question him.

Expert power. When we feel uncertain of our own skills and abilities, we often follow the advice of experts and specialists. An employee may balk when asked to perform a routine task in a new way unless the supervisor explains that the recommended change is based on a report made by a team of efficiency experts. Similarly, students may be reluctant to disagree with a teacher who seems to be an expert in his or her field. And when it comes to influencing your friends, you will find it is easier when you tell them, "I know what I'm talking about" or "I've been studying this business for several years now." People with special ability based on experience influence us because they possess **expert power**. Very few of Milgram's subjects knew much about electricity or its effects in such a situation; because they considered Mr. Williams an expert, they believed him when he said "Although the shocks may be painful, there is no permanent tissue damage" (Milgram, 1974, p. 21). The few people who were knowledgeable about electricity refused to obey.

expert power
Influence that derives from subordinates' assumption that the power holder possesses superior skills and abilities.

Social Influence Tactics

French and Raven's fivefold theory of power, as summarized in Table 9-8, does more than describe sources of power. It also suggests ways to *use* power to influence others. According to French and Raven, if you want to influence others, offer them rewards, threaten them with punishment, emphasize the legitimacy of your request, make certain the target likes, admires, and respects you, and at least try to seem like an expert.

These suggestions, however, only scratch the surface of the vast array of interpersonal strategies people can use to influence others. In earlier chapters, we saw that people often use *ingratiation* tactics to make themselves seem likable (Chapter 2) and *persuasion* to change others' attitudes (Chapter 8). Even aggression, which we consider in Chapter 13, is a social-influence tactic, albeit one that involves coercion and violence. But the social-influence arsenal includes many other useful tactics, including complaining, discussion, making requests and demands, instruction, negotiation, applying group pressure, persistence, fait accompli, manipulation, supplication, evasion, and disengagement (Alicke et al., 1992; Belk et al., 1988; Buss et al., 1987; Cowan, Drinkard, & MacGavin, 1984; Dillard & Fitzpatrick, 1985; Falbo, 1977; Falbo & Peplau, 1980; Howard, Blumstein, & Schwartz, 1986; Instone, Major, & Bunker, 1983; Kipnis, 1984; Kipnis & Cosentino, 1969; Marwell & Schmitt, 1967; Offermann & Schrier, 1985; Wheeless, Barraclough, & Stewart, 1983; Wilkinson & Kipnis, 1978; Wiseman & Schenck-Hamlin, 1981; Yukl & Tracey, 1992).

Table 9-9 lists many of the interpersonal strategies people can use to get their way. Each tactic takes a different approach to social influence. First, some of these methods are more *rational* than others. Imagine that you face this situation: Your social psychology instructor requires a 20-page paper on an approved topic. The paper is due tomorrow and you haven't even picked a topic yet. You have an appointment to see your professor about the situation.

▲ **TABLE 9-8**
Summing up: French and Raven's five bases of power

Base of Power	*Definition*
Reward	Influence based on rewards offered to the target by the power holder contingent on compliance
Coercive	Influence based on punishments or threats directed toward the target person in the event of noncompliance
Legitimate	Influence based on the target's belief that the power holder has a justifiable right to demand the performance of certain behaviors
Referent	Influence based on the target's identification with, attraction to, or respect for, the power holder
Expert	Influence based on the target's belief that the power holder possesses superior skills and abilities

Source: Adapted from French & Raven, 1959.

What can you do to get the professor to give you an extension? If you tried to reason with your professor by simply stating that you lack the time to do a good job on the paper and need an extension, you would be using a rational influence tactic. But if you tried to evade the issue by skipping your appointment and cutting class until you finished the paper, you would be using a nonrational method. Some methods are also *direct,* whereas others are more indirect. If you walked into your instructor's office and baldly stated, "I must have an extension on my paper," you would be using a strong, direct method. But if you told your teacher that your paper was stolen, you would be using deceit, which is a weak, indirect method (Falbo, 1977; Falbo & Peplau, 1980; Kipnis, 1984).

We use different tactics depending on the situation we face. We prefer, for example, to use a variety of tactics when we are working with subordinates, but when dealing with our superiors, we rely more on rational methods such as persuasion and discussion (Kipnis, 1984). When we are uncertain of our authority in the situation, we are more likely to use indirect tactics, but when we have considerable power, we rely more on strong tactics (Kipnis, 1984; Kipnis et al., 1984). A little boy may use relatively weak methods when trying to influence his father, but stronger methods when interacting with his peers (Cowan, Drinkard, & MacGavin, 1984). And a boss is more likely to use demands, threats, or promises when dealing with a subordinate, and coalition tactics when trying to influence a superior (Yukl & Falbe, 1990, 1991). Also, when the target of the influence resists, we shift to stronger and stronger tactics (Kipnis, 1984; Michener & Burt, 1975; Strong, 1991a; Strong et al., 1988).

How do people react to these various kinds of tactics? Although people may do what you want if you use strong tactics, they will like you more if you rely on the rational ones. One researcher recruited college students who claimed to use one of the tactics similar to those shown in Table 9-9 for discussion groups. When they rated one another on such factors as friendliness, consideration, and honesty, the investigator discovered that people who reported using rational influence methods were better liked than those who used nonrational methods. Thus, if you use reasoning, compromise, expertise, bargaining, or persuasion to influence others, they will probably like you more than if you use such techniques as deceit, evasion, or threats (Falbo, 1977).

Not everyone uses the full range of tactics shown in Table 9-9. People who are concerned with being accepted and liked by others use more indirect and

▲ **TABLE 9-9**
Tactics people use to influence others in everyday situations

Tactic	*Examples*
Bully	I yell at him; I criticize her work; I push him around.
Claim expertise	I let her know I'm an expert; I bury them in technical details; I rely on my experience.
Complain	I gripe about all the work I have to do; I grumble about having to study; I complain about my headache.
Demand	I insist that he stop; I demand that the problem be solved; I order her to continue.
Discuss	I give him supporting reasons; I explain why I favor the plan; we talk about it.
Disengage	I break up with her; I give him the cold shoulder; I stop talking to her.
Evade	I keep it from him; I change the subject when it comes up; I skip the meeting.
Fait accompli	I just do it; I don't get anyone's permission; I avoid going through channels.
Ingratiate	I flatter her; I try to be seductive; I compliment him on the way he looks.
Inspire	I appeal to her sense of fair play; I cheer him on; I remind her of her many good qualities.
Instruct	I teach him how to do it; I explain it in simple terms; I set an example.
Join forces	I get the boss to agree with me; I turn the group against her; I get others to take my side.
Manipulate	I lie; I get him to think it's his idea; I leave out important details.
Negotiate	I offer her a bargain; I work out a compromise; I wheel and deal.
Persist	I don't take no for an answer; I reiterate my point; I nag until she agrees.
Persuade	I coax her into it; I convert him to my side; I present all the evidence.
Promise	I promise never to do it again; I offer her a bonus; I offer to do some of his work for him.
Punish	I fire her; I slap him; I take away her toys.
Request	I say what I want; I ask him to do me a favor; I tell her what I expect.
Reward	I increase his pay; I give her a present; I fix dinner for him.
Supplicate	I plead; I cry; I beg humbly for permission.
Threaten	I tell her I'm going to leave her; I threaten legal action; I tell him that he might get fired.

rational tactics than direct and nonrational strategies. Those who enjoy manipulating others use indirect and nonrational tactics instead. Men use more of the tactics than women do, and they are likely to rely on the more direct strategies (Belk et al., 1988; Falbo & Peplau, 1980; Instone, Major, & Bunker, 1983).

Specialized Change Tactics

A final category of social influence tactics remains to be examined. These specialized tactics, as Robert Cialdini (1993) explains, exploit our tendency to respond without considering our options. Each of these techniques commits us to a course of action before we can stop to consider it. In a sense, these tactics amount to psychological jujitsu. Just as martial arts experts use their opponents' weight and momentum against them, these techniques push us into psychological motion and then take advantage of our momentum (Dillard, 1991).

The foot in the door. Have you ever noticed that some panhandlers preface their requests for money by asking the time? That telemarketers often begin by asking if you have a few moments to answer some survey questions? That car dealers do all they can to get you to test-drive the car? That political canvassers sometimes begin by asking if you will sign a petition? That people seeking money for their cults often start by asking you to take a flower as a gift?

foot-in-the-door technique A method of influence in which influencers first make a very small request with which the target will probably agree. Once the target agrees to the minor request, influencers then make the more important request.

Such tactics exemplify the **foot-in-the-door technique**. This tactic, long advocated by door-to-door salespersons, recommends first getting your foot in the door by making some small request that the target can't refuse, then following up the initial request with the real sales pitch. Investigators tested this technique by telephoning women who were homemakers with a small request (Freedman & Fraser, 1966). Claiming to be pollsters for a public service publication known as *The Guide,* they asked the women if they would be willing to answer some survey questions. If the woman consented, they asked her a few innocuous questions about household soaps and thanked her for her cooperation. Three days later came the major request. The researchers called back and claimed that the survey had been expanded: A team of five or six men would like to visit the subject's home to enumerate and classify all her household products. The men must have the run of the house, so they could go through all her cupboards and storage places, and the information they collected would be published in *The Guide.*

The researchers discovered that the foot-in-the-door method was very effective: 52.8% of the women who participated in the initial survey agreed to the outrageous second request. In contrast, only 22.2% of the women who were exposed only to the second request agreed. Similar studies have also found that the two requests called for by the foot-in-the-door technique are superior to a single request for many types of behaviors, although such factors as the sex of the influencer and the amount of time that elapses between the two requests moderate the power of the foot-in-the-door method (Beaman et al., 1983).

The door in the face. As you walk across campus, a student asks you to stop for a minute. The student asks if you would be willing to work as an unpaid counselor of juvenile delinquents as part of the Youth Counseling Program. As a counselor, you would have to put in 2 hours a week for at least two years. Thinking of your other commitments, you immediately answer that you aren't interested. Two years! That's preposterous! But before you can escape, the student makes another request: Well, would you be willing to chaperone a group on a trip to the zoo? It will only take 2 hours.

door-in-the-face technique A method of influence in which influencers first make a very large request that the target is likely to refuse. After they are turned down, influencers then make their actual, more reasonable request.

If you say yes to the second request, you may be falling victim to the **door-in-the-face technique**. Cialdini finds that this method reverses the foot-in-the-door approach by prefacing a reasonable request with an initial request so extreme it is sure to be denied. When Cialdini and his associates simply asked students if they would be willing to chaperone juveniles on a trip to the zoo, only 16.7% agreed. When they prefaced this minor request with the major request for 2 years of volunteer service, they achieved 50.0% compliance (Cialdini et al., 1975).

Cialdini suggests that the door-in-the-face technique may capitalize on a contrast effect. Just as lukewarm water feels colder if you have just had your hand in a bucket of hot water, the second request seems more reasonable when it is contrasted with the larger initial request. Cialdini suggests that a similar contrast process is at work in many sales settings. If a man tells a salesperson he wants to buy a three-piece suit and a pair of shoes, the salesperson should

▲ Despite this executive's claim, people who are concerned with being accepted and liked generally don't use direct, coercive influence tactics.

Drawing by M. Twohy; © 1993 The New Yorker Magazine, Inc.

"I like to think of myself as a nice guy. Naturally, sometimes you have to step on a few faces."

show the customer the suit first; a $150 pair of shoes will seem less expensive after he spends $400 on a suit. Similarly, realtors sometimes begin a tour of available homes with a few overpriced houses so the other houses they show will seem like attractive bargains.

lowball technique
A method of influence in which the influencer first exacts agreement from the target before revealing hidden costs or the unexpected lack of benefits.

Lowballing. A final influence tactic depends on inducing the customer to agree to the request before revealing certain hidden costs. The **lowball technique**, a favorite ploy of car salespeople, begins when the seller offers the customer a bargain on a car. Once the customer agrees—and perhaps even begins completing the necessary paperwork—the salesperson reveals the hidden costs in a variety of ways. The seller may claim that the manager refused to allow a discount; or an extra item that the customer thought was included in the quoted price may be added on after the deal has been closed; or the amount of trade-in allowance for the customer's old car may be reduced by the used-car manager. No matter what the method, the goal is the same: to induce the target to make a decision before all the drawbacks have been revealed. A more commonplace example of lowballing occurs when someone asks, "Will you do me a favor?" and gets us to say yes before revealing what is expected of us.

Lowballing works. Cialdini and his colleagues used this tactic when they telephoned students to ask whether they would be interested in participating in an experiment on thinking processes for extra credit in their psychology class. In the control condition, before asking if the subject was willing to take part, the caller admitted that the sessions were scheduled for 7 A.M. In the lowball condition, the researcher omitted this key piece of information until after the subject had agreed or refused to participate. Just as any car salesperson would predict, compliance was greater in the lowballing condition (56%) than in the control condition (31%). Furthermore, when 7 A.M. rolled around, the lowball subjects were more likely than the controls to keep the appointment. Parenthetically, before the subjects were debriefed about the study, they actually participated in the promised study of thinking processes (Cialdini et al., 1978; see also Burger & Petty, 1981).

Question authority. Cialdini warns us to beware of the tactics summarized in Table 9-10, for they can change us without our awareness. Jerry would have profited from Cialdini's advice. The One-World Crusaders used all these tactics, and more, to influence him to join their group. Their requests escalated ever so gradually, exploiting fully the foot-in-the door principle. Once he was at the seminary, they pushed him to make major commitments to the group, and when he couldn't, they asked him to make minor ones. They didn't reveal major costs associated with the group until after he had expressed significant commitment. He didn't discover, for example, that the group was linked to Reverend Moon until after he had agreed to go to the week-long retreat. They cast, he bit, and they reeled him in.

How could Jerry have defended himself against these tactics? Cialdini recommends wariness—fight the urge to respond automatically to these types of influence techniques, and base your choices on your own best interests. If a situation gets out of hand, step out of it. Recognize that consistency is expected, but that *foolish* consistency "lays us open to the maneuvers of those who want to exploit" us (Cialdini, 1992, p. 86). Recognize, too, the difference between authority and the *trappings* of authority. If you question authority, Cialdini suggests, you will be able to distinguish between those who deserve your obedience and those who do not.

Summary

Social influence occurs when other people change our feelings, thoughts, or behaviors. *Conformity,* for example, results whenever our opinions, judgments, or actions change to match the opinions, judgments, or actions of the people around us. Social influence can also result in *obedience*: When authorities give us orders, we often obey.

Isn't it our nature to rebel rather than conform? Sherif's studies using the *autokinetic effect* suggest that people will accept the opinion favored by the majority of the group over their own. Asch, using a less ambiguous task, also found that people conformed about one-third of the time. Some individuals actually accepted the group's opinion as the correct one (*conversion*) but others agreed publicly while disagreeing privately (*compliance*). Conformity pressure is greatest when the majority is unanimous and contains at least three members. *Social impact theory,* in fact, suggests that conformity increases as more members are added beyond three, but at an ever-decreasing rate. Conformity is not inevitable, however. If minorities manage to resist the majority's pressuring, they sometimes succeed in influencing the majority. Moscovici believes that a consistent minority wields the most influence, whereas Hollander's concept of *idiosyncrasy credits* recommends that minorities preface dissent with agreement. In all likelihood, both approaches are effective.

In some situations, some individuals conform more than others. Crutchfield proposed that some people are conformists, whereas others are nonconformists. One's willingness to conform depends on a number of personality factors, including dependence and self-confidence. Moreover, two types of nonconformists have been identified. *Independents* publicly express ideas that are consistent with their personal standards, irrespective of the pressure to conform. *Counterconformists,* in contrast, deliberately express ideas that clash with the dominant view, simply to oppose that view. Women conform more than men only when the situation involves face-to-face interaction.

▲ **TABLE 9-10**
Three indirect-influence tactics

Technique	*Basic Form*	*Example*
Foot in the door	First make a very small request to which you are certain the target person will agree; then make the more important request.	A door-to-door magazine salesperson asks for a drink of water.
Door in the face	First make a very large request that the target will refuse; then make the more reasonable request for what you really want.	A friend asks to borrow your car; when you refuse, he asks for a ride.
Lowballing	Get the target to agree to the request before revealing its hidden costs or unexpected lack of benefits.	You agree to give someone a ride home, then discover she lives 20 miles away.

What causes conformity? *Informational influence* occurs when other people provide us with information that we then use to make decisions and form opinions. *Normative influence* occurs when we tailor our actions to fit the social norms of the situation. *Interpersonal influence* occurs when other people selectively encourage conformity while discouraging or even punishing nonconformity. We like people who agree with us, and in some cases reject those who do not bend to the will of the group.

Some individuals in society use social *power* to influence others, even when these others try to resist their influence. Milgram's studies demonstrate that ordinary people, if put into extraordinary circumstances, can be goaded into obedience by an authority. He discovered that 65% of his subjects, when asked to deliver painful electric shocks to an innocent person, obeyed. According to French and Raven, the experimenter's power in the Milgram experiments was based on five sources: rewards and promises (*reward power*), threats and punishments (*coercive power*), status and position (*legitimate power*), attraction and respect (*referent power*), and skill and ability (*expert power*). Often, these bases are supplemented by a variety of power tactics, such as persuasion, coercion, reasoning, bargaining, or deceit. These tactics differ from one another in terms of directness and rationality. Last, in some instances, individuals make use of indirect influence techniques that take advantage of our tendency to conform unthinkingly. Influencers who use the *foot-in-the-door technique* preface a large request with a small request. With the *door-in-the-face technique,* this sequence is reversed: After first making a very large request, people tend to comply with a small request. Last, the influencer who uses the *lowball technique* first extracts a commitment from the target person before revealing hidden costs.

For More Information

• *Cults: Faith, Healing, and Coercion,* by Marc Galanter (1989), is a well-balanced and research-based analysis of the way radical religious groups operate. His discussion provided the foundation for the case study (Jerry) used in this chapter.

• *Crimes of Obedience,* by Herbert C. Kelman and V. Lee Hamilton (1989), provides a detailed analysis of the factors that sustain obedience in contemporary society.

• *The Individual in a Social World: Essays and Experiments,* by Stanley Milgram (and edited by John Sabini and Maury Silver) (1992), is a powerful and personal compendium of the late Stanley Milgram's work on conformity, obedience, and other social-psychological processes.

• *Influence: Science and Practice,* by Robert B. Cialdini (1993), is an exceptionally well-written excursus on the techniques that "compliance professionals"—salespersons, advertisers, charity workers, and panhandlers—use to influence us in our daily lives.

• *Inside the Jury,* by Reid Hastie, Steven D. Penrod, and Nancy Pennington (1983), presents a detailed social-psychological analysis of communication, influence, and decision making in juries.

• *Obedience to Authority,* by Stanley Milgram (1974), provides an authoritative explanation of why we obey some authorities and disobey others.

Application: Social Influence in Juries

Societies that follow the British legal tradition settle questions of guilt and innocence by submitting them to a jury. As early as the 11th century, the neighbors of those accused of wrongdoing in England were asked to weigh the evidence and render a verdict. In theory, the jury is the "finder of fact"—a group of representative citizens who can objectively decide whether a law has been broken and punishment is warranted (Kadish & Paulsen, 1975). More than 300,000 juries convene each year in American courtrooms, and these juries are often the final arbiters of justice.

But even though the jury system is a time-honored tradition that is guaranteed by the Bill of Rights, juries draw as much criticism as praise. The majority of most Americans, both white and black, were shocked when a jury did not convict four Los Angeles police officers charged with the videotaped assault of motorist Rodney King. Many people felt that the Florida jurors in William Kennedy Smith's trial for rape and the Indianapolis jurors who convicted boxer Mike Tyson let irrelevant personal prejudices bias their verdicts (Wrightsman, Nietzel, & Fortune, 1994). These highly publicized cases raise doubts about the wisdom of relying on ordinary people to determine guilt and innocence.

Can people put aside their personal biases and weigh the evidence objectively? Can people discuss controversial matters openly in a small, face-to-face group? Will people listen and fairly consider other people's opinions about a case? Can juries be trusted to reach a fair decision? As might be expected, social psychologists believe these questions should be settled empirically. Legal experts draw on personal experience and logic when they discuss juries; social psychologists prefer to base their conclusions on scientifically reputable studies of juries and other decision-making groups (Hastie, Penrod, & Pennington, 1983; Wrightsman et al., 1994).

These studies offer many insights into the nature of juries and their effectiveness. They indicate, for example, that a jury's deliberations tend to follow the pattern shown in Figure 9-9. Once sequestered in the jury room, the group settles on procedures for voting and discussion (Hastie, Penrod, & Pennington, 1983). Some juries elect a leader at this point, and decide whether balloting will be secret or public. Once the agenda has been set, the jurors discuss the evidence presented during the trial and take a straw poll of their initial preferences for the verdict (Davis et al., 1988; Davis et al., 1989). More than 30% of all juries reach complete consensus on the very first ballot; if so, their task is finished at this point (Penrod & Hastie, 1980). But should members disagree, they must initiate a consensus-seeking process. During this phase of the deliberation, the group may ask the judge for instructions and request additional information concerning the evidence. The group spends most of its time, however, discussing points favoring the two possible verdicts. This process eventually leads to agreement on a verdict. A hung jury—one that is unable to agree on a verdict—occurs in only about 6% of all cases (Kalven & Zeisel, 1966).

The jury process is designed to foster careful decision making and tolerance for all viewpoints. Juries meet for only a limited period of time in a highly formal setting, so the group can't become very cohesive. In all but the smallest towns, the members of a jury are strangers to one another and don't anticipate any future interactions; they therefore risk little if they don't make a good impression or win others' friendship. Jurors usually vote by secret ballot so members can express disagreement with little fear of retribution. The situation is a novel one for virtually all jurors—there are no professional jurors—yet everyone has made judgments concerning right and wrong and guilt and innocence.

This process should shield jurors from social pressure and encourage dissent. Yet the verdict favored by the majority of the jurors *before deliberation* usually corresponds to the jury's final verdict. If the majority favors guilt when the first vote is taken, a guilty verdict is returned 90% of the time. If, in contrast, the major-

▲ **FIGURE 9-9**
How do juries make decisions? This flowchart diagrams the sequence of decisions made during a jury's deliberation. The diamond-shaped symbols correspond to points in the deliberations when decisions are made. (From Hastie, Penrod, & Pennington, 1983)

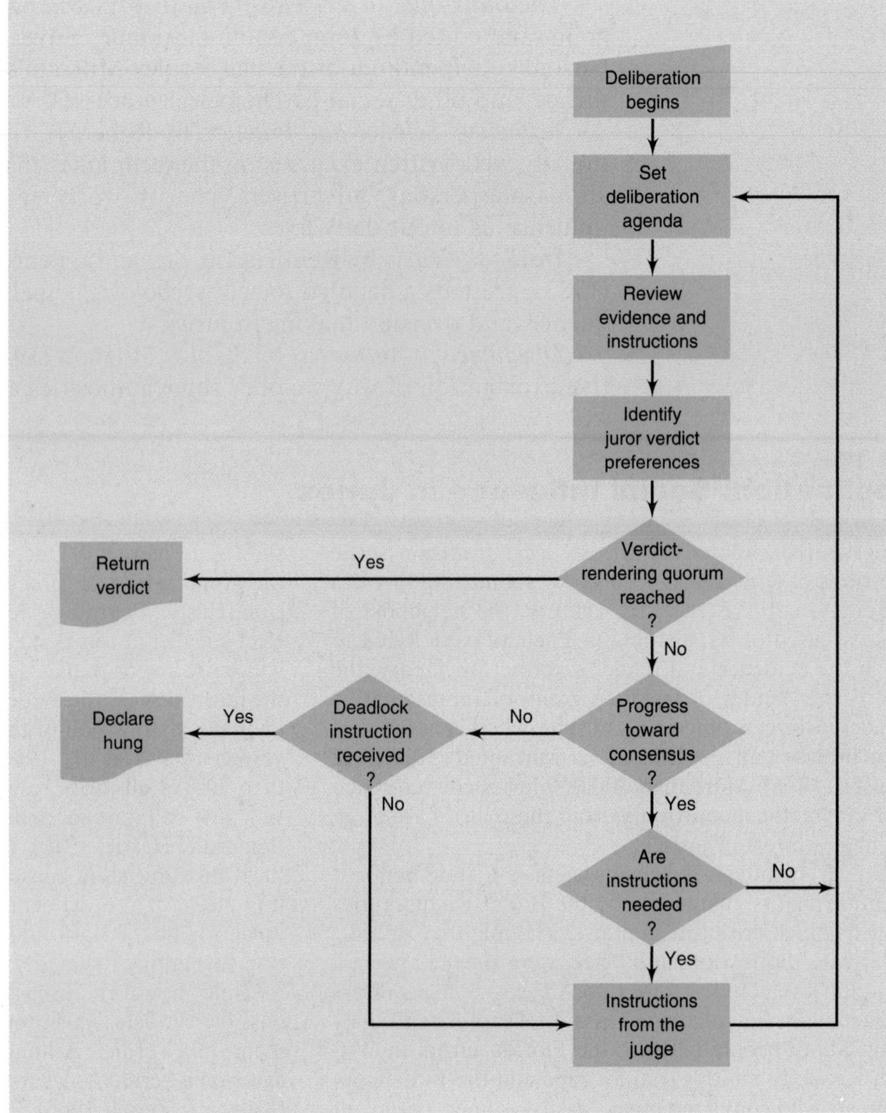

ity of the jurors favor innocence, a not-guilty verdict is returned in 86% of cases. Interviews with jurors and studies of **mock juries** (simulated juries created for research purposes) indicate that juries reach consensus by pressuring the members whose judgment is in the minority. Staunch minorities that convince the rest of the jury to change their minds are statistical rarities, occurring in less than 3% of all juries. Like the people Asch (1955) studied, the lone dissenter usually changes his or her vote so that it conforms to the majority's view. Dissenters can be more influential if they are more numerous, but even a jury that initially favors guilt or innocence by a vote of 9 to 3 is likely to return the majority's verdict. Indeed, researchers have simulated the deliberation process with a computer, which they deliberately programmed so a 3-person minority in a standard 12-person jury would be relatively weak. This computer simulation can very accurately predict the outcome of most jury deliberations (Penrod & Hastie, 1980).

Juries also tend to weigh more heavily the opinions of jurors who are wealthy, well educated, and outspoken, while discounting the opinions of people who are uneducated, poor, and reticent. Fred Strodtbeck and his colleagues documented this bias by recording communication patterns in simulated juries. He created a large number of mock juries by selecting 12 individuals from the community's pool of eligible jurors. He then simulated the pretrial-interview process known as *voir dire,* assembled the group in a courtroom, and arranged for a bailiff to play a tape recording of a trial. Except for the use of the tape-recorded trial, the groups were treated just like real juries (Strodtbeck & Hook, 1961; Strodtbeck, James, & Hawkins, 1957; Strodtbeck & Mann, 1956).

mock juries: Simulated juries created for research purposes.

Strodtbeck and his associates found that jurors with certain qualities tended to exert stronger influence in the groups. People with higher-paying jobs, such as professionals and proprietors, talked more than those who had lower-paying jobs. The higher-status individuals also provided more leadership within the group, and the low-status individuals followed their direction. In fact, a central core of high-status members usually dominated the group discussion. This core accounted for as much as 70% of the jury's communications. Their effectiveness as influencers became apparent when Strodtbeck compared the group's verdict to the jurors' private, predeliberation preferences. The correlation between the predeliberation verdict and the jury's final decision was .50 for the high-status jurors. For low-status jurors, the correlation was only .02. Men also tended to dominate the discussion, whereas women's comments focused more on the interpersonal relations among the members. Women were also more likely to express agreement with the majority (James, 1959; Strodtbeck et al., 1957).

Would these conformity pressures be less compelling if juries were smaller? Researchers raised this question in response to the 1970 Supreme Court ruling on 6-person juries. In the case of *Williams* v. *Florida* (1970), Williams sought to have his conviction overturned on the grounds that the State of Florida uses 6-person juries. The Supreme Court ruled, however, that a jury does not necessarily require 12 members. The justices concluded that 6 should be sufficient to "promote group deliberation, free from outside attempts at intimidation, and to provide a fair possibility for obtaining a representative cross-section of the community" (1970, p. 100). The Court's decision sparked a widespread revision of jury systems throughout the country.

Researchers, however, have identified a number of important changes that occur when juries are reduced in size. First, larger juries tend to deliberate longer than smaller juries. Second, communication is more evenly distributed in smaller groups, because no central core of jurors dominates the discussion. Third, conformity pressure may be greater in smaller juries. Asch argued that conformity rates remain essentially constant once the group includes 4 members, but the dissenting juror has less of a chance to find an ally in a 6-person group than in a 12-person group. The Supreme Court assumed that a 5-to-1 vote in a 6-person jury was equivalent to a 10-to-2 vote in a 12-person jury. Social psychologically, however, these two situations differ dramatically. When the vote is 10 to 2, the dissenter faces the majority with an ally. When the vote is 5 to 1, the juror faces the majority alone. Pressures to conform may be approximately equally strong in 6- and 12-person juries, but the supports for nonconformity are weaker in 6-person juries (Kerr & MacCoun, 1985; Saks, 1977).

Researchers aren't yet certain whether these differences between 6- and 12-person juries lead to differences in conviction and acquittal rates. Jurors participate more in small groups, and smaller groups are more efficient. However, dissenters may be able to form coalitions more easily in larger groups. Although preliminary evidence suggests that these advantages and disadvantages balance out in the long run, additional research is needed before any firm conclusions can be reached (Davis & Stasson, 1988; Wrightsman et al., 1994).

Many questions concerning juries remain unanswered, but applications of social psychology to juries have already proved to be particularly informative. First, researchers have been able to test many theoretically interesting hypotheses by studying the interchanges between people in juries. Studies such as Asch's represent an important first step in understanding conformity, but theories must also survive when they are tested in nonlaboratory settings. Second, by examining juries, social psychologists have contributed directly to our understanding of an important social issue. Many of the questions that legal experts debate can be answered through research. By documenting the interpersonal processes underlying human behavior in groups, we can evaluate and even improve our current methods for making legal decisions.

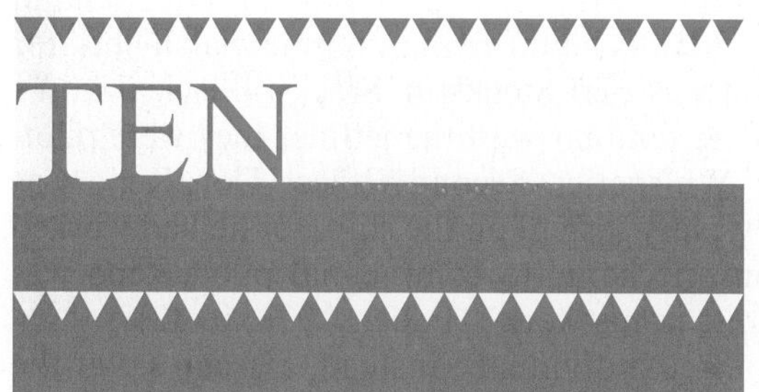

Group Dynamics

Robert Loft was the captain on Eastern Airlines Flight 401. Tall, athletic, and confident, Loft had logged nearly 30,000 hours flying commercial flights for Eastern. His first officer on the flight was Bert Stockstill. Stockstill lacked Loft's extensive experience, but he was more familiar with the jetliner they were piloting tonight—a brand-new L-1011 Whisperjet. Second Officer Don Repo was also an expert on L-1011s. He knew every system on the ship, for he had worked his way up through the ranks from mechanic to commercial pilot. Repo was "rough-hewn, popular, a perfectionist in his work" (Fuller, 1976, p. 42).

group
Two or more interdependent individuals who influence one another through social interaction.

But Flight 401 wasn't flown by three individuals; instead, a **group** sat at the jet's controls. Stockstill worked closely with Loft as the two checked systems, communicated with the air-traffic controller, and set the craft's heading. When a warning light signaled that the landing gear were malfunctioning, the captain turned to Repo for suggestions on how to remedy the problem. As Stockstill double-checked the warning light, Loft asked Repo to climb below the flight deck to inspect the landing gear visually. Each person influenced, and was in turn influenced by, every other person in the group.

Social psychologists study groups because social behavior is often group behavior. Except for the occasional street person, castaway, or recluse, we all belong to groups. These groups dramatically influence our thoughts, feelings, and behaviors. Can Loft's actions be understood if we ignore the way he, Stockstill, and Repo worked together? Can a child's actions be understood without taking into account his family's influence? Can an athlete's feelings on the day after the team's loss be predicted if we overlook her relationship with her team? Can we augment the productivity of factory workers without considering their perceptions of their group and their supervisors? We human beings are social creatures whose actions are shaped by groups.

Groups are so commonplace, so much a part of everyday experience, that we take them for granted. We spend so much time in groups—working, studying, exercising, competing, playing, performing, worshiping, and even sleeping—that we need to look at groups anew by examining their basic properties and dynamics. We must also study the way groups influence individuals as they discharge their duties within the group, and the way individuals work together to make decisions. We conclude our analysis of groups by reviewing the way leaders can enhance or undermine their groups' outcomes.

The Nature of Groups

Audiences, bands, committees, crowds, congregations, dance troupes, families, fraternities, gangs, juries, mobs, orchestras, queues, ship crews, support groups, and teams are just a few of the collections of people that surround us. Are all these collections *groups*? What, precisely, is a group?

Groups differ in many ways. Some are small, like the flight crew; others include thousands of members (for example, audiences at rock concerts, church congregations). Some groups form spontaneously for only a short time, whereas others are deliberately created for some purpose, long-lasting, and elaborately structured. Despite these wide variations, however, virtually all groups are based on interdependence among their members (Lewin, 1948). A classroom is a group: the teacher influences the students, who in turn influence the teacher and one another. Bystanders trying to free an accident victim from a car are a group. Even people standing silently in a queue can become a group when the members must prevent someone from breaking into the line. *A group is two or more interdependent individuals who influence one another through social interaction.*

We can't always divide collections of people into groups and nongroups so neatly, however. Passersby on a city street aren't a group, but they may become one when something—an accident, a street mime, a crime—links them together. Some groups, too, are so large that, although the potential for influence may exist, it is rarely realized. Whereas one collection of people may fit the definition precisely, another may possess only some of the defining features of a group.

The Characteristics of Groups

If you observed the crew of Flight 401, you might have noticed that Loft was in his fifties, that Stockstill was handsome and friendly, and that Repo knew his job inside and out. But would you have noticed the group's characteristics? Would you have noticed if two of the men were friends who disliked the third? If Loft was not just the flight's captain but also the group's respected leader? Would you have noticed the group's unity and identity? If you are to understand groups, you must examine them with an informed eye that notes their fundamental qualities (Mullen, 1987a; Turner, 1985).

Roles. Group behavior is usually orderly and predictable rather than disorganized and capricious. In every group, some people make the assignments and others carry them out. Some members are liked by nearly everyone; others

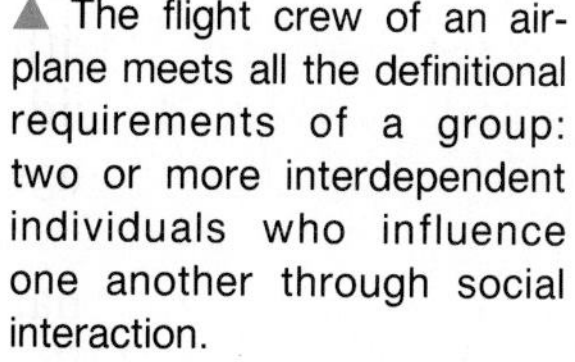

▲ The flight crew of an airplane meets all the definitional requirements of a group: two or more interdependent individuals who influence one another through social interaction.

▲ **TABLE 10-1**
Task and socioemotional (relationship) roles in groups

Role	*Function*
	Task Roles
Initiator-contributor	Offers novel ideas about the problem at hand, new ways to approach the problem, or possible solutions not yet considered
Information seeker	Emphasizes getting the facts by calling for background information from others
Opinion seeker	Asks for qualitative types of data, such as attitudes, values, and feelings
Information giver	Provides data for forming decisions, including facts that derive from expertise
Opinion giver	Provides opinions, values, and feelings
Elaborator	Gives additional information—examples, rephrasings, implications—about points made by others
Coordinator	Shows the relevance of each idea and its relationship to the overall problem
Orienter	Refocuses discussion on the topic whenever necessary
Evaluator-critic	Appraises the quality of the group's methods, logic, and results
Energizer	Stimulates the group to continue working when discussion flags
Procedural technician	Cares for operational details, such as the materials, machinery, and so on
Recorder	Takes notes and maintains records
	Socioemotional Roles
Encourager	Rewards others through agreement, warmth, and praise
Harmonizer	Mediates conflicts among group members
Compromiser	Shifts his or her own position on an issue in order to reduce conflict in the group
Gatekeeper-expediter	Smooths communication by setting up procedures and ensuring equal participation from members
Standard setter	Expresses, or calls for discussion of, standards for evaluating the quality of the group process
Observer-commentator	Points out the positive and negative aspects of the group's dynamics and calls for change if necessary
Follower	Accepts the ideas offered by others and serves as an audience for the group

Source: From Benne and Sheats, 1948.

structure
A stable pattern of relationships among the members of a group.

roles
Sets of behaviors characteristic of people in a context.

task roles
Positions in a group whose occupants are expected to perform goal-oriented, task-focused behaviors.

socioemotional roles
Positions in a group whose occupants are expected to perform supportive, interpersonally accommodative behaviors.

are barely tolerated. Some people talk to many others in the group; others hardly speak at all. These regularities reflect the group's **structure**—the underlying pattern of relationships among members (Cartwright & Zander, 1968).

Roles structure interactions by specifying the general behaviors expected of people who occupy different positions within the group. Once people take on roles, such as leader, follower, or critic, they must play their parts. Loft, for example, was the group leader, so he gave the orders, asked the questions, and made the final decisions. Repo, in contrast, was the flight engineer, so he was responsible for monitoring the plane's mechanical systems and carrying out Loft's orders.

There are many roles in groups, but most theorists draw a distinction between two basic types, **task roles** and **socioemotional roles**. As Table 10-1 indicates, people who occupy task roles focus on the work to be done in the group.

Loft's role pertained to the task: He motivated the group to work, assigned tasks to members, and provided guidance and advice. Other roles, in contrast, focus on the quality of the relationships among group members. If Stockstill joked frequently or Repo was the one who made certain that everyone enjoyed the flight, then they would be fulfilling socioemotional roles in the group. Both task and socioemotional roles are required in most groups, but very few people can fulfill both of these positions simultaneously. The leader who can both give orders and promote harmony is rare (Bales, 1950, 1970, 1980).

communication network
The pattern of communication in a group that determines who speaks most frequently to whom.

Communication. The flow of information from one person to another in groups is often structured by the group's **communication network**. Loft sent information to and received information from a variety of sources, including the ground controller, copilot, flight attendants, and engineer. Although Repo and Stockstill spoke to one another occasionally, most of their statements were directed at Loft. This type of network is *centralized* rather than *decentralized* because most information flows through one person. These types of networks tend to be most efficient so long as the communication rate is modest. If the number of messages routed through the central member becomes too great, however, then this type of network can break down (L'Herrou, 1992; Shaw, 1978).

status
Prestige in the group.

Status. Loft had more **status**, or prestige, in the group. He was, after all, officially appointed to the role of captain, and his years of experience earned him considerable respect from the other members of the crew. Status hierarchies, however, are also common in informally organized groups. People may

▲ Athletic teams, like this one, develop collaborative interdependence through extensive organization and practice.

start off on an equal footing, but over time certain individuals are accorded more prestige by others. In many cases, groups confer status on those who are exceptionally skilled and contribute the most to the group effort. In other cases, though, qualities that have little relevance to the aims of a group can also influence the rise to the top of the hierarchy. Unrecognized prejudices may prompt us to accord more status to men than to women, to whites than to blacks, and to older people than to younger people (Berger, 1992; Berger et al., 1986; Forsyth, 1990; Ridgeway, 1982, 1984).

sociometric structure Patterns of liking and disliking in the group.

Attraction. Just as some people have more status than others, some group members are better liked than others. Loft may have liked Stockstill but disliked Repo. Repo, however, may not have liked either of the pilots. These patterns of liking and disliking make up the **sociometric structure** of the group (Doreian, 1986). This term derives from *sociometry,* a technique for measuring social relationships in groups (Moreno, 1953). Researchers who use this method typically ask group members to identify who they like the most or dislike the most in their groups. Group members' choices are then summarized statistically or in a sociogram like the one shown in Figure 10-1. Popular individuals (*stars*) are singled out by virtually all the others to be the target of much affection; *isolates* are neglected by most of the group; *outcasts* are rejected by the majority of the group; the average members are liked by several others in the group (Coie, Dodge, & Coppotelli, 1982; Newcomb & Bukowski, 1983; Newcomb, Bukowski, & Pattee, 1993).

cohesiveness The strength of the relationships linking the members to one another and to the group itself.

Cohesiveness. In physics, the strength of the molecular attraction that holds particles of matter together is known as cohesiveness. Similarly, a group's **cohesiveness** is the strength of the relationships linking the members to one another and to the group itself. People in a cohesive group aren't only attracted to one another; they are also attracted to the group as a whole. They are proud to identify themselves as group members, and they defend the group against criticism. Close-knit, unified, and high in esprit de corps, a cohesive group suffers little from turnover or intragroup conflict (Cartwright, 1968; Dion, 1990).

Groups and Time

Like all living things, groups change over time. A group may begin as an assortment of unrelated individuals, but in time, roles develop and friendships form

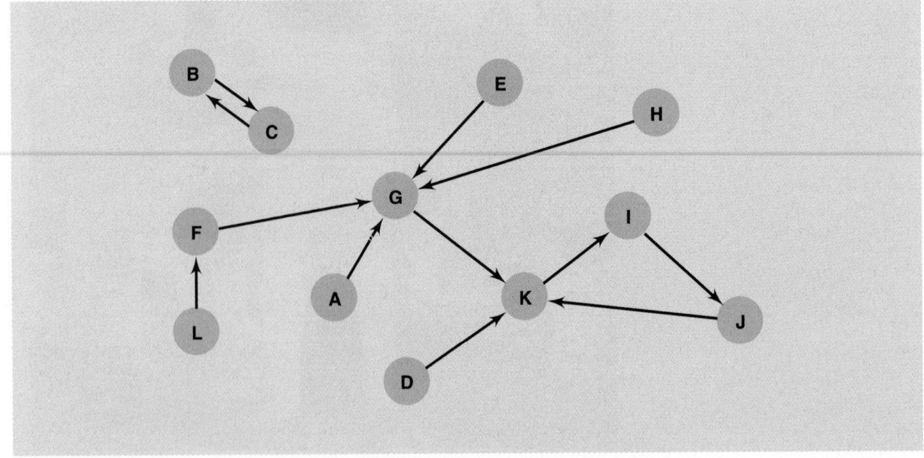

▲ **FIGURE 10-1** Are group members linked to one another by a network of rarely noticed interpersonal relations? Researchers often measure a group's structure by asking members to name people they like (or respect or talk to) in a group. These choices are then summarized in a sociogram. Lines capped with arrows represent relationships. Here, *G* is a star, *L* and *D* are isolates, *B* and *C* are a pair, and *I, J,* and *K* form a chain, or coalition.

▲ **TABLE 10-2**
Summing up: Critical characteristics of groups

Quality	*Definition*	*Examples*
Roles	A set of behaviors characteristic of people in a context	Leader, secretary, uninvolved outsider, joker, encourager.
Status	Prestige in the group	Big man on campus, resourceful contributor, disrespected innovator.
Attraction	Patterns of liking and disliking in the group	Star, isolates, outcasts, friends, enemies.
Communication	Patterns of communication that determine who speaks most frequently to whom	In Group *X* all information is sent to one person; in Group *Y* information is passed to all members.
Cohesiveness	The strength of the relationships linking the members to one another and to the group itself	Esprit de corps, feelings of we-ness, camaraderie, unity.

(see Table 10-2). New members join the group and old members leave. The group may become more cohesive or begin to lose its unity.

These changes, however, follow a predictable pattern. In most groups, the same sorts of issues arise over time; once they are resolved, the group can develop further. Bruce W. Tuckman maintains that this *group development* often involves five stages (Tuckman, 1965; Tuckman & Jensen, 1977). In the *forming* phase, the group members become oriented toward one another. In the *storming* phase, the group members find themselves in conflict, and some solution is sought to improve the group environment. In the *norming* phase, standards develop for behavior and roles that regulate behavior. In the *performing* phase, the group has reached a point where it can work as a unit to achieve desired goals. The *adjourning* stage ends the sequence of development; the group disbands (see Table 10-3). Throughout these stages, groups tend to oscillate back and forth between the task-oriented issues and the socioemo-

▲ **TABLE 10-3**
Five stages of group development

Stage	*Major Processes*	*Characteristics*
Orientation (forming)	Exchange of information; increased dependence; task exploration; identification of commonalities	Tentative interactions; polite conversation; concern over ambiguity; self-disclosure
Conflict (storming)	Disagreement over procedures; expression of dissatisfaction; emotional responding; resistance	Criticism of ideas; poor attendance; hostility; fractionation
Organization (norming)	Growth of cohesiveness and unity; establishment of roles, standards, and relationships	Agreement on procedures; reduction in role ambiguity; increased cohesion
Performance (performing)	Goal achievement; high task orientation; emphasis on performance and production	Decision making; problem solving; mutual cooperation
Dissolution (adjourning)	Termination of roles; completion of tasks; reduction of dependence	Disintegration and withdrawal; increased independence

Sources: From Tuckman, 1965; Tuckman & Jensen, 1977.

tional issues, with members sometimes working hard but at other times strengthening their interpersonal bonds (Bales, 1965).

Individuals also experience change as they pass through the group. We don't become full-fledged members of a group in an instant. Instead, we gradually become a part of the group, remain in the group, and eventually leave the group. Richard Moreland and John Levine's (1982) model of *group socialization,* shown in Figure 10-2, describes this process. During the *investigation* stage we are still outsiders, interested in joining the group, but not yet committed to it in any way. Once the group accepts us as a member, *socialization* begins: We learn the group's norms and take on different responsibilities depending on our roles. Even though we are full-fledged members at this point, changes still occur. If the group changes, our roles and responsibilities change as well. During this *maintenance* phase, we may have to learn new ways of doing things or accept responsibilities we would rather avoid. If this maintenance is successful, then we remain in this stage until the group or our membership ends as scheduled. If, however, we fail to adapt to changes appropriately, then group members may attempt *resocialization*—they remind us that, as group members, we must abide by the group's norms. If they fail, then we will probably leave the group. In any case, once membership in the group is concluded, we sometimes pass through yet another stage, *remembrance.* We are no longer members, but we still remember—sometimes with fondness, sometimes with regret—what membership in the group was like (Moreland & Brinthaupt, 1990).

Why Do Groups Matter?

Why join groups rather than remain alone? Perhaps the answer lies in the fact that groups fulfill so many basic psychological, social, and practical needs (Hill, 1987; Mullen, 1990). As we see in Chapter 11, groups help us meet our need for affiliation—contact with our own kind. When we have stressful experiences, we often turn to other people for social support—emotional support, advice, and guidance. Our groups are also an important source of information about ourselves and the social world. Our **reference groups**, for example, provide us with social-comparison information we can use to formulate attitudes, opinions, and beliefs (Singer, 1990). Our social identity also derives, in large

reference groups
A group that provides individuals with a reference point for defining their own personal attitudes and beliefs.

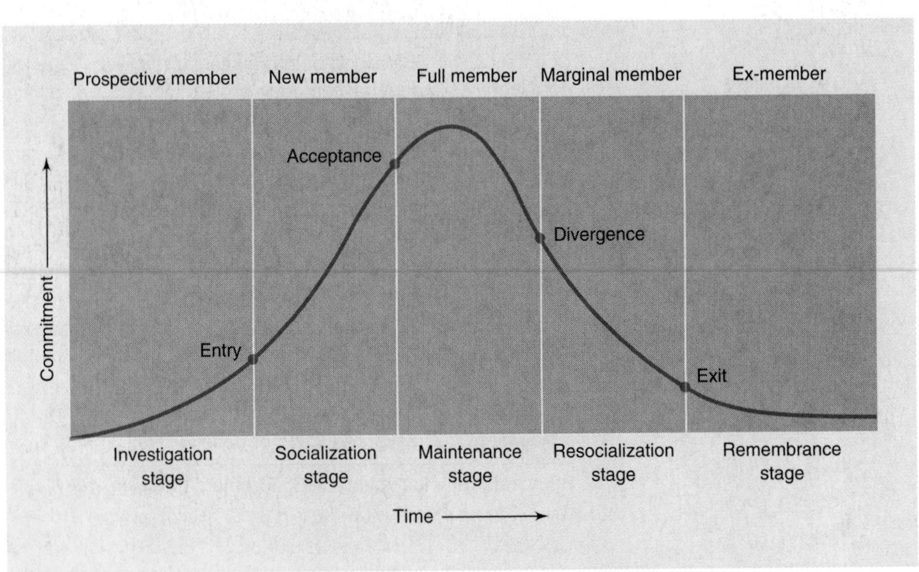

▲ **FIGURE 10-2**
What stages do we typically pass through during our tenure in groups? The Moreland and Levine model of group socialization identifies five stages demarcated by four transition points. In this hypothetical example, the individual became more committed to the group until he was granted full membership. His commitment then dropped, and he eventually left the group. (Adapted from Moreland & Levine, 1982)

part, from our memberships in social groups. Loft was not only Robert Loft, but also captain of the crew of Flight 401, pilot for Eastern Airlines, husband, and U.S. citizen (Shaver & Buhrmester, 1983). Groups are so important to us that it's no wonder people fear exclusion. When they think others will cast them out of the group, they mend their ways to regain acceptance (Baumeister & Tice, 1990; Leary, 1990).

primary groups Influential groups characterized by face-to-face interaction, interdependency, and strong group identification.

Groups also influence society and culture. The sociologist Emile Durkheim (1964) argued that most social systems are sustained, not by individuals, but by **primary groups**—small, intimate groups such as families, friendship cliques, and long-term work groups. These groups are the building blocks of society, so we must understand groups if we are to understand society and culture. Groups are also useful on a practical level (Zander, 1985). In many cases, people join together in a collaborative effort when the problems they face cannot be solved by working alone. As we see in the next two sections, and in the section "Application: The Social Psychology of Work Teams," which concludes this chapter, groups are tools. We use them to manufacture products and make decisions (Zander, 1985).

Group Performance

Much of the world's work is done by groups rather than by individuals. In office buildings, executives hold conferences to solve problems of management and production; in courthouses, juries weigh evidence to determine guilt or innocence; in factories, production lines turn out finished products; in schools, teachers work with their pupils in small learning groups; pilots pool their individual skills and efforts to fly jet airplanes. At the same time, we grumble about the inefficiency of groups. Witticisms abound, such as "An elephant is a mouse designed by a committee," "A committee is a group that keeps minutes and wastes hours," and "Too many cooks spoil the broth." As we will see next, groups can push us to reach the peak of our capabilities, but they can also promote mediocrity.

Social Facilitation

Loft, Stockstill, and Repo rapidly ran through the prelanding checklist. The three men checked brake, radar, hydraulic, and power systems with a smooth efficiency born of constant practice. Their troubles began when Loft told Stockstill to change the bulb on the landing gear indicator light. Neither Stockstill nor Loft could get the bulb out; they hadn't been trained to replace it, and in the crowded cockpit the peanut-size bulb eluded them time and again. The group that worked so well on the routine tasks failed when it tried to change a light bulb. What is it about social situations that facilitates our performance on some tasks while undermining our performance on others?

Norman Triplett examined this question in 1898. He was intrigued by the improved race times of bicyclists when they competed against other cyclists. By comparing records from bicycle races, Triplett discovered that people cycled an average of 32.6 miles per hour when they were competing with other racers, 31 miles per hour when they were paced by another cyclist, and only 24 miles per hour when they were racing alone and unpaced. Why did the racers cycle so much faster when competing and when they were paced? Triplett believed that the presence of others leads to psychological stimulation that enhances performance. He tested his hypothesis by conducting one of the first laboratory studies in the field of social psychology. He arranged for 40 children

social facilitation
Improvement in task performance that occurs when people work with other people (coaction) or in front of an audience.

to play a game that involved turning a small reel as quickly as possible. He noted that children turned the reel faster when they played the game in pairs than when they played alone. Triplett had succeeded in experimentally verifying a phenomenon that is now known as **social facilitation**: the enhancement of an individual's performance when that person works in the presence of other people.

Researchers soon began to extend Triplett's findings. Initially, it seemed that social facilitation occurred only during *coaction*—when people were working on similar tasks. Before long, however, researchers found evidence of social facilitation in the presence of a *passive audience*. Individuals who are working out with weights, for example, may suddenly find that they can lift heavier weights when others are watching them (Meumann, 1904). Investigators also discovered that social facilitation is not a uniquely human phenomenon. Puppies, chickens, mice, rats, monkeys, armadillos, ants, opossums, and even cockroaches all show signs of increased performance in the presence of other members of their species (Cottrell, 1972). One investigator went so far as to measure the excavation efforts of 36 ants working to build nests alone or in groups of 2 or 3. In line with studies of humans, each ant began to work sooner and moved more earth when it worked in the presence of other ants than when it worked alone (Chen, 1937). Similarly, hungry chickens given food in the presence of observing chicks, who watched through a clear plastic barrier, pecked 84% more often than isolated chicks (Tolman, 1968).

Working with other people, however, doesn't always facilitate performance. Indeed, sometimes a coactor or an audience undermines more than it facilitates. Students write poorer quality essays on philosophical works when they write in a group rather than alone (Allport, 1924). They also need more practice to learn a list of nonsense words when they are watched by an audience than when they work alone (Pessin, 1933). And they make more mistakes in solving multiplication problems with either an audience or a coactor than when they work in isolation (Dashiell, 1930).

Why do coactors or audiences sometimes inhibit rather than facilitate performance? Robert B. Zajonc (1965, 1980), after reviewing dozens of studies, offered a compelling explanation based on the difference between dominant and nondominant responses. *Dominant responses* are well-learned or instinctive behaviors that the organism has practiced and is primed to perform. *Nondominant responses,* in contrast, are novel, complicated, or untried behaviors that the organism has never performed before or has performed only infrequently. Zajonc noted that in some studies, subjects needed to perform only dominant responses to do well on the problems they faced; lifting weights, bicycling, and eating rapidly are all tasks that require dominant responses. Subjects in other studies needed to perform nondominant responses to succeed. When they attempted to solve mathematics problems or memorize lists of words, these people had to learn to give nondominant responses.

Zajonc hypothesized that the presence of others increases our tendency to perform dominant responses and decreases our tendency to perform nondominant responses. If the dominant response is the correct or most appropriate response in a particular situation, then social facilitation occurs—people perform better when others are present than when they are alone. If the task calls for nondominant responses, however, then the presence of other people interferes with performance. Imagine that you must memorize pairs of words. If the pairs are commonly associated, such as *blue-sky* or *clean-dirty,* then the dominant response is correct. If you hear *blue* or *clean,* the word *sky* or *dirty,* respectively, is likely to pop into your head.

▲ **FIGURE 10-3**
When do other people improve the way we perform tasks? Zajonc suggests that the presence of others increases the likelihood of dominant responses. If the situation calls for a dominant response, facilitation occurs. But if the situation calls for a nondominant response, the presence of others will interfere with performance. (From Zajonc, 1965)

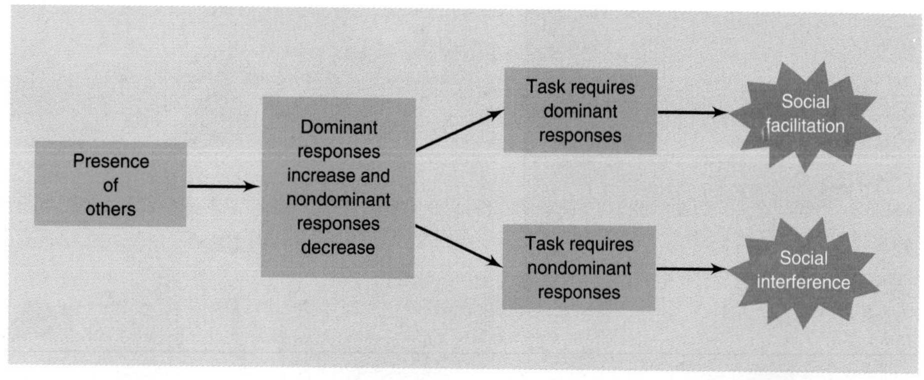

Hence, your performance will improve when other people are present. If, however, you are trying to learn some unusual associations—such as *blue-rutabaga* or *clean-discombobulation*—then you must learn to make a nondominant response, and the presence of an audience will hurt more than help (see Figure 10-3).

Zajonc tested his theory by studying cockroaches (Zajonc, Heingartner, & Herman, 1969). As anyone who has surprised a roach in the kitchen late at night knows, cockroaches run from bright lights. Therefore, Zajonc designed two mazes, each with a start box near a light and a goal box hidden from the light. One of the mazes was very simple—just a straight runway from the start to the goal. The second maze was more complex—the roaches had to turn to the right to reach their goal. Zajonc reasoned that when other roaches were present, the roaches should perform more efficiently in the simple maze than in the complex one. The results, shown in Figure 10-4, supported Zajonc's model. Cockroaches escaped the light more quickly in pairs than alone, provided the maze was simple. If the maze was complex, they escaped more quickly alone than with another cockroach. Zajonc and his colleagues also found that an observer roach, which watched from a small plastic cubicle located by the maze, facilitated performance of the simple task but interfered with performance of the complex task.

Zajonc's explanation applies to people, too. One enterprising researcher unobtrusively watched people take off their own shoes and socks and put on unfamiliar articles of clothing. People needed an average of 16.5 seconds to take off their own clothes when they were alone, but they got the job done even

▲ **FIGURE 10-4**
Are cockroaches social creatures? Do they respond differently when other cockroaches are around? As Zajonc predicted, coacting roaches traversed simple maze faster than solitary roaches. Coacting roaches took longer when the maze was complex, however. (From Zajonc, Heingartner, & Herman, 1969)

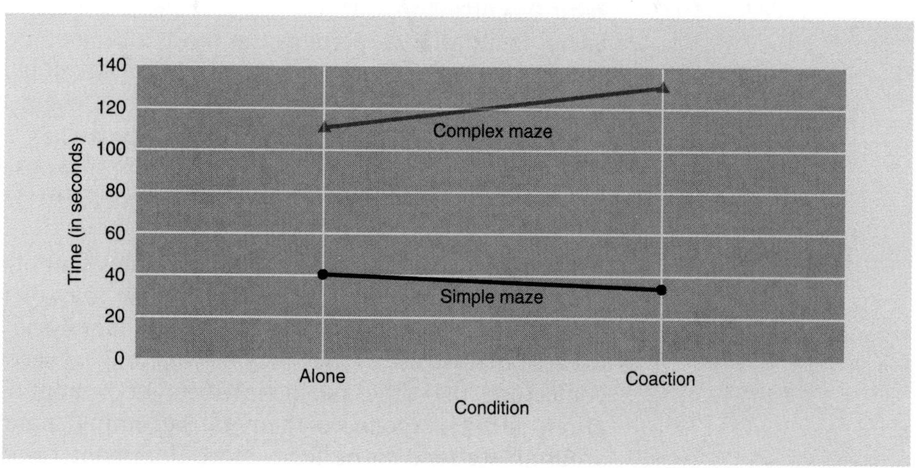

▲ What happens when a single person is joined by a second person? Studies of social facilitation suggest that as soon as another person is added to a situation, social processes begin to influence our thoughts, emotions, and actions. If the lone individual is an experienced golfer, the addition of a second person will likely enhance performance. If, however, the individual is a novice, another person's presence will likely lead to poorer performance.

faster when others were present. They needed just 13.5 seconds when someone was in the room with them and 11.7 seconds when they were watched by the person. Observers slowed them down when they put on unfamiliar clothes. People managed the unfamiliar task in 28.9 seconds when alone, but needed 32.7 and 33.9 seconds when another person was present and was watching them, respectively (Markus, 1978). Other researchers report similar findings. Indeed, a thorough review of 241 studies of social facilitation, involving nearly 24,000 human subjects, concluded that facilitation occurs primarily when people perform simple tasks that require dominant responses (Bond & Titus, 1983).

Why Facilitation?

Social facilitation is perhaps the most rudimentary of social processes. When you work alone, social forces are minimized. But add another person to the situation, and social processes immediately begin to shape your actions and outcomes. You may not even notice it, but when a situation becomes social, you change ever so subtly. Other people may arouse you. They may make you feel that you are being evaluated. They may also distract you.

Arousal. Zajonc (1965, 1980) assumes that other people arouse us whenever they are present. These other people may or may not have the slightest interest in what we are doing. They may merely be occupying the same physical area that we do, or they may be watching us very closely. No matter. Zajonc conjectures that other people introject an element of uncertainty into any situation, so we respond to them by becoming more aroused and alert. Once aroused, we tend to perform more dominant responses and fewer nondominant responses. Provided dominant responses are appropriate for the task at hand, arousal will improve performance. If nondominant responses are needed, however, this arousal will lead to a decrement in performance (see Figure 10-3). Zajonc believes that this tendency to become aroused when other people are present is an unlearned, innate reaction.

Evaluation apprehension. Imagine yourself reciting a well-memorized poem while standing before a group of fellow students. All the students are seated with their backs to you, however, and are listening to rock music through individual headphones. Your audience is paying no attention to you. They have no idea whether you are doing a good or bad job.

According to Nickolas B. Cottrell (1972), the audience wouldn't help your recital in this situation because the uncertainty produced by the mere presence of other people is insufficient to produce social facilitation. Cottrell agrees with Zajonc that we perform dominant behaviors better when we are aroused and nondominant behaviors better when we aren't aroused. Unlike Zajonc, however, Cottrell asserts that we become increasingly aroused only when we are apprehensive about being evaluated by these other people. If we know we will perform masterfully or if the other people are oblivious to us, then their presence will have a negligible effect on us. If, however, the audience engenders *evaluation apprehension,* then we will excel on easy tasks but falter on harder ones (see Figure 10-5). Who wants to experience the self-presentational predicament of seeming incompetent, particularly when the task is an easy one? To avoid that potential embarrassment, we redouble our efforts when we know that others are evaluating us (Bond, 1982).

Distraction and attention. As early as 1904, investigators noted that working in the presence of an audience or coactors can be distracting; our attention is divided as we try to concentrate on both the task and the audience's or coactors' reactions (Meumann, 1904). When people we don't know are near us, we often monitor what they are doing. This monitoring process taxes our limited cognitive resources and so prevents us from processing task-related information as thoroughly as we should (Baron, 1986; Guerin, 1983; Guerin & Innes, 1983; Mullen & Baumeister, 1987).

Distraction isn't all bad, however. When our attention is divided between the task and the other people, we work harder to try to overcome the effects of

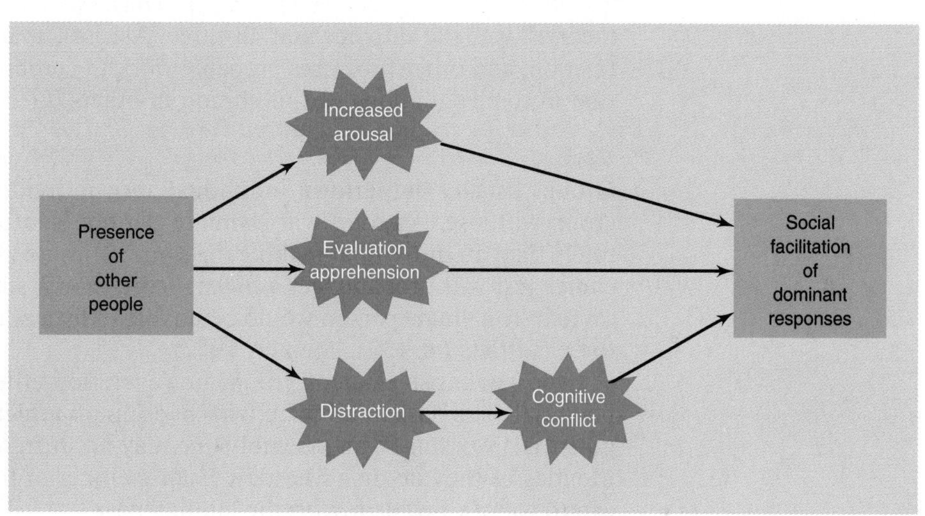

▲ **FIGURE 10-5**
Why does social facilitation occur? Investigators have identified three factors that may mediate the relationship between observers and performances. Zajonc's arousal model assumes that the presence of others increases arousal. Cottrell's explanation of social facilitation argues that evaluation apprehension (not arousal) is responsible for social facilitation when tasks are simple. Other theorists believe that the presence of other people is a distraction and that the attentional conflict their presence creates can be motivating.

▲ **TABLE 10-4**
Three possible explanations of social facilitation processes

Theory	*Mediating Processes*	*Source*
Arousal theory	The mere presence of other species members increases uncertainty, and this uncertainty generates arousal.	Unlearned reaction to uncertainty
Evaluation apprehension theory	The presence of others generates evaluation apprehension—an anxiety-toned feeling that others are evaluating us in negative ways.	Learned response to repeated evaluations
Distraction-conflict theory	When others are present, attention is divided between the other people and the task. The attentional conflict increases motivation, which facilitates performance so long as the task is a simple one.	Distraction and cognitive overload

the distraction (see Figure 10-5). If the task is so simple that the increase in motivation outweighs the decrement caused by distraction, then social facilitation will occur. But if the task is so complex that the increase in motivation cannot offset the negative consequences of attentional conflict, then the presence of others will lead to a decrement in performance (Baron, 1986; Groff, Baron, & Moore, 1983; Sanders, 1981; Sanders & Baron, 1975; Sanders, Baron, & Moore, 1978).

The causes of social facilitation. We need not select only one of the three models summarized in Table 10-4 as *the* explanation of social facilitation. Just as Zajonc suggested, we become slightly more aroused when other people are present (Cacioppo et al., 1991). This arousal, however, becomes more pronounced when observers are evaluating us (Seta & Seta, 1992). Indeed, any factor that increases evaluation apprehension—negative expectations about our performance; a large, high-status audience; or the presence of experts—makes social facilitation more likely (Sanna, 1992; Sanna & Shotland, 1990; Seta, Crisson, et al., 1989; Seta, Wang, et al., 1989). Working with others can also interfere with overt and covert practicing of material, retention, and understanding (Berger et al., 1981; Berger et al., 1982). Thus, rather than eliminate any of the theories, we take into account all three. Arousal, evaluation apprehension, distraction, and other processes probably work in combination to produce facilitation in some situations and inhibition in others (Geen, 1991).

Social Loafing

Groups usually outperform individuals. An individual in a tug-of-war with a group will lose. A group will estimate the temperature of a room more accurately than an individual making the same estimate. A group taking a multiple-choice test will probably get a higher score than a single individual taking the same test. A single person would be unable to fly a plane that requires a crew of three (Littlepage, 1991; Steiner, 1972).

Even the most efficient group, however, sometimes fails to reach its full potential. The basketball team with five superb athletes may not play up to its potential. Workers in an assembly line may not turn out as many products on a Monday as they do on a Tuesday. Each member of the crew may not do all he can to solve a problem with the landing gear.

A French agricultural engineer named Max Ringelmann (1913) documented the inefficiency of groups a century ago. Ringelmann was interested in productivity. Should you plow a field with two horses or three? Can five men turn a mill-crank faster than four? To investigate these questions, he arranged for individuals and groups to pull on a rope attached to a pressure gauge. Larger groups, he found, were stronger groups. He also noted, however, a mysterious loss of individual strength as the group grew larger. An average individual working alone was able to exert about 63 kilograms (kg) of pressure. Therefore, two people working together should have been able to exert 126 kg (63 kg + 63 kg), three people should have pulled 189 kg (63 kg + 63 kg + 63 kg), and so on. Ringelmann's groups, however, regularly fell below this level of production. Dyads managed to pull only about 1.9 times as much as one person, triads only 2.5 times as much, and eight-person groups a woeful 3.9 times the individual level. Even though the task was a simple one, the presence of other people led to inferior performances (Steiner, 1972). This intriguing tendency for individuals to become less productive as group size increases is known as the **Ringelmann effect**. (Kravitz and Martin, 1986, present a summary and interpretation of Ringelmann's work.)

Ringelmann effect
The tendency for people to become less productive when they join a group; the larger the group, the more pronounced the loss of productivity.

social loafing
The reduction of individual effort exerted when people work in groups compared to when they work alone.

What causes the Ringelmann effect? Ringelmann identified two causes. First, when people work together on tasks, **social loafing** sometimes sets in. People just don't expend as much physical effort when working on a collective endeavor, nor do they expend as much cognitive effort trying to solve problems. They get lazy (Ingham et al., 1974; Latané, Williams, & Harkins, 1979; Petty, Harkins, & Williams, 1980; Petty et al., 1977). Second, group members sometimes have trouble coordinating their individual activities and contributions, so they never reach the maximum level of efficiency (Diehl & Stroebe, 1987). Three people on a tug-of-war team, for example, invariably pull and pause at slightly different times, so their efforts aren't perfectly coordinated. In consequence, they are stronger than a single person, but not three times as strong. Ringelmann notes that work groups often sing songs in an attempt to reduce these *coordination losses*.

Bibb Latané, Kip Williams, and Stephen Harkins examined both social loafing and coordination losses in a series of clever studies (Harkins, Latané, & Williams, 1980; Williams, Harkins, and Latané, 1981). They told the men who participated in one study that they were researching "the effects of sensory feedback on the production of sound in social groups." They assigned the subjects an easy job: Make as much noise as possible by shouting when alone, in dyads, or in six-person groups. The subjects then put on blindfolds and headsets, which played a loud stream of noise that masked any noise made by other group members. Then they shouted. As Figure 10-6 indicates, individual productivity was lower in groups. Subjects who were tested alone averaged a rousing 9.22 dynes per square centimeter (about as loud as a pneumatic drill). Groups generated more noise than solitary subjects, but their productivity dropped as the groups became larger in size. In dyads, each subject worked at only 66% of capacity, and in six-person groups, at 36%. This drop in productivity is represented by the line labeled "Pseudogroups" in Figure 10-6 (Latané, Williams, & Harkins, 1979; Experiment 2).

Latané, Williams, and Harkins isolated the effects of social loafing and coordination losses by testing noise production in "pseudogroups." They told another group of subjects that other people were cheering with them, but they actually cheered alone. Because the subjects wore blindfolds and headsets, they didn't see through the deception. As Figure 10-6 indicates, when subjects thought one other person was shouting with them, they shouted only 82% as intensely, and when they thought five other people were shouting, they reached only 74% of their capacity. These losses in productivity were not due to coordination problems because no other group members were shouting; this decline in production could be attributed only to a reduction in effort—in other words, social loafing.

Increasing Group Productivity

Social loafing can have disastrous consequences. People carrying out all sorts of physical and mental tasks—including brainstorming, evaluating employees, monitoring equipment, interpreting instructions, and formulating causal judgments—were less productive when they combined their efforts in a group situation. Even worse, loafing seems to go unrecognized by group members. When people in groups are asked if they are working as hard as they can, they usually claim that they are doing their best—even though the objective evidence indicates that they are loafing. Evidently, people either aren't aware that they are loafing, or they are simply unwilling to admit it (Karau & Williams, 1993). Fortunately, steps can be taken to limit this deleterious consequence of collective action (Harkins, 1990).

Increase identifiability. People don't loaf as much if their individual contributions to the group project can be clearly identified. Williams, Harkins, and Latané (1981, Experiment 1) succeeded in eliminating social loafing in their noise-making paradigm by making each person's contributions seem identifiable. People who shouted in actual groups reached only a small fraction of their potential. They worked at only 59% and 31% of their peak efficiency in two-person and six-person groups, respectively. By creating pseudogroups (subjects worked alone but thought they were part of a group), the researchers eliminated coordination losses, but the groups still reached only 65% of their potential productivity. When people were led to believe that their individual contributions would be identifiable, however, efficiency rates soared to 95%.

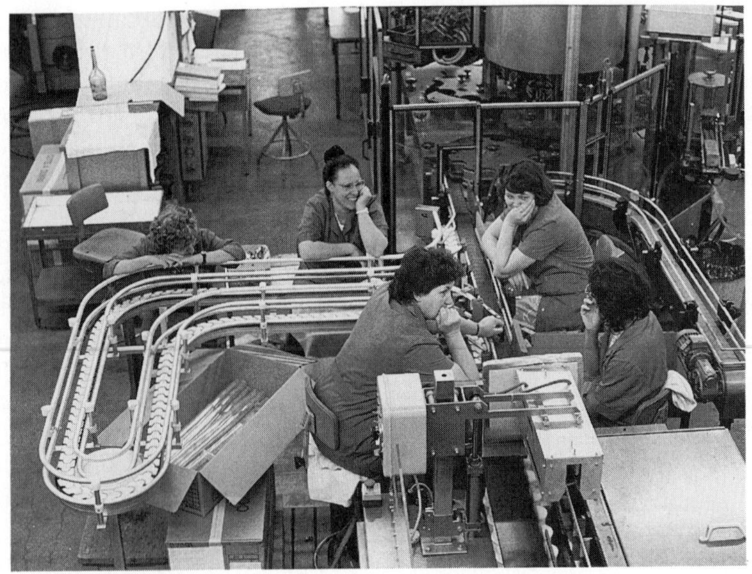

▲ Many hands make light the work, but not necessarily because people work as a team to accomplish more. The inefficiency of some groups goes beyond problems of coordination, because as the group becomes larger, its members tend to expend less energy. This process is known as social loafing.

Increasing identifiability may limit social loafing by heightening feelings of evaluation apprehension. Just as the feeling that one is being evaluated can facilitate performance on simple tasks, so evaluation apprehension can stimulate productivity on collective endeavors. If people think their individual efforts are unknown, then they need not worry about being caught when they don't work hard. But if they think their contributions can be identified and evaluated, then they are likely to work much harder (Harkins & Jackson, 1985; Jackson & Latané, 1981). Social loafing is also minimized when subjects think there are objective standards that can be used to evaluate their personal performances (Szymanski & Harkins, 1987).

social dilemma
A situation that prompts individuals to act in their own immediate self-interest to the detriment of other group members' needs or their own long-term interests.

free-rider effect
The tendency to contribute less to a collective task when one believes that other group members will compensate for one's lack of effort.

sucker effect
The tendency to contribute less to a collective task when one believes that other group members are not going to be contributing their fair share.

Undo the social dilemma. Pooling our efforts in a group is a kind of **social dilemma**—a situation that tempts individuals to act in their own self-interests to the detriment of the group's overall needs (Shepperd, 1993). For a group to function efficiently, members must sometimes put their own personal goals aside, but they may not always be as selfless as they should be. If, for example, everyone in your office is rushing about trying to meet a project deadline, will anyone notice if you slip out early or take a nap in the stockroom? If your community is doing a fantastic job recycling its used aluminum, do you need to bother? The temptation to expend less effort in the hopes that others will do your share of the work is called the **free-rider effect**. Why waste your own time, effort, and resources when you can hitch a free ride on the sweat of others' brows? The **sucker effect**, in contrast, describes your fear that you are working harder than the other members (Kerr, 1983). How would you feel if you discovered that you had worked more than everyone else in your group, that other people were napping in the back room and throwing away their soft-drink cans while you were expending your valuable energy working and recycling? Nobody likes to be the sucker, so we sometimes don't work any harder than anyone else (Jackson & Harkins, 1985).

Any factor that helps people escape from the social dilemma that collective endeavors pose will limit social loafing. People should be made to feel that their contributions are unique and essential for the group's success. Large groups, for

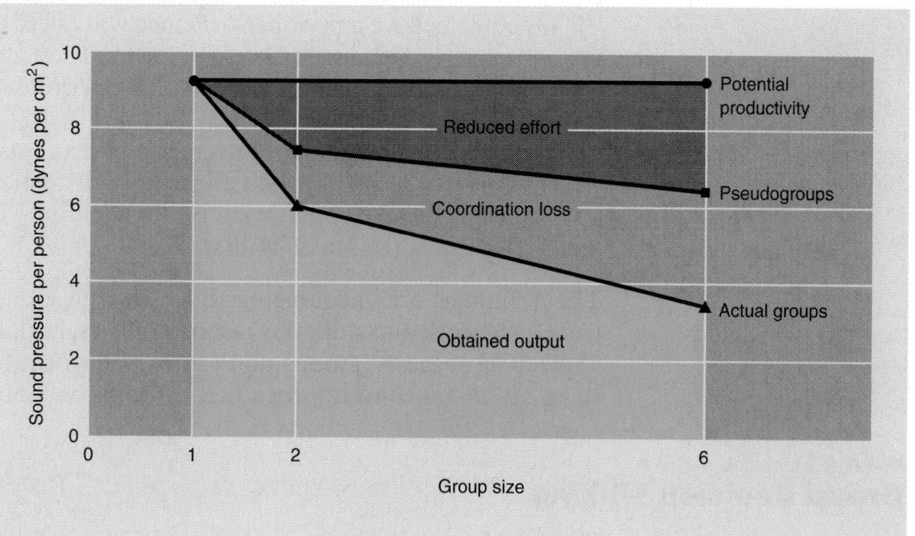

▲ **FIGURE 10-6**
Do many hands make light the work? Productivity dwindled as the groups swelled in size (the so-called Ringelmann effect). The "Actual groups" line represents the productivity of people working alone or in groups, so losses in this condition are caused by both coordination problems and loafing. "Pseudogroups" (people *thought* they were working in groups but were actually working alone) eliminated losses due to faulty coordination, so reductions in productivity could only be attributed to social loafing. (From Latané, Williams, & Harkins, 1979)

example, should be broken down into smaller ones so members won't feel anonymous or uninvolved (Kameda et al., 1992). The costs of contributing time and effort should also be minimized when possible. When researchers combated the sucker effect by convincing participants that the others in the group were both capable and willing to contribute to the group, loafing levels fell substantially (Kerr, 1983). Similarly, people who thought their partners would loaf reduced their own efforts to establish an equitable division of labor. Those who believed that their partners would be expending maximum effort, however, did not loaf even when unidentifiable (Jackson & Harkins, 1985).

collective effort model (CEM)
A theoretical explanation that traces losses of productivity in groups to diminished expectations about successful goal attainment and the diminished value of group goals.

Maximize collective motivation. The **collective effort model (CEM)** draws on classic expectancy-value theories of motivation to suggest ways to minimize social loafing (Karau & Williams, 1993). Expectancy-value theories argue that two factors determine our motivation: our expectations about reaching a goal and the value of that goal. Motivation is greatest when we think that the goal is within our reach (our expectations are high) *and* we consider the goal to be valuable. Motivation diminishes, in contrast, if our expectations are low *or* we don't think the goal is desirable. Working in a group, unfortunately, can diminish both our expectations about reaching our goal and the value we place on that goal. In groups, the link between our own effort and our chances of success is ambiguous. Even if we work hard, others may not, and the group may fail. Moreover, even if the group does succeed, we personally may not benefit much from the group's good performance. Earning a high grade on a project completed by a group may not be as satisfying as earning a high grade on a project that we completed working on our own.

Researchers recently tested the CEM's basic predictions using meta-analysis (Karau & Williams, 1993). Their review of 78 studies indicated that loafing is reduced when individuals' expectations for success are high and they feel that the goal they are seeking is a valuable one. For example:

- People who are interested in what they are doing are much less likely to loaf (Harkins & Petty, 1982; Zaccaro, 1984).
- Loafing is reduced when people work on a challenging, difficult task instead of on a task that is easily accomplished (Harkins & Petty, 1982).
- If people believe a poor performance will affect them personally, they don't loaf (Brickner, Harkins, & Ostrom, 1986). They also don't loaf when a high-quality performance will be rewarded (Shepperd & Wright, 1989; Williams & Karau, 1991).
- People who are committed to their group and its goals loaf less than people who are more interested in pursuing individualistic goals. Hence, women loaf less than men, and people from Eastern cultures loaf less than people from Western cultures (Karau & Williams, 1993).

These findings are encouraging. Even though groups offer us a place to hide from hard work and shirk our responsibilities, social loafing isn't inevitable. As Table 10-5 suggests, groups don't always perform up to our expectations, but steps can be taken to improve their productivity and efficiency.

Group Decision Making

Captain Loft immediately noticed the flashing indicator light on his landing gear monitor during the final approach to Miami. Fearing that the gear for the nose of the plane was jammed, he aborted the landing. The crew then discussed the

▲ **TABLE 10-5**
Summing up: Performance in groups

Process	*Characteristics*	*Example*	*Conditions*
Social facilitation	Task performance sometimes improves when people work with others (coaction) or before an audience. Zajonc suggests that social facilitation is most likely when tasks call for dominant (well-learned) responses rather than nondominant (novel) responses.	People undressed more rapidly when others were present, but when they donned awkward garb, their speed decreased. Roaches in groups ran for cover faster than lone roaches if the maze was simple.	Enhanced performance may be contingent on physiological arousal, evaluation apprehension, and attentional conflict.
Ringelmann effect	People are less productive in groups. The larger the group, the more pronounced the loss of productivity.	Two men pulling a rope reached 95% of their efficiency. Efficiency dropped to 83.3% in three-man groups and 49% in eight-man groups.	Two factors cause loss of productivity: coordination problems and the reduction of personal effort (social loafing).
Social loafing	People don't work as hard in groups as they do when they work alone.	People who were told to shout didn't try as hard to make noise when in groups as when alone. People in two-person groups expended 18% less effort than those working alone. People in six-person groups reduced their effort by 26%.	Social loafing can be prevented by making inputs identifiable, by helping participants solve the social dilemma that collaborative efforts can create, and by maximizing collective motivation.

problem. All of them thought the bulb was burned out because the gear had made the usual locking sounds when they were lowered. But, to be certain, they decided to replace the bulb. Loft turned on the plane's autopilot; then he and Stockstill spent some time fussing with the light. All this time they joked about their predicament: The $20 million airplane couldn't land because of a 20-cent bulb. They were still trying to change the bulb when the plane crashed.

When people must make important decisions, they turn to groups. Groups can draw on more resources than an individual. Loft may know a great deal about the L-1011, but this factual knowledge is far surpassed by the combined memories of the three crew members. Groups can also generate more ideas and possible solutions by discussing the problem. Loft may think that the only way to solve the problem is to change the light bulb, but after talking with Stockstill he may realize that they can also inspect the landing gear by going down into the bay underneath the flight deck. Groups can evaluate the options they generate during discussion more objectively as well. Before accepting a solution, a group may require that a certain number of people favor it, or that it meets some other standard of acceptability. People usually think a group's decision will be superior to an individual's decision (Hinsz, 1990; Laughlin, 1980; Paulus et al., 1993; Stasser, Kerr, & Davis, 1989; Worchel, Wood, & Simpson, 1991).

Groups, however, don't always make good decisions. Juries sometimes render verdicts that run counter to the evidence presented. Community groups take radical stances on issues before thinking through all the ramifications. Military strategists concoct plans that seem, in retrospect, ill conceived and shortsighted. The flight crew's decision to let all three members work on the landing gear problem was fatal. Why do groups sometimes fail? Two processes that can warp a group's decisions—group polarization and groupthink—are considered next.

Polarization in Groups

For centuries people assumed that groups exerted a moderating, subduing effect on their members. The common belief was that if radical members advocated a plan of action that was too risky, the group gently steered them toward more cautious solutions. Conversely, when conservative members took an extremely cautious stance on issues, then the group stepped in to suggest a bolder solution. As a result, groups were thought to be more moderate decision makers than individuals.

In the early 1960s, however, social psychologists began to question this assumption. By asking individuals to make judgments alone and then in groups, they found a surprising shift in the direction of greater riskiness after group interaction (Stoner, 1961; Wallach, Kogan, & Bem, 1962). In one study, college students read 12 story problems in which a hypothetical individual had to choose between one of two possible courses of action. In each story, the alternative that offered the more desirable rewards was also the course of action least likely to be carried out successfully. One story, for example, described an electrical engineer who had a very secure job with many benefits. The head of a newly founded company offers him a job, promising a much higher salary. The choice is risky, though, because the company might fold in the near future. Subjects were asked, "What would the probability of success have to be before you would advise the character in the story to choose the riskier course of action?"

Subjects completed the choice dilemmas questionnaire (CDQ) at the very start of the experiment, after discussing the stories with a group of four or five other subjects, and again when alone. Some subjects also completed the questionnaire again several weeks after the session. When answers were compared, the researchers found that the subjects usually advocated riskier decisions in groups than as individuals. Moreover, this group shift carried over when subjects gave their private choices following the group discussion. This change was dubbed the **risky shift** (Wallach et al., 1962).

risky shift
The tendency for individuals, when making a decision as a group, to make a riskier decision than they would have made had they made the decision alone.

In the decade from 1960 to 1970, researchers carried out hundreds of studies of the risky shift in groups. Researchers found evidence of risky shifts for all sorts of judgments, and the effect was demonstrated in many countries

▲ We often assume that consequential, complex questions are best settled through group discussion, yet groups don't always perform at peak efficiency.

DOONESBURY copyright G. B. Trudeau. Reprinted with permission of UNIVERSAL PRESS SYNDICATE. All rights reserved.

around the world (Myers, 1982; Pruitt, 1971). Occasionally, however, investigators reported a different kind of shift—toward caution rather than risk. Belatedly, researchers realized that risky shifts after group discussion are part of a larger, more general process. When people discuss issues in groups, they tend to decide on a *more extreme* course of action than would be suggested by the average of their individual judgments. Discussion doesn't moderate people's judgments after all. Instead, it leads to **group polarization**: Judgments made after group discussion will be more extreme in the same direction as the average of individual judgments made before discussion (Myers, 1982).

group polarization
The tendency for groups to polarize members' opinions and beliefs in the direction of the average of the group members' prediscussion opinions.

Imagine, for example, a group discussing solutions to a particular problem. Some of the people in the group initially favor cautious solutions, whereas others prefer riskier solutions. Indeed, if we ranked everyone on a continuum from risk to caution, some people would be closer to the risky pole, and others would be close to the cautious end of the continuum. If the average of the group members' prediscussion choices is closer to the risky pole of the continuum than to the cautious pole, a risky shift will occur. If, in contrast, the group members tend to be cautious rather than risky, a cautious shift will occur. Thus, before we can predict whether the group discussion will polarize the group, we must first know the initial opinions of the members.

Why does group discussion polarize people's judgments and opinions? Some researchers initially endorsed the *leadership hypothesis*: Individuals with more extreme opinions exercise more influence over the group members because of their greater persuasiveness, confidence, and involvement in the discussion. Other investigators felt that shifts were due to *familiarization*. As individuals discuss the problems, their uncertainty decreases and they begin advocating more extreme alternatives. *Diffusion of responsibility* may also be a factor, for people may be more comfortable endorsing extreme solutions in groups because their personal responsibility for the decision is diminished.

Overall, however, the bulk of the evidence supports the *value hypothesis*. When individuals discuss their opinions in a group, they shift in the direction they think is consistent with the values of their group or culture (Clark, 1971; Myers & Lamm, 1975, 1976). If they feel that taking risks is more acceptable than exercising caution, then they will become riskier after a discussion (Weigold & Schlenker, 1991). In France, where people generally like their government but dislike Americans, group discussion improved their attitude toward their government but exacerbated their negative opinions of Americans (Moscovici & Zavalloni, 1969). Similarly, prejudiced people who discussed racial issues with other prejudiced individuals became even more biased. Conversely, when mildly prejudiced persons discussed racial issues with other mildly prejudiced individuals, they became less prejudiced (Myers & Bishop, 1970).

Why should we shift our judgments to match the position our group initially values? Perhaps we can generate more arguments favoring the more valued alternative. This *persuasive-arguments theory* suggests that when people answer the choice dilemmas questionnaire, arguments favoring risk are more plentiful than arguments favoring caution. Similarly, anti-American students can muster many more arguments to confirm their negative image of the United States, and bigots offer more reasons to reject others rather than to accept them. The result? The group persuades itself as it develops more arguments favoring the initially preferred position (Burnstein & Vinokur, 1973, 1977; Kaplan & Miller, 1983; Stasson & Davis, 1989; Vinokur & Burnstein, 1974, 1978).

Social comparison theory offers a different explanation (Goethals & Zanna, 1979; Myers, 1978; Myers & Lamm, 1976). According to this approach, during group discussion people actively compare themselves with others. When they discover that some members of the group have stronger (or more extreme) attitudes than they do, they begin to endorse more extreme positions. Individuals who consider themselves to be risk takers may find that, compared with others in the group, they are cautious. Therefore, they shift their choices in a riskier direction. People who consider themselves to be prejudiced may find that they are relatively tolerant of others, so they express even more biased opinions. Just knowing the positions of the other people in the groups, without knowing the reasons behind them, is sometimes sufficient to produce polarization (Blascovich, Ginsburg, & Howe, 1975, 1976).

Social decision scheme theory offers yet a third explanation. This theory argues that groups adopt rules about how they will make decisions on the issues they face (J. H. Davis, 1982). Formal voting is taken for granted in some groups, but many groups use informal techniques to make decisions. A group may implicitly adopt a majority-rules scheme and accept a solution when more than 50% of the group express their approval of it. Another group may adopt a unanimity-rules scheme and insist that every single person in the group agree to the solution before the group will accept it. Interestingly, groups whose members are initially more risky seem to adopt a "risk-supported-wins" scheme. If only one person favors a risky alternative, the group won't adopt it. But if two people throw their support behind a risky alternative, then the group often accepts the recommendation. Conversely, when the majority of the group members lean toward the cautious pole, the group seems to adopt a "caution-supported-wins" scheme. If two people express support for a more conservative solution, then the group chooses that alternative (Davis, Kameda, & Stasson, 1992; Laughlin & Earley, 1982; Zuber, Crott, & Werner, 1992).

Persuasion, social-comparison, and decision schemes probably combine to generate group polarization (Isenberg, 1986; Kaplan & Miller, 1983). Other people are a critical source of information, as Chapter 9's analysis of informational influence concludes. If our group generates more arguments that favor Position *A*, then we are likely to take these arguments into consideration and come to favor Position *A* as well. Normative influence can also guide our behaviors; if discussion convinces us that the group's norms are more extreme than we initially thought, then we are likely to adopt the more extreme position. Last, our desire to be democratic and open to our group's recommendations may require that we accept a risky or conservative group decision as our own. In any case, these social processes result in more extreme, rather than more conservative, final decisions.

Groupthink

In 1961, a special advisory committee to President John F. Kennedy planned and implemented a covert invasion of Cuba at the Bay of Pigs. Even though the group spent hundreds of hours working out the details of the attack, the invasion was a total disaster. The entire attacking force was killed or captured within days, and the U.S. government had to send food and supplies to Cuba to ransom them back.

Why, Irving Janis wondered, would a group of top military and government leaders make such a terrible decision? Intrigued by this infamous failure, Janis initiated a series of extensive case studies of the groups described in Table 10-6. Each of these military or governmental groups included top-quality personnel; most had been picked for their intelligence, their dedication, and their outstanding decision-making skills. Yet when they gathered together in a group, something happened. To paraphrase Carl Jung, the individually clever heads became one big nincompoop.

groupthink
A strong concurrence-seeking tendency that interferes with effective group decision making.

Janis concluded that the members of these groups experienced **groupthink**, a distorted style of thinking that renders group members incapable of making a rational decision. According to Janis (1982), groupthink is "a mode of thinking that people engage in when they are deeply involved in a cohesive in-group, when the members' strivings for unanimity override their motivation to realistically appraise alternative courses of action" (p. 9). To Janis, groupthink is a disease that infects healthy groups, rendering them inefficient and unproductive. And like the physician who searches for symptoms that distinguish one disease from another, Janis has identified a number of symptoms that occur in groupthink situations. These danger signals, which should serve to warn members that they may be falling prey to groupthink, are discussed next.

Overestimation of the group. Groups that have fallen into the trap of groupthink are actually planning fiascoes and making all the wrong choices. Yet the members usually assume that everything is working perfectly. Indeed, they often express their enthusiasm in public statements about their wrongheaded decisions (Tetlock, 1979). Janis traces this unwarranted optimism to two types of illusory thinking, *illusions of invulnerability* and *illusions of morality*. The White House staff who took part in the Watergate cover-up, for example, were certain that Nixon would use his presidential powers to dispose of any problems that might arise. Furthermore, transcripts of the famous Nixon tapes indicate that the group felt the cover-up was a morally appropriate action; that bribes, lies, and deception were permissible so long as the president was protected.

Biased perceptions. During groupthink, members respond to people who oppose their plan with suspicion and hostility. The naval advisers and officers responsible for the protection of the U.S. Pacific Fleet based at Pearl Harbor, for example, received many warning signals indicating a possible air attack, but they managed to dismiss them all through rationalizing and stereo-

▲ In 1961, this group of experts, handpicked by President John F. Kennedy, spent months planning the invasion of Cuba at the Bahía de Cochinos (Bay of Pigs). Despite long hours and careful deliberation, the invasion failed when all 1,400 men in the attack force were either captured or killed. Janis, after conducting a thorough analysis of the event, described the decision as one of the "worst fiascoes ever perpetrated by a responsible government" (1972, p. 14).

▲ TABLE 10-6
Five fiascoes in U.S. history: Was groupthink to blame?

Group	*Fiasco*
Senior advisers to Admiral H. E. Kimmel, including 20 captains, vice-admirals, and other executive naval officers	In 1941, this group concentrated on Pearl Harbor's importance as a training base to such an extent that the base was left unprotected.
President Truman's policy-making group, including the Joint Chiefs of Staff, and members of the National Security Council	When this group authorized the crossing of the 38th parallel during the Korean War, China joined the conflagration.
President Kennedy's ad hoc advisory committee, including the secretaries of state and defense, Joint Chiefs of Staff, and top CIA officers	This group backed an ill-conceived plan to invade Cuba at the Bay of Pigs in 1961.
President Johnson's Tuesday Lunch Group, consisting of White House staff, the chairman of the Joint Chiefs of Staff, the CIA director, and several cabinet members	During lunch meetings held from 1965 to 1968, this group recommended the escalation of the Vietnam War.
President Nixon's White House staff, including John Dean, John Ehrlichman, Charles E. Colson, and H. R. Haldeman	From 1971 to 1972, this group tried to cover up the activities surrounding the Watergate break-in by destroying evidence and bribing the burglars.

Source: Janis, 1982.

typing. They convinced themselves that "weak little Japan" would never consider attacking the powerful U.S. fleet; that the Japanese would concentrate on easier targets located thousands of miles from Hawaii; that the Japanese didn't have the courage to gamble their fleet of aircraft carriers in such a bold attack; that the Japanese lacked the military know-how and expertise to carry out the attack successfully. All of these suppositions lulled the navy into a false sense of security.

Conformity pressures. Conformity is a natural and necessary aspect of a group's dynamics (see Chapter 9). But in groupthink situations, pressures to conform become overwhelming. Each member of the group experiences a personal reluctance to disagree. Members who begin to question the group's decision even engage privately in *self-censorship*—they hide their misgivings when they discuss the issue openly. Group members also become increasingly intolerant of dissent. In fact, some of the group members become self-appointed vigilantes, or *mindguards,* who try to shield the group from information that will shake the members' confidence in themselves or their leaders. Through self-censorship, pressuring dissenters, and mindguarding, the group develops an atmosphere of *unanimity*. Every person may privately disagree with what is occurring in the group, yet publicly everyone expresses total agreement with the group's policies. The planners who mounted the Bay of Pigs invasion, for example, quashed dissent, kept misgivings to themselves, and hid controversial information from the group. As a result, a "curious atmosphere of assumed consensus" characterized each session (Schlesinger, 1965, p. 250).

Defective decision-making strategies. Janis believes that groups experiencing groupthink use faulty strategies when they make decisions. In Kennedy's advisory group, discussion focused on two extreme alternatives—either endorse the Bay of Pigs invasion or abandon Cuba to communism—while ignoring all other potential alternatives. In addition, the group lost sight of its overall objectives as it became caught up in the minor details of the invasion plan. The group also avoided any information that pointed to limitations in their plans but sought out facts and opinions that buttressed their initial preferences. The group members didn't make a few small errors; they committed dozens of blunders.

What Causes Groupthink?

You probably belong to at least one group that must make decisions from time to time—a community group that must choose a fund-raising project; a union or employee group that must ratify a new contract; a family that must discuss your college plans. Can these kinds of groups experience groupthink? Yes, if the causal factors specified by Janis are present. Here we review four of the most important factors: cohesiveness, isolation, leadership style, and stress.

Cohesiveness. Cohesive groups have many advantages over groups that lack unity. People enjoy their membership much more in cohesive groups, they are less likely to abandon the group, and they work harder in pursuit of the group's goals. But extreme cohesiveness can be dangerous. When cohesiveness intensifies, members become more likely to accept the goals, decisions, and norms of the group without reservation. Conformity pressures also rise as members become reluctant to say or do anything that goes against the grain of the group, and the number of internal disagreements—so necessary for sound decision making—decreases. Janis (1982) admits that noncohesive groups can also make terrible decisions, "especially if the members are engaging in internal warfare" (p. 176), but they do not fall prey to groupthink. In a cohesive group, however, members refrain from speaking out against decisions, avoid arguing, and strive to maintain friendly, cordial relations with one another at all costs.

Isolation. Many military, industrial, and governmental groups work in secret. They avoid leaks by maintaining strict confidentiality and working only with people who are members of their group. The government advisers who planned the Bay of Pigs invasion believed that only a surprise attack would succeed, so they insulated themselves from any outside contacts. Unfortunately, their isolation limited the amount of information available to the group and prevented any type of consultation with independent experts. Military analysts could have provided fresh insights and useful criticisms of the plan, but their input was avoided. The group's isolation from important sources of information resulted in a poor plan that was never rigorously tested.

Biased leadership. Leaders can also contribute to the growth of groupthink. A biased leader who exerts too much authority over the group members can increase conformity pressures and railroad decisions. Many groups follow a rigid protocol that gives the leader considerable control over the group discussion. The leader determines the agenda for each meeting, sets limits on discussions, and can even decide who will be heard. A biased leader can discourage dissension by expressing his or her own views at the very outset, and by urging the group to strive for agreement rather than participate in critical discussion.

President Lyndon B. Johnson's actions as the leader of his advisory committee on Vietnam War strategies provide many examples of biased leadership.

Committed to escalating the Vietnam War, Johnson met each Tuesday with military experts to consider strategy and select targets for bombing. Johnson controlled the discussion at all meetings and expressed his own views forcefully and unwaveringly. He refused to allow the group to discuss deeper issues—such as ways to achieve peace through negotiation—and called dissenters such names as "my favorite dove" or "Mr. Stop-the-Bombing." Johnson also forced Secretary of Defense Robert McNamara to resign from his post because McNamara continually disagreed with the group's policies; Johnson felt that McNamara was undermining the unity of the group.

Decisional stress. As Janis (1989) notes, most of us experience stress when we must make an important decision. Important choices—such as which college to attend, which house or apartment to buy or rent, which car to buy, whom to marry—are made reluctantly and only after we have suffered through days and nights of worry, anxiety, and uncertainty.

We reduce the stress of decision making in many ways. We sometimes procrastinate for so long that we avoid the decision entirely. Or we make an arbitrary decision and then rationalize our choice. Or we deny responsibility for our choice by delegating the decision to someone else. Unfortunately, these tendencies become stronger when people make major decisions in groups than when they decide alone. The insecurity of each individual can be minimized if the group quickly chooses a plan of action, with little argument or dissension. Then, through collective discussion, the group members can rationalize their choice by exaggerating the positive consequences, minimizing the possibility of negative outcomes, concentrating on minor details, and overlooking larger issues. Naturally, these stress-reduction tactics increase the likelihood of groupthink (Callaway, Marriott, & Esser, 1985).

Combining the causes. Figure 10-7 summarizes Janis's theory of groupthink. Janis thinks several group and situational factors contribute to the development of groupthink, but he emphasizes high cohesiveness above all other causes. Once a group falls prey to groupthink, various symptoms of faulty group process begin to surface, including overestimation of the group's effectiveness, closed-mindedness, strong pressures toward uniformity, and faulty decision-making strategies. Finally, the process culminates in a fiasco.

Did the crew of Flight 401 suffer from groupthink? We can't be sure, but many of the causes identified by Janis were present as the crew struggled to solve the problem of the light (Foushee, 1984; Foushee & Helmreich, 1988). The crew was probably very cohesive, for Loft, Stockstill, and Repo liked and respected one another. Second, the crew was isolated in the cockpit, receiving information from dispatchers and controllers, but relying mostly on instrument information and crew members' judgments. Indeed, an L-1011 expert was on the plane, but they never asked him for his advice. Third, Stockstill and Repo may not have felt free to question Loft's judgment because the chain of command is very strong in such crews. This factor played a significant role in the crash of a DC-8 in 1978. Like the crew of Flight 401, the crew was checking a malfunctioning instrument. The flight engineer told the captain they were running out of fuel, but the captain dismissed the warning. The plane crashed, and investigators concluded that

> the stature of a captain and his management style may exert subtle pressure on his crew to conform to his way of thinking. It may hinder interaction and adequate monitoring and force another crewmember to yield his right to express an opinion. (NTSB, 1979, p. 27)

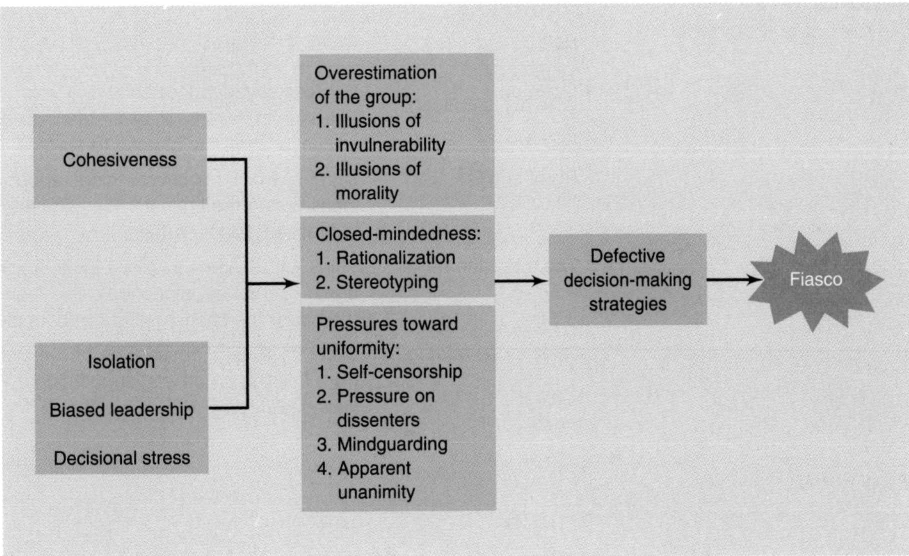

▲ FIGURE 10-7
What causes groupthink? Janis identified four key causes—cohesiveness, isolation, biased leadership, and decisional stress—that set the stage for groupthink. These causes generate the symptoms of groupthink, which eventually culminate in a poor decision. (Based on Janis, 1982)

Last, the problem with the light may have created too much stress for the crew. During the emergency, the crew was trying both to fly the plane and deal with the malfuntioning light bulb. In such situations, pilots sometimes develop tunnel vision and lock into "the most obvious hypotheses which are often at least partially incorrect" (Foushee, 1986, p. 3). Loft and his crew may have become so absorbed with fixing the light that they didn't notice their autopilot had failed (Ginnett, 1990).

Avoiding Groupthink

Researchers have succeeded in confirming many of Janis's ideas about faulty decision making in groups. Case studies of groups that made poor decisions, such as the planners of the mission to rescue the hostages held in Tehran and the team that decided to launch the space shuttle *Challenger,* identified the symptoms and causes Janis describes (Esser & Lindoerfer, 1989; Hensley & Griffin, 1986; Herek, Janis, & Huth, 1987; Smith, 1984; Tetlock et al., 1992). Laboratory studies also offer some support for the model (Callaway & Esser, 1984; Moorhead, 1982; Moorhead & Montanari, 1986). Very cohesive groups that were told to hurry their discussion failed to explore their options fully (Courtright, 1978; Turner et al., 1992). Groups led by biased leaders generated fewer solutions than groups led by leaders who adopted a more open style of leadership (Flowers, 1977; Leana, 1985).

Janis's model, however, is limited in some ways (Aldag & Fuller, 1993; Longley & Pruitt, 1980; McCauley, 1989; Park, 1990; Tetlock et al., 1992). Even though he distinguishes between symptoms and causes, these two sets of factors are difficult to distinguish empirically. Janis also overlooks some factors that may cause faulty decisions, such as the group's stage of development, and overemphasizes others (for example, cohesiveness). Despite these problems, however, Janis's model offers useful suggestions for improving decision making in groups.

Removing the causes. Janis doesn't recommend reducing the cohesiveness of the group as a means of limiting groupthink. As he notes, the impact of cohesiveness on group processes can be either negative or positive, depending on other characteristics of the group and the setting. He does, how-

▲ TABLE 10-7
The rules of brainstorming

Rule	*Content*
Open up.	Express any idea that comes to your mind, even if it seems odd, extreme, irrelevant, or pedestrian. If you censor yourself, good ideas will never have the chance to surface.
Don't criticize.	Don't say or think critical things about your ideas or anyone else's ideas during the brainstorming phase. Any idea, no matter how it's expressed, might be helpful.
The more the better.	Think and express as many ideas as possible, without worrying about overlap or uniqueness. The more ideas that are generated, the better the chances that the best idea will be discovered.
Build by borrowing.	Don't try to take possession of the ideas you offer or shy away from building on others' suggestions. The group creates the ideas; individuals don't.

Harnessing the Creativity of Groups

How can manufacturers package potato chips so they take up less space? What are some creative solutions to the problem of world hunger? What other products besides tea could be packed in bags? List as many possible uses for cardboard boxes as you can. How would the world be different if everyone had six fingers instead of five?

To solve these kinds of problems, individuals must be able to generate a range of potential solutions. Rather than restricting their focus by concentrating on only one or two solutions—as is so typical in groupthink situations—the problem solver must pursue the creative and innovative while avoiding the routine and traditional. Seeking creative solutions, governments, businesses, industry, and schools often turn to groups.

Many methods have been developed to enhance creativity through group interaction. One of the most famous, **brainstorming,** encourages freewheeling expression, a supportive atmosphere, developing many ideas, and building on others' ideas (see Table 10-7). Brainstorming encourages group members to generate as many ideas as possible, without worrying whether these ideas are good or bad. Ideas can be critiqued later, but during the brainstorming phase all ideas—no matter how half-baked or bizarre—should be expressed. Quantity counts more than quality (Osborn, 1957).

Brainstorming, however, is something of a boondoggle. Decision makers swear by it, and most people believe that brainstorming groups are productive groups (Paulus et al., 1993). Social psychologists, however, aren't at all impressed with the technique (Bond & Van Leeuwen, 1991; Mullen, Johnson, & Salas, 1991). Groups *are* more creative than individuals, but only when researchers don't give the brainstorming directions to individuals (Cohen, Whitmyre, & Funk, 1960; Meadow, Parnes, & Reese, 1959). Four-person groups, for example, generated an average of 28 ideas in their session, but 4 individuals working alone generated an average of 74.5 ideas when their ideas were pooled. Individuals also generated 79.2% of the good ideas (Diehl & Stroebe, 1987; see also Bouchard & Hare, 1970; Bouchard, Barsaloux, & Drauden, 1974; Bouchard, Drauden, & Barsaloux, 1974; Dunnette, Campbell, & Jaastad, 1963; Taylor, Berry, & Block, 1958).

Should we be shocked that groups don't brainstorm particularly well? Only if we ignore their basic dynamics. On the positive side, just the presence of others may be stimulating, and the interchange of ideas may lead to the discovery of novel solutions that individuals working alone would have never imagined (Ruback, Dabbs, & Hopper, 1984). However, on the negative side, the studies of social loafing described earlier imply that people may not work as hard when they are members of an interacting group. Brainstorming creates an ideal setting for social loafing—low identifiability, lack of rewards for personal contributions, ambiguous standards, and doubts about others' willingness to contribute. Coordination problems can also interfere with productivity, for individuals can produce ideas at an almost constant rate, whereas conversing group members must wait their turn. If this problem is minimized by encouraging participants to take notes as ideas are generated, then much of the value of group discussion is lost because members are distracted (Diehl & Stroebe, 1991).

Groupthink processes may also interfere with idea

brainstorming: A method for enhancing creativity in groups that calls for heightened expressiveness, inhibited evaluation, quantity rather than quality, and deliberate attempts to build on others' ideas.

ever, recommend several methods for dealing with the other three causes of groupthink. First, to reduce isolation, people who are not members of the decision-making group should be invited to meetings periodically and encouraged to give their opinions and criticisms of the group's plans. Also, group members should feel free to discuss the decision with trusted subordinates who aren't members of the group. Second, leaders must strive to remain impartial. They must make it clear that they expect group members to argue and criticize and should state their own preferences only after all other voices have been heard. Third, although decision making, by its very nature, tends to be stressful, groups can reduce this stress by allowing sufficient time for full discussion and routinely holding "second-chance" meetings—review sessions held after the final decision is made but before the plan is put into action. Janis recommends that these second-chance meetings be held in different, more relaxed

generation. People can rarely escape implicit pressures to conform to the group's standards of normality, so self-censorship, mindguards, and social pressure are to be expected. People in brainstorming groups also implicitly compare their own productivity to that of others, so if one person is unproductive, others may adopt that person's low-level standard (Paulus & Dzindolet, 1993).

Brainstorming can, however, be improved. Training in creative problem solving is essential. If the group members simply sit down and brainstorm without discussing procedures and dynamics, then their efforts will probably be less than satisfying (Bouchard, 1972). Each person should also record more ideas after the group session to help control social loafing (Philipsen, Mulac, & Dietrich, 1979). Talking should also be stopped periodically to allow group members to generate ideas silently. Pauses and silences during brainstorming improve the quality of the ideas generated (Ruback, Dabbs, & Hopper, 1984). Groups should also be given explicit standards that state what kind of performance is expected of them to prevent them from adopting a group norm that condones low productivity (Paulus & Dzindolet, 1993).

Brainstorming also takes time, so groups should avoid trying to rush through their task. Time pressures can motivate people to work more rapidly than they usually do, but often the quality of their products suffers. Therefore the group needs to set aside sufficient time to complete the task thoroughly, particularly during the early training stages when the group is learning to brainstorm effectively. Studies suggest that the group that hurries through this week's meeting will likely hurry again next week even if the group is given more time to accomplish its task (Kelley, 1988; Kelley, Futoran, & McGrath, 1990; Kelley & Karau, 1993).

A skilled discussion leader is also an essential ingredient for successful brainstorming (Bouchard, 1972). Group members must sometimes be stimulated before they can become creative. Facilitators should record all ideas in full view of participants and use a round-robin procedure if only a few ideas are offered. When ideas begin to dwindle, facilitators can prevent group members from giving up. They can also make use of special procedures to stimulate the group's creative juices. One such approach, the *nominal group technique,* involves four basic phases.

- The discussion leader introduces the problem or issue in a short statement that is written on a blackboard or flip chart. Once members understand the statement, they silently generate ideas concerning the issue in writing, usually working for 10 to 15 minutes.
- The members share their ideas with one another in a round-robin fashion. Each person states an idea, which is given an identification letter and written beneath the issue statement, before the next individual adds his or her contribution.
- The group discusses each item, focusing primarily on clarification.
- The members rank the five solutions they most prefer, writing their choices on an index card. The leader then collects the cards, averages the rankings to yield a group decision, and informs the group of the outcome.

Groups that use the nominal group technique often outperform those who only brainstorm (Delbecq, Van de Ven, & Gustafson, 1975; Van de Ven, 1974; but see also Pavitt, 1993).

Studies of brainstorming offer an important lesson. Even though brainstorming is thought by many to be a marvelous way to generate creative solutions, it only begins to tap the group's potential. Groups are powerful performance machines, but they must be tuned up and operated properly if they are to perform up to expectations.

settings, citing as precedent the decision-making techniques of the ancient Persians. History claims that they made all important decisions twice—once when sober and once when drunk.

Alleviating the symptoms. Even if groupthink's causes cannot be directly attacked, its symptoms can be treated. First, Janis stresses the importance of eliminating overconfidence by cataloging and reviewing the ingroup's limitations and, if relevant, the outgroup's strengths. Second, as a safeguard against closed-mindedness, group members should devote a sizable block of time to "surveying all warning signals from the rivals and constructing alternative scenarios of the rivals' intentions" (Janis, 1982, p. 268). Third, to reduce conformity pressures the group leader should (a) establish an atmosphere of open inquiry in which criticism, debate, and dissension are the norm rather than the exception; (b) ask one or more group members to play the role of devil's advocate by consistently criticizing the ideas and suggestions raised by others; and (c) break the group down into subgroups, which work independently on the decision.

Fourth, the group should always strive to use effective decision-making strategies. Even before beginning deliberations, group members should plan the process they will use to arrive at a decision. Problem-solving groups rarely devote much time to this issue—they usually jump immediately into the question under discussion. This practice is unfortunate because the more time the group spends planning its strategy, the more likely the group is to make a good decision (Hackman & Morris, 1975; Hirokawa, 1980, 1984). In addition, the group members should generate as many alternative solutions to the problem as they can, perhaps by using such special group techniques as brainstorming. (See "In Depth: Harnessing the Creativity of Groups."). All these alternatives should be painstakingly reviewed before one is chosen as the solution to the problem. The group should also explicitly adopt a decision scheme that promotes discussion and debate rather than one that promotes premature consensus seeking. Groups that use a unanimity rule to determine their final decisions are more likely to suffer from groupthink than those that use a majority-rules decision scheme (Kameda & Sugimori, 1993) (see Table 10-8).

Leadership

Scholars down through the centuries have debated the nature of leadership. In the 19th century, the historian Thomas Carlyle argued that famous figures in history—Alexander the Great, Napoleon, Cleopatra, Julius Caesar, Catherine the Great—possessed certain characteristics that destined them to be great leaders. To Carlyle, leadership was a quality that exists in some people and not in others. He advanced the *great-leader theory* of history (he called it the "great man theory"), which argued that the success and failure of nations and empires are determined by the skills and abilities of their leaders (Carlyle, 1841; Simonton, 1980).

Russian novelist Leo Tolstoy argued that, far from shaping history, great leaders are themselves shaped by situational forces beyond their control. Rejecting the idea that leaders are geniuses with unique characteristics, he proposed that the "spirit of the times"—the zeitgeist—destines them either to succeed or to fail (Tolstoy, 1869/1952).

These two perspectives—Carlyle's great-leader theory and Tolstoy's zeitgeist approach—influenced social psychologists' initial attempts to understand lead-

▲ **TABLE 10-8**
Summing up: Decision making in groups

Process	*Characteristics*	*Causes*
Group polarization	Group decisions are more extreme than individual decisions. Groups shift in the direction closest to the average of members' predeliberation opinions. A risky shift, for example, occurs when more of the group members initially favor positions on the risky side of the continuum rather than on the cautious side.	Polarization occurs because people want to adopt positions that are consistent with positions valued by their group or culture. Polarization depends on the arguments generated during discussion (persuasive arguments theory), social comparison, and the group's social decision scheme.
Groupthink	Groups sometimes display a distorted style of thinking that renders group members incapable of making a rational decision. Symptoms include illusions of invulnerability and morality, biased perceptions of the outgroup, interpersonal pressure, self-censorship, mindguarding, apparent unanimity, and defective decision-making strategies.	Cohesiveness, isolation, leadership, and decisional stress combine to cause groupthink, although cohesiveness is the most critical ingredient. Groupthink can be prevented by reducing conformity pressures, correcting judgmental errors, and using effective decision-making procedures.

ership. The great-leader theory migrated into social psychology as a *trait approach,* which argued that the ability to lead others must be related to measurable personality, intellectual, and physical characteristics. Compared to poor leaders and followers, outstanding leaders were more achievement oriented, adaptable, alert, energetic, responsible, self-confident, and sociable; they were also taller, more intelligent, older, and weighed more. The zeitgeist approach, in contrast, inspired a *situational approach* that suggested leadership is determined by a host of variables operating in the leadership situation, including the needs of the group members, the availability of resources, and, most importantly, the type of task to be performed. If a group is about to disintegrate because of heated conflicts among the members, for example, the effective leader will be someone who can improve the group's interpersonal relations (Katz, 1977). Similarly, if individuals possess skills that facilitate performance on Task *X* but undermine performance on Task *Y,* then they are likely to emerge as effective leaders only if the group is working on Task *X* (Stogdill, 1974).

Contemporary theories about leadership, true to Kurt Lewin's $B = f(P, E)$ formula discussed in Chapter 1, integrate the trait approach and the situational approach by taking an *interactional approach* to leadership (see Table 10-9). Interactionism assumes that any aspect of the leader, group member, or setting can influence, and be influenced by, every other variable in the system. Loft's personal qualities influenced the way he led, but so did the highly structured norms of the flight deck and the personal qualities of Stockstill and Repo (Hollander, 1985). Leadership is also a transactional and transformational process. Loft made suggestions and gave orders, but his crew accepted his offerings; this exchange may have inspired them to exert even more effort than they usually would (Bass, 1985a, 1985b; Bass, Avolio, & Goldheim, 1987). Leadership is a cooperative process of legitimate influence rather than one of sheer power (Grimes, 1978). Loft did not force Repo to go into the bay beneath the

▲ TABLE 10-9
Summing up: Three approaches to leadership

Approach	*Guiding Assumption*
Trait	Traits predispose certain people to become effective leaders.
Situational	Situational factors cause people with certain characteristics to lead effectively.
Interactionism	Situational factors, the leader's traits and behaviors, and followers' characteristics and perceptions interact to determine who is an effective leader.

flight deck. He told Repo to do so, and Repo obeyed, because the leader has the right to influence others (Hollander, 1985). Last, leadership is an adaptive, goal-seeking process, for it organizes and motivates group members' attempts to attain personal and group-level goals (Katz & Kahn, 1978). **Leadership**, then, is a "reciprocal, transactional, and transformational process in which individuals are permitted to influence and motivate others to facilitate the attainment of group and individual goals" (Forsyth, 1990, p. 216).

leadership
A reciprocal, transactional, and transformational process in which individuals are permitted to influence and motivate others to facilitate the attainment of group and individual goals.

Who Will Lead?

The instructor of one of your courses randomly assigns all the class members to five-person groups. These groups must complete a project within three weeks, and each group member will get whatever grade the group project earns. Your group's members are shown in the photos on page 387. Person A is very familiar with the topic of the project and offers excellent suggestions. Person B is very friendly and makes certain everyone is satisfied with the group's decisions. Person C is clearly the intellectual giant of the group; he rarely speaks, but the things he says are incredibly insightful. Person D typically sits at the head of the table and talks more than the rest of the group members. Excluding yourself, who would you predict would emerge as your group's leader?

leadership emergence
The process by which an individual becomes the leader of a formerly leaderless group.

Leadership emergence in small groups isn't a random phenomenon, for leaders differ, physically and psychologically, from their subordinates. As Table 10-10 suggests, they tend to be older, taller, and heavier than the average group member. They are usually more accomplished at the tasks facing the group, and they tend to talk more than the average member. Leaders are outgoing rather than shy and dominant rather than submissive. Leaders are more often men than women and more likely masculine than feminine in sex-role orientation (Eagly & Karau, 1991; Kenny & Zaccaro 1983; Littlepage & Silbiger, 1992; Lord, De Vader, & Alliger, 1986; Malloy & Janowski, 1992).

How do these factors influence our choices of leaders? Studies of social cognition, discussed in Chapter 3, suggest that our choices are constrained by our stereotypes about leaders and followers. When the group begins its discussion, we treat each group member's actions and characteristics as evidence attesting to the presence or absence of leadership ability. If someone in the group matches our intuitive definition of a leader—our *implicit leadership theory*—then we will probably allow that individual to lead. When we size up a person's leadership potential, our perceptions result more from our preconceptions about leadership than from the qualities the potential leader presents. Like many of the perceptual processes discussed in Chapter 3, our perceptions of leaders are more conceptually driven than data driven (Cronshaw & Lord, 1987; Foti, Fraser, & Lord, 1982; Lord, 1985).

▲ Whom would you choose to lead your group? People's choices often reveal their assumptions about leadership. In some cases they favor older, more talkative men and overlook women and minorities.

Person A, for example, may be the most qualified because she possesses more task-relevant skills, but if the group members are prejudiced against female leaders, then she may not be chosen to lead. Men are more often chosen to be leaders in all kinds of situations. The lone man in an otherwise all-female group often becomes the leader; the lone woman in an otherwise all-male group has little influence in the group (Crocker & McGraw, 1984). Even women who are quite dominant interpersonally may not be able to overcome members' leadership stereotypes. In one study, researchers created dyads that included one person who was highly dominant and one person who was low in dominance. When two men or two women were interacting, the high-dominant individual became the leader 73% of the time. But when the groups contained one man and one woman, the high-dominant man became the leader 90% of the time, but the high-dominant woman became the leader only 35% of the time (Nyquist & Spence, 1986). Sexism is alive and well in small groups (Eagly & Karau, 1991; Eagly, Makhijani, & Klonsky, 1992).

Person B probably won't be selected as the leader, either. Not only is she a woman, but the skills she displays are often devalued by group members when

▲ TABLE 10-10
Personal characteristics associated with leadership and nonleadership in small groups

Characteristic	*Leader*	*Nonleaders*
Age	Older	Younger
Weight	Heavier	Lighter
Height	Taller	Shorter
Abilities	Experienced	Inexperienced
Participation	High rate	Low rate
Personality	Extraverted	Introverted
Interpersonal style	Dominant	Submissive
Sex	Male	Female
Gender	Masculine	Feminine

they select a leader (Carbonell, 1984; Forsyth, Schlenker, et al., 1985). Person C is also an unlikely winner in the leadership race. Blacks are typically denied leadership positions in racially heterogeneous groups, even if their qualities and experiences qualify them for that role (Molm, 1986; Webster & Driskell, 1983). Person C may also be perceived as too intelligent (Simonton, 1985). Groups like leaders who are smarter than the average group member but they shy away from people who seem too intelligent; they fear they won't be able to communicate with them.

Person D, then, is the most likely leader for the group. First, Person D looks older than the others, and group members often assume that age, experience, and leadership ability go hand in hand (Stogdill, 1974). Second, in our culture the head of the table is so strongly associated with leadership that we naturally assume the person who sits there is the group leader (Nemeth & Wachtler, 1974). Third, evidence also indicates that many group members associate talkativeness with leadership (Malloy & Janowski, 1992; Sorrentino & Boutillier, 1975). In fact, it doesn't really matter whether D's comments are helpful or valuable to the group, for people seem to be more influenced by the sheer quantity of the participation rather than by its quality. Thus, for many of the wrong reasons, D would probably emerge as the leader rather than A, B, or C.

How Much Should the Leader Lead?

Which leader is most effective, the one who takes charge and directs the group with a strong hand or the one who consults with group members and lets them share the reins of leadership? Kurt Lewin, Ronald Lippitt, and Ralph White examined this question in the late 1930s (Lewin, Lippitt, & White, 1939; White & Lippitt, 1968). They put a male adult in charge of small groups of boys who were working on hobby projects after school. In some groups, the man made all the decisions for the group without consulting the boys. This *directive,* or autocratic, leader told the boys what to do, he often criticized them, and he remained aloof from the group. Other groups were guided by a *participatory,* or democratic, leader who let them make decisions as he provided guiding advice. He explained long-term goals and steps to be taken to reach the goals, but he rarely criticized the boys or gave them orders. Still other groups were given a *laissez-faire* leader who allowed the boys to work however they wished. He provided information on demand, but he didn't offer information, criticism, or guidance spontaneously.

The boys responded very differently to these three types of leaders. Groups with directive leaders spent more time working (74%) than participatory groups (50%), which in turn spent more time working than the laissez-faire groups (33%)—provided the leader remained in the room. Groups with a participatory leader kept right on working when their leader left, but the boys working under the direction of a directive leader did not. Laissez-faire and participatorily led groups were also less aggressive than groups with a directive leader. In the latter group, observers noted high rates of hostility among members, more demands for attention, more destructiveness, and a greater tendency to single out one group member to serve as the target of almost continual verbal abuse.

Lewin, Lippitt, and White's findings suggest that directive (autocratic) and participatory (democratic) leaders each have strengths and weaknesses. The strongly directive leader often succeeds in pushing the group to high levels of productivity, although at an interpersonal cost. The participatory leader, in contrast, increases feelings of satisfaction and members' involvement in the group (Stogdill, 1974). Therefore, shrewd leaders should plan their management style accordingly, depending on the situation they face and the goals they want to attain. If, for example, you are put in charge of a group of people who aren't the least bit interested in working hard to attain the group's goals, then a strong, directive style may work best. An autocratic approach is also warranted when the issues to be settled are minor ones, the group's acceptance won't impact them in any way, and when the group members are, themselves, autocratic. In general, however, your group members will be much happier if you involve them in group decisions. The decisions, too, will probably be wiser ones if you yourself are puzzled by the issues and group members have information that might be relevant (Field & House, 1990; Heilman et al., 1984; Vroom & Yetton, 1973).

What Style of Leadership Is More Effective?

Like most roles in a group, leadership breaks down into two components, task orientation and relationship orientation. Task leadership focuses on the problem at hand. Defining problems for the group, establishing communication networks, providing evaluative feedback, planning, motivating action, coordinating members' actions, and facilitating goal attainment by proposing solutions and removing barriers are key aspects of task leadership. But even in groups set up to complete tasks or solve problems, leaders must often take steps to meet the members' personal needs. Boosting morale, increasing cohesiveness, reducing interpersonal conflict, establishing leader-follower rapport, and illustrating one's concern and consideration for group members are all elements of relationship leadership (Lord, 1977).

contingency theory of leadership
Any model predicting that leadership depends on the interaction of personal characteristics of the leader and the nature of the group situation; usually used in reference to Fiedler's (1981) theory that the effectiveness of a task- or relationship-oriented leader depends on the favorability of the group situation.

Least Preferred Co-worker (LPC) Scale
A self-report method for assessing leadership style developed by Fiedler (1981); individuals who give relatively high ratings to their least-preferred co-worker tend to adopt a relationship-oriented leadership style; whereas those who give low ratings to their least-preferred co-worker tend to adopt a task-oriented style.

The contingency model. Which leader will be more effective, the one who can get the job done or the one who has interpersonal skills? Fred Fiedler's (1978, 1981) **contingency theory of leadership** offers one answer. Fiedler thinks most leaders lean toward one of these two orientations—some tend to be task oriented but others tend to be relationship oriented. To assess this tendency, Fiedler asks people to rate the person they least prefer to work with on a series of adjective pairs such as *pleasant-unpleasant, friendly-unfriendly,* and *nasty-nice.* People who get high scores on this **Least Preferred Co-worker (LPC) Scale** are assumed to be relationship oriented; after all, they even rate the person they don't like to work with positively. Low LPC scorers are assumed to be task oriented. (This scale has generated considerable controversy and debate; see Rice, 1978a, 1978b, 1979; Schriesheim, Bannister, & Money, 1979; Schriesheim & Kerr, 1977.)

Fiedler thinks different styles work better in different situations. First, is the leader on good terms with his or her followers (see Figure 10-8)? If so, he or she will have an easier time influencing them. Second, are the tasks being done by the group so structured that the leader can assess his or her subordinates' performance? Third, does the leader have the power to reward or punish group members (Smith, 1990)? To simplify, when all these factors are favorable—relations are good, the task is structured, and the leader occupies a powerful position within the group—or extremely unfavorable, Fiedler predicts that the task-oriented leader will perform most effectively. In contrast, the relationship leader should be more effective in moderately favorable or moderately unfavorable situations. The precise predictions of the theory are shown in Figure 10-8.

As an example of the model, consider a Delta flight crew and USAir flight crew. The captains of both crews are very powerful because their evaluations of their crews' performances determine the crews' salaries and chances for advancement. Second, the task is highly structured—everyone knows what he or she must do to fly the plane properly. Imagine, however, that leader/member relations differ between the two crews. The USAir captain enjoys positive relations with the crew, whereas the Delta captain and crew don't get along. Fiedler predicts that the USAir crew will perform best if their captain is task oriented. In contrast, a relationship-oriented captain is needed on the Delta crew.

Why does one style work better in a particular situation than another. Fiedler's *motivational hierarchy hypothesis* offers a possible answer. Fiedler contends that most leaders want to get the job accomplished and increase their subordinates' levels of satisfaction. Task-oriented leaders, however, give greater priority to the task than relationship-oriented leaders do, especially when they are working in stressful, unfavorable situations. Therefore, the task-oriented leader concentrates on driving the group forward to complete its task, wasting no time worrying about the group members' need for positive interpersonal relations. The relationship-oriented leader, on the other hand, may spend so much time trying to build positive relations that productivity diminishes. Fiedler also believes that when leaders find themselves in very favorable situations, they shift their attention from their primary goal to their secondary goal. So the task-oriented leader becomes more interpersonal, but the relationship-oriented leader becomes more concerned with the task. Once again, this strategy on the part of the relationship-oriented leader backfires, for productivity drops when the group members rebel against the increased work pressures. Whether or not Fiedler's analysis is accurate has not yet been determined empirically (Fiedler, 1978, 1986; Fiedler & Chemers, 1974; Fiedler & Garcia, 1987).

Fiedler's theory has been criticized, but it nonetheless offers considerable insight into leadership effectiveness (Peters, Hartke, & Pohlmann, 1985; Strube & Garcia, 1981). His theory also has interesting applications for management settings. His LEADER MATCH program, for example, seems to be a remarkably effective way to train leaders (Burke & Day, 1986; Csoka & Bons, 1978; Fiedler, 1978). Instead of telling leaders to change their personal style to fit the situation, LEADER MATCH trains them to change the group situation to fit their particular leadership style. For example, if task-oriented leaders find themselves in disadvantageous group situations, then they should change the situations until they match the leaders' styles. Leaders trained by LEADER MATCH are typically rated as more effective.

▲ FIGURE 10-8
When is a task-oriented leader more effective than a relationship-oriented leader? Fiedler's contingency model argues that effectiveness depends on the favorability of the situation: Are leader/member relations good or bad? Is the task structured or unstructured? Is the leader's position strong or weak? The task-oriented leader is most effective in favorable and extremely unfavorable group settings. (From Fiedler, 1978)

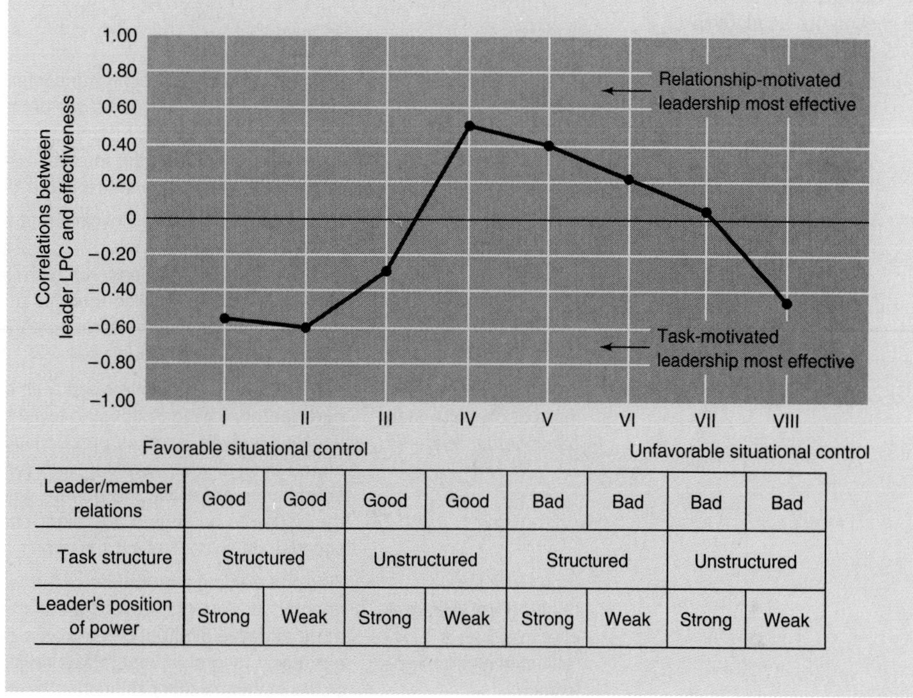

Leader/member relations	Good	Good	Good	Good	Bad	Bad	Bad	Bad
Task structure	Structured		Unstructured		Structured		Unstructured	
Leader's position of power	Strong	Weak	Strong	Weak	Strong	Weak	Strong	Weak

situational leadership theory Hersey and Blanchard's (1982) theory of leadership, which suggests that groups benefit from leadership that meshes with the maturity level of the group.

Situational leadership. Paul Hersey and Kenneth Blanchard also think that leaders must get the task accomplished and make sure the group survives intact. Their **situational model of leadership**, however, is based on the idea that leaders can be both task oriented *and* relationship oriented. This model assumes that leaders can be low or high in their task orientation and simultaneously low or high in their relationship orientation. Thus, rather than arguing for two basic types of leaders, Hersey and Blanchard view leadership as a fourfold typology.

They also agree with Fiedler that groups benefit from leadership that meshes with the needs of the group members, but their set of situational factors differs from Fiedler's. They believe that, to be effective, leaders must gauge the developmental stage of their group and make certain they meet the unique needs of the group that emerge at different times. Newly formed groups, groups beginning a new project, or groups with many new members are immature, and they require a high-task/low-relationship leader (Quadrant 1). As the group matures and begins working adequately on the task, the leader can increase relationship behavior and adopt a high/high style (Quadrant 2). Still later in the group's development, the leader can ease off on both types of leadership, starting first with task emphasis. In moderately mature groups the high-relationship/low-task style is most effective (Quadrant 3), and in fully mature work groups a low/low, laissez-faire style is appropriate (Quadrant 4). Thus, an effective leader must display four different leadership styles as the group moves through its life cycle: telling, selling, participating, and delegating. Unlike Fiedler, they recommend that leaders adjust their style until it fits the situation (Hersey & Blanchard, 1976, 1977, 1982).

Situational leadership theory's emphasis on *flexibility* as a cardinal trait in a leader is consistent with studies that have identified people who seem to rise to positions of leadership no matter what the setting (Kirkpatrick & Locke, 1991; Slater, 1955). One team of researchers, for example, asked small groups of

▲ **TABLE 10-11**
Summing up: Leadership processes in small groups

Question	*Answer*
What is leadership?	Leadership is a reciprocal, transactional, and transformational process in which individuals are permitted to influence and motivate others to facilitate the attainment of group and individual goals. It is shaped by the interaction of the situation and the qualities possessed by leaders and their followers.
Who emerges as a leader in small groups?	Individuals with certain physical and psychological characteristics (for example, men, dominant individuals, extroverts) are more likely to rise to positions of leadership. This process is determined, in part, by followers' implicit theories of leadership. People who match group members' stereotypes about leaders are usually chosen to lead the group.
Are directive leaders more successful than participatory leaders?	Lewin, Lippitt, and White's study of directive (autocratic), participatory (democratic), and laissez-faire leaders indicated that directive leaders increase productivity, but that group members are more satisfied when working with participatory leaders. Directive approaches are most appropriate when members are rebellious, the issues to be settled are minor ones, and the group's acceptance will not affect the group or its productivity.
When is a task-oriented leader more effective than a relationship-oriented leader?	Fiedler's contingency theory of leadership argues that task-oriented leaders (those who focus more on the group's goals) are more effective in situations that are either extremely unfavorable or extremely favorable, where favorability is determined by the quality of the leader/member relations, the nature of the task (structured or unstructured), and the leader's position of power. Relationship-oriented, socioemotional leaders are most effective in intermediate situations.
Are different styles of leadership more effective at different times during the group's life cycle?	Situational leadership theory recommends using a high-task and low-relationship style in new or inexperienced groups. As groups mature, leaders should shift to a participatory style (high task and high relationship) and maintain that style until the group has become task proficient. Leaders should then shift to low task and high relationship, and eventually to a delegating style (low task and low relationship).

college students to perform several kinds of tasks. Some of the tasks, such as group discussions of controversial topics, called for a leader who was good with people. Other tasks, in contrast, called for a leader who was task oriented. When the groups were asked to fold paper to make simple objects, they were more effective when someone took charge of the group and got the members working.

People didn't stay in the same groups to complete all of the tasks. When a task was completed, the researchers dissolved the groups and reformed them before assigning new tasks to each group. Yet, across all the groups and all the different tasks, the same individuals tended to emerge as group leaders. Later analysis indicated that these individuals were able to alter their behaviors to fit the demands of the situation. If their group was working on a task that required good people skills, they become more interpersonally oriented. But when the group needed a directive, task-oriented leader, these individuals stressed the task. These findings suggest that flexibility may be one of the most important qualities to look for in an effective leader (Zaccaro, Foti, & Kenny, 1991).

The Value of Groups

Not all groups, and not all leaders, are successes (see Table 10-11 for a summary). Still, let's not judge them too harshly. The crew of Flight 401, for example, didn't cause the crash. Investigators discovered a flaw in the L-1011: The autopilot would switch off if one of the pilots just nudged the steering yoke, but the instruments would not clearly indicate that it was off. Moreover, were it not for groups, the tragedy of Flight 401 would have been compounded. Within seconds of the crash, groups mobilized to help the victims. Hunters from the surrounding swamps worked with rescue squads to transport the injured to hospitals. Medical teams arrived at Levee 67A within the hour to minister to the victims. Relatives of the survivors banded together to give one another solace. Our groups may not fulfill all our expectations, but we could not live without them (Buys, 1978; Green & Mack, 1978; Kravitz et al., 1978).

Summary

Social behavior is often group behavior. Clubs, friendship cliques, work groups, military units, teams, classrooms, and assembly lines are all examples of *groups,* for each of these social settings involves two or more interdependent individuals who influence one another through social interaction. The many and varied groups we observe may seem to be unique social aggregates, but beneath the surface, groups share a common, fundamental *structure. Roles,* for example, specify the general behaviors expected of people who occupy different positions within the group. People who occupy *task roles* focus on the work to be done, whereas people in *socioemotional roles* attend to the group's interpersonal relations. Stable variations in *status,* attraction (*sociometric structure*), and communication (*communication networks*) can also be discerned, as well as varying degrees of group *cohesiveness.*

Over time groups change, moving in many cases through stages characterized by orientation (forming), conflict (storming), increased order (norming), productivity (performing), and dissolution (adjourning). People, too, go through stages during their tenure in a group. This group-socialization process can involve investigation, socialization, maintenance, resocialization, and remembrance. Groups have a remarkable impact on their members. *Reference groups* provide us with social-comparison information, and *primary groups* play a fundamental role in structuring society.

As early as 1898, social psychologists recognized that individuals sometimes work more efficiently when other people are present. This tendency, which is known as *social facilitation,* occurs when others are working nearby (coaction) and when others are watching us work (audience). Social facilitation depends, in part, on the task: Other people facilitate performance when the task is so simple that it requires only dominant responses, but they interfere when the task requires nondominant responses. Zajonc assumes that the mere presence of others automatically leads to arousal, but other theorists think individuals become aroused only when they experience evaluation apprehension or distraction. In all likelihood, several processes combine to determine task performance when others are present. The presence of others doesn't always have positive effects, however. The *Ringelmann effect,* for example, occurs on many tasks—as the group gets bigger, people become less productive. This phenomenon is caused by coordination problems and by *social loafing*—the reduction of individual effort when people work in a group. Social loafing can be prevented, however, by taking the following steps:

- Making input identifiable and increasing evaluation apprehension
- Minimizing aspects of the situation that create a *social dilemma* for participants (undoing the *free-rider effect* and the *sucker effect*)
- Maximizing the value of group goals and members' expectations about achieving those goals (*collective effort model*)

Not all groups are effective decision makers. Early studies using the choice dilemmas questionnaire revealed that individuals choose more risky alternatives in groups than when alone. This *risky shift* reflects *group polarization*—the tendency for groups to make more extreme choices than individuals. People apparently shift their opinions in the direction they think is consistent with the values of their group or culture. Three processes—persuasive arguments, social comparison, and social decision schemes—probably combine to produce this effect. Groups also blunder into poor decisions when group members strive for solidarity and cohesiveness to such an extent that any questions or topics that could lead to disputes are avoided. Janis calls this process *groupthink.* In describing the symptoms of groupthink, he emphasizes illusions of invulnerability and morality, biased perceptions of the outgroup, interpersonal pressure, self-censorship, mindguards, apparent unanimity, and defective decision-making strategies. When considering the causes of groupthink, however, he focuses on cohesiveness, isolation, leadership, and decisional stress. Turning to ways to prevent poor decision making, Janis notes that groups need not sacrifice cohesiveness to avoid the pitfalls of groupthink. Rather, Janis recommends limiting premature concurrence seeking, correcting misperceptions and errors, and improving the group's decisional methods.

Leaders play a key role in determining a group's effectiveness. Although early theorists usually took either a trait or situational approach to leadership, most modern theories emphasize the interaction among the leader's characteristics, the group members' qualities, and the nature of the situation. *Leadership,* viewed from this perspective, is a reciprocal, transactional, and transformational process in which individuals are permitted to influence and motivate others to facilitate the attainment of group and individual goals. Many factors influence *leadership emergence,* but this process depends to a large extent on group members' implicit leadership theories. People who match our intuitive expectations about leaders tend to be selected to lead our groups.

In an early study, Lewin and his colleagues found that directive, autocratic leaders are less effective than participatory, democratic leaders. Recent work, however, suggests that different situations call for different amounts of control. Similarly, Fiedler's *contingency theory of leadership* predicts performance by considering the leader's style of leadership and the favorability of the leadership setting. Like many other leadership theorists, Fiedler argues that leaders perform two basic functions in groups: they help the group members successfully complete their tasks while maintaining positive interpersonal relations within the group. Fiedler believes, however, that most leaders emphasize one of these two goals and assesses this orientation with the Least Preferred Coworker (LPC) Scale. His theory predicts that task-motivated leaders (low LPCs) are most effective in situations that are either extremely unfavorable or extremely favorable, but relationship-motivated leaders are most effective in intermediate situations. Hersey and Blanchard's *situational leadership theory,* in contrast, suggests that superior leaders know how to adapt their leadership style to the maturity level of their group.

For More Information

• *Group Dynamics,* by Donelson R. Forsyth (1990), gives a general introduction to the field of groups. Chapters deal with group structure, group development, decision making, and leadership.

• *Group Process, Group Decision, Group Action,* by Robert S. Baron, Norbert L. Kerr, and Norman Miller (1992), is a concise but thorough analysis of group performance, social influence, intergroup conflict, and groups' responses to crowded environments.

• *Group Processes: Dynamics Between and Within Groups,* by Rupert Brown (1988), is a carefully crafted analysis of the structural, interpersonal, and ingroup-outgroup processes that influence group dynamics.

• *Groups that Work (and Those that Don't),* edited by J. Richard Hackman (1990), mixes theory with the specific findings gleaned from detailed case studies of dozens of different work groups functioning across a wide range of organizational settings.

• *How Groups Work,* edited by Rupert Brown (1990), is volume 15 in the *Marshall Cavendish Encyclopedia of Human Behavior.* The 13 chapters are written by experts in the field, and the information is presented in a friendly, accessible style.

• *Leadership Theory and Research: Perspectives and Directions,* edited by Martin M. Chemers and Roya Ayman (1992), offers an up-to-date analysis of the social psychology of leadership, with an emphasis on integrating classic contingency theories and current models of charismatic and transformational leadership.

• *Teamwork: What Must Go Right/What Can Go Wrong,* by Carl E. Larson and Frank M. J. Lafasto (1989), proffers eight basic suggestions for creating successful, productive teams in organizations, including clear goals, norms that encourage productivity, and principled leadership.

• *Victims of Groupthink,* by Irving Janis (1982), takes a sobering look at the pitfalls of group decision making, while recommending many ways to avoid groupthink. Excellent reading for anyone who regularly takes part in groups that make important decisions. *Crucial Decisions,* also written by Janis (1989), provides a more general analysis of decision making.

Application: The Social Psychology of Work Teams

• In the Harwood garment factory, changes in technology require frequent changes in how employees carry out their responsibilities. Employees are unhappy with the frequent changes, production is off, and turnover is high.

• The young executives in a firm that develops computer technologies decide to redesign the corporation's management structure. The team works well until disputes arise about who will occupy each of the new positions they have created.

• The crews that paint the lines on state highways for the Department of Motor Vehicles are supposed to work from 8 A.M. to 4 P.M., but any crew that puts in more than 6 hours is ridiculed by other crews.

• Workers stacking logs for transport routinely leave the log trailers only partly filled. This small but consistent error costs the Lewell Lumber Company over a million dollars each year.

• A company that manufactures sporting goods rewards its most productive workers by promoting them to supervisory positions. Many of the newly appointed supervisors experience considerable stress when they must evaluate their former co-workers' performance.

• The executives of Central Power and Light Company, ignoring warnings from outside experts, decide to build a new nuclear plant. Cost overruns during construction amount to millions of dollars, and the facility never performs up to its design specifications.

How should businesses, governments, hospitals, and military units be organized to perform efficiently? The field of **organizational behavior (OB)** is devoted to analy-

organizational behavior (OB): A subarea of industrial-organizational psychology devoted to the analysis and improvement of complex human groups and organizations.

sis and improvement of such organizations. OB experts, depending on their special interests, study a range of practical problems that organizations encounter and must solve. What motivates people? How can jobs be designed to best match the needs of the organization and the abilities of employees? How can turnover and absenteeism be minimized? What techniques do effective managers use to communicate with their subordinates and superiors? (Mowday & Sutton, 1993; O'Reilly, 1991).

In many cases, answers to these questions can be found by studying the groups within the organization. If we are to understand why some people work harder than others, we may do well to consider their work unit's norms pertaining to productivity and their relations with fellow group members (Mitchell, 1982). Before we design a particular task, we must decide how many people are needed to carry it out, and how their various contributions can best be organized (Hackman, 1987). Turnover and absenteeism both increase when individuals don't feel committed to their work group and decrease when people like their co-workers (Cotton & Tuttle, 1986). Management questions, too, tend to be questions of leadership emergence and effectiveness (Bass, 1985b). Thus, before we can understand the dynamics of an organization—a military unit, a hospital, a factory, or an educational complex—we must understand the dynamics of the groups in that organization.

Consider, as an example, the impact of the **work team** on the modern organization (Sundstrom, De Meuse, & Futrell, 1990). Years ago many experts believed that interaction among employees should be minimized. This practice was based on the notion that people don't like to work, so they must be goaded into action by the promise of financial incentives tied to productivity, close supervision, and clear goals that they can attain with little effort. Workers were viewed as mere "adjuncts to machines," and steps were taken to prevent them from wasting time talking to one another (Taylor, 1923).

This view was shaken by the classic studies of group productivity carried out in the 1920s by Elton Mayo and his associates at the Hawthorne plant of the Western Electric Company (Landsberger, 1958; Mayo, 1945; Roethlisberger & Dickson, 1939). Mayo's research team initially assumed that productivity was shaped, in large part, by the physical characteristics of the workplace. So they sequestered a small group of workers in an experimental test room before manipulating aspects of the work environment, such as the lighting and the temperature. To their surprise, virtually all the changes led to improved work output; people worked harder when researchers increased the lighting, but they also worked hard when they dimmed the lighting. The researchers were perplexed until they realized that people weren't working harder because the room was being changed, but because they were part of a small group that responded positively and productively to their special treatment (but also see Bramel & Friend, 1981; Franke, 1979).

The group-level approach to organizational productivity implied by the Hawthorne studies has been fully realized in the widespread use of work teams in business, industry, government, education, and health-care settings. Indeed, groups are at the foundation of the modern organization. *Management and advisory groups,* such as administrative units, review panels, focus groups, committees, and advisory counsels, identify and solve problems, make decisions about day-to-day operations and production, and set the goals for the organization's future. And who creates the organization's products or delivers its services? In many cases, these tasks are carried out by small, autonomous *production groups,* including assembly lines, manufacturing teams, and maintenance crews. The organization's engineers, researchers, architects, and computer programmers may also work together in *project groups* as they develop innovative products and identify new solutions to existing problems. Last, some organizations make use of *action groups.* Sports teams, surgery teams, police squads, military units, and orchestras are specialized groups that accomplish their goals through highly coordinated actions (Hackman, 1990; Sundstrom et al., 1990).

Organizational experts often draw on social-psychological analyses of small groups to design, develop, and improve these work groups. **Team building**, for example, begins with the assumption that success in work groups results from a collaborative interdependence that develops through practice (Woodman & Sherwood, 1980). The work-group-as-team analogy is fundamental to this approach, so in many ways team building in the workplace parallels team building in sports. In most team sports, players must practice continually until they function as a single unit, and their desire for personal success must be transformed into a desire for group success. The team's coaches may create situations designed to foster a sense of team spirit, and they may encourage the players to formulate group goals, identify weaknesses in the team, and strive for cooperation and integration. Similarly, during team building in the work setting, the manager or consultant acts as the coach by helping the group develop a sense of team unity. Team building usually requires the following (Dion, 1990; Sundstrom et al., 1990):

- *Interpersonal process analysis.* Team members may complete exercises or take part in discussions that help them develop insight into the nature of their group's processes and their company's organizational dynamics. Members study the group's patterns of communication and attraction, decision-making procedures, sources of power, informal social norms, and varieties of intermember conflict.

work team: A cohesive production unit.
team building: Fostering cohesion, clarifying structure, and reducing conflict through the use of role analysis, interpersonal-skills training, communication training, retreats, and workshops.

• *Cohesion building.* The concept of team work implies a unified, close-knit work group where members like one another and are committed to their group. Team building strengthens the group's morale by encouraging interpersonal trust, cooperation, and the development of a group identity.

• *Goal setting.* Just as athletes must learn how to pool their individual abilities and energies to maximize the team's performance, employees must learn to coordinate their efforts with those of the other group members. Group goals must be set, work patterns structured, and a sense of group identity developed. In general, groups function more effectively when goals are explicit, and members regularly receive feedback about their progress toward their goals (Locke & Latham, 1990).

• *Role definition.* Teams tend to work more efficiently when the members understand the requirements of their roles. During team development, members may identify sources of role stress, which can occur when members' responsibilities are ambiguous or when other people in the group misunderstand the duties associated with their roles (House, Schuler, & Levanoni, 1983).

• *Problem solving.* Team members learn to use effective decisional methods to identify problems and their solutions. Many work teams, for example, are based on the **quality circle** model (Deming, 1975). Quality circles are small, employee-centered groups that are given decision-making authority by upper management. These teams meet to discuss problems in the workplace that are undermining productivity, efficiency, quality, or job satisfaction. Once the causes of these problems are identified, the group implements corrective changes. Should these changes prove to be ineffective, then the problem-solving process begins again.

People are usually more satisfied with their work environment when they are part of a cohesive work team. Even though team building doesn't work in all cases, across many different types of organizations and job settings, absenteeism, turnover, and employee complaints decrease after a group-focused intervention (de Meuse & Liebowitz, 1981; Sundstrom et al., 1990; Woodman & Sherwood, 1980). These increases in satisfaction and stability may not, however, always translate into increased productivity. Cohesive groups, for example, tend to be more productive than groups that lack unity (Dion & Evans, 1992; Evans & Dion, 1991). Cohesive groups, however, can be strikingly unproductive if the group's norms don't always call for high productivity. One major survey of nearly 6,000 factory workers in over 200 groups found productivity levels fluctuated less in the more cohesive groups. Everyone in a cohesive group worked at about the same rate, whereas work rates varied considerably more in the less cohesive groups. However, fairly low standards of performance had developed within some of the cohesive groups, so productivity was uniformly low among these groups. In contrast, in groups with relatively high performance goals, members of cohesive groups were extremely productive (Seashore, 1954). Thus, cohesive work teams are often enjoyable, but they aren't always more productive.

Work teams are only one of the many areas in which social psychology overlaps with the field of organizational behavior. Because most work is carried out with other people, the influence of social-psychological processes is inevitable. When managers wonder how they should intervene to help their group become more productive, they are raising questions of leadership (Hollander & Offermann, 1990). Management teams that routinely make faulty decisions after spending months reviewing the issues may be suffering from groupthink. If productivity drops when members who once worked individually now pool their efforts in a communal project, the problem may be traced to social loafing and coordination problems. The study of organizations raises questions that are imminently practical. These questions can be answered by drawing on theory and research in social psychology.

quality circle: Small, self-regulated groups of employees charged with identifying ways to improve product quality.

ELEVEN

Personal Relationships

Molly Haskell first met Andrew Sarris in 1967 at a screening of the movie *Scorpio Rising*. Molly worked at the French Film Office as a publicist, and Andrew wrote a column of film criticism for the *Village Voice*. Molly had always enjoyed Andrew's reviews, and she was entranced by the way he expressed himself with such wry wit and creativity. Andrew, Molly recollected, "took one look at my legs—these were the days of the mini-skirt—and asked . . . who I was" (Haskell, 1990, p. 87). Two years and hundreds of movies later, Molly and Andrew married.

Molly and Andrew spent the next 15 years living and working in New York City. They visited art galleries, suffered through dinners with their in-laws, discussed each other's writings, and fought whenever they played tennis together. But their happiness was threatened when Andrew, in 1984, became seriously ill. The doctor's were baffled, and Andrew's condition steadily worsened. Molly was filled with fear at the thought of losing Andrew, for after all their years together, Molly no longer thought of herself as a distinct, independent person; she was now half of a whole. As she later wrote in her book, *Love and other Infectious Diseases* (1990, p. 67):

> I was falling like a meteor; my selves, generally held together by Andrew, my center of gravity, splintered in every direction. Like a reflection in a mountain lake, in which the reflected trees are clearer and more defined than the trees themselves, I needed Andrew to give me my clarity of outline, to show me who I was.

Their love braided their lives together ever so tightly, and Molly felt that if Andrew died, she would die: "Not by suicide, but just automatically, as bees die when they are detached from the hive" (p. 159).

personal relationships Enduring, often intensely emotional relationships characterized by frequent and diverse interdependence.

We all recognize the importance of **personal relationships** in our lives. When asked, "What is it that makes your life meaningful?" most people mention their relationships—their friends, lovers, children, and parents (Klinger, 1977). And when people are asked about sources of lasting happiness and satisfaction, "a happy marriage," "a good family life," and "good friends" top the list of their answers. Career accomplishments, financial security, and material possessions pale in comparison with our relationships (Campbell, Converse, & Rodgers, 1976).

Personal relationships are not static; the fabric of our social world is torn and mended and rewoven all the time (Levinger, 1980; Levinger & Snoek, 1972). Consider one strong thread—one long-term relationship—in the social fabric of your life. Whether you have chosen to consider your link to your spouse, your lover, or your best friend, search back through time, and recall your first encounter with the stranger who became your intimate friend or

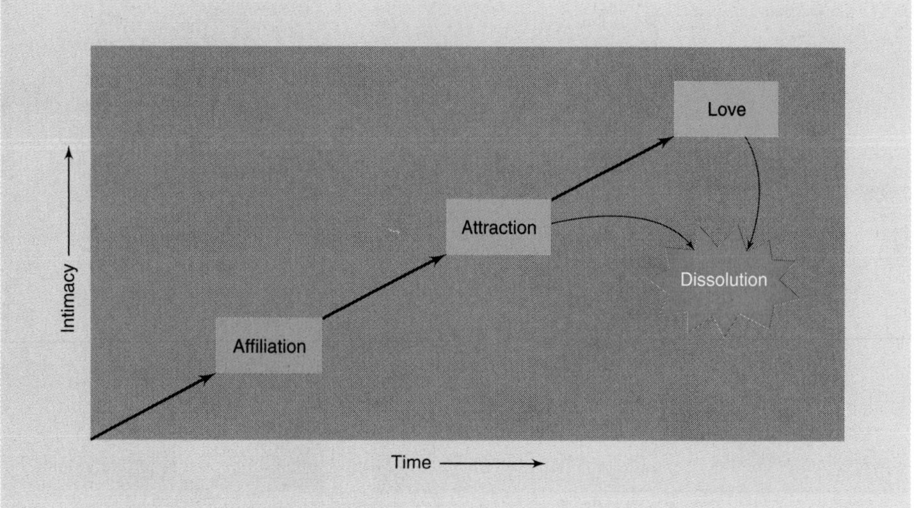

▲ **FIGURE 11-1**
How do personal relationships change over time? Many relationships follow a pattern that begins with affiliation and ends with dissolution. Affiliation sets the stage for the growth of attraction, which then ripens into a close, intimate relationship. Dissolution occurs when the relationship ends.

lover. This first encounter may have seemed uneventful at the time, but it set the stage for subsequent developments. *Affiliation* is our first topic, for if human beings didn't affiliate with other human beings, intimate relationships might never have the opportunity to form.

The second phase of personal relationships, *attraction,* begins when a feeling of liking for the other person takes root. Like Molly and Andrew, you may have met your friend or lover at a party, where many of the other people left no lasting impression. Yet something drew the two of you together, and the seeds of a longer, more intimate relationship were sown.

As feelings of attraction deepen, the bond between you becomes a close relationship, including friendship and *love.* You become more committed to each other, and you feel you can trust and rely on each other. With trust comes more intimate interaction, the sharing of personal feelings, and a desire to care for the other person. Yet close relationships also bring conflict, strain, and doubt. If these problems can't be managed, then your relationship may enter a final stage, *dissolution.* Your friend becomes a stranger, or your lover becomes an enemy. In this chapter, we chart the journey of our personal relationships from affiliation to attraction to closeness to dissolution (see Figure 11-1).

Affiliation

Aristotle, who was as much a social psychologist as a philosopher, proclaimed that humans are social animals by nature. All of us seek solitude from time to time, but we spend much of our lives in the company of other people (Latané & Bidwell, 1977; Wheeler & Nezlek, 1977).

affiliation
The act of joining together with members of one's own species.

What causes **affiliation**? What prompts us to join together with other members of our species? In part, the motivation comes from without—the situations we face may be so novel, ambiguous, or frightening that we seek company. However, the need to join with others may also come from within—our personal needs and biological instincts may push us to join together with other people (Hill, 1987). Both types of factors are examined next.

Social Comparison and Affiliation

What if you lived a life of total isolation? How would you know whether you were a success or a failure? How would you learn to appreciate art and

▲ Personal relationships follow a pattern of growth and change. A relationship begins with affiliation and attraction but may eventually ripen into a close relationship involving deep friendship or love. The relationship may last until the couple is parted by death, but it may also end in conflict. If the emotional climate becomes too negative, the relationship will not survive.

music? How would you determine the validity of your political and moral values? How would you assign meaning to everyday events and personal experiences? If you couldn't compare your own opinions, beliefs, and values with those of other people, you could never develop a conception of social reality.

Leon Festinger (1950, 1954) described the way we rely on other people for information about ourselves and the world around us. As we learned in Chapter 5, this process is known as *social comparison*. By comparing ourselves to others, we can test and validate our beliefs. Do you think New York City is a wonderful place to live? Is *The Searchers* John Wayne's best movie? Does a correlation tell you anything about causality? Through social comparison, you can answer these kinds of questions. When we lack sufficient information to form our own judgments, comparison also allows us to construct entirely new opinions, attitudes, and beliefs (Fazio, 1979; Gerard & Orive, 1987). These two goals—validation and construction—become more important when we face confusing and frightening situations.

Uncertainty and affiliation. Only when she tried to write a review of a film without Andrew did Molly realize how much she depended on him for information. She called him her "walking reference book" (p. 158). Whenever she felt uncertain about a passage she would read it to him and watch his eyes for signs of pleasure or disagreement.

Stanley Schachter studied this kind of symbiotic sharing of information in his classic studies of affiliation. The women college students he recruited for his experiment thought they would be participating in a routine psychology study. However, when they arrived at the lab, they were greeted by a serious-looking young man named Dr. Gregor Zilstein. Zilstein, who claimed to hail from the medical school's departments of neurology and psychiatry, told each subject that he was researching the question "What are the physiological effects of electric shocks?" How did he study this question? By connecting volunteers to equipment that monitored their physiological responses and then giving them electric shocks, of course. Zilstein told some women that the shocks would be painless; they would "resemble more a tickle or a tingle than anything unpleasant." But he told other women that the shocks would be very painful:

> These shocks will hurt, they will be painful. As you can guess, if, in research of this sort, we're to learn anything at all that will really help humanity, it is necessary that our shocks be intense. These shocks will be quite painful but, of course, they will do no permanent damage. (Schachter, 1959, p. 13)

Zilstein needed some time to set up his equipment, so he told each woman she would have to wait briefly. He then offered her a choice: Would she like to wait in a private room or in a room with several other people?

Schachter conducted this experiment to see whether people affiliate to reduce their uncertainty about their social environment. He surmised that, finding themselves in an ambiguous situation, his subjects would want to compare their reactions with those of the others (see Figure 11-2). Sure enough, 63% of the women who expected to receive painful shocks wanted to wait with others. Only 33% chose affiliation when Zilstein used less provocative procedures.

Schachter summed up his findings with the adage "Misery loves company." He added, however, that if other people know nothing about the situation you face, then there is no reason to affiliate with them. He tested this inference in a second study. Dr. Zilstein once again told subjects he was planning to give them painful shocks, and he gave them the chance to wait alone or with other people. Some women, however, were told that the other people they could join were also waiting to receive shocks, whereas others believed they might join people who "were waiting to talk to their professors and advisors." Schachter thought that if the subjects believed the others could provide them with no useful information about the situation they faced, then they would have no reason to affiliate with them. As predicted, 60% of the subjects wanted to wait with other subjects, but not a single subject wanted to wait with the nonsubjects. Thus we tend to compare ourselves with people who are similar to us in some way. Or, as Schachter (1959) puts it, "misery doesn't love just any kind of company; it loves only miserable company" (p. 24).

Fear and affiliation. Schachter didn't leave his subjects feeling just a bit uncertain; he also frightened them. The participants wanted to understand the situation clearly, but they also wanted to reduce their fear. Researchers examined this aspect of social comparison by interviewing people two days before their scheduled coronary bypass operations. During the interviews, researchers asked the people to choose between two kinds of roommates: one who was also waiting to have a bypass operation or one who was recovering from a bypass operation. Some preferred a roommate who was about to have the operation (17%), some had no preference (23%), but 60% wanted a roommate who was recovering from a bypass operation (Kulik & Mahler, 1989). Similarly, when

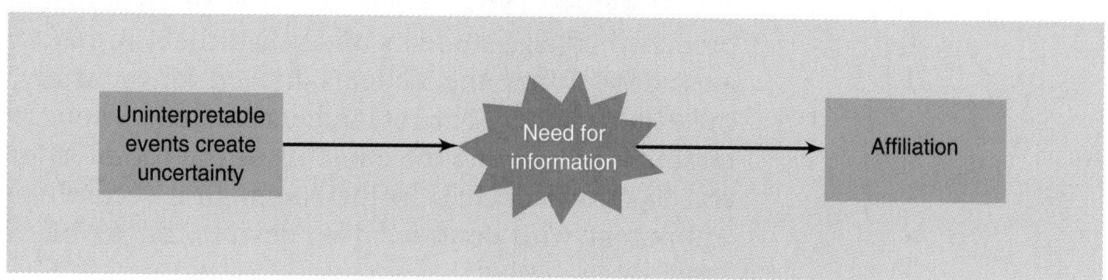

▲ **FIGURE 11-2**
Why do we affiliate with other people? Schachter believed that uninterpretable events create a need for information, which we can satisfy through affiliation. (Adapted from Schachter, 1959)

subjects who were waiting for electric shocks were asked if they wanted to wait with someone who seemed to be very fearful, moderately fearful, or calm, most chose to wait with less fearful people (Rabbie, 1963). It seems that misery sometimes loves reassuring company rather than miserable company (Affleck & Tennen, 1991; Gibbons & Gerrard, 1991).

Researchers now believe that social comparison serves two sets of goals (Suls & Wills, 1991). As Festinger (1954) and Schachter (1959) both argued, we affiliate with others because they are a rich source of information. As Chapter 3 notes, we are information seekers and processors who try to understand our social world (Miller, Gross, & Holtz, 1991). But we also strive to confirm our current ideas, reaffirm our sense of self-worth, and reduce our anxieties and fears. If we think we will have to defend our ideas, we seek out people who agree with us (Fazio, 1979; Kruglanski & Mayseless, 1990). We seek out people who are performing less well than we are—an example of *downward* social comparison—if our self-esteem is on the line (Wills, 1991; Wood & Taylor, 1991; see Chapter 5). When situations arouse our fears and anxieties, we seek out people who will assuage our fears (Kulik & Mahler, 1989; Rofé, Lewin, & Hoffman, 1987). We seek both information and reassurance from others.

Ralph L. Rosnow's (1991) studies of rumors illustrate the dual purposes of social comparison. Rumors are often viewed as idle gossip or as the distorted ramblings of the uninformed. Rosnow, however, believes that some rumors are "a reasonable and nonpainful way to obtain needed social comparison information" (Rosnow, 1980, p. 587). The accident at the Three Mile Island nuclear power plant, for example, threatened the nearby residents, but it was shrouded in ambiguity. As a result, within days, rumors that both exaggerated and minimized the danger began to circulate. Eventually authorities opened a rumor-control center to supply more accurate information to people who had heard that cows were dying, that the reactor had melted down, or that a radioactive cloud had been released. Rosnow points out that these rumors may have been factually incorrect, but they gave people a sense of being informed at a time of great anxiety (Rosnow & Kimmel, 1979). The rumors also provide reassurance by reinterpreting events in a more positive light. Even bleak, pessimistic rumors may, in the long run, reduce our anxiety by preparing us for bad news (Allport & Postman, 1947; Prasad, 1950).

Embarrassment and affiliation. If you have ever committed a social blunder in front of strangers, you have probably felt like crawling under a rock—affiliation was the last thing on your mind. Although we may want information, when other people are watching and evaluating us, we may be too embarrassed to seek it out. We sometimes choose to be confused and fearful rather than appear foolish (Rofé, 1984).

Researchers examined the muting impact of embarrassment on affiliation by telling people that they would have to perform childish acts—such as sucking on large nipples and pacifiers—either alone or in front of other people. As expected, the subjects expressed a strong desire to remain alone (Sarnoff & Zimbardo, 1961; Teichman, 1973). Experimenters in another study approached college students and asked them to participate in a study of "sexual attitudes." When the students arrived for the study, they were told to wait for the experimenter. The researchers created various levels of anxiety and embarrassment by varying the contents of the room. In one condition, they left several electrical devices in the room. In a second condition, they replaced the equipment with contraceptive devices, books on venereal disease, and color

▲ We all differ somewhat in the strength of our need to be with other people. Some prefer to stay far from the madding crowd, content in their isolation. Others, in contrast, are happiest when they are surrounded by other people.

pictures of nudes. Subjects affiliated with one another, by talking about the situation and looking at each other, when the room contained fear-provoking equipment. When the room was filled with embarrassing sexual materials, however, subjects fled. Thus misery may love company, but embarrassed misery loves privacy (Morris et al., 1976).

Joiners: The Affiliating Personality

When U.S. President John F. Kennedy was assassinated, Americans grieved in two distinct ways. When researchers asked Americans to describe their reactions to the tragedy, they found that the majority sought solace by talking to others, but about 40% wanted to be left alone (Sheatsley & Feldman, 1964).

To predict affiliation, we must go beyond the situational factors identified by social comparison theorists and consider the personality characteristics of individuals in their social settings. Even when they face the same situations, different people react in different ways. Joiners seem to seek out social stimulation, whereas loners prefer privacy to sociability (see Gangestad & Snyder, 1985).

What distinguishes the person who prefers to affiliate from the person who is more solitary? Schachter (1959) was intrigued by *birth order.* He thought that children who are born first and only children probably received greater stimulation and protective guidance from their parents, so these first-borns would be more affiliative than later-borns (Zajonc, Markus, & Markus, 1979). Sure enough, when Schachter threatened first- and later-born subjects with painful or mild electric shocks, he found that birth order made a difference. When they expected severe shocks, the first-borns were more likely than later-borns to affiliate. (Cottrell & Epley, 1977, and Warren, 1966, present divergent views on the strength of the relationship between birth order and affiliation.)

nAffiliation
The need for affiliation; the dispositional tendency to seek out others.

Other researchers have focused on the strength of various needs that make up our personalities. According to this approach, human behavior is guided by a limited number of social drives, or motives, such as the need for achievement (or *n*Achievement), the need for power (or *n*Power), and the need for affiliation (***n*****Affiliation**). When these needs are strong, they exert a pervasive influence on

▲ **FIGURE 11-3**
What is happening to the two people in this picture? Researchers often use the Thematic Apperception Test (TAT) to measure social needs. Subjects are shown a series of pictures like this one, and then asked to make up a story about each picture that describes what is happening, the relationship between the people in the picture, and the characters' thoughts and interests. Researchers who use the TAT assume that respondents will project their inner motives and needs in the stories they write about the pictures. (From Murray, 1938)

behavior across situations. When they are weak, their influence on actions is minimal (Murray, 1938).

How can we gauge the strength of these motives? In some cases, the motives can be tapped by traditional self-report methods, such as interviews or questionnaires. Many motivation researchers, however, prefer to use such projective techniques as the Thematic Apperception Test, or TAT (Atkinson, 1958). Respondents write imaginative stories about several ambiguous pictures (see Figure 11-3). The researcher then analyzes the imagery, themes, needs, actions, goals, and other key symbols in subjects' stories for evidence of each social motive. Some investigators question the validity of the TAT, but proponents of this method argue that people aren't sufficiently aware of their motivations to describe them accurately through traditional self-report methods (McClelland, 1980, 1985; McClelland, Koestner, & Weinberger, 1989).

People who are high in *n*Affiliation tend to be joiners, although they worry about their relationships more than other people do (McAdams, 1988). In general, people high in *n*Affiliation share the following:

- They are more concerned with "establishing, maintaining, and restoring a positive affective relationship" (Atkinson, Heyns, & Veroff, 1954).
- They would rather be with their friends than be alone (Wong & Csikszentmihalyi, 1991).
- They perceive themselves as compatible with other people (Mehrabian, 1976).
- They join social groups, such as clubs (Smart, 1965).
- They communicate with others in a friendly manner (Exline, 1962; Fishman, 1966).
- They are well liked by others (Mehrabian & Ksionsky, 1974).
- They display more anxiety in social settings (Byrne, 1961).
- They fear rejection by others (McAdams, 1982).
- They write more letters to friends (McAdams & Constantian, 1983).
- They willingly enter into interaction with warm, empathetic people, but they avoid interacting with people who seem unfriendly (Hill, 1991).

Overall, people who are high in *n*Affiliation depend more on other people (Bornstein, 1992).

Loners: Social Anxiety and Shyness

Henry David Thoreau spent two years secluded at Walden Pond. He would have scored very low in *n*Affiliation, for he observed:

> Society is commonly too cheap. We meet at very short intervals, not having had time to acquire any new value for each other. We meet at three meals a day and give each other a taste of that old musty cheese that we are. Certainly less frequency would suffice for all important and hearty communication. (Thoreau, 1962, p. 206)

Thoreau was a loner simply because he valued his privacy more than contact with other people (Leary, 1983).

social anxiety
A feeling of apprehension and embarrassment experienced when anticipating or actually interacting with other people.

In contrast to Thoreau, some people avoid others because they suffer from **social anxiety**. Social anxiety sets in when people want to make a good impression, but they don't think that their attempts at impression management will succeed (Leary, 1982b, 1983; Leary & Atherton, 1986; Maddux, Norton, & Leary, 1988; Schlenker & Leary, 1982b). Because of these pessimistic expectations, they experience a number of emotional, physiological, and behavioral symptoms when they encounter other people. They report feelings of tension, awkwardness, and discomfort, as well as evaluation apprehension. They may experience physiological arousal, including increases in pulse rate, blushing, perspiration, and "butterflies." This anxiety can cause them to *disaffiliate*—to "reduce the amount of social contact one individual has with another" (Leary, 1982b, p. 111). Socially anxious people can be identified by their *lack* of social behaviors; their silence in groups, downcast eyes, and low speaking voices.

Some people are more prone to social anxiety than others. As early as age 2, some children begin to display fear or timidity when they encounter a person they don't recognize (Kagan, Snidman, & Arcus, 1992). Some grade-school children consistently seek out other people, whereas others show signs of nervousness and tension when they are in groups (Asendorpf & Meier, 1993). This dispositional tendency to respond negatively in interpersonal encounters is often called **shyness** (Zimbardo, 1977). Shy people tend to agree with such statements as (Cheek & Buss, 1981):

shyness
The tendency to experience social anxiety across situations.

- I am socially somewhat awkward.
- I find it hard to talk to strangers.
- I feel tense when I'm with people I don't know well.
- When conversing I worry about saying something dumb.
- I feel inhibited in social situations.
- I have trouble looking someone right in the eye.

Most people manage to cope with their shyness (Leary, 1988; Leary & Miller, 1986). In some cases, however, this anxiety escalates into *social phobia*: "a persistent, irrational fear of, and compelling desire to avoid, situations in which the individual may be exposed to the scrutiny of others. There is also fear that the individual will behave in a manner that will be humiliating or embarrassing" (DSM-III, 1980, p. 227).

Why So Social an Animal?

Across most situations and societies, humans tend to be social rather than solitary, for affiliation offers many advantages over isolation (Mann, 1980). When we face situations that are ambiguous or frightening, by comparing ourselves to other people, we can gather information that is both informative and supportive. Affiliation also allows us to satisfy some of our most basic needs, including our craving for social contact. Indeed, when we are cut off from other

▲ **TABLE 11-1**
Summing up: Factors that affect affiliative tendencies

Factor	*Description*
Social comparison	Individuals sometimes construct and validate their beliefs (perceptions, opinions, reactions, and the like) by comparing them to beliefs expressed by the people around them. Schachter (1959) found that people seek out other people for social comparison when they are uncertain, but other studies indicate that people also seek out others to reduce their fear and sustain their self-esteem. Embarrassment limits social comparison.
Birth order	People who were born first in their families and people who are only children affiliate more than other people.
Needs	*n*Affiliation is the general need to seek out other people. People who are high in this need are more likely to affiliate, although they also tend to experience anxiety in social settings.
Social anxiety	People sometimes experience social anxiety when they are motivated to make a good impression, but their expectations for success are pessimistic. Socially anxious people reduce their social contact with other people and are inhibited in social settings. Shy people are particularly prone to social anxiety.
Instincts	Evolutionary theory argues that affiliation was necessary for survival in prehistoric times. Therefore, individuals who were genetically predisposed to affiliate were more likely to survive and pass their genes on to future generations. This natural selection process resulted in instinctive affiliation in humans.

people, we often experience disorientation, sadness, and loneliness. As the section "Application: Love, Loneliness, and Health" reveals, it is affiliation—not the proverbial "apple a day"—that keeps the doctor away.

Affiliation is also a biological necessity. Indeed, all people living today are the offspring of individuals who chose affiliation over isolation. Our ancestors were joiners, not loners, for the human reproduction cycle usually requires affiliation. If the situational and personality factors summarized in Table 11-1 did not bring two people together, then how would more intimate relationships develop?

Attraction

Molly's mother never quite understood why Molly thought Andrew was attractive. He was an urbanite who wrote a column for a small paper, and his breadwinning potential wasn't particularly great. He was tall but somewhat gangly. He was virtually unable to make small talk, and he would often raise subjects that prudent people avoided. Molly found him charming.

Affiliative forces brought Molly and Andrew together, but why was Molly attracted to Andrew? Did she like his looks? the way he dressed? the way he listened to her? his views on French films? his build? Although poets and romance novelists would have us believe that liking occurs spontaneously and capriciously, attraction is a predictable process. Initially, surface-level factors such as looks pull us toward some people and push us away from others. But just as we find another layer beneath the first when we peel an onion, when we look beneath surface factors, we find that personal qualities such as attitudes and values also influence attraction. And when we peel away this layer, we find still other layers. Indeed, at the core of the question we find that attraction is a matter of exchange—we like people who provide us with many rewards and few costs (Berscheid, 1985; Brehm, 1985; Hendrick & Hendrick, 1992).

The Power of Propinquity

When I was in the seventh grade, I hung out with Stanley Fogel; was it because he was a funny guy or because he sat next to me in homeroom? In college my girlfriend happened to live in the same apartment complex that I did. And why do I like Dr. Stasson? Is it because his office is located next to mine?

propinquity Nearness in place or in time.

The impact of **propinquity**, or close proximity, on attraction is remarkable. We may want to think that we screen our friends and lovers using such criteria as intelligence, good looks, or zest for living, but in many cases we like people who just happen to be close by. When teachers assign students to their seats alphabetically, friendships usually develop alphabetically. Forsyth likes Fogel rather than Zimmer (Segal, 1974). People assigned to rooms in dorms or apartments at random are more likely to form friendships with people who occupy nearby rooms or apartments (Nahemow & Lawton, 1975; Newcomb, 1960). Couples who live in more centrally located apartments have more friends than those who live in secluded apartments, even when the assignments are random (Festinger, Schachter, & Back, 1950). One observer writes "the chances are about 50-50 that the 'one and only' lives within walking distance" (Eckland, 1968, p. 16).

Why does physical closeness sometimes lead to emotional closeness? First, proximity removes some of the obstacles that can block the development of interpersonal attraction. We can spend time interacting with people we see frequently without expending much time or energy. Provided these interactions are enjoyable, our feelings of attraction should grow (Ebbesen, Kjos, & Konečni, 1976; Kenrick & Johnson, 1979; Riordan & Tedeschi, 1983).

Second, as Chapter 6 notes, the more frequently we are exposed to social objects, the more we tend to like them. This *mere exposure* process also works for people. When exposure to a stranger is varied from high to low, people like the stranger they have seen frequently more than the one they've seldom seen (Bornstein, Leone, & Galley, 1987; Brockner & Swap, 1976; Insko & Wilson, 1977; Saegert, Swap, & Zajonc, 1973).

Third, the proximity-attraction effect may be due to our need to maintain consistency among our various cognitions (see Chapter 6). Initially, I may not like someone whose office is located next to mine. However, admitting to myself, "I dislike Mark" and "I interact with Mark every day," would lead to dissonance. Hence I change my liking for Mark to reduce this tension (Arkin & Burger, 1980; Newcomb, 1981).

Physical Attractiveness

Folk wisdom may tell us that familiarity breeds contempt, but evidence indicates that propinquity encourages liking. Similarly, even though we may know that "beauty is only skin deep," our liking for others can be influenced by their physical appearance. We are often drawn to people whose physical attributes we admire or value.

Elaine Hatfield and her colleagues studied the impact of physical appearance on liking by setting up a computer dance open to all incoming students at the college where she taught (Walster et al., 1966). To be assigned a date, students paid a fee of $1 and completed a series of questionnaires. Hatfield convinced the young men and women that the questionnaires would be used to match them with a compatible opposite-sex date, but she actually paired them at random, with only one stipulation—the man had to be taller than the woman. Four judges rated the students' physical attractiveness on a scale from 1 (extremely unattractive) to 8 (extremely attractive) while they were standing in line to buy tickets.

On the evening of the dance, most subjects met their partners at about 8 P.M. and then talked or danced until a 10:30 P.M. intermission. The men and women then went to different locations where they rated their dates. Hatfield and her colleagues initially assumed that people would be discriminating judges—that they would like people with admirable personal characteristics such as high intellect or self-confidence—but these factors mattered very little. The only significant predictor of subjects' reactions was the date's physical attractiveness: the more beautiful or handsome the date, the higher the rating. The correlation between rating and physical attractiveness, as estimated by the objective judges, was .44 for women and .36 for men. And when subjects' own estimates of their dates' looks were used as the index of physical attractiveness, these correlations were even stronger: .78 and .69.

Other researchers have also found that, at least during initial encounters, we tend to like physically attractive people more than unattractive people (Dion, 1986; Hatfield & Sprecher, 1986b). In one study of heterosexual couples meeting for the first time, women who were talking to a handsome man not only responded more positively to him nonverbally, but they also limited their references to *other people*. They may have been trying to forge a stronger bond by implying that the "relationship was an exclusive one." When talking to a pretty woman, men were more conversational and more inquisitive. When they described their thoughts later, men also reported that they were trying harder to empathize with their partners, to see the situation from their perspective (Garcia et al., 1991, p. 43).

Our preference for good-looking people does not necessarily mean we are so shallow and insensitive that we base our judgments of others on looks alone. We may seek the company of attractive people because we have learned to associate physical attractiveness with other positive personal traits. As noted in Chapter 2, our judgments of other people are often based on a *"what is beautiful is good" stereotype* (Dion et al., 1972). We just assume that physically attractive people possess qualities that make them socially attractive as well. Good-looking people are thought to be sociable, dominant, sexual, and more interpersonally skilled than less attractive people (Feingold, 1992). To a lesser degree, our stereotypes about attractive people also suggest that they are better adjusted and more intelligent (Eagly et al., 1991).

The "what is beautiful is good" stereotype may unduly influence our perceptions of good-looking people. We may overlook qualities displayed by attractive people that don't match our expectations but remember vividly each attractive person who seems warm, well-adjusted, and sexy (Feingold, 1992). The stereotype may also function as a self-fulfilling prophecy. In a study described in Chapter 5, when a man talking to a woman on a telephone thought his partner was physically beautiful: (a) he evaluated her more positively, and (b) she *sounded* more pleasant and attractive (Snyder, Tanke, & Berscheid, 1977). This preferential treatment may explain why attractive people enjoy a more active and satisfying interpersonal life before marriage and tend to be more skillful in their dealings with other people (Sussman, Gavriel, & Romer, 1983). Attractive people—handsome men in particular—are more assertive than less attractive men and fear rejection by others less (Garcia et al., 1991; Reis et al., 1982).

Our favorable response to attractive people may also be rooted in our genetic heritage. Standards of beauty vary from culture to culture and from era to era, but people of many different races and cultures agree when identifying beautiful women and handsome men. Both men and women are attracted to people with babyfaces, particularly in nonsexual situations (Cunningham, 1986; Keating, 1985; Zebrowitz, Olson, & Hoffman, 1993; see Chapter 2). We are also attracted to people whose physical features proclaim their health, fitness, and breeding potential. Men, in particular, consider women who possess qualities that signal fertility—mature facial features, healthy skin, youth, and a slim figure—to be beautiful (Alley & Cunningham, 1991; Buss & Schmitt, 1993; Kenrick & Keefe, 1992). Women place less value on physical attractiveness and instead more highly value qualities that signal a man's maturity and status in the group (Riggio & Friedman, 1986; Sadalla, Kenrick, & Vershure, 1987). They also prefer men who seem to need nurturing. A man who is well respected by others is attractive, but the man who is well respected *and* seems approachable and vulnerable is particularly attractive (Cunningham, Barbee, & Pike, 1990).

Similarity and Attraction

Andrew was a second-generation Greek; Molly's people had lived in the South for generations. Andrew was short-tempered and always spoiling for a good argument—Molly thought of him as a "sort of reverse Will Rogers" (Haskell, 1990, p. 11). Molly did all she could to be liked and accepted by other people. Andrew and Molly's similarities, however, were more profound than these superficial dissimilarities. They endorsed virtually identical outlooks on politics, sports, art, theater, and even life. They adored films and movies, they were both writers and critics, and they were both successful. Neither wanted to pursue the dream of a family, a house in the country, and vacations at the beach with the kids. "We lived in a harmony of mutual interests and tastes, with surprisingly little friction considering our differences in background and temperament" (Haskell, 1990, p. 13).

similarity-attraction effect The tendency to like people with characteristics that are similar to our own.

We like people who endorse values and attitudes that are similar to our own. Theodore Newcomb investigated this **similarity-attraction effect** in a study of friendships. He recruited 17 male students who were transferring to the University of Michigan from other colleges. He offered them free rent if they answered his questions each week. All of the men were total strangers to one another when the study began, but four months later an assortment of friendships and rivalries had developed (Newcomb, 1960, 1961, 1979, 1981).

Newcomb found that many roommates ended up liking each other—strong evidence of the impact of propinquity on attraction. He also found, however, that cliques formed within the dormitory and that these cliques weren't based on proximity alone. The 17-man group split into two subgroups containing 9 and 7 members (one person was an outcast from both subgroups). It was as though some invisible magnet were drawing certain people together and pulling others apart.

The magnet was similarity in values, beliefs, and interests. All of the men in one of the subgroups were enrolled in the liberal arts college. They all came from cities or suburbs and they had similar aesthetic, social, theoretical, economic, political, and religious values. Most of the men in the second subgroup were engineering majors who came from small towns in the Midwest, and they, too, shared certain religious and economic values. The outcast had idiosyncratic values and interests.

The similarity-attraction effect has been confirmed in both laboratory and field situations (Brent & Granberg, 1982; Davison & Jones, 1976; Kandel, 1978). Many of the lab studies have used a paradigm developed by Donn

Byrne and his colleagues. Byrne first asks subjects to complete a questionnaire that measures their personal characteristics—attitudes, values, background, personality, and so on. Then he shows them a copy of a stranger's responses to the questionnaire. He tells the subjects that the questionnaire was completed by another subject, but the responses on the questionnaire are actually tailored to each participant. Some people encounter a stranger with very similar characteristics; others are shown a questionnaire containing very dissimilar responses. Subjects then indicate their personal feelings about the stranger and their willingness to work with him or her in an experiment. Byrne and other researchers find that attraction increases in a straight line as similarity increases (Byrne, 1971; Byrne & Nelson, 1965; Palmer & Kalin, 1985, 1991).

Similarity even promotes romantic attraction. When Byrne and his colleagues arranged blind dates between men and women who shared either 33% or 67% of their attitudes, attraction was greater among the high-agreement couples (Byrne, Ervin, & Lamberth, 1970). Married couples also tend to share a variety of personality and attitudinal characteristics (Buss, 1984). Also, despite our bias toward beautiful people, our friends and lovers usually match our own level of physical attractiveness. People with average looks may dream of capturing the heart of an extremely attractive person, but they seek out others who are also average in attractiveness (Cappella & Palmer, 1990; Feingold, 1988; Hatfield & Sprecher, 1986b; Shanteau & Nagy, 1979).

The impact of similarity on attraction is subtle but powerful. From the very outset, similarity colors our perceptions of others. As soon as we realize we have something in common with someone else, we begin to feel a sense of unity and belonging (Arkin & Burger, 1980). Our assumptions about relationships lead us to assume that our friends and loved ones will be similar to us rather than different from us (Forgas, 1993). We also tend to take similarity to be a sign that future interactions will be rewarding and free of conflict, and we usually assume that people who are similar to us will also like us (Gonzales et al., 1983). Byrne also notes that when other people agree with us, they confirm the accuracy of our beliefs. Hence the discovery of similarity in attitudes, beliefs, and values is a very rewarding experience (Byrne, 1971).

balance theory
A theoretical framework advanced by Heider (1958) that assumes interpersonal relationships can be either balanced (integrated units with elements that fit together without stress) or unbalanced (inconsistent units with elements that conflict with one another). Heider believed that unbalanced relationships create an unpleasant tension that must be relieved by changing some element of the system.

Fritz Heider's **balance theory** argues that liking similar people makes more sense to us, psychologically, than liking dissimilar people. Such relationships are "harmonious"; the elements of the situation all "fit together without stress" (1958, p. 180). Intuitively, we can recognize that the statements, "John and his best friend, Dennis, both like to fish" and "Mary avoids dressing like Ruby, whom she hates," describe balanced relationships. Unbalanced relationships, in contrast, "do not 'add up'; they seem to pull in different directions" (p. 180). For example:

> Bob thinks Jim very stupid and a first class bore. One day Bob reads some poetry he likes so well that he takes the trouble to track down the author in order to shake his hand. He finds that Jim wrote the poems. (p. 176)

This situation is unbalanced because its components are inconsistent. As the triangle at the far left in Figure 11-4 indicates, Bob (identified as *P*) dislikes Jim (*O*). However, *P* and *O* are similar in that they both like the poetry (*X*). This situation is unbalanced because the number of negative relationships is uneven. If balance is to be regained, the negative relationship must become positive (Bob must decide he likes Jim, as in the center triangle), or one of the positive relationships must become negative (Bob can decide he was wrong about the poetry or Jim can admit he didn't write it). Thus a situation is

▲ **FIGURE 11-4**
When is a relationship balanced? *P* (the perceiver), *O* (another person), and *X* (a social object) can be linked by positive (liking) or negative (disliking) relationships. Triads are unbalanced if the product of their relationships is negative. The relationship on the left is unbalanced; the others are balanced.

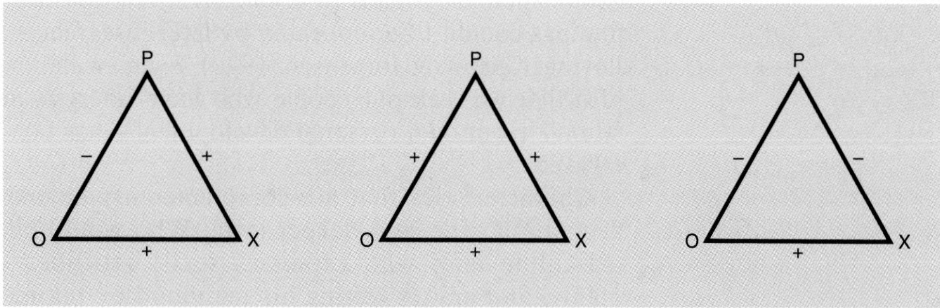

balanced only when all of the relationships among the three components of the triad are positive, or when two of the three relationships are negative, and one is positive. In all other cases, the relationship is unbalanced.

Balance theory, like cognitive dissonance theory, predicts that unbalanced relationships create an unpleasant tension that must be relieved by a change in some element of the system. Because disliking people who are similar to us and liking people who are dissimilar are both unbalanced situations, we avoid them.

Complementarity

Newcomb's finding that friendships formed between men who were similar to one another in some way lent support to the old adage "Birds of a feather flock together." But isn't it also true that opposites attract? Will a person who is intelligent be attracted to someone who is unintelligent? Will a physically attractive person seek out someone who is ugly? In most cases, no. Attraction is based on similarity, not dissimilarity.

complementarity
The hypothesis that individuals are attracted to people who are dissimilar to them provided these dissimilarities complement their own personal qualities.

But don't we like people with dissimilar characteristics that *complement* our own? Wouldn't a highly masculine person want to settle down with a highly feminine person? Wouldn't a dependent, insecure person feel happiest under the protection of a nurturing person? And isn't a masochist the perfect complement to a sadist? According to the concept of **complementarity**, we like people who possess characteristics that fulfill, or gratify, our own personal needs.

Researchers have searched diligently for evidence that supports the complementarity hypothesis. When they first found that complementarity of personality traits failed to promote attraction, some argued that people who have complementary needs should become fast friends. Yet the findings concerning needs are mixed at best; people with mutually satisfying needs aren't necessarily attracted to one another (Meyer & Pepper, 1977). Taking another path, others suggested that complementarity may become more important later in the life cycle of the relationship; similarity may bring people together, but

© 1991 by King Features Syndicate, Inc. World rights reserved.

Reprinted with special permission of King Features Syndicate.

▲ Although folklore argues that opposites attract, in most cases the similarity-attraction effect holds: an attractive woman with a great personality would probably marry an attractive man with an equally interesting personality (does that describe Lucky Eddie?).

complementarity leads to a long-term relationship. Again, initially promising findings couldn't be replicated by later researchers (Kerckhoff & Davis, 1962; Levinger, Senn, & Jorgensen, 1970). Even an elaborate pacing hypothesis—the idea that we seek out people who have interests and characteristics that will stimulate our own personal development—has fared poorly empirically (Buss, 1984).

Characteristics that are complementary at one level also turn out to reflect similarities at a deeper level. Who would be attracted to an extremely masculine man who expresses sexist attitudes, considers violence to be manly, and enjoys testing his manhood by taking risks? Why, an extremely feminine woman who believes that women should act in submissive ways, who condones violence, and who is willing to use her sexuality to influence men. Although their qualities complement one another, they are similar in that they both adopt hypertraditional sex roles (Mosher & Sirkin, 1984; Murnen & Byrne, 1991). About the only form of complementarity that consistently influences our relationships is sexual complementarity: Men tend to fall in love with women and women tend to fall in love with men (Buss, 1985).

Reciprocity of Attraction

Molly had planned to spend her energies on her career rather than on a marriage. But she hadn't figured on the power of reciprocity. Although Andrew had many annoying characteristics, he loved her. And Molly, in time, came to love him in return.

reciprocity principle
The view that attraction tends to be mutual; if A likes B, then B will tend to like A.

Attraction obeys the **reciprocity principle**: We like people who like us. If Molly discovers that Andrew likes her, she will tend to feel positive toward him (Newcomb, 1960). We are attracted to people who display nonverbal cues that signal "I like you"—high eye contact, smiling, leaning forward—and we are repelled by people whose nonverbal cues communicate their lack of interest in us (Burgoon et al., 1984). Lovers are happier in their relationships when their partners express their love openly and frequently (Byrne & Murnen, 1988). We like a person who plays hard to get by remaining aloof and uninterested provided he or she expresses positive opinions about us (Walster et al., 1973). Friendships, too, tend to be mutual. Football players, police officers, students, and dormitory residents, when asked to identify who they like, choose people who like them in return 32% to 40% of the time (Newcomb, 1960; Segal, 1979). Some people tend to like lots of people, and others dole out their affections in a more reserved fashion. Some people are liked by many; others, by only a few. When these individual differences in liking and being liked are taken into account statistically, reciprocity is even stronger (Kenny & Nasby, 1980).

Why is liking so frequently reciprocated? Balance theory suggests that disliking a positive evaluator will create an unbalanced state for most people: If Molly likes herself, and Andrew likes Molly, then Molly should like Andrew in order to achieve balance (Deutsch & Solomon, 1959; Hummert, Crockett, & Kemper, 1990; Regan, 1976). Interpersonal processes, too, may promote reciprocity. Once Molly finds out that Andrew likes her, she might be nicer to him the next time she sees him. By treating him positively, she will only make her own attraction to him more apparent, and Andrew is likely to respond more positively as well. The initial expression of approval, then, may trigger a cycle of positive reciprocal responses that gradually intensify (Curtis & Miller,

1986). Just telling people that they like one another may be sufficient to trigger this cycle.

The reciprocity principle is not inviolate, however (Mettee & Aronson, 1974). Some people who express liking for us aren't attractive to us at all—because we recognize that they are ingratiators. Sometimes, too, we are drawn to people who dislike us—perhaps because we dislike ourselves or we hope to win their affection in time. These exceptions to the reciprocity principle are considered next.

Ingratiation and reciprocity. E. E. Jones and Camille Wortman (1973) describe a young man who tries to create reciprocal attraction by telling his date that she is a "beautiful, sensitive person." Jones and Wortman admit that this expression of approval may make the man seem more likable, but if his date labels the compliment as *ingratiation*—a manipulative attempt to make oneself seem more likable—then she will probably respond negatively (see Chapter 2). The compliment will also be ineffective if she thinks the man is a nondiscerning evaluator who tends to compliment rather than complain. She may decide that her date is a nice guy, but the compliment won't generate reciprocity. She may also attribute the compliment to the situation rather than to her date. Norms of politeness require that a person be complimentary in some situations. When a friend gets a haircut, it's customary to compliment the new hairdo rather than criticize it. Complimenting people in such cases indicates that we are courteous, but our compliment may not generate the reciprocal attraction the ingratiator seeks.

What can ingratiators do to maximize the power of their compliments? Jones and Wortman offer the following suggestions:

- Play down your dependence on the target. The person who admits, "This is my first date in six months," won't seem sincere when he then says, "You are a beautiful, sensitive person."
- Express your liking for the person to a third party who you know will then repeat it to the target. Your motives can't be impugned if you don't divulge your sentiments directly.
- Repeat only positive comments made by others about the target person. The skilled ingratiator knows better than to transmit bad news to the person—this is the so-called **MUM effect**—because the negative emotions the bad news creates in the person may spread to the transmitter (Bond & Anderson, 1987).
- Avoid complimenting other people when the target person is nearby. If you compliment only the targets, they can't conclude that you are a nondiscerning evaluator who likes anyone and anything. Don't criticize other people, though. Few people are attracted to someone who seems critical (Amabile, 1983a).
- Exceed the usual standards for politeness when the situation requires a complimentary response. If the target person has just gotten a haircut, don't just say "I like your new cut." Rave about how much you like the hairdo.

MUM effect
Our general reluctance to give negative information to others, even when we are not the origin of the information.

Self-esteem and reciprocity. People who don't like themselves don't always respond positively when they discover someone likes them. If Molly doubted her own self-worth, she might not be able to recognize that Andrew actually likes her. People with low self-esteem often misinterpret others' signs of social approval, recasting them in a more negative light that matches their bleak views of themselves (Jacobs, Berscheid, & Walster, 1971). And if Andrew signals his approval clearly, Molly may not even appreciate being liked and admired. Heider's balance theory predicts that if Molly dislikes herself but Andrew likes Molly, then the relationship is unbalanced. Molly may therefore strive to regain balance by rejecting Andrew and finding someone who dislikes her as much as she dislikes herself (Jones, 1973; Shrauger, 1975).

William Swann, Jr., has studied this unusual exception to reciprocity over the last several years. His self-verification theory argues that even though people with low self-esteem respond positively to social approval at an emotional level, they nonetheless seek information that verifies their negative self-conceptions (see the section, "In Depth: Which Motive Is Stronger: The Need for Self-Esteem or the Need for Self-Consistency?" in Chapter 5). In one study, Swann and his colleagues offered people the chance to interact with either a person who had evaluated them unfavorably or a person who had evaluated them favorably. People with high self-esteem wanted to meet the adulator, but an astonishing 78% of the people with negative self-concepts wanted to meet the critic (Swann, Stein-Seroussi, & McNulty, 1992). In other studies, people with low self-esteem asked to interact with someone who disparaged them rather than perform an unrelated experiment. They also sought out information about their limitations after they received praise about some of their general characteristics (Swann, 1992).

This striving for self-verification over self-enhancement influences even our choice of friends and intimates. Swann asked married men and women to rate themselves and their partner's intelligence, physical attractiveness, athletic skill, interpersonal skill, and musical talent. He also asked them a series of questions about their commitment to their relationships: How satisfied are you, do you plan to remain in the relationship, how much time do you spend together, and so on. When he compared people with a positive self-concept to people with a negative self-concept, he discovered that those with a positive self-concept were more committed to a spouse who evaluated them favorably. However, and as Figure 11-5 indicates, people with low self-esteem were more committed to a critical spouse rather than to a supportive one. The researchers concluded that "the warmth produced by favorable feedback is chilled by incredulity, and that the reassurance produced by negative feedback is tempered by sadness that the 'truth' could not be more kind" (Swann, Hixon, & De La Ronde, 1992, p. 120).

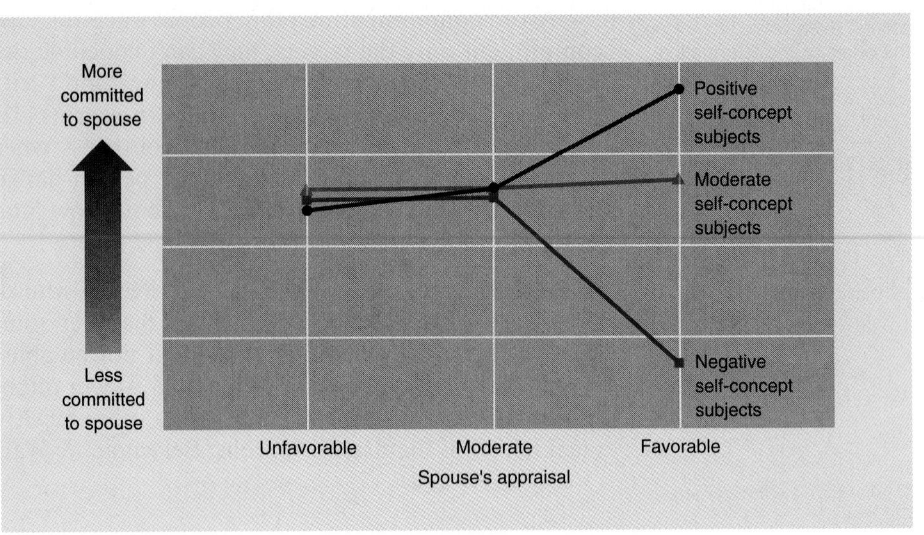

▲ **FIGURE 11-5**
Do people who have low self-esteem prefer a spouse who ridicules them or praises them? Swann and his colleagues asked married people who possessed negative, moderate, and positive self-esteem to rate their commitment to their spouses. People with negative self-esteem were more committed to spouses who rated them relatively negatively. People with positive self-esteem, in contrast, were more committed to spouses who evaluated them positively. (Adapted from Swann, Hixon, & De La Ronde, 1992)

▲ **FIGURE 11-6**
Who is liked more: the person who likes you right away or the person who becomes more positive toward you over time? When subjects rated a confederate on a scale of +10 to −10, most evaluated the confederate positively. However, a pattern of negative evaluations shifting to positive ones (gain condition) led to more attraction than uniformly positive evaluations. A pattern of positive evaluations shifting to negative ones (loss condition) led to a marginally significant reduction in attraction relative to uniformly negative evaluations. (From Aronson & Linder, 1965)

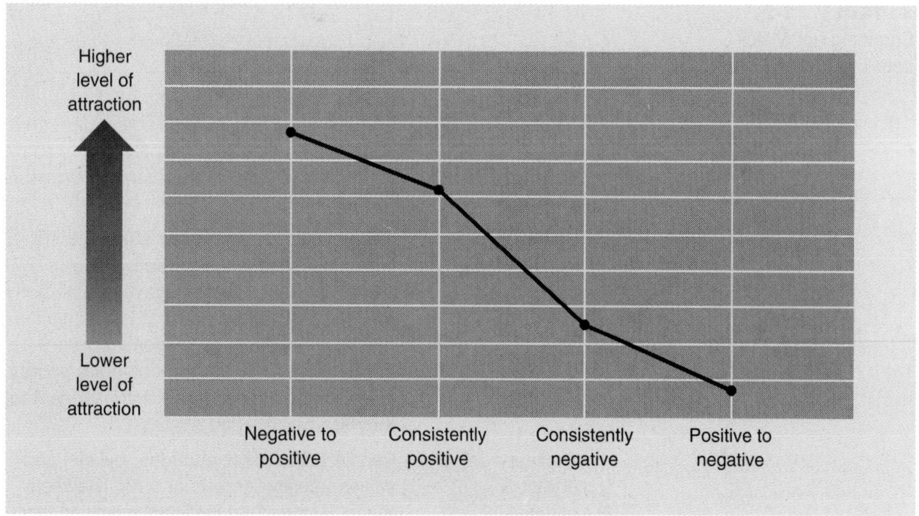

The gain-loss hypothesis. Imagine that Molly meets Andrew and Johnny on five occasions. Each time she chats with Johnny he seems warm and friendly. Andrew, in contrast, acts cold and unfriendly at first, but by the fourth and fifth encounters, he makes it very clear that he likes her. Who will she like better: Johnny, who was always positive, or Andrew, who was initially negative but eventually became positive?

gain-loss hypothesis
The prediction that evaluators who are negative initially but who gradually become positive are liked more than consistently positive evaluators, whereas evaluators who are positive initially but gradually become negative are disliked more than consistently negative evaluators.

Elliot Aronson and Darwyn Linder (1965) state that approval is nice, but winning approval from someone who is initially negative is particularly rewarding. According to their **gain-loss hypothesis**, a "gain in esteem is a more potent reward than invariant esteem, and similarly, the loss of esteem is a more potent 'punishment' than invariant negative esteem" (p. 156). In a test of this hypothesis, female college students conversed individually with another woman (a confederate of the researchers) in seven consecutive sessions. Each subject then listened as the confederate evaluated her. By controlling the confederate's remarks, Aronson and Linder created four sequences of evaluation: all positive, all negative, negative shifting to positive (the gain condition), and positive shifting to negative (the loss condition). When the subjects evaluated the confederate after all seven sessions, women in the gain condition (negative to positive) were the most positive, and women in the loss condition (positive to negative) were the most negative in their ratings of the confederate (see Figure 11-6; Aronson & Linder, 1965; Mettee & Aronson, 1974; see also Brothen, 1977; Sigall & Aronson, 1967).

The Economics of Attraction

Occasionally, social psychologists have confirmed age-old beliefs about liking and disliking. In general, however, adages and folklore aren't much help when it comes to understanding attraction. Does familiarity breed contempt? Do we refrain from judging a book by its cover? Do opposites attract? Table 11-2, which summarizes the factors that influence attraction, rejects most of these commonsense notions.

social exchange theory
An economic model of interpersonal relationships that argues individuals seek out relationships that offer them many rewards while exacting few costs.

So why do we like some people and dislike others? The answer depends, in most cases, on the rewards they offer us. **Social exchange theory** assumes that attraction depends on "the exchange of rewards and punishments that takes place when people interact" (Berscheid, 1985, p. 429). At least in the initial stages of an interpersonal relation, we act like shoppers looking for bargains.

▲ **TABLE 11-2**
Summing up: Major determinants of liking

Factor	*Description*	*Example*
Propinquity	Individuals who live or work in close proximity tend to like one another. Propinquity reduces the cost of getting acquainted (for example, time, energy) and increases mere exposure.	Roommates, even though assigned to rooms at random, come to like one another.
Physical attractiveness	People who are physically attractive are better liked than less attractive people. People assume that attractive people possess positive qualities (the "what is beautiful is good" stereotype). Evolutionary theory suggests that attractive people are sought after because their appearance suggests that they are healthy and available.	College students meeting for the first time liked their partner more if he or she was physically attractive (Walster et al., 1966).
Similarity-attraction effect	People with similar attitudes, beliefs, and values usually like one another. Balance theory argues that disliking someone who is similar (and liking dissimilar people) is an unbalanced state.	Students in a dorm who had similar values and interests became friends (Newcomb, 1960).
Complementarity	People whose qualities complement one another sometimes (although very rarely) like one another. Similarity, rather than complementarity, usually determines attraction.	Sadistic people are attracted to masochistic people (Baumeister, 1989).
Reciprocity principle	We like people who like us. Exceptions include (a) negative reactions to ingratiators; (b) low self-esteem individuals' preference for rejection; and (c) the tendency to like people who become more favorable to us over time (gain-loss).	Friendships tend to be mutual. When people name who they like, they choose people who like them in return.

When we encounter potential partners, we assess their value by enumerating their positive, rewarding features. When friends lend you money, do you a favor, buy you lunch, or give you a present, they are giving you tangible, concrete rewards. Social rewards are important as well, for we are drawn to people who validate us and our attitudes. We also shy away from people who possess negative, costly characteristics. People who live far away, who express ideas that clash with our own, or exhibit qualities that we find undesirable, such as tediousness, rudeness, and incompetence, are disliked (Gilchrist, 1952; Iverson, 1964; Leary, Rogers, et al., 1986).

minimax principle
The tendency for individuals to make choices that minimize their losses and punishments and maximize their gains and rewards.

In general, social exchange theory assumes that our choices of friends and lovers are based on a **minimax principle**. Just as we tend to select the product that offers us the best value for our money, we are attracted to people who offer us maximum rewards with a minimum of costs. As simple (and as unromantic) as this theory seems, it makes more sense than common sense does. (Adams, 1965; Altman & Taylor, 1973; Blau, 1964; Foa & Foa, 1974; Hays, 1985; Huesmann & Levinger, 1976; Kelley et al., 1983; Rusbult, 1983; and Thibaut & Kelley, 1959, are among the theorists who embrace these basic assumptions.)

Love

In her memoirs, Molly Haskell (1990) admits she was decidedly ambivalent when Andrew proposed to her. She thought of herself as an independent person who needed no one in her life, and she certainly wanted little to do with the responsibilities a traditional marriage brings. She said "yes" nevertheless, taking for granted that marriage wouldn't really be that much of a change. But then she fell deeply in love with Andrew:

> We were "everything" to each other, made for each other. . . . Like the troubadours, we were exalted as much by the expression of love—the pleasing sound of our words of praise, the exaltation of the intense feelings we had invested in each other—as by the object of our adoration; we were in love with our own lovingness. (p. 280)

Molly loved Andrew "as much as any woman can love a man" (p. 48). But what is love? Is it friendship with sexual intimacy, or a union so unique that it defies analysis? And why did Molly's relationship with Andrew ripen over time, changing from mutual liking into an impassioned and abiding bond?

What Is Love?

Andrew Capellanus (1959), who wrote a manual for lovers in the 12th century, calls love "a certain inborn suffering derived from the sight of and excessive meditation upon the beauty of the opposite sex" (p. 28). To psychotherapist Erich Fromm (1956), love is "the active concern for the life and growth of that which we love" (p. 22). Author George Bernard Shaw defines love as "a game exaggerating the difference between one person and everybody else" (quoted in Murstein, 1988, p. 14).

What is love? You may like many people—your co-workers, neighbors, and friends—but you don't love them. Rather, our loved ones are our best friends, our boyfriends and girlfriends, our parents, our spouses, and our children. What makes love such a special kind of relationship (Sternberg, 1987)?

The two sides of love. Love means different things to different people, but for centuries writers, poets, and scholars have drawn a distinction between love as an intense, often sexual need for another person and love as a gradually developing commitment to another person. Elaine Hatfield and her colleagues, for example, argue that love usually takes two forms: passionate and companionate. **Passionate love** is an emotion-laden "state of intense absorption in another" (Walster & Walster, 1978, p. 9). People in the throes of passionate love are so fascinated by their partners that their thoughts are disrupted or confused. They may feel an overwhelming need to possess or be possessed by the lover and find little satisfaction in any other social activities. If Molly were passionately in love with Andrew, she would be likely to agree with such statements as the following (Hatfield & Sprecher, 1986a, p. 391):

passionate love
An emotion-laden state of intense interest in another person.

- I would feel deep despair if Andrew left me.
- Sometimes I feel I can't control my thoughts; they are obsessively on Andrew.
- I yearn to know all about Andrew.
- I have an endless appetite for affection from Andrew.

Passionate lovers desire close physical contact with their partners, including sexual intercourse.

companionate love
A strong commitment to support and care for another person that develops gradually.

Companionate love, in contrast, is slow-moving and gradual. It often builds on friendship and respect and results in a strong mutual commitment. People who love each other are similar in some respects to very close friends: They enjoy each other's company; they respect and trust one another; they also provide one another with support and understanding. Companionate lovers care deeply for one another. They want only the best for their partners; they

▲ Writers, poets, and scholars often draw a distinction between passionate love—an intense, often sexual need for another person—and companionate love—a gradually developing commitment to another person. Passionate lovers are captivated by their lover to the point where their thoughts are disrupted, they lose interest in other activities, and they yearn for close physical contact. Companionate lovers, in contrast, enjoy each other's company, support one another, and care deeply for one another.

willingly support them when they need support, and act as their champions when others attack them. Molly's love for Andrew was the companionate kind. She writes, "Without quite realizing when it had happened, or why, Andrew had come to play not only the central role of husband/lover but that of confidant, 'best friend,' as well" (Haskell, 1990, p. 247). She would be likely to agree with such statements as these:

- I want only the best for Andrew (Shaver et al., 1987).
- I can open up to Andrew (Burgess & Huston, 1979).
- Andrew and I have a warm and comfortable relationship (Sternberg, 1988).
- Andrew would come to my aid if I needed help (Davis & Latty-Mann, 1987).
- Andrew understands my hurts and joys (Schaefer & Olson, 1981).

Companionate love is the stuff of intimate, long-term relationships (Aron, Aron, & Smollan, 1992; Berscheid, Snyder, & Omoto, 1989).

Other researchers corroborate Hatfield's distinction between passion and compassion (Davis, 1985; Davis & Todd, 1985; Driscoll, Davis, & Lipetz, 1972; Kelley, 1983; Rubin, 1973; Shaver et al., 1987). The sociologist John Alan Lee (1977), for example, collected and compared various conceptions of love dating back to Plato's recommendation of sexless love. When he examined them with the help of a panel of objective raters, he identified the six styles of loving shown in Table 11-3. The first three styles define love as an impassioned emotional experience (eros, ludus, and mania), but the other three underscore companionship, giving, and interpersonal exchange (storge, agape, pragma). Other studies of these types of love find that lovers often agree on the type of love they are experiencing. An eros man, for example, is more likely to be paired with an eros woman than with a woman experiencing agape (Hendrick & Hendrick, 1986; Hendrick, Hendrick, & Adler, 1988).

The triangle model of love. Robert Sternberg's triangle approach adds a third element to the formula for love. Sternberg, like most theorists, assumes that long-term relationships are often based on intimacy and passion. *Intimacy* is the emotional component, the "close, connected, and bonded" feelings lov-

TABLE 11-3
In different historical eras, love has been defined in a variety of ways

Name	*Style of Love*	*Characteristics*
Eros	Romantic love	The search for the ideal mate, with emphasis on physical beauty
Ludus	Game-playing	Playing the field; a search for many conquests with little long-term involvement
Mania	Possessive love	Obsessive, jealous, emotionally extreme involvement with the lover
Storge	Companionate love	Slow-developing affection and friendship love culminating in a long-term relationship
Agape	Altruistic love	Gentle, caring desire to give to another, without expectation of return
Pragma	Pragmatic love	Practical, rational relationship based on mutual satisfaction

Source: From Lee, 1977.

ers experience. This component corresponds, in many respects, to Hatfield's companionate love. *Passion* is the motivational component. Like passionate love, passion includes physical attraction, sexual desire, sexuality. But Sternberg adds a cognitive component, *decision/commitment.* Initially, this component refers to the decision to enter into a relationship. In a long-term relationship, this decision becomes a commitment to work to maintain the relationship. Words like *loyalty, responsibility, faithfulness,* and *devotion* characterize commitment (Fehr, 1988).

Sternberg uses these three dimensions to describe the following seven types of relationships (see Figure 11-7):

- *Intimacy only = Liking*: Friends who feel very close to one another, without any desire for sexual closeness or a long-term commitment from their partner.
- *Passion only = Infatuation*: People who fall in love at first sight and on one-night stands. They experience passionate desire for their partners, but these lustful feelings can dissipate as rapidly as they commenced.

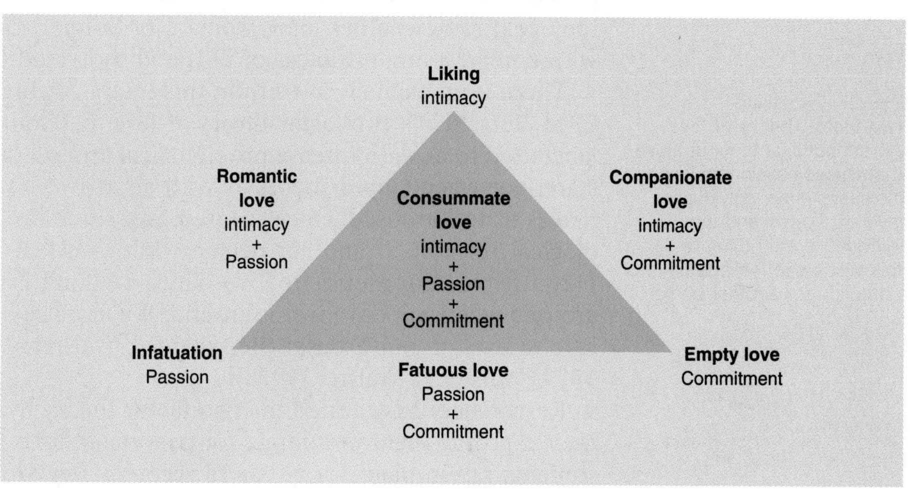

FIGURE 11-7
How do I love thee? Robert Sternberg counts seven different ways. His triangle model of love is based on three dimensions that he calls Intimacy, Passion, and Decision/Commitment. By distinguishing between relationships that are high and low on these three dimensions, he succeeds in identifying seven kinds of love: liking, infatuation, empty love, romantic love, companionate love, fatuous love, and consummate love. (From Sternberg, 1988)

▲ **TABLE 11-4**
Summing up: Most theorists believe that love has several components, including passion and companionship.

Components	*Characteristics*
Passionate love	Emotionally intense passions; fascination for one's partner; disrupted thoughts, confusion; need to possess and be possessed by lover; desire for close physical contact with the loved one.
Companionate love	Gradually developing friendship, respect, trust, and commitment; partners care and support each other. Sternberg (1987) breaks this component down into two factors: intimacy and decision/commitment.

- *Commitment only = Empty love*: Partners who remain committed to each other without warmth or passion. Examples include stagnant, worn-out marriages and many arranged marriages.
- *Intimacy + Passion = Romantic love*: Close friends who also experience sexual passion or lovers whose primarily sexual relationship develops into a warm, close friendship. Romeo and Juliet were classic romantic lovers.
- *Intimacy + Commitment = Companionate love*: People who are committed to their emotionally satisfying, long-term relationships even though they no longer experience strong sexual desire for their partner.
- *Passion + Commitment = Fatuous love*: Whirlwind romances that lead to ill-considered commitment, including marriage.
- *Intimacy + Passion + Commitment = Consummate love*: The ultimate relationship, in which the partners feel that they are close friends, passionate lovers, and lifemates.

Sternberg argues that partners experience problems in their relationship when they differ along these three dimensions. If, for example, one person is experiencing companionate love but his or her partner is experiencing romantic love, then the relationship is likely to falter (Sternberg, 1988; Sternberg & Barnes, 1985; Sternberg & Grajek, 1984; see Table 11-4 for a summary).

Falling in Love

The Romans thought they knew why lovers experience such intense, all-consuming agony and ecstasy. They blamed the roguish god Cupid, who roamed about shooting people with his gold-tipped arrows. His targets became passionately aroused and consequently fell in love with whomever or whatever they next saw, whether man, woman, or animal. Greco-Roman myth is filled with embarrassing instances of ill-timed shots and unlikely alliances.

two-factor theory of love
An attributional theory of love that traces passionate love to increases in an individual's level of arousal and the individual's attribution of this arousal to feelings of attraction for another person.

There is an element of truth in this myth. According to Elaine Hatfield and Ellen Berscheid's **two-factor theory of love**, passionate love is an attributional label used to explain intense physiological arousal (see Chapter 4). The process starts not when Cupid shoots us with an arrow, but when a situational factor makes us feel aroused. Once aroused, we search for a likely cause of our physiological turmoil. If another person whom we feel is attractive is nearby, we may attribute our arousal to love. Thus, we don't first fall in love, and then feel aroused whenever our lover is around. We first become aroused and then fall in love to explain our arousal (Berscheid & Walster, 1978; Walster & Berscheid, 1974; Walster & Walster, 1978).

Researchers have tested the two-factor theory by first arousing subjects and then exposing them to a target for passionate love. In one study, male college students ran in place for either 15 seconds (low arousal) or 120 seconds (high arousal) to create differences in arousal levels. The men then watched a videotape of a woman whom they thought they would be meeting for a brief get-

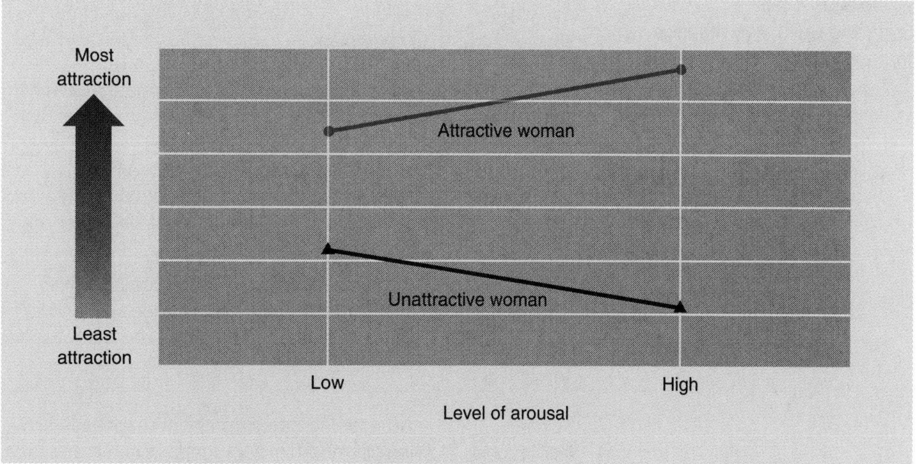

▲ **FIGURE 11-8**
Does physiological arousal fuel our passions? When heterosexual men ran in place for either 15 seconds (low arousal) or 120 seconds (high arousal) and then rated a woman they saw in a videotape, aroused men were more impassioned—in both a positive and negative sense—than unaroused men. Arousal, it seems, polarized their opinions of the woman. (From White, Fishbein, & Rutstein, 1981)

acquainted talk. Some subjects viewed a tape of the woman wearing attractive makeup and form-fitting clothes; her hair was styled, and she spoke energetically. Others saw a videotape of the same woman wearing ill-fitting clothes, a scarf, and clumsily applied makeup. In this condition, she sniffled and spoke with little enthusiasm. The men then rated the woman's physical beauty, sexiness, and how much they would like to date and kiss her. As the average ratings (shown in Figure 11-8) indicate, the men liked the attractive woman more than the unattractive woman. Arousal, however, intensified the men's reactions. These men gave very high ratings to the attractive woman and very low ratings to the unattractive woman (White, Fishbein, & Rutstein, 1981).

Other studies have yielded similar findings (Cantor, Zillmann, & Bryant, 1975; Dermer & Pyszczynski, 1978; Dutton & Aron, 1974). Men who had just read about a woman's sexual fantasies rated their own lovers more positively (Dermer & Pyszczynski, 1978). In contrast to men who were interviewed by a woman while standing on a solid wooden bridge, men interviewed while standing on a suspension bridge over a deep gorge showed signs of stronger sexual arousal and were more likely to telephone the interviewer (Dutton & Aron, 1974). When researchers convinced nonaroused subjects that they were experiencing physiological arousal, they showed exaggerated romantic responses (Valins, 1966; see Chapter 4). The two-factor theory also offers a potential explanation for the so-called **Romeo-and-Juliet effect**. Just as Romeo and Juliet fell passionately in love against their parents' wishes, researchers have shown that the more parents interfere with their children's romances, the more romantically involved their children become. The explanation? The frustration and distress caused by disputes over their romantic involvement can be misattributed to love (Driscoll, Davis, & Lipetz, 1972).

Romeo-and-Juliet effect The tendency for individuals to experience stronger passionate love for forbidden individuals.

Other factors, besides misattribution, can also promote or inhibit the experience of passionate love. Douglas T. Kenrick and his colleagues believe that passionate love is sometimes based on a reinforcement process rather than an attribution process (Kenrick & Cialdini, 1977; Kenrick, Cialdini, & Linder, 1979; Kenrick & Johnson, 1979). Kenrick notes that in most cases people can accurately identify the causes of their arousal. A businesswoman traveling by airplane may feel very much aroused during a takeoff in stormy weather, but she is likely to attribute her arousal to fear of flying rather than to the handsome flight attendant (Kenrick et al., 1979; White & Knight, 1984). The flight attendant, however, may help the woman cope with the stressful situation, so she might be drawn to him because of the rewards he offers. Kenrick's research

▲ **TABLE 11-5**
Summing up: Three theories that explain passionate love

Theory	*Description*	*Example*
Two-factor theory	Individuals experience passionate love when they affix the label *love* to their arousal. If misattribution occurs, arousal caused by some extraneous factor (such as parental interference or exercise) is erroneously attributed to the emotion of love rather than to the true cause.	Heterosexual men liked an interviewer more when they met her on a fear-provoking bridge rather than on an ordinary, nonarousing bridge.
Reinforcement theory	Individuals who help us reduce negative emotional states reward us, so we tend to like them more than individuals who do not reward us in this manner.	Men interviewed on a frightening bridge felt comforted by the attractive interviewer, so they liked her.
Social facilitation theory	Arousal facilitates dominant responses and inhibits nondominant, unpracticed responses. If responding positively to an attractive person is a dominant response, arousal will increase the likelihood that this response will occur.	Men's positive responses to an attractive woman were facilitated by arousal produced by the fear-provoking bridge.

team argues that loved ones do more than provide a target for our attributions; they also help us reduce our level of arousal. The men interviewed on solid or frightening bridges liked the interviewer on the suspension bridge because she helped them reduce their level of fear (Riordan & Tedeschi, 1983).

Kenrick and his colleagues also point out that passionate love may be a form of social facilitation. As noted in Chapter 10, when people become aroused, they are more likely to perform well-learned actions but less likely to act in novel, unpracticed ways. If we assume that feelings of attraction are dominant responses, then arousal should intensify these responses. After reviewing over a dozen studies of the two-factor theory, Kenrick's research team conclude that passionate love results more frequently from social facilitation than from misattribution (Allen et al., 1989).

The theoretical intricacies summarized in Table 11-5 aside, the two-factor theory is correct when it argues that our society has romanticized love. The two-factor process works because people assume that arousal and love go together. In America and many other Western countries, love is considered a mysterious and accidental process; something we fall into rather than nurture. Movies, television, novels, and poetry describe love as blossoming at first sight, with overwhelming intensity. We are taught that when we feel aroused and a potential partner is nearby, love must be the cause (Averill, 1985; Averill & Boothroyd, 1977; Dion & Dion, 1988, 1993).

This conception of love, however, can be misleading. Because we view love as a mixture of emotion and sexual desires, people sometimes assume that a marriage based on passionate love will be successful. Yet too many marriages based on romantic love end in divorce when the fire dies out. As the noted sociologist Willard Waller lamented many years ago:

> It is possibly very unfortunate that people must make one of their most important decisions on the basis of certain delusive emotions of adolescence. There is truth in the ancient proverb, *Amantes amentes,* lovers are mad. And the persons who have the power to excite this madness in others are by no means always the persons with whom it is possible to live happily after the knot is tied. (Waller, 1938, p. 208)

Waller believed that such a long-term relationship as marriage should be founded on mutual trust, exchange, and commitment instead of on emotion. These factors provide the foundation for companionate rather than passionate love.

Sustaining Love

Passionate love may set the stage for a relationship, but it can rarely sustain it over the long term. Passionate love can blossom (or wither) overnight, but companionate love must be nurtured. Slowly, and sometimes painfully, individuals must disclose information about themselves to develop intimacy. If a relationship is to prosper, both individuals must be willing to contribute to it without asking too much in return. They must also deal, eventually, with questions of sexual intimacy.

intimacy
The experience of psychological and emotional closeness.

self-disclosure
The process of revealing personal, intimate information about oneself to another person.

Intimacy and love. Andrew and Molly's relationship was an intimate one. They felt loved when they were together, even when they were only paying the bills or watching a movie in a darkened theater. They could talk about private, personal matters with each other, ideas that could be shared with no one else. Their lives were interconnected and closely linked: "Over the years we had grown together like two trees" (Haskell, 1990, p. 280). Such **intimacy** is fundamental to personal relationships (Clark & Reis, 1988; Helgeson, Shaver, & Dyer, 1987; Perlman & Fehr, 1987).

Intimacy often develops through a process called **self-disclosure**: the sharing of personal, intimate information between two people. When Molly first started dating Andrew, they probably talked politely but avoided saying anything too personal or provocative. In this *orientation stage,* Andrew and Molly were only trying to form a general impression of each other, and possibly to make a good impression themselves. In the *exploratory affective stage,* Andrew and Molly probably began to discuss their personal attitudes and opinions but carefully avoided intimate topics. This stage was probably followed by the *affective stage,* when a few topics remained taboo, but Andrew and Molly could now talk about very personal matters. Eventually, Andrew and Molly's relationship reached the final stage, *stable exchange,* in which all personal feelings and possessions are shared (Altman & Taylor, 1973).

Self-disclosure and the growth of intimacy are reciprocally related. Each new self-disclosure deepens the intimacy of the relationship, and this increased closeness then makes further self-disclosures possible. If this gradual cycle of deepening intimacy is disrupted, then the relationship may not mature. If Molly were to refuse to share personal information after Andrew offered his self-disclosures, or if Andrew made extremely personal self-disclosures too early in the relationship, the relationship might falter (Baxter, 1987; Chaikin & Derlega, 1974; Miller, 1990; see also Berg & McQuinn, 1986). By sharing information about yourself with others, you are telling them "I trust you enough to tell you this" (Rempel & Holmes, 1986; Rempel, Holmes, & Zanna, 1985). Self-disclosures also signal your commitment to the relationship and encourage self-disclosure in return. As a result, intimacy, self-disclosure, and satisfaction go hand in hand in most close relationships (Berg, 1984; Hendrick, 1981).

Achieving intimacy can be a challenge for some couples. Particularly during the early stages of a relationship, women readily disclose personal information; men do not (Dindia & Allen, 1992). In their same-sex friendships, men rarely share personal information about themselves, so their friendships aren't as intimate as women's (Caldwell & Peplau, 1982; Hays, 1985; Hill & Stull, 1981; Reis, Senchak, & Solomon, 1985). Even those men who disclose personal in-

© 1994, The Washington Post Writers Group. Reprinted with permission.

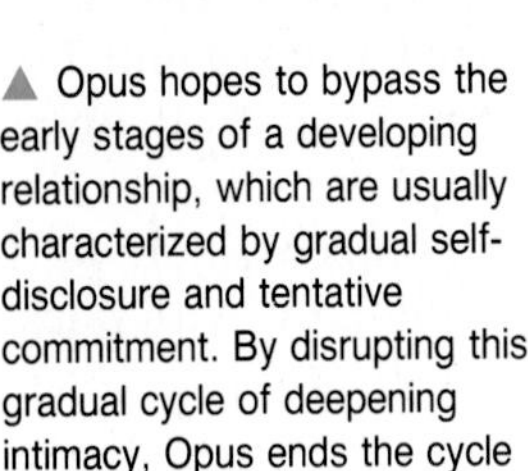

▲ Opus hopes to bypass the early stages of a developing relationship, which are usually characterized by gradual self-disclosure and tentative commitment. By disrupting this gradual cycle of deepening intimacy, Opus ends the cycle altogether.

formation at relatively high rates when they are courting a woman may become "emotionally stingy" after the relationship matures. When married people talk about their relationship, the wife does more of the talking. Wives are happier when their husbands talk more, but husbands' satisfaction with their marriages isn't related to how much they or their wives talk about their relationships (Acitelli, 1992).

Some people also seem to fear becoming too intimate with other people (Pilkington & Richardson, 1988). Cindy Hazan and Phillip Shaver trace intimacy-related problems back to early childhood experiences. Although some children form strong, secure attachments, other children display striking independence or ambivalence when responding to their parents (Ainsworth, 1979). These childhood differences emerge in adulthood in one of three **attachment styles**: secure, avoidant, or anxious/ambivalent.

attachment styles
One's characteristic approach to relationships with other people; the three basic types of styles are secure, avoidant, and anxious/ambivalent.

- *Secure* individuals are comfortable with intimacy. They enjoy forming close relationships with other people, and they don't worry about being abandoned by their loved ones.
- *Avoidant* types evade intimacy with others. They are uncomfortable relying on other people and complain that their partners ask for more intimacy than they can easily provide.
- *Anxious/ambivalent* people desire intimacy, but they worry that their loved ones will reject them. They sometimes question their partner's sincerity and demand excessive intimacy.

Hazan and Shaver (1987) report that 56% of the people they surveyed were secure, 25% were avoidant, and 19% were anxious/ambivalent. Secure people report growing up in families where parents were warm and supportive rather than cold or inconsistent (Collins & Read, 1990; Feeney & Noller, 1990).

These differences in attachment style naturally influence people's responses in their intimate relationships. Secure people experienced more warmth, trust, and friendship in their relationships than the other types. Avoidant individuals reported fearing closeness, and anxious/ambivalent people reported more jealousy, obsessive preoccupation, sexual attraction, and desire for union (Hazan & Shaver, 1987). Anxious/ambivalent and avoidant people also have more problems maintaining their relationships (Levy & Davis, 1988; Simpson, Rholes, & Nelligan, 1992; Vormbrock, 1993). When a group of young adults was asked about love, more of the avoidant types reported that they had never been in love, and those who had been, rated the experience as less intense (Feeney & Noller, 1990; see Figure 11-9). They were also less distressed when their relationships failed (Simpson, 1990). Last, two of the three types tend to seek out each other. Secure people are more likely to date secure people than are avoidant types. Anxious/ambivalent individuals, however, seem to seek out people who confirm their insecurities. They tend to date avoidant types who are uncomfortable with intimacy (Collins & Read, 1990).

Equity and exchange. Both Molly and Andrew put as much into their relationship as they took out. Molly was the active one who planned their outings, kept track of their friends, and worried about money. Andrew was the bill-payer, the entertainer, and the bon vivant. When Molly was ill, Andrew took care of her. And when Andrew was so very ill that he nearly died, Molly was always by his side.

Molly and Andrew's marriage illustrates the exchange-like nature of long-term relationships. As noted earlier, we like people who reward us in some way. A close relationship, however, depends on the *equitable* exchange of rewards between partners. Few people enter into relationships thinking they will be able to experience only rewards (companionship, sex, a home, a family, gifts, clean laundry, meals, and entertainment) without incurring any costs. Rather, they expect **equity**. They hope that the rewards they receive will be in proportion to the costs they incur. If they put a great deal into the relationship, they expect to get a great deal out of it. If they expect to invest only minimally, then they expect that they will reap only minimal rewards (Sprecher, 1992a, 1992b; Sprecher & Schwartz, 1992).

equity
Receiving rewards from a relationship that are commensurate with one's contributions to that relationship.

Equitable relationships tend to be more stable, more enjoyable, and more sexually intimate than inequitable relationships (Traupmann & Hatfield, 1981; Van Ypern & Buunk, 1990). Dating and married couples who feel they aren't getting their fair share of rewards from the relationship will experience anger and dissatisfaction (Davidson, 1984; Michaels, Edwards, & Acock, 1984). College students, explaining why they broke up with their most recent lovers, frequently complained that their relationships were inequitable (Baxter, 1986). Note, however, that people who benefit excessively from an inequitable relationship—they get more out than they put in—aren't as upset by the situation as those who benefit too little (Sprecher, 1992a). An equity theory of relationships may seem mercenary and calculating, but remember that the rewards we seek go beyond expensive gifts, sexual gratification, and excitement. Our close friends or lovers provide us with many other, more commendable rewards, including intimacy, acceptance, companionship, security, and self-worth (Drigotas & Rusbult, 1992).

Some relationships, however, may transcend the what's-in-it-for-me attitude of equity. Margaret Clark and Judson Mills argue that many couples don't

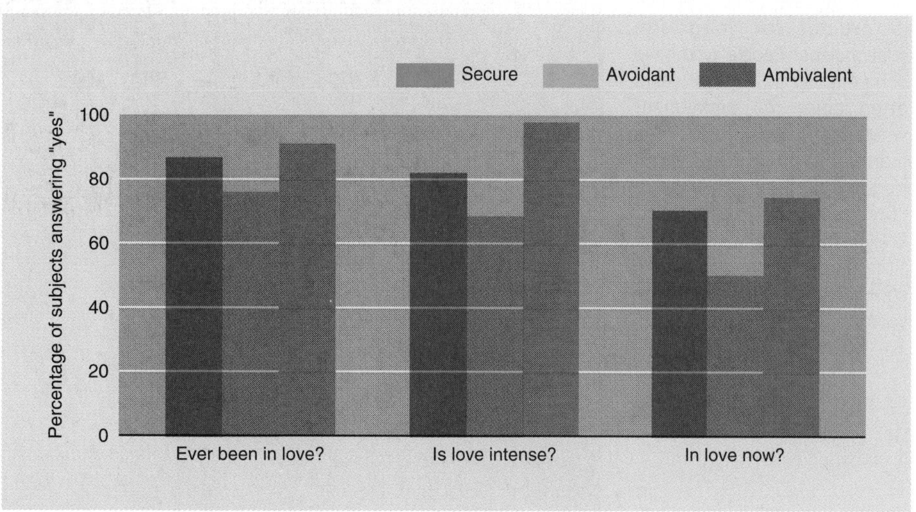

▲ **FIGURE 11-9**
Have you ever been in love? More of the secure and ambivalent individuals said yes to this question, as compared to avoidant types. The ambivalent individuals were virtually unanimous in their belief that love is a very intense emotional experience, and fewer of the avoidant individuals reported that they were in love at this time. (Adapted from Feeney & Noller, 1990)

communal relationships Interpersonal relationships between individuals who are more concerned with what their partner gets rather than with what they receive.

worry about costs and rewards. People in such **communal relationships**, they suggest, are more concerned with what their partners get rather than what they receive. Clark and Mills have explored communal and exchange relationships in a series of intriguing studies. The researchers usually introduce an unattached, male college student to a beautiful woman. In some cases, the man is told that the woman is available; she is new in town and eager to meet men. Others, however, are told that she is married and not interested in meeting new people. If the woman is married, the man's reaction is usually determined by exchange principles. He keeps track of his contributions when they work on tasks together, and he feels exploited if she doesn't reciprocate when he helps her. He also likes the woman more if she keeps track of her contributions and pays back his favors immediately. If the beautiful woman is unmarried, however, the man usually responds very differently. He helps her more readily, particularly if she seems depressed. He prefers to think of their work as a joint effort and feels disappointed if she insists on reciprocating his help. These findings suggest that, in some cases, people are more interested in giving rather than maintaining a fair balance between inputs and outcomes (Clark, 1984; Clark & Mills, 1979; Clark, Mills, & Powell, 1986; Clark & Reis, 1988; Clark & Wadell, 1985; Clark et al., 1987).

Love and sex. The concept of love, and passionate love in particular, stresses sexuality. When asked to explain the difference between romantic love and deep friendship, most people mention sexual passion. In most other respects, these two kinds of close relationships are very similar to each other. Good friends and lovers enjoy one anothers' company, they help one another, and they inspire mutual trust, understanding, and confidence. Only lovers, however, experience strong sexual desire. People in love, "want physical intimacy with the partner, wanting to touch and be touched and to engage in sexual intercourse" (Davis, 1985, p. 24). But most people realize that sexuality is not the defining characteristic of love. A one-night stand involves sex but not love, whereas deep friendship creates companionate love, but does not involve sex (Forgas & Dobosz, 1980).

▲ A deep level of commitment is crucial for long-term relationships. People who have been married for over 15 years often point to commitment when they explain why their marriages work. The most frequently offered reasons are "My spouse is my best friend," "I like my spouse as a person," "Marriage is a long-term commitment," and "Marriage is sacred" (Lauer & Lauer, 1985).

Sexuality nonetheless pervades our conception of romantic love and, for many couples, romantic involvement includes sexual intimacy. In one study, investigators charted the sexual development of 430 men and women from 1969, when they were in junior and senior high school, until 1979, when they were 23 to 25 years old. The average subject in this study was 18 years old when he or she first engaged in intercourse, and 40% of the men and 60% of the women reported that their initial sexual encounter occurred in the context of a steady dating relationship. When the subjects were asked about their reasons for engaging in intercourse, 85% mentioned sex as a way of giving and receiving love and achieving intimacy (Jessor et al., 1983).

Similar findings were obtained in the Boston Couples Study, which traced the development and decline of more than 200 heterosexual relationships over a two-year period. Eighty-two percent of the couples studied engaged in sexual intercourse (Peplau, Hill, & Rubin, 1993; Peplau, Rubin, & Hill, 1977). The men and women in these couples didn't always agree about the role of sex in their relationships, however. The men were much more likely than the women to mention sex as an important part of a relationship. They also reported more desire for sex than their partners did. In many cases, the woman restrained the couple's sexual activity. When dating couples abstained from sex, 64% of the men reported that their restraint was due to their partner's desire to refrain from sex. Fear of pregnancy and a moral code that opposed premarital sex were important reasons for refraining from sex. Other studies, as noted in the section "In Depth: Men, Women, and Sex," suggest that men's and women's attitudes about sex may reflect biological differences in mating.

Sex did not necessarily enrich the couples' relationships. All the couples, irrespective of their sexual proclivities, were equally satisfied with their relationships. This finding suggests that sexual intimacy is not a prerequisite for a happy premarital dating relationship. The sexually moderate couples tended to report stronger feelings of love than the other groups. This difference was particularly pronounced among women who had been virgins before they entered their current relationship. Sexuality was also associated with feelings of guilt and worry over unwanted pregnancy. Thus sex had both a positive and a negative impact on the relationship.

Was sexuality linked to the long-term success of the relationship? After two years, 20% of the couples had married, 34% were still dating, and 46% had broken up. Significantly, sexual intimacy was unrelated to the relationships' success. People who engaged in sexual intercourse were no more likely to remain together than people who refrained from sex. Sexual intimacy didn't help a relationship endure, but neither did it hurt the relationship's chances of success (Brehm, 1985).

Dissolution

Like the waxing and waning of the moon or the rise and fall of the tides, personal relationships follow a pattern of growth and change. Of all the people you meet, a small number will seem attractive to you. And of those, only a few will become good friends or loved ones. Fewer still will remain good friends and lovers (see Table 11-6 for a summary). Why do some of our close relationships endure and others dissolve?

The Loss of Passion

Strong positive feelings about one's partner are the hallmark of a healthy personal relationship. When we are with someone we love, we experience a range

IN DEPTH

Men, Women, and Sex

The battle between the sexes is still being waged in the arena of relationships. Men and women differ, in general, in their attitudes and values about liking, loving, and sexual behavior. Men express their love more rapidly than women do, yet they are slower to reach deeper levels of intimacy and commitment (Hatfield & Rapson, 1993). Women's friendships with women tend to be more emotionally intimate than are men's (Sherrod, 1989). Men are more influenced by physical attractiveness than are women (Buss & Schmitt, 1993). Men tend to deny their jealous feelings, but they respond to rivals with more anger than do women (Clanton & Smith, 1987). Men are more sexually permissive than women. They are more likely to approve of casual sex, sex with many partners, and sex with no strings attached. Women display a more responsible attitude toward sex (Oliver & Hyde, 1993). More than men, they feel that birth control and good communication are both part of mature sexuality (Hendrick et al., 1985). These differences emerged with much robustness when an attractive man or woman (the researchers' accomplice) approached strangers of the opposite sex and said, "I have been noticing you around campus. I find you very attractive." The accomplice then asked the stranger one of the following questions: "Would you go out with me tonight?" "Would you come over to my apartment tonight?" or "Would you go to bed with me tonight?" None of the women agreed to the third request; 75% of the men did (see Figure 11-10; Clark & Hatfield, 1989).

Experts have traced these differences to a variety of possible causes, including social learning, role expectations, psychodynamic processes, hormonal differences, and the patriarchal nature of most cultures (Huston & Ashmore, 1986; Ickes, 1993; Maccoby, 1990; Winstead & Derlega, 1993). Evolutionary theory, however, offers a particularly intriguing and parsimonious account. Inspired by Charles Darwin and sociobiology, evolutionary psychology argues that in the last 15 million years the human species has evolved socially as well as physically. Through the process of natural selection, individuals who were even slightly predisposed to engage in adaptive social behaviors were the "fittest"—they tended to survive longer and to be more successful in passing their genes along to future generations. Over countless generations, this selection process weeded out individuals who lacked these predispositions, and those who possessed them prospered. Even though these tendencies may not enhance our fitness in today's world, eons spent in harsher environments have left us genetically predisposed to perform certain social behaviors when situational cues call forth ancient instincts (Buss & Schmitt, 1993; Kenrick & Trost, 1989).

What does evolutionary psychology have to say about relationships? David Buss's *sexual strategies theory* suggests that men and women face different problems when they seek out mates, and so they often approach relationships in very different ways. His argument follows (from Buss & Schmitt, 1993, pp. 205–206):

- In virtually all societies, men and women engage in both short-term matings (affairs, one-night stands) and long-term matings (marriages) under certain conditions.
- Both short-term and long-term matings are effective ways to increase one's reproductive potential, but the two strategies have different strengths and weaknesses.
- Sex differences arise because **parental investment** is greater for women than for men. Women must carry the child in pregnancy and usually deal with child care, so their investment in their children is greater. They therefore devote a larger portion of their total mating effort to long-term mating. A father's investment is less than a mother's, plus he faces the problem of *paternity uncertainty*: No man can ever be 100% certain that he is the father of his mate's children. Men therefore "devote a larger portion of their total mating effort to short-term mating than do women."
- To be successful in short-term mating, men must be able to locate a larger number of partners who are sexually accessible and fertile. They must also identify ways to limit their commitment and costs. Women, to be successful in short-term mating, must extract resources from the man, identify short-term mates who may be good long-term mates, and select mates with good-quality genes.
- To be successful in long-term mating, men must solve the problem of paternity uncertainty and identify mates with high reproductive potential. Women must identify men who can and will make parental investments and will provide some protection. Both sexes must extract commitment from their mates, identify possible mates with parenting skills, and select ones with good-quality genes.

Buss and his colleagues have tested many predictions derived from these general principles about short-term and long-term relationships (Buss, 1985, 1987, 1988, 1989; Buss & Barnes, 1986; Buss et al., 1992; DeKay & Buss, 1992). In one study, Buss found that men, on average, reported wanting 18 different partners throughout their lifetime, whereas women wanted only 4 or 5 mates on average. He also found that men's standards for an acceptable short-term partner were lower than women's standards, presumably because they seek multiple part-

parental investment: Behavior of mothers or fathers that increases the well-being of their children at a cost to the mother or father.

of pleasant feelings—warmth, happiness, satisfaction, and sometimes sexual passion. But the fire of sexual passion tends to dwindle to a flickering afterglow over time. Excitement is replaced by routine, tedium, and boredom. A passionate love relationship is a race against time.

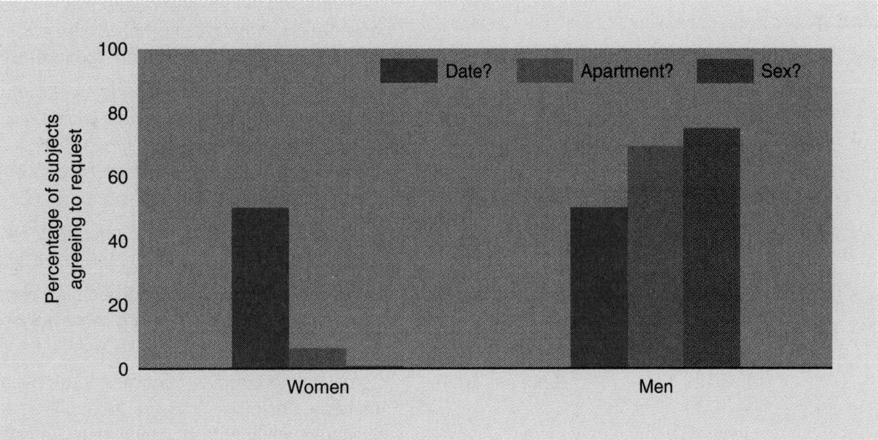

▲ FIGURE 11-10
If someone attractive asked you, "Will you go to bed with me?" what would you say? Researchers had an attractive person ask opposite-sex strangers one of these questions: "Would you go out with me tonight?" "Would you come over to my apartment tonight?" or "Would you go to bed with me tonight?" Men and women didn't differ on the date question, but many more men than women agreed to the sexually suggestive request. (From Clark & Hatfield, 1989)

ners without considering long-term investment (see also Kenrick et al., 1993). Men also value qualities that signal sexual accessibility—such as physical beauty and sex appeal—in short-term partners, but devalue these traits in long-term partners. Women, in contrast, rate a man who is willing to impart immediate resources positively but a promiscuous man negatively when considering him for short-term mating.

Buss also believes that jealousy serves different functions for men and women. Men respond negatively to the suggestion of infidelity because of their paternity uncertainty. Only by monitoring their spouse closely and demanding sexual loyalty can men be certain that their children are their offspring. Women, in contrast, respond negatively to rivals because they threaten the stability of their resources and relationship. Buss and his colleagues asked men and women: "What would upset or distress you more: (a) imagining your mate having sexual intercourse with someone else, or (b) imagining your mate forming a deep emotional attachment to someone else?" Alternative (b) provoked more jealousy for 85% of the women, but alternative (a) provoked more jealousy for 60% of the men (Buss et al., 1992).

Evolutionary psychology's explanation for sex differences in liking and loving is controversial. Some critics argue that evolutionary theory doesn't apply in modern times when men's and women's responsibilities for child-rearing have changed, and modern techniques are available for determining paternity. These arguments, however, ignore the genetic basis for these responses. The modern era is but a blink of the eye in the span of evolution, and any modern alterations have left our genetic tendencies virtually untouched. Neither does the theory assume that instincts are so powerful and undifferentiated that they control our actions in most situations. Rather, evolutionary psychology assumes that our instinctive tendencies emerge only in certain conditions and that their influence on our actions varies greatly across situations (DeKay & Buss, 1992). Nor is evolutionary theory, by necessity, a sexist theory. It suggests that the sexes differ, but it does not assign more benevolent motives to men than it does to women, or vice versa. Both are viewed as biological creatures seeking to improve their genetic destinies. Social exchange theory explains how individuals exchange rewards in their relationships; evolutionary theory explains *why* some qualities are more rewarding than others (Kenrick et al., 1993).

Researchers are only now subjecting the theory to close scrutiny, so its assumptions should be considered only skeptically. The theory is difficult to test experimentally, and too many studies conducted up to this point have relied on self-report methods that ask people to imagine how they would feel if their spouse was unfaithful or who they prefer in short-term and long-term dating situations. If people can't accurately anticipate their instinct-based reactions in such situations, then such methods may not be valid. The approach also raises as many questions as it answers. Why do some men show a preference for long-term matings rather than short-term matings (Gangestad & Simpson, 1990; Simpson & Gangestad, 1992)? Why do some women seek only short-term matings? What impact does the family have on the choice of strategy? Why do some individuals form homosexual relationships? Why do some cultures tolerate infidelity more than others? Time is needed to assess the theory's validity and potential.

▲ **TABLE 11-6**
Summing up: Factors that strengthen companionate love

Factor	*Impact on Companionate Love*
Intimacy	Successful relationships are intimate rather than emotionally neutral, characterized by psychological closeness, mutual caring, trust, and acceptance.
Self-disclosure	Individuals in successful relationships openly share personal, intimate information with one another. Self-disclosure usually becomes more intimate in stages (orientation, exploratory affective, affective, and stable exchange stages).
Attachment style	People with secure attachment styles are more successful in their relationships than avoidant types. Anxious/ambivalent individuals desire relationships, but fear rejection by others. These styles originate in the child's attachment to his or her parents.
Equity	Successful relationships are equitable: Partners' investments are in proportion to the rewards they receive and the costs they incur.
Communal relationships	Some relationships succeed because people no longer track their costs and rewards; rather, they are more concerned with what their partner gets rather than what they receive.
Sex	Some dating couples become more psychologically intimate after sexual intimacy. For other couples, sexual intimacy is an expression of their psychological intimacy. Men are more concerned with sexual intimacy than women, and heterosexual dating couples who are sexually intimate are no more likely to marry than nonintimate couples.

Is this cooling-off process inevitable? Experts aren't certain (Berscheid, 1983; Sternberg, 1987). Some argue that couples can take steps to keep the passion in their relationships; others are pessimistic. Ellen Berscheid, drawing on the two-factor theory of love, points out that passionate love requires arousal. If arousal diminishes, then love, too, must diminish. Moreover, she notes that our physiological makeup is such that we cannot maintain high levels of physiological arousal over long periods of time. "Much as one wishes to hold on to the intensely positive emotions, to retain the euphoric state, there is little that is known about the underlying dynamics of emotion and of its antecedents that suggests this is possible." She concludes that "intense emotion is not maintained—not even intense positive emotion that may be fervently desired, coddled, and encouraged" (1983, p. 158).

Coping with Conflict

No two people are perfectly compatible. Even Molly and Andrew had their differences, and these differences occasionally generated conflict. When Harold H. Kelley and his colleagues asked dating, cohabitating, or married couples to describe sources of disagreement in their relationships, they generated a list that included failure to divide domestic chores, carelessness, nagging, violence, moodiness, passivity, and lack of ambition (see Table 11-7; Kelley, Cunningham, & Stambul, 1973; Kelley, Tiggle, & Peters, 1977; cited in Kelley, 1979, p. 19). Men in heterosexual relationships are particularly bothered by sexual rejection and moodiness, whereas women are upset by men's sexual demands, emotional shallowness, and thoughtlessness (Buss, 1989). Couples, it seems, can manage to fight about just about anything.

Conflicts, if ignored, can destroy the fabric of the relationship. When positive emotions are replaced by negative ones, caring becomes hostility, warmth becomes coldness, and trust becomes jealousy. The relationship remains passionate, but in an aversive, negative sense. People in troubled marriages reveal

TABLE 11-7
What does your partner do that irritates you?

When researchers asked young, heterosexual dating and married couples to air their complaints, they obtained hundreds of responses.

Percentage Mentioning Problem	*Problem*
14.5	Carelessness, sloppiness, impulsivity
11.2	Failure to give appreciation, understanding, affection
9.7	Division and fulfillment of responsibility
9.4	Passivity, lack of confidence, lack of ambition
9.1	Conflicting preferences about leisure time, where and how to live, etc.
7.5	Inadequate and poor communication
6.4	Excessive worry, compulsivity, moodiness
5.5	Influence attempts, nagging, making decisions
4.3	Inappropriate behavior in social situations
4.1	Aggressive behavior and temper
3.7	Attitudes and behavior toward parents
3.5	Interference with partner's study, work, etc.
3.4	Independence, external involvements
3.2	Dependence, possessiveness
3.0	Attitudes and behavior toward friends

Source: From Kelley, 1979.

their negative affect by complaining, criticizing, interrupting, insulting, and disagreeing with each other (Birchler, Weiss, & Vincent, 1975). They also divulge their feelings, but these self-disclosures emphasize negative feelings; "I really care deeply for you" becomes "I don't think I can stand to live with you any longer" (Tolstedt & Stokes, 1984). Even when positive emotions are expressed, their partners rarely respond to them. Instead, they wait for their partners to express a negative emotion, and then reciprocate with an equally negative response. With all this negative affect, it is no wonder that distressed couples get into more arguments than nondistressed couples (Gottman & Levenson, 1992; Levenson & Gottman, 1983, 1985).

Distressed couples also tend to explain their conflicts in ways that worsen the problem. After reviewing nearly two dozen studies of couples' attributional explanations for their problems, Thomas Bradbury and Frank Fincham concluded that happy couples make *relationship-enhancing* attributions. When problems arise, they blame them on external, situational factors. If Andrew criticized Molly, she wouldn't think he was selfish; rather, she would assume he was troubled by his illness or had a hard day at work. Unhappy couples do just the opposite. Their *distress-maintaining* attributions cite internal, stable, and global causes. If distressed, Molly would think that Andrew's behavior was caused by his personal qualities (such as his selfishness). She would also believe that his actions were intentional and that he deserved to be blamed for them. Because of the self-serving attributional bias (discussed in Chapter 4), Andrew would probably dispute these attribution conclusions, adding one more element to an already conflictful situation (Bradbury & Fincham, 1990, 1992; Fincham & Bradbury, 1992, 1993).

People cope with their relationship conflicts in dozens of different ways, but Caryl Rusbult and her colleagues have identified four key tactics that consistently emerge (Rusbult, 1987; Rusbult & Zembrodt, 1983; Rusbult, Zembrodt, & Gunn, 1982, p. 1231):

- *Voice*: discussing problems, compromising, seeking help from a therapist or clergyman, suggesting solutions to problems, asking the partner what is bothering him or her, trying to change oneself or change the partner
- *Loyalty*: waiting and hoping that things will improve, "giving things some time," praying for improvement
- *Neglect*: ignoring the partner or spending less time together, refusing to discuss problems, treating the partner badly emotionally or physically, criticizing the partner for things unrelated to the real problem, "just letting things fall apart," (perhaps) developing extrarelationship sexual involvements
- *Exit*: formally separating, moving out of a joint residence, deciding to "just be friends," getting a divorce

Theoretically, these four tactics differ along two dimensions. Exit and voice are *active* coping responses, whereas neglect and loyalty are *passive* responses (see Figure 11-11). The second dimension is destructive-constructive.

Rusbult finds that people's use of these strategies depends on their commitment to their relationship and on their personality characteristics. People who are, in general, satisfied with their current relationship and remain committed to it use voice and loyalty rather than exit and neglect. People with attractive alternative relationships predictably display exit rather than loyalty (Rusbult et al., 1982). Sex-role orientation and self-esteem, too, are reliably linked to the four different coping methods. Men and women who adopt a masculine sex-role orientation rely more on the negative coping strategies, neglect and exit. Feminine men and women, in contrast, use voice, and if that approach fails, turn to loyalty (Rusbult, Zembrodt, & Iwaniszek, 1986). Also, when people with higher self-esteem use a negative strategy, they usually opt for exit rather than neglect (Rusbult, Morrow, & Johnson, 1987).

Which tactic is best? Rusbult finds that couples who used the negative tactics (neglect and exit) experienced more distress in their relationships. Voice, in contrast, was the best strategy to use in dealing with relatively minor relationship problems (Rusbult, Johnson, & Morrow, 1986).

Competing Relationships

Other people can also threaten the stability of our relationships. When our friends demand much of our time, our close relationship may suffer (Surra, 1985). When a married couple's first baby bursts upon the scene, conflicts multi-

▲ **FIGURE 11-11**
How do people cope with problems in their relationships? By considering whether or not the strategy is constructive or destructive and active or passive, Rusbult identified four methods: exit, voice, loyalty, and neglect. (From Rusbult, Zembrodt, & Gunn, 1982)

	Negative	Positive
Active	Exit: Actively harming the relationship (e.g., breaking up, seriously hurting the partner physically or emotionally)	Voice: Actively attempting to improve conditions (e.g., discussing the problem, proposing solutions, asking others for help or advice)
Passive	Neglect: Passively allowing conditions to deteriorate (e.g., refusing to discuss problems, spending time away from the partner)	Loyalty: Passively but optimistically waiting for conditions to improve (e.g., praying for help, defending the partner in the face of criticism)

ply and satisfactions dwindle (Hackel & Ruble, 1992). The couple's parents can also help or hinder a relationship's success (Felmlee, Sprecher, & Bassin, 1990).

Rivals, however, pose a much greater threat than friends, children, and parents. Each day our partners interact with people who could potentially take our places in our relationships. These contacts may be completely innocent or merely minor flirtations, but others culminate in extrarelationship affairs. Even though American mores condemn infidelity in committed relationships, people are not always to be trusted. Depending on the survey, between 33% and 75% of all married men report having had an extramarital affair. Are women more faithful? No. Between 26% and 70% of all married women admitted they had affairs (Buss & Schmitt, 1993).

Affairs wreak havoc on relationships. When people who are divorcing or breaking up after a long-term relationship are asked the cause of their relationship's dissolution, many point to their partner's (or their own) infidelity (Blumstein & Schwartz, 1983; Buunk & Bringle, 1987). Such affairs become particularly problematic when they are discovered. Adulterous wives, when asked if their affairs caused problems with their marriages, said "no" if the husband didn't know about the tryst. If husbands did know about the affair, 42% said the affair had serious repercussions for their relationship (Kinsey, Pomeroy, & Martin, 1948; Kinsey et al., 1953).

jealousy
A negative emotional experience (fear, resentment, distrust, suspicion) that occurs when an individual's partner is attracted to, or seems to be attracted to, a third person.

Even if our partner is faithful, we may nonetheless experience **jealousy** (White & Mullen, 1990). Jealousy is "the aversive emotional response to a partner's real, imagined, or potential attraction to a third person" (Bringle & Buunk, 1986, p. 226). Jealous people display a range of cognitive, emotional, and behavioral responses that may negatively influence their relationships. They often experience many losses—of self-esteem, of intimacy, and of fairness. Jealous people may wonder whether their limitations drove their partner into the arms of their rival, and worry that their relationship won't survive (Salovey & Rodin, 1985; White & Mullen, 1990). They also experience a range of negative emotions, the principle ones being distrust, fear, uncertainty, and loneliness (Parrott & Smith, 1993).

Satisfaction and Social Exchange

Partners in a relationship grow closer when they provide each other with the rewards they desire. But when the rewards we receive dwindle, and the costly aspects of our relationships escalate, we become dissatisfied. Dissatisfaction, however, doesn't always lead to withdrawal from the relationship. Let's consider Darienne's view of her relationship with Myron. Before they were married, Myron and Darienne spent lots of time together, enjoyed the same kinds of activities, and hardly ever disagreed. But almost from the moment they said, "I do," things started to change. Nights out on the town became rare events, saved for special occasions. Myron's job took up more of his time, and when he came home from work, he rarely did much in the way of household chores. Also, with all the bickering about money, they never seem to be in the mood for sex.

Will Darienne leave Myron? Social exchange theory assumes that the answer depends on Darienne's *satisfaction* with her current relationship, the *value of alternative relationships* (sometimes called the "comparison level for alternatives"), and her *investment* in her current relationship. Darienne's level of satisfaction is low, for the rewards she receives are too few compared with the many costs she must bear. But she may remain in the relationship, however, because the value of alternative relationships may seem low as well. Even if she gets divorced, she may not be able to find anyone better than Myron. And she doesn't like living alone. Also, she may feel that she has already put too much into this relationship to let it go. In a sense, she feels a need to recoup her losses and her *investment* in the current relationship (Kelley, 1983; Thibaut & Kelley, 1959; see Figure 11-12).

Several investigators have found that the course of friendship and romantic relationships depends on these three factors (Berg, 1984; Hays, 1985; Kurdek, 1991, 1993; Rusbult, 1983). Caryl Rusbult, for example, charted changes in these three factors over a one-year period. She began her study by recruiting college students who were just becoming involved in romantic relationships. Then, on each of 12 separate occasions, she asked these men and women to answer a series of questions that tapped perceptions of rewards, costs, satisfaction, alternatives, and investment. When the final measures were collected, she separated the subjects into three categories: *stayers* (those who remained in their relationships), *leavers* (those who terminated their relationships), and the *abandoned* (people whose partners left them). As anticipated, stayers reported increases in rewards, satisfaction, and investment over the leavers and the abandoned. Stayers' costs and alternatives also decreased. Leavers, in contrast, reported small increases in rewards but substantial increases in costs. Satisfaction and investments also declined, and their evaluations of alternative relationships became more positive over time. Rusbult concludes, "No wonder they ended their relationship!"

How did the abandoned subjects compare with these two groups? Many recognized that their relationships were unrewarding, but they had invested so much in them that they couldn't voluntarily withdraw. Their costs increased more rapidly than their rewards, so they were dissatisfied. As their alternatives declined in quality, they invested increasing amounts of emotional capital in the relationship. In fact, their investments matched those of the stayers. As a result, they became trapped in their relationships, even though they were dissatisfied (Rusbult, 1983). Rusbult believes that people who become entrapped in their relationships don't withdraw from them. Instead, they try to improve them (voice), or they just keep hoping things will improve (loyalty) (Rusbult, Zembrodt, & Gunn, 1982).

Love Across a Lifetime

Close relationships are central to everything we value—our families, our health, and even our happiness. When our close relationships are satisfying, we escape the ravages of our impersonal, ever-changing world (Hays & Oxley, 1986). But when our close relationships are disrupted, we experience psychological grief and physical disorder.

Not all relationships can endure the threats summarized in Table 11-8, but some can. With Molly's help, Andrew survived his illness and recovered com-

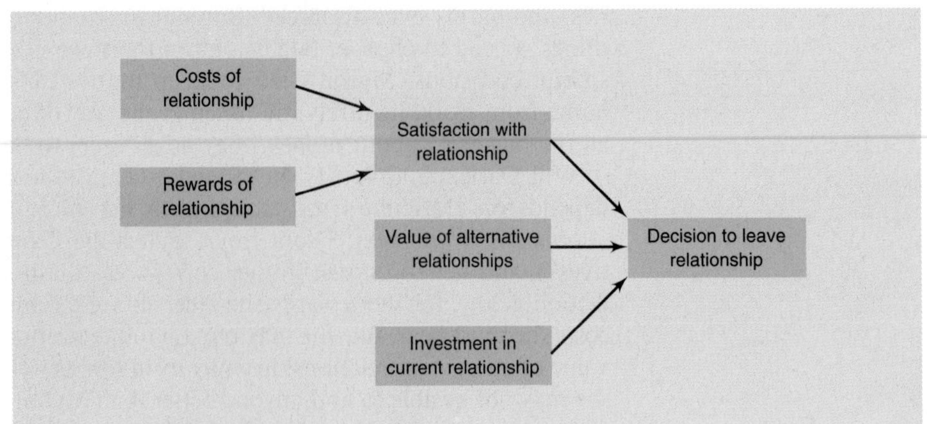

▲ FIGURE 11-12
When will we leave a relationship that isn't satisfying? Social exchange theory argues that the balance between rewards and costs determines our overall satisfaction with a relationship. However, individuals may remain in unsatisfactory relationships if no alternative relationships are available and they feel they have invested too much to withdraw.

▲ TABLE 11-8
Summing up: Factors that contribute to the dissolution of relationships

Factor	Impact on Relationship
Loss of passion	Passionate love is difficult to maintain over long periods of time. When the arousal diminishes, the relationship founders.
Conflict	Disagreements, if left unsettled, can undermine the value of the relationship. Carelessness, failure to give appreciation, disagreements over the division and fulfillment of responsibility, and lack of ambition are frequently mentioned sources of conflict.
Attributions	Distressed couples blame their problems on internal, stable, and global causes (distress-maintaining attributions) rather than on external, situational factors (relationship-enhancing attributions).
Coping strategies	Some conflict strategies are more harmful to the relationship than others (destructive-constructive), and some are more passive than active. *Exit* (ending the relationship), *voice* (actively discussing the problem and its solution), *loyalty* (delaying discussion in the hope that the situation improves), and *neglect* (avoiding the problem while exhibiting hostility in other ways) are four basic conflict-reduction strategies.
Competing relationships	Relationships with other people, including children, parents, friends, and rivals, can create tensions, conflicts, and jealousy.
Social exchange	Relationship longevity depends upon partners' satisfaction (based on rewards and costs), the value of alternative relationships, and the magnitude of one's investments in the relationship. People who experience increased satisfaction and investments remain in the relationship, whereas others leave the relationship or are abandoned.

pletely to teach, write, and love again. Their relationship encountered many obstacles—the loss of passion, conflict, jealousies, and dwindling satisfactions—but they overcame them. Molly Haskell described their love eloquently:

> We are born into the blissful twosome of mother and child, wrenched away, and seek ever after to recapture that early sensation of oneness with another, and of knowing ourselves through the other's eyes. The process of coupling and uncoupling is the dance of life, and Andrew and I, rickety on our feet perhaps, and shorter of breath, were still dancing. For some people it is that way. (1990, p. 302)

Summary

Personal relationships follow a pattern of growth and change. Initially, social and personal factors may prompt us to affiliate with others. Next, we become attracted to individuals who possess characteristics we admire or who are similar to us in some way. In time this attraction may ripen into a long-lasting close relationship involving deep friendship or love. Alternatively, the relationship may end in dissolution.

Joining together with members of our own species is known as *affiliation.* This tendency, which is very pronounced in humans, stems from a number of situational, personal, and biological factors. Schachter's studies illustrate our tendency to seek out other people in order to reduce our uncertainty about social reality and to reduce our fear. Individuals who are first-borns or only children tend to be more affiliative, as are people who are high in n*Affiliation.* Embarrassment, however, reduces the likelihood of affiliation, and people who suffer from *social anxiety* or *shyness* also tend to withdraw from contact with others.

Of all the people you meet, a small number will seem attractive to you. Initial attraction depends on surface-level factors, such as *propinquity* and physical attractiveness. However, similarity and rewards become increasingly important over time. The following tendencies underlie many of our likes and dislikes:

- Proximity and attraction: We like people who live nearby and people we see frequently.
- "What is beautiful is good": We are drawn to people who are physically attractive. This tendency, which may be biologically based, can lead to a self-fulfilling prophecy. Because we assume that attractive people are friendly, we treat them in ways that evoke positive responses.
- *Similarity-attraction effect*: We like people who are similar to us in some way, rather than people who possess qualities that complement our personal needs. *Balance theory* suggests that balanced interpersonal relations create less cognitive discomfort than others.
- *Complementarity*: We sometimes (but very rarely) like people who possess dissimilar qualities that complement ours.
- *Reciprocity principle*: We like people who like us. Disapproval, in contrast, is a powerful punishment, for it almost always leads to disliking. Individuals sometimes avoid relaying negative information to others to avoid provoking rejection (the *MUM effect*). Exceptions include disliked ingratiators, low self-esteem individuals who prefer disapproval, and the greater liking that sometimes occurs when approval is prefaced with disapproval (the *gain-loss hypothesis*).

Social exchange theory explains these findings by arguing that we like people who provide us with the maximum number of valued rewards while exacting minimum costs. Approval is a potent form of social reward, and most of our relationships are consistent with the *minimax principle.*

Close relationships are characterized by strong emotional bonds and endurance over a relatively long period of time. Close relationships can be based on *passionate love, companionate love,* or both. Both forms of love are reflected in the three components of Sternberg's triangle model of love: intimacy, passion, and decision/commitment.

How does love develop? According to the *two-factor theory of love,* passionate love results from an attributional process. When we experience physiological arousal, we search for a cause of our arousal. If we conclude that another person is the cause, then we experience love. This theory explains the *Romeo-and-Juliet effect,* but other processes—such as reinforcement and social facilitation—may also influence passionate love under such circumstances.

Companionate love develops slowly. Through gradual increases in the *intimacy* of our *self-disclosures,* we reveal personal information about ourselves while also demonstrating our trust in each other. Hazan and Shaver's theory of *attachment styles* suggests that secure people can more easily achieve intimacy compared to avoidant and anxious/ambivalent people. People also expect their close relationships to be based on *equity*: They assume that the rewards they receive will be proportional to the costs that are incurred. Some people may not seek equity, however, when they want to enter *communal relationships* characterized more by concern for their partners than themselves. Sexuality, in some cases, also plays a facilitative role in the formation and health of long-term relationships.

Why do close relationships end? Romantic alliances founded on passionate love may expire when the strong emotions that provided the foundation for the relationship cool. Everyday strains and stress can create negative emotional reactions within close relationships, particularly if couples explain these conflicts in distress-maintaining rather than relationship-enhancing ways. People also cope with conflicts in different ways, including leaving the relationship (exit), discussing problems openly (voice), delaying (loyalty), and avoiding the problem but responding negatively in other ways (neglect). Other people, such as friends, parents, and children, can also cause problems for our relationships, although *jealousy* is greatest when we worry that our partners are attracted to other people. If the emotional climate becomes too negative, the relationship may not survive. *Social exchange theory* suggests that three factors influence the longevity of a relationship: the number of rewards and costs received (or satisfaction), the value of alternative relationships, and the magnitude of one's investment in the current relationship. This theory predicts that individuals withdraw from unsatisfying relationships if alternative relationships are available and if their investment in their current relationship is not too great.

For More Information

- *How to Win Friends and Influence People,* by Dale Carnegie (1937), is a useful guide to techniques for getting along well with others. The book is also filled with insightful observations on the basic nature of our interpersonal relationships.
- *Liking, Loving, and Relating,* by Susan and Clyde Hendrick (1992), is a comprehensive overview of virtually all the major topics covered in this chapter.
- *Love and Other Infectious Diseases: A Memoir,* by Molly Haskell (1990), describes Haskell's life as she contemplated losing her husband, Andrew Sarris, to illness. Haskell's descriptions of love and relationships are both poignant and insightful.
- *Love, Sex, and Intimacy,* by Elaine Hatfield and Richard L. Rapson (1993), is a broad summary of recent research on love written by a social psychologist and a historian who happen to be married to each other. In addition to summarizing our current knowledge, the authors also offer a number of practical suggestions on how to deal with problems that arise in close relationships.
- *The Psychology of Affiliation,* by Stanley Schachter (1959), describes the methods he used to document when and why we seek out others. A model of scholarly research.
- *The Psychology of Love,* edited by Robert J. Sternberg and Michael L. Barnes (1988), is a sourcebook of information on the social psychology of long-term relationships. Chapters are written by leading thinkers in the field, including Murstein, Shaver and Hazan, Buss, Sternberg, Hatfield, Brehm, the Dions, Byrne and Murnen, Williams and Barnes, Beach and Tesser, and Berscheid.
- "Sexual Strategies Theory: An Evolutionary Perspective on Human Mating," by David M. Buss and David P. Schmitt (1993) and published in *Psychological Review,* is a masterful theoretical and empirical analysis of the intricacies of relationships—viewed from an evolutionary perspective.
- *Understanding Social Anxiety,* by Mark Leary (1983), takes a social psychological look at the anxiety that is aroused by a feeling that one cannot behave competently in social settings. Leary enumerates the causes and consequences of social anxiety and makes a number of recommendations for overcoming this problem.

Application: Love, Loneliness, and Health

Rare is the person who escapes sickness and accident entirely. The average American contacts his or her physician over five times each year and will require treatment for a medical problem twice a year on average. Illnesses cut productivity in the workplace, for 2.1 million people call in sick to work each month (Garreau, 1993). And the cost of health care is rising steadily. In 1992, Americans spent $838.5 billion on health care, and by 1994 this figure may reach $1 trillion (Jennings, 1993).

What can people do to improve their health? A physician's recommendations typically include eating sensibly, exercising regularly, getting plenty of sleep, and seeing your doctor regularly. This prescription, however, omits one important prerequisite for health—happy, satisfying relationships. People who are married are happier than single people, and they suffer fewer health problems (Burman & Margolin, 1992). Men, in particular, profit from marriage, for husbands outlive bachelors by several years (Wingard, 1982). People who are firmly embedded in a network of friends and families also tend to be healthier than more isolated individuals. Although the benefits of relationships don't emerge in all studies, many find that people with more ties to other people suffer fewer physical (for example, tuberculosis, heart disease) and psychological (for example, depression, anxiety) illnesses. One long-term study asked 7,000 people to describe their social relationships. Nine years later, the researchers found that people who did not have many ties to other people were more likely to have died than people with many ties (Berkman & Syme, 1979). Having a network of friends also helps us return to health more quickly when we are ill. Heart patients, stroke victims, and kidney patients all recovered more rapidly when their friends and loved ones visited them regularly (Wallston et al., 1983).

Why are personal relationships good for our health? In many cases, our friends, family, spouses, and lovers provide us with **social support**: personal actions and resources that help us cope with minor aspects of everyday living, daily hassles, and more significant life crises. Most forms of social support fall into one of the three categories shown in Table 11-9. *Emotional support* includes statements of approval, compliments, and expressions of caring and love. Emotional support also includes a willingness to listen to others' problems without offering criticism or advice. *Informational support* involves providing another person with information that might help her or him in some way and includes directions, advice, and social comparison data. *Tangible assistance* is also helpful, for from time to time people need help with their work, their responsibilities, and their finances (Barrera, 1986; Cutrona, 1986; Dunkel-Schetter et al., 1992; Sarason et al., 1987; Stokes & Wilson, 1984).

Social support is particularly valuable during times of stress. As noted in Chapter 4, stressful life circumstances leave us at risk for psychological and physical illness. Other people, however, often serve as a protective buffer against these negative consequences (Cohen & Wills, 1985). One study of this *buffering hypothesis* found that people who were laid off from work were more likely to retain a positive sense of self-worth if they could share their feelings with their spouse. Individuals who didn't perceive their spouses to be confidants did not maintain their self-esteem (Pearlin et al., 1981). In another study, people who weren't part of a network of social relations often coped with stress by taking drugs. People who were more firmly embedded in a social network didn't (Pakier & Wills, 1990).

Our relationships also protect us from one of the most distressing emotions known to human beings—**loneliness**. As the term is used by social psychologists, loneliness is not just isolation or being alone. Rather, we experience loneliness when our close relationships are too few or too unsatisfying (Peplau & Perlman, 1982). In some cases, loneliness occurs because we feel cut off from our network of friends and acquaintances. If you have ever moved to a new city, or entered a college located far away from your hometown, you may have experienced a period of *social loneliness. Emotional loneliness,* in contrast, occurs when we lack a meaningful, intimate relationship with another person (Russell et al., 1984; Weiss, 1973). Social and emotional loneliness lead to a common core of negative emotions. When we are lonely, we report feelings of desperation (panic, helplessness, hopelessness, vulnerability), boredom (impatience, uneasiness, anger), self-deprecation (feelings of lack of attractiveness, stupidity, shame), and depression (sadness, emptiness, isolation, self-pity) (Rubenstein & Shaver, 1982). Lonely people often feel

- unhappy doing things alone,
- as if nobody really understands them,
- completely alone,
- unable to reach out and communicate with those around them, and
- starved for company.

(These statements are paraphrased from an early version of the Revised UCLA Loneliness Scale; Russell, Peplau, & Cutrona, 1980.)

Both situational and personal factors combine to cause loneliness. On the situational side, loneliness often sets in after the loss of a spouse through divorce or death, a breakup with a lover, or repeated failure to develop an intimate relationship with another person. Personal factors, including attitudes, personality characteristics, and attributional outlook, can also promote the development of loneliness. Lonely people tend to behave passively when they talk to other people, so they have difficulty forming friendships and long-term relationships. Even in innocuous social settings, lonely people don't disclose as much personal information, they pay less attention to their conversation partners, and they display more nonverbal signs of nervousness (Solano, Batten, & Parish, 1982; Spitzberg & Hurt, 1987). Loneliness and shyness also go hand in hand, for people who feel that they lack the social skills needed to interact effectively with other people often avoid social contacts (Jones, Carpenter, & Quintana, 1985). Loneliness is also linked to the attribu-

social support: Emotional support, advice, guidance, and tangible assistance provided by other individuals.

loneliness: Feelings of desperation, boredom, self-deprecation, and depression experienced when individuals feel their personal relationships are too few or too unsatisfying.

▲ **TABLE 11-9**
Three forms of social support

Type of Support	*Examples*
Emotional support	Expressing your concern for the person's well-being Listening to the person Agreeing with the person Taking the person's side Admiring the person's personal attributes
Informational support	Suggesting solutions to a problem Demonstrating a way to perform a task Explaining how you cope in similar situations Offering helpful advice Providing useful information
Tangible assistance	Doing small favors for the person Lending the person money Helping the person with some of their tasks Giving the person gifts, presents

tions that people make about the cause of their relationship difficulties. People who blame internal, stable factors that cannot be controlled—such as basic personality traits or personal faults—are more likely to become lonely (Cutrona, 1982; Solano, 1987).

Loneliness is not some trifling problem that bothers only a few people. Loneliness is so commonly reported by individuals suffering from psychological problems that it has been called the "common cold of psychopathology" (W. H. Jones, quoted in Meer, 1985, p. 33). Loneliness may not directly cause dysfunction, but it tends to be present whenever people suffer from depression, anxiety, personality disorders, and interpersonal hostility (Jones & Carver, 1991). Prolonged periods of loneliness have been linked to such physical illnesses as cirrhosis of the liver (brought on by alcohol abuse), hypertension, heart disease, and leukemia (Hojat & Vogel, 1987). Loneliness may also attack the immune system. Individuals who are extremely lonely display elevated levels of Epstein-Barr virus and reduced levels of B lymphocytes. Both of these physical characteristics are associated with reductions in immunity and increased vulnerability to mononucleosis (Kiecolt-Glaser, Ricker, et al., 1984; Kiecolt-Glaser, Speicher, et al., 1984).

Other people shelter us from feelings of loneliness. Indeed, a poll taken in two U.S. cities indicated that people who had many connections to other people felt less lonely than people who had fewer ties (Rubenstein & Shaver, 1982). College students who eat dinner or spend weekend evenings with other people rather than alone describe themselves as less lonely (Russell et al., 1980), as do people who are satisfied with their friendships (Schmidt & Sermat, 1983). Loneliness can also be combatted by taking part in community groups, joining clubs, or by seeking therapy and counseling (Evans & Dingus, 1987; Rook, 1984; Stokes, 1985). Other ways of coping with loneliness include the following (Rook & Peplau, 1982):

- Try to increase the number of your social contacts by making an effort to talk to people in your classes or next-door neighbors, joining social organizations, or volunteering to help an acquaintance.
- Perform an activity that takes your mind off your troubles, such as going to a movie, exercising, reading a book, writing a letter.
- Remind yourself that the cure for your loneliness may not be the restoration of the loss that caused it. Rather than insist that you need a new romantic relationship to replace a terminated one, for instance, you might try to increase your circle of friends.
- Clearly enumerate all the positive, rewarding relationships you have with other people.
- Keep a diary. Studies suggest that just writing about stressful life events is therapeutic (Pennebaker, 1990). Students who wrote about their thoughts and feelings upon entering college made fewer visits to the infirmary than students who didn't keep a journal. The students who wrote down their thoughts did experience more homesickness initially, but by the year's end they were less homesick and their grades had improved (Pennebaker, Colder, & Sharp, 1990).

The problem of loneliness underscores, once again, the importance of other people in our lives. As social animals, we depend on other people for the satisfaction of many of our most basic psychological and informational needs. If these needs go unmet because we have no friends or loved ones, then we experience negative emotional, psychological, and physical consequences. Studies of loneliness also underscore our resilience. Even though we may turn to helping professionals for solutions to our problems, in most cases we can use our own personal and interpersonal resources to deal with the problem. Difficulties with our relationships are the culprits that cause our loneliness, yet our relationships also offer the cure.

TRUCK
CAFE

TWELVE

Helping

Journey back through time to an early morning in March of 1987. Mana Mashoon, a 41-year-old nutritionist, is sleeping alone in the bedroom of her apartment in New York City. Watch as Jose Figueroa, the building superintendent, uses his pass key to open the door to her apartment. Figueroa is carrying a knife. He walks down the dark hallway to Mashoon's bedroom. He pins her down, presses the blade of the knife against her throat, and orders her to lie still. Mashoon, though, struggles against him, and screams out for help.

On the floor below, Timothy Mosher is still awake. An aspiring writer, he drives a cab part-time until he can get a job in his field. He hears a thumping sound and then a woman's scream. He immediately runs into the hallway and up the stairs to the next floor. He sees no one and wonders if maybe he imagined the noise. But then he sees Mashoon's apartment door is ajar. He goes in. At the end of the hall stands the building superintendent, Figueroa, with a woman. Mosher recognizes her as one of the tenants, but he doesn't know her name. She is covered with blood.

"What's going on here?" demands Mosher.

"Someone stabbed her," answers Figueroa, who is holding Mashoon tightly by her arm.

When Mosher says, "Let her go!" she breaks free and runs out of the apartment. Figueroa then attacks Mosher, stabbing him once in the chest with the knife. Mosher, though, doesn't give up. He pulls the knife from his chest and throws it into the living room. Figueroa then runs from the apartment. Mosher finds Mashoon: She is banging on the doors of other apartments pleading for help, but no one lets her in. Mosher leads Mashoon down to his apartment and they dial 911. Their wounds are serious, but not fatal; they recover after a week's stay in New York Hospital. Figueroa is arrested and convicted of assault and attempted rape (Hunt, 1990, pp. 129–131).

Mosher's behavior, although exemplary, is perplexing. It seems almost unnatural to sacrifice ourselves for someone we hardly know. Such acts run "counter to the primal urge to do whatever increases one's chance of staying alive and to avoid doing whatever has the opposite effect" (Hunt, 1990, p. 12). Social psychologists have taken up the challenge of understanding these baffling behaviors, and this chapter examines the insights these researches offer.

We begin with an almost philosophical query about people in general: Are we prosocial creatures who help one another, or are we more often callous and cruel to other people? We then turn to the question "Why?" Why did Mosher help Mashoon, and why did so many others refuse even to open their doors to her? A glib answer, such as "Mosher was a good Samaritan" or "People who live in big cities are unfriendly" is not enough. To predict when people will help and when they will fail to help, we must take into account both the nature of the situation and the characteristics of the people caught up in that situation. Emergencies are complex social phenomena; they take place in real places and involve flesh-and-blood bystanders and victims. If we ignore either the people involved or the situation itself, our analysis will be incomplete.

What Is Prosocial Behavior?

Aristotle commented, "Everyone thinks chiefly of his own, hardly ever of the public interest." Sigmund Freud believed that humans are a rather base lot, warlike and destructive rather than "gentle, friendly creatures wishing for love" (Freud, 1930/1961). And B. F. Skinner (1971) argued that our actions are fueled by reinforcers, not by benevolent motives. But they never met Timothy Mosher. He risked his life to save another person, a person he didn't even know. Aren't we, in fact, a species capable of *both* cruelty and caring?

The Commonness of Kindness

On your way to work you give all your change to a Salvation Army Santa Claus. When a friend loses her confidence after she fails a statistics quiz, you offer words of comfort and encouragement. You don't agree with your company's decision to add a new line of products, but you do all you can to make the new venture a success. When an acquaintance in class asks to borrow your notes, you obligingly turn them over to him.

prosocial behavior
Actions that benefit other people, such as helping, cooperation, and common courtesy.

These are all examples of **prosocial behavior**. Perhaps you wanted to use your change to buy a Coke, you don't like dealing with emotional problems, other projects require your attention, or you yourself need your notes for studying. Nevertheless, you still put the other person's needs before your own. When you perform prosocial behaviors, the interests of others are as important to you as your own. Prosocial behaviors thus contrast sharply with aggression, rape, war, and violence—the kinds of **antisocial behavior** discussed in the next chapter. Prosocial actions benefit others; antisocial actions injure them.

antisocial behavior
Actions that harm other people, such as aggression, violence, and rudeness.

Many types of behaviors are prosocial: Cooperating with co-workers, sympathizing with a friend whose loved one has died, giving advice to a new employee, and even common courtesy qualify as prosocial actions. This chapter, however, concentrates on **helping behavior**. When we help other people, we use our own personal energies and resources to remedy another person's problems. In some situations, helping is a matter of life or death. Lives will be lost unless others offer assistance. We also render aid to others, however, in less serious situations. Students who volunteer to visit the elderly in nursing homes, a driver who picks up a hitchhiker, and the shopper who helps the lost child find his or her mother are all helping. Helping can also be spontaneous—for example, you suddenly decide to stop and help a motorist who has a flat tire—or it can be planned in advance. Benefits, such as concerts to help flood victims in the Midwest, and charity drives are organized forms of helping others. As Table 12-1 indicates, helping can take the form of giving something you have to others (for example, donating your time, your money, or your blood) or performing an action that has positive consequences for others (Amato, 1990; Pearce & Amato, 1980; see also McGuire, 1994). All of these responses qualify as *helping behavior* because they each benefit another person.

helping behavior
Giving assistance to another person.

Altruism is perhaps the most dramatic form of prosocial behavior. Altruists, like the good Samaritan in the *Bible,* help others for one reason and one reason only—the other person needs help.

altruism
Helpful behaviors that are motivated solely by the other person's need rather than the desire for personal gain; also the motive underlying self-sacrificing actions.

▲ **TABLE 12-1**
Helping other people takes many different forms.

Some situations are very serious, whereas others pose less of a threat to people and property. Helping can also be spontaneous or planned, and it can involve active assistance or donating one's time and money.

Distinction	*Yes*	*No*
Is the problem serious?	*Serious problem*: helping to save a town threatened by floods, assisting victims of an automobile accident, preventing an assault	*Nonserious problem*: giving change for a phone call, mailing a letter for a friend, handing back tests for the teacher
Were responses to the problem planned or unplanned?	*Planned helping*: canvassing for charity, staffing a hotline, chaperoning delinquents on a trip to the zoo	*Spontaneous helping*: rescuing a child from a fire, giving CPR to a heart attack victim
Did helping involve doing rather than giving?	*Doing*: rescuing a Jew during the Holocaust, picking up dropped packages, turning off the lights of a parked car	*Giving*: donating bone marrow, giving money to a panhandler, contributing to a religious group

Source: From Pearce & Amato, 1980.

> A certain man went down from Jerusalem to Jericho, and fell among thieves, which stripped him of his raiment, and wounded him, and departed, leaving him half dead. And by chance there came down a certain priest that way: and when he saw him, he passed by on the other side. And likewise a Levite, when he was at the place, came and looked on him, and passed by on the other side. But a certain Samaritan, as he journeyed, came where he was: and when he saw him, he had compassion on him, and went to him, and bound up his wounds . . . and took care of him. (Luke 10:30–34)

Altruistic behaviors are motivated solely by the other person's need. They are completely unselfish, for the doer expects no reward of any kind for rendering aid (Romer, Gruder, & Lizzardo, 1986; Swap, 1991).

Altruists even help when intervention is dangerous. Mosher was stabbed in the chest when he stopped Figueroa's deadly attack. Fifty-nine U.S. soldiers died during the Vietnam War when they saved others by throwing themselves on exploding hand grenades and booby traps (Blake, 1978). Thousands of people worked to hide Jews from the invading Nazi forces during World War II, and many of them were killed when the Nazis discovered their rescue efforts (Oliner & Oliner, 1988). The Carnegie Hero Fund Commission has recognized over 7,000 people who risked grave danger to save others' lives. Winners of the award include David S. Bradford, who died trying to save a friend who was drowning; Everett W. Snow, who was severely injured when he pulled a woman from a burning car; and Carl W. Edwards, Jr., who was repeatedly stabbed when he prevented the mugging of an elderly man ("Carnegie Fund," 1984).

Prosocial behaviors—and altruism in particular—raise some thorny conceptual problems. Before we can call people *altruistic,* we must know their motivations. Good Samaritans seem only to want to help a needy person, but they may secretly hope that they will be rewarded for their efforts. If they are motivated by hope of reward, then they are not altruists. And what if good Samaritans take great pleasure in helping other people? If they help others to gain personal pleasure, then they are no longer acting altruistically. Good Samaritans may also help because they know that they will be racked by guilt if they don't, or they may intervene only because their religious code insists that they help. If their actions are motivated by external concerns or personal desires, instead of the other person's need, they may be helpful, but they aren't truly altruistic.

We return to the complexities inherent in the concept of altruism later in the chapter. Most social psychologists, however, avoid these conceptual difficulties by focusing on *helping behavior* per se, regardless of the helper's reasons for helping. After all, even when helpers are motivated by greed or by some other selfish intention, at least help has been given. So what if Mosher wanted to be on television or earn a medal for helping? He helped, and Mashoon's life was saved (see Bar-Tal, 1976; Gelfand & Hartmann, 1982; Rushton & Sorrentino, 1981; Staub, 1978).

Why Do People Help Other People?

Even though our interactions with others sometimes take an antisocial turn, we are more prosocial than antisocial. During their day-to-day interactions, people constantly act in ways that further others' interests as well as their own. As Émile Durkheim (1951) noted, social life wouldn't be possible if people didn't give up their own individual needs and desires for the sake of collective peace and harmony.

Why do we help other people who are in need? This chapter answers this question in five different ways. The first explanation draws on *evolutionary psychology,* for it suggests that Mosher responded instinctively when he realized that Mashoon needed help. This approach argues that, as social creatures, human beings are genetically ready to help others rather than hurt them. The second explanation, an *individual-differences approach,* focuses on the characteristics of the particular people in the situation. Did Mosher have personality characteristics that prompted him to help people rather than ignore their suffering? The third explanation, a *decisional analysis,* focuses on the sequence of decisions that Mosher must have made before he left the safety of his apartment. How did he decide that an emergency was taking place or that he was responsible for helping? The fourth approach, a *motivational perspective,* looks closely at Mosher's emotions and motivations. How did he feel when he heard the scream, and what motivated him to rush to Mashoon's side? The final approach, a *nor-*

▲ Helping comes in many forms. Situations like the out-of-control brush fire are serious emergencies, and by intervening, the helpers risk grave injury. Other situations aren't dangerous for the helper, but they require investment of time, energy, and money. People participating in a walkathon to raise money for charity face no great danger, yet they invest their own energies and resources so others will be helped. Still other forms of helping, such as acts of common courtesy, aren't costly at all, yet they are often very much appreciated by the receiver.

mative model, points out that social norms can prompt us to respond to others who are in need. All five of these approaches indicate that whenever people need help and give help, they become part of a complex web of interpersonal processes. As social psychologists, we must dissect this complex web and ferret out the interpersonal processes that sustain and inhibit helping.

The Evolution of Altruism

Mosher himself wasn't sure why he helped Mashoon. He explained that he heard a noise and responded as if by instinct: "I don't cast myself in the role of a hero. I didn't give much thought to doing what I did; it was a situational thing, it was just something that had to be done" (Hunt, 1990, p. 131). Could it be that nature has built into each human being an instinct to help—to intervene when other members of our species face danger?

The Instinctive Roots of Helping

Evolutionists have long been puzzled by altruistic actions. Ground squirrels often give alarm calls at the approach of a predator. These calls warn other squirrels to take cover, but they also draw attention to the caller, who is then likely to be killed (Sherman, 1980). Dolphins sometimes stay near an injured dolphin and will risk their own safety to protect the injured one from a predator (Conner & Norris, 1982). Zebra stallions will attempt to defend colts against attack, even by lions (West Eberhard, 1975). According to Charles Darwin's theory of evolution, these actions make no sense. Because altruists expose themselves to greater danger than those who selfishly protect themselves, helping is a disadvantage to personal survival. More individuals who lean toward altruism should die than nonaltruists, so their altruistic tendencies cannot be passed on to the next generation. Natural selection should weigh against altruists and favor the selfish individuals who refuse to render aid. So why do animals sometimes engage in altruistic behavior?

The geneticist William D. Hamilton provided one piece of the puzzle in 1964. Hamilton pointed out that the organism's fundamental goal is not mere survival or even the survival of its offspring. Rather, the fittest individual is the one that succeeds in passing the maximum number of *genes* on to the next generation. Why, for example, do animals go to all the trouble of breeding and raising offspring? Because having children is an extremely effective means of ensuring the survival of one's genes in a future generation. Caring for offspring may seem self-sacrificing, but these actions are prompted by the gene's selfish tendency to seek survival at all costs. Even if the parent perishes protecting its young, the parent's genes will continue to flourish in its offspring. To Darwin, the fittest animal is the one that can survive longest. To Hamilton, the fittest animal is the one that maximizes the survival of its genes in future generations. This redefined concept of fitness is known as **inclusive fitness** (Hamilton, 1964).

inclusive fitness
A species member's ability to ensure the survival of its genes in future generations.

Parenting, however, is not the only way to enhance the survival of one's genes. Because copies of one's genes exist in one's relatives, Hamilton reasoned that a truly selfish gene can further enhance its fitness by helping relatives survive. Ground squirrels tend to give warning calls only when their close relatives are nearby. A dominant macaque monkey will share food with a subordinate monkey only if the two are close relatives. In many species of insects, workers and soldiers labor to protect the egg-laying queen, but they themselves never produce offspring. Individuals who help close relatives may be risking their lives, but they are also increasing the chances that their genes will survive in their relatives. This process is known as **kin selection**—the

kin selection
A form of natural selection that favors genes because of their effect in improving the reproductive success of one's relatives.

evolutionary favoring of genes that prompt individuals to help their relatives, or kin (Maynard Smith, 1964).

The concept of kin selection explains why relatives help one another, but it does not account for the good Samaritan—the Timothy Mosher who helps a total stranger. Evolutionary theory may still apply, however. Imagine that you are standing on a pier when you hear a drowning man call for help. Would you try to save the man by throwing him a life preserver? Kin selection theory says no, for he is not a relative. Sociobiologist Robert Trivers (1985), however, predicts that you might help if you think you will receive a benefit in return. The risk to you in this situation is minimal—you can save the man without harm to yourself. More important, you may benefit in some way through your action. At least, should you need help in the future when this man is nearby, he will be alive to help you. The concept of **reciprocal altruism** argues that we help others because they might help us in return (see Figure 12-1). Sociobiologists believe that reciprocal altruism is most common in social, gregarious species, for only animals that live in groups will have the opportunity to benefit from reciprocal helping (Barash, 1982).

reciprocal altruism
Helping another person so the helped individual can help in return.

Testing the Evolutionary Argument

Evolutionary psychology's emphasis on the successful projection of genes into future generations seems to apply only to ancient human societies that struggled to survive. Nowadays, if we help a stranger on the street corner, he or she will rarely be nearby when we ourselves require help. Remember, though, that the current era represents a mere instant in the span of evolution. Our world has changed rapidly in the last 200 years, but genetically we are still hunters and gatherers, living in small groups and striving to improve our chances of survival. Instinctively, we still assume that the people who live near us or look like us are kin and that they are likely to remain close by so they can help us in the future (Rushton, 1989). Evolutionary psychology also explains two intriguing aspects of altruism: Children respond sympathetically to others' distress early in their lives and helpfulness seems to run in families.

Baby altruists. Until recently, most experts believed that babies were interested only in their own satisfactions; they ate when they were hungry, slept when they were tired, and cried out when they were uncomfortable, without paying any attention to the people around them. But when developmental

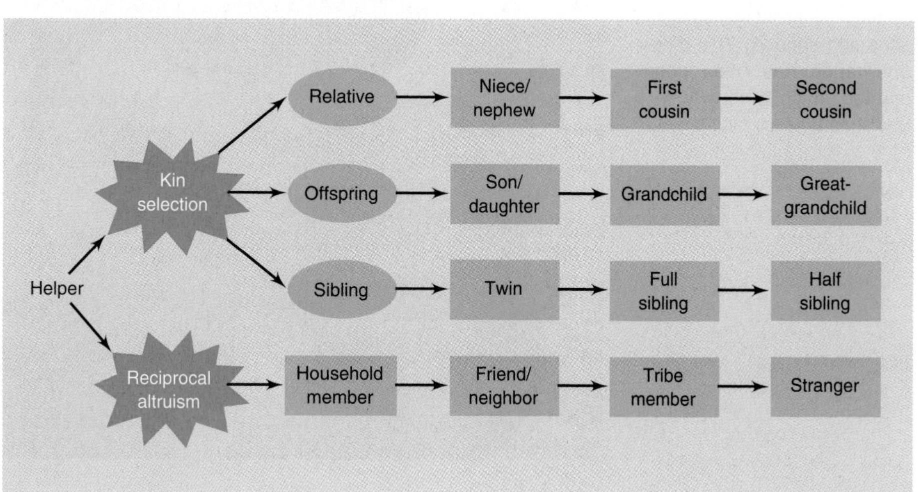

▲ **FIGURE 12-1**
Whom do we help? Evolutionary psychologists believe that *Homo sapiens* help one another for two basic reasons: (a) by helping relatives, we protect the genes we share (kin selection); and (b) helping those who aren't related to us increases the chances that they will help us when we are in distress (reciprocal altruism). Helping therefore becomes more likely when (a) those in distress are closely related to us genetically and (b) they are likely to reciprocate our help in the future.

psychologists took a closer look at babies, they noted that even very small children become upset when they see that other people are distressed (Eisenberg, 1992). When a baby hears another baby crying, he or she will often take up the call (Hoffman, 1981; Martin & Clark, 1987). Many of the 6-month-old babies in one study moved toward and tried to touch a peer who was distressed (Hays, Nash, & Pedersen, 1981). And by the time they are only a year old, some babies actively help other babies and adults. One 18-month-old girl tried to comfort a crying baby by offering him cookies, stroking his hair, and bringing him toys. An 11-month-old boy rose up to defend his mother when she made a choking sound while her physician examined her throat. A 13-month-old girl, seeing her mother's friend crying, offered the woman her favorite doll (Dunn, 1988; Radke-Yarrow, Zahn-Waxler, & King, 1979).

Older children are much more helpful than younger children. As they grow older they learn, often by direct instruction from their parents, to share their toys, to offer assistance to other children, and to weigh the consequences of their actions for themselves and for other people (Eisenberg, 1992). These changes, however, seem to build on a very basic *empathic-distress response* that is present at birth (Hoffman, 1981). As the evolutionary psychologists argue, we seem to be instinctively ready to respond to others who are in distress (Eisenberg & Fabes, 1991; Eisenberg & Miller, 1987).

Twins and helping. J. Philippe Rushton and his colleagues used a classic twin-study design to investigate the genetic bases of altruism (Rushton, 1989; Rushton et al., 1986). The logic of a twin study is quite compelling. Twins come in two varieties. Identical twins, or monozygotic (MZ) twins, result when a fertilized zygote splits in two. MZ twins are genetically identical to one another. Fraternal twins, or dizygotic twins (DZ), result when two zygotes are fertilized. DZ twins share the same amount of genetic material as any other siblings—about 50%, on average. In twin studies, researchers compare each twin with his or her other twin and then calculate their similarities and differences. If MZ twins differ from each other, then the characteristic probably isn't inherited. If, however, the twins are more similar to each other than DZ twins

▲ Children seem capable of caring acts of kindness. When they see their friends or parents in distress, they often try to help by providing reassurance and support. This caring orientation has been documented in children who are less than 2 years old.

▲ **TABLE 12-2**
Summing up: Evolutionary mechanisms that sustain helping behavior in humans

Concept	*Definition*	*Example*
Inclusive fitness	The likelihood that the individual's genes will survive in future generations	Caring for offspring requires considerable investment of personal resources, but parenting increases the survival of genetic material carried by the children.
Kin selection	The evolutionary favoring of individuals who help genetically similar individuals (kin)	An individual will be more likely to help his or her siblings when they are in danger rather than a cousin or other distant relative.
Reciprocal altruism	The evolutionary favoring of individuals who help individuals, who are likely to return the help in the future	Individuals are more likely to help their neighbors and close friends rather than strangers or friends who have moved away.
Empathic distress response	The inborn tendency to experience discomfort in response to another's distress	A news telecast featuring interviews with anguished flood victims generates distress in viewers.

are, then the similarities *might* be produced by their genetic similarity. (Other factors—particularly similarities in how the two twins were raised—can't be completely eliminated as potential causes).

Rushton and his colleagues had MZ twins and DZ twins complete a number of personality measures, including a self-report measure of helping behavior that included such items as the following (Rushton, Chrisjohn, & Fekken, 1981):

- I have helped push a stranger's car out of the snow.
- I have given directions to a stranger.
- I have made change for a stranger.
- I have given money to a charity.
- I have donated goods or clothes to a charity.
- I have done volunteer work for a charity.
- I have donated blood.
- I have delayed an elevator and held the door open for a stranger.

As evolutionary theory would predict, the MZ twins' scores were more highly correlated, on average, than the DZ twins' scores. Based on their findings, Rushton concluded that about 56% of the variability in helping is due to genetics, and the rest can be attributed to the environment and measurement error.

Do We Help Instinctively?

Are we, by nature, a helpful species? Many social psychologists dispute the evolutionists' assumptions summarized in Table 12-2. Instincts, they argue, are usually overwhelmed by the force of the social situation and by the things that the person has learned about helping in the past. The remarkable helpfulness of infants and Rushton's study of twins, however, suggest that helping may have an instinctive basis. Indeed, the evolutionary view offers a surprisingly positive view of human nature. Granted, our helpfulness is selfish at its root, for it results from natural selection's tendency to favor helping genes over nonhelping genes. We are, however, natural helpers (Cunningham, 1981; Hoffman, 1981; Ridley & Dawkins, 1980).

▲▲▲▲▲▲▲▲▲▲▲▲▲▲

People Who Give and Get Help

Dozens of people heard Mashoon cry out, but only one—Timothy Mosher—intervened. Why did Mosher help when others didn't? Was he a physically powerful man, the type who is quick to fight to settle an argument? When he was young, did his parents teach him the importance of helping others? Did the long nights driving a cab in New York City leave him so street savvy that he knew something was very wrong when he heard the thump in the apartment upstairs? Doesn't helping behavior depend on who is watching and who needs help?

The Altruistic Personality

In 1928, Hugh Hartshorne and Mark May reported some surprising inconsistencies among personality traits and prosocial behavior. They developed 33 tests to measure positive social behaviors—including helping, honesty, and resistance to temptation—and administered these tests to hundreds of children. Across these various tests, some children helped more consistently than others, but the average correlation among the various types of helping was only +.23. The child who agreed to share money with classmates was only slightly more likely to also work for the Red Cross or to send letters to hospitalized children. In explanation, Hartshorne and May offered the so-called *doctrine of specificity*: Prosocial behavior, such as honesty and helping, is situationally specific. The person who helps in one setting may walk away in another.

Subsequent studies of altruists often reaffirmed Hartshorne and May's doctrine of specificity; when individuals were observed in several different kinds of helping situations, they behaved inconsistently, sometimes helping, sometimes not (Gergen, Gergen, & Meter, 1972). Furthermore, when researchers correlated helping with many different personality traits (including authoritarianism, moral development, Machiavellianism, alienation, autonomy, and trustworthiness), the correlations were usually rather paltry; they averaged out to about .30 (Rushton, 1980).

Rushton (1981), however, believes that "there is a 'trait' of altruism. Some people are consistently more generous, helping, and kind than others" (p. 66). He notes that when multiple measures of personality are taken, the correlation between personality and helping rises markedly. If several aspects of personality are measured (such as values, moral development, and social responsibility), and these various measures are then combined to form an overall composite, the correlation between the composite score and helping ranges from .40 to .50 (Staub, 1974). Altruistic individuals tend to be empathic people; they have the ability to see situations from other people's perspectives (Archer, 1984; Underwood & Moore, 1982). Helpers also tend to be more deeply committed to personal moral standards and values than nonhelpers (Fogelman & Wiener, 1985; Staub, 1978). They are more likely to adopt an ethic of caring that stresses compassion for other people, and they also tend to be idealistic rather than pragmatic (Ford & Lowery, 1986; Gilligan, 1982; Waterman, 1988). Individuals who are self-confident also help more, as do those who are less concerned about their own personal safety (Aronoff & Wilson, 1985).

Interviews with altruists—people who rescued Jews in Nazi Germany during World War II, civil rights workers who participated in the freedom rides of the 1960s, and volunteers in community mental health centers—also suggest that helpers share certain qualities, including a sense of social responsibility, inner-directedness, self-control, flexibility, self-acceptance, empathy, independence, and strong moral values (London, 1970; Oliner & Oliner, 1988; Rosenhan, 1970). Samuel and Pearl Oliner (1988) located hundreds of people who rescued Jews from the German Nazis during the Holocaust. The Oliners then interviewed these individuals extensively and compared the interviewees' responses to a sample of people who had lived near the rescuers but hadn't helped the Jews escape. The Oliners discovered that the two groups differed little in religiousness, self-esteem, integration into the community, adventurousness, or even their opinions about Hitler and Nazism. But rescuers were more caring than nonrescuers; 76% mentioned the importance of compassion, giving, and concern for others. They were also empathic people who were moved by others' pain. They often said such things as, "I can't feel good if others around me feel sad," "Seeing people cry upsets me," and "I get very upset when I see an animal in pain" (Oliner & Oliner, 1988, p. 174). Also, rescuers were more often raised by parents who avoided the use of punishment and tried to explain to their children the importance of being good to others. These lessons must have been well learned. The Oliners found that the people who rescued the Jews were still helping others some 40 years later. Compared to the nonrescuers, the rescuers were more likely to report visiting the elderly, counseling other people, involvement in children's programs, and helping raise money for charity.

Thus personality is linked to helping. But as the concept of interactionism introduced in Chapter 1 suggests, personality characteristics interact with situational factors to produce helping or failures to help. People who empathize with others are often more helpful, but if they find that they can avoid watching the victim suffer, then the relationship between personality and helping disappears (Batson, Bolen, et al., 1986). Individuals who are usually helpful may not respond to a person in need if that person's suffering is unevocative (Carlo et al., 1991). People who are high in self-monitoring are more likely to volunteer to help blind students, but only if the helpers think helping is a socially rewarding experience (White & Gerstein, 1987). Helping behaviors, like so many other social actions, are best understood in terms of an interaction between the person and situation (Krebs & Miller, 1985).

Men, Women, and Helping

In legend, fiction, and real-life emergencies, men help more than women do. Women are less likely to stop to aid a stranded motorist (Bryan & Test, 1967; Pomazal & Clore, 1973; West, Whitney, & Schnedler, 1975), less likely to give a dime to a stranger (Kleinke, 1977), less likely to relay a telephone message for someone who has dialed the wrong number from a pay phone (Gaertner & Bickman, 1971), and more likely to ignore a victim who collapses on the subway (Piliavin, Rodin, & Piliavin, 1969). Women, however, are more helpful than men in nonemergency, everyday situations. As the section "Application: Love, Loneliness, and Health" in Chapter 11 recognizes, we constantly help our loved ones and acquaintances in a variety of ways. These everyday forms of helping include emotional sustenance, advice, favors, and reassuring feedback about our worth. And who is more likely to provide us with the social support we need? Women (Eagly & Crowley, 1986).

These sex differences may be due in part to the greater risks intervention in emergencies poses for a woman—she is more likely than a man to be attacked if she stops to aid a stranger in distress. However, sex-role socialization also influences people's reactions to emergencies and other helping situations. Some women may feel they lack the skills to help when an emergency arises. Men, in contrast, may be reluctant to provide emotional disclosures or provide reassurance. Intervention in emergencies may also be viewed as a masculine prerogative. The masculine sex role traditionally emphasizes bravery, and the feminine sex role traditionally emphasizes caring for others. Hence, women who are relatively feminine in their sex-role orientation help in emergencies less often than women who adopt some aspects of the masculine sex role—particularly a sense of personal responsibility and competence (Senneker & Hendrick, 1983; Siem & Spence, 1986). Masculine men are usually more helpful than less masculine men, provided they feel they have the skills needed to deal with the problem. When masculine men are excessively concerned with maintaining a competent social image, they sometimes assume that no help is needed to avoid embarrassment (Tice & Baumeister, 1985).

The Unresponsive Urbanite

Mosher was a New Yorker, a veteran of big-city living. But Mosher doesn't quite fit the stereotype of the apathetic urbanite because he helped. We expect people who live in big cities—who cope with the stresses of overcrowding, noise, and confusion—to become blasé or indifferent to the needs of strangers. We assume they won't help (Korte, 1978; Milgram, 1970).

Is there any truth to the stereotype of the unresponsive urbanite? Social psychologists have used a variety of field methods to examine this question. Showing considerable creativity, investigators typically stage a minor accident or make a small request of passersby in both cities and towns, and then compare the amount of helping they experienced in both environments (see Table 12-3). Stanley Milgram, for example, used the wrong-number technique to call subjects in Chicago, New York City, and Philadelphia and subjects in small towns outside these cities. In most cases, the small town residents were more helpful than the city dwellers (Milgram, 1970). When researchers dropped stamped postcards in small towns around Boston and in Boston proper, more of the postcards dropped in small towns were mailed (70% versus 61%; Korte & Kerr, 1975). When researchers deliberately overpaid clerks for small purchases, only 55% of the clerks in cities corrected the mistake, but 80% in smaller towns did so (see Korte, 1978, 1981, for a review).

Paul R. Amato (1983) studied 55 randomly selected Australian communities with populations that ranged from fewer than 1,000 to more than 3 million (Sydney). In addition, he measured six types of helping: (1) reactions to a serious emergency (Amato, wearing a bloody bandage on his leg, would fall to his knees with a cry of pain in front of an approaching passerby); (2) responses to the question "What is your favorite color?" (3) assistance given to a stranger who dropped a stack of envelopes on the ground; (4) donations to the Multiple Sclerosis Society; (5) corrections of wrong directions (see Table 12-3); and (6) refusal to participate in a compulsory census. Even after he controlled for other situational variables—such as the homogeneity of the community, residential stability, and the number of strangers (tourists) who visit the area—he found a significant relationship between helping and population density. People who lived in larger communities were less helpful than people who lived in smaller communities. This finding applied equally to all types of helping, with the exception of assistance given to someone who dropped a stack of envelopes. This individual received very little help in any community.

Why do urbanites help less? Amato found that helping rates dropped even in relatively small cities (with populations of only 20,000), so overstimulation isn't the answer. It's more likely that, as cities grow larger, the situational forces that block helping become stronger. In larger cities, urban bystanders don't know each other, and the potential for harm is also greater. Urban bystanders are also more likely to overlook someone who needs help, for the city's environment is busier than the town's, and urban dwellers more

▲ **TABLE 12-3**
Techniques social psychologists use to study helping behavior in field settings

Technique	*Procedure*	*Application*
Wrong number	A person apparently using a pay phone calls subjects. Claiming to have no more change, the caller asks the subject to make the call for him or her.	City dwellers are less likely to make the call than residents of rural areas (Milgram, 1970).
Lost letter	Stamped, addressed envelopes are dropped in public areas so they appear to have been lost by the writer before they could be mailed.	Letters dropped in cities are less likely to be mailed than letters dropped in towns (Korte & Kerr, 1975).
Overpayment	After making a purchase, the customer overpays the clerk by a small amount.	Clerks in towns are more likely to return the overpayment than clerks in cities (Korte & Kerr, 1975).
Sidewalk requests	Small requests are made of passersby; requests include money, name, directions, favorite color.	City dwellers are less likely to name their favorite color than rural dwellers (Amato, 1983).
Stranger at the door	Claiming to have lost a nearby friend's address, a stranger asks to use the telephone to call for more information.	Requester is admitted to more rural homes than urban homes (Milgram, 1970).
Wrong directions	In a public place, one stranger gives another stranger incorrect directions within earshot of the subject.	Bystanders intervene with correct directions more frequently in towns than in cities (Amato, 1983).

zealously protect their privacy by not getting involved in others' affairs. Last, the sheer number of people who need help in big cities may be too daunting for most bystanders. As Milgram (1992) puts it, "If every citizen attended to every needy person, if he were sensitive to and acted on every altruistic impulse that was evoked in the city, he could scarcely keep his own affairs in order" (p. 14).

Whom Do We Help?

Consider this simple experiment. Researchers placed a dime on the shelves in telephone booths at Kennedy Airport and Grand Central Station in New York City. They then retreated to a nearby observation point. When an unsuspecting subject entered the booth and used the dime, the experimenters returned. They tapped on the door and said, "Excuse me, I think I might've left a dime in this phone booth a few minutes ago. Did you find it?" When the experimenters were well dressed (suits), they got their dime back 77% of the time. Informally dressed experimenters (unkempt work clothes) got their dime back from only 38% of the subjects (Bickman, 1974).

If people were all perfect altruists, helping wouldn't depend on such irrelevancies as clothing. But we aren't perfect altruists—we consider the other person's looks and clothes before we offer to help. We respond more positively to people who are physically attractive (Benson, Karabenick, & Lerner, 1976; Harrell, 1978) if they are dressed attractively (Bickman, 1974; Kleinke, 1977) and if they possess no stigmatizing physical characteristics, such as unattractive birthmarks (Piliavin, Piliavin, & Rodin, 1975), eye patches, or scars (Samerotte & Harris, 1976). We also give more help to women than we do to men (Eagly & Crowley, 1986).

The similarity-helping effect. In the study conducted in telephone booths in New York City, well-dressed victims received more help than unkempt ones. Most of the bystanders were well dressed, too. Did the researchers discover a tendency to help well-dressed people or a tendency to help people who are similar to us in some way?

To an important degree, the impact of the victim's characteristics depends on the bystanders' personal characteristics. In general, if you feel that others are similar to you in some way, then you will be more likely to go to their aid. This tendency is known as the *similarity-helping effect,* and it parallels the similarity-attraction effect discussed in Chapter 11. Thus, birds of a feather not only flock together; they also help one another. Similarity may influence helping by creating a feeling of "we-ness" between bystander and victim, so the bystander feels more responsible for helping (Hornstein, 1982; Piliavin et al., 1981).

The similarity-helping relationship has been confirmed in many studies, involving such diverse attributes as attitudes, political beliefs, nationality, and race as well as dress (Dovidio, 1984). Researchers in one creative study of similarity in attitudes clipped two open envelopes together and then dropped them on the sidewalk in a Jewish section of Brooklyn, New York. Researchers put a completed opinion poll in one of the envelopes and answered it so that it seemed the person who lost the envelopes was either pro-Israel or anti-Israel. They placed a check and a contribution card for the Institute for Research in Medicine in the second envelope. If, as the researchers reasonably assumed, the finder favored Israel, the results strongly supported the similarity-helping prediction; 69% of the envelopes in the pro-Israel condition were returned, compared to only 30% of the envelopes in the anti-Israel condition (Hornstein et al., 1971). A conceptually similar study was carried out in the early 1970s. College students—who at the time were presumed to be politically liberal—were found to be less likely to turn off the headlights of a parked automobile bearing bumper stickers touting conservative values like "America—love it or leave it" than such liberal values as "Make love, not war" (Ehlert, Ehlert, & Merrens, 1973).

Race and helping. The similarity-helping effect also accounts for some racial biases in helping. As noted in Chapter 7, many bystanders help members of their own racial groups, but not members of other racial groups. When the driver of a disabled car parked by the side of the road was white, 94% of the people who stopped to help were white. When the victim was black, 97% of the people who offered help were black (West, Whitney, & Schnedler, 1975). Racial favoritism occurs about 40% of the time; it becomes particularly pronounced when the failure to help won't appear to be racially motivated (Crosby, Bromley, & Saxe, 1980). When bystanders think they are anonymous—the victim and bystander can't see or identify one another—whites are much less likely to help a black victim. If, however, bystanders and victim can see each other, then the shield of anonymity is stripped away. In such cases, whites usually help blacks. Apparently, racist bystanders don't want to appear to be prejudiced, so they help, to disconfirm this negative social image (Dovidio, 1984).

Will You Help?

As you wait for the light to change, your eyes wander to the opposite street corner. There you see a bicyclist brake to avoid a turning car. Her rear wheel locks, the bicycle slides sideways, and she falls roughly to the sidewalk. Legs

▲ **TABLE 12-4**
Summing up: Personal characteristics of people who help and people who receive help

Characteristic	*Impact on Helping*
Helper's personality	Helping is the product of situational factors (the doctrine of specificity), personality factors, and the interaction of situational and personality factors. People who are consistently helpful tend to be empathic, ethical, self-confident, and socially responsible.
Sex of helper	Men help more in emergencies, whereas women help more when other people require social support. Sex-role socialization influences the magnitude of these sex differences—more masculine individuals are more helpful in emergencies provided the possibility of embarrassment is minimal.
Urban and rural helpers	Residents of small towns usually help more when they witness minor accidents, when asked to make a telephone call (the wrong-number technique), when they find a dropped letter (the lost-letter technique), and when asked for directions or favors.
Victim's characteristics	Individuals who possess positive social qualities (for example, those who are attractive, well dressed, and unblemished) are helped more than less attractive individuals. Similarities between the helper and victim, including racial similarity, increase helping (similarity-helping effect).

tangled in the frame of the bicycle, head resting on the pavement, the bicyclist lies still for a few moments before slowly raising a hand to her head. Will you help?

Before you say yes, note that the characteristics of the people in the situation—both the victim and you, the onlooker—influence your willingness to help (see Table 12-4). Without knowing it, you may take note of the cyclist's race, physical attractiveness, and similarity to you before you go to her aid. In addition, your own personal attributes—such as your sex-role identity, your willingness to take social responsibility, your general level of empathy—may also influence your reaction. "Will you help?" is a complex question, and it requires a complex answer that takes into account the characteristics of both victim and bystander.

Deciding to Help

When Mana Mashoon cried out, Timothy Mosher came to her aid. Kitty Genovese wasn't so lucky. Winston Moseley stabbed her outside of her apartment in the Kew Gardens section of Queens, New York. When one of her neighbors shouted at him, Moseley retreated to his car. But no one called the police, and Moseley returned 20 minutes later to renew his attack. He found Genovese hiding in the stairwell of her apartment building. He raped her and stabbed her to death. The police received the first call from a witness at 3:50 A.M. They were on the scene in 2 minutes after the call, but 37 minutes after the first attack. Journalists who described the incident claimed that as many as 38 people witnessed the murder, yet no one helped.

Why didn't anyone help Kitty Genovese? Many people pointed the finger of blame at the bystanders. Some argued that the onlookers simply didn't want to get involved. Others suggested that the urbanites were cruel and selfish, lacking the moral compunction needed to compel them to act. Still others attributed the tragedy to cowardice or to an incapacitating fear of retribution. But these explanations underestimate the complexity of giving and receiving help. Rather than blaming the bystanders' lack of moral fiber or the dehumanizing effects of big cities, we must systematically study the nature of the interpersonal forces that trapped the bystanders, leaving them "fascinated, distressed, unwilling to act, but unable to turn away" (Latané & Darley, 1976, p. 310).

The Bystander Effect

When Bibb Latané and John Darley (1970) read about the murder of Kitty Genovese, they were struck by the large number of witnesses. Could it be, they wondered, that people are less likely to help if other people are also present in the situation?

They studied this possibility by creating a false emergency in their laboratory. Latané and Darley put college student volunteers (all men) to work filling out questionnaires in a small room. Then they pumped white smoke through an air vent into the test room. (The researchers got the idea from the old Camel cigarette sign in Times Square.) Some men were alone in the room; others were part of three-person groups consisting of one subject and two confederates. The confederates pretended to be subjects, but they were trained to ignore the emergency. As the room filled with smoke, they nonchalantly glanced at the vent, shrugged, and went back to their questionnaires. If the subject mentioned the smoke to them, they said merely, "I dunno." In a third condition, all three members of the group were actual subjects.

When tested alone, subjects usually left the room to report the smoke within 2 minutes; 75% reported the emergency within the 6-minute time limit. Subjects tested in groups, however, behaved very differently. Only 10% of the subjects tested with the passive confederates reported the smoke, and the percentage reached no higher than 15 when all three group members were actual subjects. By the time the 6-minute period was up, the room was so smoky that subjects couldn't see the far wall. They coughed and rubbed their eyes, but they stayed at their tables, fanning away the fumes so they could finish their questionnaires.

bystander effect
The tendency for people to help less in groups than when they are alone.

Latané and Darley had succeeded in documenting the **bystander effect**: People are less likely to help in groups than when they are alone. However, Latané and Darley's smoke study didn't involve actually helping another person who was hurt or injured. Therefore, they carried out a second study to examine a true bystander situation more closely. They ushered each volunteer into a small room that was equipped with an intercom system. A researcher then used the intercom system to explain: "I'm concerned with the kinds of personal problems faced by normal college students under pressure. To gather some general information on this topic, I would like you to discuss some of your personal concerns with other students." He also said that, in order to ensure confidentiality, all communication would take place by means of the intercom system, so no face-to-face meeting would be necessary. The conversation would be a private one—even the experimenter wouldn't be listening to the discussion.

Some of the subjects thought they were talking to only one other person. Others thought that three or six students were taking part in the discussion. In any case, each subject then gave a 2-minute description of his or her problems with studying, taking exams, missing classes, and so on. All of the participants' comments—save the real subjects' remarks—were simulated with tape recordings. And all mentioned typical difficulties except one. This individual sheepishly explained that he sometimes became so nervous when he was preparing for or taking exams that he experienced seizures.

Several minutes later, during the second round of discussion, this young man began to sound strange. His statements became increasingly garbled, until finally he complained:

> I er um think I I need er if if could er er somebody er er er er er er give me a little er give me a little help here because er I er I'm er er h-h-having a a a a real problem er right now and I er if somebody could help me out it would it would er er s-s-sure be sure be good . . . I'm . . . gonna die er help er er seizure er.

With the last word, he choked loudly and then lapsed into complete silence.

Certainly people helped. Who could ignore someone sitting in a booth just down the hall who was calling out, "I could really use some help"? But many of Latané and Darley's subjects remained in their booths when they thought other bystanders were present (see Figure 12-2). Everyone who was alone with the victim helped, and they helped quickly. People in groups were slower to respond, and some never did leave their booths to seek help. If people didn't respond within 3 minutes, they never did.

Latané & Darley's findings are surprising (and disappointing), but they have been replicated in dozens of studies of nearly 6,000 people who faced various emergencies alone or in groups. Researchers have varied the number of bystanders, the kind of danger, the setting (lab versus field), the sex of bystanders, the characteristics of the victims, and the bystanders' capacity to communicate with each other. Across all these variations about 75% of the subjects tested alone intervened, but only 53% of the subjects in groups helped (Latané & Nida, 1981).

A Decision Model of Helping

Latané and Darley discovered that bystanders help less in groups than when they are alone. They are careful to point out, however, that the bystanders who failed to help weren't apathetic or afraid to get involved. When subjects witnessed an emergency, many seemed very nervous and worried—their hands trembled, their palms were sweating, and most asked about the victim. To Latané and Darley (1976), the unresponsive bystanders "seemed more emotionally aroused than did the subjects who reported the emergency" (p. 326).

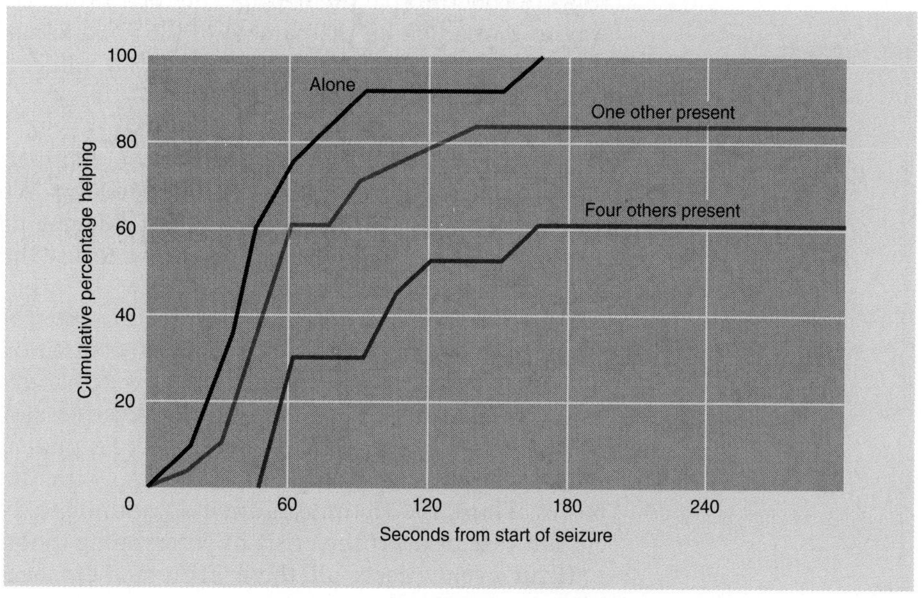

▲ **FIGURE 12-2**
Do people help less in groups than when they are alone? When Latané and Darley staged a bogus emergency, people who were alone helped more quickly and more frequently than people who knew another person was present. Helping dropped even further when subjects thought that four other people were also aware of the problem. (From Darley & Latané, 1968)

▲ **FIGURE 12-3**
What decisions must people make before they will help someone in distress? The decision model of helping, developed by Latané and Darley, suggests that bystanders must notice the event, label it an emergency, take responsibility, identify a way to help, and then implement the method of help they have chosen. If bystanders respond negatively at any point in the sequence, they will not help. (Based on Latané & Darley, 1970)

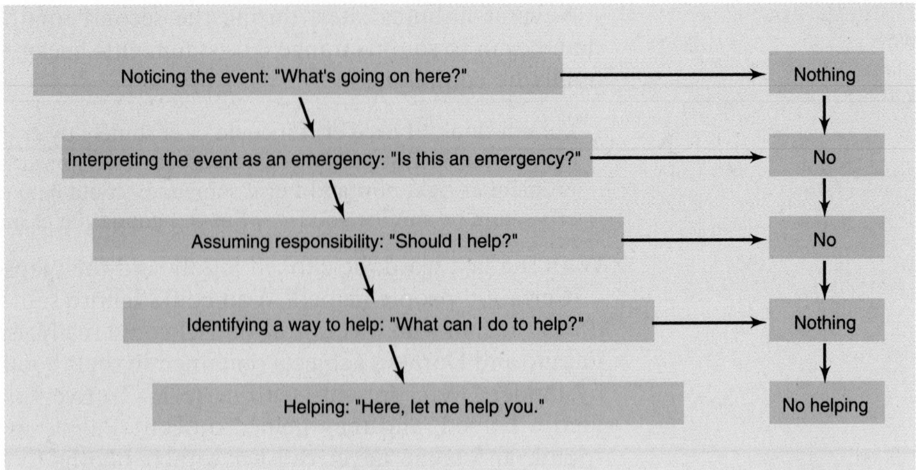

decision model of helping A theoretical framework developed by Latané and Darley (1976) that proposes individuals make a series of decisions before they offer a victim help, including noticing the event, interpreting the event as an emergency, taking responsibility, identifying a way to help, and implementing the chosen form of help.

So why didn't they help? Latané and Darley hypothesized that people who witness an emergency make a series of decisions before they actually offer help. Their **decision model of helping**, summarized in Figure 12-3, identifies five steps: (1) noticing the event, (2) interpreting the event as an emergency, (3) taking responsibility, (4) identifying a way to help, and (5) implementing the chosen form of help. If bystanders don't make a help-promoting decision at each choice point, they will remain uninvolved (Latané & Darley, 1970).

Noticing the event. Asking yourself "Is something going on here?" is the necessary first step in the helping decision. Sometimes people fail to help just because they never notice that help is needed. Imagine that you are hurrying to an appointment on a cold winter day. Off to your left, slumped in a doorway, is a person in a heavy coat. If the person groans when you pass by, will you stop to help? Not if, in your haste, you don't even notice the person. Researchers created just this kind of situation by asking seminary students to give a short speech to some other students. Passing by the groaning man, only 10% of them helped if they thought they were late; but if they had ample time to get to their talk, 63% helped. The final irony? Some subjects were on their way to give a talk on the parable of the good Samaritan, but this reminder of the moral injunction to help others had no influence on their own willingness to help (Darley & Batson, 1973).

Interpreting the event. Some of the seminary students noticed the person lying in the doorway but still failed to stop. When asked why, many gave this explanation: "I thought he was just sleeping off a drunk and didn't need any help." These individuals didn't help because they interpreted the situation as a nonemergency.

How do people distinguish between an emergency and a nonemergency? When people reviewed a list of problematic situations and identified those they thought were emergencies, their choices were based on the three characteristics listed in Table 12-5. First, emergencies occur so suddenly that the victims and bystanders are surprised and unprepared. Second, emergencies also involve an imminent threat of harm to the victim, with the harm escalating as time passes. Third, the victim can often do nothing to avoid the harm, but onlookers can ease or avert the crisis by intervening (Shotland & Huston, 1979).

If an event meets all these criteria, help becomes more likely. Irving Piliavin, Judith Rodin, and Jane Piliavin's (1969) classic study of helping on

▲ TABLE 12-5
What factors do people take into account before they label a situation an emergency?

As these examples suggest, emergencies are usually unexpected, they involve an imminent threat of harm, and victims need help from other people if they are to avoid harm.

Situation	*Characteristics*	*Examples*
Emergency	Individuals are unexpectedly exposed to imminent danger that they cannot avoid unless other people provide help.	An injured person is bleeding from a cut artery; a house is ablaze and people inside are screaming; a person lies on the ground in shock.
Possible emergency	Individuals may experience harm in the situation, but they may be able to avert the problem without help from others.	A car is broken down; leaves are burning on a windy day with no one watching; an intoxicated friend insists on driving home.
Nonemergency	Individuals find the situation bothersome, but the consequences aren't extreme or worsening with the passage of time.	A car door chips another car's paint; a telethon wants to raise money; a car is parked by a fire hydrant; a person scrapes her knee.

Source: Adapted from Shotland & Huston, 1979.

the subway provides a clear case in point. Over a period of 73 days, the trio of researchers staged 103 accidents on the Eighth Avenue Express. With two observers recording bystanders' reactions, the "victim" would take up a position near a pole in the center of the car (see Figure 12-4). At times he carried a cane and moved as though he were injured or ill. At other times he feigned drunkenness—he smelled of liquor and carried a bottle in a brown paper bag. In either case, as the train left the station, the victim would collapse on the floor.

Piliavin, Rodin, and Piliavin expected very few of the bystanders to help. In fact, to provide a positive model of helping, they had another confederate ready to go to the victim's aid. However, the model was rarely needed. On 62 of the 65 trials involving the cane-carrying victim, passengers usually intervened before 10 seconds had elapsed. The drunken confederate fared less well, but even he received help on 19 of the 38 trials. People were slower to help the drunken victim, but larger groups of bystanders responded more rapidly than smaller ones. When only one to three bystanders were near the intoxicated victim, it took nearly 5 minutes for one of the bystanders to help. If, however, seven or more bystanders were nearby, help arrived in about 1.5 minutes.

How can this reversal of the usual bystander effect be explained? According to Piliavin, Rodin, and Piliavin, when the cane-carrying confederate fell, the bystanders immediately realized he needed help. His cane and his sudden collapse unmistakably signaled *emergency.* If the bystanders can actually see the victim and they are sure of the seriousness of the crisis, then the bystander effect does not occur (Clark & Word, 1972). These studies suggest that the bystanders at the Kitty Genovese incident may have misinterpreted the situation. They may not have heard her cries clearly and simply concluded that intervention was unnecessary. One bystander actually claimed, "We thought it was a lovers' quarrel." Only 19% of the people who witnessed a staged fight between a man and a woman intervened when the woman screamed, "Get away from me, I don't know why I ever married you!" If, however, the woman clarified the nature of the incident by screaming, "Get away from me, I don't know you!" then 65% of the bystanders helped (Shotland, 1985).

The bystanders may have also taken other people's failure to respond as a sign that the situation was not an emergency. Because an emergency is such a

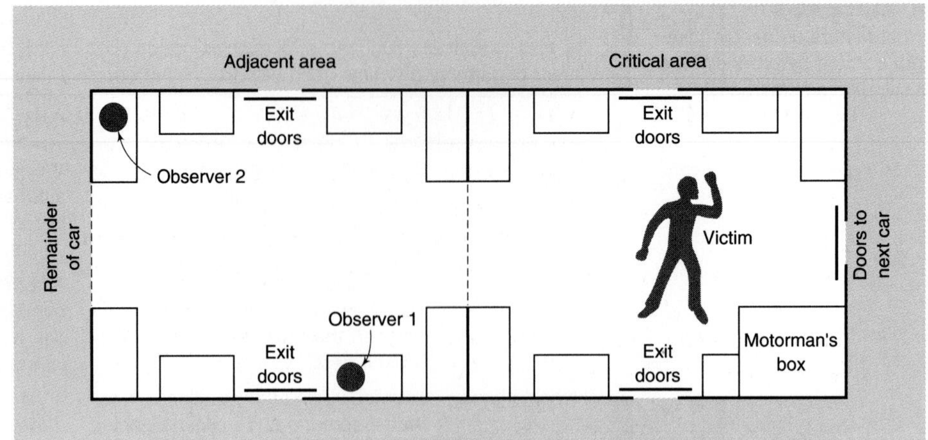

▲ **FIGURE 12-4**
If you saw a person collapse in the subway, would you go to that person's side and try to help? Piliavin, Rodin, and Piliavin positioned two observers in a subway car, and then arranged for their "victim" to quietly collapse from a standing position by a pole. The subjects were people who happened to be on the subway at that time. (From Piliavin, Rodin, & Piliavin, 1969)

novel, atypical situation, bystanders often rely on other people's reactions to understand what is happening. Unfortunately, each nonresponding bystander sends an inaccurate message to other nonresponding bystanders: "It's OK; no help is needed" (Latané & Darley, 1976).

Taking responsibility. At this point in the decision sequence Timothy Mosher has heard the scream and the thumping, and he has decided that this is not a lovers' spat—her screams convince him that she is in danger. But before he intervenes, he must ask himself, "Should I help?" If Mosher doesn't take responsibility for helping, he stays in his apartment. But if he feels that it's his responsibility to get involved, he goes into action.

diffusion of responsibility A reduction of personal responsibility that results from membership in a group.

What factors undercut and reinforce our feeling of responsibility? First, Latané and Darley's initial studies (1968) of the bystander effect point to **diffusion of responsibility**: People feel less personally responsible when they are in groups than when they are alone. When we are alone, no one else shares the burden of civic duty. But when we are in groups, the "pressures to intervene do not focus on any one of the observers; instead, the responsibility for intervention is shared among all the onlookers and is not unique to any one" (p. 378). When later asked what went through their minds, people who had witnessed a violent crime or emergency were more likely to report having thought they *weren't* responsible when they were part of a group. People who were alone, in contrast, later claimed that they had spontaneously thought about their obligation to help (Schwartz & Gottlieb, 1976, 1980). Diffusion of responsibility is minimal, however, if bystanders realize that the other bystanders either can't or won't help (Bickman, 1971, 1972b; Korte, 1970; Ross & Braband, 1973). Mosher later explained that he felt responsible for helping because most of the people who lived in the building were elderly or women, and he didn't think they would be able to prevent a violent crime.

Second, people sometimes don't help because they don't want to be blamed for contributing to the problem. This *confusion of responsibility* occurs because a potential helper realizes that other bystanders try to determine who is responsible for the victim's misfortune when they arrive on the scene of an accident. The potential helper also realizes that the onlookers may assume that anyone who helps is partially responsible for the accident itself. Imagine that you happened upon this scene: A man is lying on the ground, a pair of crutches lies nearby, and another person is lifting the man to his feet as several bystanders watch. Wouldn't you assume that the helper caused the accident in the first place? Otherwise, why did he help while others watched? Thus, bystanders refrain from helping because they don't want to be blamed by other onlookers (Cacioppo, Petty, & Losch, 1986).

Third, people help more when situational factors focus responsibility on them personally. In a study of children trick-or-treating on Halloween, researchers asked them if they wanted to give some of their candy to hospitalized children. In some groups the researcher pointed to one of the children and said, "I will put you in charge of the group here." In other cases the researcher pointed to each child, explaining, "I will be counting on you and you and you. . . ." When no mention was made of responsibility, the children donated an average of 2.2 candies. But when one person was given responsibility, that person donated 3.3 candies, and this average increased to 5.0 when all the children were made to feel responsible (Maruyama, Fraser, & Miller, 1982, pp. 660–661). Adults who were assigned responsibility were also more helpful, in an innovative study conducted at a New York beach. The research assistant spread his blanket by potential subjects and then relaxed in the sun. After about 2 minutes he turned to the bystander and said, "Excuse me, I'm going up to the boardwalk for a few minutes. Would you watch my things?" He left, and a few minutes later a woman walked up to the man's blanket. With no hesitation she grabbed the blaring radio and took off down the beach. Fully 95% of the bystanders who had been asked to "watch my things" intervened by stopping the thief or grabbing back the radio. In contrast, when the victim had said only, "Excuse me, I'm here alone and have no matches . . . do you have a light?" before leaving, 20% of the bystanders intervened when the woman took the radio (Moriarty, 1975). Other studies suggest that if people feel that they are personally responsible, they are more likely to intervene to prevent crimes (Bickman & Rosenbaum, 1977; Klentz & Beaman, 1981; Shaffer, Rogel, & Hendrick, 1975).

Identifying a way to help. Mosher heard the scream, decided someone needed help, and took responsibility. But if he had felt there was nothing he could do to help, Mashoon might have ended up like Genovese. Only people who can identify a way to help the person can implement the chosen form of help.

At this stage in the decision process, experience in emergency settings appears to be one of the primary determinants of helping. If bystanders feel they have the skills or abilities needed in the setting, they tend to help. If they think they lack the necessary know-how, they usually fail to intervene. When the emergency involves faulty or dangerous electrical equipment, people experienced in working with electricity tend to help more than those who are untrained (Clark & Word, 1974; Midlarsky & Midlarsky, 1973, 1976). In medical emergencies when a person is choking on food or bleeding from a severe wound, bystanders with first-aid training intervene more quickly than untrained observers (Pantin & Carver, 1982; Shotland & Heinold, 1985). And if a group member is overcome by a seizure, help is much more likely if the bystanders know the seizure can be treated by giving the victim the medicine he keeps in his pocket (Schwartz & Clausen, 1970).

The importance of competence as a necessary condition for helping receives dramatic support from interviews with real-life good Samaritans. One team of researchers located 32 individuals who had intervened to prevent a violent crime, such as a street mugging, armed robbery, or a bank holdup. One of the men had broken up a violent argument between a man and a woman. During the dispute, his jaw was broken by the male assailant. In another emergency, a

▲ **FIGURE 12-5**
Are you prepared to help when an emergency arises? People who intervened in violent crimes tended to be better prepared to cope with the emergency than a matched group of nonhelpers. The helpers also tended to be taller, heavier, and higher in self-rated strength and emotionality than the control group subjects. (From Huston et al., 1981)

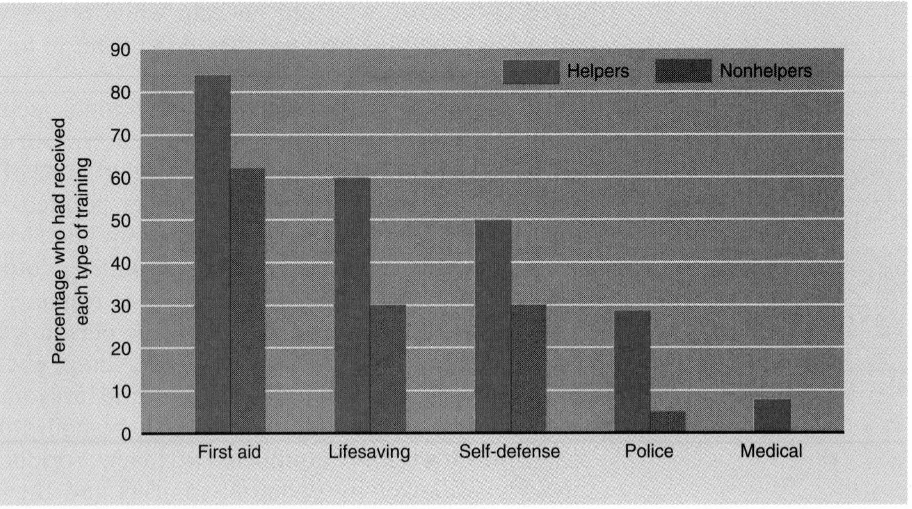

man entering a grocery store confronted a robber pointing a rifle at the salesclerk. Instantly, he disarmed the robber and was hitting him when the police arrived. In 27 of the 32 cases, the helpers were injured in some way.

Compared to a group of randomly selected people who had never intervened in a violent crime, these good Samaritans had experienced more emergencies. Not only had they witnessed more crimes, but they were also better prepared to help in the emergency. As Figure 12-5 indicates, significantly more of the good Samaritans were trained in lifesaving, first aid, medicine, self-defense, or crime prevention (Huston et al., 1981).

The final stage: Helping. With each decision in the sequence, Mosher moved closer and closer to the final step: intervention in the emergency. But even people who are ready to help sometimes fail to intervene. The situation may block their response. Mosher might have been unable to track down the source of the screams. He might also have been overcome by fear or evaluation apprehension. In many cases, people who fail to help later explain that they didn't want to look foolish by offering assistance to someone who didn't need it. The screams might have come from a television set; the bicyclist who takes a tumble might be insulted by the offer of help; the smoke might have come from an incinerator. The inhibiting effects of evaluation apprehension explain why people are less helpful in groups: More witnesses increase our worry that we will look foolish and stupid (Schwartz & Gottlieb, 1976). And why are people who are intoxicated *more* likely to help rather than to turn away in indifference? Because alcohol lessens our sensitivity to risks and relaxes our social inhibitions (Steele, Critchlow, & Liu, 1985).

A Cost-Reward Model of Helping

Latané and Darley's decision model, which Table 12-6 summarizes, assumes that helping is the end result of a series of decisions. A study conducted by Jane and Irving Piliavin (1972), however, raises questions that the original Latané and Darley model can't fully answer. A cane-carrying confederate collapses on the floor of a subway car in front of several onlookers. In some cases, he just lay on the floor, staring up at the ceiling. In other cases, a thin trickle of stage blood oozed from his mouth. Surprisingly, fewer people helped the bleeding victim. In fact, some people seemed ready to help, but stopped when they noticed the blood. Two teenage girls got up when they saw the man fall but sat down quickly when one said, "Oh, he's bleeding!"

Why didn't people help the more seriously injured person? Piliavin and her colleagues (1981) propose that Latané and Darley left out one step in the decision-making sequence—the calculation of costs and rewards. According to the **cost-reward model of helping**, people strive to minimize their costs and maximize their rewards. Once bystanders realize an emergency is occurring, they intuitively calculate the costs and rewards they can expect from helping and failing to give help. The subway riders may have identified a number of possible rewards for helping, including thanks from the victim, praise from onlookers, self-praise, and even a monetary reward or a good citizenship award. But these rewards were offset by many possible costs: lost time, embarrassment, expenditure of effort, danger, fear, revulsion caused by the sight of blood, and the possibility of infection. When the victim only collapsed, he received help nearly 90% of the time; the costs of helping were low. But when the victim bled, those costs rose, and helping dwindled to about 60%. Thus costs—both those of helping and those of failing to help—have a major impact on our reactions in emergencies (Dovidio et al., 1991).

cost-reward model of helping
An extension of the Latané-Darley decision model of helping that argues individuals also consider the costs and rewards they might experience if they help or do not help.

Research supports the amended model, for helping usually decreases as the costs of helping increase. People aren't likely to help if they fear personal injury or embarrassment (Borofsky, Stollak, & Messe, 1971; Clark, 1976; McGovern, 1976; Midlarsky & Midlarsky, 1973). Darley and Latané (1970), for example, found that 85% of the pedestrians they studied in New York City gave an answer to the cost-free question "What time is it?" Only 34% responded when asked, "Could you give me a dime?" People who joined local organizations that helped people with AIDS, only to quit a short time later, found the work just as rewarding as people who continued their volunteer service. The quitters, however, complained more about the costs of helping: They felt that their volunteer work was too time-consuming and embarrassing (Snyder & Omoto, 1992).

The costs of *not* helping, however, must also be considered (Piliavin & Piliavin, 1972; Piliavin et al., 1981). If you saw a man collapse on the subway and did not help, you might continue to worry about him. You might also feel

▲ If you saw a jogger fall to the ground and clutch his ankle, would you offer assistance? Latané and Darley's decision model of helping suggests that your response would depend on five factors: noticing the event, interpreting the event as an emergency, taking responsibility, identifying a way to help, and implementing the chosen form of help.

▲ **TABLE 12-6**
Summing up: Latané and Darley's decision model of emergency intervention describes the sequence of decisions bystanders must make before helping.

Stage	*Characteristics*	*Application*
Noticing the event	Onlookers must be aware of the problem. Individuals who are preoccupied or distracted by other features of the situation rarely help.	Students hurrying to give a lecture didn't notice a man moaning in an alley (Darley & Batson, 1973).
Interpreting the event as an emergency	Bystanders are more likely to help when the victim faces a clear threat of harm, the victim is not prepared to cope with the threat, and bystanders can ease or avert the crisis by intervening.	Subway riders were more likely to help a passenger who appeared to be ill rather than intoxicated (Piliavin et al., 1969).
Taking responsibility	People help less in groups because they feel less responsible (diffusion of responsibility) and they are concerned that onlookers will blame them for contributing to the problem (confusion of responsibility). Individuals are more helpful when they are explicitly assigned responsibility.	Children trick-or-treating on Halloween donated more candy when they were told they were responsible for helping (Maruyama et al., 1982).
Identifying a way to help	People help more when they can identify a way to help. Bystanders who are trained to help or have useful skills help more than untrained individuals.	People who intervened in emergencies were often trained in lifesaving, first aid, medicine, self-defense, or crime prevention (Huston et al., 1981).
Implementing the chosen form of help	People do not help when the situation prevents intervention or their personal reaction to the event (fear, embarrassment) inhibits helping.	Intoxicated people are more helpful because alcohol relaxes social inhibitions (Steele et al., 1985).

Source: From Latané & Darley, 1970.

ashamed and guilty for not helping, and if other people found out about your failure, you might be afraid they would criticize you. In some cities and countries, you can even be convicted of a crime for not helping. All of these costs of failure to help—empathic worry, shame and guilt, public censure, and prosecution—may combine to prompt you to help. Mosher later explained his response: "If something really bad was going on and I didn't do anything about it, I wouldn't be able to feel comfortable living with myself afterward" (quoted in Hunt, 1990, p. 130).

The cost-reward model thus argues that people are most likely to help when the costs for helping are minimal, but the costs for failure to help are substantial. Russell D. Clark III (1976) tested this hypothesis by asking college students if they would be willing to serve as a reader for a blind student who had been injured in an automobile accident. Some students thought that the blind student was hospitalized in a community clinic several miles from campus (high costs for helping); others were told that the student was in the campus health center (low costs). They were also told that the blind student had three major exams in the next week (the costs of failure to help were high) or that he just needed to keep up with his assignments (the costs of failure to help were low). Clark found that twice as many subjects helped when the costs of helping were low and the costs of failure to help were high (Clark, 1976, Experiment 2; Piliavin et al., 1981).

Motives, Emotions, and Helping

The decision models summarized in Table 12-7 explain why Mosher helped when Mashoon screamed out in the night: He rationally evaluated the situation and concluded that helping was required. But how did he *feel* as he bounded out of his apartment? Didn't the emergency create strong emotions, which then influenced the way he responded to Figueroa when he met him in the darkened hallway? The theories discussed next suggest that helping depends as much on what people are feeling as what they are thinking.

Impulsive Helping

Mosher nearly died saving someone he had never met. His act of selflessness was recognized by the Carnegie Hero Fund Commission, which honors people who ignore costs as they risk their lives to save others. What inner forces could have motivated him to ignore the danger and help?

Piliavin and her colleagues believe that bystanders often experience physiological arousal when they witness an emergency. This arousal, which can be traced back to the evolutionarily ancient *fight-or-flight* response, leaves bystanders physically ready to cope with the situation. Mild or ambiguous emergencies don't create much physiological arousal, but extreme emergencies—those in which a victim is threatened with severe injury, and the situation is worsening with each passing second—set the stage for **impulsive helping**. In extreme emergencies, onlookers bypass the decision-making process and act immediately.

impulsive helping Responding rapidly to another person's need without considering personal danger or consequences.

Russell D. Clark III and his colleagues studied this kind of helping by exposing people to a sham electrocution (Clark & Word, 1974, Experiment 1). The researchers claimed they were validating a self-report measure of mental ability when they recruited their bystanders-to-be for the study. When the subjects finished the testing and exited the building, they had to pass by a room filled with complex electrical gadgets and signs that read, "Danger: High Voltage." Just as they passed the door of the room, the electrician inside apparently received a severe electric shock: A bright light flashed, a dull buzzing sound filled the room, he cried out in pain, and knocked over his equipment as he collapsed on the floor.

Clark created four different versions of the accident to vary the ambiguity of the emergency as well as the potential costs of helping. In one condition, bystanders faced an unambiguously dangerous situation: The victim lay on several wires, and his hand clutched wires from the equipment. In a second

▲ **TABLE 12-7**
Summing up: Decision models of emergency intervention

Model	*Predictions*	*Application*
Latané and Darley decision model	Bystanders don't help unless they notice the problem, decide it's an emergency, take responsibility, identify a way to help, and implement the identified form of help.	Because of diffusion of responsibility, people are less helpful when others are present (the bystander effect).
Piliavin et al. cost-reward model	People are most helpful when the costs of helping are low, and the costs of not helping are high.	Volunteers who terminated community service found the work rewarding but too time-consuming and embarrassing (Snyder & Omoto, 1992).

condition, nonambiguous and nondangerous, the electrician fell away from the wires and equipment. In the remaining two conditions, the emergency was more ambiguous: Subjects couldn't see the electrician clearly, and either they heard him moan (moderate ambiguity) or he made no sound (high ambiguity).

In the nonambiguous situations, the amount of helping was impressive; 53 of the 54 subjects intervened by either directly assisting the confederate or locating others who could help. In contrast, only about 40% of the subjects helped when the emergency was ambiguous. Furthermore, had the electrocution been real, many of the helpful bystanders would have died. Even when they faced a deadly emergency—an unconscious victim still clutching live wires—many subjects grabbed the confederate by his feet and pulled him away from the wires. During a subsequent interview they admitted their mistake, but explained that "at the time they acted so quickly that no consideration was given to the possible harm involved" (Clark & Word, 1974, p. 286).

How did the subjects react to this stressful experience? Because of the nature of the emergency, Clark carefully debriefed all the subjects in the study. The majority were upset by the experience, but nearly all of them felt better after a thorough discussion of the study. Furthermore, over 90% of the subjects agreed that the research was very valuable, both immediately after their experience and several months later.

Opponent Processes and Emotions

What do people receive in return for the blood they donate to community blood banks? Most community agencies do not use a credit system, whereby each donor is guaranteed a proportionate amount of blood in the future. Nor do they offer payment of any sort. Instead, giving blood seems to involve only costs: lost time, a little pain, weakness, perhaps even nausea. Donors don't even know what happens to their blood: It's usually given to a community agency, so there is no victim to help. So why do people donate blood?

Piliavin and her colleagues believe that many factors prompt people to donate blood the first time: social pressure, guilt, curiosity, embarrassment, shame, whim, and so on. Once they give blood, however, a cycle of strong emotional reactions can create an addiction to donating blood. This cycle is best explained by an **opponent-process theory of emotions**. According to this model, whenever we experience a positive or negative emotion, after a short period of time we also begin to experience the opposing emotional reaction. If, for example, we discover we have won a million dollars, we will feel happy. However, our emotions will gradually become more neutral as sadder emotions develop that oppose our happiness. The same opponent process occurs where we experience a tragedy. According to the opponent-process model, this system works to keep our emotions from becoming too positive or too negative (Solomon, 1980; Solomon & Corbit, 1974).

opponent-process theory of emotions
A theoretical framework, which proposes that, after individuals experience an emotion, they begin to experience the opposing emotional reaction after a short period of time.

Piliavin and her colleagues believe that the experience of giving blood initially creates very negative emotions, which soon give rise to positive emotions. As a result, people may become addicted to the pleasure they experience when they give blood. Piliavin's research team tested their model by asking 1,846 donors to complete a questionnaire before and after they gave blood. On the pretest, people who were giving blood for the first time described themselves as uptight, dubious, fearful, skeptical, jittery, regretful, suspicious, angry, defiant, and rebellious. After giving blood, however, they described themselves as relieved, relaxed, self-satisfied, warmhearted, carefree, playful, self-centered, and even egoistic. Moreover, the more times they had given blood, the less intense were their negative feelings. With each visit they experienced less anxiety, but their positive emotions remained strong. For most people, the magic number of visits was four: By the time people had donated blood four times, their positive feelings were so much stronger than their negative ones that they became hooked. Also, Piliavin believes that once people donate blood four times they come to incorporate the blood-donor role into their personal identities. They come to think of themselves as *blood donors* rather than just people who give blood (Piliavin, 1987; Piliavin & Callero, 1991; Piliavin, Callero, & Evans 1982).

The Two-Factor Theory of Helping

Try to remember the way you felt the last time you witnessed a crisis or emergency—a minor automobile accident, a stranger stumbling on an uneven sidewalk, a child lost in a shopping mall, or even a fictional accident depicted in a television show or movie. Ignore your behavior for a moment and focus only on your feelings. How did you react emotionally when you saw someone else in need?

The *two-factor theory of emotions,* examined in Chapter 4, argues that your emotional reaction to the emergency is shaped by the thinking-feeling-acting sequence summarized in Figure 12-6. First, witnessing another person in need or distress usually causes an increase in general arousal. Second, you search for a potential cause for the arousal you are experiencing. At this point in the process, you may attribute your arousal to your concern for the other person, but you may come up with some other explanation instead. If you decide that the coffee you drank earlier caused your arousal, you may conclude that you have caffeine jitters. Third, depending on the results of your attribution search, you label your emotion and make a decision about helping. If you assign a prosocial label to your feeling, such as *concern* or *sympathy,* then you are likely to help. If, however, you assign a negative label to your emotion, such as *anger,* then you may not help.

The two-factor theory explains why we feel sorry for and help people who are victims of chance accidents, but don't feel very sympathetic when we think victims bring their suffering on themselves. Consider two bystanders who pass

▲ Some people, like this fire fighter, repeatedly risk their own safety to help others. A motivational model of helping suggests that such individuals may have responded negatively when they encountered their first emergency but that in time this negative reaction was countered by an opposing, positive reaction. Eventually, the positive emotional response dominated the negative, and the individual became committed to helping.

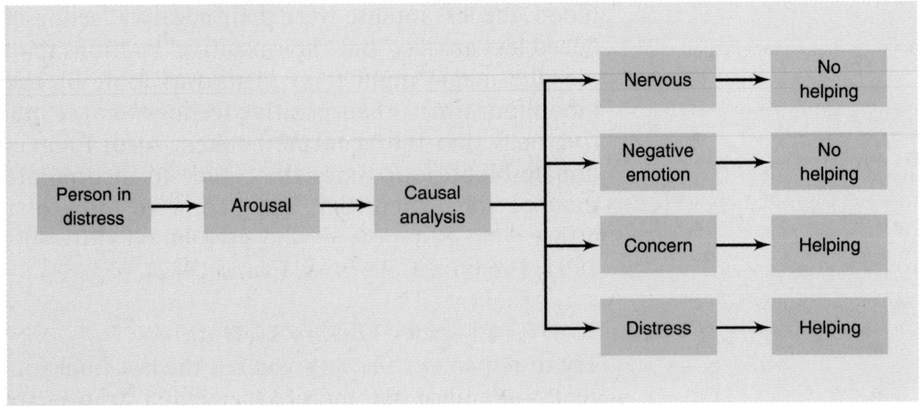

▲ **FIGURE 12-6**
How do you feel when you see someone who is upset, distressed, or suffering? Seeing others in distress is arousing, but if you attribute your arousal to some irrelevant cause, you probably won't help. You also won't help much if you attach a negative label to the arousal, such as anger or fear. You will help, though, if you attach a prosocial label to your emotion, such as concern or distress.

by an elderly man lying in a doorway on a cold winter night. The first bystander becomes aroused by the man's plight until she spies an empty wine bottle by the man's side. She thinks, "A drunk. It's his own fault if he freezes to death out here. I won't help." The second passerby, also aroused, thinks, "He's homeless, one of the city's victims. He needs my help." The first bystander fails to help because she attributes the man's misfortune to factors within the victim's control. She experiences anger and disgust rather than pity and concern. The second bystander, in contrast, intervenes, for he attributes the victim's problem to factors beyond his control.

Bernard Weiner and his colleagues have found that people experience very different emotions when they think victims are innocent sufferers rather than blameworthy miscreants. In one study, he asked students how they would feel about a classmate who asked to borrow their notes because (a) he was having trouble reading because of a severe eye infection or (b) he skipped classes and went to the beach. People who thought that the student's problem was caused by factors he could have controlled felt angrier ($r = .35$), and the more anger they felt, the less they intended to help ($r = -.58$). People who thought the student could not have controlled the cause of his problem, in contrast, felt more sympathetic ($r = -.64$), and the more sympathetic they felt, the more they helped ($r = .47$). Because attributions about controllability didn't directly influence willingness to help, Weiner concluded that emotions mediate the attribution-action relationship (Schmidt & Weiner, 1988; Weiner, 1991; see also Meyer & Mulherin, 1980; Yates, 1992).

Misattribution—attributing one's arousal to some extraneous factor rather than to the actual cause—can also break the thinking-feeling-acting sequence summarized in Figure 12-6. Researchers examined this misattribution process by giving inert pills (placebos) to subjects. They told some of the participants that the pill might increase their heart rate (arousal), but they told others that the pill might give them a headache (nonarousal). Then, as the subjects worked alone on a task, a woman working in the next room apparently injured herself by knocking over a stack of chairs. Subjects' heart rates and the length of time they waited before helping lent support to the attributional model. To simplify, increases in heart rate and speed in helping were positively correlated: People who helped immediately were much more aroused than subjects who were slow to help. But subjects who thought they had taken an arousing pill were slower to help than those who took the nonarousing pill; they apparently attributed their physiological state to the pill rather than to the victim's plight (Gaertner & Dovidio, 1977; see also Coke, Batson, & McDavis, 1978; Harris & Huang, 1973).

The Empathy-Altruism Model of Helping

A college professor is talking with a student in her office. While pleading with the professor for postponement of an upcoming test, the student begins to cry. Reacting to the student's distress, the professor becomes upset as well. The professor helps the student by postponing the test.

Daniel Batson and his colleagues believe that two different motivations may underlie the professor's behavior. First, the professor may help in order to reduce her own personal distress. She gets upset when she sees the student cry, and she helps the student to erase her own distress. Batson describes this reason for helping as *egoistic motivation* because it is self-serving; this form of helping helps the helper feel better. In contrast, the professor's behavior may spring from *empathic motivation*—an altruistic desire to reduce the distress of the person in need. Unlike the egoistic helper, the empathic helper is other-serving, for her primary goal is to help the student through the crisis.

These two motivations lead to two qualitatively distinct emotional and behavioral reactions (see Figure 12-7). Both egoistic and empathic observers become upset when they see others suffering, but empathic bystanders describe themselves as concerned, softhearted, compassionate, sympathetic, and moved. Distressed bystanders, in contrast, feel alarmed, grieved, upset, worried, disturbed, or perturbed (Batson, Fultz, & Schoenrade, 1987). These different emotional reactions also lead to differences in helpfulness. Batson and his colleagues find that egoistic people aren't particularly helpful if they can easily escape from the emergency situation. Because their distress is caused by exposure to a person experiencing a problem, they can deal with their distress by simply leaving the situation. As the section "In Depth: The Search for the True Altruist" explains, empathic people suffer because someone else is suffering. They will stay and help a person during an emergency, even if they can easily escape the situation (Batson, 1987, 1990).

Moods and Helping

Moods also play an important role in determining our reactions to emergencies. What would you do if you needed a favor? Say you want to borrow some money from Amy to pay an overdue bill. You missed a class, and you need to borrow some notes from Gliceria before the next exam. You want to take a day off from work next week, but you need to get the boss's permission. What is the best time to ask for your favor?

Social psychological research supports the wisdom of the wait-for-a-good-mood ploy. Challenge Amy to a game of tennis and lose. While she is basking

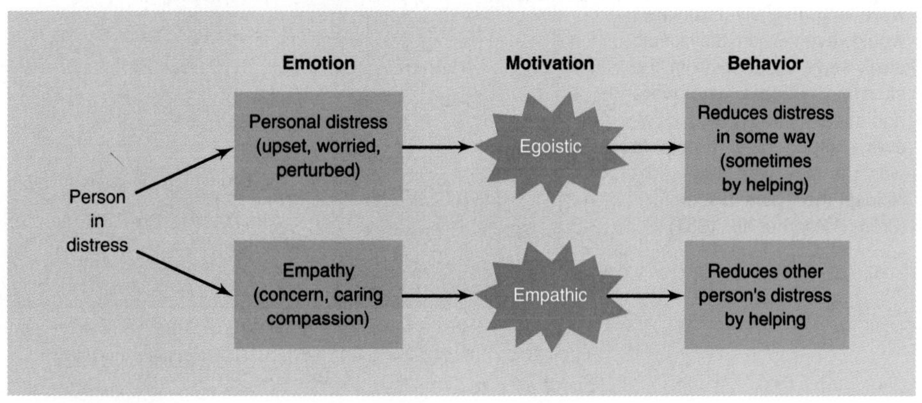

▲ **FIGURE 12-7**
When other people's suffering upsets us, do we help to relieve their discomfort or ours? Batson argues that egoists become upset when they see others suffer, but their emotions revolve around their own distress. Empathic people, in contrast, become upset when people suffer because they are concerned for the other person's welfare. Batson believes that empathic individuals will provide help more consistently than egoistic individuals will.

IN DEPTH

The Search for the True Altruist

Daniel Batson (1990, 1991) believes that people often perform benevolent actions for selfish reasons. People who pass by a panhandler on the street sometimes donate a coin because they are upset by the other person's predicament; making a small donation makes them feel less upset. Small children share their toys because they will be punished if they don't. People intervene in emergencies because they would feel guilty if they didn't. Professors let students take makeup tests because they don't want students to cry and plead in their offices.

He also believes, however, that people are capable of true altruism: They help others, not to secure some reward or ease their own distress, but because they want to ease another person's suffering. This altruistic form of helping, he believes, results from *empathy*. Empathy allows us to take other people's perspective on events and to see the situation as they see it. We also share their emotions. If they are upset or fearful, then we become distressed and worried. And we help them, not to reduce *our* distress, but to reduce *their* distress.

Batson and his colleagues initially tested this **empathy-altruism hypothesis** by studying people's reactions to others who were experiencing distress or pain. They found that urging people to "imagine how the person . . . feels about the situation and how it has affected that person's life" increased their empathy for the victim and their helpfulness. Also, if they somehow blocked people's empathic emotions—say, by telling them that a pill they had just taken might make them tense—observers weren't as helpful (Coke, Batson, & McDavis, 1978, p. 755; Toi & Batson, 1982). People who helped others were also higher than nonhelpers in *dispositional empathy*—a generalized tendency to take the perspective of other people (Archer et al., 1981; see also Archer, 1984; Batson, Coke, & Pych, 1983).

Batson, however, still doubted the motives of the subjects who helped in his early studies. Even though they empathized with the victim and subsequently helped more, their motives may have been selfish rather than selfless. They may have been motivated by the need to reduce the distress they experienced when they saw someone else suffering (egoistic motivation) rather than by an empathic concern for the other person's well-being (empathic motivation). So Batson and his colleagues (1981) compared egoistic and empathic helpers in an ingenious study that asked subjects to sacrifice their own well-being to help another person. Batson's research team told each of the college women who participated that they were studying impression-formation processes in stressful situations. They therefore wanted the woman to watch another student (Elaine) on closed-

empathy-altruism hypothesis: Batson's (1990) analysis of helping that argues empathic observers are sometimes motivated only by their desire to reduce the victim's suffering rather than by an egoistic desire to secure some reward or ease their own distress.

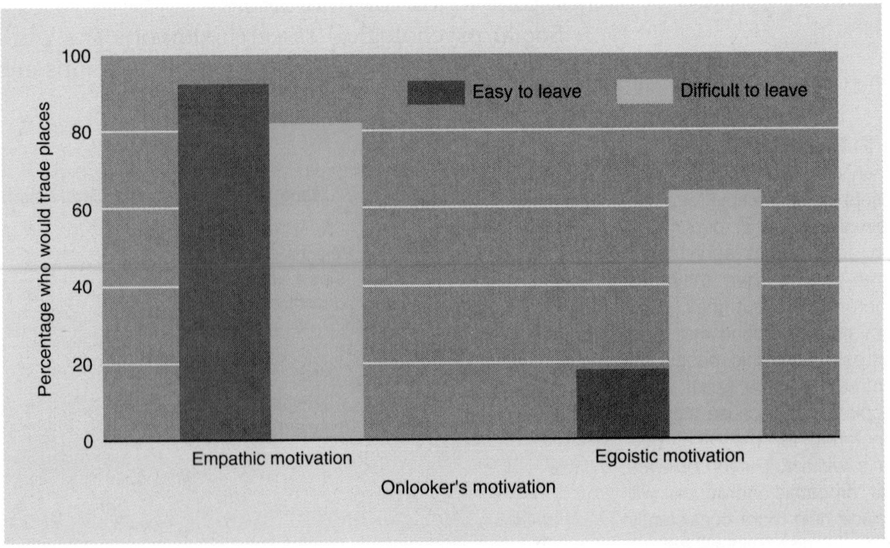

▲ **FIGURE 12-8**
Would you trade places with another person who was being given painful electric shocks? Batson found that people who were empathically motivated would, even when they could easily have escaped from the situation. People who were egoistically motivated, however, helped only if helping was the only way they could reduce their own discomfort. (From Batson et al., 1981)

circuit television as she received a series of mild electric shocks. Actually, subjects watched a carefully prepared videotape in which Elaine's reactions became so intense that after only two shocks the assistant had to stop and get her a glass of water. When the assistant returned with the water, she asked Elaine if she had ever had any prior experience with shocks. Elaine then revealed that, as a child, she had been traumatized when thrown onto an electrical fence by a horse. The assistant then suggested that they stop the experiment, but Elaine wouldn't hear of it. She had agreed to do it and didn't want to ruin the session. At this point, the assistant had an idea: Why not ask the observer if she would be willing to trade places with Elaine?

Batson's research group discovered that the observer's willingness to help depended on two factors: the amount of empathy she felt for Elaine and the ease with which she could escape from the distressing situation. First, some of the women felt considerable empathy for Elaine because they had been led to believe she was similar to them in many ways. Others, though, thought that Elaine was not like them at all, so their empathic motivation was minimal. Second, some of the women were offered an easy escape from the stressful situation. When the experimenter entered the observation room to ask them if they would be willing to change places, she explained, "If you want to continue in your role as the observer . . . all you need to do is answer a few questions about your impression of Elaine, and you'll be free to go." Others were told they would have to watch Elaine receive eight more shocks before they could escape (Batson et al., 1981, p. 295). Ease of escape didn't influence the empathic observers: Most of them volunteered to take Elaine's place (see Figure 12-8). Less empathic observers, in contrast, helped only when they couldn't get away from the situation. Apparently, their helpful responses were motivated by their desire to reduce their own discomfort rather than to save Elaine from further pain.

Batson still wasn't completely convinced that the empathic helpers were truly altruistic (Batson, 1990; Batson & Oleson, 1991). Perhaps, he suggested, they were only trying to avoid the shame and guilt that failing to help can generate. So his team carried out more studies in which they manipulated other people's awareness of the helper's response to the victim. Empathic people helped even when no one else knew that the victim needed help, so embarrassment or public shame couldn't be producing their benevolence. They also helped when the victim herself didn't know that the observer could have rendered assistance (Fultz et al., 1986). Empathic people even helped when Batson gave them a ready-made excuse for not helping. He led people to believe that, before they could take Elaine's place, they would have to pass an extremely difficult qualifying test. All people had to do to minimize their distress was skip the test or make a few mistakes, yet empathic people chose to take the test, and they answered more of the items correctly (Batson et al., 1988).

Despite Batson's diligence in searching for ulterior motives in his empathic helpers, other researchers still wonder whether true altruism exists. One group, led by Robert Cialdini, proposed that the empathic people become sad when they see others suffer, and that they help in order to make themselves feel happier. They are therefore acting selfishly: They help, not because they want to ease Elaine's suffering, but because they want to erase the sadness her suffering made them feel (Baumann, Cialdini, & Kenrick, 1981; Cialdini, Darby, & Vincent, 1973; Cialdini & Kenrick, 1976; Manucia, Baumann, & Cialdini, 1984).

Cialdini and his colleagues tested this **negative-state relief model** by changing their subjects' moods just before they had the opportunity to help the victim. In one study, Cialdini's research group used Batson's basic paradigm to offer some subjects an easy means of escaping from the situation. However, before asking whether they would be willing to trade places with the victim, some subjects were given an unexpected reward ($1) or they were lavishly complimented on their social skills. Researchers discovered that people who weren't empathizing with the victim didn't help as much when escape was easy rather than difficult, but this effect also held for empathic people whose mood had been boosted by the reward or praise (Cialdini et al., 1987). Empathic people in one study also helped less if they were led to believe that helping wouldn't change their mood because they had been given a "mood-fixing drug" (Cialdini et al., 1987), although a second study failed to replicate this result (Schroeder et al., 1988). Also, other investigators have extended Cialdini's model by suggesting that empathic people help because they want to share the joy the victims will experience when they escape their predicament (Smith, Keating, & Stotland, 1989; compare with Batson et al., 1991).

Timothy Mosher, at great risk to his well-being, saved Mana Mashoon's life. Was this an act of complete selflessness? Probably, for he passes most of the tests that Batson has used to screen out the egoists from the altruists. He could have gone to sleep; he could have blamed Mashoon's next-door neighbors; he could have looked for the source of the noise but given up before finding Mashoon's door. But he didn't. Moreover, although he might have helped just to reduce his own sadness, as the negative-state relief model suggests, he could have regained his happiness in a less life-threatening way. Some people who help might be egoists, but surely others are true altruists.

negative-state relief model: A theory of helping that suggests individuals who are in negative moods help others in order to improve their own negative mood state.

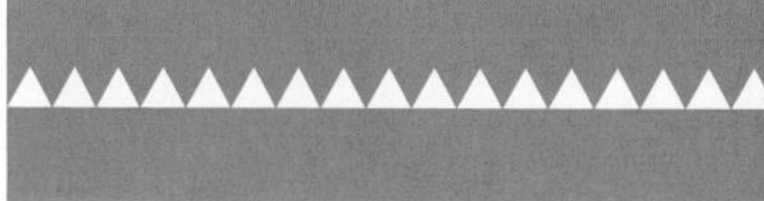

in the warm glow of success that follows victory, ask for the favor (Isen, 1970). Don't ask Gliceria for her notes on a rainy day. Wait until the sun is shining; people are usually in a better mood when the weather is pleasant (Cunningham, 1979). Catch the boss just after lunch when he is relaxed and contented (Isen & Levin, 1972). Momentary happiness usually heightens helping. When people think happy thoughts; receive compliments; find money in phone booths; win games; receive free samples; view pretty pictures; eat cookies or; listen to good news, soothing music, or a comedian, they become more helpful. A good mood apparently initiates a loop of positive thoughts and feelings, which sets the stage for prosocial behaviors (Cunningham, Steinberg, & Grev, 1980; Fried & Berkowitz, 1979; Isen, 1970; Isen, Clark, & Schwartz, 1976; Isen, Horn, & Rosenhan, 1973; Isen & Levin, 1972; Isen et al., 1978; Moore, Underwood, & Rosenhan, 1973; Veitch, de Wood, & Bosko, 1977; Weyant, 1978; Wilson, 1981; Yinon & Bizman, 1980).

Before you rush out and take advantage of the feel-good-do-good effect, be sure to consider these two important limitations. First, if your request is too troublesome, a good mood will not improve your chance of getting help. People try to maintain their good moods, so they probably won't grant your favor if it is too unpleasant (Isen & Simmonds, 1978). Second, make your request for help soon after their happiness-inducing experience, or the good mood may fade away. Immediately after the subjects in one study were given a free sample of stationery, they received a telephone call asking them to relay a message. Helpfulness peaked after 3 or 4 minutes, then quickly dropped down to a very low level (Isen et al., 1976).

The relationship between bad moods and helping is more complex, however. Initially, some investigators found that people who were depressed, sad, or unhappy were unlikely helpers. If asked to do a favor or donate to charity, they refused. Other researchers, however, confirmed a feel-bad-do-good phenomenon. Unhappy subjects—people who had just failed a test, seen a stranger receive shocks, reminisced about negative experiences, or imagined a close friend dying of cancer—tended to be *more* helpful (Rosenhan et al., 1981).

The *negative-state relief model* offers one explanation for these inconsistent findings. Robert Cialdini and his colleagues believe that when people are un-

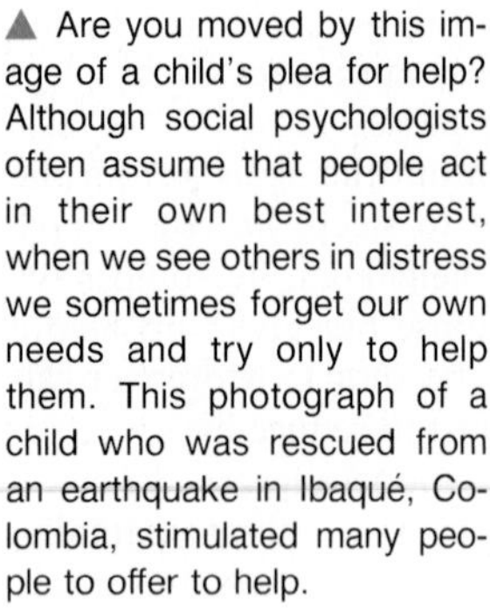

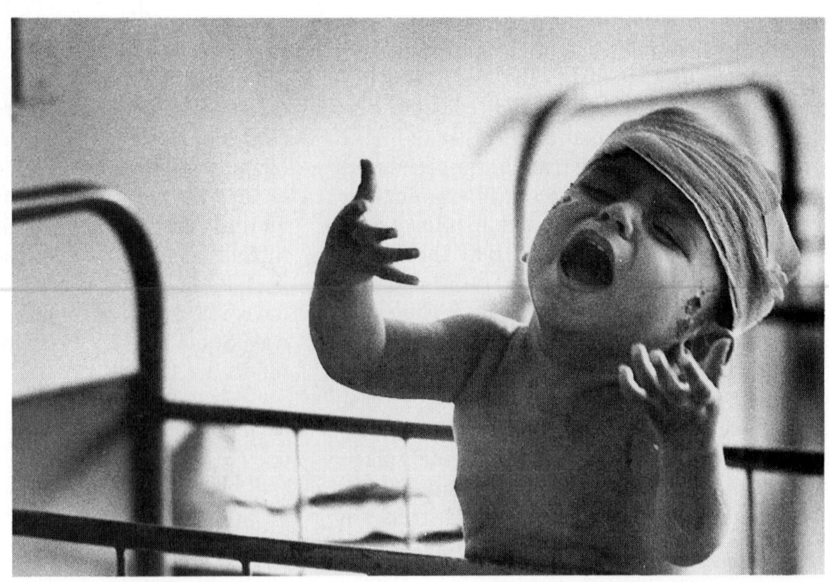

▲ Are you moved by this image of a child's plea for help? Although social psychologists often assume that people act in their own best interest, when we see others in distress we sometimes forget our own needs and try only to help them. This photograph of a child who was rescued from an earthquake in Ibaqué, Colombia, stimulated many people to offer to help.

▲ **TABLE 12-8**
Summing up: Emotions and helping

Theoretical Approach	*Characteristics*
Impulsive helping	Bystanders intervene immediately in some emergencies, presumably because emergencies are profoundly arousing.
Opponent-process theory	Helping behaviors that generate a negative emotion initially can lead to more positive emotions over the long term.
Two-factor theory of helping	Bystanders rely on situational cues to label their emotions. Individuals who attribute the victim's suffering to uncontrollable causes experience pity and concern and help more than individuals who attribute the victim's problems to controllable causes. Misattribution inhibits helping.
Empathy-altruism model	Bystanders react negatively when they see others suffering, but egoistic bystanders are motivated to reduce their personal distress, whereas empathic bystanders are motivated to reduce the victim's suffering. When bystanders can leave the situation without helping, empathic bystanders are more likely to remain to help.
Negative-state relief model	Individuals who are in good moods are more helpful than people in neutral moods. The negative-state relief model predicts that people in bad moods are more helpful if they think that helping will improve their mood.

happy, they often take steps to change their bad mood into a good mood. Furthermore, having learned that helping others is pleasant and satisfying, sad people sometimes use helping others to relieve their own sadness (Baumann, Cialdini, & Kenrick, 1981; Cialdini & Kenrick, 1976; Cialdini et al., 1973; Manucia et al., 1984).

Cialdini predicts that people who are in a bad mood will usually help others, for by doing so they help themselves. The model also predicts, however, that sad people will not help if their actions won't make them feel any better. Young children, who haven't yet learned that one of the greatest pleasures in life comes from doing things for others rather than for oneself, don't become more helpful when unhappy; they don't consider helping to be a viable method for achieving relief from their sadness (Moore et al., 1973; Rosenhan, Underwood, & Moore, 1974). Sorrowful adults who receive some unexpected money or praise just before a request for help aren't particularly helpful; they have already gained relief from their unhappiness through other means (Cialdini et al., 1973). If people believe their bad mood is highly resistant to change, they won't help; why should they help if helping won't improve their mood (Manucia et al., 1984)? People who are more concerned with their own problems than with those of the other person aren't particularly helpful, either. When bystanders' attention is focused on themselves, they tend to think, "I am the one who needs the help!" (Thompson, Cowan, & Rosenhan, 1980). Thus the negative-state relief model predicts that in most cases, a sad bystander is a helpful bystander. If, however, the helping → happiness route is obscured, blocked, or too long and difficult to follow, then sad bystanders are bad bystanders—they won't help (Cialdini & Fultz, 1990; Miller & Carlson, 1990; see Table 12-8).

Norms and Helping

We are often confronted with requests for charitable donations. A telephone caller asks if you want two tickets to a musical jamboree—it's for a good cause, he reminds you. A magazine ad asks you to "adopt" a hungry child overseas—after all, you have plenty to share. An announcer for your local public radio station thanks you for listening but reminds you to support the station by sending in a donation. In such situations, we often help because we feel we ought to—helping is guided by the norms of the situation.

The Rule of Reciprocity

reciprocity norm
A societal standard that enjoins individuals to pay back in kind what they receive from others.

In many social situations, our actions are based on a **reciprocity norm**. Simply stated, this norm enjoins us to pay back in kind what others give to us. If Norman gives you a birthday gift, then you should give him a birthday present, too. If Kara helps you with your studying, then you should help Kara when she has problems. If you give Angela a ride to class one day, you expect Angela to return the favor in the future. If Juan refuses to help you, then you won't help Juan. The reciprocity norm suggests that we help for two reasons: to pay back past favors and to create obligations for future favors.

Robert Cialdini (1993) describes how businesses and charities frequently use reciprocity to increase sales and donations. During the 1970s Hare Krishnas patrolled many public places seeking donations. Initially they weren't very successful; their odd appearance repelled passersby, who usually donated nothing more than a scowl. In time, however, the Krishnas increased their success by using a you-owe-me-one sales technique. Before asking for a donation, the Krishnas gave the passerby a gift: a book (for example, the *Bhagavad Gita*), a magazine (for example, *Back to Godhead*), or a flower. Having put the passerby in their debt, they then requested a donation. The power of the reciprocity norm is so great that many people complied.

Seasoned travelers refuse the flowers pressed on them by Krishnas, just as some people refuse an offer of help in order to avoid incurring a debt that must be paid back in the future. In one study, two-person teams were given two tasks to complete. During a practice session, subjects were led to believe that they would have trouble on Task 1 unless they received help from their partners. Some subjects thought their partners would probably need help to succeed in Task 2, but others were convinced that their partners could complete the task without their assistance. As anticipated, subjects were more likely to ask their partners for help on Task 1 when they thought they could return the favor during Task 2. Other studies supplement these findings by suggesting that people who receive help display intensely negative reactions if they cannot reciprocate that help (Greenberg & Shapiro, 1971; see Bar-tal, 1976, for a review).

Equity

Equity is a norm of justice that defines fair and unfair outcomes of relationships. As noted in Chapter 11, a relationship is equitable when those involved receive from it a return that is proportional to what they have invested in it. The relationship becomes inequitable when we receive more or less than we should, given our contribution to the relationship. Applied to helping, equity theory predicts that people who receive more than they think they should will try to give up some of their resources to reestablish equity. If, for example, Joyce feels her salary is too high considering the work she does, she may donate a portion of it to charity. If Bernard can't pay his share of the rent one month, he may feel compelled to do small favors for his roommates (Adams, 1965; Walster, Walster, & Berscheid, 1978).

Equity theory predicts not only when people will help, but also the reactions of the recipients of aid. We often naively assume other people want help and will react favorably when it is given. Helping, however, is a mixed blessing

(Fisher, Nadler, & Whitcher-Alagna, 1982). In some cases, people do appreciate receiving help because they feel that, given their inputs and outcomes, they deserve that help. When a wife helps her husband bring in the groceries, he appreciates the help because he has already contributed by going to the store. In other cases, however, helping disrupts the equity of a relationship. When people are given more than they feel they deserve, they feel so uncomfortable that they will try to restore equity in one of two ways: by altering what they put into and take out of the relationship (actual equity) or by distorting their perceptions of these inputs and outcomes (psychological equity). Thus help can lead to a range of negative consequences, including (1) a drop in self-esteem, (2) derogation of the helper (ingratitude), and (3) exaggeration of one's own misfortunes (Fisher, DePaulo, & Nadler, 1981; Nadler, 1991; Nadler & Fisher, 1986; Shell & Eisenberg, 1992).

Social Responsibility

social responsibility norm A societal standard prescribing socially commendable actions, such as helping others in need.

When others depend on us to help them, and we know that they cannot reciprocate our help, the **social responsibility norm** shapes our actions. According to this norm, helping people who are in need—the sick, the infirm, the very young, the injured—is a duty that should not be shirked.

The norm of social responsibility explains a curious reaction displayed by some helpers. Kidney donors frequently downplay their own valor (Fellner & Marshall, 1981). The statement of this 60-year-old woman is typical: "People say to me: what a brave thing to do. I say, there was no bravery connected. It was just a thing I had to do" (p. 357). Similarly, an 18-year-old man who donated a kidney to his brother said, "Some say I'm a very brave person, but bravery had nothing to do with it. Others say I must love my brother a lot, but it seemed like the thing to do at the time" (p. 362). Time and again, donors explain that they simply "had to do it."

When does the norm of social responsibility compel us to help? Consider the plight of the Joneses, whose son was stricken with cystinosis, a kidney disorder. When their son's kidneys failed, both the mother and father volunteered to be donors. However, only the father's kidney was suitable, so he was the donor. Several years later, however, the son required another kidney. In this case, his brother volunteered, explaining, "it was no big deal."

The son's willingness to be a donor can be explained through reference to the norm of social responsibility. First, his brother was counting on him to give up a kidney. Without it, he would die. Second, his brother's plight was caused by factors that were beyond his control; he couldn't be blamed for the disease. Third, the mother and father both served as models for helping behavior. Fourth, the family was quite religious and frequently noted the importance of helping others who are in need (Fellner & Marshall, 1981). Thus, the norm of social responsibility becomes stronger in the following circumstances (Berkowitz, 1972; Berkowitz & Connor, 1966; Berkowitz & Daniels, 1963; Berkowitz, Klanderman, & Harris, 1964; Bryan & Davenport, 1968; Paulus, Shaffer, & Downing, 1977):

- The victim depends on us to help.
- The victim can't be held responsible for creating his or her problem.
- Other people model compliance with the norm.
- Bystanders are explicitly reminded that helping others is a duty.

Personal Norms

Norms of reciprocity, equity, and social responsibility provide general standards for behavior, but our own personal values and beliefs also guide our actions (see

▲ **TABLE 12-9**
Summing up: Normative approaches to helping

Norm	*Characteristics*
Reciprocity	Individuals help people who have previously helped them. Organizations seeking donations sometimes give away small items to increase compliance with their request for help.
Equity	People who receive more than they have given will help others (through donations, volunteerism) to reestablish a sense of equity. Individuals who receive help sometimes react to the inequity the giving creates by derogating the giver.
Social responsibility	People often feel that those who can should help those who need help (for example, the sick, the homeless, the injured).
Personal norms	People help when helping behavior is consistent with their situated, self-based standards and personal values.

Table 12-9). Christopher always stops when he sees a disabled car at the roadside. Christina never stops to assist stranded motorists, but she regularly donates blood. Noeline doesn't give blood, but she canvasses for the March of Dimes. They all help in ways that are consistent with their own personal norms. Christopher's actions are based on the norm "I should stop to help people who have car trouble"; Christina believes "I should donate blood"; and Noeline feels obligated to "raise funds for worthwhile charities." As these examples show, **personal norms** are situated, self-based standards for specific behavior generated from internalized values (Schwartz & Howard, 1982, p. 329).

personal norm
A personal standard for specific behavior generated by one's own internalized values.

Studies conducted by Shalom Schwartz and his colleagues have repeatedly demonstrated the impact of personal norms on helping behavior (Schwartz, 1968, 1970, 1974, 1977; Schwartz & Fleishman, 1978; Schwartz & Howard, 1980, 1981). Several studies have measured subjects' specific personal norms concerning various actions (such as giving blood, tutoring blind children, and donating bone marrow) and their subsequent willingness to engage in those actions. As expected, people who strongly endorsed a personal norm pertaining to the action were far more likely to help in the particular situation. The link

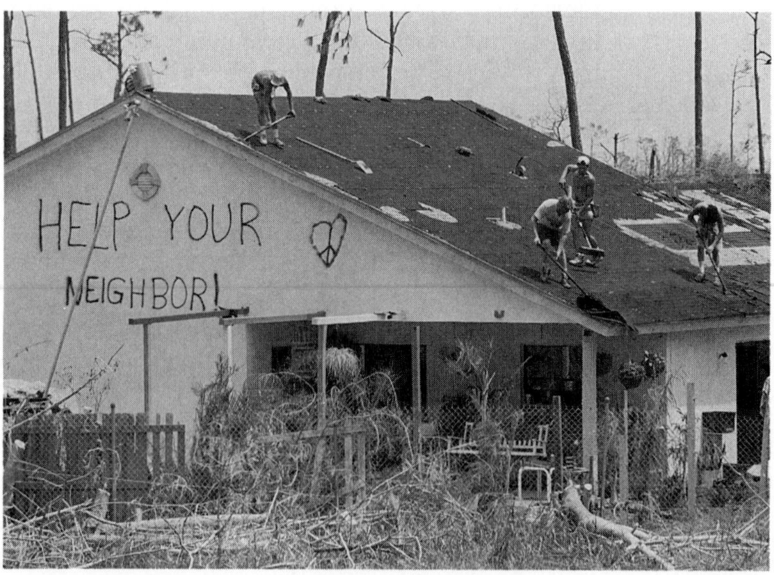

▲ The norm of social responsibility reminds us that helping one another is a social obligation that should not be shirked.

between personal norms and helping became even more apparent when other variables, such as the tendency to take responsibility for others and awareness of the consequences of one's actions to others, were taken into account (see Schwartz & Howard, 1982).

Helping: A Look Back

Why did Mosher help Mashoon? Why didn't anyone save Kitty Genovese? Prosocial behavior is complex social behavior, and each perspective summarized in Table 12-10 accounts for some, but not all, of that complexity. Mosher may have reacted instinctively to Mashoon's screams, for we are all biologically ready to respond to others' distress. He may have been the kind of person who helps people—one of those rare altruistic personalities. Mosher also decided that help was needed, whereas Genovese's neighbors decided that help was unnecessary. Many of her neighbors noticed that something was happening, but only a few thought that they were witnessing an emergency. And fewer still felt responsible for helping or identified a way to help. Their decision not to help may also have been influenced by the lack of rewards for intervening and by the high cost of getting involved in another person's problems.

We should not, however, leave out the emotional and normative side of helping. Mosher experienced empathic concern for Mashoon, but Genovese's neighbors may have blamed her instead of her attacker. And what of the norms of the setting? Did they owe Genovese their help? Would equity be served by a call to the police? Did they feel it was their personal or social duty to help Genovese? Apparently not. Norms can encourage helping, but they can also discourage it.

These factors dispel some of the mystery surrounding helping and failures to help, for they explain the nature of the forces that immobilized the bystanders. These findings also offer some practical advice should you ever find yourself in need of help. You must arouse others' empathy by making your distress clear to them. Force the bystanders to make the right decisions. Make the costs of failure to help too great to ignore. Create feelings of empathy in those who are watching. Make it clear that they will feel better if they help. And emphasize the norms that require them to help (see the section "Application: Encouraging Altruism").

Robert Cialdini (1993) explains how he once used these methods to get help when he was involved in an automobile accident. Dizzy after the collision, he watched as cars drove by without stopping.

> I remember thinking, "Oh no, it's happening just like the research says. They're all passing by!" I consider it fortunate that, as a social psychologist, I knew enough about the bystander studies to have that particular thought. By thinking of my predicament in terms of the research findings, I knew exactly what to do. Pulling myself up so I could be seen clearly, I pointed at the driver of one car: "Call the police." To a second and a third driver, pointing directly each time: "Pull over, we need help." The responses of these people were instantaneous. They summoned a police car and ambulance immediately, they used their handkerchiefs to blot the blood from my face, they put a jacket under my head, they volunteered to serve as witnesses to the accident; and one person even offered to ride with me to the hospital. (p. 114)

By destroying the situational factors that inhibit helping, Cialdini was able to secure the help he needed. It is tragic that Kitty Genovese could not achieve the same goal.

▲ **TABLE 12-10**
Summing up: Explanations of helping

Theoretical Perspective	*Source of Helping*	*When Do People Help?*
Evolutionary theory	Instincts	People give more help to those who are genetically similar to them and those who may help them in the future.
Individual-differences models	Personal qualities of individuals	Helping depends on the characteristics of the people in the situation. Individuals with a propensity to help others (for example, empathy, a sense of social responsibility) help, provided the situation does not inhibit these proclivities.
Decision models	Bystanders' decisions	Bystanders help when they notice the event, label it an emergency, feel responsible, identify a way to help, and personal or situational factors don't prevent them from implementing the help. They also help more if the costs of helping are low and the costs of failure to help are high.
Motivational models	Emotions and motivations	Emergencies are emotionally arousing events. Some emotions, such as pity and concern, facilitate helping, but others, such as anger, inhibit it. Empathy, a good mood, or a bad mood that can be improved by doing a good deed facilitate helping.
Normative models	Conformity to norms	People help because they feel obligated to reciprocate helping, they strive to maintain equity, they feel responsible for those who are in need, and their personal values require certain forms of helping.

Summary

Prosocial behaviors, in contrast to harmful, *antisocial behaviors,* benefit other people. Prosocial behavior takes many forms, including cooperation, common courtesy, and sympathy, but our willingness to use our own personal energies and resources to remedy another person's problems—*helping behavior*—is particularly intriguing. Not all help qualifies as *altruism,* for in some cases helpers are selfish rather than selfless.

Many explanations have been offered to account for our tendency to help others. Evolutionary psychology argues that *Homo sapiens* help one another for two basic reasons. First, by helping relatives we are protecting the genes that we share (*kin selection*). Second, even helping people who aren't related to us is adaptive because it increases the chances that these people will help us when we are in distress (*reciprocal altruism*). Our apparently inborn tendency to respond to others who are in pain (the empathic-distress response) and twin studies of helping lend support to this view.

Personality theorists, in contrast, look to the characteristics of the people who give and need help in order to predict prosocial behavior. Empathic, socially responsible, self-confident people usually help more than others, although their reactions are shaped in part by the nature of the emergency situations. The sexes often react differently in helping situations, for women are more helpful when other people need social support, and men give more help during emergencies. People who live in cities help less than those who live in the country, and people who possess socially desirable attributes, such as physical beauty, tend to be helped more than less attractive people. We also give more help to people who seem to be similar to us in some way (the similarity-helping effect). This bias extends to racial similarities.

Dozens of studies have confirmed the *bystander effect*: People are less likely to help in groups than when they are alone. The tragic case of Kitty Genovese illustrates the bystander effect. Even though 38 people witnessed the attack, no one helped her escape her assailant. Latané and Darley's *decision model of helping* suggests that the presence of other people can inhibit helping at any of the five steps needed for helping: noticing the event, interpreting the event as an emergency, taking responsibility, identifying a way to help, and implementing the chosen form of help. People in groups sometimes experience a reduction in personal responsibility (*diffusion of responsibility*) and worry that they will be blamed for the problem (confusion of responsibility). Bystanders may also calculate the costs and rewards associated with helping and failing to help. As the *cost-reward model of helping* predicts, helping is most likely to occur when its cost is low and the cost of failure to help is high.

Helping situations are also emotionally arousing. In some cases, people engage in *impulsive helping*: They ignore personal costs and render aid in dangerous emergencies. Some emotionally difficult forms of helping, such as donating blood, may also be maintained by the strong positive emotions that arise to oppose the negative emotions associated with the action (the *opponent-process theory*). Many researchers also believe that helping is influenced by the way we label our emotional reactions. According to the two-factor theory of emotions, when we see others in need, we become physiologically aroused. If we misattribute our arousal to some irrelevant factor, such as our nervousness, then we will not help. Helping is also unlikely when we assign a negative label to our emotion, such as anger or disgust. Helping becomes more likely when we realize that our arousal is caused by our concern for the other person. In some cases, we may help simply in order to reduce our personal distress (egoistic helping). In contrast, we may help because we want to reduce the other person's distress (the *empathy-altruism hypothesis*). Moods also play a role in producing helping behavior. We tend to be more helpful when we are in a good mood, though bad moods *sometimes* increase the tendency to help. As the *negative-state relief model* explains, if we feel that helping others will provide relief from our negative mood, then we tend to help.

Our decision to help another person may also be influenced by a desire to conform to the norms of the situation, including the *reciprocity norm,* the *equity norm,* the *social responsibility norm,* and *personal norms.*

For More Information

• *The Altruism Question: Toward a Social-Psychological Answer,* by C. Daniel Batson (1991), discusses the theoretical and philosophical underpinnings of altruism and presents the results of his attempt to test for true altruism experimentally.

• *The Altruistic Personality: Rescuers of Jews in Nazi Europe,* by Samuel P. Oliner and Pearl M. Oliner (1988), summarizes the results of hundreds of interviews with people who sheltered Jews from harm during World War II. A powerful analysis of the personality characteristics frequently exhibited by people who help rather than turn away from others who are in need.

• *The Caring Child,* by Nancy Eisenberg (1992), examines the developmental antecedents of the altruistic personality.

• *The Compassionate Beast: What Science Is Discovering about the Humane Side of Humankind,* by Morton Hunt (1990), is a compelling summary of recent studies of the roots of helping that deftly mixes research findings with material drawn from personal interviews with investigators.

• *Emergency Intervention,* by Jane Piliavin, John Dovidio, Samuel Gaertner, and Russell Clark III (1981), presents an overall framework for understanding helping behavior. The importance of costs and rewards is highlighted, but other variables—such as number of bystanders and emotional arousal—are also considered.

• *Giving Blood: The Development of an Altruistic Identity,* by Jane Allyn Piliavin and Peter Callero (1991), uses five theoretical models in an attempt to explain why people donate blood.

• *Helping and Being Helped: Naturalistic Studies,* edited by Shirlynn Spacapan and Stuart Oskamp (1992), examines a number of different helping processes, including volunteerism, self-help groups, and spousal caregiving.

• *New Directions in Helping: Help-Seeking,* edited by Bella M. DePaulo, Arie Nadler, and Jeffrey D. Fisher (1983), looks at the other side of helping by examining how the person who needs help reacts when help is given and the factors that prompt individuals to seek out help.

Application: Encouraging Altruism

In the summer of 1991, dozens of people relaxing at Meridian Hill Park in Washington, D.C., watched with "marked indifference" as a young man who was bleeding profusely from gunshot wounds collapsed on the sidewalk (Casteneda, 1991). In that same city, cars sped by a mugging victim, ignoring his cries for help. Eventually, a bus driver stopped his bus and called an ambulance for the injured man ("Bus Driver Aids," 1990). On December 28, 1991, eight people were killed in New York City when concertgoers mobbed the doors to a gymnasium. Instead of helping the injured, some crowd members stole their purses and wallets (Hampson, 1992). And no one helped Kitty Genovese when she called out for help.

Human beings may have a great capacity for kindness, but in so many situations we fail to fulfill that potential. Too often we see others in need and distress, and we turn away instead of lending a helping hand. What can be done to encourage helpful behavior and discourage indifference and mistrust?

Parents can have a profound influence on their children's prosocial tendencies. As Chapter 7's discussion of social learning theory suggests, children can learn both antisocial and prosocial behavior by watching and imitating their parents. Children who are raised by warm, empathic mothers tend themselves to be more prosocial, as are children who describe their fathers as generous and compassionate (Rutherford & Mussen, 1968; Zahn-Waxler, Radke-Yarrow, & King, 1979). As noted earlier in the chapter, Oliner and Oliner (1988) compared people who helped Jews escape from the Nazis during World War II with people who didn't help. Although both sets of people remembered that their parents stressed concepts of fairness and justice, the helpers' parents tended to act in caring, sympathetic ways toward other people. Helpers said such things as

> I did everything from my heart—I didn't think about getting something for it. My father taught me to be this way. (p. 227)
>
> My nature is the result of being raised by my mother. She was my role model. She helped a lot of people. (p. 228)
>
> [My father] taught me to love my neighbor—to consider him my equal whatever his nationality or religion. He taught me especially to be tolerant. (p. 165)

Many of the helpers mentioned their parents' openness and tolerance of other people. They thought of other people inclusively, as part of humanity in general rather than in some other group. They therefore responded altruistically when people needed help. Nonhelpers' parents, in contrast, often displayed *moral exclusion*—even though they espoused principles of fairness and justice, they did not apply these principles to people who weren't members of their group. They excluded Jews from their moral circle (Staub, 1989, 1990).

Parents who want to encourage prosocial behavior in their children must act in prosocial ways themselves instead of only preaching the importance of helping others. Children raised by parents who express prosocial values and act on these values tend to be more altruistic than children raised by parents who espouse lofty principles but don't act on them (Clary & Miller, 1986). Other suggestions include the following:

• Explain why helping others is important. Children raised by parents who express prosocial principles, such as "It's our duty to help others," but who don't discuss the reasons behind the principles, aren't as likely to be altruistic as children raised by parents who explain the reasons why they help others (Bryan & Walbek, 1970; Eisenberg-Berg & Geisheker, 1979). Explanations that stress the importance of caring and sympathy are particularly effective (Eisenberg, 1992).

• Encourage children to make internal attributions whenever they behave in unselfish, prosocial ways. Compared to children in a control condition, children who were told, on two occasions, that they were generous, helpful individuals were more likely to help a sick child (Grusec, 1991).

• Avoid using harsh punishment. When children act in negative, antisocial ways, provide them with careful explanations when you discipline them. The child who is told, "Go and share your toys with Mark. Can't you see that you made him cry?" is more likely to be helpful than the child who is spanked for not sharing (Hoffman, 1975; Zahn-Waxler, Radke-Yarrow, & Chapman, 1983).

Schools can also encourage prosocial, cooperative behavior by creating curricula that stress cooperation, sharing, and helping rather than competition, rivalry, and individual achievement. One program, the Child Development Project, teaches children to balance their own personal needs against the needs of other people. Students are taught in cooperative groups, where they discuss causes of conflicts and practice identifying other people's viewpoints. Teachers model prosocial values and introduce activities that help students see situations from others' perspectives. The children are also given many opportunities to perform helpful behaviors, such as tutoring other students or helping with classroom chores. Students who have attended such schools for several years act more prosocially than students who have attended regular classrooms (Solomon et al., 1988).

This type of educational program, although atypical for the United States, is commonly used in non-Western, collectivist countries such as the former Soviet Union, China, and Japan. The Chinese culture, for example, stresses the importance of order and harmony among people. Children are taught to avoid disputes and to respect other people's feelings. The motto of preschools in China is often "Cooperation first, competition second," and daily lessons stress the importance of sacrificing individual needs for the collective good. Educators also glorify the actions of political or storybook figures who have acted in altruistic ways. In the 1960s and 1980s, children read about Lei Feng, who supposedly acted in prosocial ways at every turn. He would go hungry so that others could eat, he gave money to the family of his friends, and he volunteered to help with community projects. His diary entries referred repeatedly to his desire to help others, his unselfishness, and the importance of helping the group (Stevenson, 1991).

The Chinese approach to encouraging prosocial behavior succeeds because Chinese society, in general, stresses interdependence rather than independence; cooperation rather than competition. Even in Western societies, however, steps can be taken to foster cooperation and interpersonal harmony. Many experts recommend using the media, including television, movies, and newspapers, to reinforce prosocial values. The television program *Mister Rogers' Neighborhood,* for example, strives to encourage prosocial values by stressing the importance of community, sharing, communication, and impulse control. Children who watched the program regularly offered more sophisticated explanations for their prosocial behaviors, and they were more likely to act in positive ways in their classrooms (Friedrich & Stein, 1973). Other programs, such as *Fat Albert and the Cosby Kids* and *Superfriends,* also had positive effects on viewers (Liebert & Sprafkin, 1988). Children who watched an episode of *Superfriends* with a prosocial message, for example, were more helpful than children who saw an episode that used punishment to illustrate the same prosocial message (Liss, Reinhardt, & Fredricksen, 1983).

In sum, many social psychologists are not content simply to study the complex of factors that prompts people to help or fail to help. Instead, they try to find ways to encourage people to be more helpful toward one another. Their work follows in the tradition of Kurt Lewin's (1951) action research, which uses social-psychological theory and research to explore and possibly solve important problems that face our groups, our communities, our countries, and the entire world (see Chapter 1). Such problems are often called *social issues,* for they raise important but debatable questions about how we should treat one another. This chapter has considered prosocial behavior, but other chapters examined such issues as sexual harassment, prejudice, intergroup conflict, rape, violence, and pollution. Social psychologists' interest in these topics underscores the field's applied side. Social psychologists are not, in all cases, dispassionate scientists who are content to remain in the so-called ivory towers of academia. Rather, they are also social activists who use their knowledge of social behavior to identify ways to enhance the quality of our social lives. They are *pro*social psychologists rather than simply social psychologists.

THIRTEEN

Aggression

Bernhard Hugo Goetz (pictured in chapter opening) leaves his New York City apartment and enters the subway station at about 1 P.M. He boards the downtown express and takes a seat next to four young men—Troy Canty, Barry Allen, James Ramseur, and Darrell Cabey. The four talk loudly among themselves until one of them, Canty, turns to Goetz and says, "How are ya?" Goetz doesn't answer. Canty stands up, walks over to Goetz, and demands, "Give me $5." Some witnesses say Goetz says, "What do you want?" Canty repeats his demand. Goetz answers, "I have $5 for each of you." He pulls a .38-caliber revolver from his jacket and shoots all four of the youths. Someone pulls the emergency cord, and the train stops. Goetz reassures two women on the subway car that he means them no harm before he jumps out of the car. He remains at large for nine days. Then, on New Year's Eve, he walks into a police station in New Hampshire and confesses to the shootings (Fletcher, 1988).

Goetz's actions are by no means unique. With an extensive and sinister arsenal of weapons—teeth, fists, clubs, spears, arrows, swords, guns, cannon, bombs, missiles, and nuclear warheads—humans have been injuring other humans for millennia. Goetz's actions flow from a long tradition of violence among the species *Homo sapiens*. Yet any act of violence, including Goetz's, raises a number of interrelated questions about aggression. We must first ask, "What is aggression?" Many of the people surveyed in the months that followed the incident approved of Goetz's actions and argued that he was justified in attacking the youths. Goetz clearly injured other people, but do we want to label his behavior *aggression*?

Second, how can Goetz's action, and violent behaviors in general, be explained? Some people dubbed him the "subway vigilante" and the "*Death Wish* gunman," calling to mind a Charles Bronson–like figure who haunted the subways in search of muggers to punish. Others felt that his actions were instinctive; that anyone, pushed too far by hoodlums, might react with violence. Still others felt that he was motivated by aggressive racist urges. The young men weren't armed, and any violence on their part was implied rather than explicit. But they were black, and Goetz was white. No matter what the answer, we want to know what causes aggression. Is it part of our instinctive heritage, or is it shaped by the social environment in which we live? Once we understand the causes of aggression, we will want to examine the factors that can decrease it. Goetz's actions led to tragedy for both Goetz and the four young people he injured. Could this incident have been prevented? Can other acts of aggression, which have become so commonplace in recent years, be eliminated?

What Is Aggression?

Intuitively, you know the difference between actions that are aggressive and actions that are not aggressive. If Goetz walked up to the men and shot them because they were noisy, then his actions would certainly be considered aggressive. But if he was only defending himself and his property—should we call his actions *aggression*? What if Goetz had given the teenagers the money, but inside had seethed with rage and fantasized about killing each of them? What if he had pushed one of the young men away, and the youth had fallen and injured his head? Would Goetz still have been aggressive if he had pulled out his gun, it jammed, and nothing happened when he pulled the trigger? What is aggression, and what are its basic forms?

Defining Aggression

The New York prosecutor charged Goetz with attempted murder, for he believed Goetz's actions met all the requirements for that crime. First, Goetz himself admitted that he was the man who shot the four youths. Second, the prosecutor believed that Goetz intended to hurt the men. In fact, one witness reported hearing Goetz say, "Here's another!" before shooting Darrell Cabey a second time. Last, Goetz's actions resulted in catastrophic consequences for the four men. All were hospitalized, and Cabey was left partially paralyzed.

The elements identified by the prosecutor—a harmful action, the intent to do harm, and negative consequences—are also the elements of a social-psychological definition of aggression. Although no clear-cut rule allows us to distinguish in all cases between acts that are aggressive and acts that are not, in most cases an action performed with the intention of harming or injuring another person qualifies as **aggression**. The key elements in this definition are action, intention, and harm (Berkowitz, 1993; Green, 1990).

aggression
An action performed with the deliberate intention of harming or injuring another person.

First, aggression is often accompanied by strong internal states, such as anger and passion, but *aggression* refers to behavior. The action may not be as manifestly damaging as shooting someone, for the behavior can be verbal or nonverbal, direct or indirect, and blatant or subtle. But the individual must do something—threaten, insult, ridicule, or attack—before the label of *aggression* can be applied.

Second, people usually call harmdoers *aggressive* when they *intend* to inflict harm on others. The clumsy passerby who bumps into you on the sidewalk isn't aggressive; neither is the careless driver who broadsides your car after running a red light. But assassins who are poor shots and muggers on the subway who are shot before they can do any damage are still aggressive because they intended to harm others (Feshbach, 1971, 1990; Tedeschi, Smith, & Brown, 1974).

Third, aggressive behaviors are antisocial—they expose others to *harmful, aversive consequences*. These aversive consequences include both physical and psychological injury. The abusive father may not hit his children, but he may terrorize and degrade them by threatening and insulting them. Aggression involves a victim who is an unwilling participant in the interaction (Baron, 1977; Baron & Richardson, 1994).

Types of Aggression and Violence

When Andrea learns that she has been passed over for promotion, she gets so angry that she shouts insults at her supervisor. The security guard twists the troublemaker's arms behind his back to control him. John strikes his wife repeatedly on the face and arms during an argument.

These actions all qualify as aggression: They are behaviors, they are intentional, and they are harmful. However, they differ from one another in many respects. Andrea's actions flow from her anger, but the security guard is using aggression as a means to an end. Also, the guard may be justified in harming the troublemaker. The troublemaker may have threatened him, so he used force to protect himself from harm. John's actions, however, are both unjust and unlawful.

Emotional versus instrumental aggression. Did Goetz act out of passion or out of reason? The prosecutor thought that Goetz was an angry, bitter man who lost control of his emotions. The defense, however, argued that Goetz was a reasonable man who defended himself. Goetz had been mugged before, and he claimed that he immediately realized that the four young men were going to attack him. So he acted first.

Aggression, in some cases, is stimulated by strong emotions. The enraged subway rider, the hate-filled bigot, the hostile rapist, and the fanatical terrorist attack others for one basic reason: They want to inflict harm and suffering on their victims. This *emotional aggression* is also called hostile, affective, irritable, impulsive, or angry aggression, for it occurs when emotionally aroused people lash out aggressively against other people (Baron, 1977; Berkowitz, 1993). *Instrumental aggression*, in contrast, occurs when people use violent actions to control and influence other people (Felson & Tedeschi, 1993; Tedeschi, Melburg, & Rosenfeld, 1981). Goetz knew that shooting the men would injure them, but perhaps his attack was just his way of protecting himself. Similarly, white racists may attack blacks to drive them out of their neighborhood. The abusive husband may assault his wife to subordinate her. The mugger may shoot his victims so they can't escape before he takes their wallets. The racist, batterer, and mugger intend to hurt their victims, but inflicting harm isn't their primary goal.

Legitimate and illegitimate aggression. We don't necessarily condemn all aggressive actions. When a soldier kills the enemy in battle, the police officer uses her nightstick to subdue a violent criminal, or the executioner pulls the switch at the electric chair, they are inflicting harm on another person. Their actions, however, are sanctioned by society—they are considered by many to be legitimate forms of aggression rather than illegitimate ones (Tedeschi, Smith, & Brown, 1974).

People weigh a number of factors before deciding whether or not an aggressive action is legitimate. In some cases, we consider an action legitimate if the perpetrator occupies certain social roles: Police officers and soldiers, for example, may use force to achieve their goals. But even these individuals, if they exceed the boundaries of their authority, will be condemned as illegitimate aggressors. The police officers who beat Rodney King claimed they were only subduing him. Perceivers who saw the videotape of the beating labeled their actions illegitimate, however. We tend to think that actions we take to defend ourselves against an aggressor are also legitimate forms of violence. Goetz claimed that he acted in self-defense, and many individuals who read about the incident agreed that he was within his rights to shoot the young men. We generally condemn the individual who starts the fight, but we tolerate the violent action of the person who responds defensively (Brown & Tedeschi, 1976).

Culture also plays a role in determining our interpretation of harmful actions. In cultures that maintain strict hierarchies of authority, such as China, superiors aren't viewed as aggressive when they insult their subordinates

(Bond et al., 1985). In Sweden, spanking your child is a criminal offense (although it carries no penalty), but parents in other countries rely on harsh means to discipline children. Husbands who assault their wives aren't uniformly condemned across all cultures.

Aggression and violence. Chapter 12 argues that we tend to be more prosocial than antisocial. But for people living in such places as Northern Ireland, the Middle East, Somalia, and many large cities in the United States, aggressive acts seem to outnumber prosocial acts, and aggression takes many forms.

Criminal violence consists of harmful, unlawful actions, such as assault, aggravated assault, rape, attempted murder, and murder itself. According to statistics, nearly 3 of every 100 Americans will be victims of violent crime, and the rates are much higher for some segments of the population (Langan & Innes, 1986; Nisbett, 1993). Murder, for example, is the leading cause of death among African American men between the ages of 15 and 34.

Sexual assault has increased by 21% since 1979 (FBI, 1989), prompting some experts to argue we are in the midst of a rape epidemic (Koss, 1992, 1993; White, 1983). Researchers are quick to point out that many women don't report incidents that legally qualify as rape, attempted rape, or sexual assault, so the actual incidence of sexual assault is likely to be higher than the reported incidence (White & Sorenson, 1992). Rape often occurs in the context of a relationship, such as dating and marriage. Fifteen percent of the college women surveyed in one study reported that they were raped by a date, and 10% of the men surveyed admitted that they had used force to subdue a date (Shotland, 1992).

In recent years the public has also become increasingly aware of *domestic violence*—child abuse, spouse abuse, and abuse of parents by their children. Tragically, the home, so long considered a haven in a heartless world, is now recognized as a setting for routine violence. Evidence suggests that aggression is an integral part of growing up in America. Ninety-three percent of all adults were spanked during childhood, 31% were punched or beaten, and more than 12% report that they were cut with a knife or threatened with a gun (Mulvihill & Tumin, 1969; Wood, 1990). Conservative estimates indicate that 1.4 to 1.9 million children between the ages of 3 and 17 will be dangerously abused this year; not just spanked or paddled, but kicked, bitten, beaten, knifed, or shot (Gelles, 1980a, 1980b). And about one-quarter of all American wives have been physically abused at least once by their husbands (Straus & Gelles, 1990; Straus, Gelles, & Steinmetz, 1980).

Youth violence has also increased, as reflected by the 85% increase of assaults in schools in the 1980s and the 40% increase in rapes. Attacks on teachers also rose dramatically, from 15,000 in 1955 to 110,000 in 1980 (Harootunian & Apter, 1983). Twenty percent of the students attending inner-city schools surveyed in one study reported that they had been threatened with a gun, and 12% reported that they had been shot at (Sheley, Smith, & Wright, 1992). One student in five admits to carrying a gun or weapon to school at least once during a typical month (CDC, 1991).

Collective violence—aggressive actions perpetrated by groups such as gangs or mobs—is also a significant social problem in many societies. Gang activity in urban areas has increased dramatically in recent years and has been blamed for an escalating number of homicides among minorities. In its most extreme form, collective violence takes an organized and deadly form—warfare. International violence, or the "use of armed force by a state against the sovereignty, territorial integrity or political independence of another state" continues to threaten the survival of the human species (United Nations, 1974). These statistics are sobering, and they compel us to search for the underlying causes of aggression in human beings.

What Causes Aggression?

Humans have lived with and died by aggression since the beginning of recorded history. Estimates suggest that about 2.6 wars have been fought each year for the last 5,600 years, yielding a total of 14,560. During the period from 1820 to 1945, about 58 million people died violently. In this century alone, nearly one million Americans have been murdered.

Why are humans aggressive? Scholars have debated this question for centuries. Some, like 17th-century philosopher Thomas Hobbes, argued that humans are naturally vicious creatures. Calling our species *Homo lupus*, or human wolf, he believed we would quickly murder one another if we were not restrained by civilization. Others, however, accepted philosopher John Locke's *tabula rasa* argument, which posits that at birth humans are blank slates on which experiences leave impressions. According to Locke, we learn to become aggressive.

Current explanations of aggression still resonate with these two arguments. Many theorists argue that aggression is part of human *nature*, for it springs from our basic physiology, our biochemistry, and instincts rooted in our evolution. Other theorists think aggression is an acquired quality; we aren't born aggressive, but learn to behave aggressively through experience. *Nurture* theorists therefore trace aggression to people's motivations, learning, and social norms. Both explanations are considered here.

Aggression and Human Nature

No discipline holds a monopoly on the study of aggression. Whereas social scientists pursue the psychological, social, and cultural causes of violence, biological scientists search for causes in physiological, biochemical, and hereditary mechanisms of individual organisms. Aggression is a complex form of behavior, but it is also a primitive one. Bernhard Goetz can solve complex problems, communicate with other people using spoken and written language, formulate plans and identify goals, and even contemplate his own mortality. But Bernhard Goetz, like all *Homo sapiens*, is an animal—a highly evolved animal, but an animal nonetheless. So we must explore the biological systems that maintain his actions and reactions.

The Brain and Aggression

Goetz may have been thinking about his plans to spend Christmas in New Hampshire as the train left the station, but when Canty confronted him, these thoughts were forgotten; a different, and more primitive, portion of his brain took control. When we are confronted by danger, our brain prepares us physiologically to either confront the source of the danger or flee from it (Cannon, 1932). This *fight-or-flight response* appears to be controlled by the **limbic system** (see Figure 13-1), which is one of the evolutionarily older portions of the brain (MacLean, 1954). This system links several brain sites (for example, the amygdala and the hypothalamus) and appears to be responsible for increasing heart rate, boosting blood flow to the muscles, slowing digestion, and stimulating the adrenal glands (Asterita, 1985). Portions of the limbic system also act as inhibitors of aggression by slowing the body's internal systems (Moyer, 1976).

limbic system
A set of interconnected brain structures, including portions of the cerebral cortex and parts of the thalamus and hypothalamus, that is believed to be responsible for emotional responses (including anger and aggression).

▲ **FIGURE 13-1**
The limbic system lies at the boundary separating the cortex (gray matter) and the evolutionarily older structures of the interior of the brain. The structures that make up this system (the cingulate gyrus, amygdala, septal nucleus, and hippocampus) appear to play a major role in producing strong emotional reactions, including anger, hostility, and fear.

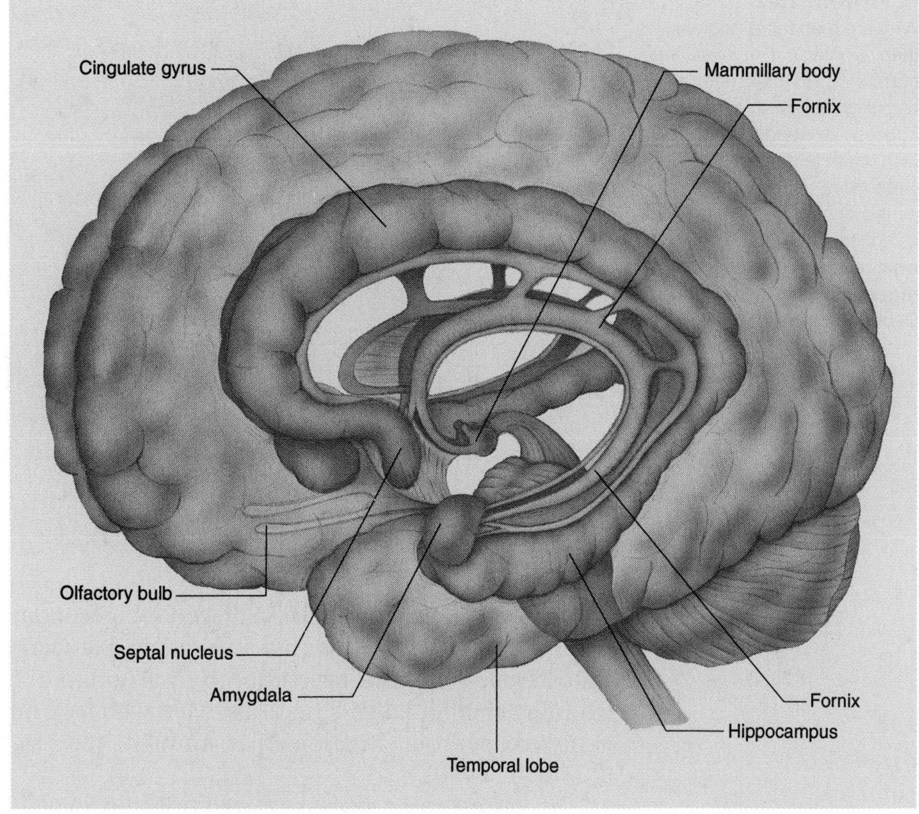

Is the limbic system the seat of aggression? Studies of nonhuman species suggest that when this portion of the brain is stimulated, passive animals respond aggressively. Moreover, studies of violent human beings often reveal abnormalities in this portion of the brain (Lewis et al., 1985). Charles Whitman, for example, displayed few outward signs of violent tendencies until the day he climbed to the top of a tower on the University of Texas campus and began shooting people with a high-powered rifle. During the next several hours, he killed 14 people and wounded dozens more. Whitman was killed by police when they stormed the tower, and an autopsy revealed a large, malignant brain tumor in the limbic area of his brain (Sweet, Ervin, & Mark, 1969). The tumor and his aggressive outburst, however, may not have been causally related.

Hormones and Aggression

The brain processes information rapidly, allowing us to respond quickly to dangerous environmental events. The endocrine system, in contrast, relies on hormones to effect physical and psychological changes more slowly. The body's glands secrete dozens of different hormones; one of them—**testosterone**—has been frequently identified as a likely contributor to aggressive behavior. Testosterone is a growth hormone that stimulates the development of sex organs and secondary sexual characters (such as facial hair) in men. This hormone, however, may also stimulate aggression. When researchers compared nearly 4,000 men who had normal levels of testosterone to approximately 500 men with elevated levels, they discovered that those with higher testosterone levels reported more childhood delinquency, criminal behavior as adults, and greater drug abuse. This relationship between testosterone and aggression, however,

testosterone
The principle androgen (male sex hormone) in humans and other mammals.

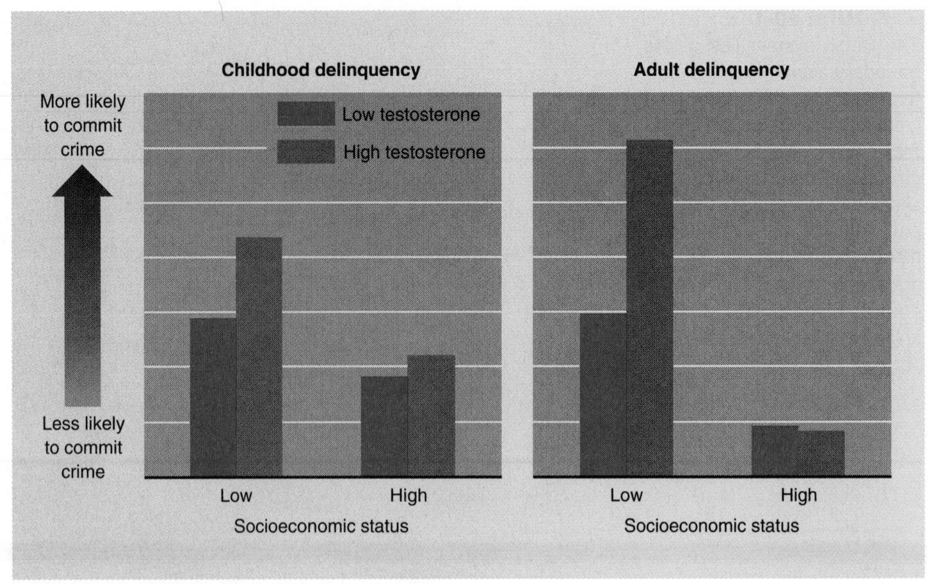

▲ **FIGURE 13-2**
Why are men more aggressive than women? The male sex hormone, testosterone, may be partly responsible for men's aggressive tendencies. Men with high testosterone levels were more likely to have committed crimes as children and as adults, but only if they came from economically disadvantaged backgrounds. (From Dabbs & Morris, 1990)

held only for men from disadvantaged socioeconomic backgrounds (see Figure 13-2). Apparently, men with considerable financial resources can control their testosterone-produced aggression by pursuing hobbies, taking vacations, and avoiding conflict-laden situations. Men who lack financial resources cannot so easily escape from situations that stimulate their aggressive tendencies (Dabbs & Morris, 1990).

The testosterone-aggression relationship explains why, in most cultures, men are more aggressive than women (Eagly & Steffen, 1986; Moghaddam, Taylor, & Wright, 1993). It also explains the greater aggressiveness of men who have the genetic abnormality known as the *XYY syndrome.* Women's 23rd chromosome is an XX pairing; for men this chromosome pairing is usually XY. But some men carry an extra Y chromosome, and these men are often prone to violence. This genetic abnormality, however, probably does not influence their aggressiveness directly. XYY men tend to be taller, heavier, and less intelligent than XY men. They also have higher levels of testosterone (Daly, 1969; Geen, 1990). As a result, they are more likely to engage in criminal behavior, and to get caught when they do so, than are XY men.

The Instinctive Roots of Aggression

Aggression is commonplace in the animal kingdom, so commonplace that Charles Darwin concluded it springs from basic survival instincts. The cat that kills a bird and the lion that hunts a gazelle are engaged in *predatory aggression*: many species attack and kill other species for food. Cats and lions, however, sometimes fight among themselves. This intraspecies, or *agonistic aggression*, is also essential for survival. The strongest, most aggressive animals occupy the top positions in the group's social hierarchy or *pecking order*. The control they are able to exercise over food, water, shelter, territory, and mating partners increases their chances of survival. Furthermore, aggression prevents overcrowding by keeping the population from outstripping the available resources; it also ensures protection of the young. Darwin believed that agonistic aggression must be adaptive, for otherwise evolution would have eliminated these aggressive behaviors through natural selection.

ethology
The study of animal behavior that emphasizes the observation of animals in their natural surroundings.

Researchers working in the field of **ethology** also argue that some forms of aggression are instinctive. They add the concept of a *releaser* to Darwin's general analysis of the instinctive roots of aggression. A releaser is an environmental cue that stimulates the display of fixed patterns of instinctive behavior. Male sticklebacks, for example, are highly territorial fish that will drive away other male sticklebacks. They will not attack, however, if the intruding fish does not have a red underbelly. Apparently this attack response is released by the red coloring of the male's underbelly, for the male stickleback will attack even a block of wood if it has a red mark painted on the bottom (Tinbergen, 1951).

The ethologist Konrad Lorenz (1966) theorized that humans also attack when releasers stimulate their aggressive instincts. Cabey's stance, his eyes, and the tone of his voice may all have signaled ATTACK at some basic level, and so Goetz responded defensively. But Lorenz also argues that human aggression, unlike aggression in other animals, tends to be more deadly because we lack the instinctive inhibitions needed to turn off aggression. In most encounters between members of the same species, aggressive encounters end before either combatant is killed. Two wolves, for example, will fight until one bares his throat to the other, signaling surrender. Humans, Lorenz argues, have no instinctive inhibition against killing. Our early ancestors lacked the brute strength, claws, and teeth needed to kill each other, so inhibitions never developed. But once humans discovered weapons, our capacity to kill overwhelmed our ability to control our aggression.

Sociobiology also argues that aggression is, in many cases, an instinctive response to a particular type of situation. Consider the plight of the recently mated male mountain bluebird (*Sialia currucoides*). He discovers another male bluebird lurking in a nearby tree when he returns home to his nest. The bluebird immediately attacks the interloper. Will he also attack his mate (Barash, 1976)?

Sociobiology assumes that aggression is a situationally specific action that maximizes the survival of its genes, or its inclusive fitness (see Chapter 12). The male bluebird will drive off the rival because the adulterer poses a great threat to his genetic fitness. He will attack his mate, however, only if her adultery threatens his reproductive potential. If the incident occurs before she has laid her eggs, then his attacks are intense, and he may drive her from the nest. But if no threat exists because she has already laid her eggs, then the male will not attack her (Barash, 1976, 1982).

Sociobiologists reject the notion of a fighting instinct that is automatically touched off by environmental signals. Instead, they hypothesize that humans behave aggressively in some situations because hostility increases inclusive fitness. Competition, for example, tends to stimulate aggression in humans. For thousands of years humans lived in small hunting-and-gathering tribes. By occasionally attacking neighboring groups, humans succeeded in acquiring extra territory, food, and mates. Fighting also occurred within the group to settle disputes. Because more aggressive individuals usually triumphed over those who were less aggressive, aggression emerged as an evolutionarily stable strategy. In consequence, modern-day humans display aggressive actions when they compete for valued resources (Maynard Smith, 1976).

Sociobiologists also challenge the idea that humans are uniquely aggressive. According to the prominent sociobiologist Edward O. Wilson, murder occurs frequently in many species besides *Homo sapiens*, including tigers, lions, langurs, gulls, macaques, gorillas, and most insects. Infanticide—the killing of infants—is very common in many species. Whenever a male langur monkey takes control of another male's harem, he systematically murders all the infants (Hrdy, 1977). Female ground squirrels sometimes murder their neighbors' infants to make room for their own offspring. Hyenas are habitual cannibals as well; if mothers don't protect their young, they are eaten by adults (Kruuk, 1972).

Wilson (1975) notes that if unbiased observers studied humans as just one more animal species, they would probably see very few aggressive actions. Most of the time, in most places, most of us are nonviolent. Only rarely do we perform an action with the intention of deliberately harming or injuring someone. He concludes that "there is no universal 'rule of conduct' in competitive and predatory behavior, any more than there is a universal aggressive instinct" (p. 247).

A Psychodynamic View

Sigmund Freud (1920/1961), like Lorenz, believed that humans are aggressive creatures. His psychodynamic approach to personality argued that hostility stems from dynamic psychological forces originating within the **unconscious**: a portion of the mind that actively directs actions and thoughts, while remaining hidden from conscious awareness. Freud felt that many primitive urges lurk within the unconscious, but he emphasized two above all others: *eros*, the life instinct, and *thanatos*, the death instinct. Eros propels us toward physical pleasures, such as sex, whereas thanatos propels us toward destruction and violence.

unconscious
Freud's term for thoughts, emotions, memories, and desires that influence everyday actions but remain hidden from conscious awareness.

Freud thought of hostile impulses in hydraulic terms; he felt that aggression builds up in the unconscious like steam in a boiler. If this psychological steam isn't vented from time to time, the strain on the system can cause psychological disorders. Therefore, healthy people discharge these aggressive urges in a process he called **catharsis**. One way to achieve catharsis is through overt aggression. If people direct their aggression outward, they injure other people; an inward aim, in contrast, leads to self-injury (depression, suicide, masochism). Catharsis can also be achieved through **displacement**: aggressive urges are displaced, or redirected, into more acceptable channels. Goetz could have drained away his aggressive motivation by watching a violent movie, dreaming that he was Charles Bronson, kicking his dog, or playing a vigorous game of tennis. Freud argued that all of us, without displacement and self-control, would become violent.

catharsis
The discharge of hostile impulses and urges, often achieved by behaving aggressively.

displacement
Achieving catharsis by diverting aggressive impulses from their original source to a substitute target.

Like the ethologists and sociobiologists, Freud believed that our need to be aggressive is instinctive, a part of human nature. He also believed, however, that the strength of this need and the way it is expressed is shaped by early childhood experiences. If Freud had been asked why Goetz shot Canty, he would have been likely to focus on Goetz's stormy relationship with his father. Goetz's father was a harsh disciplinarian, and Goetz often refused to comply with his father's demands. As an adult, Goetz openly rebelled against any form of authority. When others said or did anything that he interpreted as an attempt to control him, he resisted them both unconsciously and aggressively. Freud would probably also have suggested that, at an unconscious level, Goetz was still angry with his father, even though his father passed away four years before the incident. Because he could not release this hostility by physically or verbally attacking his father, he attacked the teenagers.

Is Aggression Part of Human Nature?

Was Goetz responding instinctively on that cold day in December? Perhaps, for portions of Goetz's brain and hormonal systems have evolved to do one thing particularly well—to ready the body for aggressive action in response to threat. His actions may have also been produced, in part, by his basic instinct to preserve his life and his genes at all costs. As he himself explained, "I became a vicious animal" (quoted in Fletcher, 1988, p. 16).

▲ **TABLE 13-1**
Summing up: Biological, hormonal, and instinctual mechanisms that sustain aggressive behavior in humans

Theory	*Explanation of Aggression*	*Example*
Physiology	The limbic system of the brain responds to threat by triggering physiological arousal (for example, increased heart rate, blood flow, and so on).	When people hear strange noises in their houses late at night, their heart rates accelerate.
Biochemistry	Hormones secreted by the body's glands influence temperament and reactivity across social situations. Testosterone, the male sex hormone, may increase aggressiveness.	XYY men are more likely to be convicted of violent crimes, *and* they tend to have high levels of testosterone.
Ethology	Aggression is adaptive, for it increases the individual's chances of survival. Environmental cues can stimulate the display of fixed patterns of aggressive behavior.	A stickleback will attack another stickleback only when the intruding fish has a red underbelly.
Sociobiology	Aggression is adaptive, for it increases inclusive fitness (the likelihood that the individual's genes will survive in future generations).	A male bluebird who observes a rival near his mate will attack his mate if she has not yet laid her eggs.
Psychodynamic	Hostility stems from instinctive aggressive urges within the unconscious. Catharsis occurs when these urges are discharged directly or through displacement.	A woman shouts obscenities at other drivers to relieve her pent-up tensions and hostilities.

The biological and instinctive bases of aggression summarized in Table 13-1, however, do not fully account for aggression. If, as Lorenz suggests, "aggression is, in man, just as much of a spontaneous instinctive drive as in most other higher vertebrates," then why is aggression so rare in some cultures? The "Yamis of Orchid Island off Taiwan, the Semai of Malaya, the Tikopia of the Western Pacific, the Land Dayaks of Sarawak, the Pellchas of Sikkim, the Papago Indians, the Hopi, the Zuni, and the Pueblo peoples generally" display little, if any, violence against other humans (Montagu, 1978, p. 5). How can people in these groups escape the binds of aggression if it is genetic in origin?

Second, even if aggression is biological in part, other factors also play a role in producing violence. As noted in Chapter 12, J. Philippe Rushton and his colleagues used a twin-study design to investigate the genetic bases of several behavioral tendencies, including aggression (Rushton et al., 1986). They found that identical (MZ) twins were more similar in their aggressiveness than fraternal (DZ) twins. Rushton attributed about 50% of the variability in aggression to genetics, but he also added that the rest must be due to nurture—the things individuals experience living in the social world. We consider these social influences in the next sections.

▲▲▲▲▲▲▲▲▲▲▲▲▲

Motives, Emotions, and Aggression

Goetz could have done many things when he boarded the subway. He could have gone to another car when he saw all the passengers had moved far away from the

▲ Instinct explanations of aggression argue that the human species, by genetic design, is an aggressive one. Yet cross-cultural researchers have identified wide variations in violence and peacefulness. Conflict is taken for granted in some societies, but in others—including many Native American cultures—aggression is a rarity.

four young men. He could have smiled and nodded his head when Canty greeted him. He could have given Canty $5 or told him that he didn't have any money to spare. Instead, he took out his gun and shot the four young men.

motivation
Wants, needs, and other psychological processes that energize certain responses, prompting us to move in one direction rather than another.

Why do people do one thing rather than another? The concept of **motivation** argues that our wants and needs often guide our behavior, prompting us to move in one direction rather than another. To predict whether or not a passerby will enter a fast-food restaurant, we must know if she is hungry. Before we can say if she will order a drink with her meal, we must know if she is thirsty. Hunger and thirst are biological *motives*, or *drives*, but other motives—such as the need for social contact, safety, achievement, and power—also guide the choices we make and the goals we seek.

John Dollard, Neal E. Miller, and their colleagues at Yale University used this motivational approach to explain aggressive behaviors. They believed that whenever external conditions thwart our attempts to reach our goals, we become frustrated. Frustration then arouses an aggressive drive, which surfaces at the behavioral level in the form of (1) an attack on the source of the frustration or (2) displaced aggression aimed at some other person or object (see Figure 13-3). Dollard and his colleagues summarized their **frustration-aggression hypothesis** by stating that "the occurrence of aggressive behavior always presupposes the existence of frustration and, contrariwise, that the existence of frustration always leads to some form of aggression" (Dollard et al., 1939, p. 1; Miller, 1941; Miller & Dollard, 1941).

frustration-aggression hypothesis
An early motivational model that argued individuals become aggressive whenever external conditions prevent them from reaching their goals.

Few social processes are as simple as they first appear, and the link between frustration and aggression is no exception. Miller and Dollard hypothesized that frustration is a necessary and sufficient cause of aggression. Aggression, they thought, occurs only when people are frustrated, and frustrated people are always aggressive. Fifty years of research, however, has clarified and extended their original explanation of aggression. We now know that a host of aversive events, in addition to frustration, can stimulate aggression. We also know that Dollard and Miller overstated the strength of the relationship between frustration and aggression. Aversive events may leave us ready to be aggressive, but frustrated and irritated people are not *always* aggressive people. Both of these refinements to their original frustration-aggression hypothesis are considered next.

▲ **FIGURE 13-3**
Why are people aggressive? The original frustration-aggression hypothesis argued that whenever we cannot achieve a goal, we experience frustration, which in turn causes us to be aggressive: Either we attack the source of our frustration or we direct our attack at some other person or object.

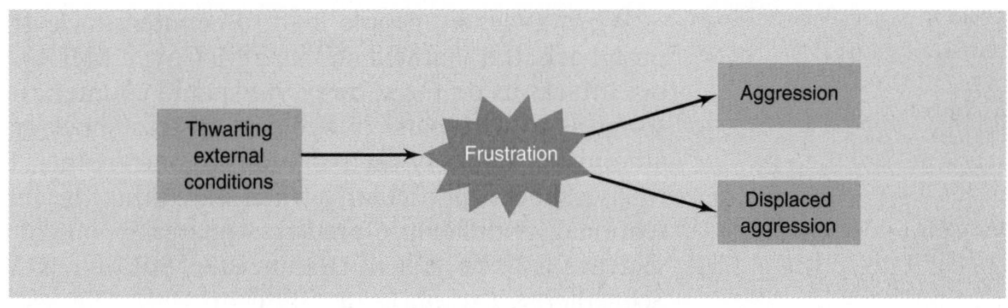

Arousing Circumstances

Experimental studies of Dollard and Miller's hypothesis confirmed that when people are frustrated, they behave aggressively. Arnold Buss (1963) frustrated college students by telling them that they had failed at a simple task or missed the chance to win some money or to improve their grade. When he then asked them to give electric shocks to another student, they delivered higher-intensity shocks than students who hadn't been frustrated. Similarly, people who were given jigsaw puzzles that couldn't be solved, callers trying to use a broken telephone in a phone booth, and group members who couldn't reach consensus tended to become aggressive (Geen, 1968; Moser & Levy-Leboyer, 1985; Burnstein & Worchel, 1962, respectively). Even hate crimes, riots, terrorism, and other forms of political instability have been blamed on the aggression-facilitating effects of frustration (Feierabend & Feierabend, 1972; Hovland & Sears, 1940).

These studies, however, also indicate that frustrating events are part of a larger family of environmental events that can set the stage for aggression. Goetz may have been frustrated on the day he shot Canty, Allen, Ramseur, and Cabey, but virtually any situational factors that lead to arousal—pain, competition, insults, and other aversive environmental events—could also have influenced his reaction (Berkowitz, 1989).

The pain-attack reaction. When they experience pain, many species of animals become very aggressive and will attack any other animal that is nearby. A rat and a mouse will share a cage in peace, but if a shock is applied to the cage floor, the rat will attack and kill the mouse immediately (Azrin, 1967). Humans display a similar *pain-attack reaction*. Leonard Berkowitz and his colleagues, for example, asked women college students to evaluate another student's work either by giving her rewards or by subjecting her to unpleasant noise. Women who carried out this task with one of their hands immersed in painfully cold water were more aggressive than women who put a hand in lukewarm water (Berkowitz, Cochran, & Embree, 1981).

Attack and counterattack. One of the best-known cases of violence in frontier America involved two families living in the valleys of Appalachia, the Hatfields and the McCoys. The two families began feuding in 1863 when a Hatfield stole some hogs from a McCoy. The McCoys countered by stealing hogs from another member of the Hatfield clan, and soon members of the two families began shooting at each other. Then, in 1865, someone—most likely a Hatfield—killed Harmon McCoy. After this incident, things quieted down until 1878 when Randolph McCoy accused Floyd Hatfield of stealing more hogs. When a jury found Hatfield guilty, full-scale violence gripped the families. In the years between 1878 and 1890, more than ten men and women were killed by the feuders (Rice, 1978).

When attacked, people tend to counterattack. If someone pushes you, you push back. If a Hatfield shoots a McCoy, a McCoy shoots a Hatfield. If someone attacks us on the subway, we should counterattack. Researchers have gone so far as to wire pairs of subjects up to a shock generator and then let them administer shocks of up to 40 volts to one another. People who get shocks tend to give shocks, particularly when they think the initial attack is arbitrary, intentional, or difficult to predict. Apparently, one of the surest ways to provoke violence is to be violent (Baumeister, Stillwell, & Wotman, 1990; Dengerink, Schnedler, & Covey, 1978; Ohbuchi, 1982; Ohbuchi & Kambara, 1985; Taylor & Pisano, 1971).

Threats. In many cases, just the threat of aggression can be sufficient to arouse aggressive motives. Canty never touched Goetz, but Goetz felt menaced by Canty's saying, "How are ya?" So Goetz mounted a preemptive strike to protect himself.

Morton Deutsch and Robert Krauss (1960) confirmed the impact of threats on conflict by asking pairs of women to play a simple game. Each woman was asked to imagine herself the owner of either the Acme or Bolt Trucking Company. Each time Acme's truck reached the destination shown in Figure 13-4, the owner earned 60 cents minus 1 cent for each second taken up by the trip. Bolt was rewarded on the same basis. Only one truck, however, could use the shorter route (Route 216) at a time, so it was to the subjects' advantage to cooperate by taking turns traveling first over the short route.

The women who played the trucking game usually cooperated with one another, and each one turned a profit of about $1. But all this changed when Deutsch and Krauss introduced the element of threat into the situation. When Acme's owner could threaten Bolt by closing a gate located at the fork in Route

▲ "An eye for an eye, a tooth for a tooth" underscores the rule of reciprocity: When people are attacked, they tend to counterattack.

The Far Side cartoon by Gary Larson is reprinted by permission of Chronicle Features, San Francisco, CA. All rights reserved.

Carl shoves Roger, Roger shoves Carl, and tempers rise.

216, neither side profited. If Bolt attempted to use the main route, all Acme had to do was close the gate, forcing Bolt to back up and enabling Acme to reopen the gate and proceed quickly to her destination. Bolt usually fought back by leaving her truck where it would block Acme's path. Bolt's losses were twice as great as Acme's, but even Acme lost more than a dollar at the game. Conflict worsened when both Acme and Bolt had gates—losses averaged $4.38. When the women could talk openly during negotiations, conflict intensified even more (Deutsch, 1973). When people exchange hostile, contentious threats, then communication can lead to, rather than settle, conflicts (McClintock, Stech, & Keil, 1983; Pruitt et al., 1993).

Competition. Competition between people sometimes sets the stage for aggression (see the section "Application: Coping with Conflict," which concludes this chapter). The Robbers Cave Experiment, discussed in Chapter 7, pitted two groups of young boys against one another in a series of games (Sherif et al., 1961). Once the games began, the boys changed rapidly from competitors to aggressors. They began to call each other names and accuse each other of cheating. Eventually this verbal abuse turned into physical violence. One group burned the other group's flag, two boys began punching each other, and several boys pushed each other. The two groups had to be physically separated to prevent them from injuring each other. Other studies indicate that when people compete with one another, they often become physiologically aroused. Their heart rates increase, as does their blood pressure (Lanzetta & Englis, 1989).

Environmental stressors. The subways of New York City are stuffy, crowded, noisy, and dirty. Could this aversive environment have contributed to Goetz's motivation for attacking the four young men?

As Chapter 14 explains, social behavior is sometimes largely shaped by the physical environment in which it occurs. Hot, crowded, and noisy places, for

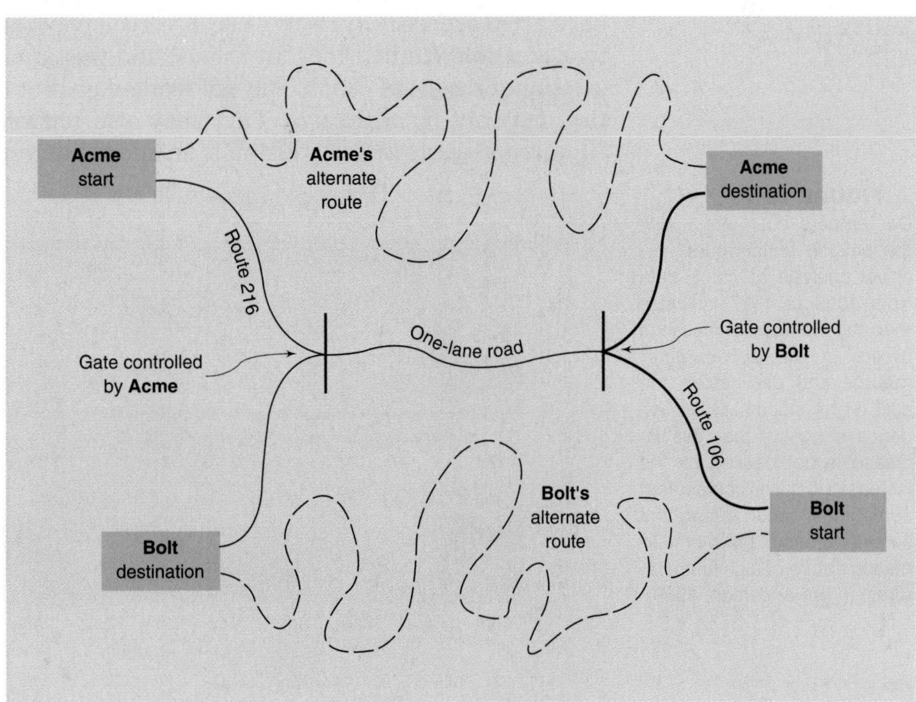

▲ **FIGURE 13-4**
Does the power to threaten other people reduce hostilities or only exacerbate them? Deutsch and Krauss studied this question by asking women to imagine themselves the owner of either the Acme or Bolt Trucking Company. Players earned more money if they took the direct route, but only one truck could use the shared route (Route 216) at a time. Deutsch and Krauss found that people worked cooperatively at this task, but if one person could threaten the other, then conflict erupted. (From Deutsch, 1973)

example, raise our level of physiological *arousal*, leaving us ready to engage in more intense forms of behavior. If the situation is extremely stimulating, we may even experience *cognitive overload*. Our ability to fully process information is disrupted; we are receiving so much information that our limited ability to process it is overwhelmed. Often, too, we may become annoyed because the place *interferes with our behavior* in some way. We can't move freely in a crowded subway or hear other people talk to us at a loud party, and the interference that our environment is causing can be very irritating. Aversive places also generate *negative affect*: Good moods can be ruined by traffic jams, loud noises, or exposure to someone's secondhand cigarette smoke (Mueller, 1983).

Heat, overcrowding, noise, and pollution have all been linked to increased violence. When Craig Anderson (1987, 1989) reviewed dozens of crime statistics, he found that violent crimes, such as murder, rape, and aggravated assault, become increasingly frequent when the temperature rises (see Figure 13-5). Laboratory studies sometimes find that people would rather escape from a hot room rather than attack other people, but field studies suggest that hot temperatures often lead to hot tempers. In one particularly clever study, researchers in Phoenix deliberately blocked an intersection on days when the temperature varied from 84° to 108°F (Kenrick & MacFarlane, 1986). Motorists honked sooner, and with more vigor, when the weather was hot rather than comfortable, but the heat-honking relationship was much stronger for people in cars without air conditioning ($r = .76$) than for people in air-conditioned cars ($r = -.12$). Anderson believes that hot weather arouses people and increases the negativity of their thoughts and emotions (Rule, Taylor, & Dobbs, 1987). Similar negative consequences have been documented in studies of noise (Geen, 1978; Geen & McCown, 1984), crowding (Welsch & Booth, 1975), pollution (Rotton & Frey, 1985), and cigarette smoke (Zillmann, Baron, & Tamborini, 1981).

Triggering Conditions

Goetz spent years living in New York City, frustrated and irritated, but never once acted aggressively. Why? Because aversive experiences don't lead directly to aggression. Rather, they arouse us, and this arousal *sometimes* leads to aggression. Frustrated people may get worked up, but if no one angers them, then they may not be aggressive. They may also remain passive if nothing in the situation suggests that aggression is an allowable response. These extra ingredi-

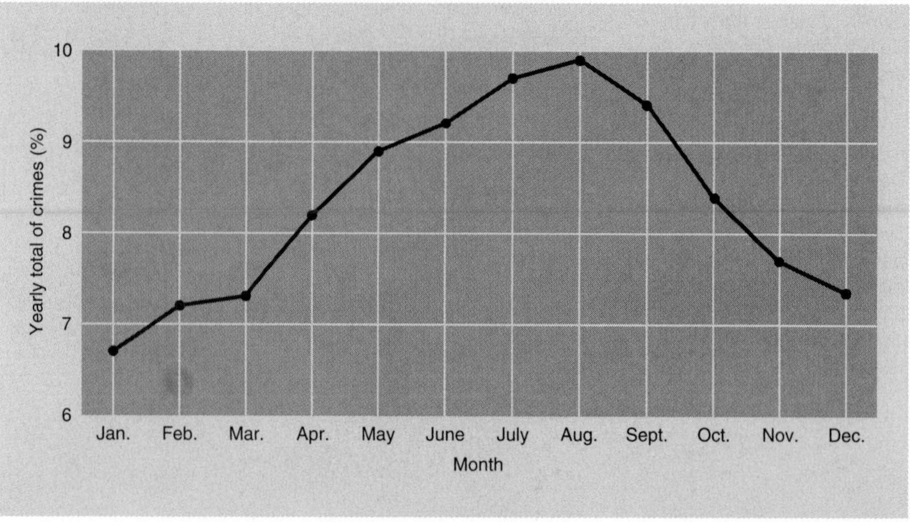

▲ **FIGURE 13-5**
Do tempers soar along with the outside temperature? Archival analysis of crime data from 1899 to 1987 indicates that the number of assaults peaks in the hot summer months and declines in the cold winter months. Other evidence suggests that this increase is not caused by the increases in social contact that sometimes occur during the summer months, but by the irritating nature of high temperatures. (From Anderson, 1989)

ents—anger, personal hostility, attributions, aggression-facilitating cues, and the like—are considered next (Berkowitz, 1981a, 1983).

Anger and aggression. Two men are arguing at the end of a difficult day that has been filled with frustrations, irritations, and inconveniences. As the argument continues, one's face grows flushed. His eyes narrow into slits, and his brows arch downward. His eyes fix in a stare, and his lips frown. His lips are drawn back and colorless. His teeth are clenched, and his hands are balled into fists. This man is angry.

Anger and aggression generally go hand in hand. When people described a time when they became angry, many admitted that their anger spilled out as aggression; 49% became verbally abusive when they were angered, and 10% said they became physically aggressive (Averill, 1983, 1993). Individuals in another study also stressed the relationship between anger and aggression. Many people reported physically attacking someone or something, losing emotional control, or imagining violence against someone else when they were angry (Shaver et al., 1987). Feelings of anger may not be the direct cause of anger. They may prime negative thoughts and memories, but it may be the ensuing cognitive associations that actually cause violence (Berkowitz, 1990, 1993). Still, anger tends to be the bridge between irritating circumstances and physical aggression (Buss & Perry, 1992).

When do people become angry? Most people report that they respond angrily when interacting with their friends and loved ones, rather than with strangers or enemies (Averill, 1983; Miller, 1991). Anger is also experienced when others treat us badly, either intentionally or through carelessness. A co-worker who deliberately spreads lies about our productivity or a friend who forgets to water our plants as promised is likely to raise our ire. Their misdeeds are unjustified, and we are within our rights to complain about them. But when others harm us accidentally or they are justified in their treatment of us, we are

▲ Frustrating circumstances can lead to aggression, but so can other unpleasant, noxious conditions. Traffic jams, work difficulties, travel, and other stressful aspects of modern life can set the stage for aggression by generating negative emotional arousal. This arousal leaves us ready to behave agressively if some aspect of the situation triggers a hostile response.

less likely to respond angrily. If our friends are late for lunch, we may not become angry if they explain their tardiness with a good excuse. We also keep our anger in check if we realize that we are partly to blame for the problem (Ferguson & Rule, 1983; Weiner, 1991).

People also vary in their propensity to respond angrily to others. Some people rarely experience anger; others become angry several times a day (Averill, 1983, 1993). Irritable people are more likely to let small aggravations bother them, and they are likely to agree with such statements as "I easily fly off the handle with those who don't listen or understand" and "It makes my blood boil to have somebody make fun of me" (Caprara, 1986; Caprara et al., 1985). They also tend to fall prey to the *hostile attributional bias*: They overlook situational causes and instead routinely assume that other people are deliberately treating them harshly (Dodge & Coie, 1987; Dodge & Crick, 1990). People who are prone to feelings of shame and guilt also anger easily, as do individuals whose self-esteem is unstable (Kernis, Grannemann, & Barclay, 1989; Tangney et al., 1992).

Type A and Type B personalities
The Type A personality is a constellation of traits and behavioral tendencies characterized by aggressive tendencies, competitiveness, and time urgency. The Type B personality is a constellation of more relaxed, easygoing qualities.

Type A individuals are also more hostile than **Type B** individuals. The Type A personality was originally documented by cardiologists who were studying the causes of heart disease (Friedman & Rosenman, 1974). These cardiologists initially thought that heart disease was linked to smoking cigarettes, obesity, and the lack of exercise, but they soon noticed that many of their patients displayed a similar personality syndrome. Aggressive, competitive, and excessively time oriented, these individuals set deadlines for themselves, pushed themselves to achieve more and more, and showed almost no sign of patience. Type Bs, in contrast, were more relaxed and low-key.

Type A people die from coronary heart disease at higher rates than Type B people, but many researchers trace the difference to Type A's greater hostility (Matthews, 1988; Miller et al., 1991; Smith & Pope, 1990). Type A individuals are "likely to experience anger often, to be bitter and resentful, and to view others with distrust." Like Goetz, they view "their interpersonal world as an irritating struggle that requires vigilance" (Smith & Frohm, 1985, p. 510). They are also more likely to behave aggressively when provoked. In one study, researchers asked Type As and Type Bs to help teach a concept to a male confederate by giving him electric shocks whenever he made a mistake. Some of the subjects were frustrated before they were seated at the controls of the shock machine; they had failed to complete a complex puzzle in 3 minutes. Others had been insulted: The confederate chided the subjects as they tried to complete the puzzle by saying such things as "I don't know what's taking you so long; it's not that difficult," and "The next move is obvious." Type Bs, as Figure 13-6 indicates, gave low-intensity shocks in all conditions. Type As, in contrast, became more aggressive when they were frustrated and when they were insulted (Carver & Glass, 1978; see also Strube et al., 1984).

Misattribution and anger. When was the last time you lost your temper and acted in a hostile, aggressive manner? A dentist, when asked this question, claimed that he never lost his temper. But when pressed, he recalled an incident that took place while he was exercising after work. He was finishing his workout by lifting weights when another weight lifter accidentally bumped into him. Suddenly enraged, he shouted, "Why don't you look where you're going, asshole? Those weights could have fallen on me!" The incident escalated into a shouting and shoving match. After recounting the incident, the dentist sheepishly admitted, "I guess I overreacted" (Tavris, 1982, p. 169).

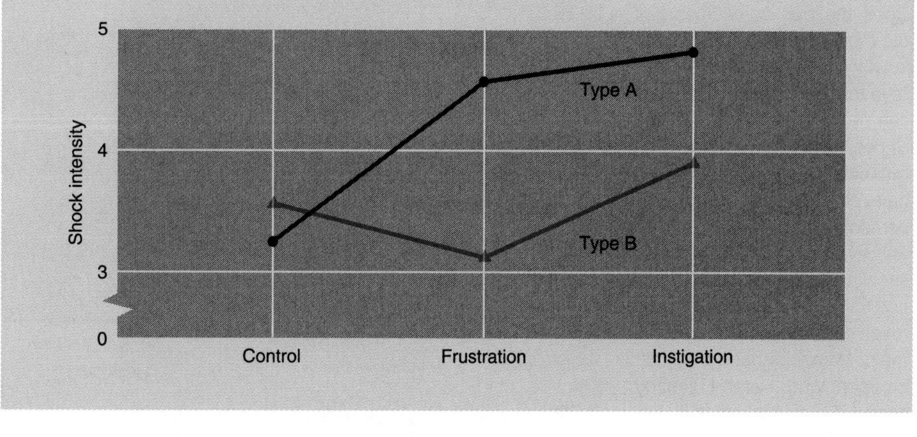

▲ **FIGURE 13-6**
Who is more likely to lose their tempers: Type As or Type Bs? When told to give electric shocks to another person (supposedly as part of a study on learning), As and Bs gave shocks of equal intensity so long as they weren't irritated (the control condition). But if they were frustrated by a previous failure or insulted by the learner, then As gave stronger shocks than the Bs did. (From Carver & Glass, 1978)

excitation-transfer theory The hypothesized tendency for arousal produced by nonviolent stimuli or events, such as high temperatures or pornography, to energize aggression when misattributed to an unrelated source.

Dolf Zillmann's **excitation-transfer theory** explains the dentist's reaction. Zillmann's theory draws on the two-factor theory of emotion, first discussed in Chapter 4. In most cases, a trivial irritation wouldn't be sufficient to motivate an aggressive action, but the dentist was already physiologically aroused. Even though this arousal was produced by his workout and had nothing to do with hostility or anger, the dentist was still in a highly excited state. This energized condition, combined with an aversive event, prompted an overly aggressive reaction. Zillmann found that excitation transfer became more likely when individuals were already predisposed to engage in aggression and when the true causes of the arousal were relatively ambiguous (Rule & Nesdale, 1976; Zillmann, 1983).

Because of excitation transfer, arousal caused by factors that have nothing to do with anger or hostility may still fan the fires of aggression. Stimulating drugs, physical exercise, pornography, and loud music can all energize aggression if excitation transfer occurs (Zillmann, 1983). Alcohol, for example, is a depressant, but in small amounts it can be physiologically arousing rather than relaxing. Alcohol also interferes with self-regulation (Critchlow, 1986; Taylor & Leonard, 1983). Therefore, people who have been drinking often behave more violently, particularly when they find themselves in situations that encourage aggression (Taylor & Sears, 1988). They are also less sensitive to situational cues that typically keep aggression in check. For example, men and women are more likely to behave violently when provoked by a male rather than a female, but when they are intoxicated, they don't discriminate based on sex—both men and women become targets (Bushman & Cooper, 1990).

Situational cues and aggression. Leonard Berkowitz (1970) believes that relatively subtle cues in the environment can also change an irritated individual into an outwardly aggressive person. Angry people who have the chance to attack someone else don't attack unless cues associated with aggression are present in the situation. People who perform badly on a puzzle may be frustrated, but when they are given the chance to give electric shocks to another subject, they don't take out their frustrations on the subject. But if they are told that the other subject is an amateur boxer, or that he has the same name as an actor who plays the role of a boxer in a violent film that is currently popular—then frustrated people become aggressive people.

Any cue associated even indirectly with aggression can stimulate violence, but Berkowitz finds that weapons are particularly powerful prompts. He demonstrated their influence on aggression in one study by telling pairs of subjects

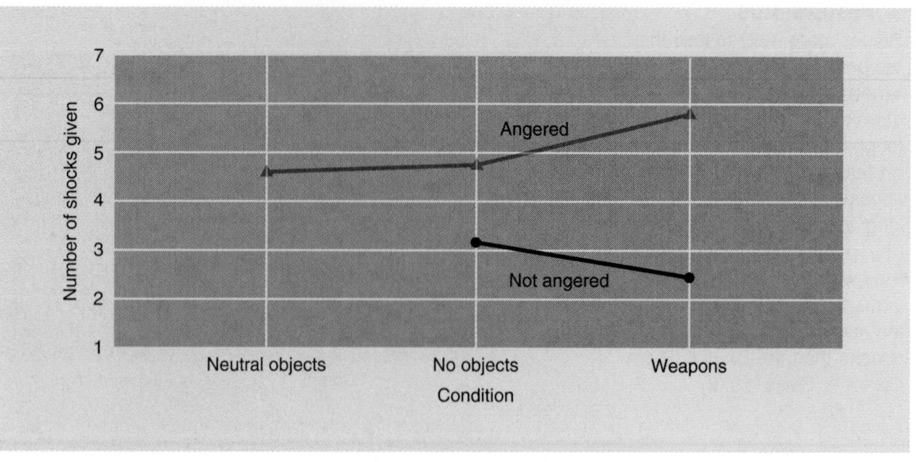

▲ FIGURE 13-7
Does the gun sometimes pull the trigger for aggression? Berkowitz and his colleagues believe that subtle situational cues can pull aggressive actions out of people who would otherwise remain nonviolent. Men who gave electric shocks to another person (supposedly as part of an evaluation) gave more shocks when they were angry *and* they could see a gun and revolver on the table next to them. Weapons had no impact on men who weren't already angry. (From Berkowitz & LePage, 1967)

that, as part of an evaluation, each would be giving the other some electric shocks. One subject (Berkowitz's confederate) gave the real subject one shock or seven shocks. When it was the subjects' turn to take over the controls of the shock machine, the angry subjects (those who had received seven shocks) meted out an average of about six shocks when a 12-gauge shotgun and a snub-nosed .38-caliber revolver lay next to the shock machine. If subjects saw only badminton rackets and shuttlecocks or no cues at all, they administered significantly fewer shocks, about 4.6. Unangered subjects administered from two to three shocks (see Figure 13-7). Berkowitz had documented the **weapons effect**: The presence of weapons makes people more aggressive than they normally would be (Berkowitz & LePage, 1967).

weapons effect
The tendency for individuals to respond more aggressively in the presence of weapons.

When Berkowitz published his findings, some researchers suggested that the subjects, skeptical about the presence of weapons in an experimental laboratory, guessed the true purpose of the study (Page and Scheidt, 1971). Berkowitz stands by his original findings, however, and cites other studies that have confirmed the weapons effect (Berkowitz, 1970, 1981b, 1983; Berkowitz & Donnerstein, 1982; Carlson, Marcus-Hewhall, & Miller, 1990). Belgian students shown pictures of weapons became more punitive (Leyens & Parke, 1975); college students at a carnival threw more wet sponges at a clown when a gun was visible near the front of the booth (reported in Turner et al., 1977); frustrated Croatian children were more likely to hit each other during a free play period after seeing toy guns (Zuzul, 1989); and drivers were more likely to honk their horns at a stalled pickup truck with a rifle in a gun rack than at one without a weapon (Turner, Layton, & Simons, 1975). All in all, these studies argue that the slogan "Guns don't kill; people do" isn't true. Berkowitz (1981c) explains: "People do have to pull the gun's trigger in order to shoot someone. But to some extent, the weapon can also pull the finger on the trigger" (p. 3).

A Motivational Model of Aggression

When Goetz confessed after the shooting, he expressed his frustration and anger in no uncertain terms. He was mugged once before, and he felt that the police had done nothing about it. He had tried to get a permit to carry a gun, but the police turned him down. He hated living in New York City; he thought of the streets as a combat zone filled with danger. Goetz was a man on the edge of aggression. When Canty angered him, and he felt the cold handle of his .38 in his hand, he responded.

TABLE 13-2
Summing up: Motivational factors that increase aggression by elevating arousal, triggering aggression in individuals who are aroused, or both

Factor	*Characteristics*	*Examples*
Aversive events	Individuals who experience irritating, negative events become aroused, and this arousal creates a readiness to respond aggressively.	Frustration Pain Attacks Threats Competition Environmental stressors
Triggering conditions	Individuals who are aroused and ready to act aggressively do so when aggression-provoking situational and psychological factors trigger an aggressive response.	Anger Personality factors (for example, Type A) Excitation transfer Misattribution Weapons and other aggression-triggering cues

arousal-aggression hypothesis
A motivational explanation of aggressive behavior that argues aversive events lead to arousal, which in turn can prompt aggression.

A motivational approach to aggression argues that the factors summarized in Table 13-2 combine to create aggressive behavior. Frustration does lead to aggression, as the original frustration-aggression hypothesis argued, but this relationship can be considered a special case of the more general motivational model shown in Figure 13-8. This **arousal-aggression hypothesis** predicts that many unpleasant and noxious conditions, including thwarting circumstances, set the stage for aggression. These aversive events generate a negatively toned emotional arousal, which is often subjectively labeled anger. This arousal, then, is the motivation that drives the subsequent aggressive actions (see Berkowitz, 1983, 1990, 1993; Berkowitz & Heimer, 1989; Ferguson & Rule, 1983; Zillmann, 1983).

Learning to Be Aggressive

Two kindergartners punch and kick each other when they both want the same toy. A father hits his baby with his closed fist. The blitzing linebacker spears the quarterback on the opposing team. Bernhard Goetz, confronted by four youths on a subway, pulls out a gun and shoots them all. Why?

Aggression may be part of human nature: When we are threatened, we respond vigorously to protect ourselves. Motivational processes may also be at work; frustrations, irritations, and other negative events can leave us ready to attack rather than retreat. But aggressive behavior is also *learned* behavior.

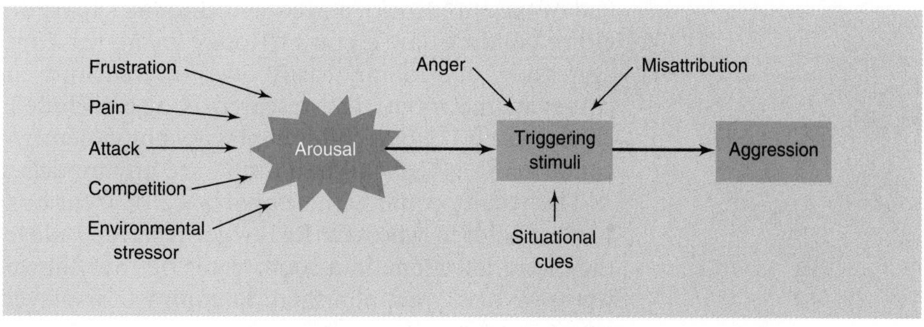

FIGURE 13-8
Why are people aggressive? The arousal-aggression model extends the original frustration-aggression hypothesis. This general motivational model argues that irritating events can leave people feeling aroused and ready to be aggressive. They will not be aggressive, however, unless personal or situational factors trigger an aggressive response.

Social Learning Theory

Albert Bandura's (1973, 1977, 1983) *social learning theory,* introduced in Chapter 7, argues that we learn through observation. Like all learning theorists, Bandura emphasizes the concept of reinforcement, for he predicts that people will become more aggressive when their hostile behavior is positively reinforced (rewarded). The child who is more aggressive is rewarded when she wins the toy. The hard-hitting football player is praised by the coach, his teammates, and the roar of the crowd. In each case, aggression is followed by a reinforcer, so it will probably occur more frequently in the future.

Social learning theory diverges from traditional models of learning when it suggests that people also learn through observation. The two children who were fighting provided an example, or model, for the other children. Watching them punch each other, their classmates were learning to be aggressive. If children are abused by their parents, then they may grow up to be abusive parents themselves (but see Widom, 1989). By watching game films, the linebacker had many opportunities to learn new ways to hurt the opposition. Thus we acquire aggressive behaviors through **observational learning**—by watching and imitating the actions of people who *model* hostile acts.

observational learning Acquiring new behaviors by watching the actions of people who model the action.

Bandura, Ross, and Ross's (1961, 1963a) classic studies of aggression in young children are discussed in Chapter 1. They exposed nursery school children to adults and cartoon characters who modeled various types of behavior. Later the children were tested to see whether they would imitate the models' actions. In one study, some children watched as an adult played quietly with Tinker Toys. Other children watched a violent model attack a plastic Bobo-the-Clown doll. The model sat on the doll and punched it, hit it with a mallet, kicked it, and exclaimed, "Sock him in the nose . . . ," "Hit him down . . . ," and "Pow . . . " (Bandura et al., 1961, p. 577). Bandura, Ross, and Ross watched when the children were later mildly frustrated and left alone in the room with Bobo. As they predicted, the children were far more aggressive if they had seen an aggressive model than if they had seen a nonaggressive model or no model at all. They had learned to be aggressive by observing aggression.

Bandura doesn't believe we imitate every action that we see other people perform. His social learning theory assumes instead that observers are sensitive to *vicarious consequences*: the rewards and punishments that the model receives after engaging in aggressive behavior. Bandura, Ross, and Ross (1963b) discovered that children are more likely to imitate an aggressive model who is reinforced than one who is punished. They showed nursery school children a short film clip of a violent encounter between two children named Rocky and Johnny. When Johnny refused to let Rocky play with his toys, Rocky hit him with a rubber ball, beat him with a baton, dragged him around the room with a hoola hoop, and eventually made him sit in the corner. At the end of the clip, Rocky played with Johnny's toys, drank 7-Up, and ate cookies. Other children saw a clip of Rocky losing the confrontation. Rocky was still aggressive, but Johnny easily overpowered him, and Rocky retreated to the corner of the room. The researchers also included a condition in which the children saw a clip of children playing nonviolently with the toys, and a control condition in which children didn't see any models at all.

The results confirm the importance of vicarious consequences (see Figure 13-9). Children who saw Rocky get rewarded played more aggressively when they were left alone in a room with the toys shown in the film clip. Children who saw Rocky get punished, in contrast, displayed a slight decrease in their aggressiveness.

Media Violence and Aggression

One of the most controversial aspects of social learning theory concerns the role of television, films, and other media as sources of vivid models of aggression. Violence pervades television programming. By one estimate, as many as 75% of all programs depict violence, and the percentage swells to 93.6 when only weekend programming is considered. With the average adolescent currently watching about 4 hours of television per day, children may witness as many as 13,000 dramatized murders by the time they reach age 16 (Gerbner et al., 1986; Signorielli, Gross, & Morgan, 1982). Does this constant diet of mayhem affect us? Correlational studies suggest that children who watch violent TV programs tend to be more aggressive. One team of researchers asked more than 700 children to describe their television-viewing habits and the number of times they engaged in such aggressive actions as fighting, delinquency, and disputes with their parents. In this study, as well as in others, children who watched more violent TV programs were more likely to report high levels of aggression (McCarthy et al., 1975).

These findings, however, don't prove that viewed violence *causes* aggression. As noted in Chapter 1, it may be that highly aggressive people seek out violent programs to view. Or a third variable may be causing increases in both aggression and the tendency to watch violent programs. Experimental studies, however, also indicate that watching violence increases aggression. Some of these studies, such as Bandura's Bobo doll studies, have been conducted in laboratory settings; others have been carried out in field settings (Goldstein et al., 1975). One team of researchers separated institutionalized delinquent boys into two groups. For five nights, one group watched violent films and the other group watched nonviolent films. During the day the boys were observed, and signs of aggression were noted. The two groups were equivalent in aggressiveness before the week of films, but during that week the boys who were shown the violent films showed higher levels of aggression (Parke et al., 1977).

These findings can also be criticized, however. Delinquents may be particularly susceptible to the effects of viewed violence. Moreover, some field studies have found that television or movie violence has little or no effect on the observer's behavior (Feshbach & Singer, 1971; Milgram & Shotland, 1973; Singer & Singer, 1980). Furthermore, these brief studies say little about the

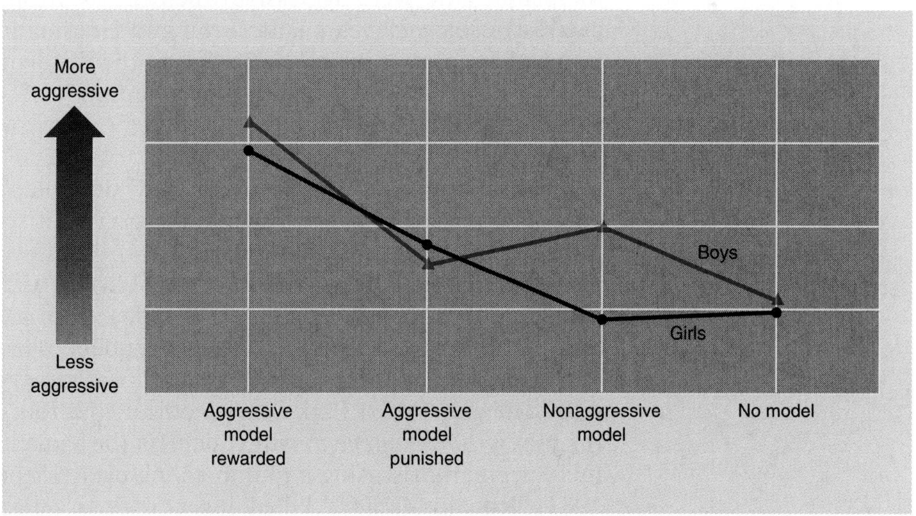

▲ **FIGURE 13-9**
When do children imitate another child who acts aggressively? Researchers tested Bandura's social learning theory by showing some children a film about a little boy named Rocky who was very aggressive. In one version, Rocky was rewarded after he acted cruelly, but in another version he was punished. Children who saw Rocky rewarded later played more aggressively themselves. (Adapted from Bandura, Ross, & Ross, 1963b)

▲ Television does more than just entertain. It also teaches viewers many lessons about social behavior, including cooperation, conflict, and aggression.

long-term effects of watching aggression. Some researchers, such as Leonard Eron and Rowell Huesmann, deal with these objections by carrying out longitudinal studies. In 1960, these researchers measured the number of violent programs watched and the overall aggressiveness of 875 third graders. These two variables were correlated ($r = .21$), suggesting that aggressive children watch violent TV. Ten years later, the researchers tracked down as many of the original subjects as possible (they found 475) and again measured these variables. Surprisingly, the correlation between aggression and television viewing was now only −.05. However, when Eron and Huesmann compared the level of TV violence the subjects had viewed in the third grade with the aggressiveness they showed as teenagers, the correlation was .31. These findings suggest that televised violence may have cumulative effects that build up gradually over time (Eron, 1982, 1987; Eron et al., 1972; Huesmann, 1982).

When Eron and Huesmann interviewed 427 of their subjects a third time, in 1982, they discovered that the TV violence they had watched back in 1960 was still systematically related to the behaviors they displayed as adults. Most of the people who were aggressive when they were in the third grade were still aggressive some 20 years later. Eron and Huesmann also found that men who watched large amounts of violent TV in the third grade were much more likely to have committed serious crimes as adults (see Figure 13-10; Eron, 1987; Eron et al., 1987).

The effects of TV violence. How do violent television programs influence viewers? First, viewers sometimes carry out specific types of actions they have seen on television (Berkowitz, 1984). An 18-year-old high school student walked into a school for beauticians in Arizona and shot four women and one child. He explained that he got the idea from news stories about Richard Speck, the man who murdered eight student nurses in Chicago (Berkowitz, 1970). In San Francisco, a 9-year-old girl was raped with a bottle by three older girls. The girls told a Park Service officer that four days earlier they had seen the movie *Born Innocent,* which depicts the violent rape of an adolescent girl by four other girls using a plumber's plunger (Liebert, Sprafkin, & Davidson, 1982). Ronald Zamora killed his next-door neighbor. His defense lawyers

▲ The relationship between watching violent programs and one's hostility may not support the argument that watching violent programming causes the viewer to be more aggressive. People who are highly aggressive may seek out violent television programs, while more pacifistic people ("sissies") are likely to avoid such programs.

ZIGGY copyright ZIGGY AND FRIENDS, INC. Dist. by UNIVERSAL PRESS SYNDICATE. Reprinted with permission. All rights reserved.

claimed that his addiction to television had distorted his understanding of reality (Liebert & Sprafkin, 1988).

Direct *copying* of specific aggressive actions has been documented in a number of studies. Children who were exposed to an aggressive model in Bandura's Bobo doll studies sometimes mimicked the precise words and actions of the model (Bandura, 1973). Evidence also suggests that reports of spectacular crimes on television and in newspapers, such as assassinations, hijackings, kidnappings, and murder-suicides, are often followed by increases in similar crimes. Even aggression against oneself, suicide, may occur in imitation of front-page suicides. One investigator examined the number of suicides in the United States between 1947 and 1968. When suicide rates in the months before and after each of 35 highly publicized suicides were contrasted, startling increases were revealed. On the average, each suicide story was followed by

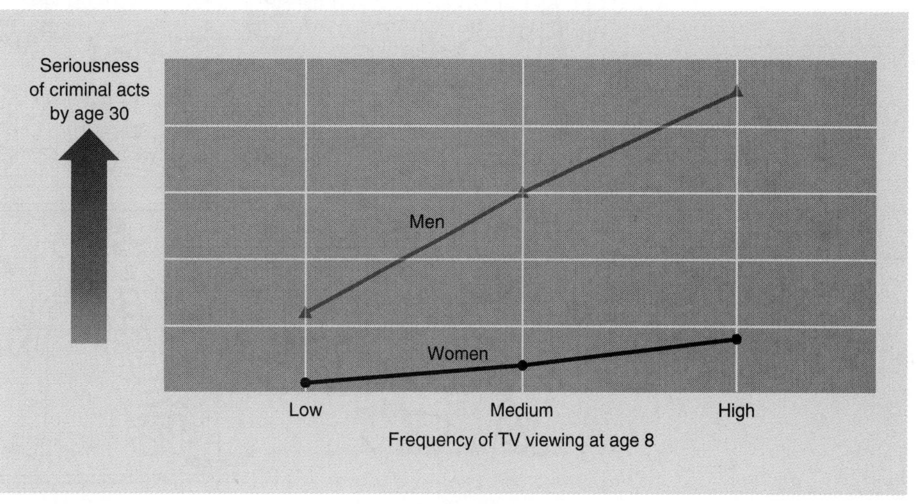

▲ **FIGURE 13-10**
Do children who watch TV violence in the third grade grow up to be criminals? When Eron tracked hundreds of people over a 20-year period, he discovered that people who committed serious crimes tended to be the ones who watched large amounts of violent TV as children. Men, in general, were more likely to have commited criminal acts by the time they were 30. (From Eron, 1987)

about 58 copycat suicides (Phillips, 1974, 1979, 1980, 1982, 1983). These findings suggest that the mass media, by giving extensive coverage to acts of violence, may actually promote violence (Bandura, 1983; Berkowitz, 1984; Phillips, 1982).

Second, viewers also become *desensitized* to real-life violence after prolonged exposure to televised violence. In two studies, children were shown an aggressive film, a nonaggressive film, or no film at all. They were then asked to monitor the actions of two children who were playing in a nearby room. When the two children began to argue and destroy each other's property, the subjects were less likely to intervene if they had just seen a violent film (Drabman & Thomas, 1974, 1976). People who are exposed to fictitious violence also show fewer signs of physiological arousal when they watch scenes depicting real violence (Cline, Croft, & Courrier, 1973; Thomas et al., 1977). Also, as noted in the section "In Depth: Pornography and Sexual Assault," men who watch movies filled with violence against women become less sensitive to women's rights and welfare.

If aliens from another planet tried to understand our civilization by watching our television shows, they would probably form a distorted view of us. After watching our situation comedies, police shows, detective thrillers, soap operas, and commercials, they would conclude that the average human being is witty, violent, deceitful, selfish, sexually driven, and vain. Third, television seems to shape the viewer's values, so that the "more time one spends 'living' in the world of television, the more likely one is to report perceptions of social reality which can be traced to (or are congruent with) television's most persistent representations of life and society" (Gerbner et al., 1980, p. 14).

Much of this *value-shaping* is related to our views of violence. Because violence plays a major role in TV life, viewers sometimes feel that murder, rape, and assault are routine, commonplace occurrences. One team of researchers asked 587 adolescents a series of questions about violence in America. Each question was followed by two alternatives: One alternative was factually correct; the other was consistent with violence rates in television programming.

CALVIN AND HOBBES copyright Watterson. Reprinted with permission of UNIVERSAL PRESS SYNDICATE. All rights reserved.

▲ An ironic illustration of the danger of desensitization brought on by watching too much televised violence.

▲ **TABLE 13-3**
Percentages of TV viewers whose answers corresponded to information provided by TV plots rather than to actual crime rates

Question	*TV Answer*	*Heavy TV Viewers (%)*	*Light TV Viewers (%)*
How many people are involved in some kind of violence each year: 3% or 10%?	10%	83	62
How many people are involved in some kind of violence each week: 1 person out of 100 or 10 people out of 100?	10	73	62
What percentage of all people commit serious crimes: 3% or 12%?	12%	88	77
Would you be afraid to walk alone in your neighborhood at night?	Yes	52	46
Is it dangerous to walk alone in a city at night?	Yes	86	79
On an average day, how many times does a policeman usually pull out his gun: less than once a day or more than five times a day?	More than five times	18	6
When police arrive at a scene of violence, how much of the time do they use force and violence: most of the time or some of the time?	Most of the time	56	45
Can most people be trusted, or do you think you can't be too careful in dealing with people?	Must be careful	62	52

Source: Adapted from Gerbner et al., 1979.

One item read, "Think about the number of people who are involved in some kind of violence each year. Do you think that 3 percent of all people are involved in some kind of violence in any given year, or is it closer to 10 percent?" The correct answer was 3%; the "television answer" was 10%. As Table 13-3 indicates, relatively more of the heavy television viewers selected the television answers. The more television you watch, the more distorted your perception of reality becomes (Gerbner et al., 1979).

A note of caution. Two scientists are driving by a flock of sheep. One scientist says to the other, "I see those sheep have just been shorn." The other looks at the sheep for a moment before replying, "On the side facing us, anyway."

This story reminds us never to be too sure we know all the answers. The factors noted in Table 13-4 suggest televised violence and aggression are linked. Children behave more aggressively after viewing violence, and adults sometimes copy aggressive actions they have seen on television or read about in the newspapers. Televised violence also reduces our sensitivity to real-world violence and may distort our perceptions of the world in which we live. All of these findings suggest that television *probably* increases the aggressiveness of some viewers. Like the skeptical scientist, however, we must remain open to alternative possibilities. The evidence is strong but not definitive (Freedman, 1984; Friedrich-Cofer & Huston, 1986; Widom, 1989; Wood, Wong, & Chachere, 1991).

Norms and Aggression

Bernhard Goetz thought that New York City was a dangerous place to live but that this danger was predictable. Even though hundreds of thousands of people crowd the city's streets and subways, their encounters are guided by social standards. These *norms* work to keep aggression in check in most cases, but they also sanction aggression in others. Goetz believed he was within his rights to defend himself from attack, for Cabey was the first to threaten violence. Actions that might be considered abnormal or extreme in any other city were allowable in New York City. Violence, Goetz believed, was just "part of the game."

Normative approaches offer a counterpoint to the instinct and motivation theories. Rather than viewing aggressive behavior as wild and uncontrolled, a norm-based approach suggests that aggressive behavior, like most behaviors, follows the rules of the situation. In many situations, aggression is "normal"; it is *the* most appropriate way to behave.

Violence in a Cross-Cultural Context

Despite Freud's claims to the contrary, violence is not a universal aspect of human existence. Anthropologists have documented whole cultures where vio-

Pornography and Sexual Assault

The characters in the movie you are watching on cable television have fallen in love. After several impassioned kisses, they begin to undress each other. Once naked, they slowly sink down to the thickly carpeted floor, where they engage in gentle but intense sexual intercourse.

Could watching two people make love possibly make you more aggressive? Yes and no. Mildly sexual material that is presented in a positive, pleasant way can actually decrease aggression. People vary greatly in their preferences for erotic material, but most people respond positively to sexually provocative images. They become slightly aroused by the material, but their feelings are pleasant and nonaggressive. If the erotic materials are too intense, however, they may engender more negative feelings, which in turn heighten aggressiveness (Ramirez, Bryant, & Zillmann, 1983; White, 1979; Zillmann et al., 1981).

A relatively new form of erotic material combines sexually explicit images with violence. These films don't usually meet the legal definition of *pornography*, yet they depict graphic violence directed at women or children, who are raped, beaten, or even killed. Rape and other forms of violence against women have a number of causes, but violent pornography has been shown to increase violence directed at women (Malamuth, 1986). Edward Donnerstein (1980) first irritated some of his male subjects by giving them mild electric shocks. He then asked them to watch a 4-minute clip of a portion of a talk show interview (neutral material), a couple engaged in sexual intercourse (erotica), or a man raping a woman at gunpoint (violent pornography). Donnerstein

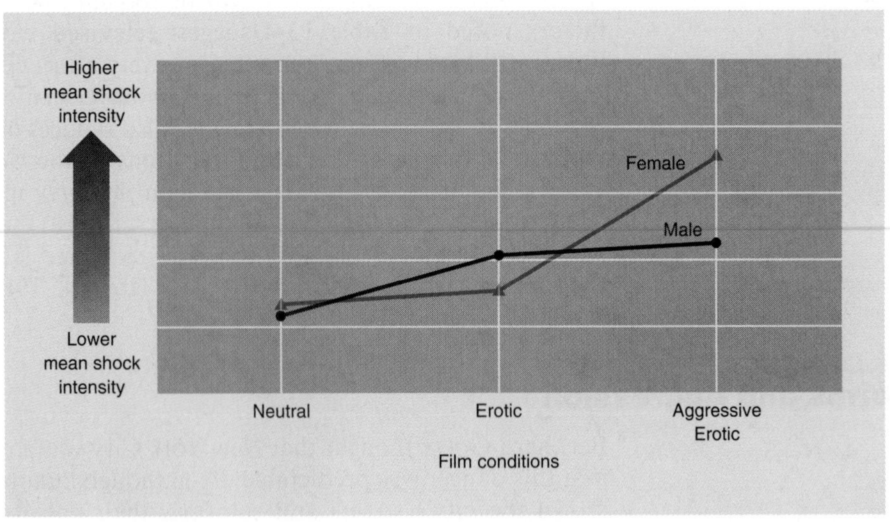

▲ **FIGURE 13-11**
Could watching films that depict sexual violence against women make men become more aggressive? Donnerstein found that men who watched clips that contained sexual material and clips that depicted sexual violence against women gave slightly more intense shocks to another man. Men gave much more intense shocks, however, to a woman when they had just been shown a film clip that depicted sexual violence against a woman. (From Donnerstein, 1980)

lence and conflict are taboo. The !Kung and the Pygmies of Africa and several Native American tribes (for example, the Blackfoot and Zuni) avoid conflict and competition, preferring to settle differences by making concessions. The members of these societies live in small groups. Rather than defend their territories when others intrude, they withdraw to more isolated areas. Men are not regarded as brave or strong when they are aggressive, and war with other groups is nonexistent (Gorer, 1968). In contrast, the Yanomanö of South America and the Mundugumor of New Guinea seem to thrive on violence (Chagnon, 1974; Mead, 1935). Anthropologist Napoleon Chagnon calls the Yanomanö the "fierce people," for they choose violence over peace at every opportunity. Among the Yanomanö, prestige is accorded to those who are most aggressive, and bravery is the most revered personal quality one can have. Villages routinely attack other villages, and personal conflicts are usually settled through violence. Chagnon reports that over one-third of the men in this society are murdered or killed during wars and battles. These widely dispa-

then arranged for the men to deliver a series of painful electric shocks either to a man or a woman, ostensibly as part of a study of learning and punishment. The men who had been given shocks themselves responded more aggressively than the men who hadn't been shocked, particularly when they had watched a sexually violent film clip. Moreover, as Figure 13-11 indicates, they also gave more intense shocks to a woman than a man after watching the violent film. In a subsequent study, Donnerstein and Berkowitz (1981) found that men were particularly aggressive toward women when the victim in the film acquiesced to the rape and seemed to enjoy it.

Other studies corroborate these laboratory findings. When researchers interviewed 930 women, nearly 10% reported an upsetting sexual experience that they felt had been caused by aggressive pornography. One woman reported that her boyfriend tied her up and beat her after getting the idea from a pornographic movie (Russell, 1984). Researchers have also found that convicted sexual offenders are heavy users of pornography, much more so than men who have never committed rape (Marshall, 1989). They are also more openly accepting of rape myths and express more positive attitudes about the use of violence against women (Scully & Marolla, 1984). In a study of men who had never been arrested for rape, Neil Malamuth (1986) discovered that men who became sexually aroused when they read a story about a violent rape were more likely to admit that they had coerced a woman into having sex with them by using force.

Other studies suggest that sexually violent films also alter viewers' acceptance of myths about rape and undermine their sympathy for women who have been raped (Linz, Wilson, & Donnerstein, 1992). Men were more likely to accept myths about rape, such as "women don't really mean it when they say 'no'," one week after they watched the movie *The Getaway,* which depicts sexual violence (Malamuth, Cheek, & Briere, 1981). Men who watched several sexually violent films over a 5-day period felt anxious on the first day, but by the last day their anxiety had diminished substantially. Their evaluation of material also changed, so that, by the last day, material that initially had been viewed as degrading was judged less harshly (Linz, Donnerstein, & Penrod, 1984). And men who were exposed to violent "slasher" films (for example, *Friday the 13th, Part 2, The Texas Chainsaw Massacre*); sexually explicit, X-rated films that depict no violence (for example, *Debbie Does Dallas, Indecent Exposure*); or R-rated teenage sex films that depict women as sexual objects (for example, *Porky's, Hots*) all became more inured to the depicted violence and degradation of women in the films over time. Also, compared to subjects who saw X-rated films and teenage sex films, men shown films depicting violent crimes against women expressed more callous attitudes about rape (Linz, Donnerstein, & Penrod, 1988).

These findings are consistent with social learning theory and a motivation model of aggression: The sexual content of the material creates arousal, and the violent content models hostile, degrading behaviors. Aggressive pornography also reinforces a number of prejudices against women (Russell, 1984):

> Porn sexually objectifies women. Women feel this degradation. Porn teaches men that women enjoy violence. It eroticizes violence for men. Porn confuses some women into believing they should experience pleasure through pain. Some men enjoy hurting women physically. It teaches women to endure rape and violence. (Wheeler, 1985, p. 385)

▲ **TABLE 13-4**
Summing up: Social learning processes that sustain aggressive behavior

Process	*Impact on Aggression*	*Example*
Observational learning	Exposure to models who engage in violent behavior increases the observers' aggressiveness if the vicarious consequences for the model are rewarding rather than punishing.	Children who watched an adult beat up a Bobo doll were more violent than children who were not exposed to an aggressive model.
Media violence	Correlational studies, field studies, experiments, and longitudinal studies suggest that increases in exposure to violence on television or in films is associated with increases in violence.	Children who watched large amounts of violent TV in the third grade were more likely to commit violent crimes as adults.
Copying	Viewers sometimes copy the specific actions depicted in TV programs and films.	Three girls attacked another girl after seeing this crime in a movie.
Desensitization	Viewers become indifferent to crimes and violence depicted frequently on TV and in films.	Men repeatedly exposed to films that included violent rape scenes became less sympathetic toward a rape victim.
Value-shaping	Individuals who watch large amounts of television come to believe that the rates of violence depicted on TV reflect the level of aggression in contemporary society.	Heavy TV watchers believed that 10% of all people in the United States are victims of violence each year; this rate matches the percentage of violence in TV plots, but the actual rate is only 3%.

rate climates of violence suggest that aggression is determined, in part, by the culture's values and norms pertaining to conflict.

Norms about aggression are also linked to gender roles in many cultures. Aggression varies across cultures, but in virtually all societies men are more aggressive than women (Segall, 1988). The Human Relations Area files, which contain comparative information on 48 different nonindustrialized societies, indicate that men are far more likely to commit violent crimes than women (Moghaddam et al., 1993). When researchers compared boys and girls growing up in Kenya, India, Mexico, Okinawa, the Philippines, and the United States, they found that the boys were more aggressive than the girls (Whiting & Whiting, 1975). This robust sex difference, as noted earlier in the chapter, may be due to hormonal differences. But normative processes may also account for this sex difference if societies differentially apply norms pertaining to toughness and aggression to boys and girls. Cross-cultural studies suggest that, in many societies, boys are more likely to be encouraged to maintain their dominance over others through physical force, whereas girls who behave violently are more likely to be punished. Indeed, when pressures to conform to social norms are minimized experimentally, women behave as aggressively as men (Lightdale & Prentice, 1994).

Subcultures of Violence

Subgroups within the larger culture can also adopt unique norms and values pertaining to violence. In the United States the Mennonites and Amish avoid interpersonal conflict and strive instead for cooperative, peaceful living. Urban youth gangs, in stark contrast, accept norms that emphasize toughness and physical strength. When conflict arises among members, violence is the pre-

▲ **TABLE 13-5**
Subcultures of violence

The percentage of Southerners and Northerners who strongly agreed with statements about men's use of aggression to defend their honor

Statement	*Southern White Men*	*Northern White Men*
A man has the right to kill a person to defend his home.	36	18
A man has the right to kill a person to defend his family.	80	67
A man should use violence to respond to various affronts.	20	12
A man who fails to use violence in response to various affronts is "not much of a man."	12	6
Most fathers would expect their son to stand and fight when confronted by a bully.	39	25

Source: Adapted from Nisbett, 1993.

ferred means of settling it. When one gang invades another gang's turf, a fight or rumble is the normal method of settling the dispute. When gang members need money, they acquire it by committing robberies or muggings. Violence is so strongly ingrained in the normative structure of the group that individuals behave aggressively simply to establish a reputation among their peers. In one study of 69 men who were convicted of violent crimes, approximately 76% claimed to use violence to create a tough-guy image (Toch, 1969, 1992). Their actions violated society's norms of behavior, but they were consistent with the unique norms that had emerged in their particular subgroup (Cloward & Ohlin, 1960; Thrasher, 1927; Yablonsky, 1962).

Richard Nisbett (1993) presents a normative analysis of regional differences in various types of violent crimes committed by white males in the United States. Murder, Nisbett notes, is a tradition down south; nearly three times as many men are murdered each year in the southern states as in other parts of the country. In explanation, Nisbett suggests that the "culture of honor" in the South encourages men to respond violently in defense of their homes, their property, and their honor. Southerners aren't more positive about aggression in general, but they are more likely to recommend aggressive responses for self-defense and in response to insults. As Table 13-5 indicates, white Southern men were more likely to approve of killing to protect their home or family. They were also more likely to advocate fighting when insulted and felt that their sons should be taught to fight (Cohen & Nisbett, 1994).

Nisbett and his colleagues went so far as to test for regional differences experimentally (Bowdle, Nisbett, & Schwarz, 1993; reported in Nisbett, 1993). They recruited white college students whose permanent home addresses were located in Southern states or Northern states. Each student first filled out a questionnaire and was told to put it on a table at the end of the hall. To reach the table, the subject had to pass by a male confederate who was filing materials in a cabinet. The confederate feigned irritation at the interruption, and when the subject passed by after dropping off the form, the confederate jostled him briefly and called him an asshole. This encounter had a much stronger impact on the Southerners than on the Northerners. Most of the Northerners were amused by the incident, whereas most of the Southerners were angered by it. The Southerners who were insulted also wrote more aggressive endings for a story that described a confrontation between a man and another man who has flirted with the first man's fiancée. Nisbett's research suggests that insulting certain people—especially those who have been taught to defend their honor—can have deadly consequences.

The Norm of Reciprocity

As noted earlier in this chapter, when people attack us, we usually counterattack. Although a motivational approach argues that our counterattack is caused by the arousal and anger produced by the initial attack, our response is also consistent with the norm of reciprocity. This norm encourages us to return, in kind, what others give to us. If others help us, we help them (see Chapter 12). But if others abuse, insult, or injure us, then we follow the rule of an "eye for an eye" and mistreat them in return (Tedeschi et al., 1974).

As the saying "Paybacks are hell" suggests, our response to an attack is often more intense than the original attack (Youngs, 1986). Reciprocity is rarely exact, with equal amounts of intensity passing between combatants. Rather, reciprocity tends to be rough, with the individual giving too much in return (overmatching). Some researchers believe that rough reciprocity causes violence to spiral. Studies of American race riots in the late 1960s reveal that the larger conflicts were preceded by a series of escalating hostile actions between police forces and black activists (L. Goldberg, 1968).

Norms and Deindividuation

Because some norms keep aggression in check, counternormative actions are sometimes also aggressive actions. Consider the case of the crowd that gathered to watch as a young woman threatened to commit suicide by jumping from a tower. Rather than assist the rescuers, the crowd pelted them with rocks as they chanted, "jump, jump." The woman was eventually rescued, despite the interference of the crowd (Mann, 1981).

deindividuation
A process by which individuals lose their sense of personal identity when they become too submerged in a group; also, the psychological state produced by this process.

Why would people behave so callously? According to Philip Zimbardo's theory of **deindividuation**, people sometimes lose their sense of personal identity when they are part of a group. Once deindividuated, they no longer feel compelled to act in accord with social norms. They also lack self-control and self-regulation, so their actions become highly emotional, impulsive, and atypical. Deindividuation rarely stimulates prosocial behaviors. Instead, it typically leads to "aggression, vandalism, stealing, cheating, rudeness, as well as a general loss of concern for others" (Zimbardo, 1969b, 1975, p. 53; see also Coleman, 1991; Diener, 1980; Prentice-Dunn & Rogers, 1983).

Anonymity is one of the most important determinants of deindividuation. You are more likely to act aggressively when "others can't identify or single you out, they can't evaluate, criticize, judge, or punish you" (Zimbardo, 1969b). Zimbardo tested this hypothesis by asking small groups of college women to deliver electric shocks to another woman as part of a learning exercise. Some of the women were clearly identifiable to one another; they wore name tags and were introduced to the other group members by name. A second group of women were disguised; they wore large lab coats and hoods over their heads. As predicted, the anonymous women gave more intense shocks than the identifiable women.

Even dressing up in a costume that disguises your identity may make you more aggressive. Researchers studied 1,352 children who went trick-or-treating at one of 27 experimental homes in Seattle, Washington. They manipulated anonymity by randomly asking some children to state their names and addresses. Others weren't asked to give their names, and because they were in costume, they should have felt anonymous. Next, the experimenter told the

▲ Aggression rises and falls across various subcultures of American society. Some subgroups, such as the Mennonites and Amish, live in small, peace-loving communities that are relatively free of conflict. Other subgroups, such as Latino gangs, display extremely high levels of aggression.

children they could each have one candy bar. She then left the room, and a hidden observer watched to see whether the children took extra candy bars or removed any money from a bowl containing pennies and nickels. Nearly 60% of the children transgressed by stealing either candy or money when they were anonymous *and* part of a group. About 20% stole something when they were anonymous *or* part of a group. Only 7.5% stole when alone. These findings explain why groups are capable of more violent acts than the individuals who make up these groups (Diener et al., 1976).

Controlling Aggression

Down through the centuries, countless millions have died, not from illness, not from disease, not from accident, but from human aggression. Given the causes of aggression summarized in Table 13-6, what suggestions do social psychologists offer for controlling violence and hostility?

Achieving Catharsis Without Aggression

Both Freud and Lorenz were pessimistic about our chances of eliminating aggression. They believed that hostile impulses build up gradually over time and that these urges must be discharged eventually. For Freud, damming up these impulses by keeping them inside is no solution, for unexpressed anger can cause depression, suicide, and other psychological abnormalities (Smyth, 1982). As noted earlier in this chapter, catharsis—the release and subsequent reduction of aggressive tensions—is inevitable.

Freud was more optimistic about our chances of *controlling* aggression. We need not release our hostile urges in negative ways. When his wife tells him he is a drunken lout, the husband need not physically abuse her—although abusing her may be cathartic. First, he could ventilate his hostility by expressing his anger and annoyance verbally. Second, because hostility can be displaced from one source to another, he could reduce his hostility by playing a sport, working out, or doing household chores. Both of these techniques should lead to catharsis.

Does ventilation work? Common sense argues that "blowing off steam" or "getting it off your chest" will reduce aggressiveness. In many cases, however, venting our hostility only heightens our psychological distress and upset. When we lose our temper and shout at our friend, we will likely regret the outburst later (Konečni, 1975a, 1975b; Konečni & Ebbesen, 1976). Ventilation can even backfire completely; by expressing anger, you can get yourself even more worked up and hostile. Children who were given the opportunity to vent their anger became more hostile as their personal restraints against aggression were lowered (Feshbach, 1956; Mallick & McCandless, 1966). The cathartic act may even become the first stage in a series of escalating aggressive interchanges. This spiraling cycle often occurs in domestic settings. Family violence usually begins with verbal hostilities. Instead of reducing aggression, complaints only fan the flames of conflict. A harsh word from the wife ("You thoughtless, inconsiderate bastard!") may lead to a rebuke from the husband ("You bitch, what do you . . ."), which in turn prompts physical violence (Straus, Gelles, & Steinmetz, 1980). Anger tends to exercise rather than exorcise hostility.

Does displacement work? Many theorists, including Freud, believe that unconscious aggressive urges can be *displaced,* or redirected into more socially acceptable activities. When you punch a pillow, scream in the closet, complain to a friend, play a rough sport, or imagine your enemy's demise, your thirst for aggression is slaked. But displacement is no panacea. Vigorous activities can drain off hostilities, but they work only under highly specific conditions. If you are angry with Catina but displace your hostility by kicking a wall or attacking Catina in your imagination, you probably will gain no relief. To investigate displacement, experimenters mildly irritated subjects by interrupting as they counted backward from 100 to 0 by 2s. Then they let some subjects vent their hostility by giving the experimenter electric shocks. People who thought they had harmed the experimenter showed less tension than people who had no cathartic experience at all. But fantasizing about harming the experimenter or giving shocks to a third party did not reduce their anger and tension (Hokanson, 1970; Hokanson & Burgess, 1962a, 1962b; Hokanson & Shetler, 1961; Hokanson, Willers, & Koropsak, 1968).

▲ **TABLE 13-6**
Summing up: Five theoretical perspectives on aggression

Theoretical Perspective	*Source of Aggression*	*Explanation*
Physiological theories	Neurological and hormonal mechanisms	Specific biological mechanisms, such as the limbic system in the brain and such hormones as testosterone, control aggressiveness.
Evolutionary theory	Instincts	Aggression increases the individual's chances for survival (ethology) or the likelihood that his or her genes will survive in future generations (sociobiology). Violence is one way of satisfying the instinctive urge to be aggressive (psychodynamic theory of catharsis).
Motivational model	Arousal and emotions	The frustration-aggression hypothesis argued that frustrating situational factors cause aggression. A more general motivational model argues that aggression occurs when irritating events generate arousal and when personal or situational factors trigger an aggressive response.
Social learning models	Reinforcement, punishment, and observation	Individuals learn to perform aggressive actions after exposure to aggressive models who are rewarded for violent behavior.
Normative models	Conformity to norms	People are violent because their culture or subculture positively sanctions aggression, when they reciprocate a harmful act, or because they feel freed from regulatory norms that typically keep aggression in check.

Undoing Aggressive Motives

Since aversive, noxious experiences can motivate us to act violently, perhaps aggression can be controlled by simply avoiding all environmental irritants. But for those of us who can't escape all the hassles that seem to fill our lives, other strategies are needed.

Controlling arousal. "Count to ten" is an ancient and insightful recommendation for controlling aggression. A cooling-off period lets your arousal drop to a more normal level. If arousal can be controlled, then aggression can be controlled. Drugs, too, can have a calming effect. Studies suggest that marijuana, which is reputed to have mellowing effects on humans, inhibits aggressive actions. Similarly, even though significant amounts of alcohol increase arousal and aggression, small amounts of alcohol inhibit aggression (see Taylor & Leonard, 1983, for a summary). Arousal can also be controlled by avoidance of sources of excitation that can energize an aggressive response. Playing a contact sport may be a poor outlet for aggression. Not only will you become aroused, but this excitation may transfer from the athletic context to an aggressive context.

Incompatible responses. The wife tickles her grumpy husband until he starts to giggle. The employee tells his boss a few anecdotes before explaining why the report is late. The handsome man who nearly caused a fender-bender flirts with the woman driving the other car.

incompatible response strategy
Reducing aggression by creating emotions that are not compatible with anger.

The **incompatible response strategy** suggests that the people in these cases avoided aggression by creating emotions that are not compatible with anger. The wife short-circuits her husband's anger by making him laugh; the employee undermines anger by creating amusement; the driver relies on mild sexual titillation. Apparently any "stimuli or conditions serving to induce responses or affective states incompatible with anger or overt aggression may be effective in deterring such reactions" (Baron, 1983, p. 174).

The incompatible response strategy works. In one study, subjects were given a chance to deliver electric shocks to a confederate who had angered them. Subjects who were shown a series of amusing cartoons before they delivered the shocks were less aggressive than subjects who saw only neutral pictures of scenery and abstract art (Baron & Ball, 1974). In this study as well as in others, mildly positive experiences tended to undermine aggression. However, hostile humor or highly arousing sexual material will not reduce aggression because the reactions they tend to generate are compatible with aggression (Baron, 1983).

Apologies and mitigating circumstances. Researchers have shown that we can sometimes interrupt the anger-aggression circuit by offering an apology or explanation for our irritating, harmful behaviors. If you treat friends rudely and they become angry, you may be able to short-circuit their anger by saying you are sorry or just by offering some explanation for your untoward behavior. When people are informed about mitigating circumstances—background factors that indicate the insult is unintentional or unimportant—they tend to moderate their aggression (Ferguson & Rule, 1983; Ohbuchi, Kamdea, & Agarie, 1989).

Mitigating information has its greatest impact on us when it is presented before the aversive event even occurs. If, before you behave rudely, you mention, "I flunked a test today," they will be likely to let the subsequent insult pass. If, however, you insult your friend before talking about the test, this mitigating information may not reduce your friend's aggression (Johnson & Rule, 1986; Kremer & Stephens, 1983; Zillmann & Cantor, 1976). When college-age men encountered a rude experimenter, but knew the experimenter had an excuse for his ill temper (for example, "He's really uptight about a midterm that he has tomorrow"), they did not evaluate him negatively if they were told about the test before they were insulted. The everyday implications of these findings are clear: If you are going to annoy people, (1) make sure they know its not your fault, and (2) give them your excuse in advance (Zillmann & Cantor, 1976).

Gun control. Leonard Berkowitz (1993), drawing on his studies of the weapons effect, argues that the sale of guns in the United States should be more closely regulated. Firearms are the weapon of choice in the United States, for they are used to commit over 9,000 homicides each year. Production and importation rates of new firearms closely parallel homicide rates, and people who live in a home were a gun is kept are more likely to be killed (often by suicide) than are people who live in gun-free homes. Berkowitz's motivational approach to aggression suggests that murders aren't often planned out well in advance. Rather, husbands, wives, lovers, and close friends become so furious that their anger—and the available handgun—combine to cause a deadly action. Berkowitz writes:

> Although reasonable arguments against gun control have been advanced . . . , I argue in favor of a gun control policy. . . . Guns can contribute to impulsive crimes of violence. The more firearms, and especially the more handguns, that there are circulating in society, the greater are the chances people in general, and not necessarily lawbreakers, will be killed. (1993, p. 332)

▲ Many Americans staunchly defend their right to own and use firearms. Unfortunately, in the United States, firearms are used to commit over 9,000 homicides each year. This statistic has prompted some to suggest stricter rules governing the sale and possession of such weapons.

Unlearning Aggression

Both social learning theory and normative approaches argue that aggressive behavior is learned through experience. And if aggression is learned, then it can be unlearned (Deutsch, 1993).

Modeling nonaggression. If little Johnny learns to punch his younger brother by watching professional wrestling on television, he can also learn *not* to punch his brother when he sees television characters turn the other cheek. Children who are repeatedly exposed to nonviolent programs display more positive, prosocial behaviors and fewer aggressive actions (Friedrich & Stein, 1973; Goldstein & Keller, 1983). Other studies suggest that TV, so long considered the source of bad habits and the erosion of cultural standards, can be used for prosocial ends. In fact, when one researcher compared the impact of antisocial programs and prosocial programs, she found that positive messages are twice as influential as negative messages (Hearold, 1986).

Child-rearing practices can also have a major impact on aggressive tendencies. Eron (1980) goes so far as to suggest that "if we want to reduce the level of aggression in society, we should also discourage boys from aggression very early on in life and reward them too for other behaviors; in other words, we should socialize boys more like girls" (p. 251). Morton Deutsch (1993) extends the responsibility for modeling cooperation over competition to school systems and community groups. He argues that students must be taught the skills they need to deal with conflicts and offers many suggestions for how to teach peace rather than violence.

Censoring aggressive models. Considerable evidence indicates that televised violence and aggression are linked and that sexually violent films can increase violence against women. Televised violence also reduces our sensitivity to real-world violence and may distort our perceptions of the world in which we live. Do these findings suggest that violence on TV and in films should be banned?

Most social psychologists don't favor a ban on film and TV violence (Hearold, 1986; Linz et al., 1992). Rather than protecting viewers through censorship or by affixing warning labels to programs, they advocate "media literacy programs" that would inoculate viewers against the harmful effects of TV (Wilson, 1987, 1989). Adults should learn to identify aggressive themes, and parents should take an active role in their childrens' television viewing. Social psychologists also suggest that the television industry should reduce "direct imitatable violence on real-life fictional children's programming or violent incidents in cartoons, and . . . provide more programming for children designed to mitigate possible effects of television violence." Other ways to control the impact of violence on TV, they note, could be identified through research (Proceedings of the American Psychological Association, 1985, p. 649).

Punishing aggression. The use of punishment to decrease aggression creates a paradox. Punishment sometimes effectively eliminates aggression, but isn't punishment itself a form of aggression? When the school principal paddles a truant, when a mother spanks her child, when the judicial system executes a murderer, their actions make the statement, "Aggression is a legitimate means to achieve your goals." Punishment can also increase feelings of anger, particularly when the punished person thinks the punishment is unfair. Last, children who don't act aggressively only because they fear punishment may never learn to use more mature, and less aggressive, means of dealing with conflict (Lore & Schultz, 1993).

Punishment, however, appears to be effective in some cases. Parents in the United States are more tolerant when their children behave aggressively; in countries such as Mexico and Kenya, parents punish their children when they play too aggressively. These countries also have lower rates of adult violence (Lambert, 1971). Studies also suggest that stronger legal sanctions for some forms of criminal violence reduce those forms of violence. For many years, domestic violence was not punished very harshly. When a man attacked and beat his wife, he was often given counseling or forced to leave the premises for a short time. In an experimental program carried out in Minnesota, however, police found that men who were arrested were much less likely to commit the same crime again (Sherman & Berk, 1984). Punishment will, in some cases, deter violence.

Norms and Society

A final prescription based on the normative approach can be added to the others summarized in Table 13-7. This approach argues that in many societies violence is not just condoned—it is expected. To eliminate aggression, these norms must change, for violence will flourish in a country where a man who shoots four unarmed teenagers is praised as a hero.

Norms are slow to change, for they can be traced back to cultural values that have defined American society for generations (Nisbett, 1993). However, changes in the legal definition of aggressive actions can, in some cases, change the way people view these acts. In recent years, many states revised their laws concerning rape, and with these changes have come changes in public tolerance of such crimes as acquaintance rape and marital rape (Goldberg-Ambrose, 1992; White & Sorenson, 1992). Researchers have also begun testing specific norm-changing programs in groups that have developed norms that sanction violence. Several of these violence-prevention programs are aimed at African American youths, and they focus on changing community norms pertaining to violence by stressing a return to such Afrocentric cultural values as collectivism, cooperation, and self-acceptance (Hammond & Yung, 1993). Last,

▲ **TABLE 13-7**
Summing up: Ways to control aggression

Theoretical Perspective	*Recommendations for Controlling Aggression*
Psychodynamic processes	Purge the urge to be aggressive by expressing anger verbally rather than physically. Channel hostility into less violent directions (displacement).
Motivational processes	"Count to ten" to let emotions cool. Take mood-altering drugs. Avoid sources of excitement and arousal. Create emotions that are incompatible with anger. Offer and accept apologies. Describe and recognize mitigating circumstances. Institute gun controls.
Social learning	Model nonaggressive, cooperative behavior in the media. Stop modeling aggressive, hostile behavior in the media. Punish aggressive behavior.
Normative models	Legislate stronger penalties for aggressive behaviors. Advocate changes in society's tolerance of aggressive behavior.

changes in the media can also effect changes in social norms pertaining to violence. Television programs need not convey violent images. Rather, they could stress prosocial, cooperative values (Liebert & Sprafkin, 1988).

Summary

Aggression is an action performed with the intention of harming or injuring another person. It takes many forms. Emotional, or hostile, aggression involves strong emotional arousal. Instrumental aggression is a less emotional means of manipulating and influencing other people. Aggression is considered legitimate when it is perceived to be justified in the social setting but illegitimate when deemed unjust and unwarranted. Contemporary forms of aggression include such violent crimes as murder and sexual assault, as well as domestic, youth, and collective violence. Many of these forms of aggression have become increasingly common in recent years.

A number of theoretical perspectives explain why humans are aggressive. Some theorists trace aggression to physiological, biochemical, and hereditary processes that are part of human nature. The *limbic system,* for example, prepares us physiologically either to confront the source of the danger or to flee from the danger (the fight-or-flight response), and the hormone *testosterone* contributes to aggressiveness in men in general and in XYY men in particular. Aggression, both predatory and agonistic, is so commonplace in the animal kingdom that many theorists assume aggression is evolutionarily adaptive. *Ethology*, for example, argues that animals are instinctively sensitive to certain types of environmental cues that serve to release aggression. Moreover, other cues turn off aggression. Lorenz argued that the use of weapons has undermined the effectiveness of these cues in humans. Sociobiology, in contrast, argues that aggression is a situation-specific action that maximizes the animal's fitness. Freud's psychodynamic approach also assumes aggression is instinctive, stemming from urges that build up gradually over time in the *unconscious*. These impulses must be discharged to achieve *catharsis*, but if *displacement* occurs, the individual can achieve catharsis nonviolently.

In contrast to Freud's psychodynamic theory, ethology, and sociobiology, social-psychological theories emphasize the impact of situational forces on aggression. Theories based on the concept of *motivation* argue that environmental factors heighten the need to be aggressive. The *frustration-aggression hypothesis*, an early motivation theory, argued that thwarting environmental conditions led to feelings of frustration, and that these feelings of frustration caused aggression. This view has been refined and extended through research, so the motivational approach now argues that many aversive environmental factors, such as pain, attacks, threats, competition, and environmental stress, can cause physiological arousal. These environmental irritants generate arousal, and aggression will then follow, provided additional personal and situational conditions are present. Anger, for example, works to trigger aggression, and individuals who are *Type A* personalities tend to be more aggressive than *Type B* individuals. Physiological arousal caused by nonaggressive stimuli or events, such as a high temperature or pornography, can also instigate aggression, according to *excitation-transfer theory*. And, as Berkowitz's studies of the *weapons effect* suggest, certain social stimuli can function as cues, which increase the likelihood that arousal will lead to aggression. Thus, the *arousal-aggression theory* argues that irritating events + aggression-triggering personal or situational factors = aggression.

Bandura's *social learning theory* assumes that individuals learn aggressive behavior through reinforcement and observation. As Bandura's Bobo doll studies show, *observational learning* occurs when children observe aggressive acts performed by peer and adult models. Bandura's social learning theory suggests that watching violence on television may cause viewers to become more aggressive. Researchers have found that children who watch violent programs tend to be more aggressive and sometimes directly copy types of violence they have observed. Heavy television viewing has also been linked to reduced sensitivity to real-world violence and to distorted perceptions of social reality. Sexually violent films that depict rapes and other forms of sexual assault also model violence. Evidence indicates that men who watch sexually violent films are more likely to attack women; these men also express more callous attitudes about sexual violence.

According to the normative approach, aggression is sometimes consistent with the standards of conduct considered appropriate in society. Anthropologists have documented cultures in which violence and conflict are either unknown or commonplace. Within cultures, certain subgroups may adopt norms that condemn violence, but others—such as urban gangs or white men living in the southern states of the United States—may adopt norms that condone violence. The norm of reciprocity suggests that violence can be legitimately met with violence, but other norms keep aggression in check. When individuals experience *deindividuation,* they tend to become violent because they no longer feel constrained by norms. Anonymity and group membership appear to be the key determinants of deindividuation.

How can aggression be controlled? Freud recommended the ventilation of anger to release hostile urges and the displacement of aggression in more socially acceptable actions. Research, however, has failed to confirm the usefulness of these suggestions. Interventions derived from the arousal-aggression model and social learning theory have been shown to be more effective. We can diminish aggression by delaying our reactions until our arousal dissipates, by employing an *incompatible response strategy,* and by offering apologies and noting mitigating circumstances. Aggression is also unlearned when children view models who engage in nonaggressive actions. Experts also feel that punishment can temporarily prevent aggression, but this technique may not be as effective as rewarding prosocial behavior. Last, the normative approach argues that aggression can be countered by the elimination of norms that encourage violence.

For More Information

• *Adult Sexual Assault,* edited by Jacquelyn W. White and Susan B. Sorenson (1992), is a volume of the *Journal of Social Issues.* The authors examine definitional and methodological issues encountered in the study of sexual violence, factors that sustain violence, and implications of these issues for changes in the law and public policy.

• *Aggression and Crimes of Violence* (2nd ed.), by Jeffrey H. Goldstein (1986), is a down-to-earth analysis of the causes of violence. Goldstein synthesizes evidence drawn from many fields of study, and he offers a particularly compelling rejection of many myths about violence.

• *Aggression: Its Causes, Consequences, and Control,* by Leonard Berkowitz (1993), summarizes two decades of empirical research into the causes and consequences of aggression and violence.

• *A Crime of Self-Defense: Bernhard Goetz and the Law on Trial,* by George P. Fletcher (1988), reviews the legal aspects of the Goetz case, including the legal basis for Goetz's claim that he acted in self-defense.

• *The Early Window: Effects of Television on Children and Youth* (3rd ed.), by Robert M. Liebert and Joyce N. Sprafkin (1988), takes a close look at the impact of television on our social lives. Liebert and Sprafkin explore the link between violent programs and aggression, and also consider television's use as an educational tool.

• *Human Aggression,* by Russell G. Geen (1990), is a thorough analysis of the interpersonal and environmental antecedents of aggression, the processes that facilitate and inhibit aggression, and the role of individual differences in producing violence.

• *Human Aggression* (2nd ed.), by Robert A. Baron and Deborah R. Richardson (1994), examines recent advances in theory and research in aggression, with special sections dealing with biological bases of aggression and aggression in natural settings.

• *Rape and Sexual Assault,* edited by Ann Wolbert Burgess (1985), studies violence against women from a variety of perspectives. Chapters deal with five basic themes: contemporary attitudes toward rape, victims of rape, family and legal issues, the rapist, and the prevention of rape.

• *The Resolution of Conflict,* by Morton Deutsch (1973), examines the way in which conflict between people can arise through competition and mistrust. Drawing on his own laboratory studies of subjects' reactions to interdependence, Deutsch offers insights into the causes and consequences of interpersonal conflict.

Application: Coping with Conflict

We cannot expect all our interactions with others to be smooth and harmonious. In business settings, employees and employers don't always agree with one another. Married people talking about vacation plans end up fighting about finances. Two close friends lose patience with each other and say things they later regret. The customer and the salesclerk argue over the fairness of the store's policy on returns. These situations are all rife with **conflict**: The actions or beliefs of one person are unacceptable to—and hence are resisted by—one or

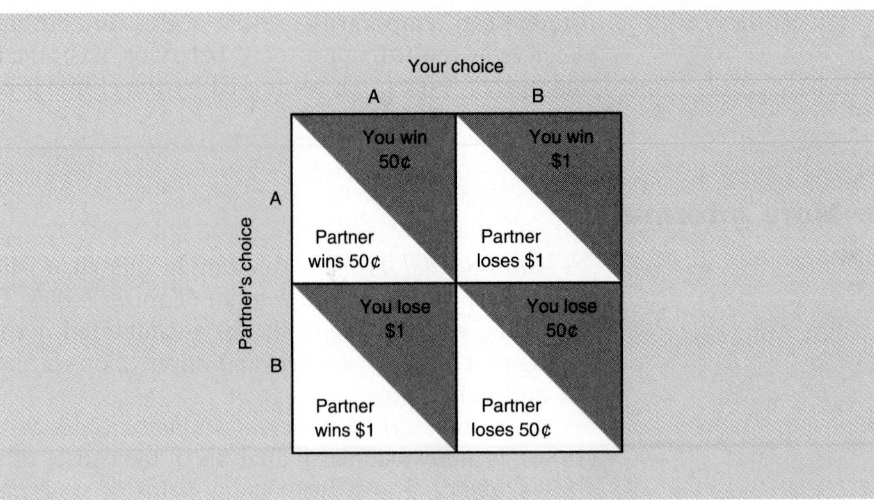

▲ **FIGURE 13-12**
If given a choice, would you choose to cooperate or compete? The prisoner's dilemma game requires players to choose either option A or option B. In each cell, your outcomes are shown above the diagonal line, and your partner's outcomes are shown below the diagonal. If you choose A and your partner chooses A, for example, you both earn 50 cents. If, however, one of you chooses A and the other chooses B, the one who picks A loses money, and the one who picks B wins money. A is the cooperative choice, whereas B is the competitive choice.

more other people. Interpersonal conflicts do not necessarily lead to hostility or aggression, but they often shake the foundations of our interpersonal relationships.

Conflict springs from many sources (Rubin, Pruitt, & Kim, 1994; Tjosvold, 1986). In many cases, the problem begins when people realize they are competing for scarce resources. When we compete, others must fail if we are to succeed. By striving for our personal goals, we interfere with others' attempts to reach their goals. Competition, by definition, creates incompatibility between people, and this incompatibility can escalate into interpersonal conflict (Deutsch, 1949a, 1949b, 1973, 1980). Reciprocity, too, may fan the fires of conflict. If our friends say something that irritates us, we may complain in return. When they respond rudely to our complaint and we respond angrily to their rudeness, we are well on our way to conflict (Gouldner, 1960). Conflict also arises when we don't trust each other. We may want to think that our friend, business partner, or spouse is acting in ways that help us, but sometimes we begin to wonder whether they have our best interests at heart (Rempel et al., 1985).

Social psychologists often use a specialized laboratory technique known as the **prisoner's dilemma game (PDG)** to study the causes of conflict. This technique derives its name from a tale about two men who are arrested by the police. The suspects are questioned in separate rooms. The police are certain the two are guilty, but they need more evidence to make their case. So they offer each man a deal. Each one is told that if he remains silent and his partner confesses, the partner will be released, and he himself will receive a stiff sentence. Alternatively, if he confesses and his partner remains silent, then he will be released and his partner will suffer. If both men confess, they will each receive a moderate sentence, and if neither confesses, they will both be tried on a minor charge that carries a fairly light sentence.

This situation creates a dilemma for each prisoner. He will end up either with no sentence or a moderate sentence if he confesses. And if he remains silent, he takes the chance of receiving a substantial sentence should his partner confess. Should he gamble that his partner will remain silent, or give in to the pressure and confess?

In the experimental version of this dilemma, the years are replaced by money or points, and the decision to confess or not becomes a choice between Option A and Option B (see Figure 13-12). Typically, players are seated in separate rooms, and they make their choices simultaneously. After the players select either A or B, they are then told about their partner's choice and the amount of money they won. In most cases, people choose between A and B a number of times. Each set of choices is called a trial.

The PDG captures the essence of a competitive conflict (see Wrightsman, O'Connor, & Baker, 1972). Imagine that you are a subject in a study that uses the matrix shown in Figure 13-12. You want to earn $1, and to win that amount, you must pick B. But you see that whenever you pick B, your partner loses money. B, then, is the *competitive* choice. Moreover, if you pick B and your partner also picks B, you both lose 50 cents. In other words, if you both make competitive choices, you both lose. A, in contrast, is the *cooperative* choice. If you look at the matrix, you can see that any time you pick A, your partner will earn some money (either 50 cents or $1). What happens if your partner, a stranger with whom you have no way of communicating, picks B when you pick A? Then you will lose $1, and your partner will earn $1. If you cooperate while your partner competes,

conflict: Disagreement, discord, and friction that occurs when the actions or beliefs of one individual or group of individuals are incompatible with and hence are resisted by another individual or group of individuals.

prisoner's dilemma game (PGD): A laboratory procedure in which players must make either cooperative or competitive choices in order to earn points or money; used in the study of cooperation, competition, and the development of mutual trust.

you will lose money. Because the PDG creates conflicting pressures to cooperate and compete, it is known as a **mixed-motive situation**: The motive to cooperate is mixed with the motive to compete.

How do people react when asked to make a choice in the prisoner's dilemma game? In most cases, actions in the PDG follow the principle of reciprocity: Cooperation begets cooperation, while competition begets competition. When people play the PDG with a partner who consistently makes cooperative choices, they also tend to cooperate. Those who encounter competitors, however, soon adopt the competitive strategy, and they, too, begin to compete. Negative reciprocity, however, is stronger than positive reciprocity. That is, a cooperative person who runs into a competitive partner is likely to begin to compete *before* the competitive person begins to cooperate (Kelley & Stahelski, 1970a, 1970b, 1970c). A partner turns into an opponent faster than an opponent turns into a partner.

People will also exploit a person who is unusually cooperative. Imagine that you are taking part in a PDG study. You have gone through 5 trials, and each time both you and your partner chose A. You cooperated with each other, and won 50 cents each time. Out of boredom or spite or curiosity, however, you decide to compete on trial 6. Your cooperative partner loses $1, and you win $1. Now, on trial 7, fearful that your partner will pay you back for your competitive choice, you once more pick the competitive option to minimize your loss. Much to your surprise, your partner once again selects A, the cooperative choice. What should you do on trial 8—reciprocate by cooperating or continue to exploit? Most people choose exploitation. Perhaps a study wasn't needed to verify this point, but the findings indicate that people are quite ready to take advantage of you if you let them (Shure, Meeker, & Hansford, 1965).

Researchers have also found that negative reciprocity and exploitation are caused by the erosion of trust that occurs during competition. The payoff matrix of the PDG makes the exploitation of a cooperating partner a tempting alternative. Recognizing this temptation, players sometimes feel that their partners cannot be trusted to make responses that benefit both players. Therefore, they make competitive choices to defend themselves, while they assume that their partners make competitive choices to exploit *their* trust. As a result, *mirror image thinking* occurs: Both players assume their opponent is the competitor who is intent upon winning, while they are only trying to defend themselves (White, 1977).

Even when they encounter a cooperative partner, players are so suspicious that they refuse to reciprocate with cooperation. In one study, people played a modified version of the PDG against a simulated partner who adopted one of four styles: (1) competitive (maximized personal winnings while minimizing the subject's winnings), (2) cooperative (maximized joint winnings), (3) individualistic (maximized personal winnings but didn't interfere with the subject's winnings), and (4) altruistic (always tried to help the subject win). When asked to describe their partners' motives, people were most accurate when their partners adopted an individualistic or competitive style and least accurate in interpreting cooperation and altruism. They recognized competition when they saw it, but they had difficulty believing that their partners were behaving in a prosocial manner (Maki, Thorngate, & McClintock, 1979; see also Kelley & Stahelski, 1970a, 1970b).

This distrust cannot be undone by having people make their choices in groups rather than alone. Just as groups sometimes make decisions that are too extreme, they also respond more competitively than individuals do. In one study, individuals who played other individuals averaged only 6.6% competitive responses over the course of the game. But when an interacting triad played another interacting triad, 36.2% of their choices were competitive. When triads played triads but communicated their choices through representatives selected from within the group, competition rose to 53.5% (Insko et al., 1987). More than individuals, groups distrust other groups. Groups also seem to be more interested in exploiting other groups (Insko et al., 1990; Schopler et al., 1993).

What does the PDG tell us about the causes and consequences of conflict? In our daily lives we constantly encounter mixed-motive situations that force us to choose between competition and cooperation. If we decide to compete, then we must realize that our choice will prompt others to compete as well. Cooperation, however, is no guarantee that others will reciprocate. If others interpret our cooperativeness as a sign of weakness, then they may exploit our selflessness. Indeed, to push a competitive partner toward cooperation, we must sometimes show our willingness to compete if necessary. We must also be wary of our competitive tendencies in intergroup settings. Even though individual group members may prefer to cooperate, when they join groups, this cooperative orientation may be replaced by a competitive one. Last, conflicts become destructive when they are clouded by misunderstandings and misperceptions. Many of the negative consequences of conflict can be avoided if we simply strive to see the situation from the other person's perspective (Deutsch, 1973).

mixed-motive situation: Performance settings in which the interdependence among interactants involves both competitive and cooperative goal structures.

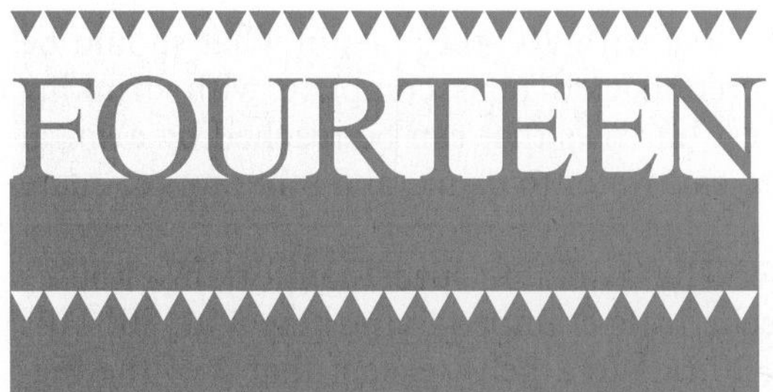

FOURTEEN

Social Environment

For the moment, you are a rat. You live with 80 other rats in what should be rat paradise—a series of four interconnected pens complete with drinking fountains, feed hoppers, and five-nest burrows that can be reached by a spiral staircase. You have plenty of food to eat, water to drink, and other rats to mate with. You should be happy.

But there is trouble in paradise. The available space comfortably houses between 50 and 60 rats, and you feel a little cramped living here with 80. This crowding wouldn't be too severe—20 rats to a pen—except that 2 of the biggest males have laid claim to the two pens that can be reached by only one ramp (see Figure 14-1). They spend most of their time dozing at the base of the ramp and waking at the approach of interlopers, whom they attack and drive away. These males keep a harem of about 10 females in their pens, and they have forced the rest of the rats into the remaining two pens. During feeding periods, as many as 60 rats crowd around the food hoppers.

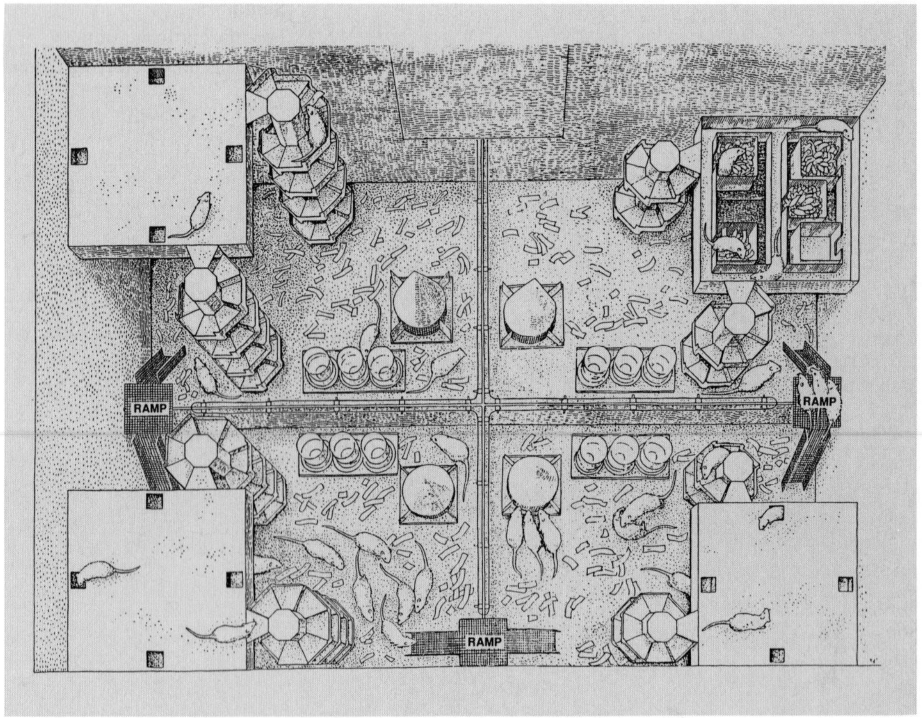

▲ **FIGURE 14-1**
If a colony of rats is given plenty of food and water, will it flourish? Calhoun's colony lived in an enclosure that contained four pens separated by electrified fences. Each of the top pens could be reached by only one ramp. The other two pens were linked by two ramps, making them very difficult to defend. All pens contained burrows (see the cutaway view of the top pen), feeders (the conelike structures), and water dishes (the cylindrical objects). (From Calhoun, 1962)

How do you react to this overcrowding? If you are a male rat, you have an outside chance of becoming one of the two dominant rats with a harem. But even the dominant males behave abnormally. They spend almost all their time defending their turf, they virtually ignore their harems and offspring, and they show an odd propensity to bite the tails of all the other rats, even the pups. Still, they are better off than you nondominant males. Some of you have become withdrawn; you spend much of your time in the burrows, ignoring the other rats, even the females. Others of you have lost the ability to distinguish between appropriate and inappropriate sexual partners, and try to mount males, females who are not ready to mate, and even sexually immature rats. You may become one of the "probers" (Calhoun, 1962). Probers are hyperactive and hypersexual males who constantly search for sexually receptive females. As a prober, you sometimes foray into one of the defended zones in search of females, but you quickly retreat when challenged. You also violate courtship rituals by attacking females in their burrows. If you are a prober, you are also a cannibal; you eat baby rats.

If you are a female rat and live in a harem, your life is fairly normal. You can mate, build a nest in the burrow, and raise your young in peace. If you live in one of the two overcrowded pens, however, you are repeatedly raped by gangs of probers. You are quite likely to die giving birth. If you survive, you are a poor mother. You fail to build a nest for your young, protect them from danger, or nourish them. Ninety-five out of 100 pups born in one of the lower pens die before they reach maturity.

territory
A specific area that an individual or group of individuals claims and defends for personal use.

personal space
The area individuals maintain around themselves into which others cannot intrude without arousing discomfort.

stressors
Environmental events that threaten an individual's existence or sense of well-being.

You are not a rat, though. You are a human being. But like the rats studied by John B. Calhoun, you are sometimes profoundly influenced by your social and physical environment. Like the dominant rats, you probably have established a **territory** that you consider to be your property. Your territory may consist of your home, a reserved parking space, or a chair in a classroom, but you defend it with as much energy as a rat defending its pen. And when you are away from your territory, you are still sensitive to how close other people approach to you. So long as people stay out of your **personal space**, you are comfortable and content, but what if a stranger comes too close? You respond, like Calhoun's rats, by withdrawing or forcing the invader to move back. Last, your actions take place in a physical location—such as a room, a home, an office, a park, or a street corner—and the design and layout of this environment influences your behavior. If too many people occupy the same space, then like the rats, you may feel crowded. Overcrowding, noise, and heat are all environmental **stressors**, for they can lead to many unhealthy consequences.

Calhoun's rats acted in bizarre ways, but their responses become understandable once we recognize that they were housed in small pens. Similarly, human behavior often seems mysterious until we look closely at the place where it occurs. The social processes we studied in earlier chapters—meeting people for the first time, working in groups, helping people, and so on—take place in an environmental context, and this context can't be ignored. This chapter examines several aspects of this *person-environment relationship,* including territoriality, personal space, and environmental stressors (McAndrew, 1993; Saegert & Winkel, 1990; Stokols & Altman, 1987).

Territoriality

Who would not be proud of the tremendous advances human beings have made in a scant 10,000 years? We have developed systems of trade and complex forms of social organization. We have constructed huge cities, assembled transportation and communication networks, and reshaped the land. We have nurtured the arts, created beautiful music, and written powerful prose and poetry. We have even visited our planet's moon.

But when it comes to territoriality, our actions follow an ancient pattern. Like so many other members of the animal kingdom, we still establish areas that only we can use and enjoy, and we strive to protect these places when others intrude. We erect doors to keep people out, post signs to warn them to keep away, hang curtains so they can't see in, and punish them if they enter. Like wolves patrolling their home range, birds defending their nests, monkeys howling warnings to intruders, or rats guarding the ramp leading to their pens, humans claim specific areas that they defend for personal use. Here we consider the nature of these territories and their impact on our social world.

The Nature of Territories

Are you territorial? Before you answer, review the different places you use during a typical day. Do you generally sleep in the same bed night after night, and do you keep to one side rather than the other? Where is this bed located? Is it in a room that you think of as yours? Do you sit in the same seat in social psychology class? When you lunch at the cafeteria or drink at a favorite bar, do you routinely sit at one table rather than another? Do you have a desk at work that is yours, and have you decorated it with pictures of friends and family?

When does a place become a territory? Calhoun decided that some of his rats had established territories when they began displaying two types of behavior. First, the more dominant rats marked their pens at regular intervals, leaving their scent by urinating here and there and by rubbing their bodies on the feeders, burrows, and ramps. Second, these rats also defended their pens against invasion by others. The dominant rats permitted females to pass freely in and out of their pens, but they attacked adult males who tried to descend the ramp. These two qualities—marking and defending—are also defining features of many humans' territories.

Marking territories. The poodle urinating on every rock, bush, fire hydrant, and tree in an area and the homeowner posting a "No trespassing" sign are both marking their turf—identifying territorial boundaries by erecting or leaving indicators that announce their spacial claims. Many species use bodily wastes or secretions from scent glands for markers; humans tend to rely more on walls, fences, and signs ("Do not enter," "Occupied"), as well as more subtle devices—a coat left on a chair, a hedge around a plush lawn, a beach towel spread out on the sand, a nameplate on a door.

Markers define the boundaries of our territories and warn others not to intrude. If we didn't see the book bag on the desk in the library, then we might

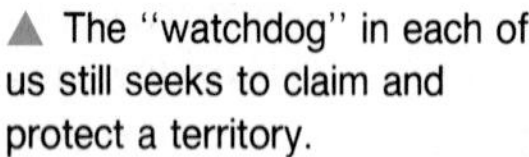
▲ The "watchdog" in each of us still seeks to claim and protect a territory.

From *Tiny Footprints and Other Drawings* by B. Kliban. Copyright 1978 by Workman Publishing. Reprinted by permission of Brentwood Licensing.

▲ Wolves mark their territories by urinating at the boundaries. Birds define their territories through song. Howler monkeys rely on their howling screams. Humans, in contrast, take a more sophisticated approach: They post signs.

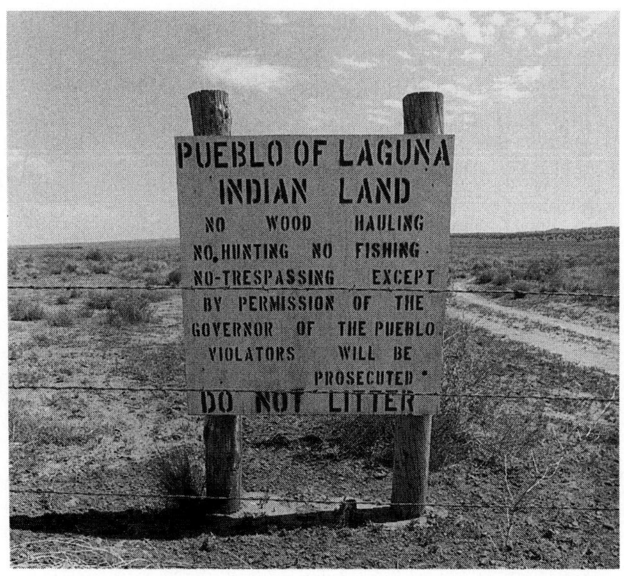

not know that someone has already staked a claim to this particular area. Robert Sommer and his colleagues studied this function of markers by placing various objects on the tables in front of unoccupied chairs in a library (Sommer, 1969; Sommer & Becker, 1969). When Sommer left personal and valuable objects on the table (a sport coat, notebooks, and pen) the chairs were never occupied during the entire 2-hour observation period. Neatly stacked magazines, in contrast, reserved the table for an average of 77 minutes, whereas randomly strewn magazines reserved the spot for an average of 32 minutes. Even when competition for a territory is great, a personal marker may still prevent intrusion. A sport coat or a book bag held a table against intrusion in a crowded bar, although the masculine markers (a sport coat and small briefcase) were more potent than the feminine markers (a jacket and a flowered book bag; Shaffer & Sadowski, 1975).

Groups also mark their claimed areas with signs, fences, and boundaries. Gangs mark the areas they control by spray-painting graffiti on the buildings, signs, and sidewalks. Markings are more plentiful near the center of the gang's sphere of control and serve to warn intruders that they are straying onto dangerous ground. Neighboring gangs, however, may occasionally invade a rival gang's territory to spray-paint their own names over the territorial marker of the home gang, or at least to append a choice obscenity to alter the meaning of the message. A study of Philadelphia gangs concluded that the weaker groups' markers were often defaced, whereas the strongest gangs' markers usually remained undisturbed (Ley & Cybriwski, 1974a).

Defending territories. When people establish a proprietary claim to a place, they usually strive to control who is allowed to enter. Nations patrol their borders to make certain that people from neighboring countries cannot enter the country easily. Property owners erect fences and plant hedges to keep others out. When people buy a new home or move into a new apartment, they often install locks and elaborate burglar alarms to prevent break-ins. Residents in many institutional settings, such as prisons, hospitals, and dormitories, strive to regulate who may enter their room, sit on their bed, or use their bathroom. Students who find someone sitting in their usual chair will ask the intruder to leave (Haber, 1980).

These territorial disputes, curiously enough, more often end with the defender of the territory vanquishing the intruder. Case studies of street gangs indicate that defending groups usually succeed in repelling invading groups, apparently because they are more familiar with the physical layout of the area and have access to necessary resources (Whyte, 1943). One member of a gang in New York explained that his group never lost a fight ("rally") so long as it took place on his group's turf:

> I don't remember that we ever really lost a rally. Don't get the idea that we never ran away. We ran sometimes. We ran like hell. They would come over to our street and charge us. We might scatter, up roofs, down cellars, anywhere. We'd get ammunition there . . . then we would charge them—we had a good charge. They might break up, and then we would go back to our end of the street and wait for them to get together again. . . . It always ended up by us chasing them back to their street. We didn't rally them there. We never went looking for trouble. We only rallied on our own street, but we always won there. (Whyte, 1943, p. 5)

Individuals, too, are often more assertive when they are within their territorial confines rather than encroaching on others' turf. Patients on psychiatric wards tend to establish their own territories and usually drive out other patients who intrude without permission (Esser, 1970). College students working with another student on a cooperative task spent more time talking, felt more "resistant to control," and were more likely to express their own opinions when they were in their own rooms rather than in their partners' rooms (Conroy & Sundstrom, 1977; Edney, 1975; Taylor & Lanni, 1981). A canvasser was less likely to convince students to sign a petition when they were within their territory (their own rooms) rather than outside their territory (Harris & McAndrew, 1986). Individuals and groups seem to gain strength and resolve when the dispute takes place on their home territory, even if they are encountering an opponent who is physically stronger or more socially dominant.

home advantage
The tendency for individuals and groups to gain an advantage over others when interacting in their home territory.

This **home advantage** also influences the outcome of sporting events, for the home team is more frequently the victor than the loser. When a basketball team must travel to the rival team's home court to play, players often make more errors, score fewer points, and end up the losers of the contest (Schwartz & Barsky, 1977). This advantage becomes even greater when the visiting team must travel longer distances, and the fans watching the game support their home team and boo the visiting opponent (Courneya & Carron, 1991; Greer, 1983). Playing at home can, however, become something of a disadvantage in rare circumstances. As Roy Baumeister and his associates suggest, when athletes play must-win games on their home field, the pressure to win may become too great. Consider professional baseball's World Series. The victor in this competition must win four games, and pressure to win becomes greater and greater with each game. When Baumeister studied the World Series games from 1924 to 1984, he found that the home team won 60.2% of the first two games of the seven-game series. But as the series wore on and the need to win intensified, the home team's play deteriorated. By the series' end, the home team's advantage became a disadvantage, for the home team won only 40.8% of the last games in the series. Baumeister calls this reversal the "championship choke." People usually feel more comfortable when they work and play in familiar settings. But when success becomes too important a goal, they may perform more poorly in familiar settings instead of more competently (Baumeister, 1984, 1985; Baumeister, Hamilton, & Tice, 1985; Baumeister & Steinhilber, 1984).

▲ **TABLE 14-1**
Three types of territories

Altman (1975) has proposed a useful typology of human territories based on control and duration of use.

Territory	*Characteristics*	*Examples*
Primary	Places we feel belong to us or our groups exclusively; these areas are central to our identities. We control them for a long period of time, and we defend them when others invade without our permission.	A bedroom, a fenced-in backyard, the interior of your car, a cubicle at work
Secondary	Areas located in public settings, which we use with such regularity that we develop a proprietary orientation toward them. Such places are usually marked with common objects, and if others intrude we sometimes relocate rather than attempt to regain the position.	Seat in a classroom, a favorite bench in the park, a stool at a neighborhood bar
Public	Public areas we control only when we are physically present in the space. These locations are rarely marked, they are not central to our identities, and they are often abandoned when others attempt to gain access.	A telephone booth, a restroom stall, a spot in line, a seat at a lunch counter

Source: From Altman, 1976.

Types of Territories

Some of your territories are more important to you than others. You may mark some of your territories intensively and defend them vigorously against encroachment, but you may abandon others if outsiders intrude. You would be likely to repel someone who tried to enter your home, but you would be less concerned when people parked their cars on the street in front of your house or walked across your college's campus. Irwin Altman (1975) explains these varying reactions by distinguishing among primary, secondary, and public territories (see Table 14-1). *Primary territories* are places that we feel belong exclusively to us or to our groups—a dorm room, a rented parking space, a home, a private office, or a cubicle at work are all primary territories. These territories are very important to us personally, and we expect to be the exclusive users of these areas.

We maintain only a moderate amount of control over our *secondary territories.* These areas are located in public settings—restaurants, streets, parks, college campuses—but because we use the areas on a regular basis, we come to consider them ours. In neighborhood bars, the regular customers often develop a preference for particular stools and tables and will ask intruding strangers to move. College students often become very territorial about their chairs, so much so that they always sit in the same place during each class period (Haber, 1980). Because these territories are established through regular use rather than legal ownership, we can't always mount a successful defense when others intrude.

Our control over *public territories* is even more limited. We can prevent intrusion when we are physically present in the situation, but we cannot expect to control access after we leave. A telephone booth, a restroom stall, a spot on the beach, a seat at a bar, or a space at a parking meter is ours when we are using it, but it becomes the next user's territory when we leave.

Primary territories play a more central role in our social lives than our secondary and public territories. When people are in their primary territories, they feel more in control, secure, and comfortable. We are at home in our primary territories (Taylor & Stough, 1978). Primary territories provide us with a place to leave our possessions (comedian George Carlin defines *home* as a "place to leave our stuff while we're out looking for more stuff"), store our food, and interact with friends and loved ones.

Because we feel a stronger sense of ownership over our primary territories, we are more likely to defend these areas vigorously (Brown, 1987). When someone intrudes into our public or secondary territories, we often withdraw rather than contest the intrusion (McAndrew et al., 1978). But invasions of primary territories are not tolerated. We do not allow other people to enter our homes, offices, or automobiles without our consent. And when such invasions occur, we respond very negatively. Many burglary victims are stunned when they discover that someone has trespassed in their home. Not only are they distressed because their property has been stolen, but because someone has entered their most closely guarded, highly controlled, and personal of places. Some victims report that they never recover from the shock of this form of invasion (Brown & Harris, 1989; Van den Bogaard & Wiegman, 1991).

The Functions of Territories

The origin of territoriality in humans has blurred with the passage of time. Some experts believe that our ancestors lived in tribes that gathered nuts, berries, and other foods from the land as they foraged. These tribes, like the !Kung, the Australian aborigines, and the Mescaleo Apache Native Americans of today, built no permanent dwellings, but they did establish control over certain geographic areas (Altman & Chemers, 1980). Other experts believe that humans became territorial only recently. They suggest that we paid little attention to boundaries until we learned to cultivate the land and domesticate animals. Only then did we become attached to a single place and resist its use by

▲ Irwin Altman identifies three types of territories. Primary territories, such as our home or private desk at the office, are places that we feel belong exclusively to us. Secondary territories are areas in public settings that we use regularly, such as a playground jungle gym or classroom seat. Public territories are areas that we control only when we are physically present in them.

other people. As we settled down and gave up our nomadic ways, our need for territories grew stronger (Reynolds, 1972).

Today we no longer defend a stand of lush berry bushes or our family farm against intruders, but we still retain our territorial ways. Why? Evolutionary psychology suggests that people who were predisposed to control their food sources against encroachment by others gained an evolutionary edge over others, and so their offspring were more likely to survive (Kaplan, 1987; Kaplan & Kaplan, 1989). But even though today's humans don't need territories to survive, territories still function for us in many ways (Edney, 1976). Territories not only systematize many of our interactions with others, but they also offer us a way of achieving privacy and a sense of identity.

Territories as social organizers. When Calhoun's rats matured, the males began to fight among themselves in contests for dominance. The fights were rarely fatal, and afterwards the loser would take a subordinate position in the social hierarchy. Through one battle after another, two rats eventually dominated the others, and these rats established their empires in the two top pens.

Humans' territories, too, reflect our social statuses. In undifferentiated societies people rarely divide up space into "yours," "mine," and "ours." The Basarawa of Africa, for example, don't make distinctions between people on the basis of age, sex, or prestige. Nor do they establish primary territories or build permanent structures (Kent, 1991). But stratified societies with leaders, status hierarchies, and classes are territorial. Moreover, the size and quality of the territories held by individuals tend to correspond to their status within society. The political and social elite in the community live in large, fine homes rather than in small, run-down shacks (Cherulnik & Wilderman, 1986). Inner-city gangs with larger territories are recognized as more powerful than those with smaller territories (J. R. Davis, 1982). Executives with large offices hold a higher, more prestigious position with the company than executives with small offices (Durand, 1977). Prison inmates who control the most desirable portions of the exercise yard enjoy higher status than individuals who cannot establish a territory (Esser, 1970).

Eric Sundstrom and Irwin Altman (1974) probed the organizational advantages of territories in a study of boys housed in a rehabilitation center. They discovered that during the first 5 weeks of the study the boys maintained fairly well-defined territories; the more dominant boys controlled the most desirable areas, and the less dominant boys were left with the lower-quality areas. During this period, such disruptive behaviors as disobedience, fighting, and stealing were minimal. The system was organized.

When Sundstrom and Altman transferred two of the most dominant boys out of the cottage and replaced them with two new boys, the group became disorganized. Like the rats fighting individual contests for dominance, for three weeks the boys seemed to be striving for control of the choicest territories. In consequence, the incidence of fighting and other forms of disruptive behavior rose dramatically. In the final few weeks of the study, territories again began to emerge, and with them came reductions in conflict and misbehavior. Apparently we fight one another for territory, but once these disputes are settled conflict becomes less likely.

Territories as privacy maintainers. We use our territories to regulate the frequency and intimacy of our contacts with other people. When you desire *privacy,* you go to one of your primary territories, such as your home or your

▲ TABLE 14-2
Percentage of dormitory residents who reported using various types of privacy-regulating mechanisms

Mechanism	Percentage
Contact-Seeking Mechanisms	
Phoning someone	74
Visiting others' rooms	71
Going to dorm lounge	70
Inviting people to own room	64
Opening door to room	64
Studying in a busy place	30
Going to student union	22
Attracting others with music	21
Using bathroom at busy time	10
Contact-Reducing Mechanisms	
Shutting door to room	92
Finding quiet place	62
Tuning out noise to sleep	59
Tuning out noise to study	52
Going for walk alone	49
Using loud music to cover noise	19
Arranging room for privacy	16
Preparing for bed in quiet place	16
Using bathroom at quiet time	12

Source: From Vinsel et al., 1980.

bedroom. But when you want to interact with people, you go to a public territory or an area that is unclaimed by any one individual. Territories can therefore be used to make "adjustments of self-boundaries to permit various levels of contact with others" (Altman, 1975, p. 31).

Irwin Altman and his colleagues explored the way people use their territories to regulate their privacy in dormitories at the University of Utah (Hansen & Altman, 1976; Vinsel et al., 1980). They found that dorm residents used several territorial techniques to strike a satisfactory balance between achieved and desired social contacts. When students wanted to increase social contact, they left their primary territories (their rooms) to visit a neighbor, they invited a neighbor into their own territories, they telephoned someone, or they went to a public area (see Table 14-2). When students wanted to avoid interactions, they used several of the privacy-enhancing strategies shown in Table 14-2, including closing off their primary territories by shutting doors, retreating to a secluded, quiet territory, and ignoring distracting noise.

Altman's research team also discovered that some students who dropped out of school after their first year (dropouts) weren't particularly adept at using their territories to maintain their privacy. These students reported using fewer contact-seeking and contact-reducing strategies than students who remained in school (stay-ins), and they also rated those they used as less effective. Even when dropouts used a territorial tactic to control their level of privacy, they usually chose one that was relatively ineffective. Stay-ins used music to increase social contact, but dropouts used loud music to drown out other sounds. Dropouts who wanted to increase their social contacts often reported going to the lounge areas; stay-ins realized that these lounges were notoriously poor

▲ We mark our various territories in different ways. We might mark a public territory, such as a table at the library, by spreading our books and papers across it so others can't find any usable space. Personal territories, such as our homes, are often marked by walls, gates, signs, and personalized touches in the yard.

places to meet people. The researchers concluded that the dropouts' inability to use their territories to achieve the level of privacy they desired may have contributed to their eventual academic demise (Vinsel et al., 1980).

Altman and his colleagues found similar benefits and limitations of territoriality in their studies of isolated groups (Altman, 1977; Altman & Haythorne, 1967; Altman, Taylor, & Wheeler, 1971). Altman and his colleagues recruited pairs of men to spend several days completely isolated in a small enclosure. Compared to men who were allowed to leave their room to eat and sleep, the isolated men became very territorial; they claimed particular chairs, spaces, and bunks within the space. Over the course of the experiment, the men used these territories to achieve privacy, and as the isolation wore on, they spent more time in their territories than in interaction. Territoriality helped some groups adapt to the situation.

> The epitome of a successful group was one in which the members, on the first or second day, laid out an eating, exercise, and recreation schedule; constructed a deck of playing cards, a chess set, and a Monopoly game out of paper; decided how they would structure their lives over the expected lengthy period of isolation. (Altman, 1977, p. 310)

Other pairs, however, failed to use their territories effectively to secure sufficient privacy. Many of these pairs refused to finish the full term, apparently because they couldn't cope with the stressful situation.

Territories and identity. Rats do not use their territories to express aspects of their identity, but people do. One self-proclaimed graffiti king commented: "I started writing . . . to prove to people where I was. You go somewhere and get your name up there and people know you were there, that you weren't afraid" (Ley & Cybriwsky, 1974b, p. 494). Homeowners decorate their houses and landscape their yards in ways that communicate information about who they are and what they value (Csikszentmihalyi & Rochberg-Halton, 1981). When perceivers are shown pictures of other people's living rooms, they can judge with some degree of accuracy the identity the residents are trying to claim (Sadalla, Burroughs, & Quaid, 1980; Sadalla, Vershure, & Burroughs, 1987). As Altman and Martin M. Chemers (1980) conclude, "territories permit people and groups to display their personalities and values through the vehicle of the physical environment" (p. 143).

Altman and his colleagues tested the identity-defining function of territorial displays in their studies of dorms (Hansen & Altman, 1976; Vinsel et al., 1980). Many students posted schedules of classes, syllabi, and calendars on their walls to help them keep track of their schoolwork. But they also used their rooms to express their personal values, including religious and political beliefs, athletic and sports interests, and entertainment preferences. Women had a greater tendency than men to decorate their space with markers emphasizing personal relationships (photographs of family and friends); men's markers tended to be more sports- and school-oriented. But students who dropped out at the end of their first year were *more* extensive markers than stay-ins. Their markings, however, were less diverse, and they were less likely to include items related to academic responsibilities. The typical stay-in's room would often include items related to a variety of topics, such as posters of rock groups, schedules of classes, reminders about when papers were due, postcards, and plants. A typical dropout's wall, in contrast, would be completely covered by pictures of Janet Jackson. Dropouts also displayed more items related to their family and home town (photographs of high school friends, drawings by siblings); stay-ins displayed more items related to the university and the surrounding area (campus and city maps, pictures of local recreational sites). The investigators concluded that dropouts marked with less diversity "because they chose to reveal only a few facets of themselves to others. Furthermore, their decorations symbolized a lack of commitment to the university and community" and a "greater commitment to their past life and to their parents and friends" (Vinsel et al., 1980, p. 114). Thus dropouts' markers broadcast their uncertainty about their new territory, whereas stay-ins used their markers to stake out their territorial claims.

Territoriality and Residential Satisfaction

Life was good for the rats who lived in the territorialized portions of the pens. The males guarded their turf, the females built nests and raised babies, and the juveniles played. Calhoun's experiment was not so kind, though, for the rats living in areas that could not be territorialized. In those pens, normal patterns of social organization disintegrated, and the mortality rate soared.

The social fabric of human communities similarly suffers when residents cannot establish territories. People who live in busy urban areas—near corner markets, playgrounds, major thoroughfares, or sports facilities—often feel that their neighborhood is unsafe and overcrowded (Bonnes, Bonaiuto, & Ercolani, 1991; Normoyle & Lavrakas, 1984). They appreciate the convenience of the city, but they resent the presence of so many strangers in their community. In contrast, people who can use the semipublic areas outside their homes enjoy their neighborhoods. In Boston, 75% of the people living in some of the most run-down parts of the city were perfectly content with their circumstances. They could sit on their front porches and visit with neighbors. Relatives lived nearby, and they often took turns watching over the children who played on the sidewalks and streets. These neighborhoods were very stable, for the majority of the families had lived there for over 20 years (Fried, 1982; see also Gates & Rohe, 1987; Rohe & Burby, 1988).

People who live in large-scale residential units, such as college dormitories, retirement communities, and urban housing projects, are also more satisfied when they can territorialize their surroundings. One team of investigators compared college students who lived in traditional dorms with students who lived in suite-style dorms. The corridor-style rooms were located along a corridor, and residents shared certain areas, such as bathrooms and lounges. Students controlled access to their rooms, but they could not claim any of the common areas as territories. In the suite-style dorm, two or three bedrooms were clustered around a small lounge and bathroom. The students who lived in the suites controlled the bedrooms *and* these common areas.

Even though the students had roughly the same amount of space and equal access to facilities in the two types of dorms, students living in the corridor building were less satisfied. They felt crowded, they complained of their inability to control their interactions with others, and they lamented the lack of privacy in the dormitory. Suite residents, in contrast, developed deeper friendships with their suite mates, worked with one another more effectively, and seemed friendlier even when they interacted with students in their classes and on campus. These differences presumably stemmed from the corridor residents' lack of control over their living area (Baum & Davis, 1980; Baum, Harpin, & Valins, 1975; Baum & Valins, 1977).

Architect and urban planner Oscar Newman (1972, 1980) believes that many large-scale housing projects suffer from the same design flaws as the corridor-style dormitories. The massive Pruitt-Igoe housing project in St. Louis included many features that designers believed would reduce crime and vandalism—open areas between buildings, special vandalism-resistant lighting fixtures, tiled walls designed to discourage graffiti—but within a few years the project was a ruined wasteland. Many of the 2,762 apartments were vacant, crime and vandalism were rampant, and most residents lived in constant fear of attack. The project was eventually torn down (Yancey, 1971).

defensible space
Semipublic areas surrounding private dwellings that residents can territorialize.

What went wrong at Pruitt-Igoe? Newman argues that many large-scale housing projects lack **defensible space**: semipublic areas surrounding the apartments that residents can territorialize. Planners strive for safe, low-cost, and easy-to-maintain housing, but they often forget that residents won't feel secure if they can't establish territories in the areas surrounding their residences. Pruitt-Igoe residents maintained primary territories within their apartments, but they could not defend any secondary territories within or around their buildings. So many people lived in each building that residents couldn't distinguish each other from outsiders, who moved freely through the buildings by using the undefended stairwells. The areas between the buildings included no barriers or other territorial markings, and the height of the buildings made surveillance of these areas impossible. In addition, some features of the project—window gratings, unpainted cinder block walls, and lack of landscaping—only served to remind residents that they lived in a low-income project that its builders expected to be vandalized.

Newman recommends several ways to increase the defensibility of spaces. First, boundaries must be established to give residents control over hallways, lobbies, and nearby streets and playgrounds. Second, residents must be able to maintain surveillance over these semipublic areas. Third, the design of the building must foster positive, protective attitudes. Fourth, if possible, the project should be built in a low-crime area. Newman tested these design recommendations by comparing two housing projects built side by side in New York City. The newer project, Van Dyke, was built in 1955 along the same lines as Pruitt-Igoe—mostly large, 14-story buildings separated by open spaces. The Brownsville project was 8 years older and featured 6-story, X-shaped buildings with some 3-story wings. Occupants entered the Brownsville buildings at the central core, where open staircases were located. Newman discovered that the Brownsville buildings were far more defensible than the Van Dyke's. Each

▲ TABLE 14-3
Number of crimes and maintenance jobs required in two urban housing projects studied by Newman

Incident	*Van Dyke*	*Brownsville*
All crimes	1189	790
Felonies, misdemeanors, and other offenses	432	264
Robberies	92	24
Other malicious mischief	52	28
All maintenance jobs	3301	2376
Maintenance jobs not involving glass repair	2643	1654
Repairs, other than glass repair, per unit	1.47	1.16
Employees needed to make repairs	9	7
Elevator breakdowns per month	280	110

Source: From Newman, 1972.

entrance was used by only a small number of families, and anyone approaching it could be observed from dozens of windows. The open stairways were easy for residents to monitor, so they let their children play in the hallways and on the landings. Residents even left their doors ajar to "keep an eye on the place." This greater defensibility was associated with stronger bonds between neighboring families, more positive attitudes toward the police, and lower crime and maintenance rates (see Table 14-3).

Newman's ideas are consistent with evolutionary analyses of people's preferences for different kinds of environments. People in many cultures, when asked to evaluate the attractiveness of various kinds of habitats, consistently prefer places that offer them *prospect*—unobstructed views of open spaces. They also prefer places with naturally occurring or built structures where they can seek *refuge* if they encounter dangers. These preferences, which can be traced to our ancestors' needs to protect themselves against attack by predators, still influence our reactions to our environments (Appleton, 1984; Kaplan & Kaplan, 1989). Researchers at Ohio State University, for example, studied the Wexner Center for the Visual Arts on that campus to find out why so many people disliked the building. They discovered that too many areas in and around this structure lacked prospect and refuge. The semipublic areas near the building were too dark at night, doors into the building were difficult to reach, and many walkways adjacent to the building led to dead ends. Pedestrians felt that the building was dangerous and avoided it at night (Fisher & Nasar, 1992).

Much of the research on defensible space is correlational and should be interpreted with caution (Holahan & Wandersman, 1987). Still, studies of territoriality and defensible space have reshaped designers' thinking about the importance of territories (Brower, Dockett, & Taylor, 1983; McCarthy & Saegart, 1979; Taylor, Gottfredson, & Brower, 1980, 1984). Urban planners and architects who focus on aesthetics rather than users' feelings of safety sometimes create unusable parks, courtyards, and buildings. Pruitt-Igoe was praised for a design with little wasted space. But people couldn't live in the complex. Similarly, the Wexner Center received architectural awards, yet people who had to use the site rated it as distressing and inaccessible (Nasar & Kang, 1989). Given these findings, experts like Robert Sommer argue that builders and city planners should consult with social psychologists before they build (Albrecht & Lim, 1986; Schneekloth, 1987). Moreover, they should constantly

▲ **TABLE 14-4**
Summing up: Territoriality and social behavior

Factor	*Description*
Characteristics	A territory is a specific area that an individual or group claims and defends for personal use. Markers define the boundaries of claimed territories, and intrusions into claimed territories can lead to conflict. The defender of the territory usually repels an intruder rather than an intruder displacing a defender.
Types	Altman identifies three types of human territories: primary (high control for extended periods of time), secondary (high control over semipublic areas for brief periods of time), and public (moderate control only when occupied).
Functions	Territories (a) systematize interpersonal relations with other people and thereby limit conflict, (b) provide a way to increase and decrease contact with other people (privacy maintenance), and (c) allow residents to express their values and claim identities. Individuals who cannot establish territories around their residences are less satisfied than individuals who can establish defensible spaces.

evaluate their buildings so they can identify and design buildings in which people prosper. Sommer (1972) writes: "When architects make mistakes, the least they can do is *learn* from them. . . . One can excuse a noisy or inadequate high school library, but not a third library no better than the first, or a twentieth no better than the third" (p. 88). (See Table 14-4 for a summary of the concept of territoriality.)

▲▲▲▲▲▲▲▲▲▲▲▲▲▲

Interpersonal Distance

What is the "hidden dimension" that influences so many of our social interactions but remains unnoticed? Space, says anthropologist Edward T. Hall (1966). We rarely pay much attention to the distance we maintain between ourselves and other people, yet this distance profoundly influences our social relations. When students enter a classroom they select seats that are a discreet distance from the teacher. People standing in slow-moving lines continually inch forward, maintaining a fixed distance between themselves and the person in front of them. And who hasn't experienced the awkwardness that comes when someone we don't know well gets too close to us?

Without even noticing it, we regulate the space that separates us from other people. This personal space, or interpersonal distance, is "the area individuals maintain around themselves into which others cannot intrude without arousing discomfort" (Hayduk, 1983, p. 293). Our personal space completely surrounds us, although it tends to be smaller behind our backs than directly in front of us. Like our territory, our personal space is an area to which we strive to control access. We also experience discomfort when violations occur. But unlike a territory, personal space is portable—it moves along with us from place to place—and is not usually marked in any detectable way (Aiello, 1987; Sommer, 1969).

How much space do people require? This question would be a simple one to answer if human beings' personal space requirements were equal and constant; if everyone liked to keep about 25 inches between themselves and others no matter what the situation. Personal space, however, varies in size depending on the situation and the people in that situation. Chapter 2 discusses impression formation: How much space do we need when we are first meeting some-

▲ TABLE 14-5
Hall's zones of interpersonal distance

Zone	*Distance*	*Activities*
Intimate	0 to 18 inches	Sex, massage, comforting, handshakes, dancing, wrestling
Personal	18 inches to 4 feet	Casual conversation, automobile travel, parties, walking
Social	4 to 12 feet	Dining, business meetings, interactions with strangers
Public	12 feet or more	Lectures, addresses, plays, recitals, sport events

Source: From Hall, 1966.

one? Chapter 10 discusses group dynamics: Do people in cohesive groups need less space than people in less cohesive groups? And don't different people need more or less space, depending on their partner in the interaction? How much space do we need when we are talking with our loved one or an enemy? (See Chapter 11.) We consider both the situational and personal determinants of interpersonal distancing before examining our reactions to too little space.

Situational Determinants of Distance

Hall (1959, 1966) watched countless interactions between people in a host of different situations before concluding that people use more than just one zone to regulate their spatial behaviors. Hall believed that we don't just notice when people are inside or outside our personal space; we also classify their distance from us in terms of four **interpersonal distance zones**: intimate, personal, social, and public (see Table 14-5).

interpersonal distance zones
Situationally determined interpersonal distances that are defined by the usual type of activity performed at that distance; the intimate zone, for example, is reserved for very private interactions.

The *intimate zone* is reserved for only our closest friends and loved ones, for in this zone personal space becomes so small that touching is considered appropriate. We may, in some cases, permit acquaintances to enter the intimate zone (for example, when we hug a visiting relative), or strangers may force their way into this zone (for example, when someone pushes us), but in general we guard this space zealously.

The *personal zone* is usually used when we are conversing with friends and acquaintances. This zone allows us to see other people's faces and hear their voices clearly, yet we can't touch them or (in most cases) smell them. Over 60% of the conversations between people who are standing take place in this zone or in the intimate zone (Altman & Vinsel, 1977).

The *social zone* is used for more formal interactions, such as dinners or meetings. In such situations, people usually keep 4 to 12 feet between each other, and their discussion concerns less personal matters. Most conversations between people who are seated, for example, in a restaurant, occur in the social zone (Altman & Vinsel, 1977). Military personnel tend to stand in the social zone when conversing with their superiors, whereas they use the personal zone when conversing with peers (Dean, Willis, & Hewitt, 1975).

The *public zone* is the site of impersonal interactions involving a large number of participants, such as lectures or speeches. Hall explains that certain nonverbal communication cues, such as eye contact and smiles, become difficult to discern at this distance, so we rely more on body posture and gestures when we communicate at this distance.

Why do we use different distances in different situations? Hall argued that distance is a form of nonverbal communication (see Chapter 2). Just as we communicate wordlessly with our eyes, our faces, and our body postures (kinesic cues), we also communicate by distancing ourselves from other people. Hall calls

proxemic cues
Distance cues that nonverbally signal the intimacy and type of situation.

distances **proxemic cues** (from the Latin *proximare*, "to approach"), and he believes they signal the intimacy of a situation. When people choose to interact in the social zone, for example, they are communicating to one another, and to anyone else who is watching, the impersonal, businesslike nature of their conversation. Conversely, when people move close to others, they are signaling interest and possibly romantic involvement. Even the most casual observer of human courting rituals knows that the first sign that one person is attracted to another is his or her move closer to the target. If the target doesn't feel equally interested, he or she signals this disinclination by moving back (Hall, 1966).

equilibrium model
An explanation of distancing behavior in interpersonal settings; argues that the amount of eye contact, the intimacy of the topic, and smiling influence the amount of personal space required by interactants.

Hall's belief that people use distance to regulate the intimacy of their interactions is consistent with the **equilibrium model** (Argyle & Cook, 1976; Argyle & Dean, 1965). This theory suggests that the intimacy of any interaction is determined by two factors: (a) the proportion of friendly, approach-oriented, nonverbal behaviors people display (for example, smiling, eye contact, body orientation, and small distances) and (b) the verbal content of the conversation. If individuals aren't smiling and are discussing business matters, then their interaction isn't intimate at all. But if people are sitting close to one another and discussing sex, then the interaction is extremely intimate (Patterson, 1975, 1976, 1982).

Equilibrium theory assumes that interactants use their nonverbal behaviors to keep the level of intimacy in a comfortable range. When discussing social psychology with classmates, interactants are likely to display positive, affiliative nonverbal cues. But if this equilibrium is disturbed, perhaps by one individual's making excessively personal comments, then interactants will compensate by reducing eye contact, changing to a more indirect body orientation, or moving farther away. Should the conversation return to more staid topics, then interactants can once more compensate by displaying friendly, warmer nonverbal behaviors. The desired level of intimacy, however, depends on the nature of the situation and the people in the situation. When talking about sex with close same-sex friends we will probably move closer and smile more frequently (Ashton, Shaw, & Worsham, 1980; Scott, 1984). But if we are asked to talk about sex with someone we have just met, then we will probably compensate for the intimate topic by reducing the intimacy of our nonverbal behavior (Aiello, 1987; Burgoon, 1983).

People and Personal Space

When researchers measure people's personal space requirements by watching where they stand in relationship to other people or by asking them to describe the shape of their personal space, they find that some people consistently need more space than others (Hayduk, 1983). Some people may feel very comfort-

▲ Hall identifies four interpersonal distance zones that vary according to the nature of our activities: intimate, personal, social, and public.

able when they talk to a friend standing only 6 inches away, but other people may find this proximity distressing and uncomfortable.

Culture. Hall was particularly interested in how our culture shapes our need for space. He recounts one amusing incident when he was sitting comfortably in an almost empty hotel lobby. Suddenly, for no apparent reason, a stranger walked up and stood so close to his chair that he could hear the man breathing. Hall refused to abandon his chair despite this invasion, and the stranger stood there until he was joined by several other people. Hall then realized that the stranger was from a Middle Eastern country and that his behavior was consistent with his cultural beliefs about space. In the Middle East, personal space zones are quite small and open to invasion, particularly in public areas.

Hall explains cultural differences in personal space by drawing a broad distinction between contact and noncontact cultures. People who grow up in *contact cultures* of the Mediterranean, Middle East, and Latin America learn to prefer strong sensory involvement with others and so seek direct social contact whenever possible. Residents of such *noncontact countries* as the United States, England, and Germany try to limit their spatial openness with others. Indeed, the distances shown in Table 14-5 pertain to Americans only and may be larger for people raised in other cultures. The French, for example, maintain very small personal spaces in trains, buses, cafés, and even in their homes, and they increase their involvement with other people by using more direct body postures and eye contact. In consequence, when Americans visit Paris, they are sometimes shocked when strangers approach so closely and stare right into their eyes. Furthermore, when Americans attempt to protect their invaded personal space, Parisians interpret their retreat as a lack of good manners.

Sex. Men and women use space differently. Women allow others to get closer to them than men do, and they approach other people more closely than males do. Women also take up less space by sitting with their arms close to their sides and by crossing their legs, but men enlarge their personal space by assuming expansive, open positions (Mehrabian, 1972). Men and women use

▲ To people raised in a noncontact culture like the United States, the seating arrangement of this sidewalk cafe may seem too crowded. The French, however, prefer to maintain small personal spaces in public places, so they experience no discomfort.

▲ **FIGURE 14-2**
Which sex tries the hardest to prevent strangers from sitting directly opposite them? Researchers went to libraries and recorded where men and women positioned books and personal possessions when they sat alone at a large table. They found that women were more protective of adjacent seating positions. Men were more likely to defend adjacent and opposite seats. (From Fisher & Byrne, 1975)

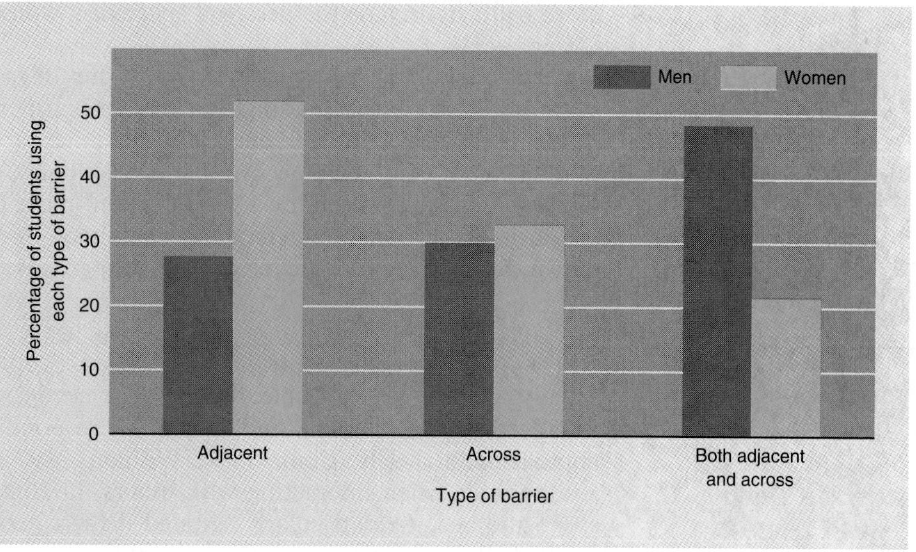

space differently even when they walk. Women carry their books in both arms, resting the edges against the stomach and chest (Jenni & Jenni, 1976). Men carry their books in one arm, with the edges resting on the hip or side of the leg.

Women also approach their friends more closely than men do. Researchers in one study first photographed pairs of adults as they walked along a city street. Then they asked the couples to describe the nature of their relationship. When the researchers used the photographs to calculate personal space size they found that women needed less space when they were close friends, but that men's spatial needs were unrelated to intimacy (Heshka & Nelson, 1972). Similarly, a man and a woman who are friends stand closer together than a man and woman who don't know one another well. The spatial intimacy of mixed-sex friends, however, occurs because women move closer to men; men tend to remain stationary (Edwards, 1972).

Men and women also respond differently when their personal space is invaded, although the point of attack makes an important difference. In one study conducted in a library, male and female confederates sat adjacent to or across from same- or opposite-sex subjects (Fisher & Byrne, 1975). When one researcher later approached the subjects and asked them to rate the confederate, men were most negative when the intruder sat across from them. Women were most negative when the intruder sat beside them. In a second study, when the investigators recorded the placement of books and belongings on library tables, they found that men erected more barriers against face-to-face invasion, and women erected barriers against adjacent invasion. As Figure 14-2 indicates, women tended to place their belongings in front of the adjacent chair. Men placed their belongings in front of adjacent chairs *and* chairs across from them. In a related study, men showed signs of greater discomfort than women when the intruder was a man who approached them from the rear (Harris, Luginbuhl, & Fishbein, 1978).

Women are more likely than men to withdraw when their space is invaded. In one study of near-collisions of men and women on a public sidewalk, the woman moved out of the man's way 63.2% of the time, the man moved out of the woman's way 15.8% of the time, and both moved 21.0% of the time (Henley, 1977). This weaker resistance to spatial invasion may explain why people more willingly invade the personal space of a woman than of a man (Riess & Salzer, 1981).

Leslie Hayduk (1983) reviewed 110 studies of men's and women's personal space needs before concluding that the sexes differ only in subtle ways. Furthermore, in discussing the source of these differences, Hayduk emphasizes the role played by socialization over biology. Women tend to be more affiliative than men, more positive toward others, and more concerned about maintaining positive interpersonal relations with others. In consequence, as women are drawn closer to others psychologically, they are also drawn to them physically.

Other personal qualities. Personal space needs are also shaped, in part, by our personalities, traits, and values. People who tend to be interpersonally oriented (for example, high in their need for affiliation, or extraverted) usually require less space, and they don't respond as negatively when others approach too closely (Cook, 1970; Williams, 1971). People who are anxious and nervous when interacting with others, in contrast, tend to require more space and become particularly agitated if their need for great distances is unfulfilled (Bailey, Hartnett, & Gibson, 1972; Karabenick & Meisels, 1972). Indeed, oddities in one's use of space may reflect oddities in personality and adjustment. Individuals whose relationships with others are disrupted, such as violent individuals, schizophrenics, and emotionally disturbed children, tend to have relatively large personal space zones (Gilmour & Walkey, 1981). One researcher walked toward violent and nonviolent prisoners from various angles until they told him to stop. The nonviolent prisoners had smaller space zones than the violent prisoners, particularly when the researcher approached from the rear rather than the front (see Figure 14-3). The nonviolent prisoners needed an average of 7.0 square feet of space, whereas the violent prisoners needed, on average, 29.3 square feet of space (Kinzel, 1970).

The size of our personal space is also affected by the qualities and characteristics of the person or persons we are approaching. We require less space when we are with friends than when we are with strangers or acquaintances (Hayduk, 1983). We also maintain smaller personal spaces when we interact with people who seem to be similar to us in race, age, and even attitudes, but again the findings are not completely consistent (Bell et al., 1990). Our personal space also shrinks in size when we interact with people who seem friendly, pleasant,

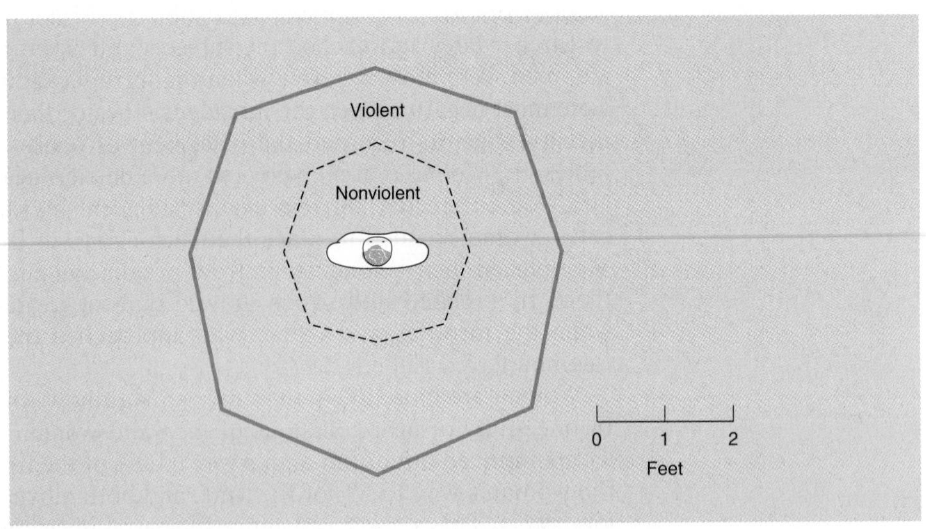

▲ **FIGURE 14-3**
Do people with a proclivity for violence keep their distance from others or do they approach others too closely? The nonviolent prisoners had smaller space zones than the violent prisoners, particularly when the researcher approached from the rear rather than the front. (From Kinzel, 1970)

cooperative, and relaxed, but it expands when we believe that the other person is unusual in some respect. We tend to maintain larger spaces between us and people who have some visible physical disability, such as extreme obesity or the loss of a limb. We also strive to isolate ourselves from individuals who are socially stigmatized, such as the mentally handicapped or maladjusted (Altman, 1975).

Reactions to Invasions of Personal Space

We expect other people to respect our boundaries and to keep out of our personal space. Keeping appropriate distances between ourselves and others is one way of controlling our social interactions, so we fight to maintain desired distances between ourselves and others (Knowles, 1980). When confederates approached too closely to people studying in libraries (Sommer, 1969), sitting outdoors, standing on escalators, or walking down the street, the targets displayed a number of negative reactions, including reduced eye contact, shifts in body posture, verbal rebukes, and withdrawal from the situation (Felipe & Sommer, 1966; Harris, Luginbuhl, & Fishbein, 1978; Konečni et al., 1975; Smith & Knowles, 1978).

Close encounters with other people can even lead to physiological arousal: Our heart rate and blood pressure tend to increase, we breathe more quickly, and we sometimes perspire more (Aiello, Epstein, & Karlin, 1975; Evans, 1979; Walden & Forsyth, 1981). One of the more creative—if ethically controversial (Koocher, 1977)—investigations of the arousal properties of personal space invasion was conducted in a men's restroom (Middlemist, Knowles, & Matter, 1977). Building on physiological research demonstrating that individuals take longer to begin urinating and urinate for a shorter period of time when they feel stressed or aroused, these researchers unobtrusively recorded the length of time before men began to urinate and the length of time they urinated across three experimental conditions: alone, moderate interpersonal distance (a confederate used the rightmost urinal when the subject was at the leftmost urinal), and close interpersonal distance (a confederate used the urinal next to the subject). As predicted, delay of urination increased from 4.9 seconds in the control (alone) condition to 6.2 seconds in the moderate distance condition and to 8.4 seconds in the close distance condition. Duration decreased in the same conditions. Stressed by a too-close companion, the men started more slowly and finished more quickly. This work has not yet been replicated with women.

Even though invasion of personal space can lead to physiological arousal, this arousal is not always experienced negatively. If a close friend, a relative, or a very attractive person enters an area we normally protect, we may experience a positive reaction rather than a negative one (Willis, 1966). We also respond positively if we think that the other person is attempting to initiate a friendly relationship or needs assistance (Baron, 1978; Murphy-Berman & Berman, 1978).

The two-factor theory of emotion, which explains such emotions as love (Chapter 11) and anger (Chapter 13), also offers insight into our reactions to personal space invasions. This theory suggests that closeness leads to arousal, which can be either stressful or pleasurable depending on our interpretation of the invasion. If we believe the invader has encroached on our space because she or he is rude or manipulative, our reaction will probably be negative. But if we attribute the encroachment to positive factors—such as the invader's desire to become more intimate or friendly with us—then we may react more favorably (Knowles, 1980; Patterson, 1976).

▲ We respond negatively when a stranger or a person we dislike invades our personal space, but our response to an intruding friend or relative or a very attractive person tends to be much more positive. Indeed, some invasions of personal space can be pleasurable.

Researchers tested this explanation by arranging for a male confederate to interview male college students while sitting either 6 or 30 inches from them. After the interview, the interviewer gave the subject either a very positive evaluation or a very negative evaluation. As Figure 14-4 shows, men were most negative when the interviewer invaded their space *and* gave them a critical evaluation. They not only reported less liking for the interviewer, but also complained that the study was uninteresting and unenjoyable. People who were positively evaluated, however, liked the space-violating interviewer more, and they also described the study in more positive terms. Thus close distances may work to intensify our feelings and emotions (Storms & Thomas, 1977, Experiment 3). (See Table 14-6 for a summary of the concept of personal space.)

Environmental Stressors

We don't live in small cages, like Calhoun's luckless rats, but our environment can challenge us nonetheless. For 24 hours each day, whether awake or asleep, we are bombarded by a flood of information about events unfolding in the

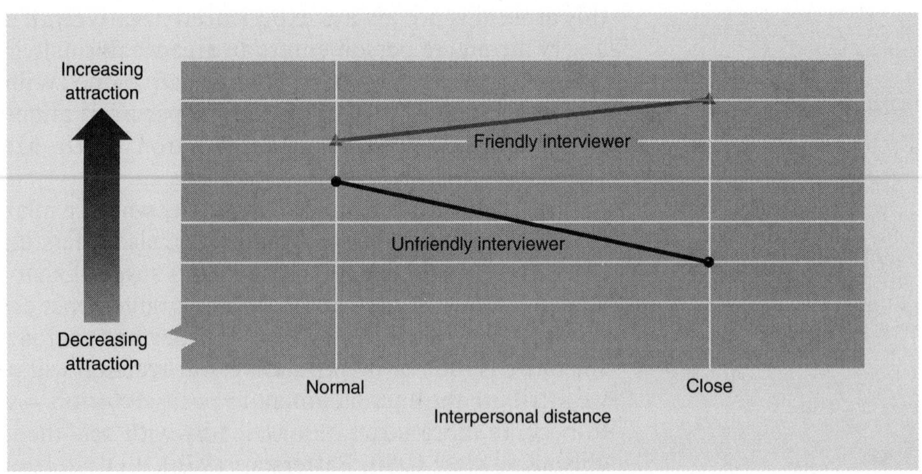

▲ **FIGURE 14-4**
Do invasions of personal space intensify our emotions and feelings? People seated at a normal distance from an interviewer liked the friendly interviewer slightly more than the unfriendly one. When their personal space was violated, subjects expressed more extreme liking or disliking. (From Storms & Thomas, 1977)

▲ **TABLE 14-6**
Summing up: Personal space and social behavior

Factor	*Description*
Characteristics	Personal space is that area around one's body that other people are not permitted to enter. This space isn't marked or linked to any specific location, and it varies in size across situations. Individuals experience physiological arousal when others approach them too closely, but in some cases this arousal is experienced as positive rather than negative.
Types	Hall identifies four interpersonal distance zones: intimate (for only our closest friends and loved ones), personal (for interacting with friends and acquaintances), social (for more impersonal settings, such as meetings), and public (for interactions involving a large number of participants).
Determinants	People regulate the intimacy of an interaction by moving closer to or farther away from others. Intimate interactions require less space than less intimate ones. Culture influences spatial needs, for people raised in contact cultures approach others more closely than people raised in noncontact cultures. Other personal qualities, such as sex, personalities, traits, and values, also influence spatial needs. Women, for example, require less space than men.

surrounding environment. Some of these environmental events are so mild that they slip by without our awareness; some are so positive that they fill us with pleasure; still others are *stressors*—environmental events that threaten, or at least seem to threaten, our well-being (Evans & Cohen, 1987).

If we are to understand social behavior, we usually need to consider the people in the place rather than the place itself. But when the environment threatens us, places rather than people shape our actions. If you are trying to work with a group of people on a project, your productivity may suffer if the space that is available is too small, too noisy, or uncomfortably hot or cold. And what happens to people whose lives are changed by traumatic environmental events, such as floods, hurricanes, and such technological disasters as the accident at the Russians' Chernobyl nuclear reactor? In this technological age, we often assume that we control our environment. Yet, in many cases, it is the environment that controls us.

Crowding

A sold-out football game; a lively party thrown in a two-bedroom apartment; a psychology class held in a large auditorium; a bar that closes its doors at 10 P.M. when its occupancy limit is reached; 80 rats living in a habitat built to house 60. These are all high-density situations: A large number of people are packed into a relatively small area. Just because the density is high, however, we cannot assume that the interactants will feel crowded. **Density** is a physical condition determined by the number of individuals present in a given area. **Crowding**, in contrast, is a psychological condition that occurs when people think density is too high (Stokols, 1972). A wild party and a football game may be high-density settings, but the interactants may not feel the least bit crowded. But the students in the large auditorium and the customers at the bar may feel very crowded. Why? Because people sometimes respond negatively to high-density situations. The students in the class may find that their ability to process information is disrupted by the large number of students, or they may feel helpless and anonymous in such a large class. The customers in the bar may enjoy being immersed in a sea of people, but they will probably begin to feel stressed if the club becomes so crowded that no one can dance or the bartend-

density
The number of individuals per unit of space.

crowding
A psychological reaction that occurs when individuals feel that the amount of space available to them is insufficient for their needs.

▲ A high-density situation (one with many people occupying a small area) may not be a *crowded* situation. If interactants retain a sense of control and the situation is designed to handle large numbers of people, then occupants will probably feel no negative effects of high density.

ers fall hopelessly behind in filling their orders. As we see next, cognitive, emotional, and behavioral factors can change a high-density situation into a crowded one.

overload
An excessive number of inputs, which come so rapidly that the information cannot be processed effectively.

Overload. As Stanley Milgram (1970) explains, crowded situations can tax our limited perceptual and mental abilities. When we walk in the country, we may notice the color of the sky, the feel of the gravel road beneath our feet, and the sound of the birds singing. But when we find ourselves on a busy street corner in New York City, Paris, or Tokyo, we can no longer take note of all that surrounds us. Indeed, the urban setting can be so complex that, in our struggle to grasp it, we experience **overload**. Cognitively, we receive so many inputs so rapidly that we lose our ability to process information effectively. Socially, we are repeatedly exposed to unwanted contact with other people. As a result, we feel crowded and stressed, and we usually respond by using one or more coping mechanisms to eliminate excessive environmental stimulation. We might screen out much of the information in our environment and focus our attention on only a restricted portion of the environment. We may, too, follow strict habits as we move through the crowded space, avoiding contact with strangers, and withdrawing whenever possible (Milgram, 1970; Saegert, 1978).

Most of the time, these coping strategies are effective: Students living in high-density dormitories who used screening strategies to limit their contacts with other people were better adjusted than those who did not (Baum et al., 1982). Withdrawal can be maladaptive, however, if taken to extremes. When researchers studied men living in overcrowded homes in Pune, India, they discovered that some of the men coped with the stress by seeking greater privacy. These men, however, were also the ones who could no longer rely on their friends, relatives, and loved ones for social support. Thus, their coping strategy backfired: The more crowded they felt, the more they withdrew, but by withdrawing they cut themselves off from the social support that would have helped them deal with their stress (Evans et al., 1989; Lepore, Evans, & Schneider, 1991).

Loss of control. Most people prefer to think that they are in control of their lives, and that the occasional setbacks that befall them can be controlled through redoubled efforts or other prophylactic precautions (Thompson, 1991). Crowded situations, however, diminish this sense of control (see Chapter 4). Prison inmates believe they have less control over their circumstances when the prison is overcrowded, and the prisoners are also likely to report more symptoms of illness and stress (Ruback & Innes, 1988). People who live in crowded homes report greater distress when the overcrowding leaves them feeling as though circumstances are beyond their control (Lepore, Evans, & Schneider, 1992). When they felt they could control their living conditions, residents of a drug rehabilitation center experienced less depression than individuals who didn't feel in control (Schutte et al., 1992).

College students, too, suffer when overcrowding in their dorms erodes their sense of control (Baum & Davis, 1980). When three students are crowded into two-person rooms, one of the roommates is often rejected by the other two. These isolated roommates tend to complain about their inability to regulate their interactions or change "the way things are"; they also report negative expectations about future opportunities to gain control in the dormitory. A higher percentage of the rejected students (43%) also reported experiencing problems in comparison to students who weren't rejected (23%) and students living in double-occupancy rooms (21%) (Aiello, Baum, & Gormley, 1981; Baum & Davis, 1980; Baum & Valins, 1979).

Because crowding becomes particularly noxious when it undermines our sense of control, reinforcing feelings of control can undo some of the deleterious effects of high-density settings. Researchers tested the benefits of increasing *cognitive control* in a study of women shopping in crowded and uncrowded New York City grocery stores. They told some of the women about the consequences of crowding (they were told that crowding makes people feel aroused and anxious), but others were given no preparation. The women who were mentally prepared coped better with the shopping experience (Langer & Saegert, 1977). Another study tested the benefits of *behavioral control.* Researchers arranged for four confederates to enter an elevator in the Yale University Library whenever a lone individual arrived to use the elevator. These confederates jockeyed the subject into either the corner opposite the control panel or the corner in front of the control panel. When subjects reached their floor and exited, they encountered another researcher who asked them a few questions about the elevator. As expected, passengers who had been able to manipulate the floor-selection buttons felt that the elevator was less crowded than those who could not reach the buttons (Rodin, Solomon, & Metcalf, 1978, Experiment 1).

Arousal and crowding. Crowding is not just a cognitive reaction to overstimulation or a loss of control. Rather, it is also a *feeling*, so the two factors highlighted in the two-factor theory of emotion—arousal and cognitive labeling—determine how we *feel* about a crowded situation. A two-factor theory approach argues that when the number of people in a setting becomes too great, we experience physiological arousal. This arousal, however, need not be experienced as crowding. If we attribute the arousal to some other source—such as fear of being attacked, anxiety over bad news, or job tension—then we will not feel crowded. But if we attribute this arousal to the excessive closeness of others, then we will label the experience *crowding.* Our subjective interpretation of this arousal, then, depends on our attributional interpretation of its cause.

▲ **FIGURE 14-5**
Can the two-factor theory of emotion explain why we don't feel crowded in some high-density situations? People seated close together usually reported feeling more crowded than subjects seated far apart. The important exception, however, occurred when subjects were led to believe that a subliminal noise playing through speakers in the room could possibly arouse them. These people felt no more crowded than those seated far apart. (From Worchel & Yohai, 1979)

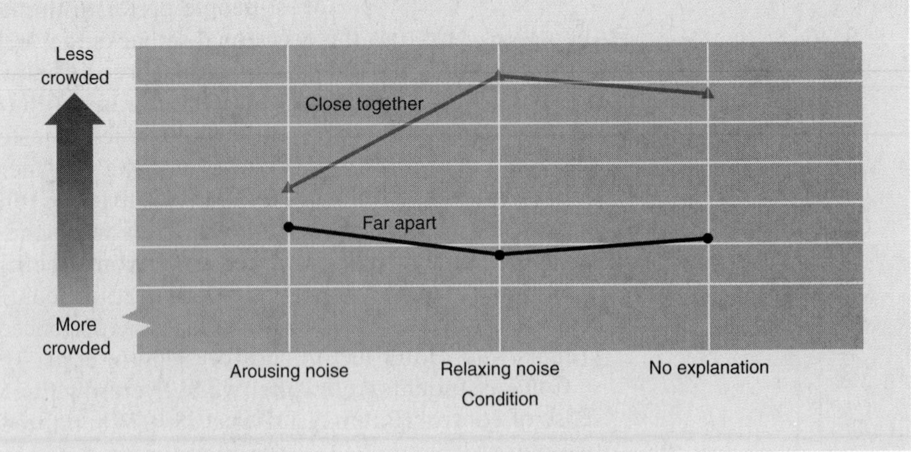

Researchers tested this two-factor theory of crowding by arranging for the members of five-person groups to sit very close together or comfortably far apart (Worchel & Yohai, 1979). They then told the subjects that they would be exposed to subliminal noise to see if inaudible sounds influenced their performance on several tasks. The subjects were never exposed to noise, but this cover story allowed the researchers to manipulate people's attributions about the causes of their arousal. Reasoning that subjects seated close together would feel less crowded if they could attribute their arousal to some other causal factor, one-third of the subjects were told that the noise might cause stressful, uncomfortable side effects. Another third of the subjects were told that the noise should be relaxing, and the final third were given no explanation of the effects of the sound (see Figure 14-5). Supporting the two-factor theory, people who attributed their arousal to the fictitious noise rather than to the high density felt less crowded than the other subjects (Worchel, 1978; Worchel & Teddlie, 1976; Worchel & Yohai, 1979).

density-intensity hypothesis An explanation of crowding; predicts that high density makes unpleasant situations more unpleasant, and pleasant situations more pleasant.

The two-factor theory of crowding also explain why, in some cases, overcrowding can actually be a pleasant rather than an unpleasant experience. As Jonathan Freedman (1973, 1975, 1979) argues, we don't automatically react negatively when we enter a place that is overcrowded. Freedman's **density-intensity hypothesis** suggests instead that crowding works to intensify our dominant emotional reaction. If we are enjoying ourselves in the particular place, then adding more people to the situation increases that level of enjoyment. The enjoyable party becomes delightful when more people arrive, and the interesting city becomes fascinating when it grows into a crowded metropolis. If something in the situation makes the group interaction unpleasant, however, then high density will make the situation seem even more unpleasant. Freedman (1975), in one test of this hypothesis, discovered that people enjoyed working with other people much more when they were complimented for their work rather than criticized. When these people worked in a high-density situation, these reactions became even stronger: People given positive feedback about their work responded even more favorably, whereas people given negative feedback responded even more unfavorably. Apparently, "crowding does not generally have negative effects on people." Rather, "it can have either good or bad effects depending upon the situation" (p. vii).

Social ecology of crowding. Ecological psychologist Roger Barker (1968, 1987) argued that the layout and design of the physical environment also influences our responses to overcrowded conditions. In some cases, a situation (or, to use Barker's term, a *behavior setting*) may be packed with people, but because the setting is designed to minimize unwanted intrusions, people may not feel all that crowded. A fast-food restaurant may use a system of guide chains and multiple cash registers to handle large numbers of customers efficiently. Hundreds of employees may work in one large, open office, but because they are separated from each other by sound-deadening partitions, they may be able to work efficiently nonetheless (Sundstrom, 1987). Airport lounges are often designed so that people aren't forced into interaction with the people around them (Sommer, 1969). But if the environment is poorly planned—if corridors are too narrow to let people move freely or if so many students attend the lecture that some must sit on the floor—then people will feel far more crowded (Heller, Groff, & Solomon, 1977; McCallum et al., 1979; Morasch, Groner, & Keating, 1979; Paulus et al., 1976).

staffing theory
An ecological analysis of behavior settings that argues both understaffing (not enough people) and overstaffing (too many people) can be detrimental.

Staffing theory is based on Barker's ecological approach to crowding (Wicker, 1979, 1987). Consider a fast-food restaurant. The typical customer wants to order a meal as rapidly as possible, and then eat the meal at the restaurant or take it to another location. The employees must take the customer's order, relay it to the kitchen, select the items when they are cooked, bag or otherwise package the items, and charge the customer for the food. If the number of employees working behind the counter is sufficient to meet the demands of the customers in a reasonable amount of time, then the behavior setting is *optimally staffed.* If, however, the restaurant is *understaffed*—one employee must perform all the counter tasks while another employee cooks all the food—then the group lacks "enough people to carry out smoothly the essential program and maintenance tasks" in the setting (Wicker, 1979, p. 71). And if the number of employees exceeds the number needed in the situation—if 15 employees are working a shift that serves only a half dozen customers—*overstaffing* exists. People who work in understaffed situations tend to experience anxiety and distress, for the demands on their time and resources are too great. To cope, they often seek out and actively recruit new members (Cini, Moreland, & Levine, 1993). People who work in overstaffed situations, in contrast, feel bored and uninvolved in their work. They are also less interested in recruiting new members. Thus, too few people can be just as damaging as too many people (Wicker et al., 1976).

Crowding and social pathology. Imagine a college professor driving into a large city for a social psychology conference. As he drives closer and closer to the heart of the city, he is exposed to so many unfamiliar surroundings, sights, and people that he begins to feel overstimulated (overload). To cope, he concentrates on finding his way to his hotel, but he misses his exit and gets lost (loss of control). As his distress mounts, he searches for a cause of his arousal (attribution), and quickly finds an obvious source—the city with its crowded highways, sidewalks, and skyline. His reaction is further intensified when a minor accident blocks the entrance to the hotel, and he discovers the parking garage is completely filled (overstaffing). Given this combination of factors, summarized in Table 14-8, the professor will probably feel very crowded in this high-density setting.

What would happen to this person if he experienced this type of environmental stress repeatedly over a prolonged period of time? Would he, like the rats studied by Calhoun, begin to display the negative effects of high density, such as increased irritability, aggressiveness, and withdrawal? The section "In Depth: Does Crowding Cause Social Pathology?" considers the impact of prolonged crowding on humans.

Noise

People don't always equate high density with crowding; the packed party may be viewed as pleasurable rather than stressful. Neither are all loud sounds noises. Sound results from changes in air pressure detected by the sensory organs of the ear; noise results from the judgment that the incoming auditory message is unpleasant, unwanted, and irritating. Thus one person's sound may be another person's noise. If you turn up your stereo so high that the plaster cracks, the sounds you are generating may be music to you but noise to your angry neighbor. **Noise** is any sound that is unwanted.

noise
Unwanted sound.

When does a sound become a noise? First, the louder a sound, the more likely it will be considered noise. Sounds in the range of 0–50 decibels (dB) are very soft, and usually produce little irritation for the listener. Sounds over 80 dB, in contrast, may be bothersome enough to be called noise (see Table 14-9). Of course, a 30-dB whisper in a movie theater may still prompt a "please be

Does Crowding Cause Social Pathology?

Crowded animals often behave in unusual and unhealthy ways. When colonies of lemmings—small furry rodents found in Scandinavian mountain regions—grow too large, the lemmings apparently commit mass suicide: They migrate into the sea where many drown (Dubos, 1965). A herd of deer living on an isolated island in Chesapeake Bay prospered for many years until overcrowding became a problem. Then the deer began dying by the score, and the size of the herd plummeted sharply (Christian, 1963; Christian, Flyger, & Davis, 1960). Calhoun's rats displayed odd, pathological behavior: disrupted courtship rituals, aberrant forms of sexuality, aggressiveness, and inadequate care of the young. Calhoun (1962) used the phrase **behavioral sink** to describe overcrowded living conditions that "aggravate all forms of pathology that can be found within a group" (p. 143).

Scientists were quick to note the parallels between Calhoun's behavioral sink and our own urban habitats. Until this century, most of the world's human population lived in small families and villages. But now the bulk of the world's population lives in high-density cities, where overcrowding is a daily occurrence. Could this crowding be responsible for some of the social problems that plague our cities? Does crowding lead to increases in divorce and out-of-wedlock births? Can increases in violent crime, including assault and rape, be attributed in part to the pressures of crowding? Do people who are living in crowded places have more physical and psychological health problems, as a result of which they die younger and experience more psychological dysfunction?

Correlational analyses of this *social-pathology hypothesis* suggest that social problems, such as crime, delinquency, rape, and suicide, are indeed more prevalent in overpopulated areas than in less crowded areas. When researchers calculated the correlation between the number of people living in an area of a U.S. city and the various indices of problematic social behaviors recorded in those areas, they found that mortality and birth rates, welfare rates, juvenile delinquency, and admissions to mental hospitals all increased as the population grew in size (Galle, Gove, & McPherson, 1972). When other investigators applied this analysis to data obtained from 65 other countries, they obtained similar results. Homicide, riots, infant mortality, and suicide were more prevalent in crowded parts of the world than in less densely populated places (Booth, 1976; see the leftmost column of correlations in Table 14-7). These relationships were even stronger when researchers measured crowding by calculating the number of people living in each room of a dwelling (inside density) rather than the number of people living in a general area of the city (outside density; Galle et al., 1972).

However, these findings must be interpreted cautiously and critically. First, very little evidence suggests that a human version of a behavioral sink develops in overcrowded cities. Social relations become more impersonal in large cities, but the percentage of people who wantonly break social norms regulating appropriate behavior remains fairly low. Milgram argues that, far from being cases of social disorganization, cities are examples of highly organized, complex patterns of human relationships. In most cities large numbers of people live and work in a small space, yet their day-to-day interactions are well regulated and free of conflict and anxiety.

Second, even though crowding and social problems are correlated, other variables that covary with over-

behavioral sink: The deterioration of various forms of adaptive behavior observed by Calhoun in his studies of overcrowded rats; any living situation characterized by both overcrowding and social dysfunction.

▲ **TABLE 14-7**
What is the relationship between crowding and some symptoms of social pathology?

Although these signs of social dysfunction increased as population sizes grew, when researchers adjusted the correlations to take into account differences in social class and ethnicity, the correlations were no longer statistically significant.

Symptom	*Correlation*	*Adjusted Correlation*
Mortality rate (% of deaths in total population)	.28	−.18
Fertility rate (number of births per 1,000 women aged 15–44)	.37	−.02
Welfare rate (% of 18-year-olds receiving welfare)	.34	−.12
Delinquency rate (% of males ages 12–16 charged with crimes)	.49	.23
Admissions to mental hospitals (number of people per 100,000 admitted for psychiatric treatment)	.35	.14

Source: Data from Galle, Gove, & McPherson, 1972.

crowding (for example, income levels, police protection, community services, and stability of communities) may be the actual causes of increases in social pathology. Indeed, when researchers controlled for several of these other variables statistically, the crowding-pathology correlations became much smaller. Once we adjust for the facts that people with lower incomes tend to live in the most crowded parts of the city and that the housing conditions in these high-density areas are substandard, the relationship between crowding and various signs of social disorganization disappear (see the rightmost column of Table 14-7; Galle et al., 1972; Sampson & Groves, 1989).

Third, people's reactions to high-density situations depend, in large part, on their culture's norms pertaining to crowding. People who grow up in cultures that don't put a premium on privacy don't react negatively to high-density situations. People who learn to associate crowding with stress, in contrast, are more likely to respond negatively when they find themselves in high-density situations. For them, crowding may lead to more negative consequences, but their cultural beliefs mediate the strength of the crowding → pathology relationship (Gillis, Richard, & Hagan, 1986; Loo, 1986; Rotton, 1986).

Last, most people can learn to cope successfully with crowded situations. Experimental studies suggest that high-density situations can be too stimulating and sometimes undermine our sense of control. But field studies—of inmates in crowded prisons, personnel serving on submarines, people living in high-density neighborhoods, workers laboring on oil-drilling platforms at sea, and people living in very small quarters—suggest that people learn to cope with crowding before it leads to any negative consequences (Evans & Cohen, 1987; Ruback & Innes, 1988). Inmates in crowded prisons feel less control over their situation, but they don't suffer more illnesses nor are they more likely to die by violence than prisoners in less crowded prisons (Ruback & Innes, 1988; compare with Cox, Paulus, & McCain, 1984). Men who spent weeks living in a confined undersea habitat enjoyed this challenging experience (Radloff & Helmreich, 1968). Researchers who studied a neighborhood in Rome called *Quartiere Aurelio* found that people didn't feel crowded in some of the highest-density sections if highways, buildings, and parks were carefully designed to promote a sense of openness (Bonnes et al., 1991). Indeed, Freedman's density-intensity hypothesis (1975) goes so far as to suggest that overcrowding may increase the pleasures of city living: "Under some circumstances high density makes people more competitive and aggressive, but under others it has the opposite effect. High density can cause people to be friendlier" (p. 8).

Does crowding threaten one's physical, psychological, and social health? The social-pathology hypothesis is intuitively appealing, but the available evidence does not confirm it. Some studies suggest that overcrowding—particularly in one's home—may set the stage for negative social processes, such as the loss of privacy, social support, and intimacy. However, other studies support Freedman's (1975) bold claim: "Overall, with other factors equated, living, working, or spending time for any reason under conditions of high density does not harm people" (p. 7). At present we can cautiously conclude that the social-pathology hypothesis, at least in its boldest form, is an exaggeration.

▲ **TABLE 14-8**
Summing up: Factors that exacerbate negative reactions to high-density situations

Factor	*Characteristics*	*Example*
Overload	Information processing capacity is exceeded when individuals are exposed to too many inputs in a short period of time. People cope by restricting their attention and limiting their contact with others.	Men who lived in small homes and apartments coped with their domestic situation by limiting their contact with family members (Lepore et al., 1991).
Control	High-density situations can diminish individuals' sense of personal control.	As density increases, prison inmates believe they have less control over their circumstances, and they report more symptoms of illness and stress (Ruback & Innes, 1988).
Arousal	High density leads to physiological arousal, which is experienced as crowding when attributed to the high density. Thus crowding can intensify our dominant emotional reaction (the density-intensity hypothesis).	Individuals who misattributed the arousal produced by high density to an irrelevant situational factor (subliminal noise) felt less crowded than people who attributed the arousal to the high-density situation (Worchel & Yohai, 1979).
Social ecology	The design of the physical space influences perceptions of crowding. If the behavior setting is designed to accommodate large numbers of people, then the individuals in that setting won't feel as crowded when density is high.	People experience tension and stress when the number of people working in an office is insufficient to meet work demands (understaffing). People experience boredom and withdrawal when the number of people greatly exceeds work demands (overstaffing) (Wicker, 1979).

quiet," and a 115-dB rock concert may evoke considerable pleasure (for reviews, see Cohen, 1980; Cohen & Weinstein, 1981).

Second, annoyance also depends on your attitudes and beliefs about the noise and its source. If you were awakened at 3:30 A.M. by your neighbor's loud music, your irritation would be great if you disliked your neighbor; felt that your neighbor was uncaring and thoughtless; believed that the music was unnecessarily loud; and thought that the disruption of your sleep would impair your health or reduce your efficiency the following day (Cohen, 1980).

Last, unpredictable, uncontrollable sounds are more irritating than controllable continuous sounds. David Glass, Jerome Singer, and their colleagues studied reactions to uncontrollable noises by asking people to work on various tasks in a noisy room. Some people, however, were told that they could control the noise by pressing a small button attached to the side of their chair. The experimenters asked the subjects to use the button only if they had to, but subjects were reminded that the button was there if they needed it. None of the subjects who were told about the button ever pushed it, but the knowledge that a means of controlling the noise was available to them served to reduce its aversiveness. Subjects with buttons rated the noise as less irritating and distracting than the subjects who weren't told anything about a button. Even a researcher working down the hall confirmed Glass and Singer's hypothesis. He complained, "I can't stand hearing that noise anymore. It's not so much the loudness as not knowing when its going to come on" (Glass, Singer, & Friedman, 1969, Experiment 2, p. 205).

▲ **TABLE 14-9**
Decibel levels of various sounds and their effects on hearing

Decibel	*Sound*	*Effect on Hearing*
0	Breathing	Hearing threshold
10	Pin dropping	Barely audible
30	Whisper at 15 feet	Very quiet
50	Light traffic in the distance	Quiet
70	Freeway at 50 feet	Difficult to hear conversation
90	Heavy truck at 50 feet	Hearing damage after 8 hours
110	Dance floor in a club	Difficult to hear a shout from more than 6 inches away
130	Jet taking off at 200 feet	Maximum limit of amplified speech
140	Planes landing on aircraft carrier deck	Painfully loud

Source: Based on Turk et al., 1974.

Gerald Gardner (1978), quite by accident, also documented the impact of controllability on noise. In 1973 and 1974 Gardner replicated Glass and Singer's results when he found that people made more errors after they were exposed to 100-dB bursts of unexpected noise. But in 1975, using almost identical procedures, he failed to find any negative aftereffects. Why did his 1975 study fail? Gardner carried out the earlier studies before new federal guidelines for research involving human beings were implemented. He always treated his subjects fairly, but none of them completed an informed consent agreement, a formal statement indicating they understood the nature of the procedures and their rights as subjects. In the later studies, Gardner added consent forms that emphasized that the subjects were free to withdraw from the experiment at any time without penalty. Gardner belatedly realized that the new consent procedures may have increased subjects' feeling of control over the noise, thereby eliminating its negative aftereffects. When he replicated his study once more, using special consent procedures that didn't underscore subjects' rights to withdraw, he confirmed Glass and Singer's results (Dill et al., 1982).

How do we respond when we live in places that are noisy? Studies of people who must endure noisy places—people who work in noisy offices, families living in homes near airports, and children on playgrounds located near major highways—usually find that the noise has a disruptive impact on their social behaviors. People are less likely to interact with other people in noisy places, and they also tend to be less helpful (Appleyard & Lintell, 1972; Korte, 1981; Loewen & Suedfeld, 1992). As noted in Chapter 13, noise can also set the stage for negative interpersonal exchanges. In one study subjects who had been given either one shock (nonangry) or nine shocks (angry) by the experimenter's male accomplice were told to shock the accomplice each time he made a mistake on a bogus learning task. Although angry subjects usually delivered more intense shocks (no shocks were actually delivered), they chose particularly strong shock levels when they were exposed to loud bursts of uncontrollable noise (Donnerstein & Wilson, 1976, Experiment 2; see Figure 14-6).

Noise is also mentally taxing, for it seems to interfere with our ability to work and learn. Glass and Singer, in their initial studies of people working on various types of cognitive and mathematical tasks, found that most people were able to

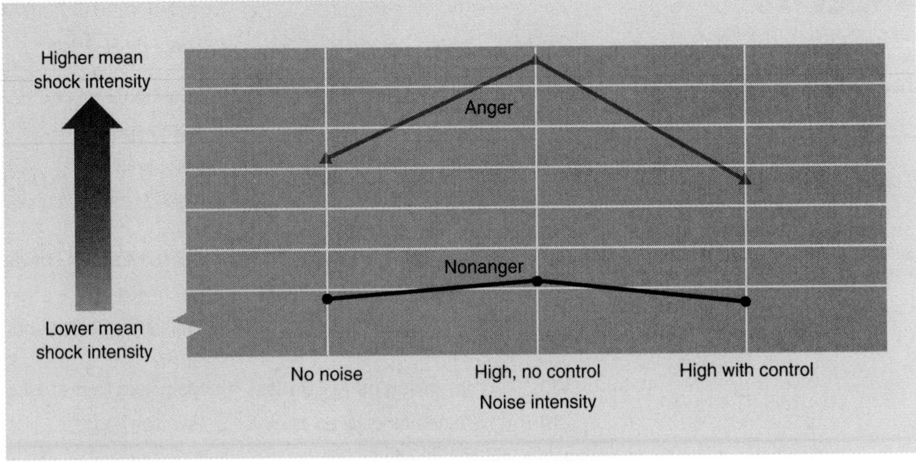

▲ **FIGURE 14-6**
Do people display more hostility in noisy places? People who were shocked nine times, when given the chance to reciprocate, gave stronger shocks than people who received only one shock. Note, however, that people who were exposed to a loud noise that they could not control were particularly hostile. They gave stronger shocks than all the other participants. (From Donnerstein & Wilson, 1976)

overcome the irritating effects of the noise and continue working effectively, but this adaptation process proved psychologically costly. As Glass and Singer experimented with highly unpredictable and uncontrollable noises, they realized that "individuals expend 'psychic energy' in the course of the adaptive process," and thus are "less able to cope with subsequent environmental demands and frustrations" (Glass, Singer, & Pennebaker, 1977, p. 134). Later investigations have sought to catalog these aversive aftereffects of exposure to noise, which include increases in physical illnesses (headaches, heart disease, allergies, and digestive disorders), infant and adult mortality rates, mental illnesses, interpersonal conflict, and even impotence (Cohen, 1980).

Noise may even be partly responsible for differences in school performance displayed by children attending schools in urban and rural settings. One team of researchers began by identifying children who attended schools located in the air corridor of the Los Angeles International Airport. Owing to the close proximity of the airport, noise levels in these schools often reached 95 dB; during a typical school day, flights passed overhead every 2.5 minutes. When these children were compared with students living in quieter areas of Los Angeles, the investigators found that they had higher blood pressure, were less likely to solve a nine-piece jigsaw puzzle, and were more likely to give up before the allotted time for the task had expired. These differences were most pronounced among children who had lived in the noisy area for three or more years, and were not erased when noise levels were reduced (as part of the settlement of a lawsuit filed against the airport). These findings clearly argue against exposing children to excessive environmental noise (Cohen, Glass, & Singer, 1973; Cohen, Evans, et al., 1981; Cohen, Krantz, et al., 1981; Cohen et al., 1986).

Temperature

Calhoun's rats lived in a climate-controlled habitat that protected them from the stress brought on by climatic changes. We are not so lucky: Humans live in places where temperatures hover at −50°F for weeks on end, yet they also thrive in desert areas with temperatures routinely reaching 120°F. Extreme temperatures are physically harmful, for the body must work hard to keep its internal temperature stable when the temperature of the ambient environment changes. When a heat wave hits a large city, the number of people who suffer from exhaustion, stroke, and heart attacks increases. But extremes in temperature also have social-psychological consequences. When we haven't had time to acclimate to an extreme temperature, we can't perform routine tasks as competently or as efficiently as acclimated individuals. We also feel more uncomfortable, irritated, and fatigued when we must live or work in places that are too hot or too cold (Bell, 1981, 1992; Bell & Greene, 1982). Our interpersonal relations also feel the effects of hot or cold temperatures. We don't help people as much when we are hot or cold; we don't like other people as much either (Bennett et al., 1983; Cunningham, 1979; Ruback & Pandey, 1992). When college students filled out various questionnaires while seated in a hot room (effective temperature 90.6°F) they reported feeling more uncomfortable and unhappy than students working in a room with a more comfortable climate (effective temperature 67.5°F). They also rated a stranger more negatively when they were hot rather than comfortable (Griffitt, 1970).

Extremes in temperature also increase our aggressiveness. Our commonsense notions about aggression are reflected in such expressions as "hot under the collar," "flaring tempers," and "that burns me up." In fact, when the U.S. Riot Commission searched for the causes of racial violence that occurred in 1968, it concluded that high temperatures were to blame. The commission warned city officials to expect trouble when long, hot summers heat the spirits and tempers of urban populations. As noted in Chapter 13, Craig Anderson's (1987, 1989) archival studies of crime statistics support the idea that increases in temperature go hand-in-hand with increases in hostility and violence. People in many different countries and climates tended to commit more crimes and act more violently when the temperature was warm rather than cold.

Anderson's work suggests that the relationship between heat and aggression is a *linear* one: The hotter the temperature, the more violent people become. Robert Baron and Paul Bell, however, have noted a possible exception to this general principle: Extremely high temperatures may work to reduce violence. Baron and Bell came to this conclusion after studying people giving shocks to one another in either a comfortable room or a hot room (Baron, 1972; Baron & Bell, 1975, 1976). Initially, they believed that people would deliver more intense shocks when the temperature in the room was in the mid-90s than when it was in the low 70s, but in these studies the high-temperature group was less aggressive. They concluded that uncomfortable heat leads to two incompatible reactions: It produces a negative affective reaction, which can increase anger, *and* a strong desire to escape from the noxious environmental setting. Thus, the heat-stressed subjects were angry, but they were so uncomfortable that their primary concern was to finish the experiment as quickly as possible. Baron, Bell, and their colleagues concluded that aggression is linked to temperature in a *curvilinear relationship*. Although moderate increases in temperature will prompt increased aggression, at extremely high levels, the need to escape from the heat will reduce aggression (see Figure 14-7).

Despite their differences, Anderson, Baron, and Bell all agree that people become more violent when temperatures rise. The two approaches disagree only when examining very high temperatures, but this disagreement may be due to differences in the situations Anderson and Baron studied. When individuals experience high temperatures routinely during the course of their daily lives, and they cannot escape from the heat, then the relationship between aggression and heat may be a linear one. If, however, people can escape from high temperatures or the heat lasts only briefly, then the relationship may be curvilinear: People leave the situation rather than act aggressively. Clearly, further research is needed to determine whether aggression drops off as Baron's approach suggests (Anderson, 1989; Anderson & DeNeve, 1992; Bell, 1992; Bell & Fusco, 1989).

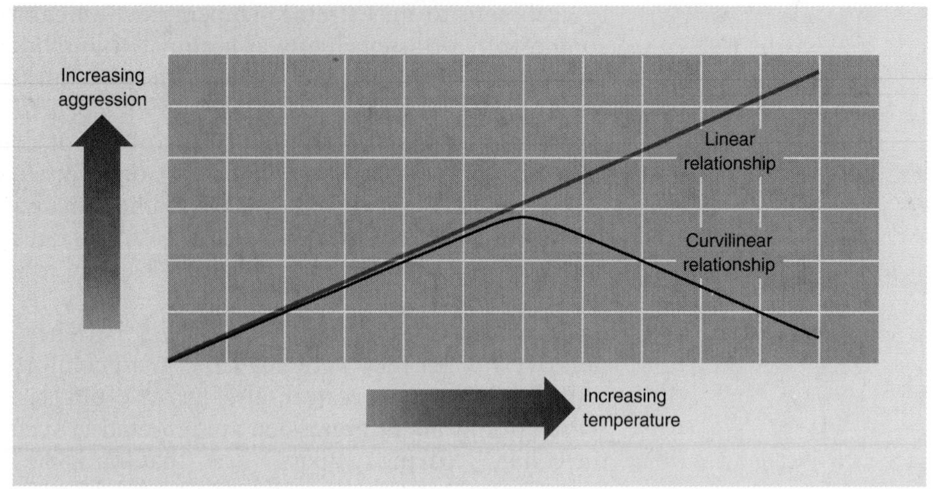

▲ **FIGURE 14-7**
When people get hotter and hotter, do they become more and more aggressive? Anderson believes that aggression and temperature are linearly related: Increases in temperature go hand-in-hand with increases in aggression. Baron and Bell, in contrast, believe that aggression and temperature are curvilinearly related. People usually become more aggressive as they get hotter, but when they become too overheated, they become less and less aggressive.

Environmental Hazards

In 1979 residents panicked when radiation was accidentally released at the Three Mile Island power plant in Pennsylvania. In 1980 Mount Saint Helens erupted, raining ash down on nearby towns and cities and temporarily changing the planet's weather cycles. In 1986 fires and explosions at a nuclear reactor in Chernobyl caused widespread nuclear pollution and death. Deaths, injuries, and property damage on a tremendous scale occurred when a major earthquake hit northern California in 1989. In 1993 the midwestern portions of the United States were inundated by flood waters.

People the world over are subjected, from time to time, to environmental hazards. Some of these, such as volcanoes, floods, hurricanes, blizzards, and typhoons, can be blamed on naturally occurring disruptions in the planet's meteorological and geological systems. Others, however, result from human error. These human-made disasters include nuclear accidents, the spilling of polluting substances, transportation accidents, fires, and industrial accidents. Environmental hazards can be deadly, for estimates suggest that about 250,000 people are killed each year in environmental disasters (Burton, Kates, & White, 1978). They also generate considerable stress for the individuals who survive (Hovanitz, 1993; Kaniasty & Norris, 1993). One comprehensive review of dozens of published studies of psychological reactions to disasters concluded that people who survive a disaster are more likely to suffer from anxiety, sleeplessness, and fearfulness. Disasters also lead to small increases in drug use and depression among people exposed to a hazard. Between 7 and 40% of the survivors of disasters will exhibit some sign of psychopathology (Rubonis & Bickman, 1991).

The aftereffects of environmental catastrophes decrease gradually over time as individuals learn to cope with their situation. In some cases, however, people continue to experience aftereffects of an environmental hazard years after the experience. Individuals who experienced a tornado or a flood reported less and less stress in the months following the event, but even 16 months later, stress levels remained abnormally high (Steinglass & Gerrity, 1990). Mothers living near the Three Mile Island power plant continued to worry, 10 years after the accident, about the effects of the radiation (Bromet, 1990). Some evidence also suggests that women, in particular, suffer longer after a traumatic event, as do people who try too hard to regain control of an uncontrollable event or who become too focused on the event (Prince-Embury, 1991).

▲ Both technologies and people pose a threat to our environment. Modern technologies—such as nuclear power plants, superhighways, and sophisticated mining methods—can create widespread pollution and permanently scar the landscape. And people, by polluting and wasting natural resources and energy, contribute to the degradation of the environment. Social psychologists are now exploring ways to discourage such environmentally destructive behavior while encouraging constructive actions, such as recycling.

The stress caused by technological disasters seems to be particularly long lasting. Natural disasters, such as earthquakes or tornadoes, are traumatic, but they are usually short in duration. Technological disasters, such as pollution or nuclear accidents, are equally damaging, but their effects can't always be clearly assessed because they take place over a longer period of time. Hence, individuals can cope with a once-in-a-lifetime hurricane, but they have a harder time adjusting when they discover their well water is contaminated by a nearby chemical waste dump. One study compared individuals who lived within a mile of a leaking waste dump, individuals whose homes had been flooded, and a control group. Even though the event had occurred 9 months before, individuals who had lived near the dump were far more distressed than individuals who had experienced a flood and the control subjects. They were more anxious and depressed, and they reported experiencing more physical symptoms. They also displayed elevated levels of stress-related hormones in their systems (Baum et al., 1992).

Because environmental hazards, like the other environmental stressors summarized in Table 14-10, threaten our physical and mental well-being, it makes good sense to try to do what we can to prevent these hazards from occurring. Although natural disasters, such as hurricanes and tornadoes, can't be controlled, many devastating environmental hazards are created by people rather than by nature. Rather than remaining complacent, in recent years people have become more actively involved in efforts to protect and sustain the natural environment. Calhoun's rats lived in a world created by Calhoun, so the rats could not change it or even escape it. We humans, however, live in places that we can tear down and rebuild. As the section "Application: Protecting the Environment" notes, people should take better care of their world.

Summary

Because social interactions occur in physical settings, our behavior is often profoundly influenced by such environmental factors as *territories*, *personal space*, and crowding and noise (*stressors*). A territory is an area of controlled access that is usually marked and defended against intrusion by others. People

▲ **TABLE 14-10**
Summing up: Environmental events that generate stress by threatening our well-being

Factor	*Description*
Crowding	High-density situations become stressful when people in the situation experience overload, a reduced sense of personal control, and they attribute their arousal to the crowded circumstances. Crowding is also more stressful when the behavior setting isn't designed to accommodate the large number of people who are present.
Noise	Noise is most stressful when it is loud, unpleasant, uncontrollable, and unpredictable. People can cope with noisy places, but prolonged exposure has been linked to increases in aggression and decreases in the quality of interpersonal relations, learning, and concentration.
Temperature	Extreme temperatures are physically harmful. Individuals perform tasks less efficiently when the temperature is too hot or cold, and they also report feeling more uncomfortable, irritated, and fatigued. Extremes in temperature also increase aggressiveness.
Hazards	People who survive a natural (for example, volcanoes, floods, hurricanes) or human-made (pollution, fires, accidents) hazard are more likely to suffer from anxiety, sleeplessness, and fearfulness. Posttraumatic stress symptoms decline gradually over time but are particularly persistent following technological disasters.

sometimes abandon their territories when others invade them, but because of the *home advantage* the defender usually succeeds in driving off intruders. According to Altman, humans maintain primary, secondary, and public territories, but control is most important in primary territories. These various types of territories serve multiple functions for humans, for they organize social relationships, help people maintain privacy, and provide a means of self-expression. Given the importance of territories, people are satisfied when they live in residences that they can territorialize in some way. Some theorists feel that increases in the amount of secondary territory surrounding buildings (*defensible space*) lead to decreases in vandalism and crime.

During social interaction, we strive to keep a comfortable distance between ourselves and others. This distance is known as personal space. Unlike territories, which are always specific to a particular geographic location, our personal space moves with us. However, we defend our personal space against intrusion just as we defend our territories. Our personal space needs are influenced by several situational and personal factors. Hall identifies four *interpersonal distance zones* that vary in accordance with the nature of our activities: intimate, personal, social, and public. Similarly, the *equilibrium model* suggests that interactants regulate interpersonal distance to keep the level of intimacy in a comfortable range. Age, sex, race, personality, and cultural background also influence personal space needs. Women and people raised in "contact cultures" require less space than men and people raised in "noncontact cultures." In contrast, violent individuals and introverted people require more space. If we cannot secure sufficient space, we tend to experience physiological arousal, but the consequences of this arousal vary depending on individuals' interpretations of the intrusions.

Aspects of our environment, including overcrowding, noise, uncomfortable temperatures, and hazards, not only threaten our well-being but also influence the way we interact with others. *Crowding*, a psychological reaction that occurs when *density* is too high, has been linked to four separate processes: *overload*, loss of cognitive or behavioral control, arousal, and the social ecology of the particular situation. It is not yet known whether overcrowding invariably leads to psychological and behavioral problems in humans. The *density-intensity hypothesis*, for example, suggests that crowding intensifies only our dominant emotional reaction, and *staffing theory* argues that crowding will have few negative consequences if the behavior setting is designed to handle large numbers of people. However, Calhoun's studies of rats suggest that large cities may become *behavioral sinks* that contribute to dramatic increases in various forms of social pathology.

When is unwanted sound labeled *noise*? When it is loud, unpredictable and uncontrollable, and your attitudes and beliefs about the source are negative. Despite the annoyance noise creates, evidence indicates that humans gradually adapt to loud noises, but at a cost. Children who attend schools in noisy areas, for example, display reduced intellectual ability and elevated blood pressure. Noise has also been linked to increases in aggression and decreases in altruism.

Extremes in temperature also influence our social interactions. Evidence indicates that we perform less effectively at very high and very low temperatures. Aggression and violence may be linked to high temperatures, but at present the precise nature of this relationship is not known. Researchers have identified both curvilinear and linear relationships between rising temperatures and violence.

Environmental hazards, both natural (for example, volcanoes, floods, hurricanes) and human-made (pollution, fires, accidents), can also threaten our physical and psychological well-being. People who survive a significant environmental hazard are more likely to suffer from anxiety, sleeplessness, and fearfulness. Posttraumatic stress symptoms decline gradually over time but are particularly persistent following technological disasters.

For More Information

- *The Environment and Social Behavior*, by Irwin Altman (1975), reviews basic studies of personal space and territoriality and organizes these topics within an original theoretical framework based on the concept of privacy.
- *Environmental Psychology*, by Paul A. Bell, Jeffrey D. Fisher, Andrew Baum, and T. E. Greene (1990), is a detailed analysis of the reciprocal relationships between humans and their environment.
- *Environmental Psychology*, by Francis T. McAndrew (1993), offers a concise appraisal of environmental psychology, with compact chapters dealing with such topics as territoriality, interpersonal distance, and work, learning, and home environments.
- *Handbook of Environmental Psychology*, edited by Daniel Stokols and Irwin Altman (1987), contains chapters written by leading researchers and theorists in the field of person-environment relations. The 22 chapters in Volume 1 focus on basic processes, and the 21 chapters in Volume 2 consider applications and cross-cultural implications.
- *Handbook of Post-Disaster Interventions*, edited by Richard D. Allen (1993), describes the psychological and social consequences of and possible remedies for such disasters as hurricanes, tornadoes, and earthquakes. The book is a special issue of the *Journal of Social Behavior and Personality*.
- "Personal Space: Where We Now Stand," by Leslie A. Hayduk (1983), in *Psychological Bulletin*, painstakingly reviews and synthesizes hundreds of studies of interpersonal distance, crowding, and personal space.
- *Personal Space*, by Robert Sommer (1969), takes an entertaining look at interpersonal distancing processes.

Application: Protecting the Environment

Human beings do not always treat the earth's lands, rivers, and skies with the respect they deserve. Technological advances have brought with them an increasing variety of environmental problems, including acid rain, smog, oil spills, and hazardous waste dumps. Pure water and unspoiled natural landscapes are becoming increasingly rare, whereas landfills, dying lakes, and pollution-spewing industrial sites are plentiful. Industrialization is also to blame for the change in the composition of the atmosphere that is creating the **greenhouse effect**. Carbon dioxide and other gases produced by manufacturing processes are raising the planet's temperature to the point that widespread climatic changes are likely (Kempton, Darley, & Stern, 1992).

Our failure to protect the environment is due, in part, to our willingness to risk long-term problems in order to secure immediate personal gains. This tendency is illustrated laconically by the *tragedy of the commons.* Families, in simpler times, grazed small flocks of sheep and other animals in a common pasture. So long as the families in the village kept only a few animals in the common, everyone benefited: the villagers, the sheep, and even the pasture. Often, however, some families would increase the size of their herds. Another sheep or goat made life easier, and the extra animals cost no more to feed. But as more and more animals were added to herds, the common became overcrowded. The herds stripped the common of its grass, and the pasture was ruined. Adding extra animals made life easier in the short run, but eventually the villagers paid the price for their selfishness. The tragedy of the commons is an example of a **social trap**: a situation in which an action that is personally advantageous is damaging to society as a whole (Hardin, 1968).

In contemporary times, we no longer fall prey to the social trap of the tragedy of the commons, for all commons have already been destroyed. Our own social traps prompt us to act in ways that are environmentally destructive: littering, cutting down forests, erecting gaudy billboards, running all-terrain vehicles through wilderness areas, polluting the air, dumping sewage into streams, turning up thermostats in winter, driving gas-guzzling cars. We act in what we perceive to be our own best interests, ignoring the long-range impact of our selfishness (Darley & Gilbert, 1985; Edney, 1980).

We often turn to technological solutions to escape environmental social traps. If we are running out of coal to fuel our power plants, we turn to nuclear energy. If rivers are being polluted, we develop better waste-treatment facilities. If cars are polluting the air, we improve their exhaust systems. Social psychologists, however, feel that technology solves only part of the problem. Although scientific advances will undoubtedly continue to play a major role in solving our environmental problems, we must also consider social-psychological solutions. We must discover ways to discourage environmentally destructive behaviors while we promote environmentally constructive behaviors; littering and polluting must give way to energy conservation and recycling (Demick & Wapner, 1990; Stern, 1992).

Educational programs aimed at increasing public awareness of environmental issues offer one means of achieving this goal (Dennis et al., 1990). Beginning in the 1970s, many public utilities and oil companies launched massive information campaigns designed to reeducate Americans about conservation. Similarly, federal agencies sought to foster proecology attitudes toward littering, pollution, and conservation through various types of educational programs. But even when these interventions increase our knowledge of environmental issues, they don't necessarily lead to changes in our behaviors. Individuals who express great concern for the environment don't always engage in positive forms of environmental action (Geller, 1992; O'Riordan, 1976). One investigator discovered that 94% of the nearly 500 people he interviewed expressed a positive attitude toward cleaning up litter; yet when they left the interview situation, only 1.4% of the subjects picked up the litter that had been planted in their path. Most assumed it was somebody else's responsibility (Bickman, 1972a). Similarly, people's general attitudes about the environment and recycling didn't predict whether or not they would participate in their neighborhood's recycling projects. Did people who thought that waste was a serious problem recycle? Did individuals who favored government regulation of recycling recycle? Did people who thought that recycling was an effective way of dealing with pollution recycle? Did people with proecology attitudes recycle? No. Only people who knew how to recycle, people who thought that *household waste* was a problem, and people who lived in neighborhoods where most households recycled regularly recycled (Oskamp et al., 1991).

Steps can be taken, however, to increase the correspondence between attitudes and behaviors (Burn & Oskamp, 1986; Kempton, Darley, & Stern, 1992; Stern, 1992). In one longitudinal study of energy conservation, investigators manipulated homeowners' commitment to energy-saving actions. After giving subjects information about energy conservation, the interviewer asked them to sign a pledge that they would try to reduce the amount of energy they used to heat their homes. Some subjects were led to believe that their names would be released to the news media at the end of the study (pub-

greenhouse effect: The gradual warming of the temperature of the planet caused by increased concentrations of carbon dioxide and other gases in the atmosphere.

social trap: A situation that tempts individuals to act in ways that will benefit them initially but will prove detrimental, over the long term, both to them and to society as a whole.

lic commitment), while others were told that their names would be kept confidential (private commitment). At the end of one year, the subjects who had publicly committed themselves to conservation were found to have used less heating fuel (natural gas) than the subjects in the private commitment condition. People whose commitment to energy conservation was kept private didn't conserve much energy at all; they used as much natural gas as homeowners in the control condition who were given no information about conservation (Pallak, Cook, & Sullivan, 1980).

Robert Cialdini and his colleagues have also used normative social influence to increase proenvironment actions (Cialdini, Kallgren, & Reno, 1991; Cialdini, Reno, & Kallgren, 1990). In their field studies of littering, they distinguish between *descriptive norms* and *injunctive norms.* Descriptive norms exert informational influence over us by defining what most people would do, feel, or think in a particular situation. "Most people don't litter" and "Very few people waste electricity" are examples of descriptive environmental norms. Injunctive norms, in contrast, include an evaluative component. "Harming the environment is wrong" and "We have a moral obligation to save the rain forests" are injunctive norms. People who do not comply with descriptive norms may be viewed as unusual, but people who violate injunctive norms are evaluated negatively.

Cialdini's research team put handbills under the windshield wipers of cars in a parking lot and then watched to see whether people threw these scraps of paper on the ground when they returned to their cars. They then manipulated the salience of norms about littering across three conditions. In the descriptive norm condition, subjects witnessed a confederate dropping a bag of trash into a garbage can. In the injunctive norm condition, subjects saw a confederate pick up a piece of litter (the same bag of trash) and dispose of it in the garbage can. In the control condition, the confederate merely walked by the subject. Subjects encountered the confederate either in the lot where the subject's car was parked or on the path leading to the parking lot.

These researchers discovered that descriptive norms are nearly as influential as injunctive norms, but that their impact wears off rapidly. If the encounter between the subject and the confederate occurred in the parking lot, only 17% of the subjects in the descriptive norm condition littered. This percentage jumped to 36%, however, if the confederate's litter-conscious actions had occurred on the path leading to the lot. In contrast, the injunctive norm became more powerful over time. No one who saw the confederate pick up litter on the path leading to the lot littered (Reno, Cialdini, & Kallgren, 1993, Study 3). These results identify two routes to increasing environmentally responsive actions: Convince people that environmentally harmful actions are the exception rather than the rule (descriptive norm) or convince people that harming the environment is immoral (injunctive norm).

Researchers have also sought to change environmental behavior directly through the use of prompts, reinforcements, and feedback (Geller, 1989). These three techniques are all based on learning theory, for they assume that we acquire our behaviors through reinforcement (see Chapter 6). *Prompts* are situational cues that convey information about appropriate behavior. Signs, for example, are often used to remind us to "help keep our community clean," "turn off the lights when you leave," and "keep off the grass." To be effective, they should be polite; a sign that is too demanding, such as "You MUST NOT litter," can actually lead to more littering by creating feelings of reactance (Reich & Robertson, 1979). Prompts are also more effective when they encourage actions that are fairly easy to perform (Geller, 1989).

Researchers have also made use of *reinforcements* by administering desirable rewards to individuals each time they engage in an environmentally constructive action. All sorts of incentives have been used to encourage proecology actions, including raffle tickets, monetary payment, decals that say "I conserve energy," and social approval (Geller, Winnett, & Everett, 1982). Reinforcement also takes more subtle forms. When we receive money back from our deposit on soda bottles, pay less on our heating bills, or drive in a commuter traffic lane because we have three passengers in the car with us, our behaviors are being reinforced.

Positive effects have also been obtained by giving people *feedback* about their level of energy consumption. Like prompts, feedback tells individuals when they need to conserve. And because feedback gives people information about how close they are to their goals, it also functions as a reinforcer. Thus feedback is among the most powerful of all learning techniques for decreasing energy consumption. In one elegant field study of feedback, researchers asked the owners of identical homes if they would participate in a study of energy conservation. In some homes, a small device that monitored the operation of the air conditioner and the outside temperature was installed by the family telephone. A blue light on the device flashed whenever the outside temperature fell below 68° and the air conditioner was running. Thus the device signaled the homeowners to shut off their air-conditioning and open their windows. If they complied, the device rewarded them by shutting off the light. Some households were also given a chart that summarized their energy conservation efforts. Three days a week for a month, a research assistant read the family's electric meter and charted the amount of energy they had "conserved" and "wasted" (Becker & Seligman, 1978). When the energy consumption rates were examined, investigators found that households with the signaling device had reduced their electricity consumption by over 15%. The chart also helped, resulting in a 9% reduction.

Changing people's environmental attitudes, increasing normative pressure to protect the environment, and creating behavioral change through prompts, reinforcements, and feedback are only three of the many social-psychological techniques we can use to combat human-made environmental problems. Although these and other social-psychological methods of promoting environmentally positive actions have yet to be applied on a wide scale, the preliminary results are promising. Questions of energy conservation are bound to become more important in the future as resources are drained and the need for conservation becomes more critical. We can only hope that we can effect large-scale changes in the way we treat our environment before it's too late.

References

ABBEY, A. (1982). Sex differences in attributions for friendly behavior: Do males misperceive females' friendliness? *Journal of Personality and Social Psychology, 42,* 830–838.

ABELSON, R. P. (1983). Whatever became of consistency theory? *Personality and Social Psychology Bulletin, 9,* 37–54.

ABELSON, R. P., ARONSON, E., MCGUIRE, W. J., NEWCOMB, T. M., ROSENBERG, M. J., & TANNENBAUM, P. H. (Eds.). (1968). *Theories of cognitive consistency: A sourcebook.* Chicago: Rand McNally.

ABELSON, R. P., & PRENTICE, D. A. (1989). Beliefs as possessions: A functional perspective. In A. R. Pratkanis, S. J. Breckler, & A. G. Greenwald (Eds.), *Attitude structure and function* (pp. 361–382). Hillsdale, NJ: Erlbaum.

ABRAMS, D. (1990). Influencing each other. In R. Brown (Ed.), *The Marshall Cavendish encyclopedia of personal relationships: Human behavior, How groups work* (Vol. 15, pp. 1836–1843). North Bellmore, NY: Marshall Cavendish Corporation.

ABRAMSON, L. Y., METALSKY, G. I., & ALLOY, L. B. (1989). Hopelessness depression: A theory-based subtype of depression. *Psychological Review, 96,* 358–372.

ABRAMSON, L. Y., SELIGMAN, M. E. P., & TEASDALE, J. D. (1978). Learned helplessness in humans: Critique and reformulation. *Journal of Abnormal Psychology, 87,* 49–74.

ACITELLI, L. K. (1992). Gender differences in relationship awareness and marital satisfaction among young married couples. *Personality and Social Psychology Bulletin, 18,* 102–110.

ADAMS, S. (1965). Inequity in social exchange. In L. Berkowitz (Ed.), *Advances in experimental social psychology* (Vol. 2). New York: Academic Press.

AD HOC COMMITTEE ON ETHICAL STANDARDS IN PSYCHOLOGICAL RESEARCH. (1973). *Ethical principles in the conduct of research with human participants.* Washington, DC: American Psychological Association.

ADORNO, T. W., FRENKEL-BRUNSWICK, E., LEVINSON, D., & SANFORD, N. (1950). *The authoritarian personality.* New York: Harper.

AFFLECK, G., & TENNEN, H. (1991). Social comparison and coping with major medical problems. In J. Suls & T. A. Wills (Eds.), *Social comparison: Contemporary theory and research* (pp. 369–394). Hillsdale, NJ: Erlbaum.

AFFLECK, G., TENNEN, H., PFEIFFER, C., & FIFIELD, J. (1988). Social comparisons in rheumatoid arthritis: Accuracy and adaptational significance. *Journal of Social and Clinical Psychology, 6,* 219–234.

AIELLO, J. R. (1987). Human spatial behavior. In D. Stokols & I. Altman (Eds.), *Handbook of environmental psychology* (Vol. 1, pp. 389–504). New York: Wiley.

AIELLO, J. R., BAUM, A., & GORMLEY, F. (1981). Social determinants of residential crowding stress. *Personality and Social Psychology Bulletin, 7,* 643–644.

AIELLO, J. R., EPSTEIN, Y. M., & KARLIN, R. A. (1975). *Field experimental research in human crowding.* Paper presented at the Annual Meetings of the Eastern Psychological Association, New York.

AINSWORTH, M. D. S. (1979). Infant-mother attachment. *American Psychologist, 34,* 932–937.

AJZEN, I. (1988). *Attitudes, personality, and behavior.* Chicago: Dorsey.

AJZEN, I., & FISHBEIN, M. (1977). Attitude-behavior relations: A theoretical analysis and review of empirical research. *Psychological Bulletin, 84,* 888–918.

AJZEN, I., & FISHBEIN, M. (1980). *Understanding attitudes and predicting social behavior.* Englewood Cliffs, NJ: Prentice-Hall.

AJZEN, I., TIMKO, C., & WHITE, J. B. (1982). Self-monitoring and the attitude-behavior relation. *Journal of Personality and Social Psychology, 42,* 426–435.

ALBA, J. W., & HASHER, L. (1983). Is memory schematic? *Psychological Bulletin, 93,* 203–231.

ALBRECHT, J., & LIM, G. C. (1986). A search for alternative planning theory: Use of critical theory. *Journal of Architectural Planning and Research, 3,* 117–132.

ALBRIGHT, L., KENNY, D. A., & MALLOY, T. E. (1988). Consensus in personality judgments at zero acquaintance. *Journal of Personality and Social Psychology, 55,* 387–395.

ALDAG, R. J., & FULLER, S. R. (1993). Beyond fiasco: A reappraisal of the groupthink phenomenon and a new model of group decision processes. *Psychological Bulletin, 113,* 533–552.

ALICKE, M. D. (1992). Culpable causation. *Journal of Personality and Social Psychology, 63,* 368–378.

ALICKE, M. D., BRAUN, J. C., GLOR, J. E., KLOTZ, M. L., MAGEE, J., SEDERHOLM, H., & SIEGEL, R. (1992). Complaining behavior in social interaction. *Personality and Social Psychology Bulletin, 18,* 286–295.

ALLEN, J. B., KENRICK, D. T., LINDER, D. E., & MCCALL, M. A. (1989). Arousal and attraction: A response-facilitation alternative to misattribution and negative-reinforcement models. *Journal of Personality and Social Psychology, 57,* 261–270.

ALLEN, R. D. (Ed.). (1993). Handbook of post-disaster interventions [Special issue]. *Journal of Social Behavior and Personality, 8.*

ALLEN, V. L., & WILDER, D. A. (1980). Impact of group consensus and social support on stimulus meaning: Mediation of conformity by cognitive restructuring. *Journal of Personality and Social Psychology, 39,* 1116–1124.

ALLEY, T. R., & CUNNINGHAM, M. R. (1991). Averaged faces are attractive, but very attractive faces are not average. *Psychological Science, 2,* 123–125.

ALLISON, S. T., MACKIE, D. M., MULLER, M. M., & WORTH, L. T. (1993). Sequential correspondence biases and perceptions of change: The Castro studies revisited. *Personality and Social Psychology Bulletin, 19,* 151–157.

ALLISON, S. T., & MESSICK, D. M. (1985). The group attribution error. *Journal of Experimental Social Psychology, 21,* 563–579.

ALLISON, S. T., WORTH, L. T., & KING, M. C. (1990). Group decisions as social inference heuristics. *Journal of Personality and Social Psychology, 58,* 801–811.

ALLOY, L. B., & ABRAMSON, L. Y. (1988). Depressive realism: Four theoretical perspectives. In L. B. Alloy (Ed.), *Cognitive processes in depression* (pp. 223–265). New York: Guilford.

ALLPORT, F. H. (1924). *Social psychology.* Boston: Houghton Mifflin.

ALLPORT, F. H., ET AL. (1953). The effects of segregation and the consequences of desegregation: A social science statement. *Minneapolis Law Review, 37,* 429–440.

ALLPORT, G. W. (1935). Attitudes. In C. Murchison (Ed.), *Handbook of social psychology*. Worcester, MA: Clark University Press.

ALLPORT, G. W. (1954). *The nature of prejudice.* Reading, MA: Addison-Wesley.

ALLPORT, G. W. (1985). The historical background of modern social psychology. In G. Lindzey & E. Aronson (Eds.), *Handbook of social psychology* (3rd ed., Vol. 1, pp. 1–46). New York: Random House.

ALLPORT, G. W., & POSTMAN, L. J. (1947). *The psychology of rumor.* New York: Henry Holt.

ALTEMEYER, B. (1981). *Right-wing authoritarianism.* Winnipeg, Canada: University of Manitoba Press.

ALTEMEYER, B. (1988). *Enemies of freedom: Understanding right-wing authoritarianism.* San Francisco: Jossey-Bass.

ALTMAN, I. (1975). *The environment and social behavior.* Pacific Grove, CA: Brooks/Cole.

ALTMAN, I. (1976). Privacy: A conceptual analysis. *Environment and Behavior, 8,* 7–29.

ALTMAN, I. (1977). Research on environment and behavior: A personal statement of strategy. In D. Stokols (Ed.), *Perspectives on environment and behavior.* New York: Plenum.

ALTMAN, I., & CHEMERS, M. M. (1980). *Culture and environment.* Pacific Grove, CA: Brooks/Cole.

ALTMAN, I., & HAYTHORNE, W. W. (1967). The ecology of isolated groups. *Behavioral Science, 12,* 169–182.

ALTMAN, I., & TAYLOR, D. A. (1973). *Social penetration: The development of interpersonal relationships.* New York: Holt, Rinehart & Winston.

ALTMAN, I., TAYLOR, D. A., & WHEELER, L. (1971). Ecological aspects of group behavior in social isolation. *Journal of Applied Social Psychology, 1,* 76–100.

ALTMAN, I., & VINSEL, A. M. (1977). Personal space: An analysis of E. T. Hall's proxemics framework. In I. Altman & J. F. Wohlwill (Eds.), *Human behavior and environment: Advances in theory and research* (Vol. 1). New York: Plenum.

ALWIN, D. F., COHEN, R. L., & NEWCOMB, T. M. (1991). *Personality and social change: Attitude persistence and changes over the life-span.* Madison: University of Wisconsin Press.

AMABILE, T. M. (1983a). Brilliant but cruel: Perceptions of negative evaluators. *Journal of Experimental Social Psychology, 19,* 146–156.

AMABILE, T. M. (1983b). *The social psychology of creativity.* New York: Springer-Verlag.

AMABILE, T. M. (1985). Motivation and creativity: Effects of motivational orientation on creative writers. *Journal of Personality and Social Psychology, 48,* 393–399.

AMABILE, T. M., & GLAZEBROOK, A. H. (1982). A negativity bias in interpersonal evaluation. *Journal of Experimental Social Psychology, 18,* 1–22.

AMABILE, T. M., HENNESSEY, B. A., & GROSSMAN, B. S. (1986). Social influence on creativity: The effects of contracted-for reward. *Journal of Personality and Social Psychology, 50,* 14–23.

AMATO, P. R. (1983). Helping behavior in urban and rural environments: Field studies based on a taxonometric organization of helping episodes. *Journal of Personality and Social Psychology, 45,* 571–586.

AMATO, P. R. (1990). Personality and social network involvement as predictors of helping behavior in everyday life. *Social Psychology Quarterly, 53,* 31–43.

AMBADY, N., & ROSENTHAL, R. (1992). Thin slices of expressive behavior as predictors of interpersonal consequences: A meta-analysis. *Psychological Bulletin, 111,* 256–274.

AMES, R. (1975). Teachers' attributions of responsibility: Some unexpected counterdefensive effects. *Journal of Educational Psychology, 67,* 668–676.

ANANND, P., & STERNTHAL B. (1990). Ease of message processing as a moderator of repetition effects in advertising. *Journal of Marketing Research, 27,* 345–353.

ANDERSEN, J. F., ANDERSEN, P. A., & LUSTIG, M. W. (1987). Opposite sex touch avoidance: A national replication and extension. *Journal of Nonverbal Behavior, 11,* 89–109.

ANDERSEN, S. M. (1984). Self-knowledge and social inference: II. The diagnosticity of cognitive/affective and behavioral data. *Journal of Personality and Social Psychology, 46,* 294–307.

ANDERSEN, S. M., & KLATZKY, R. L. (1987). Traits and social stereotypes: Levels of categorization in person perception. *Journal of Personality and Social Psychology, 53,* 235–246.

ANDERSEN, S. M., KLATZKY, R. L., & MURRAY, J. (1990). Traits and social stereotypes: Efficiency differences in social information processing. *Journal of Personality and Social Psychology, 59,* 192–201.

ANDERSEN, S. M., & ROSS, L. (1984). Self-knowledge and social inference: I. The impact of cognitive/affective and behavioral data. *Journal of Personality and Social Psychology, 46,* 280–293.

ANDERSEN, S. M., & WILLIAMS, M. (1985). Cognitive/affective reactions in the improvement of self-esteem: When thoughts and feelings make a difference. *Journal of Personality and Social Psychology, 49,* 1086–1097.

ANDERSON, C. A. (1982). Inoculation and counter-explanation: Debiasing techniques in the perseverance of social theories. *Social Cognition, 1,* 126–139.

ANDERSON, C. A. (1983). The causal structure of situations: The generation of plausible causal attributions as a function of type of event situation. *Journal of Experimental Social Psychology, 19,* 185–203.

ANDERSON, C. A. (1985). Actor and observer attributions for different types of situations: Causal-structure effects, individual differences, and the dimensionality of causes. *Social Cognition, 3,* 323–340.

ANDERSON, C. A. (1987). Temperature and aggression: Effects on quarterly, yearly, and city rates of violent and nonviolent crime. *Journal of Personality and Social Psychology, 49,* 91–97.

ANDERSON, C. A. (1989). Temperature and aggression: Ubiquitous effects of heat on occurrence of human violence. *Psychological Bulletin, 106,* 74–96.

ANDERSON, C. A., & DENEVE, K. M. (1992). Temperature, aggression, and the negative affect escape model. *Psychological Bulletin, 111,* 347–351.

ANDERSON, C. A., LEPPER, M. R., & ROSS, L. (1980). Perseverance of social theories: The role of explanation in the persistence of discredited information. *Journal of Personality and Social Psychology, 39,* 1037–1049.

ANDERSON, C. A., & SECHLER, E. S. (1986). Effects of explanation and counter-explanation on the development and use of social theories. *Journal of Personality and Social Psychology, 50,* 24–34.

ANDERSON, C. A., & SEDIKIDES, C. (1991). Thinking about people: Contributions of a typological alternative to associationistic and dimensional models of person perception. *Journal of Personality and Social Psychology, 60,* 203–217.

ANDERSON, C. A., & SLUSHER, M. P. (1986). Relocating motivational effects: A synthesis of cognitive and motivational effects on attributions for success and failure. *Social Cognition, 4,* 270–292.

ANDERSON, J. R. (1990). *Cognitive psychology and its implications* (3rd ed.). New York: W. H. Freeman.

ANDERSON, N. H. (1965). Averaging versus adding as a stimulus combination rule in impression formation. *Journal of Experimental Psychology, 70,* 394–400.

ANDERSON, N. H. (1991). A cognitive theory of judgment and decision. In N. H. Anderson (Ed.), *Contributions to information integration theory: Cognition* (Vol. 1, pp. 105–142). Hillsdale, NJ: Erlbaum.

ANTHONY, D., & ROBBINS, T. (1992). Law, social science and the "brainwashing" exception to the First Amendment. *Behavioral Sciences and the Law, 10,* 5–29.

ANTHONY, T., COPPER, C., & MULLEN, B. (1992). Cross-racial facial identification: A social cognitive integration. *Personality and Social Psychology Bulletin, 18,* 296–301.

APPLE, W., STREETER, L. A., & KRAUSS, R. M. (1979). Effects of pitch and speech rate on personal attributions. *Journal of Personality and Social Psychology, 37,* 715–727.

APPLETON, J. (1984). Prospects and refuges revisited. *Landscape Journal, 8,* 91–103.

APPLEYARD, D., & LINTELL, M. (1972). The environment quality of city streets: The resident's viewpoint. *Journal of the American Institute of Planners, 38,* 84–101.

ARCHER, D., & AKERT, R. M. (1977). Words and everything else: Verbal and nonverbal cues in social interpretation. *Journal of Personality and Social Psychology, 35,* 443–449.

ARCHER, D., IRITANI, B., KIMES, D. D., & BARRIOS, M. (1983). Face-ism: Five studies of sex differences in facial prominence. *Journal of Personality and Social Psychology, 45,* 725–735.

ARCHER, R. L. (1984). The farmer and the cowman should be friends: An attempt at reconciliation with Batson, Coke, and Pych. *Jour-*

nal of Personality and Social Psychology, 46, 709–711.

Archer, R. L., Diaz-Loving, R., Gollwitzer, P. M., Davis, M. H., & Foushee, H. C. (1981). The role of dispositional empathy and social evaluation in empathic mediation of helping. *Journal of Personality and Social Psychology, 40,* 786–796.

Argyle, M., & Cook, M. (1976). *Gaze and mutual gaze.* Cambridge, England: Cambridge University Press.

Argyle, M., & Dean, J. (1965). Eye contact, distance, and affiliation. *Sociometry, 6,* 32–49.

Arkes, H. R. (1991). Costs and benefits of judgment errors: Implications for debiasing. *Psychological Bulletin, 110,* 486–498.

Arkin, R. M., Appelman, A. J., & Berger, J. M. (1980). Social anxiety, self-presentation, and the self-serving bias in causal attribution. *Journal of Personality and Social Psychology, 38,* 23–35.

Arkin, R. M., & Baumgardner, A. H. (1985). Self-handicapping. In J. H. Harvey & G. Weary (Eds.), *Attribution: Basic issues and applications.* New York: Academic Press.

Arkin, R. M., & Berger, J. M. (1980). Effects of unit relation tendencies on interpersonal attraction. *Social Psychology Quarterly, 43,* 380–391.

Arkin, R. M., & Duval, S. (1975). Focus of attention and causal attributions of actors and observers. *Journal of Experimental Social Psychology, 11,* 427–438.

Armstrong, G. B., Neuendorf, K. A., & Brentar, J. E. (1992). TV entertainment, news, and racial perceptions of college students. *Journal of Communication, 42,* 153–176.

Aron, A., Aron, E. N., & Smollan, D. (1992). Inclusion of Other in the Self Scale and the structure of interpersonal closeness. *Journal of Personality and Social Psychology, 63,* 596–612.

Aronoff, J., & Wilson, J. P. (1985). *Personality in the social process.* Hillsdale, NJ: Erlbaum.

Aronson, E. (1968). Dissonance theory: Progress and problems. In R. P. Abelson, E. Aronson, W. J. McGuire, T. M. Newcomb, M. J. Rosenberg, & P. H. Tannenbaum (Eds.), *Theories of cognitive consistency: A sourcebook* (pp. 5–27). Chicago: Rand McNally.

Aronson, E. (1982). Modifying the environment of the desegregated classroom. In A. J. Stewart (Ed.), *Motivation and society* (pp. 319–336). San Francisco: Jossey-Bass.

Aronson, E. (1989). Analysis, synthesis, and the treasuring of the old. *Personality and Social Psychology Bulletin, 14,* 508–512.

Aronson, E. (1990). Applying social psychology to desegregation and energy conservation. *Personality and Social Psychology Bulletin, 16,* 118–132.

Aronson, E., Carlsmith, J. M., & Darley, J. M. (1963). The effects of expectancy on volunteering for an unpleasant experience. *Journal of Abnormal and Social Psychology, 66,* 220–224.

Aronson, E., & Gonzalez, A. (1988). Desegregation, jigsaw, and the Mexican-American experience. In P. Katz & D. Taylor (Eds.), *Eliminating racism.* New York: Plenum.

Aronson, E., & Linder, D. (1965). Gain and loss of esteem as determinants of interpersonal attractiveness. *Journal of Experimental Social Psychology, 1,* 156–172.

Aronson, E., & Mills, J. (1959). The effects of severity of initiation on liking for a group. *Journal of Abnormal and Social Psychology, 59,* 177–181.

Aronson, E., Stephan, C., Sikes, J., Blaney, N., & Snapp, M. (1978). *The jigsaw classroom.* Newbury Park, CA: Sage.

Asch, S. E. (1946). Forming impressions of personality. *Journal of Abnormal and Social Psychology, 41,* 258–290.

Asch, S. E. (1951). Effects of group pressure on the modification and distortion of judgments. In H. Guetzkow (Ed.), *Groups, leadership, and men.* Pittsburgh, PA: Carnegie Press.

Asch, S. E. (1955). Opinions and social pressures. *Scientific American, 193*(5), 31–35.

Asch, S. E., & Zukier, H. (1984). Thinking about persons. *Journal of Personality and Social Psychology, 46,* 1230–1240.

Aschenbrenner, K. M., & Schaefer, R. E. (1980). Minimal group situations: Comments on a mathematical model and on the research paradigm. *European Journal of Social Psychology, 10,* 389–398.

Asendorpf, J. B., & Meier, G. H. (1993). Personality effects of children's speech in everyday life: Sociability-mediated exposure and shyness-mediated reactivity to social situations. *Journal of Personality and Social Psychology, 64,* 1072–1083.

Ashmore, R. D., & Del Boca, F. K. (1981). Conceptual approaches to stereotypes and stereotyping. In D. Hamilton (Ed.), *Cognitive processes in stereotyping and intergroup behavior* (pp. 1–36). Hillsdale, NJ: Erlbaum.

Ashmore, R. D., Del Boca, F. K., & Wohler, A. J. (1984). Gender stereotypes. In R. D. Ashmore & F. K. Del Boca (Eds.), *The social psychology of female-male relations: A critical analysis of central concepts.* Orlando, FL: Academic Press.

Ashton, N. L., Shaw, M. E., & Worsham, A. P. (1980). Affective reactions to interpersonal distances by friends and strangers. *Bulletin of the Psychonomic Society, 15,* 306–308.

Aspinwall, L. G., Kemeny, M. E., Taylor, S. E., Schneider, S. G., & Dudley, J. P. (1991). Psychosocial predictors of gay men's AIDS risk-reduction behavior. *Health Psychology, 10,* 432–444.

Asterita, M. F. (1985). *The physiology of stress.* New York: Human Sciences Press.

Atkinson, J. W. (Ed.). (1958). *Motives in fantasy, action, and society.* Princeton, NJ: Van Nostrand.

Atkinson, J. W., Heyns, R. W., & Veroff, J. (1954). The effect of experimental arousal of the affiliation motive on thematic apperception. *Journal of Personality and Social Psychology, 49,* 405–410.

Atkinson, R. C., & Shiffrin, R. M. (1968). Human memory: A proposed system and its control. In K. W. Spence & J. T. Spence (Eds.), *The psychology of learning and motivation* (Vol. 2, pp. 89–105). New York: Academic Press.

Atlas, J. (1990). A psychohistorical view of crusade origins. *Journal of Psychohistory, 17,* 412–415.

Averill, J. R. (1983). Studies on anger and aggression: Implications for theories of emotion. *American Psychologist, 38,* 1145–1160.

Averill, J. R. (1985). The social construction of emotion: With special reference to love. In K. J. Gergen & K. E. Davis (Eds.), *The social construction of the person.* New York: Springer-Verlag.

Averill, J. R. (1990). Emotions as episodic dispositions, cognitive schemas, and transitory social roles: Steps toward an integrated theory of emotion. In D. J. Ozer, J. M. Healy, Jr., & A. J. Stewart (Eds.), *Perspectives in personality* (Vol. 3a, pp. 137–165). Greenwich, CT: JAI Press.

Averill, J. R. (1993). Illusions of anger. In R. B. Felson & J. T. Tedeschi (Eds.), *Aggression and violence: Social interactionist perspectives* (pp. 171–191). Washington, DC: American Psychological Association.

Averill, J. R., & Boothroyd, P. (1977). On falling in love in conformance with the romantic ideal. *Motivation and Emotion, 1,* 235–247.

Axsom, D. (1989). Cognitive dissonance and behavior change in psychotherapy. *Journal of Experimental Social Psychology, 25,* 234–252.

Axsom, D., & Cooper, J. (1985). Cognitive dissonance and psychotherapy: The role of effort justification in inducing weight loss. *Journal of Experimental Social Psychology, 21,* 149–160.

Axsom, D., Yates, S., & Chaiken, S. (1987). Audience response as a heuristic cue in persuasion. *Journal of Personality and Social Psychology, 53,* 30–40.

Azrin, N. H. (1967). Pain and aggression. *Psychology Today, 1*(5), 27–33.

Azuma, H. (1984). Secondary control as a heterogeneous category. *American Psychologist, 39,* 970–971.

Backman, C. W. (1985). Identity, self-presentation, and the resolution of moral dilemmas: Towards a social psychology theory of moral behavior. In B. R. Schlenker (Ed.), *The self and social life* (pp. 261–289). New York: McGraw-Hill.

Bagby, R. M., Parker, J. D. A., & Bury, A. S. (1990). A comparative citation analysis of attribution theory and the theory of cognitive dissonance. *Personality and Social Psychology Bulletin, 16,* 274–283.

Bagley, C., & Verma, G. (1979). *Racial prejudice, the individual, and society.* Westmead, England: Saxon House.

Bagozzi, R. P., & Burnkrant, R. E. (1979). Attitude organization and the attitude-behavior relationship. *Journal of Personality and Social Psychology, 37,* 913–929.

Bagozzi, R. P., & Burnkrant, R. E. (1985). Attitude organization and the attitude-behavior relation: A reply to Dillon and

Kumar. *Journal of Personality and Social Psychology, 49,* 47–57.

Bailey, K. G., Hartnett, J. J., & Gibson, F. W., Jr. (1972). Implied threat and the territorial factor in personal space. *Psychological Reports, 30,* 263–270.

Baldwin, J. D., & Baldwin, J. I. (1988). Factors affecting AIDS-related sexual risk-taking behavior among college students. *Journal of Sex Research, 25,* 181–196.

Baldwin, M. W. (1992). Relational schemas and the processing of social information. *Psychological Bulletin, 112,* 461–484.

Bales, R. F. (1950). *Interaction process analysis: A method for the study of small groups.* Reading, MA: Addison-Wesley.

Bales, R. F. (1965). The equilibrium problem in small groups. In A. P. Hare, E. F. Borgatta, & R. F. Bales (Eds.), *Small groups: Studies in social interaction.* New York: Knopf.

Bales, R. F. (1970). *Personality and interpersonal behavior.* New York: Holt, Rinehart & Winston.

Bales, R. F. (1980). *SYMLOG case study kit.* New York: Free Press.

Bandler, R. J., Jr., Madaras, G. R., & Bem, D. J. (1968). Self-observation as a source of pain perception. *Journal of Personality and Social Psychology, 9,* 205–209.

Bandura, A. (1969). *Principles of behavior modification.* Stanford, CA: Stanford University Press.

Bandura, A. (1973). *Aggression: A social learning analysis.* Englewood Cliffs, NJ: Prentice-Hall.

Bandura, A. (1977). *Social learning theory.* Englewood Cliffs, NJ: Prentice-Hall.

Bandura, A. (1983). Psychological mechanisms of aggression. In R. G. Geen & E. I. Donnerstein (Eds.), *Aggression: Theoretical and empirical reviews* (Vol. 1, pp. 1–40). New York: Academic Press.

Bandura, A. (1986). *Social foundations of thought and action: A social-cognitive theory.* Englewood Cliffs, NJ: Prentice-Hall.

Bandura, A., Ross, D., & Ross, S. A. (1961). Transmission of aggression through imitation of aggressive models. *Journal of Abnormal and Social Psychology, 63,* 575–582.

Bandura, A., Ross, D., & Ross, S. A. (1963a). Imitation of film-mediated aggressive models. *Journal of Abnormal and Social Psychology, 66,* 3–11.

Bandura, A., Ross, D., & Ross, S. A. (1963b). Vicarious reinforcement and imitative learning. *Journal of Abnormal and Social Psychology, 67,* 601–607.

Bandura, A., & Schunk, D. H. (1981). Cultivating competence, self-efficacy, and interest through proximal self-motivation. *Journal of Personality and Social Psychology, 41,* 586–598.

Banuazizi, A. (1981). *An evaluation of the first year's activities of the National Demonstration Title II Project.* Cambridge, MA: Basic Skills Improvement Program.

Banzai, T. (1983). The effect of observers' point of view on their causal attribution of actors' performance. *Japanese Journal of Psychology, 53,* 365–371.

Bar-Tal, D. (1976). *Prosocial behavior: Theory and research.* Washington, DC: Hemisphere.

Bar-Tal, D., Goldberg, M., & Knaani, A. (1984). Causes of success and failure and their dimensions as a function of SES and gender: A phenomenological analysis. *British Journal of Educational Psychology, 54,* 51–61.

Barash, D. P. (1976). The male response to apparent female adultery in the mountain bluebird, *Sialia currucoides*: An evolutionary interpretation. *American Naturalist, 110,* 1097–1101.

Barash, D. P. (1982). *Sociobiology and behavior* (2nd ed.). New York: Elsevier.

Barber, T. X. (1976). *Pitfalls in human research.* New York: Pergamon.

Barber, T. X., & Silver, M. J. (1968a). Fact, fiction, and the experimenter bias effect (Monograph Supplement). *Psychological Bulletin, 70,* 1–29.

Barber, T. X., & Silver, M. J. (1968b). Pitfalls in data analysis and interpretation: A reply to Rosenthal (Monograph Supplement). *Psychological Bulletin, 70,* 48–62.

Bargh, J. A. (1984). Automatic and conscious processing of social information. In R. S. Wyer & T. K. Srull (Eds.), *Handbook of social cognition* (Vol. 3). Hillsdale, NJ: Erlbaum.

Bargh, J. A. (1990). Auto-motives: Preconscious determinants of social interaction. In E. T. Higgins & R. M. Sorrentino (Eds.), *Handbook of motivation and cognition: Foundations of social behavior* (Vol. 2, pp. 93–130). New York: Guilford Press.

Bargh, J. A., Bond, R. N., Lombardi, W. L., & Tota, M. E. (1986). The additive nature of chronic and temporary sources of construct accessibility. *Journal of Personality and Social Psychology, 50,* 869–879.

Bargh, J. A., Chaiken, S., Govender, R., & Pratto, F. (1992). The generality of the automatic attitude activation effect. *Journal of Personality and Social Psychology, 62,* 893–912.

Bargh, J. A., & Pietromonaco, P. (1982). Automatic information processing and social perception: The influence of trait information presented outside of conscious awareness on impression formation. *Journal of Personality and Social Psychology, 43,* 437–449.

Barker, R. G. (1968). *Ecological psychology.* Stanford, CA: Stanford University Press.

Barker, R. G. (1987). Prospecting in ecological psychology: Oskaloosa revisited. In D. Stokols & I. Altman (Eds.), *Handbook of environmental psychology* (Vol. 2, pp. 1413–1432). New York: Wiley.

Baron, J., & Jurney, J. (1993). Norms against voting for coerced reform. *Journal of Personality and Social Psychology, 64,* 347–355.

Baron, R. A. (1972). Aggression as a function of ambient temperature and prior anger arousal. *Journal of Personality and Social Psychology, 21,* 183–189.

Baron, R. A. (1977). *Human aggression.* New York: Plenum.

Baron, R. A. (1978). Aggression and heat: The "long hot summer" revisited. In A. Baum, J. E. Singer, & S. Valins (Eds.), *Advances in environmental psychology* (Vol. 1). Hillsdale, NJ: Erlbaum.

Baron, R. A. (1979). Aggression, empathy, and race: Effects of victim's pain cues, victim's race, and level of instigation on physical aggression. *Journal of Applied Social Psychology, 9,* 103–114.

Baron, R. A. (1983). The control of human aggression: A strategy based on incompatible responses. In R. G. Geen & E. I. Donnerstein (Eds.), *Aggression: Theoretical and empirical reviews* (Vol. 2, pp. 173–190). New York: Academic Press.

Baron, R. A., & Ball, R. L. (1974). The aggression-inhibiting influence of nonhostile humor. *Journal of Experimental Social Psychology, 10,* 23–33.

Baron, R. A., & Bell, P. A. (1975). Aggression and heat: Mediating effects of prior provocation and exposure to an aggressive model. *Journal of Personality and Social Psychology, 31,* 825–832.

Baron, R. A., & Bell, P. A. (1976). Aggression and heat: The influence of ambient temperature, negative affect, and a cooling drink on physical aggression. *Journal of Personality and Social Psychology, 33,* 245–255.

Baron, R. A., & Richardson, D. R. (1994). *Human aggression* (2nd ed.). New York: Plenum.

Baron, R. M., & Harvey, J. H. (1980). Contrasting perspectives on social knowing: An overview. *Personality and Social Psychology Bulletin, 6,* 502–506.

Baron, R. S. (1986). Distraction-conflict theory: Progress and problems. In L. Berkowitz (Ed.), *Advances in experimental social psychology* (Vol. 19, pp. 1–40). New York: Academic Press.

Baron, R. S., Kerr, N. L., & Miller, N. (1992). *Group process, group decision, group action.* Pacific Grove, CA: Brooks/Cole.

Barrera, M., Jr. (1986). Distinctions between social support concepts, measures, and models. *American Journal of Community Psychology, 14,* 413–422.

Bartlett, F. A. (1932). *A study in experimental and social psychology.* New York: Cambridge University Press.

Bartolini, T., Kresge, J., McLennan, M., & Windham, B. (1988). Perceptions of personal characteristics of men and women under three conditions of eyewear. *Perceptual and Motor Skills, 67,* 779–782.

Bass, B. M. (1985a). Good, better, best. *Organizational Dynamics, 13,* 26–40.

Bass, B. M. (1985b). *Leadership and performance beyond expectations.* New York: Free Press.

Bass, B. M., Avolio, B. J., & Goldheim, L. (1987). Biography and the assessment of transformational leadership at the world-class level. *Journal of Management, 13,* 7–19.

Batson, C. D. (1975). Rational processing or rationalization? The effect of disconfirming information on a state religious belief. *Journal of Personality and Social Psychology, 32,* 176–184.

Batson, C. D. (1987). Prosocial motivation: Is it ever truly altruistic? In L. Berkowitz

(Ed.), *Advances in experimental social psychology* (Vol. 20, pp. 65–122). New York: Academic Press.

Batson, C. D. (1990). How social an animal? The human capacity for caring. *American Psychologist, 45,* 336–346.

Batson, C. D. (1991). *The altruism question: Toward a social-psychological answer.* Hillsdale, NJ: Erlbaum.

Batson, C. D., Batson, J. G., Slingsby, J. K., Harrell, K. L., Peekna, H. M., & Todd, R. M. (1991). Empathic joy and the empathy-altruism hypothesis. *Journal of Personality and Social Psychology, 61,* 413–426.

Batson, C. D., Bolen, M. H., Cross, J. A., & Neuringer-Benefiel, H. (1986). Where is the altruism in the altruistic personality? *Journal of Personality and Social Psychology, 50,* 212–220.

Batson, C. D., Coke, J. S., & Pych, V. (1983). Limits on the two-stage model of empathic mediation of helping: A reply to Archer, Diaz-Loving, Gollwitzer, Davis, and Foushee. *Journal of Personality and Social Psychology, 45,* 895–898.

Batson, C. D., Duncan, B. D., Ackerman, P., Buckley, T., & Birch, K. (1981). Is empathic emotion a source of altruistic motivation? *Journal of Personality and Social Psychology, 40,* 290–302.

Batson, C. D., Dyck, J. L., Brandt, J. R., Batson, J. G., Powell, A. L., McMaster, M. R., & Griffitt, C. (1988). Five studies testing two new egoistic alternatives to the empathy-altruism hypothesis. *Journal of Personality and Social Psychology, 55,* 52–77.

Batson, C. D., Flink, C. H., Schoenrade, P. A., Fultz, J., & Pych, V. (1986). Religious orientation and overt versus covert racial prejudice. *Journal of Personality and Social Psychology, 50,* 175–181.

Batson, C. D., Fultz, J., & Schoenrade, P. A. (1987). Distress and empathy: Two qualitatively distinct vicarious emotions with different motivational consequences. *Journal of Personality, 55,* 19–39.

Batson, C. D., & Oleson, K. C. (1991). Current status of the empathy-altruism hypothesis. In M. S. Clark (Ed.), *Review of personality and social psychology* (Vol. 12, pp. 62–85). Newbury Park, CA: Sage.

Baum, A., Calesnick, L. E., Davis, G. E., & Gatchel, R. J. (1982). Individual differences in coping with crowding: Stimulus screening and social overload. *Journal of Personality and Social Psychology, 43,* 821–830.

Baum, A., & Davis, G. E. (1980). Reducing the stress of high-density living: An architectural intervention. *Journal of Personality and Social Psychology, 38,* 471–481.

Baum, A., Flemin, I., Israel, I., Israel, A., & O'Keeffe, M. K. (1992). Symptoms of chronic stress following a natural disaster and discovery of a human-made hazard. *Environment and Behavior, 24,* 347–365.

Baum, A., Harpin, R. E., & Valins, S. (1975). The role of group phenomena in the experience of crowding. *Environment and Behavior, 7,* 185–198.

Baum, A., & Valins, S. (1977). *Architecture and social behavior: Psychological studies of social density.* Hillsdale, NJ: Erlbaum.

Baum, A., & Valins, S. (1979). Architectural mediation of residential density and control: Crowding and the regulation of social contact. In L. Berkowitz (Ed.), *Advances in experimental social psychology* (Vol. 12). Orlando, FL: Academic Press.

Baumann, D. J., Cialdini, R. B., & Kenrick, D. T. (1981). Altruism as hedonism: Helping and self-gratification as equivalent responses. *Journal of Personality and Social Psychology, 40,* 1039–1046.

Baumeister, R. F. (1984). Choking under pressure: Self-consciousness and paradoxical effects of incentives on skillful performance. *Journal of Personality and Social Psychology, 46,* 610–620.

Baumeister, R. F. (1985). The championship choke. *Psychology Today, 19*(4), 48–52.

Baumeister, R. F. (1986). *Public self and private self.* New York: Springer.

Baumeister, R. F. (1987). How the self became a problem: A psychological review of historical research. *Journal of Personality and Social Psychology, 52,* 163–176.

Baumeister, R. F. (1989). *Masochism and the self.* Hillsdale, NJ: Erlbaum.

Baumeister, R. F. (1990a). Anxiety and deconstruction: On escaping the self. In J. M. Olson & M. P. Zanna (Eds.), *Self-inference processes: The Ontario Symposium* (Vol. 6, pp. 259–292). Hillsdale, NJ: Erlbaum.

Baumeister, R. F. (1990b). Suicide as escape from self. *Psychological Review, 97,* 90–113.

Baumeister, R. F. (1991). *Escaping the self: Alcoholism, spirituality, masochism, and other flights from the burden of selfhood.* New York: Basic Books.

Baumeister, R. F., Hamilton, J. C., & Tice, D. M. (1985). Public versus private expectancy of success: Confidence booster or performance pressure? *Journal of Personality and Social Psychology, 48,* 1447–1457.

Baumeister, R. F., & Jones, E. E. (1978). When self-presentation is constrained by the target's knowledge: Consistency and compensation. *Journal of Personality and Social Psychology, 36,* 608–618.

Baumeister, R. F., & Steinhilber, A. (1984). Paradoxical effects of supportive audience on performance under pressure: The home field disadvantage in sports championships. *Journal of Personality and Social Psychology, 47,* 85–93.

Baumeister, R. F., Stillwell, A., & Wotman, S. R. (1990). Victim and perpetrator accounts of interpersonal conflict: Autobiographical narratives about anger. *Journal of Personality and Social Psychology, 59,* 994–1005.

Baumeister, R. F., & Tice, D. M. (1984). Role of self-presentation and choice in cognitive dissonance under forced compliance: Necessary or sufficient causes? *Journal of Personality and Social Psychology, 46,* 5–13.

Baumeister, R. F., & Tice, D. M. (1985). Self-esteem and responses to success and failure: Subsequent performance and intrinsic motivation. *Journal of Personality, 53,* 450–467.

Baumeister, R. F., & Tice, D. M. (1990). Anxiety and social exclusion. *Journal of Social and Clinical Psychology, 9,* 165–195.

Baumeister, R. F., Tice, D. M., & Hutton, D. G. (1989). Self-presentational motivations and personality differences in self-esteem. *Journal of Personality, 57,* 547–579.

Baumgardner, A. H., Lake, E. A., & Arkin, R. M. (1985). Claiming mood as a self-handicap: The influence of spoiled and unspoiled public identities. *Personality and Social Psychology Bulletin, 11,* 349–357.

Baumrind, D. (1964). Some thoughts on the ethics of research: After reading Milgram's "Behavioral study of obedience." *American Psychologist, 19,* 421–423.

Baxter, L. A. (1986). Gender differences in the heterosexual relationship rules embedded in break-up accounts. *Journal of Social and Personal Relationships, 3,* 389–406.

Baxter, L. A. (1987). Self-disclosure and relationship development. In V. J. Derlega & J. Berg (Eds.), *Self-disclosure: Theory, research, and therapy* (pp. 155–174). New York: Plenum.

Baxter, T. L., & Goldberg, L. R. (1987). Perceived behavioral consistency underlying trait attributions to oneself and another: An extension of the actor-observer effect. *Personality and Social Psychology Bulletin, 13,* 437–447.

Beaman, A. L. (1991). An empirical comparison of meta-analytic and traditional reviews. *Personality and Social Psychology Bulletin, 17,* 252–257.

Beaman, A. L., Cole, C. M., Preston, M., Klentz, B., & Steblay, N. M. (1983). Fifteen years of foot-in-the-door research: A meta-analysis. *Personality and Social Psychology Bulletin, 9,* 181–196.

Beauvois, J. L., & Joule, R. V. (1982). Dissonance versus self-perception theories: A radical conception of Festinger's theory. *Journal of Social Psychology, 117,* 99–113.

Becker, L., & Seligman, C. (1978). Reducing air-conditioning waste by signaling it is cool outside. *Personality and Social Psychology Bulletin, 4,* 412–415.

Beggan, J. K. (1992). On the social nature of nonsocial perception: The mere ownership effect. *Journal of Personality and Social Psychology, 62,* 229–237.

Belk, S. S., Snell, W. E., Jr., Garcia-Falconi, R., Hernandez-Sanchez, J. E., Hargrove, L., & Holtzman, W. H., Jr. (1988). Power strategy use in the intimate relationships of women and men from Mexico and the United States. *Personality and Social Psychology Bulletin, 14,* 439–447.

Bell, P. A. (1981). Physiological, comfort, performance, and social effects of heat stress. *Journal of Social Issues, 37,* 71–94.

Bell, P. A. (1992). In defense of the negative affect escape model of heat and aggression. *Psychological Bulletin, 111,* 342–346.

Bell, P. A., Fisher, J. D., Baum, A., & Greene, T. E. (1990). *Environmental psychology* (4th ed.). Fort Worth, TX: Holt, Rinehart & Winston.

Bell, P. A., & Fusco, M. E. (1989). Heat and violence in the Dallas field data: Linearity, curvilinearity, and heteroscedasticity. *Journal of Applied Social Psychology, 19,* 1479–1482.

Bell, P. A., & Greene, T. C. (1982). Thermal stress: Physiological, comfort, performance, and social effects of hot and cold environments. In G. W. Evans (Ed.), *Environmental stress.* London: Cambridge University Press.

Bem, D. J. (1965). An experimental analysis of self-persuasion. *Journal of Experimental Social Psychology, 1,* 199–218.

Bem, D. J. (1972). Self-perception theory. In L. Berkowitz (Ed.), *Advances in experimental social psychology* (Vol. 6). New York: Academic Press.

Bem, D. J., & Allen, A. (1974). On predicting some of the people some of the time: The search for cross-situational consistencies in behavior. *Psychological Review, 81,* 506–520.

Bem, S. L. (1975). Sex role adaptability: One consequence of psychological androgyny. *Journal of Personality and Social Psychology, 31,* 634–643.

Bem, S. L. (1985). Androgyny and gender schema theory: A conceptual and empirical integration. *Nebraska Symposium on Motivation, 32,* 179–226.

Bennett, R., Rafferty, J. M., Canivez, G. L., & Smith, J. M. (1983). *The effects of cold temperature on altruism and aggression.* Paper presented at the meeting of the Midwestern Psychological Association, Chicago, IL.

Benson, M. J. (1989). Attributional measurement techniques: Classification and comparison of approaches for measuring causal dimensions. *Journal of Social Psychology, 129,* 307–323.

Benson, P. L., Karabenick, S. A., & Lerner, R. M. (1976). Pretty pleases: The effects of physical attractiveness, race, and sex on receiving help. *Journal of Experimental Social Psychology, 12,* 409–415.

Bentler, P. M., & Speckart, G. (1981). Attitudes "cause" behaviors: A structural equation analysis. *Journal of Personality and Social Psychology, 40,* 226–238.

Benware, C., & Deci, E. L. (1975). Attitude change as a function of the inducement for espousing a proattitudinal communication. *Journal of Experimental Social Psychology, 11,* 271–278.

Berg, J. H. (1984). Development of friendship between roommates. *Journal of Personality and Social Psychology, 46,* 346–356.

Berg, J. H., & McQuinn, R. D. (1986). Attraction and exchange in continuing and noncontinuing dating relationships. *Journal of Personality and Social Psychology, 50,* 942–952.

Berger, J. (1992). Expectations, theory, and group processes. *Social Psychology Quarterly, 55,* 3–11.

Berger, J., Webster, M., Jr., Ridgeway, C., & Rosenholtz, S. J. (1986). Status cues, expectations, and behavior. In E. J. Lawler (Ed.), *Advances in group processes* (Vol. 3, pp. 1–22). Greenwich, CT: JAI Press.

Berger, S. M., Carli, L. C., Garcia, R., & Brady, J. J., Jr. (1982). Audience effects in anticipatory learning: A comparison of drive and practice-inhibition analyses. *Journal of Personality and Social Psychology, 42,* 478–486.

Berger, S. M., Hampton, K. L., Carli, L. L., Grandmaison, P. S., Sadow, J. S., Donath, C. H., & Herschlag, L. R. (1981). Audience-induced inhibition of overt practice during learning. *Journal of Personality and Social Psychology, 40,* 479–491.

Berglas, S., & Jones, E. E. (1978). Drug choice as a self-handicapping strategy in response to noncontingent success. *Journal of Personality and Social Psychology, 36,* 405–417.

Berkman, L. F., & Syme, S. L. (1979). Social networks, host resistance, and mortality: A nine-year follow-up study of Alameda County residents. *American Journal of Epidemiology, 109,* 186–204.

Berkowitz, L. (1970). The contagion of violence: An S-R mediational analysis of some effects of observed aggression. *Nebraska Symposium on Motivation, 18,* 95–135.

Berkowitz, L. (1972). Social norms, feelings, and other factors affecting helping and altruism. In L. Berkowitz (Ed.), *Advances in experimental social psychology* (Vol. 6). New York: Academic Press.

Berkowitz, L. (1981a). Aversive conditions as stimuli for aggression. In L. Berkowitz (Ed.), *Advances in experimental social psychology* (Vol. 15). New York: Academic Press.

Berkowitz, L. (1981b). How guns control us. *Psychology Today, 15*(6), 11–12.

Berkowitz, L. (1981c). *When the "trigger" pulls the finger.* Washington, DC: American Psychological Association.

Berkowitz, L. (1983). The experience of anger as a parallel process in the display of impulsive, "angry" aggression. In R. G. Geen & E. I. Donnerstein (Eds.), *Aggression: Theoretical and empirical reviews* (Vol. 1, pp. 103–134). New York: Academic Press.

Berkowitz, L. (1984). Some effects of thoughts on anti- and prosocial influences of media events: A cognitive-neoassociation analysis. *Psychological Bulletin, 95,* 410–427.

Berkowitz, L. (Ed.). (1988). *Advances in experimental social psychology* (Vol. 21). New York: Academic Press.

Berkowitz, L. (1989). Frustration-aggression hypothesis: Examination and reformulation. *Psychological Bulletin, 106,* 59–73.

Berkowitz, L. (1990). On the formation and regulation of anger and aggression: A cognitive-neoassociationistic analysis. *American Psychologist, 45,* 494–503.

Berkowitz, L. (1993). *Aggression: Its causes, consequences, and control.* New York: McGraw-Hill.

Berkowitz, L., Cochran, S., & Embree, M. (1981). Physical pain and the goal of aversively stimulated aggression. *Journal of Personality and Social Psychology, 40,* 687–700.

Berkowitz, L., & Connor, W. H. (1966). Success, failure, and social responsibility. *Journal of Personality and Social Psychology, 4,* 664–669.

Berkowitz, L., & Daniels, L. R. (1963). Responsibility and dependency. *Journal of Abnormal and Social Psychology, 66,* 664–669.

Berkowitz, L., & Devine, P. G. (1989a). Research traditions, analysis, and synthesis in social psychological theories: The case of dissonance theory. *Personality and Social Psychology Bulletin, 14,* 493–507.

Berkowitz, L., & Devine, P. G. (1989b). Some comment in reply: Analysis, synthesis, and contemporary social psychology. *Personality and Social Psychology Bulletin, 14,* 530–532.

Berkowitz, L., & Donnerstein, E. I. (1982). External validity is more than skin deep: Some answers to criticisms of laboratory experiments. *American Psychologist, 37,* 245–257.

Berkowitz, L., & Heimer, K. (1989). On the construction of the anger experience: Aversive events and negative priming in the formation of feelings. In L. Berkowitz (Ed.), *Advances in experimental social psychology* (Vol. 22, pp. 1–38). Orlando, FL: Academic Press.

Berkowitz, L., Klanderman, S. B., & Harris, R. (1964). Effects of experimenter awareness and sex of subject and experimenter on reactions to dependency relationship. *Sociometry, 27,* 327–332.

Berkowitz, L., & LePage, A. (1967). Weapons as aggression-eliciting stimuli. *Journal of Personality and Social Psychology, 7,* 202–207.

Berry, D. S. (1990). Taking people at face value: Evidence for the kernel of truth hypothesis. *Social Cognition, 8,* 343–361.

Berry, D. S. (1991). Accuracy in social perception: Contributions of facial and vocal information. *Journal of Personality and Social Psychology, 61,* 298–307.

Berry, D. S., & Brownlow, S. (1989). Were the physiognomists right? Personality correlates of facial babyishness. *Personality and Social Psychology Bulletin, 15,* 266–279.

Berry, D. S., & McArthur, L. Z. (1985). Some components and consequences of a babyface. *Journal of Personality and Social Psychology, 48,* 312–323.

Berry, D. S., & McArthur, L. Z. (1986). Perceiving character in faces: The impact of age-related craniofacial changes on social perception. *Psychological Bulletin, 100,* 3–18.

Berry, D. S., & Zebrowitz-McArthur, L. (1988). What's in a face? Facial maturity and the attribution of legal responsibility. *Personality and Social Psychology Bulletin, 14,* 23–33.

Berscheid, E. (1983). Emotion. In H. H. Kelley, E. Berscheid, A. Christensen, J. H. Harvey, T. L. Huston, G. Levinger, E. McClintock, L. A. Peplau, & D. R. Peterson, *Close relationships.* New York: W. H. Freeman.

Berscheid, E. (1985). Interpersonal attraction. In G. Lindzey & E. Aronson (Eds.), *Handbook of social psychology* (3rd ed., Vol. 2). New York: Random House.

Berscheid, E. (1992). A glance back at a quarter century of social psychology. *Journal of Personality and Social Psychology, 63,* 525–533.

Berscheid, E., Graziano, W., Monson, T. C., & Dermer, M. (1976). Outcome dependency: Attention, attribution, and attraction.

Journal of Personality and Social Psychology, 34, 978–989.

Berscheid, E., Snyder, M., & Omoto, A. M. (1989). The Relationship Closeness Inventory: Assessing the closeness of interpersonal relationships. *Journal of Personality and Social Psychology, 57,* 792–807.

Berscheid, E., & Walster, E. H. (1978). *Interpersonal attraction* (2nd ed.). Reading, MA: Addison-Wesley.

Bickman, L. (1971). The effect of another bystander's ability to help on bystander intervention in an emergency. *Journal of Experimental Social Psychology, 7,* 367–379.

Bickman, L. (1972a). Environmental attitudes and actions. *Journal of Social Psychology, 87,* 323–324.

Bickman, L. (1972b). Social influence and diffusion of responsibility in an emergency. *Journal of Experimental Social Psychology, 8,* 438–445.

Bickman, L. (1974). Clothes make the person. *Psychology Today, 8*(4), 48–51.

Bickman, L. (1983). Introduction: Applied social psychology and education. In L. Bickman (Ed.), *Applied social psychology annual* (Vol. 4, pp. 7–19). Newbury Park, CA: Sage.

Bickman, L., & Rosenbaum, D. P. (1977). Crime reporting as a function of bystander encouragement, surveillance, and credibility. *Journal of Personality and Social Psychology, 35,* 577–586.

Biernat, M., & Wortman, C. B. (1991). Sharing of home responsibilities between professionally employed women and their husbands. *Journal of Personality and Social Psychology, 60,* 844–860.

Biggers, T., & Pryor, B. (1982). Attitude change: A function of emotion-eliciting qualities of the environment. *Personality and Social Psychology Bulletin, 8,* 94–99.

Birchler, G. R., Weiss, R. L., & Vincent, J. P. (1975). Multimethod analysis of social reinforcement exchange between maritally distressed and nondistressed spouse and stranger dyads. *Journal of Personality and Social Psychology, 31,* 349–360.

Birnbaum, M. H. (1974). The nonadditivity of personality impression (Monograph). *Journal of Experimental Psychology, 102,* 543–561.

Bither, S. W., Dolich, I. J., & Nell, E. B. (1971). The application of attitude immunization techniques in marketing. *Journal of Marketing Research, 8,* 56–61.

Blake, J. A. (1978). Death by hand grenade: Altruistic suicide in combat. *Suicide and Life-Threatening Behavior, 8,* 46–59.

Blanchard, F. A., Adelman, L., & Cook, S. W. (1975). Effect of group success and failure upon interpersonal attraction in cooperating interracial groups. *Journal of Personality and Social Psychology, 31,* 1020–1030.

Blanchard, F. A., & Cook, S. W. (1976). Effects of helping a less competent member of a cooperating interracial group on the development of interpersonal attraction. *Journal of Personality and Social Psychology, 34,* 1245–1255.

Blanchard, F. A., Tilly, T., & Vaughn, L. A. (1991). Reducing the expression of racial prejudice. *Psychological Science, 2,* 101–105.

Blanchard, F. A., Weigel, R. H., & Cook, S. W. (1975). The effect of relative competence of group members upon interpersonal attraction in cooperating interracial groups. *Journal of Personality and Social Psychology, 32,* 519–530.

Blascovich, J., Ginsburg, G. P., & Howe, R. C. (1975). Blackjack and the risky shift: II. Monetary stakes. *Journal of Experimental Social Psychology, 11,* 224–232.

Blascovich, J., Ginsburg, G. P., & Howe, R. C. (1976). Blackjack, choice shifts in the field. *Sociometry, 39,* 274–276.

Blascovich, J., & Kelsey, R. M. (1990). Using electrodermal and cardiovascular measures of arousal in social psychological research. In C. Hendrick & M. S. Clark (Eds.), *Review of personality and social psychology* (Vol. 11, pp. 45–73). Newbury Park, CA: Sage.

Blascovich, J., Nash, R. F., & Ginsburg, G. P. (1978). Heart rate and competitive decision making. *Personality and Social Psychology Bulletin, 4,* 115–118.

Blass, T. (1991). Understanding behavior in the Milgram obedience experiment: The role of personality, situations, and their interactions. *Journal of Personality and Social Psychology, 60,* 398–413.

Blass, T., & Kaplowitz, H. (1990). A longitudinal study of the actor-observer attributional effect. *Personality and Individual Differences, 11,* 259–264.

Blau, P. M. (1964). *Exchange and power in social life.* New York: Wiley.

Bliese, J. R. (1990). The motives of the First Crusaders: A social psychological analysis. *Journal of Psychohistory, 17,* 393–411.

Blumstein, P., & Schwartz, P. (1983). *American couples.* New York: Morrow.

Bobo, L. (1983). Whites' opposition to busing: Symbolic racism or realistic group conflict? *Journal of Personality and Social Psychology, 45,* 1196–1210.

Bochner, S., & Insko, C. A. (1966). Communicator discrepancy, source credibility, and opinion change. *Journal of Personality and Social Psychology, 4,* 614–621.

Bodenhausen, G. V., Gaelick, L., & Wyer, R. S., Jr. (1987). Affective and cognitive factors in intragroup and intergroup communication. In C. Hendrick (Ed.), *Review of personality and social psychology: Group process* (Vol. 9, pp. 137–166). Newbury Park, CA: Sage.

Boggiano, A. K., & Katz, P. (1991). Maladaptive achievement patterns in students: The role of teachers' controlling strategies. *Journal of Social Issues, 47*(4), 35–51.

Bond, C. F. (1982). Social facilitation: A self-presentational view. *Journal of Personality and Social Psychology, 42,* 1042–1050.

Bond, C. F., & Anderson, E. L. (1987). The reluctance to transmit bad news: Private discomfort or public display? *Journal of Experimental Social Psychology, 23,* 176–187.

Bond, C. F., & Titus, L. J. (1983). Social facilitation: A meta-analysis of 241 studies. *Psychological Bulletin, 94,* 265–292.

Bond, C. F., & Van Leeuwen, M. D. (1991). Can a part be greater than a whole? On the relationship between primary and meta-analytic misinterpretations. *Basic and Applied Social Psychology, 12,* 33–40.

Bond, M. H. (1988). *The cross-cultural challenge to social psychology.* Newbury Park, CA: Sage.

Bond, M. H., Wan, K., Leung, K., & Giacalone, R. A. (1985). How are responses to verbal insult related to cultural collectivism and power distance? *Journal of Cross-Cultural Psychology, 16,* 111–127.

Bonnes, M., Bonaiuto, M., & Ercolani, A. P. (1991). Crowding and residential satisfaction in the urban environment: A contextual approach. *Environment and Behavior, 23,* 531–552.

Booth, A. (1976). *Urban crowding and its consequences.* New York: Praeger.

Borgida, E. (1981). Legal reform of rape laws. In L. Bickman (Ed.), *Applied social psychology annual* (Vol. 2). Newbury Park, CA: Sage.

Borgida, E., & Brekke, N. (1981). The base-rate fallacy in attribution and prediction. In J. H. Harvey, W. J. Ickes, & R. F. Kidd (Eds.), *New directions in attribution research* (Vol. 3). Hillsdale, NJ: Erlbaum.

Borgida, E., & Campbell, B. (1982). Belief relevance and attitude-behavior consistency: The moderating role of personal experience. *Journal of Personality and Social Psychology, 42,* 239–247.

Bornstein, F., Crum, L., Wittenbraker, J., Harring, K., Insko, C. A., & Thibaut, J. (1983). On the measurement of social orientations in the Minimal Group Paradigm. *European Journal of Social Psychology, 13,* 321–350.

Bornstein, R. F. (1989). Exposure and affect: Overview and meta-analysis of research, 1968–1987. *Psychological Bulletin, 106,* 265–289.

Bornstein, R. F. (1992). The dependent personality: Developmental, social, and clinical perspectives. *Psychological Bulletin, 112,* 3–23.

Bornstein, R. F., Leone, D. R., & Galley, D. J. (1987). The generalizability of subliminal mere exposure effects: Influence of stimuli perceived without awareness on social behavior. *Journal of Personality and Social Psychology, 53,* 1070–1079.

Borofsky, G. L., Stollak, G. E., & Messe, L. A. (1971). Sex differences in bystander reactions to physical assault. *Journal of Experimental Social Psychology, 7,* 313–318.

Bouchard, T. J. (1972). Training, motivation, and personality as determinants of the effectiveness of brainstorming groups and individuals. *Journal of Applied Psychology, 56,* 324–331.

Bouchard, T. J., Barsaloux, J., & Drauden, G. (1974). Brainstorming procedure, group size, and sex as determinants of the problem-solving effectiveness of groups and individuals. *Journal of Applied Psychology, 59,* 226–227.

Bouchard, T. J., Drauden, G., & Barsaloux, J. (1974). A comparison of individual, subgroup, and total group methods of problem solving. *Journal of Applied Psychology, 59,* 226–227.

Bouchard, T. J., & Hare, M. (1970). Size, performance, and potential in brainstorming groups. *Journal of Applied Psychology, 54,* 51–55.

Bourne, E. (1977). Can we describe an individual's personality? Agreement on stereotype versus individual attributions. *Journal of Personality and Social Psychology, 35,* 863–872.

Bowdle, B., Nisbett, R. E., & Schwarz, N. (1993). *Regional differences in responses to insults.* Unpublished manuscript, University of Michigan.

Bower, G. H. (1981). Mood and memory. *American Psychologist, 36,* 129–148.

Bradbury, T. N., & Fincham, F. D. (1990). Attributions in marriage: Review and critique. *Psychological Bulletin, 107,* 3–33.

Bradbury, T. N., & Fincham, F. D. (1992). Attributions and behavior in marital interaction. *Journal of Personality and Social Psychology, 63,* 613–628.

Bramel, D. (1968). Dissonance, expectation, and the self. In R. P. Abelson, E. Aronson, W. J. McGuire, T. M. Newcomb, M. J. Rosenberg, & P. H. Tannenbaum (Eds.), *Theories of cognitive consistency: A sourcebook.* Chicago: Rand McNally.

Bramel, D., & Friend, R. (1981). Hawthorne, the myth of the docile worker, and class bias in psychology. *American Psychologist, 36,* 867–878.

Branthwaite, A., & Peirce, L. (1990). The portrayal of black people in British television advertisements. *Social Behavior, 5,* 327–334.

Brawley, L. R. (1984). Unintentional egocentric biases in attributions. *Journal of Sport Psychology, 6,* 264–278.

Bray, R. M., Johnson, D., & Chilstrom, J. T., Jr. (1982). Social influence by group members with minority opinions: A comparison of Hollander & Moscovici. *Journal of Personality and Social Psychology, 43,* 78–88.

Breckler, S. J. (1984). Empirical validation of affect, behavior, and cognition as distinct components of attitude. *Journal of Personality and Social Psychology, 47,* 1191–1205.

Breckler, S. J., Pratkanis, A. R., & McCann, C. D. (1991). The representation of self in multidimensional cognitive space. *British Journal of Social Psychology, 30,* 97–112.

Breckler, S. J., & Wiggins, E. C. (1989a). Affect versus evaluation in the structure of attitudes. *Journal of Experimental Social Psychology, 25,* 253–271.

Breckler, S. J., & Wiggins, E. C. (1989b). On defining attitude and attitude theory: Once more with feeling. In A. R. Pratkanis, S. J. Breckler, & A. G. Greenwald (Eds.), *Attitude structure and function* (pp. 407–427). Hillsdale, NJ: Erlbaum.

Breckler, S. J., & Wiggins, E. C. (1991). Cognitive responses in persuasion: Affective and evaluative determinants. *Journal of Experimental Social Psychology, 27,* 180–200.

Brehm, J. W. (1956). Post-decision changes in desirability of alternatives. *Journal of Abnormal and Social Psychology, 52,* 384–389.

Brehm, J. W. (1966). *A theory of psychological reactance.* New York: Academic Press.

Brehm, J. W., & Sensenig, J. (1966). Social influence as a function of attempted and implied usurpation of choice. *Journal of Personality and Social Psychology, 4,* 703–707.

Brehm, S. S. (1985). *Intimate relationships.* New York: Random House.

Brehm, S. S., & Brehm, J. W. (1981). *Psychological reactance: A theory of freedom and control.* New York: Academic Press.

Brehm, S. S., & Smith, T. W. (1986). Social psychological approaches to psychotherapy and behavior change. In S. L. Garfield and A. E. Bergin (Eds.), *Handbook of psychotherapy and behavior change* (3rd ed.). New York: Wiley.

Brent, E., & Granberg, D. (1982). Subjective agreement with the presidential candidates of 1976 and 1980. *Journal of Personality and Social Psychology, 42,* 393–403.

Brewer, M. B. (1979). In-group bias in the minimal intergroup situation: A cognitive-motivational analysis. *Psychological Bulletin, 86,* 307–324.

Brewer, M. B. (1988). A dual process model of impression formation. In T. K. Srull & R. S. Wyer, Jr. (Eds.), *Advances in social cognition* (Vol. 1, pp. 1–36). Hillsdale, NJ: Erlbaum.

Brewer, M. B., & Kramer, R. M. (1985). The psychology of intergroup attitudes and behavior. *Annual Review of Psychology, 36,* 219–243.

Brewer, M. B., & Miller, N. (1984). Beyond the contact hypothesis: theoretical perspectives on desegregation. In N. Miller & M. Brewer (Eds.), *Groups in contact: The psychology of desegregation* (pp. 281–302). New York: Academic Press.

Brewer, W. F., & Nakamura, G. V. (1984). The nature and functions of schemas. In R. S. Wyer, Jr., & T. K. Srull (Eds.), *Handbook of social cognition* (Vol. 1, pp. 119–160). Hillsdale, NJ: Erlbaum.

Brickner, M. A., Harkins, S. G., & Ostrom, T. M. (1986). Effects of personal involvement: Thought-provoking implications for social loafing. *Journal of Personality and Social Psychology, 51,* 763–770.

Brigham, J. C. (1986). Race and eyewitness identifications. In S. Worchel & W. G. Austin (Eds.), *Psychology of intergroup relations* (2nd ed.). Chicago: Nelson-Hall.

Brigham, J. C., Maass, A., Snyder, L. D., & Spaulding, K. (1982). The accuracy of eyewitness identification in a field setting. *Journal of Personality and Social Psychology, 42,* 673–681.

Bringle, R. G., & Buunk, B. (1986). Examining the causes and consequences of jealousy: Some recent findings and issues. In R. Gilmour & S. Duck (Eds.), *The emerging field of personal relationships* (pp. 225–240). Hillsdale, NJ: Erlbaum.

Brock, T. C. (1965). Communicator-recipient similarity and decision change. *Journal of Personality and Social Psychology, 1,* 650–654.

Brockner, J. (1988). *Self-esteem at work: Research, theory, and practice.* Lexington, MA: Lexington Books.

Brockner, J., Pressman, B., Cabitt, J., & Moran, P. (1982). Nonverbal intimacy, sex, and compliance: A field study. *Journal of Nonverbal Behavior, 6,* 253–258.

Brockner, J., & Swap, W. C. (1976). Effects of repeated exposure and attitudinal similarity on self-disclosure and interpersonal attraction. *Journal of Personality and Social Psychology, 33,* 531–540.

Bromet, E. J. (1990). Methodological issues in the assessment of traumatic events. *Journal of Applied Social Psychology, 20,* 1719–1724.

Bromley, D. G. (1985). Cult facts and fiction. *VCU Magazine, 14*(2), 10–15.

Brothen, T. (1977). The gain/loss concept and the evaluator: First some good news, then some bad. *Journal of Personality and Social Psychology, 35,* 430–439.

Brower, S., Dockett, D., & Taylor, R. B. (1983). Residents' perceptions of site-level features. *Environment and Behavior, 15,* 419–437.

Brown, B. B. (1987). Territoriality. In D. Stokols & I. Altman (Eds.), *Handbook of environmental psychology* (Vol. 1, pp. 505–531). New York: Wiley.

Brown, B. B., & Harris, P. B. (1989). Residential burglary victimization: Reactions to the invasion of a primary territory. *Journal of Environmental Psychology, 9,* 119–132.

Brown, B. B., & Lohr, M. (1987). Peer group affiliation and adolescent self-esteem: An integration of ego-identity and symbolic-interaction theories. *Journal of Personality and Social Psychology, 52,* 47–55.

Brown, J(ane). D. (1985). Race and gender in rock video. *Social Sciences Newsletter, 70,* 82–86.

Brown, J(onathan). D. (1991). Accuracy and bias in self-knowledge. In C. R. Snyder and D. R. Forsyth (Eds.), *Handbook of social and clinical psychology: The health perspective* (pp. 158–178). New York: Pergamon.

Brown, J. D., & Mankowski, T. A. (1993). Self-esteem, mood, and self-evaluation: Changes in mood and the way you see you. *Journal of Personality and Social Psychology, 64,* 421–430.

Brown, J. D., Novick, N. J., Lord, K. A., & Richards, J. M. (1992). When Gulliver travels: Social context, psychological closeness, and self-appraisals. *Journal of Personality and Social Psychology, 62,* 717–727.

Brown, J. D., & Siegel, J. H. (1988). Attributions for negative life events and depression: The role of perceived control. *Journal of Personality and Social Psychology, 54,* 316–322.

Brown, R. (1988). *Group processes: Dynamics between and within groups.* New York: Blackwell.

Brown, R. (Ed.). (1990). *The Marshall Cavendish encyclopedia of personal relationships: Human behavior, How groups work* (Vol. 15). North Bellmore, NY: Marshall Cavendish Corporation.

Brown, R., Condor, S., Matthews, A., Wade, G., & Williams, J. A. (1986). Explaining intergroup differentiation in an industrial organization. *Journal of Occupational Psychology, 59,* 273–286.

Brown, R. C., Jr., & Tedeschi, J. T. (1976). Determinants of perceived aggression. *Journal of Social Psychology, 100,* 77–87.

Brown, V., & Geis, F. L. (1984). Turning lead into gold: Evaluations of men and women leaders and the alchemy of social consensus. *Journal of Personality and Social Psychology, 46,* 811–824.

Brownlow, S., & Zebrowitz, L. A. (1990). Facial appearance and credibility in television commercials. *Journal of Nonverbal Behavior, 14,* 51–60.

Brownmiller, S. (1975). *Against our will: Men, women, and rape.* New York: Simon & Schuster.

Bryan, J. H., & Davenport, M. (1968). *Donations to the needy: Correlates of financial contributions to the destitute.* Princeton, NJ: Educational Testing Service.

Bryan, J. H., & Test, M. A. (1967). Models and helping: Naturalistic studies in aiding behavior. *Journal of Personality and Social Psychology, 6,* 400–407.

Bryan, J. H., & Walbek, N. (1970). The impact of words and deeds concerning altruism upon children. *Child Development, 41,* 747–757.

Buby, C. M., & Penner, L. A. (1974). Conformity as a function of response position. *Psychological Reports, 34,* 938.

Buck, R. (1984). Emotion development and emotion education. In R. Plutchik & H. Kellerman (Eds.), *Emotions in early development.* Orlando, FL: Academic Press.

Buckhout, R. (1974). Eyewitness testimony. *Scientific American, 231,* 23–31.

Buller, D. B., Comstock, J., Aune, R. K., & Strzyzewski, K. D. (1989). The effect of probing on deceivers and truth-tellers. *Journal of Nonverbal Behavior, 13,* 155–170.

Bulman, R. J., & Wortman, C. B. (1977). Attributions of blame and coping in the "real world": Severe accident victims react to their lot. *Journal of Personality and Social Psychology, 35,* 351–363.

Burger, J. M. (1981). Motivational biases in the attribution of responsibility for an accident: A meta-analysis of the defensive-attribution hypothesis. *Psychological Bulletin, 90,* 496–512.

Burger, J. M., & Palmer, M. L. (1992). Changes in and generalization of unrealistic optimism following experiences with stressful events: Reactions to the 1989 California earthquake. *Personality and Social Psychology Bulletin, 18,* 39–43.

Burger, J. M., & Petty, R. E. (1981). The low-ball compliance technique: Task or person commitment? *Journal of Personality and Social Psychology, 40,* 492–500.

Burgess, A. W. (Ed.). (1985). *Rape and sexual assault: A research handbook.* New York: Garland.

Burgess, R. L., & Huston, T. L. (Eds.). (1979). *Social exchange in developing relationships.* New York: Academic Press.

Burgoon, J. K. (1983). Nonverbal violations of expectations. In J. M. Wiemann & R. P. Harrison (Eds.), *Sage annual reviews of communication: Nonverbal interaction* (Vol. 11). Newbury Park, CA: Sage.

Burgoon, J. K., Buller, D. B., Hale, J. L., & deTurck, M. A. (1984). Relational messages associated with nonverbal behaviors. *Human Communication Research, 10,* 351–378.

Burgoon, J. K., Coker, D. A., & Coker, R. A. (1986). Communicative effects of gaze behavior: A test of two contrasting explanations. *Human Communication Research, 12,* 495–524.

Burgoon, J. K., Newton, D. A., Walther, J. B., & Baesler, E. J. (1989). Nonverbal expectancy violations and conversational involvement. *Journal of Nonverbal Behavior, 13,* 97–120.

Burgoon, J. K., & Walther, J. B. (1990). Nonverbal expectancies and the evaluative consequences of violations. *Human Communication Research, 17,* 232–265.

Burke, M. J., & Day, R. R. (1986). A cumulative study of the effectiveness of managerial training. *Journal of Applied Psychology, 71,* 232–245.

Burke, P. A., Kraut, R. E., Dworkin, R. H. (1984). Traits, consistency, and self-schemata: What do our methods measure? *Journal of Personality and Social Psychology, 47,* 568–579.

Burman, B., & Margolin, G. (1992). Analysis of the association between marital relationships and health problems: An interactional perspective. *Psychological Bulletin, 112,* 29–63.

Burn, S. M., & Oskamp, S. (1986). Increasing community recycling with persuasive communication and public commitment. *Journal of Applied Social Psychology, 16,* 29–41.

Burnkrant, R. E., & Page, T. J. (1988). The structure and antecedents of the normative and attitudinal components of Fishbein's theory of reasoned action. *Journal of Experimental Social Psychology, 24,* 66–87.

Burns, M. O., & Seligman, M. E. P. (1991). Explanatory style, helplessness, and depression. In C. R. Snyder and D. R. Forsyth (Eds.), *Handbook of social and clinical psychology* (pp. 267–284). New York: Pergamon.

Burnstein, E., & Schul, Y. (1982). The informational basis of social judgments: The operations in forming an impression of another person. *Journal of Experimental Social Psychology, 18,* 217–234.

Burnstein, E., & Schul, Y. (1983). The informational basis of social judgments: Memory for integrated and nonintegrated trait descriptions. *Journal of Experimental Social Psychology, 19,* 49–57.

Burnstein, E., & Vinokur, A. (1973). Testing two classes of theories about group-induced shifts in individual choice. *Journal of Experimental Social Psychology, 9,* 123–137.

Burnstein, E., & Vinokur, A. (1977). Persuasive arguments and social comparison as determinants of attitude polarization. *Journal of Experimental Social Psychology, 13,* 315–332.

Burnstein, E., & Worchel, P. (1962). Arbitrariness of frustration and its consequences for aggression in a social situation. *Journal of Personality, 30,* 528–541.

Burt, M. R. (1980). Cultural myths and supports for rape. *Journal of Personality and Social Psychology, 38,* 217–230.

Burton, I., Kates, R. W., & White, G. F. (1978). *The environment as hazard.* New York: Oxford University Press.

Bus driver aids gunshot victim as others ignore cries for help. (1990, January 24). *Washington Post,* p. B5.

Bushman, B. J., & Cooper, H. M. (1990). Effects of alcohol on human aggression: An integrative research review. *Psychological Bulletin, 107,* 341–354.

Bushman, B. J., & Geen, R. G. (1990). Role of cognitive-emotional mediators and individual differences in the effects of media violence on aggression. *Journal of Personality and Social Psychology, 58,* 156–163.

Buss, A. H. (1963). Physical aggression in relation to different frustrations. *Journal of Abnormal and Social Psychology, 67,* 1–7.

Buss, A. H., & Perry, M. (1992). The aggression questionnaire. *Journal of Personality and Social Psychology, 63,* 452–459.

Buss, D. M. (1984). Toward a psychology of person-environment (PE) correlation: The role of spouse selection. *Journal of Personality and Social Psychology, 47,* 361–377.

Buss, D. M. (1985). Human mate selection. *American Scientist, 73,* 47–51.

Buss, D. M. (1987). Sex differences in human mate selection criteria: An evolutionary perspective. In C. Crawford, D. Krebs, & M. Smith (Eds.), *Sociobiology and psychology: Ideas, issues, and applications* (pp. 335–352). Hillsdale, NJ: Erlbaum.

Buss, D. M. (1988). The evolution of human intrasexual competition. *Journal of Personality and Social Psychology, 54,* 616–628.

Buss, D. M. (1989). Conflict between the sexes: Strategic interference and the evocation of anger and upset. *Journal of Personality and Social Psychology, 56,* 735–747.

Buss, D. M., & Barnes, M. F. (1986). Preferences in human mate selection. *Journal of Personality and Social Psychology, 50,* 559–570.

Buss, D. M., Gomes, M., Higgins, D. S., & Lauterbach, K. (1987). Tactics of manipulation. *Journal of Personality and Social Psychology, 52,* 1219–1229.

Buss, D. M., Larsen, R. J., Westen, D., & Semmelroth, J. (1992). Sex differences in jealousy: Evolution, physiology, and psychology. *Psychological Science, 3,* 251–255.

Buss, D. M., & Schmitt, D. P. (1993). Sexual strategies theory: An evolutionary perspective on human mating. *Psychological Bulletin, 100,* 204–232.

Butler, D., & Geis, F. L. (1990). Nonverbal affect responses to male and female leaders: Implications for leadership evaluations. *Journal of Personality and Social Psychology, 58,* 48–59.

Buunk, B. (1984). Jealousy as related to attributions for the partner's behavior. *Social Psychology Quarterly, 47,* 107–112.

Buunk, B., & Bringle, R. G. (1987). Jealousy in love relationships. In D. Perman & S. Duck (Eds.), *Intimate relationships: Development, dynamics, and deterioration* (pp. 123–147). Newbury Park, CA: Sage.

Buys, C. J. (1978). Humans would do better without groups. *Personality and Social Psychology Bulletin, 4,* 123–125.

Byrne, D. (1961). Anxiety and the experimental arousal of affiliation need. *Journal of Abnormal and Social Psychology, 63,* 660–662.

Byrne, D. (1971). *The attraction paradigm.* New York: Academic Press.

Byrne, D., Ervin, C. F., & Lamberth, J. (1970). Continuity between the experimental study of attraction and real-life computer dating. *Journal of Personality and Social Psychology, 16,* 157–165.

Byrne, D., & Murnen, S. K. (1988). Maintaining loving relationships. In R. J. Sternberg & M. L. Barnes (Eds.), *The psychology of love* (pp. 293–310). New Haven, CT: Yale University Press.

Byrne D., & Nelson, D. (1965). Attraction as a linear function of proportion of positive and negative reinforcements. *Journal of Personality and Social Psychology, 1,* 659–663.

Cacioppo, J. T., Claiborn, C. D., Petty, R. E., & Heesacker, M. (1991). A general framework for the study of attitude change in psychotherapy. In C. R. Snyder & D. R. Forsyth (Eds.), *Handbook of social and clinical psychology: A health perspective* (pp. 523–539). New York: Pergamon.

Cacioppo, J. T., Martzke, J. S., Petty, R. E., & Tassinary, L. G. (1988). Specific forms of facial EMG response index emotions during an interview: From Darwin to the continuous flow hypothesis of affect-laden information processing. *Journal of Personality and Social Psychology, 54,* 592–604.

Cacioppo, J. T., & Petty, R. E. (1979). Effects of message repetition and position on cognitive response, recall, and persuasion. *Journal of Personality and Social Psychology, 37,* 97–109.

Cacioppo, J. T., & Petty, R. E. (1982). The need for cognition. *Journal of Personality and Social Psychology, 42,* 116–131.

Cacioppo, J. T., & Petty, R. E. (1985). Central and peripheral routes to persuasion: The role of message repetition. In A. Mitchell & L. Alwitt (Eds.), *Psychological processes and advertising effects* (pp. 91–111). Hillsdale, NJ: Erlbaum.

Cacioppo, J. T., & Petty, R. E. (1989). Effects of message repetition on argument processing, recall, and persuasion. *Basic and Applied Social Psychology, 10,* 3–12.

Cacioppo, J. T., Petty, R. E., Kao, C. F., & Rodriguez, R. (1986). Central and peripheral routes to persuasion: An individual difference perspective. *Journal of Personality and Social Psychology, 51,* 1032–1043.

Cacioppo, J. T., Petty, R. E., & Losch, M. (1986). Attributions of responsibility for helping and doing harm: Evidence for confusion of responsibility. *Journal of Personality and Social Psychology, 50,* 100–105.

Cacioppo, J. T., Petty, R. E., & Morris, K. (1983). Effects of need for cognition on message evaluation, recall, and persuasion. *Journal of Personality and Social Psychology, 45,* 804–818.

Cacioppo, J. T., Rourke, P. A., Marshall-Goodall, B. S., Tassinary, L. G., & Baron, R. S. (1990). Rudimentary physiological effects of mere observation. *Psychophysiology, 27,* 177–186.

Cacioppo, J. T., & Tassinary, L. G. (1990). Inferring psychological significance from physiological signals. *American Psychologist, 45,* 16–28.

Caldwell, M. A., & Peplau, L. A. (1982). Sex differences in same-sex friendship. *Sex Roles, 8,* 721–732.

Calhoun, J. B. (1962). Population density and social pathology. *Scientific American, 206*(2), 139–148.

Callaway, M. R., & Esser, J. K. (1984). Groupthink: Effects of cohesiveness and problem-solving procedures on group decision making. *Social Behavior and Personality, 12,* 157–164.

Callaway, M. R., Marriott, R. G., & Esser, J. K. (1985). Effects of dominance on group decision making: Toward a stress-reduction explanation of groupthink. *Journal of Personality and Social Psychology, 49,* 949–952.

Campbell, A., Converse, P. E., Miller, W. E., & Stokes, D. E. (1960). *The American voter.* New York: Wiley.

Campbell, A., Converse, P. E., & Rodgers, W. L. (1976). *The quality of American life.* New York: Russell Sage Foundation.

Campbell, D. T. (1950). The indirect assessment of social attitudes. *Psychological Bulletin, 47,* 15–38.

Campbell, D. T. (1963). Social attitudes and other acquired behavioral dispositions. In S. Koch (Ed.), *Psychology: A study of a science.* New York: McGraw-Hill.

Campbell, D. T. (1965). Ethnocentric and other altruistic motives. In D. Levine (Ed.), *Nebraska Symposium on motivation* (Vol. 13). Lincoln: University of Nebraska Press.

Campbell, D. T., & Stanley, J. C. (1963). *Experimental and quasi-experimental designs for research.* Chicago: Rand McNally.

Campbell, J. D., Tesser, A., & Fairey, P. J. (1986). Conformity and attention to the stimulus: Some temporal and contextual dynamics. *Journal of Personality and Social Psychology, 51,* 315–324.

Cannon, W. B. (1932). *The wisdom of the body.* New York: Norton.

Cantania, J. A., Dolcini, M. M., Coates, T. J., Kegeles, S. M., Greenblatt, R. M., Puckett, J. D., Corman, M., & Miller, J. (1989). Predictors of condom use and multiple partnered sex among sexually active adolescent women: Implications for AIDS-related health interventions. *Journal of Sex Research, 26,* 514–524.

Cantor, J., Zillmann, D., & Bryant, J. (1975). Enhancement of experienced sexual arousal in response to erotic stimuli through misattribution of unrelated residual excitation. *Journal of Personality and Social Psychology, 32,* 69–75.

Cantor, N., & Kihlstrom, J. F. (1987). *Personality and social intelligence.* Englewood Cliffs, NJ: Prentice-Hall.

Capellanus, A. (1959). *The art of courtly love.* New York: Norton.

Cappella, J. N. (1985). Controlling the floor in conversation. In A. W. Siegman & S. Feldstein (Eds.), *Multichannel integrations of nonverbal behavior* (pp. 69–103). Hillsdale, NJ: Erlbaum.

Cappella, J. N., & Palmer, M. T. (1990). Attitude similarity, relational history, and attraction: The mediating effects of kinesic and vocal behaviors. *Communication Monographs, 57,* 161–183.

Caprara, G. V. (1986). Indicators of aggression: The dissipation-rumination scale. *Personality and Individual Differences, 7,* 763–769.

Caprara, G. V., Cinanni, V., D'Imperio, G., Passerini, S., Renzi, P., & Travagli, G. (1985). Indicators of impulsive aggression: Present status of research on irritability and emotional susceptibility scales. *Personality and Individual Differences, 6,* 665–674.

Carbonell, J. L. (1984). Sex roles and leadership revisited. *Journal of Applied Psychology, 69,* 44–49.

Carli, L. L. (1990). Gender, language, and influence. *Journal of Personality and Social Psychology, 59,* 941–951.

Carlo, G., Eisenberg, N., Troyer, D., Switzer, G., & Speer, A. L. (1991). The altruistic personality: In what contexts is it apparent? *Journal of Personality and Social Psychology, 61,* 450–458.

Carlson, J. M., & Iovini, J. (1985). The transmission of racial attitudes from fathers to sons: A study of blacks and whites. *Adolescence, 20,* 233–237.

Carlson, M., Marcus-Hewhall, A., & Miller, N. (1990). Effects of situational aggression cues: A quantitative review. *Journal of Personality and Social Psychology, 58,* 622–633.

Carlson, R. (1984). What's social about social psychology? Where's the person in personality research? *Journal of Personality and Social Psychology, 47,* 1304–1309.

Carlyle, T. (1841). *On heroes, hero-worship, and the heroic.* London: Fraser.

Carnegie, D. (1937). *How to win friends and influence people.* New York: Simon & Schuster.

Carnegie fund honors heroism of 21 people. (1984, December 15). *Richmond Times Dispatch,* p. A-7.

Cartwright, D. (1968). The nature of group cohesiveness. In D. Cartwright & A. Zander (Eds.), *Group dynamics: Research and theory* (3rd ed., pp. 91–109). New York: Harper & Row.

Cartwright, D., & Zander, A. (Eds.). (1968). *Group dynamics: Research and theory* (3rd ed.). New York: Harper & Row.

Carver, C. S., & Glass, D. C. (1978). Coronary-prone behavior pattern and interpersonal aggression. *Journal of Personality and Social Psychology, 36,* 361–366.

Carver, C. S., & Scheier, M. F. (1981). *Attention and self-regulation: A control-theory approach to human behavior.* New York: Springer-Verlag.

Carver, C. S., & Scheier, M. F. (1990). Origins and functions of positive and negative affect: A control-process view. *Psychological Review, 97,* 19–35.

Carver, C. S., & Scheier, M. F. (1991). Self-regulation and the self. In J. Strauss & G. R. Goethals (Eds.), *The self: Interdisciplinary approaches* (pp. 168–207). New York: Springer-Verlag.

Carver, C. S., Scheier, M. F., & Weintraub, J. K. (1989). Assessing coping strategies: A theoretically based approach. *Journal of Personality and Social Psychology, 56,* 267–283.

Cash, T. F. (1990). Losing hair, losing points? The effects of male pattern baldness on social impression formation. *Journal of Applied Social Psychology, 20,* 154–167.

Cash, T. F., & Janda, L. H. (1984). The eye of the beholder. *Psychology Today, 18*(5), pp. 46–52.

Casteneda, R. (1991, August). Indifference greets bloody victim in park. *Washington Post,* pp. B3–B4.

Ceci, S. J., Peters, D., & Plotkin, J. (1985). Human subjects review, personal values, and the regulation of social science research. *American Psychologist, 40,* 994–1006.

Centers for Disease Control. (1991a). *HIV/AIDS surveillance report.* Rockville, MD: National AIDS Information Clearinghouse.

Centers for Disease Control. (1991b). *Morbidity and mortality report.* Rockville, MD: Author.

Cervone, D., & Peake, P. K. (1986). Anchoring, efficacy, and action: The influence of judgmental heuristics on self-efficacy judgments and behavior. *Journal of Personality and Social Psychology, 50,* 492–501.

Chagnon, N. A. (1974). *Studying the Yanomanö.* New York: Holt, Rinehart & Winston.

Chaikin, A., & Derlega, V. (1974). Variables affecting the appropriateness of self-disclosure. *Journal of Consulting and Clinical Psychology, 42,* 588–593.

Chaiken, A. L., & Darley, J. M. (1973). Victim or perpetrator? Defensive attribution of responsibility and the need for order and justice. *Journal of Personality and Social Psychology, 25,* 268–275.

Chaiken, S. (1979). Communicators physical attractiveness and persuasion. *Journal of Personality and Social Psychology, 37,* 1387–1397.

Chaiken, S. (1980). Heuristic versus systematic information processing and the use of source versus message cues in persuasion. *Journal of Personality and Social Psychology, 39,* 752–766.

Chaiken, S. (1987). The heuristic model of persuasion. In M. P. Zanna, J. M. Olson, & C. P. Herman (Eds.), *Social influence: The Ontario Symposium* (Vol. 5, pp. 3–40). Hillsdale, NJ: Erlbaum.

Chaiken, S., & Baldwin, M. W. (1981). Affective-cognitive consistency and the effect of salient behavioral information on the self-perception of attitudes. *Journal of Personality and Social Psychology, 41,* 1–12.

Chaiken, S., Liberman, A., & Eagly, A. H. (1989). Heuristic and systematic information processing within and beyond the persuasion context. In J. S. Uleman & J. A. Bargh (Eds.), *Unintended thought* (pp. 212–252). New York: Guilford Press.

Chaiken, S., & Stangor, C. (1987). Attitudes and attitude change. *Annual Review of Psychology, 38,* 575–630.

Chapman, L. J. (1967). Illusory correlation in observational report. *Journal of Verbal Learning and Verbal Behavior, 6,* 151–155.

Chapman, L. J., & Chapman, J. P. (1967). Genesis of popular but erroneous psychodiagnostic observations. *Journal of Abnormal Psychology, 72,* 193–204.

Chassin, L., Presson, C. C., & Sherman, S. J. (1990). Social psychological contributions to the understanding and prevention of adolescent cigarette smoking. *Personality and Social Psychology Bulletin, 16,* 133–151.

Chebat, J. C., & Filiatrault, P. (1986). Preference for forms of political causal attributions. *Journal of Social Psychology, 126,* 633–638.

Cheek, J. M. (1982). Aggregation, moderator variables, and the validity of personality tests: A peer-rating study. *Journal of Personality and Social Psychology, 43,* 1254–1269.

Cheek, J. M., & Buss, A. H. (1981). Shyness and sociability. *Journal of Personality and Social Psychology, 41,* 330–339.

Chemers, M. M., & Ayman, R. (1992). Leadership theory and research: Perspectives and directions. San Diego: Academic Press.

Chen, S. C. (1937). Social modification of the activity of ants in nest-building. *Physiological Zoology, 10,* 420–436.

Cheng, P. W., & Novick, L. R. (1990). A probabilistic contrast model of causal induction. *Journal of Personality and Social Psychology, 58,* 545–567.

Cherulnik, P., & Wilderman, S. (1986). Symbols of status in urban neighborhoods. *Environment and Behavior, 18,* 604–622.

Chesterfield, Earl of (Philip Darmer Standhope). (1774/1901). Letters to his son (Walter M. Dunne, Ed.). New York: Wiley.

Christensen-Szalanski, J. J., & Beach, L. R. (1984). The citation bias: Fad and fashion in the judgment and decision literature. *American Psychologist, 39,* 75–78.

Christensen-Szalanski, J. J., & Bushyhead, J. B. (1981). Physicians' use of probabalistic information in a real clinical setting. *Journal of Experimental Psychology: Human Perception and Performance, 7,* 928–935.

Christian, J. J. (1963). Pathology of overpopulation. *Military Medicine, 128,* 571–603.

Christian, J. J., Flyger, V., & Davis, D. E. (1960). Factors in the mass mortality of a herd of Silka deer, *Cervus nippon. Chesapeake Science, 1,* 79–95.

Christie, R. (1991). Authoritarianism and related constructs. In J. P. Robinson, P. R. Shaver, & L. S. Wrightsman (Eds.), *Measures of personality and social psychological attitudes* (pp. 501–571). San Diego, CA: Academic Press.

Cialdini, R. B. (1993). *Influence: Science and practice* (3rd ed.). New York: HarperCollins.

Cialdini, R. B., Borden, R., Thorne, A., Walker, M., Freeman, S., & Sloane, L. T. (1976). Basking in reflected glory: Three (football) field studies. *Journal of Personality and Social Psychology, 34,* 366–375.

Cialdini, R. B., Cacioppo, J. T., Bassett, R., & Miller, J. A. (1978). Low-ball procedure for producing compliance: Commitment then cost. *Journal of Personality and Social Psychology, 36,* 463–476.

Cialdini, R. B., Darby, B. L., & Vincent, J. E. (1973). Transgression and altruism: A case for hedonism. *Journal of Experimental Social Psychology, 9,* 502–516.

Cialdini, R. B., & De Nicholas, M. E. (1989). Self-presentation by association. *Journal of Personality and Social Psychology, 57,* 626–631.

Cialdini, R. B., & Fultz, J. (1990). Interpreting the negative mood-helping literature via "Mega"-analysis: A contrary view. *Psychological Bulletin, 107,* 210–214.

Cialdini, R. B., Green, B. L., & Rusch, A. J. (1992). When tactical pronouncements of change become real change: The case of reciprocal persuasion. *Journal of Personality and Social Psychology, 63,* 30–40.

Cialdini, R. B., Kallgren, C. A., & Reno, R. R. (1991). A focus theory of normative conduct: A theoretical refinement and reevaluation of the role of norms in human behavior. In M. P. Zanna (Ed.), *Advances in experimental social psychology* (Vol. 24, pp. 201–234). Orlando, FL: Academic Press.

Cialdini, R. B., & Kenrick, D. T. (1976). Altruism as hedonism: A social development perspective on the relationship of negative mood state and helping. *Journal of Personality and Social Psychology, 34,* 907–914.

Cialdini, R. B., Reno, R. R., & Kallgren, C. A. (1990). A focus theory of normative conduct: Recycling the concept of norms to reduce littering in public places. *Journal of Personality and Social Psychology, 58,* 1015–1026.

Cialdini, R. B., & Richardson, K. D. (1980). Two indirect tactics of image management: Basking and blasting. *Journal of Personality and Social Psychology, 39,* 406–415.

Cialdini, R. B., Schaller, M., Houlihan, D., Arps K., Fultz, J., & Beaman, A. L. (1987). Empathy-based helping: Is it selflessly or selfishly motivated? *Journal of Personality and Social Psychology, 42,* 749–758.

Cialdini, R. B., Vincent, J. E., Lewis, S. K., Catalan, J., Wheeler, D., & Darby, R. L. (1975). Reciprocal concessions procedure for inducing compliance: The door-in-the-face technique. *Journal of Personality and Social Psychology, 31,* 206–215.

Cini, M. A., Moreland, R. L., & Levine, J. M. (1993). Group staffing levels and responses to prospective and new group members. *Journal of Personality and Social Psychology, 65,* 723–734.

Clanton, G., & Smith, L. G. (Eds.). (1987). *Jealousy.* Lanham, MA: University Press of America.

Clark, M. S. (1984). Record keeping in two types of relationships. *Journal of Personality and Social Psychology, 47,* 549–557.

Clark, M. S., & Mills, J. (1979). Interpersonal attraction in exchange and communal relationships. *Journal of Personality and Social Psychology, 37,* 12–24.

Clark, M. S., Mills, J., & Powell, M. C. (1986). Keeping track of needs in communal and exchange relationships. *Journal of Personality and Social Psychology, 53,* 94–103.

Clark, M. S., Ouellette, R., Powell, M. C., & Milberg, S. (1987). Recipient's mood, relationship type, and helping. *Journal of Personality and Social Psychology, 53,* 94–103.

Clark, M. S., & Reis, H. T. (1988). Interpersonal processes in close relationships. *Annual Review of Psychology, 39,* 609–672.

Clark, M. S., & Waddell, B. (1985). Perceptions of exploitation in communal and exchange relationships. *Journal of Social and Personal Relationships, 2,* 403–418.

Clark, R. D., III. (1971). Group-induced shift toward risk: A critical appraisal. *Psychological Bulletin, 76,* 251–270.

Clark, R. D., III. (1976). On the Piliavin & Piliavin model of helping behavior: Costs are in the eye of the beholder. *Journal of Applied Social Psychology, 6,* 322–328.

Clark, R. D., III, & Hatfield, E. (1989). Gender differences in receptivity to sexual offers. *Journal of Psychology and Human Sexuality, 2,* 39–55.

Clark, R. D., III, & Word, L. E. (1972). Why don't bystanders help? Because of ambiguity? *Journal of Personality and Social Psychology, 24,* 392–400.

Clark, R. D., III, & Word, L. E. (1974). Where is the apathetic bystander? Situational characteristics of the emergency. *Journal of Personality and Social Psychology, 29,* 279–287.

Clary, E. G., & Miller, J. (1986). Socialization and situational influences on sustained altruism. *Child Development, 57,* 1358–1369.

Clee, M. A., & Wicklund, R. A. (1980). Consumer behavior and psychological reactance. *Journal of Consumer Research, 6,* 389–405.

Cleva, G. D. (1989). *Henry Kissinger and the American approach to foreign policy.* Lewisburg, PA: Bucknell University Press.

Cline, V. B., Croft, R. G., & Courrier, S. (1973). Desensitization of children to television violence. *Journal of Personality and Social Psychology, 27,* 360–365.

Cloward, R. A., & Ohlin, L. E. (1960). *Delinquency and opportunity: A theory of delinquent gangs.* Glencoe, IL: Free Press.

Cohen, C. E. (1981). Person categories and social perception: Testing some boundaries of the processing effects of prior knowledge. *Journal of Personality and Social Psychology, 40,* 441–452.

Cohen, D., & Nisbett, R. E. (1994). Self-protection, insults, and the culture of honor: Explaining Southern homicide. *Personality and Social Psychology Bulletin.*

Cohen, D. J., Whitmyre, J. W., & Funk, W. H. (1960). Effect of group cohesiveness and training upon group thinking. *Journal of Applied Psychology, 44,* 319–322.

Cohen, S. (1980). Aftereffects of stress on human performance and social behavior: A review of research and theory. *Psychological Bulletin, 87,* 578–604.

Cohen, S., Evans, G. W., Krantz, D. S., Stokols, D., & Kelly, S. (1981). Aircraft noise and children: Longitudinal and cross-sectional evidence on adaptation to noise and the effectiveness of noise abatement. *Journal of Personality and Social Psychology, 40,* 331–345.

Cohen, S., Evans, G. W., Stokols, D., & Krantz, D. (1986). *Behavior, health, and environmental stress.* New York: Plenum.

Cohen, S., Glass, D. C., & Singer, J. E. (1973). Apartment noise, auditory discrimination, and reading ability in children. *Journal of Experimental Social Psychology, 9,* 407–422.

Cohen, S., Krantz, D. S., Evans, G. W., & Stokols, D. (1981). Cardiovascular and behavioral effects of community noise. *American Scientist, 69,* 528–535.

Cohen, S., & Weinstein, N. (1981). Nonauditory effects of noise on behavior and health. *Journal of Social Issues, 37,* 36–70.

Cohen, S., & Wills, T. A. (1985). Stress, social support, and the buffering hypothesis. *Psychological Bulletin, 98,* 310–357.

Coie, J. D., Dodge, K. A., & Coppotelli, H. (1982). Dimensions and types of social status: A cross-age perspective. *Developmental Psychology, 18,* 557–570.

Coie, J. D., Watt, N. F., West, S. G., Hawkins, J. D., Asarnow, J. R., Markman, H. J., Ramey, S. L., Shure, M. B., & Long, B. (1993). The science of prevention: A conceptual framework and some directions for a national research program. *American Psychologist, 48,* 1013–1022.

Coke, J. S., Batson, C. D., & McDavis, K. (1978). Empathic mediation of helping: A two-stage model. *Journal of Personality and Social Psychology, 36,* 752–766.

Coleman, A. M. (1991). Crowd psychology in South African murder trials. *American Psychologist, 46,* 1071–1079.

Coleman, S. R., & Gormezano, I. (1979). Classical conditioning and the "law of effect": Historical and empirical assessment. *Behaviorism, 7,* 1–33.

Collins, A. M., & Loftus, E. F. (1975). A spreading-activation theory of semantic processing. *Psychological Review, 82,* 407–428.

Collins, B. E., & Hoyt, M. F. (1972). Personal responsibility-for-consequences: An integration and extension of the "forced compliance" literature. *Journal of Experimental Social Psychology, 8,* 558–593.

Collins, N. L., & Read, S. J. (1990). Adult attachment, working models, and relationship quality in dating couples. *Journal of Personality and Social Psychology, 58,* 644–663.

Collins, R. W., Dmitruk, V. M., & Ranney, J. T. (1977). Personal validation: Some empirical and ethical considerations. *Journal of Consulting and Clinical Psychology, 45,* 70–77.

Comer, R., & Laird, J. D. (1975). Choosing to suffer as a consequence of expecting to suffer: Why do people do it? *Journal of Personality and Social Psychology, 32,* 92–101.

Condry, J. (1977). Enemies of exploration. *Journal of Personality and Social Psychology, 35,* 459–477.

Condry, J., & Condry, S. (1976). Sex differences: A study of the eye of the beholder. *Child Development, 47,* 812–819.

Conner, R. C., & Norris, K. S. (1982). Are dolphins and whales reciprocal altruists? *American Naturalist, 119,* 358–374.

Conroy, J., & Sundstrom, E. (1977). Territorial dominance in a dyadic conversation as a function of similarity of opinion. *Journal of Personality and Social Psychology, 35,* 570–576.

Contrada, R. J. (1989). Type A behavior, personality hardiness, and cardiovascular responses to stress. *Journal of Personality and Social Psychology, 57,* 895–903.

Converse, J., Jr., & Cooper, H. (1979). The importance of decisions and free-choice attitude change: A curvilinear finding. *Journal of Experimental Social Psychology, 15,* 48–61.

Conway, M., & Ross, M. (1985). Getting what you want by revising what you had. *Journal of Personality and Social Psychology, 47,* 738–748.

Conway, M. A. (1991). In defense of everyday memory. *American Psychologist, 46,* 19–29.

Cook, M. (1970). Experiments on orientation and proxemics. *Human Relations, 23,* 61–76.

Cook, S. W. (1978). Interpersonal and attitudinal outcomes in cooperating interracial groups. *Journal of Research and Development in Education, 12,* 97–113.

Cook, S. W. (1984). The 1954 social science statement and school desegregation: A reply to Gerard. *American Psychologist, 39,* 819–832.

Cook, S. W. (1985). Experimenting on social issues: The case of school desegregation. *American Psychology, 40,* 452–460.

Cook, T. D., & Campbell, D. T. (1979). *Quasi-experimentation.* Chicago: Rand McNally.

Cook, T. D., & Flay, B. R. (1978). The temporal persistence of experimentally induced attitude change: An evaluative review. In L. Berkowitz (Ed.), *Advances in experimental social psychology* (Vol. 11). New York: Academic Press.

Cook, T. D., Gruder, C. L., Hennigan, K. M., & Flay, B. R. (1979). History of the sleeper effect: Some logical pitfalls in accepting the null hypothesis. *Psychological Bulletin, 86,* 662–679.

Cooley, C. H. (1902). *Human nature and the social order.* New York: Scribner's.

Cooper, H. (1979). Statistically combining independent studies: Meta-analysis of sex differences in conformity research. *Journal of Personality and Social Psychology, 37,* 131–146.

Cooper, H. (1983). Teacher expectation effects. In L. Bickman (Ed.), *Applied social psychology annual* (Vol. 4, pp. 247–275). Newbury Park, CA: Sage.

Cooper, H., & Hazelrigg, P. (1988). Personality moderators of interpersonal expectancy effects: An integrative research review. *Journal of Personality and Social Psychology, 55,* 937–949.

Cooper, J., & Fazio, R. H. (1984). A new look at dissonance theory. In L. Berkowitz (Ed.), *Advances in experimental social psychology* (Vol. 17, pp. 229–266). Orlando, FL: Academic Press.

Cooper, J., & Fazio, R. H. (1986). The formation and persistence of attitudes that support intergroup conflict. In S. Worchel & W. G. Austin (Eds.), *Psychology of intergroup relations* (2nd ed., pp. 183–195). Chicago: Nelson-Hall.

Cooper, J., & Fazio, R. H. (1989). Research traditions, analysis, and synthesis: Building a faulty case around misinterpreted theory. *Personality and Social Psychology Bulletin, 14,* 519–529.

Cooper, J., Fazio, R. H., & Rhodewalt, F. (1978). Dissonance and humor: Evidence for the undifferentiated nature of dissonance arousal. *Journal of Personality and Social Psychology, 36,* 280–285.

Cooper, J., Zanna, M. P., & Taves, P. A. (1978). Arousal as a necessary condition for attitude change following induced compliance. *Journal of Personality and Social Psychology, 36,* 1101–1106.

Cooper, M. G. (1990). "I saw what you said": Non-verbal communications and the EAP. *Employee Assistance Quarterly, 5*(4), 1–12.

Copeland, G. A. (1989). Face-ism and primetime television. *Journal of Broadcasting and Electronic Media, 33,* 209–214.

Corrigan, J. D., Dell, D. M., Lewis, K. N., & Schmidt, L. D. (1980). Counseling as a social influence process: A review. *Journal of Counseling Psychology, 27,* 395–441.

Coser, L. A. (1956). *The functions of social conflict.* Glencoe, IL: Free Press.

Cotton, J. L., & Tuttle, J. M. (1986). Employee turnover: A meta-analysis and review with implications for research. *Academy of Management Review, 11,* 55–70.

Cottrell, N. B. (1972). Social facilitation. In C. G. McClintock (Ed.), *Experimental social psychology.* New York: Holt, Rinehart & Winston.

Cottrell, N. B., & Epley, S. W. (1977). Affiliation, social comparison, and socially mediated stress reduction. In J. M. Suls & R. L. Miller (Eds.), *Social comparison processes.* Washington, DC: Hemisphere.

Courneya, K. S., & Carron, A. V. (1991). Effects of travel and length of home stand/road trip on the home advantage. *Journal of Sport and Exercise Psychology, 13,* 42–49.

Courtright, J. A. (1978). A laboratory investigation of groupthink. *Communication Monographs, 43,* 229–246.

Cousins, S. D. (1989). Culture and self-perception in Japan and the United States. *Journal of Personality and Social Psychology, 56,* 124–131.

Covington, M. V. (1992). *Making the grade: A self-worth perspective on motivation and school reform.* New York: Cambridge University Press.

Cowan, G., Drinkard, J., & MacGavin, L. (1984). The effects of target, age, and gender on use of power strategies. *Journal of Personality and Social Psychology, 47,* 1391–1398.

Cox, V. C., Paulus, P. B., & McCain, G. (1984). Prison crowding research: The relevance for prison housing standards and a general approach regarding crowding phenomena. *American Psychologist, 39,* 1148–1160.

Coyne, J. C., Burchill, S. A. L., & Stiles, W. B. (1991). An interactional perspective on depression. In C. R. Snyder & D. R. Forsyth (Eds.), *Handbook of social and clinical psychology* (pp. 327–349). New York: Pergamon.

Craig, R. S. (1992). The effect of television day part on gender portrayals in television commercials: A content analysis. *Sex Roles, 26,* 197–211.

Crandall, C. S. (1988). Social contagion of binge eating. *Journal of Personality and Social Psychology, 55,* 588–598.

Critchlow, B. (1986). The powers of John Barleycorn: Beliefs about the effects of alcohol on social behavior. *American Psychologist, 41,* 751–765.

Crittenden, K. S., & Wiley, M. G. (1985). When egotism is normative: Self-presentational norms guiding attributions. *Social Psychology Quarterly, 48,* 360–365.

Crocker, J., & Luhtanen, R. (1990). Collective self-esteem and ingroup bias. *Journal of Personality and Social Psychology, 58,* 60–67.

Crocker, J., & Major, B. (1989). Social stigma and self-esteem: The self-protective properties of stigma. *Psychological Review, 96,* 608–630.

Crocker, J., & McGraw, K. M. (1984). What's good for the goose is not good for the gander: Solo status as an obstacle to occupational achievement for males and females. *American Behavioral Scientist, 27,* 357–369.

Cronbach, L. J. (1955). Processes affecting scores on "understanding of others" and "assumed similarity." *Psychological Bulletin, 52,* 177–193.

Cronshaw, S. F., & Lord, R. G. (1987). Effects of categorization, attribution, and encoding processes on leadership perceptions. *Journal of Applied Psychology, 72,* 97–106.

Crosby, F., Bromley, S., & Saxe, L. (1980). Recent unobtrusive studies of black and white discrimination and prejudice: A literature review. *Psychological Bulletin, 87,* 546–563.

Croyle, R. T., & Cooper, J. (1983). Dissonance arousal: Physiological evidence. *Journal of Personality and Social Psychology, 45,* 782–791.

Crutchfield, R. S. (1955). Conformity and character. *American Psychologist, 10,* 191–198.

Csikszentmihalyi, M., & Rochberg-Halton, E. (1981). *The meaning of things: Domestic symbols and the self.* Cambridge, England: Cambridge University Press.

Csoka, L. S., & Bons, P. M. (1978). Manipulating the situation to fit the leader's style—Two validation studies of Leader Match. *Journal of Applied Psychology, 63,* 295–300.

Cunningham, M. R. (1979). Weather, mood, and helping behavior: Quasi-experiments with the sunshine Samaritan. *Journal of Personality and Social Psychology, 37,* 1947–1956.

Cunningham, M. R. (1981). Sociobiology as a supplementary paradigm for social psychological research. In L. Wheeler (Ed.), *Review of personality and social psychology* (Vol. 2). Newbury Park, CA: Sage.

Cunningham, M. R. (1986). Measuring the physical in physical attractiveness: Quasi-experiments on the sociobiology of female facial beauty. *Journal of Personality and Social Psychology, 50,* 925–935.

Cunningham, M. R., Barbee, A. P., & Pike, C. L. (1990). What do women want? Facialmetric assessment of multiple motives in the perception of male facial physical attractiveness. *Journal of Personality and Social Psychology, 59,* 61–72.

Cunningham, M. R., Steinberg, J., & Grev, R. (1980). Wanting to help and having to help: Separate motivations for positive moods and guilt-induced helping. *Journal of Personality and Social Psychology, 38,* 181–190.

Curtis, R. C., & Miller, K. (1986). Believing another likes or dislikes you: Behaviors making the beliefs come true. *Journal of Personality and Social Psychology, 51,* 284–290.

Cutrona, C. E. (1982). Transition to college: Loneliness and the process of social adjustment. In L. A. Peplau & D. Perlman (Eds.), *Loneliness: A sourcebook of current theory, research, and therapy.* New York: Wiley-Interscience.

Cutrona, C. E. (1986). Objective determinants of perceived social support. *Journal of Personality and Social Psychology, 50,* 349–355.

Dabbs, J. M., Jr., & Morris, R. (1990). Testosterone, social class, and antisocial behavior in a sample of 4,462 men. *Psychological Science, 1,* 209–211.

Daly, R. F. (1969). Neurological abnormalities in XYY males. *Nature, 221,* 472–473.

Damhorst, M. L. (1990). In search of a common thread: Classification of information communicated through dress. *Clothing and Textiles Research Journal, 8*(2), 1–12.

Dane, F. C. (1988). *The common and uncommon sense of social behavior.* Pacific Grove, CA: Brooks/Cole.

Darley, J. M., & Batson, C. D. (1973). "From Jerusalem to Jericho": A study of situational and dispositional variables in helping behavior. *Journal of Personality and Social Psychology, 27,* 100–108.

Darley, J. M., & Fazio, R. H. (1980). Expectancy confirmation processes arising in the social interaction sequence. *American Psychologist, 35,* 867–881.

Darley, J. M., Fleming, J. H., Hilton, J. L., & Swann, W. B., Jr. (1988). Dispelling negative expectancies: The impact of interaction goals and target characteristics on the expectancy confirmation process. *Journal of Experimental Social Psychology, 24,* 19–36.

Darley, J. M., & Gilbert, D. T. (1985). Social psychological aspects of environmental psychology. In G. Lindzey & E. Aronson (Eds.), *Handbook of social psychology* (3rd ed., Vol. 2, pp. 949–991). New York: Random House.

Darley, J. M., & Gross, P. H. (1983). A hypothesis-confirming bias in labeling effects. *Journal of Personality and Social Psychology, 44,* 20–33.

Darley, J. M., & Latané, B. (1968). Bystander intervention in emergencies: Diffusion of responsibility. *Journal of Personality and Social Psychology, 8,* 377–383.

Darley, J. M., & Latané, B. (1970). Norms and normative behavior: Field studies of social interdependence. In J. Macaulay & L. Berkowitz (Eds.), *Altruism and helping behavior: Social psychological studies of some antecedents and consequences.* New York: Academic Press.

Darwin, C. (1872/1955). *The expression of emotions in man and animals.* New York: The Philosophical Library.

Dashiell, J. F. (1930). An experimental analysis of some group effects. *Journal of Abnormal and Social Psychology, 25,* 190–199.

Davidson, A. R., & Jaccard, J. J. (1979). Variables that moderate the attitude-behavior relation: Results of a longitudinal study. *Journal of Personality and Social Psychology, 37,* 1364–1376.

Davidson, A. R., & Morrison, D. M. (1983). Predicting contraceptive behavior from attitudes: A comparison of within- versus across-subjects procedures. *Journal of Personality and Social Psychology, 45,* 997–1009.

Davidson, A. R., Yantis, S., Norwood, M., & Montano, D. E. (1985). Amount of information about the attitude-object and attitude-behavior consistency. *Journal of Personality and Social Psychology, 49,* 1184–1198.

Davidson, B. (1984). A test of equity theory for marital adjustment. *Social Psychology Quarterly, 47,* 36–42.

Davies, M. F. (1987). Reduction of hindsight bias by restoration of foresight perspective: Effectiveness of foresight-encoding and hindsight-retrieval strategies. *Organizational Behavior and Human Decision Processes, 40,* 50–68.

Davis, D. M. (1990). Portrayals of women in prime-time network television: Some demographic characteristics. *Sex Roles, 23,* 325–332.

Davis, J. A., & Smith, T. W. (1990). *General social surveys, 1972–1990: Cumulative codebook.* Chicago: National Opinion Research Center.

Davis, J. H. (1982). Social interaction as a combinatorial process in group decision. In H. Brandstatter, J. H. Davis, & G. Stocker-Kreichgauer (Eds.), *Group decision making* (pp. 27–58). London: Academic Press.

Davis, J. H., Bray, R. M., & Holt, R. W. (1977). The empirical study of decision processes in juries: A critical review. In J. L. Tapp & F. J. Levine (Eds.), *Law, justice, and the individual in society.* New York: Holt, Rinehart & Winston.

Davis, J. H., Kameda, T., Parks, C., Stasson, M., & Zimmerman, S. (1989). Some social mechanics of group decision making: The distribution of opinion, polling sequence, and implications for consensus. *Journal of Personality and Social Psychology, 57,* 1000–1012.

Davis, J. H., Kameda, T., & Stasson, M. (1992). Group risk taking: Selected topics. In J. F. Yates (Ed.), *Risk-taking behavior* (pp. 163–199). Chichester: Wiley.

Davis, J. H., & Stasson, M. F. (1988). Small group performance: Past and present research trends. In E. J. Lawler & B. Markovsky (Eds.), *Advances in group processes* (Vol. 5, pp. 245–277). Greenwich, CT: JAI Press.

Davis, J. H., Stasson, M., Ono, K., & Zimmerman, S. (1988). Effects of straw polls on group decision making: Sequential voting pattern, timing, and local majorities. *Journal of Personality and Social Psychology, 55,* 918–926.

Davis, J. R. (1982). *Street gangs: Youth, biker, and prison groups.* Dubuque, IA: Kendall/Hunt.

Davis, K. E. (1985). Near and dear: Friendship and love compared. *Psychology Today, 19*(2), 22–30.

Davis, K. E., & Latty-Mann, H. (1987). Love styles and relationship quality: A contribution to validation. *Journal of Social and Personal Relationships, 4,* 409–428.

Davis, K. E., & Todd, M. J. (1985). Assessing friendship: Prototypes, paradigm cases, and relationship description. In S. Duck & D. Perman (Eds.), *Understanding personal relationships: An interdisciplinary approach* (pp. 17–38). Newbury Park, CA: Sage.

Davison, R., & Jones, S. C. (1976). Similarity in real-life friendship pairs. *Journal of Personality and Social Psychology, 34,* 313–317.

Dawes, R. M. (1988). *Rational choice in an uncertain world.* San Diego: Harcourt Brace Jovanovich.

Dawes, R. M., & Smith, T. (1985). Attitude and opinion measurement. In G. Lindzey & E. Aronson (Eds.), *Handbook of social psychology* (3rd. ed., Vol. 1, pp. 509–565). New York: Random House.

Dean, L. M., Willis, F. N., & Hewitt, J. (1975). Initial interaction distance among individuals equal and unequal in military rank. *Journal of Personality and Social Psychology, 32,* 294–299.

Deaux, K. (1984). From individual differences to social categories: Analysis of a decade's research on gender. *American Psychologist, 39,* 105–116.

Deaux, K. (1993). Reconstructing social identity. *Personality and Social Psychology Bulletin, 19,* 4–12.

Deaux, K., & Emswiller, T. (1974). Explanations of successful performance on sex-linked tasks: What is skill for the male is luck for the female. *Journal of Personality and Social Psychology, 29,* 80–85.

Deaux, K., & Lewis, L. L. (1984). The structure of gender stereotypes: Interrelationships among components and gender label. *Journal of Personality and Social Psychology, 46,* 991–1004.

Deaux, K., & Major, B. (1987). Putting gender into context: An interactive model of gender-related behavior. *Psychological Review, 94,* 369–389.

Deaux, K., Winton, W., Crowley, M., & Lewis, L. L. (1985). Level of categorization and content of gender stereotypes. *Social Cognition, 3,* 145–167.

DeBono, K. G., & Edmonds, A. E. (1989). Cognitive dissonance and self-monitoring: A matter of context? *Motivation and Emotion, 13,* 259–270.

DeBono, K. G., & Klein, C. (1993). Source expertise and persuasion: The moderating role of recipient dogmatism. *Personality and Social Psychology Bulletin, 19,* 167–173.

DeBono, K. G., & Packer, M. (1991). The effects of advertising appeal on perceptions of product quality. *Personality and Social Psychology Bulletin, 17,* 194–200.

deCharms, R. (1968). *Personal causation.* New York: Academic Press.

Deci, E. L., & Ryan, R. M. (1985). *Intrinsic motivation and self-determination in human behavior.* New York: Plenum.

Decision Making Information. (1986). *A national survey of adult Americans prepared for the American Coalition for Traffic Safety.* Santa Ana, CA: Author.

DeFleur, M. L., & Westie, F. R. (1958). Verbal attitudes and overt acts: An experiment on the salience of attitudes. *American Sociological Review, 23,* 667–673.

DeKay, W. T., & Buss, D. M. (1992). Human nature, individual differences, and the importance of context: Perspective from evolutionary psychology. *Current Directions in Psychological Science, 1,* 184–189.

Delbecq, A. L., Van de Ven, A. H., & Gustafson, D. H. (1975). *Group techniques for program planning: A guide to nominal group and Delphi process.* Glenview, IL: Scott, Foresman.

de Meuse, K. P. (1987). A review of the effects of non-verbal cues on the performance appraisal process. *Journal of Occupational Psychology, 60,* 207–226.

de Meuse, K. P., & Liebowitz, S. J. (1981). An empirical analysis of team-building research. *Group and Organizational Studies, 6,* 357–378.

Demick, J., & Wapner, S. (1990). Role of psychological science in promoting environmental quality: Introduction. *American Psychologist, 45,* 631–632.

Deming, W. E. (1975). On some statistical aids towards economic production. *Interfaces, 5,* 1–15.

Dengerink, H. A., Schnedler, R. W., & Covey, M. K. (1978). Role of avoidance in aggressive responses to attack and no attack. *Journal of Personality and Social Psychology, 36,* 1044–1053.

Dennis, M. L., Soderstrom, E. J., Koncinski, W. S., Jr., & Cavanaugh, B. (1990). Effective dissemination of energy-related information: Applying social psychology and evaluation research. *American Psychologist, 45,* 1109–1117.

DePaulo, B. M. (1988). Nonverbal aspects of deception. *Journal of Nonverbal Behavior, 12,* 153–161.

DePaulo, B. M. (1991). Nonverbal behavior and self-presentation: A developmental perspective. In R. S. Feldman & B. Rime (Eds.), *Fundamentals of nonverbal behavior* (pp. 351–397). New York: Cambridge University Press.

DePaulo, B. M. (1992). Nonverbal behavior and self-presentation. *Psychological Bulletin, 111,* 203–243.

DePaulo, B. M., Kenny, D. A., Hoover, C. W., Webb, W., & Oliver, P. V. (1987). Accuracy of person perception: Do people know what kinds of impressions they convey? *Journal of Personality and Social Psychology, 52,* 303–315.

DePaulo, B. M., Kirkendol, S. E., Tang, J., & O'Brien, T. (1988). The motivational impairment effect in the communication of deception. *Journal of Nonverbal Behavior, 12,* 177–202.

DePaulo, B. M., Lassiter, G. D., & Stone, J. I. (1982). Attentional determinants of success at detecting deception and truth. *Personality and Social Psychology Bulletin, 8,* 273–279.

DePaulo, B. M., Nadler, A., & Fisher, J. D. (Eds.). (1983). *New directions in helping: Help-seeking.* New York: Academic Press.

DePaulo, B. M., & Pfeifer, R. L. (1986). On-the-job experience and skill at detecting deception. *Journal of Applied Social Psychology, 16,* 249–267.

DePaulo, B. M., Stone, J. I., & Lassiter, G. D. (1985). Deceiving and detecting deceit. In B. R. Schlenker (Ed.), *The self and social life* (pp. 323–370). New York: McGraw-Hill.

DePaulo, P. J., DePaulo, B. M., Tang, J., & Swaim, G. W. (1989). Lying and detecting lies in organizations. In R. A. Giacalone & P. Rosenfeld (Eds.), *Impression management in the organization* (pp. 377–393). Hillsdale, NJ: Erlbaum.

Derlega, V. J., Hendrick, S. S., Winstead, B. A., & Berg, J. H. (1991). *Psychotherapy as a personal relationship.* New York: Guilford Press.

Derlega, V. J., Lewis, R. J., Harrison, S., Winstead, B. A., & Costanza, R. (1989). Gender differences in the initiation and attraction of tactile intimacy. *Journal of Nonverbal Behavior, 13,* 83–96.

Dermer, M. & Pyszczynski, T. A. (1978). Effects of erotica upon men's loving and liking responses for women they love. *Journal of Personality and Social Psychology, 36,* 1302–1309.

Desforges, D. M., Lord, C. G., Ramsey, S. L., Mason, J. A., Van Leeuwen, M. D., West, S. C., & Lepper, M. R. (1991). Effects of structured cooperative contact on changing negative attitudes toward stigmatized social groups. *Journal of Personality and Social Psychology, 60,* 531–544.

Deutsch, F. M. (1990). Status, sex, and smiling: The effect of role on smiling in men and women. *Personality and Social Psychology Bulletin, 16,* 531–540.

Deutsch, M. (1949a). A theory of cooperation and competition. *Human Relations, 2,* 129–152.

Deutsch, M. (1949b). An experimental study of the effects of cooperation and competition upon group process. *Human Relations, 2,* 199–231.

Deutsch, M. (1973). *The resolution of conflict.* New Haven, CT: Yale University Press.

Deutsch, M. (1980). Fifty years of conflict. In L. Festinger (Ed.), *Retrospection on social psychology.* New York: Oxford University Press.

Deutsch, M. (1993). Educating for a peaceful world. *American Psychologist, 48,* 510–517.

Deutsch, M., & Gerard, H. B. (1955). A study of normative and informational social influences upon individual judgment. *Journal of Abnormal and Social Psychology, 51,* 629–636.

Deutsch, M., & Krauss, R. M. (1960). The effect of threat upon interpersonal bargaining. *Journal of Abnormal and Social Psychology, 61,* 181–189.

Deutsch, M., & Solomon, L. (1959). Reactions to evaluations by others as influenced by self-evaluations. *Sociometry, 22,* 93–112.

Devine, P. G. (1989). Stereotypes and prejudice: Their automatic and controlled components. *Journal of Personality and Social Psychology, 56,* 5–18.

Devine, P. G., Monteith, M. J., Zuwerink, J. R., & Elliot, A. J. (1991). Prejudice with and without compunction. *Journal of Personality and Social Psychology, 60,* 817–830.

Diamond, R., & Carey, S. (1986). Why faces are and are not special: An effect of expertise. *Journal of Experimental Psychology: General, 115,* 107–117.

Diehl, M., & Stroebe, W. (1987). Productivity loss in brainstorming groups: Toward the solution of a riddle. *Journal of Personality and Social Psychology, 53,* 497–509.

Diehl, M., & Stroebe, W. (1991). Productivity loss in idea-generating groups: Tracking down the blocking effect. *Journal of Personality and Social Psychology, 61,* 392–403.

Diener, C. I., & Dweck, C. S. (1978). An analysis of learned helplessness: Continuous changes in performance, strategy, and achievement cognitions following failure. *Journal of Personality and Social Psychology, 36,* 451–462.

Diener, C. I., & Dweck, C. S. (1980). An analysis of learned helplessness: II. The processing of success. *Journal of Personality and Social Psychology, 39,* 940–952.

Diener, E. (1980). Deindividuation: The absence of self-awareness and self-regulation in group members. In P. B. Paulus (Ed.), *The psychology of group influence.* Hillsdale, NJ: Erlbaum.

Diener, E., Fraser, S. C., Beaman, A. L., & Kelem, R. (1976). Effects of deindividuation on stealing among Halloween trick or treaters. *Journal of Personality and Social Psychology, 33,* 178–183.

Dill, C. A., Gilden, E. R., Hill, P. C., & Hanselka, L. L. (1982). Federal human subjects regulations: A methodological artifact? *Personality and Social Psychology Bulletin, 8,* 417–425.

Dillard, J. P. (1991). The current status of research on sequential-request compliance techniques. *Personality and Social Psychology Bulletin, 17,* 283–288.

Dillard, J. P., & Fitzpatrick, M. A. (1985). Compliance-gaining in marital interaction. *Personality and Social Psychology Bulletin, 11,* 419–433.

Dillon, W. R., & Kumar, A. (1985). Attitude organization and the attitude-behavior relation: A critique of Bagozzi and Burnkrant's reanalysis of Fishbein and Ajzen. *Journal of Personality and Social Psychology, 49,* 33–46.

Dindia, K., & Allen, M. (1992). Sex differences in self-disclosure: A meta-analysis. *Psychological Bulletin, 112,* 106–124.

Dion, K. K. (1986). Stereotyping based on physical attractiveness: Issues and conceptual perspectives. In C. P. Herman, M. P. Zanna, & E. T. Higgins (Eds.), *Appearance, stigma, and social behavior: The Ontario Symposium* (Vol. 3, pp. 7–21). Hillsdale, NJ: Erlbaum.

Dion, K. K., & Dion, K. L. (1993). Individualistic and collectivistic perspectives on gender and the cultural context of love and intimacy. *Journal of Social Issues, 49*(3), 53–69.

Dion, K. L. (1973). Cohesiveness as a determinant of ingroup-outgroup bias. *Journal of Personality and Social Psychology, 28,* 163–171.

Dion, K. L. (1979). Intergroup conflict and intragroup cohesiveness. In W. G. Austin & S. Worchel (Eds.), *The social psychology of intergroup relations* (pp. 211–224). Pacific Grove, CA: Brooks/Cole.

Dion, K. L. (1990). Group morale. In R. Brown (Ed.), *The Marshall Cavendish encyclopedia of personal relationships: Human behavior, How groups work* (Vol. 15, pp. 1854–1861). North Bellmore, New York: Marshall Cavendish Corporation.

Dion, K. L., Berscheid, E., & Walster, E. (1972). What is beautiful is good. *Journal of Personality and Social Psychology, 24,* 285–290.

Dion, K. L., & Dion, K. K. (1988). Romantic love: Individual and cultural perspectives. In R. J. Sternberg & M. L. Barnes (Eds.), *The psychology of love* (pp. 264–289). New Haven, CT: Yale University Press.

Dion, K. L., & Evans, C. R. (1992). On cohesiveness: Reply to Keyton and other critics of the construct. *Small Group Research, 23,* 242–250.

Ditto, P. H., & Lopez, D. F. (1992). Motivated skepticism: Use of differential decision criteria for preferred and nonpreferred conclusions. *Journal of Personality and Social Psychology, 63,* 568–584.

Dixon, T. M., & Baumeister, R. F. (1991). Escaping the self: The moderating effect of self-complexity. *Personality and Social Psychology Bulletin, 17,* 363–368.

Dodge, K. A., & Coie, J. D. (1987). Social information-processing factors in reactive and proactive aggression in children's peer groups. *Journal of Personality and Social Psychology, 53,* 1146–1158.

DODGE, K. A., & CRICK, N. R. (1990). Social information-processing bases of aggressive behavior in children. *Personality and Social Psychology Bulletin, 16,* 8–22.

DOLLARD, J. R., DOOB, L. W., MILLER, N. E., MOWRER, O. H., & SEARS, R. R. (1939). *Frustration and aggression.* New Haven, CT: Yale University Press.

DOLLINGER, S. J., & CLANCY, S. M. (1993). Identity, self, and personality: II. Glimpses through the autophotographic eye. *Journal of Personality and Social Psychology, 64,* 1064–1071.

DONNERSTEIN, E. I. (1980). Aggressive erotica and violence against women. *Journal of Personality and Social Psychology, 39,* 269–277.

DONNERSTEIN, E. I. (1983). Erotica and human aggression. In R. G. Geen & E. I. Donnerstein (Eds.), *Aggression: Theoretical and empirical reviews* (Vol. 2, pp. 103–126). New York: Academic Press.

DONNERSTEIN, E. I., & BERKOWITZ, L. (1981). Victim reactions in aggressive erotic films as a factor in violence against women. *Journal of Personality and Social Psychology, 41,* 710–724.

DONNERSTEIN, E., & DONNERSTEIN, M. (1973). Variables in interracial aggression: Potential ingroup censure. *Journal of Personality and Social Psychology, 27,* 143–150.

DONNERSTEIN, E., & WILSON, D. W. (1976). The effects of noise and perceived control upon ongoing and subsequent aggressive behavior. *Journal of Personality and Social Psychology, 34,* 774–781.

DOREIAN, P. (1986). Measuring relative standing in small groups and bounded social networks. *Social Psychology Quarterly, 49,* 247–259.

DORNBUSCH, S. M., HASTORF, A. H., RICHARDSON, S. A., MUZZY, R. E., & VREELAND, R. S. (1965). The perceiver and the perceived: Their relative influence on categories of interpersonal perception. *Journal of Personality and Social Psychology, 1,* 434–440.

DOTY, R. M., PETERSON, B. E., & WINTER, D. G. (1991). Threat and authoritarianism in the United States, 1978–1987. *Journal of Personality and Social Psychology, 61,* 629–640.

DOVIDIO, J. F. (1984). Helping and altruism: An empirical and conceptual overview. In L. Berkowitz (Ed.), *Advances in experimental social psychology* (Vol. 17). New York: Academic Press.

DOVIDIO, J. F., BROWN, C. E., HELTMAN, K., ELLYSON, S. L., & KEATING, C. F. (1988). Power displays between women and men in discussions of gender-linked tasks: A multichannel study. *Journal of Personality and Social Psychology, 55,* 580–587.

DOVIDIO, J. F., ELLYSON, S. L., KEATING, C. F., HELTMAN, K., & BROWN, C. E. (1988). The relationship of social power to visual displays of dominance between men and women. *Journal of Personality and Social Psychology, 54,* 233–242.

DOVIDIO, J. F., & GAERTNER, S. L. (1986). Prejudice, discrimination, and racism: Historical trends and contemporary approaches. In J. F. Dovidio & S. L. Gaertner (Eds.), *Prejudice, discrimination, and racism* (pp. 1–34). Orlando, FL: Academic Press.

DOVIDIO, J. F., & GAERTNER, S. L. (1991) Changes in the expression and assessment of racial prejudice. In H. J. Knopke, R. J. Norell, & R. W. Rogers (Eds.), *Opening doors: Perspectives on race relations in contemporary America* (pp. 119–150). Tuscaloosa: University of Alabama Press.

DOVIDIO, J. F., PILIAVIN, J. A., GAERTNER, S. L., SCHROEDER, D. A., & CLARK, R. D., III. (1991). The arousal: Cost-reward model and the process of intervention: A review of the evidence. In M. S. Clark (Ed.), *Review of personality and social psychology* (Vol. 12, pp. 86–118). Newbury Park, CA: Sage.

DOYLE, A. C. (1938). *The complete Sherlock Holmes.* New York: Garden City.

DRABMAN, R. S., & THOMAS, M. H. (1974). Does media violence increase children's toleration of real-life aggression? *Developmental Psychology, 10,* 418–421.

DRABMAN, R. S., & THOMAS, M. H. (1976). Does watching violence on television cause apathy? *Pediatrics, 57,* 329–331.

DRIGOTAS, S. M., & RUSBULT, C. E. (1992). Should I stay or should I go? A dependence model of breakups. *Journal of Personality and Social Psychology, 62,* 62–87.

DRISCOLL, R., DAVIS, K. W., & LIPETZ, M. E. (1972). Parental influence and romantic love: The Romeo and Juliet effect. *Journal of Personality and Social Psychology, 24,* 1–10.

DSM-III: Diagnostic and statistical manual of mental disorders. (1980). Washington, DC: American Psychiatric Association.

DUBOS, R. (1965). *Man adapting.* New Haven, CT: Yale University Press.

DUCKITT, J. H. (1992). *The social psychology of prejudice.* New York: Praeger.

DUNCAN, B. L. (1976). Differential social perception and attribution of intergroup violence: Testing the lower limits of stereotyping of blacks. *Journal of Personality and Social Psychology, 34,* 590–598.

DUNKEL-SCHETTER, C., BLASBAND, D. E., FEINSTEIN, L. G., & HERBERT, T. B. (1992). Elements of supportive interactions: When are attempts to help effective? In S. Spacapan & S. Oskamp (Eds.), *Helping and being helped: Naturalistic studies* (pp. 83–114). Newbury Park, CA: Sage.

DUNN, J. (1988). *The beginnings of social understanding.* Cambridge, MA: Harvard University Press.

DUNNETTE, M. D., CAMPBELL, J., & JAASTAD, K. (1963). The effect of group participation on brainstorming effectiveness for two industrial samples. *Journal of Applied Psychology, 47,* 30–37.

DUNNING, D., GRIFFIN, D. W., MILOJKOVIC, J. D., & ROSS, L. (1990). The overconfidence effect in social prediction. *Journal of Personality and Social Psychology, 58,* 568–581.

DURAND, D. E. (1977). Power as a function of office space and physiognomy: Two studies of influence. *Psychological Reports, 40,* 755–760.

DURKHEIM, E. (1897/1951). *Suicide: A study in sociology.* New York: Free Press.

DURKHEIM, E. (1964). *The division of labor in society.* New York: Free Press.

DUTTON, D. G., & ARON, A. P. (1974). Some evidence for heightened sexual attraction under conditions of high anxiety. *Journal of Personality and Social Psychology, 30,* 510–517.

DUVAL, S., & WICKLUND, R. A. (1972). *A theory of objective self-awareness.* New York: Academic Press.

DUVAL, T. S., DUVAL, V. H., & MULILIS, J. P. (1992). Effects of self-focus, discrepancy between self and standard, and outcome expectancy favorability on the tendency to match self to standard or to withdraw. *Journal of Personality and Social Psychology, 62,* 340–348.

DWECK, C. S. (1975). The role of expectations and attributions in the alleviation of learned helplessness. *Journal of Personality and Social Psychology, 31,* 674–685.

EAGLY, A. (1974). Comprehensibility of persuasive arguments as a determinant of opinion change. *Journal of Personality and Social Psychology, 29,* 758–773.

EAGLY, A. H. (1978). Sex differences in influenceability. *Psychological Bulletin, 85,* 86–116.

EAGLY, A. H. (1987). *Sex difference in social behavior: A social-role interpretation.* Hillsdale, NJ: Erlbaum.

EAGLY, A. H. (1992). Uneven progress: Social psychology and the study of attitudes. *Journal of Personality and Social Psychology, 63,* 693–710.

EAGLY, A. H., ASHMORE, R. D., MAKHIJANI, M. G., & LONGO, L. C. (1991). What is beautiful is good, but . . . : A meta-analytic review of research on the physical attractiveness stereotype. *Psychological Bulletin, 110,* 109–128.

EAGLY, A. H., & CARLI, L. L. (1981). Sex of researchers and sex-typed communications as determinants of sex differences in influenceability: A meta-analysis of social influence studies. *Psychological Bulletin, 90,* 1–20.

EAGLY, A. H., & CHAIKEN, S. (1975). An attribution analysis of the effect of communicator characteristics on opinion change: The case of communicator attractiveness. *Journal of Personality and Social Psychology, 32,* 136–144.

EAGLY, A. H., & CHAIKEN, S. (1984). Cognitive theories of persuasion. In L. Berkowitz (Ed.), *Advances in experimental social psychology* (Vol. 17, pp. 267–359). New York: Academic Press.

EAGLY, A. H., & CHAIKEN, S. (1992). *The psychology of attitudes.* San Diego, CA: Harcourt Brace Jovanovich.

EAGLY, A. H., & CROWLEY, M. (1986). Gender and helping behavior: A meta-analytic review of the social psychological literature. *Psychological Bulletin, 100,* 283–308.

EAGLY, A. H., & JOHNSON, B. T. (1990). Gender and leadership style: A meta-analysis. *Psychological Bulletin, 108,* 233–256.

EAGLY, A. H., & KARAU, S. J. (1991). Gender and the emergence of leaders: A meta-analysis. *Journal of Personality and Social Psychology, 60,* 685–710.

EAGLY, A. H., MAKHIJANA, M. G., & KLONSKY, B. G. (1992). Gender and the evaluation of leaders: A meta-analysis. *Psychological Bulletin, 111,* 3–22.

EAGLY, A. H., & STEFFEN, V. J. (1984). Gender stereotypes stem from the distribution of women and men into social roles. *Journal of Personality and Social Psychology, 46,* 735–754.

EAGLY, A. H., & STEFFEN, V. J. (1986). Gender and aggressive behavior: A meta-analytic review of the social psychological literature. *Psychological Bulletin, 100,* 309–330.

EAGLY, A. H., WOOD, W., & CHAIKEN, S. (1978). Causal inferences about communicators and their effect on opinion change. *Journal of Personality and Social Psychology, 36,* 424–435.

EAGLY, A. H., WOOD, W., & FISHBAUGH, L. (1981). Sex differences in conformity: Surveillance by the group as a determinant of male nonconformity. *Journal of Personality and Social Psychology, 40,* 384–394.

EARLE, H. H. (1973). *Police recruit training: Stress vs. nonstress.* Springfield, IL: Charles C Thomas.

EBBESEN, E., KJOS, G., & KONEČNI, V. (1976). Spatial ecology: Its effects on the choice of friends and enemies. *Journal of Experimental Social Psychology, 12,* 505–518.

ECKLAND, B. K. (1968). Theories of mate selection. *Eugenics Quarterly, 15,* 71–84.

EDELMANN, R. J., ASENDORPF, J., CONTARELLO, A., ZAMMUNER, V., GEORGAS, J., & VILLANUEVA, C. (1989). Self-reported expression of embarrassment in five European cultures. *Journal of Cross-Cultural Psychology, 20,* 357–371.

EDINGER, J. A., & PATTERSON, M. L. (1983). Nonverbal involvement and social control. *Psychology Bulletin, 83,* 30–56.

EDNEY, J. (1975). Territoriality and control: A field experiment. *Journal of Personality and Social Psychology, 31,* 1108–1115.

EDNEY, J. (1976). Human territories: Comment on functional properties. *Environment and Behavior, 8,* 31–48.

EDNEY, J. J. (1980). The commons problem: Alternative perspectives. *American Psychologist, 35,* 131–150.

EDWARDS, A. L., & KLOCKARS, A. J. (1981). Significant others and self-evaluation: Relationships between perceived and actual evaluations. *Personality and Social Psychology Bulletin, 7,* 244–251.

EDWARDS, D. J. A. (1972). Approaching the unfamiliar: A study of human interaction distances. *Journal of Behavioral Sciences, 1,* 249–250.

EDWARDS, K. (1987). Effects of sex and glasses on attitudes toward intelligence and attractiveness. *Psychological Reports, 60,* 590.

EDWARDS, K. (1990). The interplay of affect and cognition in attitude formation and change. *Journal of Personality and Social Psychology, 59,* 202–216.

EDWARDS, W. (1968). Conservatism in human information processing. In B. Kleinmuntz (Ed.), *Formal representation of human judgment* (pp. 17–52). New York: Wiley.

EDWARDS, W. (1992). Discussion: Of human skills. *Organizational Behavior and Human Performance, 53,* 267–277.

EGETH, H. E. (1993). What do we *not* know about eyewitness identification. *American Psychologist, 48,* 577–580.

EHLERT, J., EHLERT, N., & MERRENS, M. (1973). The influence of ideological affiliation on helping behavior. *Journal of Social Psychology, 89,* 315–316.

EINHORN, H. J., & HOGARTH, R. M. (1978). Confidence in judgment: Persistence in the illusion of validity. *Psychological Review, 85,* 395–416.

EISENBERG, N. (1992). *The caring child.* Cambridge, MA: Harvard University Press.

EISENBERG, N., & FABES, R. A. (1991). Prosocial behavior and empathy: A multimethod developmental perspective. In M. S. Clark (Ed.), *Review of personality and social psychology* (Vol. 12, pp. 34–61). Newbury Park, CA: Sage.

EISENBERG, N., FABES, R. A., MILLER, P. A., FULTZ, J., SHELL, R., MATHY, R. M., & RENO, R. R. (1989). Relation of sympathy and personal distress to prosocial behavior: A multimethod study. *Journal of Personality and Social Psychology, 57,* 55–66.

EISENBERG, N., & MILLER, P. (1987). The relation of empathy to prosocial and related behaviors. *Psychological Bulletin, 101,* 91–119.

EISENBERG-BERG, N., & GEISHEKER, E. (1979). Content of preachings and power of the model/preachers: The effect on children's generosity. *Developmental Psychology, 15,* 168–175.

EISER, J. R., & VAN DER PLIGT, J. (1988). *Attitudes and decisions.* New York: Routledge & Kegan Paul.

EKMAN, P. (1985). *Telling lies: Clues to deceit in the marketplace, politics, and marriage.* New York: Norton.

EKMAN, P. (1988). Lying and nonverbal behavior: Theoretical issues and new findings. *Journal of Nonverbal Behavior, 12,* 163–175.

EKMAN, P. (1992a). Are there basic emotions? *Psychological Review, 99,* 550–553.

EKMAN, P. (1992b). Facial expressions of emotion: New findings, new questions. *Psychological Science, 3,* 34–38.

EKMAN, P., DAVIDSON, R. J., & FRIESEN, W. V. (1990). Duchenne's smile: Emotional expression and brain physiology II. *Journal of Personality and Social Psychology, 58,* 342–353.

EKMAN, P., & FRIESEN, W. V. (1975). *Unmasking the face.* Englewood Cliffs, NJ: Prentice-Hall.

EKMAN, P., FRIESEN, W. V., & BEAR, J. (1984). The international language of gestures. *Psychology Today, 18*(5), 64–69.

EKMAN, P., FRIESEN, W. V., CHAN, A., DIACOYANNI-TARLATZIS, I., HEIDER, K., KRAUSE, R., LECOMPTE, W. A., O'SULLIVAN, M., PITCAIRN, T., RICCI-BITTI, P. E., SCHERER, K., TOMITA, M., & TZAVARAS, A. (1987). Universals and cultural differences in the judgments of facial expressions of emotion. *Journal of Personality and Social Psychology, 53,* 712–717.

EKMAN, P., FRIESEN, W. V., & ELLSWORTH, P. (1972). *Emotion in the human face: Guidelines for research and an integration of findings.* New York: Pergamon.

EKMAN, P., FRIESEN, W. V., & O'SULLIVAN, M. (1988). Smiles when lying. *Journal of Personality and Social Psychology, 54,* 414–420.

EKMAN, P., FRIESEN, W. V., O'SULLIVAN, M., & SCHERER, K. (1980). Relative importance of face, body, and speech in judgments of personality and affect. *Journal of Personality and Social Psychology, 38,* 270–277.

ELDRIDGE, A. F. (1983). Pondering intangibles: A value analysis of Henry Kissinger. In D. Caldwell (Ed.), *Henry Kissinger: His personality and policies* (pp. 64–85). Durham, NC: Duke University Press.

ELIG, T. W., & FRIEZE, I. H. (1979). Measuring causal attributions for success and failure. *Journal of Personality and Social Psychology, 37,* 621–634.

ELKIN, R. A., & LEIPPE, M. R. (1986). Physiological arousal, dissonance, and attitude change: Evidence for a dissonance-arousal link and a "Don't remind me" effect. *Journal of Personality and Social Psychology, 51,* 55–65.

ELLIOT, G., & TYSON, G. (1983). The effects of modifying color-meaning concepts on the racial attitudes of black and white South African preschool children. *Journal of Social Psychology, 121,* 181–190.

ELLIOTT, G. C. (1979). Some effects of deception and level of self-monitoring on planning and reacting to a self-presentation. *Journal of Personality and Social Psychology, 37,* 1282–1290.

ELLSWORTH, P. C., CARLSMITH, J. M., & HENSON, A. (1972). The stare as a stimulus to flight in human subjects: A series of field experiments. *Journal of Personality and Social Psychology, 21,* 302–311.

ELMS, A. C. (1967). Role playing, incentive, and dissonance, *Psychological Bulletin, 68,* 132–148.

ELMS, A. C. (1986). From House to Haig: Private life and public style in American foreign policy advisors. *Journal of Social Issues, 42*(2), 33–53.

ELSTER, J. (1989). *The cement of society: A study of social order.* Cambridge: Cambridge University Press.

EMERSON, R. W. (1926). *On civil disobedience and other essays.* New York: Holt.

ENGEL, G. L. (1978). Psychologic stress, vasodepressor (vasovagal) syncope, and sudden death. *Annals of Internal Medicine, 89,* 403–412.

EPSTEIN, R., & KOERNER, J. (1986). The self-concept and other daemons. In J. Suls & A. G. Greenwald (Eds.), *Psychological perspectives on the self* (Vol. 3, pp. 27–53). Hillsdale, NJ: Erlbaum.

ERBER, R., & FISKE, S. T. (1984). Outcome dependency and attention to inconsistent information. *Journal of Personality and Social Psychology, 47,* 709–726.

ERDLEY, C. A., & D'AGOSTINO, P. R. (1988). Cognitive and affective components of automatic priming effects. *Journal of Personality and Social Psychology, 54,* 741–747.

Ernst, J. M., & Heesacker, M. (1993). Application of the elaboration likelihood model of attitude change to assertion training. *Journal of Counseling Psychology, 40,* 37–45.

Eron, L. D. (1963). Relationship of TV viewing habits and aggressive behavior in children. *Journal of Abnormal and Social Psychology, 67,* 193–196.

Eron, L. D. (1980). Prescription for reduction of aggression. *American Psychologist, 35,* 244–252.

Eron, L. D. (1982). Parent-child interaction, TV violence, and aggression in children. *American Psychologist, 37,* 197–211.

Eron, L. D. (1987). The development of aggressive behavior from the perspective of a developing behaviorism. *American Psychologist, 42,* 435–442.

Eron, L. D., Huesmann, L. R., Dubow, E., Romanoff, R., & Yarmel, P. (1987). Aggression and its correlates over 22 years. In D. Crowell, I. Evans, & C. O'Donnell (Eds.), *Childhood aggression and violence* (pp. 249–262). New York: Plenum.

Eron, L. D., Huesmann, L. R., Lefkowitz, M. M., & Walder, L. O. (1972). Does television violence cause aggression? *American Psychologist, 27,* 253–263.

Esser, A. H. (1970). Interactional hierarchy and power structure on a psychiatric ward. In S. J. Hutt & C. Hutt (Eds.), *Behavior studies in psychiatry.* New York: Oxford University Press.

Esser, J. K., & Lindoerfer, J. S. (1989). Groupthink and the space shuttle *Challenger* disaster: Toward a quantitative case analysis. *Journal of Behavioral Decision Making, 2,* 167–177.

Evans, C. R., & Dion, K. L. (1991). Group cohesion and performance: A meta-analysis. *Small Group Research, 22,* 175–186.

Evans, G. W. (1979). Behavioral and physiological consequences of crowding in humans. *Journal of Applied Social Psychology, 9,* 27–46.

Evans, G. W., & Cohen, S. (1987). Environmental stress. In D. Stokols & I. Altman (Eds.), *Handbook of environmental psychology* (Vol. 1, pp. 571–610). New York: Wiley.

Evans, G. W., Palsane, M. N., Lepore, S. J., & Martin, J. (1989). Residential density and psychological health: The mediating effects of social support. *Journal of Personality and Social Psychology, 57,* 994–999.

Evans, R. I. (1980). Behavioral medicine: A new applied challenge to social psychologies. In L. Bickman (Ed.), *Applied social psychology annual* (Vol. 1). Newbury Park, CA: Sage.

Evans, R. I. (1984). A social inoculation strategy to deter smoking in adolescents. In J. D. Matarazzo, J. A. Herd, N. E. Miller, & S. M. Weiss (Eds.), *Behavioral health: A handbook of health enhancement and disease prevention.* New York: Wiley.

Evans, R. L., & Dingus, C. M. (1987). Serving the vulnerable: Models for treatment of loneliness. *Journal of Social Behavior and Personality, 2,* 249–259.

Exline, R. (1962). Need affiliation and initial communication behavior in problem-solving groups characterized by low interpersonal visibility. *Psychological Reports, 10,* 79–89.

Exline, R., & Messick, D. (1967). The effects of dependency and social reinforcement upon visual behavior during an interview. *British Journal of Social and Clinical Psychology, 6,* 256–266.

Fairweather, G. W., & Tornatzky, L. G. (1977). *Experimental methods for social policy research.* New York: Pergamon.

Falbo, T. (1977). The multidimensional scaling of power strategies. *Journal of Personality and Social Psychology, 35,* 537–548.

Falbo, T., & Beck, R. C. (1979). Naive psychology and the attributional model of achievement. *Journal of Personality, 47,* 185–195.

Falbo, T., & Peplau, L. A. (1980). Power strategies in intimate relationships. *Journal of Personality and Social Psychology, 38,* 618–628.

Fazio, R. H. (1979). Motives for social comparison: The construction-validation distinction. *Journal of Personality and Social Psychology, 37,* 1683–1698.

Fazio, R. H. (1986). How do attitudes guide behavior? In R. M. Sorrentino & E. T. Higgins (Eds.), *The handbook of motivation and cognition: Foundations of social behavior* (pp. 204–243). New York: Guilford Press.

Fazio, R. H. (1987). Self-perception theory: A current perspective. In M. P. Zanna, J. M. Olson, & C. P. Herman (Eds.), *Social influence: The Ontario Symposium* (Vol. 5, pp. 129–150). Hillsdale, NJ: Erlbaum.

Fazio, R. H. (1989). On the power and functionality of attitudes: The role of attitude accessibility. In A. R. Pratkanis, S. J. Breckler, & A. G. Greenwald (Eds.), *Attitude structure and function* (pp. 153–180). Hillsdale, NJ: Erlbaum.

Fazio, R. H. (1990). Multiple processes by which attitudes guide behavior: The MODE model as an integrative framework. In M. P. Zanna (Ed.), *Advances in experimental social psychology* (Vol. 23, pp. 75–109). New York: Academic Press.

Fazio, R. H., Effrein, E. A., & Falender, V. J. (1981). Self-perceptions following social interaction. *Journal of Personality and Social Psychology, 41,* 232–242.

Fazio, R. H., Powell, M. C., & Herr, P. M. (1983). Toward a process model of the attitude-behavior relation: Accessing one's attitude upon mere observation of the attitude object. *Journal of Personality and Social Psychology, 44,* 723–735.

Fazio, R. H., Sanbonmatsu, D. M., Powell, M. C., & Kardes, F. R. (1986). On the automatic activation of attitudes. *Journal of Personality and Social Psychology, 50,* 229–238.

Fazio, R. H., & Williams, C. J. (1986). Attitude accessibility as a moderator of the attitude-perception and attitude-behavior relations: An investigation of the 1984 presidential election. *Journal of Personality and Social Psychology, 51,* 505–514.

Fazio, R. H., & Zanna, M. P. (1978). Attitudinal qualities relating to the strength of the attitude-behavior relationship. *Journal of Experimental Social Psychology, 14,* 398–408.

Fazio, R. H., & Zanna, M. P. (1981). Direct experience and attitude-behavior consistency. In L. Berkowitz (Ed.), *Advances in experimental social psychology* (Vol. 14, pp. 162–202). New York: Academic Press.

Fazio, R. H., Zanna, M. P., & Cooper, J. (1977). Dissonance and self-perception: An integrative view of each theory's proper domain of application. *Journal of Experimental Social Psychology, 13,* 464–479.

Feather, N. T. (1969). Attribution of responsibility and valence of success and failure in relation to initial confidence and task performance. *Journal of Personality and Social Psychology, 13,* 129–144.

Feather, N. T. (1993). Authoritarianism and attitudes toward high achievers. *Journal of Personality and Social Psychology, 65,* 152–164.

Feather, N. T., & Simon, J. G. (1971). Attribution of responsibility and valence of outcome in relation to initial confidence and success and failure of self and other. *Journal of Personality and Social Psychology, 18,* 173–188.

Federal Bureau of Investigation. (1988). *Uniform crime reports.* Washington, DC: U.S. Department of Justice.

Federal Bureau of Investigation. (1989). *Uniform crime reports.* Washington, DC: U.S. Department of Justice.

Feeney, J. A., & Noller, P. (1990). Attachment style as a predictor of adult romantic relationships. *Journal of Personality and Social Psychology, 58,* 281–291.

Fehr, B. (1988). Prototype analysis of the concepts of love and commitment. *Journal of Personality and Social Psychology, 55,* 557–579.

Feierabend, I. K., & Feierabend, R. L. (1972). Systemic conditions of political aggression: An application of frustration-aggression theory. In I. K. Feierabend, R. L. Feierabend, & T. R. Guff (Eds.), *Anger, violence, and politics* (pp. 136–183). Englewood Cliffs, NJ: Prentice-Hall.

Fein, S., Hilton, J. L., & Miller, D. T. (1990). Suspicion of ulterior motivation and the correspondence bias. *Journal of Personality and Social Psychology, 58,* 753–764.

Feingold, A. (1988). Matching for attractiveness in romantic partners and same-sex friends: A meta-analysis and theoretical critique. *Psychological Bulletin, 104,* 226–235.

Feingold, A. (1992). Good-looking people are not what we think. *Psychological Bulletin, 111,* 304–341.

Feldman, N. S., & Ruble, D. N. (1981). The development of person perception: Cognitive and social factors. In S. S. Brehm, S. M. Kassin, & F. X. Gibbons (Eds.), *Developmental social psychology* (pp. 191–210). New York: Oxford University Press.

Feldman, R. S. (1986). Introduction. The present and promise of the social psychology of education. In R. S. Feldman (Ed)., *The social psychology of education: Current research and theory* (pp. 1–13). New York: Cambridge University Press.

Feldman, R. S., Philippot, P., & Custrini, R. J. (1991). Social competence and nonverbal behavior. In R. S. Feldman & B. Rime (Eds.), *Fundamental of nonverbal behavior* (pp. 329–350). New York: Cambridge University Press.

Feldman, R. S., & Rime, B. (Eds.). (1991). *Fundamentals of nonverbal behavior.* New York: Cambridge University Press.

Felipe, N. J., & Sommer, R. (1966). Invasions of personal space. *Social Problems, 14,* 206–214.

Fellner, C. H., & Marshall, J. R. (1981). Kidney donors revisited. In J. P. Rushton & R. M. Sorrentino (Eds.), *Altruism and helping behavior.* Hillsdale, NJ: Erlbaum.

Felmlee, D., Sprecher, S., & Bassin, E. (1990). The dissolution of intimate relationships: A hazard model. *Social Psychology Quarterly, 53,* 13–30.

Felson, R. B. (1981). Self and reflected appraisals among football players: A test of the Meadian hypothesis. *Social Psychology Quarterly, 44,* 116–126.

Felson, R. B., & Tedeschi, J. T. (Eds.). (1993). *Aggression and violence: Social interaction perspectives.* Washington, DC: American Psychological Association.

Fenigstein, A., Scheier, M. F., & Buss, A. H. (1975). Public and private self-consciousness: Assessment and theory. *Journal of Consulting and Clinical Psychology, 43,* 522–527.

Ferguson, T. J., & Rule, B. G. (1983). An attributional analysis of anger and aggression. In R. G. Geen & E. I. Donnerstein (Eds.), *Aggression: Theoretical and empirical reviews* (Vol. 1, pp. 41–74). New York: Academic Press.

Ferraro, G. A. (1984). Bridging the wage gap: Pay equity and job evaluations. *American Psychologist, 39,* 1166–1173.

Feshbach, S. (1956). The catharsis hypothesis and some consequences of interaction with aggressive and neutral play objects. *Journal of Personality, 24,* 449–461.

Feshbach, S. (1971). Dynamics and morality of violence and aggression: Some psychological considerations. *American Psychologist, 26,* 281–292.

Feshbach, S. (1990). Psychology, human violence, and the search for peace: Issues in science and social values. *Journal of Social Issues, 46*(1), 183–198.

Feshbach, S., & Singer, R. D. (1971). *Television and aggression.* San Francisco: Jossey-Bass.

Festinger, L. (1950). Informal social communication. *Psychological Review, 57,* 271–282.

Festinger, L. (1954). A theory of social comparison processes. *Human Relations, 7,* 117–140.

Festinger, L. (1957). *A theory of cognitive dissonance.* Stanford, CA: Stanford University Press.

Festinger, L., Riecken, H. W., & Schachter, S. (1956). *When prophecy fails.* Minneapolis: University of Minnesota Press.

Festinger, L., Schachter, S., & Back, K. (1950). *Social pressures in informal groups: A study of human factors in housing.* New York: Harper.

Fiedler, F. E. (1978). The contingency model and the dynamics of the leadership process. In L. Berkowitz (Ed.), *Advances in experimental social psychology* (Vol. 12, pp. 59–112). New York: Academic Press.

Fiedler, F. E. (1981). Leadership effectiveness. *American Behavioral Scientist, 24,* 619–632.

Fiedler, F. E. (1986). The contribution of cognitive resources to leadership performance. *Journal of Applied Social Psychology, 16,* 532–548.

Fiedler, F. E., & Chemers, M. M. (1974). *Leadership and effective management.* Glenview, IL: Scott, Foresman.

Fiedler, F. E., & Garcia, J. E. (1987). *New approaches to leadership: Cognitive resources and organizational performance.* New York: Wiley.

Field, R. H. G., & House, R. J. (1990). A test of the Vroom-Yetton model using manager and subordinate reports. *Journal of Applied Psychology, 75,* 362–366.

Fincham, F. D., Beach, S. R., & Baucom, D. H. (1987). Attribution processes in distressed and nondistressed couples: IV. Self-partner attribution differences. *Journal of Personality and Social Psychology, 52,* 739–748.

Fincham, F. D., & Bradbury, T. N. (1992). Assessing attributions in marriage: The relationship attribution measure. *Journal of Personality and Social Psychology, 62,* 457–468.

Fincham, F. D., & Bradbury, T. N. (1993). Marital satisfaction, depression, and attributions: A longitudinal analysis. *Journal of Personality and Social Psychology, 64,* 442–452.

Fischer, K., Schoeneman, T. J., & Rubanowitz, D. E. (1987). Attributions in the advice columns: II. The dimensionality of actors' and observers' explanations for interpersonal problems. *Personality and Social Psychology Bulletin, 13,* 458–466.

Fischhoff, B. (1977). Perceived informativeness of facts. *Journal of Experimental Psychology: Human Perception and Performance, 3,* 349–358.

Fishbein, M., & Ajzen, I. (1975). *Belief, attitude, intention, and behavior: An introduction to theory and research.* Reading, MA: Addison-Wesley.

Fisher, B. S., & Nasar, J. L. (1992). Fear of crime in relation to three exterior site features: Prospect, refuge, and escape. *Environment and Behavior, 24,* 35–65.

Fisher, J. D., & Byrne, D. (1975). Too close for comfort: Sex differences in response to invasions of personal space. *Journal of Personality and Social Psychology, 32,* 15–21.

Fisher, J. D., DePaulo, B. M., & Nadler, A. (1981). Extending altruism beyond the altruistic act: The mixed effects of aid on the help recipient. In J. P. Rushton & R. M. Sorrentino (Eds.), *Altruism and helping behavior.* Hillsdale, NJ: Erlbaum.

Fisher, J. D., & Fisher, W. A. (1992). Changing AIDS risk behavior. *Psychological Bulletin, 111,* 454–474.

Fisher, J. D., Nadler, A., & Whitcher-Alagna, S. W. (1982). Recipient reactions to aid. *Psychological Bulletin, 91,* 27–54.

Fisher, J. D., Rytting, M., & Heslin, R. (1976). Hands touching hands: Affective and evaluative effects of an interpersonal touch. *Sociometry, 39,* 416–421.

Fisher, W. A., & Fisher, J. D. (1993). A general social psychological model for changing AIDS risk behavior. In J. B. Pryor & G. D. Reeder (Eds.), *The social psychology of HIV infection* (pp. 127–153). Hillsdale, NJ: Erlbaum.

Fishman, C. (1966). Need for approval and the expression of aggression under varying conditions of frustration. *Journal of Personality and Social Psychology, 4,* 155–164.

Fiske, S. T. (1992). Thinking is for doing: Portraits of social cognition from daguerreotype to laserphoto. *Journal of Personality and Social Psychology, 63,* 877–889.

Fiske, S. T. (1993). Social cognition and social perception. *Annual Review of Psychology, 44,* 155–194.

Fiske, S. T., Bersoff, D. N., Borgida, E., Deaux, K., & Heilman, M. E. (1991). Social science research on trial: The use of sex stereotyping research in Price Waterhouse v. Hopkins. *American Psychologist, 46,* 1049–1060.

Fiske, S. T., Lau, R. R., & Smith, R. A. (1990). On the varieties and utilities of political expertise. *Social Cognition, 8,* 31–48.

Fiske, S. T., & Neuberg, S. L. (1990). A continuum of impression formation, from category-based to individuating processes: Influences of information and motivation on attention and interpretation. In M. P. Zanna (Ed.), *Advances in experimental social psychology* (Vol. 23, pp. 1–74). New York: Academic Press.

Fiske, S. T., & Taylor, S. E. (1991). *Social cognition* (2nd ed.). New York: McGraw-Hill.

Fiske, S. T., Taylor, S. E., Etcoff, N. L., & Laufer, J. K. (1979). Imagining, empathy, and causal attribution. *Journal of Experimental Social Psychology, 15,* 356–377.

Fitzgerald, L. F. (1993). Sexual harassment: Violence against women in the workplace. *American Psychologist, 48,* 1070–1076.

Fleming, J. H., & Darley, J. M. (1989). Perceiving choice and constraint: The effects of contextual and behavioral cues on attitude attribution. *Journal of Personality and Social Psychology, 56,* 27–40.

Fletcher, G. J., Reeder, G. D., & Bull, V. (1990). Bias and accuracy in attitude attribution: The role of attributional complexity. *Journal of Experimental Social Psychology, 26,* 275–288.

Fletcher, G. J. O. (1984). Psychology and common sense. *American Psychologist, 39,* 203–213.

Fletcher, G. J. O., & Ward, C. (1988). Attribution theory and processes: A cross-cultural perspective. In M. H Bond (Ed.), *The cross-cultural challenge to social psychology* (pp. 230–244). Newbury Park, CA: Sage.

Fletcher, G. P. (1988). *A crime of self-defense: Bernhard Goetz and the law on trial.* New York: Free Press.

Flink, C., Boggiano, A. K., & Barrett, M. (1990). Controlling teaching strategies: Undermining children's self-determination and performance. *Journal of Personality and Social Psychology, 59,* 916–924.

Flowers, M. L. (1977). A laboratory test of some implications of Janis's groupthink hypothesis. *Journal of Personality and Social Psychology, 35,* 888–896.

Foa, U. G., & Foa, E. B. (1974). *Societal structures of the mind.* Springfield, IL: Charles C Thomas.

Fogelman, E., & Wiener, V. L. (1985). The few, the brave, the noble. *Psychology Today, 19*(8), pp. 60–65.

Foley, L. A. (1976). Personality and situational influences on changes in prejudice: A replication of Cook's railroad game in a prison setting. *Journal of Personality and Social Psychology, 34,* 846–856.

Folkman, S. (1984). Personal control and stress and coping processes: A theoretical analysis. *Journal of Personality and Social Psychology, 46,* 839–852.

Folkman, S., & Lazarus, R. S. (1988). Coping as a mediator of emotion. *Journal of Personality and Social Psychology, 54,* 466–475.

Folkman, S., Lazarus, R. S., Dunkel-Schetter, C., DeLongis, A., & Gruen, R. J. (1986). The dynamics of a stressful encounter: Cognitive appraisal, coping, and encounter outcomes. *Journal of Personality and Social Psychology, 50,* 992–1003.

Follette, V. M., & Jacobson, N. S. (1987). Importance of attributions as a predictor of how people cope with failure. *Journal of Personality and Social Psychology, 52,* 1205–1211.

Fong, G. T., Krantz, D. H., & Nisbett, R. E. (1986). The effects of statistical training on thinking about everyday problems. *Cognitive Psychology, 18,* 253–292.

Forbach, G. B., Evans, R. G., & Bodine, S. M. (1986). Gender-based schematic processing of self-descriptive information. *Journal of Research in Personality, 20,* 372–384.

Ford, M. R., & Lowery, C. R. (1986). Gender differences in moral reasoning: A comparison of the use of justice and care orientations. *Journal of Personality and Social Psychology, 50,* 777–788.

Forer, B. R. (1949). The fallacy of personal validation: A classroom demonstration of gullibility. *Journal of Abnormal and Social Psychology, 44,* 118–123.

Forgas, J. P. (1993). On making sense of odd couples: Mood effects on the perception of mismatched relationships. *Personality and Social Psychology Bulletin, 19,* 59–70.

Forgas, J. P., & Bower, G. H. (1987). Mood effect on person-perception judgments. *Journal of Personality and Social Psychology, 53,* 53–60.

Forgas, J. P., & Dobosz, B. (1980). Dimensions of romantic involvement: Towards a taxonomy of heterosexual relationships. *Social Psychology Quarterly, 43,* 290–300.

Forsterling, F. (1985). Attribution retraining: A review. *Psychological Bulletin, 98,* 495–512.

Forsterling, F. (1989). Models of covariation and attribution: How do they relate to the analogy of analysis of variance? *Journal of Personality and Social Psychology, 57,* 615–625.

Forsyth, D. R. (1981). Moral judgment: The influence of ethical ideology. *Personality and Social Psychology Bulletin, 7,* 218–223.

Forsyth, D. R. (1985). Individual differences in information integration during moral judgment. *Journal of Personality and Social Psychology, 49,* 264–272.

Forsyth, D. R. (1986). An attributional analysis of students' reactions to success and failure. In R. Feldman (Ed.), *The social psychology of education.* New York: Cambridge University Press.

Forsyth, D. R. (1988). Social psychology's three little pigs. *Journal of Social Behavior and Personality, 3,* 65–67.

Forsyth, D. R. (1990). *Group dynamics* (2nd ed.). Pacific Grove, CA: Brooks/Cole.

Forsyth, D. R., Berger, R., & Mitchell, T. (1981). The effects of self-serving vs. other-serving claims of responsibility on attraction and attribution in groups. *Social Psychology Quarterly, 44,* 59–64.

Forsyth, D. R., & Leary, M. R. (1991). Metatheoretical and epistemological issues. In C. R. Snyder & D. R. Forsyth (Eds.), *Handbook of social and clinical psychology: The health perspective* (pp. 757–773). New York: Pergamon.

Forsyth, D. R., & McMillan, J. H. (1981a). The attribution cube and reactions to educational outcomes. *Journal of Educational Psychology, 73,* 632–641.

Forsyth, D. R., & McMillan, J. H. (1981b). Attributions, affect, and expectations: A test of Weiner's three-dimensional model. *Journal of Educational Psychology, 73,* 393–401.

Forsyth, D. R., & Nye, J. L. (1990). Personal moral philosophy and moral choice. *Journal of Research in Personality, 24,* 398–414.

Forsyth, D. R., & Pope, W. R. (1984). Ethical ideology and judgments of social psychology research: Multidimensional analysis. *Journal of Personality and Social Psychology, 46,* 1365–1375.

Forsyth, D. R., Pope, W. R., & McMillan, J. H. (1985). Students' reactions after cheating: An attributional analysis. *Contemporary Educational Psychology, 10,* 72–82.

Forsyth, D. R., Riess, M., & Schlenker, B. R. (1977). Impression management concerns governing reactions to a faulty decision. *Representative Research in Social Psychology, 8,* 12–22.

Forsyth, D. R., Schlenker, B. R., Leary, M. R., & McCown, N. E. (1985). Self-presentational determinants of sex differences in leadership behavior. *Small Group Behavior, 16,* 197–210.

Forsyth, D. R., & Strong, S. R. (1986). The scientific study of counseling and psychotherapy: A unificationist view. *American Psychologist, 41,* 113–119.

Foti, R. J., Fraser, S. L., & Lord, R. G. (1982). Effects of leadership labels and prototypes on perceptions of political leaders. *Journal of Applied Psychology, 67,* 326–333.

Foushee, H. C. (1984). Dyads and triads at 35,000 feet: Factors affecting group process and aircrew performance. *American Psychologist, 39,* 885–893.

Foushee, H. C. (1986, August). *Group performance in space: Lessons learned from aviation.* Paper presented at the Annual Meetings of the American Psychological Association, Washington, DC.

Foushee, H. C., & Helmreich, R. L. (1988). Group interaction and flightcrew performance. In E. L. Wiener & D. C. Nagel (Eds.), *Human factors in modern aviation.* New York: Academic Press.

Foxman, J., & Radtke, R. (1970). Negative expectancy and the choice of an aversive task. *Journal of Personality and Social Psychology, 15,* 253–257.

Frager, R. (1970). Conformity and anticonformity in Japan. *Journal of Personality and Social Psychology, 15,* 203–210.

Franke, R. H. (1979). The Hawthorne experiments: Re-view. *American Sociological Review, 44,* 861–867.

Frazier, P. A. (1990). Victim attributions and post-rape trauma. *Journal of Personality and Social Psychology, 59,* 298–304.

Frazier, P. A. (1991). Self-blame as a mediator of postrape depressive symptoms. *Journal of Social and Clinical Psychology, 10,* 47–57.

Fredrick, A. J., & Dossett, D. L. (1983). Attitude-behavior relations: A comparison of the Fishbein-Ajzen and the Bentler-Speckart models. *Journal of Personality and Social Psychology, 45,* 501–512.

Freedman, J. L. (1965). The long-term behavioral effects of cognitive dissonance. *Journal of Experimental Social Psychology, 1,* 145–155.

Freedman, J. L. (1973). The effects of population density on humans. In James T. Fawcett (Ed.), *Psychological perspectives on population.* New York: Basic Books.

Freedman, J. L. (1975). *Crowding and human behavior.* San Francisco: Freeman.

Freedman, J. L. (1979). Reconciling apparent differences between responses of humans and other animals to crowding. *Psychological Review, 86,* 80–85.

Freedman, J. L. (1984). Effect of television violence on aggressiveness. *Psychological Bulletin, 96,* 227–246.

Freedman, J. L., Cunningham, J. A., & Krismer, K. (1992). Inferred values and the reverse-incentive effect in induced compliance. *Journal of Personality and Social Psychology, 62,* 357–368.

Freedman, J. L., & Fraser, S. C. (1966). Compliance without pressure: The foot-in-the-door technique. *Journal of Personality and Social Psychology, 4,* 195–202.

French, J. R. P., Jr., & Raven, B. (1959). The bases of social power. In D. Cartwright

(Ed.), *Studies in social power.* Ann Arbor, MI: Institute for Social Research.

Freud, S. (1920/1961). *A general introduction to psychoanalysis.* New York: Washington Square Press.

Freud, S. (1930/1961). *Civilization and its discontents.* London: Hogarth.

Freud, S. (1933). *New introductory lectures on psychoanalysis.* London: Hogarth.

Frey, D. (1981). Postdecisional preferences for decision-relevant information as a function of the competence of its source and the degree of familiarity with this information. *Journal of Experimental Social Psychology, 17,* 51–67.

Frey, D. (1982). Different levels of cognitive dissonance, information seeking, and information avoidance. *Journal of Personality and Social Psychology, 43,* 1175–1183.

Frey, D., Fries, A., & Osnabrugge, G. (1983). Reactions to failure after taking a placebo: A study of dissonance reduction. *Personality and Social Psychology Bulletin, 9,* 481–488.

Frey, D., Kumpf, M., Irle, M., & Gniech, G. (1984). Re-evaluation of decision alternatives dependent upon the reversibility of a decision and the passage of time. *European Journal of Social Psychology, 14,* 447–450.

Frey, D., & Wicklund, R. A. (1978). A clarification of selective exposure: The impact of choice. *Journal of Experimental Social Psychology, 14,* 132–139.

Fried, M. (1982). Residential attachment: Sources of residential and community satisfaction. *Journal of Social Issues, 38,* 107–119.

Fried, R., & Berkowitz, L. (1979). Music hath charms . . . and can influence helpfulness. *Journal of Applied Social Psychology, 9,* 199–208.

Friedman, H. S., & Miller-Herringer, T. (1991). Nonverbal display of emotion in public and in private: Self-monitoring, personality, and expressive cues. *Journal of Personality and Social Psychology, 61,* 766–775.

Friedman, M., & Rosenman, R. (1974). *Type A behavior and your heart.* New York: Knopf.

Friedrich, L. K., & Stein, A. H. (1973). Aggressive and prosocial television programs and the natural behavior of preschool children. *Monographs of the Society for Research in Child Development, 38*(4, Serial No. 151).

Friedrich-Cofer, L., & Huston, A. C. (1986). Television violence and aggression: The debate continues. *Psychological Bulletin, 100,* 364–371.

Frieze, I. H., Whitley, B. E., Jr., Hanusa, B. H., & McHugh, M. C. (1982). Assessing the theoretical models for sex differences in causal attributions for success and failure. *Sex Roles, 8,* 333–343.

Fromm, E. (1956). *The art of love.* New York: Harper & Row.

Fromme, D. K., Jaynes, W. E., Taylor, D. K., Hanold, E. G., Daniell, J., Rountree, J. R., & Fromme, M. L. (1989). Nonverbal behavior and attitudes toward touch. *Journal of Nonverbal Behavior, 13,* 3–14.

Fukuhara, S. (1990). The effect of eye contact and verbal content about impression on affective reactions of the other partner. *Japanese Journal of Psychology, 61,* 177–183.

Fuller, J. G. (1976). *The ghost of Flight 401.* New York: Putnam.

Fultz, J., Batson, C. D., Fortenbach, V. A., McCarthy, P. M., & Varney, L. L. (1986). Social evaluation and the empathy-altruism hypothesis. *Journal of Personality and Social Psychology, 50,* 761–769.

Funder, D. C. (1987). Errors and mistakes: Evaluating the accuracy of social judgment. *Psychological Bulletin, 101,* 75–90.

Funder, D. C., & Colvin, C. R. (1988). Friends and strangers: Acquaintanceship, agreement, and the accuracy of personality judgment. *Journal of Personality and Social Psychology, 55,* 149–158.

Funder, D. C., & Dobroth, K. M. (1987). Differences between traits: Properties associated with interjudge agreement. *Journal of Personality and Social Psychology, 52,* 409–418.

Gaertner, S., & Bickman, L. (1971). Effects of race on the elicitation of helping behavior: The wrong number technique. *Journal of Personality and Social Psychology, 20,* 218–222.

Gaertner, S. L., & Dovidio, J. F. (1977). The subtlety of white racism, arousal, and helping behavior. *Journal of Personality and Social Psychology, 35,* 691–707.

Gaertner, S. L., & Dovidio, L. (1986). The aversive form of racism. In J. F. Dovidio & S. L. Gaertner (Eds.), *Prejudice, discrimination, and racism* (pp. 61–90). Orlando, FL: Academic Press.

Gaertner, S. L., Mann, J., Dovidio, J. F., Murrell, A., & Pomare, M. (1990). How does cooperation reduce intergroup bias? *Journal of Personality and Social Psychology, 59,* 692–704.

Gaes, G. G., Kalle, R. J., & Tedeschi, J. T. (1978). Impression management in the forced compliance situation: Two studies using the bogus pipeline. *Journal of Experimental Social Psychology, 14,* 579–582.

Gaes, G. G., Melburg, V., & Tedeschi, J. T. (1986). A study examining the arousal properties of the forced compliance situation. *Journal of Experimental Social Psychology, 22,* 136–147.

Galanter, M. (1989). *Cults: Faith, healing, and coercion.* New York: Oxford University Press.

Galle, O. R., Gove, W. R., & McPherson, J. M. (1972). Population density and pathology: What are the relationships for man? *Science, 176,* 23–30.

Gallup, G. (1978). *The Gallup poll: Public opinion 1978.* Wilmington, DE: Scholarly Resources.

Gallup, G. (1993). *The Gallup poll of public opinion.* Wilmington, DE: Scholarly Resources.

Gallup, G. G., Jr. (1977). Self-recognition in primates: A comparative approach to the bidirectional properties of consciousness. *American Psychologist, 32,* 329–338.

Gallup, G. G., Jr. (1991). Toward a comparative psychology of self-awareness: Species limitations and cognitive consequences. In J. Strauss & G. R. Goethals (Eds.), *The self: An interdisciplinary approach* (pp. 121–135). New York: Springer-Verlag.

Galper, R. F. (1976). Turning observers into actors: Differential causal attributions as a function of "empathy." *Journal of Research in Personality, 10,* 328–335.

Gangestad, S. W., & Simpson, J. A. (1990). Toward an evolutionary history of female sociosexual variation. *Journal of Personality, 58,* 69–96.

Gangestad, S. W., Simpson, J. A., DiGeronimo, K., & Biek, M. (1992). Differential accuracy in person perception across traits: Examination of a functional hypothesis. *Journal of Personality and Social Psychology, 62,* 688–698.

Gangestad, S. W., & Snyder, M. (1985). "To carve nature at its joints": On the existence of discrete classes in personality. *Psychological Review, 92,* 317–349.

Garcia, S., Stinson, L., Ickes, W., Bissonnette, V., & Briggs, S. R. (1991). Shyness and physical attractiveness in mixed-sex dyads. *Journal of Personality and Social Psychology, 61,* 35–49.

Gardner, G. T. (1978). The effects of human subject regulations on data obtained in environmental stressor research. *Journal of Personality and Social Psychology, 36,* 628–634.

Garfinkel, H. (1967). *Studies in ethnomethodology.* Englewood Cliffs, NJ: Prentice-Hall.

Garreau, J. (1993, March 9). The cold facts about calling in sick. *Washington Post,* pp. C1–C5.

Gates, L., & Rohe, W. (1987). Fear and reactions to crime: A revised model. *Urban Affairs Quarterly, 22,* 425–453.

Geen, R. G. (1968). Effects of frustration, attack, and prior training in aggressiveness upon aggressive behavior. *Journal of Personality and Social Psychology, 9,* 316–321.

Geen, R. G. (1978). Effects of attack and uncontrollable noise on aggression. *Journal of Research in Personality, 12,* 15–29.

Geen, R. G. (1990). *Human aggression.* Pacific Grove, CA: Brooks/Cole.

Geen, R. G. (1991). Social motivation. *Annual Review of Psychology, 42,* 377–399.

Geen, R. G., & McCown, E. J. (1984). Effects of noise and attack on aggression and physiological arousal. *Motivation and Emotion, 8,* 231–241.

Geis, F. L., Boston, M., & Hoffman, N. (1985). Sex, of authority role models and achievement by men and women: Leadership performance and recognition. *Journal of Personality and Social Psychology, 49,* 636–653.

Gelfand, D. M., & Hartmann, D. P. (1982). Response consequences and attributions: Two contributors to prosocial behavior. In N. Eisenberg (Ed.), *The development of prosocial behavior.* New York: Academic Press.

Geller, D. M. (1982). Alternatives to deception: Why, what, and how. In J. E. Sieber

(Ed.), *The ethics of social research: Surveys and experiments.* New York: Springer-Verlag.

GELLER, E. S. (1989). Applied behavior analysis and social marketing: An integration for environmental preservation. *Journal of Social Issues, 45*(1), 17–36.

GELLER, E. S. (1992). It takes more than information to save energy. *American Psychologist, 47,* 814–815.

GELLER, E. S., WINNETT, R. A., & EVERETT, P. B. (1982). *Preserving the environment: New strategies for behavior change.* New York: Pergamon.

GELLES, R. J. (1980a). A profile of violence toward children in the United States. In G. Gerbner, C. J. Ross, & E. Zigler (Eds.), *Child abuse: An agenda for action.* New York: Oxford University Press.

GELLES, R. J. (1980b). Violence in the family: A review of research in the seventies. *Journal of Marriage and the Family, 42,* 873–885.

GERARD, H. B. (1983). School desegregation: The social science role. *American Psychologist, 38,* 869–877.

GERARD, H. B., & MATHEWSON, G. C. (1966). The effects of severity of initiation on liking for a group: A replication. *Journal of Experimental Social Psychology, 2,* 278–287.

GERARD, H. B., & MILLER, N. (1975). *School desegregation.* New York: Plenum.

GERARD, H. B., & ORIVE, R. (1987). The dynamics of opinion formation. In L. Berkowitz (Ed.), *Advances in experimental social psychology* (Vol. 20, pp. 171–202). New York: Academic Press.

GERARD, H. B., & WHITE, G. L. (1983). Post-decisional reevaluation of choice alternatives. *Personality and Social Psychology Bulletin, 9,* 364–369.

GERARD, H. B., WILHELMY, R. A., & CONOLLEY, E. S. (1968). Conformity and group size. *Journal of Personality and Social Psychology, 8,* 79–82.

GERBNER, G., GROSS, L., MORGAN, M., & SIGNORIELLI, N. (1980). The "mainstreaming" of America: Violence profile no. 11. *Journal of Communication, 30*(3), 10–29.

GERBNER, G., GROSS, L., MORGAN, M., & SIGNORIELLI, N. (1986). Living with television: The dynamics of the cultivation process. In J. Bryant and D. Zillmann (Eds), *Perspectives on media effects* (pp. 17–40). Hillsdale, NJ: Erlbaum.

GERBNER, G., GROSS, L., SIGNORIELLI, N., MORGAN, M., & JACKSON-BEECK, M. (1979). The demonstration of power: Violence profile no. 10. *Journal of Communication, 29*(3), 177–195.

GERGEN, K. J., GERGEN, M. M., & METER, K. (1972). Individual orientations to prosocial behavior. *Journal of Social Issues, 28,* 105–130.

GERRARD, M., GIBBONS, F. X., WARNER, T. D., & SMITH, G. E. (1993). Perceived vulnerability to HIV infection and AIDS preventive behavior: A critical review of the evidence. In J. B. Pryor & G. D. Reeder (Eds.), *The social psychology of HIV infection* (pp. 59–84). Hillsdale, NJ: Erlbaum.

GIBBONS, F. X. (1978). Sexual standards and reactions to pornography: Enhancing behavioral consistency through self-focused attention. *Journal of Personality and Social Psychology, 36,* 976–987.

GIBBONS, F. X. (1990). Self-attention and behavior: A review and theoretical update. In M. P. Zanna (Ed.), *Advances in experimental social psychology* (Vol. 23, pp. 249–303). New York: Academic Press.

GIBBONS, F. X., & GERRARD, M. (1989). Effects of upward and downward social comparison on mood states. *Journal of Social and Clinical Psychology, 8,* 14–31.

GIBBONS, F. X., & GERRARD, M. (1991). Downward comparison and coping with threat. In J. Suls & T. A. Wills (Eds.), *Social comparison: Contemporary theory and research* (pp. 317–346). Hillsdale, NJ: Erlbaum.

GIBBS, N. (1991, October). Office crimes. *Time,* pp. 52–64.

GIFFORD, R. (1991). Mapping nonverbal behavior on the interpersonal circle. *Journal of Personality and Social Psychology, 61,* 279–288.

GILBERT, D. T. (1991). How mental systems believe. *American Psychologist, 46,* 107–119.

GILBERT, D. T., & JONES, E. E. (1986a). Exemplification: The self-presentation of moral character. *Journal of Personality, 54,* 593–615.

GILBERT, D. T., & JONES, E. E. (1986b). Perceiver-induced constraint: Interpretations of self-generated reality. *Journal of Personality and Social Psychology, 50,* 269–280.

GILBERT, D. T., & KRULL, D. S. (1988). Seeing less and knowing more: The benefits of perceptual ignorance. *Journal of Personality and Social Psychology, 54,* 193–202.

GILBERT, D. T., KRULL, D. S., & MALONE, P. S. (1990). Unbelieving the unbelievable: Some problems in the rejection of false information. *Journal of Personality and Social Psychology, 59,* 601–613.

GILBERT, D. T., MCNULTY, S. E., GIULIANO, T. A., & BENSON, J. E. (1992). Blurry words and fuzzy deeds: The attribution of obscure behavior. *Journal of Personality and Social Psychology, 62,* 18–25.

GILBERT, D. T., PELHAM, B. W., & KRULL, D. S. (1988). On cognitive busyness: When person perceivers meet persons perceived. *Journal of Personality and Social Psychology, 54,* 733–739.

GILCHRIST, J. C. (1952). The formation of social groups under conditions of success and failure. *Journal of Abnormal and Social Psychology, 47,* 174–187.

GILLIG, P. M., & GREENWALD, A. G. (1974). Is it time to lay the sleeper effect to rest? *Journal of Personality and Social Psychology, 29,* 132–139.

GILLIGAN, C. (1982). *In a different voice: Psychological theory and women's development.* Cambridge, MA: Harvard University Press.

GILLIS, A. R., RICHARD, M. A., & HAGAN, J. (1986). Ethnic susceptibility to crowding: An empirical analysis. *Environment and Behavior, 18,* 683–706.

GILMOUR, D. R., & WALKEY, F. H. (1981). Identifying violent offenders using a video measure of interpersonal distance. *Journal of Consulting and Clinical Psychology, 49,* 287–291.

GILOVICH, T. (1981). Seeing the past in the present: The effect of associations to familiar events on judgments and decisions. *Journal of Personality and Social Psychology, 40,* 797–808.

GILOVICH, T. (1983). Biased evaluation and persistence in gambling. *Journal of Personality and Social Psychology, 44,* 1110–1126.

GINNETT, R. C. (1990). Airline cockpit crew. In J. R. Hackman (Ed.), *Groups that work (and those that don't): Creating conditions for effective teamwork* (pp. 427–448). San Francisco: Jossey-Bass.

GIOLA, D. A., & SIMS, H. P. (1985). Self-serving bias and actor-observer differences in organizations: An empirical analysis. *Journal of Applied Social Psychology, 15,* 547–563.

GLASS, D. C., & SINGER, J. E. (1972). *Urban stress.* New York: Academic Press.

GLASS, D. C., SINGER, J. E., & FRIEDMAN, L. W. (1969). Psychic cost of adaptation to an environmental stressor. *Journal of Personality and Social Psychology, 12,* 200–210.

GLASS, D. C., SINGER, J. E., & PENNEBAKER, J. W. (1977). Behavioral and physiological effects of uncontrollable environmental events. In D. Stokols (Ed.), *Perspectives on environment and behavior.* New York: Plenum.

GLEICHER, F., & PETTY, R. E. (1992). Expectations of reassurance influence the nature of fear stimulated attitude change. *Journal of Experimental Social Psychology, 28,* 86–100.

GODFREY, D. K., JONES, E. E., & LORD, C. G. (1986). Self-promotion is not ingratiating. *Journal of Personality and Social Psychology, 50,* 106–115.

GOETHALS, G. R., & ZANNA, M. P. (1979). The role of social comparison in choice shifts. *Journal of Personality and Social Psychology, 37,* 1469–1476.

GOFFMAN, E. (1959). *The presentation of self in everyday life.* Garden City, NY: Doubleday.

GOFFMAN, E. (1961). *Asylums.* Garden City, NJ: Doubleday.

GOFFMAN, E. (1963). *Stigma.* Englewood Cliffs, NJ: Prentice-Hall.

GOFFMAN, E. (1971). *Relations in public.* New York: Harper & Row.

GOLDBERG, C. (1974). Sex roles, task competence, and conformity. *Journal of Psychology, 86,* 157–164.

GOLDBERG, C. (1975). Conformity to majority as a function of task type and acceptance of sex-related stereotypes. *Journal of Psychology, 89,* 25–37.

GOLDBERG, L. (1968). Ghetto riots and others: The faces of civil disorder in 1967. *Journal of Peace Research, 2,* 116–132.

GOLDBERG, L. R. (1981). Unconfounding situational attributions from uncertain, neutral, and ambiguous ones: A psychometric analysis of descriptions of oneself and various types of others. *Journal of Personality and Social Psychology, 41,* 517–551.

Goldberg, L. R. (1993). The structure of phenotypic personality traits. *American Psychologist, 48,* 26–34.

Goldberg, P. (1968). Are women prejudiced against women? *Transaction, 5,* 28–30.

Goldberg-Ambrose, C. (1992). Unfinished business in rape law reform. *Journal of Social Issues, 48*(1), 173–185.

Goldstein, A. P., & Keller, H. R. (1983). Aggression prevention and control: Multitargeted, multichannel, multiprocess, multidisciplinary. In A. P. Goldstein (Ed.), *Prevention and control of aggression.* New York: Pergamon.

Goldstein, J. H. (1986). *Aggression and crimes of violence* (2nd ed.). New York: Oxford University Press.

Goldstein, J. H., Rosnow, R. L., Raday, T., Silverman, I., & Gaskell, G. D. (1975). Punitiveness in response to films varying in content: A cross-national field study of aggression. *European Journal of Social Psychology, 5,* 149–165.

Gollob, H. F., Rossman, B. B., & Abelson, R. P. (1973). Social inference as a function of the number of instances and consistency of information presented. *Journal of Personality and Social Psychology, 27,* 19–35.

Gollwitzer, P. M., & Wicklund, R. A. (1985). Self-symbolizing and the neglect of others' perspectives. *Journal of Personality and Social Psychology, 48,* 702–715.

Gonzales, M. H., Davis, J. M., Loney, G. L., Lukens, C. K., & Junghans, C. H. (1983). Interactional approach to interpersonal attraction. *Journal of Personality and Social Psychology, 44,* 1192–1197.

Gonzales, M. H., Manning, D. J., & Haugen, J. A. (1992). Explaining our sins: Factors influencing offender accounts and anticipated victim responses. *Journal of Personality and Social Psychology, 62,* 958–971.

Gonzales, M. H., Pederson, J. H., Manning, D. J., & Wetter, D. W. (1990). Pardon my gaffe: Effects of sex, status, and consequence severity on accounts. *Journal of Personality and Social Psychology, 58,* 610–621.

Gordon, C. (1968). Self-conceptions: Configurations of content. In C. Gordon & K. J. Gergen (Eds.), *The self in social interaction* (pp. 115–136). New York: Wiley.

Gorer, G. (1968). Man has no "killer" instinct. In M. F. A. Montagu (Ed.), *Man and aggression* (pp. 27–36). New York: Oxford University Press.

Gorsuch, R. L., & Ortberg, J. (1983). Moral obligation and attitudes: Their relation to behavioral intentions. *Journal of Personality and Social Psychology, 44,* 1025–1028.

Gottman, J. M., & Levenson, R. W. (1992). Marital processes predictive of later dissolution: Behavior, physiology, and health. *Journal of Personality and Social Psychology, 63,* 221–233.

Gouldner, A. W. (1960). The norm of reciprocity: A preliminary statement. *American Sociological Review, 25,* 161–178.

Graham, S., & Folkes, V. S. (Eds.). (1990). *Attribution theory: Applications to achievement, mental health, and interpersonal conflict.* Hillsdale, NJ: Erlbaum.

Green, J. A. (1972). Attitudinal and situational determinants of intendent behavior toward blacks. *Journal of Personality and Social Psychology, 22,* 13–17.

Green, R. B., & Mack, J. (1978). Would groups do better without social psychologists? A response to Buys. *Personality and Social Psychology Bulletin, 4,* 561–563.

Greenberg, J., & Pyszczynski, T. (1985). The effect of an overheard ethnic slur on evaluations of the target: How to spread a social disease. *Journal of Experimental Social Psychology, 21,* 61–72.

Greenberg, J., Pyszczynski, T., & Solomon, S. (1982). The self-serving attributional bias: Beyond self-presentation. *Journal of Experimental Social Psychology, 18,* 56–67.

Greenberg, J., Simon, L., Pyszczynski, T., Solomon, S., & Chatel, D. (1992). Terror management and tolerance: Does mortality salience always intensify negative reactions to others who threaten on's worldview? *Journal of Personality and Social Psychology, 63,* 212–220.

Greenberg, J., Williams, K. D., & O'Brien, M. K. (1986). Considering the harshest verdict first: Biasing effects on mock juror verdicts. *Personality and Social Psychology Bulletin, 12,* 41–50.

Greenberg, M. S., & Shapiro, S. (1971). Indebtedness: An adverse aspect of asking for and receiving help. *Sociometry, 34,* 290–301.

Greenberger, D. B., Porter, G., Miceli, M. P., & Strasser, S. (1991). Responses to inadequate personal control in organizations. *Journal of Social Issues, 47*(4), 111–128.

Greene, D., & Lepper, M. R. (1974). Effects of extrinsic rewards on children's subsequent intrinsic interest. *Child Development, 45,* 1141–1145.

Greenwald, A. G. (1975a). Consequences of prejudice against the null hypothesis. *Psychological Bulletin, 82,* 1–20.

Greenwald, A. G. (1975b). On the inconclusiveness of "crucial" cognitive tests of dissonance versus self-perception theories. *Journal of Experimental Social Psychology, 11,* 490–499.

Greenwald, A. G. (1980). The totalitarian ego: Fabrication and revision of personal history. *American Psychologist, 35,* 603–618.

Greenwald, A. G. (1988). Self-knowledge and self-deception. In J. S. Lockard & D. L. Paulhus (Eds.), *Self-deception: An adaptive mechanism?* (pp. 113–131). Englewood Cliffs, NJ: Prentice-Hall.

Greenwald, A. G. (1989a). Why are attitudes important? In A. R. Pratkanis, S. J. Breckler, & A. G. Greenwald (Eds.), *Attitude structure and function* (pp. 1–10). Hillsdale, NJ: Erlbaum.

Greenwald, A. G. (1989b). Why attitudes are important: Defining attitude and attitude theory 20 years later. In A. R. Pratkanis, S. J. Breckler, & A. G. Greenwald (Eds.), *Attitude structure and function* (pp. 429–440). Hillsdale, NJ: Erlbaum.

Greenwald, A. G. (1993). New look 3: Unconscious cognition reclaimed. *American Psychologist, 47,* 766–779.

Greenwald, A. G., & Pratkanis, A. R. (1984). The self. In R. S. Wyer, Jr., & T. K. Srull (Eds.), *Handbook of social cognition* (Vol. 3). Hillsdale, NJ: Erlbaum.

Greenwald, A. G., & Ronis, D. L. (1978). Twenty years of cognitive dissonance: Case study of the evolution of a theory. *Psychological Review, 85,* 53–57.

Greer, D. L. (1983). Spectator booing and the home advantage: A study of social influence in the basketball arena. *Social Psychology Quarterly, 46,* 252–261.

Gregory, W. L. (1989). An introduction to program evaluation. In W. L. Gregory & W. J. Burroughs (Eds.), *Introduction to applied psychology* (pp. 497–513). Boston: Scott, Foresman.

Griffin, B. Q., & Rogers, R. W. (1977). Reducing interracial aggression: Inhibiting effects of victim's suffering and power to retaliate. *Journal of Psychology, 95,* 151–157.

Griffin, D., & Buehler, R. (1993). Role of construal processes in conformity and dissent. *Journal of Personality and Social Psychology, 65,* 657–669.

Griffitt, W. (1970). Environmental effects on interpersonal affective behavior: Ambient effective temperature and attraction. *Journal of Personality and Social Psychology, 15,* 240–244.

Grimes, A. J. (1978). Authority, power, influence and social control: A theoretical synthesis. *Academy of Management Review, 3,* 724–737.

Groff, B. D., Baron, R. S., & Moore, D. L. (1983). Distraction, attentional conflict, and drivelike behavior. *Journal of Experimental Social Psychology, 19,* 359–380.

Gross, A. E., & Fleming, I. (1982). Twenty years of deception in social psychology. *Personality and Social Psychology Bulletin, 8,* 402–408.

Grube, J. W., Kleinhesselink, R. R., & Kearney, K. A. (1982). Male self-acceptance and attraction toward women. *Personality and Social Psychology Bulletin, 8,* 107–112.

Gruder, C. L., Cook, T. D., Hennigan, K. M., Flay, B. R., Alessis, C., & Halamaj, J. (1978). Empirical tests of the absolute sleeper effect predicted from the discounting cue hypothesis. *Journal of Personality and Social Psychology, 36,* 1061–1074.

Grusec, J. E. (1991). The socialization of altruism. In M. S. Clark (Ed.), *Review of personality and social psychology* (Vol. 12, pp. 9–33). Newbury Park, CA: Sage.

Guerin, B. (1983). Social facilitation and social monitoring: A test of three models. *British Journal of Social Psychology, 22,* 203–214.

Guerin, B., & Innes, J. M. (1983). Social facilitation and social monitoring: A new look at Zajonc's mere presence hypothesis. *British Journal of Social Psychology, 21,* 7–18.

Gunter, B. (1986). *Television and sex role stereotyping.* London: Libbey.

Haan, N. (1986). Systematic variability in the quality of moral action, as defined in two formulations. *Journal of Personality and Social Psychology, 50,* 1271–1284.

Haber, G. M. (1980). Territorial invasion in the classroom: Invadee response. *Environment and Behavior, 12,* 17–31.

Hackel, L. S., & Ruble, D. N. (1992). Changes in the marital relationship after the first baby is born: Predicting the impact of expectancy disconfirmation. *Journal of Personality and Social Psychology, 62,* 944–957.

Hackman, J. R. (1987). The design of work teams. In J. W. Lorsch (Ed.), *Handbook of organizational behavior* (pp. 315–342). Englewood Cliffs, NJ: Prentice-Hall.

Hackman, J. R. (Ed.). (1990). *Groups that work and those that don't: Creating conditions for effective teamwork.* San Francisco: Jossey-Bass.

Hackman, J. R., & Morris, C. G. (1975). Group tasks, group interaction process, and group performance effectiveness: A review and proposed integration. In L. Berkowitz (Ed.), *Advances in experimental social psychology* (Vol. 8, pp. 47–99). New York: Academic Press.

Hakmiller, K. L. (1966). Threat as a determinant of downward comparison. *Journal of Experimental Social Psychology 2* (Supp. 1), 32–39.

Hall, E. T. (1959). *The silent language.* New York: Doubleday.

Hall, E. T. (1966) *The hidden dimension.* New York: Doubleday.

Hall, J. A. (1984). *Nonverbal sex differences: Communication accuracy and expressive style.* Baltimore, MD: Johns Hopkins University Press.

Hall, J. A. (1985). Male and female nonverbal behavior. In A. W. Siegman & S. Feldstein (Eds.), *Multichannel integrations of nonverbal behavior* (pp. 195–225). Hillsdale, NJ: Erlbaum.

Hall, J. A., & Veccia, E. M. (1990). More "touching" observations: New insights on men, women, and interpersonal touch. *Journal of Personality and Social Psychology, 59,* 1155–1162.

Hamachek, D. (1987). *Encounters with the self.* New York: Holt, Rinehart & Winston.

Hamill, R., Wilson, T. D., & Nisbett, R. E. (1980). Insensitivity to sample bias: Generalizing from atypical cases. *Journal of Personality and Social Psychology, 39,* 578–589.

Hamilton, D. L. (1979). A cognitive-attributional analysis of stereotyping. In L. Berkowitz (Ed.), *Advances in experimental social psychology* (Vol. 12). New York: Academic Press.

Hamilton, D. L., & Gifford, R. K. (1976). Illusory correlation in interpersonal perception: A cognitive basis of stereotypic judgments. *Journal of Experimental Social Psychology, 12,* 392–407.

Hamilton, D. L., & Rose, T. L. (1980). Illusory correlation and the maintenance of stereotypic beliefs. *Journal of Personality and Social Psychology, 39,* 832–845.

Hamilton, D. L., & Sherman, S. J. (1989). Illusory correlations: Implications for stereotype theory and research. In D. Bar-Tal, C. F. Gaumann, A. W. Kruglanski, & W. Stroebe (Eds.), *Stereotyping and prejudice: Changing conceptions* (pp. 56–82). New York: Springer-Verlag.

Hamilton, D. L., Sherman, S. J., & Ruvolo, C. M. (1990). Stereotype-based expectancies: Effects on information processing and social behavior. *Journal of Social Issues, 46*(2), 35–60.

Hamilton, D. L., & Zanna, M. P. (1974). Context effects in impression formation: Changes in connotative meaning. *Journal of Personality and Social Psychology, 29,* 649–654.

Hamilton, W. D. (1964). The genetic evolution of social behavior: I and II. *Journal of Theoretical Biology, 7,* 1–52.

Hammond, W. R., & Yung, B. (1993). Psychology's role in the public health response to assaultive violence among young African-American men. *American Psychologist, 48,* 142–154.

Hampson, R. (1992, January 5). Culprit at rap event was crowd that spawned a beast. *Richmond Times Dispatch,* p. A-3.

Hampson, S. E., John, O. P., & Goldberg, L. R. (1986). Category breadth and hierarchical structure in personality: Studies in asymmetries in judgments of trait implications. *Journal of Personality and Social Psychology, 51,* 37–54.

Hans, V. P. (1989). Psychology and the law. In W. L. Gregory & W. J. Burroughs (Eds.), *Introduction to applied psychology* (pp. 327–368). Glenview, IL: Scott, Foresman.

Hansen, C. H., & Hansen, R. D. (1988a). Finding the face in the crowd: An anger superiority effect. *Journal of Personality and Social Psychology, 54,* 917–924.

Hansen, C. H., & Hansen, R. D. (1988b). How rock music videos can change what's seen when boy meets girl: Priming stereotypic appraisals of social interaction. *Sex Roles, 19,* 287–316.

Hansen, W. B., & Altman, I. (1976). Decorating personal places: A descriptive analysis. *Environment and Behavior, 8,* 491–504.

Hardin, G. (1968). The tragedy of the commons. *Science, 162,* 1243–1248.

Harding, J., Proshansky, H., Kutner, B., & Chein, I. (1969). Prejudice and ethnic relations. In G. Lindzey & E. Aronson (Eds.), *The handbook of social psychology* (2nd ed., Vol. 5, pp. 1–76). Reading, MA: Addison-Wesley.

Hardyck, J. A., & Braden, M. (1962). Prophecy fails again: A report of a failure to replicate. *Journal of Abnormal and Social Psychology, 65,* 136–141.

Hare, A. P. (1976). *Handbook of small group research* (2nd ed.). New York: Free Press.

Harkins, S. G. (1987). Social loafing and social facilitation. *Journal of Experimental Social Psychology, 23,* 1–18.

Harkins, S. G. (1990). Is teamwork always best? In R. Brown (Ed.), *The Marshall Cavendish encyclopedia of personal relationships: Human behavior, How groups work* (Vol. 15, pp. 1862–1869). North Bellmore, NY: Marshall Cavendish Corporation.

Harkins, S. G., & Jackson, J. M. (1985). The role of evaluation in eliminating social loafing. *Personality and Social Psychology Bulletin, 11,* 457–465.

Harkins, S. G., Latané, B., & Williams, K. (1980). Social loafing: Allocating effort or taking it easy. *Journal of Experimental Social Psychology, 16,* 457–465.

Harkins, S. G., & Petty, R. E. (1982). Effects of task difficulty and task uniqueness on social loafing. *Journal of Personality and Social Psychology, 43,* 1214–1229.

Harkness, A. R., DeBono, K. G., & Borgida, E. (1985). Personal involvement and strategies for making contingency judgments: A stake in the dating game makes a difference. *Journal of Personality and Social Psychology, 49,* 22–32.

Harootunian, B., & Apter, S. J. (1983). Violence in school. In A. P. Goldstein (Ed.), *Prevention and control of aggression.* New York: Pergamon.

Harrell, A. W. (1978). Physical attractiveness, self-disclosure, and helping behavior. *Journal of Social Psychology, 104,* 15–17.

Harris, B., & Harvey, J. H. (1975). Self-attributed choice as a function of the consequences of a decision. *Journal of Personality and Social Psychology, 31,* 1013–1019.

Harris, B., Luginbuhl, J. R., & Fishbein, J. E. (1978). Density and personal space in a field setting. *Social Psychology, 41,* 350–353.

Harris, M. B., & Huang, L. C. (1973). Helping and the attribution process. *Journal of Social Psychology, 90,* 291–297.

Harris, M. J., & Rosenthal, R. (1985). Mediation of interpersonal expectancy effects: 31 meta-analyses. *Psychological Bulletin, 97,* 363–386.

Harris, M. J., & Rosenthal, R. (1986). Four factors in the mediation of teacher expectancy. In R. S. Feldman (Ed)., *The social psychology of education: Current research and theory* (pp. 91–114). New York: Cambridge University Press.

Harris, P. B., & McAndrew, F. T. (1986). Territoriality and compliance: The influence of gender and location on willingness to sign petitions. *Journal of Social Psychology, 126,* 657–662.

Hartshorne, H., & May, M. A. (1928). *Studies in the nature of character.* New York: Macmillan.

Harvey, J. H., & McGlynn, R. P. (1982). Matching words to phenomena: The case of the fundamental attribution error. *Journal of Personality and Social Psychology, 43,* 345–346.

Harvey, J. H., Orbuch, T. L., & Weber, A. L. (1990). A social psychological model of account-making in responses to severe stress. *Journal of Language and Social Psychology, 9,* 191–207.

Haskell, M. (1990). *Love and other infectious diseases.* New York: Carol Publishing Group.

Hass, R. G., Katz, I., Rizzo, N., Bailey, J., & Eisenstadt, D. (1991). Cross-racial appraisal as related to attitude ambivalence and cognitive complexity. *Personality and Social Psychology Bulletin, 17,* 83–92.

Hass, R. G., Katz, I., Rizzo, N., Bailey, J., & Moore, L. (1992). When racial ambivalence evokes negative affect, using a disguised measure of mood. *Personality and Social Psychology Bulletin, 18,* 786–797.

Hastie, R., Penrod, S. D., & Pennington, N. (1983). *Inside the jury.* Cambridge, MA: Harvard University Press.

Hastorf, A. H., & Cantril, H. (1954). They saw a game. *Journal of Abnormal and Social Psychology, 49,* 129–134.

Hatfield, E., & Rapson, R. L. (1993). *Love, sex, and intimacy: Their psychology, biology, and history.* New York: HarperCollins.

Hatfield, E., & Sprecher, S. (1986a). Measuring passionate love in intimate relations. *Journal of Adolescence, 9,* 383–410.

Hatfield, E., & Sprecher, S. (1986b). *Mirror, mirror: The importance of looks in everyday life.* Albany, NY: SUNY Press.

Hattie, J. (1992). *Self-concept.* Hillsdale, NJ: Erlbaum.

Haugtvedt, C. P., & Petty, R. E. (1992). Personality and persuasion: Need for cognition moderates the persistence and resistance of attitude changes. *Journal of Personality and Social Psychology, 63,* 308–319.

Haverkamp, B. E. (1993). Confirmatory bias in hypothesis testing for client-identified and counselor self-generated hypotheses. *Journal of Counseling Psychology, 40,* 303–315.

Hawkins, S. A., & Hastie, R. (1990). Hindsight: Biased judgments of past events after the outcomes are known. *Psychological Bulletin, 107,* 311–327.

Hayamizu, T. (1984). Changes in causal attributions on a term examination: Causal dimensions. *Japanese Psychological Research, 26,* 1–11.

Hayduk, L. A. (1983). Personal space: Where we now stand. *Psychological Bulletin, 94,* 293–335.

Hays, D. F., Nash, A., & Pedersen, J. (1981). Responses of six-month-olds to the distress of their peers. *Child Development, 52,* 1071–1075.

Hays, R. B. (1985). A longitudinal study of friendship development. *Journal of Personality and Social Psychology, 48,* 909–924.

Hays, R. B., & Oxley, D. (1986). Social network development and functioning during a life transition. *Journal of Personality and Social Psychology, 50,* 304–313.

Hazan, C., & Shaver, P. (1987). Romantic love conceptualized as an attachment process. *Journal of Personality and Social Psychology, 52,* 511–524.

Hearold, S. (1986). A synthesis of 1043 effects of television on social behavior. In G. Comstock (Ed.), *Public communications and behavior* (Vol 1., pp. 65–133). New York: Academic Press.

Heatherton, T. F., & Baumeister, R. F. (1991). Binge eating as escape from self-awareness. *Psychological Bulletin, 110,* 86–108.

Heatherton, T. F., & Polivy, J. (1991). Development and validation of a scale for measuring state self-esteem. *Journal of Personality and Social Psychology, 60,* 895–910.

Heesacker, M. (1989). Counseling and the elaborational likelihood model of attitude change. In J. F. Cruz, R. A. Goncalvez, & P. P. Machado (Eds.), *Psychology and education: Investigations and interventions* (pp. 39–52). Oporto, Portugal: Portuguese Psychological Association.

Heider, F. (1958). *The psychology of interpersonal relations.* New York: Wiley.

Heilman, M. E., Hornstein, H. A., Cage, J. H., & Herschlag, J. K. (1984). Reactions to prescribed leader behavior as a function of role perspective: The case of the Vroom-Yetton model. *Journal of Applied Psychology, 69,* 50–60.

Helgeson, V. S., Shaver, P., & Dyer, M. (1987). Prototypes of intimacy and distance in same-sex and opposite-sex relationships. *Journal of Social and Personal Relationships, 4,* 195–233.

Heller, J. F., Groff, B. D., & Solomon, S. H. (1977). Toward an understanding of crowding: The role of physical interaction. *Journal of Personality and Social Psychology, 35,* 183–190.

Hendrick, C. (1977). Role-taking, role-playing, and the laboratory experiment. *Personality and Social Psychology Bulletin, 3,* 467–478.

Hendrick, C., & Hendrick, S. S. (1986). A theory and method of love. *Journal of Personality and Social Psychology, 50,* 392–402.

Hendrick, S. S. (1981). Self-disclosure and marital satisfaction. *Journal of Personality and Social Psychology, 40,* 1150–1159.

Hendrick, S. S., & Hendrick, C. (1992). *Liking, loving, and relating* (2nd ed.). Pacific Grove, CA: Brooks/Cole.

Hendrick, S. S., Hendrick, C., & Adler, N. L. (1988). Romantic relationships: Love, satisfaction, and staying together. *Journal of Personality and Social Psychology, 54,* 980–988.

Hendrick, S. S., Hendrick, C., Slapion-Foote, M. J., & Foote, F. H. (1985). Gender differences in sexual attitudes. *Journal of Personality and Social Psychology, 48,* 1630–1642.

Henley, N. M. (1977). *Body politics: Power, sex, and nonverbal communication.* Englewood Cliffs, NJ: Prentice-Hall.

Hennessey, B., Amabile, T., & Martinage, M. (1989). Immunizing children against the negative effects of reward. *Contemporary Educational Psychology, 14,* 212–227.

Hensley, T. R., & Griffin, G. W. (1986). Victims of groupthink: The Kent State University Board of Trustees and the 1977 gymnasium controversy. *Journal of Conflict Resolution, 30,* 497–531.

Herek, G., Janis, I. L., & Huth, P. (1987). Decisionmaking during international crises: Is quality of process related to outcome? *Journal of Conflict Resolution, 31,* 203–226.

Herek, G. M. (1987). Can functions be measured? A new perspective on the functional approach to attitudes. *Social Psychology Quarterly, 50,* 285–303.

Herek, G. M., & Glunt, E. K. (1993). Public attitudes toward AIDS-related issues in the United States. In J. B. Pryor & G. D. Reeder (Eds.), *The social psychology of HIV infection* (pp. 229–261). Hillsdale, NJ: Erlbaum.

Herr, P. M. (1986). Consequences of priming: Judgment and behavior. *Journal of Personality and Social Psychology, 51,* 1106–1115.

Hersey, P., & Blanchard, K. H. (1976). Leader effectiveness and adaptability description (LEAD). In J. W. Pfeiffer & J. E. Jones (Eds.), *The 1976 annual handbook for group facilitators* (Vol. 5). La Jolla, CA: University Associates.

Hersey, P., & Blanchard, K. H. (1977). *Management of organizational behavior: Utilizing human resources* (3rd ed.). Englewood Cliffs, NJ: Prentice-Hall.

Hersey, P., & Blanchard, K. H. (1982). *Management of organizational behavior* (4th ed.). Englewood Cliffs, NJ: Prentice-Hall.

Hershey, J. C., & Baron, J. (1992). Judgment by outcomes: When is it justified? *Organizational Behavior and Human Decision Processes, 53,* 89–93.

Heshka, S., & Nelson, Y. (1972). Interpersonal speaking distance as a function of age, sex, and relationship. *Sociometry, 25,* 491–498.

Hessing, D. J., Elffers, H., & Weigel, R. H. (1988). Exploring the limits of self-reports and reasoned action: An investigation of the psychology of tax evasion behavior. *Journal of Personality and Social Psychology, 54,* 405–413.

Hewstone, M., & Jaspars, J. (1983). A re-examination of the roles of consensus, consistency and distinctiveness: Kelley's cube revisited. *British Journal of Social Psychology, 22,* 41–50.

Hewstone, M., & Jaspars, J. (1987). Covariation and causal attribution: A logical model of the intuitive analysis of variance. *Journal of Personality and Social Psychology, 53,* 663–672.

Higbee, K. L., Millard, R. J., & Folkman, J. R. (1982). Social psychology research during the 1970s: Predominance of experimentation and college students. *Personality and Social Psychology Bulletin, 8,* 180–183.

Higgenbotham, H. N., West, S. G., & Forsyth, D. R. (1988). *Psychotherapy and behavior change: Social, cultural, and methodological perspectives.* New York: Pergamon.

Higgins, E. T. (1987). Self-discrepancy: A theory relating self and affect. *Psychological Review, 94,* 319–340.

Higgins, E. T. (1989a). Knowledge accessibility and activation: Subjectivity and suffering from unconscious sources. In J. S. Uleman & J. A. Bargh (Eds.), *Unintended thought* (pp. 75–123). New York: Guilford Press.

Higgins, E. T. (1989b). Self-discrepancy theory: What patterns of self-beliefs cause people to suffer? In L. Berkowitz (Ed.), *Advances in experimental social psychology* (Vol. 22, pp. 93–136). Orlando, FL: Academic Press.

Higgins, E. T., & Bargh, J. A. (1987). Social cognition and social perception. *Annual Review of Psychology, 38,* 369–425.

Higgins, E. T., King, G. A., & Mavin, G. H. (1982). Individual construct accessibility and subjective impression and recall. *Journal of Personality and Social Psychology, 43,* 35–47.

Higgins, E. T., Rhodewalt, F., & Zanna, M. P. (1979). Dissonance motivation: Its nature, persistence, and reinstatement. *Journal of Experimental Social Psychology, 15,* 16–34.

Higgins, E. T., Rholes, W. S., & Jones, C. R. (1977). Category accessibility and impression formation. *Journal of Experimental Social Psychology, 13,* 141–154.

Higgins, E. T., & Tykocinski, O. (1992). Self-discrepancies and biographical memory: Personality and cognition at the level of psychological situation. *Personality and Social Psychology Bulletin, 18,* 527–535.

Higgins, E. T., Van Hook, E., & Dorfman, D. (1988). Do self-attributes form a cognitive structure? *Social Cognition, 6,* 177–207.

Higgins, R. L., & Harris, R. N. (1988). Strategic "alcohol" use: Drinking to self-handicap. *Journal of Social and Clinical Psychology, 6,* 191–202.

Higgins, R. L., Snyder, C. R., & Berglas, S. (1990). *Self-handicapping: The paradox that isn't.* New York: Plenum.

Hill, A. (1991, October 12). Her version of the events. *Richmond Times Dispatch,* p. A-6.

Hill, C. A. (1987). Affiliation motivation: People who need people but in different ways. *Journal of Personality and Social Psychology, 52,* 1008–1018.

Hill, C. A. (1991). Seeking emotional support: The influence of affiliative need and partner warmth. *Journal of Personality and Social Psychology, 60,* 112–121.

Hill, C. E., Helms, J. E., Tichenor, V., Spiegel, S. B., O'Grady, K. E., & Perry, E. S. (1988). Effects of therapist response modes in brief psychotherapy. *Journal of Counseling Psychology, 35,* 222–233.

Hill, C. T., & Stull, D. E. (1981). Sex differences in effects of social and value similarity in same-sex friendship. *Journal of Personality and Social Psychology, 41,* 488–502.

Hilton, D. J., & Slugoski, B. R. (1986). Knowledge-based causal attributions: The abnormal conditions focus model. *Psychological Review, 93,* 75–88.

Hilton, J. L., & Fein, S. (1989). The role of typical diagnosticity in stereotype-based judgments. *Journal of Personality and Social Psychology, 57,* 201–211.

Hilton, J. L., Klein, J. G., & von Hippel, W. (1991). Attention allocation and impression formation. *Personality and Social Psychology Bulletin, 17,* 548–559.

Himelstein, P., & Moore, J. C. (1963). Racial attitudes and the action of Negro- and white-background figures as factors in petition signing. *Journal of Social Psychology, 61,* 267–272.

Hinkle, S., & Schopler, J. (1986). Bias in the evaluation of in-group and out-group performance. In S. Worchel & W. G. Austin (Eds.), *Psychology of intergroup relations* (2nd ed., pp. 196–212). Chicago: Nelson-Hall.

Hinsz, V. B. (1990). Cognitive and consensus processes in group recognition memory performance. *Journal of Personality and Social Psychology, 59,* 705–718.

Hinsz, V. B., & Tomhave, J. A. (1991). Smile and (half) the world smiles with you, frown and you frown alone. *Personality and Social Psychology Bulletin, 17,* 586–592.

Hirokawa, R. Y. (1980). A comparative analysis of communication patterns within effective and ineffective decision-making groups. *Communication Monographs, 47,* 312–321.

Hirokawa, R. Y. (1984). Does consensus really result in higher quality group decisions? In G. M. Phillips & J. T. Wood (Eds.), *Emergent issues in human decision making* (pp. 40–49). Carbondale: Southern Illinois University Press.

Hirose, Y., & Kitada, T. (1985). Actors' and observers' attributions of responsibility and attitude change in the forced-compliance situation. *Japanese Journal of Psychology, 56,* 262–268.

Hirt, E. R., Zillmann, D., Erickson, G. A., & Kennedy, C. (1992). Costs and benefits of allegiance: Changes in fans' self-ascribed competencies after team victory versus defeat. *Journal of Personality and Social Psychology, 63,* 724–738.

Hoch, S. J. (1985). Counterfactual reasoning and accuracy in predicting personal events. *Journal of Experimental Psychology: Learning, Memory, and Cognition, 11,* 719–731.

Hoch, S. J., & Loewenstein, G. F. (1989). Outcome feedback: Hindsight and information. *Organizational Behavior and Human Decision Processes, 15,* 605–619.

Hoelter, J. W. (1983). The effects of role evaluation and commitment on identity salience. *Social Psychology Quarterly, 46,* 140–147.

Hoelter, J. W. (1984). Relative effects of significant others on self-evaluation. *Social Psychology Quarterly, 47,* 255–262.

Hoffman, M. L. (1975). Altruistic behavior and the parent-child relationship. *Journal of Personality and Social Psychology, 31,* 937–943.

Hoffman, M. L. (1981). Is altruism part of human nature? *Journal of Personality and Social Psychology, 40,* 121–137.

Hogg, M. A., & Sunderland, J. (1991). Self-esteem and intergroup discrimination in the minimal group paradigm. *British Journal of Social Psychology, 30,* 51–62.

Hojat, M., & Vogel, W. H. (1987). Socioemotional bonding and neurobiochemistry. *Journal of Social Behavior and Personality, 2,* 135–144.

Hokanson, J. E. (1970). Psychophysiological evaluation of the catharsis hypothesis. In E. I. Megargee & J. E. Hokanson (Eds.), *The dynamics of aggression: Individual, group, and international analyses.* New York: Harper & Row.

Hokanson, J. E., & Burgess, M. (1962a). The effects of status, type of frustration and aggression on vascular processes. *Journal of Abnormal and Social Psychology, 65,* 232–237.

Hokanson, J. E., & Burgess, M. (1962b). The effects of three types of aggression on vascular processes. *Journal of Abnormal and Social Psychology, 64,* 446–449.

Hokanson, J. E., & Shetler, S. (1961). The effect of overt aggression on physiological arousal. *Journal of Abnormal and Social Psychology, 63,* 446–448.

Hokanson, J. E., Willers, K. R., & Koropsak, E. (1968). The modification of autonomic responses during aggressive interchange. *Journal of Personality, 36,* 386–404.

Holahan, C. J., & Wandersman, A. (1987). The community psychology perspective in environmental psychology. In D. Stokols & I. Altman (Eds.), *Handbook of environmental psychology* (Vol. 1, pp. 827–861). New York: Wiley.

Hollander, E. P. (1958). Conformity, status, and idiosyncrasy credit. *Psychological Review, 65,* 117–127.

Hollander, E. P. (1960). Competence and conformity in the acceptance of influence. *Journal of Abnormal and Social Psychology, 61,* 365–369.

Hollander, E. P. (1961). Some effects of perceived status on responses to innovative behavior. *Journal of Abnormal and Social Psychology, 63,* 247–250.

Hollander, E. P. (1981). *Principles and methods of social psychology.* New York: Oxford University Press.

Hollander, E. P. (1985). Leadership and power. In G. Lindzey & E. Aronson (Eds.), *Handbook of social psychology* (3rd ed., Vol. 2, pp. 485–537). New York: Random House.

Hollander, E. P., & Offermann, L. R. (1990). Power and leadership in organizations: Relationships in transition. *American Psychologist, 45,* 179–189.

Homer, P. M., & Kahle, L. R. (1988). A structural equation test of the value-attitude-behavior hierarchy. *Journal of Personality and Social Psychology, 54,* 638–646.

Hoorens, V., Nuttin, J. M., Jr., Herman, I. E., & Pavakanun, U. (1990). Mastery versus mere ownership: A quasi-experimental cross-cultural and cross-alphabetical test of the name letter effect. *European Journal of Social Psychology, 20,* 181–205.

Hornik, J., & Ellis, S. (1988). Strategies to secure compliance for a mall intercept interview. *Public Opinion Quarterly, 52,* 539–551.

Hornstein, H. A. (1982). Promotive tension: Theory and research. In V. J. Derlega & J. Grzelak (Eds.), *Cooperation and helping behavior.* New York: Academic Press.

Hornstein, H. A., Masor, H., Sole, K., & Heilman, M. (1971). Effects of sentiment and completion of a helping act on observer helping. *Journal of Personality and Social Psychology, 17,* 107–112.

Horowitz, L. M., Locke, K. D., Morse, M. B., Waikar, S. V., Dryer, D. C., Tarnow, E., & Ghannam, J. (1991). Self-derogations and the interpersonal theory. *Journal of Personality and Social Psychology, 61,* 68–79.

House, R. J., Schuler, R. S., & Levanoni, E. (1983). Role conflict and ambiguous scales: Realities or artifacts. *Journal of Applied Psychology, 68,* 334–337.

Hovanitz, C. A. (1993). Physical health risks associated with aftermath of a disaster: Basic paths of influence and their implications for preventative intervention. *Journal of Social Behavior and Personality, 8,* 213–254.

Hovland, C., & Sears, R. (1940). Minor studies of aggression: VI. Correlation of lynchings with economic indices. *Journal of Psychology, 9,* 301–310.

Hovland, C. I., Janis, I. L., & Kelley, H. H. (1953). *Communication and persuasion.* New Haven, CT: Yale University Press.

Hovland, C. I., Lumsdaine, A. A., & Sheffield, F. D. (1949). *Experiments on mass communication.* Princeton, NJ: Princeton University Press.

Hovland, C. I., & Weiss, W. (1951). The influence of source credibility on communication effectiveness. *Public Opinion Quarterly, 15,* 635–650.

Howard, D. J. (1990). Rhetorical question effects on message processing and persuasion: The role of information availability and the elicitation of judgment. *Journal of Experimental Social Psychology, 26,* 217–239.

Howard, J. A., Blumstein, P., & Schwartz, P. (1986). Sex, power, and influence tactics in intimate relationships. *Journal of Personality and Social Psychology, 51,* 102–109.

Howard, J. W., & Rothbart, M. (1980). Social categorization and memory for in-group and out-group behavior. *Journal of Personality and Social Psychology, 38,* 301–310.

Hrdy, S. B. (1977). Infanticide as a primate reproductive strategy. *American Scientist, 65,* 40–49.

Huesmann, L. R. (1982). TV violence and aggressive behavior. In D. Pearl, L. Bouthilet, & J. Lazar (Eds.), *Television and behavior, ten years of scientific progress and implications for the eighties.* Rockville, MD: NIMH.

Huesmann, L. R., & Levinger, G. (1976). Incremental exchange theory: A formal model for progression in dyadic social interaction. In L. Berkowitz (Ed.), *Advances in experimental social psychology* (Vol. 9, pp. 192–229). New York: Academic Press.

Hull, J. G., & Mendolia, M. (1991). Modeling the relations of attributional style, expectancies, and depression. *Journal of Personality and Social Psychology, 61,* 85–97.

Hummert, M. L., Crockett, W. H., & Kemper, S. (1990). Processing mechanisms underlying use of the balance schema. *Journal of Personality and Social Psychology, 58,* 5–21.

Hunt, M. (1990). *The compassionate beast: What science is discovering about the humane side of humankind.* New York: Morrow.

Huston, A. C., Donnerstein, E., Fairchild, H. H., Feshbach, N. D., Katz, P. A., Murray, J. P., Rubinstein, E. A., Wilcox, B. L., & Zuckerman, D. (1992). *Big world, small screen: The role of television in American society.* Lincoln: University of Nebraska Press.

Huston, T., Ruggiero, M., Conner, E. R., & Geis, G. (1981). Bystander intervention into crime: A study based on naturally occurring episodes. *Social Psychology Quarterly, 44,* 14–23.

Huston, T. L., & Ashmore, R. D. (1986). Women and men in personal relationships. In R. D. Ashmore & F. K. Del Boca (Eds.), *The social psychology of female-male relationships* (pp. 167–210). New York: Academic Press.

Hyde, J. S. (1986). Gender differences in aggression. In J. S. Hyde & M. C. Linn (Eds.), *The psychology of gender: Advances through meta-analysis.* Baltimore, MD: Johns Hopkins University Press.

Hymes, R. W. (1986). Political attitudes as social categories: A new look at selective memory. *Journal of Personality and Social Psychology, 51,* 233–241.

Iacobucci, D., & McGill, A. L. (1990). Analysis of attribution data: Theory testing and effects estimation. *Journal of Personality and Social Psychology, 59,* 426–441.

Ickes, W. J. (1984). Compositions in black and white: Determinants of interactions in interracial dyads. *Journal of Personality and Social Psychology, 47,* 230–241.

Ickes, W. J. (1993). Traditional gender roles: Do they make, and then break, our relationships? *Journal of Social Issues, 49*(3), 71–86.

Ingham, A. G., Levinger, G., Graves, J., & Peckham, V. (1974). The Ringelmann effect: Studies of group size and group performance. *Journal of Personality and Social Psychology, 10,* 371–384.

Ingram, R. E. (1990). Self-focused attention in clinical disorders: Review and a conceptual model. *Psychological Bulletin, 107,* 156–176.

Ingram, R. E. (1991). Tilting at windmills: A response to Pyszczynski, Greenberg, Hamilton, and Nix. *Psychological Bulletin, 110,* 544–550.

Insko, C. A. (1965). Verbal reinforcement of attitude. *Journal of Personality and Social Psychology, 2,* 621–623.

Insko, C. A., Pinkley, R. L., Hoyle, R. H., Dalton, B., Hong, G., Slim, R., Landry, P., Holton, B., Ruffin, P. F., & Thibaut, J. (1987). Individual versus group discontinuity: The role of intergroup contact. *Journal of Experimental Social Psychology, 23,* 250–267.

Insko, C. A., Schopler, J., Hoyle, R. H., Dardis, G. J., & Graetz, K. A. (1990). Individual-group discontinuity as a function of fear and greed. *Journal of Personality and Social Psychology, 58,* 68–79.

Insko, C. A., & Wilson, M. (1977). Interpersonal attraction as a function of social interaction. *Journal of Personality and Social Psychology, 35,* 903–911.

Institute for Social Research. (1983). Black Americans surveyed. *ISR Newsletter, 11*(1), pp. 3, 7.

Institute for Social Research. (1985). Racial attitudes. *ISR Newsletter, 13*(2), pp. 6–7.

Instone, D., Major, B., & Bunker, B. B. (1983). Gender, self-confidence, and social influence strategies: An organizational simulation. *Journal of Personality and Social Psychology, 44,* 322–333.

Isen, A. M. (1970). Success, failure, attention, and reaction to others: The warm glow of success. *Journal of Personality and Social Psychology, 15,* 294–301.

Isen, A. M. (1987). Positive affect, cognitive processes, and social behavior. In L. Berkowitz (Ed.), *Advances in experimental social psychology* (Vol. 20, pp. 203–253). Orlando, FL: Academic Press.

Isen, A. M., Clark, M., & Schwartz, M. F. (1976). Duration of the effect of good mood on helping: "Footprints in the sands of time." *Journal of Personality and Social Psychology, 34,* 385–393.

Isen, A. M., Horn, N., & Rosenhan, D. L. (1973). Effects of success and failure on children's generosity. *Journal of Personality and Social Psychology, 27,* 239–248.

Isen, A. M., & Levin, P. F. (1972). Effect of feeling good on helping: Cookies and kindness. *Journal of Personality and Social Psychology, 21,* 384–388.

Isen, A. M., Shalker, T. F., Clark, M., & Karp, L. (1978). Affect, accessibility of material in memory, and behavior: A cognitive loop? *Journal of Personality and Social Psychology, 36,* 1–12.

Isen, A. M., & Simmonds, S. (1978). The effect of feeling good on a helping task that is incompatible with good mood. *Social Psychology, 41,* 346–349.

Isenberg, D. J. (1986). Group polarization: A critical review and meta-analysis. *Journal of Personality and Social Psychology, 50,* 1141–1151.

Isser, N. (1991). Why cultic groups develop and flourish: A historian's perspective. *Cultic Studies Journal, 8,* 104–121.

Iverson, M. A. (1964). Personality impressions of punitive stimulus persons of differential status. *Journal of Abnormal and Social Psychology, 68,* 617–626.

Izard, C. E. (1980). Cross-cultural perspectives on emotion and emotion communication. In H. C. Triandis & W. Lonner (Eds.), *Handbook of cross-cultural psychology* (pp. 185–221). Boston: Allyn & Bacon.

Jackson, J. M. (1987). Social impact theory: A social forces model of influence. In B. Mullen & G. R. Goethals (Eds.), *Theories of group behavior* (pp. 112–124). New York: Springer-Verlag.

Jackson, J. M., & Harkins, S. G. (1985). Equity in effort: An explanation of the social loafing effect. *Journal of Personality and Social Psychology, 49,* 1199–1206.

Jackson, J. M., & Latané, B. (1981). All alone in front of all those people: Stage fright as a function of number and type of co-performances and audience. *Journal of Personality and Social Psychology, 40,* 73–85.

Jacobs, L., Berscheid, E., & Walster, E. (1971). Self-esteem and attraction. *Journal of Personality and Social Psychology, 17,* 84–91.

Jacobson, M., Atkins, R., & Hacker, G. (1983). *The booze merchants: The inebriating of America.* Washington, DC: Center for Science in the Public Interest.

James, K. (1986). Priming and social categorizational factors: Impact of awareness on emergency situations. *Personality and Social Psychology Bulletin, 12,* 462–467.

James, K. (1993). Conceptualizing self with in-group stereotypes: Context and esteem precursors. *Personality and Social Psychology Bulletin, 19,* 117–121.

James, R. (1959). Status and competency of jurors. *American Journal of Sociology, 64,* 563–570.

James, W. (1892/1961). *The principles of psychology.* New York: Holt.

Jamieson, D. W., & Zanna, M. P. (1989). Need for structure in attitude formation and expression. In A. R. Pratkanis, S. J. Breckler, & A. G. Greenwald (Eds.), *Attitude structure and function* (pp. 383–406). Hillsdale, NJ: Erlbaum.

Janis, I. L. (1982). *Victims of groupthink* (2nd ed.). Boston: Houghton Mifflin.

Janis, I. L. (1989). *Crucial decisions: Leadership in policymaking and crisis management.* New York: Free Press.

Janoff-Bulman, R. (1979). Characterological versus behavioral self-blame: Inquiries into depression and rape. *Journal of Personality and Social Psychology, 37,* 1798–1809.

Janoff-Bulman, R., & Schwartzberg, S. S. (1991). Toward a general model of personal change. In C. R. Snyder and D. R. Forsyth (Eds.), *Handbook of social and clinical psychology: The health perspective* (pp. 488–508). New York: Pergamon.

Janoff-Bulman, R., Timko, C., & Carli, L. L. (1985). Cognitive biases in blaming the victim. *Journal of Experimental Social Psychology, 21,* 161–177.

Jaspars, J. M. F., Hewstone, M., & Fincham, F. D. (1983). Attribution theory and research: The state of the art. In J. M. F. Jaspars, F. D. Fincham, & M. Hewstone (Eds.), *Attribution theory and research: Conceptual, developmental, and social dimensions* (pp. 3–36). London: Academic Press.

Javornisky, G. (1979). Task context and sex differences in conformity. *Journal of Social Psychology, 108,* 213–220.

Jemmott, J. B., III, & Jones, J. M. (1993). Social psychology and AIDS among ethnic minority individuals: Risk behaviors and strategies for changing them. In J. B. Pryor & G. D. Reeder (Eds.), *The social psychology of HIV infection* (pp. 183–224). Hillsdale, NJ: Erlbaum.

Jemmott, L. S., & Jemmott, J. B., III. (1991). Applying the theory of reasoned action to AIDS risk behavior: Condom use among black women. *Nursing Research, 40,* 228–234.

Jenni, D. A., & Jenni, M. A. (1976). Carrying behavior in humans: Analysis of sex differences. *Science, 194,* 859–860.

Jennings, B. (1993). Health policy in a new key: Setting democratic priorities. *Journal of Social Issues, 49*(2), 169–184.

Jessor, R., Costa, F., Jessor, L., & Donovan, J. E. (1983). Time of first intercourse: A prospective study. *Journal of Personality and Social Psychology, 44,* 608–626.

Johnson, B. T. (1991). Insights about attitudes: Meta-analytic perspectives. *Personality and Social Psychology Bulletin, 17,* 289–299.

Johnson, B. T., & Eagly, A. H. (1989). Effects of involvement on persuasion: A meta-analysis. *Psychological Bulletin, 106,* 290–314.

Johnson, B. T., & Eagly, A. H. (1990). Involvement and persuasion: Types, traditions, and the evidence. *Psychological Bulletin, 107,* 375–384.

Johnson, D. W., Johnson, R. T., & Maruyama, G. (1984). Goal interdependence and interpersonal attraction in heterogeneous classrooms: A meta-analysis. In N. Miller & M. Brewer (Eds.), *Groups in contact: The psychology of desegregation* (pp. 187–212). New York: Academic Press.

Johnson, H. G., Ekman, P., & Friesen, W. V. (1975). Communicative body movements: American emblems. *Semiotica, 15,* 335–353.

Johnson, J. T., Cain, L. M., Falke, T. L., Hayman, J., & Perillo, E. (1985). The "Barnum effect" revisited: Cognitive and motivational factors in the acceptance of personality descriptions. *Journal of Personality and Social Psychology, 49,* 1378–1391.

Johnson, T. E., & Rule, B. G. (1986). Mitigating circumstance information, censure, and aggression. *Journal of Personality and Social Psychology, 50,* 537–542.

Jones, E. E. (1964). *Ingratiation.* New York: Appleton-Century-Crofts.

Jones, E. E. (1979). The rocky road from acts to dispositions. *American Psychologist, 34,* 107–117.

Jones, E. E. (1990). *Interpersonal perception.* New York: W. H. Freeman.

Jones, E. E. (1993). Afterword: An avuncular view. *Personality and Social Psychology Bulletin, 19,* 657–661.

Jones, E. E., & Berglas, S. (1978). Control of attributions about the self through self-handicapping strategies: The appeal of alcohol and the role of underachievement. *Personality and Social Psychology Bulletin, 4,* 200–206.

Jones, E. E., & Davis, K. E. (1965). From acts to dispositions: The attribution process in person perception. In L. Berkowitz (Ed.), *Advances in experimental social psychology* (Vol. 2). New York: Academic Press.

Jones, E. E., Davis, K. E., & Gergen, K. J. (1961). Role playing variations and their informational value for person perception. *Journal of Abnormal and Social Psychology, 63,* 302–310.

Jones, E. E., & Harris, V. A. (1967). The attribution of attitudes. *Journal of Experimental Social Psychology, 3,* 1–24.

Jones, E. E., & McGillis, D. (1976). Correspondent inferences and the attribution cube: A comparative reappraisal. In J. H. Harvey, W. J. Ickes, & R. F. Kidd (Eds.), *New directions in attribution research* (Vol. 1). Hillsdale, NJ: Erlbaum.

Jones, E. E., & Pittman, T. S. (1982). Towards a general theory of strategic self-presentation. In J. Suls (Ed.), *Psychological perspectives on the self* (Vol. 1). Hillsdale, NJ: Erlbaum.

Jones, E. E., & Sigall, H. (1971). The bogus pipeline: A new paradigm for measuring affect and attitude. *Psychological Bulletin, 76,* 349–364.

Jones, E. E., & Wortman, C. (1973). *Ingratiation: An attributional approach.* Morristown, NJ: General Learning Press.

Jones, J. M. (1983). The concept of race in social psychology: From color to culture. In L. Wheeler & P. Shaver (Eds.), *Review of personality and social psychology* (Vol. 4). Newbury Park, CA: Sage.

Jones, S. C. (1973). Self- and interpersonal evaluations: Esteem theories versus consistency theories. *Psychological Bulletin, 79,* 185–199.

Jones, S. E., & Yarbrough, A. E. (1985). A naturalistic study of the meanings of touch. *Communication Monographs, 52,* 19–56.

Jones, W. H. (1985). Interview with J. Meer. *Psychology Today, 19*(7), p. 33.

Jones, W. H., Carpenter, B. N., & Quintana, D. (1985). Personality and interpersonal predictors of loneliness in two cultures. *Journal of Personality and Social Psychology, 48,* 1503–1511.

Jones, W. H., & Carver, M. D. (1991). Adjustment and coping implications of loneliness. In C. R. Snyder and D. R. Forsyth (Eds.), *Handbook of social and clinical psychology: The health perspective* (pp. 395–415). New York: Pergamon.

Josephs, R. A., Markus, H. R., & Tafarodi, R. W. (1992). Gender and self-esteem. *Journal of Personality and Social Psychology, 63,* 391–402.

Joule, R. V. (1986). Twenty-five on: Yet another version of cognitive dissonance theory? *European Journal of Social Psychology, 16,* 65–78.

Joule, R. V. (1987). La dissonance cognitive: un état de motivation? *Année Psychologique, 87,* 273–290.

Judd, C. M., & Kulik, J. A. (1980). Schematic effects of social attitudes on information processing and recall. *Journal of Personality and Social Psychology, 38,* 569–578.

Judd, C. M., & Park, B. (1993). Definition and assessment of accuracy in social stereotypes. *Psychological Review, 100,* 109–128.

Jussim, L. (1986). Self-fulfilling prophecies: A theoretical and integrative review. *Psychological Review, 93,* 429–445.

Jussim, L. (1990). Social reality and social problems: The role of expectancies. *Journal of Social Issues, 46*(2), 9–34.

Jussim, L. (1991). Social perception and social reality: A reflection-construction model. *Psychological Review, 98,* 54–73.

Kadish, S. H., & Paulsen, M. G. (1975). *Criminal law and its processes.* Boston: Little, Brown.

Kagan, J., Snidman, N., & Arcus, D. M. (1992). Initial reactions to unfamiliarity. *Current Directions in Psychological Science, 1,* 171–174.

Kahle, L. R., & Berman, J. J. (1979). Attitudes cause behaviors: A cross-lagged panel analysis. *Journal of Personality and Social Psychology, 37,* 315–321.

Kahneman, D., & Tversky, A. (1972). Subjective probability: A judgment of representativeness. *Cognitive Psychology, 3,* 430–454.

Kahneman, D., & Tversky, A. (1973). On the psychology of prediction. *Psychological Review, 80,* 237–251.

Kahneman, D., & Tversky, A. (1982). The simulation heuristic. In D. Kahneman, P. Slovic, & A. Tversky (Eds.), *Judgment under uncertainty: Heuristics and biases* (pp. 201–208). New York: Cambridge University Press.

Kahneman, D., & Tversky, A. (1984). Choices, values, and frames. *American Psychologist, 39,* 341–350.

Kalb, M., & Kalb, B. (1974). *Kissinger.* Boston: Little, Brown.

Kallgren, C. A., & Wood, W. (1986). Access to attitude-relevant information in memory as a determinant of attitude-behavior consistency. *Journal of Experimental Social Psychology, 22,* 328–338.

Kalven, H., Jr., & Zeisel, H. (1966). *The American jury.* Boston: Little, Brown.

Kameda, T., Stasson, M. F., Davis, J. H., Parks, C. D., & Zimmerman, S. K. (1992). Social dilemmas, subgroups, and motivation loss in task-oriented groups: In search of an "optimal" team size in division of work. *Social Psychology Quarterly, 55,* 47–56.

Kameda, T., & Sugimori, S. (1993). Psychological entrapment in group decision making: An assigned decision rule and a groupthink phenomenon. *Journal of Personality and Social Psychology, 65,* 282–292.

Kamptner, N. L. (1991). Personal possessions and their meanings: A life-span perspective. *Journal of Social Behavior and Personality, 6,* 209–228.

Kandel, D. B. (1978). Similarity in real-life adolescent friendship pairs. *Journal of Personality and Social Psychology, 36,* 306–312.

Kaniasty, K., & Norris, F. H. (1993). How general is the cost of good fortune? Attempting to replicate Brown and McGill (1989). *Journal of Social Behavior and Personality, 8,* 31–49.

Kanouse, D. E., & Hanson, L. R., Jr. (1972). Negativity in evaluations. In E. E. Jones, D. E. Kanouse, H. H. Kelley, R. E. Nisbett, S. Valins, & B. Weiner (Eds.), *Attribution: Perceiving the causes of behavior.* Morristown, NJ: General Learning Press.

Kaplan, M. F. (1975). Evaluative judgments are based on evaluative information: Evidence against meaning change in evaluative context effects. *Memory and Cognition, 3,* 375–380.

Kaplan, M. F., & Miller, C. E. (1983). Group discussion and judgment. In P. B. Paulus (Ed.), *Basic group processes* (pp. 65–94). New York: Springer-Verlag.

Kaplan, R., & Kaplan, S. (1989). *The experience of nature: A psychological perspective.* New York: Cambridge University Press.

Kaplan, S. (1987). Aesthetics, affect, and cognition: Environmental preference from an evolutionary perspective. *Environment and Behavior, 19,* 3–32.

Karabenick, S. A., & Meisels, M. (1972). Effects of performance valuation on interpersonal distance. *Journal of Personality, 40,* 275–286.

Karau, S. J., & Williams, K. D. (1993). Social loafing: A meta-analytic review and theoretical integration. *Journal of Personality and Social Psychology, 65,* 681–706.

Karoly, P. (1993). Mechanisms of self-regulation: A systems view. *Annual Review of Psychology, 44,* 23–52.

Kassin, S. M., & Pryor, J. B. (1986). The development of attribution processes. In J. B. Pryor & J. Day (Eds.), *The development of social cognition* (pp. 3–34). New York: Springer-Verlag.

Katz, D. (1960). The functional approach to the study of attitudes. *Public Opinion Quarterly, 24,* 163–204.

Katz, D., & Braly, K. W. (1933). Racial stereotypes of 100 college students. *Journal of Abnormal and Social Psychology, 28,* 280–290.

Katz, D., & Kahn, R. L. (1978). *The social psychology of organizations* (2nd ed.). New York: Wiley.

Katz, I. (1981). *Stigma: A social psychological analysis.* Hillsdale, NJ: Erlbaum.

Katz, I., & Hass, R. G. (1988). Racial ambivalence and American value conflict: Correlational and priming studies of dual cognitive structures. *Journal of Personality and Social Psychology, 55,* 893–905.

Katz, I., Wackenhut J., & Hass, R. G. (1986). Racial ambivalence, value duality, and behavior. In J. Dovidio & S. Gaertner (Eds.), *Prejudice, discrimination, and racism* (pp. 35–59). Orlando, FL: Academic Press.

Katz, R. (1977). The influence of group conflict on leadership effectiveness. *Organizational Behavior and Human Performance, 20,* 265–286.

Keating, C. F. (1985). Gender and the physiognomy of dominance and attractiveness. *Social Psychology Quarterly, 48,* 61–70.

Keating, C. F., Mazur, A., Segall, M. H., Cysneiros, P. G., Divale, W. T., Kilbride, J. E., Komin, S., Leahy, P., Thurman, B., & Wirsing, R. (1981). Culture and the perception of social dominance from facial cues. *Journal of Personality and Social Psychology, 40,* 615–626.

Kegeles, S. M., Adler, N. E., & Irwin, C. E., Jr. (1988). Sexually active adolescents and condoms: Changes over one year in knowledge, attitudes, and use. *American Journal of Public Health, 78,* 460–461.

Kelley, H. H. (1952). Two functions of reference groups. In G. E. Swanson, T. M. Newcomb, & E. L. Hartley (Eds.), *Readings in social psychology* (2nd ed.). New York: Holt.

Kelley, H. H. (1967). Attribution theory in social psychology. *Nebraska Symposium on Motivation, 15,* 192–241.

Kelley, H. H. (1971). Attribution in social interaction. In E. E. Jones, D. E. Kanouse, H. H. Kelley, R. E. Nisbett, S. Valins, & B. Weiner (Eds.), *Attribution: Perceiving the causes of behavior.* Morristown, NJ: General Learning Press.

Kelley, H. H. (1979). *Personal relationships: Their structures and processes.* Hillsdale, NJ: Erlbaum.

Kelley, H. H. (1983). Love and commitment. In H. H. Kelley, E. Berscheid, A. Christensen, J. H. Harvey, T. L. Huston, G. Levinger, E. McClintock, L. A. Peplau, & D. R. Peterson, *Close relationships.* New York: W. H. Freeman.

Kelley, H. H., Berscheid, E., Christensen, A., Harvey, J. H., Huston, T. L., Levinger, G., McClintock, E., Peplau, L. A., & Peterson, D. R. (1983). *Close relationships.* New York: W. H. Freeman.

Kelley, H. H., Cunningham, J., & Stambul, H. B. (1973). Unpublished data. Reported in H. H. Kelley (1979), *Personal relationships: Their structures and processes* (pp. 18–19). Hillsdale, NJ: Erlbaum.

Kelley, H. H., Tiggle, R., & Peters, M. (1977). Unpublished data. Reported in H. H. Kelley (1979), *Personal relationships: Their structures and processes* (pp. 18–19). Hillsdale, NJ: Erlbaum.

Kelley, H. H., & Stahelski, A. J. (1970a). Errors of perception of intentions in a mixed-motive game. *Journal of Experimental Social Psychology, 6,* 379–400.

Kelley, H. H., & Stahelski, A. J. (1970b). The inference of intentions from moves in the Prisoner's Dilemma Game. *Journal of Experimental Social Psychology, 6,* 401–419.

Kelley, H. H., & Stahelski, A. J. (1970c). Social interaction basis of cooperators' and competitors' beliefs about others. *Journal of Personality and Social Psychology, 16,* 66–91.

Kelley, J. A., Murphy, D. A., Sikkema, K. J., & Kalichman, S. C. (1993). Psychological interventions to prevent HIV infection are urgently needed: New priorities for behavior research in the second decade of AIDS. *American Psychologist, 48,* 1023–1034.

Kelley, J. R. (1988). Entrainment in individual and group performance. In J. E. McGrath (Ed.), *The social psychology of time: New perspectives.* Newbury Park, CA: Sage.

Kelley, J. R., Futoran, G. C., & McGrath, J. E. (1990). Capacity and capability: Seven studies of entrainment of task performance rates. *Small Group Research, 21,* 283–314.

Kelley, J. R., & Karau, S. J. (1993). Entrainment of creativity in small groups. *Small Group Research, 24,* 179–198.

Kelly, G. A. (1955). *The psychology of personal constructs.* New York: Norton.

Kelman, H. C. (1982). Ethical issues in different social science methods. In T. L. Beauchamp, R. R. Faden, R. J. Wallace, Jr., & L. Walters (Eds.), *Ethical issues in social science research.* Baltimore, MD: Johns Hopkins University Press.

Kelman, H. C., & Hamilton, V. L. (1989). *Crimes of obedience: Toward a social psychology of authority and responsibility.* New Haven, CT: Yale University Press.

Kelman, H. C., & Hovland, C. I. (1953). "Reinstatement" of the communicator in delayed measurement of opinion change. *Journal of Abnormal and Social Psychology, 48,* 327–335.

Kempton, W., Darley, J. M., & Stern, P. C. (1992). Psychological research for the new energy problems: Strategies and opportunities. *American Psychologist, 47,* 1213–1223.

Kendzierski, D. (1990). Exercise self-schemata: Cognitive and behavioral correlates. *Health Psychology, 9,* 69–82.

Kenny, D. A. (1988). Interpersonal perception: A social relations analysis. *Journal of Social and Personal Relationships, 5,* 247–261.

Kenny, D. A. (1991). A general model of consensus and accuracy in interpersonal perception. *Psychological Review, 98,* 155–163.

Kenny, D. A., & Albright, L. (1987). Accuracy in interpersonal perception: A social relations analysis. *Psychological Bulletin, 102,* 390–402.

Kenny, D. A., Horner, C., Kashy, D. A., & Chu, L. (1992). Consensus at zero acquaintance: Replication, behavioral cues, and stability. *Journal of Personality and Social Psychology, 62,* 88–97.

Kenny, D. A., & Nasby, W. (1980). Splitting the reciprocity correlation. *Journal of Personality and Social Psychology, 38,* 249–260.

Kenny, D. A., & Zaccaro, S. J. (1983). An estimate of variance due to traits in leadership. *Journal of Applied Psychology, 68,* 678–685.

Kenrick, D. T. (1986). How strong is the case against contemporary social and personality psychology? A response to Carlson. *Journal of Personality and Social Psychology, 50,* 839–844.

Kenrick, D. T., & Cialdini, R. B. (1977). Romantic attraction: Misattribution versus reinforcement explanations. *Journal of Personality and Social Psychology, 35,* 381–391.

Kenrick, D. T., Cialdini, R. B., & Linder, D. E. (1979). Misattribution under fear-producing circumstances: Four failures to replicate. *Personality and Social Psychology Bulletin, 5,* 329–334.

Kenrick, D. T., Groth, G. E., Trost, M. R., & Sadalla, E. K. (1993). Integrating evolutionary and social exchange perspectives on relationships: Effects of gender, self-appraisal, and involvement level on mate selection criteria. *Journal of Personality and Social Psychology, 64,* 951–969.

Kenrick, D. T., & Johnson, G. A. (1979). Interpersonal attraction in aversive environments: A problem for the classical conditioning paradigm? *Journal of Personality and Social Psychology, 37,* 572–579.

Kenrick, D. T., & Keefe, R. C. (1992). Age preferences in mates reflect sex differences in reproductive strategies. *Behavioral and Brain Sciences, 12,* 24–26.

Kenrick, D. T., & MacFarlane, S. W. (1986). Ambient temperature and horn-honking: A field study of the heat/aggression relationship. *Environment and Behavior, 18,* 179–191.

Kenrick, D. T., McCreath, H. E., Govern, J., King R., & Bordin, J. (1990). Person-environment intersections: Everyday settings and common trait dimensions. *Journal of Personality and Social Psychology, 58,* 685–698.

Kenrick, D. T., & Trost, M. R. (1989). Reproductive exchange model of heterosexual relationships: Putting proximate economics in ultimate perspective. In C. Hendrick (Ed.), *Review of personality and social psychology* (Vol. 10, pp. 92–118). Newbury Park, CA: Sage.

Kent, S. (1991). Partitioning space: Cross-cultural factors influencing domestic spatial segmentation. *Environment and Behavior, 23,* 438–473.

Kerckhoff, A. C., & Davis, K. E. (1962). Value consensus and need complementarity in mate selection. *American Sociological Review, 27,* 295–303.

Kerman, S., & Martin, M. (1980). *Teacher expectations and student achievement.* Los Angeles, CA: Office of the Los Angeles County Superintendent of Schools.

Kernis, M. H., Brockner, J., & Frankel, B. S. (1989). Self-esteem and reactions to failure: The mediating role of overgeneralization. *Journal of Personality and Social Psychology, 57,* 707–714.

Kernis, M. H., & Grannemann, B. D. (1990). Excuses in the making: A test and extension of Darley and Goethals' attributional model. *Journal of Experimental Social Psychology, 26,* 337–349.

Kernis, M. H., Grannemann, B. D., & Barclay, L. C. (1989). Stability and level of self-esteem as predictors of anger arousal and hostility. *Journal of Personality and Social Psychology, 56,* 1013–1022.

Kernis, M. H., & Johnson, E. K. (1990). Current and typical self-appraisals: Differential responsiveness to evaluative feedback and implications for emotions. *Journal of Research in Personality, 24,* 241–257.

Kerr, N. L. (1983). Motivation losses in small groups: A social dilemma analysis. *Journal of Personality and Social Psychology, 45,* 819–828.

Kerr, N. L., & MacCoun, R. J. (1985). The effects of jury size and polling method on the process and product of jury deliberation. *Journal of Personality and Social Psychology, 48,* 349–363.

Kiecolt-Glaser, J. K., Ricker, D., Messick, G., Speicher, C., Holliday, J., Garner, W., & Glaser, R. (1984). Urinary cortisol levels, cellular immunocompetency, and loneliness in psychiatric inpatients. *Psychosomatic Medicine, 46,* 15–24.

Kiecolt-Glaser, J. K., Speicher, C. E., Holliday, J. E., & Glaser, R. (1984). Stress and the transformation of lymphocytes by Epstein-Barr virus. *Journal of Behavioral Medicine, 7,* 1–11.

Kiesler, C. A., Nisbett, R. E., & Zanna, M. P. (1969). On inferring one's beliefs from one's behavior. *Journal of Personality and Social Psychology, 11,* 321–327.

Kiesler, C. A., & Pallak, M. S. (1976). Arousal properties of dissonance manipulations. *Psychological Bulletin, 83,* 1014–1025.

Kihlstrom, J. F., Cantor, N., Albright, J. S., Chew, B. R., Klein, S. B., & Niedenthal, P. M. (1988). Information processing and the study of the self. In L. Berkowitz (Ed.), *Advances in experimental social psychology* (Vol. 17, pp. 145–180). New York: Academic Press.

Kim, M. P., & Rosenberg, S. (1980). Comparison of two structural models of implicit personality theory. *Journal of Personality and Social Psychology, 38,* 375–389.

Kimble, C. E., Arnold, E. M., & Hirt, E. R. (1985). An attributional perspective on interpersonal attraction using Kelley's cube. *Basic and Applied Social Psychology, 6,* 131–144.

Kinder, D. R., & Sears, D. O. (1981). Prejudice and politics: Symbolic racism versus racial threats to the good life. *Journal of Personality and Social Psychology, 40,* 414–431.

Kinder, D. R., & Sears, D. O. (1985). Public opinion and political action. In G. Lindzey & E. Aronson (Eds.), *Handbook of social psychology* (3rd ed., Vol. 2, pp. 659–741). New York: Random House.

Kinsey, A. C., Pomeroy, W. B., & Martin, C. E. (1948). *Sexual behavior in the human male.* Philadelphia, PA: Saunders.

Kinsey, A. C., Pomeroy, W. B., Martin, C. E., & Gebhard, P. H. (1953). *Sexual behavior in the human female.* Philadelphia, PA: Saunders.

Kinzel, A. F. (1970). Body buffer zone in violent prisoners. *American Journal of Psychiatry, 127,* 59–64.

Kipnis, D. (1984). The use of power in organizations in interpersonal settings. In S. Oskamp (Ed.), *Applied social psychology annual* (Vol. 5, pp. 179–210). Newbury Park, CA: Sage.

Kipnis, D., & Consentino, J. (1969). Use of leadership powers in industry. *Journal of Applied Psychology, 53,* 460–466.

Kipnis, D., Schmidt, S. M., Swaffin-Smith, C., & Wilkinson, I. (1984). Patterns of managerial influence: Shotgun managers, tacticians, and bystanders. *Organizational Dynamics, 12*(3), 58–67.

Kirkpatrick, S. A., & Locke, E. A. (1991). Leadership: Do traits matter? *Academy of Management Executives, 5*(2), 48–60.

Kissinger, H. (1979). *White House years.* Boston: Little, Brown.

Klatzky, R. L., Martin, G. L., & Kane, R. A. (1982). Influence of social-category activation on processing of visual information. *Social Cognition, 1,* 95–109.

Klayman, J., & Ha, Y-W. (1987). Confirmation, disconfirmation, and information in hypothesis testing. *Psychological Review, 94,* 211–228.

Klayman, J., & Ha, Y-W. (1989). Hypothesis testing in rule discovery: Strategy, structure, and content. *Journal of Experimental Psychology: Learning, Memory, and Cognition, 15,* 596–604.

Klein, G. A., Orasanu, J., Calderwood, R., & Zsambok, C. E. (Eds.). (1993). *Decision making in action: Models and methods.* Norwood, NJ: Ablex.

Klein, S. B., & Kihlstrom, J. F. (1986). Elaboration, organization, and the self-reference effect in memory. *Journal of Experimental Psychology: General, 115,* 26–38.

Klein, S. B., Loftus, J., & Burton, H. A. (1989). Two self-reference effects: The importance of distinguishing between self-descriptiveness judgments and autobiographical retrieval in self-referent encoding. *Journal of Personality and Social Psychology, 56,* 853–865.

Kleinke, C. L. (1977). Compliance to requests made by gazing and touching experimenters in field settings. *Journal of Experimental Social Psychology, 13,* 218–223.

Kleinke, C. L. (1986). Gaze and eye contact: A research review. *Psychological Bulletin, 100,* 78–100.

Kleinmuntz, D. (1985). Cognitive heuristics and feedback in a dynamic decision environment. *Management Science, 31,* 680–702.

Kleinpenning, G., & Hagendoorn, L. (1993). Forms of racism and the cumulative dimension of ethnic attitudes. *Social Psychology Quarterly, 56,* 21–36.

Klentz, B., & Beaman, A. L. (1981). The effects of type of information and method of dissemination on the reporting of a shoplifter. *Journal of Applied Social Psychology, 11,* 64–82.

Klinger, E. (1977). *Meaning and void: Inner experience and the incentives in people's lives.* Minneapolis: University of Minnesota Press.

Knapp, M. L. (1978). *Nonverbal communication in human interaction* (2nd ed.). New York: Holt, Rinehart & Winston.

Knopke, H. J., Norell, R. J., & Rogers R. W. (Eds.). (1991). *Opening doors: Perspectives on race relations in contemporary America.* Tuscaloosa: University of Alabama Press.

Knowles, E. (1980). An affiliative-conflict theory of personal and group spatial behavior. In P. B. Paulus (Ed.), *Psychology of group influence.* Hillsdale, NJ: Erlbaum.

Knowles, E. S. (1983). Social physics and the effects of others: Tests of the effects of audience size and distance on social judgments and behavior. *Journal of Personality and Social Psychology, 45,* 1263–1279.

Knox, R. E., & Inkster, J. A. (1968). Postdecision dissonance at post time. *Journal of Personality and Social Psychology, 8,* 310–323.

Koehler, D. J. (1991). Explanation, imagination, and confidence in judgment. *Psychological Bulletin, 110,* 499–519.

Konečni, V. J. (1975a). Annoyance, type, and duration of post-annoyance activity, and aggression: The "cathartic" effect. *Journal of Experimental Psychology: General, 104,* 76–102.

Konečni, V. J. (1975b). The mediation of aggressive behavior: Arousal level versus anger and cognitive labeling. *Journal of Personality and Social Psychology, 32,* 706–712.

Konečni, V. J., & Ebbesen, E. G. (1976). Disinhibition versus the cathartic effect. Artifact and substance. *Journal of Personality and Social Psychology, 34,* 352–365.

Konečni, V. J., Libuser, L., Morton, H., & Ebbesen, E. B. (1975). Effects of violation of personal space on escape and helping responses. *Journal of Experimental Social Psychology, 11,* 288–299.

Koocher, G. P. (1977). Bathroom behavior and human dignity. *Journal of Personality and Social Psychology, 35,* 120–121.

Korte, C. (1970). Effects of individual responsibility and group communication on help-giving in an emergency. *Human Relations, 24,* 149–159.

Korte, C. (1978). Helpfulness in the urban environment. In A. Baum, J. E. Singer, & S. Valins (Eds.), *Advances in environmental psychology* (Vol. 1). Hillsdale, NJ: Erlbaum.

Korte, C. (1981). Constraints on helping in an urban environment. In J. P. Rushton & R. M. Sorrentino (Eds.), *Altruism and helping behavior.* Hillsdale, NJ: Erlbaum.

Korte, C., & Kerr, N. (1975). Response to altruistic opportunities in urban and nonurban settings. *Journal of Social Psychology, 95,* 183–184.

Koss, M. P. (1992). The underdetection of rape: Methodological choices influence incidence estimates. *Journal of Social Issues 48*(1), 61–75.

Koss, M. P. (1993). Rape: Scope, impact, interventions, and public policy responses. *American Psychologist, 48,* 1062–1069.

Kothandapani, V. (1971). Validation of feeling, belief, and intention to act as three components of attitude and their contribution to prediction of contraceptive behavior. *Journal of Personality and Social Psychology, 19,* 321–333.

Krauss, R. M., Apple, W., Morency, N., Wenzel, C., & Winton, W. (1981). Verbal, vocal, and visible factors in judgments of another's affect. *Journal of Personality and Social Psychology, 40,* 312–320.

Krauss, R. M., Morrel-Samuels, P., & Colasante, C. (1991). Do conversational hand gestures communicate? *Journal of Personality and Social Psychology, 61,* 743–754.

Kraut, R. E., & Lewis, S. H. (1982). Person perception and self-awareness: Knowledge of influences on one's own judgments. *Journal of Personality and Social Psychology, 42,* 448–460.

Kraut, R. E., & Poe, D. (1980). Behavioral roots of person perception: The deception judgments of customs inspectors and laymen. *Journal of Personality and Social Psychology, 39,* 784–798.

Kravitz, D. A., Cohen, J. L., Martin, B., Sweeney, J., McCarty, J., Elliott, E., & Goldstein, P. (1978). Humans would do better without other humans. *Personality and Social Psychology Bulletin, 4,* 559–560.

Kravitz, D. A., & Martin, B. (1986). Ringelmann rediscovered: The original article. *Journal of Personality and Social Psychology, 50,* 936–941.

Krebs, D. L., & Miller, D. T. (1985). Altruism and aggression. In G. Lindzey & E. Aronson (Eds.), *Handbook of social psychology* (3rd ed., Vol. 2). New York: Random House.

Kremer, J. F., & Stephens, L. (1983). Attributions and arousal as mediators of mitigation's effect on retaliation. *Journal of Personality and Social Psychology, 45,* 335–343.

Krosnick, J. A. (1988). The role of attitude importance in social evaluation: A study of policy preferences, presidential candidate evaluations, and voting behavior. *Journal of Personality and Social Psychology, 55,* 196–210.

Krosnick, J. A. (1989). Attitude importance and attitude accessibility. *Personality and Social Psychology Bulletin, 15,* 297–308.

Krosnick, J. A., & Alwin D. F. (1989). Aging and susceptibility to attitude change. *Journal of Personality and Social Psychology, 57,* 416–425.

Krosnick, J. A., Betz, A. L., Jussim, L. J., Lynn, A. R., & Stephens, L. (1992). Subliminal conditioning of attitudes. *Personality and Social Psychology Bulletin, 18,* 152–162.

Kruglanski, A. W., Friedland, N., & Farkash, E. (1984). Laypersons' sensitivity to statistical information: The case of high perceived applicability. *Journal of Personality and Social Psychology, 46,* 503–518.

Kruglanski, A. W., & Mayseless, O. (1990). Classic and current social comparison research: Expanding the perspective. *Psychological Bulletin, 108,* 195–208.

Kruglanski, A. W., & Webster, D. M. (1991). Group members' reactions to opinion deviates and conformists at varying degrees of proximity to decision deadline and of environmental noise. *Journal of Personality and Social Psychology, 61,* 212–225.

Krupat, E. (1977). A re-assessment of role-playing as a technique in social psychology. *Personality and Social Psychology Bulletin, 3,* 498–504.

Kruuk, H. (1972). *The spotted hyena.* Chicago: University of Chicago Press.

Kuhn, M. H. (1960). Self attitudes by age, sex, and professional training. *Sociological Quarterly, 1,* 39–55.

Kuhn, M. H., & McPartland, T. S. (1954). An empirical investigation of self attitudes. *American Sociological Review, 19,* 68–76.

Kuhn, T. (1962). *The structure of scientific revolutions.* Chicago: University of Chicago Press.

Kuhn, T. (1970). *The structure of scientific revolutions* (rev. ed.). Chicago: University of Chicago Press.

Kulik, J. A., & Mahler, H. I. M. (1989). Stress and affiliation in a hospital setting: Preoperative roommate preference. *Personality and Social Psychology Bulletin, 15,* 183–193.

Kurdek, L. A. (1991). Correlates of relationship satisfaction in cohabitating gay and lesbian couples. *Journal of Personality and Social Psychology, 61,* 910–922.

Kurdek, L. A. (1993). The allocation of household labor in gay, lesbian, and heterosexual married couples. *Journal of Social Issues, 49*(3), 127–139.

Kurtines, W. M. (1986). Moral behavior as rule governed behavior: Person and situation effects on moral decision making. *Journal of Personality and Social Psychology, 50,* 784–791.

Lachman, M. E. (1991). Perceived control over memory aging: Developmental and intervention perspectives. *Journal of Social Issues, 47*(4), 159–175.

LaFrance, M. (1985). The school of hard knocks: Nonverbal sexism in the classroom. *Theory into Practice, 24*(1), 40–44.

Lambert, W. W. (1971). Cross-cultural background to personality development and the socialization of aggression: Findings from the six culture study. In W. W. Lambert & R. Weisbrod (Eds.), *Comparative perspectives on social psychology* (pp. 49–61). Boston: Little, Brown.

Landsberger, H. A. (1958). *Hawthorne revisited.* Ithaca, NY: Cornell University Press.

Langan, P. A., & Innes, C. A. (1986). *Preventing domestic violence against women.* Washington, DC: U.S. Department of Justice.

Langer, E. J. (1975). The illusion of control. *Journal of Personality and Social Psychology, 32,* 311–329.

Langer, E. J. (1983). *The psychology of control.* Newbury Park, CA: Sage.

Langer, E. J. (1989). *Mindfulness.* Reading, MA: Addison-Wesley.

Langer, E. J., & Rodin, J. (1976). The effects of choice and enhanced personal responsibility for the aged: A field experiment in an institutional setting. *Journal of Personality and Social Psychology, 34,* 191–198.

Langer, E. J., & Saegert, S. (1977). Crowding and cognitive control. *Journal of Personality and Social Psychology, 35,* 175–182.

Lanzetta, J. T., & Englis, B. G. (1989). Expectations of cooperation and competition and their effects on observers' vicarious emotional responses. *Journal of Personality and Social Psychology, 56,* 543–554.

LaPiere, R. T. (1934). Attitudes vs. action. *Social Forces, 13,* 230–237.

Larsen, R. J., & Sinnett, L. M. (1991). Meta-analysis of experimental manipulations: Some factors affecting the Velten mood induction procedure. *Personality and Social Psychology Bulletin, 17,* 323–334.

Larson, C. E., & Lafasto, F. M. J. (1989). *Teamwork: What must go right/what can go wrong.* Newbury Park, CA: Sage.

Latané, B. (1981). The psychology of social impact. *American Psychologist, 36,* 343–356.

Latané, B., & Bidwell, L. D. (1977). Sex and affiliation in college cafeterias. *Personality and Social Psychology Bulletin, 3,* 571–574.

Latané, B., & Darley, J. M. (1970). *The unresponsive bystander: Why doesn't he help?* New York: Appleton-Century-Crofts.

Latané, B., & Darley, J. M. (1976). Help in a crisis: Bystander response to an emergency. In J. W. Thibaut, J. T. Spence, & R. C. Carson (Eds.), *Contemporary topics in social psychology.* Morristown, NJ: General Learning Press.

Latané, B., & Nida, S. A. (1981). Ten years of research on group size and helping. *Psychological Bulletin, 89,* 308–324.

Latané, B., Williams, K., & Harkins, S. (1979). Many hands make light the work: The causes and consequences of social loafing. *Journal of Personality and Social Psychology, 37,* 822–832.

Latané, B., & Wolf, S. (1981). The social impact of majorities and minorities. *Psychological Review, 88,* 438–453.

Lau, R. R. (1984). Dynamics of the attribution process. *Journal of Personality and Social Psychology, 46,* 1017–1028.

Lauer, J., & Lauer, R. (1985). Marriages made to last. *Psychology Today, 19*(6), 22–26.

Laughlin, P. R. (1980). Social combination processes of cooperative problem solving groups on verbal intellective tasks. In M. Fishbein (Ed.), *Progress in social psychology.* Hillsdale, NJ: Erlbaum.

Laughlin, P. R., & Earley, P. C. (1982). Social combination models, persuasive arguments theory, social comparison theory, and choice shift. *Journal of Personality and Social Psychology, 42,* 273–280.

Lazarus, R. S. (1984). On the primacy of cognition. *American Psychologist, 39,* 124–129.

Lazarus, R. S., & Folkman, S. (1984). *Stress, appraisal, and coping.* New York: Springer.

Leana, C. R. (1985). A partial test of Janis's groupthink model: Effects of group cohesiveness and leader behavior on defective decision making. *Journal of Management, 11,* 5–17.

Leary, M. R. (1982a). Hindsight distortion and the 1980 presidential election. *Personality and Social Psychology Bulletin, 8,* 257–263.

Leary, M. R. (1982b). Social anxiety. In L. Wheeler (Ed.), *Review of personality and social psychology* (Vol. 3, pp. 97–120). Newbury Park, CA: Sage.

Leary, M. R. (1983). *Understanding social anxiety.* Newbury Park, CA: Sage.

Leary, M. R. (1988). A comprehensive approach to the treatment of social anxieties: The self-presentation model. *Phobia Practice and Research Journal, 1,* 48–57.

Leary, M. R. (1990). Responses to social exclusion: Social anxiety, jealousy, loneliness, depression, and low self-esteem. *Journal of Social and Clinical Psychology, 9,* 221–229.

Leary, M. R., & Atherton, S. C. (1986). Self-efficacy, social anxiety, and inhibition in interpersonal encounters. *Journal of Social and Clinical Psychology, 4,* 256–267.

Leary, M. R., Britt, T. W., Cutlip, W. D., II, & Templeton, J. L. (1992). Social blushing. *Psychological Bulletin, 112,* 446–460.

Leary, M. R., & Forsyth, D. R. (1987). Attributions of responsibility for collective endeavors. *Review of Personality and Social Psychology, 8,* 167–188.

Leary, M. R., & Kowalski, R. M. (1990). Impression management: A literature review and two-component model. *Psychological Bulletin, 107,* 34–47.

Leary, M. R., & Maddux, J. E. (1987). Progress toward a viable interface between social and clinical-counseling psychology. *American Psychologist, 42,* 904–911.

Leary, M. R., & Meadows, S. (1991). Predictors, elicitors, and concomitants of social blushing. *Journal of Personality and Social Psychology, 60,* 254–262.

Leary, M. R., & Miller, R. S. (1986). *Social psychology and dysfunctional behavior: Origins, diagnosis, and treatment.* New York: Springer-Verlag.

Leary, M. R., Robertson, R. B., Barnes, B. D., & Miller, R. S. (1986). Self-presentations of small group leaders: Effects of role requirements and leadership orientation. *Journal of Personality and Social Psychology, 51,* 742–748.

Leary, M. R., Rogers, P. A., Canfield, R. W., & Coe, C. (1986). Boredom in interpersonal encounters: Antecedents and social implications. *Journal of Personality and Social Psychology, 51,* 968–975.

Leary, M. R., & Shepperd, J. A. (1986). Behavioral self-handicapping versus self-reported handicaps: A conceptual note. *Journal of Personality and Social Psychology, 51,* 1265–1268.

Leddo, J., Abelson, R. P., & Gross, P. H. (1984). Conjunctive explanations: When two reasons are better than one. *Journal of Personality and Social Psychology, 47,* 933–943.

Lee, J. A. (1977). A typology of styles of loving. *Personality and Social Psychology Bulletin, 3,* 173–182.

Lee, M. T., & Ofshe, R. (1981). The impact of behavioral style and status characteristics on social influence: A test of two competing theories. *Social Psychology Quarterly, 44,* 73–82.

Lefcourt, H. M., & Davidson-Katz, K. (1991). Locus of control and health. In C. R. Snyder and D. R. Forsyth (Eds.), *Handbook of social and clinical psychology: The health perspective* (pp. 246–266). New York: Pergamon.

Leffler, A., Gillespie, D. L., & Conaty, J. C. (1982). The effects of status-differentiation on nonverbal behavior. *Social Psychology Quarterly, 45,* 153–161.

Lehman, D. R., Lempert, R. O., & Nisbett, R. E. (1988). The effects of graduate training on reasoning: Formal discipline and thinking about everyday-life events. *American Psychologist, 43,* 431–442.

Leigh, B. C., & Stall, R. (1993). Substance use and risky sexual behavior for exposure to HIV: Issues in methodology, interpretation, and prevention. *American Psychologist, 48,* 1035–1045.

Lemyre, L., & Smith, P. M. (1985). Intergroup discrimination and self-esteem in the minimal group paradigm. *Journal of Personality and Social Psychology, 49,* 660–670.

Leone, C. (1989). Self-generated attitude change: Some effects of thought and dogmatism on attitude polarization. *Personality and Individual Differences, 10,* 1243–1252.

Lepore, S. J., Evans, G. W., & Schneider, M. L. (1991). Dynamic role of social support in the link between chronic stress and psychological distress. *Journal of Personality and Social Psychology, 61,* 899–909.

Lepore, S. J., Evans, G. W., & Schneider, M. L. (1992). Role of control and social support in explaining the stress of hassles and crowding. *Environment and Behavior, 24,* 795–811.

Lepper, M. R., Aspinwall, L. G., Mumme, D. L., & Chabay, R. W. (1990). Self-perception and social-perception processes in tutoring: Subtle social control strategies of expert tutors. In J. M. Olson & M. P. Zanna (Eds.), *Self-inference processes: The Ontario Symposium* (Vol. 6, pp. 217–238). Hillsdale, NJ: Erlbaum.

Lepper, M. R., Greene, D., & Nisbett, R. E. (1973). Undermining children's intrinsic interest with external rewards: A test of the overjustification hypothesis. *Journal of Personality and Social Psychology, 28,* 129–137.

Lerner, M. J. (1970). The desire for justice and reactions to victims. In J. Macaulay & L. Berkowitz (Eds.), *Altruism and helping behavior: Social psychological studies of some antecedents and consequences.* New York: Academic Press.

LERNER, M. J., & MILLER, D. T. (1978). Just world research and the attribution process: Looking back and ahead. *Psychological Bulletin, 85,* 1030–1051.

LEVENSON, R. W., EKMAN, P., HEIDER, K., & FRIESEN, W. V. (1992). Emotion and autonomic nervous system activity in the Minangkabau of West Sumatra. *Journal of Personality and Social Psychology, 62,* 972–988.

LEVENSON, R. W., & GOTTMAN, J. M. (1983). Marital interaction: Physiological linkage and affective exchange. *Journal of Personality and Social Psychology, 45,* 587–597.

LEVENSON, R. W., & GOTTMAN, J. M. (1985). Physiological and affective predictors of change in relationship satisfaction. *Journal of Personality and Social Psychology, 49,* 85–94.

LEVENTHAL, H., & NILES, P. (1965). Persistence of influence for varying duration of exposure to threat stimuli. *Psychological Reports, 16,* 223–233.

LEVENTHAL, H., SINGER, R., & JONES, S. (1965). Effects of fear and specificity of recommendation upon attitudes and behavior. *Journal of Personality and Social Psychology, 2,* 20–29.

LEVENTHAL, H., WATTS, J. C., & PAGANO, R. (1967). Effects of fear and instructions on how to cope with danger. *Journal of Personality and Social Psychology, 6,* 313–321.

LEVINE, J. M. (1980). Reaction to opinion deviance in small groups. In P. B. Paulus (Ed.), *Psychology of group influence.* Hillsdale, NJ: Erlbaum.

LEVINE, J. M., & GREEN, S. M. (1984). Acquisition of relative performance information: The roles of intrapersonal and interpersonal comparison. *Personality and Social Psychology Bulletin, 10,* 385–393.

LEVINE, J. M., & RANELLI, C. J. (1978). Majority reactions to shifting and stable attitudinal deviates. *European Journal of Social Psychology, 8,* 55–70.

LEVINE, J. M., & RUBACK, R. B. (1980). Reaction to opinion deviance: Impact of a fence-straddler's rationale on majority evaluation. *Social Psychology Quarterly, 43,* 73–81.

LEVINE, J. M., & RUSSO, E. M. (1987). Majority and minority influence. In C. Hendrick (Ed.), *Review of personality and social psychology: Group process* (Vol. 8, pp. 13–54). Newbury Park, CA: Sage.

LEVINE, J. M., SAXE, L., & HARRIS, H. J. (1976). Reaction to attitudinal deviance: Impact of deviate's directions and distance of movement. *Sociometry, 39,* 97–107.

LEVINE, J. M., SROKA, K. R., & SNYDER, H. N. (1977). Group support and reaction to stable and shifting agreement/disagreement. *Sociometry, 40,* 214–224.

LEVINE, R. A., & CAMPBELL, D. T. (1972). *Ethnocentrism: Theories of conflict, ethnic attitudes, and group behavior.* New York: Wiley.

LEVINE, S. V. (1984). Radical departures. *Psychology Today, 18*(8), pp. 20–27.

LEVINGER, G. (1980). Toward the analysis of close relationships. *Journal of Experimental Social Psychology, 16,* 510–544.

LEVINGER, G., SENN, D. J., & JORGENSEN, B. W. (1970). Progress toward permanence in courtship: A test of the Kerckhoff-Davis hypothesis. *Sociometry, 33,* 427–433.

LEVINGER, G., & SNOEK, D. J. (1972). *Attraction in relationship: A new look at interpersonal attraction.* Morristown, NJ: General Learning Press.

LEVY, M. B., & DAVIS, K. E. (1988). Lovestyles and attachment styles compared: Their relations to each other and to various relationship characteristics. *Journal of Social and Personal Relationships, 5,* 439–471.

LEWICKI, P. (1983). Self-image bias in person perception. *Journal of Personality and Social Psychology, 45,* 384–393.

LEWIN, K. (1936). *A dynamic theory of personality.* New York: McGraw-Hill.

LEWIN, K. (1948). *Resolving social conflicts: Selected papers on group dynamics.* New York: Harper.

LEWIN, K. (1951). *Field theory in social science.* New York: Harper.

LEWIN, K., LIPPITT, R., & WHITE, R. (1939). Patterns of aggressive behavior in experimentally created "social climates." *Journal of Social Psychology, 10,* 271–299.

LEWIS, D. O., MOY, E., JACKSON, L. D., AARONSON, R., RESTIFO, N., SERRA, S., & SIMOS, A. (1985). Biopsychological characteristics of children who later murder: A prospective study. *American Journal of Psychiatry, 142,* 1161–1167.

LEY, D., & CYBRIWSKY, R. (1974a). The spatial ecology of stripped cars. *Environment and Behavior, 6,* 53–68.

LEY, D., & CYBRIWSKY, R. (1974b). Urban graffiti as territorial markers. *Annals of the Association of American Geographers, 64,* 491–505.

LEYENS, J. P., & PARKE, R. D. (1975). Aggressive slides can induce a weapon's effect. *European Journal of Social Psychology, 5,* 229–236.

L'HERROU, T. (1992). *Interacting in electronic space: Group dynamics resulting from individual change.* Paper presented at the Fifteenth Annual Nags Head Conference on Groups, Networks, and Organizations, Highland Beach, FL.

LIBERMAN, A., & CHAIKEN, S. (1992). Defensive processing of personally relevant health messages. *Personality and Social Psychology Bulletin, 18,* 669–679.

LICHTENSTEIN, S., FISCHHOFF, B., & PHILLIPS, L. D. (1982). Calibration of probabilities: The state of the art to 1980. In D. Kahneman, P. Slovic, & A. Tversky (Eds.), *Judgment under uncertainty: Heuristics and biases* (pp. 308–334). New York: Cambridge University Press.

LIEBERT, R. M., & SPRAFKIN, J. (1988). *The early window: Effects of television on children and youth* (3rd ed.). New York: Pergamon.

LIEBERT, R. M., SPRAFKIN, J. N., & DAVIDSON, E. S. (1982). *The early window: Effects of television on children and youth* (2nd ed.). New York: Pergamon.

LIGHTDALE, J. R., & PRENTICE, D. A. (1994). Rethinking sex differences in aggression: Aggressive behavior in the absence of social roles. *Personality and Social Psychology Bulletin, 20,* 34–44.

LINDZEY, G., & ARONSON, E. (Eds.). (1985). *Handbook of social psychology* (3rd ed.). New York: Random House.

LINGLE, J. H., DUKERICH, J. M., & OSTROM, T. M. (1983). Accessing information in memory-based impression judgments: Incongruity versus negativity in retrieval selectivity. *Journal of Personality and Social Psychology, 44,* 262–272.

LINVILLE, P. W. (1982). The complexity-extremity effect and age-based stereotyping. *Journal of Personality and Social Psychology, 42,* 193–211.

LINVILLE, P. W. (1985). Self-complexity and affective extremity: Don't put all of your eggs in one cognitive basket. *Social Cognition, 3,* 94–120.

LINVILLE, P. W. (1987). Self-complexity as a cognitive buffer against stress-related depression and illness. *Journal of Personality and Social Psychology, 52,* 663–676.

LINVILLE, P. W., & JONES, E. E. (1980). Polarized appraisals of out-group members. *Journal of Personality and Social Psychology, 38,* 689–703.

LINVILLE, P. W., SALOVEY, P., & FISCHER, G. W. (1989). Stereotyping and perceived distributions of social characteristics: An application to ingroup-outgroup perception. In J. F. Dovidio & S. L. Gaertner (Eds.), *Prejudice, discrimination, and racism* (pp. 165–208). San Diego, CA: Academic Press.

LINZ, D., DONNERSTEIN, E., & PENROD, S. (1984). The effects of multiple exposures to filmed violence against women. *Journal of Communication, 34,* 130–147.

LINZ, D., DONNERSTEIN, E., & PENROD, S. (1988). Longer-term exposure to violent and sexually degrading depictions of women. *Journal of Personality and Social Psychology, 54,* 758–768.

LINZ, D., WILSON, B. J., & DONNERSTEIN, E. (1992). Sexual violence in the mass media: Legal solutions, warnings, and mitigation through education. *Journal of Social Issues, 48*(1), 145–171.

LIPE, M. G. (1991). Counterfactual reasoning as a framework for attribution theories. *Psychological Bulletin, 109,* 456–471.

LIPPMANN, W. (1922). *Public opinion.* New York: Harcourt & Brace.

LIPSHITZ, R. (1989). "Either a medal or a corporal": The effects of success and failure on the evaluation of decision making and decision makers. *Organizational Behavior and Human Decision Processes, 44,* 380–395.

LISKA, A. E. (Ed.). (1975). *The consistency controversy.* Cambridge, MA: Schenkman.

LISS, M. A., REINHARDT, L. C., & FREDRICKSEN, S. (1983). TV heroes: The impact of rhetoric and deeds. *Journal of Applied Developmental Psychology, 4,* 175–187.

LITTLEPAGE, G. E. (1991). Effects of group size and task characteristics on group performance: A test of Steiner's model. *Personality and Social Psychology Bulletin, 17,* 449–456.

LITTLEPAGE, G. E., & PINEAULT, M. A. (1981). Detection of truthful and deceptive interpersonal communications across information transmission modes. *Journal of Social Psychology, 114,* 57–68.

Littlepage, G. E., & Silbiger, H. (1992). Recognition of expertise in decision-making groups: Effects of group size and participation patterns. *Small Group Research, 23,* 344–355.

Livesley, W. J., & Bromley, D. B. (1973). *Person perception in childhood and adolescence.* New York: Wiley.

Locke, E. A., & Latham, G. P. (1990). Work motivation and satisfaction: Light at the end of the tunnel. *Psychological Science, 1,* 240–246.

Loewen, L. J., & Suedfeld, P. (1992). Cognitive and arousal effects of masking office noise. *Environment and Behavior, 24,* 381–395.

Loewenthal, K. (1986). Factors affecting religious commitment. *Journal of Social Psychology, 126,* 121–123.

Loftus, E. F. (1979). *Eyewitness testimony.* Cambridge, MA: Harvard University Press.

Loftus, E. F. (1983). Silence is not gold. *American Psychologist, 38,* 564–572.

Loftus, E. F. (1993). Psychologists in the eyewitness world. *American Psychologist, 48,* 550–552.

Loftus, E. F., Donders, K., Hoffman, H. G., & Schooler, J. W. (1989). Creating new memories that are quickly accessed and confidently held. *Memory and Cognition, 17,* 607–616.

Loftus, E. F., & Palmer, J. C. (1974). Reconstruction of automobile destruction: An example of the interaction between language and memory. *Journal of Verbal Learning and Verbal Behavior, 13,* 585–589.

London, P. (1970). The rescuers: Motivational hypotheses about Christians who saved Jews from the Nazis. In J. Macaulay & L. Berkowitz (Eds.), *Altruism and helping behavior: Social psychological studies of some antecedents and consequences.* New York: Academic Press.

Longley, J., & Pruitt, D. G. (1980). Groupthink: A critique of Janis's theory. In L. Wheeler (Ed.), *Review of personality and social psychology* (Vol. 1). Newbury Park, CA: Sage.

Loo, C. (1986). Neighborhood satisfaction and safety: A study of a low-income ethnic area. *Environment and Behavior, 18,* 109–131.

Lord, C. G. (1980). Schemas and images as memory aids: Two modes of processing social information. *Journal of Personality and Social Psychology, 38,* 257–269.

Lord, C. G. (1989). The "disappearance" of dissonance in an age of relativism. *Personality and Social Psychology Bulletin, 14,* 513–518.

Lord, C. G., Lepper, M. R., & Mackie, D. (1984). Attitude prototypes as determinants of attitude-behavior consistency. *Journal of Personality and Social Psychology, 46,* 1254–1266.

Lord, C. G., Ross, L., & Lepper, M. R. (1979). Biased assimilation and attitude polarization: The effects of prior theories on subsequently considered evidence. *Journal of Personality and Social Psychology, 37,* 2098–2109.

Lord, C. G., & Saenz, D. S. (1985). Memory deficits and memory surfeits: Differential cognitive consequences of tokenism for tokens and observers. *Journal of Personality and Social Psychology, 49,* 918–926.

Lord, R. G. (1977). Functional leadership behavior: Measurement and relation to social power and leadership perceptions. *Administrative Science Quarterly, 22,* 114–133.

Lord, R. G. (1985). An information processing approach to social perceptions, leadership, and behavioral measurement in organizations. In L. L. Cummings & B. M. Staw (Eds.), *Research in organizational behavior* (Vol. 7, pp. 87–128). Greenwich, CT: JAI Press.

Lord, R. G., De Vader, C. L., & Alliger, G. M. (1986). A meta-analysis of the relation between personality traits and leadership perceptions: An application of validity generalization procedures. *Journal of Applied Psychology, 71,* 402–410.

Lore, R. K., & Schultz, L. A. (1993). Control of human aggression: A comparative perspective. *American Psychologist, 48,* 16–25.

Lorenz, K. (1966). *On aggression.* New York: Harcourt, Brace, & World.

Lorge, I. (1936). Prestige, suggestion, and attitudes. *Journal of Social Psychology, 7,* 386–402.

Losch, M. E., & Cacioppo, J. T. (1990). Cognitive dissonance may enhance sympathetic tonus, but attitudes are changed to reduce negative affect rather than arousal. *Journal of Personality and Social Psychology, 26,* 289–304.

Lott, B., & Lott, A. J. (1985). Learning theories in contemporary social psychology. In G. Lindzey & E. Aronson (Eds.), *Handbook of social psychology* (3rd ed., Vol. 1, pp. 109–135). New York: Random House.

Lovdal, L. T. (1989). Sex role messages in television commercials: An update. *Sex Roles, 21,* 715–724.

Lowery, C. R., Denney, D. R., & Storms, M. D. (1979). Insomnia: A comparison of the effects of pill attributions and nonpejorative self-attributions. *Cognitive Therapy Research, 3,* 161–164.

Luce, T. S. (1974). Blacks, whites, and yellows: They all look alike to me. *Psychology Today, 8*(2), pp. 105–108.

Luginbuhl, J., & Palmer, R. (1991). Impression management aspects of self-handicapping: Positive and negative effects. *Personality and Social Psychology Bulletin, 17,* 655–662.

Luhtanen, R., & Crocker, J. (1992). A collective self-esteem scale: Self-evaluation of one's social identity. *Personality and Social Psychology Bulletin, 18,* 302–318.

Lunt, P. K. (1988). The perceived causal structure of examination failure. *British Journal of Social Psychology, 27,* 171–179.

Lupfer, M. B., Clark, L. F., & Hutcherson, H. W. (1990). Impact of context on spontaneous trait and situational attributions. *Journal of Personality and Social Psychology, 58,* 239–249.

Lytton, H., & Romney, D. M. (1991). Parents' differential socialization of boys and girls: A meta-analysis. *Psychological Bulletin, 109,* 267–296.

Maass, A., & Clark, R. D., III. (1984). Hidden impact of minorities: Fifteen years of minority influence research. *Psychological Bulletin, 95,* 428–450.

Maass, A., West, S. G., & Cialdini, R. B. (1987). Minority influence and conversion. In C. Hendrick (Ed.), *Review of personality and social psychology: Group process* (Vol. 8, pp. 55–79). Newbury Park, CA: Sage.

Maccoby, E. E. (1990). Gender and relationships: A developmental account. *American Psychologist, 45,* 513–520.

Mackie, D. M., & Asuncion, A. G. (1990). On-line and memory-based modification of attitudes: Determinants of message recall–attitude change correspondence. *Journal of Personality and Social Psychology, 59,* 5–16.

Mackie, D. M., Gastardo-Conaco, M. C., & Skelly, J. J. (1992). Knowledge of the advocated position and the processing of in-group and out-group persuasive messages. *Personality and Social Psychology Bulletin, 18,* 145–151.

Mackie, D. M., & Worth, L. (1989). Processing deficits and the mediation of positive affect in persuasion. *Journal of Personality and Social Psychology, 57,* 27–40.

Mackie, D. M., Worth, L. T., & Asuncion, A. G. (1990). Processing of persuasive in-group messages. *Journal of Personality and Social Psychology, 58,* 812–822.

MacLachlan, J. (1979). What people really think of fast talkers. *Psychology Today, 13*(11), pp. 113–117.

MacLean, P. D. (1954). Studies on limbic system ("viosceal brain") and their bearing on psychosomatic problems. In E. D. Wittkower & R. A. Cleghorn (Eds.), *Recent developments in psychosomatic medicine.* Philadelphia: Lippincott.

Macrae, C. N., Milne, A. B., & Bodenhausen, G. V. (1993). Stereotypes as energy-saving devices: A peek inside the cognitive toolbox. *Journal of Personality and Social Psychology, 66,* 37–47.

Madden, T. J., Ellen, P. S., & Ajzen, I. (1992). A comparison of the theory of planned behavior and the theory of reasoned action. *Personality and Social Psychology Bulletin, 18,* 3–9.

Maddux, J. E., Norton, L. W., & Leary, M. R. (1988). Cognitive components of social anxiety: An investigation of the integration of self-presentation theory and self-efficacy theory. *Journal of Social and Clinical Psychology, 6,* 180–190.

Major, B. (1981). Gender patterns in touching behavior. In C. Mayo & N. M. Henley (Eds.), *Gender and nonverbal behavior.* New York: Springer-Verlag.

Maki, J. E., Thorngate, W. B., & McClintock, C. G. (1979). Prediction and perception of social motives. *Journal of Personality and Social Psychology, 37,* 203–220.

Malamuth, N. M. (1986). Predictors of naturalistic sexual aggression. *Journal of Personality and Social Psychology, 50,* 953–962.

Malamuth, N. M., Check, J. V. P., & Briere, J. (1986). Sexual arousal in response to aggression: Ideological, aggressive, and sexual correlates. *Journal of Personality and Social Psychology, 50,* 330–340.

Malkis, F. S., Kalle, R. J., & Tedeschi, J. T. (1982). Attitudinal politics in the forced compliance situation. *Journal of Social Psychology, 117,* 79–91.

Mallick, S. K., & McCandless, B. R. (1966). A study of catharsis of aggression. *Journal of Personality and Social Psychology, 4,* 591–596.

Malloy, T. E., & Albright, L. (1990). Interpersonal perception in a social context. *Journal of Personality and Social Psychology, 58,* 419–428.

Malloy, T. E., & Janowski, C. L. (1992). Perceptions and metaperceptions of leadership: Components, accuracy, and dispositional correlates. *Personality and Social Psychology Bulletin, 18,* 700–708.

Malpass, R. S., & Devine, P. G. (1984). Research on suggestion in lineups and photospreads. In G. L. Wells & E. F. Loftus (Eds.), *Eyewitness testimony: Psychological perspectives.* New York: Cambridge University Press.

Manis, M., Gleason, T. C., & Dawes, R. M. (1966). The evaluation of complex social stimuli. *Journal of Personality and Social Psychology, 3,* 404–419.

Mann, L. (1980). Cross-cultural studies of small groups. In H. Triandis & R. Brislin (Eds.), *Handbook of cross-cultural psychology: Vol. 5. Social psychology* (pp. 155–209). Boston: Allyn & Bacon.

Mann, L. (1981). The baiting crowd in episodes of threatened suicide. *Journal of Personality and Social Psychology, 41,* 703–709.

Manucia, G. K., Baumann, D. J., & Cialdini, R. B. (1984). Mood influences on helping: Direct effects or side effects? *Journal of Personality and Social Psychology, 46,* 357–364.

Marks, G., & Miller, N. (1987). Ten years of research on the false-consensus effect: An empirical and theoretical review. *Psychological Bulletin, 102,* 72–90.

Markus, H. (1977). Self-schemata and processing information about the self. *Journal of Personality and Social Psychology, 35,* 63–78.

Markus, H. (1978). The effect of mere presence on social facilitation: An unobtrusive test. *Journal of Experimental Social Psychology, 14,* 389–397.

Markus, H. (1980). The self in thought and memory. In D. M. Wegner & R. R. Vallacher (Eds.), *The self in social psychology.* New York: Oxford University Press.

Markus, H., Crane, M., Berstein, S., & Siladi, M. (1982). Self-schemas and gender. *Journal of Personality and Social Psychology, 42,* 38–50.

Markus, H., & Kunda, Z. (1986). Stability and malleability of the self-concept. *Journal of Personality and Social Psychology, 51,* 858–866.

Markus, H., & Nurius, P. (1986). Possible selves. *American Psychologist, 41,* 954–969.

Markus, H., Smith, J., & Moreland, R. L. (1985). The role of the self-concept in the social perception of others. *Journal of Personality and Social Psychology, 49,* 1494–1512.

Markus, H., & Zajonc, R. B. (1985). The cognitive perspective in social psychology. In G. Lindzey & E. Aronson (Eds.), *Handbook of social psychology* (3rd ed., Vol. 1). New York: Random House.

Marquis, K. H., Marshall, J., & Oskamp, S. (1972). Testimony validity as a function of question form, atmosphere, and item difficulty. *Journal of Applied Social Psychology, 2,* 167–186.

Marshall, G. D., & Zimbardo, P. G. (1979). Affective consequences of inadequately explained physiological arousal. *Journal of Personality and Social Psychology, 37,* 970–988.

Marshall, W. L. (1989). Pornography and sex offenders. In D. Zillmann & J. Bryant (Eds.), *Pornography: Research advances and policy considerations* (pp. 185–214). Hillsdale, NJ: Erlbaum.

Martin, C. L. (1987). A ratio measure of sex stereotyping. *Journal of Personality and Social Psychology, 42,* 489–499.

Martin, D. N. (1989). *Romancing the brand: The power of advertising and how to use it.* New York: Amacom.

Martin, G. B., & Clark, R. D., III. (1987). Distress crying in neonates: Species and peer specifically. *Developmental Psychology, 18,* 3–9.

Maruyama, G. (1991). Meta-analyses relating goal structures to achievement: Findings, controversies, and impacts. *Personality and Social Psychology Bulletin, 17,* 300–305.

Maruyama, G., Fraser, S. C., & Miller, N. (1982). Personal responsibility and altruism in children. *Journal of Personality and Social Psychology, 42,* 658–664.

Maruyama, G. M. (1982). How should attributions be measured? A reanalysis of data from Elig and Frieze. *American Educational Research Journal, 19,* 552–558.

Marwell, G., & Schmitt, D. R. (1967). Dimensions of compliance-gaining behavior: An empirical analysis. *Sociometry, 30,* 350–364.

Maslach, C. (1979). Negative emotional biasing of unexplained arousal. *Journal of Personality and Social Psychology, 37,* 953–969.

Maslach, C., Santee, R. T., & Wade, C. (1987). Individuation, gender role, and dissent: Personality mediators of situational forces. *Journal of Personality and Social Psychology, 53,* 1088–1093.

Massaro, D. W., & Cowan, N. (1993). Information processing models: Microscopes of the mind. *Annual Review of Psychology, 44,* 383–425.

Masson, C. N., & Verkuyten, M. (1993). Prejudice, ethnic identity, contact, and ethnic group preference among Dutch young adolescents. *Journal of Applied Social Psychology, 23,* 156–168.

Matsumoto, D. (1987). The role of facial response in the experience of emotion: More methodological problems and a meta-analysis. *Journal of Personality and Social Psychology, 52,* 769–774.

Matsumoto, D., & Ekman, P. (1989). Intensity differences: American-Japanese cultural differences in intensity ratings of facial expressions of emotion. *Motivation and Emotion, 13,* 143–157.

Matthews, K. A. (1988). CHD and Type A behavior: Update on and alternative to the Booth-Kewley and Friedman quantitative review. *Psychological Bulletin, 104,* 373–380.

Maynard Smith, J. (1964). Group selection and kin selection. *Nature, 201,* 1145–1147.

Maynard Smith, J. (1976). Evolution and the theory of games. *American Scientist, 64,* 41–45.

Mayo, E. (1945). *The social problems of an industrial civilization.* Cambridge, MA: Harvard University Press.

Mazur, A. (1983). Hormones, aggression, and dominance in humans. In B. Svare (Ed.), *Hormones and aggressive behavior.* New York: Plenum.

McAdams, D. P. (1982). Experiences of intimacy and power: Relationships between social motives and autobiographical memory. *Journal of Personality and Social Psychology, 42,* 292–301.

McAdams, D. P. (1988). Personal needs and personal relationships. In S. Duck (Ed.), *Handbook of personal relationships: Theory, research, and interventions* (pp. 7–22). New York: Wiley.

McAdams, D. P., & Constantian, C. A. (1983). Intimacy and affiliation motives in daily living: An experience sampling analysis. *Journal of Personality and Social Psychology, 45,* 851–861.

McAndrew, F. T. (1993). *Environmental psychology.* Pacific Grove, CA: Brooks/Cole.

McAndrew, F. T., Ryckman, R. M., Horr, W., & Solomon, R. (1978). The effects of invader placement of spatial markers on territorial behavior in a college population. *Journal of Social Psychology, 104,* 149–150.

McArthur, L. Z. (1972). The how and what of why: Some determinants and consequences of causal attribution. *Journal of Personality and Social Psychology, 22,* 171–193.

McArthur, L. Z. (1981). What grabs you? The role of attention in impression formation and causal attribution. In E. T. Higgins, C. P. Herman, & M. P. Zanna (Eds.), *Social cognition: The Ontario Symposium* (Vol. 1, pp. 201–246). Hillsdale, NJ: Erlbaum.

McArthur, L. Z. (1982). Judging a book by its cover: A cognitive analysis of the relationship between physical appearance and stereotyping. In A. Hastorf & A. Isen (Eds.), *Cognitive social psychology* (pp. 149–211). New York: Elsevier North-Holland.

McArthur, L. Z., & Apatow, K. (1983–1984). Impressions of babyfaced adults. *Social Cognition, 2,* 315–342.

McArthur, L. Z., & Berry, D. S. (1987). Cross-cultural agreement in perceptions of babyfaced adults. *Journal of Cross-Cultural Psychology, 18,* 165–192.

McArthur, L. Z., & Friedman, S. (1980). Illusory correlation in impression formation: Variations in the shared distinctiveness effect as a function of the distinctive person's age, race, and sex. *Journal of Personality and Social Psychology, 39,* 615–624.

McArthur, L. Z., & Montepare, J. M. (1989). Contributions of a babyface and a childlike voice to impressions of moving and talking faces. *Journal of Nonverbal Behavior, 13,* 189–203.

McCallum, R. C., Rusbult, C., Hong, C., Walden, T., & Schopler, J. (1979). The effects of resource availability and importance of behavior upon the experience of crowding. *Journal of Personality and Social Psychology, 37,* 1304–1313.

McCarthy, D. P., & Saegart, S. (1979). Residential density, social overload, and social withdrawal. In J. R. Aiello & A. Baum (Eds.), *Residential crowding and design.* New York: Plenum.

McCarthy, E. D., Langner, T. S., Gerstein, J. C., Eisenberg, J. G., & Orzeck, L. (1975). Violence and behavior disorders. *Journal of Communication, 25,* 71–85.

McCaul, K. D., Veltum, L. G., Boyechko, V., & Crawford, J. J. (1990). Understanding attributions of victim blame for rape: Sex, violence, and foreseeability. *Journal of Applied Social Psychology, 20,* 1–26.

McCauley, C. (1989). The nature of social influence in groupthink: Compliance and internalization. *Journal of Personality and Social Psychology, 57,* 250–260.

McClelland, D. C. (1980). Motive dispositions: The merits of operant and respondent measures. In L. Wheeler (Ed.), *Review of personality and social psychology* (Vol. 1). Newbury Park, CA: Sage.

McClelland, D. C. (1985). How motives, skills, and values determine what people do. *American Psychologist, 40,* 812–825.

McClelland, D. C., Koestner, R., & Weinberger, J. (1989). How do self-attributed and implicit motives differ? *Psychological Review, 96,* 690–702.

McClintock, C. G., Stech, F. J., & Keil, L. J. (1983). The influence of communication on bargaining. In P. B. Paulus (Ed.), *Basic group processes* (pp. 205–233). New York: Springer-Verlag.

McCloskey, M., & Egeth, H. E. (1983). Eyewitness identification: What can a psychologist tell a jury? *American Psychologist, 38,* 550–563.

McConahay, J. (1986). Modern racism, ambivalence, and the modern racism scale. In J. Dovidio & S. L. Gaertner (Eds.), *Prejudice, discrimination, and racism: Theory and research.* New York: Academic Press.

McConahay, J., & Hough, J. (1976). Symbolic racism. *Journal of Social Issues, 32,* 23–45.

McCrae, R. E., & Costa, P. T., Jr. (1987). Validation of the five-factor model of personality across instruments and observers. *Journal of Personality and Social Psychology, 52,* 81–90.

McDougall, W. (1908). *Introduction to social psychology.* London: Methuen.

McFarland, C., & Ross, M. (1982). Impact of causal attributions on affective reactions to success and failure. *Journal of Personality and Social Psychology, 43,* 937–946.

McFarland, S. G., Ageyev, V. S., & Abalankina-Paap, M. A. (1993). Authoritarianism in the former Soviet Union. *Journal of Personality and Social Psychology, 63,* 1004–1010.

McFarlin, D. B., & Blascovich, J. (1981). Effects of self-esteem and performance feedback on future affective preferences and cognitive expectations. *Journal of Personality and Social Psychology, 40,* 521–531.

McGovern, L. P. (1976). Dispositional social anxiety and helping behavior under three conditions of threat. *Journal of Personality, 44,* 84–97.

McGraw, K. M., & Bloomfield, J. (1987). Social influence on group moral decisions: The interactive effects of moral reasoning and sex role orientation. *Journal of Personality and Social Psychology, 53,* 1080–1087.

McGuire, A. M. (1994). Helping behaviors in the natural environment: Dimensions and correlates of helping. *Personality and Social Psychology Bulletin, 20,* 45–56.

McGuire, W. J. (1964). Inducing resistance to persuasion. In L. Berkowitz (Ed.), *Advances in experimental social psychology* (Vol. 1). New York: Academic Press.

McGuire, W. J. (1968). Personality and susceptibility to social influence. In E. F. Borgatta & W. W. Lambert (Eds.), *Handbook of personality theory and research.* Chicago: Rand McNally.

McGuire, W. J. (1985). Attitudes and attitude change. In G. Lindzey & E. Aronson (Eds.), *Handbook of social psychology* (3rd ed., Vol. 2, pp. 233–246). New York: Random House.

McGuire, W. J., & McGuire, C. V. (1988). Content and process in the experience of self. In L. Berkowitz (Ed.), *Advances in experimental social psychology* (Vol. 21, pp. 97–144). New York: Academic Press.

McGuire, W. J., & Padawer-Singer, A. (1976). Trait salience in the spontaneous self-concept. *Journal of Personality and Social Psychology, 33,* 743–754.

McGuire, W. J., & Papageorgis, D. (1961). The relative efficacy of various types of prior belief-defense in producing immunity from persuasion. *Journal of Abnormal and Social Psychology, 62,* 327–337.

McNeil, B. W., & Stoltenberg, C. D. (1989). Reconceptualizing social influence in counseling: The elaboration likelihood model. *Journal of Counseling Psychology, 36,* 24–33.

McNeill, D. (1985). So you think gestures are nonverbal? *Psychological Review, 92,* 350–371.

Mead, G. H. (1934). *Mind, self, and society.* Chicago: University of Chicago Press.

Mead, M. (1935). *Sex and temperament in three primitive societies.* New York: Morrow.

Meadow, A., Parnes, S. J., & Reese, H. (1959). Influence of brainstorming instructions and problem sequence on a creative problem solving test. *Journal of Applied Psychology, 43,* 413–416.

Meeus, W. H. J., & Raaijmakers, Q. A. W. (1987). Administrative obedience as a social phenomenon. In W. Doise & S. Moscovici (Eds.), *Current issues in European social psychology* (Vol. 2, pp. 183–230). Cambridge, England: Cambridge University Press.

Mehlman, R. C., & Snyder, C. R. (1985). Excuse theory: A test of the self-protective role of attributions. *Journal of Personality and Social Psychology, 49,* 994–1001.

Mehrabian, A. (1972). *Nonverbal communication.* Chicago: Aldine.

Mehrabian, A. (1976). Questionnaire measures of affiliation tendency and sensitivity to rejection. *Psychological Reports, 38,* 199–209.

Mehrabian, A., & Ksionsky, S. (1974). *A theory of affiliation.* Lexington, MA: D. C. Heath.

Meindl, J. R., & Lerner, M. J. (1984). Exacerbation of extreme responses to an out-group. *Journal of Personality and Social Psychology, 47,* 71–84.

Meltzer, H. (1930). The present status of experimental studies on the relationship of feeling to memory. *Psychological Review, 37,* 124–139.

Merton, R. (1948). The self-fulfilling prophecy. *Antioch Review, 8,* 193–210.

Messé, L. A., Stollak, G. E., Larson, R. W., & Michaels, G. Y. (1979). Interpersonal consequences of person perception in two social contexts. *Journal of Personality and Social Psychology, 37,* 369–379.

Messick, D. M., & Mackie, D. M. (1989). Intergroup relations. *Annual Review of Psychology, 40,* 45–81.

Mettee, D. R., & Aronson, E. (1974). Affective reactions to appraisal from others. In T. L. Huston (Ed.), *Foundations of interpersonal attraction.* New York: Academic Press.

Meumann, E. (1904). Haus-und Schularbeit: Experimente an Kindern der Volkschule. *Die Deutsche Schule, 8,* 278–303, 337–359, 416–431.

Meyer, J. P., & Mulherin, A. (1980). From attribution to helping: An analysis of the mediating of affect by expectancy. *Journal of Personality and Social Psychology, 39,* 201–210.

Meyer, J. P., & Pepper, S. (1977). Need compatibility and marital adjustment in young married couples. *Journal of Personality and Social Psychology, 35,* 331–342.

Meyer, P. (1970). If Hitler asked you to electrocute a stranger, would you? Probably. *Esquire Magazine, 73*(2), pp. 128–132.

Meyers-Levy, J., & Sternthal, B. (1991). Gender differences in the use of message cues and judgments. *Journal of Marketing Research, 28,* 84–96.

Michaels, J. W., Edwards, J. N., & Acock, A. C. (1984). Satisfaction in intimate relationships as a function of inequality, inequity, and outcomes. *Social Psychology Quarterly, 47,* 347–357.

Michener, H. A., & Burt, M. R. (1975). Use of social influence under varying conditions of legitimacy. *Journal of Personality and Social Psychology, 32,* 398–407.

Middlemist, R. D., Knowles, E. S., & Matter, C. F. (1977). Personal space invasions in the lavatory: Suggestive evidence for arousal. *Journal of Personality and Social Psychology, 33,* 541–546.

MIDDLETON, R. (1976). Regional differences in prejudice. *American Sociological Review, 41,* 94–117.

MIDLARSKY, E., & MIDLARSKY, M. (1973). Some determinants of aiding under experimentally induced stress. *Journal of Personality, 41,* 305–327.

MIDLARSKY, M., & MIDLARSKY, E. (1976). Status inconsistency, aggressive attitude, and helping behavior. *Journal of Personality, 44,* 371–391.

MILGRAM, S. (1963). Behavioral study of obedience. *Journal of Abnormal and Social Psychology, 67,* 371–378.

MILGRAM, S. (1965). Some conditions of obedience and disobedience to authority. *Human Relations, 18,* 57–76.

MILGRAM, S. (1970). The experience of living in cities: A psychological analysis. *Science, 167,* 1461–1468.

MILGRAM, S. (1974). *Obedience to authority.* New York: Harper & Row.

MILGRAM, S. (1992). *The individual in a social world: Essays and experiments* (2nd ed.). New York: McGraw-Hill.

MILGRAM, S., BICKMAN, L., & BERKOWITZ, L. (1969). Note on the drawing power of crowds of different size. *Journal of Personality and Social Psychology, 13,* 79–82.

MILGRAM, S., & SHOTLAND, R. L. (1973). *Television and antisocial behavior: Field experiments.* New York: Academic Press.

MILLAR, M. G., & MILLAR, K. U. (1990). Attitude change as a function of attitude type and argument type. *Journal of Personality and Social Psychology, 59,* 217–228.

MILLAR, M. G., & TESSER, A. (1986a). Effects of affective and cognitive focus on the attitude-behavior relation. *Journal of Personality and Social Psychology, 51,* 270–276.

MILLAR, M. G., & TESSER, A. (1986b). Thought-induced attitude change: The effects of schema structure and commitment. *Journal of Personality and Social Psychology, 51,* 259–269.

MILLAR, M. G., & TESSER, A. (1989). The effects of affective-cognitive consistency and thought on the attitude-behavior relation. *Journal of Experimental Social Psychology, 25,* 189–202.

MILLER, A. G. (1986). *The obedience experiments.* New York: Praeger.

MILLER, A. G., ASHTON, W. A., & MISHAL, M. (1990). Beliefs concerning the features of constrained behavior: A basis for the fundamental attribution error. *Journal of Personality and Social Psychology, 59,* 635–650.

MILLER, A. G., & LAWSON, T. (1989). The effect of an informational option on the fundamental attribution error. *Personality and Social Psychology Bulletin, 15,* 194–204

MILLER, A. G., MAYERSON, N., POGUE, M., & WHITEHOUSE, D. (1977). Perceivers' explanations of their attribution of attitude. *Personality and Social Psychology Bulletin, 3,* 111–114.

MILLER, A. G., MCHOSKEY, J. W., BANE, C. M., & DOWD, T. G. (1993). The attitude polarization phenomenon: Role of response measure, attitude extremity, and behavioral consequences of reported attitude change. *Journal of Personality and Social Psychology, 64,* 561–574.

MILLER, D. T. (1976). Ego involvement and attributions for success and failure. *Journal of Personality and Social Psychology, 34,* 901–906.

MILLER, D. T., & ROSS, M. (1975). Self-serving biases in the attribution of causality: Fact or fiction? *Psychological Bulletin, 82,* 213–255.

MILLER, D. T., & TURNBULL, W. (1986). Expectancies and interpersonal processes. *Annual Review of Psychology, 37,* 233–256.

MILLER, F. D., SMITH, E. R., & ULEMAN, J. (1981). Measurement and interpretation of situational and dispositional attributions. *Journal of Experimental Social Psychology, 17,* 80–95.

MILLER, L. C. (1990). Intimacy and liking: Mutual influence and the role of unique relationships. *Journal of Personality and Social Psychology, 59,* 50–60.

MILLER, L. C., BETTENCOURT, B. A., DEBRO, S. C., & HOFFMAN, V. (1993). Negotiating safer sex: Interpersonal dynamics. In J. B. Pryor & G. D. Reeder (Eds.), *The social psychology of HIV infection* (pp. 85–123). Hillsdale, NJ: Erlbaum.

MILLER, L. E., & GRUSH, J. E. (1986). Individual differences in attitudinal versus normative determination of behavior. *Journal of Experimental Social Psychology, 22,* 190–202.

MILLER, N., & BREWER, M. (Eds.). (1984). *Groups in contact: The psychology of desegregation.* New York: Academic Press.

MILLER, N., & BREWER, M. B. (1986a). Categorization effects on ingroup and outgroup perception. In J. Dovidio & S. Gaertner (Eds.), *Prejudice, discrimination, and racism: Theory and research* (pp. 209–230). New York: Academic Press.

MILLER, N., & BREWER, M. B. (1986b). Social categorization theory and team learning procedures. In R. S. Feldman (Ed.), *The social psychology of education* (pp. 172–198). New York: Cambridge University Press.

MILLER, N., & CAMPBELL, D. T. (1959). Recency and primacy in persuasion as a function of the timing of speeches and measurement. *Journal of Abnormal and Social Psychology, 59,* 1–9.

MILLER, N., & CARLSON, M. (1990). Valid theory-testing meta-analyses further question the negative state relief model of helping. *Psychological Bulletin, 107,* 215–225.

MILLER, N., & DAVIDSON-PODGORNY, G. (1987). Theoretical models of intergroup relations and the use of cooperative teams as an intervention for desegregated settings. In C. Hendrick (Ed.), *Review of personality and social psychology: Group Process* (Vol. 9, pp. 41–67). Newbury Park, CA: Sage.

MILLER, N., GROSS, S., & HOLTZ, R. (1991). Social projection and attitude certainty. In J. Suls & T. A. Wills (Eds.), *Social comparison: Contemporary theory and research* (pp. 177–210). Hillsdale, NJ: Erlbaum.

MILLER, N., MARUYAMA, G., BEABER, R. J., & VALONE, K. (1976). Speed of speech and persuasion. *Journal of Personality and Social Psychology, 34,* 615–625.

MILLER, N., ROGERS, M., & HENNIGAN, K. (1983). Increasing interracial acceptance: Using cooperative games in desegregated elementary schools. In L. Bickman (Ed.), *Applied social psychology annual* (Vol. 4). Newbury Park, CA: Sage.

MILLER, N. E. (1941). The frustration-aggression hypothesis. *Psychological Review, 48,* 337–342.

MILLER, N. E., & DOLLARD, J. R. (1941). *Social learning and imitation.* New Haven, CT: Yale University Press.

MILLER, R. S. (1991). On decorum in close relationships: Why aren't we polite to those we love? *Contemporary Social Psychology, 15,* 63–65.

MILLER, R. S. (1992). The nature and severity of self-reported embarrassing circumstances. *Personality and Social Psychology Bulletin, 18,* 190–198.

MILLER, R. S., & LEARY, M. R. (1992). Social sources and interactive functions of emotion: The case of embarrassment. In M. S. Clark (Ed.), *Review of personality and social psychology* (Vol. 14, pp. 202–221). Newbury Park, CA: Sage.

MILLER, R. S., & SCHLENKER, B. R. (1985). Egotism in group members: Public and private attributions of responsibility for group performance. *Social Psychology Quarterly, 48,* 85–89.

MILLER, T. Q., TURNER, C. W., TINDALE, R. S., POSAVAC, E. J., & DUGONI, B. L. (1991). Reasons for the trend toward null findings in research on Type A behavior. *Psychological Bulletin, 110,* 469–485.

MILNER, D. (1983). *Children and race: Ten years on.* London: Ward Lock Educational.

MINARD, R. D. (1952). Race relationships in the Pocahontas coal field. *Journal of Social Issues, 8,* 29–44.

MINTZ, A. (1946). A re-examination of correlations between lynchings and economic indices. *Journal of Abnormal and Social Psychology, 41,* 154–160.

MISCHEL, W. (1984). Convergences and challenges in the search for consistency. *American Psychology, 39,* 351–364.

MITA, T. H., DERMER, M., & KNIGHT, J. (1977). Reversed facial images and the mere-exposure hypothesis. *Journal of Personality and Social Psychology, 35,* 597–601.

MITCHELL, T. E. (1985). Actor-observer differences in attributions to morality. *Journal of Social Psychology, 125,* 475–477.

MITCHELL, T. R. (1982). Motivation: New directions for theory, research, and practice. *Academy of Management Review, 5*(1), 80–89.

MIXON, D. (1977). Why pretend to deceive? *Personality and Social Psychology Bulletin, 3,* 647–653.

MIXON, D. (1979). Understanding shocking and puzzling conduct. In G. P. Ginsberg (Ed.), *Emerging strategies in social psychological research.* New York: Wiley.

MOGHADDAM, F. M., TAYLOR, D. M., & WRIGHT, S. C. (1993). *Social psychology in cross-cultural perspective.* New York: W. H. Freeman.

Molm, L. D. (1986). Gender, power, and legitimation: A test of three theories. *American Journal of Sociology, 91,* 1156–1186.

Montagu, A. (Ed.). (1978). *Learning non-aggression: The experience of non-literate societies.* New York: Oxford University Press.

Montepare, J. M., Goldstein, S. B., & Clausen, A. (1987). The identification of emotions from gait information. *Journal of Nonverbal Behavior, 11,* 33–42.

Montepare, J. M., & Zebrowitz-McArthur, L. (1988). Impressions of people created by age-related qualities in their gaits. *Journal of Personality and Social Psychology, 55,* 547–556.

Mook, D. G. (1983). In defense of external validity. *American Psychologist, 38,* 379–387.

Moore, B., Underwood, B., & Rosenhan, D. L. (1973). Affect and altruism. *Developmental Psychology, 8,* 99–104.

Moore, T. E. (1982). Subliminal advertising: What you see is what you get. *Journal of Marketing, 46,* 38–47.

Moorhead, G. (1982). Groupthink: Hypothesis in need of testing. *Group and Organization Studies, 7,* 429–444.

Moorhead, G., & Montanari, J. R. (1986). An empirical investigation of the groupthink phenomenon. *Human Relations, 39,* 399–410.

Morasch, B., Groner, N., & Keating, J. (1979). Type of activity and failure as mediators of perceived crowding. *Personality and Social Psychology Bulletin, 5,* 223–226.

Moreland, R. L., & Brinthaupt, T. (1990). Understanding a group. In R. Brown (Ed.), *The Marshall Cavendish encyclopedia of personal relationships: Human behavior, How groups work* (Vol. 15, pp. 1808–1819). North Bellmore, NY: Marshall Cavendish Corporation.

Moreland, R. L., & Levine, J. M. (1982). Socialization in small groups: Temporal changes in individual-group relations. In L. Berkowitz (Ed.), *Advances in experimental social psychology* (Vol. 15, pp. 137–192). New York: Academic Press.

Moreland, R. S., & Sweeney, P. D. (1984). Self-expectancies and reactions to evaluations of personal performance. *Journal of Personality, 52,* 156–176.

Moreno, J. L. (1953). *Who shall survive?* (rev. ed.). Beacon, NY: Beacon House.

Moriarty, T. (1975). Crime, commitment, and the unresponsive bystander: Two field experiments. *Journal of Personality and Social Psychology, 31,* 370–376.

Morris, W. N., & Miller, R. S. (1975). The effects of consensus-breaking and consensus-preempting partners on reduction of conformity. *Journal of Experimental Social Psychology, 11,* 215–223.

Morris, W. N., Worchel, S., Bois, J. L., Pearson, J. A., Rountree, C. A., Samaha, G. M., Wachtler, J., & Wright, S. L. (1976). Collective coping with stress: Group reactions to fear, anxiety, and ambiguity. *Journal of Personality and Social Psychology, 33,* 674–679.

Morse, S., & Gergen, K. J. (1970). Social comparison, self-consistency, and the concept of self. *Journal of Personality and Social Psychology, 16,* 148–156.

Morton, J., & Johnson, M. H. (1991). CONSPEC and CONLERN: A two-process theory of infant face recognition. *Psychological Review, 98,* 164–181.

Moscovici, S. (1976). *Social influence and change.* London: Academic Press.

Moscovici, S. (1980). Toward a theory of conversion behavior. In L. Berkowitz (Ed.), *Advances in experimental social psychology* (Vol. 13). New York: Academic Press.

Moscovici, S. (1985). Social influence and conformity. In G. Lindzey & E. Aronson (Eds.), *Handbook of social psychology* (3rd ed., Vol. 2). New York: Random House.

Moscovici, S., & Faucheaux, C. (1972). Social influence, conformity biases, and the study of active minorities. In L. Berkowitz (Ed.), *Advances in experimental social psychology* (Vol. 6). New York: Academic Press.

Moscovici, S., & Lage, E. (1976). Studies in social influence: III. Majority versus minority influence in a group. *European Journal of Social Psychology, 6,* 149–174.

Moscovici, S., & Nemeth, C. (1974). Minority influence. In C. Nemeth (Ed.), *Social psychology: Classic and contemporary integrations.* Chicago: Rand McNally.

Moscovici, S., & Personnaz, B. (1980). Studies in social influence: V. Minority influence and conversion behavior in a perceptual task. *Journal of Experimental Social Psychology, 16,* 270–282.

Moscovici, S., & Zavalloni, M. (1969). The group as a polarizer of attitudes. *Journal of Personality and Social Psychology, 12,* 125–135.

Moser, G., & Levy-Leboyer, C. (1985). Inadequate environment and situation control: Is a malfunctioning phone always an occasion for aggression? *Environment and Behavior, 17,* 520–533.

Mosher, D. L., & Sirkin, M. (1984). Measuring a macho personality constellation. *Journal of Research in Personality, 18,* 150–163.

Moskowitz, G. B., & Roman, R. J. (1992). Spontaneous trait inferences as self-generated primes: Implications for conscious social judgment. *Journal of Personality and Social Psychology, 62,* 728–738.

Mowday, R. T., & Sutton, R. I. (1993). Organizational behavior: Linking individuals and groups in organizational contexts. *Annual Review of Psychology, 44,* 195–229.

Moyer, K. E. (1976). *The psychobiology of aggression.* New York: Harper & Row.

Mueller, C. W. (1983). Environmental stressors and aggressive behavior. In R. G. Geen & E. I. Donnerstein (Eds.), *Aggression: Theoretical and empirical reviews* (Vol. 1, pp. 51–76). New York: Academic Press.

Mueser, K. T., Grau, B. W., Sussman, S., & Rosen, A. J. (1984). You're only as pretty as you feel: Facial expression as a determinant of physical attractiveness. *Journal of Personality and Social Psychology, 46,* 469–478.

Mullen, B. (1983). Operationalizing the effect of the group on the individual: A self-attention perspective. *Journal of Experimental Social Psychology, 19,* 295–322.

Mullen, B. (1986a). Atrocity as a function of lynch mob composition: A self-attention perspective. *Personality and Social Psychology Bulletin, 12,* 187–197.

Mullen, B. (1986b). Stuttering, audience size, and the other-total ratio: A self-attention perspective. *Journal of Applied Social Psychology, 16,* 139–149.

Mullen, B. (1987a). Introduction: The study of group behavior. In B. Mullen & G. R. Goethals, (Eds.), *Theories of group behavior* (pp. 1–19). New York: Springer-Verlag.

Mullen, B. (1987b). Self-attention theory: The effects of group composition on the individual. In B. Mullen & G. R. Goethals (Eds.), *Theories of group behavior* (pp. 125–146). New York: Springer-Verlag.

Mullen, B. (1990). Why groups matter. In R. Brown (Ed.), *The Marshall Cavendish encyclopedia of personal relationships: Human behavior, How groups work* (Vol. 15, pp. 1800–1807). North Bellmore, NY: Marshall Cavendish Corporation.

Mullen, B., Atkins, J. L., Champion, D. S., Edwards, C., Hardy, D., Story, J. E., & Vanderlok, M. (1985). The false consensus effect: A meta-analysis of 115 hypothesis tests. *Journal of Experimental Social Psychology, 21,* 262–283.

Mullen, B., & Baumeister, R. F. (1987). Group effects on self-attention and performance: social loafing, social facilitation, and social impairment. In C. Hendrick (Ed.), *Review of personality and social psychology: Group process and intergroup relations* (Vol. 9, pp. 189–206). Newbury Park, CA: Sage.

Mullen, B., & Copper, C. (1989). The privileged position of person categories: A comment on Sedikides and Ostrom. *Social Cognition, 7,* 373–388.

Mullen, B., Copper, C., & Driskell, J. E. (1990). Jaywalking as a function of model behavior. *Personality and Social Psychology Bulletin, 16,* 320–330.

Mullen, B., & Johnson, C. (1990). Distinctiveness-based illusory correlations and stereotyping: A meta-analytic integration. *British Journal of Social Psychology, 28,* 123–133.

Mullen, B., Johnson, C., & Salas, E. (1991). Productivity loss in brainstorming groups. *Basic and Applied Social Psychology, 12,* 3–24.

Mullen, B., Salas, E., & Miller, N. (1991). Using meta-analysis to test theoretical hypotheses in social psychology. *Personality and Social Psychology Bulletin, 17,* 258–264.

Multon, K. D., Brown, S. D., & Lent, R. W. (1991). Relation of self-efficacy to academic outcomes: A meta-analytic investigation. *Journal of Counseling Psychology, 38,* 30–38.

Mulvihill, D. J., & Tumin, M. M. (1969). *Crimes of violence.* A publication of the National Commission on the Causes and Prevention of Violence. Washington, DC: Government Printing Office.

Mumpower, J. L., & Cook, S. W. (1978). The development of interpersonal attraction in cooperating interracial groups: The effects of success-failure, race and competence of groupmates, and helping a less competent groupmate. *International Journal of Group Tensions, 8,* 18–50.

Munsterberg, H. (1908). *On the witness stand.* New York: Doubleday, Page.

Murdock, N. L., & Altmaier, E. M. (1991). Attribution-based treatments. In C. R. Snyder & D. R. Forsyth (Eds.), *Handbook of social and clinical psychology: The health perspective* (pp. 563–578). New York: Pergamon.

Murnen, S. K., & Byrne, D. (1991). Hyperfemininity: Measurement and initial validation of the construct. *Journal of Sex Research, 28,* 479–489.

Murphy, J., John, M., & Brown, H. (Eds.). (1984). *Dialogues and debates in social psychology.* London: Erlbaum.

Murphy-Berman, V., & Berman, J. (1978). Importance of choice and sex invasions of personal space. *Personality and Social Psychology Bulletin, 4,* 424–428.

Murray, H. A. (1938). *Explorations in personality.* New York: Oxford University Press.

Murstein, B. I. (1988). A taxonomy of love. In R. J. Sternberg & M. L. Barnes (Eds.), *The psychology of love* (pp. 13–37). New Haven, CT: Yale University Press.

Myers, D. G. (1978). The polarizing effects of social comparison. *Journal of Experimental Social Psychology, 14,* 554–563.

Myers, D. G. (1982). Polarizing effects of social interaction. In H. Brandstatter, J. H. Davis, & G. Stocker-Kreichgauer (Eds.), *Group decision making.* New York: Academic Press.

Myers, D. G., & Bishop, G. D. (1970). Discussion effects on racial attitudes. *Science, 169,* 778–789.

Myers, D. G., & Lamm, H. (1975). The polarizing effect of group discussion. *American Scientist, 63,* 297–303.

Myers, D. G., & Lamm, H. (1976). The group polarization phenomenon. *Psychological Bulletin, 83,* 602–627.

Mynatt, C. R., & Allgeier, E. R. (1990). Risk factors, self-attributions, and adjustment problems among victims of sexual coercion. *Journal of Applied Social Psychology, 20,* 130–153.

Nacoste, R. (1987). Social psychology and affirmative action: The importance of process in policy analysis. *Journal of Social Issues, 43*(1), 41–78.

Nacoste, R. (1989). Affirmative action and self-evaluation. In F. Blanchard & F. Crosby (Eds.), *Affirmative action in perspective* (pp. 103–109). New York: Springer-Verlag.

Nadler, A. (1991). Help-seeking behavior: Psychological costs and instrumental benefits. In M. S. Clark (Ed.), *Review of personality and social psychology* (Vol. 12, pp. 290–311). Newbury Park, CA: Sage.

Nadler, A., & Fisher, J. D. (1986). The role of threat to self-esteem and perceived control in recipient reactions to aid: Theory development and empirical validation. In L. Berkowitz (Ed.), *Advances in experimental social psychology* (Vol. 19, pp. 81–123). New York: Academic Press.

Nahemow, L., & Lawton, M. P. (1975). Similarity and propinquity in friendship formation. *Journal of Personality and Social Psychology, 32,* 205–213.

Nail, P. R. (1986). Toward an integration of some models and theories of social response. *Psychological Bulletin, 100,* 190–206.

Nail, P. R., & Thompson, P. L. (1990). An analysis and empirical demonstration of the concept of self-anticonformity. *Journal of Social Behavior and Personality, 5,* 151–162.

Nail, P. R., & Van Leeuwen, M. D. (1993). An analysis and restructuring of the diamond model of social response. *Personality and Social Psychology Bulletin, 19,* 106–116.

Napolitan, D. A., & Goethals, G. R. (1979). The attribution of friendliness. *Journal of Experimental Social Psychology, 15,* 105–113.

Nasar, J. L., & Kang, J. (1989). A post-jury evaluation: The Ohio State University design competition for a center for the visual arts. *Environment and Behavior, 21,* 464–484.

National Transportation Safety Board. (1979, June). *Aircraft accident report* (NTSB Report No. AAR-79-7). Washington, DC: Government Printing Office.

Neisser, U. (1967). *Cognitive psychology.* Englewood Cliffs, NJ: Prentice-Hall.

Nelson, M. L. (1993). A current perspective on gender differences: Implications for research in counseling. *Journal of Counseling Psychology, 40,* 200–209.

Nemeth, C. J. (1986). Differential contributions of majority and minority influence. *Psychological Review, 93,* 23–32.

Nemeth, C. J., & Kwan, J. L. (1985). Originality of word associations as a function of majority vs. minority influence. *Social Psychology Quarterly, 48,* 277–282.

Nemeth, C. J., & Kwan, J. L. (1987). Minority influence, divergent thinking, and detection of correct solutions. *Journal of Applied Social Psychology, 17,* 788–799.

Nemeth, C., Mayseless, O., Sherman, J., & Brown, Y. (1990). Exposure to dissent and recall of information. *Journal of Personality and Social Psychology, 58,* 429–437.

Nemeth, C., Mosier, K., & Chiles, C. (1992). When convergent thought improves performance: Majority versus minority influence. *Personality and Social Psychology Bulletin, 18,* 139–144.

Nemeth, C. J., & Wachtler, J. (1974). Creating the perceptions of consistency and confidence: A necessary condition for minority influence. *Sociometry, 37,* 529–540.

Nemeth, C. J., & Wachtler, J. (1983). Creative problem solving as a result of majority vs. minority influence. *European Journal of Social Psychology, 13,* 45–55.

Neuberg, S. L. (1988). Behavioral implications of information presented outside of conscious awareness: The effect of subliminal presentation of trait information on behavior in the Prisoner's Dilemma Game. *Social Cognition, 6,* 207–230.

Neuliep, J. W., & Crandall, R. (1993). Everyone was wrong: There are lots of replications out there. *Journal of Social Behavior and Personality, 8,* 1–8.

Newcomb, A. F., & Bukowski, W. M. (1983). Social impact and social preference as determinants of children's peer group status. *Developmental Psychology, 19,* 856–867.

Newcomb, A. F., Bukowski, W. M., & Pattee, L. (1993). Children's peer relations: A meta-analytic review of popular, rejected, neglected, controversial, and average sociometric status. *Psychological Bulletin, 113,* 99–128.

Newcomb, T. M. (1943). *Personality and social change.* New York: Dryden.

Newcomb, T. M. (1960). Varieties of interpersonal attraction. In D. Cartwright & A. Zander (Eds.), *Group dynamics: Research and theory* (2nd ed.). Evanston, IL: Row, Peterson.

Newcomb, T. M. (1961). *The acquaintance process.* New York: Holt, Rinehart & Winston.

Newcomb, T. M. (1979). Reciprocity of interpersonal attraction: A nonconfirmation of a plausible hypothesis. *Social Psychology Quarterly, 42,* 299–306.

Newcomb, T. M. (1981). Heiderean balance as a group phenomenon. *Journal of Personality and Social Psychology, 40,* 862–867.

Newcomb, T. M., Koenig, K. E., Flacks, R., & Warwick, D. P. (1967). *Persistence and change: Bennington College and its students after twenty-five years.* New York: Wiley.

Newman, L. S., Higgins, E. T., & Vookles, J. (1992). Self-guide strength and emotional vulnerability: Birth order as a moderator of self-affect relations. *Personality and Social Psychology Bulletin, 18,* 402–411.

Newman, L. S., & Uleman, J. S. (1989). Spontaneous trait inference. In J. S. Uleman & J. A. Bargh (Eds.), *Unintended thought* (pp. 155–188). New York: Guilford Press.

Newman, O. (1972). *Defensible space.* New York: Macmillan.

Newman, O. (1980). *Community of interest.* New York: Doubleday.

Newton, L. (1990). *Overconfidence in the communication of intent: Heard and unheard melodies.* Unpublished doctoral dissertation, Stanford University, Stanford, CA.

Niedenthal, P. M., Setterlund, M. B., & Wherry, M. B. (1992). Possible self-complexity and affective reactions to goal-relevant evaluation. *Journal of Personality and Social Psychology, 63,* 5–16.

Nielsen, J. M. (1990). *Sex and gender in society: Perspectives on stratification* (2nd ed.). Prospect Heights, IL: Waveland Press.

Nisbett, R. E. (1993). Violence and U.S. regional culture. *American Psychologist, 48,* 441–449.

Nisbett, R. E., & Bellows, N. (1977). Verbal reports about causal inferences on social judgments: Private access versus public theories. *Journal of Personality and Social Psychology, 35,* 613–624.

Nisbett, R. E., & Borgida, E. (1975). Attribution and the psychology of prediction. *Journal of Personality and Social Psychology, 32,* 932–943.

Nisbett, R. E., Borgida, E., Crandall, R., & Reed, H. (1976). Popular induction: Information is not necessarily informative. In J. S. Carroll & J. W. Payne (Eds.), *Cognition and social behavior.* Hillsdale, NJ: Erlbaum.

Nisbett, R. E., Caputo, C., Legant, P., & Marecek, J. (1973). Behavior as seen by the actor and as seen by the observer. *Journal of Personality and Social Psychology, 27,* 154–165.

Nisbett, R. E., & Ross, L. (1980). *Human inference: Strategies and shortcomings in social judgment.* Englewood Cliffs, NJ: Prentice-Hall.

Nisbett, R. E., & Wilson, T. D. (1977). Telling more than we can know: Verbal reports on mental processes. *Psychological Review, 84,* 231–259.

Nisbett, R. E., Zukier, H., & Lemley, R. (1981). The dilution effect: Nondiagnostic information weakens the effect of diagnostic information. *Cognitive Psychology, 13,* 248–277.

Noel, J., Forsyth, D. R., & Kelley, K. (1987). Improving the performance of failing students by overcoming their self-serving attributional biases. *Basic and Applied Social Psychology, 8,* 151–162.

Noller, P. (1985). Video primacy: A further look. *Journal of Nonverbal Behavior, 9,* 28–47.

Nord, W. R. (1969). Social exchange theory: An integrative approach to social conformity. *Psychological Bulletin, 71,* 174–208.

Nordholm, L. A. (1975). Effects of group size and stimulus ambiguity on conformity. *Journal of Social Psychology, 97,* 123–130.

Normoyle, J., & Lavrakas, P. J. (1984). Fear of crime in elderly women: Perceptions of control, predictability, and territoriality. *Personality and Social Psychology Bulletin, 10,* 191–202.

Norvell, N., & Forsyth, D. R. (1984). The impact of inhibiting and facilitating causal factors on group members' reactions after success and failure. *Social Psychology Quarterly, 47,* 293–297.

Nowak, A., Szamrej, J., & Latané, B. (1990). From private attitude to public opinion: A dynamic theory of social impact. *Psychological Review, 97,* 362–376.

Nyquist, L. V., & Spence, J. T. (1986). Effects of dispositional dominance and sex role expectations on leadership behaviors. *Journal of Personality and Social Psychology, 50,* 87–93.

Nystedt, L., Smari, J., & Boman, M. (1991). Self-schemata: Ambiguous operationalizations of an important concept. *European Journal of Personality, 5,* 1–14.

Oakes, P. J., & Turner, J. C. (1980). Social categorization and intergroup behavior: Does minimal intergroup discrimination make social identity more positive? *European Journal of Social Psychology, 10,* 295–302.

Offermann, L. R., & Schrier, P. E. (1985). Social influence strategies: The impact of sex, role, and attitudes toward power. *Personality and Social Psychology Bulletin, 11,* 286–300.

Ofshe, R., & Singer, M. T. (1986). Attacks on peripheral versus central elements of self and the impact of thought reforming techniques. *Cultic Studies Journal, 3,* 3–24.

Ogilvy, D. (1983). *Ogilvy on advertising.* New York: Random House.

Ohbuchi, K. (1982). On the cognitive integration mediating reactions to attack patterns. *Social Psychology Quarterly, 45,* 213–218.

Ohbuchi, K., & Kambara, T. (1985). Attacker's intent and awareness of outcome, impression management, and retaliation. *Journal of Experimental Social Psychology, 21,* 321–330.

Ohbuchi, K. I., Kameda, M., & Agarie, N. (1989). Apology as aggression control: Its role in mediating appraisal of and response to harm. *Journal of Personality and Social Psychology, 56,* 219–227.

Oliner, S. P., & Oliner, P. M. (1988). *The altruistic personality: Rescuers of Jews in Nazi Europe.* New York: Free Press.

Oliver, M. B., & Hyde, J. S. (1993). Gender differences in sexuality: A meta-analysis. *Psychological Bulletin, 114,* 29–51.

Olson, J. M. (1990). Self-inference processes in emotion. In J. M. Olson & M. P. Zanna (Eds.), *Self-inference process: The Ontario Symposium* (Vol. 6, pp. 17–41). Hillsdale, NJ: Erlbaum.

Olson, J. M. (1992). Self-perception of humor: Evidence for discounting and augmentation effects. *Journal of Personality and Social Psychology, 62,* 369–377.

Olson, J. M., & Cal, A. V. (1984). Source credibility, attitudes, and the recall of past behaviors. *European Journal of Social Psychology, 14,* 203–210.

Olson, J. M., & Zanna, M. P. (1993). Attitudes and attitude change. *Annual Review of Psychology, 44,* 117–154.

O'Reilly, C. A. (1991). Organizational behavior: Where we've been, where we're going. *Annual Review of Psychology, 42,* 427–458.

O'Riordan, T. (1976). Attitudes, behavior, and environmental policy issues. In I. Altman & J. F. Wohlwill (Eds.), *Human behavior and environment: Advances in theory and research* (Vol. 1, pp. 1–36). New York: Plenum.

Orne, M. T. (1962). On the social psychology of the psychological experiment: With particular reference to demand characteristics and their implications. *American Psychologist, 17,* 776–783.

Orvis, B. R., Cunningham, J. D., & Kelley, H. H. (1975). A closer examination of causal inference: The roles of consensus, distinctiveness, and consistency information. *Journal of Personality and Social Psychology, 32,* 605–616.

Osborn, A. F. (1957). *Applied imagination.* New York: Scribner's.

Oskamp, S. (1965). Overconfidence in case-study judgments. *Journal of Consulting Psychology, 29,* 261–265.

Oskamp, S. (1984). *Applied social psychology.* Englewood Cliffs, NJ: Prentice-Hall.

Oskamp, S. (1991). *Attitudes and opinions* (2nd ed.). Englewood Cliffs, NJ: Prentice-Hall.

Oskamp, S., Harrington, M. J., Edwards, T. C., Sherwood, D. L., Okuda, S. M., & Swanson, D. C. (1991). Factors influencing household recycling behavior. *Environment and Behavior, 23,* 494–519.

Ostow, M. (1991). A psychoanalytic approach to the problems of prejudice, discrimination, and persecution. In H. J. Knopke, R. J. Norell, & R. W. Rogers (Eds.), *Opening doors: Perspectives on race relations in contemporary America* (pp. 79–99). Tuscaloosa: University of Alabama Press.

O'Sullivan, M., Ekman, P., Friesen, W. V., & Scherer, K. (1985). What you say and how you say it: The contribution of speech content and voice quality to judgments of others. *Journal of Personality and Social Psychology, 48,* 54–62.

Overmier, J. B., & Seligman, M. E. P. (1967). Effects of inescapable shock upon subsequent escape and avoidance learning. *Journal of Comparative and Physiological Psychology, 63,* 23–33.

Oxford English Dictionary. (1970). New York: Oxford University Press.

Oyserman, D., & Markus, H. (1990). Possible selves in balance: Implications for delinquency. *Journal of Social Issues, 46*(2), 141–157.

Page, M. M., & Scheidt, R. (1971). The elusive weapons' effect: Demand awareness, evaluation apprehension, and the slightly sophisticated subject. *Journal of Personality and Social Psychology, 20,* 304–318.

Pagel, M. D., & Davidson, A. R. (1984). A comparison of three social-psychologial models of attitude and behavioral plan: Prediction of contraceptive behavior. *Journal of Personality and Social Psychology, 47,* 517–533.

Pakier, A., & Wills, T. A. (1990). *Life stress and social support predict illicit drug use among methadone clients.* Paper presented at the meeting of the American Psychological Association, Boston, MA.

Pallak, M. S., Cook, D. A., & Sullivan, J. J. (1980). Commitment and energy conservation. In L. Bickman (Ed.), *Applied social psychology annual* (Vol. 1). Newbury Park, CA: Sage.

Pallak, S. R. (1983). Salience of communicator's physical attractiveness and persuasion: A heuristic versus systematic processing interpretation. *Social Cognition, 2,* 158–170.

Pallak, S. R., Murroni, E., & Koch, J. (1983). Communicator attractiveness and expertise, emotional versus rational appeals, and persuasion: A heuristic versus systematic processing interpretation. *Social Cognition, 2,* 122–141.

Palmer, D. L., & Kalin, R. (1985). Dogmatic responses to belief dissimilarity in the "bogus stranger" paradigm. *Journal of Personality and Social Psychology, 48,* 171–179.

Palmer, D. L., & Kalin, R. (1991). Predictive validity of the Dogmatic Rejection Scale. *Personality and Social Psychology Bulletin, 17,* 212–218.

Pantin, H. M., & Carver, C. S. (1982). Induced competence and the bystander effect. *Journal of Applied Social Psychology, 12,* 100–111.

Paquette, L., & Kida, T. (1988). The effect of decision strategy and task complexity on decision performance. *Organizational Behavior and Human Decision Processes, 41,* 128–142.

Park, B. (1986). A method for studying the development of impressions of real people. *Journal of Personality and Social Psychology, 51,* 907–917.

Park, B., & Judd, C. M. (1989). Agreement on initial impressions: Differences due to perceivers, trait dimensions, and target behaviors. *Journal of Personality and Social Psychology, 56,* 493–505.

Park, B., & Rothbart, M. (1982). Perception of out-group homogeneity and levels of social categorization: Memory for the subordinate attributes of in-group and out-group members. *Journal of Personality and Social Psychology, 42,* 1051–1068.

Park, W. (1990). A review of research on groupthink. *Journal of Behavioral Decision Making, 3,* 229–245.

Parke, R., Berkowitz, L., Leyens, J., West, S., & Sebastian, R. (1977). Some effects of violent and nonviolent movies on the behavior of juvenile delinquents. In L. Berkowitz (Ed.), *Advances in experimental social psychology* (Vol. 10). New York: Academic Press.

Parker, I., & Shotter, J. (Eds.). (1990). *Deconstructing social psychology.* New York: Routledge & Kegan Paul.

Parker, T. (1990). *Never trust a calm dog and other rules of thumb.* New York: HarperCollins.

Parkinson, B. (1985). Emotional effects of false autonomic feedback. *Psychological Bulletin, 98,* 471–494.

Parrott, W. G., & Smith, R. H. (1993). Distinguishing the experiences of envy and jealousy. *Journal of Personality and Social Psychology, 64,* 906–920.

Passer, M. W., Kelley, H. H., & Michela, J. L. (1978). Multidimensional scaling of the causes for negative interpersonal behavior. *Journal of Personality and Social Psychology, 36,* 951–962.

Patchen, M. (1982). *Black-white contact in schools: Its social and academic effects.* West Lafayette, IN: Purdue University Press.

Patterson, M. L. (1975). Personal space—Time to burst the bubble? *Man-Environment Systems, 5,* 67.

Patterson, M. L. (1976). An arousal model of interpersonal intimacy. *Psychological Review, 83,* 235–245.

Patterson, M. L. (1982). A sequential function model of verbal exchange. *Psychological Review, 89,* 231–249.

Patterson, M. L. (1991). A functional approach to nonverbal exchange. In R. S. Feldman & B. Rime (Eds.), *Fundamentals of nonverbal behavior* (pp. 458–495). New York: Cambridge University Press.

Patterson, M. L., Reidhead, S. M., Gooch, M. V., & Stopka, S. J. (1984). A content-classified bibliography of research on the immediacy behaviors: 1965–82. *Journal of Nonverbal Behavior, 8,* 360–393.

Paulhus, D. (1982). Individual differences, self-presentation, and cognitive dissonance: Their concurrent operation in forced compliance. *Journal of Personality and Social Psychology, 43,* 838–852.

Paulhus, D. L. (1984). Two-component models of socially desirable responding. *Journal of Personality and Social Psychology, 46,* 598–609.

Paulhus, D. L., & Bruce, M. N. (1992). The effect of acquaintanceship on the validity of personality impressions: A longitudinal study. *Journal of Personality and Social Psychology, 63,* 816–824.

Paulhus, D. L., & Reid, D. B. (1991). Enhancement and denial in socially desirable responding. *Journal of Personality and Social Psychology, 60,* 307–317.

Paulus, D., Shaffer, D., & Downing, L. (1977). Effects of making blood donor motives salient upon donor retention: A field experiment. *Personality and Social Psychology Bulletin, 3,* 99–102.

Paulus, P. B., Annis, A. B., Seta, J. J., Schkade, J. K., & Matthews, R. W. (1976). Density does affect task performance. *Journal of Personality and Social Psychology, 34,* 248–253.

Paulus, P. B., & Dzindolet, M. T. (1993). Social influence processes in group brainstorm. *Journal of Personality and Social Psychology, 64,* 575–586.

Paulus, P. B., Dzindolet, M. T., Poletes, G., & Camacho, L. M. (1993). Perception of performance in group brainstorming: The illusion of group productivity. *Personality and Social Psychology Bulletin, 19,* 78–89.

Paunonen, S. V. (1991). On the accuracy of ratings of personality by strangers. *Journal of Personality and Social Psychology, 61,* 471–477.

Pavitt, C. (1993). What (little) we know about formal group discussion procedures: A review of relevant research. *Small Group Research, 24,* 217–235.

Peabody, D., & Goldberg, L. R. (1989). Some determinants of factor structures from personality-trait descriptors. *Journal of Personality and Social Psychology, 57,* 59–71.

Pearce, P. L., & Amato, P. R. (1980). A taxonomy of helping: A multidimensional scaling analysis. *Social Psychology Quarterly, 43,* 363–371.

Pearlin, L. I., Meaghan, E. G., Lieberman, M. A., & Mullan, T. J. (1981). The stress process. *Journal of Health and Social Behavior, 22,* 337–356.

Pelham, B. W., & Swann, W. B., Jr. (1989). From self-conceptions to self-worth: On the sources and structure of global self-esteem. *Journal of Personality and Social Psychology, 57,* 672–680.

Pennebacker, J. W. (1990). *Opening up: The healing power of confiding in others.* New York: Morrow.

Pennebaker, J. W., Colder, M., & Sharp, L. K. (1990). Accelerating the coping process. *Journal of Personality and Social Psychology, 58,* 528–537.

Pennebaker, J. W., & Sanders, D. Y. (1976) American graffiti: Effects of authority and reactance arousal. *Personality and Social Psychology Bulletin, 2,* 264–267.

Penrod, S., & Hastie, R. (1980). A computer simulation of jury decision making. *Psychological Review, 87,* 133–159.

Peplau, L. A., Hill, C. T., & Rubin, Z. (1993). Sex role attitudes in dating and marriage: A 15-year follow-up. *Journal of Social Issues, 49*(3), 31–52.

Peplau, L. A., & Perlman, D. (1982). Perspectives on loneliness. In L. A. Peplau & D. Perlman (Eds.), *Loneliness: A sourcebook of current theory, research, and therapy.* New York: Wiley-Interscience.

Peplau, L. A., Rubin, Z., & Hill, C. T. (1977). Sexual intimacy in dating relationships. *Journal of Social Issues, 33,* 86–109.

Perlman, D., & Fehr, B. (1987). The development of intimate relationships. In D. Perlman & S. Duck (Eds.), *Intimate relationships: Development, dynamics, and deterioration* (pp. 13–42). Newbury Park, CA: Sage.

Perlmutter, K. B., Paddock, J. R., & Duke, M. P. (1985). The role of verbal, vocal, and nonverbal cues in the communication of evoking message styles. *Journal of Research in Personality, 19,* 31–43.

Pessin, J. (1933). The comparative effects of social and mechanical stimulation on memorizing. *American Journal of Psychology, 45,* 263–270.

Peters, L. H., Hartke, D. D., & Pohlmann, J. T. (1985). Fiedler's contingency theory of leadership: An application of the meta-analytical procedures of Schmidt and Hunter. *Psychological Bulletin, 97,* 274–285.

Peterson, B. E., Doty, R. M., & Winter, D. G. (1993). Authoritarianism and attitudes toward contemporary social issues. *Personality and Social Psychology Bulletin, 19,* 174–184.

Peterson-Lewis, S., & Adams, A. (1990). Television's model of the quest for African consciousness: A comparison with Cross's empirical model of psychological Nigrescence. *Journal of Black Psychology, 16,* 55–72.

Pettigrew, T. F. (1958). Personality and sociocultural factors in intergroup attitudes: A cross-national comparison. *Journal of Conflict Resolution, 2,* 29–42.

Pettigrew, T. F. (1959). Regional differences in anti-Negro prejudice. *Journal of Abnormal and Social Psychology, 59,* 28–36.

Pettigrew, T. F. (1960). Social distance attitudes of South African students. *Social Forces, 16,* 105–112.

Pettigrew, T. F. (1975). *Racial discrimination in the United States.* New York: Harper & Row.

Petty, R. E., & Cacioppo, J. T. (1981). *Attitudes and persuasion: Classic and contemporary approaches.* Dubuque, IA: Wm. C. Brown.

Petty, R. E., & Cacioppo, J. T. (1984). The effects of involvement on responses to argument quantity and quality: Central and peripheral routes to persuasion. *Journal of Personality and Social Psychology, 46,* 69–81.

Petty, R. E., & Cacioppo, J. T. (1986a). *Communication and persuasion: Central and peripheral routes to attitude change.* New York: Springer-Verlag.

Petty, R. E., & Cacioppo, J. T. (1986b). The elaboration likelihood model of persuasion. In L. Berkowitz (Ed.), *Advances in experimental social psychology* (Vol. 19, pp. 123–205). San Diego, CA: Academic Press.

Petty, R. E., Cacioppo, J. T., & Goldman, R. (1981). Personal involvement as a determinant of argument-based persuasion. *Journal of Personality and Social Psychology, 41,* 847–855.

Petty, R. E., Cacioppo, J. T., & Heesacker, M. (1981). The use of rhetorical questions in persuasion: A cognitive response analysis. *Journal of Personality and Social Psychology, 40,* 432–440.

Petty, R. E., Cacioppo, J. T., & Schumann, D. (1983). Central and peripheral routes to advertising effectiveness: The moderating role of involvement. *Journal of Consumer Research, 10,* 134–148.

Petty, R. E., Gleicher, F., & Baker, S. M. (1991). Multiple roles for affect in persuasion. In J. P. Forgas (Ed.), *Emotion and social judgments* (pp. 181–200). Oxford: Pergamon.

Petty, R. E., Harkins, S. G., & Williams, K. D. (1980). The effects of diffusion of cognitive effort on attitudes: An information processing view. *Journal of Personality and Social Psychology, 38,* 81–92.

Petty, R. E., Harkins, S. G., Williams, K. D., & Latané, B. (1977). The effects of group size on cognitive effort and evaluation. *Personality and Social Psychology Bulletin, 3,* 579–582.

Petty, R. E., Schumann, D. W., Richman, S. A., & Strathman, A. J. (1993). Positive mood and persuasion: Different roles for affect under high- and low-elaboration conditions. *Journal of Personality and Social Psychology, 64,* 5–20.

Pfeifer, J. E. (1992). The psychological framing of cults: Schematic representations and cult evaluations. *Journal of Applied Social Psychology, 22,* 531–544.

Phares, E. J., & Wilson, K. G. (1972). Responsibility attribution: Role of outcome severity, situational ambiguity and internal-external control. *Journal of Personality, 40,* 392–406.

Philipsen, G., Mulac, A., & Dietrich, D. (1979). The effects of social interaction on group idea generation. *Communication Monographs, 46,* 119–125.

Phillips, D. (1974). The influence of suggestion on suicide: Substantive and theoretical implications of the Werther effect. *American Sociological Review, 39,* 340–354.

Phillips, D. (1979). Suicide, motor vehicle fatalities, and the mass media: Evidence toward a theory of suggestion. *American Journal of Sociology, 84,* 1150–1174.

Phillips, D. (1980). Airplane accidents, murder, and the mass media: Towards a theory of imitation and suggestion. *Social Forces, 58,* 1001–1024.

Phillips, D. (1982). The impact of fictional television stories on U.S. adult fatalities: New evidence on the effect of mass media on violence. *American Journal of Sociology, 87,* 1340–1359.

Phillips, D. (1983). The impact of mass media violence on U.S. homicides. *American Sociological Review, 48,* 560–568.

Piliavin, I. M., Piliavin, J. A., & Rodin, J. (1975). Costs, diffusion, and the stigmatized victim. *Journal of Personality and Social Psychology, 32,* 429–438.

Piliavin, I. M., Rodin, J., & Piliavin, J. A. (1969). Good Samaritanism: An underground phenomenon? *Journal of Personality and Social Psychology, 13,* 289–299.

Piliavin, J. A. (1987). Temporary deferral and donor return. *Transfusion, 27,* 199–200.

Piliavin, J. A., & Callero, P. L. (with the collaboration of L. Keating, B. Koski, & D. Libby). (1991). *Giving blood: The development of altruistic identity.* Baltimore, MD: Johns Hopkins University Press.

Piliavin, J. A., Callero, P. L., & Evans, D. E. (1982). Addiction to altruism? Opponent-process theory and habitual blood donation. *Journal of Personality and Social Psychology, 43,* 1200–1213.

Piliavin, J. A., Dovidio, J. F., Gaertner, S. L., & Clark, R. D., III. (1981). *Emergency intervention.* New York: Academic Press.

Piliavin, J. A., & Piliavin, I. M. (1972). Effects of blood on reactions to a victim. *Journal of Personality and Social Psychology, 23,* 353–361.

Pilkington, C. J., & Richardson, D. R. (1988). Perceptions of risk in intimacy. *Journal of Social and Personal Relationships, 5,* 503–508.

Plous, S. (1989). Thinking the unthinkable: The effects of anchoring on likelihood estimates of nuclear war. *Journal of Applied Social Psychology, 19,* 67–91.

Plous, S. (1993). *The psychology of judgment and decision making.* New York: McGraw-Hill.

Podsakoff, P. M., & Schriesheim, C. A. (1985). Field studies of French and Raven's bases of power: Critique, reanalysis, and suggestions for future research. *Psychological Bulletin, 97,* 387–411.

Pollis, N. P., Montgomery, R. L., & Smith, T. G. (1975). Autokinetic paradigms: A reply to Alexander, Zucker, and Brody. *Sociometry, 38,* 358–373.

Pomazal, R. J., & Clore, G. L. (1973). Helping on the highway: The effects of dependency and sex. *Journal of Applied Social Psychology, 3,* 150–164.

Povinelli, D. J. (1993). Reconstructing the evolution of mind. *American Psychologist, 48,* 493–509.

Powers, T. A., & Zuroff, D. C. (1988). Interpersonal consequences of overt self-criticism: A comparison with neutral and self-enhancing presentations of the self. *Journal of Personality and Social Psychology, 54,* 1054–1062.

Prasad, J. (1950). A comparative study of rumours and reports in earthquakes. *British Journal of Psychology, 41,* 129–144.

Pratkanis, A. R. (1989). The cognitive representation of attitudes. In A. R. Pratkanis, S. J. Breckler, & A. G. Greenwald (Eds.), *Attitude structure and function* (pp. 71–98). Hillsdale, NJ: Erlbaum.

Pratkanis, A. R., & Aronson, E. (1991). *Age of propaganda: The everyday use and abuse of persuasion.* New York: W. H. Freeman.

Pratkanis, A. R., Breckler, S. J., & Greenwald, A. G. (Eds.). (1989). *Attitude structure and function.* Hillsdale, NJ: Erlbaum.

Pratkanis, A. R., & Greenwald, A. G. (1989). A sociocognitive model of attitude structure and function. In L. Berkowitz (Ed.), *Advances in experimental social psychology* (Vol. 22, pp. 245–285). Orlando, FL: Academic Press.

Pratkanis, A. R., Greenwald, A. G., Leippe, M. R., & Baumgardner, M. H. (1988). In search of reliable persuasion effects: III. The sleeper effect is dead. Long live the sleeper effect. *Journal of Personality and Social Psychology, 54,* 203–218.

Pratto, F., & John, O. P. (1991). Automatic vigilance: The attention-grabbing power of negative social information. *Journal of Personality and Social Psychology, 61,* 380–391.

Preiss, J. J. (1968). Self and role in medical education. In C. Gordon & K. J. Gergen (Eds.), *The self in social interaction* (pp. 207–218). New York: Wiley.

Prentice, D. A. (1987). Psychological correspondence of possessions, attitudes, and values. *Journal of Personality and Social Psychology, 53,* 993–1003.

Prentice, D. A. (1990). Familiarity and differences in self- and other-representations. *Journal of Personality and Social Psychology, 59,* 369–383.

Prentice, D. A., & Miller, D. T. (1993). Pluralistic ignorance and alcohol use on campus: Some consequences of misperceiving the social norm. *Journal of Personality and Social Psychology, 64,* 243–254.

Prentice-Dunn, S., & Rogers, R. W. (1983). Deindividuation and aggression. In R. G. Geen & E. I. Donnerstein (Eds.), *Aggression: Theoretical and empirical reviews* (Vol. 2, pp. 155–172). New York: Academic Press.

Prince-Embury, S. (1991). Information seekers in the aftermath of technological disaster at Three Mile Island. *Journal of Applied Social Psychology, 21,* 569–584.

Proceedings of the American Psychological Association. (1985). *American Psychologist, 40,* 621–653.

Pruitt, D. G. (1971). Choice shifts in group discussion: An introductory review. *Journal of Personality and Social Psychology, 20,* 339–360.

Pruitt, D. G., Mikolic, J. M., Peirce, R. S., & Keating, M. (1993). Aggression as a struggle tactic in social conflict. In R. B. Felson & J. T. Tedeschi (Eds.), *Aggression and violence: Social interactionist perspectives* (pp. 99–118). Washington, DC: American Psychological Association.

Pryor, J., Gibbons, F. X., Wicklund, R. A., Fazio, R., & Hood, R. (1977). Self-focused attention and self-report validity. *Journal of Personality, 45,* 513–527.

Pryor, J. B., & Kriss, N. (1977). The cognitive dynamics of salience in the attribution process. *Journal of Personality and Social Psychology, 35,* 49–55.

Pyszczynski, T., & Greenberg, J. (1985). Depression and preference for self-focusing stimuli after success and failure. *Journal of Personality and Social Psychology, 49,* 1066–1075.

Pyszczynski, T., & Greenberg, J. (1987). Toward an integration of cognitive and motivational perspectives on social inference: A biased hypothesis-testing model. In L. Berkowitz (Ed.), *Advances in experimental social psychology* (Vol. 20, pp. 297–340). Orlando, FL: Academic Press.

Pyszczynski, T., Greenberg, J., Hamilton, J., & Nix, G. (1991). On the relationship between self-focused attention and psychological disorder: A critical reappraisal. *Psychological Bulletin, 110,* 538–543.

Pyszczynski, T., Greenberg, J., & LaPrelle, J. (1985). Social comparison after success and failure: Biased search for information consistent with a self-serving conclusion. *Journal of Experimental Social Psychology, 21,* 195–211.

Quattrone, G. A. (1982). Behavioral consequences of attributional bias. *Social Cognition, 1,* 358–378.

Quattrone, G. A. (1986). On the perception of a group's variability. In S. Worchel & W. G. Austin (Eds.), *Psychology of intergroup relations* (2nd ed.). Chicago: Nelson-Hall.

Quattrone, G. A., & Jones, E. E. (1980). The perception of variability within in-groups and out-groups: Implications for the law of small numbers. *Journal of Personality and Social Psychology, 38,* 141–150.

Rabbie, J. (1963). Differential preference for companionship under stress. *Journal of Abnormal and Social Psychology, 67,* 643–648.

Rabbie, J. M., & Horwitz, M. (1969). Arousal of ingroup-outgroup bias by a chance win or loss. *Journal of Personality and Social Psychology, 13,* 269–277.

Radke-Yarrow, M., Zahn-Waxler, C., & King, R. A. (1979). Child rearing and children's prosocial initiations toward victims of distress. *Child Development, 50,* 310–330.

Radloff, R., & Helmreich, R. (1968). *Groups under stress: Psychological research in SEALAB II.* New York: Irvington.

Rajecki, D. W. (1990). *Attitudes* (2nd ed.). Sunderland, MA: Sinauer.

Ramirez, J., Bryant, J., & Zillmann, D. (1983). Effects of erotica on retaliatory behavior as a function of level of prior provocation. *Journal of Personality and Social Psychology, 43,* 971–978.

Rankin, R. E., & Campbell, D. T. (1955). Galvanic skin response to Negro and white experimenters. *Journal of Abnormal and Social Psychology, 51,* 30–33.

Rapoport, A., & Bornstein, G. (1987). Intergroup competition for the provision of binary public goods. *Psychological Review, 94,* 291–299.

Rasinski, K. A., Crocker, J., & Hastie, R. (1985). Another look at sex stereotypes and social judgments: An analysis of the social perceiver's use of subjective probabilities. *Journal of Personality and Social Psychology, 49,* 317–326.

Raven, B. H. (1965). Social influence and power. In I. D. Steiner & M. Fishbein (Eds.), *Current studies in social psychology.* New York: Holt, Rinehart & Winston.

Raven, B. H., & Rubin, J. Z. (1976). *Social psychology: People in groups.* New York: Wiley.

Read, S. J. (1988). Conjunctive explanations: The effect of a comparison between a chosen and a nonchosen alternative. *Journal of Experimental Social Psychology, 24,* 146–162.

Read, S. J. (1989). Constructing causal scenarios: A knowledge structure approach to causal reasoning. *Journal of Personality and Social Psychology, 52,* 288–302.

Reed, J. A., & Blunk, E. M. (1990). The influence of facial hair on impression formation. *Social Behavior and Personality, 18,* 169–175.

Reeder, G. D., Fletcher, G. J. O., & Furman, K. (1989). The role of observers' expectations in attitude attribution. *Journal of Experimental Social Psychology, 25,* 168–188.

Regan, D., & Totten, J. (1975). Empathy and attribution: Turning observers into actors. *Journal of Personality and Social Psychology, 32,* 850–856.

Regan, D. T., & Fazio, R. H. (1977). On the consistency between attitudes and behavior: Look to the method of attitude formation. *Journal of Experimental Social Psychology, 13,* 38–45.

Regan, J. W. (1976). Liking for evaluators: Consistency and self-esteem theories. *Journal of Experimental Social Psychology, 12,* 159–169.

Reich, J. W., & Robertson, J. L. (1979). Reactance and normal appeal in antilittering messages. *Journal of Applied Social Psychology, 9,* 91–101.

Reich, J. W., & Zautra, A. J. (1991). Experimental and measurement approaches to internal control in at-risk older adults. *Journal of Social Issues, 47*(4), 143–158.

Reis, H. T., Earing, B., Kent, A., & Nezlek, J. (1976). The tyranny of numbers: Does group size affect petition signing? *Journal of Applied Social Psychology, 6,* 228–234.

Reis, H. T., Senchak, M., & Solomon, B. (1985). Sex differences in the intimacy of social interaction: Further examination of potential explanations. *Journal of Personality and Social Psychology, 48,* 1204–1217.

Reis, H. T., Wheeler, L., Spiegel, N., Kernis, M. H., Nezlek, J., & Perri, M. (1982). Physical attractiveness in social interaction: II. Why does appearance affect social experience? *Journal of Personality and Social Psychology, 43,* 979–996.

Reisenzein, R. (1983). The Schachter theory of emotion: Two decades later. *Psychological Bulletin, 94,* 239–264.

Rempel, J. K., & Holmes, J. G. (1986). How do I trust thee? *Psychology Today, 20*(2), pp. 28–34.

Rempel, J. K., Holmes, J. G., & Zanna, M. P. (1985). Trust in close relationships. *Journal of Personality and Social Psychology, 49,* 95–112.

Reno, R. R., Cialdini, R. B., & Kallgren, C. A. (1993). The transituational influence of social norms. *Journal of Personality and Social Psychology, 64,* 104–112.

Reyes, R. M., Thompson, W. C., & Bower, G. H. (1980). Judgmental biases resulting from differing availabilities of arguments. *Journal of Personality and Social Psychology, 39,* 2–12.

Reynolds, K. D., & West, S. G. (1989). Attributional constructs: Their role in the organization of social information in memory. *Basic and Applied Social Psychology, 10,* 119–130.

Reynolds, V. (1972). Ethology of urban life. In P. J. Ucko (Ed.), *Man, settlement, and urbanism* (pp. 401–408). London: Duckworth.

Rhodes, N., & Wood, W. (1992). Self-esteem and intelligence affect influenceability: The mediating role of message reception. *Psychological Bulletin, 111,* 156–171.

Rhodewalt, F., & Comer, R. (1979). Induced-compliance attitude change: Once more with feeling. *Journal of Experimental Social Psychology, 15,* 35–47.

Rhodewalt, F., Saltzman, A. T., & Wittmer, J. (1985). Self-handicapping among competitive athletes: The role of practice in self-esteem protection. *Basic and Applied Social Psychology, 5,* 197–209.

Rholes, W. S., Jones, M., & Wade, C. (1988). Children's understanding of personal dispositions and its relationship to behavior. *Journal of Experimental Child Psychology, 45,* 1–17.

Rholes, W. S., & Pryor, J. B. (1982). Cognitive accessibility and causal attributions. *Personality and Social Psychology Bulletin, 8,* 719–727.

Ricci Bitti, P. E., & Poggi, I. (1991). Symbolic nonverbal behavior: Talking through gestures. In R. S. Feldman & B. Rime (Eds.), *Fundamental of nonverbal behavior* (pp. 433–457). New York: Cambridge University Press.

Rice, O. K. (1978). *The Hatfields and the McCoys.* Lexington: University Press of Kentucky.

Rice, R. W. (1978a). Psychometric properties of the Esteem for Least Preferred Coworker (LPC) Scale. *Academy of Management Review, 3,* 106–118.

Rice, R. W. (1978b). Construct validity of the Least Preferred Co-worker (LPC) score. *Psychological Bulletin, 85,* 1199–1237.

Rice, R. W. (1979). Reliability and validity of the LPC scale: A reply. *Academy of Management Review, 4,* 291–294.

Ridgeway, C. L. (1982). Status in groups: The importance of motivation. *American Sociological Review, 47,* 76–88.

Ridgeway, C. L. (1984). Dominance, performance, and status in groups: A theoretical analysis. In E. J. Lawler (Ed.), *Advances in group processes* (Vol. 1, pp. 59–93). Greenwich, CT: JAI Press.

Ridley, M., & Dawkins, R. (1980). The natural selection of altruism. In J. P. Rushton & R. M. Sorrentino (Eds.), *Altruism and helping behavior.* Hillsdale, NJ: Erlbaum.

Riecken, H. W., & Boruch, R. F. (1975). *Social experimentation: A method for planning and evaluating social intervention.* Orlando, FL: Academic Press.

Riess, M., Forsyth, D. R., Schlenker, B. R., & Freed, S. (1977). Opinion conformity as an impression management tactic following performance of an unpleasant task. *Bulletin of the Psychonomic Society, 9,* 211–213.

Riess, M., Rosenfeld, P., Melburg, V., & Tedeschi, J. T. (1981). Self-serving attributions: Biased private perceptions and distorted public descriptions. *Journal of Personality and Social Psychology, 41,* 224–231.

Riess, M., & Salzer, S. (1981). *Individuals avoid invading the space of males but not females.* Paper presented at the Annual Meetings of the American Psychological Association, Los Angeles.

Riess, M., & Schlenker, B. R. (1977). Attitude change and responsibility avoidance as modes of dilemma resolution in force compliance settings. *Journal of Personality and Social Psychology, 35,* 21–30.

Riess, M., & Taylor, J. (1989). "Self-serving" attributions to valenced causal factors: A field experiment. *Personality and Social Psychology Bulletin, 15,* 337–348.

Riggio, R. E., & Friedman, H. S. (1986). Impression formation: The role of expressive behavior. *Journal of Personality and Social Psychology, 50,* 421–427.

Rime, B., & Schiaratura, L. (1991). Gesture and speech. In R. S. Feldman & B. Rime (Eds.), *Fundamentals of nonverbal behavior* (pp. 239–281). New York: Cambridge University Press.

Ringelmann, M. (1913). Research on animate sources of power: The work of man. *Annales de l'Institut National Agronomique,* 2e série, tome XII, 1–40.

Riordan, C., & Riggiero, J. (1980). Producing equal-status interracial interaction: A replication. *Social Psychology Quarterly, 43,* 131–136.

Riordan, C. A., & Tedeschi, J. T. (1983). Attraction in aversive environments: Some evidence for classical conditioning and negative reinforcement. *Journal of Personality and Social Psychology, 44,* 683–691.

Robberson, M. R., & Rogers, R. W. (1988). Beyond fear appeals: Negative and positive persuasive appeals to health and self-esteem. *Journal of Applied Social Psychology, 18,* 277–287.

Roberts, J. E., & McCready, V. (1987). Different clinical perspectives of good and poor therapy sessions. *Journal of Speech and Hearing Research, 30,* 335–342.

Roberts, T. (1991). Gender and the influence of evaluation on self-assessments in achievement settings. *Psychological Bulletin, 109,* 297–308.

Robertson, J. M., & Fitzgerald, L. F. (1992). Overcoming the masculine mystique: Preferences for alternative forms of assistance among men who avoid counseling. *Journal of Counseling Psychology, 39,* 240–246.

Robins, R. W., & Craik, K. H. (1993). Is there a citation bias in the judgment and decision literature. *Organizational Behavior and Human Performance, 54,* 225–244.

Robles, R., Smith, R., Carver, C. S., & Wellens, A. R. (1987). Influence of subliminal visual images on the experience of anxiety. *Personality and Social Psychology Bulletin, 13,* 399–410.

Rodin, J., & Langer, E. J. (1980). Aging labels: The decline of control and the fall of self-esteem. *Journal of Social Issues, 36,* 12–29.

Rodin, J., Solomon, S. K., & Metcalf, J. (1978). Role of control in mediating perceptions of density. *Journal of Personality and Social Psychology, 36,* 988–999.

Roese, N. J., & Jamieson, D. W. (1993). Twenty years of bogus pipeline research: A critical review and meta-analysis. *Psychological Bulletin, 114,* 363–375.

Roethlisberger, F. J., & Dickson, W. J. (1939). *Management and the worker.* Cambridge, MA: Harvard University Press.

Rofé, Y. (1984). Stress and affiliation: A utility theory. *Psychological Review, 91,* 235–250.

Rofé, Y., Lewin, I., & Hoffman, M. (1987). Affiliation patterns among cancer patients. *Psychological Medicine, 17,* 419–424.

Rogers, M., & Miller, N. (1981). *The effect of school setting on cross-racial interaction.* Paper presented at the Annual Meeting of the American Psychological Association, Montreal.

Rogers, R. W. (1983). A protection motivation theory of fear appeals and attitude change. *Journal of Psychology, 91,* 93–114.

Rogers, R. W., & Mewborn, R. (1976). Fear appeals and attitude change: Effects of a threat's noxiousness, probability of occurrence, and the efficacy of coping responses. *Journal of Personality and Social Psychology, 34,* 54–61.

Rogers, R. W., & Prentice-Dunn, S. (1981). Deindividuation and anger-mediated interracial aggression: Unmasking regressive racism. *Journal of Personality and Social Psychology, 41,* 63–73.

Rohe, W. H., & Burby, R. J. (1988). Fear of crime in public housing. *Environment and Behavior, 20,* 700–720.

Rokeach, M. J. (1968). *Beliefs, attitudes, and values: A theory of organization and change.* San Francisco: Jossey-Bass.

Romer, D., Gruder, C., & Lizzadro, T. (1986). A person-situation approach to altruistic behavior. *Journal of Personality and Social Psychology, 51,* 5, 1001–1012.

Ronis, D. L., & Greenwald, A. G. (1979). Dissonance theory revised again: Comment on the paper by Fazio, Zanna, and Cooper. *Journal of Experimental Social Psychology, 15,* 62–69.

Ronis, D. L., & Lipinski, E. R. (1985). Value and uncertainty as weighting factors in impression formation. *Journal of Experimental Social Psychology, 21,* 47–60.

Rook, K. S. (1984). The negative side of social interaction: Impact on psychological well-being. *Journal of Personality and Social Psychology, 46,* 1097–1108.

Rook, K. S., & Peplau, L. A. (1982). Perspectives on helping the lonely. In L. A. Peplau & D. Perlman (Eds.), *Loneliness: A sourcebook of current theory, research, and therapy.* New York: Wiley-Interscience.

Roos, P. A. (1985). *Gender and work: A comparative analysis of industrial societies.* New York: State University of New York Press.

Rosenberg, M. (1965). *Society and the adolescent self-image.* Princeton, NJ: Princeton University Press.

Rosenberg, M. (1979). *Conceiving the self* (1st ed.). New York: Basic Books.

Rosenberg, M. (1986). *Conceiving the self* (2nd ed.). Malibar, FL: Krieger.

Rosenberg, M. J. (1965). When dissonance fails: On eliminating evaluation apprehension from attitude measurement. *Journal of Personality and Social Psychology, 1,* 28–42.

Rosenberg, M. J., & Hovland, C. I. (1960). Cognitive, affective, and behavioral components of attitude. In M. J. Rosenberg, C. I. Hovland, W. J. McGuire, R. P. Abelson, & J. W. Brehm (Eds.), *Attitude organization and change: An analysis of consistency among attitude components.* New Haven, CT: Yale University Press.

Rosenberg, S., & Sedlak, A. (1972). Structural representations of implicit personality theory. In L. Berkowitz (Ed.), *Advances in experimental social psychology* (Vol. 6, pp. 235–297). New York: Academic Press.

Rosenfeld, P., Giacalone, R. A., & Tedeschi, J. T. (1984). Cognitive dissonance and impression management explanations for effort justification. *Personality and Social Psychology Bulletin, 10,* 394–401.

Rosenfeld, P., Kennedy, J. G., & Giacalone, R. A. (1986). Decision making: A demonstration of the postdecision dissonance effect. *Journal of Social Psychology, 126,* 663–665.

Rosenhan, D. L. (1970). The natural socialization of altruistic autonomy. In J. Macaulay & L. Berkowitz (Eds.), *Altruism and helping behavior: Social psychological studies of some antecedents and consequences.* New York: Academic Press.

Rosenhan, D. L., Karylowski, J., Salovey, P., & Hargis, K. (1981). Emotion and altruism. In J. P. Rushton & R. M. Sorrentino (Eds.), *Altruism and helping behavior.* Hillsdale, NJ: Erlbaum.

Rosenhan, D. L., Underwood, B., & Moore, B. S. (1974). Affect moderates self-gratification and altruism. *Journal of Personality and Social Psychology, 30,* 546–552.

Rosenkrantz, P. S., Vogel, S. R., Bee, H., Broverman, I. K., & Broverman, D. M. (1968). Sex role stereotypes and self-concepts in college students. *Journal of Consulting and Clinical Psychology, 32,* 287–295.

Rosenthal, R. (1966). *Experimenter effects in behavioral research.* New York: Appleton-Century-Crofts.

Rosenthal, R. (1969). Interpersonal expectations: Effects of the experimenter's hypothesis. In R. Rosenthal & R. L. Rosnow (Eds.), *Artifact in behavioral research.* Orlando, FL: Academic Press.

Rosenthal, R. (1986). From unconscious experimenter bias to teacher expectancy effects. In J. B. Dusek, V. C. Hall, & W. J. Meyer (Eds.), *Teacher expectancies* (pp. 37–66). Hillsdale, NJ: Erlbaum.

Rosenthal, R., & Fode, K. L. (1963). Three experiments in experimenter bias. *Psychological Reports, 12,* 491–511.

ROSENTHAL, R., & JACOBSON, L. (1968). *Pygmalion in the classroom: Teacher expectation and pupils' intellectual development.* New York: Holt, Rinehart & Winston.

ROSENTHAL, R., & ROSNOW, R. L. (1991). *Essentials of behavior research: Methods and data analysis* (2nd ed.). New York: McGraw-Hill.

ROSKOS-EWOLDSEN, D. R., & FAZIO, R. H. (1992). The accessibility of source likability as a determinant of persuasion. *Personality and Social Psychology Bulletin, 18,* 19–25.

ROSNOW, R. L. (1980). Psychology of rumor reconsidered. *Psychological Bulletin, 87,* 578–591.

ROSNOW, R. L. (1991). Inside rumor: A personal journey. *American Psychologist, 46,* 484–496.

ROSNOW, R. L., & KIMMEL, A. J. (1979). Lives of a rumor. *Psychology Today, 13*(6), pp. 88–92.

ROSS, A. S., & BRABAND, J. (1973). Effect of increased responsibility on bystander intervention: II. The cue value of a blind person. *Journal of Personality and Social Psychology, 25,* 254–258.

ROSS, E. A. (1908). *Social psychology.* New York: Macmillan.

ROSS, L. (1977). The intuitive psychologist and his shortcomings: Distortions in the attribution process. In L. Berkowitz (Ed.), *Advances in experimental social psychology* (Vol. 10). New York: Academic Press.

ROSS, L., AMABILE, T. M., & STEINMETZ, J. L. (1977). Social roles, social control, and biases in social perception processes. *Journal of Personality and Social Psychology, 35,* 485–494.

ROSS, L., & ANDERSON, C. A. (1982). Shortcomings in attribution processes: On the origins and maintenance of erroneous social assessments. In D. Kahneman, P. Slovic, & A. Tversky (Eds.), *Judgment under uncertainty: Heuristics and biases.* New York: Cambridge University Press.

ROSS, L., BIERBRAUER, G., & POLLY, S. (1974). Attribution of educational outcomes by professional and nonprofessional instructors. *Journal of Personality and Social Psychology, 29,* 609–618.

ROSS, L., GREEN, D., & HOUSE, P. (1977). The false consensus phenomenon: An attributional bias in self-perception and social perception processes. *Journal of Experimental Social Psychology, 13,* 279–301.

ROSS, L., LEPPER, M. R., & HUBBARD, M. (1975). Perseverance in self-perception and social perception: Biased attribution processes in the debriefing paradigm. *Journal of Personality and Social Psychology, 32,* 880–892.

ROSS, L., & NISBETT, R. E. (1991). *The person and the situation: Perspectives on social psychology.* New York: McGraw-Hill.

ROSS, M., & SICOLY, F. (1979). Egocentric biases in availability and attribution. *Journal of Personality and Social Psychology, 37,* 322–336.

ROTHBART, M., EVANS, M., & FULERO, S. (1979). Recall for confirming events: Memory processes and the maintenance of social stereotypes. *Journal of Experimental Social Psychology, 15,* 343–356.

ROTHBART, M., FULERO, S., JENSEN, C., HOWARD, J., & BIRRELL, P. (1978). From individual to group impressions: Availability heuristics in stereotype formation. *Journal of Experimental Social Psychology, 14,* 237–255.

ROTHBART, M., & PARK, B. (1986). On the confirmability and disconfirmability of trait concepts. *Journal of Personality and Social Psychology, 50,* 131–142.

ROTTER, N. G., & ROTTER, G. S. (1988). Sex differences in encoding and decoding of negative facial emotions. *Journal of Nonverbal Behavior, 12,* 139–148.

ROTTON, J. (1986). Determinism redux: Climate and cultural correlates of violence. *Environment and Behavior, 18,* 346–368.

ROTTON, J., & FREY, J. (1985). Air pollution, weather, and violent crimes: Concomitant time-series analysis of archival data. *Journal of Personality and Social Psychology, 49,* 1207–1220.

ROZIN, P., & FALLON, A. E. (1987). A perspective on disgust. *Psychological Review, 94,* 23–41.

RUBACK, R. B., DABBS, J. M., JR., & HOPPER, C. H. (1984). The process of brainstorming: An analysis with individual and group vocal parameters. *Journal of Personality and Social Psychology, 47,* 558–567.

RUBACK, R. B., & INNES, C. A. (1988). The relevance and irrelevance of psychological research: The example of prison crowding. *American Psychologist, 43,* 683–693.

RUBACK, R. B., & PANDEY, J. (1992). Very hot and really crowded: Quasi-experimental investigations of Indian "tempos." *Environment and Behavior, 24,* 527–554.

RUBENSTEIN, C. M., & SHAVER, P. (1982). The experience of loneliness. In L. A. Peplau & D. Perlman (Eds.), *Loneliness: A sourcebook of current theory, research, and therapy.* New York: Wiley-Interscience.

RUBIN, J. Z., KIM, S. H., & PERETZ, N. M. (1990). Expectancy effects and negotiation. *Journal of Social Issues, 46*(2), 125–139.

RUBIN, J. Z., PRUITT, D. G., & KIM, S. H. (1994). *Social conflict: Escalation, stalemate, and settlement* (2nd ed.). New York: McGraw-Hill.

RUBIN, Z. (1973). *Liking and loving.* New York: Holt, Rinehart & Winston.

RUBLE, D. N., COSTANZO, P. R., & OLIVERI, M. E. (Eds.). (1992). *The social psychology of mental health.* New York: Guilford Press.

RUBONIS, A. V., & BICKMAN, L. (1991). Psychological impairment in the wake of disaster: The disaster-psychopathology relationship. *Psychological Bulletin, 109,* 384–399.

RULE, B. G., & NESDALE, A. R. (1976). Emotional arousal and aggressive behavior. *Psychological Bulletin, 83,* 851–863.

RULE, B. G., TAYLOR, B. R., & DOBBS, A. R. (1987). Priming effects of heat on aggressive thoughts. *Social Cognition, 5,* 131–143.

RUSBULT, C. E. (1983). A longitudinal test of the investment model: The development (and deterioration) of satisfaction and commitment in heterosexual involvements. *Journal of Personality and Social Psychology, 45,* 101–117.

RUSBULT, C. E. (1987). Responses to dissatisfaction in close relationships: The Exit-Voice-Loyalty-Neglect model. In D. Perlman & S. Duck (Eds.), *Intimate relationships: Development, dynamics, and deterioration* (pp. 209–237). Newbury Park, CA: Sage.

RUSBULT, C. E., JOHNSON, D. J., & MORROW, G. D. (1986). Predicting satisfaction and commitment in adult romantic involvements: An assessment of the generalizability of the investment model. *Social Psychology Quarterly, 49,* 81–89.

RUSBULT, C. E., MORROW, G. D., & JOHNSON, D. J. (1987). Self-esteem and problem solving behavior in close relationships. *British Journal of Social Psychology, 26,* 293–303.

RUSBULT, C. E., & ZEMBRODT, I. M. (1983). Responses to dissatisfaction in romantic involvements: A multidimensional scaling analysis. *Journal of Experimental Social Psychology, 19,* 274–293.

RUSBULT, C. E., ZEMBRODT, I. M., & GUNN, L. K. (1982). Exit, voice, loyalty, and neglect: Responses to dissatisfaction in romantic involvements. *Journal of Personality and Social Psychology, 43,* 1230–1242.

RUSBULT, C. E., ZEMBRODT, I., & IWANISZEK, J. (1986). The impact of gender and sex-role orientation on responses to dissatisfaction in close relationships. *Sex Roles, 15,* 1–20.

RUSHTON, J. P. (1980). *Altruism, socialization, and society.* Englewood Cliffs, NJ: Prentice-Hall.

RUSHTON, J. P. (1981). The altruistic personality. In J. P. Rushton & R. M. Sorrentino (Eds.), *Altruism and helping behavior.* Hillsdale, NJ: Erlbaum.

RUSHTON, J. P. (1989). Genetic similarity, human altruism, and group selection. *Behavioral and Brain Sciences, 12,* 503–559.

RUSHTON, J. P., CHRISJOHN, R. D., & FEKKEN, G. C. (1981). The altruistic personality and the self-report altruism scale. *Personality and Individual Differences, 2,* 292–302.

RUSHTON, J. P., FULKER, D. W., NEALE, M. C., NIAS, D. K. B., & EYSENCK, H. J. (1986). Altruism and aggression: The heritability of individual differences. *Journal of Personality and Social Psychology, 50,* 1192–1198.

RUSHTON, J. P., & SORRENTINO, R. M. (Eds.). (1981). *Altruism and helping behavior.* Hillsdale, NJ: Erlbaum.

RUSSELL, D. (1982). The causal dimension scale: A measure of how individuals perceive causes. *Journal of Personality and Social Psychology, 42,* 1137–1145.

RUSSELL, D., CUTRONA, C. E., ROSE, J., & YURKO, K. (1984). Social and emotional loneliness: An examination of Weiss's typology of loneliness. *Journal of Personality and Social Psychology, 46,* 1313–1321.

RUSSELL, D., PEPLAU, L. A., & CUTRONA, C. E. (1980). The revised UCLA loneliness scale: Concurrent and discriminate validity evidence. *Journal of Personality and Social Psychology, 39,* 472–480.

Russell, D. E. H. (1984). *Sexual exploitation: Rape, child sexual abuse, and workplace harassment.* Newbury Park, CA: Sage.

Russell, D. W., McAuley, E., & Tarico, V. (1987). Measuring causal attributions for success and failure: A comparison of methodologies for assessing causal dimensions. *Journal of Personality and Social Psychology, 52,* 1248–1257.

Russell, J. A. (1991). Culture and the categorization of emotions. *Psychological Bulletin, 110,* 426–450.

Russell, J. A. (1994). Is there universal recognition of emotion from facial expression? A review of cross-cultural studies. *Psychological Bulletin, 115,* 102–141.

Russo, N. F., Feller, L., & DeLeon, P. H. (1982). Sex role stereotypes in television advertising: Strategies for change in the 80's. *Academic Psychology Bulletin, 4,* 117–135.

Rutherford, E., & Mussen, P. (1968). Generosity in nursery school boys. *Child Development, 39,* 755–765.

Ryan, R. M., Mims, V., & Koestner, R. (1983). Relation of reward contingency and interpersonal context to intrinsic motivation: A review and test using cognitive evaluation theory. *Journal of Personality and Social Psychology, 45,* 736–750.

Ryan, R. M., Plant, R. W., & Kuczkowski, R. J. (1991). Relation of self-projection processes to performance, emotion, and memory in a controlled interaction setting. *Personality and Social Psychology Bulletin, 17,* 427–434.

Ryen, A. H., & Kahn, A. (1975). The effects of intergroup orientation on group attitudes and proxemic behavior: A test of two models. *Journal of Personality and Social Psychology, 31,* 302–310.

Sabini, J. P., & Silver, M. (1978). Moral reproach and moral action. *Journal for the Theory of Social Behavior, 8,* 103–123.

Sabini, J. P., & Silver, M. (1983). Dispositional vs. situational interpretations of Milgram's obedience experiments: "The fundamental attribution error." *Journal for the Theory of Social Behavior, 13,* 147–154.

Sadalla, E. K., Burroughs, W. J., & Quaid, M. (1980). House form and social identity: A validity study. In R. Stough & A. Wandersman (Eds.), *Optimizing environments: Research practice and policy* (pp. 201–206). Washington, DC: Environmental Design Research Association.

Sadalla, E. K., Kenrick, D. T., & Vershure, B. (1987). Dominance and heterosexual attraction. *Journal of Personality and Social Psychology, 52,* 730–738.

Sadalla, E. K., Vershure, B., & Burroughs, J. (1987). Identity symbolism in housing. *Environment and Behavior, 19,* 569–587.

Saegert, S. (1978). High-density environments: Their personal and social consequences. In A. Baum & Y. M. Epstein (Eds.), *Human response to crowding.* Hillsdale, NJ: Erlbaum.

Saegert, S., Swap, W., & Zajonc, R. B. (1973). Exposure, context, and interpersonal attraction. *Journal of Personality and Social Psychology, 25,* 234–242.

Saegert, S., & Winkel, G. (1990). Environmental psychology. *Annual Review of Psychology, 41,* 441–477.

Safer, M. A. (1980). Attributing evil to the subject, not the situation: Student reaction to Milgram's film on obedience. *Personality and Social Psychology Bulletin, 6,* 205–209.

Sagar, H. A., & Schofield, J. W. (1980). Racial and behavioral cues in black and white children's perceptions of ambiguously aggressive acts. *Journal of Personality and Social Psychology, 39,* 590–598.

Saks, M. J. (1977). *Jury verdicts.* Lexington, MA: D. C. Heath.

Salovey, P., & Rodin, J. (1985). The heart of jealousy. *Psychology Today, 19*(9), pp. 22–25.

Salovey, P., & Turk, D. C. (1991). Clinical judgment and decision making. In C. R. Snyder & D. R. Forsyth (Eds.), *Handbook of social and clinical psychology* (pp. 416–437). New York: Pergamon.

Samerotte, G. C., & Harris, M. B. (1976). Some factors influencing helping: The effects of a handicap, responsibility, and requesting help. *Journal of Social Psychology, 98,* 39–45.

Sampson, R., & Groves, W. (1989). Community structure and crime: Testing social-disorganization theory. *American Journal of Sociology, 94,* 774–802.

Sanbonmatsu, D. M., & Fazio, R. H. (1990). The role of attitudes in memory-based decision making. *Journal of Personality and Social Psychology, 59,* 614–622.

Sande, G. N., Goethals, G. R., & Radloff, C. E. (1988). Perceiving one's own traits and others': The multifaceted self. *Journal of Personality and Social Psychology, 54,* 13–20.

Sanders, G. S. (1981). Driven by distraction: An integrative review of social facilitation theory and research. *Journal of Experimental Social Psychology, 17,* 227–251.

Sanders, G. S., & Baron, R. S. (1975). The motivating effects of distraction on task performance. *Journal of Personality and Social Psychology, 32,* 956–963.

Sanders, G. S., Baron, R. S., & Moore, D. L. (1978). Distraction and social comparison as mediators of social facilitation effects. *Journal of Experimental Social Psychology, 14,* 291–303.

Sanna, L. J. (1992). Self-efficacy theory: Implications for social facilitation and social loafing. *Journal of Personality and Social Psychology, 62,* 774–786.

Sanna, L. J., & Shotland, R. L. (1990). Valence of anticipated evaluation and social facilitation. *Journal of Experimental Social Psychology, 26,* 82–92.

Santee, R. T., & Jackson, S. E. (1982). Sex differences in evaluative implications of conformity and dissent. *Social Psychology Quarterly, 45,* 121–125.

Santee, R. T., & Maslach, C. (1982). To agree or not to agree: Personal dissent amid social pressure to conform. *Journal of Personality and Social Psychology, 42,* 690–700.

Sarason, B. R., Shearin, E. N., Pierce, G. R., & Sarason, I. G. (1987). Interrelations of social support measures: Theoretical and practical implications. *Journal of Personality and Social Psychology, 52,* 813–832.

Sarnoff, I., & Zimbardo, P. G. (1961). Anxiety, fear, and social affiliation. *Journal of Abnormal and Social Psychology, 62,* 356–363.

Sawyer, A. G. (1973). The effects of repetition of refutational and supportive advertising appeals. *Journal of Marketing Research, 10,* 23–33.

Saxe, L., & Fine, M. (1981). *Social experiments: Methods for evaluation and design.* Newbury Park, CA: Sage.

Schachter, S. (1951). Deviation, rejection, and communication. *Journal of Abnormal and Social Psychology, 46,* 190–207.

Schachter, S. (1959). *The psychology of affiliation.* Stanford, CA: Stanford University Press.

Schachter, S., & Singer, J. (1962). Cognitive, social, and physiological determinants of emotional state. *Psychological Review, 65,* 379–399.

Schachter, S., & Wheeler, L. (1962). Epinephrine, chlorpromazine, and amusement. *Journal of Abnormal and Social Psychology, 65,* 121–128.

Schacter, D. L. (1987). Implicit memory: History and current status. *Journal of Experimental Psychology: Learning, Memory, and Cognition, 14,* 501–518.

Schaefer, M. T., & Olson, D. H. (1981). Assessing intimacy: The PIR Inventory. *Journal of Marital and Family Therapy, 7,* 47–60.

Scheier, M. F., & Carver, C. S. (1977). Self-focused attention and the experience of emotion: Attraction, repulsion, elation, and depression. *Journal of Personality and Social Psychology, 35,* 625–636.

Scheier, M. F., & Carver, C. S. (1993). On the power of positive thinking: The benefits of being optimistic. *Current Directions in Psychological Science, 2,* 26–30.

Scheier, M. F., Matthews, K. A., Owens, J. F., Magovern, G. J., Sr., Lefebvre, R. C., Abbott, R. A., & Carver, C. S. (1989). Dispositional optimism and recovery from coronary artery bypass surgery: The beneficial effects on physical and psychological well-being. *Journal of Personality and Social Psychology, 57,* 1024–1040.

Scheier, M. F., Weintraub, J. K., & Carver, C. S. (1986). Coping with stress: Divergent strategies of optimists and pessimists. *Journal of Personality and Social Psychology, 51,* 1257–1264.

Schein, E. H. (1956). The Chinese indoctrination program for prisoners of war: A study of attempted "brainwashing." *Psychiatry, 19,* 149–172.

Schein, E. H. (1961). *Coercive persuasion.* New York: Norton.

Scher, S. J., & Cooper, J. (1989). Motivational basis of dissonance: The singular role of behavioral consequences. *Journal of Personality and Social Psychology, 56,* 899–906.

Schifter, D. E., & Ajzen, I. (1985). Intention, perceived control, and weight loss: An application of the theory of planned behavior. *Journal of Personality and Social Psychology, 49,* 843–851.

Schlenker, B. R. (1975). Liking for a group following an initiation: Impression management or dissonance reduction? *Sociometry, 38,* 99–118.

Schlenker, B. R. (1980). *Impression management: The self-concept, social identity, and interpersonal relations.* Pacific Grove, CA: Brooks/Cole.

Schlenker, B. R. (1985a). Identity and self-identification. In B. R. Schlenker (Ed.), *The self and social life* (pp. 65–99). New York: McGraw-Hill.

Schlenker, B. R. (Ed.). (1985b). *The self and social life.* New York: McGraw-Hill.

Schlenker, B. R., & Forsyth, D. R. (1977). On the ethics of psychological research. *Journal of Experimental Social Psychology, 13,* 369–396.

Schlenker, B. R., Forsyth, D. R., Leary, M. R., & Miller, R. S. (1980). A self-presentational analysis of the effects of incentives on attitude change following counterattitudinal behavior. *Journal of Personality and Social Psychology, 39,* 553–577.

Schlenker, B. R., & Leary, M. R. (1982a). Audience's reactions to self-enhancing, self-denigrating, and accurate self-presentations. *Journal of Experimental Social Psychology, 18,* 89–104.

Schlenker, B. R., & Leary, M. R. (1982b). Social anxiety and self-presentation: A conceptualization and model. *Psychological Bulletin, 92,* 641–669.

Schlenker, B. R., & Miller, R. S. (1977). Egocentrism in groups: Self-serving biases or logical information processing? *Journal of Personality and Social Psychology, 35,* 755–764.

Schlenker, B. R., Nacci, P., Helm, B., & Tedeschi, J. T. (1976). Reactions to coercive and reward power: The effects of switching influence modes on target compliance. *Sociometry, 39,* 316–323.

Schlenker, B. R., & Riess, M. (1979). Self-presentations of attitudes following commitment to proattitudinal behavior. *Human Communication Research, 5,* 325–334.

Schlenker, B. R., & Weigold, M. F. (1990). Self-consciousness and self-presentation: Being autonomous versus appearing autonomous. *Journal of Personality and Social Psychology, 59,* 820–828.

Schlenker, B. R., & Weigold, M. F. (1992). Interpersonal processes involving impression regulation and management. *Annual Review of Psychology, 43,* 133–168.

Schlenker, B. R., Weigold, M. F., & Doherty, K. (1991). Coping with accountability: Self-identification and evaluative reckonings. In C. R. Snyder and D. R. Forsyth (Eds.), *Handbook of social and clinical psychology: The health perspective* (pp. 97–115). New York: Pergamon.

Schlenker, B. R., Weigold, M. F., & Hallam, J. R. (1990). Self-serving attributions in social context: Effects of self-esteem and social pressure. *Journal of Personality and Social Psychology, 58,* 855–863.

Schlesinger, A. M., Jr. (1965). *A thousand days.* Boston: Houghton Mifflin.

Schmidt, G., & Weiner, B. (1988). An attribution-affect-action theory of behavior: Replications of judgments of help-giving. *Personality and Social Psychology Bulletin, 14,* 610–621.

Schmidt, N., & Sermat, V. (1983). Measuring loneliness in different relationships. *Journal of Personality and Social Psychology, 44,* 1038–1047.

Schmitt, B. H., Dube, L., & Leclerc, F. (1992). Intrusions into waiting lines: Does the queue constitute a social system? *Journal of Personality and Social Psychology, 63,* 806–815.

Schneekloth, L. H. (1987). Advances in practice in environment, behavior, and design. In E. Zube & G. T. More (Eds.), *Advances in environment, behavior, and design* (Vol. 1, pp. 307–334). New York: Plenum.

Schneider, D. J. (1991). Social cognition. *Annual Review of Psychology, 42,* 527–561.

Schneider, D. J., & Blankmeyer, B. L. (1983). Prototype salience and implicit personality theories. *Journal of Personality and Social Psychology, 44,* 712–722.

Schneider, D. J., Hastorf, A. H., & Ellsworth, P. C. (1979). *Person perception* (2nd ed.). Reading, MA: Addison-Wesley.

Schneider, D. J., & Miller, R. S. (1975). The effects of enthusiasm and quality of arguments on attitude attribution. *Journal of Personality, 43,* 693–708.

Schofield, J. W. (1978). School desegregation and intergroup relations. In D. Bar-Tal & L. Saxe (Eds.), *The social psychology of education.* Washington, DC: Halsted.

Schofield, J. W. (1979). The impact of positively structured contact on intergroup behavior: Does it last under adverse conditions? *Social Psychology Quarterly, 42,* 280–284.

Schofield, J. W., & Sagar, H. A. (1977). Peer interaction patterns in an integrated middle school. *Sociometry, 40,* 130–138.

Schönbach, P. A. (1980). A category system for account phrases. *European Journal of Social Psychology, 10,* 195–200.

Schopler, J., Insko, C. A., Graetz, K. A., Drigotas, S., Smith, V. A., & Dahl, K. (1993). Individual-group discontinuity: Further evidence for mediation by fear and greed. *Personality and Social Psychology Bulletin, 19,* 419–431.

Schriesheim, C. A., Bannister, B. D., & Money, W. H. (1979). Psychometric properties of the LPC Scale: An extension of Rice's review. *Academy of Management Review, 4,* 287–290.

Schriesheim, C. A., & Kerr, S. (1977). Theories and measures of leadership: A critical appraisal of current and future directions. In J. G. Hunt & L. L. Larson (Eds.), *Leadership: The cutting edge.* Carbondale: Southern Illinois University Press.

Schroeder, D. A., Dovidio, J. F., Sibicky, M. E., Matthews, L. L., & Allen, J. L. (1988). Empathy and helping behavior: Egoism or altruism? *Journal of Experimental Social Psychology, 24,* 333–353.

Schul, Y. (1983). Integration and abstraction in impression formation. *Journal of Personality and Social Psychology, 44,* 45–54.

Schultz, R., & Decker, S. (1985). Long-term adjustment to physical disability. *Journal of Personality and Social Psychology, 48,* 1162–1172.

Schulz, R., & Hanusa, B. H. (1978). Longer-term effects of predictability and control enhancing interventions: Findings and ethical issues. *Journal of Personality and Social Psychology, 36,* 1194–1201.

Schuman, H., Bobo, L. D., & Krysan, M. (1992). Authoritarianism in the general population: The education interaction hypothesis. *Social Psychology Quarterly, 55,* 379–387.

Schuman, H., Steeh, C., & Bobo, L. (1985). *Racial attitudes in America: Trends and interpretations.* Cambridge, MA: Harvard University Press.

Schunk, D. H. (1984). Self-efficacy perspective on achievement behavior. *Educational Psychologist, 19,* 48–58.

Schutte, N., Malouff, J., Lawrence, E., Glazer, K., & Cabrales, E. (1992). Creation and validation of a scale measuring perceived control over the institutional environment. *Environment and Behavior, 24,* 366–380.

Schwartz, B., & Barsky, S. F. (1977). The home advantage. *Social Forces, 55,* 641–661.

Schwartz, S. H. (1968). Awareness of consequences and the influence of moral norms on interpersonal behavior. *Sociometry, 31,* 355–369.

Schwartz, S. H. (1970). Elicitation of moral obligation and self-sacrificing behavior. *Journal of Personality and Social Psychology, 15,* 283–293.

Schwartz, S. H. (1974). Awareness of interpersonal consequences, responsibility denial and volunteering. *Journal of Personality and Social Psychology, 30,* 57–63.

Schwartz, S. H. (1977). Normative influences on altruism. In L. Berkowitz (Ed.), *Advances in experimental social psychology* (Vol. 10). New York: Academic Press.

Schwartz, S. H., & Clausen, G. T. (1970). Responsibility, norms, and helping in an emergency. *Journal of Personality and Social Psychology, 16,* 299–310.

Schwartz, S. H., & Fleishman, J. A. (1978). Personal norms and the mediation of legitimacy effects on helping. *Social Psychology, 41,* 306–315.

Schwartz, S. H., & Gottlieb, A. (1976). Bystander reactions to a violent theft: Crime in Jerusalem. *Journal of Personality and Social Psychology, 34,* 1188–1199.

Schwartz, S. H., & Gottlieb, A. (1980). Bystander anonymity and reactions to emergencies. *Journal of Personality and Social Psychology, 39,* 418–430.

Schwartz, S. H., & Howard, J. A. (1980). Explanations for the moderating effect of responsibility denial on the personal norms-behavior relationship. *Social Psychology Quarterly, 43,* 441–446.

Schwartz, S. H., & Howard, J. A. (1981). A normative decision making model of altruism. In J. P. Rushton & R. M. Sorrentino (Eds.),

Altruism and helping behavior. Hillsdale, NJ: Erlbaum.

Schwartz, S. H., & Howard, J. A. (1982). Normative decision making and altruism. In V. J. Derlega & J. Grzelak (Eds.), *Cooperation and helping behavior.* New York: Academic Press.

Schwarz, N., Bless, H., & Bohner, G. (1991). Mood and persuasion: Affective states influence the processing of persuasive communications. In M. P. Zanna (Ed.), *Advances in experimental social psychology* (Vol. 24, pp. 161–199). Orlando, FL: Academic Press.

Schwarzwald, J., Amir, Y., & Crain, R. L. (1992). Long-term effects of school desegregation experiences on interpersonal relations in the Israeli Defense Forces. *Personality and Social Psychology Bulletin, 18,* 357–368.

Scott, J. A. (1984). Comfort and seating distance in living rooms: The relationship of interactants and topic of conversation. *Environment and Behavior, 16,* 35–54.

Scott, W. A. (1968). Attitude measurement. In G. Lindzey & E. Aronson (Eds.), *The handbook of social psychology* (2nd ed., Vol. 2, pp. 204–273). Reading, MA: Addison-Wesley.

Scully, D., & Marolla, J. (1984). Convicted rapists' vocabulary of motive: Excuses and justifications. *Social Problems, 31,* 530–544.

Sears, D. (1988). Symbolic racism. In P. A. Katz & D. A. Taylor (Eds.), *Eliminating racism: Profiles in controversy* (pp. 53–84). New York: Plenum.

Sears D. O., & Kinder, D. R. (1985). Whites' opposition to busing: On conceptualizing and operationalizing group conflict. *Journal of Personality and Social Psychology, 48,* 1141–1147.

Seashore, S. E. (1954). *Group cohesiveness in the industrial work group.* Ann Arbor, MI: Institute for Social Research.

Sechrest, L., & Belew, J. (1983). Nonreactive measures of social attitudes. In L. Bickman (Ed.), *Applied social psychology annual* (Vol. 4, pp. 23–63). Newbury Park, CA: Sage.

Sechrest, L., & Figueredo, A. J. (1993). Program evaluation. *Annual Review of Psychology, 44,* 645–674.

Secord, P. F., & Backman, C. W. (1961). Personality theory and the problem of stability and change in individual behavior: An interpersonal approach. *Psychological Review, 68,* 21–32.

Sedgwick, J. (1982). *Night vision.* New York: Simon & Schuster.

Sedikides, C., & Ostrom, T. M. (1990). Persons as privileged categories: A rejoinder to Mullen and Copper. *Social Cognition, 8,* 229–240.

Sedikides, C., & Skowronski, J. J. (1991). The law of cognitive structure activation. *Psychological Inquiry, 2,* 169–184.

Segal, H. A. (1954). Initial psychiatric findings of recently repatriated prisoners of war. *American Journal of Psychiatry, 111,* 358–363.

Segal, M. W. (1974). Alphabet and attraction: An unobtrusive measure of the effect of propinquity in a field setting. *Journal of Personality and Social Psychology, 30,* 654–657.

Segal, M. W. (1979). Varieties of interpersonal attraction and their interrelationships in natural groups. *Social Psychology Quarterly, 42,* 253–261.

Segall, M. H. (1988). Cultural roots of aggressive behavior. In M. H. Bond (Ed.), *The cross-cultural challenge to social psychology* (pp. 208–217). Newbury Park, CA: Sage.

Seidman, S. A. (1992). An investigation of sex-role stereotyping in music videos. *Journal of Broadcasting and Electronic Media, 36,* 209–216.

Seldes, G. (1960). *The great quotations.* New York: Stuart.

Self, C. A., & Rogers, R. W. (1990). Coping with threats to health: Effects of persuasive appeals on depressed, normal, and antisocial personalities. *Journal of Behavioral Medicine, 13,* 343–357.

Self, E. A. (1990). Situational influence on self-handicapping. In R. L. Higgins, C. R. Snyder, & S. Berglas, *Self-handicapping: The paradox that isn't* (pp. 37–68). New York: Plenum.

Seligman, M. E. P., & Maier, S. F. (1967). Failure to escape traumatic shock. *Journal of Experimental Psychology, 74,* 1–9.

Senneker, P., & Hendrick, C. (1983). Androgyny and helping behavior. *Journal of Personality and Social Psychology, 45,* 916–925.

Seta, C. E., & Seta, J. J. (1992). Increments and decrements in mean arterial pressure as a function of audience composition: An averaging and summation analysis. *Personality and Social Psychology Bulletin, 18,* 173–181.

Seta, J. J., Crisson, J. E., Seta, C. E., & Wang, M. A. (1989). Task performance and perceptions of anxiety: Averaging and summation in an evaluative setting. *Journal of Personality and Social Psychology, 56,* 387–396.

Seta, J. J., Wang, M. A., Crisson, J. E., & Seta, C. E. (1989). Audience composition and felt anxiety: Impact of averaging and summation. *Basic and Applied Social Psychology, 10,* 57–72.

Shaffer, D. R., Rogel, M., & Hendrick, D. (1975). Intervention in the library: The effect of increased responsibility on bystanders' willingness to prevent a theft. *Journal of Applied Social Psychology, 5,* 303–319.

Shaffer, D. R., & Sadowski, C. (1975). This table is mine: Respect for marked barroom tables as a function of gender of spatial marker and desirability of locale. *Sociometry, 38,* 408–419.

Shanteau, J. (1992). Competence in experts: The role of task characteristics. *Organizational Behavior and Human Performance, 53,* 252–266.

Shanteau, J., & Nagy, G. F. (1979). Probability of acceptance in dating choice. *Journal of Personality and Social Psychology, 37,* 522–533.

Sharpe, D., Adair, J. G., & Roese, N. J. (1992). Twenty years of deception research: A decline in subjects' trust? *Personality and Social Psychology Bulletin, 18,* 585–590.

Shaver, K. G. (1970a). Redress and conscientiousness in the attribution of responsibility for accidents. *Journal of Experimental Social Psychology, 6,* 100–110.

Shaver, K. G. (1970b). Defensive attributions: Effects of severity and relevance on the responsibility assigned for an accident. *Journal of Personality and Social Psychology, 14,* 101–113.

Shaver, P., & Buhrmester, D. (1983). Loneliness, sex-role orientation, and group life: A social needs perspective. In P. B. Paulus (Ed.), *Basic group processes* (pp. 259–288). New York: Springer-Verlag.

Shaver, P., Schwartz, J., Kirson, D., & O'Connor, C. (1987). Emotion knowledge: Further exploration of a prototype approach. *Journal of Personality and Social Psychology, 52,* 1061–1086.

Shavitt, S. (1989). Operationalizing functional theories of attitude. In A. R. Pratkanis, S. J. Breckler, & A. G. Greenwald (Eds.), *Attitude structure and function* (pp. 311–337). Hillsdale, NJ: Erlbaum.

Shavitt, S., & Fazio, R. H. (1991). Effects of attribute salience on the consistency between attitudes and behavior predictions. *Personality and Social Psychology Bulletin, 17,* 507–516.

Shaw, M. E. (1978). Communication networks fourteen years later. In L. Berkowitz (Ed.), *Group processes.* New York: Academic Press.

Shaw, M. E. (1981). *Group dynamics: The psychology of small group behavior* (3rd ed.). New York: McGraw-Hill.

Shaw, M. E., & Sulzer, J. L. (1964). An empirical test of Heider's levels in attribution of responsibility. *Journal of Abnormal and Social Psychology, 69,* 39–46.

Sheatsley, P. B., & Feldman, J. J. (1964). The assassination of President Kennedy: A preliminary report on public attitudes and behavior. *Public Opinion Quarterly, 28,* 189–215.

Shedler, J., & Manis, M. (1986). Can the availability heuristic explain vividness effects. *Journal of Personality and Social Psychology, 51,* 26–36.

Sheley, J. F., Smith, M. D., & Wright, J. D. (1992, Nov./Dec.). Kids, guns, and killing fields. *Society, 30,* pp. 84–89.

Shell, R. M., & Eisenberg, N. (1992). A developmental model of recipients' reactions to aid. *Psychological Bulletin, 111,* 413–433.

Sheppard, B. H., Hartwick, J., & Warshaw, P. R. (1988). A theory of reasoned action: A meta-analysis of past research with recommendations for modifications and future research. *Journal of Consumer Research, 15,* 325–343.

Shepperd, J. A. (1993). Productivity loss in performance groups: A motivational analysis. *Psychological Bulletin, 113,* 67–81.

Shepperd, J. A., & Arkin, R. M. (1989). Determinants of self-handicapping: Task importance and the absence of environmental handicaps. *Personality and Social Psychology Bulletin, 15,* 101–112.

Shepperd, J. A., & Arkin, R. M. (1991). Behavioral other-enhancement: Strategically obscuring the link between performance and evaluation. *Journal of Personality and Social Psychology, 60,* 79–88.

Shepperd, J. A., & Wright, R. A. (1989). Individual contributions to a collective effort: An incentive analysis. *Personality and Social Psychology Bulletin, 15,* 141–149.

Sherif, C. W., Sherif, M., & Nebergall, R. E. (1965). *Attitude and attitude change: The social judgment approach.* Philadelphia: Saunders.

Sherif, M. (1936). *The psychology of social norms.* New York: Harper & Row.

Sherif, M. (1966). *In common predicament: Social psychology of intergroup conflict and cooperation.* Boston: Houghton Mifflin.

Sherif, M., Harvey, O. J., White, B. J., Hood, W. E., & Sherif, C. W. (1961). *Intergroup conflict and cooperation: The Robber's Cave experiment.* Norman, OK: Institute of Group Relations.

Sherif, M., & Hovland, C. I. (1961). *Social judgment: Assimilation and contrast effects in communication and attitude change.* New Haven, CT: Yale University Press.

Sherif, M., & Sherif, C. W. (1967). Attitude as the individual's own categories: The social judgment-involvement approach to attitude and attitude change. In C. W. Sherif & M. Sherif (Eds.), *Attitude, ego-involvement, and change.* New York: Wiley.

Sherman, L. W., & Berk, R. A. (1984). The specific deterrent effects of arrest for domestic assault. *American Sociological Review, 49,* 261–272.

Sherman, P. (1980). The limits of ground squirrel nepotism. In G. Barlow & J. Silverberg (Eds.), *Sociobiology: Beyond nature/nurture?* Boulder, CO: Westview.

Sherman, S. J., Judd, C. M., & Park, B. (1989). Social cognition. *Annual Review of Psychology, 40,* 281–326.

Sherman, S. J., Mackie, D. M., & Driscoll, D. M. (1990). Priming and the differential use of dimensions in evaluation. *Personality and Social Psychology Bulletin, 16,* 405–418.

Sherman, S. J., Presson, C. C., Chassin, L., Bensenberg, M., Corty, E., & Olshavsky, R. W. (1982). Smoking intentions in adolescents: Direct experience and predictability. *Personality and Social Psychology Bulletin, 8,* 376–383.

Sherrod, D. (1989). The influence of gender on same-sex friendships. In C. Hendrick (Ed.), *Review of personality and social psychology* (Vol. 10, pp. 164–186). Newbury Park, CA: Sage.

Shiffrin, R. M., & Schneider, W. (1977). Controlled and automatic human information processing: II. Perceptual learning, automatic attending, and general theory. *Psychological Review, 84,* 127–190.

Shotland, R. L. (1985). When bystanders just stand by. *Psychology Today, 19*(6), pp. 50–55.

Shotland, R. L. (1992). A theory of the causes of courtship rape: Part 2. *Journal of Social Issues, 48*(1), 127–144.

Shotland, R. L., & Heinold, W. D. (1985). Bystander response to arterial bleeding: Helping skills, the decision-making process, and differentiating the helping responses. *Journal of Personality and Social Psychology, 49,* 347–356.

Shotland, R. L., & Huston, T. L. (1979). Emergencies: What are they and do they influence bystanders to intervene? *Journal of Personality and Social Psychology, 37,* 1822–1824.

Shrauger, J. S. (1975). Responses to evaluation as a function of initial self-perceptions. *Psychological Bulletin, 82,* 581–596.

Shrauger, J. S., & Schoeneman, T. J. (1979). Symbolic interactionist view of the self-concept: Through the looking-glass darkly. *Psychological Bulletin, 86,* 549–573.

Shure, G. H., Meeker, R. J., & Hansford, E. A. (1965). The effectiveness of pacifist strategies in bargaining games. *Journal of Conflict Resolution, 9,* 106–117.

Siegal, M. (1987). Are sons and daughters treated more differently by fathers than by mothers? *Developmental Review, 7,* 183–209.

Siem, F. M., & Spence, J. T. (1986). Gender-related traits and helping behaviors. *Journal of Personality and Social Psychology, 51,* 615–621.

Sigall, H., & Aronson, E. (1967). Opinion change and the gain-loss model of interpersonal attraction. *Journal of Experimental Social Psychology, 3,* 178–188.

Sigall, H., & Page, R. (1971). Current stereotypes: A little fading, a little faking. *Journal of Personality and Social Psychology, 18,* 247–255.

Sigelman, L., & Welch, S. (1991). *Black Americans' views of racial inequality: The dream deferred.* New York: Cambridge University Press.

Signorielli, N. (1989). Television and conceptions about sex roles: Maintaining conventionality and the status quo. *Sex Roles, 21,* 341–360.

Signorielli, N., Gross, L., & Morgan, M. (1982). Violence in television programs: Ten years later. In D. Pearl, L. Bouthilet, & J. Lazar (Eds.), *Television and behavior, ten years of scientific progress and implications for the eighties.* Rockville, MD: NIMH.

Silverman, I., & Shaw, M. E. (1973). Effects of sudden mass desegregation on interracial interaction and attitudes in one southern city. *Journal of Social Issues, 29*(4), 133–142.

Silverthorne, C., Mickelwright, J., O'Donnell, M., & Gibson, R. (1976). Attribution of personal characteristics as a function of the degree of touch on initial contact and sex. *Sex Roles, 2,* 185–193.

Simon, B., & Brown, R. (1987). Perceived intragroup homogeneity in minority majority contexts. *Journal of Personality and Social Psychology, 53,* 703–711.

Simon, B., Glässner-Bayerl, B., & Stratenwerth, I. (1991). Stereotyping and self-stereotyping in a natural intergroup context: The case of heterosexual and homosexual men. *Social Psychology Quarterly, 54,* 252–266.

Simonton, D. K. (1980). Land battles, generals, and armies: Individual and social determinants of victory and casualties. *Journal of Personality and Social Psychology, 38,* 110–119.

Simonton, D. K. (1985). Intelligence and personal influence in groups: Four nonlinear models. *Psychological Review, 92,* 532–547.

Simpson, G. E., & Yinger, J. M. (1985). *Racial and cultural minorities: An analysis of prejudice and discrimination* (5th ed.). New York: Plenum.

Simpson, J. A. (1990). Influence of attachment styles on romantic relationships. *Journal of Personality and Social Psychology, 59,* 971–980.

Simpson, J. A., & Gangestad, S. W. (1992). Sociosexuality and romantic partner choice. *Journal of Personality, 60,* 31–52.

Simpson, J. A., Rholes, W. S., & Nelligan, J. S. (1992). Support seeking and support giving within couples in an anxiety-provoking situation: The role of attachment styles. *Journal of Personality and Social Psychology, 62,* 434–446.

Sinclair, R. C., Mark, M. M., & Shotland, R. L. (1987). Construct accessibility and generalizability across response categories. *Personality and Social Psychology Bulletin, 13,* 239–252.

Sinclair, W. J. (1909). *Semmelweis: His life and his doctrine.* Manchester, England: Manchester University Press.

Singer, D. G., & Singer, J. L. (1980). *Television, imagination, and aggression: A study of preschoolers.* Hillsdale, NJ: Erlbaum.

Singer, E. (1990). Reference groups and social evaluations. In M. Rosenberg & R. H. Turner (Eds.), *Social psychology: Sociological perspectives* (pp. 66–93). New Brunswick, NJ: Transaction Publishers.

Sistrunk, F., & McDavid, J. W. (1971). Sex variable in conforming behavior. *Journal of Personality and Social Psychology, 17,* 200–207.

Sivacek, J., & Crano, W. D. (1982). Vested interest as a moderator of attitude-behavior consistency. *Journal of Personality and Social Psychology, 43,* 210–221.

Skinner, B. F. (1971). *Beyond freedom and dignity.* New York: Knopf.

Skinner, B. F. (1975). The steep and thorny way to a science of behavior. *American Psychologist, 30,* 42–49.

Skowronski, J. J., Betz, A. L., Thompson, C. P., & Shannon, L. (1991). Social memory in everyday life: Recall of self-events and other-events. *Journal of Personality and Social Psychology, 60,* 831–843.

Skowronski, J. J., & Carlston, D. E. (1989). Social judgment and social memory: The role of cue diagnosticity in negativity, positivity, and extremity biases. *Journal of Personality and Social Psychology, 52,* 689–699.

Skrypnek, B. J., & Snyder, M. (1982). On the self-perpetuating nature of stereotypes about women and men. *Journal of Experimental Social Psychology, 18,* 277–291.

Slater, B., & Leighton, F. S. (1983). *Stranger in my bed.* New York: Arbor House.

Slater, P. E. (1955). Role differentiation in small groups. *American Sociological Review, 20,* 300–310.

Sloan, L. R., & Ostrom, T. M. (1974). Amount of information and interpersonal judgment. *Journal of Personality and Social Psychology, 29,* 23–29.

Slovic, P., Fischhoff, B., & Lichtenstein, S. C. (1977). Behavioral decision theory. *Annual Review of Psychology, 28,* 1–39.

Slovic, P., Fischhoff, B., & Lichtenstein, S. (1982). Facts versus fears: Understanding perceived risk. In D. Kahneman, P. Slovic, & A. Tversky (Eds.), *Judgment under uncertainty: Heuristics and biases* (pp. 463–489). New York: Cambridge University Press.

Slusher, M. P., & Anderson, C. A. (1987). Belief perseverance and self-defeating behavior. In R. C. Curtis (Ed.), *Self-defeating behaviors: Experimental research, clinical impressions, and practical implications* (pp. 11–40). New York: Plenum.

Smart, R. (1965). Social-group membership, leadership, and birth order. *Journal of Social Psychology, 67,* 221–225.

Smetana, J. G., & Adler, N. E. (1980). Fishbein's value × expectancy model: An examination of some assumptions. *Personality and Social Psychology Bulletin, 6,* 89–96.

Smith, C. A. (1991). The self, appraisal, and coping. In C. R. Snyder & D. R. Forsyth (Eds.), *Handbook of social and clinical psychology: The health perspective* (pp. 116–137). New York: Pergamon.

Smith, E. R., & Miller, F. D. (1978). Limits on perception of cognitive processes: A reply to Nisbett and Wilson. *Psychological Review, 85,* 355–362.

Smith, E. R., Stewart, T. L., & Buttram, R. T. (1992). Inferring a trait from a behavior has long-term, highly specific effects. *Journal of Personality and Social Psychology, 62,* 753–759.

Smith, J. F., & Kida, T. (1991). Heuristics and biases: Expertise and task realism in auditing. *Psychological Bulletin, 109,* 472–489.

Smith, K. D., Keating, J. P., & Stotland, E. (1989). Altruism revisited: The effect of denying feedback of a victim's status to empathic witnesses. *Journal of Personality and Social Psychology, 57,* 641–650.

Smith, M. B., Bruner, J. S., & White, R. W. (1956). *Opinions and personality.* New York: Wiley.

Smith, P. B. (1990). Leadership and management. In R. Brown (Ed.), *The Marshall Cavendish encyclopedia of personal relationships: Human behavior, How groups work* (Vol. 15, pp. 1844–1853). North Bellmore, NY: Marshall Cavendish Corporation.

Smith, R. J., & Knowles, E. S. (1978). Attributional consequences of personal space invasions. *Personality and Social Psychology Bulletin, 4,* 429–433.

Smith, S. (1984). Groupthink and the hostage rescue mission. *British Journal of Political Science, 15,* 117–126.

Smith, S. M., & Shaffer, D. R. (1991). Celerity and cajolery: Rapid speech may promote or inhibit persuasion through its impact on message elaboration. *Personality and Social Psychology Bulletin, 17,* 663–669.

Smith, T. W., & Frohm, K. D. (1985). What's so unhealthy about hostility? Construct validity and psychosocial correlates of the Cook and Medley Ho Scale. *Health Psychology, 4,* 503–520.

Smith, T. W., & Pope, M. K. (1990). Cynical hostility as a health risk: Current status and future directions. *Journal of Social Behavior and Personality, 5,* 77–88.

Smolowe, J. (1991). She said, he said. *Time, 138*(15), 36–40.

Smyth, L. D. (1982). Psychopathology as a function of neuroticism and a hypnotically implanted aggressive conflict. *Journal of Personality and Social Psychology, 43,* 555–564.

Snyder, C. R., & Forsyth, D. R. (Eds.). (1991a). *Handbook of social and clinical psychology: The health perspective.* New York: Pergamon.

Snyder, C. R., & Forsyth, D. R. (1991). Social and clinical psychology united: The health-help-health cycle. In C. R. Snyder & D. R. Forsyth (Eds.), *Handbook of social and clinical psychology: The health perspective* (pp. 3–17). New York: Pergamon.

Snyder, C. R., & Higgins, R. L. (1988). Excuses: Their effective role in the negotiation of reality. *Psychological Bulletin, 104,* 23–35.

Snyder, C. R., Irving, L. M., & Anderson, J. R. (1991). Hope and health. In C. R. Snyder & D. R. Forsyth (Eds.), *Handbook of social and clinical psychology: The health perspective* (pp. 285–305). New York: Pergamon.

Snyder, C. R., Lassegard, M., & Ford, C. E. (1986). Distancing after group success and failure: Basking in reflected glory and cutting off reflected failure. *Journal of Personality and Social Psychology, 51,* 382–388.

Snyder, C. R., Shenkel, R. J., & Lowery, C. R. (1977). Acceptance of personality interpretations: The "Barnum effect" and beyond. *Journal of Consulting and Clinical Psychology, 45,* 104–114.

Snyder, C. R., Smith, T. W., Augelli, R. W., & Ingram, R. E. (1985). On the self-serving function of social anxiety: Shyness as a self-handicapping strategy. *Journal of Personality and Social Psychology, 48,* 970–980.

Snyder, M. (1984). When belief creates reality. In L. Berkowitz (Ed.), *Advances in experimental social psychology* (Vol. 18, pp. 247–305). New York: Academic Press.

Snyder, M. (1987). *Public appearances, private realities: The psychology of self-monitoring.* New York: W. H. Freeman.

Snyder, M., & Campbell, B. H. (1982). Self-monitoring: The self in action. In J. Suls (Ed.), *Psychological perspectives on the self* (Vol. 1). Hillsdale, NJ: Erlbaum.

Snyder, M., & DeBono, K. G. (1985). Appeals to image and claims about quality: Understanding the psychology of advertising. *Journal of Personality and Social Psychology, 49,* 586–597.

Snyder, M., & DeBono, K. G. (1989). Understanding the functions of attitudes: Lessons from personality and social behavior. In A. R. Pratkanis, S. J. Breckler, & A. G. Greenwald (Eds.), *Attitude structure and function* (pp. 339–359). Hillsdale, NJ: Erlbaum.

Snyder, M., & Ickes, W. (1985). Personality and social behavior. In G. Lindzey & E. Aronson (Eds.), *Handbook of social psychology* (3rd ed., Vol. 2, pp. 883–947). New York: Random House.

Snyder, M., & Kendzierski, D. (1982). Acting on one's attitudes: Procedures for linking attitude and behavior. *Journal of Experimental Social Psychology, 18,* 165–183.

Snyder M., & Monson, T. C. (1975). Persons, situations, and the control of social behavior. *Journal of Personality and Social Psychology, 32,* 637–644.

Snyder, M., & Omoto, A. M. (1992). Volunteerism and society's response to the HIV epidemic. *Current Directions in Psychological Science, 2,* 113–116.

Snyder, M., & Swann, W. B., Jr. (1976). When actions reflect attitudes: The politics of impression management. *Journal of Personality and Social Psychology, 34,* 1034–1042.

Snyder, M., & Swann, W. B., Jr. (1978). Hypothesis-testing processes in social interaction. *Journal of Personality and Social Psychology, 36,* 1202–1212.

Snyder, M., Tanke, E. D., & Berscheid, E. (1977). Social perception and interpersonal behavior: On the self-fulfilling nature of social stereotypes. *Journal of Personality and Social Psychology, 35,* 656–666.

Snyder, M. L., & Jones, E. E. (1974). Attitude attribution when behavior is constrained. *Journal of Experimental Social Psychology, 10,* 585–600.

Solano, C. H. (1987). Loneliness and perceptions of control: General traits versus specific attributions. *Journal of Social Behavior and Personality, 2,* 201–214.

Solano, C. H., Batten, P. G., & Parish, E. A. (1982). Loneliness and patterns of self-disclosure. *Journal of Personality and Social Psychology, 43,* 524–531.

Solomon, D., Watson, M., Delucchi, K. L., Schaps, E., & Battistich, V. (1988). Enhancing children's prosocial behavior in the classroom. *American Educational Research Journal, 25,* 527–554.

Solomon, R. (1980). The opponent-process theory of acquired motivation: The costs of pleasure and the benefits of pain. *American Psychologist, 35,* 691–712.

Solomon, R., & Corbit, J. D. (1974). An opponent-process theory of motivation: I. Temporal dynamics of affect. *Psychological Review, 81,* 119–145.

Solomon, S., Greenberg, J., & Pyszczynski, T. (1991). A terror management theory of social behavior: The psychological functions of self-esteem and cultural worldviews. In M. P. Zanna (Ed.), *Advances in experimental social psychology* (Vol. 24, pp. 93–159). Orlando, FL: Academic Press.

Solomon, Z., Mikulincer, M., & Avitzur, E. (1988). Coping, locus of control, social support, and combat-related posttraumatic stress disorder: A prospective study. *Journal of Personality and Social Psychology, 55,* 279–285.

Solso, R. L. (1991). *Cognitive psychology* (3rd ed.). Needham Heights, MA: Allyn & Bacon.

SOMMER, R. (1969). *Personal space: The behavioral basis of design.* Englewood Cliffs, NJ: Prentice-Hall.

SOMMER, R. (1972). *Design awareness.* New York: Rinehart Press.

SOMMER, R., & BECKER, F. D. (1969). Territorial defense and the good neighbor. *Journal of Personality and Social Psychology, 11,* 85–92.

SORRENTINO, R. M., & BOUTILLIER, R. G. (1975). The effect of quantity and quality of verbal interaction on ratings of leadership ability. *Journal of Experimental Social Psychology, 11,* 403–411.

SPACAPAN, S., & OSKAMP, S. (Eds.). (1992). *Helping and being helped: Naturalistic studies.* Newbury Park, CA: Sage.

SPACAPAN, S., & THOMPSON, S. C. (Eds.). (1991). Perceived control in vulnerable populations. *Journal of Social Issues, 47*(4), 1–196.

SPENCE, J. T., DEAUX, K., & HELMREICH, R. L. (1985). Sex roles in contemporary American society. In G. Lindzey & E. Aronson (Eds.), *Handbook of social psychology* (3rd ed., Vol. 2, pp. 149–178). New York: Random House.

SPITZBERG, B. H., & HURT, H. T. (1987). The relationship of interpersonal competence and skills to reported loneliness across time. *Journal of Social Behavior and Personality, 2,* 157–172.

SPRECHER, S. (1992a). How men and women expect to feel and behave in response to inequity in close relationships. *Social Psychology Quarterly, 55,* 57–69.

SPRECHER, S. (1992b). Social exchange perspectives to the dissolution of close relationships. In T. L. Orbuch (Ed.), *Close relationship loss: Theoretical approaches* (pp. 47–66). New York: Springer-Verlag.

SPRECHER, S., & SCHWARTZ, P. (1992). Equity and balance in the exchange of contributions in close relationships. In M. J. Lerner & G. Mikula (Eds.), *Entitlement and the affectional bond.* New York: Plenum.

SRULL, T. K. (1983). Organizational and retrieval processes in person memory: An examination of processing objectives, presentation format, and possible role of self-generated retrieval cues. *Journal of Personality and Social Psychology, 44,* 1157–1170.

SRULL, T. K., & WYER, R. S., JR. (1980). Category accessibility and social perception: Some implications for the study of person memory and interpersonal judgments. *Journal of Personality and Social Psychology, 38,* 841–856.

SRULL T. K., & WYER, R. S., JR. (1989). Person memory and judgment. *Psychological Review, 96,* 58–83.

STAATS, A. W., & STAATS, C. K. (1958). Attitudes established by classical condition. *Journal of Abnormal and Social Psychology, 57,* 37–40.

STANG, D. J. (1976). Group size effects on conformity. *Journal of Social Psychology, 98,* 175–181.

STANGOR, C., LYNCH, L., DUAN, C., & GLASS, B. (1992). Categorization of individuals on the basis of multiple social features. *Journal of Personality and Social Psychology, 62,* 207–218.

STANGOR, C., & MCMILLAN, D. (1992). Memory for expectancy-congruent and expectancy-incongruent information: A review of the social and social developmental literatures. *Psychological Bulletin, 111,* 42–61.

STANOVICH, K. E. (1992). *How to think straight about psychology.* Boston: Scott, Foresman.

STARR, H. (1983). The Kissinger years: Studying individuals and foreign policy. In D. Caldwell (Ed.), *Henry Kissinger: His personality and policies* (pp. 3–23). Durham, NC: Duke University Press.

STARR, H. (1984). *Henry Kissinger: Perceptions of international politics.* Lexington: University Press of Kentucky.

STASSER, G., KERR, N. L., & DAVIS, J. H. (1989). Influence processes and consensus models in decision-making groups. In P. B. Paulus (Ed.), *Psychology of group influence* (2nd ed.). Hillsdale, NJ: Erlbaum.

STASSON, M. F., & DAVIS, J. H. (1989). The relative effects of the number of arguments, the number of argument sources, and the number of opinion positions in group-mediated opinion change. *British Journal of Social Psychology, 28,* 251–262.

STASSON, M. F., & FISHBEIN, M. (1990). The relation between perceived risk and preventive actions: A within subject analysis of perceived driving risk and intentions to wear seatbelts. *Journal of Applied Social Psychology, 20,* 1541–1557.

Statistical Abstract of the U.S. (1992). Bureau of Statistics, Treasury Office. Washington, DC: General Printing Office.

STAUB, E. (1974). Helping a distressed person: Social, personality, and stimulus determinants. In L. Berkowitz (Ed.), *Advances in experimental social psychology* (Vol. 7). New York: Academic Press.

STAUB, E. (Ed.). (1978). *Positive social behavior and morality: Social and personal influences* (Vol. 1). New York: Academic Press.

STAUB, M. (1989). *The roots of evil: The origins of genocide and other group violence.* New York: Cambridge University Press.

STAUB, M. (1990). Moral exclusion, personal goal theory, and extreme destructiveness. *Journal of Social Issues, 46*(1), 47–64.

STEELE, C. M. (1975). Name-calling and compliance. *Journal of Personality and Social Psychology, 31,* 361–369.

STEELE, C. M. (1988). The psychology of self-affirmation: Sustaining the integrity of the self. In L. Berkowitz (Ed.), *Advances in experimental social psychology* (Vol. 21, pp. 261–302). San Diego, CA: Academic Press.

STEELE, C. M., CRITCHLOW, B., & LIU, T. J. (1985). Alcohol and social behavior: II. The helpful drunkard. *Journal of Personality and Social Psychology, 48,* 35–46.

STEELE, C. M., HOPP, H., & GONZALES, J. (1986). Dissonance and the lab coat: Self-affirmation and the free choice paradigm. Unpublished manuscript cited in Steele, C. M. (1988). The psychology of self-affirmation: Sustaining the integrity of the self. In L. Berkowitz (Ed.), *Advances in experimental social psychology* (Vol. 21, pp. 261–302). San Diego, CA: Academic Press.

STEELE, C. M., & LIU, T. J. (1981). Making the dissonance act unreflective of the self: Dissonance avoidance and the expectancy of a value-affirming response. *Personality and Social Psychology Bulletin, 7,* 393–397.

STEELE, C. M., & LIU, T. J. (1983). Dissonance processes as self-affirmation. *Journal of Personality and Social Psychology, 45,* 5–19.

STEELE, C. M., SOUTHWICK, L., & CRITCHLOW, B. (1981). Dissonance and alcohol: Drinking your troubles away. *Journal of Personality and Social Psychology, 41,* 831–846.

STEELE, S. (1990). *The content of our character.* New York: St. Martin's Press.

STEINER, I. D. (1970). Perceived freedom. In L. Berkowitz (Ed.), *Advances in experimental social psychology* (Vol. 5). New York: Academic Press.

STEINER, I. D. (1972). *Group process and productivity.* New York: Academic Press.

STEINGLASS, P., & GERRITY, E. (1990). Natural disasters and post-traumatic stress disorder: Short-term vs. long-term recovery in two disaster-affected communities. *Journal of Applied Social Psychology, 20,* 1746–1765.

STEPHAN, W. G. (1975). Actor vs. observer: Attributions to behavior with positive or negative outcomes and empathy for the other role. *Journal of Experimental Social Psychology, 11,* 205–214.

STEPHAN, W. G. (1985). Intergroup relations. In G. Lindzey & E. Aronson (Eds.), *Handbook of social psychology* (3rd ed., Vol. 2). New York: Random House.

STEPHAN, W. G., & ROSENFIELD, D. (1978). Effects of desegregation on racial attitudes. *Journal of Personality and Social Psychology, 36,* 795–804.

STEPHAN, W. G., & ROSENFIELD, D. (1982). Racial and ethnic stereotypes. In A. G. Miller (Ed.), *In the eye of the beholder: Contemporary issues in stereotyping.* New York: Praeger.

STERN, L. D., MARRS, S., MILLAR, M. G., & COLE, E. (1984). Processing time and the recall of inconsistent and consistent behaviors of individuals and groups. *Journal of Personality and Social Psychology, 47,* 253–262.

STERN, P. C. (1992). What psychology knows about energy conservation. *American Psychologist, 47,* 1224–1232.

STERNBERG, R. J. (1985). Implicit theories of intelligence, creativity, and wisdom. *Journal of Personality and Social Psychology, 49,* 607–627.

STERNBERG, R. J. (1987). Liking versus loving: A comparative evaluation of theories. *Psychological Bulletin, 102,* 331–345.

STERNBERG, R. J. (1988). Triangulating love. In R. J. Sternberg & M. L. Barnes (Eds.), *The psychology of love* (pp. 119–138). New Haven, CT: Yale University Press.

STERNBERG, R. J., & BARNES, M. (1985). Real and ideal others in romantic relationships: Is four a crowd? *Journal of Personality and Social Psychology, 49,* 1589–1596.

STERNBERG, R. J., & GRAJEK, S. (1984). The nature of love. *Journal of Personality and Social Psychology, 47,* 312–329.

Stevenson, H. W. (1991). The development of prosocial behavior in large-scale collective societies: China and Japan. In R. A. Hinde & J. Groebel (Eds.), *Cooperation and prosocial behavior* (pp. 89–105). New York: Oxford University Press.

Stier, D. S., & Hall, J. A. (1984). Gender differences in touch: An empirical and theoretical review. *Journal of Personality and Social Psychology, 47,* 440–459.

Stiff, J. B., Miller, G. R., Sleight, C., Mongeau, P., Garlick, R., & Rogan, R. (1989). Explanations for visual cue primacy in judgments of honesty and deceit. *Journal of Personality and Social Psychology, 56,* 555–564.

Stiles, W. B., Orth, J. E., Scherwitz, L., Hennrikus, D., & Vallbona, C. (1984). Role behaviors in routine medical interviews with hypertensive patients: A repertoire of verbal exchanges. *Social Psychology Quarterly, 47,* 244–254.

St. John, N. (1975). *School desegregation: Outcomes for children.* New York: Wiley.

Stogdill, R. M. (1974). *Handbook of leadership.* New York: Free Press.

Stokes, J. P. (1985). The relation of social network and individual difference variables to loneliness. *Journal of Personality and Social Psychology, 48,* 981–990.

Stokes, J. P., & Wilson, D. G. (1984). The inventory of socially supportive behaviors: Dimensionality, prediction, and gender differences. *American Journal of Community Psychology, 12,* 53–69.

Stokols, D. (1972). On the distinction between density and crowding: Some implications for future research. *Psychological Review, 79,* 275–278.

Stokols, D., & Altman, I. (Eds.). (1987). *Handbook of environmental psychology* (Vols. 1 and 2). New York: Wiley.

Stoner, J. A. F. (1961). *A comparison of individual and group decisions involving risk.* Unpublished master's thesis, Massachusetts Institute of Technology.

Storms, M. D. (1973). Videotape and the attribution process: Reversing actors' and observers' points of view. *Journal of Personality and Social Psychology, 27,* 165–175.

Storms, M. D., Denney, D. R., McCaul, K. D., & Lowery, C. R. (1979). Insomnia and attributions. In I. H. Frieze, D. Bar-Tal, & J. S. Carroll (Eds.), *New approaches to social problems: Applications of attribution theory.* San Francisco: Jossey-Bass.

Storms, M. D., & McCaul, K. D. (1976). Attribution processes and emotional exacerbation of dysfunctional behavior. In J. H. Harvey, W. J. Ickes, & R. F. Kidd (Eds.), *New directions in attribution research* (Vol. 1). Hillsdale, NJ: Erlbaum.

Storms, M. D., & Nisbett, R. E. (1970). Insomnia and the attribution process. *Journal of Personality and Social Psychology, 16,* 319–328.

Storms, M. D., & Thomas, G. C. (1977). Reactions to physical closeness. *Journal of Personality and Social Psychology, 35,* 412–418.

Strack, F., Martin, L. L., & Stepper, S. (1988). Inhibiting and facilitating conditions of the human smile: A nonobtrusive test of the facial feedback hypothesis. *Journal of Personality and Social Psychology, 54,* 768–777.

Strack, S., Carver, C. S., & Blaney, P. H. (1987). Predicting successful completion of an aftercare program following treatment for alcoholism: The role of dispositional optimism. *Journal of Personality and Social Psychology, 53,* 579–584.

Straus, M. A., & Gelles, R. J. (Eds.). (1990). *Physical violence in American families: Risk factors and adaptation to violence in 8,145 families.* New Brunswick, NJ: Transaction.

Straus, M. A., Gelles, R. J., & Steinmetz, S. (1980). *Behind closed doors: Violence in the American family.* Garden City, NY: Doubleday.

Strauss, J., & Goethals, G. R. (Eds.). (1991). *The self: Interdisciplinary approaches.* New York: Springer-Verlag.

Stricker, L. J., Messick, S., & Jackson, D. N. (1970). Conformity, anticonformity, and independence: Their dimensionality and generality. *Journal of Personality and Social Psychology, 16,* 494–507.

Strodtbeck, F. L., & Hook, L. H. (1961). The social dimensions of a twelve-man jury table. *Sociometry, 24,* 397–415.

Strodtbeck, F. L., James, R. M., & Hawkins, C. (1957). Social status in jury deliberation. *American Sociological Review, 22,* 713–719.

Strodtbeck, F. L., & Mann, R. D. (1956). Sex role differentiation in jury deliberations. *Sociometry, 19,* 3–11.

Stroebe, W., Lenkert, A., & Jonas, K. (1988). Familiarity may breed contempt: The impact of student exchange on national stereotypes and attitudes. In W. Stroebe, A. W. Kruglanski, D. Bar-Tal, & M. Hewstone (Eds.), *The social psychology of intergroup conflict* (pp. 167–187). New York: Springer-Verlag.

Stroessner, S. J., Hamilton, D. L., & Mackie, D. M. (1992). Affect and stereotyping: The effect of induced mood on distinctiveness-based illusory correlations. *Journal of Personality and Social Psychology, 62,* 564–576.

Strohmer, D. C., & Chiodo, A. L. (1984). Counselor hypothesis testing strategies: The role of initial impressions and self-schema. *Journal of Counseling Psychology, 31,* 510–519.

Strom, J. C., & Buck, R. W. (1979). Staring and participants' sex: Physiological and subjective reactions. *Personality and Social Psychology Bulletin, 5,* 114–117.

Strong, S. R. (1968). Counseling: An interpersonal influence process. *Journal of Counseling Psychology, 15,* 215–224.

Strong, S. R. (1991a). Social influence and change in therapeutic relationships. In C. R. Snyder & D. R. Forsyth (Eds.), *Handbook of social and clinical psychology: The health perspective* (pp. 540–562). New York: Pergamon.

Strong, S. R. (1991b). Theory-driven science and naive empiricism in counseling psychology. *Journal of Counseling Psychology, 38,* 204–210.

Strong, S. R., Hills, H. I., Kilmartin, C. T., DeVries, H., Lanier, K., Nelson, B. N., Strickland, D., & Meyer, C. W., III. (1988). The dynamic relations among interpersonal behaviors: A test of complementarity and anticomplementarity. *Journal of Personality and Social Psychology, 54,* 798–810.

Strong, S. R., Welsh, J. A., Corcran, J. L., & Hoyt, W. T. (1992). Social psychology and counseling psychology: The history, products, and promise of an interface. *Journal of Counseling Psychology, 39,* 139–157.

Strube, M. J. (1985). Attributional style and the Type A coronary-prone behavior pattern. *Journal of Personality and Social Psychology, 49,* 500–509.

Strube, M. J., & Garcia, J. E. (1981). A meta-analytic investigation of Fiedler's contingency model of leadership effectiveness. *Psychological Bulletin, 90,* 307–321.

Strube, M. J., Turner, C. W., Cervo, D., Stevens, J., & Hinchey, F. (1984). Interpersonal aggression and the Type A coronary-prone behavior pattern: A theoretical distinction and practical implications. *Journal of Personality and Social Psychology, 47,* 839–847.

Struckman-Johnson, C. J., Gilliland, R. C., Struckman-Johnson, D. L., & North, T. C. (1990). The effects of fear of AIDS and gender on responses to fear-arousing condom advertisements. *Journal of Applied Social Psychology, 19,* 1396–1410.

Stryker, S., & Stratham, A. (1985). Symbolic interaction and role theory. In G. Lindzey & E. Aronson (Eds.), *Handbook of social psychology* (3rd ed., Vol. 1, pp. 311–378). New York: Random House.

Stults, D. M., Messe, L. A., & Kerr, N. L. (1984). Belief discrepant behavior and the bogus pipeline: Impression management or arousal attribution. *Journal of Experimental Social Psychology, 20,* 47–54.

Suls, J. M., & Fletcher, B. (1983). Social comparison in the social and physical sciences: An archival study. *Journal of Personality and Social Psychology, 44,* 575–580.

Suls, J. M., & Greenwald, A. G. (Eds.). (1986). *Psychological perspectives on the self.* Hillsdale, NJ: Erlbaum.

Suls, J. M., & Wills, T. A. (Eds.). (1991). *Social comparison: Contemporary theory and research.* Hillsdale, NJ: Erlbaum.

Sumner, W. G. (1906). *Folkways.* New York: Ginn.

Sundstrom, E. (1987). Work environments: Offices and factories. In D. Stokols & I. Altman (Eds.), *Handbook of environmental psychology* (Vol. 1, pp. 733–782). New York: Wiley.

Sundstrom, E., & Altman, I. (1974). Field study of dominance and territorial behavior. *Journal of Personality and Social Psychology, 30,* 115–125.

Sundstrom, E., De Meuse, K. P., & Futrell, D. (1990). Work teams: Applications and effectiveness. *American Psychologist, 45,* 120–133.

Surra, C. A. (1985). Courtship types: Variations in interdependence between partners and social networks. *Journal of Personality and Social Psychology, 49,* 357–375.

Sussman, S., Gavriel, Z. A., & Romer, D. (1983). *Attractiveness matching is good: Physical attractiveness and stereotypes about marriage.* Paper presented at the Annual Meetings of the Midwestern Psychological Association, Chicago.

Swallow, S. R., & Kuiper, N. A. (1987). The effects of depression and cognitive vulnerability to depression on similarity judgments between self and other. *Motivation and Emotion, 11,* 157–167.

Swann, W. B., Jr. (1983). Self-verification: Bringing social reality into harmony with the self. In J. Suls & A. G. Greenwald (Eds.), *Psychological perspectives on the self* (Vol. 2). Hillsdale, NJ: Erlbaum.

Swann, W. B., Jr. (1984). Quest for accuracy in person perception: A matter of pragmatics. *Psychological Review, 91,* 457–477.

Swann, W. B., Jr. (1987). Identity negotiation: Where two roads meet. *Journal of Personality and Social Psychology, 53,* 1038–1051.

Swann, W. B., Jr. (1990). To be admired or to be known: The interplay of self-enhancement and self-verification. In R. M. Sorrentino & E. T. Higgins (Eds.), *Motivation and cognition* (Vol. 2). New York: Guilford Press.

Swann, W. B., Jr. (1992). Seeking "truth," finding despair: Some unhappy consequences of a negative self-concept. *Current Directions in Psychological Science, 1,* 15–17.

Swann, W. B., Jr., Griffin, J. J., Jr., Predmore, S. C., & Gaines, B. (1987). Cognitive-affective crossfire: When self-consistency meets self-enhancement. *Journal of Personality and Social Psychology, 52,* 881–889.

Swann, W. B., Jr., & Hill, C. A. (1982). When our identities are mistaken: Reaffirming self-conceptions through social interaction. *Journal of Personality and Social Psychology, 43,* 59–66.

Swann, W. B., Jr., Hixon, J. G., & De La Ronde, C. (1992). Embracing the bitter "truth": Negative self-concepts and marital commitment. *Psychological Science, 3,* 118–121.

Swann, W. B., Jr., Pelham, B. W., & Krull, D. S. (1989). Agreeable fancy or disagreeable truth? Reconciling self-enhancement and self-verification. *Journal of Personality and Social Psychology, 57,* 782–791.

Swann, W. B., Jr., & Read, S. J. (1981a). Acquiring self-knowledge: The search for feedback that fits. *Journal of Personality and Social Psychology, 41,* 1119–1128.

Swann, W. B., Jr., & Read, S. J. (1981b). Self-verification processes: How we sustain our self-conceptions. *Journal of Experimental Social Psychology, 17,* 351–372.

Swann, W. B., Jr., Stein-Seroussi, A., & Giesler, R. B. (1992). Why people self-verify. *Journal of Personality and Social Psychology, 62,* 392–401.

Swann, W. B., Jr., Stein-Seroussi, A., & McNulty, S. E. (1992). Outcasts in a white-lie society: The enigmatic worlds of people with negative self-conceptions. *Journal of Personality and Social Psychology, 62,* 618–624.

Swap, W. C. (1991). Perceiving the causes of altruism. In R. A. Hinde & J. Groebel (Eds.), *Cooperation and prosocial behavior* (pp. 147–158). New York: Oxford University Press.

Swede, S. W., & Tetlock, P. E. (1986). Henry Kissinger's implicit theory of personality: A quantitative case study. *Journal of Personality, 54,* 617–646.

Sweet, W. H., Ervin, F., & Mark, V. H. (1969). The relationship of violent behavior to focus cerebral disease. In S. Garattini & E. Sigg (Eds.), *Aggressive behavior.* New York: Wiley.

Swim, J., Borgida, E., Maruyama, G., & Myers, D. G. (1989). Joan McKay vs. John McKay: Do gender stereotypes bias evaluations? *Psychological Bulletin, 105,* 409–429.

Swim, J. K. (1994). Perceived versus meta-analytic effect sizes: An assessment of the accuracy of gender stereotypes. *Journal of Personality and Social Psychology, 66,* 21–36.

Szybillo, G. J., & Heslin, R. (1973). Resistance to persuasion: Inoculation theory in a marketing context. *Journal of Marketing Research, 10,* 396–403.

Szymanski, K., & Harkins, S. G. (1987). Social loafing and self-evaluation with a social standard. *Journal of Personality and Social Psychology, 53,* 891–897.

Tabachnik, N., Crocker, J., & Alloy, L. B. (1983). Depression, social comparison, and the false-consensus effect. *Journal of Personality and Social Psychology, 45,* 688–699.

Tajfel, H., Sheikh, A. A., & Gardner, R. C. (1964). Content of stereotypes and the inference of similarity between members of stereotyped groups. *Acta Psychologica, 22,* 191–201.

Tajfel, H., & Turner, J. C. (1986). The social identity theory of intergroup behavior. In S. Worchel & W. G. Austin (Eds.), *Psychology of intergroup relations* (2nd ed., pp. 7–24). Chicago: Nelson-Hall.

Tanford, S., & Penrod, S. (1984). Social influence model: A formal integration of research on majority and minority influence processes. *Psychological Bulletin, 95,* 189–225.

Tangney, J. P. (1990). Assessing individual differences in proneness to shame and guilt: Development of the Self-Conscious Affect and Attribution Inventory. *Journal of Personality and Social Psychology, 59,* 102–111.

Tangney, J. P. (1991). Moral affect: The good, the bad, and the ugly. *Journal of Personality and Social Psychology, 61,* 598–607.

Tangney, J. P., Wagner, P., Fletcher, C., & Gramzow, R. (1992). Shamed into anger? The relation of shame and guilt to anger and self-reported aggression. *Journal of Personality and Social Psychology, 62,* 669–675.

Tavris, C. (1982). *Anger: The misunderstood emotion.* New York: Simon & Schuster.

Taylor, D. A., & Moriarty, B. F. (1987). Ingroup bias as a function of competition and race. *Journal of Conflict Resolution, 31,* 192–199.

Taylor, D. W., Berry, P. C., & Block, C. H. (1958). Does group participation when using brainstorming facilitate or inhibit creative thinking? *Administrative Science Quarterly, 3,* 23–47.

Taylor, F. W. (1923). *The principles of scientific management.* New York: Harper.

Taylor, R. B., Gottfredson, S. D., & Brower, S. (1980). The defensibility of defensible space: A critical review and a synthetic framework for future research. In T. Hirshi & M. Gottfredson (Eds.), *Understanding crime.* Newbury Park, CA: Sage.

Taylor, R. B., Gottfredson, S. D., & Brower, S. (1984). Understanding block crime and fear. *Journal of Research in Crime and Delinquency, 21,* 303–331.

Taylor, R. B., & Lanni, J. C. (1981). Territorial dominance: The influence of the resident advantage in triadic decision making. *Journal of Personality and Social Psychology, 41,* 909–915.

Taylor, R. B., & Stough, R. R. (1978). Territorial cognition: Assessing Altman's typology. *Journal of Personality and Social Psychology, 36,* 418–423.

Taylor, S. E., & Brown, J. D. (1988). Illusion and well-being: A social psychological perspective on mental health. *Psychological Bulletin, 103,* 193–210.

Taylor, S. E., & Fiske, S. T. (1975). Point of view and perceptions of causality. *Journal of Personality and Social Psychology, 32,* 439–445.

Taylor, S. E., & Fiske, S. T. (1978). Salience, attention, and attribution: Top of the head phenomena. In L. Berkowitz (Ed.), *Advances in experimental social psychology* (Vol. 11, pp. 249–288). New York: Academic Press.

Taylor, S. E., Helgeson, V. S., Reed, G. M., & Skokan, L. A. (1991). Self-generated feelings of control and adjustment to physical illness. *Journal of Social Issues, 47*(4), 91–109.

Taylor, S. E., & Lobel, M. (1989). Social comparison activity under threat: Downward evaluation and upward contacts. *Psychological Review, 96,* 569–575.

Taylor, S. E., & Thompson, S. C. (1982). Stalking the elusive "vividness" effect. *Psychological Review, 89,* 155–181.

Taylor, S. P., & Leonard, K. E. (1983). Alcohol and human physical aggression. In R. Geen & E. Donnerstein (Eds.), *Aggression: Theoretical and empirical reviews* (Vol. 2, pp. 77–102). New York: Academic Press.

Taylor, S. P., & Pisano, R. (1971). Physical aggression as a function of frustration and physical attack. *Journal of Social Psychology, 84,* 261–267.

Taylor, S. P., & Sears, J. D. (1988). The effects of alcohol and persuasive social pressure on human physical aggression. *Aggressive Behavior, 14,* 237–243.

Tedeschi, J. T., Gaes, G. G., Norman, N., & Melburg, V. (1986). Pills and attitude change: Misattribution of arousal or excuses for negative actions? *Journal of General Psychology, 113,* 309–328.

Tedeschi, J. T., Melburg, V., & Rosenfeld, P. (1981). Is the concept of aggression useful? In P. E. Brain & D. Denton (Eds.), *Multidisciplinary approach to aggression research.* New York: Elsevier/North Holland Biomedical Press.

Tedeschi, J. T., & Riess, M. (1981a). Identities, the phenomenal self, and laboratory research. In J. T. Tedeschi (Ed.), *Impression management theory and social psychological research.* Orlando, FL: Academic Press.

Tedeschi, J. T., & Riess, M. (1981b). Verbal strategies in impression management. In C. Antaki (Ed.), *The psychology of ordinary explanations of social behavior.* London: Academic Press.

Tedeschi, J. T., Riordan, C. A., Gaes, G. G., & Kane, T. (1983). Verbal accounts and attributions of social motives. *Journal of Research in Personality, 17,* 218–225.

Tedeschi, J. T., Schlenker, B. R., & Bonoma, T. V. (1971). Cognitive dissonance: Private ratiocination or public spectacle? *American Psychologist, 26,* 685–695.

Tedeschi, J. T., Smith, R. B., III, & Brown, R. C., Jr. (1974). A reinterpretation of research on aggression. *Psychological Bulletin, 81,* 540–563.

Teichman, Y. (1973). Emotional arousal and affiliation. *Journal of Experimental Social Psychology, 9,* 591–605.

Teigen, K. H. (1986). Old truths or fresh insights? A study of students' evaluations of proverbs. *British Journal of Social Psychology, 25,* 43–50.

Tennen, H., & Affleck, G. (1990). Blaming others for threatening events. *Psychological Bulletin, 108,* 209–232.

Tennen, H., & Affleck, G. (1991). Paradox-based treatments. In C. R. Snyder & D. R. Forsyth (Eds.), *Handbook of social and clinical psychology: A health perspective* (pp. 624–643). New York: Pergamon.

Terry, D. J., Gallois, C., & McCamish, M. (1993). *The theory of reasoned action: Its application to AIDS-preventive behavior.* New York: Pergamon.

Tesser, A. (1988). Toward a self-evalaution maintenance model of social behavior. In L. Berkowitz (Ed.), *Advances in experimental social psychology* (Vol. 21, pp. 181–227). New York: Academic Press.

Tesser, A. (1993). The importance of heritability in psychological research: The case of attitudes. *Psychological Review, 100,* 129–142.

Tesser, A., & Campbell, J. (1983). Self-definition and self-evaluation maintenance. In J. Suls & A. G. Greenwald (Eds.), *Psychological perspectives on the self* (Vol. 2). Hillsdale, NJ: Erlbaum.

Tesser, A., Campbell, J., & Smith, M. (1984). Friendship choice and performance: Self-evaluation maintenance in children. *Journal of Personality and Social Psychology, 46,* 561–574.

Tesser, A., & Shaffer, D. R. (1990). Attitudes and attitude change. *Annual Review of Psychology, 41,* 479–523.

Tetlock, P. E. (1979). Identifying victims of groupthink from public statements of decision makers. *Journal of Personality and Social Psychology, 37,* 1314–1324.

Tetlock, P. E. (1980). Explaining teacher explanations for pupil performance: An examination of the self-presentation position. *Social Psychology Quarterly, 43,* 283–290.

Tetlock, P. E. (1981). The influence of self-presentational goals on attributional reports. *Social Psychology Quarterly, 44,* 300–311.

Tetlock, P. E. (1985). Toward an intuitive politician model of attribution processes. In B. R. Schlenker (Ed.), *The self and social life.* New York: McGraw-Hill.

Tetlock, P. E., & Levi, A. (1982). Attribution bias: On the inconclusiveness of the cognition-motivation debate. *Journal of Experimental Social Psychology, 18,* 68–88.

Tetlock, P. E., & Manstead, A. S. R. (1985). Impression management versus intrapsychic explanations in social psychology: A useful dichotomy? *Psychological Review, 92,* 59–77.

Tetlock, P. E., Peterson, R. S., McGuire, C., Chanag, S., & Feld, P. (1992). Assessing political group dynamics: A test of the groupthink model. *Journal of Personality and Social Psychology, 63,* 403–425.

Tetlock, P. E., Skitka, L., & Boettger, R. (1989). Social and cognitive strategies for coping with accountability: Conformity, complexity, and bolstering. *Journal of Personality and Social Psychology, 57,* 632–640.

Thayer, S. (1988). Close encounters. *Psychology Today, 22*(3), pp. 30–36.

Thibaut, J. W., & Kelley, H. H. (1959). *The social psychology of groups.* New York: Wiley.

Thomas, C. (1991, October 12). His version of the events. *Richmond Times Dispatch,* p. A-6.

Thomas, J. R., & French, K. E. (1985). Gender differences across age in motor performance: A meta-analysis. *Psychological Bulletin, 98,* 260–282.

Thomas, M. H., Horton, R. W., Lippincott, E. C., & Drabman, R. S. (1977). Desensitization to portrayals of real-life aggression as a function of exposure to TV violence. *Journal of Personality and Social Psychology, 35,* 450–458.

Thompson, S. C. (1981). Will it hurt less if I can control it? A complex answer to a simple question. *Psychological Review, 90,* 89–101.

Thompson, S. C. (1991). Intervening to enhance perceptions of control. In C. R. Snyder & D. R. Forsyth (Eds.), *Handbook of social and clinical psychology: The health perspective* (pp. 607–623). New York: Pergamon.

Thompson, S. C., & Kelley, H. H. (1981). Judgments of responsibility for activities in close relationships. *Journal of Personality and Social Psychology, 41,* 469–477.

Thompson, S. C., & Spacapan, S. (1991). Perceptions of control in vulnerable populations. *Journal of Social Issues, 47*(4), 1–21.

Thompson, W. C., Cowan, C. L., & Rosenhan, D. L. (1980). Focus of attention mediates the impact of negative affect on altruism. *Journal of Personality and Social Psychology, 38,* 291–300.

Thoreau, H. D. (1962). *Walden and other writings.* New York: Bantam Books.

Thrasher, F. M. (1927). *The gang.* Chicago: University of Chicago Press.

Tice, D. M. (1991). Esteem protection or enhancement? Self-handicapping motives and attributions differ by trait self-esteem. *Journal of Personality and Social Psychology, 60,* 711–725.

Tice, D. M., & Baumeister, R. F. (1985). Masculinity inhibits helping in emergencies: Personality does predict the bystander effect. *Journal of Personality and Social Psychology, 49,* 420–428.

Tiller, M. G., & Fazio, R. H. (1982). The relation between attitudes and later behavior following dissonance-produced attitude change. *Personality and Social Psychology Bulletin, 8,* 280–285.

Time Magazine. (1982). *A study of the effectiveness of advertising frequency in magazines.* New York: Time, Inc.

Tinbergen, L. (1951). *The study of instinct.* Oxford: Oxford University Press.

Tindale, R. S., Davis, J. H., Vollrath, D. A., Nagao, D. H., & Hinsz, V. B. (1990). Asymmetrical social influence in freely interacting groups: A test of three models. *Journal of Personality and Social Psychology, 58,* 438–449.

Tinsley, H. E. A., Bowman, S. L., & Barich, A. W. (1993). Counseling psychologists' perceptions of the occurrence and effects of unrealistic expectations about counseling and psychotherapy among their clients. *Journal of Counseling Psychology, 40,* 46–52.

Tjosvold, D. (1986). *Working together to get things done.* Lexington, MA: Lexington Books.

Toch, H. (1969). *Violent men.* Chicago: Aldine.

Toch, H. (1993). Good violence and bad violence: Self-presentations of aggressors through accounts and war stories. In R. B. Felson & J. T. Tedeschi (Eds.), *Aggression and violence: Social interactionist perspectives* (pp. 193–206). Washington, DC: American Psychological Association.

Toi, M., & Batson, C. D. (1982). More evidence that empathy is a source of altruistic motivation. *Journal of Personality and Social Psychology, 43,* 281–292.

Tolman, C. W. (1968). The role of the companion in social facilitation of animal behavior. In E. C. Simmel, R. A. Hoppe, & G. A. Milton (Eds.), *Social facilitation and imitative behavior.* Boston: Allyn & Bacon.

Tolstedt, B. E., & Stokes, J. P. (1984). Self-disclosure, intimacy, and the depenetration process. *Journal of Personality and Social Psychology, 46,* 84–90.

Tolstoy, L. (1869/1952). *War and peace.* Chicago: Encyclopedia Britannica.

Trafimow, D., Triandis, H. C., & Goto, S. G. (1991). Some tests of the distinction between the private self and the collective self. *Journal of Personality and Social Psychology, 60,* 649–655.

Traupmann, J., & Hatfield, E. (1981). Love: Its effects on mental and physical health. In J. March, S. Kiesler, R. Fegel, E. Hatfield, & E. Shana (Eds.), *Aging: Stability and change in the family.* New York: Academic Press.

Triandis, H. C. (1990). Cross-cultural studies of individualism and collectivism. *Nebraska Symposium on Motivation, 39,* 41–133.

Triandis, H. C., McCusker, C., & Hui, C. H. (1990). Multimethod probes of individualism and collectivism. *Journal of Personality and Social Psychology, 59,* 1006–1013.

Triplett, N. (1898). The dynamogenic factors in pacemaking and competition. *American Journal of Psychology, 9,* 507–533.

Trivers, R. (1985). *Social evolution.* Reading, MA: Benjamin/Cummings.

Trope, Y. (1986). Identification and inferential processes in dispositional attribution. *Psychological Review, 93,* 239–257.

Trope, Y., & Bassok, M. (1982). Confirmatory and diagnosing strategies in social information gathering. *Journal of Personality and Social Psychology, 43,* 637, 645.

Trope, Y., & Cohen, O. (1989). Perceptual and inferential determinants of behavior-correspondent attributions. *Journal of Experimental Social Psychology, 25,* 142–158.

Trope, Y., & Higgins, E. T. (Eds.). (1993a). On inferring personal dispositions from behavior [Special issue]. *Personality and Social Psychology Bulletin, 19.*

Trope, Y., & Higgins, E. T. (1993b). The what, when, and how of dispositional inference: New answers and new questions. *Personality and Social Psychology Bulletin, 19,* 493–500.

Tucker, J. S., & Riggio, R. E. (1988). The role of social skills in encoding posed and spontaneous facial expressions. *Journal of Nonverbal Behavior, 12,* 87–97.

Tuckman, B. W. (1965). Developmental sequences in small groups. *Psychological Bulletin, 63,* 384–399.

Tuckman, B. W., & Jensen, M. A. C. (1977). Stages of small group development revisited. *Group and Organizational Studies, 2,* 419–427.

Turk, A., Turk, J., Wittes, J. T., & Wittes, R. (1974). *Environmental science.* Philadelphia: Saunders.

Turner, C. W., Layton, J. F., & Simons, L. S. (1975). Naturalistic studies of aggressive behavior: Aggressive stimuli, victim visibility, and horn honking. *Journal of Personality and Social Psychology, 31,* 1098–1107.

Turner, C. W., Simons, L. S., Berkowitz, L., & Frodi, A. (1977). The stimulating and inhibiting effects of weapons on aggressive behavior. *Aggressive Behavior, 3,* 355–378.

Turner, J. C. (1985). Social categorization and the self-concept: A social-cognitive theory of group behavior. In E. J. Lawler (Ed.), *Advances in group processes* (Vol. 2, pp. 77–122). Greenwich, CT: JAI Press.

Turner, J. C. (1987). *Rediscovering the social group: A self-categorization theory.* New York: Blackwell.

Turner, J. C., Sachdev, I., & Hogg, M. A. (1983). Social categorization, interpersonal attraction, and group formation. *British Journal of Social Psychology, 22,* 227–239.

Turner, M. E., Pratkanis, A. R., Probasco, P., & Leve, C. (1992). Threat, cohesion, and group effectiveness: Testing a social identity maintenance perspective on groupthink. *Journal of Personality and Social Psychology, 63,* 781–796.

Turner, R. G. (1978). Self-consciousness and speed of processing self-relevant information. *Personality and Social Psychology Bulletin, 4,* 456–460.

Tuthill, D., & Forsyth, D. R. (1982). Sex differences in opinion conformity and dissent. *Journal of Social Psychology, 116,* 205–210.

Tversky, A., & Kahneman, D. (1974). Judgment under uncertainty: Heuristics and biases. *Science, 185,* 1124–1131.

Tybout, A. M., & Scott, C. A. (1983). Availability of well-defined internal knowledge and the attitude formation process: Information aggregation versus self-perception. *Journal of Personality and Social Psychology, 44,* 474–491.

Tyler, T. R., & Schuller, R. A. (1991). Aging and attitude change. *Personality and Social Psychology Bulletin, 61,* 689–697.

Tzuriel, D. (1984). Sex role typing and ego identity in Israeli, Oriental, and Western adolescents. *Journal of Personality and Social Psychology, 46,* 440–457.

Underwood, B., & Moore, B. S. (1982). The generality of altruism in children. In N. Eisenberg (Ed.), *The development of prosocial behavior.* New York: Academic Press.

United Nations. (1974). *Committee on the definition of aggression.* New York: UN Printing Office.

Valentine, T. (1991). A unified account of the effects of distinctiveness, inversion, and race in face recognition. *Quarterly Journal of Experimental Psychology, 43A,* 161–204.

Valins, S. (1966). Cognitive effects of false heart rate feedback. *Journal of Personality and Social Psychology, 4,* 400–408.

Vallacher, R. R., & Wegner, D. M. (1987). What do people think they are doing? Action identification and human behavior. *Psychological Review, 94,* 3–15.

Vallerand, R. J., Deshaies, P., Cuerrier, J., Pelletier, L. G., & Mongeau, C. (1992). Ajzen and Fishbein's theory of reasoned action as applied to moral behavior: A confirmatory analysis. *Journal of Personality and Social Psychology, 62,* 98–109.

Vallone, R. P., Griffin, D. W., Lin, S., & Ross, L. (1990). The overconfident prediction of future action and outcomes by self and others. *Journal of Personality and Social Psychology, 58,* 582–592.

Vande-Berg, L. R., & Streckfuss, D. (1992). Prime-time television's portrayal of women and the world of work: A demographic profile. *Journal of Broadcasting and Electronic Media, 36,* 195–208.

Van den Bogaard, J., & Wiegman, O. (1991). Property crime victimization: The effectiveness of police services for victims of residential burglary. *Journal of Social Behavior and Personality, 6,* 329–362.

Van de Ven, A. H. (1974). *Group decision-making effectiveness.* Kent, OH: Kent State University Center for Business and Economic Research Press.

Van Egeren, L. F. (1979). Cardiovascular changes during social competition in a mixed-motive game. *Journal of Personality and Social Psychology, 37,* 858–864.

Van Heck, G. L., & Dijkstra, P. (1985). The scope and generality of self-other asymmetry in person perception. *European Journal of Social Psychology, 15,* 125–145.

Vanneman, R., & Pettigrew, T. (1972). Race and relative deprivation in the urban United States. *Race, 13,* 461–486.

Van Ypern, N. W., & Buunk, B. P. (1990). A longitudinal study of equity and satisfaction in intimate relationships. *European Journal of Social Psychology, 20,* 287–309.

Veevers, J. E. (1971). Drinking attitudes and drinking behavior: An exploratory study. *Journal of Social Psychology, 85,* 103–109.

Veitch, R., de Wood, R., & Bosko, K. (1977). Radio news broadcasts: Their effects on interpersonal helping. *Sociometry, 40,* 383–386.

Verplanken, B. (1991). Persuasive communication of risk information: A test of cue versus message processing effects in a field experiment. *Personality and Social Psychology Bulletin, 17,* 188–193.

Vinokur, A., & Burnstein, E. (1974). The effects of partially shared persuasive arguments on group-induced shifts: A group-problem-solving approach. *Journal of Personality and Social Psychology, 29,* 305–315.

Vinokur, A., & Burnstein, E. (1978). Depolarization of attitudes in groups. *Journal of Personality and Social Psychology, 36,* 872–885.

Vinokur, A., Burnstein, E., Sechrest, L., & Wortman, P. M. (1985). Group decision making by experts: Field study of panels evaluating medical technologies. *Journal of Personality and Social Psychology, 49,* 70–84.

Vinsel, A., Brown, B., Altman, I., & Foss, C. (1980). Privacy regulation, territorial displays, and effectiveness of individual functioning. *Journal of Personality and Social Psychology, 39,* 1104–1115.

Vormbrock, J. K. (1993). Attachment theory as applied to wartime and job-related marital separation. *Psychological Bulletin, 114,* 122–144.

Vreven, R., & Nuttin, J. (1976). Frequency perception of successes as a function of results previously obtained by others and by oneself. *Journal of Personality and Social Psychology, 34,* 734–743.

Vroom, V. H., & Yetton, P. W. (1973). *Leadership and decision making.* Pittsburgh, PA: University of Pittsburgh Press.

Walden, T. A., & Forsyth, D. R. (1981). Close encounters of the stressful kind: Affective, physiological, and behavioral reactions to the experience of crowding. *Journal of Nonverbal Behavior, 6,* 46–64.

Wallach, M. A., Kogan, N., & Bem, D. J. (1962). Group influence on individual risk taking. *Journal of Abnormal and Social Psychology, 65,* 75–86.

Waller, W. (1938). *The family: A dynamic interpretation.* New York: Dryden.

Wallston, B. S., Alagna, S. W., DeVellis, B. M., & DeVellis, R. F. (1983). Social support and physical health. *Health Psychology, 2,* 367–391.

Walster, E. (1966). The assignment of responsibility for an accident. *Journal of Personality and Social Psychology, 3,* 73–79.

Walster, E. (1968). Postdecision dissonance. In R. P. Abelson, E. Aronson, W. J. McGuire, T. M. Newcomb, M. J. Rosenberg, & P. H. Tannenbaum (Eds.), *Theories of cognitive consistency: A sourcebook.* Chicago: Rand McNally.

Walster, E., Aronson, V., Abrahams, D., & Rottman, L. (1966). The importance of physical attractiveness in dating behavior. *Journal of Personality and Social Psychology, 4,* 508–516.

Walster, E., & Berscheid, E. (1974). A little bit about love: A minor essay on a major topic. In T. L. Huston (Ed.), *Foundations of interpersonal attraction.* New York: Academic Press.

Walster, E., & Walster, G. W. (1978). *A new look at love.* Reading, MA: Addison-Wesley.

Walster, E., Walster, G. W., & Berscheid, E. (1978). *Equity: Theory and research.* Boston: Allyn & Bacon.

Walster, E., Walster, G. W., Piliavin, J., & Schmidt, L. (1973). Playing hard-to-get: Understanding an elusive phenomenon. *Journal of Personality and Social Psychology, 26,* 113–121.

Warner, L. G., & DeFleur, M. L. (1969). Attitude as an interactional concept: Social constraint and social distance as intervening variables between attitudes and action. *American Sociological Review, 34,* 153–169.

Warren, J. R. (1966). Birth order and social behavior. *Psychological Bulletin, 65,* 38–49.

Wasserman, D., Lempert, R. O., & Hastie, R. (1991). Hindsight and causality. *Personality and Social Psychology Bulletin, 17,* 30–35.

Waterman, A. S. (1988). On the uses of psychological theory and research in the process of ethical inquiry. *Psychology Bulletin, 103,* 283–298.

Watkins, C. E., Jr., Terrell, F., Miller, F. S., & Terrell, S. L. (1989). Cultural mistrust and its effects on expectational variables in black client-white counselor relationships. *Journal of Counseling Psychology, 36,* 447–450.

Watkins, M. J., & Peynircioglu, Z. F. (1984). Determining perceived meaning during impression formation: Another look at the meaning change hypothesis. *Journal of Personality and Social Psychology, 46,* 1005–1016.

Weary, G. (1979). Self-serving attributional biases: Perceptual or response distortions? *Journal of Personality and Social Psychology, 37,* 1418–1420.

Weary, G. (1980). Affect and egotism as mediators of bias in causal attributions. *Journal of Personality and Social Psychology, 38,* 348–357.

Weary, G., Harvey, J. H., Schweiger, P., Olson, C. T., Perloff, R., & Pritchard, S. (1982). Self-presentation and the moderation of the self-serving bias. *Social Cognition, 1,* 140–159.

Weary, G., & Mirels, H. L. (Eds.). (1982). *Integrations of clinical and social psychology.* New York: Oxford University Press.

Weary, G., Stanley, M. A., & Harvey, J. H. (1989). *Attribution.* New York: Springer-Verlag.

Webb, E. J., Campbell, D. T., Schwartz, R. D., Sechrest, L., & Grove, J. B. (1981). *Nonreactive measures in the social sciences.* Boston: Houghton Mifflin.

Webster, M., Jr., & Driskell, J. E., Jr. (1983). Processes of status generalization. In H. H. Blumberg, A. P. Hare, V. Kent, & M. F. Davies (Eds.), *Small groups and social interaction* (Vol. 1, pp. 57–67). New York: Wiley.

Wegner, D. M., & Vallacher, R. R. (1987). The trouble with action. *Social Cognition, 5,* 179–190.

Wegner, D. M., Vallacher, R. R., Macomber, G., Wood, R., & Arps, K. (1984). The emergence of action. *Journal of Personality and Social Psychology, 46,* 269–279.

Weick, K. E. (1985). Systematic observational methods. In G. Lindzey & E. Aronson (Eds.), *Handbook of social psychology* (3rd ed., Vol. 1, pp. 567–634). New York: Random House.

Weigel, R. H., & Cook, S. W. (1975). Participation in decision-making: A determinant of interpersonal attraction in cooperating interracial groups. *International Journal of Group Tension, 5,* 179–195.

Weigel, R. H., Vernon, D. T. A., & Tognacci, L. N. (1974). Specificity of the attitude as a determinant of attitude behavior congruence. *Journal of Personality and Social Psychology, 30,* 724–728.

Weigold, M. F., & Schlenker, B. R. (1991). Accountability and risk-taking. *Personality and Social Psychology Bulletin, 17,* 25–29.

Weinberg, M. S. (1966). Becoming a nudist. *Psychiatry, 29,* 15–24.

Weiner, B. (1980). *Human motivation.* New York: Holt, Rinehart & Winston.

Weiner, B. (1983). Some methodological pitfalls in attributional research. *Journal of Educational Psychology, 75,* 530–543.

Weiner, B. (1985a). An attributional theory of achievement motivation and emotion. *Psychological Review, 92,* 548–573.

Weiner, B. (1985b). "Spontaneous" causal thinking. *Psychological Bulletin, 97,* 74–84.

Weiner, B. (1991). Metaphors in motivation and attribution. *American Psychologist, 46,* 921–930.

Weiner, B., & Brown, J. (1984). All's well that ends well. *Journal of Educational Psychology, 76,* 169–171.

Weinstein, N. D. (1980). Unrealistic optimism about future life events. *Journal of Personality and Social Psychology, 39,* 806–820.

Weinstein, N. D. (1982). Unrealistic optimism about susceptibility to health problems. *Journal of Behavioral Medicine, 5,* 441–460.

Weiss, R. S. (1973). *Loneliness: The experience of emotional and social isolation.* Cambridge, MA: MIT Press.

Wellman, D. T. (1977). *Portraits of white racism.* New York: Cambridge University Press.

Wells, G. L. (1985). The conjunction error and the representativeness heuristic. *Social Cognition, 3,* 266–279.

Wells, G. L. (1993). What do we know about eyewitness identification? *American Psychologist, 48,* 553–571.

Wells, G. L., Leippe, M. R., & Ostrom, R. M. (1979). Guidelines for empirically assessing the fairness of a lineup. *Law and Human Behavior, 10,* 83–95.

Wells, G. L., & Loftus, E. F. (Eds.). (1984). *Eyewitness testimony: Psychological perspectives.* New York: Cambridge University Press.

Wells, G. L., & Murray, D. M. (1984). Eyewitness confidence. In G. L. Wells & E. F. Loftus (Eds.), *Eyewitness testimony: Psychological perspectives* (pp. 155–170). New York: Cambridge University Press.

Welsch, S., & Booth, A. (1975). The effect of crowding on aggression. *Sociological Symposium, 14,* 105–127.

West Eberhard, M. J. (1975). The evolution of social behavior by kin selection. *The Quarterly Review of Biology, 50,* 1–33.

West, S. G., Gunn, S. P., & Chernicky, P. (1975). Ubiquitous Watergate: An attributional analysis. *Journal of Personality and Social Psychology, 23,* 55–65.

West, S. G., Whitney, G., & Schnedler, R. (1975). Helping a motorist in distress: The effects of sex, race, and neighborhood. *Journal of Personality and Social Psychology, 31,* 691–698.

Westermann, R. (1988). Structuralist reconstruction of psychological research: Cognitive dissonance. *German Journal of Psychology, 12,* 218–231.

Weyant, J. M. (1978). Effects of mood states, costs, and benefits on helping. *Journal of Personality and Social Psychology, 36,* 1169–1176.

Wheeler, H. (1985). Pornography and rape: A feminist perspective. In A. W. Burgess (Ed.), *Rape and sexual assault* (pp. 374–391). New York: Garland.

Wheeler, L., & Miyake, K. (1992). Social comparison in everyday life. *Journal of Personality and Social Psychology, 62,* 760–773.

Wheeler, L., & Nezlek, J. (1977). Sex differences in social participation. *Journal of Personality and Social Psychology, 35,* 742–754.

Wheeless, L. R., Barraclough, R., & Stewart, R. (1983). Compliance-gaining and power in persuasion. In R. N. Bostrom (Ed.), *Communication yearbook* (Vol. 7, pp. 105–145). Newbury Park, CA: Sage.

White, G. L., Fishbein, S., & Rutstein, J. (1981). Passionate love and the misattribution of arousal. *Journal of Personality and Social Psychology, 41,* 56–62.

White, G. L., & Knight, T. D. (1984). Misattribution of arousal and attraction: Effects of salience of explanations of arousal. *Journal of Experimental Social Psychology, 20,* 55–64.

White, G. L., & Mullen, P. E. (1990). *Jealousy: Theory, research, and clinical strategies.* New York: Guilford Press.

White, J. D., & Carlston, D. E. (1983). Consequences of schemata for attention, impressions, and recall in complex social interactions. *Journal of Personality and Social Psychology, 45,* 538–549.

White, J. W. (1983). Sex and gender issues in aggression research. In R. G. Geen & E. I. Donnerstein (Eds.), *Aggression: Theoretical and empirical reviews* (Vol. 2, pp. 1–26). New York: Academic Press.

White, J. W., & Sorenson, S. B. (Eds.). (1992a). Adult sexual assault. *Journal of Social Issues, 48*(1), 1–195.

White, J. W., & Sorenson, S. B. (1992b). A sociocultural view of sexual assault: From discrepancy to diversity. *Journal of Social Issues, 48*(1), 187–195.

White, L. A. (1979). Erotica and aggression: The influence of sexual arousal, positive affect, and negative affect on aggressive behavior. *Journal of Personality and Social Psychology, 37,* 591–601.

White, M. J., & Gerstein, L. H. (1987). Helping: the influence of anticipated social sanctions and self-monitoring. *Journal of Personality, 55,* 41–54.

White, P. (1980). Limitations on verbal reports of internal events: A refutation of Nisbett and Wilson and Bem. *Psychological Review, 87,* 105–112.

White, P. A. (1988). Causal processing: Origins and development. *Psychological Bulletin, 104,* 36–52.

White, R. K. (1977). Misperception in the Arab-Israeli conflict. *Journal of Social Issues, 33*(1), 190–221.

White, R. K., & Lippitt, R. (1968). Leader behavior and member reaction in three "social climates." In D. Cartwright & A. Zander (Eds.), *Group dynamics: Research and theory* (3rd ed., pp. 318–335). New York: Harper & Row.

White, R. W. (1959). Competence motivation reconsidered. *Psychological Review, 66,* 297–333.

Whiting, B. B., & Whiting, J. W. (1975). *Children of six countries: A psychological analysis.* Cambridge, MA: Harvard University Press.

Whitley, B. E., & Frieze, I. H. (1985). Children's causal attributions for success and failure in achievement settings: A meta-analysis. *Journal of Educational Psychology, 77,* 608–616.

Whitley, B. E., & Hern, A. L. (1991). Perceptions of vulnerability to pregnancy and the use of effective contraception. *Personality and Social Psychology Bulletin, 17,* 104–110.

Whyte, W. F. (1943). *Street corner society.* Chicago: University of Chicago Press.

Wicker, A. W. (1969). Attitudes versus actions: The relationship between verbal and overt behavioral responses to attitude objects. *Journal of Social Issues, 25,* 41–78.

Wicker, A. W. (1979). *An introduction to ecological psychology.* Pacific Grove, CA: Brooks/Cole.

Wicker, A. W. (1987). Behavior settings reconsidered: Temporal stages, resources, internal dynamics, context. In D. Stokols & I. Altman (Eds.), *Handbook of environmental psychology* (Vol. 1, pp. 613–653). New York: Wiley.

Wicker, A. W., Kermeyer, S. L., Hanson, L., & Alexander, D. (1976). Effects of manning levels on subjective experiences, performance, and verbal interaction in groups. *Organizational Behavior and Human Performance, 17,* 251–274.

Wicklund, R. A. (1975). Objective self-awareness. In L. Berkowitz (Ed.), *Advances in experimental social psychology* (Vol. 8). New York: Academic Press.

Wicklund, R. A. (1978). Three years later. In L. Berkowitz (Ed.), *Cognitive theories in social psychology.* New York: Academic Press.

Wicklund, R. A., & Brehm, J. W. (1976). *Perspectives on cognitive dissonance.* Hillsdale, NJ: Erlbaum.

Widom, C. S. (1989). Does violence beget violence? A critical reexamination of the literature. *Psychological Bulletin, 106,* 3–28.

Wigmore, J. H. (1909). Professor Munsterberg and the psychology of evidence. *Illinois Law Review, 3,* 399–445.

Wilder, D. A. (1978). Reduction of intergroup discrimination through individuation of the out-group. *Journal of Personality and Social Psychology, 36,* 1361–1374.

Wilder, D. A. (1986). Social categorization: Implications for creation and reduction of intergroup bias. In L. Berkowitz (Ed.), *Advances in experimental social psychology* (Vol. 19, pp. 293–355). New York: Academic Press.

Wilder, D. A. (1990). Some determinants of the persuasive power of in-groups and out-groups: Organization of information and attribution of independence. *Journal of Personality and Social Psychology, 59,* 1202–1213.

Wilder, D. A., & Thompson, J. E. (1980). Intergroup contact with independent manipulations of in-group and out-group interaction. *Journal of Personality and Social Psychology, 38,* 589–603.

Wilkinson, I., & Kipnis, D. (1978). Interfirm use of power. *Journal of Applied Psychology, 63,* 315–320.

Williams, J. E., & Best, D. L. (1990). *Measuring sex stereotypes: A multination study.* Newbury Park, CA: Sage.

Williams, J. L. (1971). Personal space and its relation to extraversion-introversion. *Canadian Journal of Behavioral Sciences, 3,* 155–160.

Williams, K. D., Harkins, S., & Latané, B. (1981). Identifiability as a deterrent to social loafing: Two cheering experiments. *Journal of Personality and Social Psychology, 40,* 303–311.

Williams, K. D., & Karau, S. J. (1991). Social loafing and social compensation: The effects of expectations of co-worker performance. *Journal of Personality and Social Psychology, 61,* 570–581.

Williams, T. P., & Sogon, S. (1984). Group composition and conforming behavior in Japanese students. *Japanese Psychological Research, 126,* 231–234.

Williams v. Florida, 399 U.S. 78 (1970).

Willis, F. N. (1966). Initial speaking distance as a function of the speakers' relationship. *Psychonomic Science, 5,* 221–222.

Willis, R. H. (1963). Two dimensions of conformity-nonconformity. *Sociometry, 26,* 499–512.

Willis, R. H., & Hollander, E. P. (1964). An experimental study of three response modes in social influence situations. *Journal of Abnormal and Social Psychology, 69,* 150–156.

Wills, T. A. (1991). Social comparison process in coping and health. In C. R. Snyder & D. R. Forsyth (Eds.), *Handbook of social and clinical psychology: The health perspective* (pp. 376–394). New York: Pergamon.

Wilson, B. J. (1987). Reducing children's emotional reactions to mass media through rehearsed explanation and exposure to a replica of a fear object. *Human Communication Research, 14,* 3–26.

Wilson, B. J. (1989). Desensitizing children's emotional reactions to the mass media. *Communication Research, 16,* 723–745.

Wilson, D. K., Kaplan, R. M., & Schneiderman, L. J. (1987). Framing of decisions and selections of alternatives in health care. *Social Behavior, 2,* 51–59.

Wilson, D. K., Purdon, S. E., & Wallston, K. A. (1988). Compliance to health recommendations: A theoretical overview of message framing. *Health Education Research, 3,* 161–171.

Wilson, D. W. (1981). Is helping a laughing matter? *Psychology, 18,* 6–9.

Wilson, E. O. (1975). *Sociobiology and the new synthesis.* Cambridge, MA: Harvard University Press.

Wilson, T. D., & Dunn, D. S. (1986). Effects of introspection on attitude-behavior consistency: Analyzing reasons versus focusing on feelings. *Journal of Experimental Social Psychology, 22,* 249–263.

Wilson, T. D., Dunn, D. S., Bybee, J. A., Hyman, D. B., & Rotondo, J. A. (1984). Effects of analyzing reasons on attitude-behavior consistency. *Journal of Personality and Social Psychology, 47,* 5–16.

Wilson, T. D., Dunn, D. S., Kraft, D., & Lisle, D. J. (1989). Introspection, attitude change, and attitude-behavior consistency: The disruptive effects of explaining why we feel the way we do. In L. Berkowitz (Ed.), *Advances in experimental social psychology* (Vol. 22, pp. 287–343). Orlando, FL: Academic Press.

Wilson, T. D., & Kraft, D. (1989). The disruptive effects of explaining attitudes: The moderating effects of knowledge about the attitude object. *Journal of Experimental Social Psychology, 25,* 379–400.

Wilson, T. D., & Linville, P. W. (1982). Improving the academic performance of college freshmen: Attribution therapy revisited. *Journal of Personality and Social Psychology, 42,* 367–376.

Wilson, T. D., & Linville, P. W. (1985). Improving the performance of college freshmen with attributional techniques. *Journal of Personality and Social Psychology, 49,* 287–293.

Wilson, T. D., & Schooler, J. W. (1991). Thinking too much: Introspection can reduce the quality of preferences and decision. *Journal of Personality and Social Psychology, 60,* 181–192.

Wilson, W., & Miller, N. (1961). Shifts in evaluations of participants following intergroup competition. *Journal of Abnormal and Social Psychology, 63,* 428–431.

Wingard, D. L. (1982). The sex differential in mortality rates: Demographic and behavioral factors. *American Journal of Epidemiology, 115,* 204–216.

Winstead, B. A., & Derlega, V. J. (1993). Gender and close relationships: An introduction. *Journal of Social Issues, 49*(3), 1–9.

Winton, B. V. (1983, February 22). Vestiges of racism remain, psychologist says. *Richmond Times Dispatch,* p. D-3.

Winter, L., Uleman, J. S., & Cunniff, C. (1985). How automatic are social judgments? *Journal of Personality and Social Psychology, 49,* 904–917.

Wiseman, R. L., & Schenck-Hamlin, W. (1981). A multidimensional scaling validation of an inductively derived set of compliance-gaining strategies. *Communication Monographs, 48,* 251–270.

Witt, L. A. (1989). Authoritarianism, knowledge of AIDS, and affect toward persons with AIDS: Implications for health education. *Journal of Applied Social Psychology, 19,* 599–607.

Woike, B. A., & Baumgardner, A. H. (1993). Global-specific incongruencies in self-worth and the search for self-knowledge. *Personality and Social Psychology Bulletin, 19,* 290–295.

Wolf, S. (1985). Manifest and latent influence of majorities and minorities. *Journal of Personality and Social Psychology, 48,* 899–908.

Wolf, S. (1987). Majority and minority influence: A social impact analysis. In M. P. Zanna, J. M. Olson, & C. P. Herman (Eds.), *Social influences: The Ontario Symposium* (Vol. 5, pp. 207–235). Hillsdale, NJ: Erlbaum.

Wolf, S., & Latané, B. (1983). Majority and minority influence on restaurant preferences. *Journal of Personality and Social Psychology, 45,* 282–292.

Wong, M. M., & Csikszentmihalyi, M. (1991). Affiliation motivation and daily experience: Some issues on gender differences. *Journal of Personality and Social Psychology, 60,* 154–164.

Wood, F. W. (Ed.). (1990). *An American profile—Opinions and behavior, 1972–1989.* New York: Gale Research.

Wood, J. V. (1989). Theory and research concerning social comparisons of personal attributes. *Psychological Bulletin, 106,* 231–248.

Wood, J. V., & Taylor, K. L. (1991). Serving self-relevant goals through social comparison. In J. Suls & T. A. Wills (Eds.), *Social comparison: Contemporary theory and research* (pp. 23–50). Hillsdale, NJ: Erlbaum.

Wood, J. V., Taylor, S. E., & Lichtman, R. R. (1985). Social comparison in adjustment to breast cancer. *Journal of Personality and Social Psychology, 49,* 1169–1183.

Wood, W. (1982). Retrieval of attitude-relevant information from memory: Effects on susceptibility to persuasion on intrinsic motivation. *Journal of Personality and Social Psychology, 42,* 798–810.

Wood, W., & Eagly, A. H. (1981). Stages in the analysis of persuasive messages: The role of causal attributions and message comprehension. *Journal of Personality and Social Psychology, 40,* 246–255.

Wood, W., & Kallgren, C. A. (1988). Communicator attributes and persuasion: Recipients' access to attitude-relevant information in memory. *Personality and Social Psychology Bulletin, 14,* 172–182.

Wood, W., Rhodes, N., & Whelan, M. (1989). Sex differences in positive well-being: A consideration of emotional style and marital status. *Psychological Bulletin, 106,* 249–264.

Wood, W., Wong, F. Y., & Chachere, J. G. (1991). Effects of media violence on viewers' aggression in unconstrained social interaction. *Psychological Bulletin, 109,* 371–383.

Woodman, R. W., & Sherwood, J. J. (1980). The role of team development in organizational effectiveness: A critical review. *Psychological Bulletin, 88,* 166–186.

Worchel, S. (1978). The experience of crowding: An attributional analysis. In A. Baum & Y. M. Epstein (Eds.), *Human response to crowding.* Hillsdale, NJ: Erlbaum.

Worchel, S. (1986). The role of cooperation in reducing intergroup conflict. In S. Worchel & W. G. Austin (Eds.), *Psychology of intergroup relations* (2nd ed., pp. 288–304). Chicago: Nelson-Hall.

Worchel, S., Andreoli, V. A., & Folger, R. (1977). Intergroup cooperation and intergroup attraction: The effect of previous interaction and outcome of combined effort. *Journal of Experimental Social Psychology, 13,* 131–140.

Worchel, S., Arnold, S., & Baker, M. (1975). The effects of censorship on attitude change: The influence of censor and communication characteristics. *Journal of Applied Social Psychology, 5,* 227–239.

Worchel, S., & Austin, W. G. (Eds.). (1986). *Psychology of intergroup relations* (2nd ed.). Chicago: Nelson-Hall.

Worchel, S., Axsom, D., Ferris, F., Samaha, C., & Schweitzer, S. (1978). Factors determining the effect of intergroup cooperation on intergroup attraction. *Journal of Conflict Resolution, 22,* 429–439.

Worchel, S., & Brehm, J. W. (1971). Direct and implied social restoration of freedom. *Journal of Personality and Social Psychology, 18,* 294–304.

Worchel, S., & Norvell, N. (1980). Effect of perceived environmental conditions during cooperation on intergroup attraction. *Journal of Personality and Social Psychology, 38,* 764–772.

Worchel, S., & Teddlie, C. (1976). The experience of crowding: A two-factor theory. *Journal of Personality and Social Psychology, 34,* 30–40.

Worchel, S., Wood, W., & Simpson, J. A. (Eds.). (1991). *Group process and productivity.* Newbury Park, CA: Sage.

Worchel, S., & Yohai, S. (1979). The role of attribution in the experience of crowding. *Journal of Experimental Social Psychology, 15,* 91–104.

Word, C. O., Zanna, M. P., & Cooper, J. (1974). The nonverbal mediation of self-fulfilling prophecies in interracial interaction. *Journal of Experimental Social Psychology, 10,* 109–120.

Wrightsman, L. S., Nietzel, M. T., & Fortune, W. H. (1994). *Psychology and the legal system* (3rd ed.). Pacific Grove, CA: Brooks/Cole.

Wrightsman, L. S., O'Connor, J., & Baker, N. J. (Eds.). (1972). *Cooperation and competition: Readings on mixed-motive games.* Belmont, CA: Wadsworth.

Wrong, D. H. (1979). *Power: Its forms, bases, and uses.* New York: Harper & Row.

Wu, C., & Shaffer, D. R. (1987). Susceptibility to persuasive appeals as a function of the source credibility and prior experience with the attitude object. *Journal of Personality and Social Psychology, 52,* 677–688.

Wyer, R. S. (1974). *Cognitive organization and change.* Hillsdale, NJ: Erlbaum.

Yablonsky, L. (1962). *The violent gang.* New York: Macmillan.

Yamagishi, T., & Hill, C. T. (1981). Adding versus averaging models revisited. A test of a path-analytic integration model. *Journal of Personality and Social Psychology, 41,* 13–25.

Yancey, W. L. (1971). Architecture, interaction, and social control: The case of large-scale housing project. In J. F. Wohlwill & D. H. Carson (Eds.), *Environment and the social sciences: Perspectives and applications.* Washington, DC: American Psychological Association.

Yarbus, A. L. (1967). *Eye movements and vision.* (L. A. Riggs, Trans.) New York: Plenum.

Yates, J. (1985). The content of awareness is a model of the world. *Psychological Review, 92,* 249–284.

Yates, S. (1992). Lay attributions about distress after a natural disaster. *Personality and Social Psychology Bulletin, 18,* 217–222.

Yinon, Y., & Bizman, A. (1980). Noise, success, and failure as determinants of helping behavior. *Personality and Social Psychology Bulletin, 6,* 125–130.

Younger, J. C., Walker, L., & Arrowood, A. J. (1977). Postdecision dissonance at the fair. *Personality and Social Psychology Bulletin, 3,* 284–287.

Youngs, G. A., Jr. (1986). Patterns of threat and punishment reciprocity in a conflict setting. *Journal of Personality and Social Psychology, 51,* 541–546.

Yuille, J. C. (1993). We must study forensic eyewitnesses to know about them. *American Psychologist, 48,* 572–573.

Yukl, G., & Falbe, C. M. (1990). Influence tactics and objectives in upward, downward, and lateral influence attempts. *Journal of Applied Psychology, 75,* 132–140.

Yukl, G., & Falbe, C. M. (1991). Importance of different power sources in downward and lateral relations. *Journal of Applied Psychology, 76,* 415–423.

Yukl, G., & Tracey, J. B. (1992). Consequences of influence tactics used with subordinates, peers, and the boss. *Journal of Applied Psychology, 77,* 525–535.

Zaccaro, S. J. (1984). Social loafing: The role of task attractiveness. *Personality and Social Psychology Bulletin, 10,* 99–106.

Zaccaro, S. J., Foti, R. J., & Kenny, D. A. (1991). Self-monitoring and trait-based variance in leadership: An investigation of leader flexibility across multiple group situations. *Journal of Applied Psychology, 76,* 308–315.

Zaccaro, S. J., & Lowe, C. A. (1985). Effort attributions: Task novelty, perceptual focus, and cue utilization. *Personality and Social Psychology Bulletin, 11,* 489–501.

Zahn-Waxler, M., Radke-Yarrow, C., & Chapman, M. (1983). Prosocial dispositions and behavior. In E. M. Hetherington (Ed.), *Manual of child psychology: Socialization, personality, and social development* (Vol. 4, pp. 469–546). New York: Wiley.

Zajonc, R. B. (1965). Social facilitation. *Science, 149,* 269–274.

Zajonc, R. B. (1968). Attitudinal effects of mere exposure [Monograph]. *Journal of Personality and Social Psychology, 9,* 1–29.

Zajonc, R. B. (1980). Compresence. In P. B. Paulus (Ed.), *Psychology of group influence* (pp. 35–60). Hillsdale, NJ: Erlbaum.

Zajonc, R. B. (1984). On the primacy of affect. *American Psychologist, 39,* 117–123.

Zajonc, R. B., Heingartner, A., & Herman, E. M. (1969). Social enhancement and impairment of performance in the cockroach. *Journal of Personality and Social Psychology, 13,* 83–92.

Zajonc, R. B., Markus, H., & Markus, G. B. (1979). The birth order puzzle. *Journal of Personality and Social Psychology, 37,* 1325–1340.

Zajonc, R. B., Murphy, S. T., & Inglehart, M. (1989). Feeling and facial efference: Implications of the vascular theory of emotion. *Psychological Review, 96,* 395–416.

Zaller, J. R. (1987). Diffusion of political attitudes. *Journal of Personality and Social Psychology, 53,* 821–833.

Zander, A. (1985). *The purposes of groups and organizations.* San Francisco: Jossey-Bass.

Zanna, M. P., & Hamilton, D. L. (1977). Further evidence for meaning change in impression formation. *Journal of Experimental Social Psychology, 13,* 224–228.

Zanna, M. P., Higgins, E. T., & Herman, C. P. (Eds.). (1982). *Consistency in social behavior: The Ontario Symposium* (Vol. 2). Hillsdale, NJ: Erlbaum.

Zanna, M. P., Kiesler, C. A., & Pilkonis, P. A. (1970). Positive and negative attitudinal affect established by classical conditioning. *Journal of Personality and Social Psychology, 14,* 321–328.

Zanna, M. P., Olson, J. M., & Fazio, R. H. (1980). Attitude-behavior consistency: An individual difference perspective. *Journal of Personality and Social Psychology, 38,* 432–440.

Zanna, M. P., & Pack, S. J. (1975). On the self-fulfilling nature of apparent sex differences in behavior. *Journal of Experimental Social Psychology, 11,* 583–591.

Zebrowitz, L. A. (1990). *Social perception.* Pacific Grove, CA: Brooks/Cole.

Zebrowitz, L. A., Montepare, J. M., & Lee, H. K. (1993). They don't all look alike: Individuated impressions of other racial groups. *Journal of Personality and Social Psychology, 65,* 85–101.

Zebrowitz, L. A., Olson, K., & Hoffman, K. (1993). Stability of babyfaceness and attractiveness across the life span. *Journal of Personality and Social Psychology, 64,* 453–466.

Zillmann, D. (1983). Arousal and aggression. In R. G. Geen & E. I. Donnerstein (Eds.), *Aggression: Theoretical and empirical reviews* (Vol. 1, 75–102). New York: Academic Press.

Zillmann, D., Baron, R. A., & Tamborini, R. (1981). Social costs of smoking: Effects of tobacco smoke on hostile behavior. *Journal of Applied Social Psychology, 11,* 548–561.

Zillmann, D., & Bryant, J. (1974). Effect of residual excitation on the emotional response to provocation and delayed aggressive behavior. *Journal of Personality and Social Psychology, 30,* 782–791.

Zillmann, D., & Cantor, R. J. (1976). Effect of timing of information about mitigating circumstances on emotional responses to provocation and retaliatory behavior. *Journal of Experimental Social Psychology, 12,* 38–55.

Zimbardo, P. G. (1969a). *The cognitive control of motivation.* Glenview, IL: Scott, Foresman.

Zimbardo, P. G. (1969b). The human choice: Individuation, reason, and order versus deindividuation, impulse, and chaos. *Nebraska Symposium on Motivation, 17,* 237–307.

Zimbardo, P. G. (1975). Transforming experimental research into advocacy for social change. In M. Deutsch & H. A. Hornstein (Eds.), *Applying social psychology.* Hillsdale, NJ: Erlbaum.

Zimbardo, P. G. (1977). *Shyness: What it is and what to do about it.* New York: Jones.

Zimbardo, P. G., & Leippe, M. R. (1991). *The psychology of attitude change and social influence.* New York: McGraw-Hill.

Zimbardo, P. G., Weisenberg, M., Firestone, I., & Levy, B. (1965). Communicator effectiveness in producing public conformity and private attitude change. *Journal of Personality, 33,* 233–255.

Zuber, J. A., Crott, H. W., & Werner, J. (1992). Choice shift and group polarization: An analysis of the status of arguments and social decision schemes. *Journal of Personality and Social Psychology, 62,* 50–61.

Zucker, P., Worthington, E., & Forsyth, D. R. (1985). Empathy skills training in structured groups. *Human Relations, 38,* 247–255.

Zuckerman, M., Amidon, M. D., Bishop, S. E., & Pomerantz, S. D. (1982). Face and tone of voice in the communication of deception. *Journal of Personality and Social Psychology, 43,* 347–357.

Zuckerman, M., DePaulo, B. M., & Rosenthal, R. (1981). Verbal and nonverbal communication of deception. In L. Berkowitz (Ed.), *Advances in experimental social psychology* (Vol. 14). Orlando, FL: Academic Press.

Zuckerman, M., & Driver, R. E. (1985). Telling lies: Verbal and nonverbal correlates of deception. In A. W. Siegman & S. Feldstein (Eds.), *Multichannel integrations of nonverbal behavior* (pp. 129–147). Hillsdale, NJ: Erlbaum.

Zukier, H. (1982). The dilution effect: The role of the correlation and the dispersion of predictor variables in the use of nondiagnostic information. *Journal of Personality and Social Psychology, 43,* 1163–1174.

Zukier, H., & Pepitone, A. (1984). Social roles and strategies in prediction: Some determinants of the use of base-rate information. *Journal of Personality and Social Psychology, 47,* 349–360.

Zullow, H. M., Oettinger, G., Peterson, C., & Seligman, M. E. P. (1988). Pessimistic explanatory style in the historical record: CAVing LBJ, presidential candidates, and East versus West Berlin. *American Psychologist, 43,* 673–682.

Zunich, M. (1961). Relationship beteween maternal behavior and attitudes toward children. *Journal of Genetic Psychology,* 155–165.

Zuzul, M. (1989). *The weapon's effect and child aggression: A field experiment.* Unpublished doctoral dissertation, University of Zagreb, Croatia.

Name Index

Subject Index

Note: Boldface page numbers indicate pages on which key terms are defined.

Credits

Chapter 1: 14: Table 1-2 from Rosenberg, M., *Society and the Adolescent Self-Image.* Copyright © 1965 by Princeton University Press. Reprinted by permission of Princeton University Press; **16:** Figure 1-1 from "A Comparative Citation Analysis of Attribution Theory and the Theory of Cognitive Dissonance," by R. M. Bagby, J. D. A. Parker, and A. S. Bury, 1990, *Personality and Social Psychology Bulletin, 16,* pp. 274–283. Copyright © 1990 by the Society for Personality and Social Psychology, Inc. Reprinted by permission; **25:** Table 1-4 based on *How to Lie with Statistics,* by D. Huff, 1954. Copyright 1954 by W. W. Norton & Company; **29:** Table 1-6 from "Twenty Years of Deception in Social Psychology," by A. E. Gross, and I. Fleming, 1982, *Personality and Social Psychology Bulletin, 8,* pp. 402-408. Copyright 1982 by the Society for Personality and Social Psychology, Inc. Reprinted by permission.

Chapter 2: 42: Figure 2-1 from "Impressions of Babyfaced Adults," by L. Z. McArthur and K. Apatow, 1983–1984, *Social Cognition, 2,* pp. 315–342. Copyright 1983–1984 Guilford Publications. Reprinted by permission; **44:** Figure 2-2 from "Self-Reported Expression of Embarrassment in Five European Cultures," by R. J. Edelmann, J. Asendorpf, A. Contarello, V. Zammuner, J. Georgas, and C. Villanueva, 1989, *Journal of Cross-Cultural Psychology, 20,* pp. 357–371. Copyright © 1989 by Western Washington University. Reprinted by permission of Sage Publications; **58:** Figure 2-4 from Daniel T. Gilbert and Edward E. Jones, "Exemplification: The Self-Presentation of Moral Character," *Journal of Personality, 54:3,* pp. 593–615. Copyright Duke University Press, 1986. Reprinted with permission; **60:** Table 2-5 from "The Self-Monitoring of Expressive Behavior," by M. Snyder, 1974, *Journal of Personality and Social Psychology, 30,* pp. 526–537. Copyright 1974 by the American Psychological Association. Reprinted by permission; **62:** Figure 2-5 from "When Our Identitites Are Mistaken: Reaffirming Self-Conceptions Through Social Interaction," by W. B. Swann, Jr., and C. A. Hill, 1982, *Journal of Personality and Social Psychology, 43,* pp. 59–66. Copyright 1982 by the American Psychological Association. Reprinted by permission; **67:** Table 2-6 from "Errors and Mistakes: Evaluating the Accuracy of Social Judgment," by D. C. Funder, 1987, Psychological Bulletin, 101, pp. 75–90. Copyright 1987 by the American Psychological Association. Reprinted by permission.

Chapter 3: 85: Table 3-2 from Southworth Wells Swede and Philip E. Tetlock, "Henry Kissinger's Implicit Theory of Personality: A Quantitative Case Study," *Journal of Personality, 54:4,* pp. 617–646. Copyright Duke University Press, 1986. Reprinted with permission.

Chapter 4: 129: Figure 4-5 from "Cognitive, Social, and Physiological Determinants of Emotional State," by S. Schachter and J. Singer, 1962, *Psychology Review, 65,* pp. 121–128. Copyright 1962 by the American Psychological Association. Reprinted by permission; **136:** Figure 4-6 from "The Rocky Road from Acts to Dispositions," by E. E. Jones, 1979, *American Psychologist, 34,* pp. 107–117. Copyright 1979 by the American Psychological Association. Reprinted by permission; **150:** Excerpt adapted from "Assessing Coping Strategies: A Theoretically Based Approach," by C. S. Carver, M. F. Scheier, and J. K. Weintraub, 1989, *Journal of Personality and Social Psychology, 56,* pp. 267–283. Copyright 1989 by the American Psychological Association. Reprinted by permission; **151:** Figure 4-8 from "Improving the Performance of Failing Students by Overcoming Their Self-Serving Attributional Biases," by J. Noel, D. R. Forsyth, and K. N. Kelley, 1987, *Basic and Applied Social Psychology, 8,* pp. 151–162. Copyright 1987 Lawrence Erlbaum. Reprinted by permission.

Chapter 5: 165: Figure 5-4 from "Self-Recognition in Primates: A Comparative Approach in Bidirectional Properties of Consciousness," by G. G. Gallup, 1977, *American Psychologist, 32,* pp. 329–338. Copyright 1977 by the American Psychological Association. Reprinted by permission; **165:** Excerpt from "Public and Private Self-Consciousness: Assessment and Theory," by A. Fenigstein, M. F. Scheier, and A. H. Buss, 1975, *Journal of Consulting and Clinical Psychology, 43,* pp. 522–427. Copyright 1975 by the American Psychological Association. Reprinted by permission; **167:** Figure 5-5 adapted from "Self-Focused Attention and the Experience of Emotion: Attraction, Repulsion, Elation, and Depression," by M. F. Scheier and C. S. Carver, 1977, *Journal of Personality and Social Psychology, 35,* pp. 625–636. Copyright 1977 by the American Psychological Association. Adapted by permission; **168:** Figure 5-6 from "A Model of Behavioral Self-Regulation: Translating Intention into Action," by M. F. Scheier and C. S. Carver, 1988, *Advances in Experimental Social Psychology, 21,* pp. 303–346. Copyright 1988 by Academic Press. Reprinted by permission; **171:** Table 5-3 from "Social Comparison in Everyday Life," by L. Wheeler and K. Miyake, 1992, *Journal of Personality and Social Psychology, 62,* pp. 760–773. Copyright 1992 by the American Psychological Association. Reprinted by permission; **182:** Figure 5-7 from "The Cognitive-Affective Crossfire: When Self-Consistency Confronts Self-Enhancement," by W. B. Swann, Jr., J. J. Griffin, Jr., S. C. Predmore, and B. Gaines, 1987, *Journal of Personality and Social Psychology, 52,* pp. 881–889. Copyright 1987 by the American Psychological Association. Reprinted by permission; **186:** Figure 5-8 from "Social Comparison after Success and Failure: Biased Search for Information Consistent with a Self-Serving Conclusion," by T. Pyszczynski, J. Greenberg, and J. LaPrelle, 1985, *Journal of Experimental Social Psychology, 21,* pp. 195–211. Copyright 1985 by Academic Press. Reprinted by permission; **188:** Figure 5-9 adapted from "Friendship Choice and Performance: Self-Evaluation Maintenance in Children," by A. Tesser, J. Campbell, and M. Smith, 1984, *Journal of Personality and Social Psychology, 46,* pp. 561–574. Copyright 1984 by the American Psychological Association. Adapted by permission.

Chapter 6: 204: Table 6-3 from "Why Attitudes are Important: Defining Attitude and Attitude Theory 20 Years Later," by A. G. Greenwald, 1989, in A. R. Pratkanis, S. J. Breckler, and A. G. Greenwald (Eds.), *Attitude Structure and Function,* pp. 429–440. Copyright 1989 by Lawrence Erlbaum. Reprinted by permission; **209:** Figure 6-3 from "Specificity of the Attitude as a Determinant of Attitude-Behavior Congruence," by R. H. Weigel, D. T. A. Vernon, and L. N. Tognacci, 1974, *Journal of Personality and Social Psychology, 30,* pp. 724–728. Copyright 1974 by the American Psychological Association. Reprinted by permission; **213:** Figure 6-4 from *Attitudes, Personality, and Behavior,* by I. Ajzen, p. 118. Copyright 1988 Dorsey Press. Reprinted by permission of Brooks/Cole Publishing Co. and the author; **215:** Table 6-6 adapted from *A Theory of Cognitive Dissonance* by L. Festinger. Copyright © 1957 by the Board of Trustees of the Leland Stanford Junior University. Adapted by permission of Stanford University Press; **221:** Figure 6-7 from "The Effects of Severity of Initiation on Liking for a Group," by E. Aronson and J. Mills, 1959, *Journal of Abnormal and Social Psychology, 59,* pp. 177–181. Copyright 1959 by the American Psychological Association. Reprinted by permission; **224:** Table 6-8 from "Rational Processing or Rationalization? The Effect of Disconfirming Information on a Stated Religious Belief," by C. D. Batson, 1975, *Journal of Personality and Social Psychology, 32,* pp. 176–184. Copyright 1975 by the American Psychological Association. Reprinted by permission; **230:** Figure 6-8 from "Arousal as a Necessary Condition for Attitude Change Following Induced Compliance," by J. Cooper, M. P. Zanna, and P. A. Taves, 1978, *Journal of Personality and Social Psychology, 36,* pp. 1101–1106. Copyright 1978 by the American Psychological Association. Reprinted by permission.

Chapter 7: 239: Figure 7-3 from "Current Stereotypes: A Little Fading, A Little Faking," by H. Sigall and R. Page, 1971, *Journal of Personality and Social Psychology, 18,* pp. 247–255. Copyright 1971 by the American Psychological Association. Reprinted by permission; **240:** Figure 7-4 from "Effects of Race on the Elicitation of Helping Behavior: The Wrong Number Technique," by S. Gaertner and L. Bickman, 1971, *Journal of Personality and Social Psychology, 20,* pp. 218–222. Copyright 1971 by the American Psychological Association. Reprinted by permission; **243:** Figure 7-6 from "Deindividuation and Anger-Mediated Interracial Aggression: Unmasking Regressive Racism," by R. W. Rogers and S. Prentice-Dunn, 1981, *Journal of Personality and Social Psychology, 41,* pp. 63–73. Copyright 1981 by the American Psychological Association. Reprinted by permission; **246:** Table 7-2 from *Measuring Sex Stereotypes: A Multination Study,* by J. E. Williams and D. L. Best. Copyright 1990 by Sage Publications. Reprinted by permission; **252:** Table 7-4 ("Three Basic Aspects of Authoritarian Personality") from *The Authoritarian Personality,* by T. W. Adorno, E. Frenkel-Brunswick, D. Levinson, and N. Sanford. Copyright 1950 by the American Jewish Committee. Reprinted by permission of HarperCollins Publishers, Inc.

Chapter 8: 279: Figure 8-1 adapted from *Communication and Persuasion: Central and Peripheral Routes to Attitude Change,* by R. E. Petty and J. T. Cacioppo. Copyright 1986 by Springer-Verlag. Adapted by permission; **286:** Figure 8-5 from "Empirical Tests of the Absolute Sleeper Effect Predicted from the Discounting Cue Hypothesis," by C. L. Gruder, T. D. Cook, K. M. Hennigan, B. R. Flay, C. Alessis, and J. Halamaj, 1978, *Journal of Personality and Social Psychology, 36,* pp. 1061–1074. Copyright 1978 by the American Psychological Association. Reprinted by permission; **289:** Table 8-3 from "The Effects of Involvement on Responses to Argument Quantity and Quality: Central and Peripheral Routes to Persuasion," by R. E. Petty and J. T. Cacioppo,

1984, *Journal of Personality and Social Psychology, 46,* pp. 69–81. Copyright 1984 by the American Psychological Association. Reprinted by permission; **290:** Figure 8-6 from "The Effects of Involvement on Responses to Argument Quantity and Quality: Central and Peripheral Routes to Persuasion," by R. E. Petty and J. T. Cacioppo, 1984, *Journal of Personality and Social Psychology, 46,* pp. 69–81. Copyright 1984 by the American Psychological Association. Reprinted by permission; **293:** Figure 8-7 from "The Use of Rhetorical Questions in Persuasion: A Cognitive Response Analysis," by R. E. Petty, J. T. Cacioppo, and M. Haesacker, 1981, *Journal of Personality and Social Psychology, 40,* pp. 432–440. Copyright 1981 by the American Psychological Association. Reprinted by permission; **295:** Figure 8-8 adapted from "Fear Appeals and Attitude Change: Effects of a Threat's Noxiousness, Probability of Occurrence, and the Efficacy of Coping Responses," by R. W. Rogers and R. Mewborn, 1976, *Journal of Personality and Social Psychology, 34,* pp. 54–61. Copyright 1976 by the American Psychological Association. Adapted by permission; **308:** Table 8-6 from "The Effects of Repetition of Refutational and Supportive Advertising Appeals," by A. G. Sawyer, 1973, *Journal of Marketing Research, 10,* p. 23–33. Copyright 1973 by the American Marketing Association. Reprinted by permission.

Chapter 9: 318: Figure 9-2 adapted from "An Experimental Investigation of Group Influence," by S. E. Asch, April 15–17, Symposium on Preventive and Social Psychiatry, Walter Reed Army Institute of Research. Washington, DC: Government Printing Office. Adapted by permission of the author; **326:** Figure 9-5 from "Sex Variable in Conforming Behavior," by F. Sistrunk and J. W. McDavid, 1971, *Journal of Personality and Social Psychology, 17,* pp. 200–217. Copyright 1971 by the American Psychological Association. Reprinted by permission; **331:** Figure 9-6 adapted from a table in "Deviance, Rejection, and Communication," by S. Schachter, 1951, *Journal of Abnormal and Social Psychology, 46,* pp. 190–207. Copyright 1951 by the American Psychological Association. Adapted by permission; **332:** Table 9-5 from "Reaction to Attitudinal Deviance: Impact of Deviate's Direction and Distance of Movement," by J. M. Levine, L. Saxe, and H. J. Harris, 1976, *Sociometry, 36,* pp. 97–107. Copyright 1976 by the American Sociological Association. Reprinted by permission; **338:** Figure 9-7 adapted from *Obedience to Authority: An Experimental View,* by Stanley Milgram. Copyright © 1974 by Stanley Milgram. Reprinted by permission of HarperCollins Publishers, Inc.; **340:** Figure 9-8 adapted from *Obedience to Authority: An Experimental View,* by Stanley Milgram. Copyright © 1974 by Stanley Milgram. Reprinted by permission of HarperCollins Publishers, Inc.; **342:** Table 9-7 adapted from *Obedience to Authority: An Experimental View,* by Stanley Milgram. Copyright © 1974 by Stanley Milgram. Reprinted by permission of HarperCollins Publishers, Inc.; **352:** Figure 9-9 reprinted by permission of the publishers from *Inside the Jury* by Reid Hastie, Steven D. Penrod, and Nancy Pennington, Cambridge, Mass.: Harvard University Press, Copyright 1983 by the President and Fellows of Harvard College.

Chapter 10: 358: Table 10-1 adapted from "Functional Roles of Group Members," by K. D. Benne and P. Sheats, 1948, *Journal of Issues, 4*(2), pp. 41–49. Copyright 1948 by the Society for the Psychological Study of Social Issues. Reprinted by permission; **362:** Figure 10-2 adapted from "Socialization in Small Groups: Temporal Changes in Individual-Group Relations," by R. L. Moreland, and M. J. Levine, 1982, *Advances in Experimental Social Psychology, 15.* Copyright 1982 by Academic Press. Reprinted by permission; **365:** Figure 10-3 from "Social Facilitation," by R. B. Zajonc, 1965, *Science, 149,* pp. 269–274. Copyright 1965 by the AAAS. Reprinted by permission; **365:** Figure 10-4 from "Social Enhancement and Impairment of Performance in the Cockroach," by R. B. Zajonc, A. Heingartner, and E. M. Herman, 1969, *Journal of Personality and Social Psychology, 13,* pp. 83–92. Copyright 1969 by the American Psychological Association. Reprinted by permission; **371:** Figure 10-6 from "Many Hands Make Light the Work: The Causes and Consequences of Social Loafing," by B. Latané, K. Williams, and S. Harkins, 1979, *Journal of Personality and Social Psychology, 37,* pp. 822–832. Copyright 1979 by the American Psychological Association. Reprinted by permission; **378:** Table 10-6 adapted from Irving L. Janis, *Groupthink,* Second Edition. Copyright © 1982 by Houghton-Mifflin Company. Adapted with permission; **391:** Figure 10-8 from "The Contingency Model and the Dynamics of the Leadership Process," by F. E. Fiedler, 1978, in L. Berkowitz (Ed.), *Advances in Experimental Social Psychology,* Vol. 12. Copyright 1978 by Academic Press. Reprinted by permission of F. E. Fiedler.

Chapter 11: 403: Figure 11-2 adapted from *The Psychology of Affiliation,* by S. Schachter. Copyright © 1959 by the Board of Trustees of the Leland Stanford Junior University. Adapted by permission of Stanford University Press; **406:** Figure 11-3 reprinted by permission of the publishers from Henry A. Murray, *Thematic Apperception Test.* Cambridge, Mass.: Harvard University Press. Copyright © 1943 by the President and Fellows of Harvard College, © 1971 by Henry A. Murray; **407:** Excerpt from "Shyness and Sociability," by J. M. Cheek and A. H. Buss, 1981, *Journal of Personality and Social Psychology, 41,* pp. 330–339. Copyright 1982 by the American Psychological Association. Reprinted by permission; **416:** Figure 11-5 adapted from Table 1 in "Embracing the Bitter 'Truth': Negative Self-Concepts and Marital Commitment," by W. B. Swann, Jr., J. G. Hixon, and C. De La Ronde, 1992, *Psychological Sciences, 3,* pp. 118–121.

Copyright © 1992 by the American Psychological Society. Adapted with the permission of Cambridge University Press; **417:** Figure 11-6 from "Gain and Loss of Esteem as Determinants of Interpersonal Attractiveness," by E. Aronson and D. Linder, 1965, *Journal of Experimental Social Psychology, 1,* pp. 156–172. Copyright 1965 by Academic Press. Reprinted by permission; **419:** Excerpt from "Measuring Passionate Love in Intimate Relations," by E. Hatfield and S. Sprecher, 1986, *Journal of Adolescence, 9,* pp. 383–410. Copyright © 1986 by the Association for the Psychiatric Study of Adolescents. Reprinted by permission; **421:** Table 11-3 from "A Typology of Styles of Loving," by J. A. Lee, 1977, *Personality and Social Psychology Bulletin, 3,* pp. 173–182. Copyright 1977 by the Society for Personality and Social Psychology, Inc. Reprinted by permission of Sage Publications, Inc.; **421:** Figure 11-7 from "Triangulating Love," by R. J. Sternberg, 1988, in R. J. Sternberg and M. L. Barnes (Eds.), *The Psychology of Love,* pp. 119–138. Copyright 1988 by Yale University Press. Reprinted by permission; **423:** Figure 11-8 from "Passionate Love and the Misattribution of Arousal," by G. L. White, S. Fishbein, and J. Rutstein, 1981, *Journal of Personality and Social Psychology, 41,* pp. 56–62. Copyright 1981 by the American Psychological Association. Reprinted by permission; **427:** Figure 11-9 adapted from Table 3 in "Attachment Style as a Predictor of Adult Romantic Relationship," by J. A. Feeney and P. Noller, 1990, *Journal of Personality and Social Psychology, 58,* pp. 281–291. Copyright 1990 by the American Psychological Association. Adapted by permission; **431:** Figure 11-10 from "Gender Differences in Receptivity to Sexual Offers," by R. D. Clark, III, and E. Hatfield, 1989, *Journal of Psychology and Human Sexuality, 2,* pp. 39–55. © by The Haworth Press, Inc. All rights reserved. Reprinted with permission. For copies of this work, contact Marianne Arnold at The Haworth Document Delivery Service (Telephone 1-800-3-HAWORTH; 10 Alice Street, Binghamton, N.Y. 13904). For other questions concerning rights and permissions, contact Wanda Latour at the above address; **433:** Table 11-7 from *Personal Relationships,* by H. H. Kelley. Copyright 1979 by Lawrence Erlbaum Associates. Reprinted by permission; **434:** Figure 11-11 from "Exit, Voice, Loyalty, and Neglect: Responses to Dissatisfaction in Romantic Involvements," by C. E. Rusbult, I. M. Zembrodt, and L. K. Gunn, 1982, *Journal of Personality and Social Psychology, 43,* pp. 1230–1242. Copyright 1982 by the American Psychological Association. Reprinted by permission; **440:** Excerpt from "The Revised UCLA Loneliness Scale: Concurrent and Discriminate Validity Evidence," 1980, *Journal of Personality and Social Psychology, 39,* pp. 472–480. Copyright 1980 by the American Psychological Association. Reprinted by permission of the author.

Chapter 12: 446: Table 12-1 from "A Taxonomy of Helping: A Multidimensional Scaling Analysis," by P. L. Pearce and P. R. Amato, 1980, *Social Psychology Quarterly, 43,* pp. 363–371. Copyright 1980 by the American Sociological Association. Reprinted by permission; **451:** Excerpt from "The Altruistic Personality and the Self-Report Altruism Scale," by J. P. Rushton, R. D. Chrisjohn, and G. C. Fekken, 1981, *Personality and Individual Differences, 2,* pp. 292–302. Copyright © 1980 by J. P. Rushton. Reprinted by permission; **459:** Figure 12-2 from "Bystander Intervention in Emergencies: Diffusion of Responsibility," by J. M. Darley and B. Latané, 1968, *Journal of Personality and Social Psychology, 8,* pp. 377–383. Copyright 1968 by the American Psychological Association. Reprinted by permission; **461:** Table 12-5 adapted from "Emergencies: What Are They and Do They Influence Bystanders to Intervene?" by R. L. Shotland and T. L. Huston, 1979, *Journal of Personality and Social Psychology, 37,* pp. 1822–1824. Copyright 1979 by the American Psychological Association. Adapted by permission; **462:** Figure 12-4 from "Good Samaritanism: An Underground Phenomenon?" by I. M. Piliavin, J. Rodin, and J. A. Piliavin, 1969, *Journal of Personality and Social Psychology, 13,* pp. 289–299. Copyright 1969 by the American Psychological Association. Reprinted by permission; **464:** Figure 12-5 from "Bystander Intervention into Crime: A Study Based on Naturally Occurring Episodes," by T. Huston, M. Ruggiero, E. R. Conner, and G. Geis, 1981, *Social Psychology Quarterly, 44,* pp. 14–23. Copyright 1981 by the American Sociological Association. Reprinted by permission; **466:** Table 12-6 from Bibb Latané and John M. Darley, *The Unresponsive Bystander: Why Doesn't He Help?* © 1970, pp. 31–35. Adapted by permission of Prentice-Hall, Englewood Cliffs, New Jersey; **472:** Figure 12-8 from "Is Empathic Emotion a Source of Altruistic Motivation?" by C. D. Batson, B. Duncan, P. Ackerman, T. Buckley, and K. Birch, 1981, *Journal of Personality and Social Psychology, 40,* pp. 290–302. Copyright 1981 by the American Psychological Association. Reprinted by permission.

Chapter 13: 492: Figure 13-2 from "Testosterone, Social Class, and Antisocial Behavior in a Sample of 4,462 Men," by J. M. Dabbs, Jr., and R. Morris, 1990, *Psychological Science, 1,* pp. 209–211. Copyright © 1990 by the American Psychological Society. Reprinted with the permission of Cambridge University Press; **499:** Figure 13-4 from *The Resolution of Conflict: Constructive and Destructive Process,* by M. Deutsch. Copyright 1973 by Yale University Press. Reprinted by permission; **500:** Figure 13-5 from "Temperature and Aggression: Ubiquitous Effects of Heat on Occurrence of Human Violence," by C. A. Anderson, 1989, *Psychological Bulletin, 106,* pp. 74–96. Copyright 1989 by the American Psychological Association. Reprinted by permission; **503:** Figure 13-6 from "Coronary-Prone Behavior Pattern and Interpersonal Aggression," by C. S. Carver, and

D. C. Glass, 1978, *Journal of Personality and Social Psychology, 36,* pp. 361–366. Copyright 1978 by the American Psychological Association. Reprinted by permission; **504:** Figure 13-7 from "Weapons as Aggression-Eliciting Stimuli," by L. Berkowitz and A. LePage, 1967, *Journal of Personality and Social Psychology, 7,* pp. 202–207. Copyright 1967 by the American Psychological Association. Reprinted by permission; **507:** Figure 13-9 adapted from "Vicarious Reinforcement and Imitative Learning," by A. Bandura, D. Ross, and S. A. Ross, 1963, *Journal of Abnormal and Social Psychology, 67,* pp. 601–607. Copyright 1963 by the American Psychological Association. Reprinted by permission; **509:** Figure 13-10 from "The Development of Aggressive Behavior from the Perspective of a Developing Behaviorism," by L. D. Eron, 1987, *American Psychologist, 42,* pp. 435–442. Copyright 1987 by the American Psychological Association. Reprinted by permission; **511:** Table 13-3 adapted from "The Demonstration of Power: Violence Profile No. 10," by G. Gerbner, L. Gross, N. Signorielli, M. Morgan, and M. Jackson-Beeck, 1979, *Journal of Communication, 29*(3), pp. 177–195. Copyright 1979 by Oxford University Press. Adapted by permission; **512:** Figure 13-11 from "Aggressive Erotica and Violence Against Women," by E. Donnerstein, 1980, *Journal of Personality and Social Psychology, 39,* pp. 269–277. Copyright 1980 by the American Psychological Association. Reprinted by permission; **515:** Table 13-5 adapted from "Violence and U.S. Regional Culture," by R. E. Nisbett, 1993, *American Psychologist, 48,* pp. 441–449. Copyright 1993 by the American Psychological Association. Adapted by permission.

Chapter 14: 530: Figure 14-1 from an illustration by Bunji Tagawa in "Population Density and Social Pathology," by J. B. Calhoun, *Scientific American,* February 1962, pp. 140–141. Copyright © 1962 by Scientific American, Inc. All rights reserved. Reprinted by permission; **535:** Table 14-1 from *The Environment and Social Behavior,* by I. Altman. Copyright 1976 by Wadsworth Publishing Company, Inc. Reprinted by permission of the author; **538:** Table 14-2 from "Privacy Regulation, Territorial Displays, and Effectivenss of Individual Function," by A. Vinsel, B. Brown, I. Altman, and C. Foss, 1980, *Journal of Personality and Social Psychology, 39,* pp. 1104–1115. Copyright 1980 by the American Psychological Association. Reprinted by permission; **542:** Table 14-3 from *Defensible Space,* by O. Newman. Copyright 1972 by Macmillan, Inc. Reprinted by permission of the author; **544:** Table 14-5 from *The Hidden Dimension,* by Edward T. Hall. Copyright 1966, 1982 by Edward T. Hall. Used by permission of Doubleday, a division of Bantam Doubleday Dell Publishing Group, Inc.; **547:** Figure 14-2 from "Too Close for Comfort: Sex Differences in Response to Invasions of Personal Space," by J. D. Fisher, and D. Byrne, 1975, *Journal of Personality and Social Psychology, 32,* pp. 15–21. Copyright 1975 by the American Psychological Association. Reprinted by permission; **548:** Figure 14-3 from "Body Buffer Zone in Violent Prisoners," by A. F. Kinzel, 1970, *American Journal of Psychiatry, 127,* pp. 59–64. Copyright 1970 by the American Psychiatric Association. Reprinted by permission; **550:** Figure 14-4 from "Reactions to Physical Closeness," by M. D. Storms, and G. C. Thomas, 1977, *Journal of Personality and Social Psychology, 35,* pp. 412–418. Copyright 1977 by the American Psychological Association. Reprinted by permission; **554:** Figure 14-5 from "The Role of Attribution in the Experience of Crowding," by S. Worchel and S. Yohai, 1979, *Journal of Experimental Social Psychology, 34,* pp. 91–104. Copyright 1979 by Academic Press. Reprinted by permission; **560:** Figure 14-6 from "The Effects of Noise and Perceived Control upon Ongoing and Subsequent Aggressive Behavior," by E. T. Donnerstein and D. E. Wilson, 1976, *Journal of Personality and Social Psychology, 34,* pp. 774–781. Copyright 1976 by the American Psychological Association. Reprinted by permission.

Photo Credits

Chapter 1: 0, **7**, Brooks/Cole PhotoDisc; **12**, Reuters/Bettmann Newsphotos; **17**, (*top left*) © Spencer Grant/Stock Boston, (*bottom*) © Cary Wolinsky/Stock Boston, (*top right*) Brooks/Cole PhotoDisc; **20**, © 1963 American Psychological Association, courtesy Albert Bandura

Chapter 2: 36, Brooks/Cole PhotoDisc; **40**, UPI/Bettmann Newsphotos; **41**, Brooks/Cole PhotoDisc; **46**, (*top left*) © Barbara Alper/Stock Boston, (*top middle*) © Susan Rosenberg/Photo Researchers, (*top right*) © Bob Daemmrich/Stock Boston, (*bottom left*) © Tyrone Hall/Stock Boston, (*bottom middle*) Brooks/Cole PhotoDisc, (*bottom right*) © Elizabeth Crews/Stock Boston; **47**, AP/Wide World Photos, Inc.; **52**, Mike Theiler/Reuters/Bettmann Newsphotos; **61**, Brooks/Cole PhotoDisc; **68**, © Rick Reinhard/Impact Visuals

Chapter 3: 74, © Ulrike Welsch; **77**, © Frederic Lewis/Archive Photos; **86**, **90**, **97**, Brooks/Cole PhotoDisc; **99**, © Chester Higgins, Jr./Photo Researchers; **107**, Brooks/Cole PhotoDisc; **113**, AP/Wide World Photos, Inc.

Chapter 4: 114, **118**, Brooks/Cole PhotoDisc; **124**, © Ulrike Welsch; **127**, **131**, **139**, **140**, **145**, Brooks/Cole PhotoDisc

Chapter 5: 154, Brooks/Cole PhotoDisc; **159**, © Loren Santow/Impact Visuals; **164**, **166**, **171**, **176**, **179**, Brooks/Cole PhotoDisc; **181**, © Daniel S. Brody/Stock Boston

Chapter 6: 194, Matt Meldelshon/UPI/Bettmann Newsphotos; **199**, Brooks/Cole PhotoDisc; **201**, © Kenneth Martin/Impact Visuals; **206**, Brooks/Cole PhotoDisc; **211**, UPI/Bettmann Newsphotos; **216**, © Richard Hutchings/Photo Researchers; **220**, **224**, Brooks/Cole PhotoDisc

Chapter 7: 232, Brooks/Cole PhotoDisc; **238**, © Sam Mircovich/SIPA Press; **241**, (*right*) © Jeff Albertson/Stock Boston; **245**, (*left*) © Dave Gatley, Courtesy of Los Angeles Times; **247**, Brooks/Cole PhotoDisc; **251**, © Bill Burke/Impact Visuals; **259**, © Rick Smolan/Stock Boston; **264**, © Michael Dwyer/Stock Boston; **268**, © Ulrike Welsch

Chapter 8: 274, Brooks/Cole PhotoDisc; **278**, courtesy of Arnold Finnegan Martin; **282**, © Spencer Grant/Photo Researchers; **287**, advertisement courtesy of Loews/Sony Theatres; **293**, courtesy of American Cancer Society; **309**, © Russ Marshall/Impact Visuals

Chapter 9: 314, Brooks/Cole PhotoDisc; **321**, Bonnie Hawthorne; **324**, (*left and right*) Brooks/Cole PhotoDisc; **330**, (*top left*) © Mark Chester/Stock Boston, (*top right*) © John Coletti/Stock Boston, (*bottom*) Brooks/Cole PhotoDisc; **336**, AP/Wide World Photos, Inc.; **337**, © 1965 Stanley Milgram, from the film OBEDIENCE distributed by Penn State, PCR; **343**, Archive Photos

Chapter 10: 354, Brooks/Cole PhotoDisc; **357**, © Frank Siteman/Stock Boston; **359**, © Peter Southwick/Stock Boston; **366**, Brooks/Cole PhotoDisc; **370**, © Mike Mazzaschi/Stock Boston; **377**, UPI/Bettmann Newsphotos; **387**, Judy Blamer, Brooks/Cole

Chapter 11: 398, © Ulrike Welsch; **402**, (*left*) UPI/Bettmann Newsphotos, (*right*) Hans-Jurgen Schmidt/Reuters/Bettmann Newsphotos; **405**, Brooks/Cole PhotoDisc; **406**, Reprinted by permission of the publishers from Henry A. Murray, THEMATIC APPERCEPTION TEST, Cambridge, MA: Harvard University Press, © 1943 The President and Fellows of Harvard College, © 1971 Henry A. Murray; **420**, Brooks/Cole PhotoDisc; **428**, © Frank Siteman/Stock Boston

Chapter 12: 442, © Jeffry D. Scott/Impact Visuals; **447**, (*left*) © Lee Celano/SIPA Press, (*middle*) © Jerry Howard/Stock Boston, (*right*) © Kenneth Martin/Impact Visuals; **450**, © Jean-Claude LeJeune/Stock Boston; **465**, Frank Keillor; **469**, © Jack Paclufsky/Stock Boston; **474**, © Joanna Pinneo/courtesy Foreign Mission Board, SBC; **478**, Andy Clark/Reuters/Bettmann Newsphotos

Chapter 13: 484, © Bill Biggart/Impact Visuals; **496**, © Lionel Delevingne/Stock Boston; **501**, Brooks/Cole PhotoDisc; **508**, © Michael Weisbrot/Stock Boston; **517**, (*top*) © Michael Dwyer/Stock Boston, (*bottom*) © Frilet/SIPA Press; **521**, © Peter Menzel/Stock Boston

Chapter 14: 528, Brooks/Cole PhotoDisc; **533**, © Michael Dwyer/Stock Boston; **536**, Brooks/Cole PhotoDisc; **539**, (*left*) © Hazel Hankin/Stock Boston, (*right*) Brooks/Cole PhotoDisc; **545**, (*right*) © Alan Carey/The Image Works, Inc., (*second from right*) Brooks/Cole PhotoDisc, (*second from left*) Brooks/Cole PhotoDisc, (*left*) Brooks/Cole PhotoDisc; **546**, © Peter Menzel/Stock Boston; **550**, **552**, **563**, **563**, Brooks/Cole PhotoDisc

TO THE OWNER OF THIS BOOK:

We hope that you have found *Our Social World* useful. So that this book can be improved in a future edition, would you take the time to complete this sheet and return it? Thank you.

School and address: ______________________________

Department: ______________________________

Instructor's name: ______________________________

1. What I like most about this book is: ______________________________

____

____

2. What I like least about this book is: ______________________________

____

____

3. My general reaction to this book is: ______________________________

____

4. The name of the course in which I used this book is: ______________________________

____

5. Were all of the chapters of the book assigned for you to read? ______________________________

If not, which ones weren't? ______________________________

6. In the space below, or on a separate sheet of paper, please write specific suggestions for improving this book and anything else you'd care to share about your experience in using the book.

____

____

____

____

____

____

Optional:

Your name: ____________________________ Date: ____________________________

May Brooks/Cole quote you, either in promotion for *Our Social World* or in future publishing ventures?

Yes: __________ No: __________

Sincerely,

Donelson R. Forsyth

FOLD HERE

NO POSTAGE NECESSARY IF MAILED IN THE UNITED STATES

BUSINESS REPLY MAIL

FIRST CLASS PERMIT NO. 358 PACIFIC GROVE, CA

POSTAGE WILL BE PAID BY ADDRESSEE

ATT: *Donelson R. Forsyth*

Brooks/Cole Publishing Company
511 Forest Lodge Road
Pacific Grove, California 93950-9968

FOLD HERE